Commentary and Overview by
Rabbi Avrohom Chaim Feuer

Translation by
Rabbi Avrohom Chaim Feuer
in collaboration with
Rabbis Nosson Scherman *and* Meir Zlotowitz

TWO VOLUME EDITION

Seven Impressions . . . June, 1985 — January, 2001
Eighth Impression . . . August 2002
Nineteenth Impression . . . October 2004

Published and Distributed by
MESORAH PUBLICATIONS, Ltd.
4401 Second Avenue
Brooklyn, New York 11232

Distributed in Europe by
LEHMANNS
Unit E, Viking Business Park
Rolling Mill Road
Jarrow, Tyne & Wear NE32 3DP
England

Distributed in Australia & New Zealand by
GOLDS WORLD OF JUDAICA
3-13 William Street
Balaclava, Melbourne 3183
Victoria Australia

Distributed in Israel by
SIFRIATI / A. GITLER — BOOKS
6 Hayarkon Street
Bnei Brak 51127

Distributed in South Africa by
KOLLEL BOOKSHOP
Shop 8A Norwood Hypermarket
Norwood 2196, Johannesburg, South Africa

THE ARTSCROLL TANACH SERIES
TEHILLIM / PSALMS

ISBN
VOL 1 0-89906-060-9 (hard cover)
0-89906-061-7 (paperback)
VOL 2 0-89906-062-5 (hard cover)
0-89906-063-3 (paperback)

Typography by CompuScribe at ArtScroll Studios, Ltd.
4401 Second Avenue / Brooklyn, N.Y. 11232 / (718) 921-9000

Printed in the United States of America by Noble Book Press, Inc.
Bound by Sefercraft, Quality Bookbinders, Ltd. Brooklyn, N.Y.

Book One of Tehillim is
dedicated to the memory of
Rabbi Zev Nisson Dachs, ז״ל

לזכר נשמת
הרב זאב ניסן זצ״ל ב״ר ארי׳ לייב הי״ו דאקס

Just as a fiery and forceful locomotive, filled with energy and
drive, can move that which is cold and inert; so too, one
dynamic individual, motivated by an insatiable enthusiasm, can
stimulate many individuals and communities to actions of הַרְבָּצַת
תּוֹרָה and קִידוּשׁ הַשֵׁם.

Rabbi Zev Nisson Dachs ז״ל, was such an individual.

In his brief 33 years, Rav Zev distinguished himself as a Rebbe
at the Ner Israel Rabbinical College, as a member of the presidium
of the Bais Yaakov Hebrew Parochial School of Chicago, and as
an active force in Agudath Israel. His concern for the community
led him to institute and develop shiurim for men and women at all
levels. He was an accomplished accountant and attorney by
profession.

In addition to his many diverse involvements, Rav Zev was
sensitive and responsive to the needs of every individual. He
inspired them with his enthusiasm and warmth, and enjoyed
giving of himself to others. A true בֶּן תּוֹרָה הַשָׂמֵחַ בְּחֶלְקוֹ, his every
decision was determined by דַּעַת תּוֹרָה.

We are thankful for the few but meaningful years that we were
privileged to be with him. He will continue to be an inspiration to
all who knew him.

May הקב״ה allow Zev's wife and four children to continue their
lives guided by his hopes and aspirations.

תנצב״ה

Book Two of Tehillim
is dedicated to
the memory of
our beloved parents

ר׳ יעקב אייזיק בן ר׳ משה אליעזר קמט ז״ל
ורעיתו זלטא בת ר׳ יהודה ע״ה
Rev. Jacob and Sadie Comet ז״ל

הרב משה לייב בן ר׳ נחום בלייר ז״ל
ורעיתו פסי׳ בת ר׳ נחום מנדל ע״ה
Rabbi Morris and Pauline Blair ז״ל

From the Old World to the New,
    they brought a dedication to the study
        and observance of Torah,
a dedication they transmitted intact
    to their children and grandchildren.

May this Book serve to carry their heritage
    to tens of thousands,
        in many places and in many generations.
And may it serve as a monument
    to the Six Million whose holy memory
        lives forever.

תנצב״ה

Israel and Naomi Blair Comet

Book Three of Tehillim
is dedicated to
the memory of

Hagaon Harav Boruch Sorotzkin זצ״ל

Rosh Hayeshivah of Telshe

מוקדש לזכר נשמת
מו״ר הרה״ג
ר׳ רפאל ברוך סורוצקין זצ״ל
ראש ישיבת טלז

נפטר לעולמו י״ג שבט תשל״ט

The blessed years of his life
were a constant psalm of joy
inspired by his burning love
of Torah and Klal Yisrael.

תנצב״ה

Book Four of Tehillim
is dedicated to
the memory of

ר׳ מאיר בן החבר ר׳ משה ז״ל

Maurice M. Schweizer

Braving the terror of the Nazi regime,
he remained behind
to serve his community of Essen
and to help others flee to freedom.

A survivor of the camps, he was on a death train
when liberation came —
and then, weakened and emaciated,
he buried 100 Jews who died on the way.
Always a kind and concerned servant of his people,
he was a guide and adviser to hundreds
until his final day.

תנצב״ה

Book Five of Tehillim
is dedicated by

Joseph and Lillie Feder

— originally of Cracow, Poland —

in gratitude to the Almighty
for allowing them to build a new Torah life
in Toronto, Canada

May He grant them the continuing privilege
of serving Him
through the support of those
who study Torah
and spread its word.

May the psalms of Tehillim be a source of
merit for the souls of their parents and families

ר׳ ישראל ומרת שיינדעל

Feder and family הי״ד

ר׳ אליעזר ליפא ומרת אסתר

Turner and family הי״ד

תנצב״ה

מכתב ברכה
ממרן הגאון ר' מרדכי גיפטער שליט"א

מרדכי גיפטער
ישיבת טלז
RABBI MORDECAI GIFTER
28570 NUTWOOD LANE
WICKLIFFE, OHIO 44092

בעה"י — ה' אמר, ל"ב למטמונים, תשל"ז
אהובי חתני כבני ר' אברהם חיים, נ"י

מאד אשמח שזכית להוסיף עוד טבעת בשלשלת זהב של סדרת ארטסקרול בתרגום
וביאור כתבי הקדש לשפה המדוברת. ודבר גדול עשית בתרגום וביאור ספר תהלים, שגם בו
חלו ידים זרות בכבל כתבי הקדש. ואתה העמדת הדברים על מכונם לכל הרוצה לראות
הדברים לאמיתתם, אבל רחוק הוא מדברי רז"ל ורבותינו הקדמונים ז"ל מפני חוסר ידיעה
בלשה"ק. וגם בני תורה ששפת המדינה שגורה בפיהם ימצאו רב תועלת בדבריך, ויש לקוות
שיתקרבו מתוך כך לעיין בדברים במקורם.

מי שזכה לראות פשוטי המון עם — שלא הבינו פירוש המלות — בעת השתפכות נפשם
באמירת תהלים, הוא שראה מה הוא ספר תהלים. ואם העיון בדבריך יביא את המעיין למעין
אותה רוממות נפש, והי' זה שכרך על רב העמל וההגיעה שהשקעת בעבודה קדושה זו.

חותנך אוהבך מלונ"ח,
מרדכי

Preface to the Two-volume Edition

The Book of Psalms enjoys a very special position in Jewish life. For generations the Jew has never felt alone as long as he held a Tehillim in his hands — a faithful companion and unerring guide, giving voice to prayer, comfort in misfortune, faith in adversity, and light in the darkness. The familiar phrases of Tehillim flow constantly from Jewish lips at all times, in all seasons. Whether joy or sorrow, triumph or failure, there is always a psalm to fit the occasion. Indeed, our daily prayers draw upon these verses to give voice to our hearts' deepest desires. The psalms comprise a major portion of Jewish liturgy.

Because this is a living book, a book which covers the entire spectrum of human emotions and experiences, it deserves a living translation and commentary. This volume is an attempt to produce such a work. It is an anthology of traditional Jewish texts and commentaries which convey the inspirational message of Tehillim. The historical background of the psalms is provided in order to show how the words flowed from the personal life of David and, in turn, the life of Israel through the ages.

In this historic epoch the words of Tehillim take on new meaning and purpose. The Talmud (Yevamos 97a) teaches that when the words of a Torah scholar are repeated in This World, his lips pulsate with life even from the grave. Thus, the person who recites the psalms of David imbues him with life. Since David is the soul of his descendant the Messiah, it may well be that the recital of Tehillim helps bring the Messiah to life and hasten his arrival. May we all be privileged to greet the Messiah with psalms of joy and thanksgiving, speedily in our days.

Together with the Publishers of the ArtScroll Tanach Series, I express deep gratitude to HASHEM for the success and wide acceptance of the original five-volume edition of this work, now out of print. It is our hope that this new two-volume edition will be more convenient and thus make these holy Psalms available to many more thousands of Jewish souls. We pray for the day when Jews the world over will unite in a universal chorus proclaiming the praise of HASHEM from every corner of the earth. It is then that the Jewish nation will truly realize its historic mission. As the prophet (Isaiah 43:21) declared:

עַם זוּ יָצַרְתִּי לִי תְּהִלָּתִי יְסַפֵּרוּ

"This nation I created for Myself, to recount My praise"

Rabbi Avrohom Chaim Feuer

Miami Beach, Florida
Iyar 5745/May 1985

Acknowledgements

I offer thanks to Hashem for giving me the privilege of participating in the ArtScroll-Mesorah series of Torah publications. At the same time I express my appreciation to the many people to whom I am deeply indebted:

My parents עמו״ש always were and continue to be my most faithful source of encouragement and inspiration. No sacrifice was ever too great for them in their constant efforts to lead me towards the דֶּרֶךְ ה׳. May Hashem bless them with many long years of good health and nachas together.

My father-in-law, HAGAON RAV MORDECAI GIFTER שליט״א has been my mentor and guide from the moment I entered Telshe Yeshivah sixteen years ago. Any Torah knowledge I may have acquired during those years is a result of the patience and paternal care of my beloved Rebbe. As the Rosh HaYeshivah now goes up to Eretz Yisrael to found the Yeshivah at Kiryat Telshe-Stone, may Hashem Yisborach grant him and my dear mother-in-law much success, happiness, and good health in this new arduous and self-sacrificing endeavor to break new ground for the great Torah tradition of Telshe.

No words can adequately express my tremendous debt of gratitude to the Telshe Yeshivah, the great Makom Torah where I have spent the major part of my life.

I cannot truly call this volume my own. That it is worthy of the readers attention is because I have benefited from the scholarship and talent of RABBI NOSSON SCHERMAN. Reb Nosson painstakingly edited the entire Translation, Commentary and Overview, literally toiling over every word and phrase. In particular he made suggestions and corrections of major significance for the Translation. His contribution to this volume is immeasurable.

The moving spirit behind this publication is RABBI MEIR ZLOTOWITZ. It was he who initiated this project and saw it through every stage with complete dedication and selflessness. Like a true brother he encouraged me and gave generous support in every crucial moment. In addition, Reb Meir spent many long days with me and Reb Nosson, painstakingly editing the Translation.

The art and graphics of this volume are the final products of the consummate skill and genius of REB SHEA BRANDER. He, too, gave of his time and talents, day and night, in order to assure the beauty of this book. His optimism and good cheer kept the entire operation running smoothly.

It has been a delight to work with the staff at ArtScroll Studios. MRS. PEARL EIDLIS and MISS ESTHER HARTMAN have given selfless devotion in preparing the manuscript for completion. Working under great stress and from a very complicated manuscript, they did everything to assure the accuracy of the written page. MISS GOLDIE BORGER and MISS SUZIE WEISS provided invaluable assistance.

I must express my gratitude to my friends who helped create this book:

When writing the Overview, I turned for advice to such talmidei chachamim as RABBIS DOVID COHEN, MOSHE EISENMANN, YITZCHOK NOTIS, YERUCHAM BENSINGER, AVROHOM AUSBAND, ZEV LEFF and AHARON STEIN who provided me with scholarly opinions and suggested sources. RABBI NISSON WOLPIN graciously read the manuscript and offered suggestions.

RABBIS SHLOMO MELAMED and AVIE GOLD, and my brothers-in-law, REB BINYOMIN GIFTER and RABBI YAAKOV REISMAN, meticulously read and re-read the commentary to assure its accuracy. To all of them go my thanks.

A note of appreciation is due to my חַבְרוּתָא and very dear friend RABBI AVROHOM YISROEL FISHMAN who has been intimately involved with this project since its inception.

Last to be mentioned yet foremost in mind, is my wife מנב״ת LUBA. Her enthusiasm and buoyant spirits which always accompanied me, made every moment of work a pleasure. Only her understanding, patience and dedication made this volume possible. In her זְכוּת may we together see much nachas from our sons.

Avrohom Chaim Feuer

Wickliffe, Ohio
Erev Rosh Hashanah 5738
September, 1977

~§דברי פתיחה§~ /
Foreword

~§Overview —

Tehillim /
The Rebirth of Mankind

דברי פתיחה

מאת מרן הגאון ר' מרדכי גיפטער

ר"מ ישיבת טעלז

לב מלך הוא לב כל קהל ישראל
(רמב"ם, פ"ג ממלכים ה"ו)

מלך ישראל לא רודה ומושל הוא אלא שליח ה' בהנהגת עמו. ושרש
המלכות הוא בזה שהוא מלך על עצמו, מכיר ויודע בסתרי לבבו ונבכי
נפשו, ושולט על כחותיו ביראת אלקים. כל נפשות ישראל אחוזים
ואוחדים זה בזה באחדותו ית', ובמדה שהמלך שולט על עצמו להגיע
לאחדות נפשו ולהדבק בבורא ב"ה, בה במדה מתאחד הוא בנפש ולב
כל העם. (עיין רמב"ם פ"ב ממלכים ה"ו, ועיין שיעור דעת ,,מלוכה''
להגרי"ל זצ"ל.)

זו המלכות הוא מכלל הכחות שבהם ניחן עם ה' כולו, ולמדונו רז"ל
שכל בני ישראל מלכים הם, וזה הכח שבעם ה' כולו מסתיים בשבט
יהודה ומתיחד במלך דוד מזרע שלמה, והיא תתגלה בכל תקפה וזהרה
בביאת משיח בן דוד, אשר אז יתוקן עולם במלכות ש-די, והי' ה' אחד
ושמו אחד. זוכה הוא המלך לפתוח כח זה בקרבו ע"י דבקתו בתורה
אשר מטעם זה ,,דבקו הכתוב בתורה יתר משאר העם שנאמר כל ימי
חייו'' (רמב"ם פ"ג ממלכים ה"ו, ועיין עוד בפי"א ממלכים ה"ד).

אין פלא איפה שבלב המלך דוד פעמו כל רגשות לב בן ישראל, רגשות
שמחה ואבל, נחם ותוגה, שקט וסער, ועל ראש כולם התשוקה הבלתי
פוסקת לדביקות בה', להתבטל כל כולו באחדותו יתברך. ויפה הרגיש
אחד שלא הי' נאמן לתורת אמת כשאמר: בתורה הקדושה מדבר ה'
יתברך אל האדם, ובספר תהלים מדבר האדם אל ה' יתברך. וזה

השומע קול ה׳ מדבר אליו הוא זה שאפשר לו להגיב בדבור אל ה׳ יתברך, ותורת ה׳ משתלמת באדם קרוץ חומר בה במדה שזוכה הוא על ידי תורה להתרומם ולדבר עם בוראו.

ולכן, לא לחנם בקש דוד שדבריו בתהלים יחשבו לפניו יתברך כנגעים ואהלות (שבת ל.). סדר טהרות בש״ס הוא סדר ,,דעת״ (שבת ל.) — פנימיות עומק החכמה כפי מה שמתקשרת ידיעת החכמה בנימי הלב להעשות קנין בנפש, ובזה הסדר טומאת נגעים מקושרת בשרשה לחולי הנפש — כפי שלמדונו רז״ל — וטומאת המת מיוחדת לגוף הנפרד מאותו שרש חיים המחייהו.

ובהיות כן, בכל דור ובכל תקופה ובכל מצב מוצא נפש ישראל את ביטויו ביחסו אל ה׳ יתברך המסבב כל המסבות בדברי המלך דוד נעים זמירות ישראל.

יזכנו ה׳ יתברך בביאת גואל הצדק, משיח בן דוד, במהרה בימינו, אמן.

An Overview
Tehillim: The Rebirth of Mankind

כתיב (בראשית ה׳ א׳) זֶה סֵפֶר תּוֹלְדֹת
אָדָם, הֶעֱבִיר לְפָנָיו כל הדורות. הראהו דוד, חיים
חקוקין לו ג׳ שעות .... א״י׳ל ע׳ שנה משנותי
יהיו למזל זה .... אמר אדם יפיות זו מלכות
וזמירות הללו נתונות לו במתנה ע׳ שנה שיחיה
ויהא מזמר לפניך. (ילקוט שמעוני בראשית מ״א)
*It is written, 'This is the book of the
generations of man,' (Gen. 5:1). God displayed all future generations to Adam. He
showed him David who was inscribed to
live for only three hours .... Said Adam,
'may seventy of my years go to this
soul.' ... Adam then said, 'Sovereign of
the Universe! This beautiful one — I present him with sovereignty and songs of
praise for the seventy years of his life, so
that he should sing before You! (Yalkut
Shimoni Ber. 41).*

I. Sovereignty and Song:

*Man — A
Miniature
World*

Of all the mighty wonders which God created, the
greatest wonder is man. For man is nothing less
than a microcosm, a miniature world, composed of
all the elements found in the entirety of creation.

*Of all the mighty
wonders which
God created,
the greatest
wonder is man.
For man is nothing
less than a
miniature world.*

An echo of the fearless lion roars forth from every
human heart, together with the gentle bleating of the
timid lamb. A strong, tough vein of iron runs
through the fabric of man, interwoven with a strand
of soft, pliable reed. Animal, vegetable, mineral — all
the kingdoms are represented within man. But there
is more — side by side with the material elements of
earth, there resides within man a lofty intellect and a

holy spirit, the stuff of heaven. Truly this all-encompassing man is no less than a tiny universe.

And what is the purpose of the universe? The Psalmist proclaims:

הַשָּׁמַיִם מְסַפְּרִים כְּבוֹד אֵל וּמַעֲשֵׂה יָדָיו מַגִּיד הָרָקִיעַ

'The heavens declare the glory of God and the expanse of the sky tells of His handiwork' (Psalms 19:2).

All the world is a choir resounding with joyous song. In פֶּרֶק שִׁירָה, *'The Chapter of Song'*, the Sages describe the songs which every creature sings to the Creator. Every creature, from the mighty sun to the lowly ant, from the lilting songbird to the croaking frog, sings one or more verses of Scripture as its song of praise to God. The earth declares that it and its fullness belong to Him. The stars proclaim that God alone made the heavenly host. The horse declares that just as it looks to its master, so must all look to God.

What is the underlying message of these songs? Simply this: God's praise is sung when each and every part of creation performs its assigned task without deviation. Every creature acting out its ordained role is a fine, precision instrument. Together they form a cosmic orchestra [see *Overview, ArtScroll Shir HaShirim*].

An assemblage of the finest virtuosos does not yet make a symphonic orchestra

However, an assemblage of the finest virtuosos does not yet make a symphonic orchestra. They need a skilled conductor to harmonize the multitude of tones into a thing of exquisite beauty. If each musician improvises without regard to the fused outcome, the result will be not music, but noise.

God placed Adam on the podium and appointed him conductor and choir master of the universe. The diverse elements of creation are bidden to obey his baton. Adam, who was composed of all those diverse elements, was provided with a score to follow and instructions on how to use each creation in its proper time and place.

So said the Psalmist of the mission of man: *'You gave him dominion over the works of Your hands,*

You placed everything under his feet (Ps. 8:7). Man's dominion is not merely privilege — it is an obligation. It requires balancing, adjusting, guiding, and coaxing all of the world's divergent forces into a sublime symphony of divine service. The *Midrash* describes the talents with which Adam was endowed for the sake of accomplishing his mission as מַלְכוּת וּזְמִירוֹת *'sovereignty and song.'*

Three Hours Adam was created on the sixth day, on the eve of the first Sabbath. That day consisted of twelve hours *(Sanhedrin* 38b). In the ninth hour, God informed Adam of his duties and restrictions and commanded him to obey — and also warned of the dire consequences of disobedience. Adam's role as 'conductor' and caretaker of the world was meant to endure for only three hours, from the ninth to the twelfth. Had he not succumbed to sin during those critical hours Sabbath would have been ushered in and the world would have risen to sacred perfection (cf. *Sifsei Cohen, Bereishis* p. 22). But Adam failed to follow the divine imperative. Instead of welcoming the Sabbath into Eden in the twelfth hour, it was then that he was driven out *(Sanhedrin* ibid.).

Instead of welcoming the Sabbath into Eden in the twelfth hour, it was then that he was driven out.

Not only did he fall, he dragged the entire universe down with him. He devoted the rest of his life to repentance. Adam scoured the pages of history, searching for that one unique soul which could lead the world back to perfection. He discovered the soul of David which was inscribed to live for only three hours, symbolizing that David was destined to take over Adam's three hour mission of universal leadership and direction. Adam granted David seventy years of his life in which to fully accomplish this task. He also endowed him with the essential gifts of *'sovereignty and song'*. What was the true nature of Adam's sin and how did David plan to erase it?

The Voice and the Vision It is not adequate merely to say that Adam dwelled in Paradise, we would be more accurate to say that Paradise dwelled inside of him. He was blessed with the inner joy of security and self-assurance; he could

trust himself! The agony of self-doubt never tormented the first man. He was completely at peace with himself, confident that his every motive was pure.

Rabbi Chaim of Volozhin offers us this eloquent word-portrait of Adam: The inclination for evil did not exist inside him. There was nothing inherent in his nature which could interfere with his spiritual ascent. Only one inclination urged him on — a good and positive one. No trace of friction or struggle existed inside Adam because he was a perfect and harmonious blend of sacred forces (*Nefesh HaChaim* 1:6).

No trace of friction or struggle existed inside Adam because he was a perfect and harmonious blend of sacred forces.

Ramban (Genesis 2:9) comments: Before the sin Adam truly resembled the heavens and their hosts who are described as פּוֹעֲלֵי אֱמֶת שֶׁפְּעוּלָתָם אֱמֶת וְלֹא יְשַׁנּוּ אֶת תַּפְקִידָם *'Creatures of truth, whose achievement is truth and undeviating from their appointed mission' (Sanhedrin 42a).*

However, Adam's life was not free of trial and challenge. Although no evil impulse was found within him — there most assuredly existed a threat from without. The external inclination towards evil was personified by the נָחָשׁ; *'serpent'*.

Certainly Adam was inclined only towards good. But what is good?

Certainly Adam was inclined only towards good. But what is good? God said one thing, the serpent, another! Adam heard the word of God with his ears.

כִּי בְּיוֹם אֲכָלְךָ מִמֶּנּוּ מוֹת תָּמוּת

'For on the day that you eat of it you shall surely die' (Gen. 2:17).

But the serpent, the adroit master of persuasion, presented an appealing argument. He reinforced his words with powerful evidence clearly visible to the eyes. 'Seeing is believing' — a vision is more convincing than a voice.

וַתֵּרֶא הָאִשָּׁה כִּי טוֹב הָעֵץ לְמַאֲכָל וְכִי תַאֲוָה הוּא לָעֵינַיִם

'And the woman saw that the tree was good for food and an enticement for the eyes' (Gen. 3:6).

[For further discussion of the Sin, see *Overview*, ArtScroll edition of *Bereishis*.]

Smoke to the Eyes

Baal HaTurim (ibid.) notes that the word לָעֵינַיִם is mentioned only four times in all of Scriptures: In *Genesis*; in *I Samuel* 16:7: כִּי הָאָדָם יִרְאֶה לַעֵינַיִם *'For man sees only what appears before his eyes'*; in *Koheles* 11:17: וּמָתוֹק הָאוֹר וְטוֹב לַעֵינַיִם *'Sweet is the light and pleasing to the eyes;* and finally in *Proverbs* 10:26, וְכֶעָשָׁן לָעֵינָיִם *'And like smoke to the eyes'.*

Baal HaTurim detects a common theme in these four scattered verses: The eyes of Adam were led astray by external *'appearances'* which seemed to be *'good and enticing'*. At first *'light'* the fruit appeared to be *'sweet and pleasing'*. Ultimately, Adam realized that his eyes had been blinded by the *'smoke'* of deception.

Ultimately, Adam realized that his eyes had been blinded by the 'smoke' of deception.

In his prime, *'Adam could see from one end of the world to the other' (Sanhedrin* 38b). His intellectual scope was all-encompassing, unlimited and un-hampered by distortion. But sin clouded his vision, and brought him to the gates of death,

יֵשׁ דֶּרֶךְ יָשָׁר לִפְנֵי אִישׁ וְאַחֲרִיתָהּ דַּרְכֵי מָוֶת
'There is a way which appears straight before a man, yet its end is the ways of death' (Proverbs 14:12).

The Interrupted Melody

Adam changed profoundly after he erred. At first, not the slightest trace of evil resided within him. However, by eating of the forbidden fruit, Adam took the enemy into himself and thereby made evil an integral part of his makeup. His inner harmony was disrupted, his entire being was shattered into two rival camps.

Now Adam's life became a bitter conflict, an endless struggle between good and evil, truth and falsehood. No longer could he trust himself. He hesitated. He stumbled. He fluctuated between as-cent and descent, success and failure. No longer was man reliable and consistent like the never-changing forces of nature. No longer was he *'A creature of truth whose achievement is truth, not deviating from the path set for his appointed mission.*

To the extent that Adam's self-mastery vanished, he forfeited his מַלְכוּת, sovereignty, over the world.

To the extent that Adam's self-mastery vanished, he forfeited his מַלְכוּת *'sovereignty'* over the world.

The universal שִׁירָה 'song' he had conducted was interrupted — all but silenced.

Hearing is Believing

אָדָם אַתֶּם אֲנִי אֱלֹהֵיכֶם נְאֻם אֲדֹנָי ה׳
'You are men [lit. 'Adam'], and I am Your God' (Ezekiel 34:31).
The Children of Israel are called אָדָם *'Adam', but the gentiles are not called 'Adam'* (Yevamos 61a).

The Patriarchs — Abraham, Isaac, and Jacob — sought to regain the perfection of Adam in his prime. The Patriarchs — Abraham, Isaac, and Jacob — sought to regain the perfection of Adam in his prime. In their merit, the Children of Israel were chosen to be Adam's spiritual heirs. At Sinai, God gave Israel the opportunity to regain the dependable vision which Adam had forfeited.

וְכָל הָעָם רֹאִים אֶת הַקּוֹלֹת
'And all of the nation saw the sounds' (Ex. 20:15).

רֹאִים אֶת הַנִּשְׁמָע וְשׁוֹמְעִים אֶת הַנִּרְאֶה
'They saw what they heard and they heard what they saw' (Mechilta ibid.).

At Sinai, Israel's senses were so heightened that they became aware of the one overwhelming truth. At Sinai, Israel's senses were so heightened that they became aware of the one overwhelming truth: the word of the living God. The word of God which their ears heard was more tangible, more real than the sights of their eyes. Transitory, essentially meaningless stimuli lost all significance for them. They 'saw' the truth and the eternity of the word of God. Furthermore, that which they saw with their eyes was relatively vague and unimpressive. The eyes were suspect for they could easily be deceived just as Adam's eyes had been clouded by deception. Consequently, visual data made only a faint impression on them, like a barely heard whisper (*Nefesh HaChaim* 1:11).

Twice daily, the Jew faithfully attempts to perpetuate this message. He covers his eyes and solemnly declares שְׁמַע יִשְׂרָאֵל ה׳ אֱלֹהֵינוּ ה׳ אֶחָד *'Hear O Israel, HASHEM is our God, HASHEM is One'*. Cover up your eyes! Pay no attention to that which you see!

Live only by the truth which you *hear* about the living God and His commands!

At Sinai, Israel returned to the purity of Adam before the sin. Once again the sanctity of man rivalled that of the angels.

בְּסִינַי פָּסְקָה זוּהֲמָתָן

'At Sinai, the defilement [which the snake injected into them] *disappeared*' (Shabbos 146a).

Rabbi Jose taught (*Avodah Zarah* 5a); Israel accepted the Torah so that the Angel of Death should have no power over them, as it says, אֲנִי אָמַרְתִּי אֱלֹהִים אַתֶּם וּבְנֵי עֶלְיוֹן כֻּלְּכֶם *'I said: You are like angels, and all of you are sons of the Most High'* (Psalms 82:6).

Unfortunately, this Utopian situation did not long endure. Only forty days later they were again led astray by their eyes which imagined that they saw what they really did not see.

Only forty days later they were again led astray by their eyes which imagined that they saw what they really did not see.

בא שטן וערבב את העולם והראה דמות חשך ואפילה וערבוביא לומר ודאי מת משה.

Satan came and mixed up the world. He showed them an apparition of confusing darkness and gloom as if to say: 'Surely Moses has died' (Rashi to Ex. 32:1).

The terrible result of this deception was the sin of the Golden Calf and the spiritual decline of Israel. The immortality attained at Sinai was lost.

Alas, Israel destroyed its accomplishments!

אָכֵן כְּאָדָם תְּמוּתוּן

'In truth, you shall perish like Adam' (Ps. 82:7) (*Avodah Zarah* ibid.).

Once again the world was plunged into darkness, to await a new dawn and a fresh vision.

II. Ruddy — But With Beautiful Eyes:

The Seer

Some three and one-half centuries after Sinai, Israel entered a period of renewal — the Era of Samuel. For one full year prior to Samuel's birth a בַּת קוֹל, *'a heavenly voice'*, continually heralded the arrival of this great soul. In Samuel's time prophecy flourished all through the land as groups of his disciples learned under his tutelage to draw close to God. The new vistas of clear vision which opened up in those days are best described in the following verse:

In Samuel's time prophecy flourished all through the land as groups of his disciples learned to draw close to God.

לְפָנִים בְּיִשְׂרָאֵל כֹּה אָמַר הָאִישׁ בְּלֶכְתּוֹ לִדְרוֹשׁ
אֱלֹהִים לְכוּ וְנֵלְכָה עַד הָרֹאֶה כִּי לַנָּבִיא הַיּוֹם
יִקָּרֵא לְפָנִים הָרֹאֶה.

In earlier times in Israel [Samuel's era] when a man went to inquire of God, so would he say: 'Come and let us go to the Seer'; For that is what the Prophet was called in earlier times — the Seer (I Sam. 9:9).

Samuel himself accepted the unprecedented title, introducing himself to Saul as אָנֹכִי הָרֹאֶה *'I am the Seer' (Ibid. 9:19).*

However, the Sages tell us that God found fault with Samuel's sweeping depiction of himself. Was it he who saw? Wasn't it God who showed him? Samuel should have made perfectly clear what he knew in his heart and expected his listeners to realize as well: 'I am he who sees what God shows him' *(Harav Gifter).*

The Holy One, Blessed be He, said to Samuel: 'You call yourself the Seer? I will show you something which you will not be able to see!' When did God show Samuel this? When he sent him to anoint David! (Yalkut Shimoni ibid.).

The source of the Seer's clear vision is not his eyes, but his ears! He who cannot listen cannot see!

Indeed, Samuel knew full well that the source of the Seer's clear vision is not his eyes, but his ears! He who cannot listen cannot see! Samuel knew all too well that God had rejected Saul, the first king whom

he had anointed because he allowed himself to be enticed and entrapped by his eyes. Saul saw the handsome animals of Amalek and spared them for future offerings, rather than destroy them immediately as God had commanded (*I Samuel* 15:9-15).

וַיֹּאמֶר שְׁמוּאֵל הַחֵפֶץ לַה׳ בְּעֹלוֹת וּזְבָחִים כִּשְׁמֹעַ בְּקוֹל ה׳ הִנֵּה שְׁמֹעַ מִזֶּבַח טוֹב לְהַקְשִׁיב מֵחֵלֶב אֵילִים.

And Samuel said, 'Does HASHEM desire burnt offerings and sacrifices as much as he desires obeying the voice of HASHEM? Behold, obedience is better than sacrifice, to listen surpasses the fat of rams' (ibid. v. 22).

The Seed of Ruth

God directed the prophet to a family which had long dedicated its efforts to regaining Adam's pristine purity.

God rejected the House of Saul and commanded Samuel to anoint a new king. He directed the prophet to a family which had long dedicated its efforts to regaining Adam's pristine purity, the family of Jesse, the son of Oved, the son of Ruth.

Ruth's son was Oved.

He was called עוֹבֵד *'Oved'* [lit. *'servant'*] because he served God with a full heart. And Oved bore Jesse who was also called נָחָשׁ *'serpent' (II Sam.* 17:25). Many days passed before the Angel of Death could find a cause to take Jesse's soul away, for this man was free of all sin and guilt. God remembered the נָחָשׁ *'serpent'* who persuaded Adam and Eve to eat of the Tree of Knowledge. Because of that sin all men are condemned to die and that was the only cause of righteous Jesse's death (*Targum; Ruth* 4:21-22)..

When the Seer beheld Eliab, the eldest, he was greatly impressed.

Samuel arrived at the house of Jesse and was introduced to his seven fine sons. When the Seer beheld Eliab, the eldest, he was greatly impressed and exclaimed,

אַךְ נֶגֶד ה׳ מְשִׁיחוֹ

'Surely HASHEM's anointed is before Him' (I Sam. 16:6).

Eliab seemed to be an aristocrat of noble bearing, a

leader possessed of discipline and self-control. But hidden from Samuel's eyes, Eliab was a man of violence, given to bursts of unbridled anger (*Pesachim* 66b; *Midrash Shmuel* 19).

וַיֹּאמֶר ה' אֶל שְׁמוּאֵל אַל תַּבֵּט אֶל מַרְאֵהוּ וְאֶל גְּבֹהַּ קוֹמָתוֹ כִּי מְאַסְתִּיהוּ כִּי לֹא אֲשֶׁר יִרְאֶה הָאָדָם כִּי הָאָדָם יִרְאֶה לַעֵינַיִם וַה' יִרְאֶה לַלֵּבָב

'And HASHEM said unto Samuel, look not at his appearance or at his high stature, for I have rejected him. Things are not as man sees them, for man sees only what appears before his eyes, but HASHEM looks into the heart' (ibid. v. 7).

He Is the One

One by one God disqualified all seven of Jesse's sons. But there was one more son — the eighth. He was a mere shepherd. No one appreciated this son, no one even knew him well. So little did he seem suited for royalty that he wasn't even invited to come to welcome the Seer. But now, his brothers rejected, this son was summoned home from the flocks.

So little did he seem suited for royalty that he wasn't even invited to come to welcome the Seer

וְהוּא אַדְמוֹנִי עִם יְפֵה עֵינַיִם

'He was ruddy — with beautiful eyes' (v. 12).

When Samuel first laid his eyes on David he was alarmed. He said, 'This ruddy fellow is a bloody killer like Esau!' But the Holy One, Blessed be He, allayed Samuel's fears and said, 'No! This one is different because he is עִם יְפֵה עֵינַיִם, *'with beautiful eyes.'* Esau murders to satisfy his own desires, but David slays his foes only upon the advice and guidance of Sanhedrin [who are the עֵינֵי הָעֵדָה *'the eyes of the congregation'*] (*Bereishis Rabba* 66:3).

In truth, Samuel's basic evaluation of David was accurate. By nature, David was inclined to violence. But by listening well to the lessons of the Sages David had refined his character.

By nature, David was inclined to violence.

וַיִּשְׁאַל דָּוִד בַּה'

'And David inquired of HASHEM' (II Sam. 2:1).

David always consulted God to learn what his next step should be. He never relied on his own wisdom

and ingenuity. It was in this virtue that David surpassed Saul who acted on his own initiative (*Malbim
ibid.*).

King Saul's temperament was far more suited than
David's to perfection. Saul's nature was cool and
subdued, not given to excess. David, however, was
אַדְמוֹנִי, *'ruddy'*, and seethed with burning passions
tamed only with great effort (*Ohr Hachaim
HaKodosh, Deut.* 31:1).

By nature, David was inclined towards cruelty.
However, he disciplined himself to use his harsh
streak only when necessary — in his battles against
idolators or heretics. Towards his fellow Israelites
David acted only with kindness (*Rambam; Shemone
Perakim 7*).

It was this unique man that God designated to restore the vision of the nation.

It was this unique man whom God designated to
restore the vision of the nation:

וַיֹּאמֶר ה' קוּם מְשָׁחֵהוּ כִּי זֶה הוּא
*HASHEM said: 'Arise, anoint him, for he
is the one!' (I Sam. 16:12).*

III. Mesillas Yesharim —
The Path of the Upright

*The First
Five Rungs*

Rabbi Moshe Chaim Luzzato's slim classic on self-
mastery charts the progressive stages through
which man must pass in his ascent to perfection.
Luzzatto called his work *Mesillas Yesharim, 'The
Path of the Upright'* and he uses David as his prime
model of perfection. The author defines the many
rungs on the ladder leading up to perfection; let us
look at the first five, in the words of Luzzato:

Rabbi Pinchos ben Yair said:
*'Watchfulness' leads to 'zeal.' 'Zeal' leads
to 'Cleanliness.' 'Cleanliness' leads to
'Separation.' 'Separation' leads to 'Purity'
(Avodah Zarah 20b).*

David said, דָּבְקָה נַפְשִׁי אַחֲרֶיךָ בִּי תָּמְכָה יְמִינֶךְ 'My soul clings to You, Your right hand sustains me' (Ps. 63:9).

A man enters This World only for this purpose — to attain closeness to God by rescuing his soul from deterrents and distractions.

1) זְהִירוּת, 'Watchfulness': One should stay away from evil company which is a prime deterrent [to attaining closeness to God] .... King David emphasized this saying אַשְׁרֵי הָאִישׁ אֲשֶׁר לֹא הָלַךְ בַּעֲצַת רְשָׁעִים וּבְדֶרֶךְ חַטָּאִים לֹא עָמָד וכו'. The praises of man are that he walked not in the counsel of the wicked and stood not in the path of the sinful ... (Ps. 1:1).

What a person must do is purify and cleanse himself and keep his feet from the paths of the crowds who are immersed in the foolishness of the time.

2) זְרִיזוּת, 'Zeal': (Ch. 6,7) King David who was grateful for his portion of 'zeal' said, חַשְׁתִּי וְלֹא הִתְמַהְמָהְתִּי לִשְׁמֹר מִצְוֹתֶיךָ 'I was quick, I did not delay, in keeping your commandments (Ps. 119:60).

The man whose soul burns with love in the service of his Creator will surely not be idle in the performance of His commandments, rather his movements will be like the quick movements of a fire. The most preferred divine service is desire of the heart and longing of the soul. In this respect David exulted, כְּאַיָּל תַּעֲרֹג עַל אֲפִיקֵי מָיִם כֵּן נַפְשִׁי תַעֲרֹג אֵלֶיךָ אֱלֹהִים צָמְאָה נַפְשִׁי לֵאלֹהִים 'As a hart yearns for brooks of water so does my soul yearn for You, O God, my soul thirsts for God ...' (Ps. 42:2-3). צָמְאָה לְךָ נַפְשִׁי כָּמַהּ לְךָ בְשָׂרִי 'My soul thirsts for You, my flesh pines for You' (Ps. 63:2).

3) נְקִיּוּת, 'Cleanliness.' (Ch. 10) This man is clean of any trace of evil which lust leaves behind and will come to possess perfectly clear vision and pure discrimination.

He will not be deceived. David rejoiced in the possession of this trait and said, אֶרְחַץ בְּנִקָּיוֹן כַּפָּי וַאֲסֹבְבָה אֶת מִזְבַּחֲךָ ה' 'I will wash my hands in cleanliness and I will go around Your altar, HASHEM (Ps. 26:6).

4) פְּרִישׁוּת, 'Separation': (Ch. 15) More desirable

than anything else in respect to the attainment of *separation*, is solitude. For when one removes worldly goods from before his eyes, he removes from his heart desire for them. As David said in praise of solitude, מִי יִתֶּן לִי אֵבֶר כַּיּוֹנָה אָעוּפָה וְאֶשְׁכֹּנָה. הִנֵּה אַרְחִיק נְדֹד אָלִין בַּמִּדְבָּר סֶלָה 'Who will give me the wings of a dove . . . I would wander far off; I would lie down in the desert' (Ps. 55:7-8).

5) טַהֲרָה, *'Purity'*: (Ch. 16) Purity refers to perfection of one's heart and thoughts as indicated in David's statement לֵב טָהוֹר בְּרָא לִי אֱלֹהִים *'Create within me a pure heart, God (Ps. 51:12).*

The intent of this trait is that a man conduct himself in accordance with intelligence and fear of God, uninfluenced by sin and lust.

The intent of this trait is that a man leave no room in his deeds for evil inclination, but conduct himself in accordance with intelligence and fear of God, uninfluenced by sin and lust.

Tehillim— A Diary of Struggle

God placed man in the midst of a raging battle, for all the affairs of This World, whether for the good or for the bad, are trials to a man. Wealth on the one hand, poverty on the other, serenity on the one hand, suffering on the other. The battle rages against man to the fore and to the rear. If he is valorous and victorious on all sides, he will be the אָדָם הַשָּׁלֵם *'The Whole Man'* (Mesillas Yesharim 1).

Chovos Halevovos (Sha'ar Yichud HaMaaseh 5) tells of the pious man who greeted troops returning from battle. He said, 'You are returning from a minor skirmish to enter into the major battle — the lifelong struggle of man versus his evil inclination!' This is the struggle which David records.

'You are returning from a minor skirmish to enter into the major battle — the lifelong struggle of man versus his evil inclination!'

He composed *Psalms* in the midst of turbulence. This book was not written as a detached memoir of events long past. It is no less than a battle-front diary, recording the fierce conflict between good and evil which raged within David — and without.

Often the style of *Tehillim* is erratic and abrupt. Often it is difficult to detect a smooth flow and continuity from one verse to the next. Sudden cries, pleas for salvation, burst forth unexpectedly in the

midst of a narrative. All of this demonstrates the urgency of the situation, the tension of the moment (Harav Gifter).

אֲדֹנָי שִׁמְעָה בְקוֹלִי תִּהְיֶינָה אָזְנֶיךָ קַשֻּׁבוֹת לְקוֹל תַּחֲנוּנָי

'My Lord, listen to my voice, let Your ears be attentive to the sound of my pleas' (Ps. 130:2).

David did not ask God to heed his message, his eloquent plea. He merely begged that God hear his voice and entreaties.

מַשְׂכִּיל לְדָוִד בִּהְיוֹתוֹ בַמְּעָרָה תְפִלָּה

'A Maskil [lit. 'a song composed with intellect'] unto David, when he was in the cave, a prayer' (Ps. 142:1).

David committed all of his vast mental powers to the composition of this psalm. What did he say?

קוֹלִי אֶל ה' אֶזְעָק קוֹלִי אֶל ה' אֶתְחַנָּן

'My voice, to HASHEM will I shout, My voice, to HASHEM will I plead!' (ibid. v. 2).

Tehillim is not poetry. It is a cry for help. It is a plea for perfection (Ohr Yahel).

The Kindness of Affliction

When King Nebuchadnezzar witnessed the miraculous salvation of Chananya, Mishael and Azarya from the fiery inferno, he was so impressed that he was prepared to recite before God songs and praises of such grandeur and beauty as to put the entire Book of Psalms to shame. But an angel descended and struck him on the mouth (Sanhedrin 92b).

An amazing story! How could this coarse, evil tyrant possibly outshine the brilliant eloquence of King David? And if indeed he could, why was he not permitted to do so?

The *Kotzker* answers: Of course, this heathen

might well have composed poetry which surpassed the literary excellence of *Psalms*. There are many degenerate, immoral writers who can boast of finely polished pens! However, literary style is not the hall-

mark of *Tehillim*. It's not so much *what* David said as *when* he said it.

One can easily become ecstatic when experiencing good fortune. Anyone can rapturously extoll God when he sits securely, watching miracles occur. But it is only the rare, unique individual who can continue to sing even when he falls, even after he is crushed and beaten. God sent an angel to test the sincerity of Nebuchadnezzar's song. 'Do you really wish to make sacred music? If so, then you will sing even after the blow!'

But it is only the rare, unique individual who can continue to sing even when he falls, even after he is crushed and beaten.

Throughout his life, David incessantly begged God to care for him as a father cares for his son, to guide him on the straight path. God responded to this sincere plea and led David as a parent would lead his child.

אֲסַפְּרָה אֶל חֹק ה׳ אָמַר אֵלַי בְּנִי אַתָּה אֲנִי הַיּוֹם
יְלִדְתִּיךָ

I am obligated to proclaim: HASHEM said to me: 'You are My son, I have begotten you this day' (Ps. 2:7).

God promised David that he would continue to maintain this close relationship with his descendants as well.

אֲנִי אֶהְיֶה לּוֹ לְאָב וְהוּא יִהְיֶה לִּי לְבֵן אֲשֶׁר
בְּהַעֲוֹתוֹ וְהֹכַחְתִּיו בְּשֵׁבֶט אֲנָשִׁים וּבְנִגְעֵי בְּנֵי אָדָם.
וְחַסְדִּי לֹא יָסוּר מִמֶּנּוּ

'I will be like a father to him, and he will be like a son to me, if he will commit iniquity I will rebuke him with the rod of men and with the plagues of mankind. But my kindness shall not depart from him . . .' (II Sam. 7:14-15).

There is no kindness which surpasses that of the father who cares so much for his child that he will even beat him if that is the way to guide him to perfection.

What manner of kindness is this? Plagues and punishing rods? Yes! There is no kindness which surpasses that of the father who cares so much for his child that he will even beat him if that is the way to guide him to perfection. Any time the son strays and loses sight of his father's instructions, he receives a blow to forcefully remind him that he must conform to his father's path.

In all of the Scriptures we find no one who was afflicted as much as David. No one was so misunderstood, no one had so many enemies. Job's suffering
was intense but it lasted for only a relatively short
while. But David's entire life was an endless succession of misfortune.

*Job's suffering was
intense but it
lasted for only a
relatively short
while. But David's
entire life was an
endless succession
of misfortune.*

דָּלְפָה נַפְשִׁי מִתּוּגָה
'My soul drips from agony' (Ps. 119:28).
My soul drips from the disasters which
overwhelm me. No year passes without
calamity. No month goes by without bad
news. There is no day without misfortune.
Woe upon woe! *(Sifri).*

But, there was no one who appreciated the benefits
of affliction as much as David.

Four men were afflicted. Job lashed back and complained. Abraham laughed for joy. King Chizkiyahu
begged that the beatings stop. But David saw the
whip hanging on the wall and said, 'Why is the whip
sitting idle, beat me with it!' (*Midrash Shocher Tov
Ps.* 26:1).

David said to the Holy One, Blessed be He, 'Show
me the open gate which leads a man straight into the
World to Come.' The Holy One, Blessed be He
replied, 'David, if eternal life is your wish, then affliction must be your wish' (*Vayikra Rabbah* 30).

Rabbi Judah the Prince said: 'Which is the דֶּרֶךְ
יְשָׁרָה, *straight path*, which a man should choose
for himself? He should love rebuke! For when there
is rebuke in the world, God is pleased with the world.
Goodness and blessing then come to the world and
evil departs *(Tamid* 28a).

Every beating, every rebuke, brought forth new
waves of song from David's lips. For he loved God
who cared so much for him that He beat him onto
the straight path.

*For he loved God
who cared so much
for him that He
beat him on to the
straight path.*

מְסִלַּת יְשָׁרִים סוּר מֵרָע שֹׁמֵר נַפְשׁוֹ נֹצֵר דַּרְכּוֹ
*'The path of the upright is to stay away
from evil, he who safeguards his soul will
preserve his way' (Prov. 16:17).*

The Secret of the Harp

The more vigorously you pluck its strings — the louder its sound, the more resonant its tones.

אֶפְתַּח בְּכִנּוֹר חִידָתִי

'I will solve my riddle with the harp' (Ps. 49:5).

If you wish to discover the secret of David's soul, pay close attention to the working of the harp. The more vigorously you pluck its strings — the louder its sound, the more resonant its tones. Likewise, the more God tugged at David's heart with pain and affliction — the louder and more beautiful were his songs. עוּרָה כְבוֹדִי עוּרָה הַנֵּבֶל וְכִנּוֹר *'Awaken my soul! Awaken me O lyre and harp!' (Ps. 57:9).* The soul is aroused and stimulated in the very same way as the lyre and harp *(Ya'aros Devash).*

This is the wondrous secret of *Tehillim.* David cries out in pain, yet songs of joy pour forth from his lips. His words are those of melancholy and despair, yet a spirit of happiness fills every syllable.

David could cry out *'Every night my bed I drench, with my tears I soak my couch'* and still exult *'HASHEM has heard my plea, HASHEM will accept my prayer' (Psalms 6:7, 10).* He said them both in the *David understood* same breath, because David understood that his af-*that his affliction* fliction and his acceptance were one *(Tzidkas Ha-and his acceptance* *were one.* Tzaddik 129).

David was possessed of the Holy Spirit, but God does not allow this precious gift to descend upon one who is sunk in sadness ... it descends only as a result of the joy derived from the performance of a mitzvah *(Shabbos 30b)* as it says: וְהָיָה כְּנַגֵּן הַמְנַגֵּן וַתְּהִי עָלָיו יַד ה׳ *'And it came to pass, when the minstrel played, that the hand of HASHEM came upon him' (II Kings 3:15).*

The basis of all prayer is to allow the heart to find happiness in God, as it says, הִתְהַלְלוּ בְּשֵׁם קָדְשׁוֹ יִשְׂמַח לֵב מְבַקְשֵׁי ה׳ *'Glory in His holy Name, let the heart of those who seek HASHEM rejoice' (Ps. 105:3).* Therefore, David, King of Israel, would accompany all his prayers and songs with music in order to fill his heart with joy flowing out of his love of God' *(Sefer Chassidim 18).*

IV. The Heart of the Nation:

Internal Influence

The king is the heart of his subjects. He embodies within himself their goals and aspirations. He sets their values and standards.

The king's slightest action sends shock-waves rippling through the ranks.

The king's slightest action sends shock-waves rippling through the ranks. If the king ascends, all rise. If the king strays, all are lost!

A harp was suspended over David's bed. At midnight, a north wind would blow through it causing it to play. When David heard the music he would arise and engage in Torah study. When the people of Israel heard David's voice studying Torah, they said, 'If David, the [busy] king of Israel is studying Torah, certainly we, too, must do so.' Immediately, they engaged themselves in Torah (*Eicha Rabbasi* 2:27).

Long before, far back in time, at the very dawn of history, Adam invested David with the power to bring his heirs back to the level of perfection which preceded the sin. For this purpose he endowed him with two gifts.

יפיות זו מלכות וזמירות הללו נתונות לו במתנה

'This beautiful one — I also present him with sovereignty and songs of praise.'

The first gift was sovereignty. The king wields the scepter with which he controls the conduct of great, masses of men. Temporal monarchs can dictate only the external behavior of their subjects, but only the

The king of Israel possesses the unique ability to influence the innermost feelings of his people, for he is nothing less than their collective heart.

king of Israel possesses the unique ability to influence the innermost feelings of his people, for he is nothing less than their collective heart.

The Torah was concerned lest the king's heart be distracted as it says וְלֹא יָסוּר לְבָבוֹ 'So that his heart shall not be turned away' (Deut. 17:17). For the heart of the king is the collective heart of the entire congregation of Israel. Therefore, the Torah ex-

horted the king more than all others to concentrate his heart on Torah study, 'all the days of his life' (Rambam, Hilchos Melachim 3:6).

It was this sense of obligation to the people which especially motivated David to seek the *Mesillas Yesharim* — the Path of the Upright. He possessed an unprecedented opportunity. If he could make his own heart upright, he could make upright the hearts of the masses.

David could not tolerate the slightest flaw in his own character because he realized the effect it would have on the people. David could not tolerate the slightest flaw in his own character because he realized the effect it would have on the people. In his efforts at purification and perfection, David strove to model himself after the righteous Patriarchs.

What is the סֵפֶר הַיָּשָׁר 'The Book of the Upright'? This is the Book of Abraham, Isaac and Jacob [the Book of *Genesis*] who are called יְשָׁרִים 'upright' (Avodah Zarah 25a).

Rambam states that the Patriarchs constantly concentrated on God without distraction or interruption. God was before their eyes as they grazed their sheep and as they tilled their soil.

'The purpose of all their efforts was to promulgate God's name in the world and to make upright the hearts of men so that they should come to love Him . . . their closeness to God was such that His Name became known to the world in connection with theirs, אֱלֹהֵי אַבְרָהָם, אֱלֹהֵי יִצְחָק, וֵאלֹהֵי יַעֲקֹב 'The God of Abraham, the God of Isaac, the God of Jacob' (Guide 3:51).

David, too, sought to achieve this level of uninterrupted concentration in God's service. It was in this vein that he said, שִׁוִּיתִי ה' לְנֶגְדִּי תָמִיד כִּי מִימִינִי בַּל אֶמּוֹט 'I have set HASHEM before me always, because He is at my right hand, I shall not falter' (Ps. 16:8). I *I do not turn my thoughts away from God; He is like my right hand.* do not turn my thoughts away from God; He is like my right hand which I do not forget even for a moment on account of the ease of its motions. Therefore, I shall not be moved, I shall not fall (ibid.).

The Test

'They were tested
but you were not.'

'Rav Yehuda said in the name of Rav: A person should never ask to be put to the test, for David, king of Israel put himself to the test — and failed. He asked: 'Sovereign of the Universe, why do people say, 'The God of Abraham, the God of Isaac, the God of Jacob,' but they do not say, 'the God of David'? God replied, 'They were tested but you were not.' David responded,

בְּחָנֵנִי ה׳ וְנַסֵּנִי צָרְפָה כִלְיוֹתַי וְלִבִּי. כִּי חַסְדְּךָ לְנֶגֶד עֵינָי וְהִתְהַלַּכְתִּי בַּאֲמִתֶּךָ.

Examine me, HASHEM, and put me to the test, refine my intellect and my heart. For Your kindness is before my eyes, and I have walked in Your truth (Psalms 26: 2-3). God said: 'I will grant your request. Furthermore, I will do for you what I never did for the Patriarchs. I never warned them of the nature of their trial, but I inform you that your test will be in the realm of carnal desire [but even this warning will be to no avail for you are as yet unprepared for this test]'.

David's greatness was that he was יְפֵה עֵינַיִם, *that he possessed beautiful eyes (I Sam. 16:12)* — and it was his mission to maintain his clarity of vision no matter what the temptation. Now he demanded a test. His 'eyes' would be tested — by being confronted with a sight that would draw them from the purity of heaven to the desires of earth.

His 'eyes' would
be tested — by
being confronted
with a sight that
would draw them
from the purity of
heaven to the
desires of earth.

Immediately, *He walked on the roof of the king's palace and from the roof he saw a woman bathing, and the woman was of exceedingly beautiful appearance (II Sam. 11:2).*

As we read these lines, we sense the nature of David's failure. The moment his eyes glimpsed Bath Sheba, they were distracted from God. The Scriptures take pain to tell us that not only did he see her, he noticed well that, *'the woman was of exceedingly beautiful appearance'*. The test is over, David had

failed to imitate the Patriarchs who were never distracted from God!

The ensuing events demonstrate the serious damage which had been inflicted on David's יְפֵה עֵינַיִם *'beautiful eyes'*.

Is it possible that he sinned and yet the Holy Presence was with him?

'Whoever says that David sinned is in error. For, it says, וַיְהִי דָוִד לְכָל דְּרָכָו מַשְׂכִּיל וַה' עִמּוֹ *'And David dealt intelligently in all his ways and HASHEM was with him'* (I Samuel 18:14). Is it possible that he sinned and yet the Holy Presence was with him? If so, what is meant [by the Prophet Nathan's admonition] מַדּוּעַ בָּזִיתָ אֶת דְּבַר ה' לַעֲשׂוֹת הָרַע בְּעֵינוֹ *'Why have you disgraced the word of HASHEM to do that which is evil in His eye'* (II Sam. 12:9)? In truth it merely says לַעֲשׂוֹת הָרַע *'to do evil'* [but not that he *'did'* evil]. This teaches that David only *desired* to do evil, but, he did not actually do it' (*Shabbos* 56a; *Rashi*).

She was a virtuous woman. David's sin was in his heart.

With his hands, David took an unmarried woman, a woman who had received a bill of divorce from her husband before he went out to war [for it was the custom of David's army that soldiers divorced their wives conditionally to avoid the tragedy of women unable to remarry in the event their husbands were missing in action]. She was a virtuous woman who was perfectly suited to be the queen of a righteous king. David's sin was in his heart, and as *Rambam* stresses:

'The Torah was concerned lest the king's heart be distracted . . . For the heart of the king is the collective heart of all Israel . . .'[1]

1. And what of Uriah, whose death was brought about by the command of David? The Talmud cites three opinions: Rav said: 'When you carefully scrutinize the actions of David, you find him liable for nothing other than the death of Uriah...' Rav Yosef said: 'He is not culpable for Uriah's death, for Uriah was guilty of rebelling against the king...' Rabbi said: 'David should have tried Uriah before the Sanhedrin but he did not' (*Shabbos* 56a). The king is empowered to execute a rebel without following normal judicial procedures. Nevertheless, David should have consulted the Sanhedrin to insure that Uriah was truly to be considered as a rebel (*Tosafos* ibid.).

The haunting words of the *Midrash* loom before our eyes:

> Samuel said: He is אַדְמוֹנִי, an Esau-like ruddy killer! But the Holy One, Blessed be He said: This one is different from Esau. He is *'with beautiful eyes'*. David slays his foes only upon the advice and guidance of Sanhedrin!

Here David faltered. The ruddiness overwhelmed the beautiful eyes. Passion blurred his vision. In requesting the test he claimed: כִּי חַסְדְּךָ לְנֶגֶד עֵינָי *'For Your kindness is before my eyes'* (Ps. 26:3). Elsewhere he repeated this theme with even greater emphasis: שִׁוִּיתִי ה' לְנֶגְדִּי תָמִיד *'I placed God straight before me always'* (Ps. 16:8). But after he failed he lamented: וְחַטָּאתִי נֶגְדִּי תָמִיד *'My sin is before me always'* (Ps. 51:5).

The word חָטָא literally means *'to miss the mark'*.

Only that man who aims to achieve the perfect alignment of שִׁוִּיתִי ה' לְנֶגְדִּי תָמִיד, placing God before him always, can fully sense the heartbreak in the words וְחַטָּאתִי נֶגְדִּי תָמִיד, *My sin is before me always* (Harav Gifter).

To correct his error David turned to Adam's second gift, the gift of song.

V. The Sweet Singer of Israel

יפיות זו מלכות וזמירות הללו נתונות לו במתנה
ע' שנה שיחיה ויהא מזמר לפניך

This beautiful one — I present him with sovereignty and songs of praise for the seventy years of his life, so that he shall sing before You!

יְהִיוּ לְרָצוֹן אִמְרֵי פִי

'May the expressions of my mouth find favor' (Ps. 19:15). When David completed the *Book of Psalms* he requested of God: 'Let these psalms be studied and contemplated like נְגָעִים וְאֹהָלוֹת, [the complex

and weighty tractates of] ritual cleanliness'
(Midrash Shocher Tov).

Harav Gifter points out that it was not because of
their depth and difficulty that David specified the
tractates of ritual cleanliness. There may be other
tractates even more difficult to comprehend. He
mentioned only them because they represent the entire order of the *Mishnah* in which they appear, the
order of טָהֳרוֹת *'Purities'*. David begged that *Psalms*
should not remain a form of sacred poetry. He
wanted it endowed with the same purifying effect on
the human soul as the laws of ritual purity.

David begged that Psalms should not remain a form of sacred poetry.

The musical accompaniment to *Psalms* represents
the intellect which is a symbol of purity because it is
divorced from the material world. No other art form
is as ethereal and intangible as music [which creates
no object of substance and body, only sound waves
travelling on thin air, which swiftly fade away]
(*Ramban, Shaar haGemul* 9).

The very word זִמְרָה, *song*, alludes to the unique
properties of song and its purifying effect on the
soul. Many say that this word is related to זְמִירָה
'pruning'. The tree cannot flourish or even survive if
its vitality is sapped by dead bark and diseased
branches. Cutting away the undesirable portions assures the continued growth of a thriving tree. The
same concept applies to spiritual development.
Coarse character and low morals rot the soul. Lust
and greed squander the precious energies of the
spirit. These undesirable traits may be *'pruned'* with
the aid of זְמִירוֹת *'songs'*.

Lust and greed squander the precious energies of the spirit.

Song expresses the inner harmony of the singer
and of creation. David sings. The frog sings. The sun
sings. When they join together in the exultation of
acknowledging God's handiwork, the sway of evil is
pruned away to wither and disintegrate.

Abarbanel (I Samuel 16:23) explains that David
possessed the unique ability to play divine music
which filled the emptiness of the soul, driving
away its sin-bred melancholy. No other man could
claim this talent, because David's skill was not a
human achievement. He did not become a virtuoso

because of long hours of practice and mastery of musical techniques. His was a God-given gift bestowed upon him from above at the moment Samuel anointed him to be king. Because David was מְשִׁיחַ אֱלֹהֵי יַעֲקֹב 'The anointed of the God of Jacob' — therefore he became נְעִים זְמִרוֹת יִשְׂרָאֵל 'The sweet singer of Israel' (II Sam. 23:1).

Because David was 'The anointed of the God of Jacob', therefore he became 'The sweet singer of Israel.'

Extol virtue! Sing of kindness! Praise God and serve Him!

Denounce evil! Condemn the wicked! Pray for protection from the evil inclination!

Set your values straight with the aid of זְמִירוֹת, the 'pruning' quality of songs and you are on the unhindered path to purity.

Tehillim — Song of Repentance

As his seventy years of song drew to a close, David uttered his last exalted words, beginning: רוּחַ ה' דִּבֶּר בִּי וּמִלָּתוֹ עַל לְשׁוֹנִי, *'The spirit of HASHEM spoke through me and His word was on my lips'* (ibid. v. 2). Indeed, he had spent a lifetime as the speaker — the singer — of God's most exalted word. Before the prophet quoted David's last statement, he described the aging king — indeed, he summed up in a few phrases the essence of the man.

וְאֵלֶּה דִּבְרֵי דָוִד הָאַחֲרֹנִים נְאֻם דָּוִד בֶּן יִשַׁי וּנְאֻם הַגֶּבֶר הֻקַם עָל מְשִׁיחַ אֱלֹהֵי יַעֲקֹב וּנְעִים זְמִרוֹת יִשְׂרָאֵל

And these are the last words of David: 'So said David, son of Jesse, and so said the man lifted on high, the anointed of the God of Jacob, the sweet singer of Israel (ibid. v. 1).

The Sages comment on the words הֻקַם עָל lifted on high, that they allude to another aspect of David's greatness: הֵקִים עוּלָהּ שֶׁל תְּשׁוּבָה, *'he raised up the yoke of repentance'.* David was the first to repent and paved the way for all future penitents (*Moed Katan* 16b, see *Rashi*).

David paved the way for all future penitents.

Concerning David's role as the trailblazer on the path of repentance, *Maharal* notes that in truth there were many sinners who repented during the centuries before David's birth. Cain and Reuben are

only two examples. Adam himself bitterly repented his sin *(Eruvin* 18b). However, this repentance was limited. They were primarily concerned with improving themselves alone, as individuals. Not so the penitence of David. His goal was to bring about a spiritual renaissance for all of Israel for he was their first true king.

Furthermore, explains *Maharal,* תְּשׁוּבָה literally means *'return';* a return to the pure source of life, a rebirth, a fresh start. Adam was the beginning of human life and he bequeathed seventy years of his extraordinary life to David. Thus David alone had the unprecedented opportunity to bring mankind back to the very roots of existence, to the level of Adam before the sin *(Nesivos Olam, Nesiv HaTeshuvah* 4).

The commentaries note another aspect of David's unique excellence in the art of repentance. Most men will eventually admit mistakes, albeit grudgingly. However, at the moment when they are accused of sin their first reaction is to find some justification; the burden of guilt is too heavy to shoulder all at once. David was different. He readily accepted the harshest critique and rebuke. David received divine assistance to purify himself completely through repentance, for he never hesitated to admit his sin and willingly accepted the punishment he deserved. Not so King Saul. Nowhere in Scriptures do we find him confessing his guilt or accepting affliction. Therefore he was rejected *(Maharsha, Yoma* 22b).

Adam, too, failed to acknowledge his sin when he was first accused:

וַיֹּאמֶר הָאָדָם הָאִשָּׁה אֲשֶׁר נָתַתָּה עִמָּדִי הִוא נָתְנָה
לִי מִן הָעֵץ וָאֹכֵל

And Adam said: 'The woman whom You gave to be with me, she gave me of the tree and I ate' (Gen. 3:12).

Adam attributed his failure to the woman. Thus, by implication, he blamed not himself, but his Maker — He Who, in His mercy, presented Adam with a mate — for his guilt. He failed to acknowledge his own guilt and immediately repent. However, when

the prophet accused David of sinning with Bath Sheba, he responded simply, חָטָאתִי 'I have sinned!' (II Sam. 12:13) (Sforno ibid.).

Hymns of the Nation

'All of you are pleasing and devoted. However, it is David who will compose Tehillim through all of you.'

Ten righteous men [Adam, Malki Zedek, Abraham, Moses, David, Solomon, Assaf, and the three sons of Korach. Some add Jedusun: see *Rashi* to 1:1.] sought to compose the Book of *Tehillim*. [cf. *comm. Psalms* 1:1] The Holy One, Blessed be He, said to them, 'All of you are pleasing and devoted, praiseworthy and fit to sing a hymn before me. However, it is David who will compose *Tehillim* through all of you. Why? Because his voice is sweet! As it says, נְעִים זְמִרוֹת יִשְׂרָאֵל 'The sweet singer of Israel'. Who makes the songs of all Israel sweet? David!' (*Shir HaShirim Rabbah* 4:3).

The seventy years of David's life are the years of Adam who was fashioned by God Himself. Therefore, no man of flesh and blood, born of a mother can compare his songs with those of David who personifies the father of all men. David alone sings the songs of the entire creation (*Mabit*, Introduction to *Perek Shira*).

Many have composed exquisite hymns to God, but their verses are confined to their personal experience. Their songs are written in the singular, not the plural. Even when recording miracles and events of national import, their feelings are essentially private ones.

David transcended these narrow limitations. His universal soul blended and merged with the spirits of all men — present, past and future. He felt and understood the vast panorama of all human feelings in all situations. Every subtle nuance and variation of human emotion finds expression in these wondrous psalms. This talent too was a result of David's יְפֵה עֵינַיִם 'Beautiful eyes'.

Every subtle nuance and variation of human emotion finds expression in these wondrous psalms.

עינא דדוד הוה מרקמא מכל זיני גוונין. לא הוה
עינא בעלמא שפירא למחזי כעינא דדוד כל
גוונין דעלמא מנצצין ביה

*David's eyes were a mixture of all colors.
There was no eye in the world whose vision was as good as David's eye. All of the
colors in the world sparkled in David's
eyes (Zohar, Balak).*

*David observed
life from a
universal vantage
point; never was
his scope
constricted.*
David observed life from a universal vantage
point; never was his scope constricted. In every
event he was able to detect the broad spectrum of
colors which emerged. In his personal misfortunes he
saw a reflection of the tragedies plaguing the nation
down through the pages of history. In his victories
David caught a glimpse of the ultimate triumph and
redemption of his people. He had the ability and
genius to be stimulated and inspired so profoundly
by events that he could soar above the boundaries of
time; and sing of past, present, and future in the
same breath, with the same words.

A double strand of meaning runs through the
fabric of the psalms. Those actually written in the
singular were motivated primarily by personal
events in which David recognized traces of national
concern. Those written in the plural describe
national experiences with which David identified
personally (cf. *Pesachim* 117a).

*A Voice
for all
Mankind*
The *Netziv* of Volozhin notes that David's need to
make a special request that psalms be considered like
the tractates of purity, indicates that there was doubt
whether this request would be fulfilled [cf. *Nefesh
HaChaim* 4:2]. If so, why did he not devote himself
to the study of the tractates of purity themselves?

*His concern was
for the nation, for
the people of all
generations who
would turn to his
psalms for
enlightenment.*
Netziv answers that David had no doubt about the
exalting, purifying effect of *Tehillim* on *himself*. He
was inspired by the holy spirit; new vistas opened up
before him with every word he uttered. His concern
was for the nation, for the people of all generations
who would turn to his psalms for enlightenment and

inspiration. David's wish was that every man should find in it some parallel to his own circumstances and a vehicle for his particular need for expression (*Haamek Shaaloh, Kidmas Ha'emek* 3:5).

Adam bestowed two gifts upon David, 'sovereignty' and 'song'. In truth, both gifts are one.

Only the sovereign who is 'the collective heart of all the nation' can give sweet expression to the songs of the entire nation. Only the sovereign who is *'the collective heart of all the nation'* can give sweet expression to the songs of the entire nation. The tears rolling down from every eye flow through the heart of the king and spring forth anew as collective chants of refreshment and consolation. The laughter resounding from countless lips reverberates on the monarch's tongue as echoes of infinite shouts of praise and thanksgiving. 'Sovereignty' and 'song' are one.

VI. A Monument for Adam:

אין ישיבה בעזרה אלא למלכי בית דוד בלבד
'No one may sit in the Temple courtyard, [not even the ministering angels — they too must stand in honor of the Almighty *(Rashi)*] except for the kings of the House of David. [God Himself accorded them this honor to demonstrate that their sovereignty is complete and total *(Rashi)*] *(Sotah* 40b).

Nowhere, in all of the Scriptures or the Talmud, do we find an obligation incumbent upon the king to build himself a palace for the sake of his honor.

Where then is the seat of Davidic royalty? The Temple! Where then is the seat of Davidic royalty? The Temple! It was in this sacred palace that the *'songs'* of *'sovereignty'* were meant to be sung. And in the Temple, the songs of only one human being were ever performed — the נְעִים זְמִרוֹת יִשְׂרָאֵל, *the sweet singer of Israel (II Sam.* 23:1 see *Rashi).*

Throughout the Books of *Samuel* and *Psalms* we find again and again that David's lifelong aspiration

was to build the Beis Hamikdash. In truth, not only was this magnificent building destined to be his spiritual palace, but even the location of the Temple had a very special bond with David's soul.

The place where David and Solomon built the altar in the field of Aravna was the same place where Abraham built his altar and bound Isaac on it for the sacrifice.

Rambam quotes a tradition that the place where David and Solomon built the altar in the field of Aravna was the same place where Abraham built his altar and bound Isaac on it for the sacrifice. It was there that Noah built his altar when he left the Ark, there that Cain and Abel offered their sacrifices. And it was there that Adam offered a sacrifice when he was created, and it was from that very place that he was created. The Sages said: אָדָם מִמְּקוֹם כַּפָּרָתוֹ נִבְרָא — '*Adam was created from the place where he was destined to find atonement*' (*Hilchos Beis Ha-Bechirah* 2:2).

Psalms represents David's effort to raise Israel back to the level of Adam before the sin. These superb stanzas achieve their ultimate power when they are performed in their proper setting. The Temple Mount, the birth place of Adam, is the shrine dedicated to man in all his primeval glory. Let all who have strayed return to this shrine and contemplate the perfection of man. Let the Temple be the destination of all who seek to travel the '*Path of the Upright*'.

Let the Temple be the destination of all who seek to travel the 'Path of the Upright.'

Small wonder then that Adam's name is featured prominently in the very first words of *Leviticus*, the book devoted to Temple service.

אָדָם כִּי יַקְרִיב מִכֶּם קָרְבָּן לַה'

'*A man* [lit. '*Adam*'] *from among you who will bring a sacrifice to HASHEM*' (*Lev.* 1:2).

The more common expression אִישׁ '*man*' is deleted here in favor of the term אָדָם, *Adam*. *Rashi* explains: 'This comes to teach us that just as Adam brought a sacrifice to God entirely free of any trace of theft [because it was immediately after his creation when the world was his alone, before he sinned], so, too, for all generations should men bring sacrifices which are not the fruits of ill-gotten gain!'

How well these words complement *Ramban's* description of Adam *(Gen. 2:9):* Of Adam, King Solomon once said, עָשָׂה הָאֱלֹקִים אֶת הָאָדָם יָשָׁר *'God made Adam upright' (Ecc. 7:29).* He followed one consistent pattern of behavior. He was not tempted by a desire to acquire what was not his. But he sinned, for, וְהֵמָּה בִקְשׁוּ חִשְׁבֹנוֹת רַבִּים, *'They sought out many calculations' (ibid.).*When man was no longer satisfied with his own lot and sought to possess that which was outside his domain, his heart became filled with many inconsistent, conflicting calculations and desires.

In preparing for the construction of the Temple, David found the opportunity to rectify the flawed human desire that had been ingrained in mankind by Adam's sin — the lust for acquisition.

Chidah (Devash L'fi) explains that Adam was responsible for bringing poverty into the world. As a result of his sin mankind was cursed: *'By the sweat of your brow you shall eat bread' (Gen. 3:19).* David attempted to rectify this by impoverishing himself for the benefit of the world. He sacrificed all his possessions and dedicated all his treasures to the cause of constructing the Temple. He said of himself many times — וַאֲנִי עָנִי וְאֶבְיוֹן *'As for me, I am poor and needy' (Psalms 40:18, 70:6 86:1, 109:22).*

VII. Satisfaction and Selflessness:

When David completed the Book of Psalms he was uplifted with satisfaction [that he had succeeded in accomplishing his purpose on earth]. He said to the Holy One, Blessed be He, 'Does there exist any creature which you created anywhere in the entire universe which sings songs and praises which surpass mine?' At that moment a frog passed and said, 'David, do not be uplifted with pride, for I sing songs and praises which surpass yours! . . . Not only that, but I also perform a mitzvah. On

the seashore there is a creature which draws its sustenance from the sea. When that creature is hungry it takes me and eats me. That is my *mitzvah'* (*Introduction to Perek Shira*).

The song of the frog is:

בָּרוּךְ שֵׁם כְּבוֹד מַלְכוּתוֹ לְעוֹלָם וָעֶד

'Blessed be the name of the glory of His Kingdom forever and ever' (*Perek Shira*).

When Moses ascended to heaven he heard the ministering angels proclaiming *'Blessed be the name of the glory of His Kingdom forever and ever'*. Only they are pure enough to proclaim this statement publicly (*Midrash Parshas Vo'eschanan; Tur Orach Chaim* 610).

Do frogs actually compose songs like men? Do frogs actually compose songs like men? The very concept is beyond our comprehension, yet the song of the frog is that which is sung by the heavenly angels! Indeed frogs have no need to compose music and lyrics as we understand them. The most wonderful song a frog can sing is being itself. The most wonderful service the frog can render is to faithfully live out its life, playing its role in the biological cycle, helping maintain the harmonious order of the world. When all parts of creation merge together in perfect order, this in itself is the most impressive song of praise, extolling the magnificence of God's handiwork.

When a creation performs its function selflessly, under all circumstances, despite any obstacles, it sings a song to God and merits the description *'Creature of truth, whose achievement is truth, and who does not deviate from the path set for his mission'*. The frog gives up even its life in order not to *'deviate from the path set for his mission'*. It does not consider its own function as more important than the function of the seashore creature which devours it. *If the harmony of creation requires the frog to offer itself as food to another, it does so — and that is its glory and song!* If the harmony of creation requires the frog to offer itself as food to another, it does so — and that is its glory and its song!

In this sense, David fell short of the achievement of the lowly frog. Although one of the humblest men

who ever lived, David still could not match the total selflessness of the frog.

The function of all creatures in the life-cycle of the world is to recognize and praise God.

How did David presume to think that no creature could sing songs and praises surpassing his?

When David completed the *Book of Psalms* there was no reason for him to be *'uplifted with satisfaction'* for he had merely performed his duty! How did David presume to think that no creature could sing songs and praises surpassing his?

VIII. Beyond Psalms:

The Cycle of the Moon

The *Midrash* derives from הַחֹדֶשׁ הַזֶּה לָכֶם *'This month* [lit. *'this new moon']* shall be for you' (Ex. 12:2) that the royalty of Israel will resemble the cycle of the moon. It will endure for thirty generations just as the month has thirty days. The light of Jewish royalty began to rise in the time of the Patriarch Abraham whom the Canaanites called a *godly prince (Gen.* 23:5). David (whose name has the numerical value of 14) was fourteen generations from Abraham and resembled the nearly full moon. Solomon, was the fifteenth generation; in his days the royal house of David reached its zenith like the full moon. Then the House of David began to decline like the waning moon until its total eclipse with King Tzidkiyahu of Judea who was thirty generations from Abraham. In

In his time the royalty of David disappeared like the vanished moon.

his time the royalty of David disappeared into the darkness of exile, like the vanished moon. Nebuchadnezzar blinded King Tzidkiyahu *(II Kings* 25:7) symbolizing the total disappearance of the moon's light.

Therefore, every month, when we sanctify the new moon, we proclaim דָּוִד מֶלֶךְ יִשְׂרָאֵל חַי וְקַיָּם *'David, king of Israel lives on and endures!' (Rabbeinu Bachya, Genesis* 38:30).

Similarly, the congregation of Israel is destined to join once again with her mate, who is the Holy One,

Blessed be He, just like the moon which will renew its status as equal to the sun, as it says, 'כִּי שֶׁמֶשׁ וּמָגֵן ה 'For HASHEM is a sun and a shield' (Ps. 84:12). Therefore, it is customary to dance and celebrate when sanctifying the new moon with a merriment resembling that of an actual wedding (Rama to Shulchan Aruch, Orach Chaim 426:2).

Names of Messiah

The three letters of Adam's name represent the initials of three men

The three letters of Adam's name 'א' 'ד' 'ם' — represent the initials of three men אָדָם 'Adam', דָוִד 'David', מָשִׁיחַ 'Messiah'. What Adam began, David continued, and Messiah will complete (Zohar; Toras Chaim, Sanhedrin 107a).

The Sages offer many names for Messiah. In Rav Shila's yeshiva they said that Messiah's name was Shila. In Rav Yanai's yeshiva they said his name was Yanun. In Rav Chanina's yeshiva they said his name was Chanina (Sanhedrin 98b). These opinions are not in conflict and God forbid that they be construed as expressions of chauvinism. For, the Messiah will be a universal man who embodies the best traits of humanity. Each saint possesses an outstanding trait which singles him out from all others. But Messiah is blessed with the finest collective qualities of them all. His name is a blend of the names of them all, thus each yeshivah understood the greatness of Messiah as an embodiment of the greatness of its own sainted head (Maharal, Netzach Yisroel 41).

Each yeshivah understood the greatness of Messiah as an embodiment of the greatness of its own sainted head.

And he will have another name — the name of his illustrious forebear who united within himself the infinite virtues that were embodied in the first human on the first day of creation.

> If he will be from the living, David will be his name. If he will be from the dead, David will be his name (Eicha Rabbosi 1:57).

The characteristic of יְפֵה עֵינַיִם 'Beautiful eyes' epitomizes the kings of the Davidian line. Their eyes blaze with a multitude of colors for their shine reflects the light of countless eyes. Even in the darkest days of this royal house, its scions were blessed with this trait in extraordinary proportions:

Five men were blessed with traits which were a semblance of the Divine ... Tzidkiyahu was blessed with wondrous eyes (*Sotah* 10a).

The eyes of King Tzidkiyahu resembled those of Adam (*Yalkut Shimoni; Melachim* 252).

The stages of man in this world are three.

The stages of man in this world are three. One — Adam before the sin. Two — Adam after the sin. Three — what Adam *could* have become had he accomplished his three-hour mission and not sinned. That potential perfection will be realized by mankind in the future (*Daas Tevunos*).

Rabbi Chaim of Volozhin (*Nefesh HaChaim* 3:11) observes that in the days of Messiah, Israel will once again achieve the clarity of vision which they attained at Sinai. Their vision will not be distorted by any distractions placed before their eyes, for they shall 'see' with their *ears*, guided only by the spoken word of God! This is foretold by the prophet:

וְנִגְלָה כְּבוֹד ה׳ וְרָאוּ כָל בָּשָׂר יַחְדָּו כִּי פִּי ה׳ דִּבֵּר

'*And the glory of HASHEM shall be revealed and all flesh together shall see it, for the mouth of HASHEM has spoken*' (*Isaiah* 40:55).

'*All flesh*' will share in the Messianic gift of '*beautiful eyes*', and '*all together shall see it*'. Together — in harmony, free from dissension; in brotherhood, without jealousy or pride. Each creature will recognize its own straight path and interfere with no other. '*Creatures of truth, whose achievement is truth and who do not deviate from the path set for their mission.*'

Adam's universal melody will be struck up again — never to be interrupted. Man will discover that the *Psalms* we sing today are a rehearsal for the perfect symphony of tomorrow. Messiah will echo the timeless words of *Tehillim* and procede further and far beyond!

Man will discover that the Psalms we sing today are a rehearsal for the perfect symphony of tomorrow.

וּבְמַקְהֲלוֹת רִבְבוֹת עַמְּךָ בֵּית יִשְׂרָאֵל בְּרִנָּה יִתְפָּאֵר שִׁמְךָ מַלְכֵּנוּ בְּכָל דּוֹר וָדוֹר שֶׁכֵּן חוֹבַת כָּל הַיְצוּרִים לְפָנֶיךָ ה׳ אֱלֹהֵינוּ וֵאלֹהֵי אֲבוֹתֵינוּ

לְהוֹדוֹת לְהַלֵּל לְשַׁבֵּחַ לְפָאֵר לְרוֹמֵם לְהַדֵּר לְבָרֵךְ
לְעַלֵּה וּלְקַלֵּס עַל כָּל דִּבְרֵי שִׁירוֹת וְתִשְׁבְּחוֹת דָּוִד
בֶּן יִשַׁי עַבְדְּךָ מְשִׁיחֶךָ

*In the assemblies of the myriads of Your
people, the House of Israel; with joyous
song shall Your Name, our King, be
glorified in every generation. For this is the
duty of all creatures towards You,
HASHEM our God and God of our fathers:*

*To thank and praise,
laud and glorify,
extol and honor,
bless and exalt,
and acclaim You!*

*Even beyond all the
songs of praise of David,
son of Jesse,
Your servant, Your anointed.*

Tehillim

Moses presented Israel with the Five Books of the Torah and David presented Israel with the Five Books of Psalms. Moses concluded the Torah with the blessing אַשְׁרֶיךָ יִשְׂרָאֵל מִי כָמוֹךָ, 'How praiseworthy are you, Israel, who can compare to you?' (Deut. 33:29). David began his psalms with Moses' concluding expression, אַשְׁרֵי הָאִישׁ, 'The praises of man' (Midrash Shocher Tov; Yalkut).

God created man with this one purpose in mind — that he should enjoy great fortune in this world and the next (Sforno).

Man need not search far for his fortune; he was created as a model of perfection with the basic components for excellence within himself. For this reason, Mesillas Yesharim observes that the prime duty of man is to protect his inherent goodness from external forces which seek to corrupt it. This is known as זְהִירוּת 'watchfulness.' David emphasized this truth by beginning his formula of fortune with a warning to avoid the wicked and the sinners (v. 1).

The next step on the 'Path of the upright' is זְרִיזוּת 'zeal' i.e. the performance of God's commandments with fiery passion and enthusiasm. David stresses this in the second verse of this psalm: 'But his desire is in the Torah of HASHEM, and in his Torah he, meditates day and night.'

Finally, the Psalmist assures the person who follows these guidelines that he will surely flourish forever (v. 3).

א אַשְׁרֵי־הָאִישׁ אֲשֶׁר | לֹא הָלַךְ בַּעֲצַת
רְשָׁעִים וּבְדֶרֶךְ חַטָּאִים לֹא עָמָד וּבְמוֹשַׁב
ב לֵצִים לֹא יָשָׁב: כִּי אִם בְּתוֹרַת יהוה

1. אַשְׁרֵי — *The praises.*

This generally unfamiliar translation of אַשְׁרֵי follows *Rashi* and *Metzudos* who render אַשְׁרֵי as a plural noun meaning תְּהִלּוֹת *'praises'*. In this verse the Psalmist introduces a listing of the acts of the righteous man which make him worthy of praise.

Sforno and *Malbim* understand אַשְׁרֵי as an adjective thus rendering it *'praiseworthy is [the man].'*

Radak* and *Meiri* point out that the plural form, אַשְׁרֵי, *'praises'*, rather than the singular, denotes that a single isolated act is insufficient to make a man worthy of praise. Only that man is lauded whose good deeds are constant and consistent.

[Many translate this word as *'happy'*, *'blessed'*, *'fortunate'*, and there are traditional commentaries which lend support to this view.]

Malbim explains the difference between אֲשֶׁר, and הַצְלָחָה. הַצְלָחָה refers to successful achievement in the material and worldly realm. אֲשֶׁר, however, applies to spiritual attainments which enhance a person's share in the Hereafter.

The Sages (*Berachos* 10a) teach that the first two chapters of *Psalms* are counted as one. When a composition was particularly dear to David, he opened it with אַשְׁרֵי, and concluded it with אַשְׁרֵי [see *comm.* to 19:15.]
He began this chapter with אַשְׁרֵי הָאִישׁ and concluded with אַשְׁרֵי כָּל חוֹסֵי בוֹ.

Tosfos (ibid.) comments that this rule is not confined exclusively to the word אַשְׁרֵי. It applies to any psalm where the opening exclamatory statement is

similar to the closing one, such as תְּהִלָּה, *praise.* or הַלְלוּיָהּ, *praise God.* [This rule demonstrates that the fortunate man who sings God's praises is totally immersed in the ecstasy of God's closeness. Nothing can dampen his buoyant spirits. His joy is constant, continuing undiminished from beginning to end.]

Hirsch maintains that the root of אַשְׁרֵי is אַשּׁוּר, *a stride forward.* The wicked fancy themselves as modern and progressive in tune with the times. They condemn as primitive and backward those who cling to Torah. The Psalmist tells us here that in reality only the righteous stride forward towards meaningful development.

הָאִישׁ — *Of [the] man.*

The definitive prefix, ה, denotes *'the'* man *par excellence*, brimming with youth, vitality and desire. Yet he controls all of his inclinations and avoids the temptation to revel and carouse in bad company (*Otzar Nechmad*).

אֲשֶׁר לֹא הָלַךְ בַּעֲצַת רְשָׁעִים — *[Are] That he walked not in the counsel of the wicked.*

Ibn Ezra suggests that the verb *'walk'* is used in connection with the wicked because they are never satisfied. They constantly move on in search of gratification, as it says, וְהָרְשָׁעִים כַּיָּם נִגְרָשׁ כִּי הַשְׁקֵט לֹא יוּכָל, *For the wicked are like the trouble-tossed sea, which cannot be still* (Isaiah 57:20).

[The root of רָשָׁע is akin to רַעַשׁ, *noise*, specifically the din raised by turbulent motion.]

Radak adds that the word עֵצָה, *counsel*, is particularly suited to the

[Please note: *The source for every excerpt in the Commentary has been documented. Whenever the author has inserted a comment or explanatory remark of his own, it is framed in square brackets.*]

* *Selections attributed to* Radak *in this volume are taken from his unabridged commentary published in* Otzar Tehillos Yisrael.

The praises of Man are that he walked not in the counsel of the wicked, And stood not in the path of the sinful, and sat not in the session of scorners.

wicked because they enjoy advising and persuading others to join in their evil revelries, as if masses were a justification for their lack of righteousness.

Rav Dessler warns against seeking the advice of the wicked even in worldly matters which are completely divorced from ritual. It is impossible for the wicked man, an avowed enemy of Hashem, not to inject some of his venom into any discussion. The Sages teach that merely looking at the face of the evildoer can cause serious spiritual damage *(Megillah* 28a); how much more detrimental must it be to take the words of the wicked to heart!

וּבְדֶרֶךְ חַטָּאִים לֹא עָמָד — *And stood not in the path of the sinful.*

Hirsch analyzes the difference between the רָשָׁע, *a wicked person,* and the חוֹטֵא, *a sinful one.* The wicked רָשָׁע deliberately counsels lawlessness and disregard for Torah. The חוֹטֵא, however, errs unintentionally. [חָטָא literally means *'to miss the mark'*]. Nevertheless, he too is condemned because of his frivolous and lighthearted attitude towards God. He who regards the Divine directives with proper reverence and awe takes all necessary precautions to prevent mistakes.

וּבְמוֹשַׁב לֵצִים לֹא יָשָׁב — *And sat not in the session of the scorners.*

Ibn Ezra derives the word לֵץ,

'scorner' from מֵלִיץ *'interpreter'.* Just as the interpreter transmits the ideas of one party to another, so the ridiculer transmits the secrets of one man to another in order to shame him. He is the antithesis of the עָנָיו *'the humble man'* who would never dishonor his neighbor.

Metzudas Zion notes the similarity between the word לֵץ, *'scorner',* and מְלִיצָה, *'a polished phrase.'* The man who ridicules others takes pain to make his verbal attack more acceptable to his audience by couching his repulsive words of ridicule in finely polished phrases.

The haughty mentality of the לֵץ is summed up in the two letters which compose his name, ל, *lamed* (לָמֵד = scholar), צ, *tzaddik,* (צַדִּיק = righteous man). The arrogant לֵץ considers himself a profound scholar and a saint. He looks down upon others as his inferiors; hence, he feels he has license to ridicule them *(Panim Yafos).*[1]

Rambam (Hilchos Tum'as Tzora'as 16:10) emphasizes that although the scorners commit no crime with their bodies, they accomplish terrible things with their tongues. They begin by gathering in taverns, exchanging idle gossip. Eventually the conversation turns to scorning the righteous, and from there it descends to denouncing the authority of the prophets. Ultimately they come to deny God Himself. To

1. Rabbi Chaninah ben Teradyon says: Whenever two sit together without words of Torah between them, it is nothing but a מוֹשַׁב לֵצִים, *a session of scorners (Avos* 3:2).

Tosafos Yom Tov (ibid.) notes that the Mishnah does not say that each individual sits idly without studying Torah. Rather, he takes pains to emphasize that there is no *exchange* of Torah thoughts between them. This implies that each may be deeply engrossed in Torah study, but is oblivious to his neighbor. Why doesn't each one pause for a moment to ask his neighbor a question or to share a stimulating thought? This indicates that each one in his heart may deem such an exchange a waste of time becaue he secretly scorns the scholastic aptitude of his neighbor. Although they utter not one evil word and waste not a moment from Torah study, these two snobs are branded as לֵצִים, *'scorners',* because, their proud hearts are saturated with scorn.

ג חֶפְצוֹ וּבְתוֹרָתוֹ יֶהְגֶּה יוֹמָם וָלָיְלָה: וְהָיָה
כְּעֵץ שָׁתוּל עַל־פַּלְגֵי מַיִם אֲשֶׁר פִּרְיוֹ |
יִתֵּן בְּעִתּוֹ וְעָלֵהוּ לֹא־יִבּוֹל וְכֹל אֲשֶׁר־

the man whose soul is rotted with scorn, nothing is sacred.

According to *Midrash Shocher Tov* this verse describes Adam who lamented after his sin, 'How praiseworthy I would have been had I not stood on the path of the evil serpent! How praiseworthy I would have been had I not sat in the place where he came to scorn [the command and warning of God]!'

Rashi sums up the lesson of this verse, מִתּוֹךְ שֶׁלֹּא הָלַךְ לֹא עָמַד וּמִתּוֹךְ שֶׁלֹּא עָמַד לֹא יָשַׁב, 'Because he did not even walk [on the evil path], he did not pause. And because he did not pause he did not sit.'

2. כִּי אִם בְּתוֹרַת ה' חֶפְצוֹ — *But his desire is in the Torah of HASHEM.*

Not only does the praiseworthy man do no evil, instead he does much good, for his only desire is Hashem's Torah (*Metzudas David*).

The Talmud (*Avodah Zarah* 18b) detects a direct flow of ideas between this verse and the preceding one:

Rabbi Shimon ben Pazi taught: What is meant by the passage 'The praises of man are that he has not walked in the counsel of the wicked'? This refers to the man who has not walked to the theatres and circuses of the heathens. 'And stood not in the path of the sinful,' i.e. that he did not stand as a spectator at bestial contests. 'And sat not in the session of scorners', i.e. that he never entered their evil conspiracies. Perhaps this person may say to himself: 'Since I have not walked to the theatres and circuses, nor stood at bestial contests, I may now spend my time sleeping!' Therefore the next verse continues, 'But his desire is in the Torah of HASHEM.'

The Talmud (*Avodah Zarah* 19a)

derives a basic principle of Torah study from this verse. Levi and Rabbi Shimon, the son of Rabbi Judah the Prince, were sitting before Rabbi Judah studying Scriptures. Upon completing one book, Levi said: 'Let us now commence with the study of *Proverbs*.' While Rabbi Shimon said: 'Let us now commence with the study of *Psalms*.' Rabbi Shimon overruled Levi, and they began to study *Psalms*. When they came to the verse 'But his desire is in the Torah of HASHEM,' Rabbi Judah explained, 'One should always study the section of Torah towards which his heart is inclined and wherein lies his desire.' Thereupon, Levi remarked: 'Rabbi, with this statement you have given me permission to stop studying *Psalms*.'

וּבְתוֹרָתוֹ — *And in his Torah.*

[The pronoun 'his' refers to the diligent student, not to Hashem.] *Rashi* (based on *Avodah Zarah* 19a) comments: At first the text calls it תּוֹרַת ה' 'the Torah of HASHEM, but after the student toils to understand it, it is considered as his possession and is called תּוֹרָתוֹ, 'his Torah'.

יֶהְגֶּה — *He meditates.*

Rashi here and elsewhere in Psalms emphasizes that the word יֶהְגֶּה pertains to meditations of the heart. However, *Metzudas Zion* maintains that although the word sometimes means meditation, as in הֶגְיוֹן לִבִּי, *the thoughts of my heart* (19:15), sometimes it means speech as וּלְשׁוֹנִי תֶּהְגֶּה צִדְקֶךָ, *And my tongue shall express your righteousness* (35:28). [Perhaps *Rashi* agrees that the term יֶהְגֶּה may be used with reference to speech provided it articulates deeply held personal thoughts weighing heavily on a person's mind rather than casual, thoughtless remarks. Cf. *comm.* of

I

2-3

² *But his desire is in the Torah of HASHEM,*
and in his Torah he meditates day and night.
³ *He shall be like a tree replanted by streams of water*
that yields its fruit in due season,

Malbim to 34:9 s.v. הֲגִיגִי, where he suggests that the word refers to a developed thought ready for expression].

The Talmud (*Avodah Zaran* 19a), urges a study program in which the student first whets his appetite by acquainting himself with the entirety of the Torah text swiftly, albeit superficially, thereby making '*HASHEM's Torah his desire.*' Then, the student is urged to go back and painstakingly analyze each topic with deep deliberation, '*And in his Torah he meditates day and night.*'

יוֹמָם וָלָיְלָה — *Day and night.*

The Jewish calendar 'day' begins at nightfall and ends with the conclusion of the following day. One exception to this rule is the mitzvah of Torah study, where the obligation is renewed every morning and continues into the following night. Therefore it is written concerning Torah study, וְהָגִיתָ בּוֹ יוֹמָם וָלָיְלָה, '*And you shall meditate therein day and night*' (*Joshua* 1:8). The sacrificial service is another exception (*Chullin* 83a). In this way the usually free, undisturbed night may be used to make up for time lost from Torah study during the day due to pursuit of livelihood (*Eruvin* 65a).

3. וְהָיָה כְּעֵץ שָׁתוּל — *He shall be like a tree replanted.*

The man who studies Torah incessantly will be rewarded well. He will constantly flourish like the tree which is constantly supplied with an abundance of water (*Metzudas David*). He will always be satisfied with his lot, whether it be much or little (*Radak*).

Malbim adds, homiletically: The wicked people who are enchanted by the charms of This World are con-

sidered as נָטוּעַ '*planted*' here, i.e. rooted permanently in this earth. Therefore, they are destined to remain here forever. After they are buried, their souls shall not ascend to a higher world for such was never their goal. Not so the righteous man who is considered as שָׁתוּל '*replanted*', i.e. he has uprooted his desire for the pleasures of This World and has planted his soul in a higher realm of existence so that it derives its vitality and sustenance from the world of the spirit.

Finally, the Talmud (*Avodah Zarah* 19a) derives a principle of methodology from these words. In order to obtain a consistent fundamental knowledge of the Talmudic text, it is best to study under one teacher who will supply an accurate textual version. However, to deepen his comprehension, the student is advised to '*replant*' himself, i.e. to sit at the feet of many masters, thus broadening himself by benefitting from different points of view on a subject.

עַל פַּלְגֵי מָיִם — *By streams of water.*

The root of this word is פֶּלֶג '*split*'. It describes the stream which branches off into small channels (*Metzudas Zion*).

Rashi renders פַּלְגֵי, in Old French vernacular, as *reservoir*; i.e., an independent, self-replenishing source of water which never fails.

אֲשֶׁר פִּרְיוֹ יִתֵּן בְּעִתּוֹ — *That yields its fruit in due season.*

When the scholar's moment of maturity arrives, after achieving self-perfection, he will give the fruits of his studies to eager disciples (*Meiri*). He will be prepared to answer questions on all Torah topics, at all times (*Ibn Yachya*).

[Compare this verse with the words of the Prophet *Jeremiah* (Ch. 17:8) in

ד יַעֲשֶׂה יַצְלִיחַ: לֹא־כֵן הָרְשָׁעִים כִּי אִם־
ה כַּמֹּץ אֲשֶׁר־תִּדְּפֶנּוּ רוּחַ: עַל־כֵּן | לֹא־יָקֻמוּ
רְשָׁעִים בַּמִּשְׁפָּט וְחַטָּאִים בַּעֲדַת צַדִּיקִים:
ו כִּי־יוֹדֵעַ יהוה דֶּרֶךְ צַדִּיקִים וְדֶרֶךְ רְשָׁעִים
תֹּאבֵד:

praise of the man who places his trust in God alone:

וְהָיָה כְּעֵץ שָׁתוּל עַל מַיִם וְעַל יוּבַל יְשַׁלַּח שָׁרָשָׁיו וְלֹא יִרְאֶה כִּי יָבֹא חֹם וְהָיָה עָלֵהוּ רַעֲנָן וּבִשְׁנַת בַּצֹּרֶת לֹא יִדְאָג וְלֹא יָמִישׁ מֵעֲשׂוֹת פֶּרִי 'He shall be like the tree replanted by the water, that spreads out its roots by the river, and shall not be fearful when heat approaches, and whose leaf will be fresh; in the year of drought it will not worry nor will it cease from bearing fruit.']

וְעָלֵהוּ לֹא יִבּוֹל — Whose leaf never withers.

In the case of the righteous scholar, even the 'leaf' which is usually discarded, has value (Rashi), i.e., even the ordinary, worldly discussions of Torah scholars merit careful study (Avodah Zarah 19a).[1]

[Just as the leaf's only purpose is to protect the fruit, any worldly words of the scholar are only for the sake of maintaining his body and soul. Thus, even ordinary conversation is elevated to a spiritual level and bestowed with enduring value.[2]

וְכֹל אֲשֶׁר יַעֲשֶׂה יַצְלִיחַ — And everything he does will succeed.

[He will succeed even in worldly matters. Cf. comm. of Malbim to v. 1.] 'Whoever occupies himself with Torah

studies is prosperous in all of his undertakings' (Avodah Zarah 9b).

4. לֹא כֵן הָרְשָׁעִים — Not so the wicked.

Unlike the righteous who produce beneficial fruit, the wicked are like chaff which only irritates and damages (Radak).

[In Jeremiah (ibid. 17:6), the Prophet foretells of the doom of those who trust in themselves and not in God:

וְהָיָה כְּעַרְעָר בָּעֲרָבָה וְלֹא יִרְאֶה כִּי יָבוֹא טוֹב וְשָׁכַן חֲרֵרִים בַּמִּדְבָּר אֶרֶץ מְלֵחָה וְלֹא תֵשֵׁב 'He shall be like the juniper tree in the desert and shall not see when good comes, but he shall inhabit the parched places in the wilderness, a salt land and not inhabited.']

כִּי אִם כַּמֹּץ אֲשֶׁר תִּדְּפֶנּוּ רוּחַ — They are like the chaff which the wind drives away.

The word מֹץ is derived from מָצַץ, 'to suck'. Every drop of nutrition has been squeezed out of the chaff, so it has no value. So, too, the existence of the evil is drained of all meaning (Hirsch).

The grain stalk has three main parts. The kernel is a staple of human nutrition. The straw makes excellent animal fodder. But the dry, thorny chaff is useless. Light and flimsy, the softest gust of wind carries it away. The wicked too are useless. The slightest ill wind

1. The sin of Adam introduced decay and deterioration into the world. The man of אוֹשֶׁר 'praise' will reverse this trend. Ramban (Gen. 2:8) describes the fruit of the Garden of Eden before the sin: They were the handiwork of God, enduring forever and ever as it says, כָּל עֵץ מַאֲכָל לֹא יִבּוֹל עָלֵהוּ וְלֹא יִתֹּם פִּרְיוֹ, 'Every tree which grows for food; its leaf shall not wither, neither shall its fruit cease' (Ezek. 47:12).

The Prophet (ibid.) foretells Messianic times when the Holy Temple will be rebuilt on the place where Adam was created and a stream shall flow from it. At that time the world will regain its original perfection וְהָיָה פִרְיוֹ לְמַאֲכָל וְעָלֵהוּ לִתְרוּפָה, 'And its fruit shall be for food and its leaf for healing.'

and whose leaf never withers.

And everything he does will succeed.

⁴ *Not so the wicked:*

They are like the chaff which the wind drives away.

⁵ *Therefore the wicked shall not be vindicated
in judgment,*

*Nor the sinful in the assembly
of the righteous.*

⁶ *For HASHEM recognizes the way of the righteous,
while the way of the wicked is doomed.*

will upset their illusion of tranquility and leave them dangling insecure in thin air *(Rav Dessler).*

5. עַל כֵּן לֹא יָקֻמוּ רְשָׁעִים בַּמִּשְׁפָּט — *Therefore the wicked shall not be vindicated* [lit. 'stand up'; 'survive'] *in judgment.*

The measure of their punishment is constantly filling up and when they reach the limit they will be so guilty that nothing will save them *(Metzudas David).*

וְחַטָּאִים בַּעֲדַת צַדִּיקִים — *Nor the sinful in the assembly of the righteous.*

[I.e. the sinful will not share in the rewards destined for them in the World to Come.]

The רְשָׁעִים, *'wicked ones'* will not rise up for judgment at all. However, the חַטָּאִים *'sinful'* will arise for judgment [and eventual expiation] but they will not merit the delight of being in the assembly of the righteous *(Malbim).*

6. כִּי יוֹדֵעַ ה' דֶּרֶךְ צַדִּיקִים — *For HASHEM recognizes the way of the righteous.*

יוֹדֵעַ [lit. *'knows'*] He supervises them constantly in order to assure them the finest reward *(Radak).*

The minds of the righteous are bound inseparably to the intellect of Hashem [therefore, Hashem reciprocates and trains His attention on them] *(Malbim).*

וְדֶרֶךְ רְשָׁעִים תֹּאבֵד — *While the way of the wicked is doomed.*

The ways of the wicked are despicable to Him, so He pushes them away from His view *(Rashi).*

Nefutzos Yehudah notes that תֹּאבֵד, *'to doom'* is in feminine gender, denoting the weakness of the path which the wicked tread.

[The psalm's conclusion reinforces its opening theme. The first prerequisite of glory and praise is to avoid the temptations and distractions which draw men to their doom.]

2. *Rav Dessler* relates an anecdote to illustrate this. When his great-grandmother, Esther, was married to the renowned saint, Rav Yisrael Salanter, the groom made the following arrangement for the management of their home. He would have complete authority in spiritual matters, while she would dictate all worldly decisions. Grandmother Esther laughed when recalling this suggestion and said that for a holy man of Rav Yisrael's caliber, even the most mundane things are used in the performance of commandments and are thus transformed into spiritual concerns. Thus, Rav Yisrael had the final word over everything!

A fter describing the good fortunes of the righteous and the failure of the wicked in Psalm I, the Psalmist now answers the classical question which is posed against this thesis: 'Why then do the wicked prosper?' He replies that the success of the evil is short lived. Their doom is impending for God Himself scorns them from above. If we are not worthy of witnessing their downfall today, the world will surely see it in Messianic times.

Thus we understand why the Sages (Berachos 10a) consider the first two Psalms as one. Though technically and physically separated, they complement each other spiritually and thematically (Meiri).

Although the Sages taught that this chapter describes Messianic times, Rashi and Radak suggest that the simple reading of the text lends itself more readily to the events of David's own career, specifically the time immediately following his coronation. 'And when the Philistines heard that they had anointed David King over Israel, all of the Philistines came up to seek David' [to attack him] (II Samuel 5:17).

In reality, the two proposed settings past and future, present no contradiction. For, as explained in the Overview, this is the uniqueness of Psalms. David had the ability and the genius to be stimulated and inspired so profoundly by present events that he could soar above the boundaries of time, and sing of past, present, and future in the same breath, with the same words.

In the brazen Philistines of his day, David detected the seeds of גוג ומגוג, Gog and Magog, the arch-enemies of Messiah. The war of Gog and Magog begins when all seventy nations of the world unite against Israel (the numerical value of גוג ומגוג, is 70). All of those nations will suffer internal instability, and will be plagued by revolution, audacity, atheism, scandal, and unbridled inflation. Truth will be virtually non-existent and falsehood will prevail (Sotah 49b).

The ultimate victory of Messiah over evil will demonstrate God's supremacy as it was never displayed before. 'And David said . . . Yours, HASHEM is the greatness and the power and the glory and the victory and the majesty, for all that is in heaven and on earth is Yours. Yours, HASHEM, is the kingdom and You are exalted as Head above all (Chronicles I, 29:11).

'Exalted as head above all: This will be evident after the war of Gog and Magog' (Berachos 58a).

א לָמָּה רָגְשׁוּ גוֹיִם וּלְאֻמִּים יֶהְגּוּ־רִיק:
ב יִתְיַצְּבוּ | מַלְכֵי־אֶרֶץ וְרוֹזְנִים נוֹסְדוּ־יָחַד
ג עַל־יהוה וְעַל־מְשִׁיחוֹ: נְנַתְּקָה אֶת־
מוֹסְרוֹתֵימוֹ וְנַשְׁלִיכָה מִמֶּנּוּ עֲבֹתֵימוֹ:
ד־ה יוֹשֵׁב בַּשָּׁמַיִם יִשְׂחָק אֲדֹנָי יִלְעַג־לָמוֹ: אָז

1. לָמָּה רָגְשׁוּ גוֹיִם — *Why do the peoples gather?*

Rashi, Radak, and *Ibn Ezra* interpret רָגְשׁוּ as a gathering of human masses. *Midrash Shocher Tov* renders this word as: 'excited, raging' i.e. 'Why are the masses in turbulence?'

The *Midrash* continues: 'To what may the wicked be likened? To grasshoppers caged in a box who madly scramble to jump out, but fail' *(ibid).*

Yalkut comments: Rav Yitzchok said, 'If a person demands of his friend, "Why do you act so?" his friend will be angered. Yet, the righteous say to HASHEM, "לָמָּה, *why?*" and they are not punished. 'Why indeed are they not punished? Because their sole concern is the welfare of Israel!'

וּלְאֻמִּים יֶהְגּוּ רִיק — *And the nations talk in vain?*

When the Philistines gathered to attack the newly crowned David, they spoke with excessive pride and confidence for they had recently routed the Israelite army and slain Saul and his sons. But their threats and boasts were hollow *(Radak).*

Ibn Ezra and *Metzudos Zion* concur with *Radak* in translating יֶהְגּוּ, as 'talk'. However, *Rashi* (as in the previous chapter v.2), renders it as 'think', thus: 'The nations think of worthless plans.'

Malbim differentiates between גוֹיִם, people bound together only by geographic circumstance without a common ideology, and לְאֻמִּים, citizens sharing mutual political interests or religious beliefs. Thus רָגְשׁוּ, physical gathering, is the most appropriate description for גוֹיִם, whereas יֶהְגּוּ, 'they talk', indicating ideas or words which express inner

thoughts, fits the intellectual לְאֻמִּים who are related by common beliefs.

2. יִתְיַצְּבוּ מַלְכֵי־אֶרֶץ — *The kings of the earth take their stand.*

This translation follows the implication of *Targum* and other commentators. *Metzudas David* perceives this verse as a continuation of the incredulous question of *v.*1, rendering: *Why do the kings ... saying.*

In all of Scripture, there is no mention of Philstine 'kings' doing battle with David, only of סַרְנֵי פְלִשְׁתִּים, '*captains of the Philistines*'. Nevertheless, the Philistine adversaries are referred to here as kings, for in their conceit, these low officers fancied themselves to be mighty rulers. It is also possible that they allied themselves with powerful monarchs who joined their campaign. If so David was truly challenged by 'kings' *(Radak).*

[יִתְיַצְּבוּ, '*to take their stand*' is a more forceful term than עָמְדוּ '*they stand*'. יָצַב implies a firm, erect stance in a challenging, uncompromising position. The man so entrenched will not allow himself to be budged.]

וְרוֹזְנִים נוֹסְדוּ יָחַד — *And the lords conspire together.*

Rashi suggests that נוֹסְדוּ, is derived from סוֹד, '*secret*'. [The word רוֹזְנִים, *lords*, too, has the connotation of privy-counsellors, being privy to secrets of state, (related to רָז, *secret*).]

Radak however translates נוֹסְדוּ as '*they take counsel*', and traces the word to the root יְסוֹד, *foundation;* explaining that 'plans and counsel are the basis for all subsequent action.' Both *Radak* and *Ibn Ezra* mention that יָחַד, *together,*

*Why do the peoples gather,
and the nations talk in vain?*
² *The kings of the earth take their stand
and the lords conspire secretly,
against HASHEM and against His anointed:*
³ *'Let us cut their cords and cast off their ropes.'*
⁴ *He who sits in heaven will laugh,
the Lord will mock them.*

refers to the kings of the earth who conspire together, meeting with the lords.

עַל ה' וְעַל מְשִׁיחוֹ — *Against HASHEM
and against His anointed.*

The Philistines knew that David was chosen by God and anointed by Samuel. By attacking David, therefore, it is as if they are waging war against God Himself *(Radak).*

[*Rambam,* in Article 12 of the Thirteen Principles of Faith (commentary to the *Mishnah, Sanhedrin* 11) emphasizes the Messianic role of David:

'... To firmly believe in the advent of Messiah; although he tarries, to wait for him, nonetheless. One must believe that the excellence and prestige of Messiah will surpass that of all kings who ever lived ... Included in this article of faith is the conviction that there can be no king for all of Israel except from the House of David, specifically from the seed of Solomon. Whoever challenges the sovereignty of this family, denies the very existence of God Himself, and defies the words of His Prophets.]

3. נְנַתְּקָה אֶת מוֹסְרוֹתֵימוֹ — [*Saying:*] *'Let us cut their cords.'* The Philistines said that they would sever the bonds of the agreement which finally united Israel under the rule of David after seven years of indecision *(Radak).* Technically speaking, the מוֹסְרוֹת, refer to the bonds used to harness the oxen to the yoke *(Rashi, Metzudos).* [This describes the submission of Israel to the yoke of David's rule.]

Hirsch stresses that the yoke of God's anointed hangs heavily upon the necks of the gentile nations also. The מוֹסֵר, *cord,* of the Messiah is the מוּסָר, *moral self-discipline* which he teaches, thus inhibiting the unbridled desires of mankind and saddling man with duties. These limitations are repugnant to the nations who yearn to free their conscience from any inhibitions.

וְנַשְׁלִיכָה מִמֶּנּוּ עֲבֹתֵימוֹ — *And cast off their ropes [from ourselves].*

Malbim describes the עֲבֹת as heavy ropes which are woven of many tough strands. These bonds are most difficult to cut and so they must be thrown off.

4. יוֹשֵׁב בַּשָּׁמַיִם יִשְׂחָק — *He Who sits in heaven will laugh.*

In contrast to the kings who *'stand'* so firm below, HASHEM merely *'sits'* and watches from above *(Ibn Ezra).*

How futile and comical is their vain threat for God is high above and they are below. In any conflict, the adversary on top has the advantage even if he is weak, how much more so if he is strong, like God *(Metzudas David).*

Whenever God is described as *'sitting'* it means that he is settled permanently, enduring forever *(Radak).*

'Once it becomes clear that God has no body or corporeality, it becomes clear that no bodily actions can be attributed to Him ... He does not sit and He does not stand ... Therefore all descriptions of God's actions in the Torah and the Prophets are merely parables and allegories, such as the description *'He who sits in heaven will laugh ...'* *(Rambam, Hilchos Yesodei haTorah* 1:11-12).

יְדַבֵּר אֵלֵימוֹ בְאַפּוֹ וּבַחֲרוֹנוֹ יְבַהֲלֵמוֹ:
ו וַאֲנִי נָסַכְתִּי מַלְכִּי עַל־צִיּוֹן הַר־קָדְשִׁי:
ז אֲסַפְּרָה אֶל חֹק יְהוה אָמַר אֵלַי בְּנִי־
ח אַתָּה אֲנִי הַיּוֹם יְלִדְתִּיךָ: שְׁאַל מִמֶּנִּי
וְאֶתְּנָה גוֹיִם נַחֲלָתֶךָ וַאֲחֻזָּתְךָ אַפְסֵי־

אֲדֹנָי יִלְעַג לָמוֹ — *The Lord will mock them* [לָמוֹ — lit. *'at them'*][1]

5. אָז — *Then.* Suddenly, without prior warning (*Malbim*).

יְדַבֵּר אֵלֵימוֹ בְאַפּוֹ — *He will speak to them in His anger.* Then, when HASHEM hears their vain words, He will retort angrily (*Radak*).

יְבַהֲלֵמוֹ — *He will terrify them* [lit. *'confuse; to rush madly'*]

6. וַאֲנִי נָסַכְתִּי מַלְכִּי — [*Saying:*] *'I Myself have anointed My king.'*
HASHEM will chastise the nations: 'How dare you attempt to remove David after I have chosen and anointed him?' (*Radak*). Furthermore, rather than undermining David's authority, your rebellion will reinforce his power, for now I, HASHEM, am forced to openly display my choice of David by destroying his adversaries (*Malbim*).

עַל צִיּוֹן הַר קָדְשִׁי — *Upon Zion, My holy mountain.*
Zion was not conquered by Israel until after David rose to the throne, therefore Zion and Jerusalem are always referred to as 'David's City'. It was after this conquest that the Philistines gathered to challenge David (*Radak*).

[Cf. *I Chronicles* 11:4 'And David and all of Israel went to Jerusalem known as Jebus; there dwelled the Jebusites, the inhabitants of that land.' *Radak* (ibid) comments: David embarked upon this campaign immediately after his coronation as King of Israel so that the people of Israel should not say: 'All of the victories which David won were in the merit of Saul and by virtue of his good fortune. But now David cowers and hesitates to wage war alone!']

7. אֲסַפְּרָה אֶל חֹק — *I am obligated to proclaim.*
David now responds and says: It is my definite obligation, and a very pleasant and acceptable one, to relate the following and to proclaim it publicly (*Rashi*). *Rashi* translates חֹק, as *obligation* however *Radak* renders the word as *a set ritual* or *custom*. *Metzudos* traces the word to חָקוּק, *engraved* or *inscribed*. Thus, David says, 'I shall proclaim that which has already been inscribed in the Written Torah: that Israel is God's son.'

ה' אָמַר אֵלַי — HASHEM *said to me:* Through the words of His prophets, Nathan, Gad, and Samuel (*Rashi*).

בְּנִי אַתָּה — *'You are My son.'*
You are the leader of Israel who is

1. The Talmud (*Avodah Zara* 3b) emphasizes that this is no ordinary mockery but rather, it is the last laugh.'
'In the future the nations, motivated by Israel's rising fortunes and rewards, will become insincere converts. They will bind *tefillin* to their heads and *tefillin* to their arms, place *tzitzis* on their garments, and *mezuzos* on their doorposts. When Gog and Magog arrive to attack Messiah, these new converts will ask Gog and Magog — *'Why have you gathered?'* To which they will reply, *"Against HASHEM and against His anointed."*
Immediately all of these converts will rip off their *mitzvos* and abandon them saying, *'Let us cut their bonds.'*
And then God will laugh, *'He who sits in Heaven will laugh.'* Rav Yitzchak said: Only on that day will HASHEM truly laugh.

⁵ *Then, He will speak to them in His anger,*
and His fury will terrify them:
⁶ *'I Myself have anointed My king,*
upon Zion My holy mountain.'
⁷ *I am obligated to proclaim: HASHEM said to me:*
'You are My son,
I have begotten you this day.
⁸ *Ask of Me*
and I will make the peoples your inheritance,

called בְּנִי בְכֹרִי, *'My son, my first born'* (*Exodus* 4:22). Because they all depend on you, David, you are called My son (*Rashi*).

He who tries to resemble God in all of his ways and deeds is considered to be a son of HASHEM (*Meiri*).

אֲנִי הַיּוֹם — *I this day.* Today, on the day when I crowned you as king over My sons (*Rashi*).

יְלִדְתִּיךְ — *Have begotten you.*
So that you can be called My son, and be as dear as a son — all in the merit of the people of Israel ... Similarly we find Solomon referred to as a son, *'I will be his father and he will be My son'* (*II Samuel* 7:14). And again we find concerning David himself *'He will cry to me, You are my Father, my Lord, the Rock of my salvation. I, in return, will make him [David] My first-born'* (*Psalms* 89:27-28) (*Rashi*).

The *Targum* maintains that David was worthy of being called God's son on his own merit:

Hashem said: 'You David, are as pure and innocent today as a son on the day he is born to his father.'

Panim Yofos notes that he who recognizes Hashem's power realizes that He renews all of creation every moment and thus this man feels reborn constantly like a newborn baby

8. שְׁאַל מִמֶּנִי — *Ask of Me.*
Because you are like a son, and a father customarily bequeaths his possessions to his children, you need only to ask and I will give you the nations as your inheritance (*Metzudas David; Ibn Ezra*).

Rashi renders שְׁאַל, as a term for supplication and prayer, i.e. 'pray to me whenever you go out to fight your enemies.'

וְאֶתְּנָה גוֹיִם נַחֲלָתֶךְ — *And I will make the peoples your inheritance.*

Because the world and its inhabitants all belong to the Lord, He has the right to bequeath them to His son (*Malbim*).

This promise was fulfilled for we find that the nations were subjected to David's rule and feared him. As it is written (*I Chron.* 14:17): וַיֵּצֵא שֵׁם דָּוִיד בְּכָל הָאֲרָצוֹת וַה' נָתַן פַּחְדּוֹ עַל כָּל הַגּוֹיִם, *'And David's reputation spread throughout all of the lands and*

[It is noteworthy that the nations are described as laying *tefillin* first on their heads and then on their arms, which is the opposite of the *halachah*, which prescribes that the *tefillin* of the arm precedes that of the head. Perhaps the implication is as follows: The dedicated, believing Jew is prepared to act with his body and hands before he understands with his mind the value of the commandment. Action precedes comprehension. נַעֲשֶׂה, *we shall do* (symbolized by *tefillin* on the arm), precedes נִשְׁמַע, *we shall listen and understand* (symbolized by *tefillin* on the head). The arm precedes the head. However, these insincere converts are motivated only by the dream of reward which their mind tells them is imminent. Their bodies follow their intellectual perception leading them to convert as long as it seems profitable to do so. Thus, their heads precede their arms.]

ט אֶרֶץ: תְּרֹעֵם בְּשֵׁבֶט בַּרְזֶל כִּכְלִי יוֹצֵר

י תְּנַפְּצֵם: וְעַתָּה מְלָכִים הַשְׂכִּילוּ הִוָּסְרוּ

יא שֹׁפְטֵי אָרֶץ: עִבְדוּ אֶת־יהוה בְּיִרְאָה

יב וְגִילוּ בִּרְעָדָה: נַשְּׁקוּ־בַר פֶּן־יֶאֱנַף |

וְתֹאבְדוּ דֶרֶךְ כִּי־יִבְעַר כִּמְעַט אַפּוֹ אַשְׁרֵי

כָּל־חוֹסֵי בוֹ:

HASHEM *cast a fear of him over all of the peoples'* (Radak).

וַאֲחֻזָּתְךָ אַפְסֵי אָרֶץ — *And the ends of the earth your possession.*

אַפְסֵי — [lit. 'nothingness'] [Because the ends of the earth seem to disappear into nothingness.]

Malbim comments that often a person inherits an estate, but cannot take possession because the property is too distant. Hashem not only offers to give the entire globe to David, but also assures him of the ability to possess and exploit it.

9. תְּרֹעֵם — *You will smash them.*

God also said to me that any nations who rise up to challenge me will be smashed (Radak).

בְּשֵׁבֶט בַּרְזֶל — *With a rod of iron.*

The sword [i.e. signifying death and destruction] (Rashi).

כִּכְלִי יוֹצֵר תְּנַפְּצֵם — [*You will*] *shatter them like an earthen vessel.*

This means breaking and scattering. Thus, the analogy to earthenware which shatters into fine fragments (Rashi).

In contradistinction to רָגְשׁוּ גוֹיִם — *the gathered masses of people* (v. 1), David will disperse and scatter them with his sword (Ibn Ezra).

10. וְעַתָּה — *And now.*

[Says David: Now that you nations see that I have tremendous power to do with you as I please, be wise enough to prevent tragedy lest I exercise my strength against you.]

מְלָכִים הַשְׂכִּילוּ — *O kings, be wise.*

The prophets of Israel are men of

mercy and they take pains to warn the heathens to desist from evil. For God stretches out His hand to both the righteous and the wicked and offers them salvation (Rashi).

הִוָּסְרוּ שֹׁפְטֵי אָרֶץ — *Be disciplined, judges of the earth.*

The *kings* here refer back to the *kings of the earth* of v. 2, and the *judges* here correspond to the רוֹזְנִים, *lords who conspire*, of that verse. David's exhortation to *'be wise'* countermands their call to gather up עַל ה', *'against Hashem.'* In response to their declared resolve to cut מוֹסְרוֹתֵימוֹ, *their restraining bonds*, he calls upon them הִוָּסְרוּ, *be disciplined* (Ibn Ezra).

הִוָּסְרוּ — *Be disciplined.*

I.e. submit to מוּסָר, *self-discipline* and moral law. You, who as שֹׁפְטֵי אָרֶץ, *judges of the earth*, desire to put earthly affairs in order, must first put yourselves in order by acknowledging HASHEM's absolute truth as the one law which stands supreme above all others (Hirsch).

11. עִבְדוּ אֶת ה' בְּיִרְאָה — *Serve HASHEM in awe.*

David continues to advise the haughty kings, how to choose the wise path of serving HASHEM. If they find no pleasure in doing good, He suggests that they change their value system — 'Make your desire to do only that which God desires, and serve Him in awe' (Radak).

Ibn Ezra sees David's call for serving HASHEM in submission as a response to the rebellious, arrogant declaration of

and the ends of the earth your possession.
⁹ *You will smash them with a rod of iron,*
   shatter them like an earthen vessel.'
¹⁰ *And now, O kings be wise,*
   be disciplined, O judges of the earth.
¹¹ *Serve HASHEM in awe*
   and rejoice with trembling.
¹² *Yearn for purity,*
   lest He grow wrathful, and your way be doomed,
   for in a brief moment His anger will blaze.
Praises — for those who trust in Him.

---

the nations: *'Let us cut their cords'* (*verse 2*).

Metzudas David adds that the only meaningful way for them to serve HASHEM is by accepting the kingship of Messiah.

וְגִילוּ בִּרְעָדָה — *And rejoice with trembling.*

Mankind is destined to be seized by a trembling of which it is written: אָחֲזָה רְעָדָה חֲנֵפִים, *'Trembling has seized the insincere'* (*Isaiah 33:14*). Even in its midst you nations shall rejoice if you will have faithfully served HASHEM beforehand (*Rashi*).

Although *Rashi* views this phrase as a promise of reward, *Ibn Ezra* holds that it is a continuation of the previous warning to fear God, rendering the verse literally: *'Even when you rejoice, remember to tremble before HASHEM's presence at all times.'*

The Talmud (*Brachos* 30b) interprets:

What is meant by וְגִילוּ בִּרְעָדָה, *rejoice with trembling?*

Rav Ada bar Masna said in the name of Rav: In the very place where you rejoice there you should tremble.

Abaya was sitting before his master, Rabba, and Rabba noticed that Abaya

seemed exceptionally happy. Rabba remarked: Is it not written *'and rejoice with trembling'?* Abaya replied: I am wearing *tefillin!* [I cannot become excessively happy because *tefillin* bear testimony that the sovereignty of my Maker rests upon me (*Rashi*).][1]

12. נַשְּׁקוּ בַר — *Yearn for Purity.*

[David offers a final word of advice to the nations on how to accustom themselves to loving that which is good.]

נַשְּׁקוּ — *Yearn.* The translation follows *Metzudos.* Similarly, *Menachem,* quoted by *Rashi,* relates נַשְּׁקוּ to תְּשׁוּקָה, *desire.* בַר — *purity,* refers to purity of the unsullied heart (*Rashi*).

Rashi alternately interprets נַשְּׁקוּ as *'stimulate'*, i.e. *'bestir and arouse yourselves quickly to acquire purity of heart.'*

פֶּן יֶאֱנַף — *Lest He grow wrathful.*

If you do not mend your ways swiftly, HASHEM will destroy you in His wrath (*Radak*).

וְתֹאבְדוּ דֶרֶךְ — *And your way be doomed* [lit. *'And you will lose your way.'*]

[Compare with the conclusion of the previous Psalm וְדֶרֶךְ רְשָׁעִים תֹּאבֵד *'while*

---

1. Mar the son of Ravina made a wedding feast for his son. He noticed that the Rabbis were excessively merry. He took hold of a fine crystal vessel worth four hundred zuzim and smashed it in front of them and their spirits were sobered (*ibid.* 31a).

Tosefos comments that this is the source of the custom to break a glass at a Jewish wedding.

the way of the wicked will be doomed'
(1:6). If the wicked will not exercise
זְהִירוּת, 'watchfulness', the distractions
luring them from the straight way will
cause them to perish.]

כִּי יִבְעַר כִּמְעַט אַפּוֹ — For in a brief moment His anger will blaze.

כִּמְעַט — [lit. 'in a small while] i.e.
'suddenly' — (Rashi).

אַשְׁרֵי כָּל חוֹסֵי בוֹ — Praises — for those
who trust in Him.

Rashi, in consonance with his interpretation of Psalm 1:1 translates
אַשְׁרֵי, not as the adjective, praiseworthy,
but rather as a noun, 'praises'. 'At that
time [when God's wrath erupts suddenly against the wicked] the good fortunes
and praises of those who trust in Him
will be evident to all.'

The drama of King David's flight from his son Absalom at the age of sixty-five, took place towards the end of his life (II Samuel 15:7; Radak; Kara ibid). Thus, the placement of this chapter at the beginning of Psalms presents a problem; a puzzle which is magnified by the fact that we find psalms dealing with David's early life near the book's end.

One solution offered by the Yalkut Shimoni does away with the problem entirely: Rabbi Eleazar said: 'The portions of the Torah were purposely recorded without proper sequence, because, had they been in order, whoever read them would have had the power to revive the dead and to perform miracles. Therefore, the true order is concealed from man and known only to Hashem.' [The Torah is God's plan and blueprint for life. Our mission and challenge is to toil over it in an effort to achieve understanding. If these vital formulae were spelled out clearly and unambiguously, then anyone could know the secret of producing life and manipulating nature. (See Overview, ArtScroll edition of Bereishis I).]

Another solution, which addresses itself to the heart of this problem, is offered in the Talmud (Berachos 10a). In the previous chapter, the Messianic turbulence of Gog and Magog was described briefly. As explained in our introduction (ibid), it will be an age of anarchy and disintegration of all authority. Thus, this psalm is intended to lend credibility to the prophecies of the previous one. 'If a person should ask, "Is it then possible that a slave should rise up against his master?" then answer, "Is it not even harder to imagine that a son should rise up against his own father? But, just as such a shocking rebellion did indeed come to pass when Absalom overthrew David, so too will the uprising of Gog and Magog come about in the future!'

A true appreciation of this psalm is impossible without understanding the historical background of Absalom's revolt. See II Samuel chapters 15-19 for the full details.

א מִזְמוֹר לְדָוִד בְּבָרְחוֹ מִפְּנֵי | אַבְשָׁלוֹם בְּנוֹ:
ב יהוה מָה־רַבּוּ צָרָי רַבִּים קָמִים עָלָי:
ג רַבִּים אֹמְרִים לְנַפְשִׁי אֵין יְשׁוּעָתָה לּוֹ
ד בֵאלֹהִים סֶלָה: וְאַתָּה יהוה מָגֵן בַּעֲדִי

1. מִזְמוֹר לְדָוִד — *A song of David.*

The Sages of the Talmud (*Pesachim* 117a) interpret מִזְמוֹר לְדָוִד in its literal connotation of 'A song *to* David' and state the following rule: Wherever the name of David occurs before the phrase, *'A song'*, divine inspiration came first and the song — which was its outpouring — followed. But wherever the phrase *'A song'* precedes David's name, David elevated himself to the level of divine exultation upon the wings of his own song. Thus לְדָוִד, *'to David'* means 'when divine inspiration descended unto David,' sometimes before the song, other times as the result of the song.

Hirsch notes that in this psalm, exaltation did not descend upon David, for he was depressed by the tragedy and he had to lift himself out of his sorrow with song.[1]

Radak explains the title of this tragic psalm in the following manner:

These verses were not meant as a song at the time of their composition. Rather, after David was saved from his many adversaries, he gave all of these works to the Levites in the Temple to sing as melodies. This explains the titles of many other bleak psalms which are called *'songs.'* The *'songs'* which depict the גָּלוּת, *'exile'* of the Jewish people will be rendered as joyous musical compositions after the future redemption from exile.

בְּבָרְחוֹ מִפְּנֵי אַבְשָׁלוֹם בְּנוֹ — *As he fled from Absalom his son.*

Even as he fled, he prayed to God in song, for he already perceived through divine inspiration that his kingdom would be returned to him (*Metzudas David*).

2. ה' מָה רַבּוּ צָרָי — *HASHEM how many are my tormentors!*

To the point where even my own son rebels against me! (*Metzudas David*).

Radak suggests that רַבּוּ implies רֹב, *the majority*, because the bulk of the people of Israel followed Absalom.

רַבִּים — *The great* [lit. *'many'*].

The translation follows *Rashi* who interprets רַבִּים as qualitative rather than quantitative.

Targum and *Radak* render רַבִּים as *'many'*, in the quantitative sense.

Rashi amplifies on the greatness of these men — 'who are great in Torah, great in wisdom, great in wealth and great in physical stature: Such as Saul, the sons of Orpah (who were powerful giants, including Goliath), Doeg, and Achitophel.

3. רַבִּים — *The great.*

The translation follows *Rashi's* rendering in *v.* 2. *Radak*, in our verse as well, renders the word quantitatively, and comments that *many* [of the greatest] men of the time turned against David.

1. In view of the tragic circumstances under which this psalm was composed, the title "A song of David", seems to be totally out of place. The Talmud (*Berachos* 7b) explains:
'A song unto David', 'A Lament' would be more correct! Said Rabbi Shimon ben Avishalom, 'To what may this be likened? To a person in debt. Before he pays, he is worried and sad, but after he pays, he rejoices. So too with David. Since God had warned him, "I will raise up evil against you from out of your own house" (II Samuel 12:11) he was saddened. Perhaps a merciless slave or an illegitimate child would rise up in vengeance, without any sympathy. Now that he saw that he was menaced by his son Absalom who indeed hesitated to pursue and slaughter his father as Achitophel advised — he gave praise in song.'

III
1-4

A song of David,
    as he fled from Absalom his son.
² HASHEM, how many are my tormentors!
    The great rise up against me!
³ The great say of my soul,
    'There is no salvation for him from God.' Selah!
⁴ But You HASHEM are a shield for me —

לְנַפְשִׁי — *Of my soul* [lit. 'to my soul]

אֵין יְשׁוּעָתָה לּוֹ בֵאלֹהִים — *There is no salvation for him from God.*

Because he sinned with a married woman *(Rashi).*

Many great men including Achitophel, followed Absalom because they were convinced that David had forfeited his share in the World to Come and that, therefore, he could not regain the throne *(Radak).*

סֶלָה — *Selah.*

This word is one of the most difficult to translate in the entire book.

Targum and *Metzudas Zion* render it 'forever', thus we read here *'there is no salvation ... forever.'*

This view is supported by the Talmud *(Eruvin 54a).* 'In the academy of Rabbi Eleazar ben Yaakov they taught: Wherever the words נֶצַח סֶלָה וָעֶד are used, they mean *'forever, without an end'* ... סֶלָה as it says עַד עוֹלָם סֶלָה 'forever, Selah!' *(Psalms 48:9).*

Ibn Ezra disagrees and concludes that the word סֶלָה is always a reaffirmation of a preceding statement, i.e. 'all of the aforementioned is *true and certain.' Ibn Ezra* also offers an alternate meaning, endorsed by *Radak* as well, that *'selah'* is a musical instruction addressed to the singers of the psalm. It indicates special emphasis and a raising of the voice. This theory is supported by the fact that this word *'selah'* is only to be found in the Book of Psalms, a book of songs, and three times in the Book of Habakuk who also sings in a style very similar to Tehillim. Accordingly, the root of the

word סֶלָה is related to סוּל *to raise,* as we find in the verse סֹלּוּ סֹלּוּ הַמְסִלָּה, *'Build up, build up, the road' (Isaiah 62:10).*

[The fact that the musical note was included in the very text of the psalm denotes the significance of the melody in this book. As explained in the *Overview,* the music of Psalms was an integral part of the message David sought to convey.]

וְאַתָּה ה' מָגֵן בַּעֲדִי **4.** — *But You HASHEM are a shield for me.*

The ruination which my enemies predict for me shall not come to pass, for You Hashem are my shield and my supporter to return me to my throne *(Metzudas David).*

Chasam Sofer and *Hirsch* comment that close attention should be given to the changes in the designations of God's Name as they appear. In the previous verse, David's enemies claim that he has no salvation from אֱלֹהִים, *God* as he appears in the role of Judge, following the letter of the law strictly, unswervingly. However, David replies that there is yet hope for him, for indeed he has sinned, but he regrets it bitterly. The truly penitent man who returns with all his heart is worthy of complete pardon and protection from ה', HASHEM, the All Merciful.

According to *Rabbeinu Yonah (Shaarei Teshuvah* 4:12) it is David's serene acceptance of torment and agony at this time which makes him worthy of Divine protection. 'If the sinner is beset with hardship and visited with trouble and he justifies the punishment accorded to him and accepts the chastise-

ה כְּבוֹדִי וּמֵרִים רֹאשִׁי: קוֹלִי אֶל־יהוה
ו אֶקְרָא וַיַּעֲנֵנִי מֵהַר קָדְשׁוֹ סֶלָה: אֲנִי
שָׁכַבְתִּי וָאִישָׁנָה הֱקִיצוֹתִי כִּי יהוה

ment with good will, this will serve as a shield against the many afflictions which, by right should come upon him . . . . Our Sages of blessed memory have said with reference to the verse, "A song of David as he fled" (Psalms 3:1), שִׂמְחָה לַצַּדִּיק עֲשׂוֹת מִשְׁפָּט, The performance of justice brings joy to the righteous (Proverbs 21:15) — it is the trait of the righteous to discharge their debt and sing to the Holy One Blessed be He.

This is analogous to the tenant-farmer who, being in debt to his landlord, collected the grain for threshing and put it into a pile, which the landowner appropriated. The tenant-farmer, returning empty-handed was asked, 'You left your threshing-floor with your hands upon your head [i.e. empty-handed] and you rejoice?' He replied: 'Even so, the bill has been paid; my debt has been discharged." ' (Medrash Tehillim 79:2).[1]

כְּבוֹדִי — For my soul. [lit. — my honor]
The soul is called man's honor because it is man's supreme privilege that he has within himself a resting place for the glory of God (Malbim) [cf. comm. 30:13].

Radak renders: 'You, Hashem, are a shield for my body in this world and a shield for my soul in the World to Come.'

He offers an alternate translation of כְּבוֹדִי: 'my honor.' 'You restore my prestige which was lost when I was forced to flee from my son in disgrace.'

וּמֵרִים רֹאשִׁי — And to raise up my pride [lit. my head].

[When David fled from Absalom he covered his face and head in mourning and shame.] I am confident that you will restore my dignity and lift me up again to my throne (Metzudas David).

5. קוֹלִי אֶל ה' אֶקְרָא וַיַּעֲנֵנִי — [With] my voice I call out to HASHEM and He answers [lit. 'would or did answer'].

Ibn Ezra connects this verse to the preceding one. David sees God as his shield because he knows that to win he need not even enter into battle; rather, by merely calling out sincerely with his קוֹל, voice, to Hashem his victory and safety are assured.

וַיַּעֲנֵנִי — [And] He answers me [lit. 'He did answer me'].

The word is literally in past tense. Radak explains that David had so much

1. David refers here to Hashem as being his מָגֵן, 'shield'. This brings us to the topic of the 'Magen David', [lit. shield of David] popularly known as 'the Star of David', and regarded as a symbol of Judaism. Strangely, there is no mention of this symbol or its meaning in any authoritative Jewish book.

Harav Moshe Feinstein שליט"א, in Igros Moshe (Orach Chaim Vol. 3, Res. 15) tells us that the most convincing source for this sign is David himself. For it is clear that David did not find security in battle from any armor or shield. Only in God did he find himself securely enveloped, invulnerable from every side — above and below, east, west, north, south, — six directions in all. Thus the six-pointed symbol stands for David's true shield — God! Harav Feinstein concludes that for this reason this symbol, hallowed by centuries of traditional usage, should be respected, because it is meant to symbolize the eternal Jewish faith in God no matter what the adversity.

The term 'Magen David,' is also to be found in the Talmud (Pesachim 117b): 'And I shall make you a great name, equal to the names of the greatest (II Samuel 7:9). Rav Yosef said: This is why we say 'Magen David.' Just as we conclude the first benediction of Shemoneh Esrei by praising God as 'Magen Avraham' the Shield of Abraham, so too, we conclude the blessings of the Haftarah by praising Him as 'Magen David', the Shield of David.

for my soul, and to raise up my pride.
    5 *With my voice I call out to HASHEM,*
        and He answers me from His holy mountain.
        Selah.
    6 *I lay down and slept;*
        yet I awoke, for HASHEM supports me.

confidence in Hashem's response (and perhaps he even had a prophetic promise in regard to this) that whenever he would call upon Hashem he was sure that his wish would be fulfilled. Therefore, he felt as if God had already answered his request, and the response was a thing of the past.

מֵהַר קָדְשׁוֹ סֶלָה — *from His holy mountain, Selah.*

There is some doubt as to which mountain is meant.

Radak suggests that it might be Mount Moriah (the Temple Mount). Although at that time it was not yet sanctified it is very possible that they already knew that upon this mount the *Beis haMikdash* was destined to be built [cf. *Zevachim* 54b]. For this reason, David, fled the city by way of הַר הַזֵּיתִים, *the Mount of Olives,* and there he prostrated himself to God, because from there one has a clear, direct view of the Temple Mount. Another possibility is that the *'holy mountain'* refers to Mount Zion where the Holy Ark was deposited temporarily at that time.

6. אֲנִי שָׁכַבְתִּי וָאִישָׁנָה — *I lay down and [I] slept.*

In the darkest hour of his despair, David's heart was paralyzed and numb with worry and fear and so he retreated into senseless sleep (*Rashi*).

הֱקִיצוֹתִי — *[Yet] I awoke!*

From my worries I awoke triumphantly for I was filled with new confidence that God would support me (*Rashi*).

Radak disagrees with *Rashi* and holds that David was never gripped with panic. Each action described here introduces an additional manifestation of David's serene faith in God. Thus, 'Even when in mortal danger, I lay down to sleep normally, and I slept peacefully like a man free of all worries. Even when I awoke, I arose calmly, not like a man who falls asleep in anguish, who usually awakens abruptly, startled and perturbed by the nightmares which plague him.'[1]

Malbim emphasizes that this verse refers to the very first night of David's flight. Had Absalom but followed Achitophel's advice he could have pursued and easily wiped out David's meager force. David was well aware of this possibility, yet he went to sleep calmly, trusting that he would wake up alive the next morning, because God would surely foil Absalom's plot, as indeed happened.

כִּי ה' יִסְמְכֵנִי — *For HASHEM supports me.*

[Here again God is designated as Hashem the Merciful, and it is in that

1. One time, when the *Brisker Rav, Harav Yitzchok Zev Soloveitchik* was a refugee in Warsaw early in World War II, he was trapped in the doomed city during the murderous Nazi siege and bombardment. The imminent danger, the terror, the relentless explosions, let no one sleep. Only the Brisker Rav did not change his daily schedule. And every night he made a point of getting into bedclothes for a normal night's sleep. He explained that in times of great peril there is a special obligation to remain serene and to openly display this tranquility. Only thus can one proclaim his total confidence in the protection of Hashem. The proof for this, he concluded, is this verse which proves that David lay down and slumbered peacefully even though he faced disaster.

ז יִסְמְכֵנִי: לֹא־אִירָא מֵרִבְבוֹת עָם אֲשֶׁר
ח סָבִיב שָׁתוּ עָלָי: קוּמָה יהוה | הוֹשִׁיעֵנִי
אֱלֹהַי כִּי־הִכִּיתָ אֶת־כָּל־אֹיְבַי לֶחִי שִׁנֵּי
ט רְשָׁעִים שִׁבַּרְתָּ: לַיהוה הַיְשׁוּעָה עַל־עַמְּךָ
בִרְכָתֶךָ סֶּלָה:

capacity that David is confident of His merciful support.]

Yaaros D'vash calls attention to the manner in which David was awakened every night precisely at midnight. God aimed a north wind at the strings of David's harp and the melody thus composed would awaken him. David here sings of the fact that even now he awakens in such miraculous fashion — הֱקִיצוֹתִי, *'I awaken'*. This proves that God still loves him and yearns for his songs in the night, proving that *'Hashem supports me.'*

7. לֹא אִירָא מֵרִבְבוֹת עָם — *I fear not the myriad people.*

The masses of Israel followed Absalom with few exceptions *(Radak)*.

Because HASHEM is my support, I have no fear of even the most overwhelming odds *(Metzudas David)*.

שָׁתוּ — *Deployed against.*

Radak and *Rashi* (in alternate translations) define the word as *'place themselves'*, i.e. they take up strategic locations from all sides. *Radak* and *Ibn Ezra* explain the word as *'to make war'*. *Ibn Ezra* sees a relationship here to the word רְשָׁתוֹת, *'nets'*: thus David describes the dragnet into which his enemies entrapped him. *Rashi* prefers to render the word as *'ruined'*; *'made desolate'*.

8. קוּמָה ה' הוֹשִׁיעֵנִי אֱלֹהַי — *Rise up HASHEM, save me my God!*

Because I have unshakeable faith in You, Hashem, it is only proper that You arise to save me *(Metzudas David)*.

[In reality, true faith in Hashem does not mean that one should believe that Hashem will always cause the result which the faithful desire. Genuine faith is the conviction that whatever occurs is a response to God's wish, not a coincidence. God's will may or may not coincide with the wishes of those who trust in Him. However, David introduces us to another concept: There is a great reward for faith! By virtue of the fact that the faithful man truly believes that only Hashem's will is of significance, Hashem reciprocates and is prepared to change His original plan in order to fulfill the desire of the faithful *(Maharal, Nesivos Olam, Nesiv HaTeshuvah* 1). [Cf. footnote to 27:3.]

Therefore, David says *'Rise up, HASHEM — The Merciful'*, grant my request for mercy! But this mercy is not an undeserved kindness, rather the strict letter of the law now demands this. For this is the promised reward of the faithful. Therefore, *'Save me* אֱלֹהַי *my God'*, The Judge; even in the capacity of unbending administrator of strict justice, I merit salvation.']

7 *I fear not the myriad people*
deployed against me from every side.
8 *Rise up, HASHEM, save me my God!*
For You struck all of my enemies on the cheek,
You broke the teeth of the wicked.
9 *Salvation is HASHEM's,*
upon Your people is Your blessing. Selah.

כִּי הִכִּיתָ אֶת כָּל אֹיְבַי לֶחִי — *For You struck*
all of my enemies on the cheek.

Radak explains the shift from future
tense to past — 'I am confident that You
will rise up for me in the future, for in
the past You always have struck my
enemies.' An alternate solution is that
the usage of the past tense here repeats
the theme of *v.5* where we see that the
moment David calls out for future support, he is so sure of Hashem's response
that it is as if the aid has already come.

הִכִּיתָ ... לֶחִי — *You struck ... the cheek.*
It was a mere blow, but a slap of disgrace (*Rashi; Metzudas David*).
[The לֶחִי, specifically refers to the
jawbone which is covered by the cheek.
The jawbone moves prominently during
the act of speech, thus we have an allusion to Achitophel who was terribly disgraced when his words of advice to Absalom were rejected. So mortified was
he that he hung himself in shame, a fate
well-deserved for his treacherous
betrayal of King David.]

שִׁנֵּי רְשָׁעִים שִׁבַּרְתָּ — *You broke the teeth*
of the wicked.
Rashi interprets שִׁנֵּי, as a metaphor
for *might.*
The teeth which they grit in anger

and hatred, you have always broken
(*Metzudas David*).

9. [David concludes, declaring that the
episode of Absalom has taught a lesson
in delineating the distinctly different
roles of God and man in the shaping of
human events.]

לָה׳ הַיְשׁוּעָה — *Salvation is HASHEM's.*
[lit. *'to HASHEM is the salvation'*]
I.e. it is Hashem's responsibility to
save His servants and His people
(*Rashi*).

עַל עַמְּךָ בִרְכָתֶךָ — *Upon Your people is*
[i.e, their duty is] *Your blessing.*
It is their obligation to bless You and
to offer thanks for Your salvation
(*Rashi*).
[God derives strength, so to speak,
from the blessings and prayers of man.
The intensity of man's appreciation of
His role in the control of human events
influences God's guidance of the
destiny of the universe. רֹכֵב שָׁמַיִם בְּעֶזְרֶךָ
'He rides the heavens with your [man's]
help' (*Deut.* 33:26). David merely
repented and prayed, taking no military
action. Yet God brought about a great
salvation by foiling Absalom's plot.]

David composed this psalm, too, as he fled from Absalom (Radak).
In the previous psalm, David called to God for salvation, but in
this psalm he addressed his enemies, lecturing them to improve their
morals and ethics. In v. 5, he tells his adversaries that it is the Evil
Inclination who is the real enemy, not he. In verses 6 and 7, he rips
away the false masks of Absalom's followers, declaring that not one is
motivated by true loyalty to the young upstart. Absalom is really no
more than a puppet, a tool in their selfish hands. His supporters
merely exploit the opportunity to elevate themselves at David's expense.

The Yalkut (II Samuel, ch. 16) tells us that the most flagrant example of this selfish opportunism was Absalom's staunchest supporter,
Achitophel. This eminent counselor had a dream wherein he saw that
royalty was destined to emanate from him. He interpreted this to
mean that he would someday sit on the throne.

In truth, the dream meant that royalty would come from his seed
by way of his granddaughter, Bath-Sheba, wife of David and mother
of Solomon. In order to realize his ambitions, Achitophel urged Absalom to publicly violate his father's ten concubines. Then he advised
him to pursue and slay the king. Achitophel intended to display
'righteous zeal' by bringing Absalom to court for his atrocities. Then
after disposing of Absalom, he would be free to take the vacant
throne.

All this David sees clearly, and he implores these men to save
themselves from disaster through repentance. He displays the great
generosity of his being: instead of seeking ruthless revenge from his
enemies, he prefers reconciliation, and offers to guide them to true
fortune and happiness.

ד א-ב לַמְנַצֵּחַ בִּנְגִינוֹת מִזְמוֹר לְדָוִד: בְּקָרְאִי
עֲנֵנִי | אֱלֹהֵי צִדְקִי בַּצָּר הִרְחַבְתָּ לִּי חָנֵּנִי
ג וּשְׁמַע תְּפִלָּתִי: בְּנֵי־אִישׁ עַד־מֶה כְבוֹדִי

1. לַמְנַצֵּחַ — For the Conductor.

[This familiar introduction to many psalms appears here for the very first time.]

Radak explains that the מְנַצֵּחַ was the Levite who directed the entire Temple orchestra. Every festival, and every occasion, indeed, every day — required songs and hymns to accompany the sacrifices; the singers and musicians were directed by the 'conductor'. To this man only, David handed over his compositions. Therefore, no psalm is introduced with לַמְנַגֵּן, 'to the musician' or לַמְשׁוֹרֵר, 'to the singer', the score was given to no one but the conductor.

Rashi maintains that every Levite performer was worthy of this title, for a מְנַצֵּחַ (from the word נִצָּחוֹן, triumph) masters himself, and prevails upon his entire being to strive for a superlative service every time. This strenuous exertion to do God's will was a hallmark of the entire Levite tribe.

[Literally the root נצח can be interpreted in two ways. The first way is נֶצַח, 'eternity'. This reading suggests that David knew full well that the message of Psalms was not restricted to his day and age, but was for all times. By passing the composition on to the Levites, who in turn, transmitted it to the entire nation, David assured the propagation and perpetuation of his songs. Thus לַמְנַצֵּחַ could be rendered as 'to him who makes eternal.'

The second interpretation of the word is נָצַח, 'victorious'. It refers to this warrior-king's most efficacious military 'tactics'. David never ceased to ridicule arms and might; he saw victory only in repentance and praise of God. 'Conquer yourselves and then you shall conquer your enemies.' Therefore, when David dispatched this psalm of self-conquest to the Levite singers, he was sure that

military victory was his. Thus לַמְנַצֵּחַ may be translated as, 'to the course which insures victory.']

Finally, the Talmud interprets this word as a reference to God.

'To Him who causes victory, a song unto David.' A song to God who is Himself vanquished, but nevertheless rejoices. Observe how different the nature of Hashem is from that of mortal men. A creature of flesh and blood suffers defeat and he is sad, but Hashem is bested — and He is glad! (Pesachim 119a).

[Even when the sins of Israel anger God and cause His wrath to be kindled against them, He rejoices when a 'tzaddik' arises and allays His anger by means of prayer and good deeds. This righteous man is provided with the power to be 'victorious' over God by God Himself.]

בִּנְגִינוֹת — With instrumental music.

Ibn Ezra and Radak note that there was a particular group of instruments used in the Temple which were called נְגִינוֹת, neginos. Similarly, the elaborate Temple orchestra contained a variety of special instrument sections such as מְצַלְתַּיִם, כִּינּוֹרוֹת, נְבָלִים, etc.

Radak here delves into the subtleties and intricacies of Temple music and stresses that the art of musicology is an essential wisdom, for melodies have the power to arouse the soul as nothing else can (see Overview).

2. בְּקָרְאִי עֲנֵנִי אֱלֹהֵי צִדְקִי — When I call, answer me, God of my vindication [lit. 'my righteousness'].

Because You have always vindicated my righteousness in the past, therefore, I beseech You to be gracious to me now as well (Metzudas David).

Since David is fleeing from the false accusations hurled against him by Ab-

For the Conductor; with instrumental music.
A song of David.
² *When I call, answer me, God of my vindication,*
You have relieved me of my distress,
be gracious to me and hear my prayer.
³ *Sons of great men:*

---

salom, he appeals to אֱלֹהֵי צִדְקִי, *'God of my righteousness'*, Who knows that justice is with David (*Radak*).

בַּצָּר הִרְחַבְתָּ לִּי — *You have relieved me of my distress.*

In days gone by You have helped me when I was in distress; now too, take pity on me and hear my prayer (*Rashi*).

David's use of the past tense is another demonstration of his un-shakeable faith. Even while he prayed for assistance, he was so confident of Hashem's response that he considered it like an already accomplished fact (*Radak*). [See 3, vs. 5 and 8 in *Radak*.]

[צָר *'distress'* means lit. 'a tight, con-stricted place'; while הִרְחַבְתָּ *'relieved'* means lit. *'widened, enlarged.'*]

David said to the Holy One, Blessed be He: Master of the Universe! Every time I was constricted by difficult cir-cumstances, You 'enlarged' them and set me free. I was caught in the dilemma of Bath-Sheba and You presented me with a son, Solomon. I was caught in the distress of all Israel and You gave me the Temple [i.e., permission to begin making preparations for the construc-tion which would be undertaken by Solomon] (*Yerushalmi Taanis* 2:9).

[This declaration is an eloquent ex-pression of one of David's most cherished credos. Never be discouraged by the terrible burdens and pressures of life. Every frustrating enfeebling situa-tion is in reality a divinely given oppor-tunity to overcome adversity by fully utilizing one's talent and ability. Thus every צָר, every distress which threatens to shrink and limit an individual, can serve as הַרְחָבָה, to broaden his scope and to enlarge his soul.]

חָנֵּנִי וּשְׁמַע תְּפִלָּתִי — *Be gracious to me and hear my prayer.*

[חָנֵּנִי derives from the word חֵן, *grace,* which implies that the subject has found favor in the eyes of the observer for no real, explicable reason. Thus, the word חֵן, *grace,* is related to חִנָּם, *un-earned,* for there is nothing tangible or substantial to justify this attraction. David adheres to the principle that one should never insist that he is meritorious and deserving of God's favor. Such a proud demand can arouse intensified scrutiny by the Heavenly Tribunal to ascertain the justice of such a demand. And who can presume to survive such close scrutiny? (See *Tur Orach Chaim* 98.) Therefore, although David begins by protesting his righteousness, he concludes with a plea that God take pity on him and show him favor 'for nothing', even if he is un-deserving.]

3. בְּנֵי אִישׁ — *Sons of great men* [lit. *'man'*]

You are sons of Abraham, Isaac, and Jacob, each of whom is described by the Torah as אִישׁ, *great man* (*Rashi*).

[This word אִישׁ is used in Scriptures to denote the superior man as opposed to אָדָם, which refers to the ordinary human being.]

David is addressing the distinguished leaders of Israel who are following Ab-salom (*Radak*).

According to *Midrash Shocher Tov* this refers to Doeg and Achitophel.

You prominent scions of noble des-cent, why do you persist in shaming me instead of according me with the honor due a king? One can forgive the low-ly man of humble origins for not ap-

לִכְלִמָּה תֶאֱהָבוּן רִיק תְּבַקְשׁוּ כָזָב סֶלָה: ד
ד וּדְעוּ כִּי־הִפְלָה יהוה חָסִיד לוֹ יהוה
ה יִשְׁמַע בְּקָרְאִי אֵלָיו: רִגְזוּ וְאַל־תֶּחֱטָאוּ

preciating the value of royalty. But you who were bred with honor and dignity should understand the significance of respecting a monarch (*Metzudas David*).

You yourselves are *'sons of men'*: obedient children to your own fathers. Why, then, do you assist my son, Absalom, to degrade his father? Since you are responsible for כְּבוֹדִי לִכְלִמָּה, *'putting my honor to shame'* you will be punished measure for measure by your own sons who will disgrace you. Thus, תֶאֱהָבוּן רִיק *'your love'* (for your sons) *will be in vain'* (*Tehillas Hashem, Rav Yosef Yaavetz*).

עַד מֶה כְבוֹדִי לִכְלִמָּה — *How long will you put my honor to shame?*

Doeg and Achitophel ardently spread slander and evil tales against David (*Yerushalmi Peah* 1:1).

How long will you disgrace me by referring to me as a non-entity without personal attainment? David's enemies did not refer to him by his own name, only as a son of Jesse, implying that his stature was due solely to his distinguished father. Saul said *'You have chosen the son of Jesse'* (*I Sam.* 20:30); and *'When my son made a pact with the son of Jesse'* (*ibid.* 22:8). Doeg said *'I saw the son of Jesse'* (*ibid.* 22:9). *'And Nabal answered David's servants and said, 'Who is David? And who is the son of Jesse?'* (*ibid.* 25:10) (*Rashi*).

Tehillos Hashem questions David's complaint. Why should David take umbrage at being called the son of Jesse? On the contrary, such a name is a badge of supreme distinction, for Jesse

was one of the great men of his time, accompanied by a staggering 600,000 disciples whenever he entered and left the Beis Hamedrash (*Berachos* 58a). Furthermore, this unique 'tzaddik' was one of only four great saints who died without any trace of personal sin (*Bava Basra* 17a).

The answer is that David realized that his detractors referred to his lineage only in order not to mention his hated name, so as to obliterate him. The proof is that only in bursts of vicious anger did they call him *'son of Jesse'*; in calmer times they did call him *'David'*. Thus, David's query is rendered: *'How long will you use my honor'*, i.e. my illustrious ancestry, as a tool *'to put me to shame?'*

תֶאֱהָבוּן רִיק — *And love vanity.*

You men who desire the rule of Absalom, I warn you that his success is but temporary. It is a vain and futile attempt which cannot endure (*Radak*).

Normally a person desires to acquire a tangible object, but you strive after empty dreams and wild fantasies which can never come to be (*Be'er Abraham*).

תְּבַקְשׁוּ כָזָב — *And seek deception.*

In addition to defaming me, you search for false and evil reports about me, such as those of the Ziffim (*I Sam.* Ch. 23) who displayed friendship but secretly betrayed me to Saul (*Rashi*).[1]

The word כָזָב is used to describe something which offers great expectations at the outset but later peters out to the disappointment of all. Therefore, a river run dry is referred to as נָהָר כּוֹזֵב.

1. *Rav Simcha Bunim Sofer* sees in this verse a penetrating analysis of those who slander the righteous. They enthusiastically inflate the slightest error of the Tzaddik to grotesque proportions so as to justify and mitigate their own evil ways. David lashes out at them, 'Why do you put my honor to undue shame? Because you love vanity and falsehood, you use me as an excuse to pursue your desires.'

How long will you put my honor to shame,
and love vanity, and seek deception? Selah.
⁴ *Recognize that*
Just as HASHEM distinguished His devoted one,
HASHEM will listen when I call upon Him.
⁵ *Tremble and sin not,*

Similarly, Absalom's revolt, although it started with every indication of success, will soon fade away (*Radak*).

The *Yalkut*, also rendering כָּזָב as a temporary situation, has David confronting his enemies and saying: 'Do you think that God's departure from me will be permanent? My fortunes will change and God will once again *'Listen to me when I call out to Him'* (v. 4).

סֶלָה — *Selah.*
[A word meaning *'forever'* or a musical instruction. See *comm.* to 3:3.]

4. וּדְעוּ כִּי הִפְלָה ה׳ חָסִיד לוֹ — *Recognize that just as HASHEM distinguished His devoted one.*
וּדְעוּ, *'recognize'* [lit. *'and know'*.] [The prefix *'vov'*, indicates special emphasis on this word and denotes a command to take heed.]

Pay close attention to the fact that just as Hashem draws close to those who are devoted to Him, so, too, has He singled me out for preferential treatment, so you will never succeed against me (*Metzudas David*).

הִפְלָה, *'distinguished'* [lit. *'set apart'*.] Because God saw me to be a חָסִיד, who acts לִפְנִים מִשּׁוּרַת הַדִּין, 'beyond the basic requirements of the law', He 'separated' me to be king over His people.

The *Yalkut* maintains that David refers to the distinction he achieved by receiving a special communique, delivered orally by Nathan the Prophet, relating divine pardon for his sin: גַּם ה׳ הֶעֱבִיר חַטָּאתְךָ לֹא תָמוּת, *'Furthermore, HASHEM has wiped away your sin, you shall not die'* (II Sam. 12:13). This complete absolution confirmed David as being a חָסִיד, *'a devout person.'*

5. רִגְזוּ וְאַל תֶּחֱטָאוּ — *Tremble and sin not.*

רִגְזוּ, *'tremble'*. Tremble before the Holy One, Blessed be He, and do not sin (*Rashi*).

Said David: If you lack a sense of awe for me, your king, at least fear Hashem who endorses me — and do not rebel (*Radak*).

Homiletically, this verse exhorts Israel to tremble from the spectre of sin, to the point where sin becomes disturbing and traumatic. רִגְזוּ would thus mean *'be distressed and upset'* by the prospect of sin.

Rabbeinu Yonah of Gerondi in his *Shaarei Teshuvah* (1:4) derives one of the fundamentals of repentance from these words:

''Reflect further upon the great evil of him who defers repentence. If he would not delay, but would repent immediately, sighing in bitterness of heart, in agitation and anxiety, his eyes overflowing in sorrow, then, when his Evil Inclination would encounter him a second time and set sin before him, he would conquer his inclination. He would recall his experience with the cup of bitterness and would not venture to drink of it again, as it says, רִגְזוּ וְאַל תֶּחֱטָאוּ — which means, *'Be agitated and aggrieved over your previous sins and thus you will not sin again.'* The sin referred to in this verse is the one mentioned previously (v. 3) *'you seek falsehood.'* This interpretation is substantiated by the use of the word רִגְזוּ, meaning *'agitation'* as in אַל תִּרְגְּזוּ בַּדָּרֶךְ *'Do not be agitated on the road'* (Gen. 45:24) and וְתַחְתַּי אֶרְגָּז — *'I grow agitated where I stand'* (Habakuk 3:16). This

ו-ז אִמְרוּ בִלְבַבְכֶם עַל־מִשְׁכַּבְכֶם וְדֹמּוּ סֶלָה:
זִבְחוּ זִבְחֵי־צֶדֶק וּבִטְחוּ אֶל־יהוה: רַבִּים
אֹמְרִים מִי־יַרְאֵנוּ טוֹב נְסָה־עָלֵינוּ אוֹר
ח פָּנֶיךָ יהוה: נָתַתָּה שִׂמְחָה בְלִבִּי מֵעֵת

---

term alone signifies extreme remorse over the past and the present. It is to be noted that precisely for this reason, the word רְגָזוּ was chosen to convey this message and not יִרְאוּ, 'fear', or גּוּרוּ, 'cower'.

אִמְרוּ בִלְבַבְכֶם עַל מִשְׁכַּבְכֶם — *Reflect* [lit. 'say'] *in your hearts* [while] *on your beds.*

When one lays down to sleep he can think with clarity and objectivity because he abandons his daily pursuits and schemes. That, suggests David, is the perfect time to contemplate the plain truth of my innocence and the falsehood of my detractors (*Radak; Metzudas David*).

וְדֹמּוּ סֶלָה — *And be utterly silent, Selah.*

Put an end to your revolt. דְּמָמָה, [lit. 'petrified, frozen'] is more than שְׁתִיקָה, 'silence'. It implies a complete cessation, not only of talk, but of all sound and activity (*Radak*).

The Sages of the Talmud (*Berachos* 5a) interpret this verse homiletically. 'A person should constantly arouse his יֵצֶר טוֹב, *his good inclination*, to battle against his יֵצֶר הָרַע, *his evil inclination*, as it says, רִגְזוּ וְאַל תֶּחֱטָאוּ, 'Be agitated and do not sin.' If he succeeded in overwhelming the evil inclination, all is well. If not, he should engage in Torah study, as it says, אִמְרוּ בִלְבַבְכֶם, '*Reflect in your hearts*'. If he is victorious, all is well. If not, he should recite the portion of *Shema* [through which one accepts

the yoke of God's sovereignty] when he lies down to sleep, as it says עַל מִשְׁכַּבְכֶם, '*while on your beds*'. If he conquers, all is well. If not, he should remind himself of the awesome day of death, as it says, וְדֹמּוּ סֶלָה, '*and be utterly silent, selah*'.[1]

6. זִבְחוּ זִבְחֵי צֶדֶק — *Offer up sacrifices of righteousness.*

[As explained in the *Prefatory Remarks*, David here exposes the true motivation of Absalom's followers. No one cares for Absalom; each is concerned only with realizing his personal ambitions. Now David calls upon these men to abandon these selfish aspirations]: 'Conquer your evil inclination. Rectify your deeds, and it will be considered like an actual sacrificial offering' (*Targum; Rashi*).

Because you have sinned until now, you require a sacrifice to achieve atonement. But take care that your offering should not be an insincere token like the offerings of the wicked who return to their sins immediately, thus rendering their sacrifice an abomination before God. Rather, accompany your offerings with genuine repentance so that they will indeed be זִבְחֵי צֶדֶק, *sacrifices of righteousness* (*Radak*).

וּבִטְחוּ אֶל ה' — *And trust in HASHEM.*

Rashi tells us that this statement comes to reinforce David's call for self-sacrifice. A sinner cannot easily abandon his evil ways as long as he is

---

1. [The Sages vividly emphasize that life is not simple. It is a constant struggle; a fierce, unending battle to curb our base lusts and desires. We must not hesitate to use the most powerful weapons available to wage this war. The *Chovas haLevovos* (*Yichud haMa'aseh* 5) records that a pious man once encountered a band of soldiers coming home from the battlefront. He said to them: 'The war from which you return was only a relatively minor skirmish. Prepare yourselves now for normal, daily living which is a truly great war against the evil inclination and his agents!' (see *Overview*).]

Reflect in your hearts while on your beds,
and be utterly silent. Selah.
⁶ Offer up sacrifices of righteousness,
and trust in HASHEM.
⁷ Many always say, 'Who will show us good?'
Let the light of Your face shine upon us, HASHEM.
⁸ But in my heart You put gladness

still convinced that success and profit can be obtained only through criminal undertakings. Therefore, David reassures his prospective repenters that God can easily satisfy all their wants and needs if they will but trust in Him completely. There is no necessity for them to slander and betray David to his enemies for monetary advantages.

7. רַבִּים אֹמְרִים מִי יַרְאֵנוּ טוֹב — *Many always say: 'Who will show us good?'*

Radak ascribes these words to the supporters of Absalom who say: 'If only Absalom were victorious and David were killed! With David's downfall all of our dreams for better times would come true'.

Rashi explains that a person would always be content with his lot if he would not look around and find someone living better. Here, the people have been stirred to jealousy and yearning because they observe the prosperity and tranquility of the heathens.

נְסָה עָלֵינוּ אוֹר פָּנֶיךָ ה' — *Let the light of Your face shine upon us, HASHEM.*

[David responds to those who envy the material success of the gentiles. He pities these poor creatures who deprive themselves of all the rich experiences of Judaism which fill the devout with ecstasy and satisfaction, placing them above petty ambitions. David pleads with God to bathe these frozen souls with the warmth of His Presence. Surely, this will alter their perverted standards.]

נְסָה, [lit. 'lift up'.] This verb is derived from נֵס, a *flag* or *standard* such as הָרִימוּ נֵס, 'raise up the flag' (Isaiah

62:10). David said to them: Raise up a new standard for yourselves: the shining of God's face (*Rashi*).

[There is a special significance attached to the lesson of this verse. David is talking to fully observant and practicing Jews whose downfall is due only to their adopting a non-Jewish value system. In contemporary times we are also plagued with the phenomenon of the 'observant Jew' who is corrupted because he makes secular success and not Torah achievment his prime value.]

8. נָתַתָּה שִׂמְחָה בְלִבִּי — *But in my heart You put gladness.*

[David continues to explain why one should not live according to a non-Jewish value system.]

Although the prosperity of the gentiles fills many Israelites with envy and bitterness, I am not jealous at all. Rather their success gladdens me. For I am confident that if God bestows such bounty upon those who anger Him, how much more so will He reward those who obey His wishes [Israel] on the day of future reward (*Rashi*).

You Hashem implanted in my heart the trait of being שָׂמֵחַ בְּחֶלְקִי, 'Happy with my portion', at all times. Therefore, whatever my lot, I am even happier than are the gentiles during their joyous harvest festival (*Metzudas David*).

Radak and *Ibn Ezra* notice here the essence of David's wonderful personality. His humane reply to his enemies is: Although you wish me only misery, I am sincerely gladdened by your moments of happiness, since God

ט דְּגָנָם וְתִירוֹשָׁם רָבּוּ: בְּשָׁלוֹם יַחְדָּו
אֶשְׁכְּבָה וְאִישָׁן כִּי־אַתָּה יהוה לְבָדָד
לָבֶטַח תּוֹשִׁיבֵנִי:

has endowed my heart with gladness in the welfare of all men.

מֵעֵת דְּגָנָם וְתִירוֹשָׁם רָבּוּ — *From when their grain and wine abounded.* 'Israel said: You have rewarded the gentile nations who have maintained only the seven Noachide rules with contentment in this world. We who are obligated in six hundred and thirteen mitzvos will cetainly be showered with good rewards in the World to Come. Therefore, when we see the contentment of the gentiles we rejoice.

Rabbi Joshua ben Levi said: This may be illustrated by the parable of the king who made a great feast. At first the guests were seated by the entrance of the palace. They saw the dogs coming out of the banquet hall, their teeth clenching pheasants, stuffed birds, and calf heads. The guests said to each other: 'If even the dogs dine so sump-tuously, imagine what a lavish feast has been prepared for us!' *(Midrash Shocher Tov).*

9. בְּשָׁלוֹם יַחְדָּו אֶשְׁכְּבָה וְאִישָׁן — *In peaceful unity I could lie down and sleep.*

If only all of Israel were in peace together with me, then I would lie down and sleep with confidence without fear of any enemy *(Rashi).*

[David ends this psalm, intended as a moral lesson for his pursuers, on a note of peace and reconciliation.] The *Yalkut* explains that this type of conclusion is customary: The Congregation of Israel said before the Holy One, Blessed be He, 'All of our prophets conclude their words with an appeal for the peace and tranquility of Israel. All of our prophets begin with harsh admonition and con-clude with gentle consolation.'

from when their grain and wine abounded.
⁹ In peaceful unity I could lie down and sleep,
For You, HASHEM, will make me dwell
apart and secure.

בִּי אַתָּה ה' לְבָדָד לָבֶטַח תּוֹשִׁיבֵנִי — *For You,*
HASHEM, will make me dwell apart and
secure.

The translation follows *Rashi* who
reads the words לְבָדָד לָבֶטַח together as a
description of the ideal state of the
Jewish people. This usage is similar to
בֶּטַח בָּדָד עֵין יַעֲקֹב, *'Secure and alone the*
fountain of Jacob' (Deut. 33:28).

Radak, however, interprets לְבָדָד as
an adjective for Hashem rendering: *For*
You alone, HASHEM, לָבֶטַח תּוֹשִׁיבֵנִי *can*
bring security to my dwelling.

[This is David's final plea to the camp
of Absalom, to abandon its folly. He
refers here to their adoption of an alien
concept of monarchy. When Israel first
demanded of the Prophet Samuel that
he appoint a king for them, they were
motivated by a feeling of inferiority and
a desire to imitate the gentiles. *"Appoint*

for us a king who will rule us like all the
nations" (I Sam. 8:5). Thus Saul's ill-
conceived reign was doomed from the
start. David's monarchy was intended
to rectify this terrible distortion by
presenting an authentically Jewish
sovereignty which emphasizes the king
as a spiritual leader and a representative
of God. Those who favored Absalom
were once again reverting back to the
false, gentile notion of royalty. Young
Absalom certainly surpassed the aging
David with his external splendor, his
beautiful long hair and his impressive
retinue of fifty swift runners.

David concludes his heartfelt
remonstrance to his challengers with a
plea to find security only in God, not in
the majesty of kings. Let us live alone,
insulated from foreign concepts, thus
being assured of eternal tranquility.]

5 מזמור ה

I n the previous psalm, David spoke to the masses who followed Absalom. He admonished them for adopting alien, gentile values. In this psalm he describes the ideologists of the revolt, specifically Achitophel, whose crime surpasses that of the masses. Achitophel has not imitated foreign ways; rather he has taken the most authentic of Jewish concepts, the Holy Torah itself, and grotesquely distorted it to serve his own ends. Instead of studying Torah for the sake of pure truth which penetrates to the very core of one's being, filling it with a love and awareness of God, Achitophel learned only for the sake of presenting an outer appearance of brilliance and originality. Inwardly he yearned only for power and honor. Because he sought to impress people with his ability to be a self-made man, he never accepted the authority and discipline of a 'Rebbe', a teacher and so he had no link with tradition.

Achitophel closely resembled another arch enemy of David, Doeg the Edomite, a great prodigy and scholar. He, too, was insincere and hated the successful David with a passion. He, too, resorted to bloodshed and deceit in an attempt to obliterate David's name.

Thus, we can well appreciate why this psalm is dedicated to נְחִילוֹת, which Midrash Shocher Tov renders as נַחֲלוֹת 'an estate, an eternal inheritance.' This refers, we are told, to the Torah which is an inheritance for all of Israel, for all times. The Midrash continues: 'Rav Chanan said: The Torah mourns because Torah scholars are impoverished. Hasn't it been promised otherwise, that those who engage in Torah will receive riches and honor?' To this the Holy Spirit replies: לְהַנְחִיל אֹהֲבַי יֵשׁ, 'That I may cause those who love me to inherit a substance of value' (Proverbs 18:21). 'I keep the scholars impoverished now so that riches should not corrupt them and lure them away to material pursuits causing them to forget their Torah.'

For Doeg and Achitophel the Torah was not an 'inheritance'. They were too proud to receive it from teachers, so their Torah was not genuine. They were ruined by the lure of riches and fame and so their studies did not remain with them as an 'estate' for all time.

Since this psalm is dedicated to condemning the insincere, David presents a sharp contrast to them in the four opening verses where he describes the man of faith who calls out to God in total sincerity.

א לַמְנַצֵּחַ אֶל־הַנְּחִילוֹת מִזְמוֹר לְדָוִד:
ב אֲמָרַי הַאֲזִינָה | יהוה בִּינָה הֲגִיגִי:
ג הַקְשִׁיבָה | לְקוֹל שַׁוְעִי מַלְכִּי וֵאלֹהָי כִּי־
ד אֵלֶיךָ אֶתְפַּלָּל: יהוה בֹּקֶר תִּשְׁמַע קוֹלִי

1. אֶל הַנְּחִילוֹת — *On the Nechilos.*

Rashi quotes *Menachem* who identifies this and many similar terms (such as עֲלָמוֹת, גִּיתִּית, יְדוּתוּן), as names of musical instruments. Every psalm had a unique musical accompaniment which complemented the mood of the song with an appropriate melody which assisted in conveying the message of the psalm.

Radak in the name of *Rav Hai Gaon* suggests that נְחִיל, literally means *'a swarm of bees'*, because this instrument produced a sound resembling the droning of bees. *Meiri* explains that the נְחִיל, was a stringed instrument which produced a droning effect, achieved by a swift strumming of the strings.

Rashi offers a second translation for נְחִילוֹת [derived from נָחַל, *'stream'*], suggesting that it means *'hordes of enemy soldiers'* who attack Israel.

[Thus the stringed נְחִילוֹת instrument would be the perfect accompaniment for this song. Since the song was dedicated to a time of attack, the droning, buzzing sound of the נְחִילוֹת, captured the mood of the enemy hordes who swarmed around Israel like angry, buzzing bees.][1]

2. אֲמָרַי הַאֲזִינָה ה' — *To my sayings give ear, HASHEM.*

When I have the ability to express my wants before You orally, please hearken to my words (*Rashi*).

Midrash Shocher Tov notes that a unique blessing was bestowed upon David's tribe, the Tribe of Judah, assuring them that Hashem would always listen to their prayers. שְׁמַע ה' קוֹל יְהוּדָה, *'Listen HASHEM to the call of Judah'* (Deut. 33:7).

בִּינָה הֲגִיגִי — *Perceive my thoughts.*

But when fear and worry render me mute and incapable of putting my desires into words, please understand the thoughts sealed up in my heart (*Rashi*).

Rashi goes on to note that this is one of the rare instances where בִּינָה, is translated as a verb *'have understanding'* rather than as a noun meaning *'insight, understanding.'*

However, *Metzudas David* renders the phrase as a reinforcement of David's opening plea: *'Hearken to my words of prayer for they are uttered with the utmost sincerity and understanding of my heart.'* Thus בִּינָה is a noun, as if to say, *'my thoughts contain בִּינָה, understanding.'*

[הֲגִיגִי is explained by *Ibn Ezra* as related to הגא, *utterance*. According to *Malbim* in 39:5 the word refers to a

---

1. If the enemy hordes are not sent as agents of God they are not even as dangerous as a swarm of bees or insects. The *Midrash Tanchuma* (*Vayeshev* 3) relates: Once, Emperor Antoninus and his Roman legions arrived in Ceasaria. Rabbi Shimon saw a legionaire who was handsome and robust and as tall as the cupola which was above the high pillars. He exclaimed to Rabbi Chiya, 'How well fattened the calves of Esau are!' Rabbi Chiya led him to the market and showed him baskets of grapes and figs around which the flies swarmed. He said, 'These flies and those legions are equal!'

When Rabbi Shimon related this conversation to his father, Rabbi Judah the Prince, he said, incredulously 'Does Rabbi Chiya really esteem the legions so much? Surely he overestimates them by equating them with the flies! Because the flies are God's agents for carrying out His will whereas the legions [if not divinely authorized to wage war] are helpless and serve no purpose at all!'

V
1-4

For the Conductor; on the Nechilos.

A song of David.

² *To my sayings give ear, HASHEM,*
perceive my thoughts.

³ *Heed the sound of my outcry, my King and my God,*
for to You alone do I pray.

⁴ *HASHEM, at dawn hear my voice,*
at dawn I will prepare myself for You,

---

developed thought ready for expression. See also *comm.* to 1:2 s.v. יֶהְגֶּה.]

3. הַקְשִׁיבָה — *Heed.*

Even when I call from far away. This is a more intensive form of listening than הַאֲזִינָה, *'give ear'* which indicates only what is spoken close to the ear (Malbim).

Rav S.R. Hirsch explains that קָשֵׁב, denotes the attention awakened by the sounds penetrating the ear, stimulating an anxiety and a yearning to hear more and more. Similarly we find, וְאָזְנֵי שֹׁמְעִים תִּקְשַׁבְנָה, *'and the ears of listeners shall pay heed (Isaiah 32:3).*

מַלְכִּי וֵאלֹהָי — *My King and my God.*

You are my King, and I cry to You as a servant cries out to his master; and You are also the God of Judgment who can rescue me from the lawless (Radak).

כִּי אֵלֶיךָ אֶתְפַּלָּל — *For to You alone do I pray.*

I pray to no other savior, for there is no one besides You (Radak).

Sincere prayer is a proclamation reaffirming God's interest in this world and His complete control over it. Although one feels undeserving, he should never waver in his efforts to pray continually, for God answers prayers even when the supplicant is undeserving. The very fact that the supplicant has abandoned all other avenues of salvation and humbly turns to God may be sufficient to arouse His mercy and kindness. Thus David says, *'Heed the sound of my outcry; I proclaim that you are 'my King and my*

God', that only You care enough to supervise my life and only You have the divine power to alter the events of my existence. Of course I do not deserve this kindness, but take pity on me by virtue of the very fact that *'to You alone I pray' (Chozeh David).*

4. ה' בּוֹקֶר תִּשְׁמַע קוֹלִי — *HASHEM, at dawn hear my voice.*

The early morning, before one gets involved in mundane affairs of the world, is the best time to pray (Radak).

The very first act of my day is to arise early and engage in God's service. Never do I precede my prayers with my own personal pursuits. Because I display that God is foremost in my life I hope that He will answer my plea affirmatively (Metzudas David).

Rashi observes that בּוֹקֶר, *'dawn'* is the time when God customarily metes out justice to the wicked, as it says, *'Morning by morning I shall destroy all of the wicked of the land'* (101:8).

On the other hand *Rabbeinu Bachya* points out that the morning is also a special time of רַחֲמִים, *'mercy'* for those who deserve it. [לְהַגִּיד בַּבֹּקֶר חַסְדֶּךָ, *'To tell of Your acts of kindness in the morning'* (92:3).]

בֹּקֶר אֶעֱרָךְ לְךָ — *At dawn I will prepare myself for You.*

Rabbi Azaria Figo in *Bina L'ittim* notices here an allusion to the *Mishnah* (Berachos 30b) which relates that the the חֲסִידִים הָרִאשׁוֹנִים, *'the devout men of old'*, would meditate for a full hour in

ה בֹּקֶר אֶעֱרָךְ־לְךָ וַאֲצַפֶּה: כִּי | לֹא אֵל־חָפֵץ
ו רֶשַׁע | אָתָּה לֹא יְגֻרְךָ רָע: לֹא־יִתְיַצְּבוּ
הוֹלְלִים לְנֶגֶד עֵינֶיךָ שָׂנֵאתָ כָּל־פֹּעֲלֵי אָוֶן:
ז תְּאַבֵּד דֹּבְרֵי כָזָב אִישׁ־דָּמִים וּמִרְמָה

preparation for their prayer in order to focus their full concentration on their Father in Heaven.

וַאֲצַפֶּה — *And I anticipate.*
I hopefully wait for You to exact just punishment from the wicked (Rashi).

Chozeh David asks: How could David expect Hashem's response with such confidence? The *Talmud* says, *(Berachos 55a)*: 'Whoever prays at great length and exerts intense concentration [and feels confident that he is worthy of having his wishes fulfilled *(Rashi)* will be left with heartache and dissappointment [Becuase he relies on his merits, the heavenly host scrutinizes his claim to see if he is really worthy. And who can be found blameless in a meticulous heavenly investigation?]

David himself answers this question by carefully choosing his words, which prove that he is not confident in his personal merits. He addresses Hashem, using the four-letter name which describes the מִדַת הָרַחֲמִים, 'the Divine Attribute of Mercy.' When? בֹּקֶר, *'at dawn'*, the time of special mercy. And his plea is *Hear my voice!* In other words I have no merit other than the mere fact that I cry out to You alone for mercy.

5. כִּי לֹא אֵל חָפֵץ רֶשַׁע אָתָּה — *For You are not a god who desires wickedness.*
Radak sees here an explanation of

why David is confident of God's response. 'Because You are a God who has no desire for evil, it is inevitable that the evildoers will ultimately be destroyed.'

לֹא יְגֻרְךָ רָע — *No evil sojourns with You* (Rashi; Radak; Metzudos).

This verse introduces a major theme of Torah belief. Where there is Godliness, there can be no evil. The juxtaposition of the two is an absolute impossibility. Nothing evil can emanate from Hashem Who is the source of pure good. Evil begins when men seek to limit God's sphere of influence. When men attempt to push God out of their lives, they invite misfortune to enter, for an absence of God is synonymous with misery. This may be compared to the engineer who constructed a splendid highway, smooth, straight, and completely unobstructed. He protected it by lining the roadside with a fence of thorns. If the foolish traveler insists on straying and ensnarls himself in the thorns, is the road-builder to blame? *(Sefer haChinuch).*[1]

Malbim, however, translates this as *'intimidate You'* [as in לֹא תָגוּרוּ מִפְּנֵי אִישׁ, *'Do not be intimidated before any man'* (Deut. 1:17).] Hashem does not cower before any evil man (a similar translation is found in *Midrash Tanchumah, Tazria* 7).

1. The Sages elaborated on this concept and stressed repeatedly that all evil is banished from the heavenly realm. A few examples:
'Only angels of peace may stand before God; angels of anger are repelled to a distant location' *(Midrash Tanchumah Tazria 9)*.
"Four groups will never be allowed to stand before the Divine Presence: scorners, liars, false flatterers, and those who bear evil tales, as it says: *'No evil can sojourn with You'* " *(Sanhedrin 103a, Sotah 42a)*.
"God never allows His Name to be mentioned in connection with evil as it is written *'In all places where I cause my name to be pronounced I will come to you and I will bless you'* (Ex-

V
5-7

and I anticipate.

⁵ *For You are not a god who desires wickedness,*
     no evil sojourns with You.
⁶ *The roisterers may not stand firm before Your eyes,*
     You despise all evildoers.
⁷ *Doom speakers of deception:*

---

6. יִתְיַצְּבוּ — *Stand firm.*
[As explained in the *comm.* to 2:2 this is more than just standing upright; it implies a firm, immovable position. Those who are mentally unbalanced cannot possibly remain steadily in a stable, permanent position.]

הוֹלְלִים — *The roisterers.*
In the terminology of the *Mishna* they are called מְעוֹרְבָּבִין, 'confused' and 'disoriented' (*Rashi*).

This refers to Doeg and Achitophel, as *Midrash Shocher Tov* comments (119:118) 'Although they studied even the most minute details of Torah, nevertheless, their hearts remained full of הוֹלֵלוּת, 'roistering wildness.'
[Since the root הָלֵל also means, 'praise' we might also translate הוֹלְלִים, as 'boastful men who praise themselves.' This is substantiated by *Ps.* 52 which is based on the occasion when Doeg slandered David before Saul. Hashem cries out to Doeg (*v.* 3 ibid.) מַה תִּתְהַלֵּל בְּרָעָה הַגִּבּוֹר, 'Why do you praise yourself with evil, O mighty man?' which the Talmud (*Sanhedrin* 106b) interprets: Hashem said to Doeg: Are you not a mighty scholar of Torah? Why do you boast and praise yourself with evil?']

פֹּעֲלֵי אָוֶן — *Evildoers* [lit. 'performers, producers of evil']

This refers to Doeg and Achitophel who engaged in that which should produce truth (Torah study) and perverted it to produce evil (*Midrash Shocher Tov*).

7. תְּאַבֵּד — *Doom.*
This translation of the phrase in the imperative follows *Radak* Drive them away from Your Presence.

This refers to Doeg and Achitophel. They will not live again in the Hereafter and they will not even arise for the Final Judgment. The *Mishnah* (*Sanhedrin* 90a) teaches: Three kings and four commoners forfeited their share in the World to Come. The commoners are Bilaam, Doeg, Achitophel and Gechazi (*Midrash Shocher Tov*).
[Cf. 1:6 and 2:12 where we also learn that the way of the wicked is נֹאבֵד 'doomed'.]

דֹּבְרֵי כָזָב — *Speakers of deception.* [See comm. to 4:3]
'When Doeg and Achitophel studied Torah, they did so with deception and treachery' (*Midrash Shocher Tov* 19:2).]
'Doeg and Achitophel at first did not perform the commandments. Although they later became Torah students, they never changed and remained as empty as they were before' (*Bamidbar Rabba* 18:17).

---

odus 20:21). Similarly, *'And God called the light day, and the darkness He called night'* (*Genesis* 1:5). When referring to darkness His Name is not mentioned. Also, in the last five of the Ten Commandments (from *'You shall not kill'* onwards), God's Name is not used [as opposed to the first five where the Name appears because they do not refer to heinous crimes against mankind (Cf. *footnote* to 34:22, where the man who is רַע is described as offensive both to God and to his fellow man).] This may be likened to the king who built a magnificent palace and had his coat-of-arms emblazoned in front of every room in the house with the exception of the lavatory, a place of filth (*Tosfos, Taanis* 3a s.v. וְאֵילוּ)

ח יִתְעֵב | יהוה: וַאֲנִי בְּרֹב חַסְדְּךָ אָבוֹא
בֵיתֶךָ אֶשְׁתַּחֲוֶה אֶל־הֵיכַל־קָדְשְׁךָ
ט בְּיִרְאָתֶךָ: יהוה | נְחֵנִי בְצִדְקָתֶךָ לְמַעַן
י שׁוֹרְרָי°הוֹשַׁר לְפָנַי דַּרְכֶּךָ: כִּי אֵין בְּפִיהוּ
נְכוֹנָה קִרְבָּם הַוּוֹת קֶבֶר־פָּתוּחַ גְּרֹנָם

אִישׁ דָּמִים וּמִרְמָה — *The bloodthirsty and deceitful man.*

The *Midrash (Bereishis Rabba,* Ch. 32) tells us that David refers to Achitophel and Doeg. Achitophel advised Absalom to kill his own father (*'bloodthirsty'*) and to defile his father's concubines (*'deceit'*). Doeg was in charge of massacring the entire priestly community of Nob (*'bloodthirsty'*) and he advised Saul to take David's wife, Michal, away from him and to give her to Palti (*'deceit'*).

The *Talmud (Sandhedrin* 106b) says that Doeg and Achitophel never met. Doeg lived in the days of King Saul and Achitophel lived in the time of David's reign. Neither of them lived out even half of their days, Doeg lived only 34 years, and Achitophel 33 (a full life being at least seventy years [90:10]). This is based on the verse: אַנְשֵׁי דָמִים וּמִרְמָה לֹא יֶחֱצוּ יְמֵיהֶם, *Men of bloodshed and deceit shall not live out half their days* (55:24).

יְתָעֵב ה' — *HASHEM abhors.*
Because Hashem abhors their presence they shall not live in the hereafter nor shall they rise before Him for Final Judgment (*Bereishis Rabba,* ibid.).

8. וַאֲנִי בְּרֹב חַסְדְּךָ — *As for me, through Your abundant kindness.*
The wicked whom You abhor are pushed away from You, but as for me, because I yearn only for Your abundant kindness, I draw close to You in Your holy sanctuary (*Radak*).

אָבוֹא בֵיתֶךָ — *I will enter* [lit. *'come'*] *Your House.*
I come to Your Temple to thank You for the kindness You heaped upon me in showing me the revenge taken upon my enemies (*Rashi*).

[However, the very Temple which evoked David's noblest emotions, brought forth his enemies' lowest passions. The Talmud relates (*Zevachim* 54b): David was sitting with Samuel studying the splendor of the world (the laws of the Temple). This aroused Doeg's intense envy as it is written: כִּי קִנְאַת בֵּיתְךָ אֲכָלָתְנִי, '*Because jealousy for Your house has eaten me up*' (69:10).]

אֶשְׁתַּחֲוֶה אֶל הֵיכַל קָדְשְׁךָ בְּיִרְאָתֶךָ — *I will prostrate myself towards Your Holy Sanctuary in awe of You.*
When David says בֵיתֶךָ, '*Your House*' and הֵיכַל קָדְשְׁךָ, '*your Holy Sanctuary*', he means the Holy of Holies, the resting place of the אָרוֹן, '*the Holy Ark.*' Whoever wished to bow down to Hashem would prostrate himself in that direction (*Radak*).

בְּיִרְאָתֶךָ — *In awe of You.*
Malbim contrasts David's attitude with that of the heathen. The idol-worshipper visits his temple only when gripped by fear lest he be punished by the wrath of his deity. As he gazes upon his lifeless idol of dead wood and stone, his terror slowly subsides and departs. Not so with Hashem, the Living God. David enters His Temple out of love and yearning for God's kindness. He witnesses only endless love in every facet of creation and so he happily draws close to the Creator. Then, as he enters God's presence he is seized with trembling. Not with fear of punishment or harm, but with *awe* before God's greatness. Thus, pagan terror

**the bloodthirsty and deceitful man
HASHEM abhors.**

⁸ *As for me, through Your abundant kindness,
I will enter Your House;
I will prostrate myself toward Your Holy Sanctuary
in awe of You.*
⁹ *HASHEM, guide me in Your righteousness,
because of my watchful enemies,
Make Your way straight before me.*
¹⁰ *For in their mouth there is no sincerity,
their inner thought is treacherous,*

evaporates into indifference, whereas Jewish love amplifies itself into mighty awe. [Cf. *Rambam, Hilchos Yesodei HaTorah* 2:2.]

9. ה' נְחֵנִי בְצִדְקָתֶךָ — *HASHEM, guide me in Your righteousness.*

And as I bow before You, this is my request: Please guide me on the path of righteousness and justice, and save me from stumbling (*Radak*).

לְמַעַן שׁוֹרְרָי — *Because of my watchful enemies.*

These are my enemies who watch me carefully, hoping that I will betray You and cause You to desert me. שׁוֹרְרָי, is derived from the word שׁוּר, '*watching closely*' as in אֲשׁוּרֶנּוּ וְלֹא קָרוֹב, '*I watch closely for him, but he is not near*' (*Numbers* 24:17, *Rashi; Radak; Ibn Ezra*).

Because of their evil intentions, David begs Hashem for special providence to safeguard him from errors which his detractors could exploit maliciously (*Radak*).

הַיְשַׁר לְפָנַי דַּרְכֶּךָ — *Make Your way straight before me.*

Here we have a discrepancy between the כְּתִיב, the Masoretic spelling of the word הושר and the קְרִי, the Masoretic pronunciation which is הַיְשַׁר. The reconciliation of the two is as follows: David says, As for myself, everything

Hashem does is in perfect order. No matter how much my suffering, I realize that it is the result of Hashem's choice of the shortest, quickest way to my destiny. But I fear that my enemies will misinterpret my woes and claim that my life, so full of obstacles and pitfalls, proves their claims that I am crooked. Therefore, although I know that my path is already הוּשָׁר, '*straightened out*', I ask that לְמַעַן שׁוֹרְרָי, '*because of my enemies*' You make my life appear outwardly straight, as well, i.e. הַיְשַׁר לְפָנַי '*make straight before me*' (*Tefillos Yisroel*).

10. כִּי אֵין בְּפִיהוּ נְכוֹנָה — *For in their mouth there is no sincerity.*

The reason I must be so very careful is because these men are the most dangerous of enemies. They feign outward friendship while in their hearts they are bitter, implacable foes (*Radak; Rashi; Metzudos*).

Even though he is referring to his many enemies, the singular form פִּיהוּ, '*His mouth*' is used as if to say that not even the mouth of *one* of them is sincere (*Metzudas David*).

קִרְבָּם הַוּוֹת *Their inner thought* [lit. '*their inside*'] *is treacherous.*

Rashi renders הַוּוֹת, as '*treacherous*'.

Metzudos explains it as '*destruction*' as in עַד יַעֲבֹר הַוּוֹת, '*until destruction*

יא לְשׁוֹנָם יַחֲלִיקוּן: הַאֲשִׁימֵם | אֱלֹהִים יִפְּלוּ
מִמֹּעֲצוֹתֵיהֶם בְּרֹב פִּשְׁעֵיהֶם הַדִּיחֵמוֹ כִּי
יב מָרוּ בָךְ: וְיִשְׂמְחוּ כָל־חוֹסֵי בָךְ לְעוֹלָם
יְרַנֵּנוּ וְתָסֵךְ עָלֵימוֹ וְיַעְלְצוּ בְךָ אֹהֲבֵי
יג שְׁמֶךָ: כִּי־אַתָּה תְּבָרֵךְ צַדִּיק יהוה כַּצִּנָּה
רָצוֹן תַּעְטְרֶנּוּ:

passes by' (57:2). Thus, David says, *'their inner thoughts are destructive.'*

Hirsch comments that הַוּוֹת is the *'piel'* infinitive of הֹוֶה, *'to become'*. It is related to הָיָה, *'to be'* and הַוָּה, *'to bring into being.'* Thus הַוּוֹת denotes ceaseless planning to make something occur. They always conspire, and scheme, and therefore, there is no sincerity in them.

קֶבֶר פָּתוּחַ גְּרֹנָם — *Their throat an open grave.*

They seek to swallow the fruits of other people's labors, just as the open grave takes in the corpse (*Rashi*).

לְשׁוֹנָם יַחֲלִיקוּן — *Their tongue they equivocate* [lit. *'they make smooth or glib'*]

Malbim notes that פֶּה, *'mouth'*, refers to *'external speech'*, that which is actually vocalized to others. לָשׁוֹן, *'tongue'*, refers to what a person really feels, the message that he internally communicates to himself. These insincere foes speak of friendship with their פֶּה, *mouth*, but, אֵין בְּפִיהוּ נְכוֹנָה, *'there is no sincerity in their mouths.'* לְשׁוֹנָם יַחֲלִיקוּן, they yearn to entrap me with their *'smooth tongues.'*

[This verse vividly describes the way of Doeg and Achitophel, especially in the light of the Talmud's comment (*Sanhedrin* 106b): 'Doeg's Torah lacked depth, it was מִן הַשָּׂפָה וּלְחוּץ, *'only from the lips outward.'*

Doeg and Achitophel did not really comprehend the true meaning of their studies. They did not merit special divine assistance which is necessary in order for a scholar to arrive at a correct legal decision. Why? סוֹד ה' לִירֵאָיו *'The secret of HASHEM is revealed only to those who fear Him'* (25:14).]

11. הַאֲשִׁימֵם אֱלֹהִים — *Declare them guilty, O God!*

Bring them to justice, convict them of their guilt and cast them down from their positions of eminence (*Metzudas David*).

Ibn Ezra suggests that הַאֲשִׁימֵם means *'make them desolate'* [derived from שָׁמֵם].

יִפְּלוּ מִמֹּעֲצוֹתֵיהֶם — *Of their own schemes they will topple.*

According to *Radak* the word seems to be a contraction of two words מִמּוֹ, *'from within'* עֲצוֹתֵיהֶם, *'their own schemes.'*

Malbim, rendering *'as a result of their very schemes'*, comments that they will be punished מִדָּה כְּנֶגֶד מִדָּה, *'measure for measure'.* [1]

בְּרֹב פִּשְׁעֵיהֶם הַדִּיחֵמוֹ — *For their many sins cast them away.*

The Sages of the Talmud (*Sanhedrin* 106b) tell us that David prayed that Doeg should forget all of his learning before he died. The request was honored as it says of Doeg, *'He shall die*

1. Because Doeg and Achitophel strayed after their eyes to desire that which was not theirs; what they sought was not given to them, and even that which they already possessed was taken away! (*Sotah* 9b).

Doeg and Achitophel fell from their positions of stature because they did not keep the Torah. They fell down into Gehinnom — even though they were originally heads of Sanhedrin (*Midrash Shocher Tov* 49:2).

V

11-13

Their throat an open grave,
their tongue they equivocate.
¹¹ *Declare them guilty, O God,*
of their own schemes they will topple,
For their many sins cast them away,
for they have rebelled against You.
¹² *And all who take refuge in You will rejoice,*
forever they will sing joyously;
And You will shelter them,
and those who love Your Name will exult;
in You;
¹³ *When You, HASHEM, will bless the righteous,*
enveloping him with favor like a shield.

---

for lack of instruction' (Proverbs 5:23).

Yalkut Shimoni (I Sam. 131) describes Doeg's last moments: 'Doeg was teaching his students. As they absorbed what was said, he forgot his own words, one thing at a time. Finally his students realized that he was falsifying and distorting the law, so they tied ropes around his feet and dragged him away.'

'Three angels of destruction accosted Doeg. One caused him to forget his learning, one burned his soul, one took his ashes and scattered them in all synagogues and Houses of Study' *(Sanhedrin 106b)*.

[This symbolizes that haughty and insincere scholars have the remnants of Doeg in their hearts.]

כִּי מָרוּ בָךְ — *For they have rebelled against You.*

Because of their hatred for me they ignore Your command to accept me as King. Thus it is You, rather than me, whom they defy *(Radak)*.

12. וְיִשְׂמְחוּ כָל חוֹסֵי בָךְ — *And all who take refuge in You will rejoice.*

Then, when You topple the wicked, all who trust in You will be glad *(Rashi)*.

לְעוֹלָם יְרַנֵּנוּ — *Forever they will sing joyously.*

The proof that their joy is in God and not in material things is that *'they rejoice forever'* and the gladness endures. For material joys never last, they quickly fade away and disappear *(Shemen Lama'or)*.

וְתָסֵךְ עָלֵימוֹ — *And You will shelter them.*

This word is related to סְכָךְ, *'a covering which makes shade'* (Metzudas Zion).

וְיַעְלְצוּ בָךְ אֹהֲבֵי שְׁמֶךְ — *And those who love Your name will exult in You.*

Malbim explains that וְיַעְלְצוּ in most cases describes spiritual, not physical, joy.

Hirsch (comm. 9:3) describes the special character of עֲלִיצָה, *exultation* as an overcoming of resistance. It is related to חֲלִיצָה, *'a liberation from bonds.'* Thus, it expresses a feeling of relief from oppression and confinement. Those who love God never allow themselves to become enshackled or oppressed by the vicissitudes of living. They praise God in every mood because every mood is permeated with His love.

בָּךְ — *In You.*

They will rejoice when they see that You bless the righteous *(Rashi)*.

Radak renders *'with Your help.'* We exult in the very aid which Hashem

gives us to shelter us from our enemies.

13. כִּי אַתָּה תְּבָרֵךְ צַדִּיק ה' — *When You, HASHEM, will bless the righteous.*

כִּי, 'when'. *Radak* and *Ibn Ezra* explain that the joy of the righteous promised in the previous verse will come to pass when Hashem will bless them and surround them with good will.

כַּצִּנָּה — *Like a shield.*

A צִנָּה affords protection to its bearer from three sides (*Rashi*). [See *footnote* to 35:2.]

רָצוֹן — *Favor.*

I.e., Your satisfaction (*Rashi*).

תַּעְטְרֶנּוּ — *Enveloping him.*

Like an עֲטָרָה, 'a crown' which encircles the head (*Metzudas Zion*).

If a person gives his friend a gift of a bag of gold and a bandit comes and robs him of the bag, what value is there to the gift? However, a gift from God is different. '*When You bless the righteous one, HASHEM*' You don't provide them with the blessing alone, You also provide protection for the gift as it says '*You will surround him with Your good will like a shield*' (*Midrash Shocher Tov*).

מזמור ו

Davidavid composed this psalm when bed-ridden with a terrible illness which enfeebled his entire body. Righteous man that he was, he accepted his pains as a means to release his soul from the shackles of sin.

The *Sheminis*, the eight-stringed instrument which accompanied this psalm, relates to this theme.

Maharal and *Hirsch* discuss in many of their writings, the significance of the numbers six, seven, eight, and ten. 'Six' symbolizes the cube form covered from all sides, a three-dimensional unit, representing the total perfection of this physical world created in six days. 'Seven' always indicates the divine element connected with the physical world of creation, as we find on the Holy Sabbath, the seventh day. 'Eight', however, heralds release from this world, redemption from all bodily and moral ills, resurrection from all physical decay. This is primarily the condition of the future, when Messiah will loosen the bonds which shackle us to this world. Similarly, circumcision is performed on the eighth day, teaching that a basic prerequisite for our covenant, our *Bris*, with God is that we free ourselves from the fetters of the sensual world (symbolized by the עָרְלָה, foreskin). The harp of ten strings, however, is reserved for the day when all of the world will unite into one harmonious whole.

David's choice of the Messianic *Sheminis* instrument to accompany this particular psalm denotes terrible anguish over his desecration of his *Bris-Covenant* with God because of sin. He yearns to achieve a self-discipline of Messianic proportions, thereby liberating himself from the lusts and desires which drew him to sin.

Radak explains that David did not dedicate this psalm to himself alone; he meant it to be a prayer for every person in distress, particularly for Israel when sick and oppressed in exile.

Indeed, David's intention was fulfilled, for this psalm has been incorporated into our daily prayers as תַּחֲנוּן, 'Tachanun' a plea for forgiveness and mercy.

א לַמְנַצֵּחַ בִּנְגִינוֹת עַל־הַשְּׁמִינִית מִזְמוֹר
ב לְדָוִד: יהוה אַל־בְּאַפְּךָ תוֹכִיחֵנִי וְאַל־
ג בַּחֲמָתְךָ תְיַסְּרֵנִי: חָנֵּנִי יהוה כִּי אֻמְלַל
ד אָנִי רְפָאֵנִי יהוה כִּי נִבְהֲלוּ עֲצָמָי: וְנַפְשִׁי
ה נִבְהֲלָה מְאֹד וְאַתְּ יהוה עַד־מָתָי: שׁוּבָה

---

1. הַשְּׁמִינִית — *The Sheminis.* An eight-stringed harp (*Rashi; Radak; Ibn Ezra*).

In the Talmud (*Arachin 13b*) the phrase עַל הַשְּׁמִינִית, is interpreted to mean עַל נִימָא שְׁמִינִית, *'on the eighth string.'* It is explained there that the harp ordinarily used in the Temple had only seven strings, while the one to be used in the Messianic era will have eight, and the instrument representing the World To Come will have ten strings.

2. ה' אַל בְּאַפְּךָ תוֹכִיחֵנִי — *HASHEM, do not rebuke me in Your anger.*

Radak explains that David readily accepts Divine punishment, for surely it is well deserved. He asks only that it be not meted out all at once in a sudden, unbearable burst of fury. Rather, let it be apportioned gradually so that the suffering can be withstood.

Similarly, we find the Prophet Jeremiah asking God to save His full wrath only for those who fully deserve it. יַסְּרֵנִי ה' אַךְ בְּמִשְׁפָּט אַל בְּאַפְּךָ פֶּן תַּמְעִטֵנִי, *'Chastise me HASHEM, but in measure, not in Your anger, lest You diminish me.'* שְׁפֹךְ חֲמָתְךָ עַל הַגּוֹיִם, *'Pour out Your rage upon* אֲשֶׁר לֹא יְדָעוּךָ *the nations who know You not'* [*Jeremiah 10:24-25*] (*Meiri*).

וְאַל בַּחֲמָתְךָ תְיַסְּרֵנִי — *Nor chastise me in Your rage.*

Malbim differentiates between אַף, *'anger'* which is openly displayed, and חֵמָה, *'rage'* which is mingled with deep animosity pent up and concealed in the heart.

He defines תוֹכָחָה, as *'rebuke'* offered gently with kind words, whereas יִסּוּר, means *'bitter chastisement'* which is often accompanied by harsh corporal punishment.

Thus, David asked of Hashem: When I err and You must correct me with תוֹכָחָה, *rebuke*, please do it gently, not with אַף, *an external display of anger.* Though I realize that my deeds may call for יִסּוּר, *harsh discipline* which involves a show of anger, I pray that the chastisement be motivated not by חֵמָה, *'inner rage and animosity'*, but by Your concern and love and a desire to improve me.[1]

[It should be noted that when Moses neglected to have his son circumcised on the eighth day due to his pre-occupation with his mission to redeem Israel from

---

1. 'The Congregation of Israel said to the Holy One, Blessed be He: "Master of the Universe, although it is written כִּי אֶת אֲשֶׁר יֶאֱהַב ה' יוֹכִיחַ — *'For, he whom HASHEM loves, He rebukes'* (*Proverbs 3:12*); still, *'Do not rebuke me in Your anger.'* And, although it is written אַשְׁרֵי הַגֶּבֶר אֲשֶׁר תְּיַסְּרֶנּוּ יָּהּ, *'Fortunate is the man whom You, HASHEM, chastise'* (*Psalms 94:12*), still, *'Do not chastise me in Your rage.' "*

This may be likened to a king who was sorely angered by his son and, in his rage, swore that he would throw a huge boulder at his son's head. Later, he reconsidered his oath and thought: 'If I crush my son's head my life will be empty, and I will leave no heir. But, to ignore my royal sentence is also impossible.'

What did the king do? He smashed the huge rock into tiny pebbles and threw them at his son one at a time. Thus, his son was not harmed and his oath was fulfilled (*Midrash Shocher Tov*). [However, each pebble thrown was a painful reminder of the King's displeasure and a warning not to repeat past sins.]

For the Conductor; with instrumental music;
on the Sheminis. A song of David.
² HASHEM, do not rebuke me in Your anger,
nor chastise me in Your rage.
³ Favor me, HASHEM, for I am feeble,
heal me, HASHEM, for my bones shudder
with terror.
⁴ My soul, too, is utterly terrified,
and You, HASHEM, — how long?

Egypt (*Exodus* 4:24-26), he was attacked by two fierce angels of
vengeance named אַף, 'anger' and חֵמָה,
'rage' who threatened his life (*Nedarim*
32a).

Similarly, because David also felt that
he had not lived up to the lofty standards imposed by the *Bris*-Covenant of
the eighth day. He trembles lest God
vent his rage upon him through those
vicious angels אַף, and חֵמָה.]

3. חׇנֵּנִי ה' כִּי אֻמְלַל אָנִי — *Favor me,*
HASHEM, for I am feeble.

Have mercy and do not continue to
aggravate me, for I am already feeble
and I have had all I can bear (*Metzudas*
David).

אֻמְלַל — *'Devastated, very feeble and*
weak' as we find הַיְּהוּדִים הָאֻמְלָלִים, *'the*
feeble Jews' [*Nehemiah* 3:34] (Rashi).

[The root of אֻמְלַל, is מָל, or מָלַל, to
cut or to *crush*. David cries out that
although he desecrated the *Bris*-
Covenant by not eliminating or
crushing his evil impulses, now his illness has enfeebled him, so that he has
truly become a מָל, a cut-down, curbed
spirit.]

רְפָאֵנִי ה' — *Heal me, HASHEM.*

David asked for even more: Not only
do I beg You to hold back future
punishment, I also pray that You heal
the wounds from which I already suffer
(*Metzudas David*).

כִּי נִבְהֲלוּ עֲצָמָי — *For my bones shudder*
with terror.

'My skeleton, the framework of my
body, shudders from the tremendous
impact of my illness.' It could also be
that David's greatest pain was not
physical, but rather his mental anguish,
the thought of his sins, which haunted
him (*Radak*).

4. וְנַפְשִׁי נִבְהֲלָה מְאֹד — *My soul, too, is*
utterly terrified.

The illness has reached such proportions that even my soul is terrified lest I
die (*Radak*).

There are those who realize that
physical punishment can be a gift from
God, designed mercifully to cleanse and
mend the soiled and tattered soul. Each
bit of pain, though hurting the body,
can bring comfort to the spirit. David,
however, is terrified by the specter of
this illness because he fears that the
physical pain is beyond his endurance
and that he may die and leave the world
with an imperfect soul (*Alshich*).

Only a robust, healthy and confident
spirit can support a sick body and make
it well. As King Solomon said: רוּחַ אִישׁ
יְכַלְכֵּל מַחֲלֵהוּ וְרוּחַ נְכֵאָה מִי יִשָּׂאֶנָּה, *The*
spirit of a man will sustain his infirmity,
but a broken spirit who can bear?
(*Proverbs* 18:14). Therefore, David
moans that his spirit is not strong
enough to support his body through
this illness (*Mahari Ya'avetz haDoresh*).

וְאַתָּה ה' עַד מָתָי — *And You, HASHEM, —*
how long? [lit. 'until when'?]

How long will You watch me and not
cure me? (*Rashi; Radak*).

יהוה חָלְצָה נַפְשִׁי הוֹשִׁיעֵנִי לְמַעַן חַסְדֶּךָ:

ו כִּי אֵין בַּמָּוֶת זִכְרֶךָ בִּשְׁאוֹל מִי יוֹדֶה־לָּךְ:

ז יָגַעְתִּי | בְּאַנְחָתִי אַשְׂחֶה בְכָל־לַיְלָה

ח מִטָּתִי בְּדִמְעָתִי עַרְשִׂי אַמְסֶה: עָשְׁשָׁה

'The holy spirit hovers above the bed of the sick' (Nedarim 40a); for it is God Himself who commands the angel of affliction to continue his work of weakening the sick until they grow humble and contrite. Hence David calls out to Hashem, 'Until when will You allow him, i.e. the angel, to continue his afflictions? Please tell him, 'enough!' (Mahari Ya'avetz haDoresh).

[This may explain why the word וְאַתָּ, 'and You' is spelled without the letter ה. Although David was addressing Hashem, he referred primarily to Hashem's agent, the afflicting angel.]

5. שׁוּבָה ה' — Desist [lit. 'return'], HASHEM.

˙ Desist from Your anger against me (Rashi).

חָלְצָה נַפְשִׁי — Release my soul.

I.e. from sickness (Rashi).

My soul which should sustain me cannot do so, because it is gripped with fear. Free my soul from the clutches of terror. Thus its inner, healthy powers will be released, and these new energies will fortify my body against its illness (Hirsch).

[In Hebrew we often find antonyms, composed of the very same letters arranged differently. Thus חָלַץ, 'release', is the opposite of לַחַץ, 'oppression'. Compare: (Job. 36:15): יְחַלֵּץ עָנִי בְעָנְיוֹ וְיִגֶל בַּלַּחַץ אָזְנָם, 'He (releases) the poor man by means of his own poverty, and he opens their ears by means of oppression).]

All infirmities of the body stem from blemishes and sins of the soul. Therefore, in our prayers we request: רְפוּאַת הַנֶּפֶשׁ וּרְפוּאַת הַגּוּף, 'A cure for the soul and a cure for the body.' Similarly,

the Talmud states (Nedarim 41a) 'A person does not recover from his illness until all his sins are forgiven, as it says: הַסֹּלֵחַ לְכָל עֲוֹנֵכִי הָרֹפֵא לְכָל תַּחֲלוּאָיְכִי, 'Who forgives all of your sins, Who heals all of your diseases' (Psalms 103:3). Thus, David first requests that Hashem release his soul by forgiving his sins; only then can his battered body be saved (Imaros Tehoros).

הוֹשִׁיעֵנִי לְמַעַן חַסְדֶּךָ — Save me as befits [lit. for the sake of] Your kindness.

Sometimes Hashem heals a person because of his merits, but, those merits had been set aside for future reward in the Hereafter. David did not want to draw upon his merits and so diminish his later reward, therefore he asks Hashem to save him for no other reason than His divine kindness (Imaros Tehoros).

6. כִּי אֵין בַּמָּוֶת זִכְרֶךָ — For there is no mention of You in death.

David said: 'I will not be able to praise or even mention Your Name if I die, but if You heal me I will glorify You for all to hear. As the soul departs from a dying person, it leaves a stone-like body that will descend to the grave. The soul, however, ascends higher and higher to praise God eternally without pause. The degree of this praise is proportional to how much the soul perfected itself on earth. Therefore, the righteous have a tremendous desire for life, for only while alive can they enrich their souls in preparation for eternal bliss' (Radak).

[Cf. Berachos 63a, Rashi s.v. וִיבָרְכוּ שֵׁם כְּבוֹדֶךָ 'The relationship of This World to the World to Come resembles that of a corridor which leads into a

⁵ *Desist, HASHEM, release my soul,*
save me as befits Your kindness.
⁶ *For there is no mention of You in death;*
in the Lower World who will praise You?
⁷ *I am wearied with my sigh,*
Every night my bed I drench,
with my tears I soak my couch.

---

great hall. Therefore, engage in the recital of God's praises in this finite world so that you will be prepared to continually praise Him in the infinite World to Come.']

בִּשְׁאוֹל מִי יוֹדֶה לָּךְ — *In the Lower World who will praise You.* [Compare: לֹא הַמֵּתִים יְהַלְלוּ יָהּ וְלֹא כָּל יֹרְדֵי דוּמָה, '*The dead praise not God, neither do any who go down into silence*' (Psalms 115:17).]

7. יָגַעְתִּי בְּאַנְחָתִי — *I am wearied with my sigh.*

Our Sages say (Berachos 58b): 'A sigh breaks half of the body ... and some say the entire body.' This means that if a sinner moans and sighs in remorse for his deeds, this subdues half or even all of the desire his body had for those sins. David says: 'I am toiling to tame my body which engaged in sin. Furthermore, even my heart and eyes which were the agents to entice me to sin — these too I purify with my tears' (Alshich).

אַשְׂחֶה בְכָל לַיְלָה מִטָּתִי — *Every night my bed I drench* [lit. befoul].

I shed so many tears that my bed becomes foul and disgusting. This word is similar to סְחִי וּמָאוֹס תְּשִׂימֵנוּ, '*You*

have made us like foul refuse and disgusting matter' (Lamentations 3:45). (The שׂ, 'sin' and the ס, 'samach' are interchangeable) (Rashi).

Rashi in the name of *Menachem; Radak; Ibn Ezra;* and *Metzudos* translate אַשְׂחֶה, '*I cause to swim*'. David, figuratively speaking, says that he shed a sea of tears so large, that he sets his bed afloat in the huge pool he created. We find this word used in the same sense in כַּאֲשֶׁר יְפָרֵשׂ הַשֹּׂחֶה לִשְׂחוֹת, '*As he who swims spreads out his hands to swim*' (Isaiah 25:11).

Ibn Ezra points out that in Aramaic אַשְׂחֶה means '*I wash*'.

[Thus David seems to say: With my nightly tears I now cleanse this bed where I sinned with Bath Sheba.]

In regard to David's abundant tears the *Yalkut (Shmuel 165)* relates:

'During the twenty two years that the Holy Spirit departed from David, King of Israel, he shed a whole cupful of tears [and drank it] every single day, and he dipped his bread in ashes.'

בְּדִמְעָתִי עַרְשִׂי אַמְסֶה — *With my tears I soak my couch.*

The translation of אַמְסֶה follows *Rashi*, however, *Metzudos Zion* and *Radak* however, render this as, '*I melt*', from the word הֵמַס.[1]

---

1. David was sick and bedridden for thirteen years. He wept so profusely that his bedding had to be changed seven times each day as it says '*Every night I drench my bed, [and by day] I soak my couch with tears.*' He shed these tears in remorse over the incident of Bath Sheba. All the while his enemies tormented him, asking, 'When will he die?' This continued until David implored God to take pity on him and lift him from his sick-bed that he might be able to arise and transmit to the people the scroll which contained the instructions for building the Temple. God granted his request (*Aggadas Bereishis 38*).

ט מִכַּעַס עֵינִי עָתְקָה בְּכָל־צוֹרְרָי: סוּרוּ
מִמֶּנִּי כָּל־פֹּעֲלֵי אָוֶן כִּי־שָׁמַע יהוה קוֹל
י בִּכְיִי: שָׁמַע יהוה תְּחִנָּתִי יהוה תְּפִלָּתִי
יא יִקָּח: יֵבֹשׁוּ | וְיִבָּהֲלוּ מְאֹד כָּל־אֹיְבָי יָשֻׁבוּ
יֵבֹשׁוּ רָגַע:

8. עָשְׁשָׁה מִכַּעַס עֵינִי — *My eye is dimmed with anger.*

עָשְׁשָׁה, *dimmed,* is derived from עֲשָׁשִׁית, a smoked, translucent glass through which one can discern only shadows and silhouettes. So, too, says David, the vision of my eyes has grown distorted and unclear (*Rashi*). [Compare with *Rashi's* commentary on the verse עָשְׁשָׁה בְכַעַס עֵינִי, 'my eyes are dimmed in anger' (Psalms 31:10).]

Rashi in the name of *Menachem; Radak; Ibn Ezra;* and *Metzudos* trace this verb to עשׁ, *'rot, decay'* as in וַעֲצָמַי עָשֵׁשׁוּ, *'and my bones are wasted away'* (Psalm 31:11).

מִכַּעַס — *With* [lit. *from*] *anger.*

I am angered because my enemies rejoice over my illness (*Radak*).

[However, David fully realized that his enemies, although truly vicious, could not have harmed him if not for his own sins. Therefore, he also turns his anger towards himself and the parts of his body which participated in his sin.]

עָתְקָה — *Aged.*

Because my eyesight is dim and weak my eyes have grown old (*Rashi*).

Their weakness is caused by my tormentors, so I beg You to rid me of them (*Metzudas David*).

עָתְקָה, can also be rendered as *'moved',* as we find וַיַּעְתֵּק מִשָּׁם הָהָרָה *'And he moved from there to the mountain'* (Genesis 12:8). Because of his incessant weeping, David's eyes became dislocated. (*Rashi* in the name of *Menachem; Radak*).

[David's eyes became agents for sin, because he allowed them to stray. Now he tearfully resolved to move his eyes away from temptation.]

9. סוּרוּ מִמֶּנִּי כָּל־פֹּעֲלֵי אָוֶן — *Depart from me, all evildoers.*

Get away from me! You shall not vanquish me now that God has heard my prayers (*Metzudas David*).

'Evildoers' refers to David's tormentors (*Ibn Ezra*).

[It also refers to his eyes, heart, and desires which torment him with temptation to do evil.]

כִּי שָׁמַע ה' קוֹל בִּכְיִי — *For HASHEM has heard the sound of my weeping.*

David used the past tense because he said this after recovering from his sickness. It may also be that he said it while still ill, prophetically foretelling his recovery and speaking of it as a *fait accompli.* A person who uses this psalm as a prayer to Hashem may utter this phrase, because he too, may be confident that Hashem will answer his broken-hearted request if he prays with sincerity (*Radak*).

The *Mishnah* (*Berachos* 5:5) relates that Rabbi Chanina ben Dosa would pray for the sick and predict: 'This one will live and this one will die.' When he was asked how he knew, he replied: 'If my prayer flows smoothly from my lips then I am sure that it was accepted. However, if I hesitate and stumble over my words then I know it was rejected.' David, too, could predict from the smoothness and fluency of his prayer that 'HASHEM heard the sound of my weeping' (*Mahari Ya'avetz Hadoresh*).

David attributes the acceptance of his prayers to his tears, as the Sages said: (*Baba Metzia* 59a): 'Even when the

⁸ *My eye is dimmed with anger,*
 aged by my tormentors.
⁹ *Depart from me, all evildoers,*
  for HASHEM *has heard the sound of*
  my weeping.
¹⁰ HASHEM *has heard my plea,*
  HASHEM *will accept my prayer.*
¹¹ *Let all my foes be shamed and utterly terrified,*
  they will regret and be instantly shamed.

heavenly gates of prayer are locked, the gates of tears are not' *(Sforno).*

10. שָׁמַע ה' תְּחִנָּתִי — HASHEM *has heard my plea.*

David thanks *only* God for healing him and, therefore, attributes his recovery to his prayers, not to his physicians *(Ibn Ezra).*

ה' תְּפִלָּתִי יִקָּח — HASHEM *will accept my prayer.*

Just as Hashem has accepted my prayers now, so will He accept them in the future *(Radak).*

Yalkut Eliezer illustrates this with a parable. 'Once a kindly king had mercy on a pauper and said: "Ask of me any one wish and I will fulfill it." The clever pauper replied: "Promise me only this one thing, that every time I come before you with a request, you will fulfill it!" '

This is what David meant: 'Hashem has heard my one plea that He should accept my every prayer to him.'

11. יֵבשׁוּ וְיִבָּהֲלוּ מְאֹד כָּל אֹיְבָי — *Let all my foes be shamed and utterly terrified.*

When they witness my recovery, my enemies who hoped for my death will be shamed and terrified *(Radak).*

וְיִבָּהֲלוּ, *'terrified'.* Like a person who is bewildered and terrified when he witnesses something he thought impossible *(Metzudas David).*

יָשֻׁבוּ יֵבשׁוּ רָגַע — *They will regret* [lit. re-pent] *and be instantly shamed.*

When they see their hopes dashed,

they will regret their animosity and come to make peace with me. At that moment they will be ashamed to face me *(Radak).*

Only at that instant will they be ashamed, because I will forgive them and never again mention their deeds. Thus, I will avoid further embarrassment to them *(Metzudas David).*

Rashi quotes the Sages of the Midrash who translate יָשֻׁבוּ as *'they shall return again'* and interpret this verse homiletically:

'What is meant here by saying that they will return and be put to shame a second time? Rabbi Yochanan said: In the future, the Holy One, Blessed be He, will judge the wicked of the heathens and sentence them to Gehinnom. When they question the justice of this verdict, God will bring them back before His Presence, and show them their account of sins and merits, and try their case once more. Again they will be found guilty and returned to Gehinnom — thus, they will suffer double disgrace.

Rabbi Samuel bar Nachmeni said: In the future all the pagan nations will call out to their idols and none will answer; then they will return and cry out to Hashem. He will reply: 'Had you called out to Me first I would have answered you, but now that you have made your idols your primary salvation, and turn around to Me only in desperation, I shall not answer.' This is why it says here, *'They return and they are ashamed.'* [cf. *Psalms* 9:18]

Midrash Shocher Tov emphasizes that the fires of Gehinnom are nothing but the burning shame of the wicked who suffer the humiliation of recognizing their waywardness.

'In the future God will take the wicked and show them the Garden of Eden and its many vacant places. He will tell them: These places were reserved for you and your colleagues. But since your evil ways render you guilty you will instead acquire a portion in Gehinnom.'

[Thus, Hashem returns them to see what they forfeited in Paradise and in that instant they burn in shame.]

This Psalm is dedicated to King Saul, whom David considered his most difficult enemy (Moed Katan 16b). For, unlike the rest of his foes, Saul was a truly great and righteous man. In many ways, his excellence even surpassed that of David. Moreover, although Saul relentlessly pursued David with large armies, David could not strike back, for he, more than anyone, appreciated Saul's exalted and privileged status as 'The Anointed of God'. Although constantly in mortal danger, David never compromised his firm conviction that harming Saul would be the equivalent of defying God Himself, for God had chosen Saul to be His first king.

Twice Saul unwittingly fell into David's hands. Once, while pursuing him, Saul entered a cave not knowing that the fugitive and his men were hiding in the depths of that very cavern. David could have slain Saul easily; instead, unbeknown to Saul, he merely cut off the corner of the royal robe as evidence of the opportunity he forfeited (I Samuel, Chapter 24).

Another time David stood over the slumbering, helpless Saul but instead of slaying him, he took the king's spear as a token of what he could have done (I Samuel, Chapter 26).

In both cases, Saul, overwhelmed by David's generosity, solemnly swore never to harm him again. But he did not keep his word, for God punished him with a spiritual malady, a dark, jealous depression. 'An evil spirit from God descended upon Saul and he raved madly in the palace' (I Samuel 18:10). Saul himself admitted that he was inconsistent and untrustworthy in his dealings with David. 'And Saul said: I have sinned . . . behold I have acted like a fool and erred very much' (ibid. 26:21).

In this psalm, David proclaims that he has been completely upright and just in all of his dealings with Saul. Through it all, he has made but one minor שִׁגָּיוֹן, 'error'. Although he mourned Saul's death bitterly and eloquently eulogized him, he also sang in gladness over his personal salvation from mortal danger with the death of his pursuer. [cf. comm. Psalms 18:1. That entire psalm was inspired mainly by Saul's downfall]. David fears now that this was wrong for it displayed a lack of total grief over the demise of one so great as King Saul.

The Sages taught that this psalm was the שִׁיר שֶׁל יוֹם 'Song of the day' for Purim (Sofrim 18:2). Yaavetz gives as the reason that Mordecai was a descendant of Saul. Furthermore, the verse 'He digs a pit, digs it deep, only to fall into his own trap' (v. 16) describes Haman who was hung on the very gallows which he prepared for Mordecai. [see Prefatory Remarks, Psalms 22].

‎א שִׁגָּיוֹן לְדָוִד אֲשֶׁר־שָׁר לַיהוה עַל־דִּבְרֵי־
‎ב כוּשׁ בֶּן־יְמִינִי: יהוה אֱלֹהַי בְּךָ חָסִיתִי
‎ג הוֹשִׁיעֵנִי מִכָּל־רֹדְפַי וְהַצִּילֵנִי: פֶּן־יִטְרֹף
‎ד כְּאַרְיֵה נַפְשִׁי פֹּרֵק וְאֵין מַצִּיל: יהוה

1. שִׁגָּיוֹן לְדָוִד — *A Shigayon, of David.*

שִׁגָּיוֹן, *Shigayon. Rashi* offers a variety of explanations for this word. *Menachem* holds that this is a musical instrument used in the Levite orchestra. The only other place where we find a similar heading is in *Habbakuk* 3:1: תְּפִלָּה לַחֲבַקּוּק הַנָּבִיא עַל שִׁגְיֹנוֹת — '*A prayer of Habbakuk the prophet, upon Shigyonos.*' There also it means a musical accompaniment.

Secondly, *Rashi* quotes the Sages (*Moed Katan* 16b), who define שִׁגָּיוֹן, as מִשְׁגָּה, '*an error*'. David sang a song celebrating the downfall of Saul (*II Samuel*, Chapter 22). Now he sees this as a mistake and asks for forgiveness. However, *Rashi* notes that the contents of the entire psalm do not lend themselves to such a theme because David sings of threatening heathens and God's meting out justice to the nations, topics which have nothing to do with Saul. [However, *Radak*, adheres to this Talmudic interpretation throughout the Psalm and skillfully explains every verse in light of this theme as will be demonstrated.]

Rashi offers a third approach which he holds to be the most acceptable one, rendering שִׁגָּיוֹן as '*mistaken choice*':

The Talmud (*Sanhedrin* 95a) tells us that because of David many people died. Doeg incited Saul to massacre the entire priestly city of Nob because of David and as a result of this, eventually Doeg was killed and Saul was slain together with his sons. Any person who is the cause of so much bloodshed, although it came about inadvertently, cannot be totally free from guilt himself. God offered David a choice of punishments: either that he fall into the hands of his enemy, or that his descendants be wiped out. David chose the first option and fell into the hands of the cruel and ferocious giant Yishbi, brother of Goliath. However, just as this villain was about to impale him on a spear, David regretted his choice and saw it as a great error, for Israel could not survive without him as their monarch. Here, he prays for forgiveness for his mistaken choice. [According to this, David was originally condemned to death at the hands of the gentile enemy as punishment for his relationship with Saul, and so the contents of the Psalm do indeed fit the heading.]

Finally, *Rashi* suggests that David is referring to the poor judgment he exercised when he cut off the corner of Saul's robe (see *Prefatory Remarks*). Although David meant well, he should have chosen some other means to prove his point, for cutting the royal robe is a disgrace to the king and also a needless destruction of a good garment. [Cf. *I Kings* 1:1, where David was punished for cutting Saul's robe.]

אֲשֶׁר שָׁר לֹה׳ — *Which he sang to HASHEM.*

'The Holy One Blessed be He said to David: You sing songs over the death of Saul? If only you would be Saul and he would be David, I would have destroyed many a David for his sake' (*Moed Katan* 16b).

In matters of personal piety and self-sacrifice Saul surpassed David. However, in the management of public, royal affairs Saul failed to be an adequate

VII
1-3

A Shigayon, of David, which he sang to HASHEM, concerning Kush ben Yemini.
² HASHEM, my God, in You I seek refuge,
 save me from all my pursuers and rescue me.
³ Lest he tear my soul asunder like a lion,
 dismembering without rescuer.

leader, whereas David was a great success. God said to David: 'If only Saul could have coupled his personal piety with the leadership qualities of David, he would have been so great that even the real David could not compare to him (Anaf Yosef to Vayikra Rabba 26:7).

עַל דִּבְרֵי כוּש בֶּן יְמִינִי — Concerning Kush ben Yemini. [lit. 'the black man of Benjamin.']

In consonance with all three of Rashi's explanations that connect this psalm with David's impropriety in dealing with Saul, כּוּש בֶּן יְמִינִי refers to that great king. Thus Rashi quotes the Sages (Moed Katan 16b): 'Just as the black man stands out clearly because of the color of his skin, so too was Saul [a member of the Benjaminite tribe] outstanding by virtue of his rare righteousness.' [Cf. Numbers 12:1; Rashi ibid.]

Ibn Ezra strongly disagrees with this identification of Saul as the כּוּשִׁי, 'the black man', arguing that it is inconceivable that such an offensive term should be used to describe a tzaddik, even though it was intended as a praise. Furthermore, it is unthinkable that King Saul, the chosen monarch of Hashem, should be accused with the strong words used later in this psalm, Behold, he conceived iniquity etc. (Verse 15). Therefore, Ibn Ezra maintains that Kush was a Jew from the tribe of Benjamin, and an avowed enemy of David.

2. בְּךְ חָסִיתִי — In You I seek refuge.
The numerical value of בְּךְ is twenty-two, which leads Rabbi Yochanan to comment: 'I seek refuge in You and

Your Torah which is written with the twenty-two letters of the Aleph-Beis (Midrash Shocher Tov).

הוֹשִׁיעֵנִי מִכָּל רֹדְפַי וְהַצִּילֵנִי — Save me from all of my pursuers and rescue me.
Save me from all those who pursue me together with Saul (Radak).

הוֹשִׁיעֵנִי ... וְהַצִּילֵנִי — 'Save me ... and rescue me.' Malbim explains that יְשׁוּעָה, 'saving' means to prevent the victim from being caught, whereas הַצָּלָה, 'rescue' means to liberate the captive after he has already been seized.

3. פֶּן יִטְרֹף כְּאַרְיֵה נַפְשִׁי — Lest he [i.e. the pursuer mentioned in the previous verse] tear my soul asunder like a lion.
If You will not save me the enemy may overcome me and rip me to pieces as a lion its prey (Metzudas David).

David compares his pursuer, Saul, to a lion, for just as a lion is the king of beasts, Saul was the King of Israel (Radak).

Just as the lion sits down and thoroughly tears apart his prey, so too would Doeg and Achitophel sit down to slander and besmirch me, ripping my reputation and honor to pieces (Midrash Shocher Tov).

פֹּרֵק — Dismembering.
I.e. the forcible separation of things hitherto linked together (Hirsch).

וְאֵין מַצִּיל — Without rescuer.
Since everyone is pursuing me there is no one left to rescue me (Metzudas David).

Not even one man in all of Saul's armies has anything to say in my favor (Midrash Shocher Tov).

אֱלֹהַי אִם־עָשִׂיתִי זֹאת אִם־יֶשׁ־עָוֶל
ה בְּכַפָּי: אִם־גָּמַלְתִּי שׁוֹלְמִי רָע וָאֲחַלְּצָה
ו צוֹרְרִי רֵיקָם: יִרַדֹּף אוֹיֵב | נַפְשִׁי וְיַשֵּׂג
וְיִרְמֹס לָאָרֶץ חַיָּי וּכְבוֹדִי | לֶעָפָר יַשְׁכֵּן
ז סֶלָה: קוּמָה יהוה | בְּאַפֶּךָ הִנָּשֵׂא
בְּעַבְרוֹת צוֹרְרָי וְעוּרָה אֵלַי מִשְׁפָּט צִוִּיתָ:

4. אֱלֹהַי אִם־עָשִׂיתִי זֹאת 'ה — *HASHEM, my God, if I have done this.*

[David now proceeds to explain that he does not deserve to be abused and threatened by his enemies because he has never mistreated them.]

אֱלֹהַי 'ה — *HASHEM, my God.*

[HASHEM, the Merciful, I beg you to become אֱלֹהַי, 'my God of Judgment' and evaluate my actions to determine whether I deserve such treatment.]

אִם־עָשִׂיתִי זֹאת — *If I have done this.*

See if I have indeed commited the iniquities which I am about to enumerate (*Rashi*).

אִם־יֶשׁ־עָוֶל בְּכַפָּי — *If there is injustice in my hands.*

Hirsch points out that עָוֶל, derived from עוֹלֶה; *ascending*, is the expression for striving or rising upward; as in עוֹל, which means 'youth developing', or 'growing up'. Therefore, עָוֶל denotes the abuse of high position to which one has risen.

[In other words, David brings to mind that he often had the upper hand over Saul, but never did he exploit his opportunities unjustly.]

5. אִם־גָּמַלְתִּי שׁוֹלְמִי רָע — *If I have repaid my friends* [lit. 'those with whom I live in peace'] *with evil.*

David says: I was living peacefully with Saul who was both my father-in-law and the commander of the armies in which I served and fought. He repaid all of my friendly gestures with malice, but I always treated him well and never repaid him with evil (*Radak*).

[This is an interrogative sentence. David asks of Hashem: Did I then truly do these things which would justify my troubles?]

וָאֲחַלְּצָה צוֹרְרִי רֵיקָם — *I, who spared those who were my unprovoked* [lit. 'their emptiness' i.e. without reason.] *tormentors* [following *Ibn Ezra*].

Radak renders וָאֲחַלְּצָה as *'spare, release'*. [Compare with *Psalm* 6:5 חַלְּצָה נַפְשִׁי, *'release my soul'*]:

Not only did I refrain from dealing out to my tormentor Saul the harsh treatment he deserved, but I did even more — I spared his life when he was in danger even though I received no personal gain for having spared; my mercy was רֵיקָם, *'without reason'*, because there was no compulsion for me to do it. Once I held back my men from slaying him in the cave [*I Samuel*, 24], and again I restrained my general Avishai from running him through with his spear [*I Samuel*, 26] (*Radak*).

Rashi, however, translates וָאֲחַלְּצָה, *'I stripped of clothing'*, and רֵיקָם as *'naked, bare'*.

David asks: Even when I cut the corner of Saul's robe did I do it out of animosity in order to strip him of his garments and to leave him רֵיקָם, *without clothing, naked?*

I did it only in order to prove my loyalty, for I could have killed him and I did not.

6. יִרַדֹּף אוֹיֵב נַפְשִׁי — *Then let the enemy pursue my soul.*

The word יִרַדֹּף incorporates two grammatical forms. It means both 'to

⁴ *HASHEM, my God:*
> *If I have done this, if there is injustice*
> *in my hands;*
⁵ *If I have repaid my friends with evil,*
> *I, who spared those who were my*
> *unprovoked tormentors.*
⁶ *Then let the enemy pursue my soul and overtake it;*
Let him trample my life to the ground,
> *and lay my soul in the dust. Selah.*
⁷ *Rise up, HASHEM, in Your anger,*
> *lift Yourself up in fury against my tormentors,*
And strengthen me to mete out the Judgment
> *which You commanded.*

pursue' and 'to cause others to pursue.'
'If I have done the terrible crimes
suggested in the previous verse, then I
deserve to be chased by my enemies and
to have them urge others to join in the
pursuit, as Saul did' (Radak; Metzudas
David).

וְיִרְמֹס לָאָרֶץ חַיָּי — **Let him trample my
life to the ground.**
חַיָּי, 'my life'. Metzudas David
translates this as 'all the days of my life'.
I deserve to have my body and my
honor trampled upon, all the days of my
life, forever.

וּכְבוֹדִי לֶעָפָר יַשְׁכֵּן סֶלָה — **And lay my soul
[lit. my honor] in the dust, Selah.**
וּכְבוֹדִי, 'my soul', deserves to be
buried in dust forever. Of course, the
spirit is not buried in the earth after
death, but David speaks metaphorically. Also, David speaks here of the
punishments he deserves according to
the distorted image which his enemies
have of him. They do indeed believe
that his spirit should sink into the earth
after death and never arise (Radak).

7. קוּמָה ה' בְּאַפֶּךָ — **Rise up, HASHEM,
in Your anger.**
However, since I did not sin I do not
deserve the aforementioned afflictions,
on the contrary I deserve that You

should arise to save me from pursuit
(Metzudas David).

הִנָּשֵׂא — **Lift Yourself up.**
For when God metes out just punishment to the wicked, He is elevated and
glorified (Metzudas David).

בְּעַבְרוֹת — **In fury.**
Malbim differentiates between אַף,
'anger' and עֶבְרָה, 'fury'. אַף, is a limited,
controlled anger in a precise measure,
equal to the gravity of the sin which
aroused it. עֶבְרָה, however, is a wild fury
pouring forth uncontrolled with no
boundaries or limitations. It derives
from the root עָבַר, 'to go over'.
[Since nothing could detain my pursuers and they overcame all barriers in
order to seize me, it is only fitting that
their punishment should be measure for
measure, an unbridled fury which
knows no limits.]

צוֹרְרָי — **My tormentors.**
Rashi holds that this refers to David's
gentile enemies such as Yishbi and his
brothers, and the Philistines. According
to Radak, David had Saul in mind.

וְעוּרָה אֵלַי — **And strengthen me** [lit.
'Arouse to me'].
[Arouse in me sufficient fortitude (to
overcome my pursuers).]

ח וַעֲדַת לְאֻמִּים תְּסוֹבְבֶךָ וְעָלֶיהָ לַמָּרוֹם
ט שׁוּבָה: יהוה יָדִין עַמִּים שָׁפְטֵנִי יהוה
י כְּצִדְקִי וּכְתֻמִּי עָלָי | יִגְמָר־נָא רַע | רְשָׁעִים
וּתְכוֹנֵן צַדִּיק וּבֹחֵן לִבּוֹת וּכְלָיוֹת אֱלֹהִים
יא צַדִּיק: מָגִנִּי עַל־אֱלֹהִים מוֹשִׁיעַ יִשְׁרֵי־לֵב:

מִשְׁפָּט צִוִּיתָ — [To mete out] the judgment which You commanded.

To mete out the specific judgment which You ordered above in *Psalm 2:9*, תְּרֹעֵם בְּשֵׁבֶט בַּרְזֶל, 'Smash them with an iron rod' (*Rashi*).

8. וַעֲדַת לְאֻמִּים תְּסוֹבְבֶךָ — When the assembly of nations surrounds You.

Rashi, following his opinion that this Psalm refers to gentile enemies, sees here a plea from David to Hashem that when the heathen armies flock around God with a request for help, He should ignore them.

Ibn Ezra, according to his view that Kush was a Jewish adversary, explains that this enemy recruited his gentile vassals to entrap David. When the asembly of nations surrounded David, it was as if they surrounded God Himself, for David was the Lord's faithful servant and the Holy Presence accompanied him wherever he went. Therefore, David says to God, תְּסוֹבְבֶךָ, 'they surround You'.

Radak, who maintains that the psalm is dedicated to Saul's pursuit of David, renders וַעֲדַת, as 'the assembly of all Israel', לְאֻמִּים, 'who are divided into separate tribes which are like many individual nations.' When they all join Saul in pursuing me it is as if they are surrounding You, Hashem, and denying the fact that You anointed me to be king.

וְעָלֶיהָ — Rise up above it. [lit. on it]

Rashi sees the word as related to 'elevate', 'rise up'. 'Rise up far above them; show them that You have the upper hand.'

Metzudas Zion translates this literally as 'because of this'. I.e. 'because they surround You, do the following.'

לַמָּרוֹם שׁוּבָה — And return to Your heavenly repose.

Do not remain on earth to be involved with them. Pay no attention to them and return to where You belong, in heavenly repose (*Rashi; Metzudas David*).

Radak interprets this phrase as a metaphorical description of God's involvement in human affairs. When God overlooks a person's iniquity it is as if He descended from His Throne of Justice. But when He adheres to the letter of the law and deals out just punishment, He then rises up to His exalted Throne of Justice once again.

9. ה' יָדִין עַמִּים — HASHEM will punish [lit. 'decide the law', 'judge'] the nations.

Here it refers to a harsh and painful sentence: 'Divert it away from Israel towards the direction of the militant nations' (*Rashi*).

Radak again describes עַמִּים 'nations' as the tribes of Israel who are hostile to David. Of course, David does not wish the bulk of the people to be punished, only the malicious ones who are determined to destroy him with unprovoked animosity.

שָׁפְטֵנִי ה' כְּצִדְקִי וּכְתֻמִּי עָלָי — But judge me, HASHEM, according to my righteousness and my integrity.

Although David asks for a harsh sentence for the heathens, he prays that he and all of Israel should be judged according to their merits and not their sins (*Rashi*).

⁸ When the assembly of nations surrounds You,
Rise up above it,
  and return to Your heavenly repose.
⁹ HASHEM will punish the nations;
But judge me, HASHEM, according to
  my righteousness and my integrity.
¹⁰ Let the evil of the wicked vanish,
  but sustain the righteous,
O searcher of hearts and minds,
  O righteous God.
¹¹ I trust in God to be my shield,
  He who saves the upright of heart.

10. יִגְמָר נָא רַע רְשָׁעִים — *Let the evil of the wicked vanish* [lit. 'come to an end']

The translation follows *Rashi* who relates יִגְמָר, 'let vanish' to כִּי גָמַר חָסִיד, 'for the devout have disappeared' (Ps. 12:2).

David prays only that 'the evil of the wicked' should disappear, not the wicked people themselves. For he hopes that they will repent, thus eradicating their evil while they themselves survive (*Alshich*).

[Similarly we read יִתַּמּוּ חַטָּאִים מִן הָאָרֶץ 'Let sins cease from the earth' (Psalms 104:35), upon which the Talmud (*Berachos* 10a) comments, 'Let the חַטָּאִים 'sins' cease and perish, but not the חֹטְאִים 'the sinners'. Let them repent.]

However, *Metzudas David* and *Radak* hold that יִגְמָר is a verb 'to cause to disappear'. 'Let the evil cause themselves to be wiped out and to disappear through their own evil.' [Cf. Ps. 34:22 תְּמוֹתֵת רָשָׁע רָעָה].

וּתְכוֹנֵן צַדִּיק — *But sustain the righteous.*

This comes from the word כֵּן, 'a solid foundation'. 'Give the righteous a firm base to support and sustain them' (*Metzudas David*).

וּבֹחֵן לִבּוֹת וּכְלָיוֹת אֱלֹהִים צַדִּיק — *O Searcher of hearts and minds, O righteous God.*

וּכְלָיוֹת — [lit. 'kidneys'. However, whenever used in context with intellect it means the part of the mind which creates ideas, plans, and decisions. Thus, we find the Talmudic phrase כְּלָיוֹת יוֹעֲצוֹת, 'The mind (kidneys) advises' (*Berachos* 61a).]

Harav Gifter explains that the mind does indeed function somewhat like a kidney. The kidney is essentially a filter which cleanses the body of waste matter and allows only pure liquids to remain. Similarly, the mind, when making decisions, eliminates impractical schemes and retains only the best plan (See *comm.* to 16:7 and 44:22).

Only You, Hashem, are capable of making a thorough analysis of heart and mind to determine the man who is a genuine tzaddik for only You are אֱלֹהִים צַדִּיק, 'the righteous God' (*Radak*).

11. מָגִנִּי עַל אֱלֹהִים — *I trust in God to be my shield* [lit. my shield is upon God].

David should have said מָגִנִּי אֱלֹהִים, 'God is my shield'. What he means to say here is that he puts all of his trust in Hashem in order that Hashem should become his shield (*Radak*). [See *comm.* to 3:4.]

מוֹשִׁיעַ יִשְׁרֵי לֵב — *He Who saves the upright of heart.*

יב אֱלֹהִים שׁוֹפֵט צַדִּיק וְאֵל זֹעֵם בְּכָל־יוֹם:
יג אִם־לֹא יָשׁוּב חַרְבּוֹ יִלְטוֹשׁ קַשְׁתּוֹ דָרַךְ
יד וַיְכוֹנְנֶהָ: וְלוֹ הֵכִין כְּלֵי־מָוֶת חִצָּיו
טו לְדֹלְקִים יִפְעָל: הִנֵּה יְחַבֶּל־אָוֶן וְהָרָה
טז עָמָל וְיָלַד שָׁקֶר: בּוֹר כָּרָה וַיַּחְפְּרֵהוּ וַיִּפֹּל

Since the righteous God knows the hearts of the just (v. 10), He will certainly save them (Ibn Ezra).

12. אֱלֹהִים שׁוֹפֵט צַדִּיק — *God is the righteous Judge.*

According to *Rashi* and *Ibn Ezra*, שׁוֹפֵט, is a noun *'the Judge'*; and צַדִּיק, is an adjective describing the Judge as *'righteous'*. However, *Radak* and *Metzudas David* render שׁוֹפֵט as a verb, *'he judges'*, and צַדִּיק as a noun, *'the righteous'*, thus: He [God] judges the righteous.

וְאֵל זֹעֵם בְּכָל יוֹם — *And God is angered* [lit. *wrathful*] *every day.*
I.e. when He observes the deeds of the wicked (*Rashi*).

Radak interprets this not as a description of God, but of the evil man. וְאֵל זֹעֵם, *'he makes God wrathful'*. Thus, the entire verse reads: *'God judges the righteous, and He also judges the wicked who make Him wrathful every day.'* Specifically, this refers to Saul who infuriates God every day he pursues the righteous David.[1]

13. אִם לֹא יָשׁוּב — *If he does not repent.*
If the wicked one does not repent from his ways (*Rashi*).

Radak translates אִם as *'because'*, and interprets the rest of the verse as a description of the evil-doers' ways. Thus: *'Because he does not repent'* [and continues to …].

חַרְבּוֹ יִלְטוֹשׁ — *He will sharpen His sword.*
According to *Rashi* this refers to God who will prepare His weapons to punish the stubborn sinner if he does not repent.

Radak maintains that this refers to the evil-doer who sharpens his sword to harm David.

קַשְׁתּוֹ דָרַךְ וַיְכוֹנְנֶהָ — *He will bend and aim His bow.*
This danger is not far-off, says David. It is imminent, for the bow is already bent and the arrows are aimed, ready to shoot (*Radak*).

דָרַךְ — *He bends* [lit. *'stepped on'*].
[The hand is usually not strong enough to bend the heavy bow in order to string it. The archer bends it by stepping on it.]

14. וְלוֹ — *And for him.*
God has prepared the following afflictions for punishing the wicked (*Rashi*).
According to *Radak* it is the evil man himself who prepares the weapons now described.

חִצָּיו לְדֹלְקִים יִפְעָל — *He will use His arrows against those in hot pursuit.*
As we find כִּי דָלַקְתָּ אַחֲרָי, *'that you chased after me in hot pursuit'* (Genesis 31:36). God is ready to use His arrows against the wicked who pursue David with a 'burning' passion (*Rashi*).

1. 'And God is wrathful every day.' How long is His wrath? A fraction of a minute; 1/58,888 of an hour. This is a רֶגַע, *'a moment'*. No living creature could precisely compute when this moment occurs except for Bilaam the Wicked. However, on the day when Bilaam attempted to curse Israel, Hashem held back His wrath. And, how do we know that God's wrath is only *'a moment'*? For it is written (30:6) כִּי רֶגַע בְּאַפּוֹ , *'For His anger endures but a moment'* (Brachos 7a).

VII ¹² *God is the righteous Judge,*
12-16   *and God is angered every day.*
¹³ *If he does not repent:*
He will sharpen His sword,
   He will bend and aim His bow.
¹⁴ *And for him God has prepared deadly weapons,*
   He will use His arrows against those
   in hot pursuit.
¹⁵ *Behold, he conceives iniquity,*
   is pregnant with evil schemes,
   and brings forth falsehood.
¹⁶ *He digs a pit, digs it deep,*
   only to fall into his own trap.

Radak, however, renders: 'The evil man prepares arrows both for himself and for the others who join him in hot pursuit of David.'

15. הִנֵּה יְחַבֶּל אָוֶן — *Behold, he* [i.e. the wicked man] *conceives iniquity.*

[David compares the hatching of evil plots to the various stages of the birth process.]

יְחַבֶּל, literally means 'travails, pains' as in שָׁמָּה חִבְּלַתְךָ אִמֶּךָ, 'There your mother was in travail with you' (Shir HaShirim 8:5). It refers to the pains of the entire birth process from initial conception through pregnancy, until birth (Rashi).

וְהָרָה עָמָל — [And] *is pregnant with evil schemes.*

Malbim explains that אָוֶן means the use of physical power inequitably, and עָמָל describes the toil and exertion of the mind and spirit to develop a scheme for the practice of אָוֶן. So first יְחַבֶּל אָוֶן, the plan to act with iniquity is conceived, the seed is fertilized. Then it

develops and grows in the mind as עָמָל, like the embryo inside of a pregnant woman.

וְיָלַד שָׁקֶר —*And brings forth* [lit. *and gives birth to] falsehood.'*

But in the end the effort was for naught. Whatever is born is a disappointing failure, all expectations have proven false *(Rashi; Malbim).*

Rashi sums up the moral of this verse with a maxim: 'Everything which falsehood earns, depletion takes away.' [1]

16. בּוֹר כָּרָה וַיַּחְפְּרֵהוּ — *He digs a pit and digs it deep.*

Malbim explains that when the words כָּרָה and חָפַר are mentioned together, the former means 'to begin the excavation' and the latter means 'to dig down deep.'

וַיִּפֹּל בְּשַׁחַת יִפְעָל — *Only to fall into his own trap* [lit. *And he fell into the destruction he made].*

Malbim describes this as a deep pit which trappers dig and camouflage by

1. When Noah built the ark, even the spirits and demons entered. שִׁיקְרָא, 'Falsehood' tried to enter but was rebuffed because he had no partner. He met פֶּחְתָא, 'Depletion' who is in charge of deteriorating human resources and impoverishing men. Falsehood proposed a match. Depletion replied, 'What will you give me'? Said Falsehood, 'Everything that I earn.' And so this couple was allowed into the ark. This is why people say, 'Everything which falsehood earns, depletion takes away' *(Midrash Shocher Tov.* See also *Da'as Zekeinim* to Gen. 6:19).

יז בְּשַׁחַת יִפְעָל: יָשׁוּב עֲמָלוֹ בְרֹאשׁוֹ וְעַל
יח קָדְקֳדוֹ חֲמָסוֹ יֵרֵד: אוֹדֶה יהוה כְּצִדְקוֹ
וַאֲזַמְּרָה שֵׁם־יהוה עֶלְיוֹן:

covering over the top. The beasts who
fall into this trap are battered and killed,
thus becoming שַׁחַת, 'destroyed matter.'

Malbim sees here a continuation of
the previous verse. When the wicked
begin to conceive their scheme they
start to dig the pit. They progressively
develop the excavation until it is
finished, just as pregnancy completes
the child. But ultimately they breed only
failure for they are destroyed in the trap
they set with their own hands.

Radak notes that it appears as if
David prophesies the doom of Saul,
who died by falling on his own sword (*I
Sam.* 31:5) and thus he fell into his own
trap, i.e. the sword, which he hoped to
use against David.

[Similarly we find that the Egyptians
planned to drown the male children of
Israel and in the end they themselves
drowned in the waters of the Red Sea.

When Yisro learned of this he declared
כִּי בַדָּבָר אֲשֶׁר זָדוּ עֲלֵיהֶם which *Targum*
renders: '*They were afflicted with the
very punishment which they intended
to bring upon Israel* (*Exodus* 18:11).]

17. יָשׁוּב עֲמָלוֹ בְרֹאשׁוֹ — *His mischief
will recoil upon his own head.*

Malbim observes that David chooses
his words carefully. עָמָל, which refers to
internal mental exertion to do evil, will
fall on the רֹאשׁ, '*the head*' which is the
word used to describe the center of the
intellect, the brain complex, where all
the mental toil for evil took place.

וְעַל קָדְקֳדוֹ חֲמָסוֹ יֵרֵד — *And upon his
own skull will his violence descend.*

However, continues *Malbim*, חָמָס,
'*violence*' which is an external physical
action, will fall on the external part of
the head, the skull.

¹⁷ *His mischief will recoil upon his own head,*
and upon his own skull will his violence descend.
¹⁸ *I will thank HASHEM according to*
His righteousness,
And sing praises to HASHEM's Name, Most High.

18. אוֹדֶה ה' כְּצִדְקוֹ — *I will thank HASHEM according to His righteous-ness.*

When Hashem completes His total judgment of the wicked according to their full measure of evil, I will thank Him *(Rashi).*

Radak renders: *'according to His Justice';* i.e. that which God deals out to me.

Chozeh Zion amplifies this inter-pretation and notes that we are obligated to thank God under all cir-cumstances. Even if the benefit of a given situation is not immediately ap-parent, we must bless God for His ac-tions. Therefore, David vows to offer gratitude *'according to His Justice'* even if, in our eyes, it is not good or merciful. Thus David reaffirms his conviction that everything which God does is just

and beneficial, regardless of our ability to appreciate His actions.

וַאֲזַמְּרָה שֵׁם ה' עֶלְיוֹן — *And [I will] sing praises to HASHEM's Name, Most High.*

He deserves praises, for He is עֶלְיוֹן, *'Lord above all'* of His creations and He can do with them as He pleases *(Radak).*

No praise can do Him justice for He is far above all praise *(Metzudas David).*

However, according to *Midrash Shocher Tov,* עֶלְיוֹן, refers to the future state of the Jewish people.

Rabbi Levi said: I will sing praise to You, Hashem, when You make Israel עֶלְיוֹן, *'most high'* in the world. As it says: וּנְתָנְךָ ה' אֱלֹהֶיךָ עֶלְיוֹן עַל כָּל גּוֹיֵי הָאָרֶץ *'And HASHEM your God will make you most high over all the peoples of the earth' (Deut. 28:1).*

8 מזמור ח

*R*ambam (Hilchos Yesodei haTorah 2:2) derives from the
rapturous verses of this psalm a set of guidelines leading to the
loftiest accomplishments to which man can aspire — the love and fear
of God.

What is the path to love and reverence for God? When a person
contemplates His great and wondrous acts and creations, obtaining
from them a glimpse of God's endless wisdom which is beyond compare, then he will promptly love, praise and glorify Him, longing exceedingly to know the great Name of God, as David said, 'My soul
thirsts for God, the living God' (Psalms 42:3). When this man continues to ponder this subject in greater depth, he will be startled and
recoil in fear, filled with the realization that he is no more than a lowly, insignificant, obscure creature possessing a weak, miniscule intellect, standing in the presence of He Who is perfect in His wisdom. All
this is as David said, 'When I behold the heavens, the work of Your
fingers, the moon and the stars which You have set in place. What is
the frail human that You should keep him in mind? And what is the
son of mortal man that You should care for him? (v. 4-5).

These profound words of Rambam encourage the study of nature
as being the preferred way to come to love God. Guided by Torah,
observation of the natural phenomena can lead to an awareness of the
One Who created them (cf. Sefer HaMitzvos 3; footnote to v. 3).

The formula is: First study Torah. Then you will discern God in
the natural phenomena of the universe.

Thus, the superscription עַל הַגִּתִּית 'On the Gitis.' Meiri explains
that the Holy Ark is called 'Gitis' because it was safeguarded in the
home of Oved Edom, the גִּתִּי 'Giti' for three months. After this,
David took the Ark to its permanent abode. The King rejoiced ec-
statically in honor of the Torah. He danced and leaped with all of his
might in its honor (II Samuel 6). At that time he composed this impassioned psalm to refute all of those who deny the Torah which
demonstrates that God created and forever rules the cosmos.

How fitting that Vilna Gaon designates this as the שִׁיר שֶׁל יוֹם 'the
Song of the Day' for Simchas Torah, 'The Rejoicing of the Torah'
(Masseh Rav 234).

א-ב לַמְנַצֵּחַ עַל־הַגִּתִּית מִזְמוֹר לְדָוִד: יהוה
אֲדֹנֵינוּ מָה־אַדִּיר שִׁמְךָ בְּכָל־הָאָרֶץ
ג אֲשֶׁר־תְּנָה הוֹדְךָ עַל־הַשָּׁמָיִם: מִפִּי
עוֹלְלִים | וְיֹנְקִים יִסַּדְתָּ עֹז לְמַעַן צוֹרְרֶיךָ

1. הַגִּתִּית — *On the Gitis.*

The commentaries suggest that the *Gitis* is a special kind of musical instrument which was meant to accompany this psalm. *Meiri* adds that perhaps the name *Gitis* derives from the fact that this instrument was designed or manufactured by the musical experts in the town of גַּת, *'Gat'*. *Radak* proposes that David composed this psalm while in גַּת. *Ibn Ezra* joins *Radak* in yet another possible explanation; that David handed over this composition to be performed by the family of Oved Edom the Giti, who was a Levite [See *Prefatory Remarks*].

An entirely different approach to the word גִּתִּית, is that it refers to a גַּת, *'a wine press'*. *Rashi* cites the Rabbis of the *Midrash* who say that גִּתִּית, alludes to our enemies who are destined to be crushed by God like grapes in a wine press (*Isaiah 63:3*). However, *Rashi* raises the objection that the text of the psalm has nothing to do with such a theme.

[Actually, the gentiles are to suffer because they defied God and His Chosen People. Their pride, conceit, and selfishness made them oblivious of God's manifest presence. When they will be crushed and humbled, they too, will come to see Hashem's splendor spread all over the earth. *Hirsch* develops this line of thinking eloquently. He notes that wine pressing is only an *apparent* destruction of the grapes, for in reality the bruising pressure does not destroy at all but only brings out the fine and noble essence which was locked within the grape. This psalm demonstrates the ennobling effect of God's affliction on mankind which will ultimately lead to universal recognition of the Lord. This acknowledgement, according to an expression used by our Sages, is called יַיִן הַמְשׁוּמָר בְּעֲנָבִים, *'the wine which is treasured in the grapes'*. It will remain concealed until that great future day when it will be extracted.]

2. ה' אֲדֹנֵינוּ — *HASHEM, our Lord.*

Master over all handiworks of creation (*Radak*).

Malbim notes that the Four-Letter Name is known as the שֵׁם הַוָיָה, *'the name of perpetual bringing forth into existence,'* for it is with this Name that Hashem reveals Himself to us by means of all of the creations which He brought out into the visible world. Thus, this particular Name, which identifies Him as Master of Existence, *'Whose Name is mighty throughout the earth.'*

מָה אַדִּיר — *How mighty.*

This is an exclamatory statement uttered in amazement (*Ibn Ezra*).

Your might is beyond the measure and capacity of the creatures below who are unworthy of having Your Holy Spirit dwell in their midst (*Rashi*).

שִׁמְךָ — *Your Name.*

God's name is Himself and He Himself is His Name (*Radak*).

[The true essence of God's being, we cannot know. The names and titles we bestow upon Him are merely descriptions of the faint glimmer of God which He reveals to us through His works and creations. But even this infinitesimal fragment is אַדִּיר, *'mighty.'*]

אֲשֶׁר תְּנָה הוֹדְךָ עַל הַשָּׁמָיִם — *For it were fit that You place Your majesty above the heavens.*

It truly belongs above the heavens, for humanity is unworthy of such

VIII
1-3

For the Conductor; on the Gitis.
A song of David.
² HASHEM, our Lord,
how mighty is Your Name throughout the earth,
For it were fit that You place Your majesty
above the heavens.
³ Out of the mouths of babes and sucklings
You have established strength,

splendor and inadequate to appreciate it. Nevertheless, You, HASHEM, in Your great humility, have placed Your majesty on earth (Rashi).

Radak and Metzudas Zion render this as past tense, 'You have placed.' Thus, 'Although Your might is evident throughout the lower world, the greatest demonstration of Your majesty has been placed in the upper heavens, for the earth fades into insignificance when compared to the celestial wonders.'

Radak offers yet another insight: God has placed control of the mundane world below in the hands of spiritual forces above. Therefore, the reason God's might is so evident below is because He has placed such a remarkable and majestic operating system in heaven above.

3. מִפִּי עוֹלְלִים וְיֹנְקִים יִסַּדְתָּ עֹז — Out of the mouths of babes and sucklings You have established 'strength'.

The following is an example of how God's management is evident even in the smallest things on earth: A tiny babe enters the world and instantly, in the very mechanics of his nursing system, we witness wonders. His mother is able to nurse him and the flow of milk is regulated according to his needs, capacity, and ability to suckle. Therefore, we use the word יִסַּדְתָּ, 'You have established,' for here at the nursing stage, the basis of human life, we already have a foundation upon which to build a lifetime of recognizing God's עֹז, 'strength', meaning His powerful

control over every aspect of the universe, leaving nothing to chance (Radak).

The recognition of God is not a supernatural mystery to be fathomed only in the far-flung zones of outer space, it is a reality which proclaims itself in every small spot on earth. It is intelligible even to עוֹלְלִים, 'babes'. Even if the name of God would be erased from earth and expunged from all books of an arrogant, erring human science, still every pure, new soul born into the world uncorrupted, would on its own sense and notice God everywhere. In this way the babes are the bedrock foundation of permanently establishing God's name on the earth forever (Hirsch).

עוֹלְלִים — 'Babes'.

Rashi comments that because infants wallow in dirt and filth, they are called עוֹלְלִים, as we find וְעֹלַלְתִּי בֶעָפָר קַרְנִי — 'And I filthied my glory in dust' (Job 16:15)

Metzudas Zion observes that the babe may be called an עוֹלֵל even while still inside its mother's womb, as in the phrase, כְּעֹלְלִים לֹא רָאוּ אוֹר 'as infants who never saw light' (Job 3:16).

Rashi points out that these words are a continuation of the previous verse. God in His supreme humbleness has placed His heavenly majesty on the lowly earth. Says David: יִסַּדְתָּ, 'You have established' the Temple as the dwelling place for Your Holy presence, and it is there that You ordained that the Priests and the Levites should utter the

praises of your עֹז, 'strength'. But who
are these Priests and Levites? They are
merely men who were once עוֹלְלִים
וְיֹנְקִים, 'babes' who rolled and played in
filth and 'sucklings' whose mothers
nursed them. Yet You are humble
enough to desire the praises of creatures
so lowly!

[In a homiletical sense, the very existence and continuation of the world
depends on the mouths of innocent
babes. In the *Talmud (Shabbos* 119a)
we learn: The world exists only by virtue of the breath of תִּנוֹקוֹת שֶׁל בֵּית רַבָּן,
'*the children studying Torah from their
Rebbe.'* Rav Pappa said to Abaye: 'And
what about my Torah and your Torah?'
Abaye replied: 'There is no comparison
between (our) breath which is tainted
with sin and (their) breath which has no
trace of sin.']

לְמַעַן צוֹרְרֶיךָ — *Because of Your
tormentors.*

These crystal-clear manifestations of
God's supervision are designed to
silence those who are hostile and dare to
deny God's mastery. Although God's
loving concern for His creations is
equally evident in the skillful engineer-
ing of animals and beasts, yet only man
is endowed with the intellectual capacity to recognize and value these won-

ders, realizing that all of these marvels
are for his benefit. Therefore, man alone
has an obligation to contemplate the
wonders of the world and to offer
thanks and praise to his Maker *(Radak).*

Hirsch explains that the wicked are
deeply disturbed by God's omnipresence all over the globe. They see God
as an impediment for their ambitions in
life, so they seek to banish Him from all
aspects of everyday existence. They
desire to confine divine authority to the
temples and synagogues, and even
there, only at certain special festivals
and ceremonies. Thus, the opponents of
God are quite literally his צוֹרְרִים *'those
who limit and confine Him';* they exclude God from playing a meaningful
role in human affairs.

[Those who are hostile to God will
look up to the sky and see no evidence
of God's mastery. On the contrary, they
will worship the heavenly host in
defiance of God, as the Torah warns,
*'Lest you lift up your eyes unto heaven
and when you see the sun and the moon
and the stars, even all the host of
heaven, you will be drawn away and
will bow to them and serve them' (Deut.
4:19).]* [1]

לְהַשְׁבִּית אוֹיֵב וּמִתְנַקֵּם — *To silence foe
and avenger.*

1. The reknowned *Gaon, Harav Mordecai Pogramanski* was fond of telling the following
anecdote:
    A group of visitors crowded around an exquisite portrait in a world-famous museum. From
all sides came exclamations of rapture. 'Marvelous!', 'Incredible!' But one lone observer was
unimpressed. 'Buttermilk!' he ranted. 'This painting is nothing but a glob of buttermilk!'
    A fellow tourist noticed the true cause of the problem and advised the upset man, 'Your
spectacles are splattered with buttermilk. Clean them and then you, too, will behold the
beautiful masterpiece!'
    Harav Pogramanski concluded, God's wisdom and mastery are evident in every atom of the
universe. Every blade of grass and every molecule of matter shouts out an unmistakable message — 'The Almighty alone is our Creator!'
    But how many observers of nature have become heretics? How many myriads of scientists
have scrutinized the heavens and the earth and remained pantheists, evolutionists, and scoffers? They fail to perceive the truth because their lenses are besmirched. Lust and pride have
blinded their clear vision. Man desperately needs Torah guidance to purify his sight so that he
can see the Name of God emblazoned in fiery letters all across the expanse of the universe.

VIII
4

Because of Your tormentors:
to silence foe and avenger.
⁴ When I behold Your heavens,
the work of Your fingers,
The moon and the stars,
which You have set in place . . .

According to *Rashi* this foe is an enemy of Israel in particular and denies that God has designated the Jews as His chosen people. But the fact that God desires the praises of the representatives of Israel in the Temple shows that He cares for us more than all others and so the foes and the avengers of Israel are silenced.

4. בִּי אֶרְאֶה שָׁמֶיךָ — *When I behold Your heavens.*

After being amazed by your wondrous works on earth, I am prepared to behold and recognize Your handiwork in the heavens above, observing without doubt that only You created them and that they are not a product of evolutionary processes which *'happen'* by themselves (*Metzudas David*).

מַעֲשֵׂה אֶצְבְּעֹתֶיךָ — *The work of Your fingers.*

The celestial spheres are ten, the highest being כִּסֵּא הַכָּבוֹד, *'the throne of glory'.* Therefore they are called the work of God's ten fingers (*Ibn Ezra*).

[When demonstrating something, the finger is used to point out details with a clarity and exactness that leave no room for doubt. Whenever the term אֶצְבַּע אֱלֹהִים, *'the finger of God'*, is used in Tanach it means that God has revealed Himself with such clarity that one can literally point to the reality of His presence. He who ponders the awesome vastness of the heavens and the myriad stars witnesses this clear revelation tenfold. [1]

In verse 7, we find mention of מַעֲשֵׂי יָדֶיךָ, *'the works (plural) of Your hands'*, whereas in this verse David says מַעֲשֵׂה אֶצְבְּעֹתֶיךָ, *'the work (singular) of your fingers.' 'The works of God's hands'* is an expression that alludes to creations that are not as intricate or precisely specialized as the delicate work of the individual *'fingers'*, which suggest God's extra care. Thus, it is precisely the unique diversity of each completely dissimilar star, endowed with its own special proportions and properties, which allows it to blend harmoniously with all other stars into one uniform work of God, displaying His painstaking attention to each minute detail of creation. Each unique product of His *'fingers'* blends with all the others in one perfectly coordinated whole.]

יָרֵחַ וְכוֹכָבִים אֲשֶׁר כּוֹנָנְתָּה — *The moon and the stars which You have set in place.*

Some say that David did not mention the sun because he composed this Psalm at night while gazing at the moon and

---

1. To God, the creation of a colossal star is no more difficult than the creation of a tiny gnat. *Rav Saadiah Gaon* writes: We find the term אֶצְבַּע *'finger'* [of God] regarding the creation of three things; the stars and planets, the לֻחֹת *'tablets of the covenant'* (Ex. 31:18) and the plague of כִּנָּם *'lice'* (Ex. 8:15).

The stars represent the greatest of all physical masses, for no creation exceeds their size. The lice are among the smallest and most despicable of creations. The לֻחֹת are smaller than the stars yet far greater in splendor. Although these three differ vastly, they are all described with the identical word, אֶצְבַּע, to emphasize God's effort in creating all three was equal (*Rabbeinu Bachya; Ex. 8:9*).

ה אֲשֶׁר כּוֹנָנְתָּה: מָה־אֱנוֹשׁ כִּי־תִזְכְּרֶנּוּ וּבֶן־
ו אָדָם כִּי תִפְקְדֶנּוּ: וַתְּחַסְּרֵהוּ מְּעַט
מֵאֱלֹהִים וְכָבוֹד וְהָדָר תְּעַטְּרֵהוּ:
ז תַּמְשִׁילֵהוּ בְּמַעֲשֵׂי יָדֶיךָ כֹּל שַׁתָּה תַחַת־

stars, pondering upon the wonders of the Creator (Radak).

By day, the bright sun does not allow man to see the vastness of the universe — he sees only earth and the heavens arched over it, supplying the earth below with light, warmth, and moisture. It is at night, when the earth has receded into the shadows and the starry hosts of shining worlds are visible in the sky that the earth shrinks to a mere speck in the universe and man on this speck becomes so infinitely small (Hirsch).

5. מָה־אֱנוֹשׁ כִּי תִזְכְּרֶנּוּ — *What is the (frail) human that You should remember him?*

The term אֱנוֹשׁ denotes the weakness and fragility of man, the shortcomings and limitations imposed upon his nature because he is a lowly earthling, terribly restricted and confined as compared to the soaring celestial bodies (Malbim).

In sharp contrast to God who is described above as מָה אַדִּיר, 'how mighty', the entire value of man's existence is questioned now with the words, מָה אֱנוֹשׁ, 'how frail is man'! Of what significance is he that You should care for him? This question becomes acutely perplexing after witnessing the intellect of the heavenly bodies and the spiritual forces controlling them. One

can appreciate why divine intellect befits such lofty creations, but why should God care enough to bestow such gifts on puny man? (Radak).[1]

וּבֶן אָדָם — *And the son of mortal man.*

Malbim points out that the description בֶּן אָדָם [lit. 'son of man'] denotes man's mortality. Heavenly bodies endure eternally. Mankind however, can only assure its continued existence through reproduction, i.e. a father bearing a 'son of man'. Thus, only the species endures, while the individual passes on.

כִּי תִפְקְדֶנּוּ — *That You should be mindful of him?*

This translation follows *Metzudas Zion* who maintains that תִפְקְדֶנּוּ is synonymous with תִזְכְּרֶנּוּ.

Hirsch, however, demonstrates that the verb פָּקַד, carries the connotation of installing someone into office, appointing him for the performance of a task, as we find וַיַּפְקִדֵהוּ עַל בֵּיתוֹ, 'and he appointed him over his household' (Genesis 39:4). David wonders why God bothered to make so frail a man in His image and place him on earth to represent divine sovereignty. 'What is the son of mortal man that You have installed him in his earthly office?'[2]

1. 'Listen my brothers and my people! In order to prevent pride and arrogance a person should lift up his eyes to the heavens and say "Who created these? Who is He Who fashioned the sun and the moon, the stars and the constellations?" It is God alone in His wisdom Who created each and every one, and Who perpetuates them with the word of His lips!' (Tanna d'Bei Eliyahu 18).

2. *Rambam* (Hilchos Yesodei HaTorah 4:12) writes: 'When a person ponders over these matters and analyzes all creations — from the lofty angels to the planets down to man and his like, he comes to recognize the wisdom of God inherent in all creatures. This comprehension will cause his love of the Creator to increase. His soul will thirst and his flesh will pine to come to adore The Blessed One. He will tremble and fear his own insignificance and minuteness when he compares himself to one of those great and holy bodies.

⁵ *What is the frail human*
that You should remember him?
And what is the son of mortal man
that You should be mindful of him?
⁶ *Yet You have made him*
only a little less than the angels,
And crowned him
with a soul and a splendor
⁷ *You gave him dominion*
over the works of Your hand,

6. וַתְּחַסְּרֵהוּ מְעַט מֵאֱלֹהִים — *Yet You have made him only a little less than the angels.*

Yet, despite man's frailty, You have taken care to make him great, only a bit less than the angels. His mission in life is an intellectual experience and a glorious one. Man surpasses all living creatures by virtue of his capacity for intelligent speech and rational communication *(Metzudas David).*

[Although אֱלֹהִים is usually a reference to God, this word often refers to angels, as in our verse, rulers, a court, or other possessors of power (cf. *Gen.* 6:2, *Rashi* and ArtScroll *comm.*)].

Like the angels, man's soul is not matter, but pure spirit. The only difference is that man's soul is imprisoned in a coarse body which threatens to corrupt it *(Radak).*

Rashi elaborates upon this theme, citing examples where mortal men controlled nature as if they were angels: 'You, HASHEM, gave Joshua the power to halt the sun and to dry up the Jordan. You endowed Moses with the ability to split the sea and to rise up to heaven to receive the Torah. You dispatched Elijah on a mission to revive the dead.'

The Talmud *(Nedarim 38a, Rosh Hashana 21b)* tells us of the one mortal who came closest to attaining the divine intellect. ''Rav and Shmuel both say: Fifty gates of understanding were crea-

ted in the world and all were presented to Moses with the exception of one, as it says, 'You have made him only a little less than the angels.' [This gate is the entranceway to comprehending God Himself. No mortal can possibly grasp this. See *Overview* to Torah, *Bereishis,* ArtScroll edition.]

וְכָבוֹד — *A soul.* The crowning achievement of man's creation was the blowing of a splendid heavenly soul into his nostrils *(Radak).*

Maharam Almosnino observes that man is handicapped in comparison to the angels, for he possesses the desire to do evil, whereas they do not. However, precisely this ability to choose between good and bad gives man an advantage over the angels, who have no challenges and no victories. Thus, because God made man *'a little less than the angels'* this in itself makes man's mission more meaningful *'and crowns him with a soul and a splendor,'* which even angels lack.

7. תַּמְשִׁילֵהוּ בְּמַעֲשֵׂי יָדֶיךָ — *You gave him dominion over the works of Your hands.*

By virtue of his exalted soul, man was given mastery over the entire world *(Radak).*

Metzudas David maintains that man was given mastery over all creations. However, *Ibn Ezra* maintains that man's sovereignty is only over this planet,

ז רַגְלָיו: צֹנֶה וַאֲלָפִים כֻּלָם וְגַם בַּהֲמוֹת

ט שָׂדָי: צִפּוֹר שָׁמַיִם וּדְגֵי הַיָּם עֹבֵר אָרְחוֹת

י יַמִּים: יהוה אֲדֹנֵינוּ מָה־אַדִּיר שִׁמְךָ בְּכָל־
הָאָרֶץ:

Earth. *Radak* suggests that man may also be considered a ruler over the heavenly bodies because his intellect can grasp and master the nature of the stars and galaxies.

Ordinarily, a מוֹשֵׁל is an absolute monarch who strictly enforces his own will. *Hirsch* points out that here we must take this word in a different sense. We find that Eliezer, the servant of Abraham, is described as עַבְדּוֹ זְקַן בֵּיתוֹ הַמּשֵׁל בְּכָל אֲשֶׁר לוֹ , *"His servant, the elder of his house, who ruled over all that belonged to him [Abraham]"* (Genesis 24:2). Eliezer, 'the ruler', really had no will of his own. He was merely a steward who assigned things to their proper place in accordance with Abraham's command. Similarly, God has appointed man as His steward in the household of this terrestrial world to fulfill His purposes. Man receives this dominion as a loan, and he must answer to God for the use to which he puts his position of power.

תַּחַת רַגְלָיו — *Under his feet.*
Everything is subservient to man (*Metzudas David*).
Even that which is at his feet, the plants and the minerals beneath the earth (*Ibn Ezra*).[1]

Harav Yerucham Levovitz writes: All philosophers agree that man contains within himself all of the forces and elements which exist throughout the universe. There is a trace of all vegetable and mineral characteristics within man. Therefore, man is called an עוֹלָם קָטָן, '*a microcosm*', i.e. a miniature world. If man exercises self-discipline and rules over all that he possesses within himself — then he will have gained mastery over the entire world. This is what the Psalmist means, '*You gave him dominion over the works of Your hands.*' When? After man controls himself and gains internal mastery over all that '*You have placed* [viz. *everything*] *under his feet*' (*Da'as Chochmah U'Mussar* Vol. III, pg. 248).

8. צֹנֶה — *Sheep.*
This is a derivation of the word צֹאן, dropping the letter 'א' from the spelling (*Metzudas Zion; Radak*).

וַאֲלָפִים — *And cattle* [lit. *'and thousands'*].
Specifically, this refers to bovines, (cows), as in שְׁגַר אֲלָפֶיךָ, *'the offspring of your cattle'* (Deut. 28:4) (*Metzudas Zion*).

כֻּלָם — *Everything* [lit. *'all of them'*].

1. The Talmud (*Berachos* 60b) rules that in the morning when one puts on his shoes he should recite the blessing, '*Blessed is He who has provided me with all of my needs.*' The holy *Shaloh* quotes an explanation of this benediction in the name of *Rabbi Shlomo Luria* (the *Maharshal*). All of the world can be divided into four major categories: mineral, vegetable, animal and human, in ascending order. Each progressive category dominates the category which precedes it, and so, man is master over all. When man dons the shoes made of animal hide, he proclaims sovereignty over the animal world and all the categories beneath it, for all were provided by God to be at man's service. Accordingly, when he puts on his shoes, he says '*Blessed is He Who has provided me with all my needs.*'
This is what David meant when he said, '*You gave him dominion over the works of Your hands, You have placed everything under his feet.*'
The shoes under his feet attest to man's rule over all of God's handiworks (*Imros Tehoros*).

VIII
8-10

You placed everything under his feet.
8 *Sheep and cattle, everything,*
    even the beasts of the open field;
9 *The birds of the sky and the fish of the sea;*
    for he crosses over the paths of the sea.
10 *HASHEM, our Master,*
    how mighty is Your Name throughout the earth!

This refers to all other domesticated animals in man's possession — horses, donkeys and camels *(Radak)*.

בַּהֲמוֹת שָׂדָי — *[Even the] beasts of the open field.*

Even the non-domesticated, wild beasts are considered under man's rule because he understands them intellectually, and, if he wished, he could plan their capture *(Radak)*.

Midrash Shocher Tov enumerates the many instances where men were accorded special dominion over wildlife. King Solomon could lecture on the beasts and birds, on the fish and the reptiles. Samson trapped three hundred wild foxes to do his bidding. Daniel sat on the necks of the lions in the den and he left the pit unharmed. The ravens faithfully brought bread and meat to Elijah all the while he hid in the cave. The great fish swallowed Jonah and transported him to where he belonged.

צִפּוֹר שָׁמַיִם וּדְגֵי הַיָּם .9 — *The birds of the sky and the fish of the sea.*

Even those creatures which appear to be inaccesible, even the birds which soar freely high above, and the fish in the seas deep below, even these are within the reach of man who can plan a trap to ensnare them *(Radak; Metzudas David)*.

עֹבֵר אָרְחוֹת יַמִּים — *For he crosses over the paths of the sea.*

No living creature is beyond the grasp of man, even the fish in the most remote seas, for man has conquered the art of transportation and can build ships to cross over any waters *(Metzudas David)*.

מָה אַדִּיר שִׁמְךָ בְּכָל הָאָרֶץ .10 — *How mighty is Your Name throughout the earth!*

When David finished relating the many kindnesses which God has done for mankind and the variety of talents with which man has been endowed, he observed that despite all this, man is relatively minute and insignificant compared to the wondrous divine works which stud the heavens. So, once again, David exclaims in awe the tremendous might of the Creator *(Radak)*.[1]

---

1. Rabbi Joshua ben Levi said: When Moses ascended to heaven, the ministering angels said to the Holy One, Blessed be He, 'Sovereign of the Universe.' What business has one who is born of woman among us?' 'He has come to receive the Torah,' was the divine answer. 'What!' said the angels to Him, 'Are You about to bestow upon frail man that cherished treasure that was with You for nine hundred and seventy four generations before the world was created? *What is the frail human that You should remember him, and the son of mortal man that You should be mindful of him? HASHEM, our Master, is not Your Name [already sufficiently] mighty all over the earth? Now place Your glory above the heavens!' (Psalms 8:2-5).*

The Holy One, Blessed Be He, then called upon Moses to refute their objection ... Moses said to them: "Of what use can the Torah be to you? ...It is written, *'Remember the Sabbath and keep it holy' (Exodus 20:8)*. Are you angels doing any work that you need rest? Again it is written, *'Honor your father and mother' (Exodus 20:12)*. Have you a father and mother? And

also it is written, *'You shall not murder, you shall not commit adultery, you shall not steal'* (*Exodus* 20:13). Does jealousy exist among you? Does an evil impulse exist among you?

The angels at once confessed that the Holy One, Blessed be He, was right, for it is written (*Psalms* 8:10) *'H*ASHEM *our Master, how mighty is Your Name throughout the earth,'* and no longer is it written, *'Now place Your glory above the heavens' (Shabbos* 88b).

In the previous psalm, David sang of the Divine order manifest in the wonders of creation. God purposely made his splendid universal scheme very clear ... to establish strength because of ... tormentors, to silence foe and avenger (8:3).

But, the enemies of God are not silenced. They demand: 'If indeed the earth is the Lord's, why does He not guide the events of history in accordance with a strict pattern of justice, just as He regulates the world of nature?'

Now, David replies forcefully to his own foes and to Israel's tormentors — Goliath, Absalom, Naval, Lavan, Esau, Amalek, King Laben.

He declares: 'The key to world history is to remember that the universe was created לַבֵּן, for the son of God, Israel, whom God is determined to make לָבָן, pure and innocent [lit. white]. To test the purity of their faith, God conceals His ways (עֲלָמוֹת) from the righteous. The confusion, havoc, and ruin wrought by the wicked are but a manifestation of עֲלָמוֹת, concealment. But the joyous song of the devout is not muted by affliction or misery, they continue to sing עַל מוּת, even beyond death, עֲלָמוֹת, forever.

1. עַל מוּת לַבֵּן — *On the death of Laben.*

The translation follows *Rashi*'s final interpretation (see further) although the meaning of these enigmatic words provide a challenge to all of the commentators who toil to find an acceptable explanation.

Rashi proposes that the psalm is dedicated to the death of David's son Absalom, but he immediately dismisses that possibility because the proper usage would necessitate the words to read עַל מוּת הַבֵּן *"upon the death of the son"* and also the text of the psalm has nothing to do with such a theme. *Rashi* then quotes the opinion (mentioned also in *Radak*) that לַבֵּן, *'laben'* spells נָבָל, *'Naval'*, backwards and refers to Naval, the Carmelite, who was insolent and rude to David and died at the hands of the Lord. However, this is rejected because it seems incongruous to spell his name backwards (*Rashi*). Furthermore Naval was not an evildoer; he never hurt anyone, he was merely an inhospitable miser (*Radak*).

Yet another alternative, says *Rashi*, is the explanation of the *Pesikta* that the psalm is dedicated to the downfall of Esau and Amalek, as implied by the words, שְׁמָם מָחִיתָ לְעוֹלָם וָעֶד *'You erased their name forever and ever' (v. 6).*This victory for the Jews will occur when the pure, youthful innocence of Israel will be revived and their righteousness revealed. Thus the word לַבֵּן is related to לָבָן, *'white'*, a symbol of purity.

Rashi also quotes *Menachem* that לַבֵּן, is derived from the word בִּינָה, *'understanding'*. This psalm was given to the director of music so that he should study and understand the score and then make others understand through his lucid explanations.

Rashi concludes with the opinion of Donash (also noted in *Radak* and *Sforno*) that לַבֵּן, *'Laben'* was the name of a powerful king of David's times who conquered many nations and then came

to threaten Israel. David defeated the tyrant and sang this psalm to commemorate his death. *Rashi* warns us not to be skeptical of this explanation despite the fact that *'Laben'* is never mentioned elsewhere in Scriptures, because there are many personalties who are mentioned but once in all of the Bible.

Radak concludes that the only explanation which is faithful to the entire psalm is that לַבֵּן derives from בֵּין, *'in between'*. It refers to the Philistine giant גָּלְיָת, *'Goliath'* who is also called אִישׁ הַבֵּנַיִם, *"the man between them"* (*Samuel I* 17:23). When David killed him he offered this song of thanks (*Meiri* concurs with this opinion).

Alshich maintains that לַבֵּן means *'to a son'* and that the psalm is in memory of the first son whom Bath Sheba bore to David. The child died seven days after birth as a punishment for his father's impropriety in the affair.

Upon learning of the tragic death of this infant, David was not overwrought with grief, but rather he rose calmly, washed and changed, and went to pray before God (*II Samuel*, 12).

Because he was so severely afflicted, David rejoiced, for he knew that God was putting him through the process of repentance and forgiveness, whitening the blackness of his sins. Thus, לַבֵּן, has a double meaning: *'to the son'*, and *'to whiten'*. Precisely for this reason David does not say עַל מוּת הַבֵּן but rather לַבֵּן, in order to inject this dual message; what happened *'to the son'* caused David *'to be whitened'*. This positive attitude is further reflected by prefacing the psalm לַמְנַצֵּחַ which means literally *'to the victorious'* (see *comm. Psalm* 4:1) because David here exults in his emotional triumph over the melancholy of tragic death.

All of the above theses are based on the premise that עַל מוּת means *'upon the death'* and that these are two

IX
1-2

For the Conductor, on the death of Laben.
A song of David.
² I will thank HASHEM with all my heart,
I will proclaim all of Your wondrous deeds.

separate words. However, *Rashi* notes that the *Masorah* here makes reference to הוּא יְנַהֲגֵנוּ עַל מוּת, 'He will lead us al-mus' (Psalm 48:15). *Rashi (ibid)* renders this as one word עֲלָמוֹת which means 'young childhood'. This means that God will lead us carefully like a father who guides his young child. *Rashi (ibid)* also quotes *Menachem* who translates the word as עוֹלָמִית, 'forever' [in both עוֹלָמוֹת, 'worlds', this world and the World to Come, eternally].

The *Midrash* (ibid) renders עַל מוּת, as two words meaning 'over death', 'He leads us forth over death to immortality'.

Hirsch ties together all the above interpretations:

David presents to us here an all-encompassing overview of the entire historical experience of Israel as a whole and of her many heroes as individuals. This is a psalm which is eternal, speaking of past, present and future. It is dedicated לְבֵן, to the son of God, Israel, who enjoys a specially close filial relationship with his Father in Heaven. Thus, none of Israel's enemies will survive. Naval, Absalom, King Laben, Goliath, Amalek, Esau — God judges them all עַל מוּת, 'for death'. Israel alone survives all catastrophes being עַל מוּת, 'immortal, above death'; living in עוֹלָמוֹת, in 'two worlds', this world and the World to Come. Thus, we maintain עֲלָמוֹת, eternal youth and vigor, because we always act like God's 'young son', submitting to His guidance and discipline. This is the secret essence of our immortality. Finally, עֲלָמוֹת means 'secrecy' from the word הֶעְלֵם, 'concealment'. God is forever behind the scenes of world history manipulating it so that immortal Israel shall always overcome all odds however awesome they may be.

2. [The reader must bear in mind throughout this psalm that we will be citing three major commentaries who follow three disparate themes in the explanation of this psalm. From all of the many options offered in *comm.* to v. 1, we have culled these essential ones. According to *Rashi* the psalm refers to the future downfall of Edom-Amalek and the redemption of Israel. *Radak* dedicates it to the death of Goliath. *Alshich* attributes the Psalm to the death of David's son.]

אוֹדֶה ה' בְּכָל לְבִי — *I will thank HASHEM with all my heart.*

The victory of David over Goliath was a crucial event for David and all of Israel and so it deserved full-hearted praise *(Radak).*

A basic credo of Judaism is that one must praise God for the bad with the very same feelings of appreciation which he has for the good. So David accepts the death of his new-born son with total calm and gratitude, fully realizing that everything God does is for the best *(Alschich).*

The *Chovos Halevovos* explains in 'The Gate of Divine Service' that man often finds it difficult to thank God properly for His kindness, because man realizes that his thanks are not genuine and sincere. For, although his lips utter gratitude for past favors, in his heart he knows that he truly wishes to make new requests for future kindness. Therefore, his appreciation for the past is not whole-hearted, for he is still not satisfied and wants more. But David says here that he will thank God with all of his heart, he is totally content and asks for nothing more *(Malbim).*

אֲסַפְּרָה כָּל נִפְלְאוֹתֶיךָ — *I will proclaim all of Your wondrous deeds.*

ג אֶשְׂמְחָה וְאֶעֶלְצָה בָךְ אֲזַמְּרָה שִׁמְךָ
ד עֶלְיוֹן: בְּשׁוּב־אוֹיְבַי אָחוֹר יִכָּשְׁלוּ וְיֹאבְדוּ
ה מִפָּנֶיךָ: כִּי־עָשִׂיתָ מִשְׁפָּטִי וְדִינִי יָשַׁבְתָּ
ו לְכִסֵּא שׁוֹפֵט צֶדֶק: גָּעַרְתָּ גוֹיִם אִבַּדְתָּ

I am not like most men who thank God only for the overt, extraordinary miracles, but do not appreciate the ordinary daily operation of the world. This they attribute to nature. I am not so. My eyes have been opened wide to notice that even the most simple everyday events are נִפְלָאוֹת, 'hidden miracles' (Malbim).

Rashi says that כָּל נִפְלְאוֹתֶיךָ refers specifically to the final redemption at the end of days. That miraculous event is equal to all preceding wonders combined.

3. אֶשְׂמְחָה וְאֶעֶלְצָה — I will rejoice and exult.

Hirsch comments that שָׂמַח is related to צָמַח, 'growth', and denotes the sensation of inner expansion and of progress in emotional development. עָלַץ (which is עָלַז, strengthened by the letter ץ) indicates the overcoming of resistance and is thus related to חָלַץ, 'to free oneself from bonds'. In short, עָלַץ, is an expression for the feeling of blessed relief from oppression and confinement.

Radak adds that this exultation gave David a surge of confidence in Hashem which boosted his courage as he, the youth, went out to challenge the seasoned warrior, the giant Goliath.

בָךְ — In You.
Malbim, pursuing the train of thought of the previous verse, observes that David differs from others who

praise God in yet another way (which makes a total of three). Others rejoice over salvation because of their personal gain and thus their praise is primarily motivated by feelings of self concern. However, David says: I primarily rejoice 'in You', gladdened by the fact that God's name is sanctified when He does justice.

אֲזַמְּרָה שִׁמְךָ עֶלְיוֹן — I will sing praise to Your Name, Most High.

The real reason I am so happy, is because victory afforded me an opportunity to publicly praise Your Name and to tell everyone that you are עֶלְיוֹן, 'Most High', the Supreme Ruler over the earth.[1]

4. בְּשׁוּב אוֹיְבַי אָחוֹר — When my enemies retreat.

This refers to the entire Philistine army who turned their backs and fled in terror after seeing their champion Goliath slain by David (Radak).

Because David sorely regretted the incident with Bath Sheba, Nathan, the Prophet, informed him that Hashem had commuted his sin. David would be spared, but the newborn babe would die (II Samuel, 12:13-14). David's enemies insisted that his soul would be condemned to eternal damnation, losing its portion in the World to Come. However, the fulfillment of Nathan's prophecy, the death of the babe, verified the other half of the prophecy,

1. [See Samuel I, 17:45-47, where David addresses Goliath before they enter into battle.
'Then said David to the Philistine: You come to me with a sword and with a spear and with a javelin, but I come to you in the name of HASHEM, Lord of legions, God of the armies of Israel, whom you have taunted. This day HASHEM will deliver you into my hands and I will smite you, and take your head from you, and give the carcasses of the camp of the Philistines to the birds of the sky and to the wild beasts of the earth, that all the earth may know that there is a God in Israel. And all this assembly will know that HASHEM saves not with sword or spear, for the battle is HASHEM's and He will give you into our hands.']

³ *I will rejoice and exult in You,*
   I will sing praise to Your Name, Most High.
⁴ *When my enemies retreat,*
      they will stumble and perish
      from Your countenance.
⁵ *For You executed my judgment and my cause,*
      You sat on Your throne, O righteous Judge.
⁶ *You destroyed peoples, and doomed the wicked;*

that David was also pardoned and cleansed of the sin. This, says David, should make my enemies *'retreat from their vicious slander'* and retract their statements, for everything they say is אָחוֹר, *'backwards'*, the opposite of the truth *(Alshich)*.

יִכָּשְׁלוּ וְיֹאבְדוּ מִפָּנֶיךָ — *They will stumble and perish from Your countenance.*

Hashem did me a double kindness, not only did He cause my enemies to turn back and flee, He even caused them to stumble and perish. This double goodness deserves double praise, thus *'I will rejoice and I will exult'* (v. 3) *(Metzudas David)*.

If they continue their malicious attacks they deserve no mercy, let them slip and stumble on their own tongues and perish, losing their portion in the Hereafter as punishment for attempting to strip me of mine *(Alshich)*.

5. כִּי עָשִׂיתָ מִשְׁפָּטִי וְדִינִי — *For You executed my judgment and my cause.*

The words מִשְׁפָּט and דִין are synonymous, and this repetition of two similar words one next to the other is one of the rare occurrences in all the Scriptures *(Rashi)*.

[Or, the repetition of these nouns could be rendered as a hendiadys meaning: *'my just cause.'*]

You executed justice when You fought for me, for the circumstances of Goliath's downfall were amazing. Here stood he, shielded in heavy armor from head to toe, and You guided my rock to

enter the one minute uncovered spot on his forehead *(Radak)*.

You acted with justice when you took away my newborn son *(Alshich)*.

יָשַׁבְתָּ לְכִסֵּא שׁוֹפֵט צֶדֶק — *You sat on Your throne, O righteous Judge.*

You dealt out well deserved justice to Goliath who cursed and taunted the armies of the living God *(Radak)*.

You did not suffice with merely one judgment. Rather You sat permanently on Your throne of justice to punish the wicked incessantly until they were destroyed and total צֶדֶק, *'righteousness'* was achieved *(Malbim)*.

Taking away my newborn son, although a harsh decree, was really an act befitting a שׁוֹפֵט צֶדֶק, *'a righteous judge'*, for Your purpose was to cleanse me and to forgive me *(Alshich)*.

6. גָּעַרְתָּ — *You destroyed.*

When this word is followed by a noun prefixed with a בּ, *'beth'*, then it means *'to rebuke harshly'* — the person or thing being mentioned. However, in our verse, גָּעַרְתָּ means *'to destroy'* as we find in Psalms 68:31 גְּעַר חַיַּת קָנֶה, *'Destroy the wild beast of the reeds'* *(Radak; Ibn Ezra)*. Nevertheless, *Targum* and *Metzudos* do render this as נָזַפְתָּ, *You rebuked.*

גּוֹיִם — *Peoples.*

According to *Rashi* this refers to the people of Amalek who are described as רֵאשִׁית גּוֹיִם עֲמָלֵק, *'Amalek was first of nations* (Numbers 24:20).

ז רָשָׁע שְׁמָם מָחִיתָ לְעוֹלָם וָעֶד: הָאוֹיֵב |
תַּמּוּ חֳרָבוֹת לָנֶצַח וְעָרִים נָתַשְׁתָּ אָבַד
ח זִכְרָם הֵמָּה: וַיהוה לְעוֹלָם יֵשֵׁב כּוֹנֵן
ט לַמִּשְׁפָּט כִּסְאוֹ: וְהוּא יִשְׁפֹּט־תֵּבֵל בְּצֶדֶק
י יָדִין לְאֻמִּים בְּמֵישָׁרִים: וִיהִי יהוה מִשְׂגָּב

According to *Radak*, גּוֹיִם refers to the Philistines.

However, *Metzudas Zion* holds that even here גָּעַרְתָּ, means *'You screamed a harsh rebuke.'* *Alshich* follows this explanation. David is thanking God for not slaying him, rather God harshly rebuked him by taking his infant son. David justifies God's mercy and cites historical precedents where nations deserved death penalties yet God commuted the sentence to sharp reproach such as the דּוֹר הַפְּלָגָה, *'the scattered generation'* who rebelled against God by building the Tower of Babel. They were not completely wiped out as were the people of the דּוֹר הַמַּבּוּל, *the Generation of the Flood.* God sufficed with serious rebuke by spreading them all over the earth.

אִבַּדְתָּ רָשָׁע — *And doomed the wicked.*
Rashi explains that the wicked one referred to here is Esau, ancestor of Amalek. *Radak* holds that David refers here to Goliath. According to *Ibn Ezra* the רָשָׁע is the menacing King Laben.

שְׁמָם מָחִיתָ לְעוֹלָם וָעֶד — *You blotted out their name for all eternity.*
You erased the memory of the Philistines who were slaughtered while fleeing from David (*Radak*).
According to *Rashi*, מָחִיתָ, *'You blotted out'* is past tense which refers to the promise God made for the future כִּי מָחֹה אֶמְחֶה אֶת זֵכֶר עֲמָלֵק — *'that I shall utterly erase the name of Amalek'* (Exod. 17:14).

7. הָאוֹיֵב — *The enemy* [lit. *'O you enemy'!*] This is a vocative form and therefore the word is prefixed with a ה, the definite article. Because David had

just threatened that God would erase their names forever (verse 6), he now turns to address himself directly to the enemy (*Radak*).

הָאוֹיֵב תַּמּוּ חֳרָבוֹת לָנֶצַח — *The enemy is finished because of the eternal sword.*
The translation follows *Rashi* who renders חֳרָבוֹת as *'swords'*, and לָנֶצַח as *'eternal.'* Thus, the destructive force of hatred will eternally lay upon the enemy like a sharp חֶרֶב *'sword'*.
Radak translates חֳרָבוֹת, *'ruins'*, and explains: Just as the cities you destroyed are finished and forgotten לָנֶצַח, *forever*, so, too, will you be blotted out from human memory. He adds in his father's name: The *'ruins'* which you created in the past will cease to be. In the future you will be deprived of the power to wreak such havoc and desolation.
Ibn Ezra quotes *Donash* who found an ancient volume of *Tehillim* in which this word is vocalized with a פַּתַּח, and is read חֲרָבוֹת which can only be translated as *'swords'*. However, *Ibn Ezra* himself is confident that the proper version is חֳרָבוֹת, *'ruins'*, as it appears in our text.

וְעָרִים נָתַשְׁתָּ — *[And] as for the cities You uprooted.*
This refers to Edom (Esau and Amalek) of whom it is prophesied, *'For Edom says: 'We are made destitute, but we will return and rebuild the desolate places'; so says HASHEM, Lord of legions: 'They shall build but I will throw down'* (Malachi 1:4).

אָבַד זִכְרָם הֵמָּה — *Their every remembrance has perished.*
The remembrance of those desolate cities is so blotted out that all who view

IX
7-10

You blotted out their name for all eternity.
⁷ *The enemy is finished*
   because of the eternal sword;
As for the cities You uprooted —
   their every remembrance has perished.
⁸ *But HASHEM is enthroned forever,*
   He has prepared His throne for judgment.
⁹ *And He will judge the world with righteousness,*
   Judging the nations in fairness.
¹⁰ *HASHEM will be a tower of strength*

the ruins will exclaim: 'Are these those cities?' *(Radak).*

8. וַה' לְעוֹלָם יֵשֵׁב — *But HASHEM is enthroned* [lit. *sits*] *forever.*

The wicked will perish, but Hashem judges all forever. 'Sits' means to be permanent and everlasting *(Radak).*

כּוֹנֵן לַמִּשְׁפָּט כִּסְאוֹ — *He has prepared His throne for judgment.*

Rashi notes that only after the eradication of Amalek will God's throne and God's name be full and complete. Before that time His כִּסֵּא is an incomplete כֵּס and His name יהוה is halved into יָהּ as it is written, כִּי יָד עַל כֵּס יָהּ מִלְחָמָה לַה' בַּעֲמָלֵק מִדֹּר דֹּר, *'For God has sworn with His hand on His throne, that HASHEM will wage a war with Amalek from generation to generation' (Exod. 17:16).*

The world is not left to haphazard chance. God sits and prepares His actions and judgments with great care and concern. Because God is enthroned eternally, His decisions are not impetuous bursts of emotion; but rulings of

everlasting dimension and scope *(Ibn Yachya).*

9. תֵּבֵל — *The world.*

Radak notes that this refers specifically to the inhabited regions of the globe.

Hirsch adds that תֵּבֵל *is derived from* בָּלַל, *'to mix',* denoting the world of mankind in all of its confusion; a lawless, chaotic state. [cf. *comm. Psalms* 24:1] God will ultimately reorganize the world, setting up a permanent, secure standard of justice.

בְּמֵישָׁרִים — *In fairness.*

Malbim differentiates between צֶדֶק, *'righteousness'* and מֵישָׁרִים, *'fairness'.* To judge with *righteousness* means to adhere strictly to the letter of the law with no leniency. However, *fairness* implies לִפְנִים מִשּׁוּרַת הַדִּין, *'to go beyond the limits of the law',* to judge the accused in the most favorable light possible.[1]

10. וִיהִי ה' מִשְׂגָּב לַדָּךְ — *HASHEM will be a tower of strength for the oppressed.*

1. At the end of days God will establish a tribunal to judge mankind according to a rigid standard of absolute, undiluted justice. Until then, however, He tempers His justice with mercy. Therefore, He always seeks to judge people at the time most favorable to them, and so He judges the gentile nations when they are fast asleep in the deep of night. Only then are they totally divorced from their wicked daily pursuits *(Rashi).*

God does not desire the destruction of the wicked for they too are His creations. Which potter would wish to see the pots and vessels he created smashed and wasted? But God judges Israel in broad daylight, when they are awake because the moment the Jew awakens, he immediately hastens to the synagogue to immerse himself in prayer and Torah study *(Midrash Shocher Tov).*

יא לָדָךְ מִשְׂגָּב לְעִתּוֹת בַּצָּרָה: וְיִבְטְחוּ בְךָ
יוֹדְעֵי שְׁמֶךָ כִּי לֹא־עָזַבְתָּ דֹרְשֶׁיךָ יהוה:
יב זַמְּרוּ לַיהוה יֹשֵׁב צִיּוֹן הַגִּידוּ בָעַמִּים
יג עֲלִילוֹתָיו: כִּי־דֹרֵשׁ דָּמִים אוֹתָם זָכָר
יד לֹא־שָׁכַח צַעֲקַת עניים: חָנְנֵנִי יהוה רְאֵה

In the future, when His throne will be prepared for judgment (v. 8), He will be a high stronghold for the people of Israel who are now downtrodden (Rashi).

לָדָךְ — The oppressed.

Metzudas Zion interprets this as a person who is broken and crushed, such as we find דַּכְּאֵי רוּחַ, 'the crushed in spirit' (34:19).

Rabbi Yochanon said: Wherever, mention is made of the דָּךְ, 'oppressed', or עָנִי, 'poor', the Scriptures are referring to Israel, for poverty has haunted them since the day the Temple was destroyed (Midrash Shocher Tov).

מִשְׂגָּב לְעִתּוֹת בַּצָּרָה — A tower of strength in times of distress.

This refers to the moment of great distress when the Philistines threatened to overcome Israel (Radak).

Hirsch points out that the word זְמַן, refers to 'time' in general, however עֵת is a specific point in time. Throughout history God has fortified Israel in many such unforgettable moments of disaster and distress.

This alludes to the saying of our Sages that Hashem never brings upon a man one huge punishment to pay for all his sins together. Rather God rations out the pain in small doses administered at intervals. This is what David meant by לְעִתּוֹת בַּצָּרָה, 'in times of distress' i.e. many separate times (Tehillas Hashem; Mahari Ya'avetz).

Tehillas Hashem comments, that halachically speaking, David had no right to place his life in danger when he challenged Goliath, for one may not rely on miracles. However, because David

had previously received divine assistance against overwhelming odds, he had the right to count on supernatural salvation again. Once, God helped him to slay a ferocious lion barehanded, a second time he killed a powerful bear. Therefore, David now said: Being that twice Hashem has been my מִשְׂגָּב, my 'tower of strength', in two עִתּוֹת בַּצָּרָה, 'times of distress' for this reason I am sure that He will now strengthen me again.

11. וְיִבְטְחוּ בְךָ יוֹדְעֵי שְׁמֶךָ — And those knowing Your Name will trust in You.

It is only fitting and proper that Israel, who knows Your Name, should have trust in You now, today (Radak).

יוֹדְעֵי שְׁמֶךָ — Those knowing Your Name.

These are men of the highest calibre who comprehend God's ways with undistorted clarity. They discern God's hand guiding the world in its constant, secretly miraculous operation and they know with a certainty that God personally directs all, without intermediaries (Malbim).

כִּי לֹא עָזַבְתָּ דֹרְשֶׁיךָ ה' — For You forsake not those who seek You, HASHEM.

For they have just witnessed how You did not forsake them in their distress at the hands of the Philistines (Radak).

12. זַמְּרוּ לַה' יֹשֵׁב צִיּוֹן — Sing praise to HASHEM Who dwells in Zion.

When God returns to make Zion once again His permanent dwelling place, they will sing to Him thus (Rashi).

God dwells in Zion even after the

> *for the oppressed,*
>
> *a tower of strength in times of distress.*
>
> ¹¹ *And those knowing Your Name will trust in You,*
>
> *for You forsake not those who seek You,*
>
> *HASHEM.*
>
> ¹² *Sing praise to HASHEM Who dwells in Zion,*
>
> *proclaim among the nations His deeds.*
>
> ¹³ *For He Who avenges blood has remembered them,*
>
> *He has not forgotten the cry of the afflicted.*
>
> ¹⁴ *Have mercy on me, HASHEM,*

destruction, as the Sages say: Never did the שְׁכִינָה 'the Divine Presence', ever depart from the כּוֹתֶל הַמַּעֲרָבִי, *the Western Wall (Tehillos Hashem).*

This psalm speaks of David's encounter with Goliath. At that time Jerusalem was as yet ruled by the heathen Jebusites. Nevertheless, Israel possessed a definite oral tradition that the Temple would be built there. Zion is the pinnacle of Jerusalem, and there God's glory resides *(Radak).*

הַגִּידוּ בָעַמִּים — *Proclaim among the nations.*

Wherever you go among the nations take care to proclaim the wonders Hashem has performed for you *(Radak).*

עֲלִילוֹתָיו — *His deeds.*

Malbim explains that עֲלִילוֹת, are deeds which manifest deep emotional feelings such as mercy, vengeance or hatred; whereas מַעֲשִׂים are merely physical accomplishments which do not display the true feelings of the soul and personality.

13. כִּי דֹרֵשׁ דָּמִים אוֹתָם זָכָר — *For He Who avenges blood has remembered them.*

I.e. all of the Jewish blood which has been spilled *(Rashi).*

God investigates to keep track of every drop of Jewish blood ever shed. Although His vengeance is not swift (for He waits for the proper moment), He remembers every drop, and for each, punishment will be exacted *(Metzudas David).*

עֲנָוִים — *Afflicted —* [lit. 'the suffering poor']

This word is spelled עֲנִיִּים, 'the poor' but the *Masorah* tells us to pronounce it עֲנָוִים, 'the humble', because the poor are usually humble and meek *(Radak).*[1]

14. חָנְנֵנִי — *Have mercy on me.* The spelling of this word with three consecutive letters נ, *nun,* is very unusual. *Alshich* explains that this alludes to David's request for an extra, more generous, portion of mercy from Hashem. 'Have great mercy on me now in exile' *(Rashi).*

1. Midrash Shocher Tov explains that this phrase refers especially to the innocent blood of the עֲשָׂרָה הֲרוּגֵי מַלְכוּת, *'the ten martyrs murdered by the Roman Government'* including Rabbi Akiva, Rabban Shimon ben Gamliel, and other great tzaddikim.

The blood of these, and all others who died עַל קִידוּשׁ הַשֵּׁם, *'For sanctification of God's Name',* is especially precious. The *Midrash* concludes: God will inscribe on His royal mantle the name of every martyr who is slaughtered by the gentiles. In the future God will demand of the murderers: Why did you kill so and so? They will deny the accusation. What will the Holy One, Blessed be He, do then? He will take out His royal mantle and show them the names of their innocent victims. This fulfills the verse *'He has not forgotten the cry of the afflicted.'*

עָנְיִי מִשֹּׂנְאָי מְרוֹמְמִי מִשַּׁעֲרֵי־מָוֶת:
טו לְמַעַן אֲסַפְּרָה כָּל־תְּהִלָּתֶיךָ בְּשַׁעֲרֵי בַת־
טז צִיּוֹן אָגִילָה בִּישׁוּעָתֶךָ: טָבְעוּ גוֹיִם
בְּשַׁחַת עָשׂוּ בְּרֶשֶׁת־זוּ טָמָנוּ נִלְכְּדָה
יז רַגְלָם: נוֹדַע | יהוה מִשְׁפָּט עָשָׂה בְּפֹעַל
יח כַּפָּיו נוֹקֵשׁ רָשָׁע הִגָּיוֹן סֶלָה: יָשׁוּבוּ
רְשָׁעִים לִשְׁאוֹלָה כָּל־גּוֹיִם שְׁכֵחֵי

מִשֹּׂנְאָי — *My foes.* Goliath in particular (*Radak*).

מְרוֹמְמִי מִשַּׁעֲרֵי מָוֶת — *You who have retrieved me from the gates of death.*

You lifted me with Your redemption (*Rashi*).

Everyone was convinced that I would fall into the hands of Goliath and I was as close to death as a gate is to a house (*Radak*).

15. לְמַעַן אֲסַפְּרָה כָּל תְּהִלָּתֶיךָ בְּשַׁעֲרֵי בַת צִיּוֹן — *That I may proclaim all of Your praises in the gates of the daughter of Zion.*

When I will be saved from my enemies the proper place to go to offer thanks will be the gates of Zion, for there God Himself dwells (*Radak*).

In contrast to the gates of death which were so near, David will offer thanks at the gates of Zion (*Ibn Ezra*).

Here David says, 'In order that I may proclaim all of Your praises.' Elsewhere, he himself deems it impossible to express *all* the praises of God, מִי יְמַלֵּל גְּבוּרוֹת ה' יַשְׁמִיעַ כָּל תְּהִלָּתוֹ, 'Who can express the mighty acts of HASHEM or make all His praise to be heard?' (*Psalms* 106:2). *Radak* explains: Here David speaks of his personal experiences. He is aware of many threats which faced him and from which he was saved by openly displayed miracles. All of these he can proclaim. However, when David sings of the salvation of the entire Jewish nation throughout the generations — these are beyond recounting (many miracles occur secretly and are not apparent unless events are well scrutinized). *Norah Tehillos* adds: To merely 'proclaim' and relate the stories of God's praiseworthy deeds, is possible. But to be מַשְׁמִיעַ, 'to deeply explain and understand' with total comprehension, the true meaning and purposes of His laudable acts, this is humanly impossible.

אָגִילָה — *That I may rejoice.*

גִּילָה differs from שִׂמְחָה in that it refers to a fresh surge of joy, bursting forth anew (*Malbim*).

בִּישׁוּעָתֶךָ — *In Your salvation.*

[I rejoice, not for my personal benefit, only for the saving of Your Name and fame.]

16. טָבְעוּ גוֹיִם בְּשַׁחַת עָשׂוּ — *The peoples are mired in their self-made pit.*

David said: These words are the praise I promised to proclaim (in the preceding verse) (*Rashi; Ibn Ezra*).

The Philistines who came to make us fall, fell themselves (*Radak*).

בְּשַׁחַת — *In the pit* (see *comm. Psalms* 7:16).

This is the pit the hunters dig, into which their prey falls and is severely injured (*Malbim*).

שַׁחַת, 'the Pit,' is one of the seven names of *Gehinnom.* Our Sages tell of the query of the gentile multitudes who ask God: How will *Gehinnom* be large enough to hold all of their masses? God answers them: As your numbers grow

see my affliction by my foes,
You Who have retrieved me
from the gates of death,
¹⁵ *That I may proclaim all of Your praises*
in the gates of the daughter of Zion;
that I may rejoice in Your salvation.
¹⁶ *The peoples are mired in their self-made pit,*
in this very snare which they hid,
their own foot is caught.
¹⁷ *HASHEM became known — He executed judgment.*
Through his very own handiwork
was the wicked entrapped.
Reflect on this. Selah.
¹⁸ *To the lowest world will the wicked return,*
all the peoples that forget God.

so shall *Gehinnom* grow, for, every sin you commit digs the pit a bit deeper! This is the meaning of our verse, '*The peoples are sunk in the pit they made.*' (*Tehillos Hashem*).

בְּרֶשֶׁת זוּ טָמָנוּ נִלְכְּדָה רַגְלָם — *In this very snare which they hid, their own foot is caught.*

Furthermore, they would put a snare or net over the pit to make sure that nothing caught inside would escape (*Malbim*). [Similarly, our enemies prepared our doom with elaborate, foolproof schemes which backfired on them].

17. נוֹדַע ה' מִשְׁפָּט עָשָׂה — *HASHEM became known — He executed judgment.*

This, too, is part of God's praise — that He manifests His greatness and dominion by judging the evil with vengeance (*Rashi*).

The amazing rout of the mighty Philistines was a clear demonstration of Divine intervention. How else could so few Israelites vanquish an enemy force which surpassed them in every way? (*Radak*).

[When He executes מִשְׁפָּט, '*strict judgment*' against the evildoers and saves Israel, He is נוֹדַע ה', '*Known as HASHEM*', (the Merciful) to His people.]

בְּפֹעַל כַּפָּיו נוֹקֵשׁ רָשָׁע — *Through his very own handiwork was the wicked entrapped.*

This refers to Goliath, killed with the sword which David snatched out of the Philistine's own hands (*Radak*).

הִגָּיוֹן — *Reflect on this.*

Let the wicked keep this הִגָּיוֹן, '*reflection*' in mind at all times and they will come to recognize God's concern with this world (*Malbim*).

18. יָשׁוּבוּ רְשָׁעִים לִשְׁאוֹלָה — *To the lowest world will the wicked return.*

Gehinnom consists of seven levels, of which שְׁאוֹל is the lowest. The utterly wicked will not descend only once. Rather יָשׁוּבוּ '*they will return*' i.e. after they are completely consumed by the flames they will be re-created again so that they can be returned to the fire another time. This cycle of destruction will continue endlessly (*Rabbeinu*

יט אֱלֹהִים: כִּי לֹא לָנֶצַח יִשָּׁכַח אֶבְיוֹן תִּקְוַת
כ עֲנָוִים תֹּאבַד לָעַד: קוּמָה יהוה אַל־יָעֹז
כא אֱנוֹשׁ יִשָּׁפְטוּ גוֹיִם עַל־פָּנֶיךָ: שִׁיתָה יהוה
מוֹרָה לָהֶם יֵדְעוּ גוֹיִם אֱנוֹשׁ הֵמָּה סֶּלָה:

Bachya, Num. 16:33). [cf. *Gittin* 56b; also see *comm.* to *Psalms* 21:10]

In Hebrew, there are two ways of writing the preposition 'to', either by adding the prefix ל, 'lamed', or by concluding with the suffix ה, 'he'. The Rabbis ask, why this word has a double preposition, both the prefix and the suffix which denote 'to'? They reply: Here special emphasis is provided to stress that the wicked will return to the very lowest level of *Gehinnom*. After death they will fall down into this fiery world. Then they will be recalled to stand for final judgment and once again they will be found guilty. יָשׁוּבוּ, 'they will return' to the hell from which they came and sink to the very bottom *(Rashi).* [cf. *Psalms* 6:11 *comm.* and footnote]

19. אֶבְיוֹן — *The pauper.*

[The situation of the אֶבְיוֹן, the 'pauper', is even worse than that of the עָנִי, 'the poor man' who at least has something. The אֶבְיוֹן is תָּאֵב לַכֹּל, 'he requires and desires everything', because he possesses absolutely nothing.]

God will not forget Israel which is needy for Divine assistance to punish the nations who oppress it *(Rashi).*

עֲנִיִּים — *The afflicted.* This word is spelled like עֲנָוִים, 'the humble' but, it is pronounced עֲנִיִּים, 'the afflicted'. The afflicted (and poor) people are generally meek and humble *(Radak).* (See *comm.* v. 13).

20. קוּמָה ה' — *Arise, HASHEM.*

David prayed that Hashem answer his request swiftly *(Rashi).*

אֱנוֹשׁ — *Frail man.*

This refers to the wicked; let them not endure for an extended period of time *(Rashi).*

עַל פָּנֶיךָ — *Because of Your anger* [lit. 'on Your face']

The translation follows *Rashi* who renders עַל as 'because of' and פָּנֶיךָ as a reference to the angry countenance of God. The anger was caused by the Roman temerity in entering the Holy Temple.

Metzudas Zion renders, 'in the time of Your anger.'

21. שִׁיתָה ה' מוֹרָה לָהֶם — *HASHEM, place [Your] mastery over them.*

Rashi relates this word to מָרוּת, 'mastery', thus David is pleading to God, 'place Your mastery over them,' i.e. over the wicked. *Rashi* also suggests

19 *For the pauper shall not eternally be forgotten,*
   nor shall the hope of the afflicted forever perish.
20 *Arise, HASHEM, let not frail man be strengthened!*
   let the peoples be judged because of Your anger.
21 *HASHEM, place Your mastery over them,*
   let the peoples know that they are but frail men.
   Selah!

that מוֹרָה is derived from יָרָה *'to throw'*, thus, *'throw them down and degrade them.'* Finally *Rashi* mentions an opinion that מוֹרָה means *'razor'*. David says: *'Cut them down with a sharp razor.'*

Radak holds that this word means fear, usually spelled מוֹרָא, but which may be spelled with a ה ending as well, מוֹרָה.

The Talmud (*Sotah* 49a) says: If not for David's prayer, all of Israel would be trash peddlers, for he pleaded שִׁיתָה ה' מוֹרָה לָהֶם, *'HASHEM place them (Israel) in a position of 'mastery.'* *Rashi* (*ibid.*) explains: In *v.* 19, Israel is described as אֶבְיוֹן, *'pauper'* and עֲנִיִּים, *'poor and humble'*. Therefore, David prayed that they attain מוֹרָה, *'mastery'* and economic power.

יֵדְעוּ גוֹיִם אֱנוֹשׁ הֵמָּה סֶּלָה — *Let the peoples know that they are but frail men, Selah!*

Let those nations know their place, that they are frail creatures and not gods; so that they shall stop tyrannizing other people with their might (*Rashi*).

Midrash Tanchuma (*Va'era* 16) says that David is particularly exhorting those kings who became so enamored of themselves that they proclaimed themselves to be divine. We find this of Pharoah of Egypt, Hiram of Tyre, Nebuchadnezzar of Babylon, and Yoash of Judea. In each instance, Scriptures relate how God eventually degraded every one of them, demonstrating that they were but frail creatures of flesh and blood.[1]

1. *Rabbeinu Yonah* in *Shaarei Teshuvah* (3:167) sums up the lesson of these concluding verses:

The holy people, who are servants of the Blessed one, should not humble themselves before frail men of flesh and blood. Our Sages of Blessed memory said, "When the number of those who call evil 'good' and good 'evil' increased, they divested themselves of the yoke of heaven and caused flesh and blood to reign over them" (*Sotah* 47b). And King David, may peace be upon him said, *'Arise, HASHEM, let not frail man be strengthened, let the people be judged in the time of Your anger. HASHEM put fear into them, let them know that they are but frail men, Selah!'* (*Psalms* 9:20-21). From this we learn that when a man presumptuously exerts his might, he no longer recognizes his limitations as a mere mortal, therefore, the exercise of dominion is unbefitting a man, except if it be for the sake of heaven.

This Psalm has no introductory superscription and may be considered a sequel to Psalm 9 in terms of content. *Chida* in *Chomas Anach* cites the opinion of *Rashi* on *(Megillah 17b)* that Psalm 9 and 10 are to be counted as one [see *Tosafos ibid.*]

Hirsch points out that in Psalm 9, David tells of the tyranny and despotism which face Israel on a broad national scale which affects all of human history. However, Psalm 10 deals with everyday human relations with the degenerate man who has cast off the yoke of moral law and threatens to harm defenseless individuals.

Radak holds that David did not dedicate this Psalm to any one particular event, rather he composed it with the intention that it should be a prayer for any man who finds himself threatened by an enemy.

According to the Ashkenazic ritual recorded in *Siddur Avodas Yisrael*, it was customary to recite this psalm during עֲשֶׂרֶת יְמֵי תְּשׁוּבָה, 'The Ten Days of Repentance.'

This practice may be explained in light of the Talmud *(Rosh Hashanah 18a)* which states that God is very close to each individual during this ten day period and so it is the ideal season for sincere repentance, as the Prophet says, דִּרְשׁוּ ה' בְּהִמָּצְאוֹ 'Seek out HASHEM while He may be found' *(Isaiah 55:6)*. Thus the person who fails to feel God's proximity during these days cries out in anguish, 'Why HASHEM do You stand aloof? Hiding Yourself in times of torment?'

א לָמָה יהוה תַּעֲמֹד בְּרָחוֹק תַּעְלִים לְעִתּוֹת
ב בַּצָּרָה: בְּגַאֲוַת רָשָׁע יִדְלַק עָנִי יִתָּפְשׂוּ |
ג בִּמְזִמּוֹת זוּ חָשָׁבוּ: כִּי־הִלֵּל רָשָׁע עַל־
ד תַּאֲוַת נַפְשׁוֹ וּבֹצֵעַ בֵּרֵךְ נִאֵץ | יהוה: רָשָׁע

1. לָמָה ה' תַּעֲמֹד בְּרָחוֹק — *Why, HASHEM, do You stand aloof?*[1]

No doubt God's glory is all pervasive and is found everywhere, but when He does not display His might it seems as if He is standing far away and does not observe human events *(Ibn Ezra)*. However, notes *Radak*, when God does come to the aid of the poor who cry out for assistance, He seems to be very close, as it says אֲשֶׁר לוֹ אֱלֹהִים קְרֹבִים אֵלָיו, *'Who has a God so very close to him' (Deut. 4:7)*.

תַּעְלִים — *Hiding Yourself.*

This translation of תַּעְלִים as a declarative statement follows *Metzudas David*, *Malbim*, and the *Targum* who adds that God 'hides' Himself in the dwelling place of the holy angels (or saints) in times of trouble. However, *Rashi, Ibn Ezra*, and *Sforno* render תַּעְלִים as part of a query, *'Why do You hide Your eyes'* and avert Your gaze from our distress?

לְעִתּוֹת בַּצָּרָה — *In [lit. 'to'] times of torment.*

[In Psalm 9:10 we find a similar phrase: וִיהִי ה' מִשְׂגָּב לַדָּךְ מִשְׂגָּב לְעִתּוֹת בַּצָּרָה, *'And HASHEM will be a tower of strength for the downtrodden, tower of strength in times of torment.'* Thus David seems to say here that although there is no question that God imposes

every distress for the ultimate best, and He will finally elevate the downtrodden to a higher level of self-fortification and encouragement, yet, he asks, why must there be a terribly dark period in that distress, when things look so bleak that it seems as if God has vanished from the scene and does not care?]

2. בְּגַאֲוַת רָשָׁע — *In the wicked one's haughtiness.*

Rabbeinu Yonah writes in *Shaarei Teshuva*: Haughtiness and pride are the cause of many other sins, for pride gives a man's evil inclination the power to overcome him, as it says: *'In the wicked one's haughtiness he hunts down the poor'*. Not only is conceit a cause of other sins, but it is also itself a sin as it says: תּוֹעֲבַת ה' כָּל גְּבַהּ לֵב — *'All who are proud of heart are an abomination to HASHEM' (Proverbs 16:5)*. Because God despises this man, He does not help him at all to conquer his evil impulse.

יִדְלַק עָנִי — *He hunts down [or hotly pursues. cf. 7:14].*

יִתָּפְשׂוּ — *Who [lit. they] are caught.* As reflected in the translation following *Rashi*, the subject is the poor whom the wicked pursue.

Radak, however, interprets this phrase as a prayer to God in regard to the menace of the wicked: 'O Lord, may it be Your will, that these wicked be

---

1. *Midrash Shocher Tov* makes clear that although God does indeed seem to stand at a distance, we, Israel are the ones to blame for this, not He. When we neglect God's call to us and attempt to push Him out of our lives, He goes, as it says: *'And so, just as they did not listen when He called out, so shall they call out and I will not listen, says HASHEM, Lord of Hosts' (Zechariah 7:13).*

Rabbi Yochanan said: 'For three and one half years the Shechinah, God's Presence, stood atop the Mount of Olives and proclaimed constantly דִּרְשׁוּ ה' בְּהִמָּצְאוֹ — *'Seek out HASHEM while He may be found' (Isaiah 55:6)*. But the people paid no attention to the call.

Rabbi Chanina said: This mas be likened to the captain of a caravan. A peasant invited him to spend the night, but the captain turned down the generous offer saying: 'It is not the custom of a captain to lodge in a lowly hut.' When night fell and wrapped the captain in a

*W*hy, HASHEM, do You stand aloof;
  hiding Yourself in times of torment?
² In the wicked one's haughtiness,
  he hunts down the poor
Who are caught in the devices
  which they have contrived.
³ For the wicked man glories in his personal desires,
  and the brazen robber blesses himself for
  blaspheming HASHEM.

ensnared [יִתָּפְשׂוּ] in the very schemes which they plotted against the poor!'

3. כִּי הִלֵּל רָשָׁע — *For the wicked man glories* [lit. *'praises himself'*].

Radak sees this statement as a continuation of the preceding verse. 'Because the wicked man glories in his ability to fill all of the unbridled desires of his spirit without anyone hindering him, please show him, HASHEM, that You are Master, by trapping him in his own devices.'

Rashi, however, connects this with the query of the opening verse: 'Why, HASHEM, do You stand aloof?' Look at the terrible results of Your distance. The wicked glory in their evil, for You do not intervene!'

עַל תַּאֲוַת נַפְשׁוֹ — *In his personal desires* [lit. *'over the desire of his spirit'*]

Malbim observes that most men do not dominate their desires; their desire far exceeds their ability to fulfill it. As the Sages put it: 'Whosoever acquires one hundred, immediately desires two hundred. Whoever acquires two hundred, desires four hundred.' These people cannot glory in their desires, for

their unattainable ambitions only frustrate them. The only exception to this rule seems to be the successful, wicked man upon whom God showers an abundance which surpasses his wildest dreams [all in order to bring about his downfall]. Only he can glory and rule over his desires, because only he seems to have 'satisfied' his lusts.

וּבֹצֵעַ בֵּרֵךְ נִאֵץ ה׳ — *And the brazen robber blesses himself for blaspheming HASHEM.*

The brazen robber praises himself: 'See, I can blaspheme HASHEM and still all will be well with me' (*Rashi*).

נִאֵץ — *For blaspheming.*

There is a פְּסִיק, *'a separation line'* between נִאֵץ, and ה׳, HASHEM, in order that the word *'blasphemy'* should not be joined together with God's name (*Minchas Shai*).

According to the Talmud (*Bava Kama* 94a) בֹּצֵעַ, means *'to separate, to break bread'* and this verse refers to the commandment to separate the *'challah'*, a portion of the dough for the Priest. 'One who robs a measure of wheat, and grinds it, and kneads it and separates

deep, lonely darkness, he decided to return to the hut and ask for shelter. However, now the peasant answered from behind his bolted door: 'It is not the custom of a peasant to open his doors to unknown strangers at night. When I invited you to enter you refused, now I can no longer take you in.' So, too, HASHEM called out, pleading with Israel to return but they refused. Then God said: 'I will go and return to My abode, until they acknowledge their offense and seek out My Presence' (*Hoshea* 5:15). Once they were in the clutches of the heathens who are likened to beasts, they began to cry out, 'Why, HASHEM, do You stand aloof?' The Holy One, Blessed be He replied: 'When I sought you, you did not seek Me, now that you finally seek Me, I no longer listen to you, measure for measure.' Will this situation remain forever? No. Only until the era of the Messiah!'

כְּגֹבַהּ אַפּוֹ בַּל־יִדְרֹשׁ אֵין אֱלֹהִים כָּל־
מְזִמּוֹתָיו: יָחִילוּ דְרָכָו | בְּכָל־עֵת מָרוֹם
מִשְׁפָּטֶיךָ מִנֶּגְדּוֹ כָּל־צוֹרְרָיו יָפִיחַ בָּהֶם:
אָמַר בְּלִבּוֹ בַּל־אֶמּוֹט לְדֹר וָדֹר אֲשֶׁר
לֹא־בְרָע: אָלָה | פִּיהוּ מָלֵא וּמִרְמוֹת וָתֹךְ

ה

ו

ז

'challah' from it, and then wishes to recite a blessing over it, is not considered a man who blesses, rather he is one who blasphemes as it says וּבֹצֵעַ בֵּרֵךְ נִאֵץ ה' — *'The robber who separates and blesses, blasphemes HASHEM',* i.e. a blessing resulting from an evil deed angers God as if it were blasphemy.

4. כְּגֹבַהּ אַפּוֹ — *In the pride of his countenance* [lit. 'nose'].

The excessive pride of the heart is visible on the face. The entire face is called אַף, *nose,* for the nose is the most prominent facial feature because it protrudes outward more than any other part (*Radak; Ibn Ezra*).

The haughty man lifts up his head in his pride and his nose points upward (*Rashi*).

However, *Metzudas David* translates אַפּוֹ, *'his anger'.* [A man consumed with anger breathes heavily through his nose]. Thus: *'when his anger rises'.* Nothing can restrain the wicked from venting his rage because he says that even God will not avenge.

בַּל יִדְרֹשׁ — [*says*] *He will not avenge!* [The word *'says'* does not appear in the Hebrew but it is implied.]

No matter what I choose to do, there is no God of Judgment who will call me to account (*Rashi; Metzudas David*).

Radak holds that this phrase describes the haughty man himself. In his unbridled conceit, בַּל יִדְרֹשׁ, *'he will not seek out'* God, neither will he pray to Him.

Rabbi Chaim Vital in *Eitz Hadaas Tov* points out that the letters of רָשָׁע, allude to the following concept: רָשׁ means *to impoverish* and the letter ע, *'ayin'* stands for עַיִן, *'eye'.* The wicked

man who claims that God does not see, impoverishes, so to speak, the power of the omnipresent *'eye'* of God which sees all.

אֵין אֱלֹהִים כָּל מְזִמּוֹתָיו — *All his thoughts are: 'There is no God'.*

Rashi succinctly sums up the total *weltanschauung* of the wicked in the words: לֵית דִּין וְלֵית דַּיָּין — *'There is no judgment and there is no judge.'*

Deep down in his heart the heretic, too, recognizes the truth of God's omnipotence and this thought gives him no rest. Since the wicked man wishes to remain uninhibited and unrestricted — he feels compelled to smother the internal voice of his conscience by constantly repeating the heresy *'There is no God!'* [cf. *Psalms* 14:1] (*Harav Eliyohu Meir Bloch*).

5. יָחִילוּ דְרָכָו — *'His ways are successful'* (*Rashi; Metzudas Zion; Malbim*).

Hirsch notes that although the word is pronounced דְרָכָו, *'his ways'* (in the plural) it is spelled דַּרְכּוֹ, *'his way'* (singular), to teach that all of the evil pursuits and paths of this man truly have only one purpose, to prove that there is no God!

בְּכָל עֵת — *Always* [lit. 'at all times'].

Malbim emphasizes that this wicked man enjoys constant success, a completely extraordinary phenomenon.

An alternate translation offered by *Rashi* (and by *Rabbi Moshe HaCohen,* quoted in the *Ibn Ezra*) is based on rendering דְרָכָו as *'his desires',* because a man's desires determine his ways of living. יָחִילוּ, *'they will come to him',* i.e. the wicked man will attain all of his wishes. Similarly, we find יָחֻלוּ עַל רֹאשׁ

X
4-7

⁴ *The wicked man, in the pride of his countenance,*
says:
'He will not avenge!'
All his thoughts are: 'There is no God.'
⁵ *His ways are always successful,*
Your judgments are far removed from him.
But as for all His foes? — He puffs at them!
⁶ *He says in his heart: 'I shall never fall*
for all generations I shall not be in adversity.'
⁷ *He fills his mouth with oaths,*
with deception and malice,

יוֹאָב, *'let them come down on the head of Yoav (II Sam. 3:29).*

Radak holds that this statement refers to the victims of the wicked. יָחִילוּ, means *'they tremble and shudder'* as in רָעֲדָה אֲחָזָתַם שָׁם חִיל כַּיּוֹלֵדָה — *'Fear took hold of them there, a shuddering like a woman at childbirth'* (48:7). The ways of the wicked cause the poor to tremble because they are intimidated by them, בְּכָל עֵת, *'at all times'*, i.e. as long as the wicked exist, the poor will continue to shudder.

מָרוֹם מִשְׁפָּטֶיךָ מִנֶּגְדּוֹ — *Your judgments are far removed from him.*
Even at a time when the entire world is plunged into the agony of famine or plague which demonstrates divine wrath and retribution, this wicked man seems to lead a charmed life and nothing affects him (*Rashi; Malbim*).

יָפִיחַ בָּהֶם — *He puffs at them!*
This translation follows *Rashi* who renders this as an expression of contempt for the wicked. God merely puffs at them, and they topple over.
Radak relates יָפִיחַ to פַּח *'a trap'*. The wicked man has success with every trap which he sets for כָּל צוֹרְרָיו, *all his foes.*
From this verse we learn that there are times in history when God sees fit to give the wicked amazing, supernatural success. The Talmud (*Berachos* 7a) ad-

vises us to avoid them at these times.
Rabbi Yitzchok says: If you see a wicked man at whom 'the hour smiles', do not antagonize him as it says, *'His ways are successful at all times.'* What is more, he will emerge victorious from all trials as it says, *'Your judgments are far removed from him'* and what is more, he will even witness the downfall of his enemies: as it says, *'his foes topple over when he puffs at them.'*

6. בַּל אֶמּוֹט — *I shall never fall.*
The wicked one says, 'I shall never fall from my position of prominence' (*Radak*).

לְדֹר וָדֹר אֲשֶׁר לֹא בְרָע — *For all generations I shall not be in adversity.*
Because I shall never experience any mishap it is inevitable that I should live a long life spanning several generations (*Radak*).
The success of the wicked has implanted in him the belief that he has been eternally exempted from the usual variety of human misfortunes (*Malbim*).

7. אָלָה פִּיהוּ מָלֵא — *He fills his mouth with oaths.*
When the wicked wish to deceive people, they utter oaths with *their entire mouth*, i.e. with vehemence, without hesitation or fear, in order to convince people of their sincerity (*Radak*).

ח תַּחַת לְשׁוֹנוֹ עָמָל וָאָוֶן וָאָוֶן‬ יֵשֵׁב | בְּמַאְרַב
חֲצֵרִים בַּמִּסְתָּרִים יַהֲרֹג נָקִי עֵינָיו
ט לְחֵלְכָה יִצְפֹּנוּ: יֶאֱרֹב בַּמִּסְתָּר | כְּאַרְיֵה
בְסֻכֹּה יֶאֱרֹב לַחֲטוֹף עָנִי יַחְטֹף עָנִי
י בְּמָשְׁכוֹ בְרִשְׁתּוֹ: °וְדָכָה יָשֹׁחַ וְנָפַל

יא בַּעֲצוּמָיו °חֵלְכָּאִים: אָמַר בְּלִבּוֹ שָׁכַח אֵל

יב הִסְתִּיר פָּנָיו בַּל־רָאָה לָנֶצַח: קוּמָה יהוה

תַּחַת לְשׁוֹנוֹ — *Under his tongue.*

This refers to his heart, the thoughts of which are concealed until they are uttered by the tongue (*Radak*).

8. יֵשֵׁב בְּמַאְרַב חֲצֵרִים — *He waits in ambush near open cities.*

I.e. the open, unwalled towns on the roadside (*Radak*).

Ibn Ezra and *Be'er Avraham* point out that most robbers hide in the depths of the forest far from civilization. But this wicked man has so much confidence in his deceptive masquerade of uprightness that he lurks near the open cities, without fear of detection.

בַּמִּסְתָּרִים יַהֲרֹג נָקִי — *In hidden places he murders the innocent.*

He fears people so he commits his crimes where they cannot see, but he has no fear of God who sees all (*Radak*).

עֵינָיו . . . יִצְפֹּנוּ — *His eyes . . . spy.*

He lurks in a hidden vantage point spying on the unsuspecting wayfarers (*Radak*).

לְחֵלְכָה — *The helpless.*

Rashi quotes *Menachem*, who translates: 'wretched and hopeless'. *Metzudas David* renders: 'poor and weak'. [The word is generally used to denote a person who cannot defend himself against attack, thus 'helpless'

conveys the various connotations of חֵלְכָה].

Rashi, however, renders חֵלְכָה, a variant of חֵילָךְ, 'Your army' and it refers to Israel. (This is but one of a number of scriptural examples where the ending כָה, is used instead of the more common ךְ). ''Esau secretly lies in ambush, spying out Your people, Your army, Israel!''

Be'er Avraham notes that חַיִל also means *riches*: the robbers wait for the rich to pass by so they can be plundered.

9. יֶאֱרֹב בַּמִּסְתָּר כְּאַרְיֵה — *He lurks in hiding like a lion.*

Like the fearsome lion, he waits in secret ambush until the last possible moment before pouncing on his prey, because if he will reveal himself too soon the victim will sense the danger and escape (*Radak*).[1]

בְסֻכֹּה יֶאֱרֹב לַחֲטוֹף עָנִי — *He lurks in concealment to seize the poor.*

This also resembles the hunting techniques of the lion who חוֹטֵף, 'swiftly snatches' his prey, taking it by surprise (*Radak*).

יַחְטֹף עָנִי בְּמָשְׁכוֹ בְרִשְׁתּוֹ — *Then he seizes the poor when he draws the net.*

Now the Psalmist compares the rob-

---

1. A vicious man is far more dangerous than the most ferocious beast. For the beast only attacks the prey which it sees in its immediate vicinity. It has no mental capacity to scheme and plan an elaborate hunt. But man is endowed with a far-reaching intellect. God endowed him with this gift so that he should seek out perfection. However, man distorts his mission and uses his mind as a weapon to hurt others in ingenious ways through elaborate machinations (*Moreh Nevuchim* 1:7).

And under his tongue are mischief and iniquity.

⁸ He waits in ambush near open cities,
*   in hidden places he murders the innocent,*
His eyes spy on the helpless.
⁹ He lurks in hiding like a lion,
*   he lurks in concealment to seize the poor,*
Then he seizes the poor when he draws his net.
¹⁰ He stoops down prostrate,
*   and the helpless fall prey to his might.*
¹¹ He says in his heart:
'God has forgotten, He hides His face,
*   He will never see, forever.'*

ber to the trapper who sets his nets for the unwary birds and then sits unnoticed, at a distance, holding the strings of the nets, waiting to quickly draw them shut when the bird comes into the trap. Similarly, the robbers station one member of their band on the road, unarmed, looking innocent. When the prospective victims pass by he signals his cohorts in the forest and they close the trap (*Radak*).

10. יִדְכֶּה — *He stoops down.* [lit. *'squash or crush'* (*Metzudas Zion*)]

The *Midrash* notes that this word is spelled as a noun form וְדַכָּה, *'and the low down person'* although it is pronounced as a verb יִדְכֶּה, *'he stoops'*. The noun form *'low person'* adequately describes the wicked and tells us that, morally, he is as low, weak, and wretched as his disabled victims.

Radak comments: This, too, is one of the tricks of the criminal. He joins a caravan departing the city and makes himself appear to be feeble and weak, so as not to arouse suspicion. When they get far away from civilization, he pillages his fellow travellers.

וְנָפַל בַּעֲצוּמָיו — *Fall prey to his might* [lit. *'in his power'*].

This is a proper description for his most powerful limbs, which seize the poor (*Radak, Ibn Ezra*).

חֵלְכָּאִים — *Helpless* (see *comm. v.* 8).

Menachem, as quoted in *Rashi* here, renders this as *'weak and wretched'* as he renders לְחֵלְכָה in *v.* 8.

However, *Rashi* cites the *'Great Masorah'* that this word is one of fifteen Scriptural examples of a word spelled as but one but pronounced as two, for it is read חֵיל כָּאִים *'a broken, wretched army.'*

כָּאִים — is similar to לְמוֹתֵת לֵבָב נִכְאֶה *'and the broken of heart he was ready to slay'* (*Psalms* 109:16). Thus, the wicked defeat the wretched army בַּעֲצוּמָיו, *'with their mighty warriors'* — *Rashi* also suggests that בַּעֲצוּמָיו means *'his signals and winks of the eye'* as we find וְעֹצֵם עֵינָיו מֵרְאוֹת בְּרָע *'And he shuts his eyes from looking upon evil'* (*Isaiah* 33:15). [The wicked send secret signals of which their victims are ignorant.]

11. אָמַר בְּלִבּוֹ שָׁכַח אֵל — *He says in his heart: 'God has forgotten.'*

He admits that there is a God, but claims that He has no knowledge of human affairs (*Ibn Ezra*).

Even if God once knew, He forgot, or now does not want to see (*Radak*).

All of the wicked deeds enumerated above are the result of that which the evil man says in his heart: *'God has forgotten'* (*Metzudas David*).

הִסְתִּיר פָּנָיו בַּל רָאָה לָנֶצַח — *He hides His*

אַל נָשָׂא יָדֶךָ אַל־תִּשְׁכַּח °עֲנִיִּים: עַל־מֶה |
נִאֵץ רָשָׁע | אֱלֹהִים אָמַר בְּלִבּוֹ לֹא
תִדְרֹשׁ: רָאִתָה כִּי־אַתָּה | עָמָל וָכַעַס |
תַּבִּיט לָתֵת בְּיָדֶךָ עָלֶיךָ יַעֲזֹב חֵלְכָה יָתוֹם
אַתָּה | הָיִיתָ עוֹזֵר: שְׁבֹר זְרוֹעַ רָשָׁע וָרָע
תִּדְרוֹשׁ־רִשְׁעוֹ בַל־תִּמְצָא: יהוה מֶלֶךְ
עוֹלָם וָעֶד אָבְדוּ גוֹיִם מֵאַרְצוֹ: תַּאֲוַת
עֲנָוִים שָׁמַעְתָּ יהוה תָּכִין לִבָּם תַּקְשִׁיב
אָזְנֶךָ: לִשְׁפֹּט יָתוֹם וָדָךְ בַּל־יוֹסִיף עוֹד
לַעֲרֹץ אֱנוֹשׁ מִן־הָאָרֶץ:

face, He will never see, forever.

He hides His face in the glorious celestial world above and disdains looking down at this lowly world (*Malbim*).

12. קוּמָה ה׳ אֵל נְשָׂא יָדֶךָ — *Arise, HASHEM! O God, raise Your hand!*

In response to these heretic claims of the wicked, arise Hashem, lift up Your hand to smite him and show that You have not forgotten the poor (*Metzudas David*).

עֲנִיִּים — *The poor.*

This word is spelled עֲנִיִּים, 'poor', but it is pronounced עֲנָוִים, 'the humble' (*Minchas Shai*).

14. רָאִתָה — *But You do see.*

Despite the heretic claims of the wicked You certainly do take notice of his deeds (*Radak; Metzudas David*).

You see it, but You remain mute (*Rashi*).

כִּי אַתָּה עָמָל וָכַעַס תַּבִּיט — *For You observe mischief and vexation.*

Not only do You see the actions of the wicked but You are even aware of their inner thoughts to do עָמָל, 'mischief' and their plans for כַעַס, 'vexation' (*Malbim*).

לָתֵת — *To grant.*

You have the power to deal punishment to the wicked as they so justly deserve (*Radak; Malbim*).

Rashi, however, offers an entirely different explanation. Here David says to God that despite His complete awareness of the wicked man's deeds it is only from God that the evil receive the strength and opportunity to sin and to succeed.

יַעֲזֹב — *Rely.* The translation follows the implication of *Radak* [lit. 'abandon'] Israel abandons her burdens and leaves it to God to punish the wicked (*Rashi*).

Menachem quoted by *Rashi*, derives this word from עָזֹב תַּעֲזֹב עִמּוֹ — *'You shall surely help him'* (*Exodus 23:5*). Here it means 'he will depend on You for help.'

חֵלְכָה — *The helpless.*

Menachem, quoted by *Rashi* once again renders this as wretched and disabled, (see *comm. v. 8 and 10*). *Rashi*, however, follows his previous translation and says the word is the equivalent of חֵילֶךָ, 'Your army', meaning Israel.

יָתוֹם אַתָּה הָיִיתָ עוֹזֵר — *The orphan, You were the Helper.*

Because in early times You always aided the unfortunate orphans, now the disabled count on Your support (*Metzudas David; Rashi*).

15. זְרוֹעַ — *The strength* [lit. 'the arm'].

Shatter the might of the wicked so

X

12-18

¹² *Arise, HASHEM! O God, raise Your hand!*
    Forget not the poor!
¹³ *Why does the wicked man blaspheme God?*
Because he says in his heart:
    'You will not avenge.'
¹⁴ *But You do see!*
    For You observe mischief and vexation.
To grant is in Your power; helpless rely upon You,
    the orphan — You were the Helper.
¹⁵ *Break the strength of the wicked; the evil one —*
    You will search for his wickedness
    and find it not.
¹⁶ *HASHEM is King forever and ever,*
    when the people have perished from His earth.
¹⁷ *The desire of the humble You heard, HASHEM,*
    You direct their heart, You are attentive.
¹⁸ *To vindicate the orphan and the downtrodden,*
    so that they shall no longer terrify the frail
    from the earth.

---

that they will acknowledge You as the God of justice and retribution *(Metzudas David)*.

Specifically, David refers to the might of Esau and the wicked *(Rashi)*.

The Sages *(Megillah 17b)* refer this verse to the unscrupulous manipulators who force up the prices of food to reap profits at the expense of the poor. In the ninth benediction of the *Shemoneh Esrei* we ask: Bless for us this year and all of its species of crops, for good. The Talmud asks: Why was this benediction placed ninth? Because it is a prayer against the price-hikers, as it says, *'Break the strength of the wicked'* and David offered that prayer in the ninth Psalm (see *prefatory remarks*).

וְרָע תִּדְרוֹשׁ רִשְׁעוֹ בַל תִּמְצָא — *The evil one — You will search for his wickedness and find it not.*

When the wicked of Israel see the success of the non-Jewish wicked, they are encouraged to perpetrate more evil themselves. But when You will smash the might of the wicked, then their Jewish imitators will desist. Then, if You will search for a wicked Jew, You will not find one *(Rashi)*

16. ה' מֶלֶךְ עוֹלָם וָעֶד — *HASHEM is King forever and ever.*

After You punish the pillagers, You will be recognized as King before the eyes of the entire world and no one will dare defy You *(Radak)*.

אָבְדוּ גוֹיִם מֵאַרְצוֹ — *When the peoples have perished from His earth.*

Rashi states that Hashem will be universally proclaimed as King only after and as a result of the wicked peoples perishing from the earth.

Radak however says that first Hashem will be recognized as King and only afterward will the wicked be

destroyed and sovereignty returned to Israel.

Malbim comments that God differs from human kings who are monarchs only as long as they have subjects. A human king without a population is no longer king. Not so Hashem. *'HASHEM is King forever and ever.'* His monarchy will never change. Even, *'after the peoples perish from the earth'* and no subjects remain, God's kingship endures.

17. שָׁמַעְתָּ ה׳ עֲנָוִים תַּאֲוַת — *The desire of the humble You heard, HASHEM.*

Hashem, You have always paid attention to the desires of the humble, therefore listen to this sincere prayer uttered with genuine intentions *(Metzudas David).*

You hear the desires of their hearts even before they articulate them *(Radak).*

אָזְנֶךָ תַּקְשִׁיב לִבָּם תָּכִין — *You direct their heart, You* [lit. *'Your ears'*] *are attentive.*

You remove from their hearts their

preoccupation with the problems of this world which interfere with their concentration. Thus their prayers will be recited with such pure intentions that You will surely listen and respond *(Radak).*

[And what is their sincere prayer?]

18. וָדָךְ יָתוֹם לִשְׁפֹּט — *To vindicate the orphan and the downtrodden.* That you do justice for the helpless and save them from their tormentors *(Radak).*

Rashi says that the orphan referred to here is the nation of Israel, fatherless and oppressed.

לַעֲרֹץ — *Terrify.* [lit. *'to break or smash'* *(Rashi; Metzudas Zion)*]

[However, this word is always used to imply a breaking of the courage and spirit, to intimidate with fear. Thus *'terrify'* would come close to conveying its true meaning.]

Specifically, notes *Rashi*, let not Ishmael and Esau continue to terrify the frail and feeble children of Israel.

11 מזמור יא

T he commentaries do not agree on the specific event in David's life
to which this psalm refers. However, all agree that this chapter
represents a chronicle of treachery, recounting the slander of those
who wished to undermine David. These wicked men flatly denied the
cornerstone of our faith, הַשְׁגָּחָה פְּרָטִית, 'personal divine guidance'
and refused to accept the fact that Hashem is ever-present and intimately involved in human affairs. David's many misfortunes served
them as evidence that God abandons everyone, even the righteous.
David forcefully responds to this heresy with his own resounding
declaration of unshakeable faith.

א לַמְנַצֵּחַ לְדָוִד בַּיהוֹה | חָסִיתִי אֵיךְ תֹּאמְרוּ
א־ג °נוּדִי ק' ב לְנַפְשִׁי °נוּדוּ הַרְכֶם צִפּוֹר: כִּי הִנֵּה
הָרְשָׁעִים יִדְרְכוּן קֶשֶׁת כּוֹנְנוּ חִצָּם עַל־
ג יֶתֶר לִירוֹת בְּמוֹ־אֹפֶל לְיִשְׁרֵי־לֵב: כִּי

1. חָסִיתִי בַּה' — In HASHEM I took refuge.

Rashi says that David refers to the dark days when he was a fugitive hunted by King Saul. Once he was chased out of the Holy Land and forced to seek refuge on foreign soil. To leave *Eretz Yisrael* is to leave the Presence of God, for in this land God's holy spirit comes closest to His people. David once bitterly lamented his flight from Israel in these terms: כִּי גֵרְשׁוּנִי הַיּוֹם מֵהִסְתַּפֵּחַ בְּנַחֲלַת ה' 'for they have driven me out this day from being joined to the estate of HASHEM' (I Samuel 26:19). David now declares that he has complete trust in Hashem that once again someday he will return to the intimate closeness of God's proximity.

Meiri holds that this psalm corresponds to the events related in *I Samuel* 23, when David defended Keyilah against Philistine attack. After his victory, the inhabitants of the city locked him inside the city to turn him over to King Saul. David escaped this trap, and declared בַּה' חָסִיתִי, 'In HASHEM I find refuge', thus I do not fear your conspiracies and snares.

אֵיךְ תֹּאמְרוּ לְנַפְשִׁי — How dare you say to me [lit. 'my soul'].

Midrash Shocher Tov illustrates this trust, drawing upon another verse, 'HASHEM is mine, I shall not fear' (Psalms 118:6). This may be likened to the king who was especially fond of one of his servants. This caused great animosity and jealousy among the other attendants who glared menacingly at the favorite. But the favorite remained unafraid, saying to himself: The master's affection is mine, what man can harm me?

נוּדִי — Flee.

This word is spelled נוּדוּ, in the plural form, but it is pronounced נוּדִי, in the singular. *Radak* explains that David's enemies addressed themselves both to his body and to his soul, thus the plural form. They predicted that his body would be killed by Saul and that his soul would find no rest in heaven. Rather, it would suffer a punishment known as כַּף הַקֶּלַע, 'the slingshot', meaning that it would be 'shot' into a perpetual orbit revolving around the earth, but never rising upward to reach the coveted heavenly paradise. Also, the singular form, נוּדִי, is used because it refers to the soul alone, and the soul is the most important element for it guides and controls the body.

Rashi says that the plural form נוּדוּ, is shouted at the Jews by the gentiles. [This means that the gentiles taunt them, saying נוּדוּ, which not only means 'flee' but also 'wander' i.e. 'you wandering Jew'!]

הַרְכֶם — Your mountain.

This refers to the mountains in the territory of those who sympathized with Saul. Whenever David sought refuge in the caves or strongholds they chased him out or informed Saul of his whereabouts. David now says to them, 'Even though I am a fugitive, I trust in Hashem that He will save me, but what right have you to tell me to flee from your mountain?' (*Radak*).

According to *Meiri*, David calls the people of Keyilah to task for their treachery and audacity. 'How did you dare request of me to run swiftly to your mountain like a bird?'

For the Conductor; of David.
In HASHEM I took refuge.
How dare you say to me:
'Flee, bird, to your mountain!'?
² *For behold the wicked bend the bow,*
ready their arrow on the bowstring,
To shoot under darkness at the upright of heart.

צִפּוֹר — [*As a*] *Bird.*

Any man who must constantly travel from place to place is likened to a bird wandering from her home. (*Rashi*).

Midrash Shocher Tov points out that the Psalmist does not liken the wanderer to the יוֹנָה *'dove'* for the *'dove'* always returns home to its original nest even after its young are taken away. Rather, he is compared to all other birds, classified generally as צִפּוֹר who never return to their nests after their young are removed. Hence, they wander on and on.

Those who deny that God's guiding hand directs every step in life, liken the journeys of David, the fugitive, to the aimless flight of the bird, hopping from one perch to another (*Malbim*).

But in reality, the foundations of David's faith and conviction are solid rock, strong as a הַר, *'mountain'*. His belief and trust are not mere flights of fancy like a צִפּוֹר, *'an unstable, unsettled bird'* (*Rabbi S.R. Hirsch*).[1]

2. כִּי הִנֵּה הָרְשָׁעִים — *For, behold, the wicked.*

Just as you betray me by disclosing my hiding place to Saul, so too, will other evil men be informers wherever I flee. For the wicked are always prepared to do evil like the archer whose bow is bent with his arrows ready to shoot (*Radak*).

David refers here specifically to the wicked Doeg and the other tale-bearers

and scandal-mongers of that generation who maliciously provoked animosity between him and Saul (*Rashi*).

יִדְרְכוּן קֶשֶׁת — *Bend* [lit. *'step on'*] *the bow* .

Their tongues are likened to the bow which shoots forth arrows of falsehood. The powerful and heavy bow can be bent for stringing only by applying pressure through stepping on it (*Rashi*).

כּוֹנְנוּ חִצָּם עַל יֶתֶר — *They ready their arrow on the bowstring.*

The Sages tell us that לְשׁוֹן הָרַע *tale-bearing* is even deadlier than the lethal arrow. For an arrow only kills the victim who is near whereas slander even kills from afar. Slander spoken in Syria can destroy a person standing in Rome. An arrow cannot be aimed properly if there is insufficient light, however, the barbs of slander can be launched even in the depths of darkness. Literally יֶתֶר means *the bowstring*, however, it also means *'extra advantage'* as we find in the word יִתְרוֹן. This alludes to the fact that slanderers have all of the aforementioned advantages over the simple arrow. Thus: they ready *'arrows'* that are even more effective than those shot by a bowstring (*Tehillos Hashem*).

לִירוֹת — *To shoot.*

David is careful to say that they *prepare* to shoot but they never do so, for their plans are foiled by God in whom David trusts (*Radak*).

---

1. David is pleading for personal absolvement from sin. 'Please forgive me, O God, for that one sin (of Bath Sheba) so that people will not say הַרְכֶם *'Your mountain'* (i.e. Your greatest man, Your king) was made to wander by a צִפּוֹר *'a bird'* [a small sin] (*Sanhedrin* 107a).

ד הַשָּׁתוֹת יֵהָרֵסוּן צַדִּיק מַה־פָּעָל: יהוה |
בְּהֵיכַל קָדְשׁוֹ יהוה בַּשָּׁמַיִם כִּסְאוֹ עֵינָיו
ה יֶחֱזוּ עַפְעַפָּיו יִבְחֲנוּ בְּנֵי אָדָם: יהוה צַדִּיק
יִבְחָן וְרָשָׁע וְאֹהֵב חָמָס שָׂנְאָה נַפְשׁוֹ:

בְּמוֹ אֹפֶל — *Under darkness.* [lit. 'in darkness itself']

To shoot secretly (Rashi; Radak; Metzudos).

לְיִשְׁרֵי לֵב — *At the upright of heart.*

Both *Rashi* and *Metzudas David* hold that this refers to David and the priests of Nob who were massacred by Saul as a result of the malicious gossip-mongering of Doeg, the Edomite.

3. הַשָּׁתוֹת — *The foundations.*

[I.e. the pillars of society — law and justice; or the righteous people.] By your hand the righteous priests of Nob were murderd and they were the very foundations, the pillars of the earth (*Rashi*).

Radak and *Ibn Ezra* hold that שָׁתוֹת, is related to רְשָׁתוֹת, *nets and traps*, a reference to the tangled schemes and plots of the wicked.

צַדִּיק מַה פָּעָל — *What has the righteous man done?* [or, following *Ibn Ezra* 'What can the righteous do?']

According to *Rashi* and *Metzudas David* this is a rhetorical question: 'What have I, the righteous one, done sinfully in this entire affair? You, Saul and Doeg will pay for this crime, not I.'

Malbim interprets the 'Righteous One' as a reference to God, not David. The wicked who witness the destruction of the righteous foundations of the earth, gloat happily צַדִּיק מַה פָּעָל, What has God, the Righteous One, done about all this? Where is His הַשְׁגָחָה, His supervision and intervention?

However, *Radak* renders this entire phrase as a declarative statement: 'The wicked will not accomplish their treacherous schemes. But as for the righteous, מַה פָּעָל, 'for that which he has done' he will be rewarded with suc-

cess.' *v.* 4. [In answer to those who question God's apparent remoteness from worldly affairs, David now assures all skeptics that God indeed supervises this earth].

4. ה' בְּהֵיכַל קָדְשׁוֹ — *HASHEM is in His Holy Temple.*

And from there He observes and examines all of the deeds of the wicked (*Rashi*).

Midrash Shocher Tov tells us that הֵיכַל קָדְשׁוֹ, refers to the Holy Temple on earth. When Israel is obedient to His will, God is pleased with them and He dwells near them, on earth.

ה' בַּשָּׁמַיִם כִּסְאוֹ — *HASHEM's throne is in heaven.*

Even when He is high above He looks down to attend to human affairs (*Rashi*).

Midrash Shocher Tov continues: When the stubborness of Israel makes them repulsive to God, He leaves their intimate company and ascends to His distant throne in heaven.

עֵינָיו יֶחֱזוּ — *His eyes scrutinize.*

The root חָזָה refers to 'scrutiny', which is intellectual in nature and penetrates into the innermost recesses of the spirit (*Hirsch*).

עַפְעַפָּיו — *His pupils.*

The translation follows *Metzudas Zion*. *Hirsch* renders 'His eyelids', deriving the word from עָפַף, which is synonymous with עוּף, 'to fly' and thus describes the eyelids which are in almost perpetual motion, like wings flapping up and down.

יִבְחֲנוּ בְּנֵי אָדָם — *They examine mankind.*

Malbim concurs with *Hirsch* in rendering עַפְעַפָּיו as 'eyelids' and ex-

³ *You have torn down the foundations,*
what has the righteous man done?
⁴ *HASHEM is in His Holy Temple,*
HASHEM's throne is in heaven,
His eyes scrutinize,
His pupils examine mankind.
⁵ *HASHEM examines the righteous one,*
but the wicked and the lover of violence
He despises.

plains how they serve to examine mankind. He points out that the first two phrases of this verse systematically relate to the last two phrases.

At times, God is very near, בְּהֵיכַל קָדְשׁוֹ, *'in His Holy Temple'* and His presence and supervision make it evident that עֵינָיו יֶחֱזוּ, *'His eyes behold'* every human action clearly. But sometimes, He removes His presence from the lower world and rises בַּשָּׁמַיִם כִּסְאוֹ, *to His throne in heaven.* Then it seems as if He is closing His eyes and covering them with עַפְעַפָּיו, *'His eyelids'.* At that time, when people can delude themselves into thinking that God is not watching, then יִבְחֲנוּ בְּנֵי אָדָם, *mankind is examined.* Then God sees who seeks to do evil surreptitiously and who serves Hashem regardless without deception, out of unswerving love and faith. Thus, by covering His eyes with His eyelids, God does not detach Himself from the world, rather, He becomes more involved by testing and examining the genuine sincerity of mankind.

5. ה׳ צַדִּיק יִבְחָן — *HASHEM examines the righteous one.*

Said David to his enemies: Because I am afflicted and pursued by you, you exult and say אֱלֹהִים עֲזָבוֹ, *'God has abandoned him'* (Psalms 71:11). But this is not the case. For the way of God is to afflict and test the righteous, but not the wicked. This may be likened to the flax-maker, who, when he knows that the

flax is strong and durable, beats it vigorously. But when it is not strong he refrains from beating, lest is shred and fall apart (Rashi).

Hashem tests the righteous man in order to display his genuine goodness to the entire world and in order to cleanse him of his few sins (Radak).

[Actually, the purpose of the *'test'* is not only to bring the righteousness of the good man to the attention of the world, but also to bring it to the attention of the good man himself. *Ramban* in שַׁעַר הַגְמוּל, *'The Gate of Reward'*, explains that God tests the righteous in order to extract the latent, potential powers of faith from their inner selves and to bring it forth to fruition. God Himself knows what strength the righteous possess, but He wishes to let them know for themselves. (See *Psalms 26:2* and *Overview*)]

וְרָשָׁע וְאֹהֵב חָמָס שָׂנְאָה נַפְשׁוֹ — *But the wicked and the lover of violence He* [lit. *'His soul'] despises.*

Because He despises the wicked He conceals their well-deserved punishment for the Eternal World and then He will rain it down upon them in Gehinnom (Rashi).

If apparently undimmed happiness comes to a man who is obviously lawless and brutal, it is by no means a sign of God's favor, but quite the contrary. He is not worthy of divine discipline because he is no longer capable of profiting by it. If it were to befall

ו יַמְטֵר עַל־רְשָׁעִים פַּחִים אֵשׁ וְגָפְרִית
ז וְרוּחַ זִלְעָפוֹת מְנָת כּוֹסָם: כִּי־צַדִּיק יהוה
צְדָקוֹת אָהֵב יָשָׁר יֶחֱזוּ פָנֵימוֹ:

him, he would not mend his ways; on the contrary, he might be led to perpetuate even greater excesses (*Hirsch*).

6. יַמְטֵר עַל רְשָׁעִים — *He will rain down upon the wicked.*

The specific word denoting rain is גֶּשֶׁם. However, מָטָר, includes everything that comes down from the sky (*Hirsch*).

פַּחִים אֵשׁ — *Fiery coals.* [lit. 'coals of fire' (*Rashi*)].

However, *Radak* and *Metzudos* translate פַּחִים as 'traps' or 'nets' as in מִפַּח יָקוּשׁ, 'from the ensnaring net' (*Psalms* 91:3). Thus, פַּחִים 'nets' and אֵשׁ 'fire', are two separate objects which are destined to rain down upon the wicked.

Hirsch explains that the good which

God sends to the wicked man brings him no happiness. All the Lord's bountiness are actually פַּחִים, 'traps' upon which he treads without concern and which finally lead to his ruin. Thus we read (*Psalms* 69:23): יְהִי שֻׁלְחָנָם לִפְנֵיהֶם לְפָח 'Let their table which is before them be for a trap.' That is, they will be caught and punished as a result of their prosperity.

וְרוּחַ זִלְעָפוֹת — *A burning blast.*

The translation follows *Rashi* who relates the word to עוֹרֵנוּ כְּתַנּוּר נִכְמָרוּ מִפְּנֵי זַלְעֲפוֹת רָעָב 'Our skin is heated up like an oven, because of the burning heat of famine' (*Lamentations* 5:10).

Radak and *Metzudas Zion* suggest that זִלְעָפוֹת, means 'trembling' as in זַלְעָפָה אֲחָזָתְנִי, 'a trembling seized me' (*Psalms* 119:53).

⁶ *He will rain down upon the wicked*
  fiery coals and brimstone,
A burning blast is their alloted portion.
⁷ *For HASHEM is righteous,*
  and He loves the righteous man.
The upright will behold His face.

מְנָת כּוֹסָם — *Is their alloted portion.*

Both words mean portion; such repetition is common in Hebrew usage. Also the word מָנָה, *'portion'* denotes הַזְמָנָה, *'preparation and readiness'* (Radak).

7. צְדָקוֹת אָהֵב — *He loves the righteous man.* [lit. *'He loves righteous deeds'*]

Here it means 'He loves the man who performs righteous deeds' (Rashi; Radak).

Usually, a craftsman despises his competitors and rivals, but Hashem is not so. He is righteous Himself and yet He still loves the righteous men (Midrash Shocher Tov).

יָשָׁר יֶחֱזוּ פָנֵימוֹ — *The upright will behold His face.*

This is similar to a king of flesh and blood. Those who are his favorites are allowed to stand in his presence to behold him directly face to face (Metzudas David).

Radak suggests an opposite translation. פָנֵימוֹ, does not mean *'His face'* referring to God, rather the ending מוֹ, denotes a plural form meaning *'their faces'*, thus *'those who are upright, God will behold their faces.'*

Malbim emphasizes that the person who is the opposite of the יָשָׁר *'upright man'*, serves God in a warped, crooked fashion. His concern is only for reward. Only vaguely does he care about God. But the יָשָׁר who serves God straight forwardly, deserves to behold God's face directly in the Hereafter.

This psalm was inspired by a prophetic message foretelling an era when the wicked would succeed in overcoming the poor and the helpless. The threat manifested itself when Saul seemed to be on the verge of subduing David. It occurred again when the entire House of David was threatened with extinction at the hands of Ataliah who annihilated the entire 'royal seed' [with the exception of the infant Yoash who was hidden (II Kings 11:1-2)] (Radak).

Rashi (II Chron. 22:11) writes: David dedicated this psalm beginning עַל הַשְּׁמִינִית, 'on the eighth' to Ataliah's atrocity which occurred in the eighth generation of his dynasty (beginning with Solomon.) David thus prayed that a remnant of his family be spared, saying: 'Save me, Hashem, for the devout is no more.'

However, the psalm ends on the confident note that God will surely protect the helpless. The full realization of this wish will come to pass in Messianic times when evil will vanish in the face of the enlightenment gained through Torah study (v. 7-8). Therefore, this psalm was accompanied by the שְׁמִינִית, the eight-stringed instrument symbolizing that the forces set loose during the seven days of Creation will finally be bridled and disciplined (cf. comm. Psalm 6:1).

In this light, we understand why the Vilna Gaon prescribes this psalm as the שִׁיר שֶׁל יוֹם, 'The Song of the Day' for Shemini Atzeres.

On the seven days of the Sukkos Festival, offerings were brought symbolizing the seventy nations who surround Israel. But on the eighth day, Shemini Atzeres, the offering symbolizes only Israel who will remain alone and exalted in Messianic times as God's chosen people.

א לַמְנַצֵּחַ עַל־הַשְּׁמִינִית מִזְמוֹר לְדָוִד:
ב הוֹשִׁיעָה יהוה כִּי־גָמַר חָסִיד כִּי־פַסּוּ
ג אֱמוּנִים מִבְּנֵי אָדָם: שָׁוְא | יְדַבְּרוּ אִישׁ
אֶת־רֵעֵהוּ שְׂפַת חֲלָקוֹת בְּלֵב וָלֵב יְדַבֵּרוּ:
ד יַכְרֵת יהוה כָּל־שִׂפְתֵי חֲלָקוֹת לָשׁוֹן
ה מְדַבֶּרֶת גְּדֹלוֹת: אֲשֶׁר אָמְרוּ | לִלְשֹׁנֵנוּ

2. הוֹשִׁיעָה ה' — *'Save, HASHEM'.*
Rescue me from the hands of Saul
(*Metzudas David*).

כִּי גָמַר חָסִיד — *For the devout is no more.*
There is no longer anyone to protest
against Saul and to tell him something
favorable about me (*Metzudas David*).

Not only have the devout vanished,
but most contemporary people are sinners who plan to exploit the poor. Only
divine salvation can come to the rescue
(*Radak*).

A חָסִיד, a devout person, need not
totally withdraw from the world. Rather
he must be active, completely and
selflessly devoted to the welfare of those
about him. Today, laments the Psalmist,
there is no trace left of that type of loving concern for the happiness of others.
Whatever is done ostensibly for the
common good is actually motivated by
clever calculation of the advantages of
such acts (*Hirsch*).

פַסּוּ — *Vanished.*
This is similar to אֶפֶס *'nothing'*
(*Rashi*).

אֱמוּנִים — *Truthful men.*
No one tells Saul the truth about me;
they only incite him with false reports
(*Metzudas David*).

Everyone deceives me and secretly
betrays my hideouts to Saul (*Rashi*).

Malbim explains that the חָסִיד, *'the
devoted man'*, serves God far beyond
the call of duty. The אֱמוּנִים, *'the
truthful men'* faithfully adhere to
everything which duty demands. When
there exist many men who are
scrupulous about obeying the letter of
the law, then there is room for a few especially pious men who are so devoted
that they exceed the normal requirements. But when the masses ignore the
basic dictates of the law, then those who
devote themselves beyond the law are
mocked and ridiculed as extremists and
fanatics. Thus David says: Because the
אֱמוּנִים, *truthful*, have come down to
אֶפֶס, *'nothing'*, this caused the גָמַר, *'the
extinction'* of the special breed of pious
חֲסִידִים, *devout ones*.[1]

3. שָׁוְא — *Untruth.*
I.e., to utter with the mouth what it
not felt in the heart (*Radak*).

This *'untruth'* refers in particular to
false theological concepts in matters of
faith and belief in God (*Malbim*).

שְׂפַת חֲלָקוֹת — *Equivocal speech* [lit.
'smooth talk'; cf. 5:10.]
They cover up their false insincerity

1. When the Beis Hamikdosh was destroyed, men of genuine faith ceased to exist as it says:
'Save me HASHEM *for the devout is no more, for truthful men have vanished from mankind.'*
[These are men who place their full faith exclusively in God alone and rely on Him to do good
and never worry about any loss *(Rashi)*.]
Rabbi Yitzchak said: This refers to men who sincerely believe in the Holy One Blessed be
He. [They readily give away their money for the sake of enhancing and beautifying a mitzvah,
or for charity, or for Sabbath and festival expenses *(Rashi)*.]
As we learned: Rabbi Eliezer the Great says: He who has bread in his basket [for today] and
yet asks, 'What will I eat tomorrow?,' is a man of very limited faith! *(Sotah* 48a,b).

For the Conductor; on the Sheminis.
    A song of David.
² Save, HASHEM, for the devout is no more,
    for truthful men have vanished from mankind.
³ Each one speaks untruth to his neighbor,
    equivocal speech; they speak from
    a double heart.
⁴ May HASHEM cut off all equivocating lips,
    the tongue which speaks boastfully.
⁵ Those who have said:
'With our tongues we shall prevail,

with glib talk and smooth words. This refers specifically to dishonesty in affairs between man and his fellow man (Malbim).

Hirsch notes that חָלָק, 'smooth' is derived from חָלַק, 'to divide'. The concept of smoothness coincides with that of complete division or separation. Nothing can cleave or support itself on a surface that is entirely smooth. David laments that speech is 'polished', that words and expressions have been deprived of 'sharpness' and effect. They are polished so slippery smooth that they offer no firm support for anything. They are noncommittal.

בְּלֵב וָלֵב יְדַבֵּרוּ — They speak from a double heart [lit. 'with a heart and a heart.']

It is as if they have two hearts. They display a heart of peace and friendliness while in reality their heart is secretly full of animosity (Rashi).

4. יַכְרֵת ה' — May HASHEM cut off.

David said this as a prophecy [or perhaps this is a prayer] (Radak).

כָּל שִׂפְתֵי חֲלָקוֹת — All equivocating [lit. 'smooth'] lips, that speak deceitfully in affairs between man and his fellow man. For in Scripture, the word שְׂפָתַיִם, 'lips' always denotes external communication; the spoken word (Malbim).

לָשׁוֹן — The tongue. This term always refers to internal speech, the intimate

thoughts only between man and his Maker concerning matters of faith and philosophy (Malbim).

מְדַבֶּרֶת גְּדֹלוֹת — Which speaks boastfully [lit. 'great things'.]

These deceptive people limit the scope of their conversations only to the most important and sophisticated topics so as to deceive their listeners (Metzudas David).

The Sages equate לָשׁוֹן הָרָע, 'evil tale-bearing' to the three cardinal sins of idolatry, adultery and murder. The Scriptures describe all of these sins in the singular as גָּדוֹל, 'great,' but evil tale bearing is termed even more forcefully in the plural as גְּדֹלוֹת, 'great things' (Yer. Peah 1:1).

5. לִלְשֹׁנֵנוּ — With [lit. 'to'] our tongues .

With the impressive philosophical ideas which roll off of our לָשׁוֹן, 'the internal tongue, which talks of faith and divinity' (Malbim).

Midrash Shocher Tov explains that the main sin of the tongue is לָשׁוֹן הָרָע, 'evil tale-bearing', and this is most difficult to control:

'Come and see how powerful לָשׁוֹן הָרָע, is! The body contains many organs, some are positioned upright, some are laid flat, but none is as enclosed as the tongue which is imprisoned in the mouth and surrounded by the cheeks

ו נַגְבִּיר שְׂפָתֵינוּ אִתָּנוּ מִי אָדוֹן לָנוּ: מִשֹּׁד
עֲנִיִּים מֵאֶנְקַת אֶבְיוֹנִים עַתָּה אָקוּם יֹאמַר
ז יהוה אָשִׁית בְּיֵשַׁע יָפִיחַ לוֹ: אִמֲרוֹת
יהוה אֲמָרוֹת טְהֹרוֹת כֶּסֶף צָרוּף בַּעֲלִיל

and held in by the lips. Yet, despite all this, man cannot hold back his tongue!'

Rav Chaim Vital says that this is what is meant by the words *'with our tongues we shall prevail.'* The wicked boast that none of the precautions which God installed to hold back the tongue can deter them. Their evil tongues will prevail over the imprisoning mouth and teeth and cheeks; no obstacle will prevent it from bearing its evil tales!

שְׂפָתֵינוּ אִתָּנוּ — *Our lips are with us.'*
Our lips which speak so smoothly between man and man; they are a prime asset of ours in deceiving people (*Malbim*).

The external utterances of our lips can conceal the true intentions of our hearts (*Metzudas David*).

מִי אָדוֹן לָנוּ — *Who is master over us.*
I.e., to force us to divulge the true thoughts of our hearts, for who even suspects that out hearts contradict the words of our mouths? (*Metzudas David*).

The wicked say: God does not supervise and guide the world therefore there is no one to be master over us from above. And, by virtue of our cunning, sly manipulations, no one can master us below either! (*Malbim*).

Whosoever spreads evil tales, is as if he denies the very existence of God, as it says: *'With our tongues we shall prevail, our lips are with us, who is master over us!'* [By saying, *'who will be master over us'* they deny the sovereignty of God (*Rashi*).] (*Arachin 15a*).

6. מִשֹּׁד עֲנִיִּים — *Because of the plundering of the poor* — which I observe in the Land (*Radak*).

The poor and afflicted such as myself [David] and the priests of Nob [who were executed by Saul] (*Rashi*).

עַתָּה אָקוּם יֹאמַר ה' — *'Now I will arise'*, says HASHEM.
Hashem vows that He will arise to assist the needy (*Rashi*). David heard these words of Hashem prophetically (*Radak*).

Rabbi Pinchas says: Five times in the Book of Psalms David asked God to rise up with the words קוּמָה ה' (*Psalm 3:8, 7:7, 9:20, 10:12, 17:13*). Each time God refused and said: David, even if you constantly arouse me, I shall not arise. When then will I arise? — When I see the poor plundered and I hear the screams of the needy! As it says here *'Now I will arise'*, says HASHEM. (*Bereishis Rabbah 75*).

אָשִׁית בְּיֵשַׁע יָפִיחַ לוֹ — *'I will grant safety'* He says to him [the poor].
This translation follows *Rashi* and *Ibn Ezra* who render יָפִיחַ as *'talk'* [cf. *Habakuk 2:3*].
Malbim adds that the speech described by the term פָּח is in a low whisper. God has not yet publicized His plans to take revenge on the wicked. He whispers to Himself — if one may so express it! — lest the poor hear.
According to *Metzudas David* יָפִיחַ לוֹ means *'to blow at him'* [cf. 10:5]. God says: 'I will save anyone who arises to destroy the wicked; with a mere puff of breath, the wicked fall over.'
Others relate יָפִיחַ to פַּח *'trap'*. Thus, *'I will grant [them] safety, from those who trap them [lit. him]'* (*Radak; Menachem quoted in Rashi*).

7. אֲמָרוֹת טְהֹרוֹת — *Pure promises* [lit. *'sayings'*]. [Here the words are used to mean *'a reliable promise'*.]

our lips are with us, who is master over us?'
⁶ *Because of the plundering of the poor,*
because of the screaming of the needy,
'Now I will arise!' says HASHEM.
'I will grant safety,' He says to him.
⁷ *The promises of HASHEM are pure promises,*
like silver refined in the finest smelting earth,

They are pure truth because God has the power to do His will, unlike men who cannot guarantee to carry out their promises *(Rashi).*

Contrary to the words of man which are שָׁוְא, *'untrue and worthless'* (verse 3), God's sayings are pure, free of any ingredient which might becloud their veracity *(Hirsch).*

Because David related a prophecy of Hashem's promise to rescue the poor, he now reinforces the faith of the downtrodden in God's ability to make good his pledges *(Radak).*

[אֲמָרוֹת טְהֹרוֹת can also be translated lit. *'pure sayings,'* in reference to the words of the Torah. The prophet describes the Messianic days as a time when *'the earth will be filled with the Knowledge of HASHEM as the waters cover the Sea (Isaiah 11:9).* The waters of the sea symbolize Purity. In the future all people will recognize the perfection of the dictates of the Torah and that recognition will lead to the extinction of Evil. Now that the Psalmist hears the conclusion of this song dedicated to the eradication of Evil (see *comm. v.* 4), he describes to us the role of the pure Torah in that era.]

כֶּסֶף צָרוּף — *[Like] refined silver.*
Which has no flaws or dross. So, too, God's promises contain no shade of falsehood *(Radak).*

בַּעֲלִיל לָאָרֶץ — *In the finest smelting earth.*

Rashi offers four explanations for the word בַּעֲלִיל. One: *'revealed, open to public view; to all the earth'* as we find in *Mishnah Rosh Hashanah* 1:5 in regard to the visibility of the new moon, נִרְאֶה בַּעֲלִיל, *'it was clearly visible to all.'* Thus 'HASHEM's promise is like refined silver whose quality is visible to all.' [*Metzudas David* also renders בַּעֲלִיל as *'open, visible'* but he applies the word differently. According to him it refers to a large open smelting pit.]

Two: *In the finest of smelting earth.* The smelting furnace used in the refining process was made of the finest quality earth. *Radak* agrees with this rendition and so we have used this as our main translation above.

Three: בַּעֲלִיל derives from עֱלִי, which refers to the mortar in which metals are crushed before refining. However, *Rashi* rejects this explanation because the mortar which holds the contents is called מַכְתֵּשׁ, and it is the pestle which does the pounding which is called עֱלִי. Since the pestle is not a receptacle, one cannot say that refined silver is בַּעֲלִיל *'in the pestle'* (See *Proverbs* 27:22).

Four: בַּעֲלִיל comes from בַּעַל, *'master'.* Thus, God's words are pure, refined silver בַּעֲלִיל לָאָרֶץ, *'from the Master of the Earth'* who is flawless Himself.[1]

1. In Psalm 119:140 it is written: צְרוּפָה אִמְרָתְךָ מְאֹד — *'Your saying is very much refined.'* *Midrash Shocher Tov (ibid.)* compares this to the king who gave his silverplate to the silversmith to melt down and refine. After it emerged from the smelter once the king requested that it be smelted and refined once again. After the second time, the king repeated his request yet a third time and so on. Similarly, God refined the Holy Torah with purification after purification, seven times seven = forty nine times in all.

ח לָאָרֶץ מְזֻקָּק שִׁבְעָתָיִם: אַתָּה־יהוה
תִּשְׁמְרֵם תִּצְּרֶנּוּ | מִן־הַדּוֹר זוּ לְעוֹלָם:
ט סָבִיב רְשָׁעִים יִתְהַלָּכוּן כְּרֻם זֻלּוּת לִבְנֵי
אָדָם:

שִׁבְעָתָיִם — *Sevenfold.*

I.e., not literally seven times, but
rather many times. The number seven is
often used to mean something doubled
and redoubled many times over (Radak).

Rabbi Yehoshua of Sichnin said in
the name of Rabbi Levi: The young
children who studied Torah in David's
times were most precocious. Before they
were old enough to even have a taste of
sin, these innocent youths could explain
and clarify each law of the Torah in
than forty-nine different ways. This is
the meaning of the phrase *'clarified
sevenfold'* seven times seven equals
forty-nine! (Rashi quoting Midrash).

8. אַתָּה ה' תִּשְׁמְרֵם — *You HASHEM will
guard them.*

You will guard the poor and needy of
this generation from the slanderers and
tale-bearers who pursue them (Rashi).

According to the *Midrash* (see comm.
to the previous verse) this verse expresses David's fervent prayer and wish
for the young students of his generation:

'Master of the Universe! See how
these children cherish Your holy words.
They clarify each statement seven-fold
until it is stored flawlessly in their
hearts. Because they care enough to
guard Your words in their hearts, please
guard them in Your heart and protect
them from the degenerate influence of
vicious, unscrupulous tale-bearers.

תִּצְּרֶנּוּ — *You will preserve them.*

נְצִירָה, *'preservation'* is more effective
than simple שְׁמִירָה, *'guarding'* (Malbim).

First David uses the plural form
תִּשְׁמְרֵם, now he uses the singular תִּצְּרֶנּוּ,
to emphasize that HASHEM watches
over and protects each individual
pauper with special personalized care
(Radak).

9. סָבִיב רְשָׁעִים יִתְהַלָּכוּן — *The wicked
walk on every side* [lit. *'all around'*; or:
'in circles'.]

To hide traps which make me stumble (Rashi).

These words offer a general description of the futile lifestyle of the wicked,
which is nothing but a vicious cycle,
leading nowhere. They eat and drink in
order to have the strength to earn
money. They earn money in order to eat
and drink again (Chasam Sofer).

*Rav Yosef Yozel Horowitz of
Novaradok* likened the wicked to the
drunken wagon-driver who ventured
out on a dark, frozen night. For hours
he toiled and sweated, beating his team
furiously in order to swiftly reach his
destination. However, much to his dismay, when dawn broke and the weary
driver became sober, he discovered that
he had spent the entire night travelling
around and around one small, slippery
patch of land — ending exactly where he
started.

clarified sevenfold.

8 You, HASHEM, will guard them,
You will preserve them from the wicked,
such as are in this generation.
9 The wicked walk on every side,
when the basest of men are elevated.

כְּרֻם — *When ... are elevated.*

[רום is not merely a high position; it means the highest of posts. When the wicked achieve supremacy, they dare to threaten the righteous.]

Rashi quotes *Menachem* who relates רֵם to the רְאֵם, *R'eim* [cf. 22:22], a huge wild beast which is זָלַת, *extremely hungry* [cognate to the word זוֹלֵל, *glutton*; (*Deut.* 21:20).] Our verse, therefore, means: the wicked walk around the poor, helpless victim, waiting for an opportunity to devour him, just as the *R'eim* stalks its prey before attacking.

זֻלַּת — *The basest* [related to זוּל, *cheap, degraded.*]

When the lowly, wicked villains are elevated to positions of power, this is is referred to as זֻלַּת בְּנֵי אָדָם, *a degradation of all of mankind* (*Radak*).[1]

לִבְנֵי אָדָם — *Of* [lit. 'to'] *men.*

Rashi explains that David himself was once regarded as the lowest of mankind for he engaged in the most insignificant of all pursuits: shepherding. When David was suddenly catapulted to greatness, the wicked were envious of his meteoric rise and surrounded him from all sides. Elsewhere, David metaphorically describes that unpleasant situation, saying: אֶבֶן מָאֲסוּ הַבּוֹנִים הָיְתָה לְרֹאשׁ פִּנָּה, *the rock which the builders rejected has become the main cornerstone* [118:22].

[This is a final allusion to the Messianic Era. When David and all of Israel who were hitherto downtrodden and persecuted, will be acknowledged as the leading citizens of the world. For this reason, this psalm was accompanied by the Messianic instrument, the *Sheminis* (see *comm.* to 6:1).]

1. The *Talmud* [*Berachos* 6b] interprets these words homiletically: 'There are commandments which are of great importance [such as prayer (*Rashi*)] and stand בְּרוּמוֹ שֶׁל עוֹלָם, *at the pinnacle of the universe,'* and yet people treat these commandments with levity, and make them זֻלַּת, *degraded..'*

Of all the suffering endured by Israel during its history, the one that stands the longest is גָּלוּת, Exile. In exile, Israel is prey to the dominant evil forces which subject their helpless victims to an infinite variety of torments.

The agony of Exile penetrates yet deeper. If there is hope in a man's heart, then his tenacity and endurance are unlimited. As long as, man can dream and pray for God's assistance, then his powers have no end.

But the depressing gloom of Exile seems like a long, dark night with no hope for a dawn. Israel appears abandoned for all time, as if God has forsaken it forever.

As the exhausted nation feels its energy ebbing, and it sinks into despair, it summons its last traces of strength and cries out again and again, עַד אָנָה, how long? [The musical note on two of the repetitions of this plaint is the שַׁלְשֶׁלֶת (lit. long chain), a drawn out sound suggesting an action which continues for an extended period of time. See Genesis 19:10 וַיִּתְמַהְמָהּ; Genesis 39:8 וַיְמָאֵן.]

Such fervent pleading does not go unheeded. Thus the psalm concludes on a confident note, showing that God responds to those who truly seek Him, even in Exile, causing the Psalmist to exclaim, my heart will exult in Your salvation, I will sing to HASHEM for He dealt kindly with me (v. 6).

א-ב לַמְנַצֵּחַ מִזְמוֹר לְדָוִד: עַד־אָנָה יהוה
תִּשְׁכָּחֵנִי נֶצַח עַד־אָנָה | תַּסְתִּיר אֶת־פָּנֶיךָ
ג מִמֶּנִּי: עַד־אָנָה אָשִׁית עֵצוֹת בְּנַפְשִׁי
יָגוֹן בִּלְבָבִי יוֹמָם עַד־אָנָה | יָרוּם
ד אֹיְבִי עָלָי: הַבִּיטָה עֲנֵנִי יהוה אֱלֹהָי
ה הָאִירָה עֵינַי פֶּן־אִישַׁן הַמָּוֶת: פֶּן־יֹאמַר

1. לַמְנַצֵּחַ מִזְמוֹר לְדָוִד — *For the Conductor, a song of David.*

Both *Rashi* and *Radak* maintain that this Psalm is dedicated to the future misery of the entire Jewish people when they are sent into exile.

2. עַד אָנָה — *How long.* [lit. 'until when' (*Radak; Metzudos*).]

David repeats this query עַד אָנָה 'how long' four times, for each query corresponds to one of the four exiles through which Israel must suffer. David wrote this psalm for the benefit of all Israel (*Rashi*).[1]

תִּשְׁכָּחֵנִי נֶצַח — *Will You forget me, forever.*

When God does not redeem a man from his oppressors, it seems as if God has completely forgotten him (*Ibn Ezra*).

You leave me in exile so long that people will say that You have forgotten me (*Radak*).

עַד אָנָה תַּסְתִּיר אֶת פָּנֶיךָ מִמֶּנִי — *How long will You hide Your countenance* [lit. face] *from me?*

Even if You did not forget me and are aware of my plight, You hide Your face from me as if You don't wish to see me (*Rashi*).

Malbim explains that one of the most agonizing forms of divine retribution against the sinner is for God to abandon him. This can be accomplished in two ways. One is סִילוּק הַהַשְׁגָּחָה, *'a total removal of divine supervision'*, wherein the Almighty abandons the sinner to the whims of haphazard, chance nature. Another, less harsh, form is הֶסְתֵּר פָּנִים, *'a concealment of God's face'.* The man punished with הֶסְתֵּר פָּנִים continues to be supervised by direct divine providence, yet God conceals Himself and leaves no trace or clue of His presence. Thus any mishap which the man suffers seems to be a chance accident, not a message from on high.

In reference to the first state of total abandonment the Psalmist laments here, *'How long will You forget me [completely]?'* In reference to the second state of concealment he moans, *'How long will You hide Your face from me?'*

3. עַד אָנָא אָשִׁית עֵצוֹת בְּנַפְשִׁי — *How long must I set schemes in my spirit?* How long will I have to seek ways to escape from the despair which lurks in my heart and spirit all day (*Metzudas David*).

יָגוֹן בִּלְבָבִי יוֹמָם — *Melancholy in my*

---

1. Rabbi Yitzchok says: All of these laments are justly ordained, measure for measure. Said the Holy One, Blessed be He, 'I called out to you, Israel, four times with the cry עַד אָנָה, 'How long' and you did not respond.

⋅§ עַד אָנָה מֵאַנְתֶּם לִשְׁמֹר מִצְוֹתַי וְתוֹרֹתָי — *How long do you refuse to observe My commands and My instructions' (Exodus 16:28).*

⋅§ עַד אָנָה יְנַאֲצֻנִי הָעָם הַזֶּה וְעַד אָנָה לֹא יַאֲמִינוּ בִי — *'How long will this nation blaspheme Me and how long will they not believe in Me?' (Numbers 14:11).*

XIII
1-4

For the Conductor.
A song of David

² How long will You forget me, forever;
how long will You hide Your countenance
from me?
³ How long must I set schemes in my spirit;
melancholy in my heart even by day?
How long will my enemy triumph over me?
⁴ Look! Answer me HASHEM, my God;

heart even by day?

By day a person ordinarily can leave behind his cares and worries as he immerses himself in worldly affairs and pursuits. I am not so. My sighs of anguish never cease, even by day *(Radak)*.

Malbim explains that יוֹמָם, *'by day'*, refers to the moment of success. This corresponds to the Psalmist's previous lament *(v. 2)* *'How long HASHEM will You forget me?'* For, the man whom God has totally forsaken, even though he has been treated kindly by the whims of nature, tastes no real joy in his success. A gloomy shadow is cast over this lonely man for he intuitively senses that despite all good fortune, he is lost. This man cries out, *'How long must I set schemes in my spirit, melancholy in my heart even by day.'*

עַד אָנָא יָרוּם אֹיְבִי עָלָי — *How long will my enemy triumph over me?*

This part of the verse echoes the words of the man who is still supervised by God, but in concealed fashion (הֶסְתֵּר פָּנִים). The same man who first moaned *(v. 2)* *'How long will You hide Your countenance from me'*, now continues to wonder why God has vanished from his life and has allowed his enemies to dominate him *(Malbim)*.

4. הַבִּיטָה — *Look.*

[After uttering four expressions of despair, the Psalmist now makes three requests which will dispel his loneliness and estrangement from God. These requests correspond to the prior exclamations of agony. In response to the questions *'How long will You forget me?'* and *'How long will You hide Your countenance from me?'* David now requests *'Look at me, take notice!'* *(Radak; Ibn Ezra; Malbim).*]

עֲנֵנִי — *Answer me.*

[Whereas David previously bemoaned the fact that he alone must *'set schemes in my spirit'* to rescue himself from despair, he now calls upon God to respond to his problems by providing a solution for his dilemma.]

הָאִירָה עֵינַי — *Enlighten my eyes.*

I am in the gloom of exile and oppression and only You can illuminate the darkness *(Radak).*

Light up my vision with a brilliant plan to outwit the enemies who threaten me *(Metzudas David).*

[This final request is an impassioned plea for great spiritual advancement. The phrase *'enlighten my eyes'* always has a spiritual connotation as in *'The*

⦿§ עַד מָתַי לָעֵדָה הָרָעָה הַזֹּאת — *'How long will this evil assembly continue to exist?'* (Numbers 14:26).

Therefore you will be condemned to call out to me four times עַד אָנָה, *'How long'*, in the exile of Babylon, the exile of Media, the exile of Greece, and the exile of Rome (Edom)' *(Midrash Shocher Tov).*

יג
ו

וֹ אֹיְבִי יְכָלְתִּיו צָרַי יָגִילוּ כִּי אֶמּוֹט: וַאֲנִי|
בְּחַסְדְּךָ בָטַחְתִּי יָגֵל לִבִּי בִּישׁוּעָתֶךָ
אָשִׁירָה לַיהוה כִּי גָמַל עָלָי:

command of HASHEM is flawless, it enlightens the eyes' (19:9) or 'By Your light we shall see light' (35:10). David wishes to begin viewing the events of life in a purely spiritual perspective; as part of a complex divine plan designed for maximum human welfare. The limited, flesh and blood perspective fails to recognize this. Thus, these words correspond to the dismal cry 'How long will my enemy triumph over me.' For, the inspired person who appreciates the divine scheme of things can discern hidden benefits even in the victory of the enemy.]

פֶּן אִישַׁן הַמָּוֶת — Lest I slumber into death [lit. 'lest I die'].

Rashi comments that death is called slumber as we find וְיָשְׁנוּ שְׁנַת עוֹלָם וְלֹא יָקִיצוּ, 'They shall sleep a perpetual sleep, and not awake' (Jer. 51:57).

If I do not outwit my enemies and they trap me, it will mean my death (Metzudas David).

Every man who enjoys God's closeness is endowed with a spark of divine vitality which flickers in his soul and illuminates it. But when God abandons the sinner, the flame slowly sinks and the soul is soon left shriveled and lifeless. David pleads, 'Enlighten

my spiritual vision to discern the presence of the divine, lest my soul sink into spiritual death' (Malbim).

5. פֶּן יֹאמַר אֹיְבִי יְכָלְתִּיו — Lest my enemy, boast [lit. 'say'], 'I have overcome him.'

This word is derived from יְכוֹלֶת, 'ability, power' (Metzudas Zion), and is a contraction of the words יָכֹלְתִּי לוֹ (Radak).

[Thus the word literally means 'I have had power over him']

צָרַי יָגִילוּ כִּי אֶמּוֹט — Lest my tormentors rejoice when I falter.

Malbim points out the difference between אוֹיֵב, 'foe', and צָר, 'tormentor'. The foe merely bears hatred in his heart, but has not yet inflicted any actual harm upon those whom he hates. The צָר, 'tormentor', has already acted maliciously. Here the man whom God has abandoned bemoans his sorry state. He is so hopelessly forlorn that even the אוֹיֵב, 'foe', who ordinarily would not have the courage to harm him, now threatens to attack, and gloat יְכָלְתִּיו, 'I have overcome him.' If he is indeed successful, then the צָר, 'tormentor', who ordinarily fights and injures, will be free to 'rejoice when I collapse' at the hands of the usually passive אוֹיֵב.

enlighten my eyes, lest I slumber into death.
⁵ *Lest my enemy boast: 'I have overcome him!'*
  Lest my tormentors rejoice when I falter.
⁶ *As for me, I trust in Your loving-kindness;*
  my heart will exult in Your salvation.
I will sing to HASHEM, for He dealt kindly with me.

6. וַאֲנִי בְּחַסְדְּךָ בָטַחְתִּי — *[And] as for me, I trust in Your loving-kindness.*

My enemies think that I have no savior; however I trust in Your loving-kindness to save me, even though I do not deserve it *(Radak).*

[When I am endowed with the enlightened spiritual perspective (described in *v.* 4), then I will have the ability to perceive the presence of Your loving-kindness even in the darkest gloom and I will certainly place my complete trust in it.]

יָגֵל לִבִּי — *My heart will exult.*

Malbim explains that גיל, 'joy', refers to a sudden, unexpected piece of good news which one never dared to hope for. David says: Although I always trusted in Your loving-kindness and thus salvation should not come as a surprise, nevertheless, when the יְשׁוּעָה 'salvation' actually occurs, I will rejoice as if it were an unexpected bonanza. The

reason is because I am undeserving of anything, even kindness, so any merciful blessing is truly a surprise.

בִּישׁוּעָתֶךָ — *In Your salvation.*

David and Israel do not say that their hearts will rejoice בִּישׁוּעָתֵנוּ, *in our own salvation* rather, בִּישׁוּעָתֶךָ, *in Your salvation.* 'God's victorious salvation is our salvation; we are one!' *(Midrash Shocher Tov).*

אָשִׁירָה לַה׳ כִּי גָמַל עָלָי — *I will sing to HASHEM for He dealt kindly with me* [lit. *'when He recompenses me']*

And did not let me fall into the slumber of death *(Radak).*

I consider myself undeserving of reward on my own merit, anything I receive seems to be the result of God's charity and kindness. If God will inform me that I am indeed worthy of גְמוּל, *'due wage'* for my faithful service then I will be doubly happy and I will sing for joy *(Malbim).*[1]

1. *Midrash Shocher Tov* traces the four expressions of jubilation contained in this verse to the four exiles from which we yearn to be redeemed. 'As for me, I trust in Your loving kindness' — In Babylon. 'My heart will rejoice in Your salvation' — In Media. 'I will sing to HASHEM' — In Greece. 'For He deals kindly with me' — In Edom (Rome).

14 מזמור יד

David composed two songs, Psalms 14 and 53, which deal with the very same topic and are very similar in language (Rashi). This one is dedicated to the destruction of the First Temple at the hands of Nebuchadnezzar, and the second psalm deals with the destruction of the Second Temple by Titus. Here David prophesies that Nebuchadnezzar will enter the Sanctuary to defile and destroy it, and not one of his soldiers will attempt to protest or restrain him.

Malbim notes that this psalm is an example of the multi-dimensional aspect of David's compositions. David created this psalm primarily in response to the enemies of his day. In later generations when new enemies and tragedies arose, however, Israel saw that the words of David applied to the problems of their times as well. And so we have a psalm endowed with both personal meaning for David and with national, historical meaning for all Israel. (Malbim interprets the prophetic aspect of this psalm not as a reference to Nebuchadnezzar, but to Sancherib of Assyria and his siege against King Chizkiyahu of Judea).

א לַמְנַצֵּחַ לְדָוִד אָמַר נָבָל בְּלִבּוֹ אֵין אֱלֹהִים
הִשְׁחִיתוּ הִתְעִיבוּ עֲלִילָה אֵין עֹשֵׂה־טוֹב:
ב יְהוָה מִשָּׁמַיִם הִשְׁקִיף עַל־בְּנֵי־אָדָם
לִרְאוֹת הֲיֵשׁ מַשְׂכִּיל דֹּרֵשׁ אֶת־אֱלֹהִים:
ג הַכֹּל סָר יַחְדָּו נֶאֱלָחוּ אֵין עֹשֵׂה־טוֹב אֵין
ד גַּם־אֶחָד: הֲלֹא יָדְעוּ כָּל־פֹּעֲלֵי אָוֶן אֹכְלֵי

1. נָבָל — *The degraded man.*

This follows the translation of *Metzudas David.*

Ibn Ezra describes this man as the opposite of a wise person because he is degraded and foolish enough to think that there is no God.

Hirsch translates this word as ' *to wither, to wear out*', as in Yisro's warning to Moses, נָבֹל תִּבֹּל, '*You shall certainly be worn out*' (*Exodus* 18:18). A withered leaf has no life nor potential for growth. It is at the mercy of outside forces and winds which blow it as they wish. So, too, has all moral strength disappeared from the heart of the נָבָל. He has totally succumbed to the influence of external lusts and passions; therefore, his own personal power to master and control his urges and desires has withered. It was the ability to choose for himself which made him similar to the image of God; but since the divine spark has faded away, he says in his once-inspired heart, '*there is no God*'.

Thus we can well appreciate the words of *Midrash Shocher Tov*: הָרְשָׁעִים בִּרְשׁוּת לִבָּן וְהַצַּדִּיקִים לִבָּן בִּרְשׁוּתָן, 'The wicked are controlled by their hearts, whereas the righteous control their hearts.' [The wicked have no control over the passions which rule them, whereas the righteous dominate their passions with a firm hand].

אֵין אֱלֹהִים — *There is no God.*

The נָבָל, '*degraded man*', referred to here is the King of Babylon, who dared to harm Israel only because he thought that there is no God, no judge, no retribution, no one to punish a sinner (*Radak*).

Rashi notes that Nebuchadnezzar boasted: אֶעֱלֶה עַל בָּמֳתֵי עָב אֶדַּמֶּה לְעֶלְיוֹן — '*I will ascend above the heights of the clouds, I will be like the Most High*' (*Isaiah* 14:14) (*Rashi*).

Harav Eliyahu Meir Bloch observed that the most eloquent proof of the true existence of God is the very fact that the wicked man must constantly soothe his conscience by declaring, '*there is no God!*'

הִשְׁחִיתוּ — *They acted corruptly.*

I.e., both Nebuchadnezzar and his people; thus the plural form (*Radak*; *Metzudas David*).

This is meant to describe the future, but David viewed these events prophetically and, therefore, saw them as if they had already transpired, hence the use of past tense (*Metzudas David*).

אֵין עֹשֵׂה טוֹב — *Not one does good.*

I.e., all of them are thoroughly corrupt (*Radak*).

2. ה' מִשָּׁמַיִם הִשְׁקִיף עַל בְּנֵי אָדָם — *From heaven HASHEM gazed down upon mankind.*

Although God dwells high above them He looks down to probe mankind [and particularly Babylon] (*Radak*).

מַשְׂכִּיל — *One who reflects.*

Who understands enough to protest against the evil of destruction (*Metzudas David*).

דֹּרֵשׁ אֶת אֱלֹהִים — *One who seeks out God.*

XIV
1-4

For the Conductor; of David.
The degraded man says in his heart,
    'There is no God!'
They acted corruptly and despicably,
    not one does good.
² From heaven HASHEM gazed down upon mankind,
    to see if there be one who reflects;
    one who seeks out God.
³ They have all gone astray,
    together become depraved,
    none does good, not even one.
⁴ Do they not realize, all those evildoers? —
They who devour my people
    as they would devour bread,

I.e., someone who seeks to see God in the role of אֱלֹהִים, 'Supreme Judge' (Radak; Metzudas David).

3. הַכֹּל סָר — They have all gone astray.
I.e. from the right path (Radak; Metzudas David).

Not one of his soldiers does the proper thing, which is to protest (Rashi).

Radak quotes an opinion that relates סָר, to the word סָג, which is used in its stead in the corresponding verse of the very similar Psalm 53 (v. 4). There it means 'they retreat'; here סָר, most precisely means 'they turn their faces away' (The letters ג, gimel, and ר, reish, are interchangeable in the alphabetical system of א״ת בַּ״שׁ, which assumes a relationship between the forward and backward orders of the alphabet i.e., the first letter with the last [א״ת], the second letter with the second from the last [בַּ״שׁ] and so on. Thus the third letter, ג, is interchangeable with ר, the third letter from the end).

Some relate סָר to the Aramaic וְסָרִי, which means decayed and putrified.

יַחְדָּו נֶאֱלָחוּ — Together become depraved.

As we find נִתְעָב וְנֶאֱלָח, 'abominable and rotten' (Job 15:16).

4. הֲלֹא יָדְעוּ — Do they not realize? [lit. 'Do they not know?']

[If we read this as an interrogative statement (as Radak does) then the word הֲלֹא is a contraction of the words הַאִם לֹא, 'is it then possible that they do not?'] I.e., do these evildoers not realize that there is indeed a God Who gazes down upon mankind? How can they lack the wisdom to realize the truth? How can these evildoers think that no one sees them? (Radak).

Rashi renders הֲלֹא as the beginning of a declarative statement, 'for indeed'. Thus, 'For indeed the evildoers will ultimately find out what happens to those of their kind.'

אֹכְלֵי עַמִּי אָכְלוּ לֶחֶם — They who devour My people as they would devour bread.

Radak explains: These enemies devour Israel as effortlessly as one consumes a piece of bread. An alternate rendition is based on the literal meaning of אָכְלוּ לֶחֶם, which is 'they ate bread'. The enemy is self-confident and self-righteous for he has mercilessly devoured my people and yet no punish-

ה עַמִּי אָכְלוּ לֶחֶם יהוה לֹא קָרָאוּ: שָׁם |
ו פָּחֲדוּ פַחַד כִּי־אֱלֹהִים בְּדוֹר צַדִּיק: עֲצַת־
ז עָנִי תָבִישׁוּ כִּי יהוה מַחְסֵהוּ: מִי יִתֵּן
מִצִּיּוֹן יְשׁוּעַת יִשְׂרָאֵל בְּשׁוּב יהוה שְׁבוּת
עַמּוֹ יָגֵל יַעֲקֹב יִשְׂמַח יִשְׂרָאֵל:

ment has befallen him. Furthermore, his prosperity endures and he still has bread to eat.

Rashi says that this verse refers to Nebuchadnezzar's descendant, King Belshazzar, who *'ate bread'*, alluding to the lavish banquet described in *Daniel 5*.

[The feast was inspired by Belshazzar's mistaken calculation of the end of the prophetically foretold seventy years of Jewish exile in Babylon. He thought that the seventy years had elapsed and since Israel had not been redeemed, he assumed that redemption would never come. He rejoiced over his new-found opportunity to devour them without restraint].

In his *comm.* to the next verse, *Rashi* quotes the opinion of the Rabbis who hold that this phrase refers to all gentiles who oppress Israel: 'Only those who devour my nation know the real, wonderful taste of bread.' Thus, part of our punishment is that the gentiles have greater incentive to exploit Israel than any other nation.[1]

ה' לֹא קָרָאוּ — *They who call not upon HASHEM.*

As they devoured Israel, they never dreamt that Hashem was watching, and so they never called out to Him. They imagined that there is no Judge and no judgment and so they were never even frightened into repentance (*Radak*).

Nebuchadnezzar had taken the holy vessels out of the Beis HaMikdash when he destroyed it, but no one dared to use these most sacred objects for profane, personal purposes. On the night of that fateful banquet, however, Belshazzar forgot all of God's awesome wonders and miracles. *'He did not call out to HASHEM'*, and so he was brazen enough to use the holy vessels for his debauchery (*Rashi*).

5. [David now proclaims that the time will yet come when God will punish the evildoers.]

שָׁם — *There.*

In the place of their glory and pride, in that very location *'they will be stricken with terror'* (*Radak*).

That very night, at that very same banquet, Belshazzar was given his just punishment and he was filled with terror and awe as described in *Daniel 5*. For in the midst of the raucous festivities there suddenly appeared the eerie, frightening sight of a man's hand which wrote an undecipherable message, the proverbial 'handwriting on the wall', [which in reality foretold the doom of Belshazzar and his empire].

Belshazzar's sheer terror is vividly described:'*The king's appearance changed, and his thoughts became confused and the joints of his loins were loosened and his knees were knocking one against another'* (*Daniel 5:1*) (*Radak*).

כִּי אֱלֹהִים בְּדוֹר צַדִּיק — *For God is with the righteous generation.*

---

1. 'Rabbi Samuel interprets this verse as referring to the gentile hordes who poured into the Temple at the time of its destruction. When they entered the Sanctuary they found lambs ready for the daily sacrifice and they slaughtered and ate them. Then they found the showbread arranged on the golden table and they ate that too' (*Midrash Shocher Tov*).

they who call not upon HASHEM.
⁵ There they will be stricken with terror,
for God is with the righteous generation.
⁶ You put to shame the plans of the poor,
because HASHEM is his refuge.
⁷ O, that out of Zion would come Israel's salvation!
When HASHEM returns the captivity of His nation,
Jacob will exult, Israel will rejoice.

I.e. the generation of King Yechan-yah which was righteous *(Rashi).*

[Eleven years before the destruction of the first Beis HaMikdash under the reign of King Tzidkiyahu, Nebuchad-nezzar exiled King Yechanya together with ten thousand of the most pheno-menal, unchallenged Torah scholars of that day *(II Kings,* 24:10-16). The Sages of the Talmud *(Gittin* 88a) describe this as a great divine kindness, for the scholars who did not suffer the horrors of the destruction were free to establish a solid spiritual life in Babylon so that when their wretched, downtrodden brethren arrived years later there was an organized Jewish communtiy run by scholars and pious men to greet them. The Talmud *(Megillah* 29a and *Rashi ibid.)* relates that the exiles of Yechan-yah took with them stones from their beloved Jerusalem and carried them all the way to Babylon where they built a great synagogue. The holy spirit of God always hovered over this sanctuary and never departed it. Thus, we see clearly that Yechanyah exemplifies the princi-ple that *'God is with the righteous generation'.*]

6. עֲצַת עָנִי תָבִישׁוּ — *You put to shame the plans of the poor.*

You mock the plans of Israel who are poor and afflicted *(Rashi).*

כִּי ה' מַחְסֵהוּ — *Because HASHEM is his refuge.*

I.e. you scoff at Israel's reliance on God's help because you deny His ex-istence.

Since you have not yet been punished, you taunt and shame these poor ones for this and ask, 'Where is your God?' *(Radak).*

7. מִי יִתֵּן — *O that* [an idiomatic Hebrew expression occurring many times in Scriptures meaning literally 'O who would give?']

The term is used to denote a yearning for the event to occur very soon *(Radak; Metzudas David),* as *Targum* renders: הַלְוַאי.

מִצִּיּוֹן — *Out of Zion.*

Zion is the capital of the Jewish kingdom and it is there that God's glory dwells. David, therefore, wishes that this location would be the source of the salvation *(Radak).*[1]

1. Rabbi Levi said: All blessings, consolations, and bounties which the Holy One, Blessed Be He, brings upon Israel, emanate from Zion. Torah from Zion, as it says: כִּי מִצִּיּוֹן תֵּצֵא תוֹרָה *'For the Torah shall come forth from Zion'* (Isaiah 2:3). Blessing from Zion, as it says: יְבָרֶכְךָ ה' מִצִּיּוֹן *'HASHEM will bless you from Zion'* (134:3). Revelation from Zion, as it says: מִצִּיּוֹן מִכְלַל יֹפִי אֱלֹהִים הוֹפִיעַ (50:2), *'Out of Zion, the perfection of beauty, God appeared.'* Sup-port from Zion, as it says: וּמִצִּיּוֹן יִסְעָדֶךָּ *'And from Zion He will support you'* (20:3). Life from Zion as it says: צִיּוֹן כִּי שָׁם צִוָּה ה' אֶת הַבְּרָכָה חַיִּים עַד הָעוֹלָם *'Zion; for there HASHEM has commanded the blessing, life forever'* (133:3). Greatness from Zion, as it says: ה' בְּצִיּוֹן גָּדוֹל, *'HASHEM is great in Zion'* (99:2). Salvation from Zion, as it says: מִי יִתֵּן מִצִּיּוֹן יְשׁוּעַת יִשְׂרָאֵל *'O, that out of Zion would come the Israel's salvation'* (14:7).

בְּשׁוּב ה' —When HASHEM returns [lit. 'brings back']

This refers to those taken captive in David's times or perhaps to the entire Jewish nation which is now in exile and we await their return from foreign captivity (Ibn Ezra).

Radak and Metzudas David offer an alternate translation of בְּשׁוּב, 'to bring to rest, to calm down and set at ease.' When, in the future, Hashem will bring שְׁבוּת עַמּוֹ, 'the captives of His people' back to their former tranquility and peace of mind, then it will be noticeable that this is the work of Hashem, for no human could accomplish such a feat.

יָגֵל יַעֲקֹב יִשְׂמַח יִשְׂרָאֵל — Jacob will exult, Israel will rejoice.

Then, when Israel proves the success of it's plan to find security only in God, at that time, the gentiles, who once disgraced it for its faith, will have to confess that Israel was correct. This will be a source of great joy to us (Metzudas David).

יָגֵל ... יִשְׂמַח, 'exult ... rejoice.' Hirsch explains that גִיל, 'elation', is the vocal expression of joy. It is a much more intensive emotion than שִׂמְחָה which is related to צְמִיחָה, 'growth' and connotes serenity; a feeling of unhampered, continual inner maturity and blossoming, which persists and endures. First, one is overwhelmed by גִיל, 'elation', later he settles down to continual lifelong gladness and well-being, שִׂמְחָה. [Perhaps גִיל, derives from גַל, 'a rolling wave', for this elation bursts upon a person suddenly, in a surging wave of joy.] For this reason we frequently find the word שִׂמְחָה following גִיל as in אָגִילָה וְאֶשְׂמְחָה בְּחַסְדֶּךָ 'I will be elated and rejoice in Your loving-kindness' (31:8).

Malbim differentiates between these two words in the very same way and adds a dash of his own. We know that the name יַעֲקֹב, Jacob, always describes the Jewish masses, the common folk. However יִשְׂרָאֵל, Israel, denotes the elite, the aristocracy, the scholars and saints who guide the masses. The great men, Israel, never ceased to trust in the future redemption. To them it was always a definite reality, a tangible fact of life. When the redemption occurs, it will not at all take them by surprise, for they have been waiting. Not so Jacob, the unlearned masses who lacked this clear faith. The redemption will burst upon them like a sudden thunderbolt and they will be overwhelmed with ecstasy and elation, thus, יָגֵל יַעֲקֹב. However, Israel will take it all in stride and continue with their constant serene state of gladness and joy, יִשְׂמַח יִשְׂרָאֵל.

15 מזמור טו

This psalm gives us eleven cardinal principles of observance which David stressed and taught (Maccos 24a). They are examples of לִפְנִים מְשׁוּרַת הַדִּין 'beyond the letter of the law', i.e. service of God beyond the Torah's minimum requirements. In order to instill in people a love for the law itself, they must be taught to go even beyond it with extra devotion and sacrifice.

All eleven principles deal with בֵּין אָדָם לַחֲבֵירוֹ, man's relationship with his fellow man. David's subjects were weak in this area. As the Sages said, 'The people of David's generation were all righteous and observant. Yet, they would fall in battle because they harbored slanderers and tale-bearers. The people of King Achav's generation were wicked idolators, yet, because they had no slanderers and tale-bearers in their ranks, they entered battle and emerged victorious, with no casualties' (Yerushalmi, Peah 1:1).

Einei Yitzchak notes that the masses were corrupted by the example of depraved leaders. Doeg and Achitophel, two prominent personalities of that period, were vicious men who engaged in vile slander and wanton bloodshed.

Hirsch makes a final observation. This psalm opens, 'HASHEM, who will reside in Your tent?', implying that the topic of Godly service will be discussed. But the Psalmist launches into a discussion of man's obligations towards his fellow man. This proves that the person who aspires to come close to God cannot hope to do so until he has first made himself acceptable to his brethren.

א מִזְמוֹר לְדָוִד יהוה מִי־יָגוּר בְּאָהֳלֶךָ מִי־
ב יִשְׁכֹּן בְּהַר קָדְשֶׁךָ: הוֹלֵךְ תָּמִים וּפֹעֵל
ג צֶדֶק וְדֹבֵר אֱמֶת בִּלְבָבוֹ: לֹא־רָגַל | עַל־

1. מִי יָגוּר — *Who may sojourn.*

This implies permanent residence as opposed to יִשְׁכֹּן *'may dwell'* which means temporarily (*Malbim*).

Hirsch, however, translates these words in exactly opposite fashion: יָגוּר implying temporary sojourn. [See Passover Haggadah where Jacob's family is said to have come to Egypt to dwell temporarily for the verse says לָגוּר בָּאָרֶץ בָּאנוּ, *we have come to sojourn in the land* (Gen. 47:4).]

בְּאָהֳלֶךָ — *In Your tent.*

This refers to the heavens which are stretched out like a pitched tent (*Radak*).

Metzudas David says that אָהֳלֶךָ, *'Your tent'*, refers to the Temple. Not everyone is worthy of entering it, and now David lays down the requirements for such a privilege.

בְּהַר קָדְשֶׁךָ — *On Your Holy Mountain.*

This refers to Mount Moriah upon which the Beis HaMikdash was built. It is the location of the most sacred place on earth (*Radak; Ibn Ezra*).

Radak goes on to explain that the verbs יָגוּר *'to sojourn'*, and יִשְׁכֹּן *'to dwell'*, pertain not to the body but to the heavenly soul. He who practices the good deeds outlined in this psalm is assured that after he dies, his soul will reside in a glorious divine dwelling.

2. הוֹלֵךְ תָּמִים — *He who walks in perfect innocence.*

This is the man who engages in the pursuits of this world with innocence. He will not become involved in complicated schemes and calculations in order to assure his success (*Radak*).

[This person will never hurt or swindle anyone in order to accomplish his goals because he innocently trusts that

HASHEM will guide his affairs to a successful conclusion without the aid of his machinations. See *Deut.* 18:13: תָּמִים תִּהְיֶה עִם ה' אֱלֹהֶיךָ, *'You shall be perfectly innocent with HASHEM, your God!'* *Rashi (ibid.)* explains: 'Walk before Him whole-heartedly, put your hope in Him and do not attempt to investigate the future, but whatever comes upon you accept with whole-hearted innocence. Then you will be as one with Him and become His portion.']

In illustrating the eleven principles of this psalm, the Talmud (*Maccos* 24a) draws upon a number of the renowned heroes of Jewish history each of whom personify one of these traits: The man who best typifies הוֹלֵךְ תָּמִים is Abraham of whom God said: הִתְהַלֵּךְ לְפָנַי וֶהְיֵה תָמִים *'Walk before Me and be perfect in innocence'* (Gen. 17:1).

וּפֹעֵל צֶדֶק — [And] *does what is right.*

Radak explains that the Torah contains positive and negative commands. There are three different ways to fulfill each of these categories; with thoughts, with words, and with actions. David begins by enumerating the praises of the man who is scrupulous in acting righteously in his deeds. Thus, פֹּעֵל, is a verb meaning *'he does'*.

However, according to the Talmud (*Maccos* 24a) פֹּעֵל is a noun meaning *'a worker'*, and together with צֶדֶק, it refers to a worker who is scrupulously righteous and honest.

The personification of this trait is Abba Chilkiyah whose piety is described at length (*Ta'anis* 23 a-b). Once the country was in need of rain and two rabbis were sent to ask him to pray. They went out to the field where they found him hoeing. They greeted him but he did not even turn his face to

A song of David.

HASHEM; Who may sojourn in Your Tent?
Who may dwell in Your Holy Mountain?
² — He who walks in perfect innocence,
does what is right,
and speaks the truth from his heart;
³ Who has no slander on his tongue,

---

them. Later, after the day was done, he explained to the rabbis that he was a day-laborer and would be cheating his employer if he so much as greeted them at a time when he was being paid to work. The Talmud relates many other pious practices).

וְדֹבֵר אֱמֶת בִּלְבָבוֹ — *And speaks the truth from* [lit. *'in'*] *his heart.*

Radak continues: David proceeds to describe how this man is careful with his thoughts and words. The true, sincere thoughts of his heart — that is all he speaks, nothing else. Furthermore, if he merely made a mental decision to do some good deed, even though he never made an oral commitment, he will still fulfill his decision. It goes without saying that he never deviates from that which he actually said openly. Most important, this man forever nurtures truth in his heart, i.e. he never stops thinking about God's reality, supremacy and omnipotence, for this is the ultimate, absolute source of all truth.

No man fit the description of וְדֹבֵר אֱמֶת בִּלְבָבוֹ, speaking truth in his heart, as well as Rav Safra. Rav Safra put up an article for sale. Once, while he was reciting the Shema, a man came to him and said, 'Sell me that article for such and such an amount.' Rav Safra did not reply because he was in the middle of Shema, but the buyer interpreted his silence as a refusal to sell for so low a price. He offered a higher bid. When Rav Safra completed the Shema he told the man, 'Take the article for the first price which you proposed, because at the time you made the original offer, I

made a mental decision to sell it for that price and so I can no longer change my mind' (*Shiltos d'Rav Achai, Vayechi* 36).

3. לֹא רָגַל עַל לְשֹׁנוֹ — *Who has no slander on his tongue.*

This refers to לָשׁוֹן הָרַע, 'evil tale-bearing' (Rashi; Ibn Ezra; Metzudas Zion).

Radak continues: David now lauds this man's achievement in carefully avoiding the transgression of negative commands. He demonstrates his care in speech and action, but he does not find it necessary to describe how he safeguards his heart. This is because in the previous verse this man is said to have his heart permeated with incessant thoughts of God's truth so that it is absolutely impossible for him to harbor any wicked ideas in his mind.

First of all this man never utters a slanderous word. This is especially praiseworthy for he is already described as a man who never holds back the truth (*v*. 2). Nevertheless, if the truth about someone is slanderous and damaging, he will not allow his zeal for truth to bring about harm to someone else.

The Talmud (*Maccos*, ibid.) puts the main emphasis on the fact that he is a man of truth and takes pains not to speak deceitfully. Jacob the Patriarch was such a person as he told his mother when he objected to impersonating Esau, *'perhaps my father will feel me and I shall seem to him like a deceiver'* (*Genesis* 27:12). Although the blessing was precious to Jacob, truth was even dearer.

לְשֹׁנוֹ לֹא־עָשָׂה לְרֵעֵהוּ רָעָה וְחֶרְפָּה
ד לֹא־נָשָׂא עַל־קְרֹבוֹ: נִבְזֶה | בְּעֵינָיו נִמְאָס
וְאֶת־יִרְאֵי יהוה יְכַבֵּד נִשְׁבַּע לְהָרַע וְלֹא
ה יָמִר: כַּסְפוֹ | לֹא־נָתַן בְּנֶשֶׁךְ וְשֹׁחַד עַל־

Rashi explains that he agreed to this masquerade only after his mother assured him that she had received a prophetic message to engage in the deception.

לְרֵעֵהוּ — [To] his friend.
I.e. the people with whom he comes in contact, his neighbors. Of course, he is gentle even with those who are not friends and neighbors, but Scriptures discuss ordinary circumstances. In the above statement David includes the entire gamut of Torah restrictions against evil deeds between man and his fellow man (Radak).

The Talmud says that this trait refers specifically to the man who never competes unfairly with his business rivals and never illegally encroaches on their rights.

וְחֶרְפָּה לֹא נָשָׂא — Nor cast [lit. 'take up'] disgrace.
The translation follows Radak and Ibn Ezra.

עַל קְרֹבוֹ — Upon his intimate.
Radak explains that קָרוֹב refers to a closer and more intimate friend than does רֵעֵהוּ, the more common word for friend or neighbor. Although usually translated 'relative', the word קָרוֹב here denotes social intimacy and closeness rather than blood relationship. Now we observe how careful this man is not to transgress a negative command with his tongue. Even if his friends and intimates curse and insult him, he will not retaliate with harsh, ugly words. [Generally, people are freer to insult those who are dear to them rather than those whose displeasure they fear or who are protected by social niceties.]

Rashi interprets this statement dif-

ferently. If this man notices his very close intimate (or relative) committing a sin for which he is liable to a court punishment, he will not overlook it. He will bring the culprit to his just punishment. Thus, no man can later insult this pious man and accuse him of concealing the crimes perpetrated by his close friends. Accordingly, נָשָׂא means 'carry' וְחֶרְפָּה לֹא נָשָׂא עַל קְרֹבוֹ 'He does not carry the disgrace on him of the crimes committed by his close friends.'

According to the Talmud, not only does this man not disgrace his close ones, he goes out of his way to establish even closer relations with them at all times. He is מְקָרֵב אֶת קְרוֹבָיו, 'he draws his near ones even nearer.'

4. נִבְזֶה בְּעֵינָיו נִמְאָס — In whose eyes the despicable is repulsive [i.e. who shows his contempt for the despicable.]

Therefore, he will not falsely flatter and condone such a wicked person (Metzudas David).

Rashi quotes the Talmud (Maccos 24a) which explains that Chizkiyah, King of Judea, best fits this title. His father, King Achaz, was an idolator. When Achaz died, the righteous son gave his father no rites of honor. Instead, he dragged his father's bones on a bed of ropes to display how despicable the wicked were in his eyes, even if it be his own father.

Radak, however, interprets this statement as a description of how this superbly righteous man evaluated himself. He was not proud of his lofty moral accomplishemnts, although a bit of pride would seem to be justified. Rather נִבְזֶה בְּעֵינָיו נִמְאָס, 'he is despicable in his own eyes; repulsive' For, he realizes that no matter how

who has done his friend no evil,
nor cast disgrace upon his intimate;
⁴ *In whose eyes the despicable is repulsive,*
but those who fear HASHEM he honors;
one who does not retract,
though he has sworn to his hurt;
⁵ *Who lends not his money at interest,*

---

much he does, he has not yet accomplished even one thousandth of what he should do in honor of his Creator. *Ibn Ezra* adds: Such is always the custom of the righteous; they are never self-satisfied, rather they constantly strive to go higher and higher on the ladder of sanctity.

וְאֶת יִרְאֵי ה' יְכַבֵּד — *But those who fear HASHEM He honors.*

[Some people, when they find fault with themselves, like to drag others down with them. They attempt to show that just as they are deficient in their service of God, so are all others. This is false humility. In his Thirteen Principles of pure character traits, *Rabbi Yisrael Salanter* describes עֲנָוָה, 'humility', thus: 'To recognize your own shortcomings but to overlook the faults of others.' Although the *tzaddik* is despicable in his own eyes, he sees only the good and praiseworthy virtues in others and finds those who fear Hashem to be honorable and above all reproach.]

The Talmud applies this to Jehoshaphat, King of Judea, who, upon seeing a Torah scholar, would rise from his throne, kiss him, and cry out joyously, 'My father, my father! My master, my master! My teacher, my teacher!'

נִשְׁבַּע לְהָרַע — *[Though] he has sworn to his own hurt* [lit. 'to do bad']

The *tzaddik* pledges to neglect his body through fasting and abstinence from luxuries. Also, he has vowed to deplete his resources by giving large sums to charity. An oath is necessary

because such deprivation is difficult. The righteous person knows that his evil inclination will harass him incessantly in an effort to make him abandon his abstinence. He uses the solemn oath as a means of reinforcing his resolve (*Radak*).

According to the Talmud (*Maccos* 24a) this describes Rabbi Yochanan who avoided the honor of dining at the home of the נָשִׂיא, 'the prince', of Israel. Therefore, he would take an oath not to partake of food until he arrived at his own home. This vow provided him with the fortitude not to eat anywhere else in violation of his principles of humility. [Cf. *Rambam Hilchos Shavuos* 12:12.]

5. כַּסְפּוֹ לֹא נָתַן בְּנֶשֶׁךְ — *Who lends not his money at interest.*

As mentioned, this pious man has not inflicted any form of harm on his friend. He hasn't cheated or robbed. Now David says that he has not taken advantage even of his fellow's full consent and encouragement. An example of this is lending money at interest; a situation where the borrower is eager to get a loan even for a price.

Radak comments that since the Torah bans the taking of interest, it cannot be that David offers such praise to one who simply refrains from what is expressly forbidden. *Radak*, therefore, interprets the verse as a reference to a case where a non-Jew has done a Jew a kindness. As an expression of appreciation, the Jew should present him with a gift — but, our verse tells us, an interest-free loan is preferable because many are

נָקִי לֹא־לָקָח עֲשֵׂה אֵלֶּה לֹא יִמּוֹט
לְעוֹלָם:

ashamed to accept gifts but readily would accept a free loan to help them in their distress. This is the type of kindness referred to here.

This opinion is supported by the Talmud (*Maccos* 24a) which also emphasizes that this man does not take interest even from a gentile, for as *Rashi* (*ibid.*) explains, once you become accustomed to taking interest, you can easily slip into taking it from Jews as well.

וְשֹׁחַד עַל נָקִי לֹא לָקָח — *Nor takes a bribe against the innocent.*

The righteous person refuses to accept a bribe even though the money is given him willingly. The bribe described here is not one which was given for the sake of influencing the judge to distort truth and justice. We already know from *v.* 3 that this *tzaddik* will do no harm or injustice to his fellow man. Rather, the bribe discussed here was offered to the judge to free an innocent man whom he intended to exonerate anyway. Even under such circumstances, the *tzaddik* refuses a bribe (*Radak*).

The Talmud (*Maccos, ibid.*) says that Rabbi Ishmael ben Yose personifies the man who takes every precaution against being influenced by bribes. The following incident is related (*Kesubos* 105b):

XV

nor takes a bribe against the innocent.
Whoever does these shall forever not falter.

Rabbi Ishmael ben Yose had a sharechopper who brought him a basket of fruits every Friday as payment. Once, the sharecropper brought the fruits on Thursday. Rabbi Ishmael asked why he had altered his routine. The sharecropper explained that he had to appear before Rabbi Ishmael's court that day in any case and, therefore, brought the basket with him. Rabbi Ishmael refused to accept the fruits even though they were his. He felt that this kindness done him in advancing payment by a day might influence him in favor of the sharecropper and as such would constitute bribery.

עָשָׂה אֵלֶּה לֹא יִמּוֹט לְעוֹלָם — *Whoever does these things shall forever not*

falter.

Even if he would by chance falter, his collapse will not be forever. He collapses and rebounds to climb high once again *(Rashi).*

Even after death he will not fall, because his soul will dwell in a place of celestial glory *(Radak).*

When Rabban Gamliel would come to this passage, he would weep saying: 'Does this mean that only one who performed *all* these shall not falter, but if he performed but one of them he still may falter?' Whereupon Rabbi Akiva said that even one who performs one of these is safeguarded, for it does not say עָשָׂה כָּל אֵלֶּה, he who does 'all' of these; instead it says עָשָׂה אֵלֶּה, 'he who does [even one] of these' *(Maccos, ibid.).*

16 מזמור טז

*I*n this psalm we find eloquent expression of David's humility, a virtue which crowned him majestically.

Strength, Torah, and humility — all three could be found in David (Midrash Shocher Tov 18:28).

David's eyes wre always cast downward for he feared to look upwards out of awe before God in heaven. When he walked in the midst of his subjects his heart was never lifted with pride (Zohar).

When God told David that He had chosen him to be king, David prostrated himself before God, and cried, 'I have done nothing worthy; all of my accomplishments were entirely Your doing' (Tanna d'Bei Eliyahu 18).

Taking no credit for himself, David appreciated everything granted him, finding happiness in every moment of life. Portions have fallen to me in pleasant places, indeed, my estate was lovely to me (v. 6).

Aching with a constant yearning for God's Presence, David looks forward to eternal bliss when he will savor the fullness of joys in Your Presence. There is delight at Your right hand for eternity (v. 11).

א מִכְתָּם לְדָוִד שָׁמְרֵנִי אֵל כִּי־חָסִיתִי בָךְ:
ב אָמַרְתְּ לַיהוה אֲדֹנָי אָתָּה טוֹבָתִי בַּל־
ג עָלֶיךָ: לִקְדוֹשִׁים אֲשֶׁר־בָּאָרֶץ הֵמָּה
ד וְאַדִּירֵי כָּל־חֶפְצִי־בָם: יִרְבּוּ עַצְּבוֹתָם
אַחֵר מָהָרוּ בַּל־אַסִּיךְ נִסְכֵּיהֶם מִדָּם וּבַל־

1. מִכְתָּם — *A Michtam.*

Rashi offers a number of explanations for this word. He maintains that the מִכְתָּם was a special musical arrangement for this psalm. [*Radak* in his comm. to 4:1 describes the מִכְתָּם *Michtam* as a unique instrument.]

Rashi also suggests as an alternate translation 'a crown'. David was accustomed to constantly repeat the following plea: 'Protect me, O God, for in You I take refuge' until it enveloped and encircled him like a crown.

Ibn Ezra relates מִכְתָּם to כֶּתֶם as in רֹאשׁוֹ כֶּתֶם פָּז, 'His head is the finest gold' (*Songs* 5:11), hence this title describes this psalm as being an extraordinarily fine and significant composition.

[The Talmud homiletically renders מִכְתָּם as two words: מָךְ, *humble*, and תָּם, *innocent*, i.e. David was humble and small to all, and perfectly innocent with all. Furthermore, just as in the days before his ascendancy to the throne he belittled himself before his Torah masters, so did he continue to belittle himself even after he was king (*Sotah* 10b).

Bearing this interpretation in mind, we can bring all the aforementioned interpretations together. The lesson that even the mightiest of kings must humble himself in the recognition that all is from Hashem, is the most precious lesson of David's career. Thus it resembles כֶּתֶם פָּז, 'the finest of fine gold'. Hence, this psalm deserved an especially wonderful melody to be accompanied by the most splendid of instruments, all called מִכְתָּם because of their exceptional quality.]

שָׁמְרֵנִי אֵל כִּי חָסִיתִי בָךְ — *Protect me, O God for in You have I taken refuge.*

In You and in no other (*Radak*).

Even if a person lacks good deeds, thus not meriting divine protection by their virtue, the mere fact that he returns only to God for salvation makes him deserving of God's protection (*S'fas Emes*).

2. אָמַרְתְּ לַה׳ — *You have said to HASHEM.*

The word אָמַרְתְּ, is in the feminine gender for David is addressing his soul (a feminine word) (*Rashi; Metzudas David*).

Rashi also suggests that David is talking to כְּנֶסֶת יִשְׂרָאֵל, the 'Congregation of Israel', and it is they who have made the following testimony to Hashem.

אֲדֹנָי אָתָּה — *You are my Master.*

I admit that You are my sole Master and that I am obligated to serve You and to succumb before You (*Ibn Ezra; Metzudas David; Radak*).

טוֹבָתִי — *To benefit me* [lit. 'my good'].

בַּל עָלֶיךָ — *You are not obliged* [lit. 'is not upon you']

Since I am no more than a servant who must obey, I do not deserve any reward for serving You. Anything good which You do is sheer חֶסֶד, 'kindness' (*Rashi; Radak; Metzudas David*). [Again, David in his humility takes no credit for his good deeds.] This is similar to *Pirkei Avos* (1:5): 'Do not be like servants who serve for the sake of receiving a reward' (*Ibn Ezra*).

Radak cites his father's interpreta-

A Michtam of David.

Protect me, O God, for in You have I taken refuge.
² You have said to HASHEM, 'You are my Master,
You are not obliged to benefit me.'
³ [But] for the holy ones who are in the earth,
for the mighty — all my desires are due to them.
⁴ May their sorrows multiply,
they who hurry after another;
I shall not pour out their libations of blood,

---

tion: טוֹבָתִי — 'My good', i.e. the good deeds which I perform; בַּל עָלֶיךָ — 'is not near You' i.e. they do not affect You for how can my actions be of consequence to You?'

3. לִקְדוֹשִׁים אֲשֶׁר בָּאָרֶץ הֵמָּה — [But] for the [sake of] the holy ones who are [buried] in the earth.

'I also realize that the kindness You have shown me is for the sake of those holy men who once walked before You with sincerity and who are now buried in the earth (Rashi).

This is a continuation of the testimony of the soul which began in the previous verse. Just as the soul bends before Hashem, it must likewise give recognition to the holy men of early times and follow their example, because emulation of their ways will lead to new heights of love for God (Radak).

וְאַדִּירֵי — [And] for the mighty.
I.e. those who were mighty in their fear of Hashem (Metzudas David).

כָּל חֶפְצִי בָם — All my desires are due to them [lit. 'all of my desire is in them'].

All of my desires and needs are fulfilled in their merit (Rashi; Metzudas David).

My one and only desire is to be like them (Ibn Ezra).

4. יִרְבּוּ עַצְּבוֹתָם — May their sorrows multiply.

David now says to God: May sor-

rows multiply for all who deny Your sovereignty (Rashi).

[The opposite is true of those who follow Hashem: בִּרְכַּת ה' הִיא תַעֲשִׁיר וְלֹא יוֹסִף עֶצֶב עִמָּה 'The blessing of HASHEM, it enriches, and no sorrows will increase with it' (Proverbs 10:22).]

אַחֵר — Another, i.e., another god.

מָהָרוּ — They [who] hurry.
The translation follows Rashi and Radak. Others offer another translation of מָהָרוּ relating it to מוֹהַר 'the bride's dowry' as in כְּמֹהַר הַבְּתוּלֹת — 'the dowry of virgins' (Exodus 22:16). Metzudas David explains: These men pay a costly price to their other gods because they futilely offer many sacrifices. But they do not realize that as they increase their sacrifices, You multiply their sorrows.

בַּל אַסִּיךְ נִסְכֵּיהֶם מִדָּם — I shall not pour out their libations of blood. I will not follow their example and sprinkle blood offerings in honor of the idol (Rashi).

נִסְכֵּיהֶם — Their libations. Libations are customarily poured with wine. They, however, offer stolen blood instead. Evil deeds render burnt sacrifices meaningless despite all their libations (Radak).

Hirsch explains that it is akin to spiritual suicide to offer sacrifices to natural forces because it is a denial of man's similarity to God, a quality which raises him high above nature. Of the sacrifice presented improperly the

ה אֶשָּׂא אֶת־שְׁמוֹתָם עַל־שְׂפָתָי: יְהוָה
מְנָת־חֶלְקִי וְכוֹסִי אַתָּה תּוֹמִיךְ גּוֹרָלִי:
ו חֲבָלִים נָפְלוּ־לִי בַּנְּעִמִים אַף־נַחֲלָת
שָׁפְרָה עָלָי: ז אֲבָרֵךְ אֶת־יְהוָה אֲשֶׁר יְעָצָנִי
ח אַף־לֵילוֹת יִסְּרוּנִי כִלְיוֹתָי: שִׁוִּיתִי יְהוָה

Torah writes דָּם יֵחָשֵׁב לָאִישׁ הַהוּא דָּם שָׁפָךְ, 'blood will be attributed to that man, he has shed blood' (Lev. 17:4).

וּבַל אֶשָּׂא אֶת שְׁמוֹתָם עַל שְׂפָתָי — Nor [shall I] carry their names upon my lips.

Not only will I not sacrifice to their idols, I will not even mention their names (Rashi; Metzudas David).

I will not even mention the names of the idol worshippers (Radak).

5. [David now emphasizes that he has taken God as his only fortune in life, not like those who seek material forms of worldly success].

מְנָת חֶלְקִי וְכוֹסִי — My allotted portion and my share.

The translation follows Malbim who is of the opinion that כּוֹס in this verse does not mean 'cup' but, 'share'. It is what a person has actually prepared for himself as we find תָּכֹסּוּ עַל הַשֶּׂה you shall count [i.e. prepare] your shares for the lamb (Exodus 12:4). He continues to explain that חֶלְקִי (when used as a noun) means 'my allotment,' which fell to me without my effort or intervention. A גּוֹרָל, 'lot,' also demands no effort, however, it differs from the חֵלֶק in this way. חֲלָקִים, 'allotments' are first precisely measured for uniformity and then disbursed to all recipients equally,

but things which fall by גּוֹרָל, 'lot' can be distributed unevenly to the recipients, some getting more and some less.[1]

אַתָּה תּוֹמִיךְ גּוֹרָלִי — You guided my destiny [lit. 'you supported my lot.']

Rashi offers two translations for תּוֹמִיךְ. The word indicates that Hashem guided David's hand to his proper lot. It can mean 'you put down' as in יִמַּךְ הַמְּקָרֶה, 'the rafters fall down' (Ecc. 10:18). Here, too, God put my hand down on my good lot. Or it can mean 'to uplift, to support', as in וַיִּתְמֹךְ יַד אָבִיו 'and he lifted up his father's hand' (Genesis 48:17). God lifted my hand and guided it in the direction of my lot. This is like the father who has one son whom he favors above all the others. He places his hand on the best portion and says, 'Here, choose this one for yourself'.

Metzudas David explains the intent of David's words: 'Hashem You have inspired me and aroused within my soul the desire to place my faith only in You!'

Radak further comments as to why David was worthy of this: This is as the Sages of the Talmud say: (Yoma 38b) הַבָּא לְטַהֵר מְסַיְיעִין אוֹתוֹ 'He who comes to purify himself, receives heavenly assistance'.

1. 'Each and every man who has come into this world, if his spirit will inspire him and if his intellect will give him understanding, has the opportunity to separate himself to stand before God to attend and serve Him. If he will truly understand God and follow the straight path and remain as God has originally made him; if he will cast off his neck the burden of the many contrivances and calculations which men seek out, then, indeed, this man will be truly sacred, a holy of holies, and God will be his portion and his estate forever and for all eternity. In this world he will be allotted an amount which will suffice for his needs just as God has provided amply for the priests and the Levites. This is as David, of blessed memory said: 'HASHEM is my share, You guided my destiny' (Rambam, Shmita V'Yovel 13:13).

XVI
5-7

nor carry their names upon my lips.
⁵ *HASHEM is my allotted portion and my share,*
You guided my destiny.
⁶ *Portions have fallen to me in pleasant places,*
indeed, my estate was lovely to me.
⁷ *I will bless HASHEM who has advised me,*
even in the nights my intellect rebuked me.

[Although a cardinal rule of Jewish theology is the existence of בְּחִירָה חָפְשִׁית, 'free will', this means only that Hashem does not force men to act in a certain way, leaving them with no power of self-determination. However, He does help to influence someone after a man has made the decision to go in a particular direction. If the man is himself inclined to repent and return to God, God will certainly help him to accomplish this worthy goal and plant in his heart the courage and fortitude to overcome all obstacles.]

6. חֲבָלִים — *Portions.* [lit. *'ropes'*] Sections of land are called חֲבָלִים, because they are measured off and demarcated with ropes. *(Metzudas Zion).*

'Where do we find that Israel is the portion of God? As it is written: כִּי יַעֲקֹב בָּחַר לוֹ יָהּ 'for HASHEM has chosen Jacob for Himself' (Psalms 135:4). כִּי חֵלֶק ה' עַמּוֹ יַעֲקֹב חֶבֶל נַחֲלָתוֹ 'For HASHEM's share is His nation, Jacob is the portion of His estate' (Deut. 32:9 Sifrei ibid.).

נָפְלוּ לִי בַּנְּעִמִים — *Have fallen to me in pleasant places.* When it fell to my lot that You, Hashem, would be my share in life, this was indeed a most pleasant portion to receive *(Rashi).*

אַף — *Indeed.* [lit. *'even'*].

[This word is used here for emphasis because David is really repeating that which was already said in his first statement.]

נַחֲלָת — *My estate.* The letter ת is substituted for the customary ה in נַחֲלָה, 'estate' *(Radak).*

שָׁפְרָה עָלָי — *Was lovely to me.* I envy not any other person's portion for I find mine to be perfectly suitable and sufficient for me *(Radak).*

7. אֲבָרֵךְ אֶת ה' אֲשֶׁר יְעָצָנִי — *I will bless HASHEM Who has advised me.* It was He who guided me in choosing my lot and taking Him for my God *(Radak; Metzudas David).*

Rashi who is of the opinion that until now David was speaking in reference to כְּנֶסֶת יִשְׂרָאֵל, 'the congregation of Israel' (see *comm.* verse 2) says that David has now ended that phase of the psalm and here begins to speak of himself. 'I, too, will bless God who advised me to choose life and to follow in His ways.'

אַף לֵילוֹת — *Even in the nights.* Night is when one can escape the affairs of the world and go into private solitude. Then his thoughts are undisturbed *(Ibn Ezra; Radak; Metzudas David).*

According to *Radak,* אַף לֵילוֹת, 'even in the nights' refers back to אֲשֶׁר יְעָצָנִי, 'Who has advised me' meaning that Hashem's advice and guidance came to me first at night when my mind was uncluttered.

כִּלְיוֹתָי — *My intellect.* [lit. *'my kidneys'.* See *comm.* Psalm 7:10].

Radak continues: and even by day, at all times, my own intellect incessantly rebuked me to follow Hashem's advice

ט לְנֶגְדִּי תָמִיד כִּי מִימִינִי בַּל־אֶמּוֹט: לָכֵן |
שָׂמַח לִבִּי וַיָּגֶל כְּבוֹדִי אַף־בְּשָׂרִי יִשְׁכֹּן
י לָבֶטַח: כִּי | לֹא־תַעֲזֹב נַפְשִׁי לִשְׁאוֹל לֹא־

and to cling to His way tenaciously with all my might.

However, according to *Metzudas David*, אַף לֵילוֹת, is linked together with יִסְּרוּנִי כִלְיוֹתָי. 'It was at night, when my mind was undisturbed, that my intellect began to reprimand me.'

8. שִׁוִּיתִי — *I have set.*

I.e. I am always aware.

Hirsch traces the root of the word to שָׁוָה, *'to smooth out, to even out'*. In Isaiah 28:25 we find the term שִׁוָּה פָנֶיהָ, meaning *'to level an expanse of soil'*, to remove all unevenness from its surface. David declares that he has leveled out any obstruction to his clear, straight vision of Hashem's presence. Furthermore, there are those who labor under the delusion that God must be conceived as a towering figure far above and removed from the lowly earthly sphere and who cares little if any for petty human affairs. 'But as for me', says David, 'I clearly perceive God's presence on the level of my own earthly existence. I need not seek him high above in concealed heights. I have set Him before my eyes in everything I do on earth. Nothing here below is too small or insignificant for Him.'

ה' לְנֶגְדִּי תָמִיד — *HASHEM before me always.*

It is as if He was positioned directly in front of me so that I cannot take my eyes and my thoughts off Him even for a moment (*Radak*).

The *Baal Shem Tov* derives שִׁוִּיתִי from שָׁוֶה *'equal'*. Thus, שִׁוִּיתִי — *'I have made all things even and equal.'* In assessing the events of my life, I accept and appreciate everything which happens to me with complete detachment. It makes no difference whether it is 'good' or 'bad'. Why? Because ה'

לְנֶגְדִּי תָמִיד, *'Hashem is before me always'*. In every single occurrence I clearly see the guiding hand of Hashem who, without a doubt, always does what is best for me even though I do not always see why. Therefore, all things are equally 'for the best'.]

Rambam, in the *'Guide'*, finds in our verse some of the most essential philosophies of Judaism. *Rambam's* interpretation of our verse is quoted by *Rama* in the opening words of his gloss on *Shulchan Aruch* (*Orach Chaim* 1:1).

David says: *'I have set HASHEM before me always, because He is at my right hand, I shall not falter.'* I do not turn my thoughts away from God. He is like my right hand, which I never can forget even for a moment. This is an essential principle for all of the Torah and for achieving the lofty heights of the righteous. For we do not sit, move, and occupy ourselves when we are alone at home in the same manner we do in the presence of the king. We speak and open our mouths as we please when we are with the people of our own household and our own relatives, but not so when we are in a royal assembly. If we desire to attain human perfection and to be truly men of God, we must awaken from our sleep and bear in mind that the great King Who is always over us and is always joined to us is greater than any earthly king, greater than David and Solomon. His glory fills the world and He perceives our every deed. When the perfect bear this in mind, they will be filled with the fear of God, humility and purity; with a true — not merely an apparent — reverence and respect for God.'

כִּי מִימִינִי בַּל אֶמּוֹט — *Because He is at my right hand I shall not falter.*

Because I never cease to con-

8 *I have set HASHEM before me always,*
   because He is at my right hand I shall not falter.
9 *Therefore, my heart rejoices and my soul is elated,*
   my flesh, too, rests in confidence.
10 *Because You will not abandon my soul*
   to the lower world,

centrate my thoughts on Hashem; He in turn never leaves me, and He is always at my right side assuring me that His support will prevent me from every fall (*Metzudas David*).

Rashi, however, interprets: 'Because God is always at my right side to aid me [and He never falters], therefore, I keep His Presence before my view always.'[1]

9. לָכֵן — *Therefore.*

I.e. because I have set You before me always (*Radak*).

I have good cause for this confidence that you will not let me fall, for, even after I sinned with Bath Sheba, You still accepted my repentance and informed me of it through Nathan the Prophet (*Rashi*).

לִבִּי — *My heart.*

This refers to the intellect (*Radak; Ibn Ezra*).

It rejoices in complete confidence that its desires will be fulfilled (*Metzudas David*).

וַיָּגֶל — *Is elated.* [see *comm.* to 14:7]

כְּבוֹדִי — *My soul.* [lit. *'my honor'*]

It is called כָּבוֹד, because it is the glory and the honor of the body. I am confident that when my soul departs from my body it will cleave unto its Maker (*Radak*).

Malbim here calls our attention to the difference between שִׂמְחָה and גִיל (already discussed in *comm.* to 14:7). Ordinarily, שִׂמְחָה 'constant joy', fol-

lows a burst of גִיל, *'elation'*. Here, however, first, שָׂמַח לִבִּי, *my heart rejoices* constantly because it always manages to steadily overcome the evil inclination. Then, וַיָּגֶל כְּבוֹדִי, *my soul is elated* because it is climbing higher and higher and experiences new thrills of spiritual rapture from time to time.

בְּשָׂרִי — *My flesh.*

I.e. the body (*Ibn Ezra*).

יִשְׁכֹּן לָבֶטַח — *Rests in confidence.* [lit. *'will rest in confidence'*]

It will be calm and tranquil because it is fused to a higher, all mighty force and this will preserve the body from all sickness no matter what changes occur in the future (*Ibn Ezra*).

This refers to the body while living. However, the Sages learned from here that even after death, David's flesh was undisturbed and untouched by worms and decay (*Radak*).

[Actually, a Talmudic debate exists on this point (*Bava Basra* 17a): 'There were seven people whose bodies were untouched by decay and worms, Abraham, Isaac, Jacob, Moses, Aaron, Miriam, and Benjamin. Some include David, as he said, *'my flesh, too, rests in confidence'*. However, others maintain that this was merely a request not a prophecy, and there is no evidence that his request was fulfilled.]

10. כִּי לֹא תַעֲזֹב נַפְשִׁי לִשְׁאוֹל — *Because You will not abandon my soul to the lower world.*

1. 'The king must possess two Torah scrolls, one he guards in his treasure room, the other he takes with him wherever he goes. He attaches it to his arm like a charm and from there it hangs at all times, as it says: *'I have set HASHEM before me always, because He is at my right hand I shall not falter'* (*Sanhedrin* 21b).

יא תִּתֵּן °חֲסִידֶיךָ לִרְאוֹת שָׁחַת: תּוֹדִיעֵנִי
אֹרַח חַיִּים שֹׂבַע שְׂמָחוֹת אֶת־פָּנֶיךָ
נְעִמוֹת בִּימִינְךָ נֶצַח:

°חֲסִידְךָ ק'

Having explained why his flesh rests in confidence, David now explains why his soul is elated by the prospect of death (Ibn Ezra).

For, although my body will be deposited in the earth, my soul will not follow it in that direction, to sink down into the grave and the lower world. You will certainly lift up my soul to the place of Your glory (Radak).

לֹא תִתֵּן חֲסִידְךָ לִרְאוֹת שָׁחַת — Nor allow your devout one to witness Destruction.

A repetition of the previous thought couched in different terms (Radak, Metzudas David).

Malbim notes that שָׁחַת in Scriptures usually refers to premature death as in: וְאַתָּה אֱלֹהִים תּוֹרִדֵם לִבְאֵר שַׁחַת אַנְשֵׁי דָמִים וּמִרְמָה לֹא יֶחֱצוּ יְמֵיהֶם 'And You O God shall lower them to the pit of destruction, men of blood and deceit they shall not live out half their days' (55:24).

Rabbi Yehoshua ben Levi said that שַׁחַת is one of seven names for Gehinnom: שְׁאוֹל, אֲבַדּוֹן, בְּאֵר שַׁחַת, בּוֹר שָׁאוֹן, טִיט הַיָּוֵן צַלְמָוֶת, אֶרֶץ תַּחְתִּית. The name בְּאֵר שַׁחַת, is derived from our verse (Eruvin 19a).

11. תּוֹדִיעֵנִי — You will reveal to me.

According to Rashi this is neither a prayer nor a request. It is a prophetic statement about the future of the soul.

Ibn Ezra further explains that when the soul departs the body, God will reveal to it the path by which to ascend to the heavens to be with the celestial angels. The revelation can be made to the soul only after it rids itself of the mundane cares of this lower world and is free to see the truth eye to eye and face to face.

However, Radak and Metzudas David do interpret this as a request and a prayer for the immediate future. According to them, תּוֹדִיעֵנִי, means תֵּן, 'endow me with the wisdom' to know חַיִּים אֹרַח, 'the proper course of life to follow throughout my lifetime', so that my soul will merit eternal bliss in the Hereafter.

שֹׂבַע שְׂמָחוֹת — The fullness of joys. [lit. 'the satisfaction and contentment of all joys']

This is the joy that has no limit and no end; the joy of the future (Rashi).

Metzudas David adds that this joy is described by the Sages (Berachos 17a) in

*Nor allow Your devout one
to witness destruction.*
¹¹ *You will reveal to me the path to life,
the fullness of joys in Your Presence.
There is delight at Your right hand for eternity.*

glowing terms: 'The righteous will sit with their crowns on their heads and enjoy the bliss of beholding the splendor of the Holy Presence!'

In a number of places the Sages say that in a homiletical sense the word שֹׂבַע, *'fullness'*, should be read as שֶׁבַע, *'seven'*, for seven denotes the achievement of a full spectrum of spiritual good. For instance: 'This refers to the seven categories of righteous men who are destined to behold God's Presence.' Another explanation: This refers to the seven foremost divisions of Torah: Pentateuch, Prophets, Writings, Mishnah, Tosefta, Gemara, Aggadah *(Shocher Tov).*

Or, this refers to the Festival of Succos which is filled with seven joyous commandments: the four species, the succah, the Chagigah sacrifice, and the sacrifice of rejoicing *(Vayikra Rabba 30:2).*

אֶת פָּנֶיךָ — *In Your presence.*
Accord to me the unique joy of being in the select group of those who sit closest to God *(Rashi).*

נְעִמוֹת — [There is] *delight* [lit. *'delights']*

I.e. the special pleasures of the revelations of the World to Come *(Metzudas David).*

בִּימִינְךָ — *At your right hand* [lit. *'in Your right hand'].*
This may be likened to the benefactor who presents delightful gifts with his right hand to his favorite *(Ibn Ezra).*

Radak explains that פָּנֶיךָ, *'in Your immediate Presence'* and בִּימִינְךָ, *'at Your right hand'* are the most distinguished positions of honor that a righteous man can hope to attain before Hashem.

נֶצַח — *For eternity.*
The gifts of divine revelation will never cease. Thus, we have in this psalm a complete picture of the future reward of the righteous *(Ibn Ezra).*

Malbim concludes: The word נֶצַח describes the eternal existence of spiritual forces which are totally divorced from the limitations of time and far above it. That which is endless, only relative to the confines of this lower world of time, is called לְעוֹלָם, *'forever'.*

17 מזמור יז

David composed this Psalm after commanding Yoav to bring about the death of Uriah, the husband of Bath Sheba. The army was then in the land of Ammon, besieging the capital, Rabbat (II Samuel, Ch. 11).

At this moment, when Israel's military security hung in the balance, David, the humble penintent feared that the army might be struck by catastrophe because of his personal sins. In the event of such a calamity, David knew that the evil neighbors of Israel — the Philistines, Moab, Edom, all would swiftly seize the opportunity to pounce on the crippled nation, and so he prayed fervently.

Mahari Yaavetz HaDoresh explains the connection between this Psalm and the preceding one. In Psalm 16, David speaks in ecstasy of his assured portion in the World to Come and he looks forward to the delights of 'the fullness of joys in God's presence' and the 'delights at God's right hand forever' (verse 11). But after he sinned, doubts about his spiritual hereafter started to crop up in his mind. In this Psalm which he composed after he repented his sin, David pleads for a return to full grace and affection before HASHEM. He ends with great confidence that his intimacy with God has been restored and his hereafter is secure: 'In righteousness I shall behold Your face, upon awakening I will be made satisfied by Your form' (verse 15).

א תְּפִלָּה לְדָוִד שִׁמְעָה יהוה ׀ צֶדֶק הַקְשִׁיבָה
רִנָּתִי הַאֲזִינָה תְפִלָּתִי בְּלֹא שִׂפְתֵי מִרְמָה:
ב מִלְּפָנֶיךָ מִשְׁפָּטִי יֵצֵא עֵינֶיךָ תֶּחֱזֶינָה
ג מֵישָׁרִים: בָּחַנְתָּ לִבִּי ׀ פָּקַדְתָּ לַּיְלָה
צְרַפְתַּנִי בַל־תִּמְצָא זַמֹּתִי בַּל־יַעֲבָר־פִּי:
ד לִפְעֻלּוֹת אָדָם בִּדְבַר שְׂפָתֶיךָ אֲנִי שָׁמַרְתִּי
ה אָרְחוֹת פָּרִיץ: תָּמֹךְ אֲשֻׁרַי בְּמַעְגְּלוֹתֶיךָ

1. שִׁמְעָה ה׳ צֶדֶק — *Hear, HASHEM what is righteous.*

Hear me for my words are righteous and I know You will not listen to falsehood (*Ibn Ezra*).

רִנָּתִי — *My cry* [lit. *'my raised voice, my shout'.*]

The word can be used in a number of ways, as shouting in prayer or shouting out a declaration or wailing aloud (*Radak*). [See *comm.* to 33:1.]

בְּלֹא שִׂפְתֵי מִרְמָה — *From lips without deceit.* [lit. *'without lips of deceit'*], i.e, from my lips which convey the true feelings of my heart (*Radak*).[1]

2. מִלְּפָנֶיךָ מִשְׁפָּטִי יֵצֵא — *May my judgment be dismissed* [lit. *'go away'*] *from before You.*

Radak quotes his father who renders יֵצֵא in the lit. sense of *go away*, and explains that David composed this prayer in connection with the incident of Bath Sheba. David requests of HASHEM that He should not bring this case up before His tribunal for judgment, but should dismiss it instead.

עֵינֶיךָ תֶּחֱזֶינָה מֵישָׁרִים — *May your eyes behold uprightness.*

David dares request such an absolution from guilt because of the many upright deeds he has performed which should merit him a lenient acquittal. *'May Your eyes behold [my] uprightness'* and be oblivious to my sins (*Radak*).

3. בָּחַנְתָּ לִבִּי — *You have examined my heart.*

You have already tested and examined my heart and found it lacking, therefore, I know that if you will try my case in your tribunal of justice I will be condemned because of my sins (*Rashi*).

פָּקַדְתָּ לַּיְלָה — *[You have] been mindful* [lit. *'made inspection'*] *by night.*

At night, You inspected me through the incident with Bath Sheba as it says: *'And it came to pass at evening time and David arose from his bed and walked upon the roof of the king's house and from the roof he saw a woman bathing, and the woman was very beautiful to look upon'* (II Samuel 11:2) (*Rashi*).

The night is the ideal time to inspect the true, undisturbed feelings of the heart for then it is free from the external interference of daily cares (*Radak; Metzudas David*).

1. *Midrash Shocher Tov* notes five separate statements in this one verse. (*'A prayer'*, *'O hear'*, *'attend'*, *'give ear'*, *'from lips without deceit'*) and ponders the significance of this number.

Why did David include five statements in this introductory verse and then follow these with *'may my judgments be dismissed'* (v. 2)?

David said: O God if You will judge me early on the Day of Atonement, Yom Kippur, I cannot possibly survive. But after I have recited the Shema and offered the four prayers (Shacharis, Musaf, Minchah, Neilah), I then ask: *'May my judgment be dismissed from before You.'*

XVII
1-5

A prayer of David:
 Hear, HASHEM, what is righteous,
   attend to my cry.
Give ear to my prayer from lips without deceit.
² May my judgment be dismissed from before You;
   Your eyes behold uprightness
³ You have examined my heart,
   been mindful by night,
   have tested me without success.
May my scheming no more cross my lips.
⁴ That human deeds accord with the word
   of Your lips,
I warily guarded lawbreakers' paths.
⁵ Let my steps be steadfast in Your circuits,

צְרַפְתָּנִי — *You have tested me (following Rashi)* [lit. 'You have put me through the refining process,'] i.e., purged me.

בַּל תִּמְצָא — *Without success* [lit. You will not find.']. You did not find that which You sought (*Rashi*). You did not find me to be completely free of flaw (*Radak*).

זַמֹּתִי — *My scheming.*

This refers to deep thoughts and intricately fabricated plans. In most cases these thoughts are evil ones because once a person makes elaborate, complicated machinations straying from innocence and simplicity, he is bound to become ensnared in some crooked scheme (*Malbim*).

בַּל יַעֲבָר פִּי — *No more cross my lips.*

May such presumptous ideas no longer be uttered by my mouth (*Radak*).

Rashi here quotes the 'presumptuous words' to which David was referring as recorded by the *Talmud* (*Sanhedrin* 107a):

'Rav Yehuda said in the name of Rav: A person should never bring a test upon himself, for David, King of Israel brought himself to trial and he failed. He once asked of God: Why in prayer do the people say 'The God of

Abraham, the God of Isaac, the God of Jacob' and they do not say, 'the God of David'? God replied, 'They were tested and you were. David pleaded: בְּחָנֵנִי ה' וְנַסֵּנִי, '*Examine me HASHEM and put me to the test*' (*Psalm 26:2*).

After David failed the test in the incident with Bath Sheba he remorsefully recited this verse regretting his presumptuous request. [See *Overview*.]

4. בִּדְבַר שְׂפָתֶיךָ אֲנִי שָׁמַרְתִּי — *The word of Your lips I warily guarded.*

According to *Rashi*, this means that David watched his own actions carefully. However, *Radak* explains this to mean that he supervised the deeds of others to prevent them from erring.

Ibn Ezra adds that this was spurred by David's great love of HASHEM which made it unbearable for him to witness others treading upon HASHEM's commands.

אָרְחוֹת פָּרִיץ — *The lawbreakers' paths.* Although I once broke the law myself in regard to the commandment לֹא תִנְאָף 'You shall not commit adultery,' from then on I have taken care not to stray (*Rashi*).

5. בְּמַעְגְּלוֹתֶיךָ — *In Your circuits.*

יז
ו-י

ו בַּל־נָמוֹטוּ פְעָמָי: אֲנִי־קְרָאתִיךָ כִי־תַעֲנֵנִי
ז אֵל הַט־אָזְנְךָ לִי שְׁמַע אִמְרָתִי: הַפְלֵה
חֲסָדֶיךָ מוֹשִׁיעַ חוֹסִים מִמִּתְקוֹמְמִים
ח בִּימִינֶךָ: שָׁמְרֵנִי כְּאִישׁוֹן בַּת־עָיִן בְּצֵל
ט כְּנָפֶיךָ תַּסְתִּירֵנִי: מִפְּנֵי רְשָׁעִים זוּ שַׁדּוּנִי
י אֹיְבַי בְּנֶפֶשׁ יַקִּיפוּ עָלָי: חֶלְבָּמוֹ סָגְרוּ

מַעְגָּל is a circular path circumscribing our acts to prevent us from leaving the bounds of God's law *(Hirsch)*.

Malbim explains that although a person should always strive to keep to the straight path, there are times when an emergency demands that a roundabout path be taken. For example, the proper and straight path is mercy and humility. However, there are times when one must employ force, pride, and audacity in combatting the terrible menace of the wicked, especially when repelling those who viciously mock and ridicule the Torah. But this path is treacherous. One can easily stray from uprightness forever if he is not wary. Therefore David pleads for special support on these 'circuits', so that his steps remain straight and so that his feet should not falter.

[The case at hand, the incident of David, Bath Sheba and Uriah, is a classic example of a righteous man who pursued a circuitous path in order to achieve upright aspirations, and strayed in the process [see *Overview*.]

נָמוֹטוּ — *Falter*, i.e., stumble and totter on the verge of falling.

6. כִּי תַעֲנֵנִי אֵל — *Because You will answer me, O God.*

Because I trust in Your willingness and ability to respond, I called out to you *(Radak)*.[1]

7. הַפְלֵה חֲסָדֶיךָ — *Withdraw* [lit. 'separate'] *Your kindness.*

Withdraw Your kindness from the wicked who do not deserve it *(Radak)*.

מוֹשִׁיעַ חוֹסִים — *O savior of those who seek refuge.*

It is only fitting that You should reserve Your kindness exclusively for those who seek refuge in You and not for the wicked who ignore You *(Metzudas David)*.

מִמִּתְקוֹמְמִים בִּימִינֶךָ — *From those who rise up against Your right hand.*

Show them that the monarchy truly belongs to me and that those who challenge me are challenging You *(Radak)*.

8. כְּאִישׁוֹן בַּת עָיִן — *'As the apple* [or: 'pupil'] *of Your eye'.* This refers to the dark part of the eye which controls vision because the light enters through it. Because it appears to be black it is called אִישׁוֹן a synonym for חֹשֶׁךְ, darkness.

1. David said to the Holy One, Blessed be He: 'If not for Your support, I could not have stood up in this world!' To what can this be likened? — To a very tall [and shaky] ladder which has a precious crown at its top. The king proclaimed, 'Whoever can climb up to the top shall have the crown!'

The first man to make an attempt climbed only two rungs and slipped down. The second man met the same fate — and so did the third.

Along came a wise man. When he got to the second rung, he too began to fall, but he cried out 'My king, my master, please hasten to my aid!' The king responded, 'Had I offered such help to the first men, they would not have fallen down and died!'

'The difference is this,' the wise man explained. 'The others did not call out to you, but I do. Please come to my aid and save me!'

Similarly, the Evil Inclination is like that ladder. The Generation of the Flood came — and

so that my feet will not falter.
⁶ I have called out to You,
because You will answer me, O God;
Bend Your ear to me,
hear my saying.
⁷ Withdraw Your kindness,
O Savior of those who seek refuge,
From those who rise up against Your right hand.
⁸ Guard me as the apple of Your eye,
in the shadow of Your wings hide me
⁹ from the wicked who have plundered me.
The enemies who threaten my soul surround me.

The Holy One Blessed be He has prepared a wonderful protection for this sensitive pupil, the eyelid and the lashes which always cover it. [Thus David asks to be protected in the same constant fashion] (Rashi).

Radak and Metzudas David also translate אִישׁוֹן as pupil, but they trace the root of the word to אִישׁ, 'a man'. The suffix וֹן is added to Hebrew words in order to express amplification of the main word, such as in the word שַׁבָּתוֹן which denotes a more intense and increased sanctity of the ordinary שַׁבָּת, rest. Or, וֹן may be appended in order to express diminution, such as in the word אִישׁוֹן which means 'a small man.' For, if you look into someone's eyes you will see your own reflection appearing like a small man.

[Harav Gifter derives from this a moral lesson: Most people observe others for the sake of finding fault with them, thus boosting their own egos by feeling smug and superior. This is not the proper way. Rather, when you look at someone else you should see only yourself, realizing what an אִישׁוֹן, a 'small man', you are compared to your neighbor.]

Hirsch maintains that בַּת עַיִן is synonymous with בָּבַת עַיִן as in Zechariah 2:12. The word בָּבָא in Chaldean (Aramaic) means a 'gate' and, therefore, the בָּבַת עַיִן would be best rendered as the 'eyelid' which opens and closes over the eye like a door.

9. מִפְּנֵי רְשָׁעִים — From the wicked.

The protection requested in the previous verse is against the wicked (Rashi).

זוּ שַׁדּוּנִי — Who have plundered me.

זוּ, is similar to אֲשֶׁר 'who have' (Radak).

Ibn Ezra translates שַׁדּוּנִי as 'who encircle me'.

אֹיְבַי בְּנֶפֶשׁ — The enemies who threaten my soul [lit. 'my enemies to the soul']

Their goal is no less than to take my life (Radak).

Ohel Yaakov translates this as 'my

---

they were swept away; the Generation of the Dispersion came — and they were swept away. The people of Sodom came — and they too were swept away. David came, after the incident with Bath Sheba, and his Evil Inclination sought to overwhelm him. He therefore pleaded that God should come to his aid.

'Had I assisted the previous generations,' God replied, 'they, too, would not have been swept away.'

Said David: 'They did not call out to You for aid, but as for me, I have called out to You for You will answer me, O God, bend your ear to me, hear my saying' (17:6). David thus declared, 'Hashem, had You not grasped my hand, I could have not stood my ground!' (Yalkut Machiri, citing Tanchuma).

פִּימוֹ דִּבְּרוּ בְגֵאוּת: אַשֻּׁרֵנוּ עַתָּה °סְבָבוּנִי יא
עֵינֵיהֶם יָשִׁיתוּ לִנְטוֹת בָּאָרֶץ: דִּמְיֹנוֹ יב
כְּאַרְיֵה יִכְסוֹף לִטְרֹף וְכִכְפִיר יֹשֵׁב
בְּמִסְתָּרִים: קוּמָה יהוה קַדְּמָה פָנָיו יג
הַכְרִיעֵהוּ פַּלְּטָה נַפְשִׁי מֵרָשָׁע חַרְבֶּךָ:
מְמְתִים יָדְךָ | יהוה מִמְתִים מֵחֶלֶד חֶלְקָם יד
בַּחַיִּים °וּצְפוּנְךָ תְּמַלֵּא בִטְנָם יִשְׂבְּעוּ

יא־יד
°סְבָבוּנוּ ק׳
°וּצְפוּנֶךָ ק׳

---

enemies in the soul', referring to the evil inclination and natural desire for pride, pleasure, and other lusts which fill the heart and soul. These are indeed the 'enemy from within' which threatens man most and which harmed David more than any of his external enemies of flesh and blood.

10. חֶלְבָּמוֹ סָגְרוּ — *They are enclosed in their own fat.*

Their excessive corpulence has closed up their hearts and their eyes preventing them from beholding Your acts and from fearing You (*Rashi*).

According to *Radak* and *Metzudas David* these words should be read together with the following word פִּימוֹ, 'their mouth', meaning that their fat has stuffed up their mouths, i.e., their excessive preoccupation with materialism symbolized as 'fat' prevents them from speaking of spiritual concerns.

Thus:

דִּבְּרוּ בְגֵאוּת — *They have spoken proudly.*

Because their mouths are stuffed with the 'fat' of luxury and opulence, they speak in haughtiness (*Radak, Metzudas David*).

11. אַשֻּׁרֵנוּ עַתָּה סְבָבוּנוּ — *They now encircle our footsteps.*

From this verse *Rashi* derives his opinion that David composed this psalm when threatened by enemies all around. He feared that he might fall into their hands as a punishment for the episode

of Bath Sheba (see *Prefatory Remarks*).

עֵינֵיהֶם יָשִׁיתוּ — *They fix their gaze* [lit. 'they set their eyes']

They watch our movements carefully (*Radak*).

לִנְטוֹת בָּאָרֶץ — *To spread over the land.*

They send out men all over (*Rashi*). They prepare to spread out a net to ensnare us (*Radak*).

12. דִּמְיֹנוֹ כְּאַרְיֵה — *His* [i.e. the enemy referred to in the previous verse] *likeness is that of a lion.*

Hirsch suggests that דִּמְיֹנוֹ is the outer appearance of a person with an inflated self-image as in *Ezek.* 31:2: *'To whom do you liken yourself* [דָּמִיתָ] *in your greatness'*. This man proudly compares himself to a powerful, rapacious lion and tries to live up to his imagined role.

13. קוּמָה ה׳ — *Rise up, HASHEM.*

When the enemy comes to prey on me (*Radak*).

קַדְּמָה פָנָיו — *Confront him.*

Before he gets to me (*Radak*).

הַכְרִיעֵהוּ — *Bring him to his knees* [lit. 'make him bow down' (from בְּרְעַיִם, knees).]

Knock his feet out from beneath him and, he will bow and fall (*Rashi*).

חַרְבֶּךָ — *Your sword.*

You empowered the wicked to mete out punishment to the guilty. Thus the wicked become Your weapon and sword (*Rashi*).

¹⁰ *They are enclosed in their own fat,*
with their mouths they have spoken proudly.
¹¹ *They now encircle our footsteps,*
they fix their gaze to spread over the land.
¹² *His likeness is that of a lion*
yearning to tear asunder,
Like a young lion lurking in hiding.
¹³ *Rise up HASHEM,*
confront him and bring him to his knees;
Rescue my soul from the wicked — Your sword.
¹⁴ *Better for those whose death is by Your hand,*
HASHEM,
from those who die of old age,
Whose portion is eternal life,
and whose innards You fill with Your
concealed treasure,
Who are satisfied with sons,

---

14. מִמְתִים יָדְךָ ה' — *Better for those whose death is by your hand, HASHEM.*

David [facing death at this moment as a result of his sins] explains that he wishes to die not at the hands of the wicked, but by God's own hand *(Rashi; Radak; Ibn Ezra).*

מִמְתִים מֵחָלֶד — *From those who die of old age.*

Rashi relates חָלֶד to *'rust'*. Thus David asks to be one of those who dies of old age when he becomes *'rusty'*. However, according to *Radak* and *Ibn Ezra*, David is mentioning the fashion in which he does *not* wish to die. He spurns the thought of resembling men whose life was dedicated to the mundane material pleasures of חָלֶד, *'the transitory, temporal world.'* We find this word used thus in 49:2: כָּל יֹשְׁבֵי חָלֶד, *'all who dwell in the temporary world.'*

חֶלְקָם בַּחַיִּים — *Whose portion is eternal life.*

Rashi holds that this describes the righteous who will be rewarded with eternal existence. David yearns to join them after death. But *Radak* and *Ibn Ezra* interpret this to mean the people who ask only for a portion in the 'good life' of this world and have no interest in the Hereafter.

וּצְפוּנְךָ תְּמַלֵּא בִטְנָם — *And whose innards You fill with Your concealed treasure.*

This translation follows *Rashi*, but according to *Radak* and *Ibn Ezra* they desire only to fill their bellies with the good things tucked away in this world.

יִשְׂבְּעוּ בָנִים — *Who are satisfied with sons.*

Among the good things David asks for is to be one of those people who receives satisfaction from fine, decent children *(Metzudas David).*

According to *Radak* and *Ibn Ezra* this refers to those whom David abhors for they live only for this world and enjoy

בָּנִים וְהִנִּיחוּ יִתְרָם לְעוֹלְלֵיהֶם: אֲנִי טו
בְּצֶדֶק אֶחֱזֶה פָנֶיךָ אֶשְׂבְּעָה בְהָקִיץ
תְּמוּנָתֶךָ:

stuffing their sons along with themselves.

וְהִנִּיחוּ יִתְרָם לְעוֹלְלֵיהֶם — *And who bequeath their abundance to their babes.*
Not only does David request fine
children, but he even asks for the added
pleasure of leaving his riches to his little
children [who need it most] after he passes on *(Metzudas David).*

Radak and *Ibn Ezra* maintain that
עוֹלְלֵיהֶם refers to the *'little ones'* of their
sons, i.e., their grandsons. After they
finish stuffing their sons these wicked
people wish to leave the surplus over to
their grandchildren.

15. אֲנִי בְּצֶדֶק אֶחֱזֶה פָנֶיךָ — *[As for me] in
righteousness I shall behold Your face.*
In the future *(Rashi).*

David said: I am not like the wicked
who have no desire for the World to
Come. My desire is to behold Your
Presence there accompanied by the
righteousness which I have performed
in this world *(Radak).*

Rav Dustoi ben Rav Yannai taught: Come
and see how different the ways of God are
from the ways of flesh and blood. If a man
will bring a gift to a king there is first a doubt
whether the gift will ever be accepted. Even if
it is accepted, it is still doubtful whether he
will be granted a royal audience. With God it
is not so. A man gives a gift of a mere penny
to a pauper and he is assured of beholding
the divine presence as it is written, *'In* צֶדֶק,
*charity, I shall behold Your face. Upon
awakening I will be satisfied by Your form.'*

Rabbi Elazar would first give a penny to a
poor man and then he would pray as it says,
'In charity I shall behold Your face.'[1]?

1. The Talmud *(Berachos* 3b) relates that David would arise at midnight and sing songs of
Tehillim until the crack of dawn. Then the Sages of Israel would enter and meet with him to
discuss ways of helping those who were economically deprived.

Why did they come so early — even before David had a chance to recite his morning
prayers?

and who bequeath their abundance to their babes.
¹⁵ *In righteousness I shall behold Your face,*
upon awakening I will be satisfied by Your form.

אֶשְׂבְּעָה בְהָקִיץ תְּמוּנָתֶךְ — *Upon awaken-ing I will be satisfied by beholding Your form.*

When the dead will be revived, and awakened from, their death-slumber, then I wish to be made content by beholding Your form *(Rashi).*

The wicked are concerned with mundane self-contentment for themselves and their sons as expressed in the previous verse יִשְׂבְּעוּ בָנִים. However I desire only spiritual satisfaction *(Radak).*

The vision of God's form is not in a dream but rather when awake. It is not a form visible to the eye, rather it is a clarity of intellectual comprehension which affords a true concept of God. These matters can be understood only by one who is versed in the wisdom of the soul *(Ibn Ezra).*

תְּמוּנָתֶךְ — *Your form.*

Malbim explains that the word תְּמוּנָה never refers to the original object. It describes a mere copy which is designed along the lines of the original as in תְּמוּנַת כָּל סָמֶל, *'the similarity of any figure' (Deut.* 4:16).

Thus, the soul of man who was made 'In God's image,' bears a similarity to the true intellect of God.

[In the future, when man will perceive his soul which was hitherto concealed by his body, this will afford him a glimpse of the essence of God Himself after which the soul is designed.]

Rav Nachman ben Yitzchak said: This verse describes the Torah scholars who in this world drive sleep away from their eyes in order to stay awake and study. For this they will merit that God will satisfy their eyes with the splendid 'form' of the Holy Presence in the Hereafter *(Bava Basra* 10a).

Because David himself said *'In charity [righteousness] I behold Your face'* (17:15). David, therefore, scheduled these meetings — which were for the purpose of doing charity with all of Israel — to set a personal example that before one *'beholds God's face'*, through prayer, one should first perform a righteous act of charity.

This extraordinary Psalm popularly known as שִׁירַת דָּוִד, 'the Song of David' was composed in his old age after a life full of trial and tribulation (Rashi). Specifically, it was recited on the day that David's army swore that their old and venerable king would no longer be allowed to expose himself to the dangers of the battlefield with them (II Sam. 21:17) (Ibn Ezra).

This Psalm has the distinction of being the only chapter in Scriptures which is recorded twice: here and in II Samuel Ch. 22. Abarbanel, in his commentary to Samuel, is of the opinion that David originally composed this song in his youth when he was still deeply enmeshed in his many problems and misfortunes. He created this song to be an all-inclusive one which would relate to every woe which could possibly occur in his life. Throughout his long life David kept this psalm at hand, reciting it on every occassion of personal salvation.

The original version appears in Samuel. This version, composed at the end of David's life, differs from the original in a number of minor variations enumerated in Soferim 18.

This second version is not a triumphant song of personal victory. David made a gift to Israel of his personal feelings as a prayer and a consolation in times of distress. He who seeks to meditate in solitude, he who seeks private communion with his Maker, he who seeks to pour out his anguished soul in fervent prayer, all of these will find in it the precise words with which to express the depths of his feelings.

The Vilna Gaon designates this psalm as the שִׁיר שֶׁל יוֹם, 'Song of the Day', for the Seventh Day of Passover.

Harav Gifter explains that the universal and eternal nature of this psalm is particularly suited to the Seventh Day of Passover when God split the Sea representing the climax of Redemption and the forerunner of all future Redemption.

א לַמְנַצֵּחַ לְעֶבֶד־יהוה לְדָוִד אֲשֶׁר דִּבֶּר |
לַיהוה אֶת־דִּבְרֵי הַשִּׁירָה הַזֹּאת בְּיוֹם |
הִצִּיל־יהוה אוֹתוֹ מִכַּף כָּל־אֹיְבָיו וּמִיַּד
ב-ג שָׁאוּל: וַיֹּאמַר אֶרְחָמְךָ יהוה חִזְקִי: יהוה |

---

1. לְעֶבֶד ה׳ — *Of the servant of HASHEM.*

Midrash Shocher Tov emphasizes the significance of this title:

You will find that in all of the Torah, whoever called himself *'God's servant'* was later addressed as such by God Himself Who endorsed this title. [Anyone who is not worthy of this title would not dare to call himself thus.] We find this to be true of Abraham, Jacob, and Moses. David also described himself as כִּי אֲנִי עַבְדְּךָ אֲנִי עַבְדְּךָ בֶּן אֲמָתֶךָ *'For I am Your servant the son of Your maidservant'* (Psalms 116:16).

In the beginning of *Joshua* we read: *And it came to pass after the death of Moses, the servant of HASHEM. Radak* (ibid.) comments: Whosoever places all of his might, concentration, and interest in the blessed Name of God, and keeps his thoughts on God even when he engages in worldly pursuits, this man deserves the title *'Servant of Hashem,'* as we find: *Abraham My servant; David My servant; the prophets My servants.*

Meir Tehillos explains that David here is demonstrating that the attitude of a servant of God is quite different from that of a slave of men. The latter is deeply bitter and perpetually grumbles over his lot. The former is joyful and sings songs of praise precisely because he is bound to the service of the divine. Such service is not a burden, but a blessing. It is not a restriction but a release. David himself says at the conclusion of the verse quoted above (Psalms 116:16) פִּתַּחְתָּ לְמוֹסֵרָי, *'You have released my bonds.'*

לְדָוִד — *Of David.*

This is the third word in this verse beginning with the letter ל, *lamed*: לַמְנַצֵּחַ...לְעֶבֶד...לְדָוִד. *Baal Haturim*

(Deut 17:20) explains that this alludes to three aspects of David's monarchy. The tribe of Jewish royalty is יְהוּדָה *'Judah'* whose name has the same numerical value as ל, thirty. The House of David possesses thirty special royal privileges [*Avos* 6:6, *Biur haGra* ibid.] Finally, David ascended to the throne at the age of thirty [*II Sam.* 5:4].

אֲשֶׁר דִּבֶּר — *Who spoke.*

Norah Tehillos notes that since this Psalm is a song the words אֲשֶׁר שָׁר, *'who sang'* would have been more appropriate here. Similarly, in *Samuel* this song begins וַיְדַבֵּר דָּוִד *'And David spoke.'* The words lend support to the translation of the *Targum* in both places, who adds the word בִּנְבוּאָה *'in prophecy.'* This teaches that David was not merely singing triumphantly. Rather he was also uttering a prophetic statement of major significance.

הַשִּׁירָה הַזֹּאת — *This song.*

The *Yalkut Shimoni* (Joshua 20) reckons this song among the ten major songs offered to HASHEM throughout all of history.

[Actually, the *Yalkut* makes specific mention of the version appearing in *II Sam.* This corroborates *Abarbanel's* opinion (quoted in Prefatory Remarks) that only the *Samuel* version is considered as a true שִׁירָה.][1]

Midrash Shocher Tov adds:

'Rabbi Semon said: Whoever is saved miraculously and responds with a song to God is assured that all of his sins are forgiven and he is considered as if he was born anew.'

מִכַּף כָּל אֹיְבָיו — *From the hand of all his enemies.*

---

1. [All references to *Abarbanel* are taken from his commentary to *Samuel*.]

XVIII
1-2

For the Conductor; of the servant of HASHEM,
of David,
Who spoke the words of this song to HASHEM,
On the day that HASHEM delivered him
from the hand of all his enemies,
and from the hand of Saul.
² And he said: I will love You, HASHEM, my strength.

The Sages tell us (Midrash Shmuel, Parsha 26) that David waged eighteen wars in his lifetime. Thirteen were primarily for national purposes, to ward off the enemies of Israel. Five were 'private' wars to protect himself from his own enemies. Therefore David made this Psalm the eighteenth composition in this Book in order to allude to the eighteen wars he fought against all kinds of adversaries (Tehillah l'David).

וּמִיַּד שָׁאוּל — And from the hand of Saul.
Saul is singled out to indicate that he was equal to all of David's enemies combined (Rashi; Radak).

Alshich explains that all of David's enemies posed only a physical threat whereas Saul presented a grave spiritual danger. Saul was a great tzaddik, the anointed king chosen by Hashem. Therefore, David could only flee to elude him, never could he strike back lest he sin by defying the man whom God had enjoined all of Israel to obey.

Abarbanel elaborates on this theme and adds the words of the Midrash (7) 'Just as David prayed that he should not fall into the hands of Saul, so did he pray that Saul should not fall into his hands.'

The Talmud (Moed Kattan 16b) says that David composed this psalm specifically after the downfall and death of Saul, and God criticized David severely for rejoicing over the demise of such a great tzaddik. To atone for his error David composed Psalm 7, which is entitled שִׁגָּיוֹן לְדָוִד 'an error unto David' (see 7, Prefatory Remarks, and comm. to v. 1).

[In Samuel we read וּמִכַּף שָׁאוּל 'and from the palm of Saul'.

To be in someone's palm means to be in his clutches. In Samuel, when Saul was still alive, David could only rejoice each time he narrowly escaped actual capture in Saul's palm. But the joy was half-hearted for Saul's יַד, 'hand' was still outstretched to catch him. Only now, later in life, after Saul's death, could David rejoice that he no longer had to fear that hand at all.]

2. אֶרְחָמְךָ — I will love you.
This word is the Aramaic expression for love. Cf. Targum to וְאָהַבְתָּ in Lev. 19:18 (Rashi).

Radak describes what love for Hashem means:

'Love means when a person makes every attempt to draw as close to God as is possible in this material world. Fear of God precedes love. Only after a person grows accustomed to fearing God can he ascend to the level of serving out of love without desire for reward.'

Radak also quotes some commentaries (see Ibn Ezra) who translate אֶרְחָמְךָ, I will request mercy (רַחֲמִים) from you.

ה' חִזְקִי — HASHEM, my strength.
I love Hashem because He allows me to be His servant and He gives me the strength to overpower my evil inclination which wishes to interfere, as the Sages of the Talmud (Kiddushin 30b) said: 'A man's evil inclination seeks to overwhelm him every day and desires to slay him. If not for the assistance of the Holy One, Blessed be He, no man could withstand the test' (Alshich).

סַלְעִי וּמְצוּדָתִי וּמְפַלְטִי אֵלִי צוּרִי
אֶחֱסֶה־בּוֹ מָגִנִּי וְקֶרֶן־יִשְׁעִי מִשְׂגַּבִּי:
ד מְהֻלָּל אֶקְרָא יהוה וּמִן־אֹיְבַי אִוָּשֵׁעַ:
ה אֲפָפוּנִי חֶבְלֵי־מָוֶת וְנַחֲלֵי בְלִיַּעַל

Abarbanel notes that this entire verse is missing from the first version in *Samuel*. He explains that here this second version is not a song of praise for the past (as in *Samuel*) but rather a prayer for the future (see *Prefatory Remarks*). He translates אֶרְחָמְךָ, *I plead with You for future* רַחֲמִים, *mercy.'* ה׳ חִזְקִי *'in order that You will be my future strength.'*

3. ה׳ סַלְעִי — *HASHEM is my rock.*
He protects me like a fortress hewn from impregnable rock (*Radak; Metzudas David*).

Rashi tells us that David is alluding to God's miraculous intervention at the סֶלַע הַמַּחְלְקוֹת *'the rock of division'* (*I Sam. 23:28*).[1]

וּמְצוּדָתִי — *[And] my fortress*, i.e., a high, strongly fortified tower (*Metzudas Zion*).

וּמְפַלְטִי — *And my rescuer.*
Although a rock and a fortress provide defense, nevertheless sometimes they fail to hold back the enemy. But I have found protection in Your Name many a time and You never failed to rescue me (*Radak*).

Abarbanel notes that in *Samuel* the word לִי *'for me'* appears after וּמְפַלְטִי but here it does not. He explains that the personal reference is omitted here because now David revised the song as a prayer for all, not for himself alone.

צוּרִי — *My rock.*
This is a repetition of the first concept of this verse ה׳ סַלְעִי using a different phrase (*Radak; Metzudas Zion*).

אֶחֱסֶה בּוֹ — *In Whom I take refuge* [lit. *'I shall take refuge in Him'*]
Because He is 'my rock' I take refuge in Him (*Radak*).
I shall try to be covered by His shadow. This is similar to what we read וּמִבְּלִי מַחֲסֶה חִבְּקוּ צוּר *'for want of shelter they embrace a rock'* (*Job 24:8*). The rocky crags serve travelers as a shelter

1. *Midrash Shocher Tov* (quoted by *Radak* and the *Yalkut* in *I Sam. 23*) gives us a deeper insight into the entire episode. The treacherous people of Zif revealed David's mountain hideaway to Saul. Saul's army encircled the mountain from all sides leaving no avenue of escape. In his despair, David asked Hashem 'Where is the promise You made to me when Samuel anointed me to be king?' God responded, assuring David that every word uttered by Samuel would come true.
Suddenly a messenger angel appeared before Saul saying, *'Hurry away for the Philistines have spread out to attack the land.'* Saul's advisers were divided on which course of action to take. Some urged him to neglect all dangers and to seize this unprecedented opportunity to kill David. Others, however, wisely counseled that the security of all Israel is the king's foremost obligation. Saul heeded the latter advice and swiftly departed to pursue the marauding Philistines. Because his counselors were divided on this spot they called the mountain סֶלַע הַמַּחְלְקוֹת, *'the rock of division'.*
Others say it was so called because Hashem miraculously split the rock in two leaving David and his warriors on one side and Saul and his army on the other. Thus the victim was out of the reach of his pursuer. A final explanation for the name of this rock is that in later years whenever David and his legions would pass by this location, he and the six hundred men who were in his original band at the time of the miracle would separate ['divide'] themselves from the rest of the army divisions and prostrate themselves on the ground reciting the benediction, 'Blessed is He Who performed a miracle for us in this place.' Because of this separation the rock was called *'the rock of division'.*

XVIII
3-5

3 *HASHEM is my rock, my fortress, and my rescuer.*
My God, my rock, in Whom I take refuge;
my shield, and my horn of salvation;
my stronghold.
4 *As the One Who is praised, I call out to HASHEM,*
and am saved from my enemies.
5 *The pains of death encircled me,*

---

and protection against the stormy wind and pouring rains (Rashi).

וְקֶרֶן יִשְׁעִי — *And my horn of salvation.*

The Scriptures often refer to a source of power as a קֶרֶן, *horn*, which attacks and butts the enemy until victory and salvation are in sight (Radak).

According to *Midrash Shocher Tov* the word 'horn' is to be taken literally. For, when Samuel came to anoint David's brothers, he attempted to pour the holy oil on their heads, but the oil miraculously flowed in a different direction. However, when Samuel finally came to David, the oil bubbled and flowed out of the horn and onto David's head by itself. This amazing sign demonstrated that David was truly God's choice.

According to *Mahari Kara (Samuel)* 'horn' refers to the trumpets which are blown by the victorious army after the battle.

מִשְׂגַּבִּי — *My stronghold.*

The soaring mountain peaks afford a position of safe height (Radak).[1]

4. מְהֻלָּל אֶקְרָא ה׳ — *As the One Who is praised, I call out to HASHEM.*

With praises I call out to Him and pray before Him. In other words, even before the victory and salvation, already

I praise God as if the victory was an accomplished fact (Rashi).

וּמִן אֹיְבַי אִוָּשֵׁעַ — *And am saved from my enemies.*

According to *Rashi* this explains why David called out in advance to declare God's praises: It is because he had total confidence in the future salvation from the enemy. However, *Radak* and *Metzudas David* translate, 'after I call out the praises of HASHEM, then I will certainly be saved.' Thus, salvation is a result, not a cause of the praise.

Nir l'David comments: David says that the source of his salvation will come 'from my enemies', i.e., from the very hands of the enemies themselves, as we find that David used Goliath's own sword to decapitate the giant.

5. אֲפָפוּנִי — *Encircled me.*

Rashi traces this word to a similar usage in כִּי אָפְפוּ עָלַי רָעוֹת'*For calamities encircled me*' (40:13).

Midrash Shocher Tov notes a number of possible homiletic derivations: David says, My misfortunes are so many that they reach my אַף, 'nose' [i.e., they threaten to snuff out my very breath of life.] They constantly roll over me, like a never-ending אוֹפָן, 'wheel'; misfortunes never visit me one at a time, they come in pairs like the אַפְפוּן, 'the

---

1. 'Ten enemies fell before David. Five from Israel: Saul, Doeg, Achitophel, Sheva ben Bichri, and Shimi ben Gera; and five from the gentiles: Shovach, Goliath, and his three brothers. Therefore, David sang to God with ten different words of praise, חִזְקִי, סַלְעִי, וּמְצוּדָתִי. Rabbi Yehudah said: For this reason David וּמְפַלְטִי, אֵלִי, צוּרִי, מָגִנִּי, וְקֶרֶן יִשְׁעִי, מִשְׂגַּבִּי, וּמְנוּסִי concluded the Book of Psalms with ten forms of Halleluyah (Midrash Shocher Tov).

[Actually the word מְנוּסִי appears only in II Sam. (22:2-3), where it is followed by the words מֹשִׁיעִי מֵחָמָס תֹּשִׁעֵנִי 'My savior, from violence You will save me.' See Abarbanel there for a lengthier discussion of the Midrash.]

ו יְבַעֲתוּנִי: חֶבְלֵי שְׁאוֹל סְבָבוּנִי קִדְּמוּנִי
ז מוֹקְשֵׁי מָוֶת: בַּצַּר־לִי | אֶקְרָא יהוה וְאֶל־
אֱלֹהַי אֲשַׁוֵּעַ יִשְׁמַע מֵהֵיכָלוֹ קוֹלִי
ח וְשַׁוְעָתִי לְפָנָיו | תָּבוֹא בְאָזְנָיו: וַתִּגְעַשׁ
וַתִּרְעַשׁ | הָאָרֶץ וּמוֹסְדֵי הָרִים יִרְגָּזוּ
ט וַיִּתְגָּעֲשׁוּ כִּי־חָרָה לוֹ: עָלָה עָשָׁן | בְּאַפּוֹ

doubled thread of the loom'; finally, interpret this word as if it were spelled עָפָפוּנִי, i.e., misfortunes *'fly and soar'* over my head like עוֹפוֹת, *'birds'*.

חֶבְלֵי מָוֶת — *The pains of death.*

This word is usually associated with the travails of birth as in חֶבְלֵי יוֹלֵדָה *'the pains of a woman in labor'* (Hosea 13:13). The *Targum* here amplifies the thought, 'Like a woman suffering in labor who is on the verge of birth, yet is in mortal danger because she lacks the strength to push out the baby.' We also find this word used as חֶבֶל, *camp* [or *group*] (I Sam. 10:5). Thus David says, *'I was encircled by camps of death.'*

[In *Samuel*, the phrase is מִשְׁבְּרֵי מָוֶת *'smashing waves of death'* (see *Radak ibid.*)]

וְנַחֲלֵי — *And torrents.* This refers to the masses of soldiers who pour forth like a swift, wild torrent (*Rashi*).

However, *Radak* and *Metzudos Zion* suggest that this word refers to חוֹלִי, *'sickness'* as in נַחְלָה מַכָּתֵךְ *'Your wound is sick'* (Nachum 3:19).

בְּלִיָּעַל — *Godless men* [lit. *'those lacking a yoke'*]

Although וְנַחֲלֵי, *'and torrents'* is plural, בְּלִיָּעַל is singular because it refers to the unique Godlessness of each and every one of David's enemies (*Radak*).

6. חֶבְלֵי שְׁאוֹל סְבָבוּנִי — *Bands of wicked surrounded me.*

The translation follows *Rashi* and *Targum* here and in *Samuel*.

Radak and *Metzudas David* however, translate חֶבְלֵי as *'pains and travails'*,

and שְׁאוֹל, as *'of the lower world'*.

קִדְּמוּנִי מוֹקְשֵׁי מָוֶת — *They confronted me with snares of death.* [This explains why the wicked here are referred to as שְׁאוֹל, *'the lower world'* because they threatened to bring about David's death and to drag him down to the lower world.]

Rabbi Yitzchak Chajes notes that the numerical value of מוֹקְשֵׁי מָוֶת equals 902. (456+446=902). The *Talmud* (*Berachos* 8a) says that there are 903 forms of death in this world, the very best being מִיתָה שֶׁל נְשִׁיקָה, *'death by the divine kiss'* for which the righteous yearn. David bemoans the fact that his enemies always sought to do away with him by means of the 902 other forms of death.

7. בַּצַּר לִי אֶקְרָא ה׳ — *In my distress I would call upon HASHEM.*

When I am distressed by the aforementioned threats I call to Hashem and to none other (*Radak*).

Midrash Shocher Tov interprets these words as referring to the national calamities which befell the entire nation. Nevertheless, David describes all of them in the singular in order to minimize them as if they were only one misfortune. This is the way all prophets speak as we find בַּצַּר לְךָ *'When you* [in the sing. form] *are in a distress'* (Deut. 4:30).

יִשְׁמַע מֵהֵיכָלוֹ קוֹלִי — *From His Sanctuary He would hear my voice.*

Although He is in heaven, He hears me whenever I call (*Radak*).

Abarbanel points out that in *Samuel*

and torrents of Godless men would frighten me.
⁶ *Bands of wicked surrounded me,*
they confronted me with snares of death.
⁷ *In my distress I would call upon HASHEM,*
and to my God would I cry for salvation.
From His Sanctuary He would hear my voice,
my cry to Him would reach His ears.
⁸ *The earth quaked and roared,*
the foundations of the mountains shook,
they trembled when His wrath flared.
⁹ *Smoke arose from His nostrils,*

the text reads וַיִּשְׁמַע, *and He heard* [past tense] because David sang of past victories. However, this version, because it is a universal prayer for the salvation of all men, is changed to the future tense יִשְׁמַע *He would* [lit. *will*] *hear.'*

וְשַׁוְעָתִי לְפָנָיו תָּבֹא בְאָזְנָיו — [*And*] *my cry to Him would reach His ears.* He hears it instantly, without delay, and comes to save me (*Radak*).

8. וַתִּגְעַשׁ — [*And*] ... *quaked'.* This refers to violent shaking and convulsion as in כִּנְהָרוֹת יִתְגָּעֲשׁוּ מֵימָיו, *'like the rivers whose waters toss themselves'* (Jer. 46:7) (*Metzudas Zion*).
The violence depicted in this verse and the ones which follow describes in allegorical terms the fate of the personal enemies of David and those of all Israel. For instance, their agitation is illustrated as quaking and roaring; similarly, David describes their punishments as *'darkness', 'gloom', 'flaming coals',* etc. (*Radak*).
Abarbanel adds that God will go to any lengths to save the deserving righteous, even as far as overturning the earth and toppling mighty kingdoms. Thus, He created a crater in the earth to swallow up Korach and his assembly who threatened Moses and Aaron.

וַתִּרְעַשׁ הָאָרֶץ — [*And*] *the earth ...*

roared'. We find that in Egypt the very earth roared because it was afflicted with ten plagues (*Sforno*).
'Why do earthquakes convulse the earth? When the Holy One, Blessed be He looks down to earth, He sees the theatres and circuses full of gentiles sitting smugly in security and tranquility. He also sees the Holy Temple in ruins and His sons [Israel] suffering in oppression. Immediately, He vents His anger on the world and shakes the firmament' (*Midrash Shocher Tov*).

וּמוֹסְדֵי הָרִים יִרְגָּזוּ — [*And*] *the foundations of the mountains shook.* This describes Pharoah and his officers (*Metzudas David*).

כִּי חָרָה לוֹ — *'His wrath flared up'.*
When God came to take revenge from Pharoah and his nation on behalf of Israel His people, then the earth quaked and roared (*Rashi*).

9. עָלָה עָשָׁן בְּאַפּוֹ — *Smoke arose from His nostrils.*
This depicts His wrath. God is described here in human terms, because the heat of anger makes it seem as if smoke is coming out of the nostrils. Similarly, we find יֶעְשַׁן אַפְּךָ, *'Your nostrils smoke'* (Psalm 74:1) (*Metzudas Zion*).

וְאֵשׁ־מִפִּיו תֹּאכֵל גֶּחָלִים בָּעֲרוּ מִמֶּנּוּ:

י וַיֵּט שָׁמַיִם וַיֵּרַד וַעֲרָפֶל תַּחַת רַגְלָיו:

יא וַיִּרְכַּב עַל־כְּרוּב וַיָּעֹף וַיֵּדֶא עַל־כַּנְפֵי־

יב רוּחַ: יָשֶׁת חֹשֶׁךְ | סִתְרוֹ סְבִיבוֹתָיו סֻכָּתוֹ

יג חֶשְׁכַת־מַיִם עָבֵי שְׁחָקִים: מִנֹּגַהּ נֶגְדּוֹ

יד עָבָיו עָבְרוּ בָּרָד וְגַחֲלֵי־אֵשׁ: וַיַּרְעֵם

בַּשָּׁמַיִם | יְהוָה וְעֶלְיוֹן יִתֵּן קֹלוֹ בָּרָד

וְאֵשׁ מִפִּיו תֹּאכֵל — [And] a devouring fire from His mouth.

This consumed the enemy (Radak).

גֶּחָלִים בָּעֲרוּ מִמֶּנּוּ — Flaming coals blazed forth from Him. To burn the enemy (Radak).

10. וַיֵּט שָׁמַיִם וַיֵּרַד — He bent down the heavens and descended. He descended so swiftly that it seemed as if He bent down the heavens in order to come with greater speed; when He passed over the land of Egypt (Rashi).

וַיֵּרַד — And descended, i.e, a derivation of רָדַד 'to beat down flat' (Rashi).

וַעֲרָפֶל תַּחַת רַגְלָיו — [And] thick darkness was beneath His feet.

He made it dark for them when they were crushed beneath His feet as he tread on them in anger (Radak).

11. וַיִּרְכַּב — He mounted. In order to come in haste, without delay (Ibn Ezra; Metzudas David).[1]

עַל כְּרוּב — On a cherub, i.e., an angel. Since their facial features resemble those of a young child, they are called cherubs, for the Sages (Chagiga 13) say that in Aramaic כְּרַבְיָא means 'resembling a youngster' (Metzudas Zion).

וַיֵּדֶא — He soared.

Similarly we read כַּאֲשֶׁר יִדְאֶה הַנֶּשֶׁר, 'as the eagle soars down' (Deut. 28:49) (Rashi; Radak; Metzudas Zion).

עַל כַּנְפֵי רוּחַ — On the wings of the wind.

Radak notes that in Samuel the verse reads וַיֵּרָא עַל כַּנְפֵי רוּחַ, 'and He appeared on the wings of the wind.' David compares the movement of the wind to the flight of a bird (Radak).

12. יָשֶׁת חֹשֶׁךְ סִתְרוֹ — He made darkness His concealment.

'Darkness' refers to all the woes and misfortunes which God visits upon the enemy and which serve to conceal His Presence from them (Radak).

[The Targum renders סִתְרוֹ as שְׁכִינְתֵיהּ, 'His Holy Presence'. Thus the verse reads, 'He placed His Holy Presence into darkness.] [2]

סְבִיבוֹתָיו סֻכָּתוֹ — And enveloped Himself in His shelter (Targum).

This is another way of saying that God conceals Himself from the enemy (Radak).

חֶשְׁכַת מַיִם — Dark waters.

In II Sam. 22:12 the phrase is חַשְׁרַת מַיִם which means a gathering and a knotting together of clouds. When

---

1. 'To what may this be likened? To the king whose son was kidnapped by bandits. His servants began to harness his many horses to his carriage. The king said: 'If I wait until they finish these lengthy preparations my son will be lost.' What did the king do? He grabbed one horse and mounted it and swiftly gave chase. Similarly, the Holy One Blessed be He grabbed a cherub from those which support His throne of Glory and descended to battle the Egyptians' (Midrash Shocher Tov).

a devouring fire from His mouth,
flaming coals blazed forth from Him.
¹⁰ *He bent down the heavens and descended,*
thick darkness was beneath His feet.
¹¹ *He mounted a cherub and flew,*
He soared on the wings of the wind.
¹² *He made darkness His concealment,*
and enveloped Himself in His shelter —
dark waters and thick clouds.
¹³ *Because of the brilliance before Him*
His clouds passed on,
Hailstones and flaming coals.
¹⁴ *HASHEM thundered at them in the heavens,*
the Most High cried out,

this happens it grows dark and overcast *(Radak)*.

עָבֵי שְׁחָקִים — *And thick clouds.*
Thick clouds hold the abundance of water vapor which creates darkness. This is the *'darkness'* wrapped around God *(Rashi)*.

[Misfortunes will pour upon the wicked like a furious, dark storm and blot all recognition of God out of their line of vision.]

13. מִנֹּגַה נֶגְדּוֹ — *Because of the brilliance before Him.*
I.e. because of the bright splendors which God waits to bestow upon His loved ones *(Radak; Metzudas David)*.

According to *Rashi* the *'brightness'* here refers to the bolt of lightning sent forth by God to crash over the heads of the Egyptians at the Red Sea.

עָבָיו עָבְרוּ — *His clouds passed on.*
Therefore, He passed His clouds of disaster on to their enemies *(Radak; Metzudas David)*.

Rashi, however, renders *'the lightning broke through the clouds and passed over'* [the Egyptians at the Red Sea]. *Midrash Shocher Tov* also interprets this verse as referring to the punishment of Egyptians: 'When God came to battle the Egyptians at the sea, His ministering angels came down to assist Him. Some armed with swords, some with bows and others with spears. But God dismissed them, saying: 'I need no assistance!' At that moment 'His clouds passed on.'

בָּרָד וְגַחֲלֵי אֵשׁ — *Hailstones and flaming coals.*
These clouds tossed a fierce barrage of hailstones and flaming coals on the enemy *(Radak; Metzudas David)*.

14. וַיַּרְעֵם בַּשָּׁמַיִם ה' — *HASHEM thundered at them in the heavens.*
Hashem did everything to frighten them and make them tremble, just as a person trembles upon hearing a thunder-clap *(Radak)*.

2. Earthiness is a great barrier which prevents the human intellect from gaining a true comprehension of God Who is pure and spiritual. The prophets describe this dark, turgid חוֹמֶר *'earthliness'* as clouds, or gloom or darkness as David said, עָנָן וַעֲרָפֶל סְבִיבָיו *'Clouds and darkness are around Him'* (97:2). This is an allegorical figure of speech. No clouds surround God; it is the mind of man which is enclosed by the darkness of flesh and matter. Similarly David said עֶשֶׁת חֹשֶׁךְ סִתְרוֹ *'He then made darkness His concealment'* (Moreh Nevuchim 3:9).

טו וְגַחֲלֵי־אֵשׁ: וַיִּשְׁלַח חִצָּיו וַיְפִיצֵם וּבְרָקִים
טז רָב וַיְהֻמֵּם: וַיֵּרָאוּ | אֲפִיקֵי מַיִם וַיִּגָּלוּ
מוֹסְדוֹת תֵּבֵל מִגַּעֲרָתְךָ יהוה מִנִּשְׁמַת
יז רוּחַ אַפֶּךָ: יִשְׁלַח מִמָּרוֹם יִקָּחֵנִי יַמְשֵׁנִי

Mahari Kara in his commentary to *II
Samuel* 22:14 says that David is referring to a miracle involving the prophet,
Samuel. '*And as Samuel was offering
up the burnt-offering, the Philistines
drew near to battle against Israel, but
HASHEM thundered with a great
thunder upon the Philistines on that day
and panicked them and they were smitten down before Israel*' (I Samuel 7:10).

Dorash Moshe draws our attention to
the words of the Talmud (*Berachos*
49a).

'God created the mighty thunderclap
for the sole purpose of straightening out
the crookedness of the heart.' [i.e. the
sudden, frightening shock humbles the
proud heart and stirs it towards repentance.]

[From the Talmud (*Chullin* 86a) we
learn that natural calamities cease in the
presence of the righteous. When the
pious Rabbi Chiya and his sons came to
Eretz Yisrael, suddenly there was an end
to the lightning and thunder, earthquakes and hurricanes which had
previously plagued the Holy Land. This
indicates that the natural calamities
which come upon people to arouse them
to repent, become unnecessary, for the
presence of the devout can better arouse
people to humility and repentance.]

בָּרָד וְגַחֲלֵי אֵשׁ — *Hailstones and flaming
coals.*

Although these are mentioned in the
preceding verse, the repetition emphasizes that hail and brimstone, although incompatible, descended together at the very same moment at the
bidding of God (*Ibn Ezra*).

Together with the thunderous
sounds, come harsh punishments which
inflict pain like hailstones and flaming
coals (*Radak*).

Alshich reminds us that long before
David was born God was already at
work, preparing for his eventual appearance. David was a descendant of
Moab, the son who was born to Lot
after he was saved from Sodom. Lot was
saved mainly because David was
destined to come from his seed.
Therefore, the fire and brimstone, hail
and thunder, described here refer to the
destruction of Sodom from which no
one escaped except for Lot and his
daughters. David thanks God for this
salvation now and in subsequent verses.

15. וַיְפִיצֵם — *And scattered them.* i.e.
the enemies (not the arrows) (*Rashi*).

רָב — *Many.*

The translation follows *Targum* who
renders this as an adjective modifying
lightning. Others (*Radak; Ibn Ezra,
Metzudos*) translate it as a verb, רָב 'to
shoot' as in רֹבֶה קַשָּׁת 'an archer'
(*Genesis* 21:20).

16. וַיֵּרָאוּ אֲפִיקֵי מַיִם — *Streams of water
became visible.* *Metzudas Zion* derives
this from strong streams, as in כַּאֲפִיקִים
בַּנֶּגֶב, '*like streams in the desert*' (*Psalms*
126:4) This refers to the splitting of the
sea for Israel (*Rashi*).

וַיֵּרָאוּ — *Became visible,* i.e. the dry land
of the sea-bed which became visible
after the waters of the sea divided (*Metzudas David*).

The waters mentioned here are symbolic of the tragedies and dangers which
befell David. The drowning person may
be rescued in two ways. The first is
through a wondrous parting of the
swirling waters as described here, a
simile for the enemies being repelled,
thwarted, and routed into retreat. The

XVIII
15-17

Hailstones and flaming coals.

15 He sent forth His arrows and scattered them;
many thunderbolts and frenzied them.
16 Streams of water became visible,
the foundations of the earth were laid bare
by the breath of Your nostrils.
17 He sent from on high and took me,
He drew me out of deep waters.

second way is described in verse 17 (Radak).

וַיִּגָּלוּ מוֹסְדוֹת תֵּבֵל — *And the foundations of the earth were laid bare.* Rashi comments that this alludes to the fact that when the Red Sea split, every other body of water in the entire world split at the same time. *Metzudas David* holds that this refers to the sea bed which also burst open when the waters of the sea divided.

[The seas are called *'the foundations of the earth'* as we read כִּי הוּא עַל יַמִּים יְסָדָהּ — *'For He has founded it upon the seas'* (Psalms 24:2).]

Midrash Shocher Tov adds that not only did natural bodies of water split, but even the water contained in pitchers and cisterns divided. *Ohel Moed* uses this fact to explain why the text in *II Samuel* 22:16 reads אֲפִקֵי יָם *'streams of the sea'* whereas here it reads אֲפִיקֵי מָיִם *'streams of water'.* This teaches us that Hashem wanted the entire world to know that He was splitting *'the streams of the sea'* for the sake of Israel and therefore, He publicized the miracle by splitting every *'stream of water'* [i.e. water in receptacles] in the world.

17. יִשְׁלַח מִמָּרוֹם — *He sent from on high.*

He sent His messenger angels down to rescue Israel from the sea and from the Egyptians (Rashi). Rashi on *v.* 21 adds another explanation, saying that this refers to the episode of *'the rock of division'* (See comm. to *v.* 3) when God saved David by sending an angel with

an urgent message to make Saul abruptly end his pursuit of David.

יִקָּחֵנִי — *And took me.*

According to *Alshich* this refers to the angels which God sent to save Lot from Sodom in order that David should emanate from his seed.

Targum refers to God's choice of David which is described אֲנִי לְקַחְתִּיךָ מִן הַנָּוֶה מֵאַחַר הַצֹּאן, *'I took you from the pasture from behind the sheep' (II Sam. 7:8).*

מִמַּיִם רַבִּים — *Out of deep waters.*

He rescued me from the pursuers who give chase like swiftly flowing waters (Metzudas David).

This describes the second avenue of divine intervention which is likened to the drowning man who is plucked out of the waters. Similarly, Hashem may simply extract the endangered man from the grasp of his enemies without harming them at all (cf. *v.* 16). David praises God for having saved him in both ways (Radak).

Alshich explains that David thanks God for saving his ancestor Nachshon ben Aminadav, who was the first man to plunge into the Red Sea even before it split. When the waters reached his nose and he was on the verge of drowning, God divided the waters as a reward for Nachshon's faith. The *Yalkut* in *Parshas Beshallach* states that David ascended to the throne only in the merit of his illustrious ancestor. Therefore, he now sings *'He drew me out of the deep waters.'*

יח מִמַּיִם רַבִּים: יַצִּילֵנִי מֵאֹיְבִי עָז וּמִשֹּׂנְאַי

יט כִּי־אָמְצוּ מִמֶּנִּי: יְקַדְּמוּנִי בְיוֹם־אֵידִי

כ וַיְהִי־יהוה לְמִשְׁעָן לִי: וַיּוֹצִיאֵנִי לַמֶּרְחָב

כא יְחַלְּצֵנִי כִּי חָפֵץ בִּי: יִגְמְלֵנִי יהוה כְּצִדְקִי

כב כְּבֹר יָדַי יָשִׁיב לִי: כִּי־שָׁמַרְתִּי דַּרְכֵי יהוה

כג וְלֹא־רָשַׁעְתִּי מֵאֱלֹהָי: כִּי כָל־מִשְׁפָּטָיו

18. מֵאֹיְבִי עָז — *From my mighty foe.*

'Foe' is in the singular because it refers to the instances when David was threatened by a single adversary (rather than an army) such as Goliath or Yishbi at Nob (*Radak*).

Midrash Shocher Tov holds that the singular form best describes Pharoah as it says, אָמַר אוֹיֵב אֶרְדֹּף אַשִּׂיג, *'The foe* [Pharoah] *said: I will pursue, I will overtake* (Exod. 15:9).

Nora Tehillos reminds us that in the very beginning of this psalm, David divided his adversaries into two categories, Saul and all the rest. Here, the singular אֹיְבִי refers to his main foe, Saul, and the plural שֹׂנְאַי, refers to the rest.

וּמִשֹּׂנְאַי כִּי אָמְצוּ מִמֶּנִּי — *And from my enemies when they overpowered me.*

When they were about to overcome me in battle God came to my rescue (*Metzudas David*).

19. יְקַדְּמוּנִי בְּיוֹם אֵידִי — *They confronted me on the day of my misfortune.*

[The word אֵיד denotes a special time designated for disaster or misfortune as in כִּי קָרוֹב יוֹם אֵידָם, *'For the day of their misfortune is near'* (Deut. 32:35)]

Radak quotes *Targum Yonasan* in Samuel (also to be found in *Targum* here) who renders אַקְדִּימוּ לִי בְּיוֹם טִלְטוּלִי, *'They confronted me on the day of my wandering and exile.'* This describes enemies such as the Ziffim who betrayed David when he was a wandering fugitive.

However, *Rashi* and *Metzudas David* render יְקַדְּמוּנִי, as *'they hastened to come early'* to do me harm on my day of misfortune. They imagined that once I began to fall I would probably never again arise.

וַיְהִי ה' לְמִשְׁעָן לִי — *But HASHEM was my support.*

But they are mistaken for, as I fall, God assists me to arise (*Metzudas David*).

20. וַיּוֹצִיאֵנִי לַמֶּרְחָב — *He brought me out into broad places.*

He took me out of the narrow place where I was in the enemy's grasp to a large area where I could elude him (*Metzudas David*).

כִּי חָפֵץ בִּי — *For He desires me.*

Sometimes a person is released from one distress only to find himself in another. The captive who gives away his entire fortune as a ransom leaves captivity only to find himself in dire poverty. Similarly, a person may receive divine assistance at the expense of some of his merits for which he would have been rewarded in the Hereafter. David thanks God for saving him at no expense, merely because he is God's chosen servant (*Kli Chemda*).

21. יִגְמְלֵנִי ה' כְּצִדְקִי — *HASHEM recompensed according to my righteousness.*

Rashi says: This refers to the righteousness and perfect trust of Israel who left Egypt and unquestioningly followed God into a barren wilderness.

18-22

XVIII ¹⁸ *He saved me from my mighty foe,*
and from my enemies
when they overpowered me.
¹⁹ *They confronted me on the day of my misfortune,*
but HASHEM was my support.
²⁰ *He brought me out into broad spaces,*
He released me for He desires me.
²¹ *HASHEM recompensed me*
according to my righteousness,
And He repaid me
befitting the cleanliness of my hands.
²² *For I have kept the ways of HASHEM*
and I have not departed wickedly from my God.

The statement also refers to David himself who displayed great restraint and righteousness when he had Saul in his power and could have slain him easily but cut the corner of his cloak instead (*I Sam.* 24:4).[1]

22. כִּי שָׁמַרְתִּי דַּרְכֵי ה' — *For I have kept the ways of HASHEM.*

I have fulfilled the positive commandments (*Ibn Ezra*).

Because I am diligent of God's commands, He keeps watch over me, protecting me from my enemies (*Radak*).

I erect safeguards to keep from laxity in fulfilling God's commands (*Chozeh David*).

וְלֹא רָשַׁעְתִּי מֵאֱלֹהָי — *And I have not departed wickedly from my God.*

I have not transgressed the negative commandments (*Ibn Ezra*).

I have never departed from His ways intentionally or wickedly. Any sins I committed were purely unintentional. Furthermore, I was careful in my dealings with Saul. Although he pursued me relentlessly, I never harmed him even when I could have killed him (*Radak*).

I was scrupulous in the observance of God's commandments whether He appeared to me as Hashem [i.e. the Attribute of Mercy] or as אֱלֹהִים [i.e. the Attribute of Justice] (*Eretz HaChaim*).

[David, unlike Saul, was blessed with the divine power of arriving at clear, truthful halachic decisions (*Eruvin* 53a). Therefore, Scriptures say of Saul, וּבְכֹל אֲשֶׁר יִפְנֶה יַרְשִׁיעַ 'And wherever he turned, he did wrong' (*I Sam.* 14:47). David now thanks God for saving him from transgressing the halachah וְלֹא רָשַׁעְתִּי מֵאֱלֹהָי 'And I have not wickedly departed from my God'.]

1. This may also refer to וַיְהִי דָוִד עֹשֶׂה מִשְׁפָּט וּצְדָקָה לְכָל עַמּוֹ 'And David performed justice and charity for all of his nation' (*II Sam.* 8:15). The Talmud (*Sanhedrin* 6b) explains that if a rich man and a poor man came to David for judgment, David would first be scrupulous to render a verdict according to the strict letter of the law. If the rich man proved to be in the right David would decide in his favor and would not be swayed by his compassion for the pauper. However, after 'justice' was done and the pauper paid the wealthy man, David then exercised 'charity' and reimbursed the poor man in the amount he had been required to give the rich one.

כד לְנֶגְדִּי וְחֻקֹּתָיו לֹא־אָסִיר מֶנִּי: וָאֱהִי
כה תָמִים עִמּוֹ וָאֶשְׁתַּמֵּר מֵעֲוֹנִי: וַיָּשֶׁב־יהוה
כו לִי כְצִדְקִי, כְּבֹר יָדַי לְנֶגֶד עֵינָיו. עִם חָסִיד
כז תִּתְחַסָּד עִם־גְּבַר תָּמִים תִּתַּמָּם: עִם־נָבָר

23. כִּי כָל מִשְׁפָּטָיו לְנֶגְדִּי — *For, all His judgments are before me.*

I have always placed them before my eyes (*Rashi*); I never forgot them (*Radak*).

If you wish to understand how I could restrain myself from harming Saul and how I managed to accept all the trials of life with joy, it is because I never forgot for a moment that every occurrence is the result of God's perfect judgment. I accepted all miseries with the full knowledge that I deserved them because of my sins (*Mahari Ya'avetz haDoresh*).

וְחֻקֹּתָיו לֹא אָסִיר מֶנִּי — *And I shall not remove His statutes from myself.*

I never averted the focus of my full concentration to other matters. I constantly stood on guard with all my might to prevent any wrongdoing (*Radak*).

24. וָאֱהִי תָמִים עִמּוֹ — *I was perfectly innocent with Him.*

Ibn Ezra comments that David proclaimed his fulfillment of the commandment, תָּמִים תִּהְיֶה עִם ה' אֱלֹהֶיךָ, *'You shall be perfectly innocent with HASHEM your God'* (*Deut.* 18:13).

Malbim elaborates on this important theme and portrays the תָּמִים as one whose entire being is perfectly attuned to the performance of God's will.

Neither in his mind nor in his body, does there exist the slightest obstacle or hindrance to interfere with his service of God. [This was the status which David yearned to achieve all of his life — that of Adam before the sin (see *Overview*).]

Radak explains: Even when Saul pursued me I did not question God's ways or deny His prophecy to me. I did not ask, 'How could God decree that I will be king if Saul stands over me constantly and threatens to kill me every day?[1]

וָאֶשְׁתַּמֵּר מֵעֲוֹנִי — *And I was vigilant against my sin.*

I guarded myself from the sin of harming King Saul (*Radak*).

עֲוֹנִי, indicates *'my personal sin'*. Every person is different and is tempted with a particular sin for which he has a weakness. He is challenged to conquer his own shortcoming (*Hirsch*).

25. וַיָּשֶׁב ה' לִי כְצִדְקִי — *[And] HASHEM repaid me according to my righteousness.*

For Saul and his family perished and vanished, but I survived and my royal dynasty endures (*Radak*).

כְּבֹר יָדַי לְנֶגֶד עֵינָיו — *According to the cleanliness of my hands before His eyes.*

I display the cleanliness of my hands only before God; to boast before men

1. This seems to contradict David's remarks as recorded in *Midrash Shocher Tov* on v. 3: 'When Saul's army trapped David on top of the סֶלַע הַמַּחְלְקוֹת, *'the rock of division'*, David lamented, 'It was for naught that Samuel anointed me in God's Name! Where is His promise now?' We see this [doubt] from David's own words: אֲנִי אָמַרְתִּי בְחָפְזִי כָּל הָאָדָם כֹּזֵב, *'I said in my haste, every man is false'* (116:11).

Perhaps the answer to this question lies in the word בְחָפְזִי, *'in my haste.'* David never denied God's promise. He merely recorded his *initial* reaction to the hopeless situation. The very first hasty thought which flew through his mind was 'What of the prophecy?' However, he immediately blotted this flicker of heresy from his mind and fortified his heart with *'perfect innocence.'* He assured himself that ultimately God's prophecy would undoubtedly be fulfilled.

²³ *For all His judgments are before me,*
and I shall not remove His statutes from myself.
²⁴ *I was perfectly innocent with Him,*
and I was vigilant against my sin
²⁵ *HASHEM repaid me in accordance*
with my righteousness,
According to the cleanliness of my hands
before His eyes.
²⁶ *With the devout You act devoutly*
with the wholehearted man
You act wholeheartedly.

would be presumptuous and proud (*Metzudas David*).

This verse corroborates the statement of the *Zohar* that all of a person's sins and merits are etched into the lines of his hands, both for good and for bad (*Eretz HaChaim*).

26. עִם חָסִיד תִּתְחַסָּד — *With the devout You act devoutly.*

This is the way of God, to repay מִדָּה כְּנֶגֶד מִדָּה, 'measure for measure' (*Rashi*).

Just as the devoted go beyond the letter of the law, so do You repay them with generosity surpassing the extent of their deeds (*Radak*).

Hirsch adds: God reveals Himself to every person according to his character. The חָסִיד, *the devout man*, dedicates himself selflessly to God; he is rewarded with God's devoted love. For the חָסִיד, *devout person*, places God's every חֶסֶד, *lovingkindness*, in the service of human progress.

[It has been said that for this reason the performance of kindness to another man is called גְּמִילוּת חֶסֶד, literally 'the repayment of a kindness.' It is difficult to understand the concept of 'repayment' as used here because often the recipient of a kindness is a total stranger to whom his benefactor is not beholden. However, the performance of kindness, as *Hirsch* explains, stems from a feeling of indebtedness to Hashem for His countless kindnesses. It is an attempt to repay God in some small way by bestowing kindness on God's beloved creations.]

Rashi, based on the *Targum*, notes that David had a special חָסִיד in mind here, Abraham, who is the example of the devout man par excellence.

Ralbag comments that David was a חָסִיד whereas Saul was not. Therefore, Saul was rejected for one sin and David, even though his sin was more severe, was forgiven. Every moment of David's life was devoted to serving God; his own will did not exist. Only once, with Bath Sheba, did his evil inclination overcome him, but he immediately accepted even harsh rebuke and repented. As a devout חָסִיד he was worthy of God's kindness and forgiveness. Saul was not so. Even after Samuel chastised him he attempted to excuse and explain his actions, stubbornly refusing to admit his guilt for which he was not ashamed. Lacking חֲסִידוּת, Saul was not worthy of God's חֶסֶד and was not forgiven. [Cf. *Maharsha, Yoma* 22a.]

עִם גְּבַר תָּמִים תִּתַּמָּם — *With the wholehearted man You act wholeheartedly.*

According to *Targum*, the Patriarch Isaac is the classic example of the תָּמִים.

[Isaac allowed himself to be made into a human sacrifice without question. In

כח תִּתְבָּרָר וְעִם־עִקֵּשׁ תִּתְפַּתָּל: כִּי־אַתָּה
עַם־עָנִי תוֹשִׁיעַ וְעֵינַיִם רָמוֹת תַּשְׁפִּיל:
כט כִּי־אַתָּה תָּאִיר נֵרִי יהוה אֱלֹהַי יַגִּיהַּ
ל חָשְׁכִּי: כִּי־בְךָ אָרֻץ גְּדוּד וּבֵאלֹהַי אֲדַלֶּג־

recognition of his perfectly innocent faith, God treated Isaac as an עוֹלָה תְּמִימָה, *'a perfect creature consecrated to be a burnt sacrifice'*. For this reason Isaac was never allowed to leave the Holy Land. This may explain the extra word here, גֶּבֶר *'man'*. It emphasizes that if one perfects himself with innocent faith, he can be considered a קָרְבָּן עוֹלָה, *'a burnt sacrifice'* even though he is a living person.]

27. נָבָר — *Trustworthy.*

This literally means *'clean'* as in כְּבֹר יָדַי, *'according to the cleanliness of my hands'* (v. 25) (Radak).

This refers to our father, Jacob who was completely true and trustworthy to You and so You chose his children from among all the nations and You cleansed his seed of all impurities. [Unlike the offspring of Abraham and Isaac, all of his sons were righteous.] (Targum).

וְעִם עִקֵּשׁ תִּתְפַּתָּל — *And with the crooked You act perversely.*

This describes Pharoah and the Egyptians who planned 'crooked', evil schemes against Israel, Your nation. Ultimately You confounded and twisted their plans (Targum).

Tehillas Hashem points out that both of these characteristics of God are included in the verse to emphasize that Hashem has the ability to act according to two contradictory patterns at one and the same time. At the same moment that He was tricking the Egyptians to plunge into the sea, He was fulfilling His trust to rescue Israel.

It is written, *'And Jacob told Rachel that he was her father's brother'* (Gen. 29:12). But was he not really Lavan's nephew? Rather he was telling her 'I am your father's brother [his match] in

trickery' i.e. if he attempts to trick me I can match his deviousness and protect myself. Is it then permissible for a *tzaddik* to act deviously? Yes, as we read, *'With the trustworthy You act trustworthy, and with the crooked You act perversely'* (Megillah 13b), [i.e. if he is forced to resort to trickery in order to protect himself from the wiles of the wicked, it is permissible.]

28. עַם עָנִי — *The afflicted nation.*

You are with Israel in the darkness of exile (Targum).

"Come and see how the ways of the Holy One, Blessed be He, differ from the ways of flesh and blood. If a man is rich and has a poor relative he tries to deny this relationship. Whenever he sees the pauper he hides because he is ashamed to talk to him. God is not so! Who is His nation? עַם עָנִי *'the poor, afflicted nation'*! When He sees the poor He always strives to join them" (Midrash Shmos Rabba 31:13).

Rabbi Yochanan said: If you see a generation which is wasting away in poverty, wait for the Messiah's imminent arrival, as it says: *'For you will save the poor nation'* (Sanhedrin 98a).

וְעֵינַיִם רָמוֹת תַּשְׁפִּיל — *And haughty eyes You bring down low.*

In the future You will deign to redeem the exiles and crush the mighty nations who overwhelmed Israel (Targum).

David relates haughtiness to the eyes for they are the main cause of conceit and sin (Radak).

Dorash Moshe observes that all misery stems from the fact that people are dissatisfied with their own lot and they cast an envious eye on their neighbor's possessions. If everyone were content

27 *With the trustworthy You act trustingly*
and with the crooked You act perversely.
28 *For You save the afflicted nation*
and haughty eyes You bring down low.
29 *For it is You Who will light my lamp,*
HASHEM, my God, will illuminate my darkness.
30 *For with You I smash a troop,*

---

with his own portion, then poverty would not be a disgrace. Therefore, David says that Hashem will save the poor, afflicted nation by lowering the envious eyes which always look up to those who are wealthier. When envy disappears, imagined poverty will go with it.

29. כִּי אַתָּה תָּאִיר נֵרִי — *It is You Who will light my lamp.*

You are the master of illumination and so You kindle a ray of light for Israel in exile (*Targum*).

Misfortune is the darkness; salvation from it is the light (*Radak*).

Rashi explains that this verse refers to the time when David fought all night against the bands of Amalek who attacked Ziklag as it is written וַיַּכֵּם דָּוִד מֵהַנֶּשֶׁף וְעַד הָעֶרֶב לְמָחֳרָתָם, *'And David smote them from the evening until the dusk of the next day'* (I Sam. 30:17).

Midrash Shocher Tov explains that David battled Amalek for two nights and one day, and God provided miraculous illumination throughout that time. The *Midrash* concludes: 'The Holy One Blessed be He said: My light [i.e. the commandments] is entrusted in your hands, and your light [i.e. the soul] is entrusted in My hands. If you will guard My light I will guard yours.'

Ohel Moed points out that in *Samuel* the words read כִּי אַתָּה נֵירִי *'For You are my lamp.'* This teaches us that sometimes God Himself serves as the lamp and personally illuminates man's way. Therefore, נֵירִי is spelled with an additional י as a *'full'* word (מָלֵא) because when God Himself is the lamp the light

is completely adequate. But sometimes God does not involve Himself in a man's affairs and sends light through intermediaries: He merely *'lights it'*, but does not serve as the *'lamp'*. Then the light is deficient, as indicated by the 'incomplete' spelling of נֵרִי [without the *'yud'*] in our verse.

יַגִּיהַּ חָשְׁכִּי — *Will illuminate my darkness.*

When Israel is redeemed, Hashem will console them and make them shine in the World to Come (*Targum*).

When a person learns Torah with pure intentions, spurred by the realization that Torah is God's lamp to light up the world, then God will respond by endowing this man with a clear understanding of Torah. All doubts, resembling darkness, will be resolved, and he will be able to issue clear halachic decisions. (*Shiltei Gibborim* to *Tractate Shabbos*, 2).

Malbim directs us to his *comm.* on *Isaiah* 59:9 where he explains at length the difference between אוֹר and נוֹגַהּ. אוֹר refers to a body which is itself a source of illumination, such as the sun. נוֹגַהּ refers to a body which merely reflects brightness emanating from elsewhere, such as the moon. [Thus, in our verse, the lamp lights with אוֹר, its own light. The darkness which has no light of its own, will be יַגִּיהַּ, it will shine from a reflection of external light.]

30. כִּי בְךָ — *For with You* [lit. *'for in You'*]

With my faith in You (*Rashi; Metzudas David*).

With Your assistance (*Radak*).

לא שׁוּר: הָאֵל תָּמִים דַּרְכּוֹ אִמְרַת־יהוה
לב צְרוּפָה מָגֵן הוּא לְכֹל| הַחוֹסִים בּוֹ: כִּי מִי
אֱלוֹהַּ מִבַּלְעֲדֵי יהוה וּמִי צוּר זוּלָתִי
לג אֱלֹהֵינוּ: הָאֵל הַמְאַזְּרֵנִי חָיִל וַיִּתֵּן תָּמִים

אֲרֹץ — *I smash.*

This is derived from רָצַץ *'to shatter'*
(*Radak; Ibn Ezra*).

Both commentaries offer an alternate
translation, deriving this word from רָץ,
'to run'. Thus David says: 'I charge into
an armed troop, armed with my faith in
You.' An example of this is David's encounter with Goliath: וַיָּרָץ הַמַּעֲרָכָה
לִקְרַאת הַפְּלִשְׁתִּי, *'And he charged into
the line of battle, towards the Philistine'*
(*I Sam.* 17:48).

וּבֵאלֹהַי — *And with my God* (*Metzudas
David*).

אֲדַלֶּג שׁוּר — *I leap a wall.*

The word *'leap'* denotes the extraordinary speed and ease with which David
captured even the most heavily fortified
cities (*Radak*).

Rashi cites the words of *Midrash
Tehillim:* When David began his campaign against the Jebusites who were
fortified in Jerusalem, he proclaimed
'Whosoever will be the first to smite the
Jebusim will be made a leader and a
general' (*I Chron.* 11:6). What did Joab
do? He brought a fresh sapling and
placed it firmly beside the wall. He then
bent the pliable sapling far back and
David held on to its top to hold it in
place. Joab jumped over David's head
and sat on the top of the sapling which
was released, catapulting Joab over the
wall. [David was disappointed because
he wanted the privilege of being the
first to smite the Jebusites.]

What did God do? He lowered instantly the entire wall and David easily
jumped over it. [Thus entering the city
before Joab who was still soaring in the
air.]

Yevakesh Ratzon explains this according to *Radak* who says that they

had a tradition that he who would lead
the victory in the capture of Jerusalem
would reign over Israel forever. Since
David was confident that the prophecy
of Samuel concerning his monarchy
would come true, he was sure that he
would lead the battle into the city and
would therefore be Israel's eternal
leader and general. He bent the sapling
to catapult himself when suddenly Joab
jumped over his head in an attempt to
be the first and thus assured of eternal
sovereignty. But Hashem foiled his attempt by lowering the wall, enabling
David to lead the attack.

31. הָאֵל — *The God.*

He who possesses all of the might and
ability (*Radak*).

תָּמִים דַּרְכּוֹ — *Whose way is perfect.*

Everything He does is with perfect
equity. He repays each man in accordance with his deeds (*Radak*).

אִמְרַת ה' צְרוּפָה — *The promise of
HASHEM is pure.*

It is like כֶּסֶף צָרוּף, *refined silver,*
which is completely free of impurities.
When God promises, nothing goes to
waste, every word comes true (*Metzudas David*).

[Although אִמְרַת literally means *'the
saying'* here it is translated as *'the
promise.'* It also refers to the *mitzvos* of
Hashem.]

God derives no benefit from our
mitzvah performance. Only the man
who fulfills them gains. Just as the
craftsman who refines silver intends to
extract the impurities and dross, so are
the *mitzvos* intended to rid our hearts of
low character traits and false beliefs.
The *Midrash* cites the example of the
humane laws of ritual slaughter to
emphasize another point, that we

and with my God I leap a wall.
31 The God Whose way is perfect,
the promise of HASHEM is flawless,
He is a shield for all who take refuge in Him.
32 For who is God besides HASHEM,
and who is a rock except for our God?
33 The God Who girds me with strength
and Who kept my way perfect.

should not think that the prohibition against cruelty to animals is because of God's concern for these creatures per se. It is not them He cares about, it is us. He is concerned lest we become cruel and insensitive to their suffering. Therefore, He commanded us to be humane in order to refine our soul with noble characteristics *(Ramban, Deut. 21:6; Chinuch 545).*

מָגֵן הוּא לְכָל הַחוֹסִים בּוֹ — *He is a shield for all who take refuge in Him.*

In order to purify a man, God must sometimes send painful afflictions upon him. But those who trust Him will always be protected so that their suffering does not destroy them *(Hirsch).*[1]

32. כִּי מִי אֱלוֹהַּ מִבַּלְעֲדֵי ה' — *For who is God besides HASHEM?*

Who can nullify His promises or interfere with His decrees? *(Radak; Ibn Ezra).*

When You will perform miracles for Messiah and the remnants of Your people who will be with him, all peoples and nations will Praise You and proclaim *'There is no God besides HASHEM'.* Israel will respond, *'There is no strong rock except our God'* *(Targum).*

33. הָאֵל — *The God.* He is the master of all might and He dispenses might *(Radak).*

הַמְאַזְּרֵנִי חָיִל — *Who girds me with strength.* This word is related to אֵזוֹר *'a belt, a girdle' (Metzudas Zion).*

The Talmud *(Yoma 47a, Niddah 31a)* explains the difference between this verse and the version in *Samuel,* which has וַתַּזְרֵנִי חָיִל [without an א, *aleph*].

The human embryo is not conceived from any random drop of semen. Rather, God carefully selects the purest one. The Yeshiva of Rabbi Ishmael likened this to the farmer winnowing his grain. He selects the edible kernels and discards the chaff. Similarly, Rabbi Abahu would take note of the variation between these two verses. It is written וַתַּזְרֵנִי חָיִל *(II Sam. 22:40)* and also, הָאֵל הַמְאַזְּרֵנִי חָיִל in our verse. This variation teaches that David said two things to the Holy One Blessed be He. In *Samuel,* he used a word related to זֵרִיתַנִי, *You winnowed me.* Thus: 'first You winnowed (chose) me from the purest drop, then, in *Psalms,* David said, 'You girded me with strength.'

וַיִּתֵּן תָּמִים דַּרְכִּי — *And Who kept my way perfect.*

He removed every obstacle and stumbling block from my path so that all was smooth and perfect *(Rashi).*

My [military] campaign was perfect and complete, for not one of my men was lost in battle *(Radak; Metzudas David).*

1. *Rabbeinu Yonah (comm.* to *Prov.* 3:25) points out that this verse is repeated almost verbatim in *Proverbs* 30:5 כָּל אִמְרַת אֱלוֹהַּ צְרוּפָה מָגֵן הוּא לַחוֹסִים בּוֹ. He explains: 'David and Solomon composed this theme together in order to teach that if a man safeguards the word of Hashem and trusts in Him, he will merit divine protection from all troubles'.

לד דַּרְכִּי: מְשַׁוֶּה רַגְלַי כָּאַיָּלוֹת וְעַל בָּמֹתַי

לה יַעֲמִידֵנִי: מְלַמֵּד יָדַי לַמִּלְחָמָה וְנִחֲתָה

לו קֶשֶׁת־נְחוּשָׁה זְרוֹעֹתָי: וַתִּתֶּן־לִי מָגֵן

יִשְׁעֶךָ וִימִינְךָ תִסְעָדֵנִי וְעַנְוַתְךָ תַרְבֵּנִי:

לז תַּרְחִיב צַעֲדִי תַחְתָּי וְלֹא מָעֲדוּ קַרְסֻלָּי:

---

34. מְשַׁוֶּה רַגְלַי כָּאַיָּלוֹת — *Who straightened my feet like the hinds.*

מְשַׁוֶּה is derived from שָׁוֶה 'equal, straight' (*Rashi*). The feet of the אַיָּלוֹת, the females, are better aligned than those of the males. Therefore, the females are swifter.

Thus, I was able to pursue the enemy with maximum speed (*Metzudas David*).

Even if it occurred that I had to flee from battle to save myself, God made me as swift as the hind so that no enemy could overtake me (*Radak*).

וְעַל בָּמוֹתַי יַעֲמִידֵנִי — *And stood me on my heights.*

Through victory, You elevated me to prominence and height (*Metzudas David*).

Even when I flee in defeat, the place of refuge which You provide is high and secure (*Radak*).

35. מְלַמֵּד יָדַי לַמִּלְחָמָה — *Who trained my hands for battle.*

When I succeeded in battle I did not take credit for my powers and skills, rather I attributed all to Hashem Who trained and accustomed my hands in the martial arts (*Radak*).

God taught me military strategy and tactics (*Metzudas David*).

וְנִחֲתָה — *To bend.*

As in כִּי חִצֶּיךָ נִחֲתוּ בִי 'For Your arrows are shot at me' (38:3). [lit. 'they are bent at me' as the bow is pulled back and poised] (*Rashi*).

קֶשֶׁת נְחוּשָׁה זְרוֹעֹתָי — *A bow of copper . . . my arms.*

A great many copper bows were hanging in David's palace. When the gentile kings would visit and see them on display they would say to each other, 'Do you really think that David has the strength to bend and string these? Of course not! They are here merely to frighten us!' Hearing this, David would proceed to bend the bows in their presence (*Rashi*).

Midrash Shocher Tov adds: It was easier to bend a copper bow than to bend David's mighty arm. Furthermore, David's bow is called נְחוּשָׁה because he was a descendant of the illustrious נַחְשׁוֹן. [The name נַחְשׁוֹן is etymologically related to נְחֹשֶׁת, copper. I.e. the source of David's strength was not in his physical prowess but in his illustrious forebear. See *comm.* to *v.* 17.]

36. וַתִּתֶּן לִי מָגֵן יִשְׁעֶךָ — *You have given me Your shield of salvation.*

In all of my battles Your salvation was my shield for I was never defeated (*Radak*).

וִימִינְךָ תִסְעָדֵנִי — *And Your right hand has upheld me.*

All credit for this uninterrupted success is due to the fact that Your right hand has constantly upheld me (*Radak*).

וְעַנְוַתְךָ תַרְבֵּנִי — *You have treated me* [lit. 'You have amplified toward me'] *with great humility.*

You have amplified Your usual trait of humility in all of Your dealings with me (*Rashi*).

34 *Who straightened my feet like the hinds,*
and stood me on my heights.
35 *Who trained my hands for battle*
and my arms to bend a copper bow.
36 *You have given me Your shield of salvation,*
and Your right hand has sustained me.
You have treated me with great humility.
37 *You have widened my stride beneath me,*
and my ankles have not faltered.

'In Your excessive humility You have always given me more than I deserve and You granted my handful of men victories which would befit large armies.' Thus, תַּרְבֵּנִי means, 'You have *made me greater*' than my massive enemies (*Radak*).

Abarbanel gives these words a different twist. Most warriors who experience victory give themselves the credit and become overly proud. David sees this as one of the gravest dangers of war and thanks God for instilling in him massive humility to counteract this natural tendency towards pride.[1]

37. תַּרְחִיב צַעֲדִי תַחְתָּי — *You have widened my stride beneath me.*

The man who widens his stride does not fall easily (*Rashi*).

קַרְסֻלָי — *My ankles.* [The Song of David is the only place in Scriptures where this word appears.] *Rashi* says that the word describes the leg from the knee downwards. (However, *Rashi* in *Samuel* translates the word as עֲקֵבִי, '*my heel*'). *Radak* and *Metzudas Zion* render it as knee and base their view on the phrase אֲשֶׁר לוֹ כְרָעַיִם '*which has knees*' (*Lev.* 11:21) which *Onkelos* renders as קַרְסוּלִין, and *Targum Yonasan* renders as רְכוּבָתֵּי, '*the knees*'.

However, from *Oholos* (1:8) which describes the positions of the 248 bones in the body it is clear that קוּרְסָל is the ankle. (See *Bertinoro*, *Tosefos Yom Tov* and *Tiferes Yisroel ibid.*). *Hirsch* also translates '*ankle*' and observes that a קֶרֶס is a '*hook*' or '*clasp*' (*Ex.* 26:11). Therfore, קַרְסוּל describes the ankle which is a type of clasp joining the foreleg to the foot. [עיין חזון איש הלכות קר״ש סימן ט״ז אות ח׳ ובשו״ת רבי עקיבא איגר תנינא סימן כ״ח.]

1. Various *Midrashim* offer examples of God's extraordinary humility in His relations with man.

A master and his disciple walk at night, who carries the lantern? Is it not the disciple? But the Holy One Blessed be He walked before Israel and held the pillar of fire like a lantern before them. The custom of the world is that the master calls out and the disciple responds. Not so with God, for we find, '*Moses spoke and God replied to him aloud*' (*Exodus* 19:19). Furthermore, under normal circumstances the master bids the disciple to wait for him at a certain place. But we find that God told Ezekiel to go out to the valley where He would be waiting for him (*Midrash Shocher Tov; Tanchuma Parshas Ki Tisa* 15).

When a disciple is sick and the master comes to visit him, the other disciples come first to announce the master's arrival. Not so Hashem. When Abraham was recuperating from his *circumcision*, the Holy One Blessed be He visited first; only later did the messenger angels whom He sent to Abraham arrive (*Tanchuma ibid.*).

לח אֶרְדּוֹף אוֹיְבַי וְאַשִּׂיגֵם וְלֹא־אָשׁוּב עַד־
לט כַּלּוֹתָם: אֶמְחָצֵם וְלֹא־יֻכְלוּ קוּם יִפְּלוּ
מ תַּחַת רַגְלָי: וַתְּאַזְּרֵנִי חַיִל לַמִּלְחָמָה
מא תַּכְרִיעַ קָמַי תַּחְתָּי: וְאֹיְבַי נָתַתָּה לִּי עֹרֶף
מב וּמְשַׂנְאַי אַצְמִיתֵם: יְשַׁוְּעוּ וְאֵין־מוֹשִׁיעַ
מג עַל־יְהוָה וְלֹא עָנָם: וְאֶשְׁחָקֵם כְּעָפָר עַל־
מד פְּנֵי־רוּחַ כְּטִיט חוּצוֹת אֲרִיקֵם: תְּפַלְּטֵנִי
מֵרִיבֵי עָם תְּשִׂימֵנִי לְרֹאשׁ גּוֹיִם עַם־לֹא־

38. אֶרְדּוֹף אוֹיְבַי וְאַשִּׂיגֵם — *I pursued my foes and overtook them.*

As in the campaign against Amalek (*Radak*).

וְלֹא־אָשׁוּב עַד כַּלּוֹתָם — *And returned not until I had annihilated them.*

David destroyed the entire army of Amalek with the exception of four hundred young men who escaped on swift camels (*I Sam.* 30:17).

39. וְלֹא יֻכְלוּ קוּם — *And they could not rise.*

[Since only a handful of Amalekites survived, they did not recover from this mortal blow.]

40. וַתְּאַזְּרֵנִי חַיִל לַמִּלְחָמָה — *You girded me with strength for battle.*

You gave the limbs of my body the strength to endure the terrible hardships of war (*Ibn Ezra*). [See *comm.* to v. 33.]

41. וְאֹיְבַי נָתַתָּה לִּי עֹרֶף — *You presented the back of my enemies' necks to me.*

[I.e., they turned and retreated, showing me the backs of their necks.] [1]

42. יְשַׁוְּעוּ וְאֵין מוֹשִׁיעַ — *They cried out, but there was no savior.*

Those who deny the Torah cried out to their idols but they had no power to offer assistance (*Rashi*).

עַל ה' — *To HASHEM* [lit. 'on Hashem']

This really means 'to HASHEM' as we find in a similar sense וַתִּתְפַּלֵּל עַל ה' *'and she prayed to HASHEM'* (*I Sam.* 1:11) (*Radak*).

וְלֹא עָנָם — *But He answered them not.*

Because they called out insincerely, only with their mouths. Their hearts were not in it (*Radak*).

43. וְאֶשְׁחָקֵם — *I pulverized them.*

As we find וְשָׁחַקְתָּ מִמֶּנָּה הָדֵק *'and you should grind from it very fine'* [*Exod.* 30:36] (*Metzudas Zion*).

אֲרִיקֵם — *I poured them out.*

The translation follows *Rashi* who relates the word to *Gen.* 42:35: *They were pouring* [מְרִיקִים] *out the contents of their sacks'.*

Radak suggests that אֲרִיקֵם be

---

1. This refers to Goliath, of whom it says: *'And the stone sunk into his forehead and he fell down to the ground on his face'* (*I Sam.* 17:49). Such a frontal blow should cause the victim to topple over backwards, why then did he fall on his face? An angel came and pushed him down frontwards, for the Holy One Blessed be He said: 'Let the foul mouth which blasphemed and insulted me now bite the dirt.' Another reason Goliath fell frontwards is because Hashem wished to save David the effort of taking extra steps when he beheaded him, for now he fell before David's feet. Goliath was six cubits and one finger-length in height. Had he fallen backwards his head would have rested altogether twelve cubits and two finger lengths from David's position.

Also, Goliath had an image of his idol, Dagon engraved on his heart. He fell forward on top of the idol to fulfill the curse *'and I shall place your corpse on top of the corpse of your idols'* (*Lev.* 26:30) (*Midrash Shocher Tov*).

38 I pursued my foes and overtook them
    and returned not until I had annihilated them.

39 I struck them down and they could not rise
        they fell beneath my feet.

40 You girded me with strength for battle,
        You bring my adversaries to their knees
        beneath me

41 You presented the backs of my enemies' necks to me
        and my antagonist I cut down.

42 They cried out, but there was no savior,
        to HASHEM, but He answered them not.

43 I pulverized them like dust
        in the face of the storm,
    Like the mud of the streets
        I poured them out.

44 Rescue me from the strife of the nation,
    Place me at the head of the peoples,

---

translated *'I will flatten (or thin) them out'* as we find רַקּוֹת בָּשָׂר *'thin of flesh'* (Gen. 41:19) and רְקִיקֵי מַצּוֹת *'flat matzah wafers'* (Ex. 29:2).

Metzudas David derives this word from רֵיק *'empty'*.

The mud in the streets is ground to a powder by the traffic and eventually the wind blows it all away and the streets are emptied of it. So too will be the fate of the enemy: אֲרִיקֵם, *'I will empty them out'*.

In *Samuel* the version, reads אֲדִקֵּם אֶרְקָעֵם, *'I will flatten them and beat them out flat'*. Mahari Kara there comments that this refers to the verse which describes Israel's victory over Moab: *'And he smote Moab, and measured them with the line, making them lie down flat on the ground'* (II Sam. 8:2).

44. תְּפַלְּטֵנִי מֵרִיבֵי עָם — *Rescue me from the strife of the nation.*

David prays for future rescue from involvement in their arguments and litigations: 'If I judge them, I fear that I risk punishment either for passing an unjust sentence or for wielding my authority too forcefully (*Rashi*).

According to *Radak*, David is speaking of the past and offering thanks. *Radak* notes that in *Samuel* the text varies slightly and reads not עָם *'the nation'*, but rather עַמִּי *'my nation'*. 'You rescued me from [internal] strife of my own nation, i.e., from Saul, Absalom, and my fellow Jews, who pursued me.

תְּשִׂימֵנִי לְרֹאשׁ גּוֹיִם — *Place me at the head of the peoples.*

According to *Midrash Shocher Tov*, when David asked to be released from the awesome responsibility of judging Israel and settling their quarrels, God lashed back, 'Do you then want to sit and do nothing'? David replied, 'Place me at the head of the [gentile] peoples.' Let me judge them, for in judging them there are no great risks involved (see *Rashi*).

Radak interprets this phrase, too, as a thanks for past victories over the

מה יָדַעְתִּי יַעַבְדוּנִי: לְשֵׁמַע אֹזֶן יִשָּׁמְעוּ לִי

מו בְּנֵי־נֵכָר יְכַחֲשׁוּ־לִי: בְּנֵי־נֵכָר יִבֹּלוּ

מז וְיַחְרְגוּ מִמִּסְגְּרוֹתֵיהֶם: חַי־יהוה וּבָרוּךְ

מח צוּרִי וְיָרוּם אֱלוֹהֵי יִשְׁעִי: הָאֵל הַנּוֹתֵן

מט נְקָמוֹת לִי וַיַּדְבֵּר עַמִּים תַּחְתָּי: מְפַלְּטִי
מֵאֹיְבָי אַף מִן־קָמַי תְּרוֹמְמֵנִי מֵאִישׁ חָמָס

foreign enemies. In his commentary to *II Sam.* 22:44 he reconciles the text here with the variant reading there, which is תִּשְׁמְרֵנִי לְרֹאשׁ גּוֹיִם, *'You have guarded me at the head of the peoples.'* Thus, David said: 'You have protected me so well that I finally was placed at the head of the peoples.'

The Vilna Gaon reconciles these two versions. The Talmud (*Moed Katan* 16b) states that when David did battle he shot one arrow and brought down eight hundred enemies in one blow. Yet he was dissatisfied and moaned over the fact that he lacked two hundred additional victims, as it is written *'How it could it be that one pursues one thousand'* (*Deut.* 32:30). When David lamented over the two hundred, a heavenly voice would cry out, *'Only on account of the incident of Uriah the Hittite'* [the husband of Bath Sheba] (*I Kings* 15:5). *Rashi* comments that as a result of that sin, David lost the additional victims. On what does *Rashi* base his comment? It is possible that this calculation may be derived from the variation between the version in *Samuel* and the version in *Psalms.* The version in *Samuel* was composed in David's youth before he sinned. Therefore he says there תִּשְׁמְרֵנִי, *guard me,* which has the numerical value of 1,000 alluding to the fact that he killed 1000 of the enemy with one blow. However, in *Psalms,* which was composed at the end of his life, after the sin, he says תְּשִׂימֵנִי, deleting the letter ר *resh,* whose numerical value is 200, alluding to his loss of 200 victims.

[The above is quoted in *Kol Eliyahu.* See also the introduction of the grandchildren of the Gaon to his comm. on *Shulchan Aruch.* The commentary of *Tosfos HaRosh* on *Moed Katan* which was written some 600 years ago but was not published until the 1930's, reconciles these variations in the same way. (See also *comm.* to 25:18-19 for a sequel to this discussion).]

עַם לֹא יָדַעְתִּי יַעַבְדוּנִי — *A nation unknown to me* [lit. *'I did not know'*] *will serve me.*

Even from far away places they come to serve me (*Metzudas David*).

45. לְשֵׁמַע אֹזֶן — *As soon as they hear.*
Even when they are not in my presence, but merely hear of my wishes through a messenger (*Rashi*).

יִשָּׁמְעוּ לִי — *They will obey me* (*Rashi*).
Radak and *Abarbanel* translate: *They gather around me,* as we find, *And Saul gathered* [וַיְשַׁמַּע] *all of the nation'* [*I Sam.* 23:8].

יְכַחֲשׁוּ לִי — *Will cringe before me* [lit. *'they lied to me'*]
Because they fear me they lie and deny their participation in the wars waged against me. Or, *'they betrayed',* for they deserted their allies because they feared me (*Radak*).

46. בְּנֵי נֵכָר יִבֹּלוּ — *Foreigners will wither away.*
I.e. fear will wear them out (*Radak*).

וְיַחְרְגוּ — *And be terrified.*
This word has no counterpart in all of Scriptures (*Ibn Ezra*).
However, the words וּמֵחֲדָרִים אֵימָה [*Deut.* 32:25] are translated by Targum as וּמִתַּוָּנַיָא חַרְגַת מוֹתָא *'and from within the chambers, the terror of death'* (*Rashi; Radak*).

מִמִּסְגְּרוֹתֵיהֶם — *By their imprisonment* [lit. *'their enclosure.'*]

a nation unknown to me, will serve me.
⁴⁵ *As soon as they hear they will obey me,*
   foreigners will cringe before me.
⁴⁶ *Foreigners will wither away*
   and be terrified by their imprisonment.
⁴⁷ *HASHEM lives and blessed is my rock!*
   may the God of my salvation be exalted.
⁴⁸ *The God who grants me vengeance*
   and subjugates nations beneath me,
⁴⁹ *Rescues me from my foes*
   and raises me even above my adversaries,
From the man of violence He delivers me.

When I imprison them they will suffer the tortures of incarceration (*Rashi*).

Rashi also quotes *Menachem* who translates this as a *'belt'* (which encloses a person). וְיַחְרְגוּ, too, is related to the customary word for belt which is חֲגוֹרָה, although the letters are in a different order. Thus, *'their belts'* [which when tightly girded symbolize strength] *'will be loosened'*. However, *Donash* translates this phrase: 'They will limp and hop because of the מִסְגְּרוֹת, *tight bonds* placed on their feet.' The *Targum* of פִּסֵחַ *'lame'* is חֲגִיר (*Lev.* 21:18).

47. חַי ה' — *HASHEM lives.*

All of the aforementioned successes happen because my God is the living God who has the power to perform miracles (*Radak*).

וְיָרוּם אֱלוֹהֵי יִשְׁעִי — *May the God of my salvation be exalted.*

Minchas Shai notes that this is the only instance in Scriptures where אֱלוֹהֵי, is spelled *'full'* with a ו, *vav*. In the *Midrash* of חֲסֵרוֹת וְיְתֵרוֹת [a catalogue of words spelled *'missing'* or *'full'*], the reason is explained: 'When the salvation of God will occur, then all things which are *'missing'* will become *'full'*.

48. הָאֵל הַנּוֹתֵן נְקָמוֹת לִי — *The God who grants me vengeance.*

He grants me the strength to take revenge (*Rashi; Radak*).

וַיַּדְבֵּר — *And subjugates.*

Targum to *Gen.* 31:18 renders וַיִּנְהַג, *'and he led'* as וּדְבַר. God led the nations to come and subject themselves to me (*Radak; Rashi*).

עַמִּים תַּחְתָּי — *Nations beneath me.*

Rashi also relates וַיַּדְבֵּר to דֶּבֶר, *pestilence*, and translates תַּחְתָּי as *'instead of me'*. Thus: 'You afflicted the nations, and not me, with pestilence.'

49. אַף מִן קָמַי תְּרוֹמְמֵנִי — *And raises me* [lit. 'You raised me'] *even above my adversaries.*

God does not merely rescue me from my enemies, He even places me high above them (*Radak*).

מֵאִישׁ חָמָס תַּצִּילֵנִי — *From the man of violence He delivers me* [lit, 'You deliver me']

This describes Saul. After I was rescued from him I achieved all of my glory (*Radak*).

נ תַּצִּילֵנִי: עַל־כֵּן | אוֹדְךָ בַגּוֹיִם | יהוה
נא וּלְשִׁמְךָ אֲזַמֵּרָה: מַגְדִּל יְשׁוּעוֹת מַלְכּוֹ
וְעֹשֶׂה חֶסֶד | לִמְשִׁיחוֹ לְדָוִד וּלְזַרְעוֹ עַד־
עוֹלָם:

50. עַל כֵּן אוֹדְךָ בַגּוֹיִם ה׳ — *Therefore I will thank You among the peoples, HASHEM.*

I will proclaim before all of the peoples who serve and obey me that my right to rule is drawn from You, Hashem (*Radak*).

51. מַגְדִּל יְשׁוּעוֹת מַלְכּוֹ — *He magnifies the victories of His king.*

The following is the song of Your praise which I shall sing before the peoples, as I promised in the previous verse (*Metzudas David*).

In *Samuel* the word is written מגדיל and is pronounced מִגְדּוֹל.

Midrash Shocher Tov explains: Rabbi Yudan says, 'The redemption of this nation will not come about all at once. Rather it will appear little by little. Therefore, it is described in Psalms as מַגְדִּל *He makes great* (constant present

tense) meaning that it gradually becomes greater and greater. This is like the dawn which breaks slowly, for if the sun were to rise all at once its fiery light would blind all. So, too, will be the redemption: If it would come all at once the people of Israel who for so long have been accustomed only to oppression could not endure the experience and it would overwhelm them. In *Samuel* the word מִגְדּוֹל is used because it also means 'a tower.' Messiah will be a tower of strength for Israel as it says, *A tower* [מִגְדַּל] *of might is the Name of Hashem; with it the righteous will run and be elevated* (*Prov.* 18:1).

וְעֹשֶׂה חֶסֶד לִמְשִׁיחוֹ — *And does kindness with His anointed.*

The victories were granted purely because of Your kindness; I did not deserve them (*Metzudas David*).

⁵⁰ *Therefore, I will thank You among the peoples,*
HASHEM,
and to Your Name will I sing.
⁵¹ *He magnifies the victories of His king,*
and does kindness with His anointed,
to David and his seed, forever.

לְדָוִד וּלְזַרְעוֹ עַד עוֹלָם — *To David and his seed, forever.*

[This was the solemn promise which God made through the prophet Nathan to David: *'When your days are filled and you shall lay to rest with your fathers, I shall set up your seed after you, he who shall come from your body, and I will establish his kingdom. He will build a house to my name and I will establish the throne of his kingdom forever ... And your house and your kingdom shall be made secure before you, forever, your throne will be established for all time'* (II Sam. 7:12,13,16).]

Abarbanel draws our attention to the three different names mentioned in this verse מַלְכּוֹ, מְשִׁיחוֹ, דָוִד, *David, His anointed, His king.* They correspond to three separate periods in David's life. He sings that God was with him at his zenith, when he was מַלְכּוֹ *'the king'* acknowledged by all. God was also with him even before when he was merely מְשִׁיחוֹ *'His anointed'*, by the act of Samuel, but was not yet crowned. Finally, God was his support even when he was but a poor shepherd named David. Therefore David asks that God be with his offspring, too, at all times.[1]

1. *Meorei Or* makes the following calculations: The number of words in the first and second *'Tablets'* containing the Ten Commandments total 365. Likewise, there are 365 words in the Song of David, 365 words in the Song of Chanah and 365 words in the Song of Devora (until וַתִּשְׁקֹט הָאָרֶץ, *and the land was tranquil*). Finally, all this corresponds to the secret of the קְטוֹרֶת, *the holy incense*, which contained 365 מָנִים *measures*.

The vast heavenly bodies orbiting with flawless precision in the skies are a clear manifestation of the infinite wisdom and power of the Creator. Nevertheless, the celestial panorama is not the ultimate form of divine revelation. It is the study of God's will as revealed in the Torah which presents the clearest available perception of the Creator.

Malbim assures the diligent scholar that if his quest for God is sincere, he will be assisted in his studies by a holy spirit, a divine ecstasy which resembles prophecy. In this chapter, the Psalmist proves in six ways that the comprehension of God gained through Torah scholarship surpasses the perception gained through scientific research. Moreover, even the astronomical secrets of the heavens are unlocked before the Torah sage.

Shmuel bar Abba said, 'I know the pathways of the skies as well as I know the streets of my own city, Nehardea.' Did Shmuel fly up to the heavens to learn this? Rather, because he toiled incessantly in the study of Torah, all of the wisdom of the skies was revealed to him (Midrash Shocher Tov).

The study of Torah reveals not only the pathways of heaven, but man's way on earth, as well. Before his sin, Adam led a life which was straight and pure; as predictable as the orbit of the sun and stars. Sin warped man. Only Torah study can right him once again (see Overview).

First the Psalmist extols the unerring precision of the heavenly spheres. Then he turns to man and exhorts him to follow the example he sees in the sky, saying in effect: 'Learn Torah and return to what you should be!' The Torah of HASHEM is perfect, it brings back the soul. The Torah is 'upright' and 'it enlightens the eyes' and 'it is pure.' Accept the Torah and imitate Adam before the sin.

Small wonder that the Vilna Gaon (Ma'aseh Rav 196) designated this psalm to be the שִׁיר שֶׁל יוֹם, 'the Song of the Day' for the festival of Shavuos when we celebrate the presentation of the Torah to Israel at Mount Sinai.

א־ב לַמְנַצֵּחַ מִזְמוֹר לְדָוִד: הַשָּׁמַיִם מְסַפְּרִים
ג כְּבוֹד־אֵל וּמַעֲשֵׂה יָדָיו מַגִּיד הָרָקִיעַ: יוֹם
לְיוֹם יַבִּיעַ אֹמֶר וְלַיְלָה לְּלַיְלָה יְחַוֶּה־
ד דָּעַת: אֵין־אֹמֶר וְאֵין דְּבָרִים בְּלִי נִשְׁמָע

2. הַשָּׁמַיִם מְסַפְּרִים כְּבוֹד אֵל — *The heavens declare the glory of God.*

Are the heavens capable of speech? No. But they can stimulate men to articulate the praises of God.

The Psalmist explains this concept in v. 4, *'There is no speech and there are no words, their sound is unheard.* There is no verbal communication between the heavens and humanity. Rather, because the light of the celestial bodies pervades the earth and illuminates it, mankind is stirred to declare the glory of God's work and to praise and bless Him for the heavenly lights *(Rashi; Radak; Targum).*

However, *Radak* and *Metzudas David* suggest that the *equivalent* of speech may be attributed to the heavens. Their astoundingly precise orbits declare the glory of HASHEM in the most vivid and eloquent manner. Indeed, their testimony to God's greatness is such that, as *Ibn Ezra* remarks, one cannot truly appreciate the celestial wonders described in this Psalm if he is not well-versed in the science of astronomy.[1]

הָרָקִיעַ — *The expanse of the sky.*

[Something flattened out and spread over a wide area is known as רָקִיעַ as in וַיְרַקְּעוּ אֶת פַּחֵי הַזָּהָב, *'And they beat flat the plating of gold'* (Exodus 39:3. See *Rashi ibid,* and cf. *comm.* to *Bereishis* 1:6.)]

Rashi says that David refers specifically to the stars and constellations which were fashioned by God's hands and placed in the skies for a sign as described in *Genesis* 1:14-18.

Malbim provides a very clear differentiation between שָׁמַיִם, *heaven,* and רָקִיעַ, *expanse* or *firmament.* שָׁמַיִם refers to the upper heavens, the extra-terrestrial reaches where the planets and stars orbit. רָקִיעַ refers to the sky where evaporated moisture forms clouds and becomes precipitation. This part of the atmosphere, although rarefied, still contains sufficient air to support breathing and is therefore considered part of earth. Beyond it, the 'heavens' begin.

Malbim goes on to explain the difference between הַגָּדָה and סִפּוּר. סִפּוּר means the declaration of a long-established fact which occured in the past. The stars and planets in the high heavens declare that long ago God created a glorious universe of staggering dimensions. However, the man who merely gazes at the stars will see no evidence of God's continual, never-ending involvement with the affairs of this earth; the שָׁמַיִם, 'heavens' are מְסַפְּרִים,'declaring' only the ancient 'glory of God'.

However, he who scrutinizes the wonders of the precipitation cycle which supports all life systems at every moment, is convinced of God's providential and constantly renewed control over every aspect of life. הַגָּדָה is the excited telling of a fresh new occurrence [as in וַחֲדָשׁוֹת אֲנִי מַגִּיד, *'of new matters I tell'* (Isaiah 42:9)] and only the person who observes the רָקִיעַ *'the lower sky'*is able to sense the excitement of constant renewal on earth.

3. יוֹם לְיוֹם יַבִּיעַ אֹמֶר — *Day following day brings expressions of praise.*

1. All stars and celestial bodies possess a spirit and an intellect and knowledge. They are alive and they exist with a comprehension of 'He who spoke and brought the world to be'. Each one of these, according to his individual level, praises and lauds the Creator like the ministering angels *(Rambam, Hilchos Yesodei HaTorah 3:9).*

XIX
1-4

For the Conductor; a song of David.
² The heavens declare the glory of God,
and the expanse of the sky tells of His handiwork.
³ Day following day brings expressions of praise,
and night following night bespeaks wisdom.
⁴ There is no speech and there are no words;
their sound is unheard.

יַבִּיעַ — [lit. 'to talk'] as in יַבִּיעוּן בְּפִיהֶם, 'they talk with their mouths' (Psalms 59:8) (Metzudas Zion).

The daily renewed works of creation beginning with the rising and setting of the sun stir mankind to speak and express God's praises (Rashi).

According to Radak the days do not cause man to speak, rather it is as if they themselves speak. When man observes the unchanging order of the earth's rotation cycle, he is convinced that this meticulous order will continue tomorrow and forever. Thus 'One day speaks of the next day that will follow it', testifying that as it is today so shall it be forever.

Rashi also quotes Menachem (whose view is shared by Ibn Ezra) who interprets יַבִּיעַ as 'to flow' [as in נַחַל נֹבֵעַ, 'a flowing stream' (Proverbs 18:4)]. Thus the Psalmist says: 'From day to day, words of God's praise will flow forth incessantly like an endless stream.'

וְלַיְלָה לְלַיְלָה יְחַוֶּה דָּעַת — And night following night bespeaks wisdom.

Night after night, the sun sets beneath the horizon, only to rise and set again on the morrow. [This continual pattern attests to divine wisdom and control] (Rashi).

The order displayed by the setting sun on one night foretells a repetition on the next (Radak).

Midrash Shocher Tov interprets this verse to mean that both day and night identify their onset to the person who has lost track of time.

'When Moses went up for forty days to receive the Torah it was always light before the Divine Presence. How did he know when it was day or night? When God taught him the Written Law, (the Scriptures) he knew that it was day. When God instructed him in the Oral Law (the Mishna) he knew that it was night.'

אֵין אֹמֶר וְאֵין דְּבָרִים בְּלִי נִשְׁמָע קוֹלָם .4 — There is no speech and there are no words, their sound is unheard.

[Cf. Rashi, Radak v. 2.]

Ibn Ezra explains that אֹמֶר, 'speech' refers to a complete statement which transmits a message. דְּבָרִים, 'words' are individual words which convey no message. קוֹל, 'sound' is the sound of individual letters. The heavens possess no means of verbal communication. Yet, the inner soul of man, through the perception of his spirit and intellect, can discern their message clearly.[1]

1. The Vilna Gaon cites a Talmudic passage (Yoma 20b) which seems to contradict this verse because it states that the sound of the sun is loud and audible. Rabbi Levi said, 'Why isn't a man's voice heard as clearly in the daytime as it is at night? Because of the orbiting sun which slices its way through the heavens like a carpenter who saws through cedars ... The Rabbis taught: Three sounds travel from one end of the earth to the other. The first one is the sound of the sun in orbit ...'

The Gaon reconciles the contradiction explaining that the sun's orbit does not make sounds audible to the human ear, but it does cause agitation and turbulence in the atmosphere. The

ה קוֹלָם: בְּכָל־הָאָרֶץ | יָצָא קַוָּם וּבִקְצֵה
תֵבֵל מִלֵּיהֶם לַשֶּׁמֶשׁ שָׂם־אֹהֶל בָּהֶם:
ו וְהוּא כְּחָתָן יֹצֵא מֵחֻפָּתוֹ יָשִׂישׂ כְּגִבּוֹר
ז לָרוּץ אֹרַח: מִקְצֵה הַשָּׁמַיִם | מוֹצָאוֹ
וּתְקוּפָתוֹ עַל־קְצוֹתָם וְאֵין נִסְתָּר

5. קַוָּם — *Their line.*

In the course of construction a plumb line is used to insure accuracy. The perfection of the celestial structures is referred to as a line which is stretched out to the ends of the earth. This means that the precision of the cosmos is evident all over the earth to any observer (*Radak*).

Rabbi S.R. Hirsch relates this word to קַו הַמִּדָּה *'the measuring line'* (*Jeremiah* 31:38) which stakes off a certain territory for a specific purpose. Here it means that the heavenly forces control and set limits and boundaries for the development of everything existing on earth.

תֵבֵל — *Land.* This word describes the inhabited areas of the earth, the civilized lands (*Ibn Ezra, Malbim*).

מִלֵּיהֶם — *Their words.* The performance of the heavenly bodies speaks of God's wisdom with greater eloquence than the spoken word (*Radak*).

Wherever men dwell, their conversations are filled with words of praise for the wonders of the heavens (*Malbim*).

אֹהֶל — *A tent.*

This refers to the תיק *'case'* of the sun which envelopes it. [If the sun were not cloaked in a protective case, its tremendous heat would burn the earth to a crisp in a flash. Perhaps this *'case'* refers to the various atmospheric levels which surround the globe like a shield, and filter out the undesirable elements of the sunlight before they reach earth] (*Rashi*).

According to *Ibn Ezra* and *Metzudas David* אֹהֶל, *'tent'* symbolizes a permanent home or dwelling place. The sun, which is the central force of the solar system, is set in a permanent axis in the sky just like a tent pitched firmly in place.

6. וְהוּא כְּחָתָן יֹצֵא מֵחֻפָּתוֹ — *The sun is like a groom coming forth from his bridal chamber.*

Radak explains: Just as everyone joyfully comes out to greet the groom, so does all of creation rejoice every morning when the light of the sun rises forth anew. *Radak* also quotes the words of his father: A groom who leaves the bridal chamber yearns to go back in as soon as possible. Similarly, the sun eagerly returns to sink beneath the horizon at the end of its daily route, for it was from beneath the horizon that it rose forth in the morning.[1]

light waves emanating from the moving sun stir up air waves which interfere with the normal air waves which carry sounds down on earth. It is not the sound of the sun itself, but rather its interruption of other sounds, which is heard all over the globe (*Avnei Eliyahu*).

◄§ "Only twice a year, at the equinoxes of Spring and Autumn are both day and night completely equal. Otherwise, night is lengthened and borrows time from the day, or the day is lengthened and 'borrows' from the night. Each one eventually repays the other faithfully and graciously without any form of proof or document or court order. But down on earth, when one man lends to another, how many documents and arguments and shouts and court cases are necessary to keep things under control. Thus, *'One day after another . . . and one night after another. . .'* They give and take constantly. Yet, *'There is no speech, and there are no words their voice is unheard'* " (*Midrash Shocher Tov*).

⁵ *Their line goes forth throughout the earth,*
  and their words reach the farthest ends of the land.
In their midst He has set up a tent for the sun.
⁶ *The sun is like a groom coming forth from his*
  bridal chamber
  rejoicing like a warrior to run the course.
⁷ *Its source is the end of the heavens*
  and its circuit is to their end;
  nothing escapes its heat.

יָשִׂישׂ כְּגִבּוֹר לָרוּץ אֹרַח — *Rejoicing like a* *warrior to run the course.*

In the blessing of the קִידּוּשׁ הַלְּבָנָה, 'the sanctification of the New Moon' we praise the heavenly spheres as שָׂשִׂים וּשְׂמֵחִים לַעֲשׂוֹת רְצוֹן קוֹנָם, 'They rejoice and are glad to do the will of their Master (Sanhedrin 42a). This description is derived from the words יָשִׂישׂ כְּגִבּוֹר, 'rejoicing like a warrior' (Rashi ibid).]

The warrior rejoices at the opportunity to go out to war for he has confidence in his strength. So too, the sun is confident that it will run its course with no interference (Metzudas David).

The rising of the sun and its shining is its rejoicing (Radak).

7. מִקְצֵה הַשָּׁמַיִם מוֹצָאוֹ — *Its source is the end of the heavens. The sun comes* up over the horizon which appears to be the end of the sky (Metzudas David).

וּתְקוּפָתוֹ עַל קְצוֹתָם — *And its circuit is to* *their end* [lit. 'to their other end']. Every day it rises from the extreme end of the eastern sky and sets in the extreme end of the western sky (Metzudas David).

וְאֵין נִסְתָּר מֵחַמָּתוֹ — *[And] nothing es-* *capes its heat.*

The rays of the sun reach every place on earth without exception, even though their intensity is not the same everywhere.

The Psalmist chooses his words carefully. He does not say that nothing escapes the sun's *light*; indeed a person can take shade from its light. However, even if one were to incarcerate himself in the deepest, darkest, best-insulated chamber, he would still be affected by the heat of the sun which warms all of the air on earth (Rashi).[2]

Rashi takes note of the fact that there are seven levels to the sky [see *Chagigah* 12b]. The first level, closest to earth, is called וִילוֹן, 'curtain'. The second is רָקִיע, 'sky'. In this level God placed the sun and the moon, the stars and all

1. חָתָן דּוֹמֶה לְמֶלֶךְ, 'A groom may be likened to a king': Just as a king does not go out in public unattended, so too the groom may not venture forth alone. Just as the king dons royal garments, so must the groom be dressed in splendor on all the seven days of feasting. Just as all shout the praises of the king, so must all laud the groom. Just as a king's face shines like the sun, so should the countenance of the groom glow with joy, as it says: 'The sun is like the groom coming forth from his bridal chamber' (Pirkei d'Rabbi Eliezer, Ch. 16).

2. The Roman Emperor Antoninus came to Rabbi Judah the Prince and asked that he pray for him. The Rabbi responded: 'May you be saved from the bitter cold.'

Said Antoninus: 'This is a worthless prayer. Just put on another warm garment and the cold will have no effect.' So, Rabbi Judah prayed again: 'May you be spared from the scorching heat which burns the earth.'

'Ah', said Antoninus, satisfied, 'This is a true prayer. May this prayer be heard, for Scripture says 'and nothing escapes its heat' " (Yerushalmi Sanhedrin 10:5).

ח מֶחֲמָתוֹ: תּוֹרַת יהוה תְּמִימָה מְשִׁיבַת
נָפֶשׁ עֵדוּת יהוה נֶאֱמָנָה מַחְכִּימַת פֶּתִי:
ט פִּקּוּדֵי יהוה יְשָׁרִים מְשַׂמְּחֵי־לֵב מִצְוַת

celestial bodies. The Psalmist praises
God for moving the sun at least one
level away from earth, for if the sun
were closer, its heat would be unbearable 'and nothing escapes its heat.'

8. תְּמִימָה ה' תּוֹרַת — *The Torah of
HASHEM is perfect.*

After completing his description of
the heavenly wonders which proclaim
the wisdom of God, the Psalmist proceeds to declare that there exists a
testimony to God's greatness which
far surpasses the heavens. That testimony is the Torah which is perfect
(Ibn Ezra; Metzudas David; Malbim).

All Five Books of Moses are called
Torah, not only the commandments,
but even the stories and narratives. All
of these are a מוֹרֶה, '*guide*' showing the
proper way to come close to Hashem
(Radak).

After depicting the illumination of
the sun, the Psalmist tells of the Torah
which also '*enlightens the eyes*' (v. 9),
as it says אוֹר וְתוֹרָה מִצְוָה נֵר כִּי '*For the
command is a lamp and the Torah is
light*' (Proverbs 6:23) (Rashi).

'When is the Torah of HASHEM
perfect? When it comes from the
mouths of those who are perfect' [when

it is studied with sincerity for noble, un-
selfish purposes] *(Midrash Shocher
Tov).*[1]

נָפֶשׁ מְשִׁיבַת — *It restores the soul.*

Torah removes the soul from the
pathway leading to death, and restores
it to the pathway leading to life *(Rashi).*

Just as the heavenly lights sustain the
earth, so does the Torah provide
sustenance for the soul. Like a stranger
in a foreign land who has no helpful
friends or support, so is the soul a
stranger in the human body. The
physical body has many helpers, to aid
it in its relentless pursuit of lust and
desire. But the soul is a lonely, forsaken
captive. Only the Torah provides
guidance toward the straight path and
restrains man from worldly lusts and
countless obstacles. Thus, the Torah
redeems the soul from its captivity and
brings it back to its spiritual source; the
place of its original glory.

Torah is more beneficial than the sun.
The sun can damage certain materials,
but Torah is perfect for all. A person
who is overexposed to the sun can die of
sunstroke. Not so the Torah, the more
one basks in its warmth, the more it
refreshes the soul *(Radak v. 10)*[2]

1. *Tosafos (Megillah* 32a s.v. גּוֹלְלוֹ) tells of the following custom:
When the Torah is taken out of the Ark it is customary to recite the verses beginning with
תְּמִימָה ה' תּוֹרַת, *(Psalms* 19:8-11), because they record the rewards of Torah study ('*it restores
the soul*', '*it makes the simple one wise*' etc.). There are forty words in this section of the psalm
(see gloss of the *Bach ibid.)* which correspond to the forty days in which the Torah was given
at Sinai. Then the reader says, יַחְדָּו שְׁמוֹ וּנְרוֹמְמָה אִתִּי לַה' גַּדְּלוּ '*Magnify HASHEM with me and
we will raise up His name together*' which contains six (Hebrew) words corresponding to the
sets of six steps at a time taken by those who carried the Holy Ark up to Jerusalem in the time
of David *(II Sam.* 6:13).

2. *Rashi* makes reference to the *Midrash Shocher Tov* which describes the superiority of
Torah over the dangerous sun:
'There is no Gehinnom in the future other than the sun itself. Today the sun is enveloped in
its protective case and kept at a distance in the רָקִיעַ, second heavenly level. But on the Day of
Judgment, the sun will be removed from its insulation and brought down to the lower sky
near earth. The wicked will be judged and burnt as is said: '*For behold, the day comes, it burns
as a furnace, and all the proud and all that do evil shall be stubble and the day that comes shall
set them ablaze (Malachi* 3:19). Furthermore, it is said: '*... And nothing escapes its heat.*'

XIX
8-9

8 *The Torah of HASHEM is perfect,*
it restores the soul,
The testimony of HASHEM is trustworthy,
making the simple one wise.
9 *The orders of HASHEM are upright,*
gladdening the heart.

עֵדוּת ה' נֶאֱמָנָה — *The testimony of HASHEM is trustworthy.* All of the mitzvos of the Torah are called עֵדוּת, 'testimony' because they attest to the אֱמוּנָה, 'faith', of the people who fulfill them *(Metzudas David)*.

There are a number of holy objects bearing testimony to the fact that Israel has chosen HASHEM for their God and that God has chosen them for His treasured people. They include the אֲרוֹן הָעֵדוּת, 'The Ark of the Testimony' which contains the Tablets of the Law *(Exodus* 40:3) and the אֹהֶל הָעֵדוּת, 'The Tent of the Testimony' *(Numbers* 17:23), i.e., the Tabernacle. They perpetuate the memory of the giving of the Law at Mount Sinai, a testimony which was transmitted from father to son throughout Jewish history. Some commandments are also called 'witnesses', such as the Sabbath and the 'Shemitah', seventh year, both of which bear witness to the fact that God rested on the seventh day from His work of creation *(Radak)*.

'When is the testimony of Hashem trustworthy? When it comes from the mouth of the trustworthy [teacher]' *(Midrash Shocher Tov)*.

מַחְכִּימַת פֶּתִי — *Making the simple one wise.*

The Torah is completely beneficial, but the heat of the sun can sometimes affect the mind adversely and drive a person mad *(Metzudas David, Radak, v.* 10).

Every facet of the Tabernacle, known as *'Tent of the Testimony'*, testified to intellectual brilliance. The building and its parts were a universe in microcosm, reflecting the heavenly and the earthly worlds. Therefore, it is called by the wise men עוֹלָם הָאֶמְצָעִי *'the intermediate world'*.

Similarly, those who study well the testimony commandments (see above) will grow wise in their comprehension of the secrets of God's creation *(Radak).* [1]

9. פְּקוּדֵי — *The orders.*
This word is derived from פְּקוּדָה *'order, command'* and is also related to פִּקָּדוֹן *'deposit' (Hirsch).*

The Lord has incorporated and deposited into the very soul of man a tendency to appreciate the importance of these divine orders and the intellect to naturally and instinctively undertand their significance *(Ibn Ezra; Rada).*

יְשָׁרִים — *Are upright.*
Because the intellect is naturally attracted to these orders, they appear to be the proper and upright thing to do *(Radak).*

מְשַׂמְּחֵי לֵב — *Gladdening the heart.*
The wise man will rejoice when his

At that time the Torah will protect the righteous who engage diligently in its study, as it is said: '... *It restores the soul'*; and it is further said: *'But unto you that fear my name, the sun of righteousness shall arise with healing in its wings' (Malachi* 3:20).

1. The *Shaloh HaKadosh* asked: How can the Torah possibly *'make the simple ones wise?'* Does it not say יָהֵב חָכְמְתָא לְחַכִּימִין *'He gives wisdom only to the wise' (Daniel* 2:21)? Rather, this means that through Torah study even the unintelligent person will appreciate wisdom enough to realize that he is simple and far from wise.

י יהוה בָּרָה מְאִירַת עֵינָיִם: יִרְאַת יהוה |
טְהוֹרָה עוֹמֶדֶת לָעַד מִשְׁפְּטֵי־יהוה אֱמֶת
יא צָדְקוּ יַחְדָּו: הַנֶּחֱמָדִים מִזָּהָב וּמִפַּז רָב

straight and upright intellect will dominate the lowly passions of the body and steer him properly (Radak).

God's commands gladden the heart unlike the sun which can bring fear and worry to the heart, for man is concerned lest the heat of the sun should harm him (Metzudas David; Radak v.10).

Rabbi Chanina, the Deputy High Priest said: Whoever takes the words of Torah to heart merits that all disturbing thoughts and fears should not molest him. He is freed from anxiety over violence and hunger, mad illusions and erotic fantasies, evil impulses of sin and adultery, worthless thoughts and fears of oppression by others. This is as it says: 'The orders of HASHEM are upright, gladdening the heart (Avos d'Rabbi Nathan Ch. 20).

בְּרָה 'ה מִצְוַת — The command of HASHEM is clear.

Every command is flawless and free of imperfection (Radak).

This refers to the positive commandments (Ibn Ezra).

מְאִירַת עֵינָיִם — Enlightening the eyes.

But those who live without the commandments stumble in darkness, for only God's commands light the way before those who strive to ascend to His glory (Radak).

Torah lights up the eyes beneficially and never hurts them, but prolonged staring at the sun injures the eyes (Metzudas David; Radak v. 10).

10. טְהוֹרָה 'ה יִרְאַת — The fear of HASHEM is pure.

This refers to the negative commandments. The person who is careful not to transgress them is pure for he has not sullied himself with sin (Ibn Ezra).

There are many sins which the Torah cautions against with the warning וְיָרֵאתָ מֵאֱלֹהֶיךָ, 'and you shall fear your God.' These are the crimes which can be committed in secrecy, such as robbery and cheating on weights and measures, etc. The man who refrains from evil when no human is looking, and controls himself only because he recognizes God's presence, truly deserves to be called 'one with a pure fear of God' (Radak).

לָעַד עוֹמֶדֶת — Enduring forever.

[What proves the purity of a man's fear? The fact that it endures without lapse or interruption.]

Radak observes that many commandments are limited to special occasions or specific circumstances. But the fear of God must be experienced at all times and in all places. It is a concept which always remains in the mind, pure and bright. Thus it surpasses the illumination of the sun which can be obscured by clouds in the day and which disappears completely at night.[1]

יַחְדָּו צָדְקוּ — Altogether righteous.

There is no contradiction between one law of the Torah and another, whereas in civil law one will very often

1. We find of a man who has studied all of the Torah, Midrash, Halachos and Aggados, that if he has no fear of sin then he has nothing. This is be likened to a man who told his neighbor: 'I possess one thousand measures each of grain, wine, and oil.'

His neighbor said: 'If you have vessels in which to preserve them safely, then you do indeed possess everything. If not, however, you have nothing. So too, we say to the man who has studied all of the Torah, 'If you have acquired fear of sin, then all is indeed yours.' So said the prophet (Isaiah 33:6): אוֹצָרוֹ הִיא 'ה יִרְאַת 'the fear of HASHEM is its [Torah's] storage house' (Midrash Shemos Rabbah 30:14).

The command of HASHEM is clear,
enlightening the eyes.
¹⁰ *The fear of HASHEM is pure, enduring forever.*
The judgments of HASHEM are true;
altogether righteous.
¹¹ *They are more desirable than gold,*
— than even much fine gold;

---

find inconsistencies and conflicts between different statutes *(Ibn Ezra).*

The sun, too, seems to be self-contradictory. When it functions in one place, it ceases to function elsewhere. When the sun shines on one side of the earth it is dark on the other *(Metzudas David).*

The praises of Torah enumerated in verses 8-10 follow six themes: תּוֹרַת, *the Torah;* עֵדוּת, *testimony (v. 8);* פִּקּוּדֵי, *orders;* מִצְוַת, *command (v. 9);* יִרְאַת, *fear;* מִשְׁפְּטֵי, *judgments (v. 10).* The six themes correspond to the שִׁשָׁה סִדְרֵי מִשְׁנָה *'the Six Orders of the Mishna.'* Each theme is described in five words (including God's Name) corresponding to the Five Books of Torah. Now the Psalmist concludes צָדְקוּ יַחְדָּו, *they are altogether righteous:* all these themes are perfectly integrated with kindness and truth. [The Oral Law is inseparably linked to the Written Law] *(Rashi v. 8).*

11. הַנֶּחֱמָדִים מִזָּהָב — *They are more desirable than gold.*

The Psalmist has concluded his comparison of the light of the Torah to the celestial lights. He has demonstrated how the light of Torah is far more beneficial to man's spirit than the heavenly lights, and how it will bring man fortune in the World to Come. Now he proceeds to show how Torah surpasses all of the luxuries of earth. Men desire gold and precious stones because they are durable and of un-diminishing value, but Torah surpasses them. Man cannot take gold to the grave, but Torah wisdom accompanies

him in this world and in the next *(Ibn Ezra).*

The Torah is more valuable and en-during than any earthly treasure. Precious possessions may be stolen or lost, but nothing can deprive a man of his knowledge. When a man spends his money it is no longer his. But when he shares his Torah with others his own resources are not depleted. On the con-trary, students make their teacher wiser *(Radak).*

וּמִפַּז רָב — *Than even much fine gold.*

[Some say that פַּז is the purest form of refined gold. Others say that פַּז is a precious gem. The word רָב may refer to either quality i.e. *'very fine'*, or quantity i.e. *'an abundance'.*]

Precious gems or metals only retain their high value when they are scarce and hard to get. Once they cease to be rare they lose all importance as we find, *'In the days of Solomon silver was not worth anything' (I Kings 10:21).*

Not so Torah. If the face of the earth were covered with knowledge and every man were a Torah scholar, this would only serve to make the Torah still more precious to man. Thus, Torah is truly dearer *'than even much fine gold' (Ohel Yaakov).*

[*Rashi* in *Yoma* 45a says that פַּז is מַרְגָּלִית, *'a pearl'.* In *Avodah Zara* 11b, *Rashi* states that פַּז is an extremely rare gem. This rarity is confirmed by the *Talmud* in *Gittin* 58a which relates that since creation only two *'selah measures'* of פַּז descended to this world; one is in Rome and one is spread over the rest of the world.]

יב וּמְתוּקִים מִדְּבַשׁ וְנֹפֶת צוּפִים: גַּם־עַבְדְּךָ
יג נִזְהָר בָּהֶם בְּשָׁמְרָם עֵקֶב רָב: שְׁגִיאוֹת
יד מִי־יָבִין מִנִּסְתָּרוֹת נַקֵּנִי: גַּם מִזֵּדִים | חֲשֹׂךְ
עַבְדֶּךָ אַל־יִמְשְׁלוּ־בִי אָז אֵיתָם וְנִקֵּיתִי

וּמְתוּקִים מִדְּבַשׁ — [And] sweeter than honey.

To the human taste, honey is the sweetest of all delicacies. Yet its taste lingers for but a brief moment. Furthermore, if one eats too much, it will make him sick. Not so wisdom — it endures forever, and the more one ingests, the better. (Radak).

[Solomon said in his wisdom 'Have you found honey? Eat only as much as is necessary, lest you become overstuffed and vomit it' (Prov. 25:16). But an abundance of Torah is always beneficial.]

וְנֹפֶת צוּפִים — 'Than dripping from the combs'.

Rashi quotes Menachem who translates נֹפֶת as 'a drop'.

Metzudas Zion defines צוּפִים as 'honeycombs' as in צוּף דְּבַשׁ, 'a honeycomb' (Proverbs 16:24).

According to the Talmud (Sotah 48b) נֹפֶת refers to a נָפָה 'a flour sifter' and צוּפִים is the finest grade of flour which is צָפָה 'floats to the top' of the sifter and tastes as sweet as a dough mixed with honey and oil. The Talmud laments the fact that this high-grade flour became extinct (together with many other outstanding natural phenomena) after the destruction of the Temple (when the entire universe lost its high standard of quality and perfection). Another opinion offered in the Talmud says that נֹפֶת צוּפִים is the finest honey gathered by rare bees who fly to the highest mountains to suck the sweetest nectar

of the freshest, most remote flowers.

12. גַּם עַבְדְּךָ נִזְהָר בָּהֶם — Even Your servant is careful of them.

The previous verse declared that wise men appreciate and desire Torah more than all earthly delights. Now David says that he has the same regard for Torah. Although he does not reckon himself among the wise men, he is a servant of God and attempts to observe every commandment (Radak).

בְּשָׁמְרָם עֵקֶב רָב — For in observing them there is great reward.

This translation follows Rashi who renders עֵקֶב as 'because' as in the verse עֵקֶב אֲשֶׁר שָׁמַע אַבְרָהָם בְּקֹלִי 'Because Abraham obeyed My voice' (Gen. 26:5). David said: Even I am very careful with Your mitzvohs עֵקֶב 'because' in keeping them there is רָב 'great' reward.

In an alternate interpretation, Rashi notes that עֵקֶב means heel. Thus, it can be rendered 'the end', for the heel is at the end of the body. Hence, our verse says that at the end of days, Torah scholars will achieve רָב 'the great', recognition which is due to them.[1]

Just as the heel is the body's end, so, too, reward will come only at the end of a man's life when he can no longer perform commandments (Radak).

Rabbeinu Bachya notes that we find the word עֵקֶב translated as 'end' in other places. הוֹרֵנִי ה' דֶּרֶךְ חֻקֶּיךָ וְאֶצְּרֶנָּה עֵקֶב, 'Guide me HASHEM in the way of Your statutes and I will safeguard them to the end' (Psalms 119:33). And again,

---

1. In Psalms 49:6 David says: עֲוֹן עֲקֵבַי יְסוּבֵּנִי 'The iniquity of my heels surrounds me'. The Talmud (Avodah Zara 18a) interprets this homiletically: 'The transgressions which a person tramples underfoot with his heels in this world will surround and accuse him in the Hereafter'. Here David says that the opposite is also true. בְּשָׁמְרָם עֵקֶב 'If you safeguard the commandments which are usually trodden by the heel' [i.e. neglected and abused], the result will be רָב, 'great reward'.

XIX
12-14

Sweeter than honey,

— than dripping from the combs.

12 Even Your servant is careful of them,

for in observing them there is great reward.

13 Yet, who can discern mistakes?

From unperceived faults cleanse me.

14 Also from intentional sins, restrain Your servant;

let them not rule me.

'I נָטִיתִי לִבִּי לַעֲשׂוֹת חֻקֶּיךָ לְעוֹלָם עֵקֶב bent my heart to perform Your statutes forever, to the end' (ibid. v. 112). [See Targum and commentaries ibid.][1]

13. שְׁגִיאוֹת מִי יָבִין — *Yet, who can discern mistakes?*

True, I have made every effort to exercise utmost care in keeping Your commands, yet who can be so careful that he never errs unintentionally? (*Rashi; Radak*).

Hirsch points out that שְׁגִיאָה is not the same as שְׁגָגָה, an error due to carelessness and criminal neglect. Rather שְׁגִיאָה denotes an error due to imperfect understanding and reasoning from which no man is immune and of which he is unaware. These errors are נִסְתָּרוֹת 'unknown' and thus, being unaware of them, it is impossible for one to correct them. Only divine assistance can protect a person from these inborn human flaws.

מִנִּסְתָּרוֹת נַקֵּנִי — *From unperceived faults cleanse me.*

I ask you to grant me this wish: Please cleanse me of unwittingly committed sins, and do not punish me for them (*Radak*).

14. גַּם מִזֵּדִים חֲשֹׁךְ עַבְדֶּךָ — *Also from intentional sins restrain Your servant.*

[Our translation, as always, follows *Rashi* who interprets זֵדִים as *intentional sins.*]

[This request is puzzling because we know that God does not interfere with a person's free choice and He does not exert control over his ability to decide between good and evil.] *Ibn Ezra* [apparently in response to this difficulty] explains that David's request is not for direct intervention but that God make the external circumstances of his life conducive to good and devoid of temptations to do bad. Accordingly, *Ibn Ezra* interprets זֵדִים as *wanton sinners*, and renders *'Guide me away from wanton sinners and let them not dominate me'.*

אַל יִמְשְׁלוּ בִי — *Let them not rule me.*

[*Radak* lays down another principle concerning instances where one can merit divine assistance in choosing good.]

'Do not let my evil inclination overpower me. I will try with all my strength to fight it, therefore You can assist me in this choice. For, God helps those whose hearts yearn to do what is right and proper.' [cf. *Yoma* 38b].

---

1. The Gaon of Vilna interprets this verse homiletically: As the Psalmist declared in the previous verses, Torah study purifies the diligent student to the point where his radiance rivals that of the sun and stars. This brilliant light pervades his entire body, even down to the coarsest, lowest part, the עֵקֶב 'heel'. Thus the student comes to resemble Adam of whom the Talmud says (*Bava Basra* 58a) as שְׁנֵי עֲקֵיבָיו דּוֹמִים לִשְׁנֵי גַּלְגַּלֵּי חַמָּה 'His two heels resembled two sun-globes'. The Psalmist uses the word נִזְהָר here in the sense of זוֹהַר 'brilliant light'. Thus: 'Even Your own servant [i.e. David] נִזְהָר, glows with brilliant light', because by keeping the Torah even his עֵקֶב 'heel' becomes רַב 'great' and radiant.' [See *Shaloh, Maseches Shavuos* in the name of *Mahari Padua*].

טו מִפֶּשַׁע רָב: יִהְיוּ לְרָצוֹן אִמְרֵי־פִי וְהֶגְיוֹן
לִבִּי לְפָנֶיךָ יהוה צוּרִי וְגֹאֲלִי:

אָז אֵיתָם — *'Then I shall be perfect'.*

אֵיתָם is a contraction of two words אֶהְיֶה תָמִים, *'I shall be perfect' (Rashi).*
This word could have been spelled without the letter 'י' after the 'א'. Homiletically, the extra letter is explained according to its numerical value which is ten, representing the symbol of universal perfection, the Ten Commandments (*Radak*).

וְנִקֵּתִי מִפֶּשַׁע רָב — *And [I will be] cleansed of great transgression.*

The man who intentionally indulges in a forbidden pleasure because he is overwhelmed by an uncontrollable lust has committed a זָדוֹן. פֶּשַׁע is a much more serious offense. It denotes a transgression motivated by an urge to rebel against God, to deny His sovereignty, and to anger Him, even if the sinner derives no physical pleasure from his transgression. [See *comm.* 32:1].

The man who habitually commits זָדוֹן by allowing his passions to overcome him, will ultimately commit פֶּשַׁע, an open rebellion against God. [In order to rationalize his constant failures to control his lust, the intentional sinner must attempt to rid his conscience of its heavy burden of guilt. Therefore, he may totally deny God's right to impose restrictions upon mankind].

David says to God: If You will help me to control passion, I will certainly never be motivated to mutiny against You. [רָב, *great*, is used in conjunction with פֶּשַׁע because every mutiny is a very great and serious offense] (*Radak*).

Rashi quotes *Midrash Shocher Tov* which sums up the past verses:

'To what may David be likened? To Samaritan beggars who make rounds from door to door. The Samaritans are the slyest, most clever, beggars of all. First, they ask for a mere drink of water, something which costs nothing. Having finished the water, the beggar asks for another trifle, a tiny onion. When that is given, he asks, 'Ah, can one eat an onion without a pinch of salt?' After that is provided, the beggar finally makes his main request, 'You know, onion without bread is so sharp it can do harm to the heart, could I have some please?' So too, David first requested forgiveness for slight mistakes, then for intentional sins and finally, even for mutinous transgressions.' [I.e. in seeking God's forgiveness, the penitent dares not have the audacity to ask that his major transgressions be forgiven while he is still sullied by smaller ones. To be content to remain with 'minor' flaws because they are 'insignificant' is not to repent at all for he continues to flout the will of God. He must purge himself level by level.]

15. יִהְיוּ לְרָצוֹן אִמְרֵי פִי—*May the expressions of my mouth find favor.*

XIX	*Then I shall be perfect*
15	*and cleansed of great transgression.*

¹⁵ *May the expressions of my mouth and the thoughts of my heart find favor before You, HASHEM, my Rock and my Redeemer.*

David requested: 'Let my words be favorably inscribed as a legacy for all time, for all generations. Let them not be read casually like the poems of Homer, rather let these Psalms be studied and contemplated like words of Torah, like נְגָעִים וְאֹהָלוֹת the weighty laws of purity and impurity' (Midrash Shocher Tov, Psalms 1:1. See Overview).

This verse, יִהְיוּ לְרָצוֹן אִמְרֵי פִי can be interpreted as a request for the acceptance of prayers already uttered in the past or it can be rendered as a petition for the kind reception of future prayers. Why then did the Rabbis ordain that it be recited as the concluding prayer of the Shemoneh Esrei, 'The Eighteen Benedictions' (as a request for past prayers) and not as an introductory request that the service be accepted? Rabbi Yehuda the son of Rabbi Shimon ben Pazi said: Since David said this verse after eighteen Psalms, the Rabbis placed

it at the end of the *Eighteen Benedictions.* Is it then at the end of the eighteenth Psalm? It is after the nineteenth! Therefore, we must say that the first two Psalms are counted as one [rendering Psalm 19 as, in reality, Psalm 18] (Berachos 9b).[1]

וְהֶגְיוֹן לִבִּי — *And the thoughts of my heart.*

Please do not limit Your attention to the requests which I express orally. Be aware of the many inner thoughts that crowd my mind which I am incapable of expressing (Radak).

ה' צוּרִי — *HASHEM, my Rock'.*

I lean on You to be my strength in fulfilling my petition (Radak).

וְגֹאֲלִי — *And my Redeemer.*

You redeem me from mistakes and intentional sins (Radak).

---

1. Maharsha (ibid.) explains the common practice to separate the first Psalm in contradiction to the Talmud. Originally Shemoneh Esrei consisted of only Eighteen Benedictions, so the concluding verse of our Psalm indeed corresponded to the conclusion of the eighteenth blessing. At a later date, however, Rabban Gamliel of Yavne added a nineteenth benediction to the Shemoneh Esrei. In order that the concluding verse would still correspond to its placement in Tehillim, Psalm 1 was divided into two, making our psalm the nineteenth.

This psalm was placed after Psalm 19 in order to express the firm conviction that the salvation of Israel depends not on physical power but on prayer (Berachos 4b).

Rabbi Yochanan said: 'Who is assured of a share in the World to Come? He who juxtaposes the benediction of גְּאוּלָה, 'redemption' with תְּפִילָה 'prayer'. Rashi (ibid.) comments: David, in the Book of Psalms alludes to this juxtaposition. He concludes Psalm 19 with 'prayer', יִהְיוּ לְרָצוֹן אִמְרֵי פִי וְהֶגְיוֹן לִבִּי לְפָנֶיךָ ה' צוּרִי וְגֹאֲלִי, 'Let the words of my mouth and the thoughts of my heart find favor before You, HASHEM, my rock and my redeemer' (v. 15). Thereupon, he immediately begins Psalm 20 with 'redemption' יַעַנְךָ ה' בְּיוֹם צָרָה, 'May HASHEM answer you on the day of the distress'.

Yerushalmi (Berachos 1:1) emphasizes this unique relationship between 'redemption' and 'prayer': To whom can we compare the man who recites the benediction requesting גְּאוּלָה, redemption, but then fails to follow it with immediate תְּפִילָה, prayer? — To the king's favorite who knocked on the door of the royal chambers but did not wait for the king to answer. When the king came to answer the knocking, the favorite had already turned his back and departed. What did the king do? He also turned away and departed! Therefore, the proper procedure is that a person should first draw God near to himself by reciting His praises and blessing Him for the 'redemption' from Egypt. Then, while God is still near at hand, he should make his personal requests through prayer.

Another application of this juxtaposition is found in the weekday שַׁחֲרִית, the Morning Service when supplications of distress are permissible. After concluding Shemone Esrei with the verse יִהְיוּ לְרָצוֹן אִמְרֵי פִי 'May the expressions of my mouth find favor', we recite Psalm 20: יַעַנְךָ ה' בְּיוֹם צָרָה 'May HASHEM answer you on the day of distress between אַשְׁרֵי, and וּבָא לְצִיּוֹן.

This practice is based on Midrash Shocher Tov: 'Rabbi Shimon bar Abba said, 'We find eighteen psalms from the beginning of this book up to this point [Psalms 1 and 2 are counted as one; cf. Prefatory Remarks, Psalm 2]. These correspond to the eighteen benedictions of the Shemoneh Esrei. When a person concludes the Shemoneh Esrei, we wish him well, saying, 'May your prayers be answered. So, too, after David concluded eighteen psalms he was encouraged and he proclaimed, יַעַנְךָ ה' בְּיוֹם צָרָה 'HASHEM will answer you on the day of distress'.

א־ב לַמְנַצֵּחַ מִזְמוֹר לְדָוִד: יַעַנְךָ יהוה בְּיוֹם
ג צָרָה יְשַׂגֶּבְךָ שֵׁם | אֱלֹהֵי יַעֲקֹב: יִשְׁלַח־
ד עֶזְרְךָ מִקֹּדֶשׁ וּמִצִּיּוֹן יִסְעָדֶךָּ: יִזְכֹּר כָּל־

1. לַמְנַצֵּחַ מִזְמוֹר לְדָוִד — *For the Conductor; A song of David.*

[All of the psalms preceding this one have generally been in first person, clearly the words of David with reference to himself. However, the first five verses of this psalm are addressed to a second party, a fact which aroused the commentators to search for the true identity of the author and the person to whom he speaks.]

Radak; Ibn Ezra, and *Metzudas David* suggest that this psalm was composed by one of the musicians and it was recited by the Temple choir לְדָוִד, 'for the sake of David', when he went out to battle his enemies.

Ibn Ezra adds that it might have been written for the future Messiah, the scion of David, to aid him in his wars.

Rashi maintains that these verses were composed by David himself when he sent forth his general, Joab, and all of the armies of Israel to battle and he himself remained in Jerusalem to pray for their victory. We find (*II Samuel* 18) that David's men feared for his safety and begged him to stay behind and not to enter the dangers of battle. They said, *'It is better that you should be a support for us from the city'* (ibid. verse 3). (This is explained by *Targum* as: 'better that you should aid us with your prayers from the city'). The Rabbis also said: 'If not for the merit of David [who stayed behind to study and teach Torah] Joab could not have been successful in war' (*Sanhedrin* 49a).

Malbim suggests that this psalm was inspired in particular by the events depicted in *II Samuel* 21 where we find David in mortal danger, almost brutally slain by Yishbi, the Philistine giant, at Nob. Miraculously, Avishai ben Zeruya sped from Jerusalem on David's horse and saved the king at the last moment (*Sanhedrin* 95a). At that time David's men pleaded with him henceforth to stay behind and not endanger himself.

2. יַעַנְךָ ה׳ — *May HASHEM answer you.*

'May HASHEM accept your prayer' (*Targum*).

May HASHEM Himself answer, not one of His intermediaries. May He respond instantly, on the very day of distress, not afterwards when it is too late (*Malbim*).

בְּיוֹם צָרָה — *On the day of distress.*

When the lines of the enemy are drawn up against you and the danger is imminent (*Metzudas David; Radak*).

Midrash Shocher Tov quotes the following verse which expresses Hashem's response to Israel's call. יִקְרָאֵנִי וְאֶעֱנֵהוּ, *'He will call out to me and I will answer him' (Psalms* 91:15). Said the Holy One Blessed be He: 'When misfortune threatens Israel and they express concern for the preservation of My honor as well as their own, then I will surely respond, for עִמּוֹ אָנֹכִי בְצָרָה *"I am with him* [Israel] *in his distress" ' (Psalms* ibid.) [When Israel realizes that they represent God and that their downfall is tantamount to the disgrace of His Name, then God will surely save them, for His own honor is at stake.][1]

---

1. The *Midrash* instructs us on how to detect the true *'day of distress'*:

A father and his son were travelling the roads. The exhausted son asked his father impatiently, 'And where then is the city?' The father replied: 'My son, take note of the following sign. When you will see a graveyard before your eyes then you will know that you have reached the outskirts of the city and that it is not far.' So too, the Holy One Blessed be He says to Israel: 'When you see misfortunes covering you all over, rest assured that you are about to be redeemed as it says '*HASHEM will answer you on the day of distress'.*

XX
1-3

For the Conductor;
A song of David.
² May HASHEM answer you
on the day of distress,
May the Name of Jacob's God
make you impregnable.
³ May He dispatch your help from the Sanctuary,
and support you from Zion.

יְשַׂגֶּבְךָ — *May . . . make you impregnable.*

— As one who is protected in a towering fortress out of the grasp of the enemy (*Radak*).

Metzudas David translates: 'May you be strengthened' [as Jacob was when he confronted Laban].

שֵׁם אֱלֹהֵי יַעֲקֹב — *The name of Jacob's God.*

When Jacob left Israel to go to Charan, the home of Laban, God promised to protect him. Therefore, the expression, 'Jacob's God' is used here (*Rashi*).

Jacob found himself in situations of distress throughout his lifetime, more than did Abraham and Isaac. Therefore, Jacob said לָאֵל הָעֹנֶה אֹתִי בְּיוֹם צָרָתִי, 'to the God who answers me on the day of my distress' (*Gen.* 35:3). Furthermore, Abraham had another son, Ishmael; Isaac had Esau, but Jacob was the father of the Jewish people exclusively. Therefore, when we seek salvation we call upon the God of Jacob. Also, the name of Jacob refers not only to the individual patriarch, but to the entire people of Israel collectively, as we often find in Scriptures (*Radak*).

The *Midrash* adds that from here we learn that when many men are carrying a beam, the owner should lift the heaviest, thickest part [Jacob is considered the Patriarch who bears the greatest responsibility for Israel because he was the father of the twelve tribes.]

Lachmei Todah brings to our attention the fact that in five places in Scriptures יַעֲקֹוב is spelled מָלֵא 'full', with a 'ו' and אֵלִיָה, is spelled חָסֵר, 'deficient' i.e. without the customary 'ו' vav. The Sages explain homiletically that Jacob took the vav from the name of Elijah as a 'security' to assure that Elijah would return to announce the arrival of Messiah (*Rashi; Lev.* 26:42). Therefore, it is written here 'may you be securely elevated by the name of [the God of] Jacob' for the name of Jacob, יַעֲקֹוב [spelled with a 'vav'] will assure that 'He will send your help out of the holy place' (v. 3) through His emissary, Elijah.

3. יִשְׁלַח עֶזְרְךָ מִקֹּדֶשׁ — *May He dispatch your help from the Sanctuary* [lit. 'holy place.']

From the Holy of Holies inside the Temple where the Holy Ark rests and where God's spirit dwells. From there will go forth divine aid in battle (*Radak*).

The *Midrash* also illustrates this verse with the parable of a mother who was angered by her daughter, yet when the daughter was giving birth and crying out from the intense labor pains, the mother sympathized so much with her daughter that she forgot her quarrel and screamed along with her agonized child. So, too, although God destroyed the Temple because His children of Israel angered Him, still He replies when they call in distress. The *Midrash* also takes note of the fact that this psalm contains exactly nine verses (excluding the introductory verse) which correspond to the nine months of pregnancy. 'May He who answers the pregnant mother in labor, answer you.'

ה מִנְחֹתֶיךָ וְעוֹלָתְךָ יְדַשְּׁנֶה סֶלָה: יִתֶּן־לְךָ
ו כִלְבָבֶךָ וְכָל־עֲצָתְךָ יְמַלֵּא: נְרַנְּנָה |
בִּישׁוּעָתֶךָ וּבְשֵׁם־אֱלֹהֵינוּ נִדְגֹּל יְמַלֵּא

Malbim explains that עֵזֶר, *'help'*, refers to the main cause of salvation which helps one in distress, whereas סָעַד refers to secondary, auxiliary support. David prays that his primary aid should emanate מִקֹּדֶשׁ, *'out of the holy place'* and not from unholy sources such as the hands of gentile kings and armies which might fight on his side. It is the holiness of the Jewish people themselves, their sacred deeds and words, that is their main ally in battle.

וּמִצִּיּוֹן יִסְעָדֶךָ — *And support you from Zion.*

Malbim continues: Although armies march out of Zion [the capital city] to do battle, these are merely a סָעַד, *'a secondary support'* to the mainstay of the battle — the קֹדֶשׁ, *'holiness'* which assures the Israelites their victory.

Rabbi Levi said: All goodness and blessing and consolation that the Holy One Blessed be He is destined to send to Israel, will go forth only from Zion (*Vayikra Rabba* 24:4).[Cf. footnote to 14:7.]

4. יִזְכֹּר כָּל מִנְחֹתֶיךָ — *May He remember all your offerings.*

Ibn Ezra comments: Why should God help you? Because He will remember all of your offerings. Some say that special offerings were always brought before entering battle because divine mercy is needed in times of danger. So we find in the case of Saul who was commanded to wait for Samuel to offer up the עוֹלָה *'burnt offering'* before engaging the enemy (*I Sam.* 13:8-12).

[The need for God's remembrance in wartime is also found in the Torah: *'When you will go into battle in your land against the enemy who oppresses you, you shall blow upon the trumpets*

and you shall be remembered before HASHEM, your God, and you shall be saved from your foes' (*Numbers* 10:9). The very next verse (ibid. 10:10) orders that the trumpets be sounded over the sacrifices in the Temple. This juxtaposition suggests that the blast of the trumpets in battle reminds God of Israel's sacrifices which were also accompanied by trumpets.]

Radak translates יְזַכֵּר *'may He smell'* the scent of your sacrifice as in *Lev.* 6:8: רֵיחַ נִיחֹחַ אַזְכָּרָתָהּ לַה', *'The savory scent is its remembrance to God'.*

Rashi, however, explains that מִנְחֹתֶיךָ and עוֹלָתְךָ refer not to sacrifices but to the prayers that were offered while the army was at war.

Malbim adds: If one is saved by another man of flesh and blood and offers him a gift in appreciation, certainly the recipient need not pay the donor back, because he has already done his share by aiding the weak man in battle. Not so with the Holy One, Blessed be He. When Israel offers sacrifices or prayers in order to be saved in war, God not only grants them the desired victory, He even remembers the sacrifices and prayers which they offered and rewards them for these devotions as well.

Elsewhere David says: זִבְחֵי אֱלֹהִים רוּחַ נִשְׁבָּרָה *'God's preferred sacrifice is shattered pride'* (*Psalm* 51:19). It is this total sacrifice of the ego that God will remember most favorably in times of crisis (*Rav Yeibi*).

יְדַשְּׁנֶה — *Consider generous* [lit. *'fat'*.]

דָּשֵׁן is a word for rich fat as in *Deut.* 31:20: וְאָכַל וְשָׂבַע וְדָשֵׁן, *'and he will eat, and be contented, and grow fat.'* May God accept your prayers willingly as if they were choice burnt sacrifices (*Rashi*).

⁴ *May He remember all your offerings,*
  and consider your burnt sacrifices generous.
  Selah.
⁵ *May He grant you your heart's desire,*
  and fulfill your every plan.
⁶ *That we may sing for joy at your victory,*
  and raise our banner in the name of our God;

However, *Ibn Ezra* and *Metzudas David* render the derivation of this word from דֶשֶׁן, 'ashes'. *Radak*, agreeing with this translation, adds that the ultimate sign of God's good will is when He sends down a fire from heaven to consume the sacrifice. Thus, 'may God display his pleasure with your sacrifice by burning it to ashes'.

5. יִתֶּן לְךָ כִלְבָבֶךָ — *May He grant you your heart's desire.* [lit. *May He give you according to your heart.*] 'According to your thoughts' (*Targum*).

When one is saved by man, the savior designs the rescue any way he wishes, even if it is not the scheme most favorable or desirable to the one in danger. Not so, the Holy One, Blessed be He. He brings about the victory exactly according to the wishes of those being saved (*Malbim*).[1]

וְכָל עֲצָתְךָ יְמַלֵּא — *And fulfill your every plan,* i.e., every execution of tactic and strategy will be successful (*Radak*).

6. נְרַנְּנָה בִּישׁוּעָתֶךָ — *That we may sing out for joy at your victory* [lit. 'salvation'.]

When God will grant all of your desires and you will successfully return from war then we will shout out for joy (*Radak*).

Ibn Ezra notes the singular form of יְשׁוּעָתֶךָ, 'your' *salvation*, and comments that this triumphant wish was exclaimed by the devoted army to their beloved leader, David.

When one must call for the assistance of another man, he cannot proudly exult in the ultimate victory, for he has shown weakness by calling for outside support. Not so he who calls upon God for help. He may glory in the victory as if it was his own personal achievement [because he deserves credit for being wise and faithful enough to call upon God rather than rely upon his own strength or allies] (*Malbim*).

וּבְשֵׁם אֱלֹהֵינוּ — *And in the name of our God.*

With the help of God's name which aids us in battle and guarantees victory (*Radak; Metzudas David*).

Another reason why the recipient of divine assistance may proudly proclaim the victory as his own, is in order to let the gentile nations see the might of God's help and thus bring them to fear His power (*Malbim*).

נִדְגֹּל — *[We shall] raise our banner.*

[As a sign of victory, the conquering army hoists its flag over the captured enemy positions].

According to *Rashi* this means: 'We

1. Once, Rabban Gamliel asked the righteous Chalafta ben Keruyah to pray for him. Chalafta responded: 'May He give you your heart's desire'. Concerning this incident, Rav Huna bar Rav Yitzchak said: The aforementioned request is one that cannot be made for an ordinary person, for who knows what thoughts are in his heart! Perhaps he plans to steal or sin! However, since Chalafta was familiar with Rabban Gamliel's integrity, he trusted that he would never utter an unbecoming request before God, and so he added the prayer of *v.* 6, 'May HASHEM fulfill all your requests' (*Midrash Shocher Tov*).

ז יהוה־כָּל־מִשְׁאֲלוֹתֶיךָ: עַתָּה יָדַעְתִּי כִּי
הוֹשִׁיעַ| יהוה מְשִׁיחוֹ יַעֲנֵהוּ מִשְּׁמֵי קָדְשׁוֹ
ח בִּגְבוּרוֹת יֵשַׁע יְמִינוֹ: אֵלֶּה בָרֶכֶב וְאֵלֶּה
בַסּוּסִים וַאֲנַחְנוּ| בְּשֵׁם־יהוה אֱלֹהֵינוּ
ט נַזְכִּיר: הֵמָּה כָּרְעוּ וְנָפָלוּ וַאֲנַחְנוּ קַמְנוּ
י וַנִּתְעוֹדָד: יהוה הוֹשִׁיעָה הַמֶּלֶךְ יַעֲנֵנוּ
בְיוֹם־קָרְאֵנוּ:

shall gather around our standards during the battle in order to renew our strength to make war'.

Midrash Shocher Tov explains that in the wilderness each tribe had its own uniquely colored and designed flag to differentiate it from the other tribes. But in the future all such divisions will be banished when all of Israel unites homogeneously under God *and in the name of God [only] we raise our banner'.*

יְמַלֵּא ה' כָּל מִשְׁאֲלוֹתֶיךָ — *When HASHEM fulfills all your requests.* [lit. *May HASHEM fulfill all of your requests*].

The translation follows *Radak* and *Ibn Ezra.* At that time, the banners of victory will be raised. *Metzudas David* offers a slight variation. 'After you will raise banners in God's name, [then] HASHEM will fulfill all of your requests'.

When Hashem will fulfill your request for victory, He will not suffice with that alone. Rather, He will continue to grant your many desires and wishes in all matters (*Malbim*).

Rabbi Shmelke of Nikolsburg would translate יְמַלֵּא ה' 'May God's Name be made full'. In exile the Four-Letter Name יהוה is fragmented and reduced to יה. More than being concerned about his own personal welfare, the Jew should yearn for the redemption of the holy Name. Once this comes to pass, everything else will be perfect and you, the individual, will realize כָּל מִשְׁאֲלוֹתֶיךָ 'all of your [personal] requests'.

7. עַתָּה יָדַעְתִּי — *Now I know,* i.e. now I know something hitherto unknown.

The words of this verse are the song of joy, referred to in verse 6, which will be on the lips of all when Joab and the army of Israel return victorious (*Rashi; Radak*).

According to *Ibn Ezra,* these are the words of the inspired psalmist who foresees in his holy spirit [a future victory.]

כִּי הוֹשִׁיעַ ה' מְשִׁיחוֹ — *That HASHEM has made His anointed one victorious.*

Now I [David] know that God still desires me, His anointed one. For the victorious salvation of Joab and the army is indeed nothing less than my own personal salvation (*Rashi*).

Before this decisive victory, רַבִּים אֹמְרִים לְנַפְשִׁי אֵין יְשׁוּעָתָה לּוֹ בֵאלֹהִים סֶלָה, 'There are many who say of my soul, there is no salvation for him from God, Selah' (Psalm 3:3). But now that You have clearly saved me they must all admit that I am your chosen, preferred, anointed one (*Radak*).

בִּגְבוּרוֹת יֵשַׁע יְמִינוֹ — *With the omnipotent victories of His right arm.*

For with a handful of men the army of Israel would rout tens of thousands. Such amazing victories can be attributed only to God's right hand which intervened to bring about salvation (*Radak*).

There is a victory which comes through natural channels and is attributed to God's left hand. But when supernatural intervention is evident,

When HASHEM fulfills all your requests.

*⁷ Now I know that HASHEM has made
His anointed one victorious,
He will answer him from His sacred heaven,
with the omnipotent victories of His right arm.
⁸ Some through chariots, and some through horses,
But we—in the Name of HASHEM, our God,
call out.
⁹ They slumped and fell,
but we arose invigorated.
¹⁰ HASHEM save!
The King will answer us on the day we call.*

then the salvation is attributed to His right hand, such as here *(Malbim).*

8. אֵלֶּה בָרֶכֶב וְאֵלֶּה בַסּוּסִים — *Some through chariots and some through horses.*

Some of our attackers place their trust in strong iron chariots, and some place trust in the strength of their horses *(Rashi).*

On the verse סוּס וְרֹכְבוֹ רָמָה בַיָּם, *'the horse and his rider He threw into the sea' (Exodus 15:1)* the *Midrash (Shemos Rabbah 23:14)* comments that *'horse'* describes the degenerate, animalistic nation of Egypt and *'rider'* refers to their special שַׂר, *'guardian angel'* who controls their affairs in heaven. The Psalmist says here that some attack us relying on רֶכֶב *'the rider'*, meaning their guardian angel above who will fight for them. Others depend on סוּסִים, *'horses'*; meaning the brute animal strength of the soldiers on earth. But none put their faith in God *(Rav Yeibi).*

Tikkunei Zohar notes that this psalm contains exactly seventy words, corresponding to the seventy nations who surround us on earth and their seventy guardian angels above. *Maharam Ibn Gabbei* in *Tola'as Yaakov* adds that there is an encouraging allusion as well: The letters in the psalm amount to 310 corresponding to the שַׁי עוֹלָמוֹת *'the 310 worlds'* which are concealed and awaiting every *tzaddik* as his portion in the Hereafter *(Uktzin 3:12).*

וַאֲנַחְנוּ בְּשֵׁם ה' אֱלֹהֵינוּ נַזְכִּיר — *But we in the Name of HASHEM, our God, call out.*

Now that I know that God manages my affairs supernaturally *(v. 7)* I will no longer concern myself with the standard armaments of war. Although the enemy comes armed with chariots and war horses; I need only mention God's name to overcome him *(Malbim).*[1]

נַזְכִּיר — *[We] Call out.*

Rashi comments that this refers to offerings of קְטֹרֶת, *'incense', (and prayer) as in* מַזְכִּיר לְבֹנָה *'he offers*

---

1. *Rabbeinu Bachya (Gen. 49:12)* writes: 'If you will scrutinize the blessing which Jacob gave to his son Judah, you will find all of the letters of the Hebrew alphabet represented in those short sentences. Only the letter 'ז' is missing, for זַיִן means *'weapons'*. The tribe of Judah is the tribe of royalty. The Torah wishes to emphasize that the power and sovereignty of the Jewish king does not depend on his military prowess. The sword is the inheritance of Esau, not Jacob. The kings of Judah triumph through God's Name and assistance. Therefore, we find the Name of God יהוה contained in the letters of יהודה. The additional ד in Judah's name alludes to the fact that he was the fourth son to be born to Jacob.'

incense' (Isaiah 66:3). Thus: 'Because we offer prayer to Hashem like fragrant incense, therefore our enemies bow down and fall.'

9. הֵמָּה כָּרְעוּ — *They slumped.*
I.e. the enemy charioteers (*Ibn Ezra*).

וְנָפָלוּ — *And fell.*
This refers to the enemy riders, as we read וַיִּפֹּל רֹכְבוֹ אָחוֹר, *so that his rider falls backwards'* (Gen. 49:17; *Ibn Ezra*).

וַאֲנַחְנוּ קַמְנוּ — *But we arose.*
We, who originally fell before the enemy, arose and boldly overwhelmed him when we mentioned Hashem's name (*Radak*).

וַנִּתְעוֹדָד—[And] *we were invigorated.*
This is similar to מְעוֹדֵד עֲנָוִים ה', *'HASHEM invigorates the humble* (Psalms 147:6; *Rashi; Metzudas Zion*). [This term is used to denote the encouragement and reinforcement of someone whose spirits are lagging.]

10. ה' הוֹשִׁיעָה — *HASHEM, save!*
This is what they would shout out in battle as stated previously, 'we [trust]

in the name of HASHEM our God [which we] call out' (v. 8) (*Radak*).

הַמֶּלֶךְ — *The King.*
I.e. Hashem who is King, He will answer . . . (*Radak*).
Some say that הַמֶּלֶךְ refers to King David and thus the word is connected with the opening words of this verse: ה' הוֹשִׁיעָה הַמֶּלֶךְ *HASHEM! Save the King!* But this interpretation is incorrect, for there is an אֶתְנַחְתָּא *'a pause'* beneath הוֹשִׁיעָה separating it from the following word הַמֶּלֶךְ the *King.* Thus, it should read, *HASHEM, save! The King* [*HASHEM*] *will answer'* (*Ibn Ezra*).

יַעֲנֵנוּ בְיוֹם קָרְאֵנוּ —[He]*will answer us on the day we call.*
Midrash Shocher Tov sums up this psalm with a long list of quotations which demonstrate how Israel and her leaders are answered only when they call out in prayer. For this reason, our nation is called תּוֹלַעַת יַעֲקֹב, *'the worm, Jacob'* (Isaiah 41:14). 'Just as the tiny worm attacks the mighty cedar, boring holes with nothing more than its mouth, so, too, Israel is armed with nothing more than the prayers [of her mouth.]

מזמור כא 21

This psalm is dedicated to two kings, David and Messiah (Rashi). Indeed, the future redeemer of Israel is also called David as the prophet says וְדָוִד עַבְדִּי נָשִׂיא לָהֶם לְעוֹלָם, 'And David, My servant, will be a prince for them forever' (Ezekiel 37:25).

Both suffer from enemies who deny their sovereignty: David by those who taunt him about Bath Sheba (Rashi), and Messiah by Gog and Magog (Radak; cf. Prefatory Remarks, Psalm 2).

Ultimately, both overcome their enemies and are universally accepted. Rambam describes the magnificence of Messiah: 'That king who will arise from the seed of David will possess wisdom surpassing that of Solomon and he will be a great prophet, close to the level of Moses. Therefore, he will teach the entire nation and guide them on the path of God. And all of the gentile nations will assemble to listen to him' (Hilchos Teshuvah 9:2).

Finally this psalm teaches that the splendor of true kings is not an ordinary, earthly glow. It is a reflection of the great faith in Hashem which radiates from their ever-confident hearts כִּי הַמֶּלֶךְ בֹּטֵחַ בַּה 'For the king trusts in Hashem'. This is the true power behind the throne.

לַמְנַצֵּחַ מִזְמוֹר לְדָוִד: יהוה בְּעָזְּךָ יִשְׂמַח־
מֶלֶךְ וּבִישׁוּעָתְךָ מַה־יָּגֶל מְאֹד: תַּאֲוַת
לִבּוֹ נָתַתָּה לּוֹ וַאֲרֶשֶׁת שְׂפָתָיו בַּל־מָנַעְתָּ
סֶּלָה: כִּי־תְקַדְּמֶנּוּ בִּרְכוֹת טוֹב תָּשִׁית
לְרֹאשׁוֹ עֲטֶרֶת פָּז: חַיִּים | שָׁאַל מִמְּךָ

2. בְּעָזְּךָ יִשְׂמַח מֶלֶךְ — *In Your might the king rejoices.*

Messiah rejoices in the might You bestowed upon him (*Metzudas David*).

Chomas Anach notes that the letters of the word יִשְׂמַח are the same as those of מָשִׁיחַ i.e. joy and the advent of Messiah are synonymous.

Midrash Shocher Tov adds that God will deign to strengthen Messiah with a semblance of His own exalted glory as it is written, *'And it shall come to pass on that day, that the root of Jesse that stands up as a standard for the nations, unto him the nations shall seek, and his resting place shall be glorious'* (Isaiah 11:10).

God differs from all mortal rulers. No flesh and blood king allows his subjects to use his horse, his throne, or his scepter. Not so God, of whom the Scriptures relate that He lets His chosen ones [including Messiah] use the symbols of sovereignty. [For, the enhancement of Messiah's glory in no way detracts from the glory of God. On the contrary, since Messiah is totally dedicated to Hashem, every addition to his honor increases the honor of Hashem.]

The *Midrash* continues to emphasize that the success of Messiah is dependent on Torah which is called עֹז 'strength' as it is written: ה' עֹז לְעַמּוֹ יִתֵּן 'HASHEM will give strength to His nation' (Psalms 29:11). Kingship is also called עֹז as in וְיִתֶּן עֹז לְמַלְכּוֹ וְיָרֵם קֶרֶן מְשִׁיחוֹ, 'and He gives strength to His king and raises the pride of His anointed (I Sam. 2:10).

וּבִישׁוּעָתְךָ מַה יָּגֶל מְאֹד — *And in your salvation how greatly does he exult.*

מַה ... מְאֹד, 'how greatly'. Ordinarily

a king who must come to another king for aid is dejected and in low spirits in realization of his own weakness. Not so, he who comes to God for help. He will exult greatly (*Malbim*).

These two words form a double amplification, denoting that his joy experiences increase after increase. David composed this psalm when he first established his kingdom in the temporary capital of Hebron. He prayed there that his shaky, challenged rule should finally be firmly entrenched. At that future time of stability, David would certainly exult exceedingly (*Meiri*).

3. תַּאֲוַת לִבּוֹ נָתַתָּה לּוֹ — *You have granted him his heart's desire.*

He who requests aid from a savior of flesh and blood is ashamed to enumerate all of his wants. Not so the man who turns to God, Who grants every last one of this man's wishes (*Malbim*).

This is a prophecy for the future, but, as in many instances, that which is foretold by the holy spirit is considered as already accomplished, so the past tense נָתַתָּה 'You have granted him' is used (*Radak*).

The wicked are never satisfied with what they already have, they long only for what they have not. If they possess one hundred they yearn for two. If they finally acquire two hundred, they desire four. But the righteous man is different. He has no interest in what he has not because he is thrilled with what God has already bestowed upon him. Thus, *'You have granted him his heart's desire'* i.e. what you have already granted Him is his heart's sole desire (*Ramban*).

XXI
1-4

For the Conductor;
A song of David.
² HASHEM, in Your might the king rejoices,
and in Your salvation how greatly does he exult.
³ You have granted him his heart's desire,
and the utterance of his lips
You have not withheld.
⁴ You preceded him with blessings of good;
You placed on his head a crown of pure gold.

וַאֲרֶשֶׁת — *The utterance.*
Rashi explains that this word describes speech and utterances of the lips. No word similar to it [in this sense] appears anywhere in Scriptures.

Metzudas Zion notes that this word is used in the liturgy of *Rosh Hashanah:* אֲרֶשֶׁת שְׂפָתֵינוּ *'the utterance of our lips.'* [Specifically this *'utterance'* expresses a deep wish or desire. The word may be related to אֵרוּסִין, the initial act of marriage.]

Midrash Shocher Tov derives this word from רְשׁוּת, *'authority, sovereignty'.* [Hashem has granted His chosen Messiah limitless authority to issue requests to Him which will be fulfilled promptly.]

בַּל מָנַעְתָּ — *You have not withheld.*
Even before the righteous open their mouths to pray, God already has fathomed their innermost desires and has agreed to them, as it says: *'You have granted him his heart's desire'.* Nevertheless, although it is not necessary, God still yearns greatly for the prayers of the righteous and so, does not interfere with them: *'and the utterances of his lips You have not withheld'* (Maharam Almosnino).

The *Mishnah* (Berachos 5:5) relates that if the words of prayer flow smoothly from the mouth of the tzaddik without hindrance, it is a sign that his request has been accepted in heaven. David says: Since *'the utterances of his lips You have not withheld'*, it is a sign

that *'You have granted him his heart's desire'.*

4. כִּי תְקַדְּמֶנּוּ בִּרְכוֹת טוֹב — *You preceded him with blessings of good.*
David said: Even before I had a chance to ask of You, You preceded me by offering Your blessings, as You did through Nathan, the prophet, who said in Your Name, *'And I will raise up your offspring after you . . . and I will establish the throne of his kingdom forever'* (II Sam. 7:12-13).

The bulk of the blessings due to the righteous is stored away in the Hereafter which is called טוֹב, *good',* as the Sages say (*Avos* 6:4): וְטוֹב לָךְ *'and good for you':* in the World to Come. But this stock of good deeds is like the 'principle' of an investment which constantly produces *'fruits'* or *'interest'.* God is pleased to bestow this additional reward upon the deserving in this world. Thus, *'You preceded him with blessings of good'* (Alshich).

תָּשִׁית לְרֹאשׁוֹ עֲטֶרֶת פָּז — *You placed on his head a crown of pure gold.*
Rashi explains that this took place After David and Joab conquered Rabat the capital of Ammon: וַיִּקַּח אֶת עֲטֶרֶת *'And* מַלְכָּם מֵעַל רֹאשׁוֹ ... וַתְּהִי עַל רֹאשׁ דָּוִד *they removed the crown of their king [of Ammon] from his head ... and it was placed on David's head'* (II Sam 12:30).

[The Torah and good deeds which one performs in this world are a glorious crown for him in the Hereafter,

וֹ נָתַתָּה לּוֹ אֹרֶךְ יָמִים עוֹלָם וָעֶד: גָּדוֹל
כְּבוֹדוֹ בִּישׁוּעָתֶךָ הוֹד וְהָדָר תְּשַׁוֶּה עָלָיו:
ז כִּי־תְשִׁיתֵהוּ בְרָכוֹת לָעַד תְּחַדֵּהוּ
ח בְשִׂמְחָה אֶת־פָּנֶיךָ: כִּי־הַמֶּלֶךְ בֹּטֵחַ
ט בַּיהוה וּבְחֶסֶד עֶלְיוֹן בַּל־יִמּוֹט: תִּמְצָא
יָדְךָ לְכָל־אֹיְבֶיךָ יְמִינְךָ תִּמְצָא שֹׂנְאֶיךָ:

as the Talmud (*Berachos* 17a) says of the future: 'The righteous sit with their crowns on their head and bask in the divine glory.' David assures us here that even though Hashem awards the righteous the '*fruits*' of their good deeds in this world, this does not detract one iota from the purity and perfection of their spiritual crown in the Hereafter.]

5. חַיִּים שָׁאַל מִמְּךָ — *Life, he asked of You.*

Rashi interprets that David asked not merely for physical life, but for the opportunity to live in Eretz Yisrael. David said: When I had to flee from Saul and seek refuge in a foreign land, I would pray אֶתְהַלֵּךְ לִפְנֵי ה' בְּאַרְצוֹת הַחַיִּים '*I will walk before HASHEM in the land of the living*' i.e. the Land of Israel (*Psalms* 116:9).

Radak comments that David is asking for long life in this world.

Actually, David was supposed to live only three hours after birth and then die like a נֵפֶל, '*a nonviable child*'. [See *Overview*] For this reason Messiah is sometimes referred to as בַּר נַפְלֵי, '*son of My nonviable child*.' But his soul requested life and Adam donated seventy years of his life to David. Not only did David merit normal life, but even more, he was promised that his descendants would rule forever (*Zohar Parshas Pekudei; Midrash Chachomim*).

נָתַתָּה לּוֹ — *You gave it to him.*

For You returned the Land of Israel (*Rashi*).

אֹרֶךְ יָמִים עוֹלָם וָעֶד — *Length of days forever and ever.*

Rashi comments that the royal line of David will endure, as God told him through the Prophet Nathan וְכֹנַנְתִּי אֶת כִּסֵּא מַמְלַכְתּוֹ עַד עוֹלָם — '*I will establish the throne of his kingdom forever*' (*II Sam.* 7:13).

This refers to the eternal '*length of days*' in the Hereafter (*Radak*).

6. גָּדוֹל כְּבוֹדוֹ בִּישׁוּעָתֶךָ — *Great is his glory in Your salvation.* When You will save him from his enemies, the nations will have additional respect for him (*Radak*).

הוֹד וְהָדָר — *Majesty and splendor.*

[The Halacha requires that the king tend to his physical splendor for he represents the majesty of God. *Rambam* (*Hilchos Melachim* 2:5) writes: 'The king must have his hair cut every day. He must take care of his appearance and adorn himself with beautiful, majestic garments, as it is said: מֶלֶךְ בְּיָפְיוֹ תֶּחֱזֶינָה עֵינֶיךָ '*Your eyes shall behold the king in his splendor*' (*Isaiah* 33:17).]

Midrash Shocher Tov comments: 'In regard to men of flesh and blood, if you find might in one, he lacks beauty. If he is endowed with beauty, he lacks might. Only Hashem has both, majesty and splendor. God bestowed majesty upon Moses and Solomon. He bequeathed splendor to Joshua. However, He will endow Messiah with both. And this double gift is not reserved for Messiah exclusively. Anyone who toils over the study of Torah is bequeathed both majesty and splendor.'

תְּשַׁוֶּה — *You conferred.*

Rashi quotes *Menachem* who

⁵ *Life, he asked of You, You gave it to him,*
length of days forever and ever.
⁶ *Great is his glory in Your salvation;*
majesty and splendor You conferred upon him.
⁷ *For You made him a blessing forever.*
You gladdened him
with the joy of Your Presence.
⁸ *For the king trusts in HASHEM*
and in the kindness of the Most High,
That will not falter.
⁹ *Your hand will find all of Your foes,*
Your right hand will find Your enemies.

---

translates this word like תָּשִׁים and תָּשִׁית:'*to place upon*'. [In the context of this sentence it means '*You conferred*'.]

7. כִּי תְשִׁיתֵהוּ — *For You made him* [lit. '*You placed him*']

בְּרָכוֹת לָעַד — *A blessing forever* [lit. '*blessings forever*'] As God told Abraham, וֶהְיֵה בְּרָכָה '*and be for a bless-ing*' (*Gen.* 12:2) meaning that when one wishes to bless his friend he will say, '*may you be like Abraham*'. So too will David and his offspring be a blessed ex-ample forever, even after David's death (*Ibn Ezra; Metzudas David; Radak*).

תְּחַדֵּהוּ — *You gladdened him.*
From the word חֶדְוָה (*Rashi; Ibn Ezra*) as in וַיִּחַדְּ יִתְרוֹ, '*and Yisro was glad*' (*Ex-odus* 18:9).

בְּשִׂמְחָה — *With the joy* [lit. '*in joy*']
The extra term of joy is added to emphasize and reinforce the sense of gladness conveyed here (*Radak*).

אֶת פָּנֶיךָ — *Of Your Presence* [lit. '*Your face*']
This refers to God's presence in the future paradise of the Garden of Eden. According to the Sages who interpret this verse as referring not to David but to Messiah, this means that God will draw Messiah near to Himself (*Rashi*).

These words describe David's con-cept of success. '*When You, Hashem, show Your face, shining with sat-isfaction, this is the greatest joy pos-sible for him. He does not rejoice in his many troops nor does he find gladness in his wealth of silver and gold. He finds happiness only in the fact that, since he sees that You help him to succeed in all of his undertakings he knows that You shine Your face on him*' (*Radak*).

Mahari Yaavetz in *Tehillos Hashem* observes that ordinarily a person who accepts charity or favors from another is ashamed to face his benefactor. David emphasizes here that with God, such is not the case. '*Even though You shower man with blessings forever, nevertheless, You still gladden him with the joy of beholding Your countenance.*'

8. כִּי הַמֶּלֶךְ בֹּטֵחַ בַּה׳ — *For the king trusts in HASHEM.*
He puts no faith in great armies, only in HASHEM (*Radak; Ibn Ezra*).

וּבְחֶסֶד עֶלְיוֹן בַּל יִמּוֹט — *And in the kindness of the Most High that will not falter.*
He trusts that Hashem's mercy will endure without pause (*Rashi*).
Because God is Most High, He has all of the power necessary to do kindness

י   תְּשִׁיתֵמוֹ ׀ כְּתַנּוּר אֵשׁ לְעֵת פָּנֶיךָ יהוה
יא בְּאַפּוֹ יְבַלְּעֵם וְתֹאכְלֵם אֵשׁ: פִּרְיָמוֹ
יב מֵאֶרֶץ תְּאַבֵּד וְזַרְעָם מִבְּנֵי אָדָם: כִּי־נָטוּ
יג עָלֶיךָ רָעָה חָשְׁבוּ מְזִמָּה בַּל־יוּכָלוּ: כִּי
    תְּשִׁיתֵמוֹ שֶׁכֶם בְּמֵיתָרֶיךָ תְּכוֹנֵן עַל־
יד פְּנֵיהֶם: רוּמָה יהוה בְּעֻזֶּךָ נָשִׁירָה
    וּנְזַמְּרָה גְּבוּרָתֶךָ:

without interference; therefore the king trusts that this structure of kindness shall not falter (Radak).

It is precisely this unshakable faith in Hashem's mercy that assures the perpetuation of God's goodness forever (Metzudas David).

9. תִּמְצָא יָדְךָ לְכָל אֹיְבֶיךָ — Your hand will find all of Your foes.

תִּמְצָא — It will find. This translation follows Rashi who adds, 'all the blows that Your hand can possibly bring upon Your enemies, let them come forth.'

Radak and Metzudos render תִּמְצָא as תַּסְפִּיק 'let it suffice'. In other words, the king himself is now being addressed with the blessing that since 'he trusts in HASHEM' (v. 8) 'may the strength of your own hands be sufficient to smite your enemies without need for the aid of others.' [Similarly, we read הֲצֹאן וּבָקָר יִשָּׁחֵט לָהֶם וּמָצָא לָהֶם, 'Can enough sheep and cattle be slaughtered to suffice for them?' (Numbers 11:22)].

10. תְּשִׁיתֵמוֹ — Make them.
Let this be their lot perpetually (Metzudas David).

כְּתַנּוּר אֵשׁ — As a fiery furnace [lit. 'like a furnace of fire'].

After the firewood is consumed, only the roaring fire remains in the furnace. Similarly, let them be devoured so completely that nothing at all remains of them (Radak).

In the past the cruel oppressors of Israel made them burn, as we read: עוֹרֵנוּ כְּתַנּוּר נִכְמָרוּ מִפְּנֵי זַלְעֲפוֹת רָעָב 'Our skin is hot like an oven, because of the burning famine' (Lam. 5:10). This vividly describes death by starvation whereby one slowly devours himself; his fat, his muscles, his flesh; until he is self-consumed, all burnt to produce energy. Measure for measure, let these oppressors suffer the same gruesome fate in the time of Messiah when starvation will turn them into furnaces of hungry fire (Tehillos Hashem).

Alshich explains that reference is made here to Titus the wicked, the Roman general responsible for the burning of the Second Beis HaMikdash and the total destruction of Jerusalem. The Sages (Gittin 56b) relate that on his deathbed Titus gave the following instructions: 'After death burn my body and scatter the ashes over the seven seas so that the God of the Jews will not be able to find me to bring me before His Tribunal of Justice.' The Talmud concludes that Titus did not succeed in his attempt to escape divine retribution. Indeed, the very sentence which he passed upon himself is meticulously fulfilled. Every day, his ashes are gathered and he is judged and burned again and the ashes are scattered over seven seas. This fulfills David's request here 'make them burn like a fiery furnace'. For, the sentence of Titus resembles the fate of the furnace which is rekindled daily after dying down to ashes on the day before.

¹⁰ Make them as a fiery furnace
    at the time of Your anger.
May HASHEM consume them in His wrath;
    let a fire devour them.
¹¹ Destroy their children from the earth,
    and their offspring from the sons of men.
¹² For they have directed evil against You,
    they have devised evil plots
    which they cannot carry out.
¹³ For You shall place them as a portion apart,
    with Your bowstring
    which You aim at their faces.
¹⁴ Be exalted, HASHEM, in Your might;
    we shall sing and chant the praise
    of Your omnipotence.

לְעֵת פָּנֶיךָ — At the time of Your anger [lit. 'Your face'].

This term is often used in reference to anger as in פְּנֵי ה' חִלְּקָם 'The anger [lit. 'face'] of HASHEM has divided them' (Lam. 4:16) (Ibn Ezra; Radak).

בְּאַפּוֹ יְבַלְּעֵם ה' — May HASHEM consume them in His wrath.

This is not a prophecy but a prayer (Rashi).

11. פִּרְיָמוֹ מֵאֶרֶץ תְּאַבֵּד — Destroy their children [lit. 'their fruit'] from the earth.

David prayed that the Holy One, Blessed be He destroy the children of Esau the wicked (Rashi).

This refers in particular to the seed of Amalek who are to be utterly obliterated from the face of the earth in Messianic times (Midrash Chachamim).

12. כִּי נָטוּ עָלֶיךָ רָעָה — For they have directed evil against You.

Rashi comments that this refers to Titus. The Talmud (Gittin 56b) relates that Titus slashed the sacred פָּרוֹכֶת, 'curtain' which hung before the Holy of Holies, with his sword, and blood began to flow from it. In his haughty foolishness, Titus imagined that he had

slain God Himself. [The real reason for the bleeding, explains Tosefos (ibid.), was because Hashem wished to show His great sorrow over the destruction of the Temple, as if He were bleeding in anguish].

חָשְׁבוּ מְזִמָּה בַּל יוּכָלוּ — They have devised evil plots which they cannot carry out.

Rabbi Shimon bar Yochai said: When the Roman Emperor Hadrian entered the area of the Holy of Holies he began to talk with excessive pride and blasphemed the name of God. Rabbi Chiya bar Abba said: David declared before God: Sovereign of the Universe, let it be known before You that if they could fell the tallest cedars and build ladders to assault heaven, they would. But since they can't, they leave You alone and attack us instead! (Midrash Shemos Rabba 51:5).

13. כִּי תְּשִׁיתֵמוֹ שֶׁכֶם — For you shall place them as a portion apart.

שֶׁכֶם — A portion. As we find שְׁכֶם אַחַד 'one extra portion' (Gen. 48:22) (Metzudas Zion).

Now the Psalmist explains why they will be unable to carry out their evil

plots (v. 12). It is because God will separate them from Him and they will be a group apart, totally divorced from Hashem and His aid (Radak).

Rashi also translates שֶׁכֶם as 'a portion'. However, he interprets the verse in reference to the future defeat of the nations when their spoils will be presented to Israel as its portion.

14. רוּמָה ה׳ בְּעֻזֶּךְ — Be exalted HASHEM in Your might.

All of Israel will say this to Hashem, bearing testimony that the final victory over the nations is due to His might only, and not theirs (Radak).

נָשִׁירָה וּנְזַמְּרָה גְּבוּרָתֶךְ — We shall sing and chant the praise to Your omnipotence.

When You will endow us with Your might and strength we will sing Your praises, acknowledging You as the source of all strength (Radak).

[This will be the fulfillment of the declaration made referring to the King Messiah in verse 2: 'HASHEM in Your might the king rejoices'.]

22 מזמור כב

T his Psalm, although entitled מִזְמוֹר לְדָוִד, 'A song of David'
primarily deals with events which were destined to occur
hundreds of years after David's time. David, with his רוּחַ הַקּוֹדֶשׁ 'holy spirit' foresaw the bleak Babylonian and Persian exiles in general,
and in particular, the terrible threat of Haman and Ahasueros against
the entire Jewish nation, personified by Queen Esther. Although
there are countless events in Jewish history which David does not discuss in the Book of Psalms, Alshich explains that David dedicated a
Psalm to Esther because he personally had a hand in the salvation of
Israel in her days. When David fled from Absalom, Shimi ben Gera
of the tribe of Benjamin went out to viciously curse David. Yet,
David would not allow his men to kill Shimi although he deserved
death for blaspheming the king (II Sam. 16:5-13). The Talmud
(Megilla 13a) says that David foresaw that Mordecai [and Esther] was
destined to descend from Shimi ['Mordecai, son of Yair, son of Shimi'
(Esther 2:5)] and being that the salvation of Israel was at stake, David
forfeited his own dignity for the sake of saving his people.

Therefore, David was inspired to compose a psalm in honor of the
Purim miracle, for without him it could not have come to pass.

It was the custom of the Vilna Gaon to recite this psalm as the שִׁיר
שֶׁל יוֹם, 'the daily song' on the day of Purim (Maaseh Rav no. 250).

א לַמְנַצֵּחַ עַל־אַיֶּלֶת הַשַּׁחַר מִזְמוֹר לְדָוִד:
ב אֵלִי אֵלִי לָמָה עֲזַבְתָּנִי רָחוֹק מִישׁוּעָתִי
ג דִּבְרֵי שַׁאֲגָתִי: אֱלֹהַי אֶקְרָא יוֹמָם וְלֹא
ד תַעֲנֶה וְלַיְלָה וְלֹא־דוּמִיָּה לִי: וְאַתָּה

1. אַיֶּלֶת הַשַּׁחַר — *Ayeles Hashachar.*

The commentaries offer numerous explanations for these words.

Many say that this was a type of musical instrument (*Rashi; Radak; Ibn Ezra; Metzudos*). Or, this refers to *'the morning star'* (*Radak*).

Meiri combines these interpretations, explaining that these very melodious instruments start with a subtle, low sound and slowly gather strength and volume, just as the light of early dawn rises slowly until it reaches a climax with the appearance of the dazzling sun. [This is another example of how the instruments which provided musical accompaniment for the psalms were chosen carefully so that their unique musical properties complemented the theme of the psalm. See *Psalms 5:1 comm.*]

Rashi comments that it is also a term of endearment towards Israel which is called אַיֶּלֶת אֲהָבִים *'a lovely hind'* (*Prov.* 5:19). At the same time the word אַיֶּלֶת denotes strength and salvation as in (*v.* 20) אֱיָלוּתִי לְעֶזְרָתִי חוּשָׁה *'O my strength, hasten to my assistance'* (*Rashi; Radak*).

Ultimately, all of these themes find expression in the personality of Esther, who represents the slow dawning of the light of redemption for the Jews who were engulfed in the darkness of exile. *Midrash Shocher Tov* explains that immediately before the rise of the morning star the night is at its darkest, for the moon and bright stars have already begun to fade and recede. Similarly, Esther arrived at Israel's darkest hour. Through her great love for God (אַיֶּלֶת

(אֲהָבִים) she gathered the tremendous strength (אֱיָלוּתִי) to fast for three days and to enter Ahasueros' court unsummoned although this meant certain death.[1]

Furthermore, the Talmud (*Yoma* 29a) adds: 'Just as the female deer (אַיָּלָה) is always enticing to her mate, so did the lovely Esther arouse Ahasuerus' passions at each meeting as if it was the first time he was with her. Also, just as the horns of a deer continue to grow as it ages, the prayers of the righteous are more readily heard the more they increase them. Finally, just as the אַיֶּלֶת הַשַּׁחַר, *'the morning star'* marks the end of the night, so does the miracle of Esther mark the last of the miracles recorded in the Scriptures'.

[*Yalkut Shimoni (Megillas Esther* 1053) explains that the name Esther is derived from *'Istahar'*, a very bright star.]

2. Esther's Prayer

The fateful letters sealing the doom of the Jews were signed and sent out on the thirteenth day of Nissan. Esther commanded that all Jews should fast, pray, and repent for three days: the thirteenth, fourteenth, and fifteenth of Nissan (*Pirkei d'Rabbi Eliezer* Ch.50, see gloss of *Rashash* to *Talmud Megillah* 15a). Mordecai protested to Esther, 'But these days of fasting include the first day of Passover?' [and fasting is prohibited on the festival]. She replied: 'If there will be no Israel then certainly there will be no Passover!' (*Midrash*).

1. *Vilna Gaon* explains that the word שַׁחַר *'morning, dawn'* is related to שָׁחוֹר *'black, dark'*, because the moment immediately preceding the dawn is the blackest, darkest period of the night (*Avnei Eliyahu*).

For the Conductor; on the Ayeles Hashachar.
A song of David.
[2] My God, my God, why have You forsaken me?
So far from saving me,
from the words of my roar?
[3] O my God!
I call out by day and You do not answer;
by night there is no respite for me.

'Now it came to pass on the third day, Esther donned royalty' (Esther 5:1). The Talmud (Megillah 15a) explains that this refers not only to royal apparel but also to spiritual royalty i.e. the holy [prophetic] spirit clothed her.

But on her way to the king's throneroom Esther passed through a chapel filled with the king's idols — and suddenly the holy spirit departed from her. In her anguish she uttered these verses.

אֵלִי אֵלִי — My God, my God.

Repetition is customary for those who cry out emotionally, as in 'Answer me, HASHEM, answer me!' (I Kings 18:37) (Radak, Metzudas David).[1]

רָחוֹק מִישׁוּעָתִי דִּבְרֵי שַׁאֲגָתִי — So far from saving me, from the words of my roar.

Esther is emphasizing that her con-

cern is not for herself, but for all of Israel. She declares: 'My anguished roar is motivated by thoughts far removed from concern over my personal salvation' (Turei Zahav).

Esther laments: Ordinarily, God does not reject the fasting and prayers of an entire congregation. Rather, 'Before they call, I already answer' (Isaiah 65:24). But here, even after I roar there is no answer, and salvation is far off (Baalei Bris Avrohom).

אֱלֹהַי אֶקְרָא יוֹמָם וְלֹא תַעֲנֶה וְלַיְלָה וְלֹא .3
דוּמִיָּה לִי — O my God! I call out by day and You do not answer and there is no respite [lit. 'silence'] for me.

Rabbi Joshua ben Levi derived the following law from this verse: A person is obligated to recite the Megillah in the

---

1. Among the י״ג מִדּוֹת שֶׁל רַחֲמִים 'the Thirteen Divine Attributes of Mercy' we find אֵל (Exodus 34:6). Rashi (ibid.) notes that it is certainly a name denoting God's mercy for we find that in this Psalm, Esther cried out to God addressing Him as אֵל and pleading 'why have You forsaken me?' One cannot ask such a question of מִדַּת הַדִּין 'the Divine Attribute of Justice.'

Sifsei Chachamim ibid. emphasizes that the concept of mercy expressed by the name אֵל is more generous and powerful than the simple mercy of the name ה', HASHEM [cf. Rashi Ex. 15:11].

The Sefer Hameoros on Tractate Berachos devotes an entire treatise to a thorough discussion of the Thirteen Attributes and defines אֵל as, 'strength and power in times of distress as we find concerning Esther. It is the third Attribute of Mercy after ה' ה', HASHEM, HASHEM, to teach us that this Name is reserved for the perfectly righteous who never sinned or for penitents who have completely atoned for every one of their sins.'

Some open the blessing following the reading of the Megillah with הָאֵל הָרָב אֶת רִיבֵנוּ, the אֵל [God] Who fights our battle, and conclude it with the blessing הָאֵל הַמּוֹשִׁיעַ, the אֵל [God] Who saves. Bayis Chadash (Orach Chaim 692) explains that this frequent use of the divine name אֵל is a reminder of the fact that the Purim miracle came about in the merit of Esther who twice called out אֵלִי אֵלִי. By invoking this powerful Attribute of Mercy, she transformed the fate of the Jews, which was already sealed in heaven, from doom to glorious triumph over their foes.]

ה קָדוֹשׁ יוֹשֵׁב תְּהִלּוֹת יִשְׂרָאֵל: בְּךָ בָּטְחוּ
ו אֲבֹתֵינוּ בָּטְחוּ וַתְּפַלְּטֵמוֹ: אֵלֶיךָ זָעֲקוּ
ז וְנִמְלָטוּ בְּךָ בָטְחוּ וְלֹא־בוֹשׁוּ: וְאָנֹכִי
תוֹלַעַת וְלֹא־אִישׁ חֶרְפַּת אָדָם וּבְזוּי עָם:
ח כָּל־רֹאַי יַלְעִגוּ לִי יַפְטִירוּ בְשָׂפָה יָנִיעוּ
ט רֹאשׁ: גֹּל אֶל־יהוה יְפַלְּטֵהוּ יַצִּילֵהוּ כִּי

evening and then repeat it again on the following day (*Megillah* 4a); this recalls the circumstances of the miracle when they cried out continually in their distress, day and night (*Rashi*).

4. וְאַתָּה קָדוֹשׁ יוֹשֵׁב תְּהִלּוֹת יִשְׂרָאֵל — *Yet You are the Holy One, enthroned upon the praises of Israel.*

Why do You not answer my call? Are You not the God Who saved Israel in the past and listened to their resultant songs of praise? Are You not as capable of saving us now as You were then? (*Radak; Metzudas David*)

According to *Rashi* יוֹשֵׁב literally means 'sitting' i.e. God sits to hear praises. *Radak* and *Metzudas David* maintain that the word יוֹשֵׁב is used figuratively to denote the permanence of God's strength which remains *sitting* i.e. unchanged for all eternity as in אַתָּה ה' לְעוֹלָם תֵּשֵׁב 'You HASHEM, are permanent forever (*Lam.* 5:19).

After reading the Megillah in the evening, the congregation recites the prayer וּבָא לְצִיּוֹן גּוֹאֵל, *May the redeemer come to Zion*, omitting the opening verses and beginning with וְאַתָּה קָדוֹשׁ יוֹשֵׁב תְּהִלּוֹת יִשְׂרָאֵל, *You are the Holy One* . . . (*Orach Chaim* 693:1).

Hagohos Maimoni (*Hilchos Megillah*) derives this custom from our psalm. The preceding verse which speaks of the obligation to read the Megillah is followed immediately by this verse which begins וְאַתָּה קָדוֹשׁ.

5. בְּךָ בָּטְחוּ אֲבֹתֵינוּ בָּטְחוּ וַתְּפַלְּטֵמוֹ — *In You our fathers trusted, they trusted and You delivered them.*

Our fathers in Egypt displayed their faith by stubbornly refusing to change their language and their names. Because of their faith You helped them to escape from their bondage (*Sforno*).

6. אֵלֶיךָ זָעֲקוּ — *To You they cried out.*

Midrash Shocher Tov refers this to the Jewish experience in Egypt: 'The children of Israel sighed because of the bondage and they cried out' (*Ex.* 2:23).

Also, they cried out when they were trapped by the sea (*Alshich*).

וְנִמְלָטוּ — *And were rescued.*

'As it says: 'On that day HASHEM saved Israel from the hand of Egypt' (*Ex.* 14:30).

בְּךָ בָטְחוּ וְלֹא בוֹשׁוּ — *In You they trusted and were not shamed.*

The final stage of their total faith was when they followed You out into the barren wilderness with no provisions for food or shelter. Yet, You did not embarrass them by forsaking them. Instead, You generously took care of all their needs for forty years (*Sforno*).

7. וְאָנֹכִי תוֹלַעַת וְלֹא אִישׁ — *But I am a worm and not a man.*

The Psalmist describes the degradation of Israel in Exile. All the nations look down upon Israel as a subhuman species, on the same level as a worm (*Radak*).

Midrash Shocher Tov emphasizes that despite the pitiful weakness of the worm it does have strength in one area. Armed with nothing more than its mouth, the worm destroys the mighty cedars. Thus, this soft and flexible

⁴ Yet You are the Holy One,
        enthroned upon the praises of Israel!
⁵ In You our fathers trusted,
        they trusted and You delivered them.
⁶ To You they cried out and were rescued,
        In You they trusted and were not shamed.
⁷ But I am a worm and not a man,
        scorn of humanity, despised of nations.
⁸ All who see me, deride me;
        they open their mouths, they wag their heads.
⁹ 'Reliance on HASHEM. He will deliver him!

organism can topple the rigid and hard tree. Similarly, Israel smites the nations, armed with nothing more than the prayers in their mouths.

The Holy One, blessed be He, said to Israel: I desire you alone because even when I shower you with greatness, you humble yourselves before Me. I bestowed greatness upon Abraham, and he said to Me, וְאָנֹכִי עָפָר וָאֵפֶר, *'I am dust and ash'* (*Gen.* 18:27). I bestowed greatness upon Moses and Aaron and they said, וְנַחְנוּ מָה, *'And what are we?'* (*Ex.* 16:7). I bestowed greatness upon David and he said, וְאָנֹכִי תוֹלַעַת וְלֹא אִישׁ, *'But I am a worm and not a man'.* However, when I elevate the nations to greatness, they grow excessively proud (*Chullin* 89a).

חֶרְפַּת אָדָם — *Scorn of Humanity.*
People use me as a term of insult. When they wish to degrade someone else they say, 'You are as low and despicable as he is' (*Metzudas David*).

וּבְזוּי עָם — *Despised of nations* [lit. *'nation']*.
Not only individuals use me as a term for insult, even nations disparage one another using my name (*Metzudas David*).

8. כָּל רֹאַי יַלְעִגוּ לִי — *All who see me deride me.*
Midrash Shocher Tov suggests that

the preceding verses describe the Jews in Esther's times. They put their faith in God and shouted and fasted to nullify Haman's decree. Esther displayed her unswerving faith by fearlessly coming to the king, unsummoned. This verse depicts the vicious sons of Haman who derided the Jews, shaking their heads and taunting, 'Tomorrow you shall die.'

יַפְטִירוּ — *Open.*
As in פֶּטֶר רֶחֶם *'the opening of the womb'* [*Ex.* 13:16] (*Rashi*).

9. [Now the Psalmist responds to the derision of those who mock his faith, and expresses complete confidence in God's salvation.]

גֹּל אֶל ה' — *Reliance on HASHEM!*
The translation follows *Radak* and *Metzudas David* who render that the Psalmist exhorts the downtrodden person or nation to ignore its mockers and place its destiny in the hands of God.

Literally, גֹּל means *'to roll over'* a burden to someone else (*Rashi*).

יְפַלְּטֵהוּ — *He will deliver him.*
Midrash Shocher Tov comments that God promised to help Israel escape from their burden of sin. If they will only repent and thus *'roll over'* their sins to God, their complete pardon is assured. [Israel has just completed three days of

י חָפֵץ בּוֹ: כִּי־אַתָּה גֹחִי מִבָּטֶן מַבְטִיחִי עַל־
יא שְׁדֵי אִמִּי: עָלֶיךָ הָשְׁלַכְתִּי מֵרָחֶם מִבֶּטֶן
יב אִמִּי אֵלִי אָתָּה: אַל־תִּרְחַק מִמֶּנִּי כִּי־צָרָה
יג קְרוֹבָה כִּי־אֵין עוֹזֵר: סְבָבוּנִי פָּרִים רַבִּים

fasting and repentance in response to Haman's decree of annihilation. Esther now exhorts them to have confidence in the power of repentance and God's boundless mercies.]

כִּי חָפֵץ בּוֹ — *For He desires him.*

The phrase is ambiguous because the subjects of the pronouns are not clarified. It may mean that God desires this man, or it may mean that this man desires only God, and by virtue of this unyielding love God will respond and save him (*Radak*).

10. גֹחִי — *Drew me.*

As in בְּגִיחוֹ מֵרֶחֶם יֵצֵא — '*When he is drawn out from the womb, he goes forth*' (*Job* 38:8).

Esther alludes to the tragic circumstances of her birth. 'When Esther's mother conceived her, her father died. At childbirth her mother died' (*Megillah* 13a). Thus, as she was leaving her mother's womb, her life was in mortal danger, and only because God drew her out of the birth passage did she survive (*Alshich; Midrash Shocher Tov*).

[In truth, her orphan status was an asset many years later. For, the Megillah tells us that '*Esther would not reveal her birthplace and her nation*' (*Esther* 2:19). The enigma of her silence intrigued Ahasueros and made her even more attractive to him. Thus, the *Talmud* (*Megillah* 13a) says: 'Every nation of the empire claimed her to be theirs.' Hence, her true identity was shrouded and therein rested the key to salvation.

Divrei Shaul offers a novel explanation of how it could be that no one knew Esther was Jewish. It was well-known that she was an orphan who was raised

by Mordecai. Therefore, it was thought that she might have been a non-Jewish foundling who was taken in by the merciful Mordecai.]

מַבְטִיחִי עַל שְׁדֵי אִמִּי — *You made me secure on my mother's breasts,* [i.e. my trust in God began from earliest infancy.]

This alludes to the *Midrash* which relates that when Mordecai adopted the new-born Esther, he could not find a wet-nurse for her. Hashem miraculously caused milk to gush forth from Mordecai's own breasts and he nursed her, as the *Megillah* relates, '*And he was a nurse for Hadassah, she is Esther, his cousin, for she had no father and mother* [Esther 2:7] (*Alshich*).

[See *Talmud* (*Shabbos* 53b) and gloss of *Tosefos Yeshonim, ibid.*]

11. עָלֶיךָ הָשְׁלַכְתִּי מֵרָחֶם — *I was cast upon You from birth.*

[As explained in the preceding verse, Esther was an orphan from birth and God is '*the father of orphans*' (*Psalms* 68:6).]

Rashi interprets this as referring to the entire Jewish nation. The moment the twelve tribes were born, the nation was formed. From that time on, God carried and guided them, as it says, '*Listen to me O House of Jacob, and all of the remnant of the House of Israel, who are borne by Me from birth, who are carried from My womb*' (*Isaiah* 46:3).

מִבֶּטֶן אִמִּי אֵלִי אָתָּה — *From my mother's womb You have been my God.*

Yerushalmi (*Yoma* 8:4) offers a striking illustration of how certain infants

XXII
10-13

He will save him, for He desires him!'

¹⁰ *Because You drew me forth from the womb,*
and made me secure on my mother's breasts.
¹¹ *I was cast upon You from birth,*
from my mother's womb You have been my God.
¹² *Be not aloof from me for distress is near,*
for there is none to help.
¹³ *Many bulls surround me,*

---

realize their divine obligations even while yet in the womb.

'A pregnant woman who is seized by an uncontrollable craving to eat on Yom Kippur may be fed until she is revived. Two such women came to Rabbi Tarfon. He dispatched two disciples to whisper in the ear of each woman, 'Today is the great fast day.' One child responded to this and immediately stopped [gnawing at his mother's innards]. The other child did not. Rabbi Tarfon praised the one who stopped and described him with the verse, *'from my mother's stomach You have been my God.'*

[Esther has already cried out אֵלִי twice (v. 2). Now she addresses God with this Name for the third time. *Midrash Shocher Tov* says that she wished to allude to the fact that she had always scrupulously observed the three commandments which God designated specifically for women נִדָּה, חַלָּה, הַדְלָקַת הַנֵּר, 'ritual purity, separating challah, and lighting the Sabbath candles.']

12. אַל תִּרְחַק מִמֶּנִּי — *Be not aloof from me.*

You have been close to me since my conception and birth, and You continued to guide me throughout my development. Please do not suddenly desert me in my distress (*Radak*).

כִּי צָרָה קְרוֹבָה — *For distress is near.*

Midrash Shocher Tov describes the

circumstances under which Esther said this:

When she dared to approach the king's throne room unsummoned, she had to pass through seven antechambers. She passed through three of them unharmed, but when she entered the fourth (the middle one) Ahasueros noticed and began to grind his teeth in wrath. He cried, 'Alas, I sorely miss the former queen who is gone but not forgotten. When I called for Vashti [to display herself] she maintained her dignity and refused to come. But this one, Esther, comes on her own, like a low woman soliciting for herself!'

At that moment Esther froze in fear. Sentries appeared from all sides and wished to pounce on her, but the middle ante-chamber was not under their jurisdiction and they were forced to pause. Esther called to God, *'Be not aloof from me for distress is near.'*

13. סְבָבוּנִי פָּרִים רַבִּים — *Many bulls surround me.*

Ahasueros' soldiers and bodyguards (*Midrash Shocher Tov*).

This alludes to the many agents who were sent out by Ahasueros to be סוֹבְבִים בָּעִיר, *'Circling all around the city'* to bring in the most beautiful maidens for the competition to decide who would be the queen. One of these searches uncovered Esther who was taken forcibly, against her will, to the palace (*Alshich*).

יד אַבִּירֵי בָשָׁן כִּתְּרוּנִי: פָּצוּ עָלַי פִּיהֶם
טו אַרְיֵה טֹרֵף וְשֹׁאֵג: כַּמַּיִם נִשְׁפַּכְתִּי
וְהִתְפָּרְדוּ כָּל־עַצְמוֹתָי הָיָה לִבִּי כַּדּוֹנָג
טז נָמֵס בְּתוֹךְ מֵעָי: יָבֵשׁ כַּחֶרֶשׂ | כֹּחִי וּלְשׁוֹנִי
יז מֻדְבָּק מַלְקוֹחָי וְלַעֲפַר־מָוֶת תִּשְׁפְּתֵנִי: כִּי
סְבָבוּנִי כְּלָבִים עֲדַת מְרֵעִים הִקִּיפוּנִי

אַבִּירֵי בָשָׁן — *Bashan's mighty ones.*
The פָּרִים, 'bulls' are the fat and powerful enemies. Bashan was a location in Eretz Yisroel where the pastureland was lush and abundant. The animals which grazed there grew strong and thick with fat. This description emphasizes the power of the foe (*Radak*).

According to *Midrash Shocher Tov* this refers to the sons of Haman.

כִּתְּרוּנִי — *Encircle me.* [lit. 'they crown me']
They surround me as a crown encircles the head (*Rashi*).

This refers to the agents who discovered Esther and sought to have her crowned (*Alshich*).

14. אַרְיֵה — *Like a lion.*
The word should be prefixed with a כ' הַדִּמְיוֹן, 'a letter כ' denoting comparison', but it is customary to delete that כ' when men are described in terms of animals (*Radak*).

According to *Rashi* this describes King Nebuchadnezzar.

[The Talmud (*Megillah* 12a) interprets the verse עָלָה אַרְיֵה מִסֻּבְּכוֹ 'the lion has come up from his thicket' (Jer. 4:7) as referring to Nebuchadnezzar. The Talmud (*Shabbos* 150a) tells us that Nebuchadnezzar used to ride a male lion with a serpent tied to its head for a bridle.]

טֹרֵף וְשֹׁאֵג — *Tearing [and] roaring.*
After the lion tears its prey to pieces it roars proudly for joy. Although bulls usually are not meat eaters, these bulls

which surround (v. 13) me are like lions (*Radak*).

The agents who forcibly brought Esther to the palace saw that she was miserable. They tried to cheer her up, saying, 'You have won the most coveted prize, the royal crown! Why don't you roar for joy like the lion who has seized his prey?' (*Alshich*).

15. כַּמַּיִם נִשְׁפַּכְתִּי — *I am poured out like water*, i.e. a metaphor meaning that my fear melted my resolve as if it were running water (*Radak*).

Tehillos HASHEM applies the verse to Esther's reaction to the news of Haman's decree against the Jews: וַתִּתְחַלְחַל הַמַּלְכָּה מְאֹד 'and the Queen was greatly distressed' (Esther 4:4) [lit. 'she became full of hollow spaces'] Rav said: she became ritually unclean; Rav Yirmiya said her stomach was loosened (and melted like water) (*Megillah* 15a).

וְהִתְפָּרְדוּ כָּל עַצְמוֹתָי — *[And] all my bones became disjointed.* Instead of enjoying the blessing of 'good tidings fatten the bones' (*Prov.* 15:30), my bones are undermined by tragedy. Instead of cohesion, as in 'all my bones will say [Your praise]' (*Psalms* 35:10), my bones have come apart (*Alshich*).

This alludes to Esther whose bones were racked with pain when her terror caused her to menstruate (*Tehillos HASHEM*).

הָיָה לִבִּי כַּדּוֹנָג — *My heart is like wax.* Like wax melted by heat (*Rashi*).

Some say Esther's heart became weak and she fainted (*Tehillos HASHEM*).

Bashan's mighty ones encircle me.
¹⁴ They open their mouths against me
like a tearing, roaring lion.
¹⁵ I am poured out like water,
and all my bones became disjointed.
My heart is like wax,
melted within my innards.
¹⁶ My spittle is dry like baked clay,
and my tongue sticks to my palate.
In the dust of death You set me down.
¹⁷ For dogs surround me,
a pack of evil-doers encloses me,

נָמֵס בְּתוֹךְ מֵעָי — *Melted within my innards.*

The word מֵעַי often refers to the embryo carried inside a pregnant woman. This alludes to the opinion (*Midrash Esther Rabba* 8:3) that Esther was pregnant but miscarried upon hearing the terrible news (*Tehillos HASHEM*).

16. כֹּחִי — *My spittle.*

In the *Talmud* we find saliva and mucus described as כִּיחוֹ וְנִיעוֹ (*Radak, quoting his father; see Bava Kama* 3b, and *Rashi* and *Tosefos* there).

Ibn Ezra explains that the saliva and all of the liquids and enzymes secreted by the body are primary factors in lubricating the various organic systems. This smooth functioning enhances the body's כֹּחַ 'strength'. Hence, these liquids are called כֹּחִי [lit. 'my strength'].

Radak and *Ibn Ezra* also quote an opinion which holds that כֹּחִי is the same as חִכִּי 'my palate'. When this is as dry as clay it is difficult to speak.

מַלְקוֹחָי — *My palate.*

This word derives from לוֹקֵחַ 'to

take,' because when the teeth chew, the palate helps to take in the food (*Metzudas Zion*).

Since the gums surround the tongue, when the mouth is parched and dry, the tongue sticks to the gums which encircle it (*Rashi*).

וְלַעֲפַר מָוֶת — *In* [lit. 'to] *the dust of death'.*

The dust of the grave (*Radak*).

תִּשְׁפְּתֵנִי — *You set me down.* This term is always used to describe the setting of a pot on the stove as in שְׁפֹת הַסִּיר 'set down the pot' [Ezek. 24:3] (*Rashi*).

Esther bemoans her passive acquiescence in living with Ahasueros as if she were 'set down like the dust which is dead and insensitive' [cf. אֶסְתֵּר קַרְקַע עוֹלָם *Sanhedrin* 74b] (*Alshich*).

17. כִּי סְבָבוּנִי כְּלָבִים — *For Dogs surround me.*

This describes Israel in the Exile of Bavel, surrounded by hostile enemies, with no avenue of escape (*Radak*).

Specifically this refers to the sons of Haman (*Midrash Shocher Tov*).[1]

1. The Rabbis often equated the seed of Amalek with that of a dog. 'He is called עֲמָלֵק because it is a contraction of the words עַם שֶׁבָּא לָלוּק, 'the nation that came to lick' the blood of the Jews, like a blood-thirsty dog' (*Tanchuma Ki Teitzei*).

Yalkut Shimoni (ibid.) illustrates the obligation to remember Amalek's wickedness with this

יח כָּאֲרִי יָדַי וְרַגְלָי: אֲסַפֵּר כָּל־עַצְמוֹתָי
יט הֵמָּה יַבִּיטוּ יִרְאוּ־בִי: יְחַלְּקוּ בְגָדַי לָהֶם
כ וְעַל־לְבוּשִׁי יַפִּילוּ גוֹרָל: וְאַתָּה יהוה אַל־
כא תִּרְחָק אֱיָלוּתִי לְעֶזְרָתִי חוּשָׁה: הַצִּילָה
כב מֵחֶרֶב נַפְשִׁי מִיַּד־כֶּלֶב יְחִידָתִי: הוֹשִׁיעֵנִי

כָּאֲרִי יָדַי וְרַגְלָי — *Like a lion on my hands and [my] feet.* [lit. 'like a lion, my hands and my feet'] The hunting strategy of the lion is as follows. He walks around a specific portion of the forest dragging his tail on the ground, marking off his territory. The animals found in this circle are petrified with fear. Instead of running, they draw in their hands and feet and prepare themselves to fall prey to the lion. So too, in Bavel, we were incarcerated in a dangerous captivity helplessly enclosed in the territory marked off by our enemies *(Radak)*.

18. אֲסַפֵּר כָּל עַצְמוֹתָי — *I count all my bones* [lit. 'I tell of all my bones'] i.e. the pains afflicting my bones *(Rashi)*.

'I am so starved and emaciated that my bones stick out and can be counted' *(Radak)*.

'My flesh is devoured and only my bones remain to be counted' *(Sforno)*.

I try to tell the high and mighty authorities of the persecutions and injustices I suffer at the hands of the low masses. But they only look back at me with scorn *(Radak)*.

'I count the broken fragments of my bones which fell to pieces (v. 15) *(Ibn Ezra)*.

This psalm contains exactly 248 words, a figure which corresponds to the 248 limbs of the human body. As Esther prepared herself to confront Ahasueros, she raised herself to a level of spiritual ecstasy. When she examined herself and counted her limbs, she found that every part of her body was suffused with רוּחַ הַקּוֹדֶשׁ *'the holy spirit'* (Rabbeinu Eliezer of Worms).

הֵמָּה יַבִּיטוּ יִרְאוּ בִי — *They look on and gloat over me* [lit. 'see me']. They rejoice over my misfortunes *(Rashi)*.

They look at me with scorn and derision as in אַל תִּרְאֻנִי שֶׁאֲנִי שְׁחַרְחֹרֶת *'Do not look at me with derision for I am blackened'* (Songs 1:6) *(Radak)*.

19. יְחַלְּקוּ בְגָדַי לָהֶם — *They divide my garments among them.*

'When Esther began to walk to the king unsummoned, she apparently sealed her doom. All of the palace courtiers eyed her valuables covetously. This one said: I will take her garments. Another said: I want her jewels! A third said: Her necklaces are mine! A fourth cried: I claim for myself her royal mantle!' *(Midrash Shocher Tov)*.

וְעַל לְבוּשִׁי יַפִּילוּ גוֹרָל — *And [they] cast lots for my clothing.*

According to *Midrash Shocher Tov* this specifically refers to the most

parable: 'This may be likened to a king who placed a mad dog at the entrance of his orchard to guard against thieves. Once, the king's favorite secretly went to steal some fruit and the mad dog pounced on him and ripped his clothing. Whenever the king wished to remind his favorite of this incident (without embarrassing him too much), he would say, 'Remember how crazy that dog was, the one who ripped your clothing!' Similarly, the Jews once cried out, 'Is HASHEM in our midst or is He not? (Ex. 17:7). [They thought Hashem was not watching over them just as the favorite thought that the king's orchard was not watched.] Immediately they were attacked by Amalek! (Ex. 17:8). Moshe did not want to embarrass them by reminding them of their lack of faith so he said 'Remember what Amalek did to you' (Deut. 25:17), like that mad dog by the gate!'

like a lion on my hands and my feet.
¹⁸ *I count all my bones,*
they look on and gloat over me.
¹⁹ *They divide my garments among them,*
and cast lots for my clothing.
²⁰ *But You, HASHEM, be not far from me.*
O my strength, hasten to my assistance!
²¹ *Deliver my soul from the sword,*
my only one from the grip of the dog.
²² *Save me from the lion's mouth*

significant article of clothing, the royal mantle, which may be worn only by the royal family (see *Malbim*).

20. אַל תִּרְחָק — *Be not far from me.*

Midrash Shocher Tov interprets this as a plea from Esther, asking that the scepter of Ahasuerus be elongated to touch her so as to authorize her to enter before him; thus, 'let his scepter not be far from me.'

אֱיָלוּתִי — *My strength.* Zohar (*Parshas Teruma*) interprets this as my אַיָל 'hart'. Israel begs God 'Be not far from me'. Even if our sins should force Your presence to depart from our midst, nevertheless, 'be like the hart which always returns home no matter how far afield it flees'.

21. הַצִּילָה מֵחֶרֶב נַפְשִׁי — *Deliver my soul from the sword.*

Abudraham on the laws of Purim notes that the initials of these three words form the name הָמָן 'Haman'. The initials of the next three words form מַכִּי 'who smites me'. (See *Maharsha* on *Megillah* 15b s.v. וְאָמְרָה.)[1]

מִיַד כֶּלֶב — *From the grip of the dog.*

This too refers to Haman for the Talmud equates the slanderer to a dog, 'Whoever speaks evil gossip, deserves to be thrown to the dogs' (*Pesachim* 118a). The Talmud (*Megillah* 13b) also says 'There was never anyone who could spread slander as well as Haman' (*Tehilla L'David*).

יְחִידָתִי — *My only one.*

This describes the soul which is the lone spiritual force dwelling in a physical, material body of flesh and blood (*Radak*).

[In the Talmud (*Menachos* 18a) we find that Rabbi Elazar loved his student Yoseif the Bavli עַד לְאַחַת 'until one'. *Tosefos* (ibid.) explains this to mean that he loved him to the very depths of his own soul which is called יְחִידָה 'the only one'.

The *Pnei Yehoshua* on *Berachos* 10a explains that according to the kabbala the soul is divided into five different levels through which a man ascends in the course of his existence. The highest level is called יְחִידָה and this can only be

1. [When Jacob feared his encounter with Esau, Haman's ancestor, he pleaded הַצִּלֵנִי נָא מִיַד 'Deliver me from the hand [of Esau]' (Gen. 32:11); there, too, the initials form הָמָן. Again we find the verse לְהַצִּיל מִמָּוֶת נַפְשָׁם 'To deliver their souls from death' (Psalms 33:19) in which the initials (starting with the 'ה' of הַצִּיל) form Haman. Interestingly, that verse ends with the words וּלְחַיּוֹתָם בָּרָעָב, which literally means 'to keep them alive with hunger. The numerical value of בָּרָעָב is 274 which equals 'Mordecai' (מָרְדְּכַי = 274). It was Mordecai's hunger and penitent fasting for three days which delivered the souls of Israel from the death planned by Haman.]

מִפִּי אַרְיֵה וּמִקַּרְנֵי רֵמִים עֲנִיתָנִי:

כג אֲסַפְּרָה שִׁמְךָ לְאֶחָי בְּתוֹךְ קָהָל אֲהַלְלֶךָּ:
כד יִרְאֵי יהוה | הַלְלוּהוּ כָּל־זֶרַע יַעֲקֹב
כה כַּבְּדוּהוּ וְגוּרוּ מִמֶּנּוּ כָּל־זֶרַע יִשְׂרָאֵל: כִּי
לֹא־בָזָה וְלֹא שִׁקַּץ עֱנוּת עָנִי וְלֹא־
הִסְתִּיר פָּנָיו מִמֶּנּוּ וּבְשַׁוְּעוֹ אֵלָיו שָׁמֵעַ:

realized after death when the soul is fused together once again and unites inseparably with its Maker.]

22. וּמִקַּרְנֵי רֵמִים — 'And from the horns of the Reimim'.

[Many English translations have been offered for the word רְאֵם. Ox, bison, buffalo, unicorn and reindeer are among the most popular. One thing is clear, the רְאֵם derives its name from its majestic horns which are its most precious asset. The horns are רָם 'most high, exalted', taller than those of all other animals (this would make reindeer a very appropriate identity for the mysterious r'eim). Ibn Ezra bases this fact on the verse וַתָּרֶם כִּרְאֵים קַרְנִי 'You have exalted my horn like that of the R'eim' (Psalms 92:11).

Radak explains that all of the animals described in these verses i.e. dog, lion, r'eim, refer to Nebuchadnezzar and his officers. Each one is compared to an animal which corresponds to his rank.

23. אֲסַפְּרָה שִׁמְךָ לְאֶחָי — I will proclaim Your Name to my brethren.

When You will save me from the creatures of the Babylonian Exile, the dogs, lions, and r'eimim, I will relate this to my brothers who were not in this Exile, meaning the Jews of the Ten Lost Tribes of Israel who were in Chalach and Chabur, far from the dominion of Nebuchadnezzar. Furthermore, I am presently exiled amongst my brothers, i.e. אֱדוֹם 'Edom' [Rome] and יִשְׁמָעֵאל 'Ishmael' [Arabs] who are both descendants of my forefather, Abraham. I will

tell them, too, of Your salvation (Radak).

בְּתוֹךְ קָהָל אֲהַלְלֶךָּ — In the midst of the congregation will I praise You.

Alshich comments: The Talmud (Megillah 14a) explains that one reason we do not recite the Hallel on Purim even though the salvation from death would warrant such a recital is because the reading of the Megillah itself takes the place of Hallel. Therefore, Esther says: 'I will proclaim Your Name to my brethren' by reading the Megillah publicly and this will be considered as if 'I will praise You' [i.e., equivalent to reciting Hallel], in the midst of the congregation'.

24. יִרְאֵי ה׳ — You, who fear HASHEM.

These are the גֵּרִים, converts (Rashi).

[Similarly, on the verse יִרְאֵי ה׳ בִּטְחוּ בַה׳ 'Those who fear HASHEM trust in HASHEM' (115:11). Rashi identifies them as the converts. This alludes to the many gentiles who converted after witnessing the miraculous salvation of the Jews. 'And many of the people of the land became Jewish, for the fear of the Jews fell upon them' (Esther 8:17).]

הַלְלוּהוּ — Praise Him.

When the salvation of Hashem appears, everyone will laud Him differently. Each man will offer praise in accordance with his personal degree of closeness to God. Moreover, the very act of praise will have an inspiring effect. Those who originally served only

as You have answered
from the horns of the Reimim.
²³ I will proclaim Your Name to my brethren;
in the midst of the congregation will I praise You.
²⁴ You, who fear HASHEM, praise Him!
All of you, the seed of Jacob, glorify Him!
Be frightened of Him all you seed of Israel.
²⁵ For He has neither despised nor loathed
the screams of the poor,
nor has He concealed His face from him,
But when he cried to Him for help,
He heard.

out of fear i.e. 'יְרְאֵי ה, 'those who fear HASHEM', will come to serve God out of love and adoration, i.e. כָּל זֶרַע יַעֲקֹב כַּבְּדוּהוּ, 'all you, the seed of Jacob, glorify Him' (Radak).

כָּל זֶרַע יַעֲקֹב כַּבְּדוּהוּ — All of you, the seed of Jacob, glorify Him! I.e., the twelve sons of Jacob (Midrash Vayikra Rabba, 3:5).

וְגוּרוּ מִמֶּנּוּ כָּל זֶרַע יִשְׂרָאֵל — Be frightened of Him all you seed of Israel.

I.e., the tribe of Benjamin (Midrash ibid.). Benjamin merits the name 'seed of Israel' by virtue of his being the only one of the tribes born after Jacob wrestled with the angel who bestowed upon him the additional name, Israel, which denotes sovereignty (Ha'amek Davar, Gen. 33:7).

Maharal adds that Benjamin has the only one of Jacob's sons who was born in the land of Israel. Therefore the holy spirit dwelled in Benjamin's territory and it was there that the Temple was built.

[Benjamin was also the only tribe which was not humiliated by bowing down before Esau in fear, because Benjamin had not yet been born. The Midrash (Esther Rabba 7:9) explains that precisely for this reason Mordecai, the Benjaminite, refused to bow down before Haman, the descendant of Esau. Therefore it can truly be said of Benjamin that he fears God only. Thus, 'Be frightened of Him (and Him only) all you seed of Israel (Benjamin).]

[See comm. to 33:8 for the difference between גורו and יְרְאוּ.]

25. עֱנוּת עָנִי — The screams of the poor.

This follows Rashi who also suggests that it can be interpreted as 'submission' as in עַד מָתַי מֵאַנְתָּ לַעֲנֹת מִפָּנָי 'How long will you refuse to be submissive before Me' (Ex. 10:3). Radak holds that עֱנוּת describes the poor man's poverty and affliction, or it derives from עוֹנֶה 'answer, response' and refers to the prayers of the poor.[1]

1. Once, King Agrippa decided to offer 1000 burnt sacrifices in one day. He gave strict orders to the High Priest, 'Today, no one will bring any sacrifices except for me!' A poor man came to the High Priest and gave him two turtledoves, saying, 'Please sacrifice these for me.' When the High Priest refused the poor man said, 'My master, I trap four birds every day. Two I dedicate for sacrifice and two I keep for my livelihood. If you will not accept these two from me you will be undermining my entire income [because I am able to catch the two birds for my livelihood only in the merit of the two that I dedicate]. The High Priest relented and offered up

כו מֵאִתְּךָ תְהִלָּתִי בְּקָהָל רָב נְדָרַי אֲשַׁלֵּם
כז נֶגֶד יְרֵאָיו: יֹאכְלוּ עֲנָוִים | וְיִשְׂבָּעוּ יְהַלְלוּ
כח יהוה דֹּרְשָׁיו יְחִי לְבַבְכֶם לָעַד: יִזְכְּרוּ |
וְיָשֻׁבוּ אֶל־יהוה כָּל־אַפְסֵי־אָרֶץ

26. מֵאִתְּךָ תְהִלָּתִי בְּקָהָל רָב — *You are the cause of my praise; in the great congregation.*

The *'great congregation'* refers to the multitude of gentile nations before whom Israel will recite God's praises. They will say, 'The praises we offer are not empty words. God truly deserves them, because it was His wondrous salvation which inspired this acclaim' (*Radak*).

Previously the Psalmist said, *'Those who fear HASHEM, praise Him'* (v. 24). Now the Psalmist speaks for those men and demonstrates that their praise consists of but one word מֵאִתְּךָ *'From You'* i.e. Hashem, You alone are the source of all salvation (*Rav Yeibi*).

On Purim, all Jews hear the Megillah in vast congregations. However, Israel attributes this scroll (so full of praise) to God, saying, *'From You'* Hashem came the miracle itself and the divine inspiration to record it as one of the Holy Scriptures (*Alshich*).

נְדָרַי אֲשַׁלֵּם נֶגֶד יְרֵאָיו — *I will fulfill my vows before those who fear Him.*

This refers to all of the gentile nations who will ultimately come to fear God when they witness His salvation. At that time I will praise You and fulfill my vows in their presence (*Radak*).

This also alludes to the many vows David made for the benefit of the Tem-

ple treasury. He would always dedicate the spoils of war to the sacred task of constructing the *Beis HaMikdash* (*Rav Yeibi*).

27. יֹאכְלוּ עֲנָוִים וְיִשְׂבָּעוּ — *The humble will eat and be satisfied.*

When I fulfill my vows (v.26) then the humble will join me in eating the תּוֹדָה שַׁלְמֵי *'peace-offerings of thanksgiving'* (*Metzudas David*).

Rashi comments that this describes the future era of Messiah when abundance of food will fill the earth.

Radak explains that *'the humble'* referred to here are the Jews who were downtrodden in the exile of the haughty Babylonians. When the Babylonian Empire was overthrown by Darius and Cyrus, Cyrus took the treasures of the *Beis HaMikdash* which had been the proud possession of the Babylonians and returned it to the Jews along with permission to rebuild the Temple. Thus Israel will *'eat and be content'* with the return of its most precious possession.

[It was Ahasueros, the successor of Cyrus, who commanded that the construction of the Temple come to a halt. Esther prays that she should have the power to influence Ahasueros to rescind his decree. Ahasueros never did this. Nevertheless, Esther ultimately did realize her wish when Darius II, the son she bore to Ahasueros, ascended the

the birds. At that moment King Agrippa had a vision in which he was told, 'The offering of the poor trapper preceded all of your offerings.' He immediately called for the High Priest who explained the matter to him. The righteous Agrippa responded: 'You did the proper thing!'

Another incident occurred where a man was dragging his ox to be sacrificed but the animal balked. Along came a poor man, a stranger, and with the small bundle of vegetables he was carrying in his hand he coaxed and enticed the ox to follow him to the altar. The owner of the ox was told in a vision, 'God appreciated the vegetables which the poor man sacrificed for His sake more than the ox itself.'

Thus, we see that *'He has neither despised nor loathed the screams* [the sacrifices or prayers] *of the poor'* (*Midrash Vayikra Rabba* 3:5-6).

XXII
26-28

²⁶ *You are the cause of my praise;*
    in the great congregation.
I will fulfill my vows
    before those who fear Him.
²⁷ *The humble will eat and be satisfied,*
    those who seek HASHEM will praise Him.
May your hearts be alive forever.
²⁸ *All the ends of the earth will remember*
    and turn back to HASHEM,

---

throne and gave orders to renew construction of the Temple in the year 3408.]

יְהַלְלוּ ה' דּורְשָׁיו — *Those who seek HASHEM will praise Him.*

[Only a handful of people responded to Cyrus' invitation to return to Israel (which was then desolate) to rebuild the Temple. These hardy pioneers may be called 'Those who seek HASHEM.' The rest sought the security and comfort of their established homes. Mordecai has amongst those who returned with Zerubavel in the year 3390 to rebuild the Temple. However, the construction was quickly halted as a result of the vicious slander (accusing the Jews of treason) spread by Haman and his sons.]

This statement alludes to the Talmud (*Megillah* 12b) which says: After the gentiles eat and drink they start to talk of obscene things. At Ahasueros' feast they started to quarrel about the beauty of their women. Ahasueros himself claimed that his wife, Vashti, was the most splendid of all and so he commanded her to appear unclothed. However, the Talmud emphasizes that by Jews the opposite is

true: 'After they eat and drink they begin to discuss matters of Torah and sing praises to God!'

Therefore it says here, 'The humble (Israel) will eat and be satisfied' and then, 'those who seek HASHEM will praise Him' (Tehillos Hashem).

יְחִי לְבַבְכֶם לָעַד — *May your heart[s] be alive forever.*

May the spirit of prophecy dwell in your hearts for all times! (*Targum*).

Metzudas David explains that when the heart is depressed it is as if it is dead. Thus we find of Nabal the Carmelite when he heard of his impending doom: 'and his heart died within him' (I Sam. 25:37). But, *Ibn Ezra* notes, when the spirits are lifted, the heart comes to life. The Scripture describe how Jacob, after twenty-two years of depression, was spiritually revived upon learning that his beloved son Joseph was still living, 'and the spirit of their father Jacob came alive' (Gen. 45:27).[1]

28. יִזְכְּרוּ — *They will remember.*

When the nations of the earth see the good which will come to us in the future they will remember our previous poverty and degradation (*Rashi; Radak*).

---

1. *Midrash Shocher Tov* says that Haman's treasures were divided into three parts. One third went to Mordecai and Esther. One third went to those who toiled in Torah study. And one third went to construct the Temple. All three are implied in this verse '*The humble will eat and be satisfied*' refers to Mordecai and Esther. '*Those who seek HASHEM will praise Him*' refers to those who toil in Torah study. '*May your hearts be alive forever*' refers to the Temple of which it says elsewhere '*My eyes and heart shall be there forever*' (II Chron. 7:16).

כט וְיִשְׁתַּחֲווּ לְפָנֶיךָ כָּל־מִשְׁפְּחוֹת גּוֹיִם: כִּי
ל לַיהוה הַמְּלוּכָה וּמֹשֵׁל בַּגּוֹיִם: אָכְלוּ
וַיִּשְׁתַּחֲווּ | כָּל־דִּשְׁנֵי־אֶרֶץ לְפָנָיו יִכְרְעוּ
לא כָּל־יוֹרְדֵי עָפָר וְנַפְשׁוֹ לֹא חִיָּה: זֶרַע
לב יַעַבְדֶנּוּ יְסֻפַּר לַאדֹנָי לַדּוֹר: יָבֹאוּ וְיַגִּידוּ
צִדְקָתוֹ לְעַם נוֹלָד כִּי עָשָׂה:

וַיָּשֻׁבוּ אֶל ה' — *And [they will] turn back to HASHEM.*

This will arouse them to repent and return to God *(Rashi; Radak).*

29. כִּי לַה' הַמְּלוּכָה — *For, the Kingship belongs to HASHEM.*

When they see the sovereignty returning to Hashem they will return to Him *(Rashi).*

וּמֹשֵׁל בַּגּוֹיִם — *And He rules the nations.*

The *Vilna Gaon* makes the following differentiation: מֶלֶךְ, 'king,' is the leader who is accepted by his subjects of their own free will. Thus, in reference to Israel who accept Hashem gladly, it says, 'For the kingship belongs to Hashem.

However, the מוֹשֵׁל is the 'ruler' who forces himself upon the people without their consent. Therefore, in regard to the nations who don't wish to submit to God's wishes the Psalmist says 'and He rules the nations.' But in the future וְהָיָה ה' לְמֶלֶךְ עַל כָּל הָאָרֶץ 'and HASHEM will be the king for all of the earth' *(Zech.* 14:9) and even the nations will accept Him willingly.

[Esther took pains to publicize the miracle of Purim throughout the world,

in all 127 provinces of Ahasueros. She also had the wondrous event inscribed in a special scroll for all times. (Cf. *Megillah* 7a, Esther sent a message to the Sages, כְּתָבוּנִי לְדוֹרוֹת Record my story for all future generations').She was not concerned with her own glory, only with the sanctification of God's Name. Esther hoped that her contribution to Jewish history would be of universal significance, bringing the entire world closer to its ultimate goal of recognizing Hashem as the one and only God.

Her wish to be perpetuated in Jewish history was fulfilled as the *Megillah* 9:28 itself attests, 'Consequently, these days should be remembered and celebrated by every single generation, family, province and city; and these days of Purim should never cease among the Jews, nor shall their remembrance perish from among their descendants.']

30. אָכְלוּ וַיִּשְׁתַּחֲווּ כָּל דִּשְׁנֵי אֶרֶץ — *They will eat all the fat of the land and bow down* [lit. 'all the fat ones of the earth will eat and bow down']

Rashi comments that this verse refers back to *v.* 27, and that its sequence is in-

All the families of nations will bow down before You.
²⁹ *For the kingship belongs to HASHEM*
and He rules the nations.
³⁰ *They will eat all the fat of the land and bow down;*
All who go down to the dust will kneel before Him,
but He will not revive his soul.
³¹ *By the seed who will serve Him*
the Lord will be proclaimed to the generation.
³² *They will come and tell of His righteousness;*
to the newborn nation, that which He has done.

verted. He renders: *They* [i.e. *the humble ones* mentioned in *v. 27*] *will eat the fat of the land* [i.e. the finest produce of the earth] *and bow down* [i.e. to praise and thank God.]

However, *Radak* (quoting his father) says that דִּשְׁנֵי אֶרֶץ refers to people, not goods. The Psalmist is uttering a prophecy that even the fat and contented Persians and Medes will eventually return to Hashem and humble themselves before Him.

לְפָנָיו יִכְרְעוּ כָּל יוֹרְדֵי עָפָר — *All who go down to dust will kneel before Him.*

But there are some who will not be accepted even if they repent and kneel before Hashem. These are the enemies of Torah (*Rashi*), or those who shed Jewish blood (*Radak*). Their souls *'go down to the dust'*, meaning to Gehinnom, never to be released (*Rashi; Radak*).

וְנַפְשׁוֹ לֹא חִיָּה — *But He will not revive his soul* [lit. *'but his soul, He did not keep alive'*]

Rashi quotes the Rabbinic statement on this verse (*Sifri, Parshas B'haaloscha*): כִּי לֹא יִרְאַנִי הָאָדָם וָחָי, *'For*

no man will see me and stay alive' (*Ex. 33:20*). God said: Only when man is alive, he will not see me, but he will see me at the moment of death when the soul departs. This is derived from the verse, *'all who go down to dust kneel before Him'* i.e., before death men see God in front of them *'for then HASHEM no longer keeps his soul alive.'*

31. זֶרַע יַעַבְדֶנּוּ — [*By*] *the seed* [*who*] *will serve Him.*

I.e. the seed of Israel who constantly worship Hashem (*Rashi; Radak*).

יְסֻפַּר לַאדֹנָי לַדּוֹר — *The Lord will be proclaimed to the generation.*

The seed of the earlier generation will tell the later generation of the wonders He performed for them (*Rashi*).

32. יָבֹאוּ וְיַגִּידוּ צִדְקָתוֹ — *They will come and tell of His righteousness.*

The early generations will come to tell the later ones (*Rashi*).

Those who come up from exile in all the corners of the earth will relate God's goodness to their children who never saw God's great acts (*Radak*).

David composed this famed psalm during one of the most
dangerous and discouraging periods of his life. He was a forlorn
fugitive, fleeing from King Saul and his army. In desperation, David
hid himself in a barren, desolate forest called יַעַר חָרֶת (I Samuel 22:5),
so named because it was parched and dry, like חֶרֶס, 'baked
earthenware.' But God did not forsake David. He soaked this dry
forest with a moisture which had the flavor of the World to Come,
making even the grass and leaves of the forest succulent and edible
(Midrash). This showed David that God supports and nourishes at all
times even when their chances of survival seem to be non-existent.

David does not confine his inspiration to himself; he utilizes it to
sing for all of Israel, recalling how God provided for the entire nation
throughout its forty-year sojourn in the wilderness.

Mishnah Berurah (Orach Chaim 166:1) cites a custom to recite this
psalm between נְטִילַת יָדַיִם, the washing of the hands before the meal,
and the recital of the blessing over bread (cf. Eliyahu Rabba ibid.).

Arizal explains the connection between Psalm 23 and the meal. The
psalm contains fifty-seven words, the numerical equivalent of the
word זָן 'nourishes'. Furthermore, it contains 227 letters, the
numerical equivalent of בְּרָכָה 'blessing'. Arizal concludes that those
who recite this psalm and live by its message will always be blessed
with ample provisions.

מִזְמוֹר לְדָוִד יהוה רֹעִי לֹא אֶחְסָר: א
בִּנְאוֹת דֶּשֶׁא יַרְבִּיצֵנִי עַל־מֵי מְנֻחוֹת ב

1. רֹעִי — My shepherd.

This term describes God as the Supreme Provider of all human needs. The *Targum* translates it, זָן יַת עַמֵּהּ בְּמַדְבְּרָא *'He provided all of His nation's needs in the wilderness.'* In *Psalms* 80:2 we find another example of this title רֹעֵה יִשְׂרָאֵל הַאֲזִינָה נֹהֵג כַּצֹּאן יוֹסֵף *'Shepherd (Targum: 'Provider) of Israel, listen, You who led the people of Joseph like sheep.'* The entire nation is identified with Joseph because he supported them and provided for all their needs during the famine (*Rashi*).

Similarly, Jacob said of God: הָאֱלֹהִים הָרֹעֶה אֹתִי (*Gen.* 48:15) which *Targum* (ibid.) renders as 'the God who provided for me'. *Midrash Shocher Tov* comments: "There is no occupation which is more degrading and lowly than that of the shepherd who trudges about all day carrying his stick and his knapsack. Yet David dared to call God a shepherd! David declared, 'I take a lesson from my ancestors! Jacob called God his shepherd and so I call Him that too!' "[1]

לֹא אֶחְסָר — I shall not lack.

David felt like the sheep who has no reason to care for his own welfare because he knows that his shepherd (God) will provide for all of his needs (*Radak*).

Ibn Ezra (v.5) explains that David dedicated this Psalm to those servants of God who forsake all worldly desires and

rejoice in their own lot, whatever it may be. They appreciate their simple bread and water more than all of the delicacies of this world, for their attention is focused on the spiritual pleasures of the World to Come.

Panim Yofos makes the following observation: The rewards of the Hereafter are spiritual and are reserved for the world of the spirit. Nevertheless, it is possible for those spiritual riches to be converted to material rewards in This World. To squander them on the petty momentary luxuries of This World, however, is shortsighted — even criminal. Therefore, in the בִּרְכַּת הַמָּזוֹן, 'Grace After Meals', when asking for continued abundance, we add a condition: וּמִכָּל טוּב לְעוֹלָם אַל יְחַסְּרֵנוּ, 'From all of the goodness of the World (to Come) do not deprive us', i.e. do not give us material blessing at the cost of later spiritual reward. Therefore, David emphasizes here that although Hashem has provided him with every material necessity, nevertheless, לֹא אֶחְסָר, 'I am sure that this will not deprive me of my share in the Hereafter.'

Midrash Shocher Tov elaborates on how these words לֹא אֶחְסָר, 'I shall lack nothing' describe God's boundless generosity towards the Israelites in the wilderness. Elsewhere, we find a similar statement, זֶה אַרְבָּעִים שָׁנָה ה' אֱלֹהֶיךָ, עִמָּךְ לֹא חָסַרְתָּ דָּבָר, 'These forty years, HASHEM your God has been with you,

1. [David spent the early, formative years of his life as a shepherd. He was proud of those years which played such an important role in developing his leadership abilities. The *Midrash* (*Shmos Rabba* 2:3) sets down a rule: 'The Holy One Blessed be He does not elevate anyone to a great position of leadership until He first tests him in small, lowly matters. So we find Moses and David, who were shepherds prior to their ascent to greatness. God tested David with sheep and David proved his integrity. He always grazed his flocks in the wilderness in order to keep them far away from pastures belonging to others.

The *Midrash* (78:70) adds that David took special pains for each animal. He let the kids eat the tender tops of the grass, to the mature rams he gave the main part of the blade of grass, and to the old sheep he gave the roots.

God said to him, 'You have been found trustworthy with the sheep of others, now come and lead my flock of Israel!' [cf. *Rambam, Hilchos Melachim,* 2:6.]

XXIII
1-2

A song of David:
HASHEM is my shepherd, I shall not lack.
² In lush meadows He lays me down,
    beside tranquil waters He leads me.

you have lacked nothing' (Deut. 2:7).
Rabbi Judah said in the name of Rabbi
Elazar: 'Travel has three detrimental effects. It wears out clothing, it exhausts
the body, and it forces one to skimp on
food (due to the great financial burden
of travel). None of these deprivations
befell Israel, who lacked nothing in the
wilderness. Furthermore, it is human
nature that when a person welcomes a
guest, on the first day of his visit he
slaughters a fat calf for him. On the second day, a sheep. On the third, a hen.
On the fourth day, he serves beans, and
on the fifth day even less. Not so in the
wilderness, as it says *'These forty
years'*, i.e. the entire period, from beginning to end. On the last day of the forty
years God was just as generous as on
the first. Rabbi Nechemiah said: They
lacked for nothing. All they had to do
was say a word and their wish was immediately fulfilled. If they so much as
said, 'let the Manna taste like calf's
flesh', so it did. Or, they could give it
the taste of rich oil, or fine flour, or
spiced wine, or sweet cakes.
The Rabbis say: 'It was not even
necessary for them to speak. All they
had to do was to think, and their heart's
desire came to pass immediately.'

2. בִּנְאוֹת דֶּשֶׁא — *In lush meadows.*
[נְאוֹת is the plural form of נָאֶה *'pleasant, luxuriant, lush.'* The letter 'ו', *vav*,
is often added to this word for greater

emphasis as in 33:1, לַיְשָׁרִים נָאוָה תְהִלָּה,
*'For the upright it is pleasant to give
praise.'*]

Rashi, Ibn Ezra, and *Metzudos* relate
נְאוֹת to נָוֶה *'dwelling, abode',* as it refers
to pastureland of the sheep which is its
abode.

David continues his comparison of
God to a shepherd, likening Him to one
who seeks out choice grazing grounds
for his flock *(Metzudas David).*

According to *Midrash Shocher Tov*
David alludes to God's generosity in
providing the necessities and comforts
of the Jews in the desert. In particular
he refers to בְּאֵרָה שֶׁל מִרְיָם, *the well of
Miriam,* a fresh-water spring that followed the Jews wherever they went in
the parched desert, thanks to the merit
of the righteous prophetess.

This well would cause verdant meadows and vast, flourishing forests to
spring up miraculously from the arid desert wherever Israel encamped. Hence,
'He lays me down in lush meadows.'

מֵי מְנֻחוֹת — *Tranquil waters.*
The waters of the tranquil stream are
clear and sweet, whereas those of the
torrential river are turgid and muddy
(Metzudas David).

יְנַהֲלֵנִי — *He leads me.*
Rabbi Chaim of Volozhin observes
that David teaches how to make the best
of even uncomfortable situations.

The *Midrash (Bereishis Rabba* 39:11) says that David as king issued a coin. On one side, it
portrayed him as a shepherd holding his stick and knapsack. On the reverse side was an
engraving of the Tower of David.

Finally, the *Midrash (Bereishis* 59:5) notes: "David was the shepherd of Israel, as God says,
'You will be the shepherd of my nation Israel' (I *Chronicles* 11:2). Who was David's
shepherd? HASHEM himself! As David says, *'HASHEM is my shepherd!' "*

The *Talmud (Succah* 52b) states: 'There are seven shepherds [i.e. men who led the world on
the path of righteousness]. In their midst is David. On his right are Adam, Seth, and
Methusaleh. On his left are Abraham, Jacob, and Moses.

יְנַחֲנִי: נַפְשִׁי יְשׁוֹבֵב יַנְחֵנִי בְמַעְגְּלֵי־צֶדֶק ג
לְמַעַן שְׁמוֹ: גַּם כִּי־אֵלֵךְ בְּגֵיא צַלְמָוֶת ד
לֹא־אִירָא רָע כִּי־אַתָּה עִמָּדִי שִׁבְטְךָ
וּמִשְׁעַנְתֶּךָ הֵמָּה יְנַחֲמֻנִי: תַּעֲרֹךְ לְפָנַי | ה

Sometimes, a person yearns to move on, to travel, to change. But his attempts are frustrated and he is tied down to one place. 'You must realize that this is God's will,' says David. 'You must feel as if this is the very best place on earth for you!' Thus, if *'He lays me down'* I must feel that this place is as wonderful as if I were *'in lush meadows.'*

Conversely, sometimes a person yearns to sink down roots in one place, to establish himself securely. But circumstances force him to move on, to flee, and he never realizes his desire to rest. 'This too is for the best!' says David. 'Accept it gladly!' Thus, if *'He leads me'*, i.e. forcing me to move on, I must feel as if I am in calm repose *'beside tranquil waters.'*

3. יְשׁוֹבֵב — *He restores.*

This translation follows *Rashi* who explains: My spirits have become faint as a result of great trials and tragedies, but Hashem revives me and restores my vigor. [Thus this word is derived from שָׁב *'return'.*]

However, *Radak* and *Ibn Ezra* render this as *'He leads tranquilly'* as in בְּשׁוּבָה וָנַחַת *'with tranquility and calm'* (Isaiah 30:15). God is not inconsiderate of His 'flock', driving it rapidly from one grazing area to another. He leads it slowly so that the sheep never become exhausted.

In a deeper sense, David offers thanks to God for preserving the equanimity of his soul despite the abundance of material blessings described above. The Sages taught (*Avos* 2:8): 'He who increases wealth increases his worries.' [Rabbi Ovadiah of Bertenora (*ibid.*) quotes a devout man who would pray that God should not 'afflict' him

with wealth, saying: 'May it be Your will that I be saved from פִּזּוּר הַנֶּפֶשׁ *'scattering of the soul'.* For if I have properties in many places, my attention will be constantly diverted as a result of anxiety and concern over my possessions.'] Furthermore, increased wealth has a tendency to breed a desire for even more riches. Therefore, David gives special thanks for his divinely inspired complacency and satisfaction with his lot (*Norah Tehillos*).

Finally, *Midrash Shocher Tov* reveals how such tranquility of the soul is accomplished. 'Through Torah study! As David himself says: תּוֹרַת ה׳ תְּמִימָה מְשִׁיבַת נָפֶשׁ *'The Torah of HASHEM is perfect, it restores the soul* (19:8).

בְמַעְגְּלֵי צֶדֶק — *On paths of justice.*

The considerate shepherd will not fatigue his sheep by taking them on difficult, roundabout routes. Rather, he leads them on the straightest, easiest path (*Radak; Ibn Ezra*).

Similarly, we often find that God miraculously shortened the length of a journey for the righteous ones, as He did for Jacob on his way to the house of Laban (*Norah Tehillos*).

[Also, we find that in the wilderness the עֲנָנֵי הַכָּבוֹד *'Clouds of Glory'* which surrounded the Jews smoothed the path before them, leveling mountains and raising up deep gorges so that the Israelites could follow a straight path uninterrupted by detours or obstacles.]

4. בְּגֵיא צַלְמָוֶת — *In the valley overshadowed by death.*

The *Targum* says that this refers to גָּלוּת, *'exile'*, in general. *Radak* explains that this describes a place of danger which is as dark and forbidding as the grave. *Rashi* maintains that David had a

³ *He restores my soul.*
He leads me on paths of justice
for His Name's sake.
⁴ *Though I walk in the valley overshadowed by death,*
I will fear no evil, for You are with me.
Your rod and Your staff, they comfort me.
⁵ *You prepare a table before me*

specific place in mind here, the Wilderness of Zif, where he was treacherously betrayed and came face to face with the specter of death at the hands of Saul (*I Sam.*, 23:19-29). Never in his life was David closer to the grave.

לֹא אִירָא רָע — *I will fear no evil.*

Chovos Halevovos tells that a devout person was once found sleeping alone in the middle of a barren and forbidding wilderness. When he was asked,'Are you not afraid of the many wild beasts?', he replied, 'I am too ashamed before God to be afraid of anything in the world except for Him!' Similarly, David's heart was so filled with the fear of God that there was no room left for the fear of anything else. Therefore, he declared, 'Even though I go through the most threatening valleys overshadowed with death, still I cannot possibly fear any evil, for the fear of God is constantly with me' (*Yalkut Eliezer*).

כִּי אַתָּה עִמָּדִי — *For You are with me.*

My confidence in You is so strong that I know that You will always stand by me in times of need (*Radak*).

שִׁבְטְךָ — *Your rod.*

This alludes to afflictions as in וּפָקַדְתִּי בְשֵׁבֶט פִּשְׁעָם, 'And I will punish their transgression with the rod' (89:33) (*Midrash Shocher Tov; Rashi*).

וּמִשְׁעַנְתֶּךָ — *And Your staff.*

I count on Hashem's mercy to be my staff for support in times of affliction (*Rashi*).

According to the *Targum* and *Midrash Shocher Tov*, Hashem's staff

is His Torah, as in the phrase בִּמְחֹקֵק בְּמִשְׁעֲנֹתָם 'with the lawmakers scepter, with their staff' (*Numbers* 21:18).

[Others explain that the rod of affliction is itself the staff of support. For, only through affliction can man atone for his sins in this world so that he may stand upright to receive his reward in the Hereafter. Furthermore, without afflictions one cannot merit the comprehension of Torah, as David himself said: 'Fortunate is the man who is afflicted by HASHEM and from His Torah He teaches Him' (94:12).]

Radak notes that both words, שִׁבְטְךָ וּמִשְׁעַנְתֶּךָ, ... *rod and ... staff,* refer to the same stick because a shepherd, uses one stick for two purposes; as a rod to beat the sheep into place and as a staff upon which to lean his weary body when he stops to rest.

הֵמָּה יְנַחֲמֻנִי — *They comfort me.*

[הֵמָּה 'they' actually means both of them together, as one; for God provides an equal balance of affliction and support, blending them skillfully to achieve the desired effect. This follows the idea mentioned previously that the affliction itself is a support. We find that this idea is a source of comfort in the words of the Prophet, 'I give thanks to You HASHEM for You were angry with me. May Your wrath subside and You will comfort me (*Isaiah* 12:1) (*Shaarei Dimah*).]

5. תַּעֲרֹךְ לְפָנַי שֻׁלְחָן — *You prepare a table before me.*

The *Midrash* (*Shmos Rabba* 25:7) says that these words are directed

שֻׁלְחָן נֶגֶד צֹרְרָי דִּשַּׁנְתָּ בַשֶּׁמֶן רֹאשִׁי
ו כּוֹסִי רְוָיָה: אַךְ | טוֹב וָחֶסֶד יִרְדְּפוּנִי כָּל־
יְמֵי חַיָּי וְשַׁבְתִּי בְּבֵית־יהוה לְאֹרֶךְ יָמִים:

towards the nations of the world who saw Israel leave Egypt and enter the wilderness. They gloated, 'This nation will surely perish in this desert!' The Psalmist records their words, הֲיוּכַל אֵל לַעֲרֹךְ שֻׁלְחָן בַּמִּדְבָּר *'Is God able to prepare a table* [for them] *in the desert?'* (78:19). What did God do? He surrounded them with protective clouds and rained down so much manna that it piled up high in the sky for all the nations to see. As Israel relaxed and ate they offered praise to God, fulfilling the verse *'You prepare a table before me in full view my tormentors.'*[1]

נֶגֶד צֹרְרָי — *In full view of* [lit. *opposite*] *my tormentors.*

They seek to deprive me of my sustenance by driving me out into the desolate wilderness (such as יַעַר חֶרֶת; see *Prefatory Remarks*) but You foiled them (*Sforno*).

דִּשַּׁנְתָּ בַשֶּׁמֶן רֹאשִׁי — *You anointed my head with oil.*

דִּשַּׁנְתָּ literally means *'to saturate with fat, to moisten with oil.'* David used this odd term to describe his anointment as king because many of his enemies conceded that he had been chosen king, but that his sins had invalidated the choice — that it was as if the anointing oil had become dry. Therefore, David stresses that the anointment is still 'moist' on his head, i.e. just as valid as when Samuel poured it on him (*Alshich*).

The *Midrash (Shemos Rabba* 25:7) comments that דִּשַּׁנְתָּ *'You saturate with fat'* alludes to the שְׂלָיו *'the fat pheasants'* which God sent to Israel in the desert. [These succulent birds were a lethal curse only for those who demanded them lustfully and improperly (*Numbers* 11:31-34); for the righteous, however, the birds were a blessing.]

כּוֹסִי רְוָיָה — *My cup overflows.*

This is a metaphor describing contentment (*Rashi*), as in תְּלָמֶיהָ רַוֵּה *'Satisfy its plowed furrows* [with rain]' (65:11) (*Metzudas Zion*).

God's provisions are not meager; they are generously given (*Sforno*).

The *Midrash (Shemos Rabba, ibid.)* interprets this as referring to the free-flowing, never-ending waters of Miriam's well.

The *Talmud (Yoma* 76a) states that David's cup in the World to Come will have a capacity of 221 '*lug*' measures the numerical equivalent of רְוָיָה = 221.

Siach Yitzchak (ibid.) explains that the numerical value of כּוֹס '*cup*' is 86 which is exactly the same as אֱלֹהִים, the name indicating God's *'Attribute of Justice'.* Just as a cup holds a precise measure, strict justice also adheres to an exact standard of recompense, i.e. measure for measure with no leniency. However, when God's kindness overcomes strict justice, He acts generously, beyond the letter of the law. Thus it is

---

1. The Talmud (*Ta'anis* 25a) relates that Rabbi Chaninah bar Dosa, who was famous for his piety, was so destitute that he did not even possess the barest necessities for the Sabbath. He prayed for divine assistance and a hand from heaven gave him a golden leg from a golden table. Later, he was shown in a dream that in the World to Come the righteous are destined to use a golden table with three legs, but his would only have two because the third leg was given him for sustenance in this world. Rabbi Chaninah immediately prayed that the leg be taken back to heaven.

Thus, David expresses confidence that despite the many bounties that God showered upon him, his 'golden table' in the Hereafter remains intact and fully prepared (*Alshich*). [Cf. *comm. v.* 1 s.v. לֹא אֶחְסָר.]

in full view of my tormentors.
You anointed my head with oil,
my cup overflows.
⁶ *May only goodness and kindness pursue me*
all the days of my life,
And I shall dwell in the House of HASHEM
for long years.

as if the precisely measured *'cup'* of justice now *'overflows'* with mercy.

[This also alludes to the *Talmudic* statement *(Berachos 7b)* 'Why was she called רות *'Ruth'*? Rabbi Yochanan said: Because she was privileged to have David descend from her, and David רִוָּהוּ לְהַקָּבָּ"ה בְּשִׁירוֹת וְתִשְׁבָּחוֹת *'provided the Holy One, blessed be He, with an overflowing abundance of songs and praises.'*]

[The *'cup'* symbolizes David's heart which brimmed over with love and appreciation of God. Anyone who gives thought to God's infinite goodness and blessing, should be overwhelmed. If so, why don't the *'cups'* overflow as did David's? Because most men have allowed bitterness and disillusionment to creep in, making 'cracks' in their once-perfect hearts. No matter how much goodness God showers on them, they have lost the capacity for commensurate gratitude.]

6. אַךְ טוֹב וָחֶסֶד יִרְדְּפוּנִי כָּל יְמֵי חַיָּי — *May only goodness and kindness pursue me all the days of my life.*

According to *Midrash Shocher Tov,* 'goodness' and 'kindness' refer to material success. However, David

prefaces his request with the diminutive אַךְ *'only'*, a small amount, to emphasize that he asks only a bare minimum of worldly goods, lest unnecessary luxury deprive him of his full share in the World to Come.

Ibn Ezra (v. 5) explains that טוֹב, *'good'*, refers to spiritual self-enrichment. חֶסֶד, *'kindness'*, describes a deep concern for the spiritual welfare of others which is manifested in an effort to teach them the ways of God. These two activities should become a constant, irreversible way of life. So much so, that the ingrained nature to do only good would not allow even a momentary lapse. Thus his noble inclinations will *'pursue'* him relentlessly to continue on the path of *'good'* and *'kindness'*.[1]

וְשַׁבְתִּי — *And I shall dwell.*

The *Targum* and *Metzudas David* maintain that שַׁבְתִּי indicates *'to sit, dwell permanently'*. The *Brisker Rav,* Harav Yitzchak Zev Soloveitchick commented that this alludes to the law that no one may sit in the Temple courtyard except for kings from the House of David *(Sotah 40b).* (See *comm.* of *Alshich* on 27:4).

Radak disagrees, rendering וְשַׁבְתִּי *'I*

1. A wealthy magnate who was noted for his extraordinary generosity, once became completely overwhelmed by the countless requests for assistance which were addressed to him incessantly. He consulted the saintly Chofetz Chaim on this matter. As the man entered the room, the Chofetz Chaim happened to be explaining this very verse. He expounded, 'No man can live out the days of his life in complete tranquility. Everyone is pursued by worrisome bother. Often it is serious, as when pursued by enemies, or police, or bill collectors or sickness. Fortunate is the man who discharges his 'obligation' by being pursued by institutions of charity which harass him continually for support. This is what David meant when he said, *'May only goodness and kindness pursue me all the days of my life.'*

The magnate understood the message. He returned home reassured and doubled his charitable efforts. (Heard from a grandchild of the philanthropist).]

will be tranquil', as in בְּשׁוּבָה וָנַחַת 'with tranquility and calm' (Isaiah 30:15, cf. v. 3, יְשׁוּבָב and in Radak).

Radak also suggests that the word may be derived from שָׁב 'to return' meaning that David asks to return to the house of God again and again without impediment.

בְּבֵית ה׳ — In the House of HASHEM.

The Targum identifies this as the Holy Temple. In this verse, David yearns to be released from the burdens of monarchy: the wars, the economics, the politics. His desire is to retire to the isolated solitude of the Temple, there to concentrate on God's service un-disturbed (Radak).

לְאֹרֶךְ יָמִים — For long years [lit. 'for the length of days'].

David uses these words to convey his desire for a long life. Earlier, he had asked for goodness and kindness for as long as he lived. Now he pleads that he be granted a long life (Radak).

[Rambam (Hilchos Teshuvah 8:4) says that בֵּית ה׳ 'the House of HASHEM' is one of the Scriptural figures of speech describing the World to Come. Thus, David is requesting a share of the Hereafter 'for the length of days' i.e. for all eternity, without end (see comm. 27:4).[1]

---

1. In I Sam. 23 we find that HASHEM promised David that even if his descendants were to sin, they would be punished and temporarily removed from the throne, but the monarchy will never be permanently removed from the House of David. Harav Chaim HaLevi Soloveitchik proves that this covenant applies only to David's offspring. However, if David himself were to sin, he could be rejected by God and the monarchy conferred on a different family. Indeed, had it not been for HASHEM's special goodness and kindness, the sin of Bath-Sheba could have disqualified David. Rav Chaim's son, Harav Yitzchak Zev HaLevi Soloveitchik explains this verse in light of that covenant. 'May only goodness and kindness pursue me all the days of my life' i.e. even if I sin, may I not be rejected. David then speaks of the time after his death when God's covenant goes into effect and the monarchy will remain in his family forever: 'I, i.e. my royal line, will dwell in the House of HASHEM all of my life', i.e. for all times.

As explained in the Overview, David dedicated his entire life to the goal of bringing mankind back to the purity of Adam before the Sin. For this reason, God commanded him to prepare for the construction of the Temple on Mount Moriah, the place from which Adam was created. This location was intended to serve as an inspiration for humanity to emulate the spotless virtue of the first man at the time of his creation.

In this psalm, David sings, 'Who can ascend the mountain of HASHEM, and who can stand in His holy place? He whose hands are clean, and whose heart is pure' (v. 3-4).

Midrash Shocher Tov comments: Rav Shmuel said, David composed four psalms which were truly worthy of being written by Adam himself. One of them is Psalm 24, 'The earth is HASHEM's.'

The psalm was composed on the day David purchased the land of the Temple site from Aravna, the Jebusite. At that time, David erected a temporary altar upon which he offered sacrifices of thanksgiving (II Sam. 24:18-25).

David's intention was that this psalm should be recited on the day of the inauguration of the Temple. God's Presence, which is spread throughout the entire world, would then be concentrated in the holiest of places, to dwell upon the Holy Ark in permanent repose (Radak; Ibn Ezra). For this reason, this psalm is recited by the congregation as they accompany the Torah scroll back to the synagogue Ark following the reading of the portion (on all occasions except for Sabbath morning when Psalm 29 is recited. Cf. comm. ibid.).

So basic and profound is the message of this psalm, that it was chosen to be the שִׁיר שֶׁל יוֹם 'Song of the Day' for the first day of the week.

א לְדָוִד מִזְמוֹר לַיהוה הָאָרֶץ וּמְלוֹאָהּ תֵּבֵל
ב וְיֹשְׁבֵי בָהּ: כִּי־הוּא עַל־יַמִּים יְסָדָהּ וְעַל־
ג נְהָרוֹת יְכוֹנְנֶהָ: מִי־יַעֲלֶה בְהַר־יהוה וּמִי־

1. לְדָוִד מִזְמוֹר — *Of David—a song.*

This is one of the few psalms which begin with the superscription לְדָוִד מִזְמוֹר 'Of David: A song' instead of מִזְמוֹר לְדָוִד 'A song of David.' This introduction shows that David wrote this psalm not to raise his depressed spirit to sublime heights. Instead, he was already inspired and expressed his Godly feelings through this song (*Pesachim* 117 a; see also *comm.* to 3:1). We can well imagine the pitch which David's ecstasy reached before he sang this psalm, because its verses contain the most profound truths that any mortal lips were ever privileged to utter concerning the ways of God in the history of man (*Hirsch*).

הָאָרֶץ — *The earth.*

Radak says that this means the entire globe of the earth.

However, *Rashi* says that in this case it refers to 'the earth' par excellence, which is Eretz Yisrael, 'the land (earth) of Israel'.

[Although God's Presence pervades the entire globe, it saturates the atmosphere of the Holy Land. Furthermore, Eretz Yisrael is like a funnel through which all of the sanctity which descends from above is channeled and dispersed throughout the world.]

וּמְלוֹאָהּ — *And its fullness.*

Rabbi Akiba says, On the first day of the week, the Levites sang the psalm HASHEM's is the earth and its fullness' This teaches that God took possession of the [newly created] world Himself, for the sake of transferring possession [to Mankind.] Yet, He alone remains the sole Master of the world (*Rosh Hashanah* 31a, *Rashi, ibid.*).

Midrash Shocher Tov comments: There is a man who owns a ship but he does not own the cargo it carries; and if the cargo is his, he does not own the ship. But the Holy One, Blessed be He is not so. He owns the earth and all which it contains. Furthermore, a mortal of flesh and blood builds a house fifty cubits high and he himself takes up a height of only three cubits. The Holy One, blessed be He, is not so. He created the world and He Himself fills it, as it says, מְלֹא כָל הָאָרֶץ כְּבוֹדוֹ *'The whole earth is filled with His glory'* (Isaiah 6:3).

The Talmud (*Berachos* 35a) derives from here the principle that all of the earth is God's sanctuary and therefore even material objects have sanctity.

Rav Yehudah said in the name of Shmuel: 'Whosoever derives pleasure from this world without offering the appropriate blessing is as if he derived illegal pleasure from a sacred, dedicated object [which belongs to the Beis HaMikdash], as it says, 'HASHEM's is the earth and its fullness.' Rav Levi noted an apparent contradiction between two verses. Here it says, 'HASHEM's is the earth and its fullness.' Elsewhere it is written, 'The heavens are heavens for HASHEM and the earth He gave to mankind' (115:16). However, this really presents no difficulty. Before one recites a blessing, all objects belong to God; after the blessing they belong to man.[1]

[There is no lack of material abundance in God's heavenly treasury. However, the Creator waits for man to recognize His sovereignty before He renews earth's depleted blessings. When a man partakes of the fruits of this world and blesses God, he causes a new flow of material abundance to stream down from heaven to replace the fruit which he consumed. Therefore, although the earth belongs to HASHEM, its replenishment depends on man.]

XXIV

1-2

O f David — a song.
HASHEM's is the earth and its fullness,
the inhabited land and those who dwell in it.
² For He founded it upon seas,
and established it upon rivers.

תֵּבֵל — *The inhabited land (Radak).*

Hirsch explains that all the places where men now reside are a result of the work of God which began at בְּבֶל the Tower of Babel. There he בּוֹלֵל *'confused'* all of their tongues and scattered them over the face of the earth. Thus, the derivation of the word תֵּבֵל: 'the land to where they were mixed up and scattered.'

According to *Rashi* (in the context of this verse) תֵּבֵל refers to all lands outside of Eretz Yisrael.

וְישְׁבֵי בָהּ — *And those who dwell in it.*
I.e., the people who fill the תֵּבֵל *'inhabited land' (Radak).*

2. כִּי הוּא עַל יַמִּים יְסָדָהּ — *For He founded it upon seas.*
At first the entire globe was covered with water until part of it became dry land. According to this עַל יַמִּים literally means *'on seas'*, i.e., the habitable land was placed upon the waters. However, Rabbi Moshe says that עַל may also mean *'with'* or *'near'* seas, for all of civilization is dependent on bodies of water *(Ibn Ezra).*
Wise men say that there is no in-

habited place in the world which is more than eighteen days distance from the sea, the moisture of which is essential for the survival of all creatures *(Radak).*

Rashi (pursuing his opinion that these verses refer specifically to Eretz Yisrael) quotes the Talmud (*Bava Basra* 74b) that the Land of Israel was founded with seven seas surrounding it. They are the seas of Tiberias (Kinneret), Sodom (The Dead Sea), Chillis, Chilta, Sivchi, Aspamia and the Great Sea (The Mediterranean).

וְעַל נְהָרוֹת יְכוֹנְנֶהָ — *And established it upon rivers.*

[The יְסוֹד, *'foundation'* is the basic element, the most essential prerequisite. That is the sea which supplies the moisture and precipitation without which any form of survival is impossible. However, in order to establish a nation which thrives on a solid base of agriculture and commerce, riverways of fresh water are imperative.]

The Talmud (*ibid.*). interprets this as the four rivers of Eretz Yisrael; the Jordan, Yarmuk, Karmiyon and Figa *(Rashi).*

---

1. Rabbi Chiya bar Abba said: I was once the guest of a wealthy householder in Ludkiya. His meal was brought before him on a golden table held by sixteen silver chains. The table was laden with an assortment of plates and goblets, trays and jars, all filled with every type of delicacy and fragrance which was created in the six days of creation. In the middle of the table stood a small child who proclaimed, *HASHEM's is the earth and its fullness.'* The child made that announcement as the meal was served. As the table was taken away at the end of the repast, the child declared, *'The heavens are heavens for HASHEM, and the earth He gave to mankind.'* Why did the householder do all this? So that his wealth should not cause him to be overwhelmed with pride.

I asked him, 'By virtue of what good deed did you merit this wealth?' He replied. I was once a butcher. Whenever I came across a choice cut of meat I did not sell it [although I could have realized a great profit.] Instead, I set it aside, saying, 'This is for the Sabbath.'

I said to him, 'You are fortunate, for you merited this. Blessed is the Creator who rewarded you so!' *(Shabbos 119a; Rabba 11:4).*

כד

ד יָקוּם בִּמְקוֹם קָדְשׁוֹ: נְקִי כַפַּיִם וּבַר־לֵבָב
ד־ו °נַפְשִׁי ק'
אֲשֶׁר לֹא־נָשָׂא לַשָּׁוְא °נַפְשׁוֹ וְלֹא נִשְׁבַּע
ה לְמִרְמָה: יִשָּׂא בְרָכָה מֵאֵת יהוה וּצְדָקָה
ו מֵאֱלֹהֵי יִשְׁעוֹ: זֶה דּוֹר דֹּרְשָׁו מְבַקְשֵׁי

3. מִי יַעֲלֶה בְהַר ה' — *Who may ascend the mountain of HASHEM?*

[Beginning with this verse, the Psalmist tells us of the unique sanctity of the Temple. Although God's glory is spread throughout the world, its greatest intensity is in the Temple. Only those who have undergone special purification can behold this splendor properly.] Although all of the earth's inhabitants are creations of God, not all are worthy of coming close to Him (*Rashi*).

This refers to Mount Moriah, the location of the Temple. David composed this psalm when he purchased the site from Aravna, the Jebusite [see *Prefatory Remarks*] (*Ibn Ezra*).

The special sanctity of this site is due to the fact that it directly faces the celestial throne of God (*Radak* v.1).

וּמִי יָקוּם בִּמְקוֹם קָדְשׁוֹ — *And who may stand in the place of His sanctity* [or: 'His holy place']

Some say that this is not the same place as 'the Mountain of HASHEM', mentioned earlier. Rather it refers to the קֹדֶשׁ הַקֳּדָשִׁים, *Holy of Holies*, where the Holy Presence is greatest because it rests upon the Holy Ark (*Chozeh David*).

[Others suggest that both parts of this verse refer to the same place, i.e., the Temple mount, however, the people who are described are different. There is a vast difference between the man who is 'ascending' and the one who is 'standing'. Often, a person is capable of elevating his spirits in a brief spasm of enthusiasm and ectasy, but he lacks the inner conviction, the emotional endurance, to make this inspiration last. After a shortlived burst, he falls. Only the sincere and devout person, who

makes a painstaking, systematic preparation, can gain a sturdy foothold and stand firm forever in the place of Hashem where the requirements for His service are so intense and demanding.

This opinion is supported by *Sifri* (*Deut.* 1:10) which classifies the two sections of this verse separately. 'Seven groups of righteous people are destined to dwell in the celestial Garden of Eden … The sixth group consists of those 'who ascend the mountain of HASHEM.' The seventh [highest] group consists of those 'who stand in His holy place'.]

4. נְקִי כַפַּיִם — [Only] *One with clean hands.*

[The Psalmist, speaking for God in first person, now answers the rhetorical question posed in v. 3].

The first prerequisite is that he be a man of impeccable integrity, his hands clean of all unlawful gain (*Metzudas David*).

Hirsch notes that the word כַּף literally means the *'palm'*, for it is there that one actually takes possession of an object and holds it firmly. The righteous man described here holds on to no such ill-gotten gains.

וּבַר לֵבָב — *And pure heart.*

In his mind he harbors no impure ideas or beliefs (*Malbim*).

His heart is permeated only with fear of Hashem and trembles before no other force (*Metzudas David*).

Hirsch defines נָקִי as superficial cleanliness, freedom from surface dirt. בַּר is inner purity, a soul from which every impure element has been 'picked out'; from בּוֹרֵר, 'choosing'.

אֲשֶׁר לֹא נָשָׂא לַשָּׁוְא נַפְשִׁי — *Who has not sworn in vain by My soul.*

We find this phrase used to express

³ *Who may ascend the mountain of HASHEM,*
    and who may stand in the place of His sanctity?
⁴ *One with clean hands and pure heart,*
    who has not sworn in vain by My soul
    nor has he taken an oath deceitfully.
⁵ *He will receive a blessing from HASHEM*
    and just kindness from the God of his salvation.
⁶ *This is the generation of those who seek Him,*

'swearing in vain' in the second of the Ten Commandments *(Exod. 20:7)*: לֹא תִשָּׂא אֶת שֵׁם ה' אֱלֹהֶיךָ לַשָּׁוְא *'You shall not swear in vain by the name of HASHEM, your God' (Radak).*

The קְרִי, *traditional pronunciation,* of the word is נַפְשִׁי, *My* [i.e, God's] *soul,* although the כְּתִיב, *traditional spelling,* is נַפְשׁוֹ, *his* [i.e., man's] *soul.* Hirsch, incorporating both into his translation renders, *'Who has not lifted up his soul which is mine unto vanity.'* This man respects his own soul and does not use it improperly because he realizes it belongs to Hashem and so it must be kept clean and unsullied *(Hirsch).*

וְלֹא נִשְׁבַּע לְמִרְמָה — *Nor has he taken an oath deceitfully.*

Radak notes the inference that he *has* taken an oath in truth and righteousness, and that oath is a *mitzvah* for those who fear God, as it says, *'You shall fear HASHEM, your God, and you shall serve Him, and you shall take an oath by His Name' (Deut. 10:20).*

Radak goes on to say that this man

has thus been found flawless in three major areas; speech (no false oaths), thoughts (pure of heart), and action (clean hands).[1]

5. יִשָּׂא בְרָכָה מֵאֵת ה' — *He will receive* [lit. *'carry away'*] *a blessing from HASHEM.*

Because he did not *'lift up'* God's Name in a vain oath *(v. 4)* he deserves, measure for measure, to *'lift up'* a blessing from that very Name he sought to preserve from disgrace *(Ibn Ezra).*

According to *Metzudas Zion,* a more precise translation of יִשָּׂא is *'he will take'* as in וַיִּשְׂאוּ לָהֶם נָשִׁים, *They took wives for themselves' (Ruth 1:4).*

וּצְדָקָה מֵאֱלֹהֵי יִשְׁעוֹ — *And just kindness from the God of his salvation.*

This person can expect that God will give him whatever will serve his genuine welfare. For this man looks to God for his salvation *(Hirsch).*

6. זֶה דוֹר דֹּרְשׁוֹ — *This is the generation of those who seek Him.*

זֶה, *'this man',* and his like embody

---

1. When the infant is yet an embryo curled up inside his mother's womb, he experiences the very best period of all his life. An angel descends to teach him the Torah in its entirety. However, as the child is about to be born, the angel strikes him on the mouth and he forgets it all.

Before he is allowed to leave the womb, they make him take an oath, 'Swear that you will be righteous and not wicked, and even if the entire world tells you that you are righteous, look upon yourself as wicked. Always bear in mind that the Holy One, Blessed be He, is pure and His ministering angels are pure, and the soul which God deposited within you is also pure. If you safeguard it in purity, fine and well. If not, I will take it back from you. 'This is the meaning of the verse [describing the righteous man who fulfilled his prenatal oath], *'He whose hands are clean and whose heart is pure, who has not sworn by My soul in vain, nor has he taken an oath deceitfully' (Niddah 31b).*

Malbim explains that it is a figurative oath describing the ethical and moral instincts which are deeply ingrained in the fibre of the Jewish character, impelling the Jew towards righteousness with the binding force of an oath.

ז פָּנֶיךָ יַעֲקֹב סֶלָה: שְׂאוּ שְׁעָרִים | רָאשֵׁיכֶם
וְהִנָּשְׂאוּ פִּתְחֵי עוֹלָם וְיָבוֹא מֶלֶךְ הַכָּבוֹד:

the generation of those who are completely dedicated to seeking out God
(Rashi).

David now addresses himself to the
generation which followed his, the people who were privileged to ascend
Hashem's mountain to build the Temple
(Ibn Ezra).

Radak takes note of the pronuncia-
tion (קְרִי) here being the plural דּוֹרְשָׁיו,
'His [many] seekers', whereas the spelling (כְּתִיב) is the singular דֹרְשׁוּ, 'His
seeker'.

Hirsch explains that this discrepancy
serves to emphasize the universal role of
the Temple as a Messianic institution
which unites mankind for a common
purpose. Each nation while retaining its
distinctive characteristics, must use
them in obedience to God's supreme
law. This subordination to God unites
all diverse peoples and cultures into one
harmonious whole. It converts דּוֹרְשָׁיו,
'the many seekers' into דֹּרְשׁוּ, 'a single
seeker' after God's truth.[1]

מְבַקְשֵׁי פָנֶיךָ — Those who strive for Your
Presence [lit.'those who search for Your
face']

Now David addresses himself to
Hashem, telling Him the praises of that
unique generation depicted here (Ibn
Ezra).

יַעֲקֹב — Jacob.

This refers to all of Israel, the offspring of the Patriarch Jacob (Radak).

Here we refer to Israel in exile among
the other nations of the world and so
they are not described with their name
of sovereignty, 'Israel', but with their
name of subservience and trial, 'Jacob'
(Hirsch).

[The human face is a reflection of the
image of God. No human was a more
perfect replica of the divine dimensions
of man than Jacob, about whom the
Torah itself testifies that he was תָּם,
'perfect' (Gen. 25:27). Therefore, his
face is etched in God's celestial throne
of glory to represent mankind. Consequently, if one strives to seek out God's
image in an effort to emulate Him
perfectly, let him seek out the face of
Jacob and make the patriarch his
model.]

7. שְׂאוּ שְׁעָרִים רָאשֵׁיכֶם — Raise up your
heads, O gates.

David speaks to the gates allegorically as if they were hosts about to receive
a mighty and exalted king. 'Raise your
heads in honor of your distinguished
guest' (Radak).[2]

וְהִנָּשְׂאוּ — And be uplifted.
[See comm. v. 9 s.v. וּשְׂאוּ פִּתְחֵי עוֹלָם].

1. דּוֹרְשָׁיו may also be translated as 'preachers, teachers, leaders.' Thus, this verse teaches us of
the relationship which exists between the דוֹר 'the people of the generation' and דּוֹרְשָׁיו 'their
leaders.' Concerning this, the Talmud (Arachin 17a) cites a debate between Rabbi Judah the
Prince and the Rabbis. 'One said that the characteristics of the people will follow those of their
leaders. If the leaders are tough and stubborn, the people will act likewise. If they are soft and
humble, the generation will follow suit. The other opinion holds that the opposite is true. The
leader conforms to the personalities of his constituents.'

2. The Talmud (Shabbos 30a) describes the circumstances which prompted the composition
of this verse.
Rav Yehudah said in the name of Rav: 'What is meant by the passage, Display for me a sign
for good so that those who hate me may see it and be shamed' (86:17). Thus said David to the
Holy One, Blessed be He: 'Sovereign of the Universe, forgive me this sin [of Bath Sheba].'
'You are forgiven', answered the Lord. David then requested, 'Show me a sign to this effect

*those who strive for Your Presence — Jacob.
Selah.*

⁷ *Raise up your heads, O gates,
and be uplifted, you everlasting entrances,
So that the King of Glory may enter.*

פִּתְחֵי עוֹלָם — *You everlasting entrances.*
Until the construction of the Temple, the Ark had no permanent abode. Now it was passing through the Temple gates in order to find eternal repose in the Holy of Holies. For this reason those gates are called *'everlasting entrances'* (*Radak*).

Furthermore, the sanctity of these gates and entrances is for all time (*Rashi*).

Radak explains additionally that שַׁעַר refers to the door-frame which consists of the threshold, doorposts, and lintel. The פֶּתַח is the air-space of the entrance way. Even after the door is shut the entrance way still remains indented and recessed and thus an opening of sorts always remains, hence the word פֶּתַח which literally means *'open'*.

The *Midrash* (*Eichah Rabbasi* 2:13) offers yet another explanation: טָבְעוּ בָאָרֶץ שְׁעָרֶיהָ, *'Her gates are sunk*

into the ground' (*Lam.* 2:9). Rav Huna said, in the name of Rabbi Yosi, The gates gave honor to the Ark as it says *'Raise up your heads, O gates, and be uplifted you everlasting entrances.'* Therefore, the hand of no enemy was permitted to grasp and destroy them, rather they sunk into the ground [protected forever.]

[The gates exemplify the main purpose of the Temple. This temporary, material world is known as חַיֵּי שָׁעָה, *'temporary existence.'* The eternal, spiritual existence of the Hereafter is called חַיֵּי עוֹלָם, *'everlasting existence.'* The function of the Temple is to serve as a channel through which eternal spiritual forces can filter down to this world from above, serving as a source of sacred inspiration to all mankind. Therefore, the gates are appropriately called פִּתְחֵי עוֹלָם, *'entrance ways for the everlasting'.*]

while I am still alive!' Whereupon the Lord replied, 'During your lifetime I shall not make it known, but during the life of Solomon, your son, I shall make your pardon public.'

After Solomon concluded the construction of the Temple, he desired to bring the Ark into the Holy of Holies. However, the gates became fastened to each other [and they could not be opened]. Solomon then offered twenty-four רְנָנוֹת *'cries of prayer'* but still he was not answered. He then began to recite these verses, *'Raise up your heads O gates, and be uplifted, you everlasting entrances, so that the King of Glory may enter.'* Thereupon the gates ran after him and opened their mouths to swallow him, saying *'Who is the King of Glory?'* [They thought that Solomon haughtily meant himself.] Solomon replied, *'HASHEM, the mighty and strong.'*

He then repeated [his plea] and said, *'Raise up your heads O gates, and raise up, you everlasting entrances so that the King of Glory may enter. Who then is the King of Glory? HASHEM of legions, He is the King of Glory, Selah.'*

Still Solomon was not answered. But as soon as Solomon said, *'O God, turn not away the face of Your anointed, remember the pious deeds of David, Your servant'* (*II Chron.* 6:12), he was immediately answered, and the gates opened. At that moment the faces of David's enemies turned black [with humiliation] like the bottom of a [burnt] pot. 'Then it became known to all that the Holy One, Blessed be He, had forgiven David that sin.'

ח מִי זֶה מֶלֶךְ הַכָּבוֹד יהוה עִזּוּז וְגִבּוֹר יהוה

ט גִּבּוֹר מִלְחָמָה: שְׂאוּ שְׁעָרִים | רָאשֵׁיכֶם

י וּשְׂאוּ פִּתְחֵי עוֹלָם וְיָבֹא מֶלֶךְ הַכָּבוֹד: מִי

הוּא זֶה מֶלֶךְ הַכָּבוֹד יהוה צְבָאוֹת הוּא

מֶלֶךְ הַכָּבוֹד סֶלָה:

8. מִי זֶה מֶלֶךְ הַכָּבוֹד — *Who is this King of Glory?*

The gates ask, 'Who is this exalted king to whom we are asked to pay homage?' (*Radak*).

ה' עִזּוּז וְגִבּוֹר ה' גִּבּוֹר מִלְחָמָה — *HASHEM, the mighty and strong, HASHEM, the strong in battle.*

[With this description David provides an answer to the preceding question.] The Psalmist describes God who dwells upon the Holy Ark in martial terms because until then, the Ark always accompanied them into battle and its presence assured them of victory over their enemies for God's mighty spirit travelled with it (*Radak*).

9. שְׂאוּ שְׁעָרִים רָאשֵׁיכֶם — *Raise up your heads, O gates.*

These words are already mentioned in v. 7. This repetition alludes to the fact that the Ark was destined to be removed from the Holy of Holies and then to be returned through these very same gates at a later time. The Ark was not returned at the time of the Second Temple (*Yoma* 21b), so this must allude to its return in the days of the Messiah (*Ibn Ezra*).

וּשְׂאוּ פִּתְחֵי עוֹלָם — *And raise up you everlasting entrances.*

This terminology implies that the gates will lift up voluntarily, whereas

the earlier wording, וְהִנָּשְׂאוּ, 'and be uplifted' (*v.*7), suggests that the gates must be uplifted against their will. *Ohel Yaakov* explains that previously the Psalmist discussed the Temple in the pre-Messianic world of violence and force, a world wherein God appears as mighty and strong in battle (*v.*8) to force the wicked to bend to His will. Therefore, the spiritual splendor of God does not enter the portals of this world easily. Israel must figuratively force open the gates and coerce them to be lifted in order to allow the Holiness to enter. This can only be accomplished by Israel's own holy actions. However, the future Messianic world will be so saturated with human spirituality that the gates will open by themselves to welcome God Who no longer needs to appear as the mighty God of vengeance. Now He appears as Lord of obedient Hosts which willingly accompany Him. [See *Shiurei Da'as, Menuchas haNefesh*, by *Harav E. M. Bloch*.]

10. מִי הוּא זֶה — *Who then is?* [lit. 'Who is he?'.]

[This differs from *v.* 8 where the wording is simply מִי זֶה, 'Who is'? The usage here adds greater emphasis to the rhetorical question and stresses that God is the one and only 'King of Glory'. This realization will become completely clear only in the future.]

XXIV 8 *Who is this King of Glory?*
8-10   *— HASHEM, the mighty and strong,*
              HASHEM, the strong in battle.
          9 *Raise up your heads, O gates,*
              and raise up, you everlasting entrances,
          So that the King of Glory may enter.
          10 *Who then is the King of Glory?*
          HASHEM, of Legions, He is the King of Glory.
              Selah!

ה' צְבָאוֹת — *HASHEM of legions.*

This answer also differs from the one given in *v.* 8, where God is described as mighty and strong in battle. No such temporal force is necessary because the verse describes the divine revelation in the time of Messiah, when all nations will voluntarily flock to serve God. Then the words of the prophet will come true, *'And they shall beat their swords into plowshares and their spears into pruning hooks, nation shall not lift up sword against nation, neither shall they learn war anymore' (Michah 4:3).* The 'legions' mentioned here refer not to armies, but to the heavenly bodies *(Ibn Ezra).*

Radak agrees that the term *'HASHEM of legions'* cannot be given a militaristic connotation. Once the Ark was brought to rest in the Temple it was never again removed and so it was no longer associated with war. The *'legions'* mentioned here refer to the multitudes of Israel who faithfully made their pilgrimage to the Temple to offer sacrifices to the Lord.

הוּא מֶלֶךְ הַכָּבוֹד סֶלָה — *He is the King of Glory, Selah.*

[The purpose of this psalm is to demonstrate that God saturated this world with endless opportunities to recognize His glory and mastery (see *Prefatory Remarks*). This idea becomes most evident when we see that God is prepared to share His own splendor and glory with human beings.]

Why is God called *'the King of Glory'*? Because He gives of His glory to those who fear Him. A mortal king lets no one sit on his throne nor ride his steed. Yet, the Holy One, Blessed be He, let Solomon sit on His throne and mounted Elijah on the stormy wind which is His steed. He allowed Moses to use His scepter in the form of the divine staff which Moses carried in his hand. God cloaked Israel in His royal mantle which is His might, and He is destined to place His crown on the head of the King Messiah. Finally, no mortal king would let anyone use his title, but God addressed Moses by His own title, saying *'Behold I have made you* אֱלֹהִים *'Elohim', [Judge] over Pharoah' (Exod.* 7:1). Therefore, God is correctly called the *'King of Glory'* because He shares His glory with others *(Shemos Rabba* 18:1).

T his psalm presents us with one of the finest examples of David's lifelong struggle to keep to the מְסִילַת יְשָׁרִים, 'The Path of the Upright' (see Overview). David begs for divine assistance to help him keep his ways straight, pure, and truthful. As such, this psalm may be considered as an introduction to Psalm 26 wherein David asks to be tested to demonstrate whether he has succeeded in reaching the Mesillas Yesharim.

Radak notes that this is the first psalm which is arranged according to the Aleph-Beis, i.e. the first letters of the respective verses are in alphabetical order. Radak comments that the reason for this order is not known. Perhaps it was put into David's mouth that way when he was inspired by the holy spirit. More likely the alphabetical sequence demonstrates the importance of the psalm [showing that the lessons of the psalm are a fundamental program for life as basic and essential as the alphabet itself.] The sequence lacks the letters ב, ו, ק, beth, vav, and kuf; and two verses begin with ר, 'reish'. Some say that the ב, 'beth' of בְּךָ, and the ו, 'vav' of וְלַמְּדֵנִי (v. 5) are considered opening letters even though they do not appear at the beginning of the respective verses.

לְדָוִד אֵלֶיךָ יהוה נַפְשִׁי אֶשָּׂא: אֱלֹהַי בְּךָ א-ב
בָטַחְתִּי אַל־אֵבוֹשָׁה אַל־יַעַלְצוּ אוֹיְבַי לִי:
גַּם כָּל־קֹוֶיךָ לֹא יֵבֹשׁוּ יֵבֹשׁוּ הַבּוֹגְדִים ג
רֵיקָם: דְּרָכֶיךָ יהוה הוֹדִיעֵנִי אֹרְחוֹתֶיךָ ד
לַמְּדֵנִי: הַדְרִיכֵנִי בַאֲמִתֶּךָ | וְלַמְּדֵנִי כִּי־ ה

1. נַפְשִׁי אֶשָּׂא — *I uplift my soul.*

I uplift it in prayer (*Targum*).

This is achieved by concentrating all of my thoughts on Hashem (*Rashi*).

Rabbi Vidal Hatzorfati in *Otzar Nechmad* sees in these words a connection between this psalm and the previous one. David says in 24:4 that the righteous man is the one אֲשֶׁר לֹא נָשָׂא לַשָּׁוְא נַפְשִׁי [lit. 'Who has not uplifted My soul for naught.'] Now he continues, 'To You, HASHEM. I uplift my soul.'

Some render אֶשָּׂא 'I offer a present' as in וַיִּשָּׂא מַשְׂאֹת 'And he offered presents' (*Gen.* 43:34). Thus David proclaims that he is prepared to offer [i.e. sacrifice] his life as a gift for God and to die for the sanctification of His Name (*Rabbi Moshe* as quoted by *Ibn Ezra*; *Radak*).

When the Temple stood a person who sinned would offer up a sacrifice and achieve atonement. Now that we no longer have the opportunity to give sacrifices we can only offer our very souls to You and we are completely dependent upon Your mercy (*Midrash Shocher Tov*).

Ibn Ezra translates this phrase: 'My soul depends on You' as we find with regard to the commandment that a day-laborer must be paid on the same day on which he toils: וְאֵלָיו הוּא נֹשֵׂא אֶת נַפְשׁוֹ 'and on this his soul depends' (*Deut.* 24:15).

2. אֱלֹהַי בְּךָ בָטַחְתִּי — *My God, in You I trust.*

Midrash Shocher Tov illustrates this with a parable. 'One night the royal watchmen seized a traveler, suspecting him of a crime. He pleaded with them,

'Don't beat me, for I am a member of the King's household'. In the morning they presented the traveler to the King. The King asked him, 'My son, do you even know me?' 'No', was the reply. 'However,' the traveler pleaded 'I placed all of my trust in you, O King. If I had not claimed to be under your protection, they would have beaten me'. The King was impressed and said, 'Because he placed his trust in me, let him go free'. [Similarly, he who places his trust in Hashem will be spared affliction by virtue of this trust alone, even if he is not worthy of being a member of the divine 'household'.]

אַל אֵבוֹשָׁה — *Let me not be shamed.*

I have placed all of my trust in You alone. If You do not respond, my faith will be put to shame and my enemies will exult (*Radak*).

I am not concerned over the fulfillment of my personal wish for my own sake. I am troubled only lest the wicked use my failure as evidence to deny the value of faith in God (*Malbim*).

3. גַּם כָּל־קֹוֶיךָ לֹא יֵבֹשׁוּ — *Also, let no one hoping in You be shamed.*

David asks not only for himself; he requests that Hashem answer all the faithful (*Radak*).

According to *Metzudas David*, this statement is a continuation of David's plea for himself. He argues that if Hashem will answer him, all those who place their hope in God will be inspired not to waver in their faith and to be confident that they too will not be put to shame.

Even if they are not worthy, as long as they place their hope in You, they

O f David:

    To You HASHEM I uplift my soul.
² *My God, in You I trust.*
Let me not be shamed,
    let not my enemies exult over me.
³ *Also, let no one hoping in You be shamed,*
    let the traitors to the destitute be shamed.
⁴ *Your ways, HASHEM, make known to me;*
    teach me Your paths.
⁵ *Lead me in Your truth and accustom me,*

will not be disappointed *(Divrei Shlomo, Dorash Moshe).*

הַבּוֹגְדִים רֵיקָם — *The traitors to the destitute* [lit. 'empty']

The translation follows *Rashi* who says that David refers to criminals who deal treacherously with רֵיקָם, the poor, defenseless people.

Radak holds that these בּוֹגְדִים, 'traitors', are those who betray God, not their fellow man. They do it רֵיקָם 'for naught', for no good reason. *Metzudas Zion* points out that we find a similar use of this word in וָאֲחַלְּצָה צוֹרְרִי רֵיקָם, 'And I released those who oppressed me for no reason' (7:5).

4. דְּרָכֶיךָ ה' הוֹדִיעֵנִי — *Your ways, HASHEM, make known to me.*

Moses made a similar request, הוֹדִעֵנִי נָא אֶת דְּרָכֶךָ וְאֵדָעֲךָ, 'Please make Your ways known to me so that I may know You' (Exod. 33:13).

This refers to an intimate and complete comprehension of the ways of nature, i.e. to thoroughly understand creation and how all is intertwined under Hashem's guidance. This is the first step towards knowing the real truth about God *(Radak).*

The word דֶּרֶךְ 'way' refers to the main course of a person's actions. The Sages often encouraged us to model ourselves after God's ways. 'Just as God is merciful, you be merciful, just as God

is kind, you be kind' *(Shabbos 133b).* This is the דֶּרֶךְ which David seeks to know *(Malbim).*

אֹרְחוֹתֶיךָ לַמְּדֵנִי — *Teach me Your paths.*

The אֹרַח is a narrow path which branches off from the דֶּרֶךְ, the main road. It is a private path for individuals, not a public thoroughfare. This metaphorically describes the ways of the Divine. Although God generally acts towards men with mercy and kindness (as described above) there are times when He must abandon this way for certain individuals who require special, abnormal treatment, such as when He must be cruel to the wicked. David asks to be taught to understand these exceptions to the general rule as well as the rule itself *(Malbim).*

5. הַדְרִיכֵנִי בַּאֲמִתֶּךָ — *Lead me in Your truth.*

We find that Moses also made a second request הַרְאֵנִי נָא אֶת כְּבֹדֶךָ, 'Please show me Your glory' (Exod. 33:18).

The understanding of nature which Moses and David requested (as described in the previous verse) is merely a דֶּרֶךְ, 'a way', a means towards the ultimate truth, but it is not in itself the truth about God's glory. This revelation of God through nature is the most man can achieve while he is still shackled to his body. The essence of Hashem's glory can be perceived by the soul only when it is liberated from the flesh and

אַתָּה אֱלֹהֵי יִשְׁעִי אוֹתְךָ קִוִּיתִי כָּל־הַיּוֹם:
זְכֹר־רַחֲמֶיךָ יהוה וַחֲסָדֶיךָ כִּי מֵעוֹלָם
הֵמָּה: חַטֹּאות נְעוּרַי | וּפְשָׁעַי אַל־תִּזְכֹּר
כְּחַסְדְּךָ זְכָר־לִי־אַתָּה לְמַעַן טוּבְךָ יהוה:

blood. Therefore, David asks God to treat him like a father who slowly trains his infant to take small steps until he can walk himself [i.e. lead me to slowly perceive You in this physical world so that I can eventually see the whole truth by myself in the world of the spirit] (Radak).[1]

In the previous verse David asks to know the characteristics of God which can be observed by anyone paying close attention to God's dealings with men. Now he desires to know the concealed truth of His being which is a secret revealed only to the most righteous through prophecy (Malbim).

[David's request, 'lead me in Your truth' was fulfilled in another significant way. The Talmud (Eruvin 53a) relates that David studied Torah with such clarity that he could render true, authoritative halachic decisions, something which Saul could not do (see Rashi ibid.)]

וְלַמְּדֵנִי — And accustom me [lit. 'and teach me']

Here it means 'let me grow accustomed' to your gradual training, so that I will be prepared for the ultimate revelation of truth (Radak).

כִּי אַתָּה אֱלֹהֵי יִשְׁעִי — For You are my God, my Savior.

Just as You save me and supply me with my physical needs, so too, I am sure that You will provide me with the knowledge necessary to satisfy my spiritual and intellectual requirements (Malbim).

כָּל הַיּוֹם — All the days [lit. 'all of the day']

This refers to all of the days of This World which is like a bright day for the gentiles [whom God rewards in this world] but like a dark night for Israel [whom God rebukes in preparation for the rewards of the Hereafter] (Rashi).

6. זְכֹר רַחֲמֶיךָ ה' וַחֲסָדֶיךָ — Remember Your mercies, HASHEM, and Your kindness.

You displayed Your mercy from the very first moment of my conception in my mother's womb throughout my embrionic development. Your mercy persisted in accompanying me at birth and throughout the subsequent years of my growth and maturity. Therefore, I call upon You now to remember the boundless mercy and to continue it (Radak).

1. Rabbi Yechezkel Landau (preface to Tzelach, Berachos) explains the value of learning even those areas of Torah which are almost incomprehensible (such as the Aggadah, the homiletical parables). He likens this to the toddler who studies the Aleph Beis. The constant drilling and memorization of letters and vowels would seem to be a waste of time. When the child finally learns to read and comprehend, however, he begins to fully appreciate the value of the time he spent on fundamentals.

Similarly, if we wish to understand and delight in the secrets of Torah in the Hereafter, we must prepare ourselves in this world by studying the basic texts even though we cannot fully fathom their meaning.

[Midrash Tanchumah (Ki Savo 4) conveys a similar message: The Torah should not have been given to Israel in This World. Because they are destined to learn it [properly and with full comprehension] in the World to Come from the mouth of God Himself. Why then was it given to them here? So that when they arrive in the World to Come they should at least recognize the portion which God is teaching.]

for You are my God, my savior,
to You have I hoped all the days.
⁶ *Remember Your mercies, HASHEM,*
and Your kindnesses,
for they are from the beginning of the world.
⁷ *The sins of my youth and my rebellions*
remember not;
According to Your kindness, HASHEM,
may You remember for me
for the sake of Your goodness, HASHEM

כִּי מֵעוֹלָם הֵמָּה — *For they are from the beginning of the world.*

God's mercies to mankind started from the very day that Adam was created. God warned Adam *'On the day you eat from the tree you shall surely die' (Gen. 2:17).* After Adam sinned, God did indeed give him only one day to live, but that day was not an ordinary one. It was a divine day which is equivalent to one thousand years *(Rashi).*

[Hashem, You created the world because You desired to do kindness to man, as it says עוֹלָם חֶסֶד יִבָּנֶה, *'The world was built in kindness' (89:3).* Therefore, You should always keep that kindness and mercy in mind.]

According to *Radak,* מֵעוֹלָם refers not to the beginning of creation, but to the first moment when David himself was conceived.

7. חַטֹּאות נְעוּרַי וּפְשָׁעַי — *The sins of my youth and my rebellions.*

The sins one commits in his youth are called חַטֹּאות [lit. *'errors, misjudgments'*] because they are the result of immaturity and an undeveloped intellect. However, at twenty the intellect is considered developed and capable of true understanding. Henceforth, the sins committed are considered as intentional acts of rebellion. David begs forgiveness for both categories of guilt i.e. error and rebellion *(Radak).*

[Although one becomes Bar Mitzvah at thirteen and is then liable to the justice of the earthly courts, he is not responsible to the Heavenly Tribunal until he is twenty years old *(Shabbos 89b).* Heaven does not punish before that time, even for intentional sins because until twenty the intellect is still immature and unstable. Therefore, until that time, all sins are considered חַטֹּאות נְעוּרַי, *'the sins of my youth'*, unintentional mistakes.]

כְּחַסְדְּךָ — *According to Your kindness.*
Remember to my credit all of the good deeds I performed which are worthy of being rewarded with Your mercy *(Rashi).*

[David pleads with God that, in consonance with His holy mercy, recall the good which David has done.]

לְמַעַן טוּבְךָ ה' — *For the sake of Your goodness, HASHEM.*

Because You are a prime source of mercy and a well-spring of good, it befits You to act thus *(Ibn Ezra).*

According to *Midrash Shocher Tov,* טוּבְךָ, *'Your goodness',* refers to the rewards of the Hereafter as we find מָה רַב טוּבְךָ אֲשֶׁר צָפַנְתָּ לִּירֵאֶיךָ, *'How great is Your goodness which You have hidden for those who fear You' (31:20).* If God will not forgive the sins and rebellions of mankind, there will be no one left unscathed to enjoy that goodness which He prepared.

ח טוֹב וְיָשָׁר יהוה עַל־כֵּן יוֹרֶה חַטָּאִים
ט בַּדָּרֶךְ: יַדְרֵךְ עֲנָוִים בַּמִּשְׁפָּט וִילַמֵּד
י עֲנָוִים דַּרְכּוֹ: כָּל־אָרְחוֹת יהוה חֶסֶד
יא וֶאֱמֶת לְנֹצְרֵי בְרִיתוֹ וְעֵדֹתָיו: לְמַעַן־שִׁמְךָ
יב יהוה וְסָלַחְתָּ לַעֲוֹנִי כִּי רַב־הוּא: מִי־זֶה

8. טוֹב וְיָשָׁר ה׳ — *Good and upright is HASHEM.*

Because He is good and upright he does not despise and utterly reject the sinners. Rather, if they wish to repent He will accept them and guide them on the straight path (*Radak*).

עַל כֵּן יוֹרֶה חַטָּאִים בַּדָּרֶךְ — *Therefore, He guides sinners on the way.*

בַּדָּרֶךְ, [spelled with בַּ, a contraction of בָּה, in 'the'] indicates 'the' way 'par excellence': the way to repentance. God showed mankind this path at the very dawn of creation when He guided Cain, the sinner, with the words אִם תֵּיטִיב שְׂאֵת, 'If you do good [i.e.. if you repent] you will be elevated' (Gen. 4:7; *Radak*).

How does God show the sinners the path? By afflicting them with pain and sickness which turn their hearts to repentance. Therefore, one should graciously accept all difficulties visited upon him, as they stem from God Who is 'good and upright' (*Sha'arei Orah*).

What did David mean when he said 'Good and upright is HASHEM, therefore, He guides the sinners on the way'? He is acknowleging the fact that God sends prophets to the people to make them aware of God's ways and to bring them back to repentance. Furthermore, God endowed them with the capacity to study and to comprehend. There is a characteristic which is inherent in every man: that when he is drawn to the ways of wisdom and righteousness, he yearns for them and pursues them. This is what the Sages meant when they said הַבָּא לְטַהֵר מְסַיְיעִין אוֹתוֹ, 'He who comes to purify himself receives divine assistance', i.e., he will discover that he is aided in this endeavor' (*Rambam, Hilchos Teshuvah* 6:5).

Also, we can interpret this verse in reference to those who murder unintentionally, and must flee to an עִיר מִקְלָט, 'a city of refuge'. The Torah commands תָּכִין לְךָ הַדֶּרֶךְ, 'prepare the way for yourself' (Deut. 19:3). The Talmud (*Maccos* 10b) explains that roadsigns indicating the city of refuge must be clearly posted, especially at the crossroads, in order to guide the sinners on the way (*Rashi*).

[The Talmud (*ibid.*) concludes: If Hashem takes such pains to guide even the sinful, then certainly He will guide the righteous.]

9. יַדְרֵךְ עֲנָוִים בַּמִּשְׁפָּט — *He leads the humble with justice.*

This refers to those who humble themselves before God by regretting their sins. God responds by leading them in accordance with the just rules of repentance (*Radak*).

He helps them to grow so accustomed to the right way that it becomes second nature to them. This habit grows as strong as an unbreakable מִשְׁפָּט, 'law' (*Ibn Ezra*).

וִילַמֵּד עֲנָוִים דַּרְכּוֹ — *And will teach the humble His way.*

The way of God is to punish and afflict in order to weaken the stubborn heart. Only the humble are prepared to accept such treatment without complaint even without a clear understanding of why they must suffer this particular pain at this particular time. However, God will eventually 'teach the humble His way' and clearly demonstrate to them the precise reason of each affliction (*Tehillos Hashem*).

XXV
8-11

⁸ *Good and upright is HASHEM,*
therefore, He guides sinners on the way.
⁹ *He leads the humble with justice*
and will teach the humble His way.
¹⁰ *All the paths of HASHEM are kindness and truth,*
for those who guard His covenant
and His testimonies.
¹¹ *For the sake of Your Name, HASHEM,*
You will pardon my guilt for it is great.

10. כָּל אָרְחוֹת ה' חֶסֶד וֶאֱמֶת — *All the paths of HASHEM are kindness and truth.*

Even if the paths are strewn with difficulty and pain, if the afflictions are sent to atone for prior sin, then they are אֱמֶת, 'truth', justly deserved. If they were not prompted by sin but come to test the sufferer in order to bring him closer to Hashem, they are חֶסֶד, 'kindness'; a generous opportunity provided by a loving God (*R' Bachya*).

Also, although the afflictions are אֱמֶת, truly deserved, nevertheless, God does not mete out the full measure of punishment in one furious blow. Rather, he doles out the pain little by little, and this is חֶסֶד, 'kindness' (*Kesef Mezukak*).[1]

לְנֹצְרֵי בְרִיתוֹ וְעֵדֹתָיו — *For those who guard His covenant and His testimonies.*

Radak comments that for them, everything the Torah commands seems straight and worthwhile. But to the stubborn sinners all seems warped and crooked because they are not capable of seeing the truth. Similarly it says, כִּי יְשָׁרִים דַּרְכֵי ה' וְצַדִּקִים יֵלְכוּ בָם וּפֹשְׁעִים יִכָּשְׁלוּ בָם *'For the ways of HASHEM are straight, and the righteous do walk in them but the transgressors shall stumble in them'.* (Hosea 14:10).

11. לְמַעַן שִׁמְךָ ה' — *For the sake of Your name, HASHEM.*

For, You are called by the name טוֹב וְסַלָּח, *'good and forgiving'* (*Radak*).

I ask You for kindness so that Your Name will become known and acknowledged for its greatness (*Ibn Ezra*).

וְסָלַחְתָּ לַעֲוֹנִי כִּי רַב הוּא — *You will pardon my guilt for it is great.*

Because Your Name and reputation for forgiveness is great, it is fitting that You pardon my guilt which is also great. A great sin requires a great God for forgiveness (*Rashi*).

David refers here to his error, the sin of Bath Sheba. He says: 'Although I have already asked on countless occasions that this guilt be wiped away, I repeat my request once again because that sin was very great' (*Radak*).

1. Sometimes it appears as if the evil visited upon this world exceeds the good. This is a mistake ... Most of the misfortunes which befall men are self-inflicted. Men make wrong choices and suffer the consequences but blame their woes on God. They are truly man's doing, however, as it says, עָשָׂה הָאֱלֹקִים אֶת הָאָדָם יָשָׁר וְהֵמָּה בִקְשׁוּ חִשְּׁבֹנוֹת רַבִּים, *'God made man upright, but they sought out many calculations'* (Ecc. 7:29). Wise men of distinction understand this, as David said, *'All the paths of HASHEM are kindness, for those who guard His covenant and testimonies.'* They who preserve the normal nature of things and safeguard the commandments and are aware of their purpose in life — these men see only the benevolent aspect of God's nature (*Rambam, Guide* 3:12).

הָאִישׁ יְרֵא יהוה יוֹרֶנּוּ בְּדֶרֶךְ יִבְחָר:

יג־יד נַפְשׁוֹ בְּטוֹב תָּלִין וְזַרְעוֹ יִירַשׁ אָרֶץ: סוֹד

טו יהוה לִירֵאָיו וּבְרִיתוֹ לְהוֹדִיעָם: עֵינַי

תָּמִיד אֶל־יהוה כִּי הוּא־יוֹצִיא מֵרֶשֶׁת

טז רַגְלָי: פְּנֵה־אֵלַי וְחָנֵּנִי כִּי־יָחִיד וְעָנִי אָנִי:

12. מִי זֶה הָאִישׁ — *Who is this, the man.*
'The man' par excellence (Ibn Ezra).

יְרֵא ה' — *Fearful of HASHEM.*

This is Abraham who is called הָאִישׁ,
'the man' (Gen. 20:7) and of whom it is
written (ibid. 22:12): כִּי עַתָּה יָדַעְתִּי כִּי
יְרֵא אֱלֹהִים אַתָּה 'For now I know that
you fear God (Midrash Shocher Tov).

יוֹרֶנּוּ בְּדֶרֶךְ יִבְחָר — *He will show him the
way he should choose.*

Hashem guided Abraham to come to
recognize His name and His way as it
says (Gen. 17:1): הִתְהַלֵּךְ לְפָנַי וֶהְיֵה תָמִים
'Walk before Me and be perfect'
(Midrash Shocher Tov).

If a person sincerely seeks to dedicate
his life to righteousness God will certainly assist him in choosing the proper
way to achieve his goal. As the Talmud
(Yoma 38b) says: הַבָּא לַטָּהֵר מְסַיְּעִין לוֹ,
'He who tries to purify himself, receives
every assistance' (Metzudas David).

Some men fear only God's punishment, others fear God Himself, i.e., they
realize His awesome greatness and their
own petty weakness and so they refrain
from sin. The former are concerned
only with protecting themselves. The
latter are truly concerned about God
and are fittingly called יְרְאֵי ה'.
Therefore, only they receive divine assistance to choose the proper path

leading to Hashem (Rav Abraham
Azulai).

13. נַפְשׁוֹ בְּטוֹב תָּלִין — *His soul will rest
in goodness.*

If he will choose only good in his
lifetime, then, when he rests in the
grave — the time of the ultimate good
reward — his soul will be blessed with
goodness (Rashi; Radak).

וְזַרְעוֹ יִירַשׁ אָרֶץ — *And his descendants
will inherit the land.*

In the merit of his righteousness
Hashem will bless his descendants
(Radak).

The man who is concerned with the
enrichment of his soul so that it will
eternally rest in goodness, engages in
the mundane matters of this world only
for the sake of perpetuating his seed. He
dedicates his best efforts to insure that
his children will survive to serve God
after he is gone (Malbim).

14. סוֹד ה' לִירֵאָיו — *The secret of
HASHEM is for those who fear Him.*

He will not reveal the secrets of His
Being to anyone other than the scholars
who study His Torah. This study must
be accompanied by fear of God and
scrupulous observance of the commandments (Radak).[1]

The full secret will not be revealed

1. Rabbi Yehudah bar Shalom said: Moshe desired that even the Mishnah, the Oral Law,
should be set down in writing. But the Holy One, Blessed be He, foresaw that in the future the
nations would translate the Scriptures into Greek and claim, 'This belongs to us and we are the
true Israel'. So God said to Moses, אֶכְתָּב לוֹ רֻבֵּי תּוֹרָתִי כְּמוֹ זָר נֶחְשָׁבוּ 'If I will write for him
[Israel] the major part of my Torah [the vast Oral Law] they will be considered as strangers'
[when the gentiles expropriate the Torah for themselves and claim that they are Israel] (Hosea
8:12) And why is God so concerned about protecting the Mishnah? Because it is His מִסְטוֹרִן,
'secret mystery' which is revealed only to the righteous who deserve it, as it says, 'The secret
of HASHEM is for those who fear Him' (Midrash Tanchumah, Vayerah 5).

12 *Who is this, the man fearful of HASHEM,*
   He will show him the way he should choose.
13 *His soul will rest in goodness,*
   and his descendants will inherit the land.
14 *The secret of HASHEM is for those who fear Him,*
   and His covenant is to let them know.
15 *My eyes are constantly towards HASHEM,*
   for He will free my feet from the snare.
16 *Turn Your face to me and show me favor,*
   for I am alone and I am afflicted.

until after *'the soul rests in goodness'*
(v. 13), i.e. after death *(Ibn Ezra).*

[Many times the Sages describe
natural phenomena with which they
could not possibly have had a personal
acquaintance. The Talmud explains
their amazing knowledge with this
verse, *'The secret of HASHEM is for* [i.e.
revealed to] *those who fear Him'* (see
Sotah 4b, *Sanhedrin* 48b, *Niddah* 20b)]

וּבְרִיתוֹ לְהוֹדִיעָם — *And His covenant is
to let them know.*

God has struck a pact with the soul,
promising to enlighten it with the true
understanding of His glory after it
departs from the body *(Radak).*

God said to Abraham: 'If you will
perform the בְּרִית מִילָה, *'the covenant of
circumcision'* then I will let you know
the סוֹד, *'secret'* which has a numerical
value of seventy (סוֹד = 70). Seventy
souls will descend from you and go to
Egypt. Seventy will be the members of
the Sanhedrin. Moses will teach Your
offspring Torah in seventy languages'
(Aggadas Bereishis, 16).

15. כִּי הוּא יוֹצִיא מֵרֶשֶׁת רַגְלָי — *For He
will free my feet from the snare.*

This refers either to the snare of sin

or to the snares set by my enemies. Until
this point David concentrated on requesting spiritual needs, henceforth he
asks for his physical needs. He is particularly concerned that his body should
be rescued from his foes as he mentions
at the outset of this psalm *'let my
enemies not exult over me'* (v. 2). In
truth, this too is a spiritual necessity, for
the soul which is agitated by the threat
of harm cannot properly concentrate on
serving God *(Radak).*[1]

16. כִּי יָחִיד ... אָנִי — *For I am alone* [lit.
'For I am an individual'].

Although I am a King of a great nation, I still regard myself as no more
than a solitary individual. I put no faith
in the multitude of soldiers, only in You
Hashem *(Radak).*

David said this verse when he was afflicted with leprosy. The Talmud tells
us that at that time the Sanhedrin abandoned him for the Torah specifically
commands that the leper sit alone outside the camp *(Sanhedrin* 107a).
Therefore he said *'I am alone and I am
afflicted'* *(Tehillas Hashem).*

וְעָנִי אָנִי — *And I am afflicted.*

Precisely because I am the King I am

---

1. כְּשׁוֹשַׁנָּה בֵּין הַחוֹחִים כֵּן רַעְיָתִי בֵּין הַבָּנוֹת, *'As a rose among thorns, so is my beloved among the
daughters (Songs 2:2).* The north wind blows at the rose and bends it down southward and
the thorn pierces its petals. The south wind bends it northward and yet another thorn tears it.
Yet, despite this, its inner parts remain intact and upright. So, too, with Israel. Although the
nations bend and oppress them with staggering taxes and levies, still their hearts remain
focused upward to their Father in Heaven. Why is this so? Because, *'My eyes are constantly
towards HASHEM, He will free my feet from the snare'* *(Shir HaShirim Rabbah 2:1).*

יז צָרוֹת לְבָבִי הִרְחִיבוּ מִמְּצוּקוֹתַי
יח הוֹצִיאֵנִי: רְאֵה עָנְיִי וַעֲמָלִי וְשָׂא לְכָל־
יט חַטֹּאותָי: רְאֵה־אוֹיְבַי כִּי־רָבּוּ וְשִׂנְאַת חָמָס
כ שְׂנֵאוּנִי: שָׁמְרָה נַפְשִׁי וְהַצִּילֵנִי אַל־
כא אֵבוֹשׁ כִּי־חָסִיתִי בָךְ: תֹּם־וָיֹשֶׁר יִצְּרוּנִי
כב כִּי קִוִּיתִיךָ: פְּדֵה אֱלֹהִים אֶת־יִשְׂרָאֵל
מִכֹּל צָרוֹתָיו:

afflicted with the sins of the entire people who all depend on me. Therefore,
although I am but one man, please turn
to me Hashem in answer to my prayer,
for it concerns the salvation of all Israel
(Rashi).

Radak renders עָנְיִי as 'humble, subdued'. David says: 'Although I am the
King I have not waxed proud. I still turn
to You humbly.'

17. צָרוֹת לְבָבִי הִרְחִיבוּ — *The troubles of
my heart have spread.*

Malbim offers an alternate translation 'The troubles have spread and
broadened my heart'. At first, my heart
[i.e. my desires and horizons] was constricted by a lust for the pleasures of
this world. But now, affliction has rid
me of these frivolous cares and the interests of my heart have spread into
greater things. The scope of my soul has
expanded [see comm. 4:2].

18. רְאֵה עָנְיִי וַעֲמָלִי — *Behold my
affliction and my toil.*

עָנְיִי describes my 'humility' (v. 16)
and עֲמָלִי refers to my 'toil' and exertion
when waging war on behalf of Israel
(Radak).

Ibn Ezra ascribes this statement to
David's war with the יֵצֶר הָרָע: 'See how
I suffer and toil to restrain my evil in-
clination from dragging me to sin.'

Alshich translates עָנְיִי as 'my poverty.' This refers to another statement
once made by David: וְהִנֵּה בְעָנְיִי
הֲכִינוֹתִי לְבֵית ה' זָהָב כִּכָּרִים מֵאָה אֶלֶף וְכֶסֶף
אֶלֶף אֲלָפִים כִּכָּרִים וכו' 'And behold, in

my poverty I have prepared for the
House of HASHEM one hundred
thousand ingots of gold and one thousand thousand ingots of silver etc.' (I
Chronicles 22:14). The Rabbis of the
Midrash comment: 'Was David then a
pauper? Rather, he acted like a poor
man, foregoing all of the customary
royal luxuries. He subsisted on a diet of
vegetables and hoarded the money he
saved in a special treasury designated
for the construction of the Temple.
Now David beseeches God to take note
of this self-afflicted poverty and let it
serve as an atonement to 'take away all
of my sins.' The עָמָל 'toil' which David
refers to is the 'toil' of arduous, incessant Torah study.

וְשָׂא לְכָל חַטֹּאותָי — *And take away all
my sins* [lit. 'and lift off all of my sins'].

Please let the virtue of the affliction
and toil which I have suffered while
waging war for the benefit of Israel be
an atonement for my sins (Radak).

19. רְאֵה אוֹיְבַי כִּי רָבּוּ — *Behold my foes
for they have become many.*

Philistine, Edom, Ammon, Moav, and
Aram (Radak).

The verses of this psalm appear in
alphabetical order as explained in the
Prefatory Remarks. However, the
repitition of the letter ר' at the beginning of vs. 18 and 19 is puzzling. The
Vilna Gaon explains: The Talmud
(Moed Katan 16b) relates that before
David sinned he would smite a thousand of the enemy with one blow. After

¹⁷ *The troubles of my heart have spread,*
release me from my distress.
¹⁸ *Behold my affliction and my toil*
and take away all my sins.
¹⁹ *Behold my foes for they have become many*
and they hate me with unjustified animosity.
²⁰ *Guard my soul and rescue me,*
let me not be shamed
for I have taken refuge in You.
²¹ *Let perfect innocence and uprightness protect me,*
for I have hope for You.
²² *Redeem Israel, O God, from all its distress.*

the sin he could smite only eight hundred at once and David was sorely grieved over the loss (see *comm.* 18:44). The numerical value of the letter 'ר' 'reish' is two hundred and so David dedicated two verses beginning with 'ר' to plead for a return to his former ability. In the first verse he asks Hashem *'take away all of my sins'* which caused me to lose two hundred victims. In the next verse he explains why he is so concerned, *'Behold my foes, because they have become many'* i.e. there are two hundred still alive who should have been smitten with my blow.

וְשִׂנְאַת חָמָס שְׂנֵאוּנִי — *And they hate me with unjustified animosity.*

The translation follows *Rashi* and *Radak.* However, *Metzudas David* renders חָמָס as *'violence'* or *'robbery'.* David says: 'They hate me as if I was a violent criminal'.

חַמְסָן is one who takes an article by force and then pays for it. Esau claims that Jacob was just such a חַמְסָן in regard to the sale of the *'birthright'*. Esau protested that he only sold the birthright under extreme duress, forced to do so by hunger. This situation was exploited by Jacob, who, despite his payment, is considered a thief. David

bemoans the fact that this false accusation is what breeds unwarranted שִׂנְאַת חָמָס [i.e. animosity based on an accusation of חָמָס, a sale by force] in Esau down through the ages (*Chozoh Zion*).

20. וְהַצִּילֵנִי — *And rescue me.*

For they plan to ambush me. These enemies are exceptionally vicious now because of the failure of previous plots to incite Israel to rebel against me (*Radak*).

21. תֹּם — *The perfect innocence,* i.e., my trusting heart (*Ibn Ezra*).

וָיֹשֶׁר — *And uprightness,* i.e., the integrity of my deeds (*Ibn Ezra*).

יִצְּרוּנִי — *Let them protect me.*

From straying off of God's straight path and thus I will be safe from my enemies as well (*Ibn Ezra*).

22. פְּדֵה אֱלֹהִים אֶת יִשְׂרָאֵל — *Redeem Israel, O God.*

I am concerned not only with my own salvation; I yearn for the redemption of all Israel (*Ibn Ezra*).

Redeem them both in my lifetime and continue to do so even after I die (*Radak*).

26 מזמור כו

The essence of David's lifelong aspiration is condensed into this brief psalm. Perfect innocence, purity, clarity of vision, truth, separation from evil, cleanliness, zeal — all of these find expression in this composition. David yearned for these traits so that he would be deemed worthy of constructing the shrine of human perfection, the Beis HaMikdash. 'HASHEM, I love the House in which You dwell, and the place in which Your glory resides' (v. 8).

Late in his career, after a lifetime of arduous preparation, David thought that he had attained the perfection of the patriarchs, Abraham, Isaac and Jacob. He asked God to let him prove his worth by testing him.

God acquiesced by tempting David with Bath Sheba, a test that showed that David had not yet achieved flawlessness (see Overview for broader discussion of this episode).

Psalm 26 was composed after David's failure and he uses its verses to convey a double message. On the one hand, David requests a test and explains why he feels ready for it. On the other hand, he expresses his feelings of repentance and remorse after his failure.

1. שָׁפְטֵנִי ה׳ — *Judge me, HASHEM!*

According to *Midrash Shocher Tov*, these are the opening words of David's lengthy request for a divine test.

Four men were afflicted. One who was afflicted kicked back and complained; this was Job who rejected God's beating. The second one was afflicted and laughed for joy. This was Abraham. His situation may be compared to the king who swore that he would discipline his son with beatings. The son said: 'You have every right to do so.' The father beat him and beat him, thinking the son would cry out 'enough'. However, the brave son never uttered so much as a groan of complaint. Eventually, the king himself was forced to stop the whipping and to say 'enough!' The third one was King Chizkiyahu who, when afflicted, begged that the beating be stopped. The fourth was David who saw the whip hanging on the wall and said, 'Why is the whip standing idle, beat me with it!, as he says here: שָׁפְטֵנִי ה׳, '*Judge me (afflict me) HASHEM.*' David also said אַשְׁרֵי הַגֶּבֶר אֲשֶׁר תְּיַסְּרֶנּוּ יָּה '*Lucky is the man whom HASHEM afflicts*' (94:12). And Solomon echoed this, saying, אֹהֵב מוּסָר אֹהֵב דָּעַת, '*He who loves affliction (rebuke) loves wisdom*' (Proverbs 12:1).[1]

[David purposely brought himself into trying situations, Abraham did not. The patriarch waited for God to initiate the test. The Talmud (*Sanhedrin* 107a)

cautions against David's approach because of its inherent danger. How can a man presume to claim that he can withstand temptation?

Other commentaries interpret the words '*Judge me, HASHEM*' as a request for benign judgment and forgiveness after David's failure.]

Rashi points out that elsewhere David makes a contradictory request: וְאַל תָּבוֹא בְמִשְׁפָּט אֶת עַבְדֶּךָ כִּי לֹא יִצְדַּק לְפָנֶיךָ כָל חָי '*Do not bring Your servant to judgment for no one living can emerge from before You all righteous*' (143:2). Therefore, we must explain David's request here as follows: 'HASHEM, judge me only after You judge the wicked, because compared to them I appear to be righteous. But when you judge the righteous, '*Do not bring Your servant to judgment.*' [I.e. David now admits that he cannot compare himself to the virtuous Patriarchs.]

The *Midrash* suggests two other ways to reconcile this apparent contradiction: Judge me before the final sentence is passed [when Your full anger has not yet been kindled and there is still room for compromise (*Zayis Raanan*)] but not after the final sentence. Judge me in this world [where You can exercise Your מִדַּת הָרַחֲמִים, '*the Attribute of Mercy*', and You are prepared to consider charity and good conduct to soften the sentence (*Eretz HaChaim*)] but not in the World to

1. The *Messilas Yesharim* explains this yearning in Ch. 19, titled חֶלְקֵי הַחֲסִידוּת, '*The Components of Devotion.*'

'This man's love of God will not weaken because of any pressure or pain, but, to the contrary, will grow stronger and steadily increase. Those with true understanding, however, do not even need this explanation, for they are entirely unmotivated by self-interest, their sole aspiration being to magnify the honor of God and to give Him pleasure. The more deterrents that cross their path requiring more of themselves to counteract them, the more will their hearts fortify themselves and rejoice to show the strength of their faith; just as a general famed for his strength will always thrust himself into the heart of battle, where a victory will serve to reveal all the more his prowess. The joy that comes with every opportunity to express the intensity of one's love is known to every lover of flesh and blood.'

XXVI Of David.

1-2   *Judge me, HASHEM,*

        for I have walked in my perfect innocence,

    And in HASHEM have I trusted,

    I shall not waver.

      ² *Examine me, HASHEM, and test me,*

Come [where all are judged according to the strict letter of the law and it is too late to repent.]

Alshich notes that David's request for a more merciful verdict is implied by the use of the words שָׁפְטֵנִי ה' — 'ה being the Name that indicates His *Attribute of Mercy.*

Tehillos Chaim points out that here David requests to be judged and punished by God Himself. In the other verse (143:2) David emphasizes that he does not want to be *'brought'* to judgment by agents of God. For, once God assigns the task of punishment to His ferocious agents, they are unbridled and indiscriminate, and execute their task without mercy. (See *Talmud Baba Kamma* 60b).

[Compare this verse with text and comm. to *Psalm* 17:2 where David makes a similar request for repentance מִלְפָנֶיךָ מִשְׁפָּטִי יֵצֵא עֵינֶיךָ תֶּחֱזֶינָה מֵישָׁרִים *'Let my judgment go forth from Your Presence, let Your eyes behold uprightness.'*]

כִּי אֲנִי בְּתֻמִּי הָלַכְתִּי — *For I have walked in my perfect innocence.*

[Perfect innocence and unshakable faith are prime prerequisites in overcoming a trial as evidenced by Abraham, who succeeded in overcoming Satan's arguments and temptations only by walking with God in perfectly innocent faith. David speaks here in the past tense claiming that he has already achieved this lofty level of perfection. His failure of the test proved that he really had not. However, in *v.* 11 of this psalm, David confidently looks to the future with strong aspirations, promis-

ing וַאֲנִי בְּתֻמִּי אֵלֵךְ, *'As for me, I will walk in perfect innocence'.*]

Sforno, interpreting the verse as a plea for forgiveness, says that David emphasizes that he did not intentionally involve himself in this sin. He was innocently walking on the roof of his palace, and by chance he happened to look down and notice the beautiful Bath Sheba bathing *(II Sam.* 11:2). This unpremeditated encounter sparked the ensuing events.

לֹא אֶמְעָד — *I shall not waver.*

The word מְעָד, literally means *'to slip'* or *'to be jerked out of place' (Metzudas Zion).*

[David expresses complete confidence that he will not stumble and err as a result of the נִסָּיוֹן he requests.]

2. בְּחָנֵנִי ה' וְנַסֵּנִי — *Examine me HASHEM and test me.*

Malbim in his *comm.* to *Malachi* 3:10 makes a very clear distinction between a בְּחִינָה and a נִסָּיוֹן. As an illustration, he draws upon the analysis of a specimen of gold. If the metal is being examined to discover whether and to what degree it has the properties commonly associated with gold, the analysis is called a בְּחִינָה. However if you are making innovative experiments with gold to ascertain unknown facts, this entry into the realm of the unknown is termed a נִסָּיוֹן, *'test.'*

Utilizing the *Malbim's* definitions we may paraphrase David's request here in the following manner: 'Hashem examine me to see if I have the purity of heart You can expect from any man.

וְנַסֵּנִי °צָרְפָה כִלְיוֹתַי וְלִבִּי: כִּי־חַסְדְּךָ ג ק׳ צָרְפָה°

לְנֶגֶד עֵינָי וְהִתְהַלַּכְתִּי בַּאֲמִתֶּךָ: לֹא־ ד

יָשַׁבְתִּי עִם־מְתֵי־שָׁוְא וְעִם נַעֲלָמִים לֹא

אָבוֹא: שָׂנֵאתִי קְהַל מְרֵעִים וְעִם־רְשָׁעִים ה

Then proceed to test me in order to discover new and unique spiritual powers which may lie dormant deep inside me. Bring these to the surface so that I can use these new-found talents and strengths to better serve You.'

צָרְפָה כִלְיוֹתַי וְלִבִּי — *Refine* [i.e. *purge*; (eradicate all that is gross, vulgar, or merely common)] *my intellect and my heart.*

David's desire for נִסָּיוֹן was motivated by an ambition to be like Abraham who is described (in the *Midrash*) as follows: "His two כְּלָיוֹת *'kidneys'* (sources of intellect) were overflowing with wisdom and taught him Torah." David sought a similar refinement of his own intellect (*Eretz HaChaim*).

Radak explains that this statement was uttered in the time of David's repentance: David says: Upon examination You will find my thoughts as pure as refined silver. כִלְיוֹתַי [lit. *'my kidneys'*] refers to the intellect, the source of advice and planning (see. *comm.* 16:7). לִבִּי, *'my heart'* refers to thoughts and desires.

David asks: Judge me according to my heart and mind for they are always upright even though my actions don't always conform to my intellectual values and innermost desires. In regard to his actions, not his thoughts, David once requested *'Do not bring Your servant to judgment'* (143:2).

[Compare this verse with text and comm. to 17:3.]

3. כִּי חַסְדְּךָ לְנֶגֶד עֵינָי — *For Your kindness is before my eyes.*

The reason why my heart has never strayed from You is because I always

train my eyes to observe Your kindness and to serve You out of a sense of appreciation. Therefore, I always tread the straight path of Your truth (*Radak*; *Malbim*).

[Once again we hear a reference to Abraham, who exemplified the trait of חֶסֶד, *'kindness'* in all of his ways. Therefore, God always reciprocated by treating him with kindness. The ultimate divine kindness was עֲשָׂרָה נִסְיוֹנוֹת, the series of ten tests through which Abraham was put. A person can appreciate tests and hope to grow with their aid only if he sees them as a kind opportunity offered to him by a loving God, not as a cruel, capricious blow dealt by an indifferent, callous Creator. David feels ready to ask for tests because he feels that he is prepared for them due to the fact that he recognizes God's mercy before his eyes constantly.

Furthermore, man's very first sin was a direct result of Adam's failure to constantly remember God's boundless generosity to him. The Talmud criticizes him as a כָּפוּי טוֹבָה *'one who fails to appreciate kindness'*, because when God accused him of eating the forbidden fruit he replied, *'The woman that You gave to be with me, she gave me of the tree and I did eat* (Gen. 3:12). Adam blames God for giving him a faulty mate. If Adam had not lost sight of the fact that in truth God had generously given him a wonderful mate, he never would have lost sight of God's command not to eat of the fruit.]

וְהִתְהַלַּכְתִּי בַּאֲמִתֶּךָ — *And I have walked earnestly in Your truth.*

This translation of *'walked earnestly'*

XXVI

3-5

refine my intellect and my heart.
³ For Your kindness is before my eyes.
    and I have walked earnestly in Your truth.
⁴ I did not consort with false men,
    nor with hypocrites have I associated.
⁵ I hated the company of evildoers,
    and with the wicked I will not sit.

---

follows *Hirsch* who refers to the parallel use of the verb הִתְהַלֵּךְ in *Genesis* 17:15.

[The purpose of נִסָּיוֹן, *a test*, is to drive one closer to the absolute, ultimate truth that only in Hashem lies real salvation. But this helps only for the man who already turns to God for help in all situations. For him the test serves as an opportunity to demonstrate with even greater clarity that he is totally dependent on God. But, for the man who often seeks other vehicles of assistance when in distress, the test can very possibly serve as a further incentive to become more deeply involved and dependent on these false forms of support. Therefore, in requesting a test David assures Hashem that it is safe to test him because he always follows only truthful avenues of salvation.]

4. מְתֵי שָׁוְא — *False men.*

The word מְתֵי refers to men or people, as in מְתֵי מִסְפָּר *'few in number of people'* (Gen. 34:30) (*Metzudas Zion*).

Targum and *Ibn Ezra* render שָׁוְא as *'falsehood'*. I have not sat with such men to learn from their bad ways (*Radak*).

[Once again David looks to Abraham for inspiration. *Midrash Tanchumah* describes how Abraham exemplified the person who never sat with *'men of untruth'*. When the people went to build

the great מִגְדָּל *'tower'* to challenge God (*Gen.* 11:4), they invited Abraham to join in their rebellion and he flatly refused. David assures Hashem that in his quest for perfection he can walk in truth, imitating Abraham, and stay away from the influence of men of untruth (see *comm.* v.3).] [1]

נַעֲלָמִים — *Hypocrites* [lit. 'the concealed']

Men who take care to commit their crimes under cover of darkness (*Rashi*).

Some trace the root of this word to עֶלֶם *'youth'* meaning someone who, like young people, enjoys loves laughter and mockery, common traits of untrustworthy people (*Ibn Ezra*).

לֹא אָבוֹא — *I have not associated* [lit. 'I have not come']

Not only have I not committed concealed crimes, I have not even come together with such criminals in their hidden places (*Radak*).

5. וְעִם רְשָׁעִים לֹא אֵשֵׁב — *And with the wicked I would not sit.*

Rather I make my permanent place, the House of God, which I visit constantly (*Radak*).

David is careful of where he walks (only *'in Your truth'* v. 3), with whom he associates (not with *'secret sinners'* v. 4), and where he resides (*'And with the wicked I would not sit'*) (*Ibn Ezra*).

---

1. The very first rung on the spiritual ladder discussed by *Mesillas Yesharim* is זְהִירוּת *'watchfulness.'* Ch. 5 describes the factors which detract from *watchfulness*: The third deterrent to *'watchfulness'* is evil companionship, that is the companionship of fools and sinners ... King David said in this connection: *'The praises of a man are that he has not walked in the counsel of the wicked, nor stood in the path of the sinners etc.'* (1:1). And again, *'I did not consort with false men, nor with hypocrites have I associated'* (26:4).

ו לֹא אֵשֵׁב: אֶרְחַץ בְּנִקָּיוֹן כַּפָּי וַאֲסֹבְבָה
ז אֶת־מִזְבַּחֲךָ יהוה: לַשְׁמִעַ בְּקוֹל תּוֹדָה
ח וּלְסַפֵּר כָּל־נִפְלְאוֹתֶיךָ: יהוה אָהַבְתִּי
ט מְעוֹן בֵּיתֶךָ וּמְקוֹם מִשְׁכַּן כְּבוֹדֶךָ: אַל־

6. אֶרְחַץ בְּנִקָּיוֹן כַּפָּי — *I wash my hands in innocence* [following *Targum*; lit. 'in cleanliness']

I make no offerings to God until I first cleanse myself from all sin *(Radak)*.

In all of the mitzvos that I fulfill I make sure that there is no shred of ill-gotten gain which would invalidate them as we find, for instance, that a stolen lulav is unfit for performing the mitzvah *(Rashi)*.

Norah Tehillos offers a different interpretation: David claims some people wash themselves with penitence only when they see the filth of undiluted sin on their hands. 'Not I', says David! '*I wash my hands in cleanliness.*' Even when they seem clean I never cease my penitence, but purify myself more and more.'[1]

וַאֲסֹבְבָה אֶת מִזְבַּחֲךָ ה' — *That I might circle around Your altar, HASHEM.*

Thus, free of all sin, I will circle Your altar to offer up sacrifices to You. Not like the wicked who bring sacrifices with their hands full of bloodshed *(Radak)*.

Dorash Mosheh provides a deeper insight into David's words. God loves looking at the pure and innocent man. He watches over him fondly, from all sides. But, when man sins, the wicked deed stands as a barrier between him and God in that direction [i.e. in the aspect of his being affected by the sin], so God averts His view from that side. David claims that he has cleansed himself of sin so thoroughly through repentance, that he can stand before the presence of God, by His altar, and circle it from all sides and yet be constantly under God's watchful eye with no barrier of sin causing obstruction.

[In the sense that David requests a test, he is trying to convince God that he is fully prepared for the challenge. Therefore David argues that his preparedness can be supported by the fact that never did he make an offering or perform a commandment without being fully cleansed and ready. In the sense that he begs forgiveness for failure, he is demonstrating here how he has washed himself of his sin.]

7. לַשְׁמִעַ בְּקוֹל תּוֹדָה — *Giving voice to thanks* [lit. 'making thanks heard with a loud voice']

לַשְׁמִעַ here means לְהַשְׁמִיעַ, 'to make heard' *(Rashi; Ibn Ezra; Radak)*.

My main purpose in circling the altar is to proclaim loudly before the entire holy congregation assembled there, my thanks to You for Your infinite kindness and the many wonders You performed when rescuing me in times of distress *(Radak)*.

[David's goal was that his trial, with God's help, would afford him ample opportunity to sing God's praises publicly.

וּלְסַפֵּר כָּל נִפְלְאוֹתֶיךָ — *And recounting all Your wondrous deeds.*

This is the recital of the Hallel in which praise is offered for all miracles; for those of the past and also for those expected in the future. In Hallel, reference is made to the wonders of the War of Gog and Magog, the wonders of

1. *Mesillas Yesharim (ibid.)* continues his discussion of the factors which detract from 'watchfulness': What a person must do, then, is to purify and cleanse himself, and keep his feet from the paths of the crowd who are immersed in the foolishness of the time, and turn to the precincts of God and His dwelling places. As David himself concludes (26:6): '*I wash my hands in innocence, that I might circle around Your alter, HASHEM'.*

⁶ *I wash my hands in innocence,*
that I might circle around Your altar, HASHEM.
⁷ *Giving voice to thanks,*
and recounting all Your wondrous deeds.
⁸ *HASHEM, I love the House in which You dwell*
and the place in which Your glory resides.

the days of Messiah, and the wonders of the Hereafter *(Rashi).*

[The source of this *Rashi* is *Vayikra Rabba* 30:5 which explains which verses of Hallel refer to the specific events mentioned by *Rashi.*]

Furthermore, the *Midrash* says that Hallel was recited every day of Succos when they encircled the temple altar with their *lulavim* in hand. Thus, this verse relates to the preceding one *'and I will circle around Your altar HASHEM.'*[1]

8. מְעוֹן בֵּיתֶךָ — *The House in which You dwell* [lit. 'the dwelling of Your house']

This refers to the Beis HaMikdash where the Holy Ark is at rest and where the Priests and the Levites serve Hashem *(Radak).*

I have not sat with men of untruth (v. 4) but I do sit in the house where You dwell, for there the truly righteous congregate to serve You *(Ibn Ezra).*

[The pinnacle of Abraham's success in trial was when he merited to serve God by binding his son to the altar on

the holiest spot on earth, Mount Moriah, the location of the Beis HaMikdash. David's most cherished dream was also bound up with the construction of the Beis HaMikdash. Here David expresses the hope that the test will elevate him enough to be worthy of fulfilling his ambition to build a dwelling place for Hashem].[2]

וּמְקוֹם מִשְׁכַּן כְּבוֹדֶךָ — *And the place where Your glory resides.*

Various Midrashic statements relate this verse to the Tabernacle constructed in the wilderness.

The מִשְׁכָּן, *'Tabernacle'* was constructed as a microcosm, a miniature model of the entire physical world. Thus it demonstrated that just as God's Presence completely filled up this small abode, so does His Presence penetrate and reach out to the most remote corners of the universe. The curtains and tapestries covering the Tabernacle correspond to the heavens. The פְּרוֹכֶת, *'curtain'* which served as a partition in front of the Holy of Holies corresponds to the skies which separate between

1. It is impossible to recount all of God's praises. Any attempt to number them would only detract from God's greatness *(Berachos* 30b). This may be likened to the king who is praises as possessing thousands of silver pieces when in reality his fortune consists of millions of gold coins.

For this reason, David chooses his words with great care. He does not presume to relate all of God's miracles and praises, only the נִפְלָאוֹת which the *Targum* renders as פְּרִישׁוּתָךְ *'the outstanding acts.'* These are the unique wonders through which God revealed Himself to Israel with unprecedented clarity. These rare instances can be counted, indeed they were meant to be counted, as they were in Hallel!]

2. Nowadays (when the Temple is no longer) God dwells in the בָּתֵּי כְנֵסִיוֹת *Houses of Prayer,* and בָּתֵּי מִדְרָשׁוֹת *Houses of Study.* Abaye would study in one place and pray in another. However, after he completed the verse: *HASHEM, I love the House in which You dwell,* he was inspired to combine both loves together and he studied Torah and prayed in the same place *(Megillah* 29a).

תֵּאֱסֹף עִם־חַטָּאִים נַפְשִׁי וְעִם־אַנְשֵׁי
דָמִים חַיָּי: אֲשֶׁר־בְּידֵיהֶם זִמָּה וִימִינָם
מָלְאָה שֹּׁחַד: וַאֲנִי בְּתֻמִּי אֵלֵךְ פְּדֵנִי
וְחָנֵּנִי: רַגְלִי עָמְדָה בְמִישׁוֹר בְּמַקְהֵלִים
אֲבָרֵךְ יהוה:

the upper waters and the lower waters.
The בִּיוֹר, 'wash basin' reminds us of the
waters which were gathered as the seas
on the third day. The golden מְנוֹרָה
'candelabra' resembles the many
celestial luminaries set in the heavens on
the fourth day.

The winged כְּרוּבִים, 'cherubs' correspond to animal and bird life created on
the fifth day. The holy priests the כֹּהֲנִים,
sons of Aaron, represent Adam, the
splendid first man, created on the sixth
day. And finally just as God rested and
sanctified the seventh day of Shabbos
so did His presence come to rest and
dwell in the Tabernacle making it most
holy (Midrash Shocher Tov, Tanchuma
Pikudei 2).

9. אַל תֶּאֱסֹף עִם חַטָּאִים נַפְשִׁי — *Gather
not my soul with sinners.*

תֶּאֱסֹף, *gather*, is the word used to
describe death (Metzudas Zion), [as in
וַיֵּאָסֶף אֶל עַמָּיו, *'and he was gathered
unto his nation'* (Gen. 25:8).

[David is aware of the pitfalls inherent in a trial. There is much to gain,
but, in the event of failure, much to
lose. Therefore, he asks that even if he
stumbles and errs, he should not be considered equally with common sinners
whose sins are a result of their worthlessness.]

10. זִמָּה — *Conspiracy* [lit. *'plots,
schemes'*]

When this word is used in Scriptures
it refers to 'schemes' sometimes good
ones, and sometimes bad (Rashi).

[Here it refers to evil thoughts which
breed crimes בְּידֵיהֶם, *'in their hands'*.]

The crime here is murder or assault
with which they bloody their hands
[and become *'men of bloodshed'* (v. 9)].
Or it is bribery with which they fill their
hands (Radak).

According to *Midrash Shocher Tov*
the words *'In whose hands is conspiracy'* describe those who play cards
and gamble. They hold up their *'hands'*
of cards with the left hand supported by
the right, and cheat and steal from one
another.

11. וַאֲנִי בְּתֻמִּי אֵלֵךְ — *As for me, I will
walk in my perfect innocence.*

[Now David expresses his hopes in
the future.] I will engage in no
falsehood or trickery, whether in
thought or deed (Radak).

These words were on the lips of
Abraham as he went to the Akeida, the
altar where he was to offer Isaac
(Sanhedrin 89b). Satan made a her-
culean effort to pursuade him to turn
back: *'How do you slaughter your own
son, the precious gift for which you
waited 100 years?'* (Maharsha ibid.) But
Abraham turned a deaf ear to all of
Satan's arguments, saying in simplicity,
*'As for me, I will walk in my perfect in-
nocence.*

XXVI

9-12

⁹ *Gather not my soul with sinners;*

nor my life with men of bloodshed,

¹⁰ *In whose hands is conspiracy,*

and whose right hand is full of bribery.

¹¹ *As for me, I will walk in my perfect innocence,*

redeem me and show me favor.

¹² *My foot is set on the straight path,*

in assemblies I will bless HASHEM.

12. רַגְלִי עָמְדָה בְמִישׁוֹר — *My foot is set on the straight path.*

[The true יְשָׁרִים, 'straight or upright ones' are the Patriarchs. The entire Book of Genesis is dedicated to them and is called the סֵפֶר הַיָשָׁר 'The Book of Uprightness.' David thought that his way of divine service was perfect (v. 1), but his failure proved otherwise. In the preceding verse he rededicated hginself to the future quest of perfection, echoing the words of Abraham. Now he repeats his commitment to abandon his previous concept of righteousness and to follow only the example of the Forefathers.][1]

Rabbi Yitzchak Chajes adds a mystical note. Zohar teaches that God's heavenly throne is held up by a מֶרְכָּבָה 'carriage' an allegorical reference to the Patriarchs who are the three 'legs' upholding God's Presence. But, a throne held up by only three legs is unstable. Therefore David is destined to join them, to make the position of God's throne firm and permanently solid. The sacred kabbalistic work *Megalleh Amukos* figures the numerical value of the words מֶרְכָּבָה שְׁלֵימָה 'complete carriage' to be 652 which is precisely the numerical value of the four names אַבְרָהָם, יִצְחָק, יַעֲקֹב, דָוִד.

בְּמַקְהֵלִים אֲבָרֵךְ ה' — *In assemblies I will bless HASHEM.*

In the congregation of the righteous (*Targum*).

Because You have always supported my foot to stand on the straight way and not slip, therefore I will bless You, HASHEM, in public (*Radak*).

[In the Sabbath prayers we echo David's words: 'In the assemblies of the tens of thousands of Your people the house of Israel, with joyous song shall Your Name, our King be glorified in every generation ... even beyond all the songs of praise by David, son of Jesse, Your servant, Your anointed.' See Overview.]

1. *Tehillos Hashem* offers an insight into the straightness and perfection which David ultimately achieved. In *Psalm 119:59* he says: חִשַּׁבְתִּי דְרָכָי וָאָשִׁיבָה רַגְלַי אֶל עֵדֹתֶיךָ *'I planned my ways, yet I returned my feet to Your testimonies.'* The *Yalkut Shimoni* (890) comments: David said to the Holy One, Blessed be He, "Every day I would plan my schedule and say, 'Today I will travel to this place or I will visit that person's house.' But my feet would not take me there. They would carry me to the houses of prayer and study." This is what is meant here *'My foot stands on the straight way'*. It walks directly to the House of God and nowhere else.

W ith this psalm, Jews all over the world usher in the spirit of the
יָמִים נוֹרָאִים, 'The Days of Awe.' It is recited at the conclusion of
services throughout the month of Elul and during the Ten Days of
Repentance. Many continue to recite it throughout the Festival of
Succos.

At first glance it would seem that Psalm 51 would be more appropriate for creating a mood of repentance. It is that psalm which
records, with unsurpassed eloquence, David's broken-hearted confession of sin and his profound remorse over his guilt.

This psalm says nothing of repentance. Nevertheless, it combats
sin by teaching how to prevent it at its source.

David declares that the mind which is fully engrossed in single-
minded dedication to God's service, has no room for sin — and he exhorts us not to be distracted from concentration on this one goal.
'One thing I asked of HASHEM, that shall I seek: That I dwell in the
house of HASHEM' (v. 4).

[As a Torah giant once had this to say about the phenomenal Gaon
of Rogatchov: 'I testify that he never so much as had one impure
thought in all his life. He is so totally engrossed in his study of Torah
and service of God that he has no time to spare for anything else!']

א לְדָוִד ‖ יהוה ‖ אוֹרִי וְיִשְׁעִי מִמִּי אִירָא

ב יהוה מָעוֹז־חַיַּי מִמִּי אֶפְחָד: בִּקְרֹב עָלַי ‖

מְרֵעִים לֶאֱכֹל אֶת־בְּשָׂרִי צָרַי וְאֹיְבַי לִי

ג הֵמָּה כָשְׁלוּ וְנָפָלוּ: אִם־תַּחֲנֶה עָלַי ‖

מַחֲנֶה לֹא־יִירָא לִבִּי אִם־תָּקוּם עָלַי

1. אורי ה׳ — HASHEM is my Light.

Since distress is like darkness, David describes salvation as light (Radak).

Although God is the ultimate source of all illumination, the psalm refers to spiritual light, as David says, נֵר לְרַגְלִי דְבָרֶךָ וְאוֹר לִנְתִיבָתִי 'Your word is a lamp to my feet, and a light to my path' (119:105).

Midrash Shocher Tov comments: David said: 'When I begin to study Torah I grasp only a small amount, but gradually the wellspring of understanding starts to flow (like the light of a lamp which is limited by its size and intensity). However, when I reach the level of total immersion in learning, many great gateways open wide before me (and I perceive endless light for my path).' [God provides light in direct proportion to a person's desire and striving for it.]

The Midrash (Vayikra Rabba 21:3) interprets homiletically: God is אוֹרִי, 'my light', on Rosh Hashanah.

[The first day of Tishrei, the Jewish New Year, corresponds to the sixth day of the creation of the world, when the first man, Adam, was formed. His divine intellect fully comprehended every aspect of the entire universe. All was revealed to him; no shadowy doubts, or dark ignorance existed for him. But, lust blinded him and sin extinguished the light (see Overview). Therefore, God established the first of Tishrei as a day of judgment and repentance for all time. Mercifully, He aids our repentance on Rosh Hashanah by revealing the majesty of His sovereignty with clarity and brilliance on that day].

וְיִשְׁעִי — And my Salvation.

Some say that God is 'a light' in the night and 'a salvation' in the day. Others say He is 'a light' for the soul and 'a salvation' for the body (Ibn Ezra).

The Midrash (Vayikra Rabba ibid) explains: 'God is יִשְׁעִי 'my salvation' on Yom Kippur. [After perceiving the light and the truth on Rosh Hashonah the soul yearns to repent fully and to be completely cleansed of sin. This requires special divine assistance which God provides on the Day of Atonement when He offers man purification and salvation. (The Vilna Gaon emphasizes that יְשׁוּעָה 'salvation' denotes assistance which is provided to someone who is unable to help himself)].

מִמִּי אִירָא — Whom should I fear?

[Similarly David said: ה׳ לִי לֹא אִירָא מַה יַּעֲשֶׂה לִי אָדָם 'HASHEM is for me, I shall not fear, what can any man do to me?' (118:6).]

Malbim defines יִרְאָה as the fear of a clearly perceived danger. David says: 'If they strike in the night when I am unprepared and cannot see, I trust Hashem to be אוֹרִי, 'my light'. If they attack in the day with superior numbers and greater force, I am still confident that God will be יִשְׁעִי 'my salvation'.

The Midrash (Bamidbar Rabba 11:3) comments: Rabbi Shimon bar Yochai said, 'Before a person sins, Hashem makes others afraid of him. But after a person sins, Hashem makes him afraid of others. Before David committed his sin [concerning Bath Sheba], he said 'whom should I fear?' But after he sinned we find him fleeing timidly from Absalom his son.'

XXVII O*f David.*

1-3
HASHEM is my light and my salvation,
whom shall I fear?
HASHEM is the source of my life's strength,
whom should I dread?
² *When evildoers approach me to devour my flesh,*
my tormentors and my foes against me —
It is they who stumble and fall.
³ *Though an army would besiege me,*
my heart would not fear.
Though war would arise against me,

ה' מָעוֹז חַיַּי — *HASHEM is the source of my life's strength.*

He binds my body to my soul [and thus permeates my being with strength] (*Ibn Ezra*).

מִמִּי אֶפְחָד — *Whom should I dread?*

Malbim defines פַּחַד as fear of an unknown threat, i.e., a suspicion of lurking danger, of concealed enemies. But David feels secure: 'God is the source of my strength, nothing can harm me!'

2. בִּקְרֹב עָלַי מְרֵעִים — *When evildoers approach me* [lit. 'come close to me']

Our translation interprets קרב as 'come close'. It can also be related to קְרָב 'battle' and rendered, '*when evildoers come to do battle*' (*Radak; Ibn Ezra*).

The *Midrash* (*Vayikra Rabba* 21:2) refers the verse to Goliath of whom it is written, '*And the Philistine approached [the Israelite camp] early in the morning and in the evening, and so he stood firm for forty days*' (*I Sam.* 17:16).

לֶאֱכֹל אֶת בְּשָׂרִי — *To devour my flesh.* '*And the Philistine said to David, "Come to me and I will give your flesh to the birds of the sky and the beasts of the field"'* (*I Sam.* 17:44; *Midrash ibid.*).

צָרַי וְאֹיְבַי לִי — *My tormentors and my foes, against me.*

This translation follows *Radak* who renders לִי as a modifier of צָרַי וְאֹיְבַי, i.e. 'they are hostile and threatening to me.'

According to the *Midrash*, however, לִי may be rendered as '*they are in my power.*' Thus, David announces that, due to his faith in God, he was able to defeat the mammoth Goliath: '*And he struck the Philistine in his forehead and the stone sunk into his forehead and he fell on his face to the earth*' (*I Sam.* 17:49; *Midrash ibid.*).

הֵמָּה כָּשְׁלוּ וְנָפָלוּ — *It is they who stumble and fall.* The *Midrash* (*ibid.*) notes that even before Goliath fell down on his face he already had '*stumbled*' into a trap. God miraculously made his feet sink into the ground beneath them, completely immobilizing him. Therefore, the giant was forced to call out to David, challenging him to come and do battle. Goliath could not chase his opponent.

3. אִם תַּחֲנֶה עָלַי מַחֲנֶה לֹא יִירָא לִבִּי — *Though an army would besiege* [lit. encamp against] *me, my heart would not fear.*

Now that I have witnessed God's miraculous assistance against Goliath, I know that I need not fear anything, not even an army (*Midrash ibid., Radak*).

מִלְחָמָה בְּזֹאת אֲנִי בוֹטֵחַ: אַחַת | שָׁאַלְתִּי ד
מֵאֵת־יהוה אוֹתָהּ אֲבַקֵּשׁ שִׁבְתִּי בְּבֵית־
יהוה כָּל־יְמֵי חַיַּי לַחֲזוֹת בְּנֹעַם־יהוה
וּלְבַקֵּר בְּהֵיכָלוֹ: כִּי יִצְפְּנֵנִי | בְּסֻכֹּה בְּיוֹם ה

בְּזֹאת אֲנִי בוֹטֵחַ — *In this I trust.*

I trust in the motto expressed in verse
1: *'HASHEM is my Light and my
Salvation, whom should I fear?' (Rashi;
Radak).*

According to *Ibn Ezra* and *Sforno,*
the trust is in that which is expressed
in the following verse: I trust in God
because I have always requested only
spiritual success and nothing vain and
worthless.

Alshich explains that if fear besets a
man, it is an indication of guilt. The
Talmud (*Berachos* 60a) tells of the student who walked in the street shaking
with fear. His teacher called out to him,
"You are surely a sinner, for it is written, *'The sinners were frightened in
Zion, trembling seized the insincere'*"
(Isaiah 33:14).

Similarly we read, *'And Jacob was
very fearful and sorely distressed'* (Gen.
32:7). How does fear differ from distress? Fear gripped Jacob as he prepared
to encounter his hostile brother, Esau.
Jacob felt that this excessive fear was
proof of his own guilt — and therefore
he became *'sorely distressed'.*

On the contrary, David's spirits were
buoyed by a good omen. Even when a
mighty enemy host encamped against
him, he felt no fear. This clearly indicated that he could place his trust in
God for he was free of sin.[1]

4. אַחַת שָׁאַלְתִּי — *One thing I asked of
HASHEM.*

David said: Man's desires are in a
constant state of flux and change. Each
moment breeds new whims and fresh
requests. I am not so. Past experience
has proven that I always limited myself
to one request (*Malbim*).

אוֹתָהּ אֲבַקֵּשׁ — *That shall I seek.*

Malbim continues: What I requested
in the past is what I still want and will
continue to desire in the future, because
this one request embodies all of my
desires! שְׁאֵלָה is an expressed request,
whereas בַּקָּשָׁה is the unspoken desire of
the heart. Some people ask for one thing
with their lips while desiring something
different in their heart. I ask only that
for which my heart yearns. [Similarly,
Queen Esther said to Ahasuerus שְׁאֵלָתִי
וּבַקָּשָׁתִי *'My verbal request which is indeed my heart's true desire' (Esther
5:7)*].

Furthermore, my request is that I remain consistent in my hopes and
desires. Thus, *'One thing I asked of
HASHEM, [namely] that I shall seek
[only this].* Save me from vacillation
and instability, from endless changes of
heart!

שִׁבְתִּי בְּבֵית ה' — *That I dwell* [lit. *'my
dwelling.'*] *in the House of HASHEM.*

Midrash Shocher Tov says: מַלְכוּת

---

1. *Chazon Ish* in *Emunah u'Vitachon* 2:1, takes great pains to correct the common misconception that בִּטָּחוֹן, *'trust'*, means the conviction that God will fulfill all the wishes of believers.
On the contrary, trust does not imply that God is held hostage to the wishes of the pious.
What it does mean is the belief that every aspect of life is controlled by God and that events
take only the course He ordains. But the wishes of God and the wishes of man do not necessarily coincide.

He concludes by quoting this verse, particularly the words *'In this I place my trust.'* It
teaches us that those who place *all* of their trust in Hashem will merit a special kindness — that
His wish will be to fulfill *their* wish. 'And a holy spirit will fill their hearts with a mighty surge
of confidence, assuring them that indeed, God will save!' (ibid. 2:7) [cf. comm. 3:8].

in this I trust.

4 One thing I asked of HASHEM,
that shall I seek:
That I dwell in the House of HASHEM
all the days of my life.
To behold the delight of HASHEM
and to meditate in His Sanctuary.

שָׁאַל, *'David asked for royalty!'* [Why did he need this; he was already a king? The Talmud (*Megillah* 15a) explains the verse וַתִּלְבַּשׁ אֶסְתֵּר מַלְכוּת, *And Esther donned royalty (Esther* 5:1) to mean 'she was enveloped by the Holy Spirit'. This is true royalty, to share in the spiritual sovereignty of God, and it was this higher form of royalty to which David aspired.]

Radak, too, emphasizes that David had no interest in the temporal powers and privileges of monarchy. Although God made him victorious in all military campaigns (*v.* 3), he nevertheless yearned to abandon the worries and cares of war in order to devote himself exclusively to serving God in the Temple where the Holy Ark rests, in the company of the pious priests and holy prophets. *Ibn Ezra* suggests that David formulated this request at the end of his reign after his army took an oath to prevent him from accompanying them into the dangers of battle (*II Sam.* 21:17).

Alshich notes the word שִׁבְתִּי [lit. *'my sitting'*], explaining it in light of the *halachah* that, 'No man may sit in the Temple courtyard except for kings from the House of David' (*Sotah* 40b) [God gave this extraordinary privilege to David's dynasty to show clearly that their sovereignty was total (*Rashi*).] David longed to sit in the Temple courtyard so that he could demonstrate to his detractors that God had indeed chosen him as Israel's king.

לַחֲזוֹת בְּנוֹעַם ה׳ — *To behold the delight of HASHEM.*

[This can only be perceived through Torah study as Solomon says, דְּרָכֶיהָ דַרְכֵי נֹעַם, *Her* (i.e., the Torah's) *ways are ways of delight (Prov.* 3:17).]

Midrash Shocher Tov relates: The Holy One, Blessed be He, said to David, 'First you said, 'Only one thing I asked of HASHEM, then you proceed to ask for many things, i.e., 'to behold the delight of HASHEM' and also 'to meditate in His sanctuary'! David replied, 'Sovereign of the Universe! Should not the servant imitate the ways of his master? First You asked for but one thing, 'And now Israel, what does HASHEM your God ask of you, except that you should fear HASHEM your God?' (Deut. 10:12). But then you proceded to demand many things, 'to go in all His ways and to love Him and to serve HASHEM' etc. (Deut. ibid.). [I.e., God's many commands really have but one goal — that we should fear him. So, too, all David's petitions have but one purpose — that he constantly dwell in the presence of God.]

וּלְבַקֵּר בְּהֵיכָלוֹ — *And to meditate* [lit. search] *in His Sanctuary.*

The translation follows *Menachem*, quoted by *Rashi*, *Radak* and *Metzudas Zion*. The term בִּיקוּר implies a critical examination to understand and differentiate as in לֹא יְבַקֵּר בֵּין טוֹב לָרַע *'He shall not search whether it be good or bad' (Lev.* 27:33). Thus, David asked that he be enabled to meditate in God's Sanctuary in order to discover the truth in all its depth. *Dunash*, quoted in *Rashi*, relates the word to בֹּקֶר, *'morn-*

רָעָה יַסְתִּרֵנִי בְּסֵתֶר אָהֳלוֹ בְּצוּר
יְרוֹמְמֵנִי: וְעַתָּה יָרוּם רֹאשִׁי עַל אֹיְבַי
סְבִיבוֹתַי וְאֶזְבְּחָה בְאָהֳלוֹ זִבְחֵי תְרוּעָה
אָשִׁירָה וַאֲזַמְּרָה לַיהוָה: שְׁמַע־יהוה
קוֹלִי אֶקְרָא וְחָנֵּנִי וַעֲנֵנִי: לְךָ | אָמַר לִבִּי

ו

ז

ח

ing', Thus: 'let me be seen in His sanctuary every morning.'[1]

According to *Rambam (Hilchos Teshuvah* 8:4) all of the places mentioned in this verse refer not to this world but to the bliss of the Hereafter: 'In the Scriptures we find the World to Come described metaphorically with a number of names: הַר ה' *'the mount of HASHEM',* מְקוֹם קָדְשׁוֹ, *'the place of His holiness',* דֶּרֶךְ הַקֹּדֶשׁ *'the sacred way',* חַצְרוֹת ה', *'the courtyards of HASHEM',* נֹעַם ה' *'the delight of HASHEM',* אֹהֶל ה' *'the tent of HASHEM',* הֵיכַל ה', *'the sanctuary of HASHEM,* בֵּית ה' *'the house of HASHEM'* and שַׁעַר ה' *'the gateway of HASHEM'.*

Rav Gifter asks: If these terms refer to the Hereafter, how can David ask to experience them כָּל יְמֵי חַיַּי *'all the days of my life',* meaning his life on earth? The Rosh haYeshiva explains this according to the words of *Ramban* in his famous ethical letter to his son, *Iggeres haRamban:* 'When you will act with humility to be respectfully ashamed of every man, and when you will truly fear Hashem and be afraid to sin, then you will be permeated with the spirit of

God's Presence and the splendid glow of its glory and the life of the World to Come.' Thus the man who sanctifies himself by eradicating his proud ego and selfish desire for sin can actually immerse himself in the bliss of the Hereafter even while he still walks upon this earth. This was David's desire.

5. כִּי יִצְפְּנֵנִי — *Indeed, He will treasure me.*

[The verb צָפַן, [lit. *concealment*], is never used in connection with something trivial. It is used only to denote the storage of something very precious, especially a spiritual treasure. Thus the word מַצְפּוּן for conscience. David is confident that HASHEM will safeguard him carefully as befits a spiritual treasure.]

Rashi notes that David is sure that HASHEM will shelter not only him but his offspring as well. 'We learn in *Seder Olam* that this verse refers to King Yoash ben Achazya who was the sole survivor of the Davidic line after Ataliah murdered all of the royal family. His aunt, Yehosheva, hid him as an infant in the attic above the Holy of

1. [לְבַקֵּר may also be translated as *to visit.* The visitor realizing that his trip is a short one, lets not a minute go to waste. Likewise, David says: Although I ask to dwell in God's house forever, I do not wish to do so like a permanent resident who does not feel the compulsion to use his time wisely. My wish, therefore, is that I should feel like an excited visitor to whom every moment is precious.

Rabbi Tzvi Pesach Frank of Jerusalem interpreted David's request this way. David was not the kind of person who felt that one can serve God only in a closed, withdrawn environment. On the contrary, he sang, *'I shall walk before HASHEM in the land of the living'* (116:9), which the *Midrash (ibid.)* explains to mean 'even in the market places and boulevards of the great city.' Therefore, David's first request in this verse was: 'Let Your holy spirit accompany me wherever I go, so that even if I live in the worst of places, my home will be dedicated to Hashem.' However, at regular intervals the soul needs spiritual refreshment. Therefore, David asked for the additional privilege of periodically visiting the main הֵיכַל *'sanctuary'* of God to draw inspiration from the fountainhead.]

⁵ Indeed, He will treasure me in His Shelter
on the day of distress
In the concealment of His Tent,
He will lift me upon a rock.
⁶ Now my head is raised up
high above my enemies around me
I will offer in His Tent offerings of rejoicing.
I will sing and chant praise to HASHEM.
⁷ Hear, HASHEM, my voice when I call'
favor me and answer me.

Holies where he remained concealed for six years' (*II Kings* 11:1-3). [We find that the Temple is called סֻכַּת דָּוִיד *'the shelter of David'* in *Amos* 9:11].

בְּסֻכֹּה — *In His Shelter.*
[This word is spelled בְּסֻכָּה *'in a shelter'* but it is pronounced בְּסֻכּוֹ *'in His Shelter.'* David declares: Often, when I am in danger, *'a shelter'* seems to appear as if by chance. I am not misled. I am fully aware of the fact that God Himself has provided this salvation and that it is *'His Shelter.'*][1]

בְּיוֹם רָעָה — *On the day of distress.*
[The day when the entire House of David was nearly annihilated by Ataliah].

6. וְעַתָּה יָרוּם רֹאשִׁי עַל אֹיְבַי סְבִיבוֹתַי — *Now my head is raised up high above my enemies around me.*
David says: Now all this will come to pass at the moment when my fondest dreams are realized. That will be when I build the Temple and merit to have God's Presence dwell there. The same will happen when I sit down in the Temple courtyard alone, something no other man can do [for only kings of the House of David may sit there (*Sotah* 40b).] At that time [referred to as *'now'* i.e. a very special moment] all of my

detractors will shrink in shame and I will rise above them (*Alshich*).

בְּאָהֳלוֹ — *In His Tent.*
Targum translates this as מַשְׁכְּנֵיה *'His Tabernacle'* (which was called אֹהֶל מוֹעֵד *'the tent of meeting'*), [It refers, however, to the Temple, the permanent stone structure which David longed to build.]

זִבְחֵי תְרוּעָה — *Offerings of rejoicing.*
I will accompany my offerings with shouts of praise and thanksgiving in gratitude for salvation from my foes (*Radak*).
The words תְּרוּעָה and הִתְרוֹעֵעַ are frequently used in the Scriptures to express loud, exultant joy (*Psalms* 60:10, 65:14, 108:10; *Job* 8:21 and elsewhere) (*Hirsch*).
Ibn Ezra comments that this may be a literal תְּרוּעָה *'trumpet blast'* as we read, *'Also on the day of your joy ... you shall blow with your trumpets over your burnt-offerings and over the sacrifices of your peace offerings* (*Numbers* 10:10).

7. שְׁמַע ה' קוֹלִי אֶקְרָא — *Hear HASHEM my voice, when I call.*
In this verse David seems to have lost the tremendous confidence which he displayed in the preceding lines. The

---

1. Some say that the word בְּסֻכֹּה is the source of the custom to recite this psalm throughout the festival of *Succos. Vilna Gaon* finds many allusions to the commandments of Succos in this verse and the next (*Be'er Abraham*).

ט בַּקְשׁוּ פָנָי אֶת־פָּנֶיךָ יהוה אֲבַקֵּשׁ: אַל־
תַּסְתֵּר פָּנֶיךָ | מִמֶּנִּי אַל תַּט־בְּאַף עַבְדֶּךָ
עֶזְרָתִי הָיִיתָ אַל־תִּטְּשֵׁנִי וְאַל־תַּעַזְבֵנִי
י אֱלֹהֵי יִשְׁעִי: כִּי־אָבִי וְאִמִּי עֲזָבוּנִי וַיהוה
יא יַאַסְפֵנִי: הוֹרֵנִי יהוה דַּרְכֶּךָ וּנְחֵנִי בְּאֹרַח

reason is that previously David discussed the wars he waged against the armies of flesh and blood. In those battles David is confident of divine salvation. Now David turns his attention to the most difficult struggle of all, the conflict against the Evil Inclination — and he requires unprecedented assistance (Otzar Nechmad).

David directs his plea to HASHEM, the 'Attribute of Mercy.' David realizes that if he is judged strictly he will not deserve to be pardoned. He cannot verbally express himself in order to plead his cause. His thoughts are in disarray and he cannot organize them. All he can do is scream out wordlessly with his קוֹל 'voice' and plead for help (Tehillos Hashem; Yosef Tehillos. See Overview).[1]

The letters of שְׁמַע are the initials of שַׁחֲרִית, מִנְחָה, עַרְבִית 'the morning prayer, the afternoon prayer, and the evening prayer'. David asks God to hear him every time he calls out in prayer, thrice daily (Tehilla L'David).

8. לְךָ אָמַר לִבִּי בַּקְשׁוּ פָנָי — In Your behalf my heart has said, 'Seek My Presence' [lit. My Face].

Although David's one great request is lofty and praiseworthy (v. 4), he takes no credit for it; he attributes all to HASHEM. David declares that it was God Himself who implanted in his heart this noble aspiration and it was as if his

heart spoke to him as God's emissary (Rashi; Radak).

Meiri maintains that David said בַּקְשׁוּ פָנָי 'seek out my presence' in reference to himself. David insisted that his subjects should seek an audience with him so that they could pay him homage. But he did not do this for his own honor. Rather, his intention was that once they sought out his presence and were under his influence, he would teach them to seek out the Presence of God.

בַּקְשׁוּ פָנָי, can also be translated as 'seek out My face.' Before a person seeks out God's countenance, he must first purify and cleanse his own appearance to make sure that his features still are a semblance of צֶלֶם אֱלֹהִים 'God's image' (Eitz Hadaas Tov).

In this verse and in ther following one the word פָּנִים 'face' is mentioned three times. The Vilna Goan interprets from the Zohar that this alludes to the שָׁלֹשׁ רְגָלִים, the Three Festivals, when Israel is obligated to come to the Temple to present itself before the Face of God (Be'er Avraham).

אֶת פָּנֶיךָ ה' אֲבַקֵּשׁ — Your Presence, HASHEM, I do seek.

I hearken to the heavenly message implanted in my heart and I seek out Hashem (Rashi).

9. אַל תַּסְתֵּר פָּנֶיךָ מִמֶּנִּי — Conceal not Your Presence from me.

My heart yearns for Your Presence,

---

1. Vilna Gaon explains that this verse alludes to the Days of Awe. שְׁמַע ה' קוֹלִי, 'Hear HASHEM my voice' refers to Rosh Hashona when we blow the קוֹל שׁוֹפָר 'the sound (voice) of the shofar.' אֶקְרָא 'when I call' refers to Yom Kippur, which the Prophet describes as קְרָאֻהוּ בִּהְיוֹתוֹ קָרוֹב 'Call to Him when He is near' (Isaiah 55:6). What do we plead for on Yom Kippur? וְחָנֵּנִי וַעֲנֵנִי, 'show me favor and answer me' (Be'er Abraham).

8 *In Your behalf, my heart has said,*
   'Seek My Presence.'
Your Presence, HASHEM, I do seek.
9 *Conceal not Your Presence from me,*
   repel not Your servant in anger.
You have been my Helper,
Abandon me not, forsake me not,
   O God of my salvation.
10 *Though my father and mother have forsaken me,*
   HASHEM will gather me in.
11 *Instruct me, HASHEM, in Your way*
   and lead me on the path of integrity

but there are two ways in which my hopes can be dashed. The first way is that You will conceal Yourself from me (*Malbim*).

Sometimes God is angry with a sinful person and wishes to deny him a share in the Hereafter. For this reason, He rewards him for his good deeds in This World. The recipient sees that God is showing him a benign and friendly face and imagines that he enjoys God's favor. The truth, however, is the reverse — God is concealing his anger behind this friendly appearance. David requested that God's feelings should be revealed to him; that God's true Presence never be hidden from him (*Panim Yofos*).

אַל תַּט בְּאַף עַבְדֶּךָ — *Repel* [lit. *turn away*] *not Your servant in anger.*

The second way to prevent me from coming close is by becoming so angry at me that the punishment will break my faith and take away my desire to cling to such a wrathful God (*Malbim*).

עֶזְרָתִי הָיִיתָ — *You have been my Helper.*

In the past You helped me fill all my physical needs. Do not disappoint me when I ask for my spiritual needs (*Radak*).

אַל תִּטְּשֵׁנִי וְאַל תַּעַזְבֵנִי — *Abandon me not, forsake me not.*

Do not allow me to become preoccupied with the affairs of this world which breed only frustration and disappointment (*Radak*).

עֲזִיבָה, *'forsaking'* indicates a complete severing of all ties. It is far more serious than נְטִישָׁה, *'abandonment'*, which is only a partial estrangement (*Alshich*).

10. כִּי אָבִי וְאִמִּי עֲזָבוּנִי — *Though my father and mother have forsaken me.* After youth and adolescence they sent me out on my own (*Sforno*).

11. הוֹרֵנִי ה' דַּרְכֶּךָ וּנְחֵנִי בְּאֹרַח מִישׁוֹר — *Instruct me HASHEM in Your way and lead me on the path of integrity* [lit. *'uprightness'*].

Continuing his request to come before the presence of God (v. 8 & 9), David now asks that HASHEM show him the way. However, the routes leading to HASHEM are many. Some are direct, some indirect. Some have obstacles and dangerous pitfalls, some don't. Therefore David asks, 'In my pursuit of Your Presence, lead me on the straight path' (*Akeida*).

[Cf. *Psalms 86:11* הוֹרֵנִי ה' דַּרְכֶּךָ אֲהַלֵּךְ בַּאֲמִתֶּךָ *'Instruct me HASHEM in Your way so that I may walk in Your truth.'* Rambam comments (*Hilchos Teshuva 6:4*): in their prayers, the

יב מִישׁוֹר לְמַעַן שׁוֹרְרָי: אַל־תִּתְּנֵנִי בְּנֶפֶשׁ
צָרָי כִּי קָמוּ־בִי עֵדֵי־שֶׁקֶר וִיפֵחַ חָמָס:
יג לוּלֵא הֶאֱמַנְתִּי לִרְאוֹת בְּטוּב־יהוה
בְּאֶרֶץ חַיִּים: קַוֵּה אֶל־יהוה חֲזַק וְיַאֲמֵץ
לִבֶּךָ וְקַוֵּה אֶל־יהוה:

righteous people and the prophets ask God to assist them in perceiving the truth, as David said, 'Instruct me HASHEM in Your way.' In other words, he requested, 'Do not let my sins prevent me from following the true path which leads to an understanding of Your ways and the Oneness of Your Name.']

לְמַעַן שׁוֹרְרָי — Because of my watchful foes.

I.e. in order to frustrate my enemies who enviously and maliciously seek out my flaws and scrutinize my ways [from שׁוּר, to stare] in order to wound me with vicious criticism. They claim that I have no share in HASHEM (Radak).

Ibn Ezra offers this pithy comment: One of the wise of heart once said, 'He who wishes to overcome his enemies should overwhelm them by increasing his service of God'. [Therefore David asks that God show him the most preferred form of service.]

12. בְּנֶפֶשׁ צָרָי — To the wishes [lit. 'soul'] of my tormentors.

We find the word נֶפֶשׁ in the phrase אִם יֵשׁ אֶת נַפְשְׁכֶם 'If it is Your wish (Genesis 23:8; Metzudas Zion).

Do not let them realize their heart's desire which is to engage me in battle so that I am prevented from concentrating on perfection of the soul (Radak).

וִיפֵחַ חָמָס — Who breathe [lit. and breather of] violence.

This describes speech which depends upon הַפָּחַת הָרוּחַ 'the breath of the mouth' (Metzudas Zion).

These false witnesses testify that I am a man of חָמָס, 'violence' and bloodshed

and am thus cut off from God (Radak).

It is written יָפִיחַ כְּזָבִים עֵד שֶׁקֶר 'The lying witness breathes falsehoods' (Prov. 6:19). This refers to Doeg, the Edomite, and the people of Zif who slandered David (Ibn Yachya).

13. לוּלֵא הֶאֱמַנְתִּי לִרְאוֹת בְּטוּב ה' — Had I not believed in beholding [lit. 'to see'] the goodness [lit. 'in the goodness'] of HASHEM.

If not for my faith, these false witnesses would have destroyed me long ago. I never stopped believing that I too am worthy of a portion in the World to Come, and so I ignored them and continued to serve God with devotion (Rashi; Radak).

However, the Talmud (Berachos 4a) relates that although David did not take the slanderous, false accusations of his enemies to heart, he never doubted that he was, indeed, guilty of some wrongdoing and this did, indeed, shake his confidence. It is taught in the name of Rabbi Yosi, 'Why are special dots placed on the word לוּלֵא? David said to the Holy One, Blessed be He. Sovereign of the Universe! I firmly believe that You will give just reward to the righteous in the World to Come. However, I do not know if I will be among them, for I am fearful that my sins may cause me to be repelled'! (Maharsha ibid. explains that only the letters לא are dotted from top and bottom, whereas the others are dotted only at the top. This suggests that the word may be read also לֹא הֶאֱמַנְתִּי 'I did not believe' which alludes to David's self-doubt aroused by his sins).[1]

XXVII — because of my watchful foes.

12-14 12 Deliver me not to the wishes of my tormentors.
For there have arisen against me false witnesses
who breathe violence.
13 Had I not believed in beholding
the goodness of HASHEM in the land of life —
14 Place confidence in HASHEM, strengthen yourself
and He will give you courage;
And place confidence in HASHEM.

בְּאֶרֶץ חַיִּים — *In the land of life.*

Metzudas Zion holds that this world is called 'the land of life'. *Malbim* identifies it as the Land of Israel. These lines were uttered after false witnesses incited Saul's jealousy to such a violent intensity that David was forced to flee from the Holy Land. But he never wavered in his faith in God's promise that someday he would return to be King of Israel in the 'Land of Holy Life.'

Rambam (Hilchos Teshuva 8:7) follows the opinion of the Talmud (*Berachos* 4a) that 'the land of life' refers to the World to Come. *Radak* explains that although the Hereafter is a purely spiritual experience, the Scriptures try to offer us a glimpse of its wonders by describing them with terms and illustrations drawn from the material world. The Garden of Eden is an actual place on earth, indeed, it is the finest place. Therefore, the Paradise of the Hereafter is often likened to it. Similarly, David here calls the Hereafter 'the land of life'. In the same vein, the fiery inferno of Hell, which is reserved for punishing the souls of the wicked, is called גֵּיהִנָּם *Gehinnom* after גֵּי בֶן הִנֹּם *'The Valley of Ben Hinnom* near Jerusalem (*Eruvin* 19a), a disgusting garbage dump where people would throw putrid carcasses and unclean objects to be burned in a fire which raged

there perpetually. No place on earth could provide a better illustration of the eternal flame which will burn the repulsive sinners in the Hereafter.

14. קַוֵּה אֶל ה' — *Place confidence in* [lit. *hope to*] *HASHEM.*

Because of my boundless faith in HASHEM I hope for His aid at all times and pay no heed to my enemies (*Radak*).

חֲזַק וְיַאֲמֵץ לִבֶּךָ — *Strengthen yourself and He will give you courage* [lit. *make your heart strong*].

If you make every effort to strengthen yourself in HASHEM's service, He will reciprocate by instilling courage in your heart so that your enemies will not weaken your resolve (*Radak*).

Just as 'He who strives to purify himself is given assistance' (*Yoma* 38b); so too, he who strives to strengthen himself in faith is assisted from above in gaining strength (*Alshich*).

Malbim observes that hoping for God's help is greatly different from hoping for the aid of man. Woe unto the unfortunate soul who must beg for the favors of others! Heartache, despondency, and disillusionment are his lot. Not so with God. Hoping for Him is an exhilarating experience which brings encouragement and renewed strength.

1. The word לוּלֵא spelled backwards becomes אֱלוּל, *'Elul'* the month preceding *Rosh Hashanah*. This alludes to the custom of reciting this Psalm throughout the entire month of *'Elul'*.

וְקַוֵּה אֶל ה' — *And place confidence in HASHEM.*

The Talmud (*Berachos* 32b) interprets this verse as referring to the techniques of prayer. 'Rabbi Chama bar Chanina said: If one prays but is not answered let him reinforce himself and pray again as it says *'Place confidence in HASHEM'* — [but if the first hopeful prayer doesn't help] *'strengthen yourself and He will give you courage and* [you will once again] *place confidence in HASHEM* [and pray].

Four pursuits require חִזוּק, *'constant exertion and effort with all of one's might' (Rashi).* They are Torah study, performance of good deeds, prayer, and pursuit of a livelihood. We learn, from the above verse, that prayer needs constant devotion.

Malbim continues to explain how placing confidence in HASHEM differs from putting one's faith in man: Hoping for the aid of flesh and blood is certainly not a goal to be desired. At best it can be tolerated as an unpleasant means towards an end. Indeed, one longs for the realization of the end purpose so that this means will no longer be necessary. Such is not the case with hoping for HASHEM. This hope is itself a desirable goal as it demonstrates an intensive level of pure faith. Thus, the Psalmist continues to repeat that he hopes for HASHEM even though he has already hoped and was fortified with an answer.

Harav Yitzchak Zev HaLevi Soloveitchik, the Brisker Rav, explains the repitition in the light of a statement by the *Chovos Halevavos (Sh'aar Habitachon)* who describes בִּטָחוֹן *'trust'* in HASHEM as the most wonderful experience which life has to offer, far surpassing all earthly fortunes. Since trusting in HASHEM is the highest commandment, it deserves a proportionately great reward. This world can offer nothing which is as great as *'trust'* itself. Thus, David declares, *'Place confidence in HASHEM'* and your reward will be that God will strengthen your heart to achieve even higher levels of intense faith; *'and place* [even more] *confidence in HASHEM!'*

מזמור כח 28

The theme of this psalm is similar to that of the preceding one. Once again David calls upon Hashem to release him from temporal responsibilities so that he can devote himself completely to God's service. This tranquility will enable him to fully repent his past sins and will afford him the opportunity to ascend ever higher and closer to Hashem (Radak).

א לְדָוִד אֵלֶיךָ יהוה | אֶקְרָא צוּרִי אַל־
תֶּחֱרַשׁ מִמֶּנִּי פֶּן־תֶּחֱשֶׁה מִמֶּנִּי וְנִמְשַׁלְתִּי
ב עִם־יוֹרְדֵי בוֹר: שְׁמַע קוֹל תַּחֲנוּנַי בְּשַׁוְּעִי
ג אֵלֶיךָ בְּנָשְׂאִי יָדַי אֶל־דְּבִיר קָדְשֶׁךָ: אַל־
תִּמְשְׁכֵנִי עִם־רְשָׁעִים וְעִם־פֹּעֲלֵי אָוֶן
דֹּבְרֵי שָׁלוֹם עִם־רֵעֵיהֶם וְרָעָה בִּלְבָבָם:

1. לְדָוִד — *Of David.*

This psalm was composed either by David or by one of the Temple musicians who dedicated it to him (*Ibn Ezra*).

אֵלֶיךָ ה׳ אֶקְרָא — *To You HASHEM I call.*

Israel says: 'We have no portion other than Hashem.' Hashem says: 'I have no portion other than Israel.' Therefore, when Israel prays, Hashem answers them immediately, as it says 'To You, HASHEM, I call' [fully confident of Your instant response.] (*Midrash Shocher Tov*).

צוּרִי — *My rock.* The Talmud (*Megillah* 14a) expounding on the verse אֵין צוּר כֵּאלֹהֵינוּ, 'There is no rock like our God' (*I Samuel* 2:2) comments: 'Do not read this word as צוּר 'rock' but as צַיָּיר 'artist, sculptor'. A man draws a form on a wall but he cannot endow it with life, but the Holy One, Blessed be He creates a form within a form [an embryo inside the mother] and bestows it with breath and a soul, internal organs and intestines. Therefore, there is no creative 'sculptor' like our God. David echoes those words in this verse, saying, צוּרִי (צַיָּירִי) 'my sculptor', 'since You took the pains to be my צַיָּיר, 'artist' who meticulously fashioned every atom of my body with loving care, it is not fitting that now You should abandon me — for I am Your creation (*Tehillos Hashem*).

אַל תֶּחֱרַשׁ מִמֶּנִּי — *Be not mute to me* i.e. do not be silent and oblivious to my prayer (*Metzudas Zion*).

[חֵרֵשׁ is a 'deaf-mute'. Therefore *Radak* explains that David requests that

God not be deaf to his plea, because then He inevitably will become mute and unresponsive as well.]

פֶּן־תֶּחֱשֶׁה מִמֶּנִּי — *For should You be indifferent* [lit. 'lest if You be silenced'] *to me.*

Malbim notes that תֶּחֱשֶׁה 'You are silenced' is the opposite of voicing an opinion. David says: Do not be mute when the time comes to reply and react to the insults hurled at me by my enemies, and do not refrain from speaking out in my favor when that becomes necessary.

וְנִמְשַׁלְתִּי עִם יוֹרְדֵי בוֹר — *[And] I would be likened to those who have gone down to the pit.*

I fear that if You will be deaf to my pleas, You will lose all interest in me and then I will resemble those for whom You have no concern at all, i.e. those who descend to the grave and never arise again to be in Your presence (*Radak*) [cf. 55:24.]

I fear that You will cease to supervise my life intimately and that You will leave me at the mercy of the unguided course of nature. I prefer that You roar harsh words of rebuke at me, than to let me be a great success with Your face concealed from me and Your lips mute (*Nir L'David*).

2. בְּנָשְׂאִי יָדַי — *When I lift up my hands.*

Like a helpless person who stretches out his hands in desperation, gesturing to others to grasp his hands and save him (*Radak*).

To You, HASHEM, I call,
   my Rock, be not mute to me.
For should You be indifferent to me
   I would be likened to those
   who have gone down to the pit.
² Hear the sound of my pleading
   when I cry out to You for help,
When I lift up my hands
   towards Your Holy Sanctuary.
³ Draw me not to the wicked
   and to those who perfom wrong-doing;
Those who speak peacefully with their companions
   though evil is in their hearts.

אֶל דְּבִיר קָדְשֶׁךָ — *Towards Your Holy Sanctuary.*

I.e. the קוֹדֶשׁ הַקֳדָשִׁים, *'the Holy of Holies'* where the Holy Ark containing the Tablets of the Covenant rested. That is where God's presence dwells. Or perhaps this refers to the heavens, the place of God's throne. The hands raised up high, symbolize a ladder upon which prayers ascend skyward (*Radak*).

3. אַל תִּמְשְׁכֵנִי עִם רְשָׁעִים — *Draw me not to* [lit. *with*] *the wicked.*

Let me not be drawn into their company, to be accustomed to their ways. Help the circumstances of my life work out in such a way that my path does not cross theirs (*Rashi; Ibn Ezra*).

However, according to *Radak* and *Metzudas David* this means, 'Do not draw me away from this world together with the wicked when they are dragged away to death and punishment in the Hereafter.'

Eretz HaChaim explains that often God purposely makes problems for the righteous because He desires the prayers which they utter in pure sincerity as a result of distress. However, David asks God not to treat him thus. He requests that God should

hear his plea immediately (*v.* 2). Otherwise, his enemies will interpret his incessant affliction as a sign of divine displeasure and this will strengthen their false claims that he is among the wicked. This is the meaning of David's prayer, *'Draw me not to the wicked'* i.e. do not treat me like them so that my enemies will have no opportunity to identify me with them.

וְרָעָה בִּלְבָבָם — *Though* [lit. *'and'*] *evil is in their hearts.*

The לֵב, *'heart'* has two opposite elements, the desire for good and the desire for evil. Wherever the Scriptures wish to describe this duality, the word is spelled with a double 'ב' as לֵבָב. David tells us that these men are so thoroughly corrupted that even the erstwhile good half of their לֵבָב, *'heart'* is filled with רָעָה *'evil'* (*Chomas Anoch*).

Alshich explains: The רְשָׁעִים are evil towards God; the פֹּעֲלֵי אָוֶן act criminally towards their fellow men. But *'those who speak peacefully with their companions though evil is in their heart'* are the hypocrites who are the most dangerous of all. [King Yannai gave his wife the following advice before he died. 'Have no fear of the [righteous]

ד תֶּן־לָהֶם כְּפָעֳלָם וּכְרֹעַ מַעַלְלֵיהֶם
כְּמַעֲשֵׂה יְדֵיהֶם תֵּן לָהֶם הָשֵׁב גְּמוּלָם
ה לָהֶם: כִּי לֹא יָבִינוּ אֶל־פְּעֻלֹּת יהוה וְאֶל־
ו מַעֲשֵׂה יָדָיו יֶהֶרְסֵם וְלֹא יִבְנֵם: בָּרוּךְ
ז יהוה כִּי־שָׁמַע קוֹל תַּחֲנוּנָי: יהוה | עֻזִּי
וּמָגִנִּי בּוֹ בָטַח לִבִּי וְנֶעֱזָרְתִּי וַיַּעֲלֹז לִבִּי
ח וּמִשִּׁירִי אֲהוֹדֶנּוּ: יהוה עֹז־לָמוֹ וּמָעוֹז

Pharisees or the [unrighteous] Sadducees. Fear only the צְבוּעִין, 'the painted ones' who masquerade as Pharisees [but are truly irreligious]. Their evil deeds are like those of Zimri, (the wicked prince) yet they seek rewards fit for Pinchos [the righteous zealot] (*Sotah* 22b)].

4. פָּעֳלָם .... מַעַלְלֵיהֶם .... מַעֲשֵׂה יְדֵיהֶם — *Their deeds ... their malice ... their handiwork.*

Malbim gives a precise definition for each of these words. פָּעַל refers to the effort exerted to achieve something. מַעֲשֶׂה, describes the final accomplishment. עֲלִילָה, denotes a deed which was stimulated by a deep character trait or an emotion which found expression through this action. Here the עֲלִילָה was spurred by the malicious streak inside the perpetrators.

הָשֵׁב גְּמוּלָם לָהֶם — *Render* [lit. 'return'] *to them their recompense.*

Repay them for their evil deeds immediately and in full measure. The *Midrash* (*Ruth* 1:5) teaches: 'The Merciful One never begins His retribution by taking a human life.' God first warns man by depriving him of his property, his house, his clothes. Only after that, if man does not repent, does God smite him in his person. David argues that these men are so corrupt and oblivious to God that they surely will never heed preliminary warnings. Therefore, God may give them their fully deserved

punishment immediately (*Yosef Tehillos*).

5. כִּי לֹא יָבִינוּ אֶל פְּעֻלֹת ה׳ — *For they comprehend not* [to] *the deeds of HASHEM.*

They use their intellectual endowments to understand the foolish, worthless trifles of this world but they completely neglect the service of God. To inspect and scrutinize the wonders of nature and creation is an essential aspect of serving God, for in this way one fortifies his faith in God as Creator and First Cause (*Radak*). [See Psalm 8, Prefatory Remarks.]

Midrash Shocher Tov describes a number of ways by which they neglect the deeds of Hashem: They pay no heed to the wonders of the interplanetary rotation and the order of seasons. They do not study the 'Agaddos' [the homiletical stories of the *Talmud* which instill fear of God]. They do not recite the blessings of the Shema, in which we bless God as יוֹצֵר אוֹר, 'the Creator of light.'

יֶהֶרְסֵם — *May He tear them down.*

David prays that since the evildoers neglect God's works and consider them to be worthless, may their own projects and undertakings be demolished, measure for measure (*Radak*).

6. בָּרוּךְ ה׳ — *Blessed be HASHEM.*

The prayers uttered by men on earth add strength and blessings to Hashem in heaven above (*Eretz HaChaim*).

XXVIII ⁴ *Give them according to their deeds*
and according to the evil of their malice;
According to their handiwork give them;
render to them their recompense.
⁵ *For they comprehend not the deeds of* HASHEM
nor His handiwork.
May He tear them down and not rebuild them.
⁶ *Blessed be* HASHEM,
for He has heard the sound of my pleading.
⁷ HASHEM *is my strength and my shield,*
my heart trusts in Him,
I was helped and my heart exulted,
with my song I give Him thanks.

כִּי שָׁמַע קוֹל תַּחֲנוּנָי — *For He has heard the sound of my pleading.*

David here is prophetically foretelling the future as if it had already occurred. Indeed, God did fulfill David's great wish for tranquility in his old age. This took place when David's warriors swore that they would no longer allow him to expose himself to danger and they insisted that he stay home while they waged his battles for him (II Sam. 21:17) (Radak).

7. ה' עֻזִּי וּמָגִנִּי — HASHEM *is my strength and my shield.*

When He saved me from the giant Yishbi at Nob. ('... *The weight of his spear was three hundred shekalim of copper and he was girded with a new sword'* — II Sam. 21:16) (Radak).

בּוֹ בָטַח לִבִּי — *My heart trusts in Him.*

Although I was in mortal danger I never doubted that He would save me (Radak).

וְנֶעֱזָרְתִּי וַיַּעֲלֹז לִבִּי — [And] *I was helped and my heart exults.*

It would be superfluous to say that David's heart rejoiced when he was saved from death, therefore, we must

say that לִבִּי refers to David's mind, which now rejoiced in its new-found freedom. As mentioned previously, after David narrowly escaped a gruesome death at the hands of the vicious giant Yishbi, his troops reacted with loyalty '*Then the men of David swore to him, saying, "You shall no longer go out with us to battle so that you will not extinguish the lamp of Israel"'* (II Sam. 21:17). This finally freed David's mind from worldly problems and afforded his intellect an opportunity to enrich itself in spiritual study. Therefore his mind now rejoiced (Radak).

וּמִשִּׁירִי אֲהוֹדֶנּוּ — *With* [lit. *'and from']* *my song I give Him thanks.*

Rabbi Moshe HaCohen (quoted by Ibn Ezra) explains this as '*From more than this one song I shall give Him thanks'.*

David said: I know clearly that the songs of praise which I sing to God, help me more in battle than all weapons of war. Therefore, I shall use these very songs of prayer and praise to give God thanks for victory (Mahari Yaavetz Hadoresh).

ט יְשׁוּעוֹת מְשִׁיחוֹ הוּא: הוֹשִׁיעָה| אֶת־עַמֶּךָ
וּבָרֵךְ אֶת־נַחֲלָתֶךָ וּרְעֵם וְנַשְּׂאֵם עַד־
הָעוֹלָם:

8. עֹז ה' — *HASHEM is strength.*

Now that David was free to remain in the House of God, he devotedly prayed for the welfare of Israel, specifically that they should continue to be strong of heart and courageous despite his absence from their ranks. He assures Israel that Hashem is their strength whether or not he, David is among them (*Radak*).

לָמוֹ — *To them* i.e. to those who depend upon Him (*Rashi*).

Ibn Ezra explains this to be a contraction of לְעַמּוֹ *'to His nation'*.

9. הוֹשִׁיעָה אֶת עַמֶּךָ וּבָרֵךְ אֶת נַחֲלָתֶךָ — *Save Your nation and bless Your estate.*

'Save' them from their enemies in war, and *'bless'* their handiwork in peace (*Radak*).

The first time the land of Israel was apportioned as a נַחֲלָה *'estate'* it was done by a human being, Joshua, whose accomplishments lasted for only a limited time. This was because God knew that the people were destined to be exiled and deprived of their inheritance. But, in the future, God Himself will redeem Israel and return them from exile.

Since this future re-settlement will endure for all time, the eternal God will Himself apportion the everlasting נַחֲלוֹת *'estates'*, not entrusting this task to a mortal man.

Thus we read: *'Save Your nation'* from exile, *and bless Your estate*, i.e., the one which You apportion personally. For Your *'tend them and elevate them forever'* and place them above their enemies, and so their inheritance will never again be taken away from them (*Shevet Me Yisrael*).[1]

XXVIII ⁸ *HASHEM is strength to them,*
8-9   *He is the stronghold of salvation*
     for His anointed.
     ⁹ *Save Your nation, and bless Your estate,*
     tend them and elevate them forever.

וּרְעֵם — *Tend them.*

This is similar to מִרְעֶה, *'pasture, grazing land' (Rashi).* [i.e. Treat them gently as a shepherd who grazes and tends to his flocks.]

The word רְעֵם, may also be derived from רֵעַ, *'friend, dear one'.* David asks Hashem to treat Israel lovingly as a cherished friend *(Kiflayim L'Sushiya).*

וְנַשְׂאֵם — *And elevate them.*

Above their enemies *(Radak).*

Be like the shepherd who brings his flock to high terrain to save them from beasts of prey *(Ibn Ezra).*

עַד הָעוֹלָם — *Forever.*

My prayer for Israel is not only for my days; I desire their success until the end of time *(Radak).*

1. *Tehillas Hashem* explains this verse according to a story related by the Talmud *(Kesubos* 112a): Rabbi Yehoshua ben Levi visited the town of Gavla and saw giant clusters of grapes which looked like calves. He said: 'There seem to be calves walking among the vines!' The local people told him, 'Those are not calves, those are the giant clusters of grapes.' Rabbi Yehoshua exclaimed 'Eretz, Eretz! Land, O land! Take back your fruits! For the sake of whom do you bring forth your fruits? For these Arabs who stand as oppressors over us because of our sins?' At the end of the year Rav Chiya visited the same place and the clusters appeared to be like small goats [they had shrunk considerably as a result of Rabbi Yehoshua's request]. He said, 'There seem to be goats walking among the vines!' The local people shouted, 'Go away from here! Don't do to us what your colleague did!'

Therefore David prays to Hashem *'Save Your nation'* and return them from exile to their land of Israel. *'And bless Your estate.'* Then, when the gentiles are expelled and the rightful owners return, the land which is Israel's rightful inheritance can be blessed and give forth its full richness.

T his psalm is related to the preceding one in which David vowed to thank God for giving him might, 'HASHEM is my might and my shield … and from my songs I shall give him thanks' (28:7). Rashbam maintains that this magnificent psalm was composed to fulfill that vow. It also serves as an introduction to the following one which is dedicated to חֲנֻכַּת הַבַּיִת לְדָוִד 'The inauguration of the House [i.e. the Temple] to David.'

The words of this Psalm bear a striking resemblance to the songs which David sang as he transferred the Holy Ark from its temporary shelter in the house of Oved Edom to its permanent abode in Jerusalem. At that time he sang: הָבוּ לַה' מִשְׁפְּחוֹת עַמִּים הָבוּ לַה' כָּבוֹד וָעֹז. הָבוּ לַה' כְּבוֹד שְׁמוֹ שְׂאוּ מִנְחָה וּבֹאוּ לְפָנָיו הִשְׁתַּחֲווּ לַה' בְּהַדְרַת קֹדֶשׁ (I Chron. 16:28-29).

Those words are almost an exact replica of the first two verses of this Psalm. This strongly implies that this Psalm was sung when the ark traveled to Jerusalem in preparation for the inauguration of the Temple (haMikra V'haMesora 5).

א מִזְמוֹר לְדָוִד הָבוּ לַיהוה בְּנֵי אֵלִים הָבוּ
ב לַיהוה כָּבוֹד וָעֹז: הָבוּ לַיהוה כְּבוֹד שְׁמוֹ
ג הִשְׁתַּחֲווּ לַיהוה בְּהַדְרַת־קֹדֶשׁ: קוֹל
יהוה עַל־הַמָּיִם אֵל־הַכָּבוֹד הִרְעִים יהוה

1. 'הָבוּ לַה — *Prepare for HASHEM.*

This translation follows *Rashi* and *Malbim* who quote similar examples of this usage as in לוֹ נִתְחַכְּמָה הָבָה *'Prepare yourselves let us plan wisely against them'* (Ex. 1:10 see *Rashi*, ibid.)

However, many commentaries render the word הָבוּ as *'give'*, as in אֶת הָבָה אִשְׁתִּי, *'give me my wife'* (Gen. 29:21) (*Radak, Ibn Ezra, Menachem, Metzudos*). Here it means *'give words of praise to HASHEM.'*

בְּנֵי אֵלִים — *You sons of the powerful.*

Similarly, we find (Ex. 15:15) אֵילֵי מוֹאָב, *'the powerful ones of Moab'* (*Metzudas Zion*). According to *Rashi*, אֵלִים are *'officers, nobles'*. *Ibn Ezra* says that it refers to the stars which are called בְּנֵי אֱלֹהִים (Job 38:7).

The *Targum* renders this as כָּתֵּי מַלְאֲכַיָּא בְּנֵי אֵלִים, *'The groups of angels, the sons of the powerful.'* It is the ministering angels who are called upon to give praise to God.

The Sages say that אֵלִים refers to the Patriarchs who were 1) אֵלִים — *powerful in their faith.* 2) אֵילִים — *rams.* Because they allowed themselves to be slaughtered like animals for God's sake, particularly Isaac who was prepared to allow himself to be sacrificed by Abraham (*Midrash Shocher Tov*). 3) Read it as if it were אִלְּמִים — *'mute':* Often the Patriarchs could have spoken back to God audaciously and refused to obey his commands, but they remained silent (*Midrash Bereishis Rabba* 56:10).

Finally, the Talmud (*Megillah* 17b) asks: 'From where do we have an allu-

sion upon which to base the first benediction of the *Shemoneh Esrei*, which is dedicated to the *Avos*, Patriarchs? From this Psalm which begins "Prepare for HASHEM, you sons of the powerful [Patriarchs]."[1]

'הָבוּ לַה' כָּבוֹד וָעֹז — *Prepare for HASHEM honor and might.*

The same words appear in *Psalms* 96:7 and *I Chronicles* 16:28.]

Praise God and proclaim: 'Glory and might belong to HASHEM!' (*Metzudas David*).

Radak (translating הָבוּ as *'give'*) cites similar verses as in תְּנוּ לַה' אֱלֹהֵיכֶם כָּבוֹד, *'Give glory to HASHEM your God'* (Jer. 13:16), and תְּנוּ עֹז לֵאלֹהִים, *'Give might to God'* (Psalms 68:35).

The Talmud (*Megillah* 17b) continues:

'How do we know that the second benediction of *Shemoneh Esrei* is dedicated to God's גְּבוּרוֹת, *'His might'*? [The benediction begins גִּבּוֹר אַתָּה לְעוֹלָם ה', *'You are mighty forever HASHEM'*] Because the second phrase of psalm 29 is *'Prepare for HASHEM glory and might.'*

2. הָבוּ לַה' כְּבוֹד שְׁמוֹ — *Prepare for HASHEM the honor due His Name.*

This tells us that we must be prepared to sanctify and glorify God's Name. His Name is repeated eighteen times in this Psalm and therefore the Rabbis included eighteen benedictions in the *Shemoneh Esrei* (*Rashi*).

הִשְׁתַּחֲווּ לַה' בְּהַדְרַת קֹדֶשׁ — *Prostrate*

1. [The Sages noted the astounding strength and stamina which the Patriarchs exercised in the service of HASHEM. This strength was derived from their daily prayers which infused them with a divine vigor. Centuries later, when the Sages formulated a uniform, universal liturgy consisting of eighteen benedictions, they modeled their prayers after those of the Avos. In doing so, they drew heavily upon this psalm as a source of inspiration as will be demonstrated.]

A song of David:
Prepare for HASHEM, you sons of the powerful,
prepare for HASHEM, honor and might.
² Prepare for HASHEM the honor due His Name,
prostrate yourselves before HASHEM,
in the splendor of holiness.
³ The voice of HASHEM is upon the waters,

---

yourselves before HASHEM, in the splendor of holiness.

הָדָר literally means 'honor' as in וְהָדַרְתָּ פְּנֵי זָקֵן, 'honor the presence of the elder' (Lev. 19:32). This verse may be paraphrased: 'Give verbal homage and honor to HASHEM' [through prayer] (Radak).

'How do we know that the third benediction of *Shemoneh Esrei* is dedicated to HASHEM's קְדוּשׁוֹת sanctities? [אַתָּה קָדוֹשׁ וְשִׁמְךָ קָדוֹשׁ, 'You are holy and Your Name is holy'] Because the third phrase in psalm 29 is 'Prepare for HASHEM the glory due His Name, bow down to HASHEM in sacred (sanctified) splendor' (Megillah ibid.).

The Rabbis of the Talmud (*Berachos* 30b) derive yet another principle of prayer from this verse. 'One should rise to pray only when he is in a mood of solemnity and seriousness ... Rabbi Yehoshua learns this from the words הִשְׁתַּחֲווּ לַה' בְּהַדְרַת קֹדֶשׁ. Don't read the word as הַדְרַת 'splendor' but rather as חֶרְדַּת 'trembling and awe' [in the presence of קֹדֶשׁ, 'sancitity'].

3. קוֹל ה' עַל הַמָּיִם — *The voice of HASHEM is upon the waters.*

The first קוֹל refers to the waters of the Red Sea which were parted by God's voice (Rashi).

Or it describes the mighty rainwaters which are the source of all growth (Ibn Ezra).

In this psalm, seven קוֹלוֹת, 'voices', of Hashem are described. They symbolize the seven main forms through which He reveals himself on earth.

Rashbam demonstrates how each 'voice' corresponds to the development of creation on the first five days before the advent of man. The first: 'Voice of HASHEM over the waters', alludes to the first day of creation when, 'the spirit of God hovered on the face of the water' (Genesis 1:2).

[The Mussaf service of the Sabbath contains only seven benedictions. The Talmud (*Berachos* 29a) says that this number is based on the seven 'voices' of God recorded in this psalm. Furthermore, after the Torah reading on the Sabbath, the Torah is accompanied back to the Ark while the congregation recites this psalm. *Tur* and *Bayis Chadash* in *Orach Chaim* 284 explain that since the seven benedictions of the Mussaf service (which follows immediately after replacing the Torah in the Ark) are derived from this Psalm, and this Psalm itself describes the giving of the Torah in detail, therefore its recital at this time is most appropriate.] [1]

---

1. The Talmud (*Sukkah* 55a) rules that the Levites should recite this psalm in the Temple on the first intermediate·day of *Succos* as the שִׁיר שֶׁל יוֹם, 'Song of the Day.' *Rashi (ibid.)* explains that this psalm describes the שִׂמְחַת בֵּית הַשּׁוֹאֵבָה, 'The Rejoicing of Drawing the Water', which began on the first night of the Intermediate Days. The exhortation 'Prepare for HASHEM honor and might' (v. 1) describes the mighty effort which was made to glorify God's Name with incomparable celebration at that time.

Rambam, Hilchos Lulav 8:15 cites David as the perfect example of how one should

ד עַל־מַיִם רַבִּים: קוֹל־יהוה בַּכֹּחַ קוֹל יהוה
ה בֶּהָדָר: קוֹל יהוה שֹׁבֵר אֲרָזִים וַיְשַׁבֵּר

אֶל הַכָּבוֹד הָרְעִים — *The God of glory thunders.*

In regard to the splitting of the sea, David said previously 'ה בַּשָּׁמַיִם וַיַּרְעֵם, וְעֶלְיוֹן יִתֵּן קֹלוֹ, 'HASHEM thundered at them in the heavens and the Most High sent forth His voice' (Psalms 18:14) (Rashi).

[Originally, the אַנְשֵׁי כְנֶסֶת הַגְדוֹלָה, *Sages of the Great Assembly,* instituted only eighteen benedictions. However, after the destruction of the Second Temple, Israel was plagued by heretics who sought to convert Jews to Christianity by threatening to slander them to the merciless Roman government. At that time, Rabban Gamliel of Yavne introduced a nineteenth benediction cursing the מַלְשִׁינִים *'slanderous tale-bearers.'* The Talmud (Berachos 28b) finds an allusion to that additional benediction in the words *'the God of glory thunders',* i.e., against the heretics who arouse His full wrath.]

ה' עַל מַיִם רַבִּים — *HASHEM is over vast waters.*

Radak cites the opinion of the Sages that this verse depicts the great voice of God which descended from heaven on the day the Torah was given at Sinai, first travelling over the vast waters. *Radak* concludes with his own opinion that the Psalm describes the Messianic era. The gentile nations are likened to the seas because in this world they are as calm and placid as the peaceful sea, lulled contentedly by abundance and covering the earth like the vast oceans. This serenity will cease in Messianic times.

4. קוֹל ה' בַּכֹּחַ — *The voice of HASHEM in strength!*

This alludes to the second day of Creation when God separated between the upper and lower waters thus beginning the precipitation cycle. Because the rains are always described as גְבוּרוֹת גְּשָׁמִים, *'the might of the rain'* [Ta'anis 2a] the verse says, *'The voice of HASHEM in strength'* (Rashbam).

According to *Rashi* and *Midrash* (Shemos Rabba 5:9, 29:1, 34:1) this describes God's revelation at Sinai when He taught Israel the Torah. If it had said קוֹל ה' בְּכֹחוֹ, *'the voice of HASHEM is in its (full) strength',* then the people would surely have perished, for they cannot withstand such force. Now that it says simply *'in strength',* it means that God modulated His voice (and the intensity of the revelation) in accordance with the כֹּחַ, capacity of each individual: Old men according to their strength, young men according to theirs; women according to their strength and pregnant ones according to theirs. Suckling infants heard on their level and even Moses himself heard according to his unique capacity. But God then said to Israel, 'Just because you have heard many voices, do not be misled into thinking that there are many gods. Know that אָנֹכִי ה' אֱלֹהֶיךָ, *'I [alone] am HASHEM your God'* (Ex. 20:5). From here we learn that Hashem never overwhelms His creations with excessive demands; He considers their individual abilities in assigning them their individual missions.

Radak continues to interpret this psalm as a prophecy of Messianic times

celebrate at the שִׂמְחַת בֵּית הַשּׁוֹאֵבָה. He notes that when David has bringing the Ark up to Jerusalem he was leaping and dancing בְּכָל עֹז לִפְנֵי ה', *'with all his might before HASHEM'* (II Sam. 6:14).

Rashi continues to point out the relationship of this particular verse to the water libation. *'The voice of HASHEM is over the waters ... HASHEM is over vast waters'* alludes to the waters poured on the altar at the time of the celebration.

XXIX
4-5

the God of Glory thunders,
HASHEM is upon vast waters.
⁴ *The voice of HASHEM in strength!*
The voice of HASHEM in splendor!
⁵ *The voice of HASHEM breaks the cedars,*

when mankind will come to recognize God's invincible strength and their own pitiful frailty. The revelation of God's might is likened to a voice, which is invisible and intangible. God does not mete out punishment with conventional weapons, rather He uses His voice which only the soul can perceive. It has the power to deeply disturb the unworthy hearer, causing mental agitation and sudden collapse.

קוֹל ה' בֶּהָדָר — *The voice of HASHEM in splendor!*

'God's voice [was heard] in splendor' on the third day of creation when plant growth began to bloom in infinite varieties (*Rashbam*).

This also describes God's revelation at Mount Sinai when He appeared as a venerable, merciful old sage. Old age is called הָדָר, 'honor, splendor' (see. *comm. v.* 2, בְּהַדְרַת קֹדֶשׁ). But, at the Splitting of the Sea, Hashem appeared as a young, powerful warrior: בַּכֹּחַ, 'in strength'.

The *Mechilta (Parshas Yisro)* says that this could cause confusion and give the heretics the opportunity to claim that there are two gods. Therefore, God proclaimed at Sinai, 'I [alone] am HASHEM Your God' (*Gevul Binyamin*).

Radak comments that these words describe the deadly voice of God which will destroy our enemies in the future Messianic War of Gog and Magog. But, at the very same time, the voice will leave Israel completely unharmed.

Thus, the very same voice which is בַּכֹּחַ, 'in [devastating] *strength*' for our enemies will be בֶּהָדָר, 'in *splendor*' [and salvation] for us.

5. קוֹל ה' שֹׁבֵר אֲרָזִים — *The voice of HASHEM breaks the cedars.*

On the third day of Creation the first trees sprang up, and so the voice of Hashem could now 'break the cedars' (*Rashbam*).

Rashi comments that this refers to the high and mighty monarchs, the enemies of Hashem. At Sinai, Israel heard God's voice [each according to his capacity] and lived. But the gentiles who heard, died. We also find that God smashed the Philistine host with His voice: '*And HASHEM thundered at them with a great noise*' (I Samuel 7:10). He slew the army of Sennacherib with His voice, '*From the voice of HASHEM Assyria trembles*' (Isaiah 30:32).

Here, Hashem's Name is mentioned for the ninth time in this psalm. *Yerushalmi (Berachos 2:4)* comments on this: Rabbi Alexandri said, 'Why does the ninth benediction of the *Shemoneh Esrei* bless Hashem as מְבָרֵךְ הַשָּׁנִים '*He Who gives blessing to the years*'? — This corresponds to the verse: '*the voice of HASHEM breaks the cedars*', meaning that He will destroy the powerful men who manipulate food prices and gouge the poor with exorbitant costs [thus, the years will be blessed with an abundance of inexpensive foodstuffs.] [1]

1. *Tanna d'Bei Eliyahu* (Ch. 2) offers another interpretation:
This refers to men who are clever and adept in all the ways of the world; skilled in all crafts and professions and business affairs. But they lack one thing, Torah knowledge. They are likened to the cedar. The cedar is tall and mighty, but it bears no fruit. So too, these men bear no fruit [they make no lasting contribution to posterity.]

יְהֹוָה אֶת־אַרְזֵי הַלְּבָנוֹן: וַיַּרְקִידֵם כְּמוֹ־ ו
עֵגֶל לְבָנוֹן וְשִׂרְיוֹן כְּמוֹ בֶן־רְאֵמִים: קוֹל־ ז
יְהֹוָה חֹצֵב לַהֲבוֹת אֵשׁ: קוֹל יְהֹוָה יָחִיל ח
מִדְבָּר יָחִיל יְהֹוָה מִדְבַּר קָדֵשׁ: קוֹל יְהֹוָה| ט
יְחוֹלֵל אַיָּלוֹת וַיֶּחֱשֹׂף יְעָרוֹת וּבְהֵיכָלוֹ
כֻּלּוֹ אֹמֵר כָּבוֹד: יְהֹוָה לַמַּבּוּל יָשָׁב וַיֵּשֶׁב י

אַרְזֵי הַלְּבָנוֹן — *The cedars of Lebanon.*
This is a forest in Eretz Yisrael where
many tall cedars grow. Although
mighty cedars grow elsewhere as well —
perhaps even to loftier heights — the
prophets always drew their illustrations
from that which was near them in their
times. Similarly, in the next verse the
Psalmist refers to the mountains in
Israel, which were in his vicinity
(Radak).

6. וַיַּרְקִידֵם כְּמוֹ עֵגֶל — *He makes them
prance about like a calf.*
The young calf is exceptionally light
on its feet, constantly running and skip-
ping (Radak).
The cedars and the mountains which
came to witness and hear the giving of
the Torah shook at that time (Rashi).
[Specifically the *prancing calf* describes the cedars of the previous verse,
and the *young R'eimim* describe the
mountains.]

לְבָנוֹן וְשִׂרְיוֹן — *[The mountains of] Lebanon and Siryon.*
These mountains represent the
mighty kings who will be deposed from
their positions just as the calf always
jumps from its place (Radak; Metzudas
David).

בֶן רְאֵמִים — *The young R'eimim.*
[בֶן when used in conjunction with a
species of wildlife describes the young
ones. See *comm.* to 22:22 for discussion
of the identity of the R'eim.]

7. קוֹל ה׳ חֹצֵב לַהֲבוֹת אֵשׁ — *The voice of
HASHEM cleaves with shafts of fire.*
This alludes to the fourth day of

Creation when God placed the fiery
celestial luminaries in the sky
(Rashbam).
When God spoke at Sinai, each commandment came forth from His mouth
as a flame in the shape of visible letters
and words. These letters penetrated the
stone tablets and engraved themselves
on the stone (Rashi).
In the future, God's wrath will pour
down upon His enemies like a bolt of
fiery lightning which rends the air
asunder (Radak).

8. יָחִיל — *Convulses.*
Rashi comments that this word describes the writhing and convulsing of a
woman in labor, as in חִיל כַּיּוֹלֵדָה *'convulsions like a woman in labor'*
(48:7).
This *'voice'* and the next one, יְחוֹלֵל
אַיָּלוֹת (*v.* 9) describe the birth of animal
life on the fifth day of creation
(Rashbam).

מִדְבָּר *The wilderness.*
Since the wilderness is flat and open,
without visual obstructions, one can
more readily observe the convulsions of
the earth there (Radak).

מִדְבַּר קָדֵשׁ — *The wilderness of Kadesh.*
Rashi quotes the Talmud (*Shabbos*
89b): Rabbi Yose bar Chanina said: The
wilderness of Sinai has five names
[which describe the events which took
place there]. It is called Tzin, Kedemos,
Paran, Sinai, and Kadesh. It is called
'Kadesh' because in that wilderness
Israel became קָדוֹשׁ, 'Kadosh', holy.
According to *Radak*, these words

HASHEM shatters the cedars of Lebanon!
⁶ He makes them prance about like a calf;
    Lebanon and Siryon like young R'eimim.
⁷ The voice of HASHEM cleaves with shafts of fire.
⁸ The voice of HASHEM convulses the wilderness.
    HASHEM convulses the wilderness of Kadesh.
⁹ The voice of HASHEM frightens the hinds,
    and strips the forests bare;
While in His Temple all that is His say, 'Glory!'
¹⁰ HASHEM sat enthroned at the flood,

---

refer to the kingdoms of God's enemies which are as worthless as vast, barren wastelands.

9. יְחוֹלֵל — Frightens.

The translation follows *Rashi*. Others say it is similar to יָחִיל 'shake, convulse', as in the previous verse *(Metzudas Zion)*.

Rashi suggests yet another translation: יְחוֹלֵל 'to bring forth'. The voice of God in the thunder helps the hind to bring forth its young. The birth canal of the hind is too narrow for its offspring to pass through, but thunder frightens the hind and arouses strong contractions which open the birth canal and propel its baby outward.

Hirsch observes: 'Even while it wreaks havoc upon forests, the storm [rains] causes the birth of much good. So too, the voice of Hashem brings to the world a renewed understanding of the Lord even while His voice is destroying all life which opposes His will.'

אַיָּלוֹת — The hinds.

This refers to the gentiles who now stand firm, just as the female אַיָּלָה, hind, is exceptionally surefooted. Those who now stand firm in their arrogance are destined to be terrified and shaken *(Rashi)*.

Since the Psalmist compared the land of the enemy to a barren wilderness, he compares them to the wild hinds which inhabit such places *(Radak)*.

וַיֶּחֱשֹׂף — And strips bare.

As in מַחְשֹׂף הַלָּבָן 'the peeled white streaks' (Gen. 30:37) *(Rashi)*.

According to *Rashi* it is the bark of the trees which will be stripped bare. However, *Radak* interprets this to mean that all of the trees in the forest will be toppled, thus stripping the entire wooded area and leaving it bare.

יְעָרוֹת — The forests.

The gentiles who are compared to mighty cedar forests will be stripped of their power and pride *(Rashi)*.

וּבְהֵיכָלוֹ — While in His Temple.

The Temple which God will build in Jerusalem *(Rashi)*. Or, God's celestial sanctuary where the angels offer praise *(Ibn Ezra)*.

[The translation of כֻּלּוֹ, 'all that is His', follows *Hirsch*.]

אֹמֵר כָּבוֹד — Say, 'Glory!'

All those who will visit the Temple will exclaim, 'Behold, now we truly see God's glory!' *(Metzudas David; Rashi)*.

10. ה' לַמַּבּוּל יָשָׁב — HASHEM sat [enthroned] at the Flood.

At the time of the great Flood in Noah's days, God sat alone on high *(Rashi)*.

When God is described as יוֹשֵׁב, 'sit-

יא יהוה מֶלֶךְ לְעוֹלָם: יְהוה עֹז לְעַמּוֹ יִתֵּן
יהוה | יְבָרֵךְ אֶת־עַמּוֹ בַשָּׁלוֹם:

ting enthroned', it means that He is permanent and unchanged. Therefore, the Psalmist says 'HASHEM *sat at the Flood*': despite the cataclysmic upheaval of the earth below, God remained unchanged above (*Rambam, Moreh* I:11).[1]

וַיֵּשֶׁב ה' מֶלֶךְ לְעוֹלָם — *'HASHEM sits [entroned] as king forever.*

So, too, when God will eradicate the idolators, His own kingship will not be affected (*Rashi*).

Before the Flood, the nations were oblivious of God and neglected Him as if He did not exist. But those who survived the Flood recognized God very clearly. Similarly, after the advent of Messiah the idolators will take notice of God as the eternal king (*Radak*).

11. ה' עֹז לְעַמּוֹ יִתֵּן — *HASHEM will give might to His nation.*

The idolators will vanish but those who serve God will grow even mightier and will be blessed with peace (*Rashi*).

[עֹז also means 'audacity, stubborness, toughness.' This trait is a prime prerequisite in maintaining the faith, as the Talmud (*Beitza* 25b) says: 'The Torah was given to Israel only because they are עַזִּים.' The *Shulchan Aruch*, the *Code of Jewish Law*, opens with the famous statement of Rabbi Yehudah ben Tema in *Avos* 5:20, 'Be always עַז כַּנָּמֵר, "*bold and tough as a leopard*" ... to do the will of your father in heaven.']

ה' יְבָרֵךְ אֶת עַמּוֹ בַשָּׁלוֹם — *HASHEM will bless His nation with peace.*

After the advent of Messiah there will no longer be wars (*Radak*). [This corresponds to the very last benediction of *Shemoneh Esrei* which is הַמְבָרֵךְ

1. This may be likened to a king who planted a splendid orchard with perfect rows of figs, palms, grapevines, apples, and pomegrantes. He put it in the care of a sharecropper and left. A while later the king returned to inspect his orchard and found it in ruins, full of thorns and brambles.

As he was about to command his axe-men to chop down and destroy the desolate ruins, he spotted one beautiful rose amongst the briars. He took it and smelled it and calmed down, his soul refreshed. He declared: 'Because of this one rose, the entire orchard will be saved!'

So too, God created the world only so that His Torah and instructions should be obeyed. But twenty-six generations after creation, God evaluated the world and saw the generations worthy of a Flood. He prepared the destructive forces for this as it says 'HASHEM יָשַׁב (lit. 'returned to') the Flood.' But then He noticed one beautiful rose, Israel, and smelled its fragrance when they willingly accepted the Ten Commandments. His soul was revived when they proclaimed 'We will do and we will listen.' So God announced, 'In the merit of one rose the orchard is saved. In the merit of Israel the entire world will be saved!'' (*Midrash Vayikra Rabba* 23:3).

XXIX

11

HASHEM sits enthroned as King forever.
11 HASHEM will give might to His nation,
HASHEM will bless His nation with peace.

אֶת עַמּוֹ יִשְׂרָאֵל בַּשָּׁלוֹם *'He who blesses His nation Israel with peace'.*]

Rabbi Shimon ben Chalafta said: 'The Holy One, Blessed be He, could find no container which would hold Israel's blessings as well as peace, as it says: *'HASHEM will give might to His nation, HASHEM will bless His nation with peace']* (*Uktzin 3:12*).[1]

Rashi quotes the Rabbis (*Zevachim* 116a) who explain these last three verses as referring to the revelation at Sinai:

When the Torah was given to Israel, God's mighty voice travelled around the earth and all of the heathen kings were gripped with terror. They all burst forth in song in honor of God as it says, *In His Temple they all say 'Glory'.* Afterwards, they gathered around the evil [prophet] Bilaam and asked, 'What is the nature of the awesome roar which we heard? Perhaps God is bringing another Flood upon Mankind?' (*'Is HASHEM to the Flood,* יֵשֵׁב, *returning?'*) 'No', he replied. 'God already swore never to bring another flood upon the earth, *'forever'* [*HASHEM sits as king, forever*].

But they protested, 'This oath only precludes a deluge of water but not one of fire! Bilaam retorted, 'No! He has sworn never to destroy all of mankind again by any means. The tremendous roar you heard is the sound of the Torah being revealed. It is a precious treasure which God safeguarded in His storehouse for 974 generations before Creation and now He is giving it to Israel, His children, as it says *'HASHEM will give might [Torah] to His nation'.* Immediately all of those assembled burst forth and said, *'May HASHEM bless His nation with peace!'*

[This was not meant as a blessing for Israel. Rather, the gentiles were so relieved to hear that their existence was not threatened and that they were still free to sin as they pleased, that they said 'Let Israel keep this restrictive "treasure" in peace, as long as God allows us our freedom!']

1. [On Friday evening it is customary to usher in the Sabbath by reciting six psalms corresponding to the six days which precede the Sabbath. This psalm is the last of the six because it speaks of seven divine קוֹלוֹת, *'voices'*, which allude to the holiness of the seventh day. The final words of this psalm capture the essence of the Sabbath delight, *'HASHEM will bless His nation with peace.'* The tranquility of the Sabbath provides us with a glimpse of the eternal peace of Messianic times and the World to Come when God's blessing will be completely fulfilled.]

This Psalm is reserved for the occasions of innovation; be it the new first-fruit, or newly dedicated Temple. It is both a prayer for success, 'To You, HASHEM, I called and to my Lord I appealed' (v. 9) and a confident declaration of eternal thanksgiving, 'HASHEM, my God, I will offer You thanks forever' (v. 13).

This psalm, once used to inaugurate the Temple, is used today to inaugurate our daily prayers at the outset of Psukei D'Zimra — Verses of Praise; for the synagogue is a מִקְדָּשׁ מְעַט 'a miniature Temple' and our prayers take the place of the sacrifices. While the Temple stood, this psalm was recited during the ceremonies which took place when the Temple courtyard was expanded. The song of thanksgiving was accompanied by musical instruments at every corner and on every great rock in Jerusalem, and they sang, 'I will exalt You on High, HASHEM' (Shavuos 15b).

Also, the Mishnah (Biccurim 3:4) relates that when the multitudes of Israel carried their baskets of בִּכּוּרִים 'first-fruits' to Jerusalem for the festival of Shavuos, they were greeted at the Temple courtyard by the choir of Levites who sang this psalm. Maseches Sofrim 18:2 designates this as the שִׁיר שֶׁל יוֹם 'The Song of the Day' for Chanukah.

א מִזְמוֹר שִׁיר־חֲנֻכַּת הַבַּיִת לְדָוִד:

1. מִזְמוֹר שִׁיר — *A song with musical accompaniment.*

Each of these words, when used alone can be translated simply as 'song'. When they are used together, however, the word שִׁיר refers to the lyrics of the composition, be they poetry or prose and the word מִזְמוֹר describes the accompaniment of כְּלִי זֶמֶר 'musical instruments' (*Siddur Baal haTanya*).

[Perhaps this definition can serve to explain the following enigmatic words of *Midrash Shocher Tov:*

'Two terms describing song are used here because the Temple was built and inaugurated twice — once in the days of Solomon and again in the days of Ezra. מִזְמוֹר refers to the First Temple, שִׁיר refers to the Second.'

How does each one of these words pertain to the respective Temples? The answer is that the dedication of Solomon's Temple was an experience of total joy. Not only were there inspired words of שִׁיר; song, but there was also מִזְמוֹר; exalted, melodious musical accompaniment.

The scene at Ezra's dedication, however, was dramatically altered. Some priests attempted to play with trumpets and cymbals, but they were drowned out by the wailing of old Jews who still remembered the splendor of the First Temple and were grief-stricken when they saw the small, impoverished Second. Therefore, all that could be heard was the שִׁיר as its words were loudly chanted, but not the joyous מִזְמוֹר, the musical accompaniment (see *Ezra* 3:10-13 and *Rashi ibid.*).]

חֲנֻכַּת הַבַּיִת לְדָוִד — *For the inauguration of the Temple; by David.*

[Since, it was Solomon, not David

who built the Temple, why is the inauguration ascribed to David?]

Rashi explains: David composed the song to be sung later, in Solomon's days, at the inauguration.

In this connection *Etz Yosef* notes that the 'initials' of מִזְמוֹר שִׁיר חֲנֻכַּת הַבַּיִת לְדָוִד form the word לְמָשְׁחָה 'anointment for greatness' which describes the kings of David's dynasty. Furthermore, the 'initials' of the words (with the exception of חֲנֻכַּת) form the name שְׁלֹמֹה 'Solomon', alluding to the fact that Solomon was destined to make the חֲנוּכָה 'inauguration'.

Midrash Shocher Tov offers two solutions: One: since it was David's idea to build the Temple and he took the pains to prepare for the construction [cf. *Succah* 53a, *Zevachim* 24a], it is therefore referred to as his.[1]

Two: one of David's Psalms was sung to accompany every sacrifice offered in the Temple. Thus, David is considered as alive and a participant in the never-ending, daily re-dedication of the Temple.

Alshich cites the fact that Solomon's entire inauguration ceremony was halted by the refusal of the Temple gates to open for him until he appealed to them to open in honor of David (*Shabbos* 30a. See *Psalms* 24:1,7 and *comm. ibid.*). Thus, it was David who was responsible for the successful completion of the inauguration (see *comm. v.* 4).

Ibn Ezra mentions an opinion that David composed this psalm not for the inauguration of the First Temple, but for a later Temple. [See *Maharshah, Shavuos* 15b.] *Tehillos Hashem* explains this according to the *Yalkut Shimoni* (II Sam. 145) "David asked

---

1. *Siddur Tzilusa D'Avraham* says that for this reason this psalm was included in the daily prayers as the conclusion of the recital of קָרְבָּנוֹת, 'the order of sacrifices'. The Talmud (*Menachos* 110) preaches that if one studies the Torah portions dealing with the Temple offerings, it is considered as if he actually brought them. This psalm proves the point, because it considers the inauguration to have been done by David — not because he actually built it but because he *desired* to build it and prepared for it.

XXX
1

Asong with musical accompaniment
for the inauguration of the Temple; by David.

God: 'Why can I not build the Holy
Temple?' God answered: 'Because if
you build it, it will endure and never be
destroyed.' Said David: 'That is certainly all the better!'

'God replied: "It is clearly revealed to
me that Israel is destined to sin, but instead of destroying them, I will vent my
rage on the beams and stones of the
Temple, and Israel will be spared."'
Therefore, David could not participate
in the first construction and inauguration, and his psalm of dedication was
reserved for the eternal Temple of the
future.

[Another problem arises here. The
psalm discusses David's sickness and
mourning and does not deal with the
Temple or its inauguration.]

— According to the opinion cited in
Ibn Ezra that this psalm refers to a
future Temple, the 'sickness' describes
the tragic, downtrodden state of Israel
during the exiles preceding its construction. Or, it may be that the edifice of
which David wrote is not the Temple at
all, but his palace of cedars which he
built after suffering a grave illness. This
is indicated by his reference to חֲנֻכַּת
הַבַּיִת, the inauguration of the *house*,
rather than בֵּית ה', 'the House of God'.

— *Iyun Tefillah* ascribes this Psalm to
the events detailed in *II Sam.* Ch. 24 and
I Chron. Ch. 21. In his old age, David
committed the serious error of counting
the population of Israel and Judea for
his own pride and glory. An angel of
destruction slew 70,000 men of Israel,
and was about to devastate Jerusalem,
but God restrained him at the last moment. God dispatched the Prophet Gad
to tell David to build an altar at the site
of the future Temple — the field of
Aravna, the spot where the Angel was
halted. David did so, and offered up
sacrifices to inaugurate and consecrate
the location. '*And David said: This is
the House of HASHEM, the God, and
this is the altar of sacrifice for Israel*' (I

Chron. 22:1). It was then that he composed this psalm, thanking God for
rescuing Israel from the deadly plague.

— The *Brisker Rav*, Harav Yitzchak
Zev haLevi Soloveitchik, explains that
David's sickness interfered with his
preparations for the Temple construction. David possessed a scroll containing the secret instructions for the construction of the Temple. It could be
given over only while both transmitter
and recipient were standing (*Midrash*,
cf. 41:11 for complete details). David
praises God '*for You have raised me up*'
(*v.* 2) and have given me the strength to
stand while transmitting the scroll —
hence the connection between David's
illness and the inauguration of the Temple.

—Radak is of the opinion that the illness described here is a חוֹלִי הַנֶפֶש, '*a
sickness of the soul*', for David's sin
made him sick at heart, especially since
his enemies predicted his doom. But
when David foresaw that the son who
was born from that very woman
(Solomon, son of Bath Sheba) would
build and inaugurate the Holy Temple,
he knew that he had merited divine
forgiveness — and so his soul was cured.

— Finally, *Malbim* suggests that the
house mentioned is not the Temple,
since it is not called בֵּית ה' '*the House of
HASHEM*', merely הַבַּיִת '*the house* (see
Ibn Ezra above). Rather, it refers to the
human body which houses the soul.

[*Harav Gifter* notes that the Torah
considers the human body, if it has been
sanctified, to be a miniature Temple, as
it says וְעָשׂוּ לִי מִקְדָּשׁ וְשָׁכַנְתִּי בְּתוֹכָם '*And
they shall make for me a sanctuary and I
shall dwell within them*' i.e. not within
it [the sanctuary], but within *them* [the
people themselves] (*Exod.* 25:8)].

Therefore, while David was ill, the
'house' was tottering towards collapse.
But now that he was cured it is as if it
was rebuilt and required joyous inauguration, especially since his enemies

ב אֲרוֹמִמְךָ יהוה כִּי דִלִּיתָנִי וְלֹא־שִׂמַּחְתָּ
ג אֹיְבַי לִי: יהוה אֱלֹהָי שִׁוַּעְתִּי אֵלֶיךָ
ד וַתִּרְפָּאֵנִי: יהוה הֶעֱלִיתָ מִן־שְׁאוֹל נַפְשִׁי
ה חִיִּיתַנִי °מִיּוֹרְדִי־בוֹר: זַמְּרוּ לַיהוה חֲסִידָיו
ו וְהוֹדוּ לְזֵכֶר קָדְשׁוֹ: כִּי רֶגַע | בְּאַפּוֹ חַיִּים

°מִיָּרְדִי ק׳

---

had already rejoiced over his imminent demise.

לְדָוִד — *By David.*

According to *Rashi* this term refers to the authorship of this psalm. However, in the opinion of *Midrash Shocher Tov* it ascribes the Temple dedication to David who made the initial preparations for its construction.

2. אֲרוֹמִמְךָ — *I will exalt You on high.*

[I will extol Your virtues with the highest of praise.]

כִּי דִלִּיתָנִי — *For You have raised me up from the depths.*

[This word is derived from דָּלָה, 'to draw up' water from the deep well'].

David's reputation sank low when his enemies claimed he had no portion in the World to Come. But when Solomon dedicated the Temple and the gates did not open until David's name was invoked, his honor [cf. *Psalms* 24:1,7], was lifted out of disgrace (*Rashi*).

In normal usage, the word הִגְבַּהְתַּנִי would be more appropriate. David used the obscure form דִלִּיתָנִי, as an allusion to the דַּלְתֵי הַבַּיִת 'the doors of the Temple' whose miraculous opening was the means by which his prestige was raised up (*Yoseif Tehillos, Baal haTanya*).

According to *Iyun Tefillah* the allusion to 'doors' refers to the plague which killed 70,000 people. 'You raised me from the gates ('doors') of death by holding back the lethal sword of the angel saying, "Enough, now hold back Your hand"' (*II Sam.* 24:16).

Alshich traces this word to the root דַּל 'impoverished, ravished with pain.' David thanks God for the tremendous suffering he had endured for it cleansed his soul and allowed him to rise above the accusation of his enemies.

Ibn Ezra observes that if we wish to appreciate the threat which David's enemies posed against him in his sickness we should study psalm 41 at length. [There the invalid is described as דַּל, *impoverished* (v. 2). Here David gives thanks כִּי דִלִּיתָנִי 'for You have raised me up from that lowly state'.]

וְלֹא שִׂמַּחְתָּ אֹיְבַי לִי — *And You have not gladdened my foes over me.*

When they saw the miracle of the gates at the inauguration, their faces turned dark with shame, like the blackened bottom of a burnt pot (*Rashi*).

The initials of these four words from the name שָׁאוּל 'Saul', David's most difficult enemy (*Chazah Zion*).

3. שִׁוַּעְתִּי אֵלֶיךָ — *I cried out to You.*

I sought a cure for my ills only from You and not from any physician. I realized that the source of my misfortunes was spiritual, not physical in nature (*Ibn Ezra; Malbim*).

[When the soul is profaned and deprived of its sanctity, the body which houses it becomes sick. Perhaps the word חוּלֶה 'sick' is related to חוּל 'profane'.]

Malbim explains the difference between the near synonyms שְׁוָעָה and צְעָקָה, both of which mean 'outcry': שְׁוָעָה is derived from יְשׁוּעָה 'salvation, help'. It is an articulate cry that describes where the salvation is needed. צְעָקָה, however, is a cry for help lacking an intelligible message.

² *I will exalt You, HASHEM,*

for You have raised me up from the depths,

and not let my foes rejoice over me.

³ *HASHEM, my God, I cried out to You*

and You healed me.

⁴ *HASHEM, You have raised up my soul*

from the Lower World, You have preserved me

lest I descend to the Pit.

⁵ *Sing to HASHEM, His devoted ones,*

and give thanks to His holy Name.

וַתִּרְפָּאֵנִי — *And You healed me.*

You accepted my repentance and forgave my sin, as it says, וְשָׁב וְרָפָא לוֹ *'he shall repent and be healed'* [Isaiah 6:10] (Rashi).

You assured my health by holding back the angel of the plague (Iyun Tefillah).

[According to those who comment that David composed the psalm with reference to his own grave illness, this verse, as well as several others, can best be understood quite literally.]

4. הי הֶעֱלִיתָ מִן שְׁאוֹל נַפְשִׁי — *HASHEM, You have raised up my soul from the lower world.*

שְׁאוֹל *'Lower World'*, describes Gehinnom, as does the word בוֹר *'pit'* (Radak).

Harav Yerucham Levovitz asks: David was still alive when he uttered these words — how could he speak as if he had already descended to Gehinnom which is a place of punishment for sinner after death? From this we learn that one can suffer in purgatory even while alive! As the Talmud (Nedarim 22a) teaches, כָּל הַכּוֹעֵס כָּל מִינֵי גֵיהִנָּם שׁוֹלְטִין בּוֹ *'Whoever flares up in anger is subjected to all types of Gehinnom'*. The flames of frustration, anguish, and melancholy which smolder within the heart of the depressed man are the equivalent of the fires of Gehinnom. Throughout the Book of Psalms, most references to *'falling into the Lower World'* refer to this type of inferno.

David thanks God for lifting up his spirits from this raging purgatory, and for instilling in his heart joy, the equivalent of Paradise (Daas Chochma, u'Mussar Vol. III pp. 20; 252).

[שְׁאוֹל may also allude to שָׁאוּל *'Saul'*, David's most implacable foe.]

Iyun Tefillah says that שְׁאוֹל refers to the grave. Seventy thousand victims of the plague had already been buried and David feared lest the remainder of Israel would soon join them. He now rejoices over their salvation.

מִיָּרְדִי בוֹר — *Lest I descend to the pit.*

[This translation follows the קְרִי reading, which is מִיָּרְדִי. However, the כְּתִיב spelling, is מִיּוֹרְדֵי בוֹר *'from those who will descend into the pit,'* which describes David's doomed enemies who sought to drag him down with them. Or it may refer to the victims of the plague, who were already dead and buried.]

5. זַמְּרוּ לַהי חֲסִידָיו — *Sing to HASHEM, His devoted ones.*

Upon witnessing my salvation, all men devoted to God should rejoice over the power of repentance and the magnitude of His mercy which redeems the righteous repenter, despite the seriousness of his transgression (Radak).

לְזֵכֶר קָדְשׁוֹ — *[To] His Holy Name* [lit. *'remembrance.'*]

This refers to His Name, for the titles which we bestow upon God are merely a means of remembering Him. There is

ז בִּרְצוֹנוֹ בָּעֶרֶב יָלִין בֶּכִי וְלַבֹּקֶר רִנָּה: וַאֲנִי

ח אָמַרְתִּי בְשַׁלְוִי בַּל־אֶמּוֹט לְעוֹלָם: יְהֹוָה

בִּרְצוֹנְךָ הֶעֱמַדְתָּה לְהַרְרִי עֹז הִסְתַּרְתָּ

ט פָנֶיךָ הָיִיתִי נִבְהָל: אֵלֶיךָ יְהֹוָה אֶקְרָא

י וְאֶל־אֲדֹנָי אֶתְחַנָּן: מַה־בֶּצַע בְּדָמִי

no name which truly describes God, for His essence is beyond our comprehension (Radak).

6. כִּי רֶגַע בְּאַפּוֹ — *For His anger endures but a moment* [lit. 'for a moment in His anger']

The devoted ones should sing Hashem's praises for His anger, although thoroughly justified, lasts only a brief moment. For example, all of the י"ג מדות הרחמים, 'The Thirteen Attributes of God's Mercy', depict God's kindness. Following them there is only one attribute that is threatening: 'He remembers the sins of the fathers to their children', and even this goes no further than 'the third and fourth generation.' However, God's kindness is לָאֲלָפִים 'for two thousand generations' (Radak). [See comm. 7:12: וְאֵל זֹעֵם, בְּכָל יוֹם, And God is wrathful every day, a wrath which the Talmud describes as enduring no more than the minutest fraction of a minute.]

[God meant to ravage the nation with three days of raging plague, but He stopped it much earlier. It lasted only מֵהַבֹּקֶר וְעַד עֵת מוֹעֵד 'From the morning until the appointed time (II Sam. 24:15). Some say this means until the next morning [a twenty-four hour period] (Abarbanel; Metzudas David).

Rabbi Yochanan says it lasted only from the morning until noon time of that day, and according to Shmuel it was even less: the time between the slaughter of the morning sacrifice and the sprinkling of its blood, which was done almost instantly (Berachos 62b). Targum; Rashi; Mahari Kara, and others (ibid.) adopt Shmuel's view.

Thus God's anger literally lasted only a few brief moments!]

חַיִּים בִּרְצוֹנוֹ — *Life results from His pleasure.*

I.e. by pleasing God and gaining His good will, one assures long life (Rashi).

Even during that brief flash of anger, God intends the punishment to make the sinner worthy of eternal life (Shaloh).

Similarly, *Isaiah* (54:7, 8) declares, *For a small moment I have forsaken you* [in order that] *in great mercies I will gather you in. In the overflowing of furious wrath I hid my face from you for a moment* [in order that] *with everlasting faithful love I will have mercy on you; so says your redeemer,* HASHEM' (Kli Poz).

בָּעֶרֶב יָלִין בֶּכִי וְלַבֹּקֶר רִנָּה — *In the evening one lies down weeping, but with dawn — a cry of joy!*

This world is compared to the darkness, the next world is the bright dawn. Similarly, this world is but a brief moment of anger compared to the future eternal bliss (Radak).

[Hashem makes man cry in this world so that he may rejoice in the Hereafter.]

Iyun Tefillah explains this according to the opinion of *Abarbanel* (see above) that the plague raged from morning through the evening and suddenly stopped on the following morning. Thus, all went to sleep that evening weeping, but with dawn came joy!

7. וַאֲנִי אָמַרְתִּי בְשַׁלְוִי בַּל אֶמּוֹט לְעוֹלָם — *I had said in my serenity 'I would never falter.'*

But I was mistaken because con-

XXX

6-9

> 6 *For His anger endures but a moment;*
>
> *life results from his pleasure;*
>
> *in the evening one lies down weeping,*
>
> *but with dawn — a cry of joy!*
>
> 7 *I had said in my serenity,*
>
> *'I would never falter'.*
>
> 8 *But HASHEM, it was Your good will alone*
>
> *that supported my greatness with might.*
>
> *You but conceal Your face,*
>
> *I would be terrified.*
>
> 9 *To You, HASHEM I would call*
>
> *and to my Lord I would appeal.*

tinued serenity is not in my hands, only in the hands of God, Who, can *'support my greatness with might'* or *'conceal His face' (v. 8)* i.e., withdraw His support from me, as He wishes *(Rashi)*.

8. עז לְהַרְרִי הֶעֱמַדְתָּה בִּרְצוֹנְךָ 'ה — *But HASHEM, it was Your good will alone that supported my greatness* [lit. *'my mountain']* *with might.*

When I experienced a period of serenity I was mistaken to assume that it was in my own hands to perpetuate that ideal, tranquil state. Now I fully realize that only You have the ability to assure my continued success *(Radak)*.

You strengthened my intellect, which is הַרְרִי *my greatness; my highest attribute,* to be mighty against the wily persuasions of Evil Inclination which sought to deceive me into sin *(Radak)*.

Siddur Tzilusa D'Abraham interprets הַרְרִי as *'my kingship'* as in הַגָּדוֹל הַר *'the great monarch' (Targum; Zech. 4:7)*.

נִבְהָל הָיִיתִי פָנֶיךָ הִסְתַּרְתָּ — *Should You but conceal Your face I would be terrified.*

There were moments when You concealed Your truth from my intellect, either because I boasted of my righteousness and You sought to test me (see 26:2), or in order to punish me for my sins. At those times my mind became

confused and overcome with fright, and my better judgment was overwhelmed by my Evil Inclination *(Radak)*.

[This describes David's misjudgment which brought about the misery of the plague. *'And Satan arose against Israel and he persuaded David to count Israel'* (II Chron. 21:1). *Radak* (ibid.) explains that Satan is the evil impulse in the heart of man which first confuses him and tricks him into sin and then is transformed into the הַמָּוֶת מַלְאָךְ *'the Angel of Death'* who kills the sinner with his lethal sword in punishment for the sin. (Cf. *Bava Basra* 16a).]

9. אֶקְרָא 'ה אֵלֶיךָ — *To You, HASHEM, I would call.*

When sin overcame me, what did I do? I called out only to You, fully realizing that I could not be healed without Your assistance. I understood that I deserved death and suffering in Gehinnom but I appealed to You saying, *'Of what value would my death be?' (v. 10) (Radak)*.

אֶתְחַנָּן אֲדֹנָי וְאֶל — *And to my Lord I would appeal.*

Alshich notes that David's manner of approaching God with a request followed the halachically prescribed procedure of prayer [cf. *Berachos* 34a]. One begins with God's praises in the first three benedictions of *Shemoneh*

בְּרִדְתִּי אֶל שָׁחַת הֲיוֹדְךָ עָפָר הֲיַגִּיד
אֲמִתֶּךָ: שְׁמַע־יהוה וְחָנֵּנִי יהוה הֱיֵה־עֹזֵר יא
לִי: הָפַכְתָּ מִסְפְּדִי לְמָחוֹל לִי פִּתַּחְתָּ שַׂקִּי יב
וַתְּאַזְּרֵנִי שִׂמְחָה: לְמַעַן | יְזַמֶּרְךָ כָבוֹד יג
וְלֹא יִדֹּם יהוה אֱלֹהַי לְעוֹלָם אוֹדֶךָ:

Esrei. Then he continues with the middle benedictions which are appeals for heavenly assistance i.e. first קְרִיאָה *'calling'*, then תְּחִנָּה *'appealing'.*

10. מַה בֶּצַע בְּדָמִי — *What gain is there in my death* [lit. *'what profit would be gained from my blood?'*]

The word דָּמִי, *'my blood',* refers to the soul for the purpose of physical existence is to become worthy of the life of the soul in the World to Come. David asks, Of what value was my existence on this earth if I am destined to fall into Gehinnom? Life in this world is of no value if it does not prepare man for the World to Come. For after death nothing at all remains of the sinners, as it says, *'And the dust returns to the ground as it was' (Ecc. 12:7) (Radak).*

'If דָּמִי *'my blood'* which was shed throughout my numerous afflictions at least assures me of a glorious Hereafter, then there was value to my pain, but if I descend to Gehinnom, *'my blood'* was wasted *(Dorash Moshe).*

הֲיוֹדְךָ עָפָר — *Will the dust acknowledge You?*

[As it is written בִּשְׁאוֹל מִי יוֹדֶה לָּךְ, *'In the Lower World who will acknowledge You?' (6:6).*]

הֲיַגִּיד אֲמִתֶּךָ — *Will it tell of Your Truth?*

The truth of Torah which establishes the veracity of Your wonders *(Sforno).*

The soul which descends to dust cannot utter one word of God's praise, only the soul which rises heavenward can, as it says *'While the soul returns to God who gave it' (Ecc. 12:7) (Radak).*

Midrash Shocher Tov (4:1) seems to contradict these words of *Radak.* 'God's praises rise forth from the mouth's of those condemned to Gehinnom with an intensity which surpasses the praises rising forth from those who bask in the Garden of Eden!' In addition, the Talmud *(Eruvin 19a)* records the words of those condemned to purgatory who declare, 'Sovereign of the Universe! Your verdict is just and proper!'

Iyun Tefillah explains that praise indeed pours forth from the lips of those who burn in the netherworld, but it is not genuine and sincere. The wicked ones do not pronounce praises of their own free will. Only the pain and duress of the excruciating punishments wrenches the truth from their stubborn hearts. Remove the pain and their lips will fall silent. Hashem has no interest in such meaningless expressions.

11. שְׁמַע ה' וְחָנֵּנִי — *Hear HASHEM and favor me.*

David appealed to *'HASHEM', 'the Divine Attribute of Mercy'* and asked for an undeserved favor and not strict judgment *(Alshich).*

12. הָפַכְתָּ מִסְפְּדִי לְמָחוֹל לִי — *You have changed for me my lament to dancing.*

This translation of מָחוֹל as *'dancing'* follows *Targum* and *Metzudos.* [However from the *comm.* of *Radak* it would seem that מָחוֹל may be related to מְחִילָה, *'forgiveness'.*]

I was mourning over the spectre of my soul perishing because of my sins, but You gladdened me by sending the Prophet Nathan with good tidings: *'HASHEM has also forgiven your sin, you shall not die' (II Sam. 12:13).* Accordingly, our verse would be rendered: *'You have changed my lament to forgiveness' (Radak).*

10 *What gain is there in my death,*
in my descent to the Pit?
Will the dust acknowledge You?
Will it tell of Your Truth?
11 *Hear, HASHEM, and favor me*
HASHEM, be my helper!
12 *You have changed for me my lament into dancing,*
You undid my sackcloth and girded me with joy.
13 *So that my soul might sing to You*
and not be stilled, HASHEM my God,
forever will I thank You.

In times of tragedy, Scriptures reverse the idiom of dancing as a representation of joy: שָׁבַת מְשׂוֹשׂ לִבֵּנוּ נֶהְפַּךְ לְאֵבֶל מְחוֹלֵנוּ 'Gone is the joy of our hearts, our dancing has turned into mourning' (Lam. 5:15) (Tehillos HASHEM).

[I was mourning over the tens of thousands who died in the plague and You transformed this time of sorrow into the pinnacle of joy by showing me where to establish the foundations of the Temple.]

פִּתַּחְתָּ שַׂקִּי וַתְּאַזְּרֵנִי שִׂמְחָה — *You undid my sackcloth and girded me with joy.*

פִּתַּחְתָּ literally means 'You have opened the knot' i.e. that secures the sackcloth of my mourning as in פִּתַּחְתָּ לְמוֹסֵרָי 'You have opened my bonds' (Psalms 116:16) (Metzudas Zion).

When I mourned over my sins I donned sackcloth as a sign of contrition. But now I am enveloped by the joy which took its place (Radak).

[This refers to the plague: 'And David lifted up his eyes and saw the angel of HASHEM standing between the earth and the heaven with a drawn sword in his hand stretched out over Jerusalem; then David and the elders clothed in sackcloth fell upon their faces' (I Chron. 21:16).]

13. לְמַעַן יְזַמֶּרְךָ כָבוֹד וְלֹא יִדֹּם — *So that my soul might sing to You and not be stilled.*

כָּבוֹד — *Soul.* [lit. 'glory']. The translation follows Radak and Metzudas Zion who explain that the soul is called כָּבוֹד, lit. glory, because it is the most glorious part of a human being. Thus: 'My soul will sing to You forever if You will not drag me down to the dust' (a reference to *will the 'dust' acknowledge You' v.* 10).

כָּבוֹד is a description of the soul because it emanates from God's כִּסֵּא הַכָּבוֹד 'Throne of Glory'.

Harav Yerucham Levovitz explains that the soul is called כָּבוֹד, glory, because its only function is to give כָּבוֹד 'honor and glory' to God, its Maker. Just as the king appoints courtiers whose sole responsibility is to praise his royal majesty, so has God endowed man with a divine soul in order that it sanctify His name (Daas Chochmah u'Mussar Vol. II pg. 38).

Iyun Tefillah comments that כָּבוֹד, glory, refers to the glory of God's presence which will dwell forever in the Temple as a result of the inauguration, as it says, כִּי מָלֵא כְבוֹד ה' אֶת בֵּית ה' 'For the glory of HASHEM filled the House of HASHEM' (I Kings 8:11).

Rabbi Israel of Rizhin explained this verse: Some people complain when God afflicts them. Others accept pain more graciously and make no utterance. However, inwardly they seethe with anger and resentment. A much higher level of resignation to God was achieved by Aaron the High Priest whose reaction to the death of his two sons, Nadav and Avihu, was וַיִּדֹּם אַהֲרֹן *and Aaron was completely still' (Lev.* 10:3). [שְׁתִיקָה means external *'silence'*, דְּמָמָה means to be internally *'still'* like a דּוֹמֵם *'an inanimate object'.]* He accepted God's action with complete calm. But David was even greater. He did not merely accept punishment, he welcomed it, for he saw with clarity the tremendous benefits reaped by his soul as a result of God's criticism and rebuke. As God smote him, he sang לְמַעַן יְזַמֶּרְךָ כָּבוֹד, *'So that my soul will sing to You'.* וְלֹא יִדֹּם *'and I will not be still'* i.e. like Aaron, *'HASHEM* the Merciful, even when You are אֱלֹהַי *'my God'* of Judgment — i.e. under all circumstances, both good and bad — לְעוֹלָם אוֹדֶךָ *'Forever will I thank You.'*[1]

1. *Rashi (v.* 12) draws our attention to the *Pesikta (Pesikta Rabbosi* 18:6, *Pesikta D'Rav Kahana* 8) which interprets this entire psalm as referring to the miracle of Purim.

'When Mordecai mounted Ahasueros' steed he exclaimed, *'I will exult You on high HASHEM, for You have raised me up from the depths...'* Mordecai's disciples continued: *'Sing to HASHEM, His devoted ones ...For His anger endures but a moment...'* Haman mourned, *'I had said in my serenity 'I would never falter.'* Esther rejoiced, *'To You HASHEM I called', 'What gain is there in my death'* [cf. 22:2]. Mordecai and all of Israel concluded, *'You have changed for me my lament to dancing, You undid my sackcloth and girded me with joy.'* Rabbi Pinchas said, 'When Haman came to mount Mordecai on the King's horse, Mordecai was in the midst of reciting the *Shema* and he refused to interrupt as it says, *'So that my soul might sing to You and not be stilled.' ''*

The Talmud *(Megillah* 4a) states: One is obligated to recite the *Megillah* at night and to repeat it again by day as it says, *'So that my soul might sing to You'* [by day *(Rashi)*], *'and not be stilled'* [by night *Rashi*].

Rashi (ibid.) also cites the *Pesikta* quoted above. The *Maharsha (ibid.)* elaborates on the relationship between this psalm and the events of Purim, and concludes that the words, *'HASHEM, my God, forever I will thank You'* alludes to the Rabbinic statement that 'Even if all of the festivals were to be nullified, the holiday of Purim would endure forever.'

D avid composed this psalm while he was fleeing from the wrath of Saul (Radak), who pursued him relentlessly. Although the psalm does not specify particular episodes, the commentators find in it allusions to various instances when David was in mortal danger at Saul's hands.

Once while playing music to soothe Saul's troubled spirit, David was the target of a spear hurled at him by the king. It missed him only by a hair's-breadth (Sforno). The persecution forced David to flee from Eretz Yisrael. The prophet Gad called upon him to return to the Land (I Samuel 22:5). Then, a divine message sent David to the town of Ke'ila to save its inhabitants from the invading Philistines. The townspeople treacherously betrayed David to Saul and planned to lock him inside their fortified walls to prevent his flight. Divinely forewarned, David escaped this trap and hid in the Desert of Ziph. Once again his whereabouts were betrayed to Saul (I Samuel, ch. 23) this time by the inhabitants of this wilderness (Malbim).

David's most precarious plight was when he was trapped by Saul's army while on the סֶלַע הַמַּחְלְקוֹת, the rock of division (ibid.) again God intervened to dave him.

In each of these episodes David sought aid and refuge in God alone. In gratitude, he dedicated this psalm to God, his Savior.

א־ב לַמְנַצֵּחַ מִזְמוֹר לְדָוִד: בְּךָ־יהוה חָסִיתִי
אַל־אֵבוֹשָׁה לְעוֹלָם בְּצִדְקָתְךָ פַלְּטֵנִי:
ג הַטֵּה אֵלַי | אָזְנְךָ מְהֵרָה הַצִּילֵנִי הֱיֵה לִי |
לְצוּר־מָעוֹז לְבֵית מְצוּדוֹת לְהוֹשִׁיעֵנִי:
ד כִּי־סַלְעִי וּמְצוּדָתִי אָתָּה וּלְמַעַן שִׁמְךָ
ה תַּנְחֵנִי וּתְנַהֲלֵנִי: תּוֹצִיאֵנִי מֵרֶשֶׁת זוּ טָמְנוּ
ו לִי כִּי־אַתָּה מָעוּזִּי: בְּיָדְךָ אַפְקִיד רוּחִי

2. בְּךָ ה' חָסִיתִי — *In You, HASHEM, I took refuge.*

When I was trapped in Saul's palace where he attempted to slay me, I sought no avenue of escape other than Your salvation (*Sforno*) for I trusted in Your word (*Targum*), i.e., the assurances You gave to see me safely to the royal throne.

Later, I was forced into exile. I could have assured my safety by indefinitely remaining in a foreign sanctuary. Yet, when You sent Gad the Prophet to call me back to the Holy Land, I disregarded my personal security and hastened to return, seeking refuge only in Your merciful protection (*Malbim*).

אַל אֵבוֹשָׁה לְעוֹלָם — *Let me not be shamed, ever.*

By virtue of the confidence I have in Your word, spare me from humiliation and disappointment (*Radak*).

בְּצִדְקָתְךָ פַלְּטֵנִי — *In Your righteousness provide me escape.*

The fact that I sought refuge only in You should make me worthy of Your salvation. But if I am still undeserving, then please let me be saved by virtue of Your righteousness (*Metzudas David*).

3. הַטֵּה אֵלַי אָזְנְךָ מְהֵרָה הַצִּילֵנִי — *Incline to me Your ear, quickly rescue me.*

I pray that You hear my plea without delay and respond swiftly to my call, for I ask no harm for my pursuers — only that I be rescued from their murderous threat (*Alshich*).

הֱיֵה לִי לְצוּר מָעוֹז — *Become for me a mighty rock.*

Reinforce my steadfast resolve to act properly in all my relations with Saul. Do not let anger or frustration overwhelm me lest I be aroused to slay him (*Alshich, Eretz HaChaim*).

לְבֵית מְצוּדוֹת לְהוֹשִׁיעֵנִי — *A fortress to save me.*

The expression בֵּית מְצוּדוֹת [lit. *house of fortresses*] is most unusual. *Alshich* perceives it as an allusion to David's two-fold dilemma. He was threatened *physically* if he did not kill Saul, for the jealous king was determined to kill him, and he was endangered *spiritually* if he killed Saul, God's anointed monarch. David asks for *fortresses* to protect him against both dangers.

[While hiding from Saul, David and his band lived in *fortresses*. It was in such a stronghold that Gad the Prophet found David (*I Samuel* 22:4-5). David hid in a stronghold once again when he fled from Ke'ilah to the wilderness of Ziph (ibid. 23:14,19).]

Chazah David interprets בֵּית מְצוּדוֹת figuratively as a reference to the two Holy Temples which were fortresses of faith for the Jewish people, and the source of their salvation.

4. כִּי סַלְעִי וּמְצוּדָתִי אָתָּה — *For my rock and my fortress are You.*

[Cf. 18:3 and commentary s.v. ה' סַלְעִי וּמְצוּדָתִי.]

Here David continues his plea of the

XXXI
1-6

For the Conductor, a song unto David.
² *In You HASHEM, I took refuge,*
let me not be shamed, ever.
In Your righteousness provide me escape.
³ *Incline to me Your ear; quickly rescue me,*
become for me a mighty rock,
a fortress to save me.
⁴ *For my rock and my fortress are You,*
for Your Name's sake guide me and lead me.
⁵ *Remove me from this net they have hidden for me*
for You are my stronghold.
⁶ *In Your hand do I entrust my spirit —*

previous verse. His reference to God as סַלְעִי, *my rock*, corresponds to צוּר מָעוֹז, *a mighty rock*, in the previous verse. מְצוּדָתִי, *my fortress*, corresponds to בֵּית מְצוּדוֹת, *a fortress*. [Thus, he proclaims that he seeks refuge and protection only in God because he recognizes Him as the Sole source of salvation to the exclusion of all other defenses.] *(Ibn Ezra).*

Alshich explains that there are two types of defenses. A soldier warding off a frontal assault may stand with his back against a *rock* to protect him against attack from behind. But the *fortress*, because it provides walled protection from all four sides, is superior to the *rock*.

תַּנְחֵנִי וּתְנַהֲלֵנִי — *Guide me and lead me.*
[In *Exodus* 15:13 we read נָחִיתָ בְחַסְדְּךָ ... נֵהַלְתָּ בְעָזְּךָ, *You guided with Your kindness ... You led with Your might. Malbim* (ibid.) explains that he who *guides* does so with the full approval of his followers (נָחִיתָ is cognate

with נֹחַ or נַחַת, *pleasant). However, the* one who *leads* does so even with force.

Here David asks God to *guide* him gently, but, if necessary, he hopes that God will *lead* him forcefully to the proper destination.]

5. תּוֹצִיאֵנִי מֵרֶשֶׁת זוּ טָמְנוּ לִי — *Remove me from this net they have hidden for me.*

When David composed this psalm, he was not yet ensnared in the traps of his foes, but the wicked people of Ziph gloated as if he had already fallen into their hands. Now he requests that these enemies be shown that he is far removed from their control *(Radak).*

6. בְּיָדְךָ אַפְקִיד רוּחִי — *In Your hand do I entrust my spirit.*

I am not frightened by the nets they spread to capture me because I have entrusted my life to You for safekeeping and You will undoubtedly redeem me *(Radak).*[1]

1. Often it happens that an object which is entrusted to another person, is accidentally exchanged for a different one. But with the Holy One, Blessed be He, this never happens. Does it ever occur that upon rising in the morning one finds that God has exchanged his soul with someone else's?

Rabbi Alexandri said: A man of flesh and blood is entrusted with a new article and he returns it later worn and tattered. But the Holy One, Blessed be He, is not so. The laborer toils

ז פָּדִיתָה אוֹתִי יהוה אֵל אֱמֶת: שָׂנֵאתִי
הַשֹּׁמְרִים הַבְלֵי־שָׁוְא וַאֲנִי אֶל־יהוה
ח בָּטָחְתִּי: אָגִילָה וְאֶשְׂמְחָה בְּחַסְדֶּךָ אֲשֶׁר
ט רָאִיתָ אֶת־עָנְיִי יָדַעְתָּ בְּצָרוֹת נַפְשִׁי: וְלֹא
הִסְגַּרְתַּנִי בְּיַד־אוֹיֵב הֶעֱמַדְתָּ בַמֶּרְחָב
י רַגְלָי: חָנֵּנִי יהוה כִּי צַר לִי עָשְׁשָׁה בְכַעַס

פָּדִיתָה אוֹתִי ה' אֵל אֱמֶת — *You redeemed me, HASHEM — O God of truth.*

Since the Psalmist spoke of entrusting his spirit to God, he now elaborates that He is אֱמֶת, a true and reliable guardian *(Ibn Ezra).*

Every night when we go to sleep we entrust our souls to God. Although our debt to God is great, He does not hold back the soul as payment. He is אֱמֶת, *true,* to His role as guardian of souls, and returns them in the morning *(Zohar; Ketzos HaChoshen 4:1).*

David is confident that God will redeem him from his enemies in order to be true to His promise that David would become king *(Radak, Sforno).* [See commentary of *Harav Yitzchak Zev Soloveitchik of Brisk* to *Haftorah of Chayei Sarah.*]

7. שָׂנֵאתִי הַשֹּׁמְרִים הַבְלֵי שָׁוְא — *I despise those who anticipate worthless vanities.*

I.e., those who turn to worthless idols for salvation *(Rashi),* or, those who depend on astrology or divination to determine the most propitious time for going to war.

David said: When I fled from Saul my life was in constant uncertainty. Yet, never did I turn to the seers and astrologers to clarify the future and allay my doubts. Rather, I spurned these vain and worthless soothsayers and blindly placed my faith in God, with no concern for the future *(Radak).*

[In this respect David's conduct excelled Saul's. When confronted by the Philistine army, Saul was so distraught that, in desperation, he sought out the witch of Ein Dor to communicate with the spirit of Samuel, in order to discover the future.]

The translation of הַשֹּׁמְרִים, *those who anticipate,* is based on *Rashi,* who departs from the common meaning of *watchmen. Rashi* derives this translation from וְאָבִיו שָׁמַר אֶת הַדָּבָר, *and his father [Jacob] anticipated the matter* [i.e., the fulfillment of Joseph's dreams] *(Genesis 37:11).*

וַאֲנִי אֶל ה' בָּטָחְתִּי — *As for me — in HASHEM do I trust!*

Midrash Shocher Tov and *Shemos Rabbah* 7:4 interpret his homiletically as the cry of the Garden of Eden which proclaims: Send me no wicked men, for *I despise those who anticipate worthless vanities.* Let the wicked descend to Gehinnom where they will be welcomed! *As for me — I welcome only*

all day and at night he falls asleep and deposits his worn and weary soul with his Maker. In the morning his soul is returned to his body refreshed as if newly created as it says, *They are renewed every morning, great is Your faithfulness (Lamentations 3:23).* Rabbi Shimon said in the name of Rabbi Semon: From the phenomenon of our renewal every morning we learn to have faith in Your future redemption [and renewal] of Israel *(Midrash Shocher Tov).*

Based on this *Midrash,* the *Talmud (Berachos 5a)* states: Although a Torah scholar need not recite the *Shema* at bedtime [to protect him from evil thoughts and spirits, for he is protected by the Torah thought which occupy his mind], nevertheless he should at least recite the verse: *In Your hand do I entrust my spirit, You redeemed me, HASHEM, O God of truth.*

XXXI
7-10

You redeemed me HASHEM, O God of truth.
⁷ *I despise those who anticipate worthless vanities.*
As for me — in HASHEM do I trust!
⁸ *I will exult and be glad at Your kindness,*
in noting my affliction,
You know the troubles of my soul,
⁹ *And delivered me not to the grip of the foe,*
but stood my feet expansively.
¹⁰ *Favor me HASHEM, for I am distressed,*
dimmed in anger are my eyes, my soul

---

the righteous men who declare — *in HASHEM do I trust!.*

8. אָגִילָה וְאֶשְׂמְחָה בְּחַסְדֶּךָ — *I will exult and be glad at Your kindness.*

Hirsch explains that גִיל, *exultation*, is the vocal expression of joy. It is a far more intensive emotion that שִׂמְחָה, *gladness*, which is related to צְמִיחָה, *growth*, and connotes serenity, a feeling of continued inner maturity and blossoming. Usually a person is first overwhelmed by a wave [גַל] of גִיל, *exultation*, and later he settles down to a constant, quiet gladness [שִׂמְחָה]. [See *commentary* to 14:7.]

אֲשֶׁר רָאִיתָ אֶת עָנְיִי — *In noting* [lit. *that you noted*] *my affliction.*

You ordained my suffering for You determined it to be in my best interest. I accept Your concern for my welfare as a *kindness* over which *I will exult and be glad (Kiflayim L'tushiah).*

יָדַעְתָּ בְּצָרוֹת נַפְשִׁי — *You know the troubles of my soul.*

[You realize that my soul is plagued with sin and so You seek to cure me with the therapy of *affliction*.]

And despite the shortcomings of my troubled soul You still do not abandon me to my foes *(Tzafnas Paneach).*

9. וְלֹא הִסְגַּרְתַּנִי בְּיַד אוֹיֵב — *And* [*You*] *delivered me not to the grip of the foe.*

This is the translation according to

Rashi, Radak, and *Metzudos.* This refers to the people of Ziph, who betrayed David and revealed his whereabouts to Saul *(Radak).* However, *Menachem* renders *You have not closed me up* [an allusion to the incident at Ke'ila when he was locked in the fortified city].

הֶעֱמַדְתָּ בַמֶּרְחָב רַגְלָי — [*But*] *stood my feet expansively.*

Not only have You released me from confinement, You have even widened my stride. I enjoyed complete freedom of movement and I traveled wherever my heart desired *(Ibn Ezra).*

10. חָנֵּנִי ה׳ כִּי צַר לִי — *Favor me HASHEM, for I am distressed.*

But the freedom and mobility of the previous verse are now a thing of the past. Once again my enemies dog my footsteps and threaten to incarcerate me. Moreover, I am stricken with a debilitating disease *(Ibn Ezra).*

עָשְׁשָׁה בְכַעַס עֵינִי — *Dimmed in anger are my eyes.*

[Cf. 6:8, עָשְׁשָׁה מִכַּעַס עֵינִי.]

Radak translates עָשְׁשָׁה, *consumed with rot and decay.*

Metzudas Zion notes that the usage of עָשְׁשָׁה as *consumed* is derived from the noun עָשׁ which is the name of a worm which eats garments as in הֵן כֻּלָּם כַּבֶּגֶד יִבְלוּ עָשׁ יֹאכְלֵם, *They will all be*

יא עֵינִי נַפְשִׁי וּבִטְנִי: כִּי כָלוּ בְיָגוֹן חַיַּי
וּשְׁנוֹתַי בַּאֲנָחָה כָּשַׁל בַּעֲוֹנִי כֹחִי וַעֲצָמַי
יב עָשֵׁשׁוּ: מִכָּל־צֹרְרַי הָיִיתִי חֶרְפָּה וְלִשֲׁכֵנַי
מְאֹד וּפַחַד לִמְיֻדָּעָי רֹאַי בַּחוּץ נָדְדוּ
יג מִמֶּנִּי: נִשְׁכַּחְתִּי כְּמֵת מִלֵּב הָיִיתִי כִּכְלִי
יד אֹבֵד: כִּי שָׁמַעְתִּי | דִּבַּת רַבִּים מָגוֹר

worn out like a garment, a worm will consume them (Isaiah 50:9).

נַפְשִׁי וּבִטְנִי — *My soul and my belly.*
Radak explains that נֶפֶשׁ here refers to the 'spirit of desire' in man which yearns to eat and drink. Many times while fleeing Saul, David had nothing to eat or drink. The threat of starvation was so great that Achimelech of Nob was compelled to give David the sacred לֶחֶם הַפָּנִים, *show-bread,* in order to save David's life (I Samuel 21:7). In those difficult times not only were his *eyes* consumed with *rot* [i.e. pain], but also his *soul* and his *belly* were overcome by hunger and thirst.

11. כִּי כָלוּ בְיָגוֹן חַיַּי — *For my life is spent with grief.*
From the moment that I killed Goliath and the women came out to sing: *Saul has slain his thousands and David his tens of thousands* (I Samuel 18:7), Saul's jealousy was kindled and my life became an endless succession of agony and grief (*Radak*).

וּשְׁנוֹתַי בַּאֲנָחָה — *And my years with sighing.*
The sighs which I utter because of Saul's persecution rob my body of its vitality; as the *Talmud* (*Berachos* 58b) states: A sigh breaks half of the body (*Radak*).

כָּשַׁל בַּעֲוֹנִי כֹחִי — *Because of my iniquity my strength has failed.*
I deserve these afflictions to atone for

my sins, otherwise God would not have allowed them to befall me (*Radak*).

Rabbi Tanchuma bar Chiya said that four things rob a person of his strength: sin, travel, fasting, and exile. Sin, as it says: *Because of my iniquity my strength has failed* (*Midrash Shocher Tov*).

12. הָיִיתִי חֶרְפָּה — *I became an insult.*
[If a person wished to insult another he would call him 'David'.]

וְלִשֲׁכֵנַי מְאֹד — *And to my neighbors exceedingly.*
My neighbors, more than anyone else, witness the humiliation and insults that I suffer at the hands of my tormentors (*Ibn Ezra*).

According to *Radak*, David's humiliation is at the hands of his *neighbors,* i.e. his fellow Jews, for it is they who revile and insult him.

וּפַחַד לִמְיֻדָּעָי — *A fright to those who know me.*
[A close friend is a מוֹדָע; as in וּמֹדָע, לַבִּינָה תִקְרָא, *and call understanding a close friend* (Proverbs 7:4).]

רֹאַי בַּחוּץ נָדְדוּ מִמֶּנִּי — *Those who see me outside flee* [lit. *wander*] *from me.*
They run away from me as from the plague (*Metzudas David*).

According to *Radak,* this phrase refers to David's dear friends who are pained by his plight. נָדְדוּ means *they shake and tremble* , as they commiserate with the effect that this terrible situation has upon him.

and my belly.

¹¹ *For my life is spent with grief*
and my years with sighing,
Because of my iniquity my strength has failed
and my bones are consumed.
¹² *From all my tormentors have I become an insult,*
and to my neighbors exceedingly;
A fright to those who know me,
those who see me outside flee from me.
¹³ *I became as forgotten as the dead from the heart,*
I became like a lost vessel.
¹⁴ *For I have heard the connivance of the multitude,*

---

13. נִשְׁכַּחְתִּי כְּמֵת מִלֵּב — *I became as forgotten as the dead from the heart.*

My acquaintances are so afraid for me *(v.* 12) that they have given up hope that I will survive Saul's persecution, just as no one hopes that the dead will come back to life *(Radak).*

According to *Ibn Ezra* it is God who has forgotten and abandoned David.[1]

כִּכְלִי אֹבֵד — *Like a lost vessel.*

[The Psalmist likens the body to a coarse vessel of flesh and blood which houses a precious, noble spirit. As long as it protects its contents, the receptacle is important, but if the soul is corrupted, the body loses its significance. It perishes and is immediately forgotten like a useless vessel.]

Rashi notes that whenever the Scriptures refer to a lost article, they never refer to the owner as having lost his property, but in terms of the object which *becomes lost* from its owner.

Thus we find: *So you shall do with every lost thing of your brother's which gets lost from him (Deuteronomy* 22:1).

[Similarly, God never abandons any of His human creations; it is they themselves who become lost from God as we read *(Psalms* 1:6): וְדֶרֶךְ רְשָׁעִים תֹּאבֵד, *And the way of the wicked goes lost.*]

14. דִּבַּת רַבִּים — *The connivance of the multitude.*

The translation follows *Rashi* who renders the word דִּבַּת as *advice,* i.e., the results of a council to discuss plans to deal with a problem.

Metzudas Zion, however, renders דִּבַּת as an *evil report,* by which a person slanders his foe as in וַיָּבֵא יוֹסֵף אֶת דִּבָּתָם רָעָה אֶל אֲבִיהֶם, *and Joseph brought their evil report to their father (Genesis* 37:2).

Radak combines both versions: This

---

1. The *Talmud (Berachos* 58b) observes:
Rav said: The deceased are forgotten only after twelve months have elapsed from the date of death; as it says. *I became forgotten as the dead from the heart, I became like a lost vessel.* [An owner usually gives up hope and forgets about his lost vessel after twelve months; as it is taught *(Bava Metzia* 28a): Whoever finds a lost vessel or any other article must announce this publicly during the course of three festivals which cover a period of an entire year. Afterwards, he can terminate his efforts, for the owner is assumed to have given up hope of recovering his property, thereby relinquishing his ownership *(Rashi).*]

מִסָּבִיב בְּהִוָּסְדָם יַחַד עָלַי לָקַחַת נַפְשִׁי
טו זָמָמוּ: וַאֲנִי | עָלֶיךָ בָטַחְתִּי יהוה אָמַרְתִּי
טז אֱלֹהַי אָתָּה: בְּיָדְךָ עִתֹּתָי הַצִּילֵנִי מִיַּד־
יז אוֹיְבַי וּמֵרֹדְפָי: הָאִירָה פָנֶיךָ עַל־עַבְדֶּךָ
יח הוֹשִׁיעֵנִי בְחַסְדֶּךָ: יהוה אַל־אֵבוֹשָׁה כִּי
קְרָאתִיךָ יֵבֹשׁוּ רְשָׁעִים יִדְּמוּ לִשְׁאוֹל:

refers to David's enemies who first held counsel together to plot against David and then slandered David before Saul with false reports of alleged evil.

מָגוֹר מִסָּבִיב — *Terror all around.*
The danger does not appear from one direction, it rises against me from all sides (*Radak*).

בְּהִוָּסְדָם יַחַד עָלַי — *When they consult together against me.*
Consultation is likened to the יְסוֹד, *foundation,* of a building because all future action is based on the original plan (*Metzudas Zion*).

15. וַאֲנִי עָלֶיךָ בָטַחְתִּי ה' — *But as for me — in You have I trusted, HASHEM.*
Although my enemies taunt me and say that You have forgotten me, my trust in You remains steadfast and I say, 'You are my God' (*Ibn Ezra*).

Only You have control over my destiny (*Radak*).

16. בְּיָדְךָ עִתֹּתָי — *In Your control* [lit. hand] *are my times.*
The different periods of danger which I have undergone were all preordained by Your order and decree (*Rashi*).
All of the *times,* i.e., occasions, when my enemies seek to harm me are in Your hands and under Your control, and so I ask You to deliver me (*Radak*).
Ibn Ezra notes that David makes this statement in defiance of those who heed the advice of the vain and worthless astrologers (*v.* 7) who consult their

horoscopes to find a propitious time to harm him. 'As for me', David declares, 'all of my times are in God's hands and, so, whatever time He chooses for my salvation is acceptable to me.'

Gevul Binyomin calls our attention to the *Midrash* (*Va'eschanan* 2:10) which says that different types of prayer are answered at different times. Some prayers are answered only after forty days, some after twenty, some after three, some after a full day, some after half a day. Some prayers are answered even before a person utters them.

Therefore, David says to God: You know the acceptable time for my prayer, but I do not. Therefore, I rely upon You to answer it at whatever You deem to be the most favorable time.

הַצִּילֵנִי מִיַּד אוֹיְבַי וּמֵרֹדְפָי — *Rescue me from the control* [lit. *hand*] *of my foes and my pursuers.*
The *Vilna Gaon* says that the word מִיַּד is superfluous, as it would suffice to say מֵאוֹיְבַי, *from my foes.* The extra word יַד alludes to David whose name [דָוִד] has the numerical value of יַד, fourteen. David is symbolized by the moon which becomes full after fourteen days. Furthermore, there were fourteen generations from Abraham until David, who culminated the ascent to greatness which was begun by Abraham. Thus, David represented climax and perfection, like the full moon. After David there were fourteen generations of descent until King Zidkiyahu in whose time the Temple was destroyed, similar

XXXI	*terror all round,*
15-18	*When they consult together against me,*
	to take my life have they plotted.

¹⁵ *But as for me — in You have I trusted, HASHEM.*
     I said, 'You are my God.'

¹⁶ *In Your control are my times,*
     rescue me from the control of my foes
     and my pursuers.

¹⁷ *Shine Your face upon Your servant,*
     save me in Your kindness.

¹⁸ O *HASHEM, let me not be shamed*
     after having called upon You!
Let the wicked ones be shamed —
     be silenced in the nether world.

---

to the waning moon which vanishes after fourteen days.

The twenty-eight periods of life enumerated in *Koheles* (3:2-8) contain fourteen positive, ascendant times and fourteen negative, descendent times, corresponding to the waxing and waning of the moon. David's life too, consisted of fourteen periods of salvation and goodness, and fourteen periods of bleakness and agony. This verse contains exactly twenty-eight letters corresponding to the twenty-eight time periods (*Tehilla L'David*). [Cf. *Rabbeinu Bachya* to *Genesis* 38:30 quoted in *Overview,* part VIII].

17. הָאִירָה פָנֶיךָ עַל עַבְדֶּךָ — *Shine Your face upon Your servant.*

Danger and fear shroud me in gloom. Save me and light up my life (*Ibn Ezra*).

Show me Your favor by accepting my petition out of kindness, even if I am unworthy of Your grace (*Sforno*).

18. O — ה' אַל אֵבוֹשָׁה כִּי קְרָאתִיךָ *HASHEM, let me not be shamed after having called upon You.*

Tehillos Hashem cites the *Talmud* (*Bava Kama* 93a) which states that he

who is מוֹסֵר דִּין, *invokes heavenly judgment,* against his fellow is himself punished first, as in the case of Sarah who invoked heavenly judgment upon Abraham and, as a result, predeceased him. For it was taught: punishment is meted out first to the one who cries, and is more severe than for the one against whom justice is invoked.

Rashi (Rosh Hashanah 16b) explains that the Heavenly Court, on being invoked, declares: Let us consider whether this appellant is worthy that his neighbor be punished on his account.

David, who now invokes heavenly judgment, anticipates the negative reaction which his charges may elicit. Therefore he begs that he not be shamed by his own invocation because he demands Justice sincerely, for the sake of God, and not for his own honor, as he cries out in the next verse, *Let them be silenced —* those lying lips, those which *speak malicious falsehood of the righteous.*

יִדְּמוּ לִשְׁאוֹל — *[Let them] be silenced in the nether world.*

This translation follows *Rashi.*

יט תֵּאָלַמְנָה שִׂפְתֵי שָׁקֶר הַדֹּבְרוֹת עַל־צַדִּיק

כ עָתָק בְּגַאֲוָה וָבוּז: מָה רַב טוּבְךָ אֲשֶׁר־

צָפַנְתָּ לִּירֵאֶיךָ פָּעַלְתָּ לַחֹסִים בָּךְ נֶגֶד

כא בְּנֵי אָדָם: תַּסְתִּירֵם | בְּסֵתֶר פָּנֶיךָ מֵרֻכְסֵי

כב אִישׁ תִּצְפְּנֵם בְּסֻכָּה מֵרִיב לְשֹׁנוֹת: בָּרוּךְ

However, *Radak* and *Metzudos* render
יִדְמוּ, *Let them be cut off*, based on *Jeremiah* 51:16.

19. תֵּאָלַמְנָה שִׂפְתֵי שָׁקֶר — *Let them be silenced — those lying lips.*

David said: *I have heard the connivance of the multitude* (v. 14), now I ask that their treacherous words be silenced (*Ibn Ezra*).

Radak explains that David was especially eager to silence the liars who accused him to Saul of boasting that he had already become king.

הַדֹּבְרוֹת עַל צַדִּיק עָתָק — *Those which speak malicious falsehood of the righteous.*

These villains attempt to convince Saul that the truly righteous David seeks to harm him (*Rashi*).

The evil also speak against God who is צַדִּיקוֹ שֶׁל עוֹלָם, *the Righteous Ruler of the Universe* (*Yerushalmi, Chagigah* 2:1).

עָתָק — *Malicious falsehood.*

This translation follows *Rashi* who renders עָתָק as something which is not there, based on *Genesis* 12:8, וַיַּעְתֵּק מִשָּׁם, *and he moved away from there.*

Dunash (quoted by *Rashi*) and *Radak* translate עָתָק, *strong,* as in *Psalms* 94:4, עָתָק יְדַבְּרוּ, *they speak strong words* [against the righteous].

20. מָה רַב טוּבְךָ — *How abundant is Your goodness.*

The abundance which God will bestow upon the righteous is beyond the power of mortal man to describe. The Psalmist can but exclaim: *How abundant!*

Rambam emphasizes that in this finite, material world we cannot conceive of the infinite spiritual rewards stored in the Hereafter. Just as the blind man has no conception of colors nor the deaf man an idea of sound, similarly, our limited senses have no way of sensing this spiritual bliss as long as we are enclosed in the body which restricts our soul. [Therefore, the Torah never makes promises of spiritual rewards for obeying its commands, for they are indescribable] (*Commentary to Mishnah, Sanhedrin* 11:1).

אֲשֶׁר צָפַנְתָּ — *Which you have treasured.*

[The verb צָפַן usually refers to a spiritual treasure which is hidden away; as in בְּלִבִּי צָפַנְתִּי אִמְרָתֶךָ, *In my heart I treasured Your sayings* (*Psalms* 19:11). The customary word for the concealment of a material object is טָמַן: as in וַיִּטְמְנֵהוּ בַּחוֹל, *and he hid him* (i.e., the dead body of the Egyptian taskmaster) in the sand (*Exodus* 2:12).]

This refers to the rewards stored away for the righteous in the World to Come. The wicked, who speak against them with falsehood and contempt, have no idea of the wonderful treasures that await the righteous (*Radak*).[1]

---

1. *Chovos Halevovos (Shaar Habitachon* 4) writes:
   There are two kinds of good deeds. Some, like the duties of the heart, are concealed; they are known only to the Creator. Other good deeds entail physical action and are, therefore, apparent to all. For the fulfillment of external duties, the Creator bestows a reward which is visi-

XXXI
19-21

¹⁹ *Let them be silenced —*
those lying lips,
Those which speak malicious falsehood of the
righteous,
with arrogance and contempt.
²⁰ *How abundant is Your goodness*
which You have treasured for Your reverent ones,
That You performed for those who seek refuge in You,
in the presence of men.
²¹ *Protect them — when Your Presence is concealed*
— from bands of wicked men.
Treasure them in an abode
from the quarreling of tongues.

פָּעַלְתָּ לַחוֹסִים בָּךְ נֶגֶד בְּנֵי אָדָם — *That You performed for those who seek refuge in You, in the presence of men.*

In addition to the spiritual treasures reserved for the future, You have often greatly rewarded the righteous in This World, not secretly, but openly, for all to see (*Radak*).

Tosefos Yom Tov lays down this principle: For performance of מִצְוֹת בֵּין אָדָם לַמָּקוֹם, *Mitzvos between man and God,* one receives no compensation in This World, only in the Hereafter. But for מִצְוֹת בֵּין אָדָם לַחֲבֵירוֹ, *Mitzvos between man and his fellow man,* a person is rewarded in This World as well [see *Rambam, Mishna Peah* 1:1.] Thus David says: For those who fear You [i.e. who observe the commandments relating directly to You] Your abundant treasure is reserved for the future. But if we see God executing great miracles in This World, for people *who seek refuge* in Him it is surely by virtue of the deeds they perform נֶגֶד

בְּנֵי אָדָם, *towards their fellow man* (*Shaarei Chaim*).

21. תַּסְתִּירֵם בְּסֵתֶר פָּנֶיךָ — *Protect them — when Your Presence is concealed.*

I know that abundant good is treasured for the reverent ones in the World to Come, but I ask You to provide them with security even in This World where *Your Presence is concealed* and the wicked surround the righteous from all sides (*Rashi*).

מֵרֻכְסֵי אִישׁ — *From bands of* [wicked] *men.*

Save the devout from the conspiracies of the wicked who join together to harm them (*Rashi*).

[Cf. *Exodus* 28:28, וְיִרְכְּסוּ, *and they will join together. Rashi* (ad loc.) cites our verse to corroborate his translation.]

תִּצְפְּנֵם בְּסֻכָּה — *Treasure them in an abode* [lit. *booth*]

Alshich notes that a סֻכָּה is a flimsy, temporary shelter. Thus, when God

ble in This World, but for the fulfillment of internal duties, God gives recompense in the World to Come.

David refers to concealed rewards in the verse, *How abundant is Your goodness which You have treasured for Your reverent ones.*

יהוה כִּי הִפְלִיא חַסְדּוֹ לִי בְּעִיר מָצוֹר: כג וַאֲנִי | אָמַרְתִּי בְחָפְזִי נִגְרַזְתִּי מִנֶּגֶד עֵינֶיךָ אָכֵן שָׁמַעְתָּ קוֹל תַּחֲנוּנַי בְּשַׁוְּעִי אֵלֶיךָ: כד אֶהֱבוּ אֶת־יהוה כָּל־חֲסִידָיו אֱמוּנִים נֹצֵר

wishes to protect someone, even the flimsiest of shelters is adequate to the task.[1]

מֵרִיב לְשֹׁנוֹת — *From the quarreling of tongues.*

[There was no reason for two righteous men such as David and Saul to quarrel. It was only the slanderous tongues of quarrelsome men who fanned the flames of dissension.]

The *Vilna Gaon* observes that each letter of the word סֻכָּה involves one of the four main areas of verbal pronunciation. ס, *Samech,* represents the hissing sounds controlled by the teeth. ו, *Vav,* represents the sounds formed by the lips. כ, *Kaf,* is sounded by the tongue and the upper palate. ה, *Hey,* is a guttural sound emanating from the throat. All of these vocal passageways control and modify the articulation of the tongue. Therefore, the Sages say that the *mitzvah* of סֻכָּה, *Tabernacles,* is a powerful agent in controlling the inclination to speak evil. This idea is alluded to here: You HASHEM treasure the tongue, in the letters of the סֻכָּה, *succah,* in order to control the quarreling of tongues.

22. בָּרוּךְ ה' כִּי הִפְלִיא חַסְדּוֹ לִי — *Blessed be HASHEM, for He has been wondrously kind to me.*

David thanks God for the wondrous kindness shown him when he was trapped inside the walls of Ke'ila (*Rashi*).

When he and his men were locked in Ke'ila, David asked two questions of God through the אוּרִים וְתֻמִים, the breastplate of the High priest, 'Will the people of Ke'ila betray me to him? Will Saul come [to attack me]?' (*I Samuel 23:11*).

The *Yerushalmi (Yoma 7:3)* says that ordinarily only one question at a time may be asked of the *Urim v'Tumim.* If two inquiries are made, together, some hold that one will be answered while others say neither will be answered. However, concludes the *Yerushalmi,* both questions posed by David were answered because he pleaded for extraordinary divine kindness, as it says 'HASHEM, my God please inform Your servant' [*I Samuel 23:11*] (*Divrei Shlomo*).]

בְּעִיר מָצוֹר — *In the city besieged.*

This refers to Ke'ila of which Saul said, *God has delivered him into my hand for he is shut in, by entering a city that has gates and bars* [*I Samuel 23:7*] (*Rashi*).

23. וַאֲנִי אָמַרְתִּי בְחָפְזִי — *But I said in my panic.*

1. The *Midrash* relates that God once saved David's life with the most fragile of shelters. It happened that David asked God, 'Of what value is the spider? It spins and weaves its web all year, yet it never wears the fruit of its loom?'

Said the Holy One, Blessed be He, 'By your life, the day will come when you yourself will need the services of a cobweb!'

When David and his men hid in a cave while fleeing from Saul and his armies [as a result of a רִיב לְשֹׁנוֹת, *quarreling of tongues*] God summoned a spider to quickly weave a web over the mouth of the cave. Saul saw the web and said to himself: 'Certainly David cannot be here for he would have broken the fragile web upon entering.' Thus, God demonstrated to David that no part of creation is superfluous, for David's own life had been saved by the insect he reviled.

22 *Blessed be HASHEM, for He has been wondrously kind to me in the city besieged.*
23 *But I said in my panic, 'I am cut off from Your sight!' But in truth, You heard the sound of my pleas when I cried to You.*
24 *Love HASHEM, all His devout ones! The truthful, HASHEM safeguards!*

This verse refers to the time when David was on the mountain, surrounded on all sides by Saul's men. Scripture says of that incident: וַיְהִי דָוִד נֶחְפָּז לָלֶכֶת מִפְּנֵי שָׁאוּל, *And David was hurrying to depart because of Saul* [I Samuel 23:26] (Metzudas David).

[See *Midrash Shocher Tov* partially quoted in footnote to *Psalms* 18:3. When Saul had him surrounded, David's plight was so hopeless that he cried out: 'It was for naught that Samuel anointed me to be king! How will his promise be fulfilled now?'

Where do we find an allusion to this statement? From the verse אֲנִי אָמַרְתִּי בְחָפְזִי כָּל הָאָדָם כֹּזֵב, *I said in my haste, 'All men are deceitful'* (Psalms 116:11).]

נִגְרַזְתִּי — *I am cut off.*

Dunash traces the root of this word to גרז which contains the same letters as גָּזַר, *to cut.* Thus, the axe or hatchet which cuts down the tree is called a גַּרְזֶן. However, *Menachem* relates this word

to נִגְרַשְׁתִּי, *I am chased*, and claims that its form is unique and is not found elsewhere in Scripture (Rashi).

אָכֵן שָׁמַעְתָּ קוֹל תַּחֲנוּנַי בְּשַׁוְּעִי אֵלֶיךָ — *But in truth You heard the sound of my pleas when I cried to You.*

[The doubt which I cast upon Samuel's prophecy was the result of panic and confusion. In truth, O God, *You heard my pleas* and saved me through a messenger angel (I Samuel 23:27). See footnote to *Psalms* 18:24.]

24. אֶהֱבוּ אֶת ה' כָּל חֲסִידָיו — *Love HASHEM, all His devout ones.*

With these words the Psalmist is issuing a command (Ibn Ezra).

David says: when you witness all the wonders which God performed for me, it becomes incumbent upon you to intensify your love for God (Radak).[1]

אֱמוּנִים נֹצֵר ה' — *The truthful, HASHEM safeguards.*

[See *commentary* to *Psalms* 12:2

1. *Rabbi Akiva Eiger* observed:

In the portion of *Shema* (Deuteronomy 6:4) the Torah commands: וְאָהַבְתָּ אֵת ה' אֱלֹהֶיךָ, *And you shall love HASHEM, your God.* This precept is difficult to comprehend because love is an emotional response which cannot be forced by a command.

We must understand this commandment in a different light. When a person realizes that he is the object of another person's affection and concern, it is only natural and instinctive that this will evoke from his heart a reciprocal feeling of tenderness and love. Thus, we are obligated to discover the countless ways whereby God demonstrates His boundless love for us, for this will strike a responsive chord in our hearts which, in turn, will be filled naturally with adoration for God.

For this reason, the benediction immediately preceding the recital of *Shema* begins with a recounting of God's concern for us '...אַהֲבָה רַבָּה אֲהַבְתָּנוּ ה' אֱלֹהֵינוּ, *With abounding love have You loved us, HASHEM, our God ...'* This awareness prepares us to accept the exhortation *And you shall love HASHEM, your God.*

כה יהוה וּמְשַׁלֵּם עַל־יֶתֶר עֹשֵׂה גַאֲוָה: חִזְקוּ
וְיַאֲמֵץ לְבַבְכֶם כָּל־הַמְיַחֲלִים לַיהוה:

---

where *Malbim* explains that the אֱמוּנִים are people who adhere faithfully to everything which duty demands. Since they are truthful to God by scrupulously safeguarding His law, God safeguards them, measure for measure, with utmost care.]

וּמְשַׁלֵּם עַל יֶתֶר עֹשֵׂה גַאֲוָה — *But He pays with precision him who acts with arrogance.*

Rashi explains that the word יֶתֶר,

literally a *bowstring*, denotes precision because the arrow must be perfectly positioned on the string in order to hit the mark. A יֶתֶר is also a *measuring rope* used to make exact calculations.

Another interpretation of יֶתֶר [cognate with יוֹתֵר] is *excessive pride* [*see Isaiah* 15:7]. God punishes the proud and arrogant measure for measure. He unleashes His full power and fury against them and, thus, He appears to act with *excessive pride.*

XXXI
25

But He pays with precision
him who acts with arrogance.
²⁵ *Be strong, and firm your hearts,*
all who wait for HASHEM.

---

25. חִזְקוּ וְיַאֲמֵץ לְבַבְכֶם כָּל הַמְיַחֲלִים לַה׳ —
Be strong and firm your hearts, all who
wait for HASHEM.

[David concludes by saying that the
example of his danger-filled life should
serve as an inspiration to others.]

The *Sefer Ha'Ikkarim* observes:
When a person puts all of his hope in
God, his heart is fortified with courage

and strength; as David says, קַוֵּה אֶל ה׳
Place confi- חֲזַק וְיַאֲמֵץ לְבֶּךְ וְקַוֵּה אֶל ה׳
dence in HASHEM, *strengthen yourself*
and He will give you courage; and place
confidence in HASHEM (27:14). And
the prophet Isaiah says: וְקֹוֵי ה׳ יַחֲלִיפוּ
כֹחַ, *Those who place confidence in*
HASHEM *shall renew their strength*
(*Isaiah* 40:31).

32 מזמור לב

Once of David's greatest teachings was that of the difficult art of repentance. David was מֵקִים עוּלָה שֶׁל תְּשׁוּבָה, he who lifted the burden of repentence (Moed Katan 16b); he demonstrated that forgiveness is accessible to all who sincerely seek it. [See Overview].

Of the many psalms addressed to this topic, this is the first. In it, David explains that there is more to repentance than simply attaining Divine forgiveness.

Rabbeinu Yonah of Gerona (Shaarei Teshuvah 1:9) summarizes the essence of this psalm:

There are many levels of repentance by which one draws closer to the Holy One, Blessed be He. Although every type of repentance brings about at least some forgiveness, the soul cannot become completely purified to the extent that the sins are regarded as never having been committed, unless the heart is cleansed and the spirit is properly conditioned; as it is written, 'Praiseworthy is the man to whom HASHEM does not account iniquity and whose spirit is without deceit (v. 2). The soul may be compared to a garment that needs cleansing. A little washing will suffice to remove the surface dirt, but only after repeated washings will it become entirely clean. Therefore, it is written that the penitent says: Wash me thoroughly from my iniquity (51:4).

The highest level of purity and forgiveness is achieved on Yom kippur; as the Torah states: For on this day He shall atone for you to purify you from all your sins, before HASHEM shall you be purified (Leviticus 16:30).

Verse 5 of this psalm tells how Nathan the Prophet informed David that God had completely forgiven his transgression with Bath Sheba. The Zohar (Bereishis 8b) says that Nathan made this pronouncement on Yom Kippur.

The Vilna Gaon designates this psalm as the שִׁיר שֶׁל יוֹם, the Song of the Day, for Yom Kippur (Maaseh Rav 216). The Ashkenazic custom, as recorded in Siddur Avodas Yisrael, is to recite this psalm on Shabbos Shuvah, the Sabbath preceding Yom Kippur.

א לְדָוִד מַשְׂכִּיל אַשְׁרֵי נְשׂוּי־פֶּשַׁע כְּסוּי
ב חֲטָאָה: אַשְׁרֵי־אָדָם לֹא יַחְשֹׁב יהוה לוֹ

1. מַשְׂכִּיל — *A Maskil.*

Rashi quotes *Pesachim* 117a: Any psalm introduced with the word *Maskil* was said through a תּוּרְגְמָן *Turgeman,* an orator who translated and interpreted the psalm for the benefit of the assemblage.

[מַשְׂכִּיל is derived from שֵׂכֶל, *wisdom, good sense, enlightenment.* The message of this psalm is so essential that David took great care to assure that it would be accurately transmitted to the entire nation so that all would properly be enlightened.]

Ibn Ezra attributes the use of this unique superscription to the fact that verse 8 of this psalm contains the promise אַשְׂכִּילְךָ וְאוֹרְךָ, *I will enlighten you and I will instruct you.*

Meiri, in accord with his interpretation on other superscriptions, holds that a *maskil* is a musical instrument. It derives its name from its capacity to enlighten the human intellect. The chords of the *maskil* focused the mind upon what was being said. Futhermore it inspired the heart to repentance. Thus, the medium truly complemented the message.

Finally, *Midrash Shocher Tov* quotes the verse אֹרַח חַיִּים לְמַעְלָה לְמַשְׂכִּיל, *The path of life is upwards for the wise* (Proverbs 15:24); and explains that the מַשְׂכִּיל is he who is מִסְתַּכֵּל לְמַעְלָה, *trains his gaze only upward.*

אַשְׁרֵי — *Praiseworthy.*
[See commentary to 1:1.]

נְשׂוּי פֶּשַׁע — *Whose transgression is forgiven* [lit. *whose rebellious sin is lifted*].

The *Talmud* (Yoma 36b) classifies three main categories of transgression: פֶּשַׁע is a sin committed with the intention of rebelling against God and casting off His sovereignty. עָוֹן, too,

refers to an intentional sin, but one which results from weakness in face or desire rather than from rebelliousness. חֲטָאָה is an unintentional sin as a result of carelessness. It requires repentance and forgiveness because if more care had been exercised, the mistake would not have occurred. The *Talmud* goes on to explain God's forgiveness, which is one of His Thirteen Attributes of Mercy: נֹשֵׂא עָוֹן וָפֶשַׁע וְחַטָאָה, *He forgives iniquity, transgression and sin* (Exodus 34:7):

Moses said to the Holy One, Blessed be He, 'Sovereign of the Universe. When the children of Israel sin against You, please consider their intentional transgressions (עָוֹן וָפֶשַׁע) as if they were merely unintentional errors (חֲטָאָה'.

[God surely exercises His Attribute of Mercy towards one who sincerely repents. Therefore, our verse may be interpreted: אַשְׁרֵי נְשׂוּי פֶּשַׁע, *fortunate is he whose intentional rebellion is removed through repentance,* thus it becomes כְּסוּי חֲטָאָה, *covered over,* i.e. its severity is mercifully obscured, and it is considered חֲטָאָה, *an unintentional sin*].

Meiri holds that the intentional sin discussed here is removed only through painful affliction; as we find וְהֵם יִשְׂאוּ עֲוֹנָם, *and they will suffer for their iniquity* (Numbers 18:23). He goes on to explain that in these two verses David enumerates four different groups of people who will enter the Hereafter cleansed of sin, however their means of achieving this state differ greatly. The man described as נְשׂוּי פֶּשַׁע, i.e., cleansed through affliction, represents the first group. [The rest will be described as the commentary progresses.]

Bereishis Rabbah 22 translates נְשׂוּי as *lifted above,* and comments that it refers to the potential sinner and not to the sin. *Fortunate is he who is נְשׂוּי פֶּשַׁע,*

To David, A Maskil:
Praiseworthy is he whose transgression is forgiven,
whose sin is covered.
² Praiseworthy is the man to whom
HASHEM does not account iniquity,

---

lifted above his sin, [and able to overcome the evil impulse which entices him] and whose sin is not above him [more powerful than he].

כְּסוּי חֲטָאָה — Whose sin is covered.

Radak (v. 1) quotes his father who explains that this refers to the man who has an abundance of merits and righteous deeds to his credit, but has also committed a חֲטָאָה, a relatively minor sin. The misdeed is covered by his countless merits and is not visible, like a lone kernel of millet which fell into many bushelfuls of wheat.

Meiri holds that the relatively slight חֲטָאָה, sin, is covered by a proportionally mild punishment. This is the second group which enters the Hereafter in cleanliness.

The Talmud (Yoma 86b) teaches, Rav noted that the following verses seem to be in contradiction. Our verse reads: Fortunate is he whose transgression is removed, whose sin is covered, yet elsewhere it is written, He who covers his transgressions will not succeed, but whoever confesses and forsakes them shall have mercy (Proverbs 28:13). Rav explained that there is really no difficulty. The verse in Proverbs refers to a sin which is well-known to the public [so it is better that the sinner should confess publicly and shame himself rather than deny his transgression (Rashi).] Our verse refers to a sin committed privately [it is preferable not to reveal it for the sake of preserving God's honor, for, to publicize the fact that a transgression was committed, detracts from God's honor and awe (Rashi).] Rav Zutra bar Tuvia said in the name of Rav Nachman, that the

verse in Proverbs refers to a sin committed against one's fellow. [If the victim refuses to forgive the sinner, other people may be informed so that they may try to induce the victim to accept the apology of the penitent (Rashi).] Our verse, however, refers to a sin committed against God. [See Rabbeinu Yonah, Shaarei Teshuvah; and Rambam, Kesef Mishneh and Lechem Mishneh, Hilchos Teshuvah 2:5. See also commentary to v. 5.]

2. אַשְׁרֵי אָדָם — Praiseworthy is the man.

[Unlike Verse 1 which discusses the various sinners, the subject of this verse is אָדָם, the man, par excellence: a person who is free of sin].

לֹא יַחְשֹׁב ה' לוֹ עָוֹן — To whom HASHEM does not account iniquity.

Although he has sinned, this man has repented so sincerely that God ascribes no sin to him, having forgiven him completely (Radak).

Quoting his father, however, Radak gives a different interpretation. He derives יַחְשֹׁב from מַחֲשָׁבָה, thought. This verse is in praise of the righteous who has never even had a thought of iniquity.

Meiri identifies this as the third category of righteous people. It consists of those who never sinned in deeds but who did allow improper thoughts to enter their minds. God's reaction to these thoughts is לֹא יַחְשֹׁב לוֹ, [lit. He gives it not a thought] for the Talmud (Kiddushin 40a) establishes the rule that מַחֲשָׁבָה רָעָה אֵין הקב"ה מְצָרְפָהּ לְמַעֲשֶׂה, God does not consider an evil thought to be equivalent to an evil deed.

ג עָוֺן וְאֵין בְּרוּחוֹ רְמִיָּה: כִּי־הֶחֱרַשְׁתִּי בָּלוּ
ד עֲצָמָי בְּשַׁאֲגָתִי כָּל־הַיּוֹם: כִּי | יוֹמָם
וָלַיְלָה תִּכְבַּד עָלַי יָדֶךָ נֶהְפַּךְ לְשַׁדִּי
ה בְּחַרְבֹנֵי קַיִץ סֶלָה: חַטָּאתִי אוֹדִיעֲךָ וַעֲוֺנִי
לֹא־כִסִּיתִי אָמַרְתִּי אוֹדֶה עֲלֵי פְשָׁעַי
לַיהוה וְאַתָּה נָשָׂאתָ עֲוֺן חַטָּאתִי סֶלָה:

עָוֹן וְאֵין בְּרוּחוֹ רְמִיָּה — *And whose spirit is without deceit.* [lit. *and there is not in his spirit deceit*].

Rashi and *Radak* hold that this is a requisite quality of the man *to whom HASHEM does not account iniquity,* i.e., his repentance is so completely sincere as to assure that he will never again repeat this transgression. [Otherwise, his very repentance is deceitful and is compared to *a dog who returns to (eat) his vomit (Proverbs* 26:11).]

According to *Meiri,* this is the fourth and final category of righteous people. It is composed of those who have never even contemplated deceitful acts.

3. כִּי הֶחֱרַשְׁתִּי — *When I kept silent.*

I refrained from confessing my sins before You (Rashi).

בָּלוּ עֲצָמָי — *Away wasted my bones.*

This deterioration resulted from my constant sighing and groaning as I worried about my sins and the inevitable punishment for them *(Rashi).*

[Similarly we read דְּאָגָה בְלֶב אִישׁ יַשְׁחֶנָּה, *Worry in a man's heart lets him diminish it (Proverbs* 12:25). The *Talmud (Sotah* 42b) recommends two courses of dealing with worry. Either one should attempt to forget his worries by being optimistic, or he should relieve his anxiety by discussing his problems and fears with others. However, David says that he repressed his worries, 'הֶחֱרַשְׁתִּי, *I kept silent* — and suffered silent frustration and torture. Consequently, בָּלוּ עֲצָמָי, *my bones,* [i.e., *my very essence*] *wasted away.*'

בְּשַׁאֲגָתִי — *Through my anguished roar.*

According to *Rashi,* the absence of repentance caused David to worry over his fate and to roar in anguish, i.e., to groan. This groaning caused his bones to waste away. However, *Metzudas David* says that anxiety had deteriorated his bones and the pain caused him to roar in anguish.

כָּל הַיּוֹם — *All day long.*

The *Talmud (Bava Metzia* 4b) relates that Rabbi Elazar ben Rabbi Shimon bar Yochai, wishing to purify himself from the slightest trace of a certain sin actually sought pain and affliction. However, he only welcomed the pains at night while he slept. When dawn broke, he addressed his suffering saying: 'My brothers and my friends, depart so as not to deter me from Torah study'. Since Rabbi Elazar could exercise such control over these pains, obviously they were יִסּוּרִין שֶׁל אַהֲבָה, *afflictions of love,* inflicted by God to bring the sufferer closer to his Maker. However, David had no such control over his pains and they caused him to groan כָּל הַיּוֹם, *all day long,* thus proving that they were a harsh punishment and not afflictions of love (Kesef Mezukak).

4. כִּי יוֹמָם וָלַיְלָה תִּכְבַּד עָלַי יָדֶךָ — *For day and night You hand was heavily upon me.*

Day and night I anticipate Your dreaded punishment *(Radak).*

נֶהְפַּךְ לְשַׁדִּי — *My freshness* [lit. *moisture*] *was transformed.*

and whose spirit is without deceit.
3 *When I kept silent, away wasted my bones*
through my anguished roar all day long.
4 *For day and night Your hand was heavily on me,*
my freshnesss was transformed
by summer dryness, Selah.
5 *My sin I make known to You*
my iniquity I do not hide.
I said, 'I will confess my transgressions to HASHEM'
but You had forgiven my iniquitous sin, Selah.

My flesh shriveled and my weight decreased as anxiety sapped my strength. לְשֻׁד refers to the internal fat and moisture which provide vitality; as we find in *Numbers* 11:8 that the manna tasted like לְשַׁד הַשָּׁמֶן, *a cake soaked in oil* (*Radak; Dunash* quoted by *Rashi*).

However *Menachem* (quoted by *Rashi*) renders: *I was turned over to be plundered;* לְשַׁדִּי being derived from שׁוֹד, *plunder.* (See 12:6, 17:9.)

בְּחַרְבֹנֵי קָיִץ — *By* [lit. *through*] *summer's dryness.*

The Sages teach that the flesh of a totally righteous person will not decay after death even if it is exposed to intense heat. In his humility and distress over his sins David bemoans his inferior state of purity, for he is sure that his fat would deteriorate if it were left in the summer heat (*Kesef Mezukak*).

[The person who thrives in God's favor flourishes like a plant nourished by abundant water (see 1:3). Not so the sinner who is parched and withered because of divine neglect.]

5. חַטָאתִי אוֹדִיעֲךָ — *My sin I make known to You.*

This statement is in the present tense to indicate that David continuously confesses his sins and seeks forgiveness for them (*Rashi*).

Although all is apparent to God, it is still incumbent upon man to confess his sins [not because God needs the information, but so that man should recognize and take responsibility for his deeds] (*Radak*).

וַעֲוֹנִי לֹא כִסִּיתִי — *My iniquity I do not hide.*

The *Beis HaLevi* observes that David seems to contradict himself, for in *verse* 1 he said: *Praiseworthy is he whose sin is covered,* whereas here he prides himself on his courage in revealing his sin. This may be explained according to *Rashi* (*Yoma* 86b), who says that it is best not to reveal a sin of which the public has no knowledge, for every sin is a disgrace to God and detracts from the glory of the Sovereign of the Universe. However, says the *Beis HaLevi,* this is only before the sinner is punished. But if the sinner is afflicted and is publicly acknowledged to be a righteous man, it is commendable to inform the public of the reason for his suffering, lest they come to complain that God has unjustly punished a *tzaddik.* Indeed, the more he promulgates his crime and punishment, the more God's name will be sanctified for the masses will recognize that His justice shows no favor, even to the righteous. [See *commentary* to verse 1 and 38:18-19].

אָמַרְתִּי אוֹדֶה עֲלֵי פְשָׁעַי לַה' וְאַתָּה נָשָׂאתָ עֲוֹן חַטָאתִי סֶלָה — *I said: 'I will confess my*

ו עַל־זֹאת יִתְפַּלֵּל כָּל־חָסִיד | אֵלֶיךָ לְעֵת
מְצֹא רַק לְשֵׁטֶף מַיִם רַבִּים אֵלָיו לֹא
ז יַגִּיעוּ: אַתָּה | סֵתֶר לִי מִצַּר תִּצְּרֵנִי רָנֵּי
ח פַלֵּט תְּסוֹבְבֵנִי סֶלָה: אַשְׂכִּילְךָ | וְאוֹרְךָ

transgressions to HASHEM', but You had forgiven my iniquitous sin. Selah!

Rashi and Sforno comment that this alludes to the harsh rebuke which Nathan the Prophet hurled against David after he sinned concerning Bath Sheba. The penitent David responded with a heartfelt confession which consisted of but two words חָטָאתִי לַה׳, I have sinned to HASHEM (II Samuel 12:13). [1]

6. עַל זֹאת יִתְפַּלֵּל כָּל חָסִיד אֵלֶיךָ — For this let every devout one pray to You.

At every opportune time, let the penitent recite the prayer given at the conclusion of our verse (Rashi).

Now that it is evident to all that You heard my prayer and removed my sin, let every devoted man follow suit and pray for forgiveness, if ever he should err and sin (Radak).

לְעֵת מְצֹא — At a time of accessibility.

There are moments when God is more accessible as the prophet said דִּרְשׁוּ אֶת ה׳ בְּהִמָּצְאוֹ, Seek out HASHEM when He is found [Isaiah 55:6] (Ibn Ezra).

Or לְעֵת מְצֹא may mean when the penitent finds his heart free of all disturbance and preoccupation and feels fully prepared to concentrate on sincere repentance (Radak; Ibn Ezra).

In a similar statement David said, עַל כֵּן מָצָא אֶת לִבּוֹ לְהִתְפַּלֵּל אֵלֶיךָ אֶת הַתְּפִלָּה הַזֹּאת, Therefore Your servant has found his heart ready to pray to You this very prayer [II Samuel 7:27] (Rav Yaavetz HaDoresh).

[In accord with the commentary of the Vilna Gaon to the preceding verse, we may interpret לְעֵת מְצֹא as the time [when You, God] find his heart to be purified with sincere, total repentance. This is a status for which every man of devotion should pray.]

רַק לְשֵׁטֶף מַיִם רַבִּים אֵלָיו לֹא יַגִּיעוּ — Only that the flooding, mighty waters not overtake him.

David likens his many enemies to a flood and pleads that he not fall into their hands. Similarly, after David's sin of counting the population of Israel he prayed (II Samuel 24:14): And David said to [the prophet] Gad: 'I am sorely distressed! Let me fall into the hand of HASHEM, for His mercies are greater, but let me not fall into the hands of men' (Rashi).

He should not pray that afflictions (which are likened to the raging waters) should not reach him at all, for without affliction one cannot be cleansed of his sins. Rather, he should pray that he should not be overwhelmed by a sudden wave of tragedy (Metzudas David).

1. The Vilna Gaon elaborates on this, noting that the words חָטָאתִי לַה׳ are followed by a פִּסְקָא, a pause, i.e., an open space left after the word לַה׳. This indicates that, originally, David had intended to continue his confession, but Nathan interrupted him. For, the confession of the penitent should consist of at least three words חָטָאתִי עָוִיתִי פָּשַׁעְתִּי, I have sinned [unintentionally], I have committed iniquity [intentionally], I have rebelled (Rambam, Hilchos Teshuva 1:2). But after David said, 'חָטָאתִי, I have sinned...', Nathan stopped him, as we read, And Nathan said to David: 'HASHEM also has forgiven your sin, you shall not die (ibid.). Most penitents cannot express their total remorse adequately without using these three words because even if they believe their sin was unintentional, they must suspect that subconscious-

⁶ *For this let every devout one pray to You*
at a time of accessibility:
Only that the flooding, mighty waters
not overtake him.
⁷ *You are shelter for me.*
From distress You preserve me.
With glad song of rescue
You envelop me, Selah!
⁸ *I will make you wise and enlighten you*
in the proper path to travel,

Sforno interprets: Let the devout man begin to pray לְעֵת מְצֹא, at the very moment he finds himself starting to be afflicted. He dare not wait until it is too late and he is engulfed in an overwhelming flood of misfortunes.

According to *Radak* this is not a prayer but rather a promise to all the devout who learn the art of repentance from David. They will surely escape a torrent of punishment.

7. אַתָּה סֵתֶר לִי — *You are shelter* [lit. *concealment*] *for me*.

I find shelter in Your shadow from my fearsome enemies *(Rashi)*.

You constantly perform concealed miracles for me, therefore I should envelop myself in endless exclamations of praise for Your kindness *(Zekan Aharon)*.

מִצַּר תִּצְּרֵנִי — *From distress You preserve me*.

You protect me from tormentors, danger and illness *(Ibn Ezra)*.

רָנֵּי פַלֵּט תְּסוֹבְבֵנִי סֶלָה — *With glad song of rescue You envelop me, Selah!*

Whereas I was previously surrounded by my enemies, now I will be encircled by many exclamations of joy at having escaped from them *(Radak)*.

So said the Holy One, Blessed be He, to David: 'If you wish Me to safeguard you from distress (מִצַּר תִּצְּרֵנִי), then you must keep My Torah, as it says נִצְּרֶהָ כִּי הִיא חַיֶּיךָ, *safeguard it, for it is your life! (Proverbs 4:13)*. If you wish Me to help you escape from the wicked, then cry out joyously before Me; as it says, *With glad song of rescue You envelop me, Selah! (Midrash Shocher Tov)*.

8. אַשְׂכִּילְךָ וְאוֹרְךָ בְּדֶרֶךְ זוּ תֵלֵךְ — *I will make you wise and enlighten you in the proper path to travel* [lit. *in this way you will go.*]

I have traveled down the arduous path of self-improvement and I have experienced the efficacy of prayer and penitence. Therefore I can instruct you

ly they might have wanted to commit the transgression. But God told Nathan to declare that He Who knows the heart of man knows that David's sin was truly unintentional, a mere חֲטָאָה, and nothing more. Therefore, David has no need to continue his confession. David refers to this event in saying, חַטָּאתִי אוֹדִיעֲךָ, *I acknowledged my sin to You*, וַעֲוֹנִי לֹא כִסִּיתִי, *and did not [wish to] conceal*, i.e., I wished to continue my confession, by saying, 'My iniquity,' אָמַרְתִּי אוֹדֶה עֲלֵי פְשָׁעַי לַה', *I said (to myself) "I will confess my rebellion to HASHEM."* But before I could do so, Nathan informed me that "You had already removed the iniquity (the suspicion of premeditation) *of my sin'* [See *Avi Ezri*, by Eliezer Schach, Hilchos Teshuva 1:2].

ט בְּדֶרֶךְ־זוּ תֵלֵךְ אִיעֲצָה עָלֶיךָ עֵינִי: אַל־
תִּהְיוּ | כְּסוּס כְּפֶרֶד אֵין הָבִין בְּמֶתֶג־וָרֶסֶן
י עֶדְיוֹ לִבְלוֹם בַּל קְרֹב אֵלֶיךָ: רַבִּים
מַכְאוֹבִים לָרָשָׁע וְהַבּוֹטֵחַ בַּיהוה חֶסֶד
יא יְסוֹבְבֶנּוּ: שִׂמְחוּ בַיהוה וְגִילוּ צַדִּיקִים
וְהַרְנִינוּ כָּל־יִשְׁרֵי־לֵב:

on how to follow my example (Metzudas David).

אִיעֲצָה עָלֶיךָ עֵינִי — I will signal you with
my eye.

Rashi comments that אִיעֲצָה refers to
a signal given by winking the eye as in
עֹצֶה עֵינָיו, he winks his eyes (Proverbs
16:30).Thus the Psalmist promises his
followers that he will continue to guide
them by means of whatever signals are
at his disposal; he will not allow them to
grope aimlessly.

However, Radak and Metzudos relate
אִיעֲצָה to עֵצָה, advice and render: I will
advise you of what I have witnessed
with my own eyes.

7. אַל תִּהְיוּ כְּסוּס כְּפֶרֶד אֵין הָבִין — Be not
like a horse or mule, uncomprehending.

They cannot differentiate between a
person who is treating them well and
one who is causing them harm. When
one inserts a bit in their mouths to make
them work they clamp their jaws shut
and eagerly chew it. But when one
combs and grooms them to cleanse and
beautify them, they react angrily and
must be muzzled to prevent them from
biting (Rashi).

But you, whom I am instructing,
please don't imitate these dumb
creatures. Appraise well and appreciate
the afflictions which come upon you
and repent (Radak).

Malbim comments: The Psalmist uses
the simile of the horse and mule when
exhorting man because the flesh and
blood of man resemble that of the beast.
The principle difference between them
is that man possesses an intelligent soul
which muzzles and bridles his beastly
nature, coaxing it to do God's bidding.
If the beastly body is not reined, i.e.,
kept in check, it can damage the soul
just as an untamed horse can throw and
injure its rider [cf. Malbim to 36:7
אָדָם וּבְהֵמָה תּוֹשִׁיעַ ה'].[1]

בְּמֶתֶג וָרֶסֶן — With muzzle and bridle.

The translation follows Targum,
בְּזָמָא וּבְפְרוּמְבְּיָא. Rashi, Radak, and
Metzudos follow this opinion, rendering מֶתֶג and רֶסֶן as approximately the
same type of equipment, designed to
restrain the animal's mouth in particular.

Other Scriptural references, however,
indicate that מֶתֶג is similar to a stick,
whip, or riding crop; as we find: שׁוֹט

1. The Torah warns us, You shall not despise the Egyptian. for you were a sojourner in his
land (Deuteronomy 23:8). [Even though the Egyptians drowned your sons in the Nile,
nevertheless, you must still appreciate them for providing you with a haven in time of famine
(Rashi).]
    Harav Yisroel Ordman of Telz noted Leo Tolstoy's comment that the above verse expresses
the pinnacle of human civilization, the highest moral level to which man can possibly aspire;
i.e. to appreciate the favor performed by a hated oppressor. To that same precept, however,
the Midrash cites the admonition of our verse: Be not like a horse, or mule, uncomprehending.
    To our Sages, basic decency demands gratitude for every kindness, even that of an oppres-
sor. To do otherwise is to sink to the level of an uncomprehending animal. What Tolstoy considered the height of morality was, to our Sages, a basic element of human behavior.

I will signal you with my eye.
⁹ *Be not like a horse or mule,*
uncomprehending;
Restrained with muzzle and bridle
when being adorned
to keep them from approaching you.
¹⁰ *Many are the agonies of the wicked —*
but he who trusts in HASHEM,
kindness surrounds him.
¹¹ *Be glad in HASHEM and rejoice, O righteous.*
Cry out in joy, all upright of heart.

לַסּוּס מֶתֶג לַחֲמוֹר וְשֵׁבֶט לְגֵו כְּסִילִים, *a whip for the horse, a stick for the mule, and a rod for the back of fools* (Proverbs 26:3); and, וַיִּקַּח דָּוִד אֶת מֶתֶג הָאַמָּה מִיַּד פְּלִשְׁתִּים, *and David seized the ruler's staff from the hands of the Philistines* (II Samuel 8:1, Rashi ibid.)

Meiri and Ibn Yachya render מֶתֶג as the sharp iron spur attached to the rider's boot which he uses to prod the mule.

Meiri and Rambam (comm. to Mishnah Sanhedrin 11) emphasize that herein lies the main difference between the man and the beast. The dumb beast can be aroused or restrained only by external threats or blows. Man, however can be motivated by his sense of right and propriety. He requires no outside goads or whips to spur him to mend his ways. [This echoes Talmud Berachos 7a: 'One self-inflicted blow of rebuke inside the heart of a man is far more effective than many external beatings.']

עֶדְיוֹ — *When being adorned* [lit. 'his adornment'].

This follows Rashi who renders עֶדְיוֹ as *his beautification* [as we find וַיִּתְנַצְּלוּ בְנֵי יִשְׂרָאֵל אֶת עֶדְיָם מֵהַר חוֹרֵב, *And the children of Israel stripped themselves of their ornaments from Mount Horeb* (Exodus 33:6).] While one beautifies the beast by combing, grooming, and cleaning, it incorrectly suspects harm and must be muzzled (לִבְלוֹם) lest it bite.

Ibn Ezra, Radak, and Metzudos render עֶדְיוֹ as *his mouth*, as in הַמַּשְׂבִּיעַ בַּטּוֹב עֶדְיֵךְ, *he satisfies your mouth with goodness* (103:5 cf. Radak ibid.)

לִבְלוֹם — *Restrained* [lit. *to muzzle*].

As we find תֹּלֶה אֶרֶץ עַל בְּלִימָה *He hangs the world on nothingness* (Job 26:7), which the Talmud (Chullin 89a) interprets to mean: The world endures by the virtue of he who muzzles his mouth in a quarrel [and makes himself like nothing] (Rashi, Metzudas Zion).

בַּל קְרֹב אֵלֶיךָ — *To keep them from approaching* [lit. *not to approach you*].

They must be restrained lest they inflict physical damage upon you (Rashi).

Maharit interprets these words homiletically. Do not act like the dumb beasts who respond only to the whip, for your intellect is incomparably loftier than theirs, they cannot *approach* to your level of comprehension.'

10. רַבִּים מַכְאוֹבִים לָרָשָׁע — *Many are the agonies of the wicked.*

He who places his trust in his power and wealth rather than in God and is oblivious to his own shortcomings will be afflicted with incurable suffering (Radak).

וְהַבּוֹטֵחַ בַּה' חֶסֶד יְסוֹבְבֶנּוּ — *But he who trusts in HASHEM, kindness surrounds him.*

Contrary to the wicked who are sur-

rounded by pain, the person who trusts in God is surrounded by kindness (*Radak*).

[Many take note of the fact that the אֶתְנַחְתָּא, a cantillation which indicates the end of a phrase, is placed on the word בָּה', *in HASHEM*. This indicates that the verse is to be read: *many are the agonies of the wicked and he who trusts in HASHEM*, thus implying that the wicked and the righteous suffer the same lot. It would have seemed more logical for the cantillation to connect the person of faith to the blessing of kindness with which the verse concludes. The construction of the verse suggests that we read these words: 'Many are the afflictions of the wicked, and included among them is he who trusts in HASHEM.' Nothing enrages the wicked more than the sight of the righteous man whose very behavior is a denunciation of the evil of the wicked.]

Another possible reading suggested by the placement of the אֶתְנַחְתָּא sign is: *Many agonies afflict the wicked and also the one who trusts in Hashem*. If so, what is the difference between the wicked and the righteous? The trusting man does not feel the suffering as much as the wicked one because he is confident that every affliction is for his good in accordance with the Divine Will. The Chofetz Chaim explained this concept with a parable. In earlier times medicines were bitter and harsh. Later, pharmacists discovered how to cover their foul tasting drugs with a sugar coating. The potency and taste of the medicine remained the same, but never

came in contact with the taste buds. Similarly, the severity of the pains which cleanse the righteous may be equal to those which punish the wicked, but the suffering does not make the righteous melancholy for it does not affect their emotional well-being. They realize that the result of the suffering will be to cleanse them and make them worthy of the World to Come. This knowledge 'sugar-coats' the bitter medicine!

Ibn Ezra defines the בּוֹטֵחַ בַּה' as the man who seeks no cures from doctors. The ultimate Healer is God; His therapy is to strengthen the soul and increase in the patient's heart the sense of heavenly awe. He who trusts in God is granted relief from his maladies. [See *commentary* of *Ibn Ezra* to *Exodus* 21:19 וְרַפֹּא יְרַפֵּא, *and he shall surely heal*].

11. שִׂמְחוּ בַה' וְגִילוּ צַדִּיקִים — *Be glad in HASHEM and rejoice, O righteous*.

You who trust in Hashem rejoice in that confidence and in the goodness you have achieved as its result (*Radak*).

וְהַרְנִינוּ כָּל יִשְׁרֵי לֵב — *Cry out in joy, all upright of heart*.

הַרְנִינוּ literally means *make others cry out in joy*. As the righteous rejoice over their own good fortune, let them share their experiences with all men of upright hearts so that they, too, may be made happy by the knowledge of God's goodness (*Radak*).

[See *Malbim* to 33:1, for detailed definition of צַדִּיק and יָשָׁר as they apply to this verse].

Malbim *introduces this psalm by saying that God controls the world in two ways. 1) Through the laws of nature which are pre-ordained and unchanging; 2) through* הַשְׁגָחָה,Hashgachah, *His* personal supervision and intervention. The manner of Hashgachah *changes constantly, for it is totally dependent on the deeds of man, for better or for worse.*

The laws of nature serve to conceal the true supervision of the Creator. One who perceives only this external cloak, sees an arbitrary, capricious world without justice or mercy. The challenge of mankind is to penetrate the mist and see the internal order dictated with precision by the Almighty.

All who truly seek this revelation will be elevated. The wicked will become good and the good will become better. They will all rejoice with musical instruments, because the symmetry and coordination of all the forces in the universe resemble the harmony and precision of superbly tuned instruments playing a well orchestrated symphony.

א רַנְּנוּ צַדִּיקִים בַּיהוה לַיְשָׁרִים נָאוָה
ב תְהִלָּה: הוֹדוּ לַיהוה בְּכִנּוֹר בְּנֵבֶל עָשׂוֹר
ג זַמְּרוּ־לוֹ: שִׁירוּ־לוֹ שִׁיר חָדָשׁ הֵיטִיבוּ נַגֵּן

1. רַנְּנוּ — *Sing joyfully.*

Let your voices be heard! *(Ibn Ezra).*

Hirsch notes that רִנָה, usually translated as a joyous cry, or joyous song, can also express sadness as in קוּמִי רֹנִי בַלַּיְלָה, *Arise, cry out at night* *(Lamentations* 2:19). Generally רָנַן implies the articulation of powerful emotions and thoughts evoked by some external stimulus. Therefore a form of פָּצַח, *bursting forth* [of emotions], frequently appears with רַנֵּן as פִּצְחוּ וְרַנֵּנוּ, *burst forth and sing joyfully* (98:4), but פָּצַח never appears in conjunction with any other word.

צַדִּיקִים — *O righteous.*

Malbim explains: The יָשָׁר *upright, straight,* man is on a higher level than the צַדִּיק, *righteous* man, because in his mind God's control over the universe is *straight,* i.e., plain and obvious. Consequently, he sees his own path in life clearly, i.e., to follow in God's ways. Therefore, the יָשָׁר, *upright one,* never deviates. However, the צַדִּיק, *righteous one,* has not yet attained that level of stability. In his mind there still exist doubts to be resolved. In his heart, conflicting emotions and desires are still at war. Nevertheless, to his great credit, he disciplines himself rigidly and so his external deeds are in complete conformity with the divine dictates.

The previous psalm ended with the exhortation שִׂמְחוּ בַה' וְגִילוּ צַדִּיקִים וְהַרְנִינוּ כָּל יִשְׁרֵי לֵב, *Be glad in HASHEM and rejoice, O righteous. Cry out in joy all upright of heart.* The highest level of joy bursts forth in song. In the previous psalm only the *upright* attained that level of intense happiness. This Psalm tells that when the *righteous* study God's supervision, they too will rise to the level of רַנְּנוּ, *singing joyfully.*

[This concept resolves a difficulty raised by many commentators: Why does the Psalmist say בַה', *because of HASHEM,* rather than לַה', *to HASHEM?* The usage is intended to emphasize that they *sing joyfully* precisely *because* they have found an enhanced understanding of God.]

בַה' — *Because of* [lit. *in*] *HASHEM.*

Because of His words [the Torah] *(Targum).*

Let only HASHEM be your joy and praise, nothing else *(Radak).*

לַיְשָׁרִים נָאוָה תְהִלָּה — *For the upright praise is fitting.*

The *upright* can best judge God's greatness; therefore they should praise him most *(Radak).*

Malbim continues: the *upright* who always accepted God's ways, always sang His praises joyfully. Further *it is fitting to give praise* to the *upright* in recognition of their spiritual greatness.

נָאוָה — *It is fitting.*

From the word נָאֶה, *comely, proper.* Praise is appropriate for them because they neither pursue nor glorify mundane, material things *(Radak).*

The Sages *(Sotah* 9a) stress that just as the upright are perfect, their works are perfect and everlasting: Do not read the verse נָאוָה, but נָוֶה, *abode.* This teaches that the Sanctuaries built by Moses and David, the *upright* ones, were never desecrated by the enemy. We find that the gates of the Temple sank into the ground before the enemies could destroy them. [The gates were a monument to David because, he made the preparations for the construction of the Temple and because, when the Temple was consecrated, the gates

Sing joyfully, O righteous, because of HASHEM;
for the upright, praise is fitting.
² Thank HASHEM with the Kinor,
with the Neivel Ossor sing to Him.
³ Sing Him a new song,

---

opened in David's honor (Shabbos 30a).]

Furthermore, the Tabernacle built by Moses, was also preserved for all times, because when the Jews constructed the First Temple they hid the tent, beams, poles and sockets of Moses' Tabernacle in the caves beneath the Holy Mount.

2. בְּכִנּוֹר — With the Kinor.

[Although there are many opinions concerning the exact translation of 'Kinor' most commentaries agree that it is a harp.] [1]

The Psalmist refers to the use of instruments in praising God because music arouses the inner spirit of the intellect and enhances its faculties (Radak).

בְּנֵבֶל עָשׂוֹר — With the Neivel Assor.

Rashi comments that neivel and assor [lit. ten] are both descriptive names for the same instrument, i.e., a neivel-instrument which produces עָשׂוֹר, ten different tones. Targum describes it as having ten strings. Rabbi Moshe quoted by Ibn Ezra says it was a wind instrument with ten holes.

However, Ibn Ezra himself holds that the neivel and the assor are two separate instruments, the proof being

עֲלֵי עָשׂוֹר וַעֲלֵי נָבֶל, On the Assor and on the Neivel (92:4). Elsewhere, Ibn Ezra agrees that although the neivel and assor are not identical, still the neivel also had ten holes (see his commentary to 150:3 and Isaiah 5:12).

The Talmud (Arachin 13b) says that the כִּנּוֹר, harp, of the Temple had seven strings, in Messianic times it will have eight, and in the World to Come, ten. It derives the last fact from our verse and explains it thus: 'That which is now a seven-stringed kinor will then become a ten-stringed assor, of a beauty rivaling that of the hitherto unsurpassed neivel. This proves that the neivel and the assor are two different instruments. Rashi (ibid.) says that the neivel derives from נֵבֶל יַיִן, a leather wine bag (filled with air and squeezed to produce sound).

The Midrash on 81:3 provides a different source for this name: It is called neivel because its exquisite music makes all other instruments seem to be נָבֵל, worn out, disgraced, withered.

3. שִׁירוּ לוֹ שִׁיר חָדָשׁ — Sing Him a new song.

Continue to compose new songs of praise at all times (Radak).

Rashi (Arachin 13b) quotes the

---

1. In support of this translation, Shiltei Hagibborim (Chapter 9) cites Berachos 3b: A 'Kinor' was suspended over David's bed. At midnight the north wind would blow through its strings and it would play by itself. The only known instrument whose strings could be strummed by the wind is a harp.

The author goes on to say that the name כִּנּוֹר is derived from כֵּן, straight, (see I Kings 7:31), because the harpstrings are positioned with great precision. כֵּן also means base (Exodus 38:8), referring to the wide base of the harp which provides stability for this heavy instrument.

Eretz HaChaim and Zera Yaakov note that, kabbalistically, kinor symbolizes the soul. Rearranged, the letters of כִּנּוֹר can be made to form כ״ו and נֵר: כ״ו, twenty-six is the numerical value of the Four-Letter Name, and נֵר, flame, is the soul as we find נֵר ה' נִשְׁמַת אָדָם, a flame of HASHEM is the soul of man (Proverbs 20:27).

ד בִּתְרוּעָה: כִּי־יָשָׁר דְּבַר־יהוה וְכָל־
ה מַעֲשֵׂהוּ בֶּאֱמוּנָה: אֹהֵב צְדָקָה וּמִשְׁפָּט
ו חֶסֶד יהוה מָלְאָה הָאָרֶץ: בִּדְבַר יהוה
ז שָׁמַיִם נַעֲשׂוּ וּבְרוּחַ פִּיו כָּל־צְבָאָם: כֹּנֵס
כַּנֵּד מֵי הַיָּם נֹתֵן בְּאוֹצָרוֹת תְּהוֹמוֹת:

Midrash which notes that throughout Scriptures the word for song is שִׁירָה in the feminine form, for in This World of misery, after every song of joy, a new tragedy is born, just as the female gives birth to one child after another. But the song of the World to Come is called שִׁיר in a masculine form because this will be the final song after which no more misfortunes will be born.

הֵיטִיבוּ נַגֵּן בִּתְרוּעָה — *Play well with sounds of deepest feeling.*

[The word *teruah* implies 'shattering', thus it is used to denote short sounds similar to the anguished sighs or tearful whimpers of people who cannot catch their breath (*Rosh Hashanah* 26b). The *Midrash* tells us that it symbolizes the person broken by affliction and pain as in תְּרֹעֵם בְּשֵׁבֶט בַּרְזֶל, *You will smash them with a rod of iron* (22:9).

In this world it is difficult to sing joyfully over the תְּרוּעָה, *shattering affliction*, but in the future, when the divine plan of history will be revealed, men will see the purpose of even the worst pains and they will make happy music (i.e., a new song) to God even out of the *teruah* blast.]

4. כִּי יָשָׁר דְּבַר ה' — *For upright is the word of HASHEM.*

God's decrees are all upright and just, therefore, the righteous rejoice over *His every deed*, for better or for worse (*Radak*).

וְכָל מַעֲשֵׂהוּ בֶּאֱמוּנָה — *And His every deed is done with trust.*

This refers to the natural forces which God set up to guide the world. They are reliable and unchanging so that one need not live in constant fear of upheaval and disaster (*Malbim*).

5. אֹהֵב צְדָקָה וּמִשְׁפָּט — *He loves charity and justice.*

God sometimes exercises charity, and, at other times, strict justice (*Radak*).

Sforno explains that צְדָקָה, *charity*, denotes a combination of God's Attribute of Mercy and His Attribute of Justice (see *commentary* to 35:24).

חֶסֶד ה' מָלְאָה הָאָרֶץ — *The kindness of HASHEM fills the earth.*

צְדָקָה *charity*, is a limited form of mercy for it is restricted within the bounds of justice (*Sforno*). [However, חֶסֶד, *kindness*, knows no bounds, *it fills the earth.*]

God's relationship to mankind is based on the three traits enumerated in this verse. He utilizes each in the proper time and hopes that mankind will follow His example. As the Prophet says: *For I am HASHEM who performs kindness, justice, and charity on the earth, for it is these that I desire* [man to imitate] (*Jeremiah* 9:23) (*Radak*). [1]

6. בִּדְבַר ה' שָׁמַיִם נַעֲשׂוּ — *By the word of HASHEM the heavens were made.*

As we find throughout the story of

1. *Eitz Yoseif* explains this verse with the words of *Yalkut Shimoni* (Ki Sisah): Ilfah (a Talmudic sage) explained why God's attribute of רַב חֶסֶד, *abundant in kindness*, precedes that of אֱמֶת, *strict truth* (*Exodus* 34:6). This may be likened to a man who owed a king a great sum of money but could not pay. The king was merciful and placed the entire amount into a purse and secretly threw it into the debtor's house. Just as the debtor was beginning to rejoice over

play well with sounds of deepest feeling.
⁴ *For upright is the word of HASHEM,*
  and His every deed is done with trust.
⁵ *He loves charity and justice,*
  the kindness of HASHEM fills the earth.
⁶ *By the word of HASHEM the heavens were made,*
  and by the breath of His mouth all their host.
⁷ *He assembles like a mound the waters of the sea,*
  He places in vaults the deep waters.

Creation וַיֹּאמֶר אֱלֹהִים, *And God said* (Radak).

[The *word of God* refers to the Torah which has been transmitted to Israel. Without the constant study of Torah, the universe would cease to exist as the prophet said: *'If not for my covenant of day and night* [i.e., the constant study of Torah] *I would not have set up the order of heaven and earth'* (Jeremiah 33:25). This process of creation continues, for the word of God, in the form of Torah continues to perpetuate creation.]

וּבְרוּחַ פִּיו כָּל צְבָאָם — *And by the breath of His mouth all their host.*
From this verse the *Talmud* (Chagigah 14a) derives: 'Each word which went forth from God's mouth at Creation, brought another ministering angel into being.' [Every physical creation on earth has a spiritual force above which controls it.]

Radak finds allusions in these verses to the four basic elements of creation.

Fire is the basis of the heavens (and the luminaries). *Air* is the breath of God's mouth. *Water* is in the seas and deep waters (next verse). *Earth* is where God's kindness abounds (v. 5).

7. כֹּנֵס כַּנֵּד מֵי הַיָּם — *He assembles like a mound the waters of the sea.*
Similarly, in reference to the Splitting of the Sea, the constrained water is described as a נֵד, *mound:* נִצְּבוּ כְמוֹ נֵד, *they stood upright like a mound* [Exodus 15:8] (Rashi).

Originally, water covered the face of the entire earth. Afterwards, God gathered the waters into the seas, where He commanded that they remain. There is sufficient water in the seas and ocean to cover the entire face of the earth, but God keeps it confined as if the water were piled up in an immovable mound (Radak).

נֹתֵן בְּאוֹצָרוֹת תְּהוֹמוֹת — *He places in vaults the deep waters.*
The waters of the sea should inundate

his new-found fortune, the king sent his guards to demand immediate payment of the long outstanding debt. The man was left as poor as before, but at least his debt was paid. So, too, a person commits a sin for which the heavenly penalty is death. But God is kind and does not exact payment immediately. He waits until the man marries and bears children, then the Lord snatches the life of the young child to pay for the father's sin. This man has discharged his debt to heaven in a most painful manner, but he at least survives to repent and improve himself.

Our verse conveys the same message. God loves to do צְדָקָה, *charity.* Yet, there are times when a man's deeds are such that God must punish him with מִשְׁפָּט, *justice.* Nevertheless, God is compassionate. First, he showers an abundance of kindness upon him. Then, He exacts punishment by snatching away that very kindness. The sinner is disappointed, but, in truth, he is now no worse off than he was initially.

ח יִירְאוּ מֵיהוה כָּל־הָאָרֶץ מִמֶּנּוּ יָגוּרוּ כָּל־
ט יֹשְׁבֵי תֵבֵל: כִּי הוּא אָמַר וַיֶּהִי הוּא־צִוָּה
י וַיַּעֲמֹד: יהוה הֵפִיר עֲצַת־גּוֹיִם הֵנִיא
יא מַחְשְׁבוֹת עַמִּים: עֲצַת יהוה לְעוֹלָם
יב תַּעֲמֹד מַחְשְׁבוֹת לִבּוֹ לְדֹר וָדֹר: אַשְׁרֵי
הַגּוֹי אֲשֶׁר־יהוה אֱלֹהָיו הָעָם | בָּחַר

the dry land, but God's rules of nature keep them as if in *vaults*. The waves and the tides furiously thunder upon the shore but then subside and dare not go beyond their boundaries (*Radak*).

Rashi refers this to the waters deep beneath the earth's surface. In the subterranean world there are both sweetwater and salt-water pools, yet God stores them so that they never mix (*Bamidbar Rabbah 18:22*). *Alshich* also notes that if the tremendous reservoirs of underground water should ever erupt and shoot to the surface, they would flood the earth [*Succah* 51b.] It is God who keeps them pent up. [1]

8. יִירְאוּ מֵה׳ כָּל הָאָרֶץ — *Fear HASHEM, all the earth.*

God in His wisdom, fashioned the world in such a way that man should never feel totally secure and complacent. Every man must be humbled by the fact that there exist forces of nature which are beyond his control. Therefore, the seas were made in such a way that it should be plain that only a miracle keeps the mighty, endless waters from overwhelming the earth. This instills fear in the hearts of man (*Alshich*).

יִירְאוּ . . . יָגוּרוּ — *Fear . . . be in dread.*

Malbim explains that יִרְאָה is fear of an external threat, while יָגֹר is a much more powerful emotion for it is a man's

inner dread when he trembles lest he be punished for his deeds (see *commentary* to 22:24). [Even animals can experience יִרְאָה, *fear*, but only יֹשְׁבֵי תֵבֵל, *the* (human) *inhabitants of the world*, can feel pangs of conscience and fear of punishment.]

9. כִּי הוּא אָמַר וַיֶּהִי — *For He spoke and it became.*

Creation came into being at His word and exactly as He commanded. This can also be interpreted as a prologue to the succeeding verses: the plans of the nations are doomed to frustration because they go counter to His will (*Radak*).

[This reflects the first of *Maimonides* Thirteen Principles of Faith: The Creator, Blessed be His Name, creates and rules all creations and He alone made, makes and will make all works.]

הוּא צִוָּה וַיַּעֲמֹד — *He commanded and it stood firm.*

[When God created the world it spread out and expanded like the threads stretching out through the loom until God roared and the earth stood firm (*Chagigah* 12a). This is why God is called שַׁדַּי, *Shaddai* [lit. *it is enough*] because it was He who halted the expansion of the world by roaring דַּי, *enough!*

Since God is perfect and complete, everything He creates should be fully developed and complete. However, the

1. Rabbi Eliezer, sees here an allusion to the entire water cycle which sustains the earth. What causes נִתַּן בְּאוֹצָרוֹת, [*The grain*] *to be placed in storehouses?* — the תְּהוֹמוֹת, *deep waters*, which evaporate from מֵי הַיָּם, *the sea*, and are כֻּנָּס כַּנֵּד, *gathered into clouds*, like liquid in a נֹאד, *water bag, gourd*. Then they rain down as precipitation, through condensation (*Taanis* 9a).

8 *Fear HASHEM, all the earth;*
of him be in dread, all inhabitants of the world.
9 *For He spoke and it became,*
He commanded and it stood firm.
10 *HASHEM annuls the counsel of peoples,*
he balks the designs of nations.
11 *But the counsel of HASHEM stands forever,*
the designs of His heart for all generations.
12 *Praiseworthy is the people whose God is HASHEM,*
the nation He chose for His own estate.

Creator ordained that the world remain imperfect in order to provide mankind in general and Israel in particular with the task of completing and perfecting the world (*Beis HaLevi, Lech Lecha*).]

10. ה' הֵפִיר עֲצַת גּוֹיִם — *HASHEM annuls the counsel of peoples.*

Now that we understand that the command of God stands firm and invincible forever (*v.* 9) we realize that every effort to challenge Him is futile and will be nullified (*Ibn Ezra*).

Specifically, this refers to the coalition of all the peoples of the earth who planned to build the Tower of Babel as a challenge to God (*Genesis* 11:1-4). They came together and adopted a simple *counsel*. Not only the physical structure of the Tower of Babel collapsed, but also the intellectual faculties which designed it were hampered. God confused the minds of its builders and deprived them of common speech and the power to communicate with one another (*Sforno*).

הֵנִיא מַחְשְׁבוֹת עַמִּים — *He balks the designs* [lit. *thoughts*] *of nations.*

Malbim explains that הַפָרָה, *annulment*, applies to something which has already come into existence whereas הֵנִיאָה, *foiling*, means preventing its ever taking effect.

11. עֲצַת ה' . . . מַחְשְׁבוֹת לִבּוֹ — *HASHEM's counsel. . . the designs of*

His heart.

This verse contrasts God's counsel to that of humans (*v.* 10). The counsel of the peoples is nullified, but HASHEM's counsel stands forever. Their designs are balked, but the designs of HASHEM endure eternally (*Ibn Ezra, Radak*).

Etz Yoseif quotes the *Vilna Gaon* who differentiates between עֵצָה, the *counsel* that one person receives from another, and מַחְשָׁבָה, *design*, which a person decides on his own. The plans of God always supercede those of man and therefore we read, רַבּוֹת מַחֲשָׁבוֹת בְּלֶב אִישׁ וַעֲצַת ה' הִיא תָקוּם, *Many are the designs in the heart of man*, [which he devises himself] *but the counsel of HASHEM will stand* (*Proverbs* 19:21). This means that after all of man's own personal designs, God will implant in his mind His advice and counsel, and that will be the one that will eventually win out over the rest.

12. אַשְׁרֵי הַגּוֹי אֲשֶׁר ה' אֱלֹהָיו — *Praiseworthy is the people whose God is HASHEM.*

Any people which would put their faith in God would be praiseworthy, for then He would provide them with His הַשְׁגָּחָה, *supervision* (*Malbim*).

הָעָם בָּחַר לְנַחֲלָה לוֹ — *The nation He chose for His own estate.*

But Israel is even more fortunate than others. For not only has Israel made

יג לְנַחֲלָה לוֹ: מִשָּׁמַיִם הִבִּיט יהוה רָאָה
יד אֶת־כָּל־בְּנֵי הָאָדָם: מִמְּכוֹן־שִׁבְתּוֹ
טו הִשְׁגִּיחַ אֶל כָּל־יֹשְׁבֵי הָאָרֶץ: הַיֹּצֵר יַחַד
טז לִבָּם הַמֵּבִין אֶל־כָּל־מַעֲשֵׂיהֶם: אֵין־
    הַמֶּלֶךְ נוֹשָׁע בְּרָב־חָיִל גִּבּוֹר לֹא־יִנָּצֵל
יז בְּרָב־כֹּחַ: שֶׁקֶר הַסּוּס לִתְשׁוּעָה וּבְרֹב
יח חֵילוֹ לֹא יְמַלֵּט: הִנֵּה עֵין יהוה אֶל־יְרֵאָיו

HASHEM their God, but He has also chosen them for His nation. He reveals Himself to them with miraculous Providence (Malbim).

13. מִשָּׁמַיִם הִבִּיט ה׳ רָאָה אֶת כָּל בְּנֵי הָאָדָם — From heaven HASHEM looks [lit. looked] down, seeing [lit. He saw] all of mankind.

In this verse and the next the Psalmist discusses the two forms of divine supervision. Our verse, in describing God as 'looking down', implies that He is distant and relatively uninvolved in earthly affairs. This is הַשְׁגָּחָה טִבְעִית, supervision through nature, i.e., the law of nature by which heavenly forces exercise control over the universe within a set of fixed laws (Malbim).

14. מִמְּכוֹן שִׁבְתּוֹ הִשְׁגִּיחַ אֶל כָּל יוֹשְׁבֵי הָאָרֶץ — From His dwelling-place He supervises all inhabitants of earth.

From the more general הִבִּיט, looks, of the previous verse the Psalmist changes to the more intense הִשְׁגִּיחַ, oversees, which implies הַשְׁגָּחָה פְּרָטִית, individual supervision, of all inhabitants of earth. God observes each, not from the distant heavens, but rather מִמְּכוֹן שִׁבְתּוֹ, from His dwelling-place, i.e., where He sits in judgment on each individual according to his unique situation (Malbim).

Etz Yoseif notices in the initials of the words מִמְּכוֹן שִׁבְתּוֹ הִשְׁגִּיחַ the name מֹשֶׁה, Moses, and explains that it was by virtue of the Torah transmitted by Moses that God granted us the privilege of receiving His personal attention.

15. הַיֹּצֵר יַחַד לִבָּם הַמֵּבִין אֶל כָּל מַעֲשֵׂיהֶם — He Who fashions their hearts all together, Who understands all of their deeds.

Because He alone fashioned their hearts, only He can truly understand them (Radak).

[Although He made them all together, each has a unique personality and must be understood according to his particular characteristics. As the Sages teach: just as no two faces are alike so are no two personalities alike (Berachos 58a).

Elsewhere God is praised: A man mints many coins with one form and they all emerge alike, but the King of Kings, the Holy One, Blessed be He, minted all of mankind with the mold of Adam, yet no man looks exactly like his neighbor (Sanhedrin 37a).]

Alshich interprets the words their hearts all together, as an allusion to the diverse elements which God has fused together in the human heart. Within man are both good and evil inclinations which are in perpetual conflict. Therefore, He understands all of their deeds, realizing man's inherent inconsistency.

16. אֵין הַמֶּלֶךְ נוֹשָׁע בְּרָב חָיִל — A king is not saved by a great army.

History furnishes ample proof of God's intervention on behalf of His chosen ones. By the laws of nature and logic, the mighty army should always crush the tiny one, yet many a king has

XXXIII
13-18

¹³ *From heaven HASHEM looks down,*
seeing all of mankind.
¹⁴ *From His dwelling-place He oversees*
all inhabitants of earth,
¹⁵ *He Who fashions their hearts all together,*
Who comprehends all their deeds.
¹⁶ *A king is not saved by a great army,*
nor is a hero rescued by great strength;
¹⁷ *A sham is the horse, for salvation;*
despite its great strength, it provides no escape.
¹⁸ *Behold, the eye of HASHEM is on those*
who fear Him,

---

been defeated despite the superiority of his forces. For example, King Sennacherib of Assyria conquered almost all of the inhabited world, and he arrogantly blasphemed God and besieged Jerusalem. Then, in a single night, the angel of God smote the entire Assyrian army of 185,000 men (*Radak*).

גִּבּוֹר לֹא יִנָּצֵל בְּרָב כֹּחַ — *Nor is a hero rescued by great strength.*

Though his entire army was annihilated, the mighty Sennacherib was spared, only to be assassinated by his own sons. All his strength was of no avail. Similarly, the giant Goliath fell before the young shepherd, David. Thus, history shows that victory depends not on physical strength but on the will of God (*Radak*).

17. שֶׁקֶר הַסּוּס לִתְשׁוּעָה — *A sham is the horse for salvation.*

The horse's might emanates from God who can deprive him of it at will (*Radak*).

Furthermore, it is often difficult to maneuver the powerful steed and thus the rider is vulnerable to enemy attack, whereas the foot soldier exercises greater control over his own movements (*Alshich*).

וּבְרֹב חֵילוֹ לֹא יְמַלֵּט — *Despite its great strength, it provides no escape.*

The strength of the horse provides no assurance that it will carry its rider away from danger (*Radak*).

Often a frenzied horse will carry its rider right into the camp of the enemy instead of galloping in the direction of escape. Or the horse terrified by battle, will throw and trample its own rider. Thus, its great strength can be a curse instead of a boon (*Alshich*).

The mighty horse may not even be able to save itself from destruction (*Ibn Ezra*).

18. הִנֵּה עֵין ה׳ אֶל יְרֵאָיו — *Behold, the eye of HASHEM is on those who fear Him.*

Those who trust in their military prowess stumble, but those who place their trust in HASHEM merit His protection (*Radak*).

The *Midrash* observes: When Israel performs according to the will of God, He looks at them with two eyes, as it says עֵינֵי ה׳ אֶל צַדִּיקִים, *The eyes* [plural] *of HASHEM are upon the righteous ones* (34:16); but when they do not perform according to His will, He looks only with one eye, as in our verse,

יט לַמְיַחֲלִים לְחַסְדּוֹ: לְהַצִּיל מִמָּוֶת נַפְשָׁם
כ וּלְחַיּוֹתָם בָּרָעָב: נַפְשֵׁנוּ חִכְּתָה לַיהוה
כא עֶזְרֵנוּ וּמָגִנֵּנוּ הוּא: כִּי־בוֹ יִשְׂמַח לִבֵּנוּ כִּי
כב בְשֵׁם קָדְשׁוֹ בָטָחְנוּ: יְהִי חַסְדְּךָ יהוה
עָלֵינוּ כַּאֲשֶׁר יִחַלְנוּ לָךְ:

Behold, the eye of HASHEM is on those who fear Him (Shir HaShirim Rabbah 8:12).

The commentaries explain the superiority of the *righteous* of 34:16 to *those who fear Him* of our verse. One may fear God but serve Him only half-heartedly to avoid punishment and acquire reward, as this and the next verse continue: *upon those who await His kindness, to rescue their soul from death, sustain them in famine.*

However, the *Zohar (Naso)* interprets the supervision with one eye as the highest level of divine attention. When two eyes are watching, the right one symbolizes *mercy*, and the left one *strict justice*. But he who ascends to the highest level is supervised by but one eye, that of *mercy*. [1]

19. לְהַצִּיל מִמָּוֶת נַפְשָׁם — *To rescue from death their soul.*

In times of war (Radak).

וּלְחַיּוֹתָם בָּרָעָב — *And sustain them* [lit. *keep them alive*] *in famine.*

1. *Ramban,* in his commentary to *Job* (36:6) explains the verse לֹא יִגְרַע מִצַּדִּיק עֵינָיו, *He does not withdraw His eyes from the righteous.* He describes the truly devout who train all of their thoughts upon God without interruption. Commensurate with the intensity of their concentration on God, He trains His eyes on them and elevates them to a lofty sphere of existence, totally insulated from the chance happenings of life; as it says in *Psalms: the eye of H ASHEM is on those who fear Him.*

upon those who await His kindness,
¹⁹ To rescue from death their soul,
and sustain them in famine.
²⁰ Our soul longed for HASHEM —
our help and our shield is He.
²¹ For in Him will our hearts be glad
for in His Holy Name we trusted.
²² May Your kindness, HASHEM, be upon us,
just as we awaited You.

By virtue of this man's confidence in God's ability to protect, God will cause him to be fed even in time of severe famine (Radak).

[In Job 5:20 we read בְּרָעָב פָּדְךָ מִמָּוֶת, Through famine He redeems you from death. Malbim (ibid.) explains: When the All Merciful decrees that a country is about to be destroyed by an earthquake or a similar holocaust, what does He do? He visits a devastating famine upon the land, forcing the inhabitants to flee in time to escape the catastrophic upheaval of the earth. Thus, the harsh curse of famine was truly a blessing in disguise, for it limited the extent of the later catastrophe.

Based on this we may render our verse as וּלְחַיּוֹתָם בְּרָעָב, and sustain them, i.e., save their lives, through famine.]

20. נַפְשֵׁנוּ חִכְּתָה לַה׳ — Our soul longed [lit. waited] for HASHEM.

Because we saw that those who fear God and await His help are answered, we too look to Him for help (Ibn Ezra).

21. כִּי בוֹ יִשְׂמַח לִבֵּנוּ — For in Him will our hearts be glad.

When He will save us from all the evils which threaten us, we will rejoice in the knowledge that our salvation stems from Him (Radak).

22. יְהִי חַסְדְּךָ ה׳ עָלֵינוּ כַּאֲשֶׁר יִחַלְנוּ לָךְ — May Your kindness, HASHEM, be upon us just as we awaited You.

[This re-emphasizes the concept that God's beneficience rests upon man in proportion to his sincere trust in God.]

34 מזמור לד

T o truly appreciate this psalm we must be aware of the events
which inspired it. Midrash Shocher Tov provides the essential
background:

Koheles says: He made everything beautiful in its proper time (Ec-
clesiates 3:11). David said to the Holy One, Blessed be He:'All that
You created is beautiful, and wisdom is the most beautiful of all.
However, I fail to appreciate the value of madness. What satisfacton
can You derive from a lunatic walking about, ripping his clothing,
chased by little children and mocked by all?'

God replied: 'David, by your life, I promise that you will some day
need this madness which you now criticize. As Solomon said, He who
despises something will be punished by it (Proverbs 13:13). Furthermore, David, I promise that you will even pray that I give this
madness to you.'

A short time later, David, forced to escape from the wrath of Saul,
fled to the land of the Philistines with nothing but the sword of
Goliath, which he took from the giant after slaying him. Goliath's
brothers were the bodyguards of Achish, King of the Philistine city of
Gath. They recognized David and the sword of their recently slain
brother. They asked the king for permission to avenge Goliath by
killing David. After some hesitation, the king agreed. Upon hearing
this, David prayed for help.

'What do you wish?', God asked.

'Please give me a measure of that madness which I once criticized'.

David assumed the role of a madman, acting strangely. He wrote
on the city gates, 'King Achish owes me one hundred myriad [coins]
and his wife owes fifty myriads.' The mother and daughter of Achish
also went mad. They shouted and raved insanely inside the palace and
David ranted outside. Exasperated, Achish drove David away, saying: Am I lacking in mad people that you bring this fellow to rave in
my presence? (I Samuel 21:16). Then David composed this Psalm in
gratitude for his madness.

א לְדָוִד בְּשַׁנּוֹתוֹ אֶת־טַעְמוֹ לִפְנֵי אֲבִימֶלֶךְ
ב וַיְגָרְשֵׁהוּ וַיֵּלַךְ: אֲבָרְכָה אֶת־יהוה בְּכָל־
ג עֵת תָּמִיד תְּהִלָּתוֹ בְּפִי: בַּיהוה תִּתְהַלֵּל

1. בְּשַׁנּוֹתוֹ — *When he disguised* [lit. *changed*].

When he feigned idiocy by drooling, with saliva running down his beard (*I Samuel* 21:14) (*Rashi*).

Zais Ra'anan asks why David had to ask God to send a fit of madness upon him — could he not have pretended to be berserk? He answers that David's primary request was not that he become mad, but that Achish's mother and daughter should also be seized with lunacy; for that, too, was essential for the success of his deception (see Prefatory Remarks). However, *Yaavetz Hadoresh* holds that feigned idiocy is easily detected. Hence, David asked for true madness in order to be convincing.

טַעְמוֹ — *His sanity.*

Metzudas Zion refers this to the ability to communicate ideas logically and intelligibly as in the verse, וְטַעַם זְקֵנִים יִקָּח [טַעַם], *He takes away the* [טַעַם] *understanding of the aged* (*Job* 12:20). [Or as in, טוֹב טַעַם וָדַעַת לַמְּדֵנִי, *Good understanding and wisdom, teach me* (119:6-6)]

לִפְנֵי אֲבִימֶלֶךְ — *Before Abimelech.*

Although in *I Samuel,* this king is called Achish, perhaps he had two names (*Ibn Ezra*); or Abimelech was the generic title of all Philistine kings, and Achish was his given name. Similarly, all Egyptian kings bore the royal title Pharoah (*Rashi*). [See *Rashbam* to *Genesis* 41:10.]

Midrash Shocher Tov explains that Achish was called Abimelech because, since he released David unharmed, he resembled an earlier Philistine King Abimelech, who acted righteously towards Abraham and Isaac, sending them away from his land safely.

וַיְגָרְשֵׁהוּ — *Who drove him out.*

Yaavetz Hadoresh explains that this, too, was a miracle because Achish should have suspected that David's madness might be only, even if genuine, temporary. Logically he should have killed David lest his sanity return making him once again a dangerous enemy.

וַיֵּלַךְ — *And he left.*

That David was able to leave Gath was another miracle, notes *Yaavetz Hadoresh,* because even after Achish released him, only Divine intervention prevented the furious, vengeful brothers of Goliath from pursuing the helpless David and killing him.

Alshich observes a different wonder here. The moment David turned his back on Achish his Divinely imposed lunacy ended, and וַיֵּלַךְ, *he left,* calmly and normally. Nevertheless, Achish allowed him to go.

Radak notes that the verses of this psalm are arranged according to the alphabet with the exception of the letter ו, *vav,* which appears in the middle of *v.* 6, and not at the beginning.

Chazah Zion explains that David now realized that just as each letter is vital, so does every situation in life, even lunacy, play an essential role in the development of God's universal scheme.

2. אֲבָרְכָה אֶת ה' — *I shall bless HASHEM.*

David's harrowing experience and his miraculous escape taught him that under no circumstances should one complain against God, for all His ways are infused with kindness and mercy. Therefore, he dedicated the rest of this psalm to God's praises (*Sforno*).

XXXIV
1-3

To David:
When he disguised his sanity before Abimelech
who drove him out and he left.
² I shall bless HASHEM at all times,
always shall His praise be in my mouth.
³ In HASHEM does my soul glory,

בְּכָל עֵת — *At all times.*

Now that I recognize that He constantly performs miracles for me, I must bless Him at all times *(Radak).*

Even in times of tragedy I realize that there is reason to bless God, for what could seem more tragic than being afflicted by lunacy, yet for me this was the ultimate blessing *(Kedushas Levi).*

[Koheles (3:2-8) lists twenty-eight different types of עִתִּים, *times.* Some are happy; some are sad. David vows to bless God in all of these diverse times, for he has come to realize that God directs the world at all times for the benefit of the wise and righteous.]

Rambam in the introduction to *Commentary on Mishnah* (Ch. 6), asks why God created so many fools who are without intellect and who live only to pursue their lusts. He answers that the world was created exclusively for those who seek God and despise material comforts. In order to facilitate their survival, God created countless common men who are afflicted with the lunacy of pursuing wealth and security. As a result, they settle and cultivate the earth, toiling incessantly and risking their lives for a pittance, while the wise man reaps the fruits of their labors. David praises this form of productive madness, too.

תָּמִיד תְּהִלָּתוֹ בְּפִי — *Always shall His praise be in my mouth.*

The blessings of God are so sweet to my tongue, that even after the words are concluded the taste of the praise lingers *(Eretz Hachaim).* [1]

3. בַּה' תִּתְהַלֵּל נַפְשִׁי — *In HASHEM does my soul glory.*

I feel personally glorified and praised because I have so great a Patron to save and protect me *(Rashi).*

David was once described to Saul in glowing terms: *He is adept in playing an instrument, a mighty warrior, a man of war, wise in speech, handsome of form and HASHEM is with him (I Samuel* 16:18). Now David declares that the only one of those flattering descriptions which matters to him is the one which attributes all of his outstanding talents to the fact that *HASHEM is with him (Eretz HaChaim).*

Malbim adds that although self-glorification is repulsive, the essence of humility is to feel that one has no personal worth except for that with which God has endowed him. Thus, ego fades entirely and disappears into the splendor of God; as it says: וַיִּגְבַּהּ לִבּוֹ בְּדַרְכֵי ה', *And his heart was lifted up in the ways of HASHEM (II Chronicles* 17:6).

1. When a man realizes that God created everything in the world for His honor, he must desire to honor God at all times, to sanctify Him in all his actions, and to extol, thank, and bless Him always; as it says, *I shall bless HASHEM at all times, always shall His praise be in my mouth.* Whatever he utters, to friends or strangers, must be proper so that God is sanctified through his words. He should extol the great value of serving and fearing God and praise those who do so. In this manner a person can attain heavenly merit through the meditation of his heart and the utterance of his lips, without physical exertion. This is among the main purposes for which man was created *(Shaarei Teshuva, III:148).*

ד נַפְשִׁי יִשְׁמְעוּ עֲנָוִים וְיִשְׂמָחוּ: גַּדְּלוּ
ה לַיהוה אִתִּי וּנְרוֹמְמָה שְׁמוֹ יַחְדָּו: דָּרַשְׁתִּי
אֶת־יהוה וְעָנָנִי וּמִכָּל־מְגוּרוֹתַי הִצִּילָנִי:
ו הִבִּיטוּ אֵלָיו וְנָהָרוּ וּפְנֵיהֶם אַל־יֶחְפָּרוּ:
ז זֶה עָנִי קָרָא וַיהוה שָׁמֵעַ וּמִכָּל־צָרוֹתָיו

יִשְׁמְעוּ עֲנָוִים וְיִשְׂמָחוּ — *May humble ones hear and be glad.*

David's friends were the humble people [for he himself was the epitome of humility] and so they rejoiced upon learning of his salvation. Not so the haughty people who were David's enemies (*Radak*).

The humble are generally those who are downtrodden and beset by misfortune and tragedy. Now that they hear that David's tragedy was turned into wondrous salvation, they too may become encouraged to recognize the blessings concealed in their woes (*Kedushas Levi*).

4. גַּדְּלוּ לַה׳ אִתִּי — *Declare the greatness of HASHEM with me.*

David now addresses his sympathizers, the humble ones (v.3), and asks them to join him in lauding God (*Radak*).

וּנְרוֹמְמָה שְׁמוֹ יַחְדָּו — *And let us exalt His Name together.*

I.e., when I return safely to *Eretz Yisrael*, from the land of the Philistines (*Sforno*).

Alshich says that David's call to join him in exalting God alludes to the obligation upon one who is miraculously saved from danger to recite בִּרְכַּת הַגוֹמֵל, *the Blessing of Thanksgiving.* The *Talmud* (*Berachos* 54b) derives this duty from the verse, וִירוֹמְמוּהוּ בִּקְהַל עָם, *They will exalt Him in the congregation of the nation* (107:32).

Malbim differentiates between the

words גָּדוֹל and רָם. גָּדוֹל describes one who is elevated, or great, yet who remains accessible and within human reach. רָם, however, denotes one exalted beyond the human sphere. The gentile cannot conceive of a deity who descends to supervise the lowly affairs of men. To him, God is רָם, *exalted*, as it says, רָם עַל כָּל גּוֹיִם ה׳ עַל הַשָּׁמַיִם כְּבוֹדוֹ, *Exalted above all of the peoples is HASHEM, His glory is upon the heavens* (113:4). Israel, however, knows that although the true essence of Hashem's Being is beyond human comprehension, He is intimately involved in shaping human affairs. Thus, God may well be described as גָּדוֹל, *great,* as we find ה׳ בְּצִיּוֹן גָּדוֹל וְרָם הוּא עַל כָּל הָעַמִּים, *HASHEM is great in Zion, and exalted above all of the nations* (99:2).

Continuing this theme, David challenges those who deny God's *greatness* [i.e., His accessibility to humans and His concern with earthly affairs], for God involves Himself even with madmen, as He did to effect David's rescue from Achish. Therefore, David proclaims, גַּדְּלוּ לַה׳ אִתִּי, *declare the greatness of HASHEM with me.*

David continues his address, saying: For my part, I am prepared to agree with you that God, in His true essence, is indeed totally removed from us. His Name, i.e., His real identity and Being, is רָם, *exalted.* Therefore I invite you to join me וּנְרוֹמְמָה שְׁמוֹ יַחְדָּו, *And let us exalt His Name* [His true Being] *together.*[1]

---

1. Three who eat together are obligated to respond and recite the Grace after Meals in unison. From where is this derived? Rav Assi said: From the verse, *Declare the greatness of HASHEM with me and let us exalt His Name together.*

may humble ones hear and be glad.
⁴ *Declare the greatness of HASHEM with me,*
and let us exalt His Name together.
⁵ *I sought out HASHEM and He answered me,*
and from all my terrors He delivered me
⁶ *They look to Him and become radiant,*
and their faces were not shamed.
⁷ *This poor man called and HASHEM hears—*

5. דָּרַשְׁתִּי אֶת ה' — *I sought out HASHEM.*

When I was in the hands of Achish I pleaded with God to save me from that danger and all similar threats (*Radak*).

וּמִכָּל מְגוּרוֹתַי הִצִּילָנִי — *And from all my terrors He delivered me.*

Not only from Achish but also from Saul who threw a spear at me a number of times and later sent men to my house to kill me (*Radak*).

מְגוּרוֹתַי describes fear as in *Numbers* 22:3, וַיָּגָר מוֹאָב, *And Moab was terrified* (*Rashi*).

[Indeed, Moab's fear of Israel was unfounded, for God delivered them from destruction in the merit of David who was destined to descend from Moab via Ruth.]

6. הִבִּיטוּ אֵלָיו — *They look to Him.*

I.e., all those who were motivated to turn to God because of their woes (*Rashi*).

Although the verb is in past tense, *Radak* interprets it as a reference to the future, describing what will happen to those who *will* look to God.

וְנָהָרוּ — *And become radiant.*

Similarly we find וְאַל תּוֹפַע עָלָיו נְהָרָה, *let the radiance not shine upon it* (*Job* 3:4).

Radak and *Ibn Ezra* suggest that the

word is related to נָהָר, *river.* Until they looked to God they were paralyzed with fear, but now they are infused with new courage, surging ahead confidently like a mighty river.

Hirsch combines both definitions explaining that נְהָרָה is a *stream of light* flowing from its source [light travels in waves which resemble a river]. He notes that the word נֵר, *candle, lamp,* is derived from נוּר or נְהָרָה.

וּפְנֵיהֶם אַל יֶחְפָּרוּ — *And their faces were not shamed.* [See commentary to 35:4.]

A person whose request is refused is humiliated, but these were answered and therefore, not put to shame (*Metzudas David*).

7. זֶה עָנִי קָרָא — *This poor man called.*

David humbly described himself as a helpless pauper, wanting for the mercies of God (*Radak*).

God's concern for David may be illustrated with a parable: There was a king who was extremely fond of a certain pauper. Once, the poor man made a modest feast to celebrate with his sons. Suddenly, the king himself entered and protested against his exclusion from the banquet. The pauper excused himself, explaining that he was ashamed to invite the great king to so meager a repast. The king declared to his dear friend,

Rav Chanan bar Abba said: From where do we know that he who answers Amen should not raise his voice above that of the one who recited the blessing? From the verse, *Declare the greatness of HASHEM with me and let us exalt His Name together* [with the same volume] (*Berachos* 45b).

ח הוֹשִׁיעוֹ: חֹנֶה מַלְאַךְ־יהוה סָבִיב לִירֵאָיו
ט וַיְחַלְּצֵם: טַעֲמוּ וּרְאוּ כִּי־טוֹב יהוה אַשְׁרֵי
י הַגֶּבֶר יֶחֱסֶה־בּוֹ: יִרְאוּ אֶת־יהוה קְדֹשָׁיו

'You have no cause for shame. I swear that your simple fare is far more dear to me than the most lavish banquets of the noblemen.' [Similarly, God prefers the prayers of the humble people who pray with genuine sincerity] (*Aggadas Bereishis*). [See also *Rashi, Numbers* 29:35.]

וַה' שָׁמֵעַ — *And HASHEM hears.*

It does not say that Hashem *heard* (in the past tense), but *hears* (in the present tense). This emphasizes that at the very moment that the poor man calls, before his prayer is even ended, God hears and responds; as in *Isaiah* 65:24, עוֹד הֵם מְדַבְּרִים וַאֲנִי אֶשְׁמָע, *While they still speak, I will hear* (*Rav Chaim Vital*).

8. חֹנֶה מַלְאַךְ ה' סָבִיב לִירֵאָיו — *The angel of HASHEM encamps around His reverent ones.*

David refers to the fact that he was surrounded by the men of Achish and yet God sent His angel to release him (*Ibn Ezra*).

Similarly we find that Daniel [a descendant of David] was thrown into the den of lions but emerged unscathed, for Hashem dispatched His angel to muzzle the lions' mouths (*Radak*).

וַיְחַלְּצֵם — *And he releases them.*

I.e., the angel of God removes the righteous from the menace of the surrounding foe (*Ibn Ezra, Radak, Metzudas David*).

Malbim translates *he armed them with weapons* [as in חָלוּץ לַמִּלְחָמָה, *armed for war (Numbers* 32:29).] He explains this entire verse as an allusion to yet another kindness which God bestowed upon David. After he fled from Achish, David was alone and defenseless. He hid in the cave of Adullam and immediately he was joined by four hundred God-fearing and well-armed men (*I Sam.* 22:1-2).[1]

9. טַעֲמוּ — *Taste.*

Utilize your intellect and fully understand this (*Radak*). [See commentary to v. 1.]

וּרְאוּ — *And see.*

Comprehend this concept intellectually and examine it empirically with your eyes (*Radak*).

Taste with your senses and *see* with your intellect (*Sforno*).

כִּי טוֹב ה' — *That HASHEM is good.*

According to *Yalkut Shimoni* every time one tastes of the delicacies of the physical world it is an opportunity to experience the wonders of the spiritual force which created it:

1. The Rabbis taught: Beloved are the people of Israel, for the Holy One, Blessed be He, has surrounded them with *Mitzvos*: *Tefillin* (phylacteries) on their heads and arms; *Tzitzis* (fringes) on their garments, and *Mezuzos* on their doorposts. Anyone who is encircled by all these *mitzvos* is assured that he is protected against sin; as it says:— *The angel of HASHEM encamps around His reverent ones and he releases them* (*Menachos* 43b).

A person should be very scrupulous about the *mitzvah* of *Mezuzah*. Every time he enters and exits and notices the Unity of the Holy One, Blessed be He, he is reminded of His love, and he awakens from his 'slumber' and erring ways in the transitory existence of This World. Then he will know that nothing exists forever and for all eternity except the knowledge of the Eternal Savior. Realizing this, he will immediately return to his good sense and follow the straight path. The Sages said: Whosoever is surrounded by *Tefillin, Tzitzis* and *Mezuzah* is assured of protection from sin for he has many reminders, and these are the very 'angels' which save him from sin; as it says: *The angel of HASHEM encamps around His reverent ones, and he releases them* (*Rambam, Hilchos Mezuzah* 6:13).

and from all his troubles He saved him.
⁸ The angel of HASHEM encamps around His
reverent ones.
and he releases them.
⁹ Taste and see that HASHEM is good —
praiseworthy is the man who takes
refuge in Him.
¹⁰ Fear HASHEM, you — his holy ones,

Said the Holy One, Blessed be He, 'If you eat of the fruit of the earth or the trees, make a blessing first, otherwise, you are considered as stealing the fruits from their Maker. But if you first bless properly and then eat, it is as if you crowned their maker as King as it says, *Taste — and see that HASHEM is good.'*[1]

אַשְׁרֵי הַגֶּבֶר יֶחֱסֶה בּוֹ — *Praiseworthy is the man who takes refuge in Him.*

After comprehending and experiencing God's goodness, one can appreciate the good fortune of the one who places his trust in God *(Radak).*

[Only after a person *tastes* and *sees* the generosity of God in providing for all, can he appreciate His kindness. And if God is so generous even to those who have not asked for His assistance, how much more magnanimous must He be to those who actually *take refuge in Him.*]

10. יִרְאוּ אֶת ה׳ — *Fear HASHEM..*

This is a command: *stand in fear before God (Rashi).*

Fear of God falls into two categories. One is יִרְאַת הָעוֹנֶשׁ, *fear of punishment.* This is an inferior dimension of fear, for it is entirely motivated by self-concern. It has in it a מַחְסוֹר, *a deficiency.* The more desirable form of fear expresses itself in יִרְאַת הָרוֹמְמוּת, a sense of awe and reverence for God's greatness and perfection, i.e., יִרְאַת ה׳, *Fear of the Name.* The person who rises to this level of God-fearing, is a קָדוֹשׁ, *holy one.* Because his fear is perfect, he will experience no deficiencies in his life. This is the sense of our verse: Fear HASHEM in such a lofty manner that you can be considered holy; then you will lack nothing *(Zekan Aharon).*

קְדֹשָׁיו — *His holy ones.*

These are people who restrain themselves from indulging their lusts,

1. The *Yerushalmi (Kiddushin* 4:12) relates: In the Hereafter a person will be brought to judgment for every species of plant which his eye saw but which he failed to eat. Rabbi Eleazer was scrupulous about fulfilling this dictate and, therefore, he would frugally save in order to buy at least one fruit from every species at least once a year [so that he could bless God for creating such a wide variety of species in This World *(Korban Hoeida, Pnei Moshe)*].

Similarly, we find that Rabbi Judah the Prince mourned when a thousand recipes for figs were partially forgotten *(Nedarim* 50b). Why? Because each recipe brought out a different flavor in the food and exhibited the incredible abundance with which God blessed this world *(Rav Gifter).*

[The difference between a great *tzaddik* and an ordinary man was once described thus: The average person sees and apple and his appetite is whetted. He wants to eat the succulent fruit but remembers that it is forbidden to eat unless a blessing is recited — so he recites a blessing in order *to taste.* However, the *tzaddik* observes an apple and is filled with admiration for the Master of Creation who fashioned so marvelous a fruit. He desires to pronounce the blessing for fruits, but it is not permissible to do so if one does not eat. So he *tastes* the apple in order to be permitted to recite the blessing.]

יא כִּי־אֵין מַחְסוֹר לִירֵאָיו: כְּפִירִים רָשׁוּ
וְרָעֵבוּ וְדֹרְשֵׁי יהוה לֹא־יַחְסְרוּ כָל־טוֹב:
יב לְכוּ־בָנִים שִׁמְעוּ־לִי יִרְאַת יהוה

as we find that the Torah refers to the *Nazir*, who abstains from wine, as קָדֹשׁ, *holy* [*Numbers* 6:5] (*Radak*).

Reishis Chochmah (*Shaar Hakedushah*, 1) explains: Although the holy person is not divorced from normal life, he goes to great lengths to isolate himself from the areas of life which have the potential for sin. Because he is a יְרֵא ה', *one who fears HASHEM*, he avoids sin strenuously and erects safeguards to separate himself from the possiblity of evil. Therefore he is called קָדֹשׁ, *holy*, [lit. *one who abstains and separates.*]

Malbim contrasts the gentile concept of the saint with the Jewish ideal of sanctity. To them holiness implies a monastic existence, that excludes joy. The underlying motivation of such a course is a wish to run from the dangers and challenges of life. But those who seek God through Torah are totally involved in all aspects of life, for by experiencing every phase of life in accord with the commands of the Torah one meets the living God.

כִּי אֵין מַחְסוֹר לִירֵאָיו — *For there is no deprivation for His reverent ones.*

David addresses the people who have consecrated themselves to Hashem, saying that they need fear Hashem alone and nothing else, for He will provide all of their needs. David was moved to make this pronouncement after he was lost among the hostile Philistines with not a friend in the land to offer him food or lodging. Nevertheless, because he feared only God, David lacked nothing (*Radak*).

11. כְּפִירִים — *Young lions.*

Some render this as כּוֹפְרִים, *unbelievers*, but the proper reading is *young lions*. It describes those who exert themselves excessively [like ferocious beasts] to acquire their sustenance. Some say that Achish's men starved David after they captured him yet God sustained him miraculously as He did Elijah who lived in a desolate cave and subsisted on the food brought him by the ravens (*Ibn Ezra*).

רָשׁוּ וְרָעֵבוּ — *May want and hunger.*

Rabbeinu Bachya in *Kad Hakemach* (*Middas HaBitachon*) observes:

God provides for all of the weak creatures such as the embryo inside its mother's womb or the chick inside the unhatched egg. God sustains the bird in the sky and the fish in the sea — He even nourishes the tiny ant. But God may well deprive mighty creatures of their food; as we read concerning the strongest of animals, *Young lions may want and hunger*. [He does this to demonstrate that it is not might or skill which assures man of his sustenance, only the will of God.]

וְדֹרְשֵׁי ה' לֹא יַחְסְרוּ כָל טוֹב — *But those who seek HASHEM will not lack any good.*

[The Psalmist speaks from personal experience, as he said earlier (*v. 5*), דָּרַשְׁתִּי אֶת ה' וְעָנָנִי, *I sought out HASHEM and He answered me*.] [1]

1. The *Shaloh Hakadosh* observes: It does not say, *Those who seek out HASHEM possess all good things*, but that they *will not lack any good*. They feel no lack because they are happy without unnecessary baubles which superficial people pursue. This may be compared to a man who pitied his neighbor who had no medicines. The neighbor laughed at him, since the absence of medicine was a blessing, because it was an indication of good health rather than sickness. [Cf. *Avos* 4:1, *Who is rich? He who rejoices in his lot.*]
Similarly, an ordinary person observing the home of a Torah scholar bereft of luxuries may

for there is no deprivation for His reverent ones.
¹¹ *Young lions may want and hunger,*
but those who seek HASHEM will not lack
any good.
¹² *Go, O sons, heed me,*
the fear of HASHEM will I teach you.

12. לְכוּ — *Go*
[If the Psalmist wanted people to
come and listen, he should have said
בֹּאוּ, *come,* rather than לְכוּ, *go.*]

Radak answers that sometimes לְכוּ
denotes encouragement to accomplish a
goal and does not actually mean an exhortation to walk away.

Chazah Zion takes the word לְכוּ
literally: Go forth and travel to the
yeshivas to pursue your Torah studies
in order to fulfill the Rabbinic dictum,
'Exile yourself to a place of Torah'(*Avos*
4:14).

However, if you do not educate
yourselves in accordance with my advice, you will not *go* through life
without stumbling as the Psalmist says
(82:5): *They do not know, nor do they
understand, they walk on in darkness*
(*Lachmei Todah*).

This verse speaks of לִמוּד, *learning,*
and so, most appropriately it begins
with the letter ל, *lamed,* which literally
means *learning.* For this very reason,
lamed is the tallest of all the letters, to
show that the study of how to fear God
is the loftiest of all pursuits (*Sefer Chassidim*).

בָּנִים — *O sons.*
Although he is addressing adults,
David calls them *sons,* for they are mere
novices in the discipline of heavenly
fear, and so they resemble children.
[Furtheremore, all students of a teacher
are considered as his sons (cf. *II Kings*
2:3)] (*Ibn Yachya*).

Or, he does not mean that they are his
sons, rather they are God's sons by virtue of the fear of heaven they attempt to
acquire, as the *Talmud* (*Bava Basra* 10a)
says: When Israel does the will of God
they are called sons, but when they do
not do the will of God they are called
slaves! (*Shaarei HaYashar*).

Malbim adds: In other religions, the
study of theology and fear of God is
reserved for advanced priests. The
Jewish ideal strives to inculcate the fear
of God into the children at the earliest
possible age when they are still impres-
sionable בָּנִים, *sons.*

This is especially true in regard to the
sin of slander (*v.* 14). If a father does
not train his son to guard his tongue in
his early youth, the hapless child will
develop vicious speech habits which
will cripple him for a lifetime (*Siach
Yitzchak*).

שִׁמְעוּ לִי — *Heed me.*
If you hearken to my teachings you
will be לִי, *unto me,* i.e., my devoted disciples who accompany me both in This
World and the Hereafter [where I will
share with you all new revelations of
divine wisdom which are granted to me]
(*Chazah Zion*).

יִרְאַת ה' אֲלַמֶּדְכֶם — *The fear of HASHEM
will I teach you.*
The masses fear sin only because they
dread אֱלֹהִים, *the Dispenser of Strict
Justice,* who punishes for transgressions. They fail to realize that the act of

be concerned about the latter's welfare. The scholar, however, rejoices because he is not sick
with a desire for luxurious trappings. He does not miss the luxuries which ordinary men attain
only with sweat and toil. Hence, David rightly says: *Those who seek HASHEM will not lack
any good* (*Lev Eliyahu* Vol. I).

יג אֲלַמֶּדְכֶם: מִי־הָאִישׁ הֶחָפֵץ חַיִּים אֹהֵב

יד יָמִים לִרְאוֹת טוֹב: נְצֹר לְשׁוֹנְךָ מֵרָע

טו וּשְׂפָתֶיךָ מִדַּבֵּר מִרְמָה: סוּר מֵרָע וַעֲשֵׂה־

sin in itself is harmful to both body and soul. I will teach you that 'ה, *HASHEM*, *the Dispenser of Mercy*, is the author of the prohibition against sin because in His boundless Mercy He is concerned for our welfare. You will learn to fear sin because HASHEM has determined it to be harmful, just as a kind father orders his son away from the thorns (*Eitz Yoseif*).

13. [Now David turns to a matter very close to his heart because it was the cause of much suffering for him and for others. Evil men constantly slandered him to Saul and kept the flames of the king's jealousy burning. While David fled to Achish, Doeg the Edomite was hastening to tell Saul of David's visit to Nob, the city where he was hospitably received by the priests who thought he was still one of Saul's favorites. Doeg distorted the facts and convinced Saul that the priests were conspiring with David in rebellion against the throne. Thus misled, the angry Saul had the in-

habitants of the city executed as rebels.

The *Yerushalmi* (*Peah* 1:1) teaches that David's generation was generally God-fearing, but its people fell in battle because they were lax with their tongues. The *Talmud* (*Shabbos* 56a) cites an opinion that even David was *once* guilty of accepting a slanderous report. Therefore, David expounds upon the evils of לָשׁוֹן הָרַע, *evil speech*.]

מִי הָאִישׁ הֶחָפֵץ חַיִּים — *Which man desires life?*

The eternal life of the World to Come (*Sforno*).

[In truth, the man who guards his tongue is assuring himself life and longevity in This World as well. The *Baal Shem Tov* said that every man is alloted only a certain amount of words for his entire lifetime. Once he has used up his quota, he must depart from this world.] [1]

אֹהֵב יָמִים — *Who loves days.*

I.e., the fleeting *days* of This World which are insignificant in comparison

1. The *Talmud* (*Avodah Zarah* 19b) relates:
Rabbi Alexandri went about shouting like a peddler hawking his wares, 'Who wants life, who wants life!'
Everyone crowded around him and pleaded 'Give us life.' He quoted our verse: *Which man desires life, who loves days of seeing good? Guard your tongue from evil, and your lips from speaking deceitfully.*
Perhaps a person will say, 'Now that I have avoided evil I can rest and sleep,' therefore, the following verse says, *Turn away from evil and do good*; there is no *good* but Torah study, as it says, *I have given you a good lesson, do not forsake my Torah* (*Proverbs* 4:2).
What was the novelty of Rav Alexandri's message? Surely his listeners were familiar with the verse from *Psalms*! Indeed, they knew the verse, but they considered it to be a homiletical formula intended for exalted scholars and pious saints. Rabbi Alexandri meant to demonstrate that David's words should be taken quite literally — by zealously protecting the purity of his speech, one does indeed assure himself of earthly reward (*Rav Eliyahu Meir Bloch, Shiurei Daas*).
[In spreading his message as if he were a peddler, Rabbi Alexandri may have intended to portray the contrast between himself and a slanderer. The Torah portrays the slanderer as a רָכִיל, *peddler*, (*Leviticus* 19:16), because he goes from house to house bartering tales and offering malicious talk like a peddler selling his wares. Rabbi Alexandri wished to show that the same character trait could be used for good. As Solomon said, *Death and life are in the power of the tongue* (*Proverbs* 18:21). The gossip peddles death, Rabbi Alexandri peddled life.]

XXXIV
13-15

13 *Which man desires life,*
who loves days of seeing good?
14 *Guard your tongue from evil,*
and your lips from speaking deceitfully.
15 *Turn from evil and do good,*

with the eternity of the World to Come (*Sforno*).

Again, stresses the *Malbim*, we see that the lessons of fearing God are meant for those who love the fullness of life, not for those who shun it.

[This alludes to the fact that the man who does not guard his tongue is actually shortening the days of his life (as if he does not love his days), for the *Talmud (Arachin* 15b) states: לָשׁוֹן הָרָע, *evil speech*, kills three people: the speaker, the listener, and the subject.]

לִרְאוֹת טוֹב — *Of seeing good.*

[This alludes to the fact that those who slander will lose even the merit of the good deeds which they performed, as *Chovos Halevavos* says in *Shaar Hakniah* 7:

On the day of reckoning many people will find unearned merits inscribed in their ledgers. They will say, 'We have not performed these good deeds.'

They will be told, 'These are the good deeds of people who spoke against you.' The people whose merits were taken away will be told, 'You forfeited your good deeds when you spoke against others.'

Similarly, some will find offenses in their ledgers that they never committed. They will be told, 'These are the offenses committed by the people you have spoken against.']

14. נְצֹר לְשׁוֹנְךָ מֵרָע — *Guard your tongue from evil.*

Radak observes that in these two verses David discusses three categories of sin; sins of thought, of speech, and of deed. The first category, transgressions of the evil tongue, includes not only slander, but also false testimony, cursing parents, judges, kings, and certainly, God Himself.

The *Midrash (Vayikra Rabbah* 33:1) relates: Rabbi Shimon ben Gamliel told Tavi, his servant, 'Go to the marketplace and buy some good food.' Tavi went to the market and returned with a tongue. Afterward, Rabbi Shimon said to Tavi, 'Go to the marketplace and buy some bad food.' Tavi again returned with a tongue.

'What is this?' asked Rabbi Shimon. 'When I told you to buy food that is good you bought tongue, and when I told you to buy food that is bad, you also bought tongue?'

Tavi replied, 'From a tongue can come good and bad. When a tongue is good, there is nothing better. But when a tongue is bad, there is nothing worse.'

וּשְׂפָתֶיךָ מִדַּבֵּר מִרְמָה — *And your lips from speaking deceitfully.*

Deceit is the second category of sin which includes the evil thoughts which the deceptive man contrives while his mouth speaks words of friendship (*Radak*).

Not only outright slander is forbidden, but there are instances when it is forbidden even to speak in praise of another man (*Arachin* 15b), for laudatory description can easily lay the groundwork for a listing of the admired man's flaws as well. To slyly recount someone's virtues as an excuse for discussing his vices is true מִרְמָה, *deceit* (*Chazah David*).

15. סוּר מֵרָע — *Turn from evil.*

This is a warning against the third area of sin, the performance of evil actions (*Radak*).

Indeed, the Psalmist warns that it is

טז טוֹב בַּקֵּשׁ שָׁלוֹם וְרָדְפֵהוּ: עֵינֵי יהוה אֶל־
יז צַדִּיקִים וְאָזְנָיו אֶל־שַׁוְעָתָם: פְּנֵי יהוה
יח בְּעֹשֵׂי רָע לְהַכְרִית מֵאֶרֶץ זִכְרָם: צָעֲקוּ
יט וַיהוה שָׁמֵעַ וּמִכָּל־צָרוֹתָם הִצִּילָם: קָרוֹב
יהוה לְנִשְׁבְּרֵי־לֵב וְאֶת־דַּכְּאֵי־רוּחַ

insufficient to merely refrain from offensive actions. One must *turn away* from evil and shun everything that can lead to it. One should erect safeguards to prevent himself from sinning (*Avos* 1:1), thereby abstaining from any act that may eventually result in evil, even if that particular act happens to be permissible.

Furthermore, one must remember that the performance of good begins only after abstinence from evil; one may never do evil to accomplish good. The ends do not justify the means. Never should one delude himself into thinking that his good deeds will make amends for his evil ones, as long as he has not repented from evil (*Hirsch*).

וַעֲשֵׂה טוֹב — *And do good.*

This is an exhortation to perform the positive commandments (*Radak*).

[In regard to evil speech, merely to *turn from evil* by refraining from slander is considered a positive accomplishment. The *Vilna Gaon* in *Iggeres HaGra* cites the *Midrash* which says: For every second that a person remains silent, he will merit a reward of a magnitude that is even beyond the comprehension of the celestial angels].

However, *Hirsch* cautions that although we are obligated to make every personal sacrifice for the sake of peace, disregarding personal interest, advan-

tage, and honor in the name of harmonious accord — nevertheless we may not abandon our duties to God even if they arouse the hostility and opposition of the entire world. We cannot *seek peace* at the expense of the principle of סוּר מֵרָע וַעֲשֵׂה טוֹב, *turn from evil and do good*.

בַּקֵּשׁ שָׁלוֹם — *Seek peace.*

Where you live (*Rashi*).

One who spreads slander creates conflicts and quarrels. The holy *Ari* promises that one who does not slander others will merit, measure for measure, that others will not speak about him. Thus his life will be peaceful.

וְרָדְפֵהוּ — *And pursue it.*

Elsewhere, too! (*Rashi*).

The *Talmud* (*Berachos* 6b) states: Rav Chelbo said in the name of Rav Huna, Whoever knows that his friend is accustomed to greet him, should make an effort to greet that friend with a blessing of 'Shalom' first (in order to enhance their friendship) as it says, *Seek peace (shalom) and pursue it.*[1]

16. עֵינֵי ה' אֶל צַדִּיקִים — *The eyes of HASHEM are toward the righteous.*

This is the reward of the God-fearing man described above: God constantly takes note of him and protects him (*Radak*).

1. Hillel said: Be among the disciples of Aaron; love peace and pursue peace, love people and draw them close to Torah (*Avos* 1:12).

This dictum is elaborated upon in *Avos D'Rabbi Nathan* (12:3):

When Aaron would happen to meet a wicked man on the street he would greet him warmly. On the morrow when the wicked man had an urge to sin, he would restrain himself saying, 'How can I do this? I won't be able to look my dear friend, Aaron, in the eye the next time he greets me!' So Aaron's 'Shalom' restrained this man from sin.

seek peace and pursue it.
¹⁶ The eyes of HASHEM are toward the righteous,
and His ears to their cry.
¹⁷ The face of HASHEM is against evildoers,
to excise from earth their memory.
¹⁸ They cried out and HASHEM hears
and from all their troubles He rescues them.
¹⁹ HASHEM is close to the brokenhearted;
and those crushed in spirit, He saves.

The People of Israel determine the intensity and intimacy of God's relationship with His nation. When they choose to neglect God, He neglects them in return. But when they search Him out, He eagerly responds in like fashion, as Daniel prayed, *My God, turn Your ear and hear, open Your eyes and see* (Daniel 9:18). Thus, in our verse, too, the eyes of God are upon His righteous ones when they cry out to Him, thereby demonstrating their closeness to Him (*Kedushas Levi*).

וְאָזְנָיו אֶל שַׁוְעָתָם — *And His ears, to their cry.*

If some mishap were to befall the *tzaddik*, God would immediately hear his cry (*Radak*).

Alshich asks: If God's eyes carefully supervise and protect every step of the righteous, how can any mishap befall them? He answers: God loves to hear the prayers of the righteous. He sometimes allows a mishap to occur in order to increase their prayers, and thereby carry their souls to otherwise unattainable heights.

17. פְּנֵי ה׳ — *The face of HASHEM.*

Rashi comments that this usage always describes a countenance of anger as God says of the man who sacrifices

his son to Molech, וְשַׂמְתִּי אֲנִי אֶת פָּנַי בָּאִישׁ הַהוּא, *Then I will set my face (of anger) against that man* (Leviticus 20:5).

לְהַכְרִית מֵאֶרֶץ זִכְרָם — *To excise from earth their memory.*

[The *Talmud* (Sanhedrin 110b) cites a number of opinions as to how the wicked are uprooted from the world. Not only are their bodies destroyed, so are their souls. Not only do *they* vanish, their young children are also cut off. And, although the remembrance of their sins endures, God makes every effort to blot out any trace of their good deeds. He quickly repays them in This World for every good deed, so that He can eradicate all their merits for entry in the World to Come.]

18. צָעֲקוּ — *They cried out.*

The righteous ones (*Rashi*), and the repentant sinners (*Ibn Ezra*).

וַה׳ שָׁמֵעַ — *And HASHEM hears.*

Even if words cannot express their anguish and their cry remains stifled in their hearts, Hashem still hears (*Sfas Emes*). [See also v. 7.]

19. קָרוֹב ה׳ לְנִשְׁבְּרֵי לֵב — *HASHEM is close to the brokenhearted.*

The singular form נִשְׁבַּר לֵב would have been sufficient to describe the

When Aaron heard that two men were quarreling, he would go and sit next to one, saying: 'I just saw that other fellow beating his breast and tearing his clothes in anguish and remorse, crying out that he is at fault in your quarrel.' Aaron did not leave until the man was appeased. He repeated this procedure with the other party, too. Later, when these two men chanced to meet, they hugged and kissed each other in total reconciliation.

כ יוֹשִׁיעַ: רַבּוֹת רָעוֹת צַדִּיק וּמִכֻּלָּם יַצִּילֶנּוּ

כא יהוה: שֹׁמֵר כָּל־עַצְמוֹתָיו אַחַת מֵהֵנָּה לֹא

כב נִשְׁבָּרָה: תְּמוֹתֵת רָשָׁע רָעָה וְשֹׂנְאֵי צַדִּיק

כג יֶאְשָׁמוּ: פּוֹדֶה יהוה נֶפֶשׁ עֲבָדָיו וְלֹא
יֶאְשְׁמוּ כָּל־הַחֹסִים בּוֹ:

broken heart. The plural form emphasizes that one break is not enough; the
truly contrite heart should be broken
into many pieces. The more shattered
the heart, the closer is God (*Turei
Zahav*).

Rabbi Alexandri said: To use broken
dishes and utensils is a disgrace even for
the most simple of men. Nevertheless,
God prefers to use broken vessels in His
service, as it says, HASHEM *is close to
the heartbroken*; and, *The sacrifices of
God are a broken spirit, a broken and
crushed heart, God will not despise*
[51:19] (*Midrash, Vayikra Rabbah* 7:2).

20. רַבּוֹת רָעוֹת צַדִּיק — *Many are the
mishaps of the righteous man.*

Grammatically the word צַדִּיק, *righteous man*, should have been preceded
by the prepositional prefix לְ, *to*, or *of*.
By omitting it, the Psalmist alludes to an
additional lesson: רַבּוֹת רָעוֹת, *from
many mishaps* — צַדִּיק, there emerges a
righteous man i.e., greatness is a
product of challenges and the effort to
surmount them (*Sfas Emes*).

וּמִכֻּלָּם יַצִּילֶנּוּ ה׳ — *But from them all
HASHEM rescues him.*

Radak observes that God constantly
tests the *tzaddik* with many a difficult
נִסָּיוֹן, *trial*, in order to elevate him and to

demonstrate to others the loyalty of the
tzaddik so that they will be inspired by
his example. However, God will rescue
the *tzaddik* from any real danger and
will not allow him to stumble.

21. שֹׁמֵר כָּל עַצְמוֹתָיו אַחַת מֵהֵנָּה לֹא נִשְׁבָּרָה
— *He guards all his bones, even one of
them was not broken.*

The term *bones* is used to describe the
entire body because the skeletal structure is the body's mainstay (*Radak*).

The *tzaddik* has scrupulously observed all of God's 613 commands
which correspond to the 248 organs and
365 sinews, ligaments and tendons; a
total of six hundred thirteen. Hashem
reciprocates and watches over all 613
parts of his body (*Tehillos Hashem*).[1]

22. תְּמוֹתֵת רָשָׁע רָעָה — *The death blow
of the wicked is evil.*

תְּמוֹתֵת is the same as תָּמִית, *will slay*.
The evil of the wicked man will kill him
(*Rashi*).

The *tzaddik* is rescued from רַבּוֹת
רָעוֹת, *many evils* (v. 20), but even one
רָעָה, *evil*, is sufficient to undo the
wicked man. As Solomon said (*Proverbs*
24:16) *The tzaddik falls seven times and
rises up again, but the wicked are ensnared in [one] evil* (*Siach Yitzchak*).

The very evil which he plots against

1. *Sefer HaBris* (Part I, Essay 11, Chapter 10) states that the entire body disintegrates after
death with the exception of one indestructible bone at the top of the spinal column. This bone,
called *Luz* or *Nasqui*, can be neither shattered by hammers nor consumed by fires (*Midrash,
Vayikra Rabbah*). When God resurrects the dead, this surviving bone will be used as the
starting point for the restoration of the rest of the body. The Psalmist alludes to this
phenomenon saying, *He safeguards all of his* (the *tzaddik's*) *bones*, i.e., even after the skeleton
turns to dust. This will be so because אַחַת מֵהֵנָּה לֹא נִשְׁבָּרָה, *one of them* [i.e., the *Luz*] *was
never broken*. However, this is not the case with the wicked who are totally corrupted. They
shall not be resurrected for even their *Luz* bone rots in the dust, לְהַכְרִית מֵאֶרֶץ זִכְרָם, *to excise
from earth their memory* (v. 17).

XXXIV ²⁰ *Many are the mishaps of the righteous man,*
but from them all HASHEM rescues him.
²¹ *He guards all his bones,*
even one of them was not broken.
²² *The death blow of the wicked is evil,*
and the haters of the righteous
will be condemned.
²³ *HASHEM redeems the soul of His servants,*
and all who take refuge in Him
will not be condemned.

the righteous will lash back and kill him instead, as in *Psalms 7:17: He falls into the very trap which he set (Radak).*

Based on verses 21-22, *Rabbeinu Yonah (Shaarei Teshuvah 4:13)* expounds on two forms of Divine punishment: The afflictions which God brings upon the wicked are יִסּוּרֵי נָקָם, *afflictions of revenge,* so to speak, which have the purpose of destroying those who are unworthy of mercy. When they are punished, the afflictions merited for even a *single* sin are enough to destroy them, for the entire punishment is brought upon them at once as we read, תְּמוֹתֵת רָשָׁע רָעָה, *The death blow of the wicked is evil* (in the singular form). Their other transgressions remain unatoned for and continue to blemish their souls.

The righteous, however, have earned the privilege of being punished by gradual, bearable degrees. Thus, all of their transgressions are eventually atoned for. The Sages *(Avodah Zarah 4a)* liken this to a lender's policy with his borrowers. From his antagonists whom he does not trust, he demands prompt and total payment. From his friends, he is satisfied with partial payments within their means.

יֶאְשָׁמוּ — *Will be condemned.*

This translation follows the *Targum* (יִתְחַיְּבוּן). *Radak* and *Metzudas David* render *they will be made desolate,* deriving the word from שְׁמָמוֹן, *desolation.* Similarly, we find, עֶדְרֵי הַצֹּאן נֶאְשָׁמוּ, *the flocks of sheep were devastated (Joel 1:18).*

23. פָּדָה ה' נֶפֶשׁ עֲבָדָיו — *HASHEM redeems the soul of His servants.*

The misfortune which was originally prepared for the righteous is diverted from its path and directed towards the wicked instead, as Solomon said *(Proverbs 11:8):* צַדִּיק מִצָּרָה נֶחֱלָץ וַיָּבֹא רָשָׁע תַּחְתָּיו, *The righteous man is released from trouble and the wicked man comes in his stead (Eitz Yoseif).*

Mordechai was redeemed from the gallows and Haman hung in his place.

When Adam ate from the Tree of Knowledge, all his organs derived pleasure from this sin, and were condemned. Only the *Luz* refused to absorb any part of this forbidden fruit and remained immortal.

After the three generous Sabbath meals, the body is surfeited and derives no physical pleasure from the *Melaveh Malkah* eaten after the Sabbath ends. Only the *Luz* is nourished by this meal exclusively, for it is eaten only for the sake of enriching the immortal spirit. The *Melaveh Malkah* is call *the feast of King David,* for *David, King of Israel lives on and endures!* It is he who will restore the immortality of Adam for he will bring the Messianic era which will be followed by the resurrection of the dead (whose formation is based on the *Luz* bone) for all eternity.

Chananyah, Mishael, and Azariyah emerged from the furnace alive, while their executioners were burned instead (Vilna Gaon).

Sforno interprets: Hashem redeems His servants from sin, i.e., He guides their footsteps away from temptation and error.

וְלֹא יֶאְשְׁמוּ כָּל הַחֹסִים בּוֹ — All who take refuge in Him will not be condemned.

Targum and Ibn Ezra translate יֶאְשְׁמוּ here as they do in the previous verse, will be condemned.

Rashi paraphrases: Those who ask God to rescue them from sin will never have cause to regret their actions and cry out in remorse, 'אָשַׁמְנוּ, We are guilty!'

[David sought refuge in God while in the grip of his Philistine enemies. The Philistines found him guilty and sought to condemn him for the death of Goliath, but God redeemed the righteous David and set him free.]

D avid concluded the preceding psalm with the hopeful declaration
of his belief that פּוֹדֶה ה׳ נֶפֶשׁ עֲבָדָיו, HASHEM redeems the soul of
His servants. Now, he requests that this Divine attribute be put into
practice, and he pleads with God to redeem him from the menace of
his many enemies (Tehillas Hashem).

Radak comments that David composed this psalm while fleeing
from Saul. According to Sforno, these verses record David's pleas as
he fled from his rebellious son, Absalom.

א לְדָוִד | רִיבָה יהוה אֶת־יְרִיבַי לְחַם אֶת־
ב לֹחֲמָי: הַחֲזֵק מָגֵן וְצִנָּה וְקוּמָה בְּעֶזְרָתִי:
ג וְהָרֵק חֲנִית וּסְגֹר לִקְרַאת רֹדְפָי אֱמֹר
ד לְנַפְשִׁי יְשֻׁעָתֵךְ אָנִי: יֵבֹשׁוּ וְיִכָּלְמוּ

1. רִיבָה ה׳ — *Fight, HASHEM.*

Radak explains this term as a command. *Midrash Shocher Tov* elaborates on its implications:

Is it conceivable that a flesh and blood servant should order his master, 'Go out and fight my enemies for me?' Yet we find that the Holy One ,Blessed be He, said to David, 'You immerse yourself in Torah study and I will fight your wars.' This is what Moses meant in the verse, עַל כֵּן יֵאָמַר בְּסֵפֶר מִלְחֲמֹת ה', *Therefore it shall be said in the Book of HASHEM's wars* (Numbers 21:14). Hashem said: 'If you are בְּסֵפֶר, [immersed] *in the Book* [of Torah study], then מִלְחֲמֹת ה' [your wars will become] *the wars of HASHEM* [and I, HASHEM, will fight them for you].'

יְרִיבַי ... לֹחֲמָי — *My adversaries* [lit. those who fight me] ... *my attackers* [lit. those who declare war on me.]

David emphasizes that the quarrel is only one-sided. He does not say that *he* fights *them*, rather *they* fight *him*, but he does not reciprocate their hostility (*Hirsch*).

According to *Yaavetz Hadoresh*, the word יְרִיבַי describes David's main adversaries, such as Saul or Absalom. Had the feud been limited only to these individuals, it would have been a mere רִיב, *quarrel*. But now that many others joined forces with the principal antagonists, the limited *quarrel* turned into מִלְחָמָה, *war*. David refers to these outside interlopers as לֹחֲמָי, literally *those who declare war against me*.

Midrash Chachamim suggests that the difference between these words may be understood in light of the fact that

every war which flares up on earth is evidence of a tremendous spiritual struggle between celestial forces representing each side. David asks that Hashem first vanquish his adversaries above, יְרִיבַי, and consequently this will spell the doom of those who make actual war below, לֹחֲמָי, his *attackers*.

2. הַחֲזֵק — *Take hold.*

Grasp it tightly, with חֹזֶק, *strength* (*Radak*).

מָגֵן וְצִנָּה — *Shield and armor.*

[These two words, which appear to be synonymous, warrant deeper scrutiny. On the verses כַּצִּנָּה רָצוֹן תַּעְטְרֶנּוּ, *You will surround him with Your favor like a shield* (5:13), *Rashi* describes the צִנָּה as a shield which protects from only three sides. However, on the verse צִנָּה וְסֹחֵרָה אֲמִתּוֹ, *Like encircling armor is His truth* (91:4) *Rashi* explains that צִנָּה surrounds the wearer from almost four sides. Similarly, we read כִּי שֶׁמֶשׁ וּמָגֵן ה', *for HASHEM is a sun and a shield* (*ibid.*) on which the *Midrash* comments: A מָגֵן is a shield which protects from only three sides. From where do we know that Hashem guards even from the fourth side? From the verse כַּצִּנָּה רָצוֹן תַּעְטְרֶנּוּ. This indicates that צִנָּה is indeed a four-sided protective armor.

Interestingly, *Targum* always renders מָגֵן as תְּרִיסָא. Also, whenever צִנָּה is mentioned alone the *Targum* translates it as תְּרִיסָא. But, when the words מָגֵן וְצִנָּה come together, as in this verse, the *Targum* for צִנָּה changes to עֲגִיל, *a round encircling armament*. This leads us to conclude that when the word צִנָּה is used alone it is the same as מָגֵן (i.e., a three-sided shield), and thus it should be translated as *shield*. But when it appears in conjunction with מָגֵן it indicates greater protection than a shield and should be translated as *armor*. The *Targum* of צִנָּה וְסֹחֵרָה is תְּרִיסָא וַעֲגִילָה and, according to *Rashi* (*ibid.*), the second word is

XXXV
1-4

To David: Fight, HASHEM, my adversaries,
      battle my attackers.
² Take hold of shield and armor,
      and rise up in my defense.
³ Draw the spear,
      and barricade before my pursuers;
Say to my soul,
      'Your salvation am I.'
⁴ May they be shamed and disgraced,

---

an adjective, and so the phrase is translated *encircling armor*. Perhaps the word צִנָּה has some relationship to צִנְעָה, *privacy, secrecy, enclosure.*]

וְקוּמָה בְּעֶזְרָתִי — *And rise up in my defense* [lit. *help.*]

Since I do not rely on my own shield and armor, only Yours, it is proper that You should defend me (*Ibn Ezra*).

Paamonei Zahav offers a general explanation of this psalm which records David's repeated requests for the destruction of his enemies. Elsewhere, David preached a different message, as we find יִתַּמּוּ חַטָּאִים מִן הָאָרֶץ, *Let sins cease to be on earth* (104:35), which the *Talmud (Berachos* 10a) interprets as meaning 'let sins cease but not the sinners,' i.e., do not pray for the death of the people who sin; rather pray that they should repent and consequently sin will cease. However, the wicked discussed here are so corrupt that the paths of repentance are sealed before them. Their hearts are consumed with hatred as is evidenced by the fact that they hate without any reason. Such fierce, bitter animosity can never be cured. Similarly we find in the *Talmud (Gittin* 7a) that the righteous Mar Ukava was gratuitously threatened and cursed by violent men and Rabbi Elazar advised him to pray morning and evening for their destruction.

3. וְהָרֵק — *Draw.*

[This comes from רֵיק, *empty.* When a spear or sword is drawn, its sheath or scabbard is emptied of it, as we find אָרִיק חַרְבִּי, *I draw my sword (Exodus* 15:9).]

It also means *to arm* as in וַיָּרֶק אֶת חֲנִיכָיו, *And he armed his trained men (Genesis* 14:14).

חֲנִית — *The spear.*

Here David alludes to the spear which Saul threw at his head, narrowly missing him [*I Samuel* 18:11] (*Chazah Zion*), and also to the spear which was lying by the head of the sleeping Saul which David did not use to kill him [*I Samuel* 26:7-9] (*Zera Yaakov*). [Because David did not defend himself against the spears of Saul out of fear that he might harm God's anointed, he calls upon God Himself to do him justice.]

אֱמֹר לְנַפְשִׁי יְשֻׁעָתֵךְ אָנִי — *Say to my soul, 'Your salvation, am I.'*

Inject strength, fortitude and courage into my heart so that it should not fear the enemy (*Radak*).

4. [*Malbim* traces the various levels of humiliation documented in this verse.]

יֵבֹשׁוּ — *Be shamed.*

This an inner, self-generated shame.

יִכָּלְמוּ — *Be disgraced.*

This embarrassment is more severe and is inflicted by others.

מְבַקְשֵׁי נַפְשִׁי יִסֹּגוּ אָחוֹר וְיַחְפְּרוּ חֹשְׁבֵי
ה רָעָתִי: יִהְיוּ כְּמֹץ לִפְנֵי־רוּחַ וּמַלְאַךְ יהוה
ו דּוֹחֶה: יְהִי־דַרְכָּם חֹשֶׁךְ וַחֲלַקְלַקֹּת
ז וּמַלְאַךְ יהוה רֹדְפָם: כִּי־חִנָּם טָמְנוּ־לִי
ח שַׁחַת רִשְׁתָּם חִנָּם חָפְרוּ לְנַפְשִׁי: תְּבוֹאֵהוּ
שׁוֹאָה לֹא־יֵדָע וְרִשְׁתּוֹ אֲשֶׁר־טָמַן תִּלְכְּדוֹ

יִסֹּגוּ אָחוֹר — *Retreat* [lit. *fall back*].

This is more intense than shame, but it is a turnabout which comes from the person's own realization of his defects.

וְיַחְפְּרוּ — *Be humilated.*

This is the most intense embarrassment which is caused by others.

The word is related to the root חפר, *to dig,* and suggests that the victim is so humiliated that he desires to bury himself. [In the Yiddish idiom this intense humiliation is called *'tzu bagrubben a mentsch lebedigerheit,'* to bury a person alive.]

5. יִהְיוּ כְּמֹץ לִפְנֵי רוּחַ — *May they be like chaff before the wind.*

[Compare with 1:4: לֹא כֵן הָרְשָׁעִים כִּי אִם כַּמֹּץ אֲשֶׁר תִּדְּפֶנּוּ רוּחַ, *Not so the wicked, they are like the chaff which the wind drives away.*]

Tanchuma (Bamidbar 4) compares the Children of Israel, who are well nourished with *mitzvos,* to the nutritious grain heaped in abundant piles, whereas the empty, meaningless lifestyle of heathens makes them similar to worthless chaff.

וּמַלְאַךְ ה' דוֹחֶה — *With the angel of* HASHEM *driving them on.*

Sometimes the flight of the blown chaff is aborted by an obstacle in its path, but these wicked men will be relentlessly pursued by angels who will give them no respite (*Radak*).

Maharam Markado suggests that this refers to the angel who drove Saul away from David when he was trapped on the סֶלַע הַמַּחְלְקֹת, *mountain of division* [I Samuel 23:27-28].

6. חֹשֶׁךְ וַחֲלַקְלַקֹּת — *Dark and exceedingly slippery.*

Ibn Ezra notes that חָלָק alone means *smooth, slippery,* but here part of the root is repeated as חֲלַקְלַק to give it increased emphasis.

Rashi explains that when both of these difficulties come together, they spell disaster. The wicked stumble on the slippery spots. Had it been light, they could avoid the danger, but because it is dark they cannot see where they are going.[1]

Rabbeinu Yonah (Shaarei Teshuvah 3:192) says: It is written וּפֶה חָלָק יַעֲשֶׂה מִדְחֶה, *A smooth* [i.e., false] *mouth causes stumbling* (Proverbs 26:28). A smooth mouth is likened to a slippery road. Just as a slippery road causes a person to stumble, so a smooth mouth, i.e., insincere flattery, causes one to falter. Regarding this, David said: יַכְרֵת ה' כָּל שִׂפְתֵי חֲלָקוֹת, *May* HASHEM *cut off all smooth lips* (12:4).

1. The wicked represent darkness as it says: *And their deeds are in the darkness* (Isaiah 29:14). Therefore God punishes them in the darkness of night. The angels arrived to overturn Sodom at night. The first-born of Egypt were smitten at midnight. Sennacherib's army was destroyed at midnight. Belshazzar was slain at night. Haman's downfall began when the King Ahaseurus could not sleep at night. So, too, in the future the wicked will be covered by darkness, but the righteous will be bathed in light; as it says (Proverbs 4:18), *And the path of the righteous is like a shining light* (Yalkut Shimoni).

those who seek my life;

Let them retreat and be humilated,
those who plot my harm.
⁵ *May they be like chaff before the wind,*
with the angel of HASHEM driving them on.
⁶ *May their way be dark and exceedingly slippery,*
with the angel of HASHEM pursuing them.
⁷ *For without cause,*
they hid me in a pit with their net;
Without cause
they dug to kill me.
⁸ *May darkness come upon him, unaware,*
and his own net which he concealed —
may it ensnare him. In darkness may he fall.

וּמַלְאַךְ ה׳ רֹדְפָם — *With the angel of HASHEM pursuing them.*

This completes the catastrophe. A person walking on slippery ground in the dark can at least walk very cautiously and slowly and thereby avoid falling, but now that they are pursued by the angels they must run recklessly and slip (*Radak*).

7. טָמְנוּ לִי שַׁחַת רִשְׁתָּם — *They hid for me a pit [with] their net.*

They prepare a deep pit which destroys all who fall into it, and camouflage it by covering it with a net [see *comm.* to 7:16]. They try every possible trick and deception in order to kill me (*Radak*).

Sforno suggests that this refers to Achitophel's advice to Absalom. He urged Absalom to pursue and trap David in order to destroy him on the first night of his flight (*II Samuel* 17:2).

8. תְּבוֹאֵהוּ — *May [it] come upon him.*

David now changes from the plural form to the singular, because he addresses each enemy individually or because he refers to Saul, the one principal enemy (*Radak*).

Sforno holds that this refers to Achitophel who was confident that Absalom would follow his advice to pursue David, until he was suddenly thrust into *darkness* by the unexpected counsel of Chushai who successfully convinced Absalom to cautiously restrain himself.

שׁוֹאָה — *Darkness.*

Rashi and *Metzudos* translate here שׁוֹאָה as *darkness*. However, *Rashi* renders יוֹם שֹׁאָה וּמְשׁוֹאָה [*Zephaniah* 1:15] as *a day of desolation* [from שְׁמָמוֹן, *utter desolation.*]

Radak translates שׁוֹאָה as *turmoil and confusion*. In Ezekiel 38:9, *Radak* renders this word as *a roaring, sudden, tidal wave*. Both in *Ezekiel* and *Zephaniah*, the *Targum* of this word is אִתְרְגוּשְׁתָּא or אִתְרְלוּשָׁא, from רְגַשׁ, *agitation* or *turbulence*. According to *Ibn Ezra*, the devastation which befalls each enemy will be so staggering that all who hear will be מִשְׁתָּאֶה, *amazed, dumb-struck*.

וְרִשְׁתּוֹ אֲשֶׁר טָמַן תִּלְכְּדוֹ — *And his own net which he concealed — may it ensnare him.*

ט בְּשׁוֹאָה יִפָּל־בָּהּ: וְנַפְשִׁי תָּגִיל בַּיהוה
י תָּשִׂישׂ בִּישׁוּעָתוֹ | כָּל עַצְמֹתַי | תֹּאמַרְנָה
יהוה מִי כָמוֹךָ מַצִּיל עָנִי מֵחָזָק מִמֶּנּוּ
יא וְעָנִי וְאֶבְיוֹן מִגֹּזְלוֹ: יְקוּמוּן עֵדֵי חָמָס
יב אֲשֶׁר לֹא־יָדַעְתִּי יִשְׁאָלוּנִי: יְשַׁלְּמוּנִי רָעָה

Achitophel sought to ensnare David with his counsel, but precisely because his counsel was rejected he was so dejected that he hung himself (Sforno).

9. [Now David describes how he will react to the downfall of his enemies.]

תָּגִיל ... תָּשִׂישׂ — Exult ... rejoice.
Malbim explains that גִילָה is inner joy, whereas שָׂשׂוֹן describes the external manifestations of gladness.

10. כָּל עַצְמֹתַי תֹּאמַרְנָה — All my limbs [lit. bones] will say.
Radak comments that David chose the bones to symbolize the entire body because they are its mainstay. The ecstatic shaking and swaying of the body during the recital of prayers, is itself an eloquent expression of praise. Also, when one studies the wonders of the human anatomy, he is moved to laud the Creator who fashioned the organs with such wisdom.
The halachic implications of this verse are recorded in Berachos [4:3]: The daily prayers contain eighteen benedictions corresponding to the eighteen vertebrae in the spine. During prayer one must bow down and bend them all, as it says, All of my limbs will say ...
The Midrash [Vayikra Rabbah 30:14] relates the Four Species of Sukkos to the four major organs:
—The Lulav (palm-branch) resembles the spine.
—The Hadas (myrtle leaf) resembles the human eye.
—The Aravah (willow leaf) resembles the mouth.

—The Esrog (citron) resembles the heart.
David said: 'These four major organs are fundamental to the rest of the body and soul, I therefore select them to praise God; All my limbs will say ...
The Pesikta cites numerous verses from Psalms which demonstrate that David praised God with every single organ of his body. This alludes to the Talmudic dictum, that here are 248 organs corresponding to the 248 positive commandments. Thus, the performance of each commandment, in effect, involves its organ, as it were, in the praise of God.
Tehillas Hashem adds that the organs representing the respective commandments are destined to proclaim the praises of their possessors who so lavishly embellished them with spiritual finery.

ה' מִי כָמוֹךָ — HASHEM, who is like You?
All of my limbs were endangered by my enemies and my debilitating sickness (Malbim), only You, Hashem, could provide salvation against such odds (Metzudas David).

מַצִּיל עָנִי מֵחָזָק מִמֶּנּוּ — Deliverer of the poor from one mightier than he.
God protects Israel in its exile among the nations where it resembles a lamb among seventy hungry wolves. How could Israel survive if not for Hashem Who delivers it every moment? (Pesikta 9:2)

וְעָנִי וְאֶבְיוֹן מִגֹּזְלוֹ — Of the poor and needy from him who robs him.
The Pesikta (ibid.) homiletically

9 *Then my soul will exult in* HASHEM,
rejoice in His salvation.
10 *All my limbs will say,*
'HASHEM, *who is like You?*
Deliverer of the poor from one mightier than he,
of the poor and needy from him who robs him.'
11 *Extortive witnesses rise up;*
what I know not, they demand.
12 *They repay me evil for good,*

refers this to the יֵצֶר הַטוֹב, *Good Inclination,* which is impoverished of good deeds. It is overpowered by the יֵצֶר הָרַע, *Evil Inclination.* The *Good Inclination* must toil long and hard before it can accomplish even one mitzvah, but then the temptation to sin deprives it of all it had earned. Is there any robber more dangerous than this?

11. יְקוּמוּן עֵדֵי חָמָס — *Extortive witnesses rise up.*

[The *Targum* renders חָמָס as חַטוֹפִין, *those who seize by force.* The word usually describes someone who will go to any lengths, even violence, to extract a desired object from its owner.]

Radak comments that among David's many enemies was a group which sought to extort money from him. Though there is no record of such people in the Book of *Samuel,* this is implied by our verse.

Sforno says that this alludes to Absalom, who would stand at the gates of Jerusalem and greet all who came to David to seek justice. Absalom would tell them: *Your cause is just, however, the king will never listen to you. If only I could be the judge over the land, then I*

would deal righteously with all (II Samuel 15:2). [Thus he bore false testimony against his father in order to extort and usurp the throne.]

The *Tosefta (Bava Kamma* 7:3) states: There are seven categories of thieves, the worst of which is the גוֹנֵב, דַּעַת הַבְּרִיּוֹת *one who tricks others by means of misrepresentation.* Thus Absalom was called a thief for he stole the hearts of all Israel [by falsely slandering David and misrepresenting himself.]

What was the result of Absalom's treachery? Absalom deceived three hearts by means of deceit, the heart of his father, of the Sanhedrin, and of all Israel. Therefore, he died with three javelins piercing his heart (*Sotah* 9b).

12. וַיְשַׁלְּמוּנִי רָעָה תַּחַת טוֹבָה — *They repay me evil for good.*

David had acted kindly towards them, but they betrayed his friendship (*Radak*).

According to *Sforno,* this refers to the elders of the Sanhedrin, who were David's friends, but who later joined Absalom and concurred in Absalom's plot to kill David immediately.[1]

1. *Yerushalmi (Sotah* 1:8) relates how Absalom lured the elders to his cause. Prior to his revolt, Absalom told his father that he wished to go to Hebron to offer up special sacrifices. Absalom slyly requested of his father, 'Assign two elders to accompany me so that I may be guided by their counsel.'
David acceded and asked, 'Which elders shall I command to accompany you? I will write their names on this letter with my order!'
Absalom cunningly replied, 'Leave the spaces blank and I will insert the names of

יג   תַּחַת טוֹבָה שְׂכוֹל לְנַפְשִׁי: וַאֲנִי | בַּחֲלוֹתָם
לְבוּשִׁי שָׂק עִנֵּיתִי בַצּוֹם נַפְשִׁי וּתְפִלָּתִי
יד   עַל־חֵיקִי תָשׁוּב: כְּרֵעַ־כְּאָח   לִי
הִתְהַלָּכְתִּי כַּאֲבֶל־אֵם קֹדֵר שַׁחוֹתִי:
טו   וּבְצַלְעִי שָׂמְחוּ וְנֶאֱסָפוּ נֶאֶסְפוּ עָלַי נֵכִים

שְׂכוֹל לְנַפְשִׁי — *Death for my soul.*

These men stop at nothing, not only will they take my money, they will even take my soul (*Radak*).

Since שְׂכוֹל usually refers to the death of children in the lifetime of their parents (see *Genesis* 42:36), support is lent to *Sforno's* commentary. The treacherous elders, who misguided Absalom, eventually caused David to be שָׂכוֹל, *bereft*, of his son Absalom who was killed as a result of his rebellion.

13. וַאֲנִי בַּחֲלוֹתָם לְבוּשִׁי שָׂק עִנֵּיתִי בַצּוֹם נַפְשִׁי — *But as for me, when they were ill my clothing was sackcloth, I afflicted myself* [lit. *my soul*] *with fasting.*

[These men rejoiced over his tragedies, but David acted nobly toward them. Although earlier in the psalm we find David requesting the destruction of his enemies, that was only after he was convinced that there was no hope for them to repent. Here, however, he discusses his initial, compassionate reaction to their evil. His foes were great scholars, but they did not work on the refinement of their characters. Absalom pandered to their pride and ambition and enmeshed them in his plot.]

The *Talmud* (*Berachos* 12b) states that whoever refrains from praying for divine mercy on behalf of his friend and does not do so is called a sinner ... And if the friend is a Torah scholar, then he who prays should become sick with misery over the scholar's plight ... As David said (in reference to Doeg and Achitophel, who were Torah scholars): *When they were ill, my clothing was sackcloth, I afflicted myself with fasting.*

From this verse *Midrash Hane'elam* learns that one should pray for the spiritual recovery of the wicked whose souls are sick. By no means should he pray for their destruction, however; for if God had removed the idol-worshiper, Terach, from the world, there never would have been an Abraham, or the twelve tribes, or David, or Messiah. The Torah would not have been given and all of the righteous, the devout, and the prophets would never have arrived on this world.

וּתְפִלָּתִי עַל חֵיקִי תָשׁוּב — *As for my prayer, upon my own bosom let it return.*

My profuse supplications wre motivated by concern for my own safety. My paranoid enemies, however, claim that my sole desire was to influence God to harm them. It that be true, may the suffering which I allegedly wished them descend upon me (*Rashi; Radak*).

whomever I wish!' Absalom then approached pair after pair of the heads of Sanhedrin in every city of the realm and convinced them that the king had no respect for them, as evidenced by the fact that he wrote them a strict order without even according them the honor of referring to them by name! Absalom, however, esteemed them so highly that he chose them as his elite honor guard. In this treacherous manner, Absalom gathered not just two, but two-hundred elders for this entourage. All who witnessed this grand processsion exclaimed with joy: 'Observe how truly dignified Prince Absalom is! Surely he is worthy of the throne!'

XXXV *death for my soul.*

13-15 *¹³ But as for me, when they were ill,*
    my clothing was sackcloth
    and I afflicted myself with fasting.
  As for my prayer,
    upon my own bosom let it return.
  ¹⁴ As if for a companion, as if for my own brother,
    I went about;
  As if in mourning for a mother
    I bleakly bent over.
  ¹⁵ But when I limped they rejoiced and gathered,
    against me gathered the lame — I now not why.

14. כְּרֵעַ כְּאָח לִי — *As if for a companion, as if for my own brother.*

I mourned for my enemies as if they were dear friends or brothers — as if I were personally affected, because the closer a tragedy strikes, the more one must be concerned, not only for the victim, but for himself. As the *Talmud* states (*Shabbos* 106a): Rabbi Yochanan said, If one of the brothers dies, all the rest should worry [fear death (*Rashi*).] If one member of a group dies, all of the others should worry (*Eretz HaChaim*).

כַּאֲבֶל אֵם — *As if in mourning for a mother.*

David uses the example of the mother because a person grieves more over the loss of his mother than of his father. For, he is conceived in her womb, nursed at her breast, raised and nurtured at her side until he is grown. Even in later life she is always ready to provide for her son's needs, his food, and his drink (*Radak*).

When a father dies, the blow is softened by the inheritance he leaves behind, which provides at least partial consolation, not so the departure of the mother, who usually leaves over nothing (*Meiri*).

קֹדֵר — *Bleakly* [lit. *black, dark.*]

Because of his pain and anguish, the face of the mourner loses its glow, and seems darker. Also, the mourner wears dark clothing (*Radak*).

15. שָׂמְחוּ וְנֶאֱסָפוּ — *They rejoiced and gathered.*

When they heard of my mishap they gathered to savor the details and rejoice over them (*Radak*).

נֶאֶסְפוּ עָלַי נֵכִים — *Against me gathered the lame.*

The translation follows *Rashi*. *Radak*, however, translates this as *lowly people* who are beaten and mistreated because of their miserable state. [Thus נֵכָה, is related to מַכָּה, *blow.*]

I went to visit these wretched people when they were bedridden. Now they reciprocate by gathering around my bed to applaud my pains (*Ibn Ezra*).

These cripples have their own problems about which to be concerned, yet when they see me disabled, they forget their own woes and rejoice over mine (*Meiri*).

וְלֹא יָדַעְתִּי — *I know not why* [lit. *I did not know.*]

I cannot understand why they desire

טז וְלֹא יָדַעְתִּי קָרְעוּ וְלֹא־דָמוּ: בְּחַנְפֵי לַעֲגֵי

יז מָעוֹג חָרֹק עָלַי שִׁנֵּימוֹ: אֲדֹנָי כַּמָּה תִרְאֶה

הָשִׁיבָה נַפְשִׁי מִשֹּׁאֵיהֶם מִכְּפִירִים

יח יְחִידָתִי: אוֹדְךָ בְּקָהָל רָב בְּעַם עָצוּם

יט אֲהַלְלֶךָּ: אַל־יִשְׂמְחוּ־לִי אֹיְבַי שֶׁקֶר שֹׂנְאַי

כ חִנָּם יִקְרְצוּ־עָיִן: כִּי לֹא שָׁלוֹם יְדַבֵּרוּ וְעַל

my injury for I never did them any harm (*Radak*).

קָרְעוּ — *They tore.*

Rashi, following *Sanhedrin* 107a, interprets this as referring to David's flesh which was being torn.[1]

Radak observes: When one howls in laughter he opens his mouth so wide it seems to be tearing apart. *Radak* adds an explanation from his father: When one commits a terrible wrong which cannot be righted, it resembles a gash that can never be mended.

וְלֹא דָמוּ — *And they would not be silenced.*

Rashi cites the *Talmud's* homiletical explanation deriving דָמוּ from דָם, *blood.* Thus, despite the tearing of David's flesh, his blood did not drip (*Rashi*).

16. בְּחַנְפֵי לַעֲגֵי — *Because of flattery and mockery.*

David's enemies fawned upon his adversaries, particularly Saul. David laments: They flatter my enemies and mock me. (*Rashi; Metzudas David*).

What is the difference between the לֵץ, *one who ridicules* (*Psalms* 1:1) and the חוֹנֵף, *the flatterer?* What is good, the mocker calls bad. What is bad, the flatterer calls good (*Tzidkas HaTzaddik*).

מָעוֹג — *A meal* [lit. *a cake.*]

Although מָעוֹג means *cake*, it is used to describe eating in general. Thus, these men fawn upon Saul in order to get free meals from him.

Radak renders מָעוֹג as *worthless talk* in which they engage.

חָרֹק עָלַי שִׁנֵּימוֹ — *They grind their teeth at me.*

This term describes the gleeful grinding of the teeth by one who gains revenge over his enemy, as in וַיַּחַרְקוּ שֵׁן, *they grind* [their] *teeth* (*Lamentations* 2:16) (*Radak; Metzudas Zion*).

17. כַּמָּה תִרְאֶה — *How much can You bear?* [lit. *look on*].

How much patience do You have that You are able to restrain Yourself after seeing all this? (*Rashi*).

מִשֹּׁאֵיהֶם — *From their darkness.*
[See *comm.* to v. 8.]

1. David said to the Holy One, Blessed be He: 'It is well-known and revealed to you that even if my enemies would tear my flesh, my blood would not drip to the earth.' [The sin born of lust is symbolized by surging, racing blood. Now, as he repented his sin, David froze his passions and his blood.]

Furthermore, David said, that even when his enemies engaged in the study of complex laws of leprosy and ritual purity, they would turn to him and say derisively, 'What is the form of the death penalty of David the adulterer?' [Even though leprosy is a heavenly inflicted punishment for slander and evil tale-bearing, their study of those laws does not deter them for one moment from viciously slandering my name (*Maharsha*).]

David answered that the adulterer dies by חֶנֶק, *choking*, but at least he still can hope for a share in the World to Come. However, he who disgraces another man in public forfeits his portion in the World to Come.

XXXV
16-20

They tore at me
and would not be silenced.

¹⁶ *Because of flattery and mockery offered for a meal,*
they grind their teeth at me.

¹⁷ *My Lord,*
how much can You bear?
Return my life from their darkness;
from the young lions, my soul.

¹⁸ *I will thank You in a great congregation,*
before a mighty throng I will praise You.

¹⁹ *Let them not rejoice over me, my foes,*
for false cause;
Or those who hate me baselessly,
let them not wink their eyes.

²⁰ *For it is not peace that they speak,*

מִכְּפִירִים — *From young lions.*

I.e., save my life from the foes who are as ferocious, powerful, and hungry as young lions (*Radak; Metzudas Zion*).

יְחִידָתִי — *My soul* [lit. *my only one.*]

This is a description of the soul (*Radak*). [See *comm.* to Psalms 22:21.]

18. אוֹדְךָ בְּקָהָל רָב — *I will thank You in a great congregation.*

David vowed (*Ibn Ezra*) to give thanks before all of Israel after God will save him from his enemies (*Radak*). [Compare 103:31-32.]

בְּעַם עָצוּם — *Before a mighty throng.*

This denotes a tremendous number of people. David vowed that his gratitude to God would be expressed openly (*Metzudas Zion*).

19. אֹיְבַי שֶׁקֶר — *My foes for false cause.*

They hate me because of the very lies which they fabricated about me. They attribute to me crimes so outlandish that they would never even enter my mind (*Rashi*).

יִקְרְצוּ עָיִן — *[Let them not] wink their eyes.*

The adverb אַל, *not*, at the beginning of the verse refers to this final phrase as well (*Rashi; Metzudas David*).

The expression קְרִיצַת עָיִן describes the opening and closing of the eyelid in a suggestive manner in order to silently mock someone (*Radak*).

20. כִּי לֹא שָׁלוֹם יְדַבֵּרוּ — *For it is not peace that they speak.*

This refers to Absalom who promised to bring everyone peace, but whose true intention was to massacre all those who favored David (*Sforno*).

[At birth, David gave this son the name אַבְשָׁלוֹם, literally, *father of peace.* David recognized fully the violent nature of this son. However, he hoped to channel Absalom's violence in a beneficial direction by making him a great military leader who would subdue the nations in the Name of God, and thus bring about universal peace. Unfortunately, Absalom did not share his father's peaceful intentions.]

Chazah David suggests that these words describe the enemies of David who harped on the fact that he was a descendant of Ruth the Moabite. They

רִגְעֵי־אֶרֶץ דִּבְרֵי מִרְמוֹת יַחֲשֹׁבוּן:

כא וַיַּרְחִיבוּ עָלַי פִּיהֶם אָמְרוּ הֶאָח | הֶאָח

כב רָאֲתָה עֵינֵנוּ: רָאִיתָה יהוה אַל־תֶּחֱרַשׁ

כג אֲדֹנָי אַל־תִּרְחַק מִמֶּנִּי: הָעִירָה וְהָקִיצָה

כד לְמִשְׁפָּטִי אֱלֹהַי וַאדֹנָי לְרִיבִי: שָׁפְטֵנִי

כה כְצִדְקְךָ יהוה אֱלֹהָי וְאַל־יִשְׂמְחוּ־לִי: אַל־

יֹאמְרוּ בְלִבָּם הֶאָח נַפְשֵׁנוּ אַל־יֹאמְרוּ

refused to accept the correct halachic ruling that all restrictions mentioned in the Torah against Moab apply only to male converts and their offspring, and not to female converts. Therefore, in their false righteousness they were most scrupulous in practicing against David the Biblical prohibition concerning Moab, לֹא תִדְרֹשׁ שְׁלֹמָם וְטֹבָתָם כָּל יָמֶיךָ לְעוֹלָם, You shall not seek their peace or their well-being all of your days, forever (Deuteronomy 23:7) and so they never extended the greeting of שָׁלוֹם, peace, to David.

רִגְעֵי אֶרֶץ — The broken people of the earth.

This refers to David's followers whom Absalom hoped to break when he was victorious over them (Sforno).

However, according to Radak, this phrase is translated, 'those who rest peacefully in the earth,' the word רִגְעֵי being related to מַרְגוֹעַ, rest.

The Targum similarly elaborates: They deceitfully scheme to say false things about the righteous men who have come to their eternal rest in the Hereafter.

Alshich explains that, in particular, they cast aspersion on the words of Samuel, [then 'at rest' because he was no longer living], who announced that David was God's chosen king and that the monarchy had been taken away from Saul.

דִּבְרֵי מִרְמוֹת יַחֲשֹׁבוּן — They scheme

deceitfully [lit. they think deceitful things.]

Chazah David, continues his trend of thought in this verse: By their false claims that Ruth was unfit to enter the congregation of Israel, they falsely slandered my holy forebears, Boaz, Oved, and Jesse (who now rest peacefully in the earth), claiming that Boaz transgressed the prohibition of the Torah, 'No Ammonite or Moabite shall enter the congregation of HASHEM' [Deuteronomy 23:4], and thus, Oved and Jesse were born of an illicit relation.

21. וַיַּרְחִיבוּ עָלַי פִּיהֶם — They broadly opened their mouths against me.

They opened their mouths with laughter and scorn when they saw me miserably wandering in exile from place to place (Radak). [Perhaps this alludes to Shimi ben Gera who 'opened his mouth' to curse David as he fled from Absalom.]

הֶאָח הֶאָח — Aha! Aha!

This is the exclamation of joy which they utter when they witness the realization of their hearts' desire (Rashi).

22. רָאִיתָה ה׳ — You have seen, HASHEM.

This is in response to their claim, Our own eyes have seen! (Ibn Ezra).

אַל תֶּחֱרַשׁ — Do not be mute.

You have seen their joy; do not be

and against the broken people of the earth
      they scheme deceitfully.
   ²¹ They broadly opened their mouths
      against me.
   They say,
      'Aha! Aha! Our own eyes have seen!'
   ²² You have seen, HASHEM, do not be mute;
      my Lord do not stand far from me.
   ²³ Arouse Yourself and awaken for my judgment,
      my God and my Lord, for my cause.
   ²⁴ Judge me according to Your righteousness,
      HASHEM, my God,
      and let them not rejoice over me.
   ²⁵ Let them not say in their hearts,
      'Rejoice our souls!'
   Let them not say,

---

mute from exacting vengeance from them on my account *(Metzudas David)*.

23. הָעִירָה וְהָקִיצָה — *Arouse Yourself and awaken.*

[In the Sabbath prayer נִשְׁמַת כָּל חַי we find God described as הַמְעוֹרֵר יְשֵׁנִים וְהַמֵּקִיץ נִרְדָּמִים, *He arouses sleepers and awakens slumberers.* This indicates that the implication of *to arouse* is not as forceful an act as *to awaken.* The word מֵקִיץ is derived from the word קֵץ, *end.* In the context of our verse, it literally means to put an end to deep slumber. See *Malbim* on *Habakuk 2:19.*]

Rashi holds that David is invoking divine assistance to arouse the Heavenly Tribunal of angels to mete out justice against his enemies.

Sforno comments: Arouse Your Attribute of Mercy to hear my prayer sympathetically. Awaken Your Attribute of Justice to vigorously support my cause.

מִשְׁפָּטִי ... רִיבִי — *My judgment ... my cause.*

Malbim here (and in *Isaiah 3:13*) explains that רִיב describes the preliminary arguments of a court case, when each side advocates its cause; while מִשְׁפָּט refers to the cross-examination and deliberation of the judges which lead to their final decision.

אֱלֹהַי וַאדֹנָי — *My God and my Lord.*

Radak translates these words literally, *my Judge and my Master.*

I come to You for judgment for You are the only judge whom I acknowledge. I ask You to defend my cause because You are my master, and ordinarily a master desires that his servant be dealt with equitably.

24. שָׁפְטֵנִי כְצִדְקְךָ ה' אֱלֹהָי — *Judge me according to Your righteousness HASHEM, my God.*

When מִדַּת הָרַחֲמִים, *the Attribute of Mercy,* expressed in the Name ה', and the מִדַּת הַדִּין, *the Attribute of Justice,* expressed in the name אֱלֹהִים, are joined together, the result is צֶדֶק, *righteousness* *(Sforno).*

כו בְּלַעֲנוּהוּ: יֵבֹשׁוּ וְיַחְפְּרוּ | יַחְדָּו שְׂמֵחֵי
רָעָתִי יִלְבְּשׁוּ־בֹשֶׁת וּכְלִמָּה הַמַּגְדִּילִים
כז עָלָי: יָרֹנּוּ וְיִשְׂמְחוּ חֲפֵצֵי צִדְקִי וְיֹאמְרוּ
תָמִיד יִגְדַּל יהוה הֶחָפֵץ שְׁלוֹם עַבְדּוֹ:
כח וּלְשׁוֹנִי תֶּהְגֶּה צִדְקֶךָ כָּל־הַיּוֹם תְּהִלָּתֶךָ:

26. יִלְבְּשׁוּ בֹשֶׁת וּכְלִמָּה — *May they be clothed in shame and disgrace.*

After they leave this world, the wicked are clothed in garments fashioned from their own wicked deeds. They are covered with the spiritual refuse and putrefaction which disgrace them (*Rav Yeibi*).

הַמַּגְדִּילִים עָלָי — *Those who are glad over my misfortune* [lit. *over me.*]

This describes Shimi ben Gera who rose up to curse David as he fled from Absalom, thus magnifying his own im-

portance as he degraded David (*Sforno*).

27. יִגְדַּל ה׳ — *Be glorified, HASHEM!* [lit. *May HASHEM be great!*]

May the *Attribute of Mercy* overwhelm the *Attribute of Justice* [in favor of David] (*Sforno*).

28. וּלְשׁוֹנִי תֶּהְגֶּה צִדְקֶךָ — *Then my tongue will express Your righteousness.*

Midrash shocher Tov comments: When do the people of Israel rejoice? Only when they see their king im-

XXXV   *'We have swallowed him.'*

26-28   ²⁶ *May they be shamed and humiliated together,*
           those who are glad over my misfortune;
      May they be clothed in shame and disgrace,
           those who glorify themselves against me.
      ²⁷ *May they sing in joy and be glad,*
           those who want my vindication;
      Let them always say, 'Be glorified, HASHEM!
      He who wants the peace of His servant!'
      ²⁸ *Then my tongue will express Your righteousness;*
           all the day, Your praise.

mersed in Torah study! The preceding verse says, *May they sing in joy and be glad, those who want my vindication.* When? *When my tongue will express Your righteousness* [by uttering words of Torah.] Similarly we read, יְרֵאֶיךָ יִרְאוּנִי וְיִשְׂמָחוּ, *Those who fear You, see me and are glad* [119:74]. When? When they see me engaged in Torah study!

[*Rambam* -(*Hilchos Melachim* 3:3) emphasizes that the king's obligation to engage in Torah study surpasses that of all other Jews, for his heart is the collective heart of all Israel and requires greater righteousness. The *Midrash* relates that when the nation observed David rising in the middle of the night to delight in Torah study, they were all aroused to follow his example (See *Overview* Part IV).

The theme of this psalm is that the enemies of David are truly enemies of God. They hate David because he represents Hashem. The proof of this is that all those who love and fear God, love His chosen king. Only through David can Israel realize the goal of יִגְדַּל ה', *HASHEM be glorified!*]

36 מזמור לו

This Psalm portrays the stark contrast between those who defy God and those who serve Him. According to Radak, the villain of the Psalm is the יֵצֶר הָרָע, the Evil Inclination, which succeeds in convincing the wicked that there is no supreme Master over the affairs of this world. The Psalmist diametrically opposes such a heresy. David proudly calls himself עֶבֶד ה׳, the servant of HASHEM, a vassal totally submissive to God's will.

Mesillas Yesharim (Chap. 24) describes the devoted servant of Hashem who lives in awe of His Divine Majesty: he constantly fears lest some trace of the Evil Inclination might have intruded into his actions and rendered them inconsonant with the grandeur of the Blessed One's honor and the glory of His Name. Fear of sin is an essential element of his being and no circumstance in life can shake him from his incessant trembling before God.

Such a man is happy and fortunate as Solomon said, Praiseworthy is the man who fears always (Proverbs 28:14). King David exulted in his possession of the trait of unshakeable fear, saying, '[Even while] Princes pursued me for naught, my heart feared [only] at Your word' (119:161).

א־ב לַמְנַצֵּחַ ׀ לְעֶבֶד־יהוה לְדָוִד: נְאֻם־פֶּשַׁע
לָרָשָׁע בְּקֶרֶב לִבִּי אֵין־פַּחַד אֱלֹהִים לְנֶגֶד

1. לְעֶבֶד ה' — *For the servant of HASHEM.*

[See *commentary* to 18:1].

Anyone who successfully withstands his evil inclination merits a song of exultation, but this is especially true of a person of lofty spiritual stature. The *Talmud (Succah* 52a) teaches: כָּל הַגָּדוֹל מֵחֲבֵירוֹ יִצְרוֹ גָדוֹל הֵימֶנּוּ, *The greater the person, the greater his inclination [for evil].* Therefore, David's spiritual struggle was far more intense than that of an ordinary person. His ultimate victory, too, was sweeter, and the resultant song of gratitude was all the more heartfelt *(Alshich).*

That David assumed the title עֶבֶד ה', *servant of HASHEM,* should not be considered boastful, for there is not a word in all of *Tehillim* that David uttered of his own accord. The Psalmist was enveloped by a holy spirit and his every word is an expression of the thoughts of God Himself *(Tehillas Hashem).*

Midrash Shocher Tov identifies the villain of this Psalm, not as the Evil Inclination, but as Goliath, who symbolizes all of David's human enemies. God wages war for Israel and emerges triumphant. Nevertheless, He ascribes all victories to His nation. Israel in turn refuses to accept the honor and attributes all success to God.

We find that after David slew Goliath, the daughters of Israel were divinely inspired to sing, *Saul has slain his thousands, and David his tens of thousands (I Samuel* 18:7). But David, in this Psalm, refuses to accept the honor, in effect saying to God, 'You are the cause of this victory and so I shall attribute it to Your name!' Therefore David dedicated this Psalm לַמְנַצֵּחַ, literally: *to He who causes victory* [from נִצָּחוֹן, *victory*] (see *commentary* to 4:1).

Victory for whom? לְעֶבֶד ה' לְדָוִד, *for the servant of HASHEM, for David.*

2. נְאֻם פֶּשַׁע לָרָשָׁע — *The words of transgression to the wicked.*

פֶּשַׁע, *transgression,* is the Evil Inclination within man *(Metzudas Zion).*

Malbim interprets the Psalm as an attempt to refute the efficacy of doing good. [We will present his comments during the course of the Psalm as they appear.] Two arguments are offered to justify performance of the commandments: 1 — They are a response to the wish of God. Like a servant obeying his master, it is not for us to decide whether or not the deed will benefit us personally, for we are beholden to carry out His command. 2 — The commandments were formulated by God in His infinite wisdom to benefit us. Like a patient following his doctor's orders, we obey for our own sake, entirely apart from a desire to serve God. The evil inclination seeks to negate both arguments. (See also *Shiurei Daas of Telshe,* vol. I, p. 117).

Midrash Shocher Tov relates this verse to the encounter of David and Goliath (see *I Samuel* Chapter 17):

When David saw the giant warrior armed with every type of weapon, he thought, 'Who can overcome such a man?' But when he heard Goliath blaspheming God, he said, 'Now I can vanquish him for he has no fear of HASHEM!' As it says in our verse: *There is no dread of God before his eyes.* From this we learn that God does not punish the wicked until they remove all fear of God from their hearts.

The *Talmud (Sotah* 42b) teaches: Why was he called גָּלְיָת? Because he stood בְּגִלּוּי פָּנִים, *brazenly,* before God. He approached the camp of Israel with

For the Conductor, for the servant of HASHEM,
for David.
² The words of transgression to the wicked
are in my heart;
There is no dread of God
before his eyes.

his blasphemy and taunts every morning and evening. Why? In order to prevent Israel from reciting the Shema [by which they accept the yoke of God's rule.] So he did for forty days, corresponding to the forty days during which Moses was at Sinai being taught the Torah which Goliath mocked.

Sforno attributes this evil speech to Achitophel who cunningly persuaded Absalom to violate his father's concubines *(II Samuel 16:21)*. Achitophel personifies פֶּשַׁע, the seductive Evil Inclination, Absalom is the רָשָׁע, the *wicked* person who commits the sin. Achitophel's baseness proved that although he was a Torah scholar *there is no dread of God before his eyes.* [See *Psalm 5* for a full description of Achitophel's insincerity.]

בְּקֶרֶב לִבִּי — *[Are] in my heart*
The Psalmist says: I imagine the Evil Inclination arguing this point to the victim whom it seduces to sin *(Rashi; Ibn Ezra).*

[Or this may refer not to the imaginative heart of the Psalmist, but to the corrupted heart of the wicked man. One chamber of the heart receives blood from the body. It symbolizes the evil inclination which fills man with passions and lust. A second chamber pumps oxygen-filled blood, symbolizing the good impulse which cleanses man of his vices. Therefore, the heart is often called לֵבָב, (the double ב, *Beis*, alluding to the two functions of this organ). Our verse quotes the evil-doer as speaking of לִבִּי, *my heart*, in the singular. This implies that wickedness dominates his entire heart.] [1]

אֵין פַּחַד אֱלֹהִים לְנֶגֶד עֵינָיו — *There is no dread of God before his eyes.*
The Evil Impulse coaxes: 'Do whatever your heart desires and pay no attention to threats of a future *Gehinnom* which no one has ever seen. Disregard any threat that is not visible to the human eye' *(Alshich).*
Furthermore, the Evil Inclination argues: 'If you feel that one should do the mitzvos because the King has so commanded, then why doesn't He display His power of punishment against those who disobey Him?' *(Malbim).*
According to *Rabbeinu Yonah of Gerona (Shaarei Teshuva*, Gate III: 169) this verse describes the בַּת עוֹזְבֵי ה', *the class of those who foresake God.* These men fancy themselves to be observers of

---

1. Rabbi Yose HaGallili said: The good inclination completely rules the righteous as David said וְלִבִּי חָלַל בְּקִרְבִּי, *my heart is dead within me* (109:22). [The section of the heart usually reserved for the evil impulse has been deadened within me for I have overcome it completely *(Rashi)*]. However, the wicked are ruled entirely by their evil inclination, as David says, *There is no dread of God before his eyes.*

Good and evil reign jointly over the average person because he vacillates, sometimes acting nobly and sometimes wickedly. Rava declared, 'I am an example of such an ordinary person.'

To this Abaye responded, 'If this is so, the master [Rava] has left no hope for any other person.' [If even *you* are considered as merely ordinary then there is no one who can be considered completely righteous *(Rashi)*] *(Berachos* 61b).

ג עֵינָיו: כִּי־הֶחֱלִיק אֵלָיו בְּעֵינָיו לִמְצֹא
ד עֲוֹנוֹ לִשְׂנֹא: דִּבְרֵי־פִיו אָוֶן וּמִרְמָה חָדַל
ה לְהַשְׂכִּיל לְהֵיטִיב: אָוֶן | יַחְשֹׁב עַל־
מִשְׁכָּבוֹ יִתְיַצֵּב עַל־דֶּרֶךְ לֹא־טוֹב רָע לֹא

the mitzvos, however all of their actions are performed automatically and routinely without any inner conviction. Fear of heaven does not weigh heavily upon them. Therefore, when the evil inclination attempts to entice these weak men, they succumb immediately and transgress. So far removed are they from contemplation of the truth that they do not even sigh or worry over their sin. They give it no second thought. Of them, the Psalmist said, 'There is no dread of God before his eyes.'

3. כִּי הֶחֱלִיק אֵלָיו בְּעֵינָיו — *For it smoothed the way before him.*

With smooth words and facile talk, the rebellious spirit makes sin seem attractive to the wicked (*Rashi; Radak*).

The eye is the Evil Inclination's source of strength, as the *Talmud* (*Sotah* 8a) teaches: We have a tradition that the evil inclination can induce a person to sin only when the object of desire is visible to his eye. This was how the snake, the symbol of evil, coaxed Eve into the first sin: *And when the woman saw that the tree was good for food and that it was desirable to the eyes ... she took of its fruit and did eat* [Genesis 3:6] (*Tehillah L'David*). [See Overview, Vol. I, Part I.]

Sforno notes that initially Absalom hesitated to publicly violate his father's concubines. However, Achitophel cunningly made the abominable deed seem like the logical course of action. He counseled: *And all of Israel shall hear that you are repulsive to your father, then all the hands of those who joined you shall be strengthened* [i.e., the more

repulsive the deed, the more powerful its effect] (*II Samuel* 16:21).

לִמְצֹא עֲוֹנוֹ לִשְׂנֹא — *Causing him to find his iniquity, to hate him.*

[The Evil Inclination is man's worst enemy]. He lures man to sin so that God should discover the wrongdoing and hate the sinner for it (*Rashi*).

Midrash Shocher Tov describes the spirit which drives the wicked: They search with their eyes and ponder in their hearts to find sins which God will find hateful so that they can then commit them out of spite.

According to *Malbim*:

Now the spirit of *Transgression* addresses itself to those who perform commandments and avoid sins because they feel that God's commands are fashioned to benefit man. The Evil Inclination counters by presenting sin in a favorable light, and challenges the observant *to find what there is in his iniquity to be hateful.*

Radak offers another explanation: The wicked indulge their desires to such an unbridled extent that, in time, even they *find iniquity to be hateful.*

4. דִּבְרֵי פִיו אָוֶן וּמִרְמָה — *The words of his mouth — evil and deceit.*

Achitophel's evil words were both contrary to the Torah and treacherously deceitful to Absalom. Achitophel's true intention was to create an irreparable rift between father and son, for if they were ever to become reconciled, Achitophel would have been blamed by both for having advised Absalom to rebel (*Sforno*).

חָדַל לְהַשְׂכִּיל לְהֵיטִיב — *He has ceased contemplating to do good.*

³ *For it smoothed the way before him,*
  causing him to find his iniquity, to hate him.
⁴ *The words of his mouth — evil and deceit —*
  he has ceased contemplating to do good.
⁵ *Evil does he devise on his bed.*
  He stations himself on a path of no good —
  evil he does not disdain.

The wicked person does not allow himself to draw a moral lesson from any incident lest it influence him to mend his ways (*Rashi*).

Although he does not utilize his mental gifts for the pursuit of goodness, nevertheless, his intellectual faculties work for evil, as the Prophet says, *They are wise to do evil, but to do good they have no understanding* [*Jeremiah* 4:22] (*Otzar Nechmad*).

Having come under the influence of פֶּשַׁע, *transgression*, this person ceased לְהַשְׂכִּיל, *to contemplate*, God's awesome sovereignty. Therefore, he fails to realize that it is incumbent upon him, as God's servant, to do His will. Furthermore, he fails to realize that whatever God commands us to do is לְהֵיטִיב, *for doing good*, i.e., for our own benefit (*Malbim*).

5. אָוֶן יַחְשֹׁב עַל מִשְׁכָּבוֹ — *Evil does he devise on his bed.*

When a person lays awake in bed, his mind is not distracted. That is the best time to think and scheme (*Radak*).

Man can intuitively recognize the sovereignty of God, both through his intellect and through his natural inclinations toward good. However, the wicked man strives to corrupt his innocence. One method of doing so is by developing the habit of seeking to find the benefits of evil rather than those of good (*Malbim*).

יִתְיַצֵּב עַל דֶּרֶךְ לֹא טוֹב — *He stations himself on a path of no good.*

At night he schemes on his bed and in

the morning he arises to execute his plans (*Ibn Ezra*).

His wrongdoing is not intermittent. He is מִתְיַצֵּב, *he stands firm and permanent* on that road (*Alshich*).

Malbim continues his above interpretation by citing a second means by which the wicked person corrupts himself. He perverts his instinct for good by acting immorally. Thus he combines evil thoughts with evil deeds, thereby corrupting himself.

Why does the Psalmist say *no good*, instead of describing *evil* in a direct manner as *bad*? One reason is in order not to repeat himself since the word רָע, *bad*, begins the next phrase. Secondly, some bad things have a good side as well, but this man's way is completely corrupt without any redeeming virtue. Thirdly, Scripture often indicates that people should attempt to avoid using foul or derogatory expressions — 'not good' is preferable to 'bad'. [See *Pesachim* 3a; also *Genesis* 7:8; *Deuteronomy* 23:11; *I Samuel* 20:26] (*Radak*).

The Psalmist reveals the psychology of the villain. He will never admit to himself that his way is evil; instead he will rationalize that his course is merely לֹא טוֹב, *not (so) good* (*Yoseif Tehillos*).

רָע לֹא יִמְאָס — *Evil he does not disdain.*

[How can a person objectively appraise his way to determine whether it is good or not? By gauging the extent of his hatred for evil. The truly pure heart will despise it, as it says, אֹהֲבֵי ה', שִׂנְאוּ רָע, *Those who love HASHEM, hate evil* (97:10). One who finds himself to

ו יִמְאָס: יהוה בְּהַשָּׁמַיִם חַסְדֶּךָ אֱמוּנָתְךָ
ז עַד־שְׁחָקִים: צִדְקָתְךָ | כְּהַרְרֵי־אֵל
מִשְׁפָּטֶיךָ תְּהוֹם רַבָּה אָדָם וּבְהֵמָה

be sympathetic or apologetic towards evil has a clear indication that his own lifestyle is not far removed from sin.]

6. ה' בְּהַשָּׁמַיִם חַסְדֶּךָ אֱמוּנָתְךָ עַד שְׁחָקִים —
HASHEM, to the heavens has Your kindness gone, Your faithfulness till the upper heights.

I, *the servant of HASHEM,* recognize that Your kindness is all encompassing and streams forth faithfully from שָׁמַיִם *the heavens (Ibn Ezra).*

But, if this kindness is not always apparent, it is the fault of the wicked who force You to remove Your goodness from the lower world of man and to place Your faithfulness in the שְׁחָקִים, *upper heights (Rashi).*

Radak defines אֱמוּנָה, *faithfulness,* with reference to God and His constant provision of the necessities required for the preservation of each general species of life. [*Sefer HaChinuch,* Mitzvah 548, cites a divine assurance that no living species will ever become extinct.]

חֶסֶד, *kindness,* refers to His mercy in making the sustenance of each creature accessible with a minimum of effort. Furthermore, the more essential a substance is to survival, the more abundant its supply. Because water is a more urgent necessity than solid food, it is found in greater quantities and does not require preparation. Air, the most basic essential for supporting life, is the most abundant of all resources.

Malbim explains: There are two heavens. The material one including the planetary forces is called שָׁמַיִם. The spiritual heaven which controls the miraculous, supernatural course of events is known as שְׁחָקִים. The constant and reliable course of natural events is denoted as אֱמוּנָה, *faithfulness,* while God's supernatural deeds are called

חֶסֶד, *kindness.* Most people associate חֶסֶד, God's supernatural *kindness,* exclusively with שְׁחָקִים, *the spiritual heaven;* and אֱמוּנָה, *the natural course of events,* with שָׁמַיִם, *the lower heaven.* This belief, however, is a manifestation of פֶּשַׁע, *Transgression,* referred to in verse 2, for it claims that one may do as he pleases because God's intervention is not visible in the natural world. This view is false, however, because even our daily, natural existence is but a series of hidden miracles (see *Ramban to Exodus* 13:16).

Furthermore, every deed on earth, for good or evil, elicits a spiritual reaction although it may not be apparent to human beings. The Psalmist indicates all of this by juxtaposing אֱמוּנָה, *natural faithfulness,* with שְׁחָקִים, *spiritual heavens;* and חֶסֶד, *supernatural kindness,* with שָׁמַיִם, *the natural order of the heavens.*

7. צִדְקָתְךָ כְּהַרְרֵי אֵל — *Your righteousness is like the mighty mountains.*

Radak notes that Scripture customarily emphasizes the great size of an object or a geographic area by appending to it the word לָאֵל, *to God,* or an equivalent. Thus, the Assyrian capital, *Nineveh,* is described as עִיר גְּדוֹלָה לֵאלֹהִים, *a great city unto God (Jonah* 3:3; see also *Genesis* 10:9).

Radak goes on to explain how this verse is a continuation of the previous one. Although God's *kindness* and *faithfulness* both encompass the entire world, when the time of judgment arrives, the Almighty differentiates between the righteous and the wicked. Upon the righteous He bestows charities as great as the *mighty mountains* while the wicked descend to the lowest depths of *the vast deep waters.*

6 HASHEM, to the heavens has Your kindness gone —
Your faithfulness till the upper heights.
7 Your righteousness is like the mighty mountains —
Your judgments are like the vast deep waters.
Man and beast You save, HASHEM.

The abundance of good is compared to a lofty mountain peak because there, one is safe from those evil forces which seek to snatch away the rewards which he has earned in his lifetime.

Ibn Ezra observes: Just as the highest peaks are inaccessible to man, so too is full comprehension of God's goodness beyond human reach.

Midrash Shocher Tov adds: Just as the mountains are countless, so are God's charities infinite.

Rashi concludes: But if we find that God's charities are far removed from us like the remote, mighty mountains, it is because the evil men drive Him away from earth. However, when God acts charitably towards someone, He raises and fortifies him like the mighty mountain.

מִשְׁפָּטֶיךָ תְּהוֹם רַבָּה — *Your judgments are like the vast deep waters.*

The punishment of the wicked is likened to the deep, because there is no escape from its grip *(Radak)*. [1]

The Psalmist notes that God's control of nature takes two forms. Sometimes we witness *revealed miracles* which are as evident as *the mighty mountains.* Most of the time, however, we must maintain our faith in God's control of nature which is as hidden as *the vast deep waters.* The reason for this will soon be explained *(Malbim).*

אָדָם וּבְהֵמָה תּוֹשִׁיעַ ה׳ — *Man and beast You save, HASHEM.*

However, there are times when instead of exercising His Attribute of Justice towards the wicked, God allows them to share in the good things of This World. Let it be known that this resembles the kindness which God bestows upon the beast who also does not recognize Him. For the rebellious heretic or the foolish skeptic is nothing more than a beast disguised in the form of a man *(Radak).*

Malbim continues: Every man has within himself both *man* and *beast.* His body is like that of the animal, whereas his human soul embodies the spirit of God. If he were only a soul, he would be like an angel, fit to witness God's glorious revelation all day long. But since his soul is concealed in a body, God's presence has been hidden from him as well. The challenge facing man is to discover God's judgment and control even in *the vast deep waters* [i.e., the murkiness of this material world] and

---

1. The *Talmud (Arachin* 8b) comments: *Your righteousness is like the mighty mountains,* this describes נִגְעֵי אָדָם, *the leprous spots which appear on the human body.* [For it can be determined within one week whether they are clean or unclean *(Rashi).*]

Your judgments are like the vast, deep waters refers to the leprous signs appearing in a house [for their accurate identification and classification may require as much as three weeks *(Tosfos ibid.).*].

This statement is puzzling, for the leprosy of the body would seem to be less of a charity and more of a punishment than those which merely afflict the house. *Harav Chaim Shmulewitz* explains that to be in doubt is itself equivalent to torture. It is better to suffer the restrictions of leprosy of the body after only one week, than to remain in doubt over the status of a house for three weeks.

ח תּוֹשִׁיעַ יהוה: מַה־יָּקָר חַסְדְּךָ אֱלֹהִים
ט וּבְנֵי אָדָם בְּצֵל כְּנָפֶיךָ יֶחֱסָיוּן: יִרְוְיֻן
י מִדֶּשֶׁן בֵּיתֶךָ וְנַחַל עֲדָנֶיךָ תַשְׁקֵם: כִּי־
עִמְּךָ מְקוֹר חַיִּים בְּאוֹרְךָ נִרְאֶה־אוֹר:

thus come to discover the soul of God buried deep within himself. [1]

8. מַה יָּקָר חַסְדְּךָ אֱלֹהִים — *How precious is Your kindness, O God!*

In this world, God may sometimes shower His goodness on the righteous *man* and on unworthy *beastly* men alike (v. 7), but in the reward reserved for the World to Come evil people will not share. The word מַה [lit. *how much*] is used to emphasize that precious good which endures forever. Of it the Prophet says, *No eye has ever seen it except for You, O God! (Isaiah 64:3).* For this reason the Almighty is referred to here as אֱלֹהִים, the Name which denotes the strict *Attribute of Justice*, for in the Hereafter there will be no undeserved kindness for the wicked *(Radak).*

וּבְנֵי אָדָם — *The sons of man.*

Those who enjoy the bliss of the Hereafter are the true *sons of man*, i.e. human beings as they were meant to be, not *beasts* disguised in human form! *(Radak).*

The אָדָם, man, who has raised his soul above the בְּהֵמָה, *beast* part of his nature (v. 7), sees the חֶסֶד, *kindness* of Divine Providence. He realizes (v. 6) that God benignly watches over man more than over anything else in the universe, and shelters him in *the shadow of His wings (Malbim).*

בְּצֵל כְּנָפֶיךָ יֶחֱסָיוּן — *In the shadow of Your wings take refuge.*

Rabbi Avun said: Come and consider how great is the power of the righteous

and those who perform acts of kindness. They do not find their shelter in the shadow of the dawn nor in the shadow of the wings of the earth, nor in the shadow of the sun, nor in the shadow of the wings of the *holy beasts,* or the *cherubs* or the *fiery angels.* Under whose wings do they find shelter? — Under the shadow of He at Whose word the world came to be, as it says, *How precious are those who perform Your kindness, O God! These sons of man will take refuge in the shadow of Your wings (Midrash Ruth Rabbah 5:4).* [2]

9. יִרְוְיֻן — *They will be sated.*

The translation follows *Metzudas Zion* who relates this word to רָוָה, *satisfy, overflow.*

Ibn Ezra identifies this with יִרְבְּיוּן, derived from the root רוב, *many, much,* meaning, *they will have a great abundance.*

מִדֶּשֶׁן בֵּיתֶךָ — *From the abundance of Your house.*

These men will contemplate the ways of God in the solitude of their homes and this divine service will enrich their souls immensely *(Ibn Ezra).*

Malbim explains that the man who recognizes God's kindness on earth deserves to rise above the laws of nature. His bread will come not from the grain grown by nature, but from God's spiritual abundance. Similarly, his water will come from a higher, celestial source; it will quench the thirst of his soul, not merely that of his parched

---

1. The Talmud *(Chullin 5b)* interprets this homiletically as referring to the righteous who devote themselves wholeheartedly to God's service: This describes people who have unbridled intellectual power [like אָדָם, *Adam,* the first man *(Rashi)*], yet humble themselves, like the בְּהֵמָה, *beast* [which is humble and obedient to its master *(Rashi).*]

8 *How precious is Your kindness, O God!*
The sons of man, in the shadow of Your wings
take refuge.
9 *They will be sated*
from the abundance of Your house;
And from the stream of Your delights
give them to drink.
10 *For with You is the source of life —*
by Your light shall we see light.

throat. Thus this righteous man is no longer subject to the limitations of this earth; rather he *takes refuge under God's wing (v. 8)*.

According to *Radak*, however, this spiritual enrichment will be experienced only in the World to Come, which is the world of souls without bodies where the righteous are like angels. The Scriptures refer to the future world of the spirit by a variety of names: *House of HASHEM, Sanctuary of HASHEM, Mountain of HASHEM.* [*See* commentary to 24:3 and 27:4; *Rambam, Hilchos Teshuva* 8:4.]

וְנַחַל עֲדָנֶיךָ תַשְׁקֵם — *And from the stream of Your delights give them to drink.*

The true knowledge of God will provide incessant delight for the devout in the Hereafter, like a stream which flows endlessly *(Ibn Ezra)*.

The phrase *You will give them to drink* is a simile meaning that You will assist them to come to understand Your ways *(Radak)*.

[However, only in proportion to one's thirst for God in This World will

he be satiated with the waters of true wisdom in the Hereafter. One who yearns only for worldly gain, will never be able to quench his thirst, for, like a man drinking salt water, he grows thirstier with every swallow. See 42:2 where the yearning to comprehend God's ways is described in terms of thirst rather than hunger.]

10. כִּי עִמְּךָ מְקוֹר חַיִּים — *For with You is the source of life.*

The source of life refers to the existence of the soul which derives its vitality from above *(Ibn Ezra)*.

The man who has perceived the true meaning of existence, sees that nature itself can breed no meaningful life. That can emanate only from the Divine Source above, just as all temporal light must stream from the celestial source of illumination *(Malbim)*.

Literally, מְקוֹר means *a fountainhead,* or the *source of a flowing spring,* for the life of the soul flows on eternally into the Hereafter. It is life not followed by

2. In his work on the precepts of performing acts of kindness, the *Chafetz Chaim* explains the above *Midrash*:

When the heavenly tribunal conducts a trial, there are many angels of mercy among the Sanhedrin. They comprise the majority and stand at the right side of the Divine throne seeking merit for the person standing in judgment, and are called נְדִיבִים, *generous ones*, according to *Sha'arei Orah*. Nevertheless, they too, act in accord with strict justice; they do not plead for totally undeserved mercy. However, when HASHEM sits alone in judgment, His pure mercy and kindness hold sway. Hence the Psalmist says, (118:9): טוֹב לַחֲסוֹת בַּה' מִבְּטֹחַ בִּנְדִיבִים, *It is better to seek refuge in HASHEM than to trust in generous ones*, i.e., even the generous angels.

However only those who have themselves performed acts of kindness in This World will be judged exclusively by God's kindness and find shelter under his wings *Ahavas Chesed,* 2:4).

יא מְשֹׁךְ חַסְדְּךָ לְיֹדְעֶיךָ וְצִדְקָתְךָ לְיִשְׁרֵי־
יב לֵב: אַל־תְּבוֹאֵנִי רֶגֶל גַּאֲוָה וְיַד־רְשָׁעִים
יג אַל־תְּנִדֵנִי: שָׁם נָפְלוּ פֹּעֲלֵי אָוֶן דֹּחוּ וְלֹא־
יָכְלוּ קוּם:

death; light never extinguished by darkness (Radak).

בְּאוֹרְךָ נִרְאֶה אוֹר — By Your light shall we see light.

When You afflict us with Your strict Attribute of Justice we shall perceive a light which will illuminate our minds to comprehend the purpose of the suffering. In the merit of our acceptance of this light, the inner illumination of the Torah will be revealed to us and we will be filled with the abundance of Your house (Alshich).[1]

According to Sforno, this is a prayer: May Israel understand Absalom's rebellion in the light of God so that Achitophel will not succeed in blinding the eyes of the wise (Exodus 23:8) to stray after his counsel.

11. מְשֹׁךְ חַסְדְּךָ — Extend Your kindness i.e., endlessly (Sforno).

Radak translates: turn Your kindness towards us as in עַל כֵּן מְשַׁכְתִּיךְ חָסֶד, Therefore I have turned kindness towards you (Jeremiah 31:2).

Keep directing Your spiritual kindness towards those who make good use of it and utilize every manifestation of Your kindness in order to know You better and to see that You control all of nature (Malbim).

לְיֹדְעֶיךָ — To those who know You.

Be kind to them in This World so that

they may be free to pursue knowledge and mitzvos without interference. Or this may refer to the World to Come, יֹדְעֶיךָ being those who strived to know God with all their strength and ability in This World. Through God's kindness they will realize their passionate wish in the Hereafter (Radak).

וְצִדְקָתְךָ לְיִשְׁרֵי לֵב — And Your charity to the upright of heart.

The upright of heart are not as great as יֹדְעֶיךָ, those who know You. While the former perform the commandments, their deeds are in the nature of carrying on the tradition received from their forebears. They lack the clear conception of God which can be achieved only through intensive, intellectual effort (Radak; Ibn Ezra).

12. אַל תְּבוֹאֵנִי רֶגֶל גַּאֲוָה — Bring me not the foot of the arrogant.

When God metes out the reward of the righteous in the Hereafter, may these haughty, wicked men not share in the good fortune of deserving people (Rashi).

Radak translates אַל תְּבוֹאֵנִי, let them not overtake me. David prays that his enemies not be enabled to disturb the contemplation and service of God, which he pursued in solitude.

Sforno agrees with this translation, but interprets these words as referring

1. Rabbi Chaim of Volozhin (Ruach Chaim, Avos 6:1), interprets this as a description of the special quality of Torah study. Through seeking the light of Torah one merits the perception of even more Torah light. This may be likened to the man who enters the king's treasury which is aglow with the glitter of dazzling jewels. The most wonderful thing revealed by their light, however, is not the jewels themselves, but a door leading to an even more splendid treasure chamber. And so the visitor goes deeper and deeper in into the innermost rooms of the palace until arriving at the king's throne room, he sees an indescribable splendor. So, too, each truth of Torah leads to deeper revelations until one comes to perceive the presence of God Himself.

XXXVI
11-13

11 *Extend Your kindness to those who know You,*
and Your charity to the upright of heart.
12 *Bring me not the foot of the arrogant,*
and let the hand of the wicked not move me.
13 *There they fell, the practitioners of evil,*
thrust down and unable to rise.

to the arrogant and ambitious Achitophel who advised Absalom not to allow the fleeing king to slip out of his grasp. Achitophel said, *'Let me now choose twelve thousand men and I will arise and pursue David this very night. And I will overtake him while he is weary and weakhanded and I will make him afraid, and all the people who are with him shall flee and I will smite the king alone'* (II Samuel 17:1-2).

According to *Malbim*, גַּאֲוָה, *arrogance*, refers not to the enemy from outside but rather to the enemy within. The most potent weapon utilized by פֶּשַׁע, *the spirit of transgression*, to trap the unwary is the trait of pride. Arrogance blinds man, preventing him from recognizing God's accomplishments, because in his erroneous pride, he considers His achievements to be his own.

[Many commentaries note that the רָאשֵׁי תֵּיבוֹת, *initials*, of the words אַל תְּבוֹאֵנִי רֶגֶל גַּאֲוָה, form the word אֶתְרֹג, *esrog*. This alludes to the fact that, according to the *Midrash*, the esrog is shaped like a human heart. Just as the esrog must be perfect and unblemished, so must people strive to cleanse their

hearts of all flaws, of which the most serious is the ugly blemish of pride.] [1]

וְיַד רְשָׁעִים אַל תְּנִדֵנִי — *And let the hand of the wicked not move me.*

Rashi comments: In the future, the righteous will inherit a double portion — their own and that forfeited by the wicked as a result of their sins. So said the Prophet, לָכֵן בְּאַרְצָם מִשְׁנֶה יִירָשׁוּ, *Therefore in their land they shall inherit a double portion* (Isaiah 61:7). The Psalmist now prays that the wicked will not be allowed to move away the righteous by reclaiming the portion which had originally been intended for them, but which they forfeited.

Do not let the wicked force me to move from the solitary retreat where I serve God (*Radak*).

Do not let Achitophel force me to flee from my position when he attempts to overtake me (*Sforno*).

13. שָׁם נָפְלוּ פֹּעֲלֵי אָוֶן — *There they fell, the practitioners of evil.*

[נָפְלוּ, *they fell*, is written in past tense because the wicked have already fallen into ruin in This World. However, they will not recognize or admit their failure

---

1. The *Midrash (Bereishis Rabbah* 15:7) relates this verse to Adam. After he sinned, Adam realized that he was naked. He tried to gather leaves from the trees to cover himself and Eve, but one tree after another said, 'This is the thief who deceived his Creator! Take no leaves from me!' As it says, *Bring me not the foot of the arrogant* — this refers to Adam who lacked humility in his conduct toward God. *And let the hand of the wicked not move me* — Adam shall remove no leaves from my tree! Only the fig-tree allowed him to take its leaves, because it was the forbidden fruit [according to one version in the *Midrash*]. Adam's experience is likened to that of the prince who seduced one of the palace maids. When the king, his father, banished him, he vainly sought refuge with the other maids, but all shut their doors in his face. Only the maid servant who had caused his disgrace would allow him in. (Cf. *Tosafos Sanhedrin* 70b s.v. בה נתקנו).

until they arrive in the world of truth, the World to Come.]

Radak notes that prophets often refer to events foretold for the future as if they had already occurred.

דֹּחוּ וְלֹא יָכְלוּ קוּם — *Thrust down and unable to rise.*

[Similarly, David said: *Therefore the wicked shall not stand up in judgment nor shall the sinners arise in the assembly of the righteous* (1:5).]

The wicked begin with the free-willed ability to choose between right and wrong, as it says *the practitioners of evil will fall* [into sin of their own choice]. But once they become ac-customed to vice, habit forces them to err and they are without hope of escape. When they lock themselves into a vise-like pattern of sin, *they will be thrust down and unable to rise up (Reishis Da'as).*

Sforno concludes his commentary on this Psalm: Absalom rejected the counsel of Achitophel and accepted that of Chushai HaArki. Achitophel was thrust down into such disgrace that he hung himself and from this ig-nominious death, he was *unable to rise up.* [This alludes to the opinion of the *Mishnah (Sanhedrin* 11:1) that Achitophet forfeited his portion in the Hereafter and will not rise up to share in the bliss of the World to Come.]

37 מזמור לז

T his is a sequel to Psalm 36. There, David described the forces of
evil which strive to convince mankind that there is no God Who
masters our destinies. The wicked point to their own success as
forceful evidence that there is no Supreme Being concerned with the
enforcement of the principles of righteousness and justice. Seeking to
counteract this argument, the Psalmist concluded Psalm 36 by
pleading with God to frustrate His adversaries and reward His
faithful.

This psalm records the response to David's plea. God sternly admonishes the righteous not to be impressed with the prosperity of
sinners, for it is empty and transient (Meiri, Meir Tehillos). Radak (v.
40) explains that this theme is repeated frequently in this rather
lengthy Psalm because most people feel an overpowering temptation
to imitate the successful ways of the wicked; therefore their faith requires constant reinforcement.

א לְדָוִד | אַל־תִּתְחַר בַּמְּרֵעִים אַל־תְּקַנֵּא
ב בְּעֹשֵׂי עַוְלָה: כִּי כֶחָצִיר מְהֵרָה יִמָּלוּ
ג וּכְיֶרֶק דֶּשֶׁא יִבּוֹלוּן: בְּטַח בַּיהוה וַעֲשֵׂה־

1. לְדָוִד — To David.

Whenever the superscription of a psalm is merely לְדָוִד, *to David* then it is neither a song nor a prayer. It is the רוּחַ הַקּוֹדֶשׁ, *the holy spirit*, speaking through David *(Zohar, Parshas Vayechi).*

Ostensibly, the message of this psalm seems geared to the unintelligent masses, who must be cautioned to avoid the company of the wicked lest they be adversely influenced by their success. However, this assumption is false. Even the greatest people may be unduly impressed by the prosperity of sinners. Therefore, the psalm is dedicated *To David* in order to emphasize that even a person of David's stature must take care not to be impressed by evildoers *(Alshich).*

אַל־תִּתְחַר — Do not compete [see *Proverbs* 24:19].

Do not attempt to compete with the success of the wicked, or to imitate their corruption in order to achieve prosperity like theirs. Similarly we read וְאֵיךְ תְּתַחֲרֶה אֶת הַסּוּסִים, *How do you compete with the horses? (Jeremiah* 12:5) *(Rashi; Radak; Ibn Ezra; Metzudos).*

The *Talmud (Berachos* 7b) adds a further interpretation: Do not quarrel with the evil men.

[This warning applies only when they enjoy extraordinary success. That indicates that for the moment it is God's will that they should be rewarded and that the righteous should be punished. To abstain from attacking them at such a time is not a display of cowardice, but a humble submission to God's will.]

Ibn Ezra and *Meiri*, offer yet another translation of אַל־תִּתְחַר in consonance with the above theme. They derive the word from חָרוֹן *anger*. Thus, 'Do not be

angered by the success of the evil!'

Sforno comments that David composed the psalm while inspired with a prophetic vision of the tragedy which was destined to split the Jewish nation. David foresaw the rebellion of Jeraboam ben Nabat who would take away the Ten Tribes of Israel, while only the tribes of Judah and Benjamin remained loyal to Rechavom, son of Solomon. David cautions Rechavom not to quarrel with the rebels. A civil war pitting Jew against Jew is to be avoided at all costs. David assures Rechavom that the success of the rebels will be short-lived provided that he concentrates his efforts on repentance.

[*Sforno* relates every verse of the psalm to an event in the long struggle between the kingdoms of Judah and Israel. However his entire commentary is beyond the scope of this work.]

בַּמְּרֵעִים — The evil men.

These are villains who are not satisfied with doing evil, but seek to subvert others as well. [They are not merely רַע, *evil*, they are מֵרִיעַ, (i.e., the transitive *Hiph'il* form), *they make others evil*, by enticing them to imitate their ways.] *(Nora Tehillos).*

אַל־תְּקַנֵּא — Be not envious.

Similarly Solomon says, אַל־יְקַנֵּא לִבְּךָ בַּחַטָּאִים, *Do not let your heart be envious of the sinners (Proverbs* 23:17). What then should you envy? כִּי אִם בְּיִרְאַת ה' כָּל הַיּוֹם, *Only the fear of HASHEM, all day long (Midrash Shocher Tov).* [Envy is basic to human nature. We cannot demand that a person should obliterate it from his character, we can only sublimate his envy, directing it towards loftier aspirations. Thus, the Sages *(Bava Basra* 22a) praise envy of superior Torah know-

XXXVII **T**o David: Do not compete with the evil men;
1-3 be not envious of evildoers.
² For like grass will they be swiftly cut,
and like green vegetation will they wither.
³ Trust in HASHEM and do good,

ledge for it serves to spur further Torah study.][1]

בְּעֹשֵׂי עַוְלָה — *Of evildoers.*

These men sin, but do not influence others. Nevertheless, the Psalmist warns us not to envy their success (*Nora Tehillos*).

2. כֶחָצִיר — *Like grass.*

The חָצִיר is a species of grass which dries out and withers sooner than others (*Malbim*).

The wicked thrive as easily as grass, which sprouts wherever there is some soil. But do not fret. Though they proliferate quickly they fail to develop deep, hardy roots and so they will fade away as quickly as they have grown (*Hirsch*).

וּכְיֶרֶק דֶשֶׁא — *And like green vegetation.*

Grass consists of two parts, the roots and the blades. Animals usually eat the blades and leave the root intact. Similarly, the green sprout will shrivel and dry, but the root remains intact to send forth new blades of grass. The flourishing wicked are likened to the sprouts which thrive only temporarily. (*Radak*).

יִבּוֹלוּן — *Will they wither.*

The 'soil' from which the Jewish soul sprouts is heaven, and even when it is on earth, the soul is still connected to its celestial roots. But sin can sever the shoot from its roots; such is the lot of the wicked. You may ask, 'If they have been severed from the roots of life, how can they still live and thrive?' The answer is that they resemble the blade of grass which, because of its accumulated moisture, remains green even after it is cut. Similarly, the wicked man, although cut off from his heavenly source, can still thrive on the handful of merits which he once stored away. But as those merits 'dry up', he will surely wither to death (*Alshich*).

The מְרֵעִים who subvert others will meet their dismal fate at the hands of others. They are like the חָצִיר which is cut down by an outside hand. Also, their end comes swiftly, in one stroke. The עֹשֵׂי עַוְלָה who sin only privately, wither away by themselves; slowly and gradually (*Ibn Yachya*).

3. בְּטַח בַּה' וַעֲשֵׂה טוֹב — *Trust in HASHEM and do good.*

Unlike the evil ones whose roots lie in

1. *Midrash Shocher Tov* continues: Said the Holy One, Blessed be He: Employ envy for My sake! For, without envy no man would bother to take himself a wife or to build himself a home. If Abraham had not been envious (i.e., zealous) on My behalf he would not have spread My Name all over heaven and earth. Once he met Malchizekek [Shem, the son of Noah] and asked him, 'By virtue of which merit did you survive the great Flood?' Malchizedek replied, 'By virtue of the charity and kindness which we practiced towards the helpless animals in the Ark! We did not close our eyes all night as we hurried to provide food for every single animal, beast, and bird. One time only were we late and, instantly, father Noah was bitten [by a lion.]'

Upon hearing this, Abraham said to himself, 'If these men survived by virtue of the kindness they displayed to lowly animals, how much greater would my salvation be if I would act charitably towards all men, who are created in God's Own image'? Immediately, Abraham established an inn to provide food, drink, and company for travelers. Therefore, Solomon observed: *And I saw that all labor and all skillful enterprise spring from man's rivalry with his neighbor (Koheles 4:4).*

the earth, sink your own roots in HASHEM, the source of all good (Hirsch).

The עֹשֵׂי עַוְלָה, evildoers (v. 1) are the victims of their own lack of trust. Do not copy this — counteract it by strengthening your trust and resolving to do good (Ibn Yachya).

Trust in HASHEM, thereby you will avoid evil and do good. Do not say to yourself, 'If I do not rob and steal or if I give my money to charity — how will I make a living and survive?' (Rashi). [1]

According to Radak and Ibn Ezra, however, this stich should be understood in the reverse order: learn to trust in God by doing good. Do good, and in the merit of your good deeds, you can trust in HASHEM to reward and protect you.

Divrei Shlomo comments that it is not enough to think or say that you trust God. Genuine trust must lead to action! If you are willing to take a risk or make a sacrifice as a result of trust, then you know that your convictions are strong and sincere. Thus, Trust in HASHEM [so firmly that] you will do good.

Ramban derives many fundamentals of faith from this verse. Like Rashi, he emphasizes that faith is the prime cause of all good deeds. One should be confident that if he is determined to perform mitzvos, God will help him do good.

Ramban continues that trust is mentioned before do good in order to emphasize that even a sinner who has not yet done any good has the right to trust in the mercy of God Who assists even those who are unworthy of reward. Whether you are righteous or wicked, trust in HASHEM. Then, after God has responded favorably to your trust, you should show your appreciation by doing good (Ha'Emunah V'ha'Betachon ch. 1).

שְׁכָן אֶרֶץ — [That you may] dwell in the land.

Your reward for doing good will be to dwell in the land, in endless tranquility (Rashi).

Ramban continues: Once you have decided to dedicate yourself to doing good, you may wish to withdraw from mundane pursuits and to abandon your occupation. Such a course of action is not desirable for the average person, since he will probably fear the lack of a source of livelihood. Therefore do not be excessively enthusiastic; instead, dwell in the land i.e., cultivate and exploit it to earn a living.

The Talmud (Berachos 35b) states that only a select handful of men like the saintly Rabbi Shimon bar Yochai can abandon all worldly pursuits in favor of exclusive Torah study [for they were not concerned with ther bodies, only with their souls]. Others must always engage in an occupation [despite their spiritual aspirations].[2]

וּרְעֵה אֱמוּנָה — And be nurtured [lit. pastured] by faith.

This translation follows Rashi who derives רְעֵה from מִרְעֶה, pasture, grazing land. Thus: [As a reward for trusting in HASHEM and doing good], you will eat and be nourished plentifully.

You will resemble sheep who graze in lush pastures, never worrying about the future. They have complete faith that just as there is grass today, so will there be grass tomorrow (Malbim).

Not only will your body be

1. The Talmud (Sotah 48b) asks: 'Who are the אַנְשֵׁי אֱמֻנָה, men of faith?'

Rabbi Yitzchak says: They are the people who sincerely believe in the Holy One, Blessed be He, [and therefore freely spend money to enhance a mitzvah, for charity, or for Sabbath and festival expenses (Rashi)].

As Rabbi Eliezer HaGadol taught: Whoever has bread in his basket today, yet asks, 'What will I eat tomorrow?', is among the קְטַנֵּי אֲמָנָה, people of meager faith.

*that you may dwell in the land and be nurtured
by faith.*

⁴ *Take delight in HASHEM,*

nourished, but even your אֱמוּנָה, *faith*,
will grow stronger and stronger
(Tanya).

Radak relates רְעֵה to the רוֹעֶה,
shepherd who takes the animals out to
the pasture. He explains: Do not content yourself with personal good deeds.
Go out and be a shepherd, a guide, a
teacher to others. This is the most
desirable service you can render to God!
By being a shepherd, who teaches
others good, you counteract the influence of the מְרֵעִים *(v. 1)* who teach
others to do evil *(Ibn Yachya)*.

Ramban translates רְעֵה as guard (for
a shepherd guards the sheep) and comments: 'Now that you, the average man,
are destined to be שְׁכָן אֶרֶץ, i.e., one who
cultivates the earth, you may be bitter
that you are condemned to an empty life
of material pursuit. This is not so! A
great spiritual challenge confronts those
who earn a living. רְעֵה אֱמוּנָה,
guard your faithfulness! Take care to
deal with honesty and integrity. Each
day that you pass this test will be well
spent in a profound state of spiritual accomplishment!'

Ramban also suggests that רְעֵה is
related to רֵעַ, *friend, companion*. Always put yourself in the company of
faith and wisdom, for that is the key to
coming close to God.

Rabbeinu Bachya concludes: This
verse begins with בִּטָּחוֹן, *trust*, and ends
with אֱמוּנָה, *faith*, in order to teach that
faith is merely one aspect of the broader
concept called *trust* and is subordinate
to it. *Faith* is a simple intellectual concept, a belief that God can control every
aspect of life. *Trust* involves translating
this lofty concept of faith into action.
Therefore, *Ramban* lays down the
postulate כָּל הַבּוֹטֵחַ מַאֲמִין אֲבָל לֹא
כָּל הַמַּאֲמִין בּוֹטֵחַ, *Everyone who trusts
has faith, but not everyone who has
faith, trusts.*

4. וְהִתְעַנַּג עַל ה׳ — *Take delight in
HASHEM*

If you are nourished only by faith,
you will take delight exclusively in
HASHEM *(Nora Tehillos)*. In His service
you will find the fulfillment of every
delightful wish for which you ever
yearned *(Radak)*.

You may demand these [spiritual]
delights from HASHEM for you are like
a worker who has the right to request
his pay *(Ibn Ezra)*.

But the main delight is reserved for
the World to Come *(Ibn Yachya)*.

The *Talmud (Shabbos* 118b) states:
Whoever makes the Sabbath delightful
is granted all of his heart's desires as it
says, *Take delight in HASHEM that He*

2. *Chovos Halevavos* relates the following tale: Once a saintly man traveled to a distant land
to seek out a livelihood. He arrived at a city whose inhabitants were all idol-worshipers. He
fiercely rebuked them, 'Fools! Why do you worship helpless images of wood and stone? Join
me and worship the living, all powerful God who feeds and supports all of mankind!'

The pagans retorted, 'Your actions contradict your own words! If indeed your God supports all men at all times in all places, why then did you yourself put your life into jeopardy to
travel so very far in order to seek your fortune? Stay home and let your God provide for you
there!'

Upon hearing this rebuke, the pious man immediately resolved never again to leave his land
in order to search for sustenace.

Based on this parable, *Tehillas Hashem* notes that even if one engages in earning a living he
has the opportunity to demonstrate this trust in HASHEM by being שְׁכָן אֶרֶץ *dwelling in* (his
own) *land* [i.e., *limiting the extent of his pursuit of a livelihood.*]

ה עַל־יהוה וְיִתֶּן־לְךָ מִשְׁאֲלֹת לִבֶּךָ: גּוֹל
עַל־יהוה דַּרְכֶּךָ וּבְטַח עָלָיו וְהוּא יַעֲשֶׂה:
ו וְהוֹצִיא כָאוֹר צִדְקֶךָ וּמִשְׁפָּטֶךָ כַּצָּהֳרָיִם:
ז דּוֹם | לַיהוה וְהִתְחוֹלֵל לוֹ אַל־תִּתְחַר
ח בְּמַצְלִיחַ דַּרְכּוֹ בְּאִישׁ עֹשֶׂה מְזִמּוֹת: הֶרֶף

will grant you the desires of your heart.
The Sabbath is a day of delight as we
read וְקָרָאתָ לַשַּׁבָּת עֹנֶג, And you shall call
the Sabbath a delight (Isaiah 58:13)

[If you take delight in HASHEM then
you will not envy the material success
of the wicked. It is not easy to attain
such spiritual contentment during the
work week, but on the Sabbath even the
humblest Jew is like a king and capable
of perceiving the futility of envy for
material benefit.]

וְיִתֶּן לְךָ מִשְׁאֲלֹת לִבֶּךָ — That He may
grant you the desires of your heart.

When God sees that you take delight
only in Him, He will surely fulfill your
every request, because whatever you
desire will be put to His service (Divrei
Shlomo).

5. גּוֹל עַל ה' דַּרְכֶּךָ — Cast [lit. roll] your
way upon HASHEM.

Shift your burdens from yourself and
put them on God. Trust Him to attend
to your every need (Rashi, Radak).

The use of the singular form דַּרְכֶּךָ,
your way, conveys a message. The
righteous man knows with a certainty
that the only route to good fortune is by
way of Hashem. But the evildoer who
has no faith in God must toil incessantly
to care for himself. He tries not one, but
many different ways to search for his
road to success (Malbim).

[If you are determined to follow in
the way of Hashem, be prepared to exert
yourself to clear away all obstacles in
your path. Roll them to the side, as the
prophet said, סֹלּוּ סֹלּוּ פַּנּוּ דָרֶךְ הָרִימוּ
מִכְשׁוֹל מִדֶּרֶךְ עַמִּי, Raise up, raise up,
prepare the way, lift up the stumbling

block out of the way, My nation (Isaiah
57:14).]

וּבְטַח עָלָיו וְהוּא יַעֲשֶׂה — Rely on Him and
He will act.

As we read, הַשְׁלֵךְ עַל ה' יְהָבְךָ וְהוּא
יְכַלְכְּלֶךָ, Cast upon HASHEM your burden and He will provide for you [55:23]
(Ibn Ezra).

[Now that the righteous man is assured that his every wish will be fulfilled, there is no reason for him to
imitate or envy the wicked.]

6. וְהוֹצִיא כָאוֹר צִדְקֶךָ — And He will
reveal [lit. He will bring forth] your
righteousness like a light.

Your righteousness will be displayed
to the entire world as clearly as a bright
light (Radak).

Evildoers resort to the lowest of tricks
in order to foil the righteous. With
vicious slander they cast aspersions on
the honesty of righteous people and the
purity of their motives. But David assures good men that ultimately they will
be cleared of all false accusations
(Hirsch).

The righteous are not ashamed of
their actions, but the evildoers must
perform all of their deeds in darkness
lest they be caught and disgraced
(Malbim).

וּמִשְׁפָּטֶךָ כַּצָּהֳרָיִם — And your judgments
like high noon.

The righteous man fears no tribunal.
He has nothing to hide from the inquiry
of a court. Not so the evildoer who
trembles before the glaring, revealing
light of justice (Malbim).

[The plural form מִשְׁפָּטֶיךָ (lit.

that He may grant you the desires of your heart.
⁵ *Cast your way upon HASHEM,*
  rely on Him and He will act.
⁶ *And He will reveal your righteousness like a light,*
  and your judgments like high noon.
⁷ *Be mute before HASHEM*
  and wait with longing for Him.
Do not compete with him who prospers,
  with the man who executes malicious plans.

judgments) appears in the authoritative Rodelheim edition of the *Psalms*. However, *Hirsch* uses the singular מִשְׁפָּטֶךָ based on older editions of *Psalms*.]

7. דּוֹם לַה' — *Be mute before HASHEM.*

This translation follows the *Targum, Menachem,* and *Dunash* who relate this to וַיִּדֹּם אַהֲרֹן, *And Aaron was silent* (Leviticus 10:3).

The realization that your fate comes only from God should end all doubts, and silence all protests *(Hirsch)*.

However, *Rashi, Radak,* and *Metzudos* render דּוֹם as *wait, tarry* as in דֹּמּוּ עַד הַגִּיעֵנוּ אֲלֵיכֶם, *Wait until we reach you* (I Samuel 14:9). [Do not be overwhelmed by present events, wait patiently for future developments which will make God's providence clearly evident.] [1]

וְהִתְחוֹלֵל לוֹ — *And wait with longing for Him.*

This is derived from תּוֹחֶלֶת, *waiting, longing.* [See *Proverbs* 13:12] *(Ibn Ezra, Radak, Metzudos).*

Similarly it says: טוֹב וְיָחִיל וְדוּמָם לִתְשׁוּעַת ה', *It is good to wait in silence for the salvation of HASHEM (Lamentations 3:26).* If God brings afflictions upon you, accept them with hope *(Yalkut Shimoni).*

Some relate this word to חִיל *pain* as in חִיל כַּיּוֹלֵדָה *a pain like a woman in labor* (48:7). Thus: prepare to suffer pain and torments for His sake *(Radak).*

And even be ready to endure חֳלִי, *sickness* if that is God's wish *(Tehillos Hashem).*

Or הִתְחוֹלֵל may be related to חָלָל *corpse* i.e. prepare to give up your life, to become a corpse, for His sake. Similarly we read הֵן יִקְטְלֵנִי לוֹ אֲיַחֵל, *Though they slay me, for Him I* [am prepared to] *become a* (חָלָל) *corpse (Tanchuma Hayashan, Devarim 4).*

אַל תִּתְחַר בְּמַצְלִיחַ דַּרְכּוֹ — *Do not compete with him who prospers*

[Never seek to emulate the seemingly successful ways of the wicked. Though your attempts at righteousness result in failure and misfortune, never stop hoping for eventual salvation by Hashem.]

1. The *Talmud* (*Gittin* 7a) interprets דּוֹם homiletically as a reference to דִּמְדּוּמֵי חַמָּה, *the dim light of the sun* i.e. early morning and late afternoon which are times of prayer. The *Talmud* relates that the Babylonian Exilarch, Mar Ukva, was harassed by rebels who flouted his authority and insulted him. He had the authority to turn these rebels over to the Babylonian government for punishment but he was reluctant to do so. He sought the advice of Rabbi Elazar who responded דּוֹם לַה', *pray to HASHEM, in the early morning and late afternoon,* וְהִתְחוֹלֵל לוֹ, and He will topple your enemies before you like so many חֲלָלִים, *corpses!*

מֵאַף וַעֲזֹב חֵמָה אַל־תִּתְחַר אַךְ־לְהָרֵעַ:

ט כִּי־מְרֵעִים יִכָּרֵתוּן וְקֹוֵי יהוה הֵמָּה

י יִירְשׁוּ־אָרֶץ: וְעוֹד מְעַט וְאֵין רָשָׁע

יא וְהִתְבּוֹנַנְתָּ עַל־מְקוֹמוֹ וְאֵינֶנּוּ: וַעֲנָוִים

יב יִירְשׁוּ־אָרֶץ וְהִתְעַנְּגוּ עַל־רֹב שָׁלוֹם: זֹמֵם

יג רָשָׁע לַצַּדִּיק וְחֹרֵק עָלָיו שִׁנָּיו: אֲדֹנָי

יד יִשְׂחַק־לוֹ כִּי־רָאָה כִּי־יָבֹא יוֹמוֹ: חֶרֶב |

---

8. הֶרֶף — *Give up.*

This is synonymous with הֶרֶף, *let loose,* (Rashi); and is related to רָפָה, *weak* (Metzudas Zion).

מֵאַף — *From anger.*

Desist from evil so as to prevent God's anger from pouring down on you (Rashi).

Subdue your own frustration and anger despite your failure to realize your ambitions (Radak).

Resist the temptation to join the company of the prosperous man who angers God (Metzudas David).

וַעֲזֹב חֵמָה — *And forsake wrath.*

Calm yourself. Do not let the prosperity of the wicked upset you (Ibn Ezra).

Not only must you subdue your אַף, *external anger,* but even your חֵמָה, *inner rage,* [see comm. 6:2], should be controlled (Malbim).

אַךְ תִּתְחַר אַךְ לְהָרֵעַ — *Do not compete; it will bring but harm.*

Think carefully before you join the wicked; you may lose more than you gain. Remember, pure faith in Hashem is more precious than any other possession. Better to be a pauper with trust than a wealthy man without it (Malbim).

Perhaps you wish to associate with the wicked in order to bring them back to Hashem. Nevertheless, do not become intimate with them. The dangers of doing so are great, but the potential benefits are extremely doubtful (Alshich).

9. כִּי מְרֵעִים יִכָּרֵתוּן — *For the evil men shall be cut off.*

Don't be taken in by their success, for it is short-lived (Radak).

וְקֹוֵי ה' הֵמָּה יִירְשׁוּאָרֶץ — *But those who hope to HASHEM shall inherit the earth.*

After the wicked are swept away, the righteous shall arise to take over their possessions, as it says (Job 27:17): יָכִין וְצַדִּיק יִלְבָּשׁ *He* [the wicked one] *prepares, but the righteous one dons* [his clothing] (Radak).

10. וְעוֹד מְעַט — *Just a little longer.*

Pay no heed to the present. In but a short while all will change and the evil will vanish (Rashi).

וְאֵין רָשָׁע — *And there will be no wicked.*

He will die and leave This World (Eretz Hachaim).

וְהִתְבּוֹנַנְתָּ עַל מְקוֹמוֹ וְאֵינֶנּוּ — *You will contemplate his place and he will be gone.*

His place will be left permanently vacant. Even his immediate heirs will not inherit his position (Otzar Nechmad).

If you consider it you will realize that not only has the evildoer left This World, but he has forfeited his place in the World to Come. And who will receive that portion? The righteous! As it says in the very next verse, *but the humble shall inherit the earth* (Eretz HaChaim).

⁸ *Give up anger and forsake wrath.*
        Do not compete; it will bring but harm.
⁹ *For the evil men shall be cut off,*
        but those who hope to HASHEM shall inherit
        the earth.
¹⁰ *Just a little longer and there will be no wicked,*
        you will contemplate his place and he will
        be gone.
¹¹ *But the humble shall inherit the earth*
        and delight in abundant peace.
¹² *The wicked man plots against the righteous*
        and gnashes his teeth at him.
¹³ *But my Lord laughs at him*
        for He sees that his day approaches.

11. וַעֲנָוִים יִירְשׁוּ אָרֶץ — *But the humble shall inherit the earth.*

Those who had previously been downtrodden and humbled by the wicked (*Radak*).

וְהִתְעַנְּגוּ עַל רֹב שָׁלוֹם — *And they shall delight in abundant peace.*

The haughty never enjoy the delight known as 'peace of mind.' In their excessive pride they imagine that they never have enough; that they deserve more and more. But the humble are delighted with what they have and consider it to be שָׁלֵם, *complete*, i.e., enough (*Yalkut Eliezer*).

Rav said: For four reasons the property of the wealthy householders suddenly disappears. They pay their laborers only with great reluctance. They don't pay their laborers at all. They shirk all communal responsibility. They are haughty. And haughtiness is as bad as all of those sins combined. However, the humble are different, as it says: *but the humble shall inherit the land and they shall delight in abundant peace* (*Succah* 29b).

12. זֹמֵם רָשָׁע לַצַּדִּיק — *The wicked man plots against the righteous.*

Do not be overawed by the wicked even when they hatch seemingly foolproof plots against the righteous (*Malbim*).

וְחֹרֵק עָלָיו שִׁנָּיו — *And gnashes his teeth at him.*

[Even when they gnash their teeth in gleeful anticipation of the downfall of the *tzaddik*, pay no heed. See 35:16 and 112:10.]

This alludes to the encounter of the two estranged brothers, Esau and Jacob. The Sages teach that when Esau fell on Jacob's neck, ostensibly to kiss him, he tried to inflict a mortal wound by biting. However, God turned Jacob's neck to marble, and Esau blunted his own teeth. Thus, the wicked Esau plotted to bite the righteous Jacob, but ground his own teeth instead (*Tehillas Hashem*).

13. אֲדֹנָי יִשְׂחַק לוֹ — *[But] my Lord laughs at him.*

The Lord to whom the future is revealed, already foresees the futility of the evildoer's schemes. God laughs at the very outset, for the plots will never succeed (*Ibn Ezra, Radak*).

Or יִשְׂחָק may mean *to show* פָּנִים שׂוֹחֲקוֹת, *a smiling contenance.* Don't be

פָּתְחוּ רְשָׁעִים וְדָרְכוּ קַשְׁתָּם לְהַפִּיל עָנִי

וְאֶבְיוֹן לִטְבוֹחַ יִשְׁרֵי־דָרֶךְ: חַרְבָּם תָּבוֹא טו

בְלִבָּם וְקַשְׁתוֹתָם תִּשָּׁבַרְנָה: טוֹב־מְעַט טז

לַצַּדִּיק מֵהֲמוֹן רְשָׁעִים רַבִּים: כִּי זְרוֹעוֹת יז

רְשָׁעִים תִּשָּׁבַרְנָה וְסוֹמֵךְ צַדִּיקִים יהוה:

יוֹדֵעַ יהוה יְמֵי תְמִימִם וְנַחֲלָתָם לְעוֹלָם יח

---

dismayed if God seems to treat the wicked person benevolently. Rest assured that God has prepared his present success to be the cause of his eventual downfall (Malbim).

כִּי יָבֹא יוֹמוֹ —That his day approaches.

Though the wicked one plots against the righteous, God knows that his plan will never come to fruition, because the day of his own doom draws near (Radak).

14. חֶרֶב פָּתְחוּ רְשָׁעִים — The wicked drew [lit. opened] a sword.

When it is sheathed, the sword appears to be locked into its cover; when it is drawn, it is opened and released (Radak, Ibn Ezra).

Or פָּתְחוּ may be rendered they sharpened as in חֶרֶב פְּתוּחָה לְטֶבַח מְרוּטָה, the sword is sharpened, polished for the slaughter (Ezekiel 21:33).

This implies that the wicked initiated hostilities without prior provocation (Rashi).[1]

15. חַרְבָּם תָּבוֹא בְלִבָּם — Their sword will pierce their own heart.

Instead of succeeding in their designs against the righteous, the wicked would

die of their own devices. Then it will be evident why God laughed at them (v. 13) when He foresaw their doom (Malbim).

The degraded one says in his heart, 'There is no God' (14:1). God responds: 'Since the degenerate rebelled against me in his heart, I will punish him measure for measure by aiming for his heart.' As it says, Their sword will pierce their own heart (Midrash Shocher Tov).

16. טוֹב מְעַט לַצַּדִּיק — Better a few with the righteous [lit. The little which the righteous one has is good].

The handful of men who rally to the call of the tzaddik, are superior to the wicked masses (Rashi).

Radak renders מְעַט literally as a small amount, i.e., the tzaddik is content even with meagre resources.

He understands that excessive wealth is often detrimental to one's faith and character because wealth can lead a man to forget that God is the ultimate source of all blessing. Therefore, he prefers to have little, because in that way he remains conscious of his dependence on God (Tehillos Hashem).

---

1. Various Midrashim trace violence back to the provocation of the wicked. Rabbi Yehoshua of Sichnin in the name of Rabbi Levi said: It is written, The wicked drew a sword, and bent their bows, this refers to Cain. To bring down the poor and needy, to slaughter those of upright path, this describes his brother, Abel. Their sword will pierce their own heart, this is Cain's punishment of exile and wandering over the earth (Bereishis Rabbah 22:9).

Another Midrash (Bereishis Rabbah 42:1) expounds that the wicked instigated the world's first large-scale war: The wicked drew a sword, this refers to King Amraphel and his allies. To bring down the poor and needy, this is Lot. To slaughter those of upright path, this is Abraham. Their sword will pierce their own heart, this describes their ultimate defeat at the hands of Abraham.

14 *The wicked drew a sword*
and bent their bow
To bring down the poor and the needy,
to slaughter those of upright path.
15 *Their sword will pierce their own heart,*
and their bows be broken.
16 *Better a few with the righteous*
than a multitude of many wicked.
17 *For the arms of the wicked will be broken,*
but the support of the righteous ones is HASHEM.
18 *HASHEM is aware of the days of the perfect,*
their inheritance will endure forever.

מֵהֲמוֹן — *Than a multitude* [lit. *more than the many*].

הָמוֹן refers to a vast army, derived from הָמָה, *to make noise*, describing the clamor of the mob (*Hirsch*).

Amraphel and his allies started the first major world war in order to capture Lot and and antagonize Abraham [see footnote v. 14.] He threatened Abraham with a הָמוֹן, *a multitude*, but the handful of men who accompanied Abraham surpassed the mighty armies of the wicked and destroyed them (*Rashi*).

According to *Radak*, הָמוֹן refers to מָמוֹן, *money*. Abundant wealth will never satisfy the wicked who incessantly crave for more, as Solomon said, *The righteous man eats to satisfy his soul, but the belly of the wicked shall always feel want* (*Proverbs* 13:25).

רְשָׁעִים רַבִּים — *Many wicked*.

In this verse the righteous are referred to in the singular form as צַדִּיק, *righteous one*, whereas the wicked ones are described in the plural. Herein lies the secret strength of the righteous. Although they are few, they unite together as one powerful unit. But the wicked ones can never agree on anything. Each one selfishly seeks to preserve his own personal interests. So, despite their vast numbers, they remain a weak, fragmented force (*Maharam Markado*).

17. כִּי זְרוֹעוֹת רְשָׁעִים תִּשָּׁבַרְנָה — *For the arms of the wicked will be broken.*

Just as their bows will be broken (v. 15) so will their arms, for the bows can kill only because of the strong arms which string and bend them (*Ibn Ezra*).

They will not have the strength to harm the righteous (*Radak*).

18. יוֹדֵעַ ה׳ יְמֵי תְמִימִם — *HASHEM is aware of the days of the perfect.*

God is concerned with their daily good deeds (*Rashi*), and providentially lengthens their lives (*Radak*).

The *Midrash* (*Bereishis Rabbah* 58:1) comments, 'Just as the righteous are

Finally, *Midrash Tanchuma* (*Lech Lecha* 7) applies these words to the life of David himself. In *II Samuel* Chapter 10, the Scriptures relate how David sent two emissaries to console Chanun ben Nachash, King of Ammon, after the death of his father. But the King opened hostilities by treating the emissaries in a most degrading fashion. He shaved off half of their beards and ripped their garments in two. The Ammonite King then hired Aram to join him in battle against Israel. Said the Holy One, Blessed be He, 'Wicked one, you started the fight with a sword, your own sword shall pierce your heart!' Thereupon, David's generals, Yoav and Avishai arose and slew them all.

יט תִּהְיֶה: לֹא־יֵבֹשׁוּ בְּעֵת רָעָה וּבִימֵי רְעָבוֹן
כ   יִשְׂבָּעוּ: כִּי רְשָׁעִים | יֹאבֵדוּ וְאֹיְבֵי יהוה
כא כִּיקַר כָּרִים כָּלוּ בֶעָשָׁן כָּלוּ: לֹוֶה רָשָׁע

---

perfect and complete, so are their days perfect and complete.' [This can be understood in two ways. One, that the lifetime allotted to the righteous is in units of complete years. They will die on a birthday so that their years will literally be 'complete.' However, only a select few are so perfectly righteous that they can be placed in this category.

A second interpretation is that the above statement applies not to God, but to the philosophy of all devout people. To them, every day presents a unique opportunity for accomplishment, and they exploit this opportunity fully. Thus, the devout end their lives with their special mission accomplished perfectly.]

Every commandment perfects the limb which performed it. Every sin distorts the organ which was used for the spiritual perversion. Thus, *the arms of the wicked will be broken* (v. 17), whereas the days and the bodies of the righteous will achieve spritual perfection (*Ahavas Shalom*).

וְנַחֲלָתָם לְעוֹלָם תִּהְיֶה — *Their inheritance will endure forever.*

Their God-given reward is eternal. [Since they never wasted an opportunity to accomplish good, every act they did was of enduring significance.]

19. לֹא יֵבֹשׁוּ בְּעֵת רָעָה — *They will not be shamed in times of calamity.*

I.e., in times of plague, war, or attack by beasts (*Radak*).

[A calamity which descends upon a community points an accusing finger at the inhabitants and their improper ways. Thus, those who are afflicted are shamed. But the perfectly innocent will remain unscathed, for their ways are above reproach.]

20. כִּי רְשָׁעִים יֹאבֵדוּ — *For the wicked will perish.*

The downfall of the wicked is imperative so that the perfect will never be shamed by calamity (*v.* 19) at their hands (*Radak*).

וְאֹיְבֵי ה' — *And the foes of HASHEM.*

Wicked people are generally those who have been overcome by their lusts. Since they lost self-control, their measure-for-measure punishment is יֹאבֵדוּ, literally, *they become lost*. But, like any lost article which can be sought and recovered, they can repent and return. However, *the foes of HASHEM* are those who wish to obliterate God's presence from their lives. Therefore, they themselves will be made to vanish forever (*Tehillos Hashem*).

כִּיקַר כָּרִים — *Like a light flashing on pastures.*

This follows *Rashi* who relates יְקַר to יְקָרוֹת, *bright light* (*Zechariah* 14:16) and כָּרִים to כַּר נִרְחָב, *broad pasture* (*Isaiah* 30:23). The first rays of the morning sun spread out all across the broad horizon, dazzling the beholder by their contrast to the darkness they displace. But the spectacle is soon over. Similarly, the spectacular success of the wicked does not endure.

Rashi, Radak, Ibn Ezra, and *Metzudos* also suggest a different translation. כָּרִים means *sheep*, and יְקָר, *glory*, is its rich flesh and fat. The sheep which is being fattened for the slaughter glories in its growing weight and size not realizing which is precisely this fattening that is the prelude to its doom. So too, the prosperity of the wicked is the first step towards their destruction.

Chovos Halevavos (Shaar Avodas HaElohim, Ch. 6) observes: He who

19 *They will not be shamed in times of calamity,*
in days of famine they will be satisfied.
20 *For the wicked will perish,*
And the foes of HASHEM —
like a light flashing on pastures;
consumed, like smoke they are consumed.
21 *The wicked one borrows but repays not,*

---

denies the existence of God and fails to recognize His abundant kindness suffers a complete decline in his personal status. No longer is he considered to be an intelligent human being. Rather, he sinks to the level of the dumb animals as it says, *And the foes of HASHEM are like the fattened sheep.*[1]

כָּלוּ בֶעָשָׁן כָּלוּ — *Consumed, like smoke they are consumed.*

David said: 'Accord to the wicked the honor reserved for the fattened sheep.' The sheep are slaughtered and hung high above the fire to be smoked' (*Yalkut Shimoni*).

Other materials leave behind some residue after burning in the form of ashes, but if fat is burned [such as the fat of the sheep mentioned here], it is completely consumed by the flames. The same is true of the wicked who will perish and leave behind no remnant (*Hirsch*).

21. לֹוֶה רָשָׁע וְלֹא יְשַׁלֵּם — *The wicked one borrows, but repays not* [lit. *and he will not repay*].

Having lost all their possessions, the wicked will be forced to borrow money

even though they have no means of repayment (*Rashbam*).

It does not say וְלֹא מְשַׁלֵּם, *and he does not pay*, i.e., later when the debt becomes due. Rather it says וְלֹא יְשַׁלֵּם, *and he 'will' not pay*, i.e., when he first borrowed the money he had no intention of ever repaying (*Yalkut Shimoni*).

Rambam (*Hilchos Malveh* 1:3) derives a halachic principle from this verse: It is forbidden to borrow money with the intention of squandering it for no worthwhile purpose. For if the money is wasted then no assets will be available from which the creditor can extract payment. The debtor who acts so carelessly and inconsiderately is called רָשָׁע, *wicked*, as it says, *The wicked man borrows and he will not repay.* Furthermore, the Sages warned, יְהִי מָמוֹן חֲבֵרְךָ חָבִיב עָלֶיךָ כְּשֶׁלָּךְ, *Let the money of your friend be as dear to you as your own.* (*Avos* 2:17).

Hirsch elaborates on the deeper message contained in these words: Whatever gain we receive on earth is a loan granted by God in order to help us advance the common welfare in accordance with His will. The greater the

---

1. To what may this be likened? To the farmer who owned a piglet, a donkey and its foal. He fed the piglet all it wanted. But to the foal and the donkey he gave measured portions. Said the foal to its mother, 'What a fool our master is. We toil and sweat for him and he gives us only limited rations, yet the piglet does nothing and he gives it all it wants!'

The donkey replied, 'Do not be upset, the day will come and your will see that the pig was pampered for its doom not for its good.'

Sure enough, when the holiday season arrived, they dragged the fat pig away to its slaughter. The master then put barley into the feedbag of the foal who shook its head and refused to eat, [thinking that it, too, was being fattened for the kill.] But the wise mother reassured it, 'Have no fear little one! It is not the feeding which marks the creature for slaughter, but idleness from productive work' (*Midrash Esther Rabbah* 7:1).

כב וְלֹא יְשַׁלֵּם וְצַדִּיק חוֹנֵן וְנוֹתֵן: כִּי מְבֹרָכָיו

כג יִירְשׁוּ אָרֶץ וּמְקֻלָּלָיו יִכָּרֵתוּ: מֵיהוה

כד מִצְעֲדֵי־גֶבֶר כּוֹנָנוּ וְדַרְכּוֹ יֶחְפָּץ: כִּי־יִפֹּל

כה לֹא־יוּטָל כִּי־יהוה סוֹמֵךְ יָדוֹ: נַעַר הָיִיתִי

'loan' granted an individual, the greater his obligation to give something in return. The wicked person who accumulates largesse for himself with no concern for the needs of others, becomes more and more indebted to the shared inventory of common good. The righteous person, however, does all in his power to benefit others, and for this — the world is indebted to him. The classic example is that of Rabbi Chanina ben Dosa of whom a heavenly voice proclaimed every day: 'All the world is sustained by virtue of My son, Chanina, but My son, Chanina, contents himself with but one measure of carob fruit from one Sabbath eve to the next' (Berachos 17b).

This is the meaning of the Mishnah (Avos 3:16): 'The store [this world] is open, and the proprietor [God] issues [materials and resources] on credit. The ledger is open and the hand [of God] records. Whoever wishes to come and borrow is welcome to do so, but the collectors [angels of punishment and death] constantly make their rounds and extract payment from the debtors, both with and without their knowledge.'

וְצַדִּיק חוֹנֵן וְנוֹתֵן — While the righteous one graciously gives [lit. shows kindness and gives].

God, who is the Righteous One of the world kindly repays the lender the money which the wicked borrower refuses to return (Rashi).

Therefore the Mishnah (Avos 2:9) says: He who takes a loan from a man is as if he took a loan from God, for God guarantees repayment (Bertenoro ibid.).

The righteous man is continuously benevolent. Even after the wicked man defaults on his debts frequently, the righteous man still gives him loans. Nor does he wait to be asked; for on his own he goes to the wicked and offers him the loan, as it says while the righteous one graciously gives (Midrash Halttamari).

The righteous one first shows kindness by making the loan. Later, he has mercy on the debtor and gives the loan money away, by canceling the debt (Yalkut Shimoni).

22. כִּי מְבֹרָכָיו יִירְשׁוּ אָרֶץ — For those blessed by Him shall inherit the earth.

Because they give generously of their wealth, righteous people will be blessed by God and they will inherit more resources with which to do even more good. Their good fortune will be permanent, just as an inheritance remains permanently in a family (Radak, Rashi).

וּמְקֻלָּלָיו יִכָּרֵתוּ — While those cursed by Him will be excised.

Their wealth will not endure and they will be cut off from this world and the next (Radak).

23. מֵה' מִצְעֲדֵי גֶבֶר כּוֹנָנוּ — By HASHEM, the footsteps of a strong man are made firm.

The word גֶבֶר derives from גְבוּרָה, strength: this is the man whose faith is strong (Rashi) by virtue of his heroic accomplishments in Torah study (Metzudas David).

Or, the righteous man firmly rejects the influence of the wicked with his good deeds (Radak).

וְדַרְכּוֹ יֶחְפָּץ — His way shall He approve.

When the tzaddik meets with success, it proves to him that God is pleased with his way (Radak).

while the righteous one graciously gives.
²² *For those blessed by Him shall inherit the earth,*
while those cursed by Him will be excised.
²³ *By HASHEM, the footsteps of a strong man are firm;*
his way shall He approve.
²⁴ *Should he fall, he will not be cast off,*
for HASHEM supports his hand.
²⁵ *I have been a youth and also aged,*

[God often limits the choice of ordinary people who are called אָדָם and אִישׁ (see *Jeremiah* 10:23) because they are under the sway of the Evil Inclination and their preferences and choices are therefore suspect. Not so the גֶּבֶר, *strong man*, who controls his evil impulse. Because he chooses only good, God approves his way and assists him thereon. This is as we read, מִי זֶה הָאִישׁ יְרֵא ה' יוֹרֶנּוּ בְּדֶרֶךְ יִבְחָר, *Who is this, the man fearful of HASHEM? He will show him the way he should choose* (25:12).]

24. כִּי יִפֹּל לֹא יוּטָל — *Should he fall he will not be cast off.*

Radak comments that even if God should cause the righteous man to fall into poverty and misfortune, He will not cast him away nor reject him entirely. His misfortune is a rebuke which emanates from Hashem's love and concern. This is the main difference between the righteous and the wicked. When the wicked fall, they are completely *excised* (v. 22), never to arise. But of the righteous it is written, שֶׁבַע יִפּוֹל צַדִּיק וָקָם, *The righteous one shall fall seven times yet [still] arise* (*Proverbs* 24:16).

כִּי ה' סוֹמֵךְ יָדוֹ — *For HASHEM supports his hand.*

[Even as he falls, God is already supporting him, for the purpose of the decline is eventually to raise the righteous person even higher. Similarly we read, סוֹמֵךְ ה' לְכָל הַנֹּפְלִים, *HASHEM*

supports all those who fall (145:14).]

25. נַעַר הָיִיתִי גַם זָקַנְתִּי — *I have been a youth and also aged.*

Ibn Ezra and *Radak* attribute this statement to the Psalmist who declares, 'After experiencing all phases of life, from beginning to end, I am equipped to make the following observation.'

However, the *Talmud* (*Yevamos* 16b, quoted by *Rashi*) maintains that such a sweeping observation can be made only by one who can evaluate all of human history, not just one short lifetime. Although God Himself exists forever, we cannot attribute this verse to Him, for the word 'aged' cannot be used in reference to the Eternal. Rather this observation was made by Mitatron, the chief of all angels who is called שַׂר הָעוֹלָם, *Officer of the World.*

The *Midrash* (*Tanchuma Mikeitz* 6) follows this opinion: *The Officer of the World* said, '*I have been a youth*, from the time of Adam, *and also aged*, until the days of the Messiah. Yet never did I see that God should forsake the world by leaving it devoid of righteous men. In every generation He raises up *tzaddikim.*

Tehillas Hashem lends support to those who attribute these words to David. The Sages say that Adam, David and Messiah share the same mission as if they were the same person [see *Overview*, Part 8. Thus, the youth of David started when, as Adam, he was 930 years old, making him *a youth and also aged* at one and the same time.

כו גַּם־זָקַנְתִּי וְלֹא־רָאִיתִי צַדִּיק נֶעֱזָב וְזַרְעוֹ
מְבַקֶּשׁ־לָחֶם: כָּל־הַיּוֹם חוֹנֵן וּמַלְוֶה
כז וְזַרְעוֹ לִבְרָכָה: סוּר מֵרָע וַעֲשֵׂה־טוֹב
כח וּשְׁכֹן לְעוֹלָם: כִּי יהוה | אֹהֵב מִשְׁפָּט

וְלֹא רָאִיתִי צַדִּיק נֶעֱזָב — *But I have not seen a righteous man forsaken.*

To be *forsaken* means to lack the barest essentials of life i.e., food and clothing (*Radak; Tanchuma Vayeitze* 3). We find that Jacob asked God to always provide him with these two staples (*Genesis* 28:20). God responded by pledging: כִּי לֹא אֶעֱזָבְךָ *For I will not forsake you* (*Genesis* 28:15).

A righteous man may suffer misfortune, but God will surely have mercy on his children (*Malbim*).

The *Midrash* (*Tanchuma Mikeitz* 6) comments: Before God brings a famine upon the world He prepares a means of proper sustenance for the righteous. For instance, before God brought a drought upon the land of Israel in fulfillment of Elijah's prophecy, He prepared a cave where the prophet could hide from Ahab, and ravens to bring him his daily meals.

וְזַרְעוֹ מְבַקֶּשׁ לָחֶם — *Nor his children* [lit. seed] *begging for bread.*

Rabbi Yosi said: We have a tradition that a scholar will not become impoverished. His students asked him, 'But is it not a fact that many of them are impoverished?'

He replied, 'Even if they should fall into poverty we are assured that they will never sink to such utter destitution as to be forced to go begging from door

to door' (*Shabbos* 151a).

Midrash Tanchuma (*Vayeitze ibid.*) interprets these words homiletically: Even if it happened that the children of the *tzaddik* had to go begging, yet never did I see their righteous father, נֶעֱזָב, *forsaken*, of his unshakeable faith in the Holy One, Blessed be He.[1]

As *Anaf Yosef* explains, I have never seen a righteous man *consider himself forsaken* even if his children must beg for bread. Whatever his lot in life, he trusts that God brings it upon him for a constructive and merciful purpose.

Hirsch observes that the verse does not say that no righteous man would ever be reduced to poverty; were that the case, it would equate poverty with wickedness — a patent falsehood. Rather, the verse says that no righteous person will be completely forsaken even if he must beg alms for his sustenance. Since Jews are obligated to help one another, it is no disgrace for one to require the help of another.

26. כָּל הַיּוֹם — *All the days.*

This means at all times, as in אוֹתְךָ קִוִּיתִי כָּל הַיּוֹם, *You I hoped all the days* (25:5). Even in times of financial difficulty, the righteous man shared his meagre resources to the best of his ability (*Radak*). [See comm. 41:2, s.v. בְּיוֹם רָעָה.]

1. The *Midrash* (*Koheles Rabbah* 2:17) relates that Rabbi Meir was a scribe who earned three *selahs* a week. He spent one *selah* on food and drink, another on clothing, and the third he gave away for the support of scholars.

[Noticing that he never had any money], his disciples asked him: 'What are you doing to provide for your children?'

He answered: 'If they are righteous, then it will be as David said, I have not seen the righteous man forsaken, not his children begging for bread [i.e., God will provide for them]. However, if they are not righteous, then why should I leave my possessions to the enemies of God!'

But I have not seen a righteous man forsaken,
nor his children begging for bread.
²⁶ All the days he graciously lends,
and his children are a blessing.
²⁷ Turn from evil and do good,
that you may dwell forever.
²⁸ For HASHEM loves justice

Since this generous man wishes to benefit others, even if he depletes his own wealth for charitable purposes *all the days*, he will nevertheless be blessed with enough to leave over for his offspring.

חוֹנֵן וּמַלְוֶה — *He graciously lends* [lit. *he shows kindness and lends*].

The verse implies that kindness and lending are called for in addition to generosity. It is not enough merely to give a donation to the poor. The benefactor should display *kindness* by encouraging him as well. As the *Talmud (Bava Basra* 9b) says, 'He who gives a penny to the poor man is blessed with six blessings, but he who comforts him with kind words is blessed with eleven.' Also, a loan is preferable to an outright gift, for it will help set the fallen man back on his feet with dignity *(Dorash Moshe).*

וְזַרְעוֹ לִבְרָכָה — *And his children are a blessing.*

The children learn to emulate the charitable deeds of their righteous father and become a blessing to all who deal with them. We find that Hashem said to Abraham וֶהְיֵה בְּרָכָה, *and you shall be a blessing (Genesis* 12:2), i.e., you will share your blessings with others through charity and kindness.

Also, the children will have numerous well-wishers who will say, 'May you be blessed by God in the merit of your fine father' *(Radak).*

The *Talmud (Nedarim* 82b) echoes these words, emphasizing that the poor home of an honest father is a palace. The Sages taught that Torah will go forth from the children of the poor *(Hirsch).*

[The Psalmist concludes that not only will the children of the righteous not be forsaken (*v.* 25), but they will thrive despite their lack of wealth.][1]

27. סוּר מֵרָע וַעֲשֵׂה טוֹב — *Turn from evil and do good.*

[See 34:15]. Avoid transgressing the negative commandments, and pursue the positive commandments *(Ibn Ezra).*

Now that the success of the righteous has been clearly demonstrated, follow in their ways and turn away from the wicked paths of ruin and failure *(Radak).*

וּשְׁכֹן לְעוֹלָם — *That you may dwell forever.*

You will abide in perpetual security without fear or loss *(Radak).*

28. כִּי ה' אֹהֵב מִשְׁפָּט — *For HASHEM loves justice.*

You may dwell securely (*v.* 27)

---

1. The *Chasam Sofer* devoted virtually every waking moment to his yeshiva, attending to the affairs of his rabbinate and responding to the countless halachic inquiries which were addressed to him from all over the world. A disturbed relative once complained that he neglected the training of his children. The *Chasam Sofer* replied, 'About that I need not be concerned, for David has made a promise to those who give away all of their time for the benefit of others. *All the days he graciously lends* [his precious time and effort to worthy causes. For this God repays him]; *and his children are a blessing.*

וְלֹא־יַעֲזֹב אֶת־חֲסִידָיו לְעוֹלָם נִשְׁמָרוּ

כט וְזֶרַע רְשָׁעִים נִכְרָת: צַדִּיקִים יִירְשׁוּ־אָרֶץ

ל וְיִשְׁכְּנוּ לָעַד עָלֶיהָ: פִּי־צַדִּיק יֶהְגֶּה

לא חָכְמָה וּלְשׁוֹנוֹ תְּדַבֵּר מִשְׁפָּט: תּוֹרַת

לב אֱלֹהָיו בְּלִבּוֹ לֹא תִמְעַד אֲשֻׁרָיו: צוֹפֶה

לג רָשָׁע לַצַּדִּיק וּמְבַקֵּשׁ לַהֲמִיתוֹ: יהוה לֹא־

לד יַעַזְבֶנּוּ בְיָדוֹ וְלֹא יַרְשִׁיעֶנּוּ בְּהִשָּׁפְטוֹ: קַוֵּה

---

without fear of unexpected upheaval, because God acts according to fixed rules of justice and propriety which insure uninterrupted tranquility for the deserving ones (*Malbim*).

וְלֹא יַעֲזֹב אֶת חֲסִידָיו — *And does not forsake His devout ones.*

חֲסִידוּת, *devotion*, surpasses מִשְׁפָּט, *justice*, because it denotes kindness which goes beyond the letter of the law. After a person accustoms himself to adhere to the strict dictates of truth and justice, he will develop a desire to go beyond the boundaries of strict justice by acting kindly even toward those who are undeserving according to the strict standard of justice (*Radak*).

לְעוֹלָם נִשְׁמָרוּ — *Eternally they will be protected.*

It is written, רַגְלֵי חֲסִידָיו יִשְׁמֹר, *He guards the feet of his devoted ones* [i.e. from sin] (I Samuel 2:9). It is really necessary to guard the devoted? This can be understood with the folk-saying, 'To the fenced-in area you add more fence and to the breached wall you add more breaches'. Similarly it says: *His devout ones, eternally they will be guarded* (*Tanchuma, Vayeshev* 14).

וְזֶרַע רְשָׁעִים נִכְרָת — *But the children of the wicked will be excised.*

Not only are the wicked themselves destroyed, but even their seed is uprooted (*Radak*).

29. צַדִּיקִים יִירְשׁוּ אָרֶץ — *The righteous will inherit the earth.*

They will inherit the estates of the wicked who have been excised (*Malbim*).

וְיִשְׁכְּנוּ לָעַד עָלֶיהָ — *And dwell forever upon it.*

The *Midrash* (*Bereishis Rabbah* 19:17) comments that after the wicked drive the שְׁכִינָה, *God's Presence*, from the world with their repulsive deeds, the righteous will merit that His Presence return to dwell in their midst by virtue of their goodness.

30. פִּי צַדִּיק יֶהְגֶּה חָכְמָה — *The mouth of the righteous man utters wisdom.*

Rashi here follows his opinion [see comm. to 1:2] that יֶהְגֶּה does not refer to verbal articulation, but to the thoughts of the heart. [Although the word פִּי, *mouth*, is used here in conjunction with יֶהְגֶּה, *Malbim* to 39:4 explains that the הִגָּיוֹן is a thought which is on the verge of being expressed i.e. 'on the tip of the tongue' therefore it is considered as if it is in the *mouth*.]

Not only does the righteous man do kindness by lending out his material wealth (*v.* 26), but he is even eager to share his intellectual abundance by instructing others (*Ibn Ezra; Radak*).

וּלְשׁוֹנוֹ תְּדַבֵּר מִשְׁפָּט — *And his tongue speaks justice.*

Not only does the righteous man speak intelligently on purely theological topics, but he is just in settling affairs between man and his fellow man (*Radak*).

XXXVII
29-33

and does not forsake His devout ones —
Eternally they will be protected,
but the children of the wicked will be excised.
²⁹ *The righteous will inherit the earth*
and dwell forever upon it.
³⁰ *The mouth of the righteous man utters wisdom,*
and his tongue speaks justice.
³¹ *The Torah of his God is in his heart;*
his footsteps do not falter.
³² *The wicked one watches for the righteous*
and seeks to execute him.
³³ *But HASHEM will not forsake him to his power,*
nor let him be condemned in his judgment.

32. תּוֹרַת אֱלֹהָיו בְּלִבּוֹ — *The Torah of his God is in his heart.*

What he expresses with his mouth is truly what he feels in his heart, for he is no hypocrite (*Radak*).

[He is not like Doeg and Achitophel whose Torah was *only from the lips outward,* (*Sanhedrin* 106b), i.e., insincere eloquence, while their hearts were full of treachery and pride (see 5:7, 10).]

לֹא תִמְעַד אֲשֻׁרָיו — *His footsteps do not falter.*

[Therefore the sincere scholar will not suffer a tragic downfall like those of Doeg and Achitophel.]

32. צוֹפֶה רָשָׁע לַצַּדִּיק — *The wicked one watches for the righteous.*

When he realizes that the *tzaddik* enjoys success while he is a failure, jealousy and hatred spur him to plot against the life of his righteous rival. If he cannot kill him, he will watch for an opportunity to libel the *tzaddik* to the authorities so that they should execute him (*Ibn Ezra; Radak*).

וּמְבַקֵּשׁ לַהֲמִיתוֹ — *And seeks to execute.*

The *Talmud* (*Sukkah* 52a) identifies the רָשָׁע of this verse as wickedness par

excellence, i.e., the Evil Inclination who is man's deadliest enemy. The Evil Inclination renews its powerful attack on man every day and tries to kill him as it says, *The wicked one watches for the righteous and seeks to execute him.* Were it not for God's assistance, no man could survive the onslaught, as it says, *But HASHEM will not forsake him to his power.*

33. ה׳ לֹא יַעַזְבֶנּוּ בְיָדוֹ — *But HASHEM will not forsake him to his power.*

God will foil the plot of the wicked. He will not abandon the *tzaddik* to the custody of the authorities before whom he has been slandered (*Radak*).

Olelos Yehudah interprets this in reference to the Evil Inclination: 'Even when you have made a habit of sin and are addicted to its enticement, still God will deliver you from its grip [if you sincerely desire to be released.]

וְלֹא יַרְשִׁיעֶנּוּ בְּהִשָּׁפְטוֹ — *Nor let him be condemned in his judgment.*

Ramban (*Deuteronomy* 19:19) explains that if a legitimate Jewish court executes a condemned criminal, that constitutes the most convincing proof of his guilt. God would never allow

אֶל־יהוה | וּשְׁמֹר דַּרְכּוֹ וִירוֹמִמְךָ לָרֶשֶׁת

לה אֶרֶץ בְּהִכָּרֵת רְשָׁעִים תִּרְאֶה: רָאִיתִי

רָשָׁע עָרִיץ וּמִתְעָרֶה כְּאֶזְרָח רַעֲנָן:

לו וַיַּעֲבֹר וְהִנֵּה אֵינֶנּוּ וָאֲבַקְשֵׁהוּ וְלֹא נִמְצָא:

לז שְׁמָר־תָּם וּרְאֵה יָשָׁר כִּי־אַחֲרִית לְאִישׁ

לח שָׁלוֹם: וּפֹשְׁעִים נִשְׁמְדוּ יַחְדָּו אַחֲרִית

לט רְשָׁעִים נִכְרָתָה: וּתְשׁוּעַת צַדִּיקִים

מ מֵיהוה מָעוּזָם בְּעֵת צָרָה: וַיַּעְזְרֵם יהוה

וַיְפַלְּטֵם יְפַלְּטֵם מֵרְשָׁעִים וְיוֹשִׁיעֵם כִּי־

חָסוּ בוֹ:

---

righteous judges to be duped by false witnesses into shedding innocent blood, because He promised that His spirit will reside in every court to guide it towards the truth. Secondly, God would never abandon a guiltless man to the wicked who seek to condemn him falsely, as it says, *But HASHEM will not forsake him to his power, nor let him be condemned in his judgment.*

34. קַוֵּה אֶל ה' וּשְׁמֹר דַּרְכּוֹ — *Hope to HASHEM and safeguard His way.*

[If you will do what is expected of you by safeguarding God's way, He will reciprocate by helping you realize your hopes. But if you don't fulfill God's wishes, what can you hope for?]

וִירוֹמִמְךָ לָרֶשֶׁת אֶרֶץ בְּהִכָּרֵת רְשָׁעִים תִּרְאֶה — *Then He will raise you high to inherit the earth. Upon excision of the wicked, you will see it.*

This verse refers to Noah whose hopes were directed towards God because He [God] safeguarded his way. God raised him high above the flood waters while the wicked drowned. When the waters subsided, Noah emerged from the Ark to inherit the earth (*Tanchuma, Berachah* 6).

35. רָאִיתִי רָשָׁע עָרִיץ — *I saw a ruthless wicked man.*

I observed a wicked man who intimidated everyone with his might (*Radak*).

וּמִתְעָרֶה — *Well-rooted.*

The translation follows *Rashi* who relates it to עָרוֹת עַל יְאוֹר, *roots by the river* (Isaiah 19:7). *Radak* renders this word as *well-watered, thriving.*

כְּאֶזְרָח רַעֲנָן — *Like a native evergreen.*

The sturdy, well-watered tree is called *native* because it is outstanding and noticeable to all by virtue of its unique beauty. It resembles the native citizen of a settlement who is well-known to all (*Radak*).

The well-established citizen who enjoys the security of having a powerful family backing him in all phases of community life resembles the flourishing tree with many spreading branches. But the גֵּר, *stranger*, is isolated and alone like a גַּרְגִּיר, *fragment; splinter*, which is cut off from the tree (*Ibn Ezra*).

The powerful villain is reinforced by a solid financial status (*Rashi*).

36. וַיַּעֲבֹר וְהִנֵּה אֵינֶנּוּ — *Yet he vanished*

XXXVII
34-40

³⁴ *Hope to HASHEM and safeguard His way,*
then He will raise you high to inherit the earth.
Upon excision of the wicked,
you will see it.
³⁵ *I saw a ruthless wicked man,*
well-rooted like a native evergreen.
³⁶ *Yet he vanished, and behold! he was no more;*
then I sought him, but he was not found.
³⁷ *Safeguard the perfect and watch the upright,*
for there is a destiny for the man of peace.
³⁸ *The sinners shall be destroyed together,*
the destiny of the wicked is to be excised.
³⁹ *But the salvation of the righteous is from HASHEM,*
their might in time of distress.
⁴⁰ *HASHEM helped them*
and caused them to escape,
He will cause them to escape from the wicked
and He will save them,
for they took refuge in Him.

[lit. *he passed*] *and behold! he was no more.*

He disappeared without prior warning (*Metzudos David*).

His body departed from this world (*Malbim*).

וָאֲבַקְשֵׁהוּ וְלֹא נִמְצָא — *Then I sought him, but he was not found.*

No trace of him remains. His residence has disappeared; even his children have vanished (*Radak*).

His body departed from this world but his soul did not pass on to the World to Come. It has been cut off so it is nowhere to be found (*Malbim*).

[Similarly we read, אֲנִי רָאִיתִי אֱוִיל מַשְׁרִישׁ וָאֶקּוֹב נָוֵהוּ פִּתְאֹם, *I have seen the foolish man taking root, but suddenly I beheld his habitation cursed (Job 5:3).*]

37. שְׁמָר תָּם וּרְאֵה יָשָׁר — *Safeguard the perfect and watch the upright.*

Pay heed to their enviable life-style so that you may be inspired to emulate them, and not the wicked (*Rashi*).

כִּי אַחֲרִית לְאִישׁ שָׁלוֹם — *For there is a destiny* [lit. *aftermath*] *for the man of peace.*

Although his beginning is unimpressive [i.e., downtrodden and oppressed], he is destined to enjoy a great reward after his sojourn in This World has ended (*Rashi*).

38. וּפֹשְׁעִים נִשְׁמְדוּ יַחְדָּו — *The sinners shall be destroyed together.*

When they die, both their bodies and their souls will be destroyed and nothing will remain (*Malbim*).

אַחֲרִית רְשָׁעִים נִכְרָתָה — *The destiny of the wicked is to be excised.*

Thus will any temptation to emulate their ways cease, for they will no longer

exist. Any temptation to copy them may be momentarily successful in this world, yet the result of their labors is doomed to failure *(Malbim)*.

39. וּתְשׁוּעַת צַדִּיקִים מֵה' — *But the salvation of the righteous is from HASHEM.*

They will enjoy an everlasting salvation in the presence of Hashem in the eternal Hereafter *(Malbim)*.

מָעוּזָם בְּעֵת צָרָה — *Their might in time of distress.*

Even though the bulk of their reward is reserved for the future, the righteous can still hope for God to deliver them from the perils of this world *(Malbim)*.

40. וַיַּעְזְרֵם ה' וַיְפַלְּטֵם — *HASHEM helped them and caused them to escape.*

We have seen Him do this for many righteous people in the past *(Ibn Ezra)*.

יְפַלְּטֵם מֵרְשָׁעִים וְיוֹשִׁיעֵם — He will cause them to escape from the wicked and He will save them.

There is no doubt that He will continue to do so in the future *(Ibn Ezra)*.

These words and this theme are continually repeated in this psalm, in order to fortify the faith of the righteous, so that they should not succumb to the lure of the success of the wicked. Since most people are envious of the fruits of evil, the Psalmist concludes with this final exhortation to uphold one's faith in God's ultimate salvation *(Radak)*.

מזמור לח 38

The series of four psalms concluding with Psalm 41 (the final psalm of the First Book) deals with one theme — the illness with which David was afflicted as a result of his sins. Rather than viewing his sickness as a purely negative experience, David sought to learn from it and share with posterity the lessons and insights which he gained from his suffering.

According to many commentators this psalm also contains a deeper message, as it expresses the feelings of the entire nation of Israel which suffers from the ravages of the long, dark exile. It concludes with a hopeful plea for swift redemption.

מִזְמוֹר לְדָוִד לְהַזְכִּיר: יְהוה אַל־בְּקֶצְפְּךָ א-ב
תוֹכִיחֵנִי וּבַחֲמָתְךָ תְיַסְּרֵנִי: כִּי־חִצֶּיךָ ג
נִחֲתוּ בִי וַתִּנְחַת עָלַי יָדֶךָ: אֵין־מְתֹם ד
בִּבְשָׂרִי מִפְּנֵי זַעְמֶךָ אֵין־שָׁלוֹם בַּעֲצָמַי

1. מִזְמוֹר לְדָוִד לְהַזְכִּיר — *A song unto David; For Remembrance.*

Rashi comments that David had all of Israel in mind when he composed this psalm. He intended it as a reminder to God to pay heed to the misfortunes of His nation in times of distress.

Radak and *Metzudas David*, however, maintain that David intended the psalm for the suffering individual. Therefore, he added the superscription, *For remembrance*, in order to encourage and remind every afflicted man to pray to God using these very words of supplication. *Radak* also suggests that לְהַזְכִּיר might be directed to the accompanist to indicate a special musical embellishment.

Malbim interprets this Psalm as David's response to the sickness which afflicted him after his sin concerning Bath Sheba. He intended its tragic theme to serve as a constant reminder of his sins.

Alshich adds that for anyone other than David, the superscription of so tragic a work would have been קִינָה, a *lament*. But David could see with perfect clarity the purifying effect of pain which atones for sin. Therefore, he entitled this psalm מִזְמוֹר, a *song* [full of hope and joy] לְהַזְכִּיר, *to remind* all men to accept misfortune as gratefully as they accept the good.

2. ה' אַל־בְּקֶצְפְּךָ תוֹכִיחֵנִי — *HASHEM, in Your wrath rebuke me not.*

[In 6:2 David prayed, ה' אַל בְּאַפְּךָ תוֹכִיחֵנִי, *HASHEM, rebuke me not in Your wrath.*] *Malbim* says that אַף and קֶצֶף are synonymous terms for *wrath*. Both terms represent anger openly dis-

played, while חֵמָה refers to anger kept hidden in the heart. Thus: 'although You rebuke me, let Your words of rebuke be soft, not harsh utterances of wrath'.

וּבַחֲמָתְךָ תְיַסְּרֵנִי — *Nor in Your rage chasten me* .

The translation follows *Radak* and *Metzudos* who comment that the word אַל, 'do not', in the first half of the verse modifies the second half as well. [Thus we have a repetition of the second half of 6:2 which reads וְאַל בַּחֲמָתְךָ תְיַסְּרֵנִי.]

Malbim however, observes that אַל is intentionally deleted in the second half of the verse, for this statement means something very different from that of 6:2. Here, after his sin, David readily accepted the fact that he must suffer. But suffering can come in one of two ways. The wrathful words of God's תּוֹכֵחָה, *rebuke*, may shroud the soul in melancholy bitterness (בְּקֶצְפְּךָ תוֹכִיחֵנִי). Or it may be only the body which is afflicted with physical יִסּוּרִים, *chastisement*, (בַחֲמָתְךָ תְיַסְּרֵנִי) for the sake of atonement. David feels that he possesses the strength to overcome either of these afflictions when applied separately, but he pleads that he is incapable of withstanding both at once. *HASHEM, rebuke me not in Your wrath*, while simultaneously *chastening me in Your rage*, i.e., I cannot endure the chastisement of both physical pain and mental anguish together.

3. חִצֶּיךָ — *Your arrows.*

Radak to our verse comments that heaven-sent ailments are like arrows of God [in that they go unerringly to fulfill

A song unto David. For Remembrance.
² HASHEM, in Your wrath, rebuke me not,
nor in Your rage chasten me.
³ For Your arrows were shot into me,
and down upon me is Your hand.
⁴ There is no perfection in my flesh
because of Your wrath,
No peace in my bones

God's objective]. In *Habakuk* 3:11 he explains that lightning is the arrow of God. The wicked are struck down by it, while the righteous make use of its light.

The angels of fury which do God's bidding by punishing the guilty with swift accuracy are called His *arrows* (*Alshich*).

The first *arrow* with which You pierced my heart was the frightful prophecy of Nathan which followed the incident with Bath Sheba: *Therefore the sword shall not depart from your house ... Behold, I will raise up evil against you from out of your own house (II Sam.* 12:10-11) (*Sforno*).

נִחֲתוּ בִי — *Were shot into me.*

Literally נִחַת means to step down on the bow in order to bend and string it. This is the main preparation for the shooting of the arrows [cf. *commentary* to 18:35] (*Rashi*).

וַתִּנְחַת עָלַי יָדֶךָ — *And down upon me is Your hand.*

תִּנְחַת is derived from נָחָה, *to come down to rest* (*Rashi*).

The Psalmist laments that he feels the hand of Hashem weighing down upon him heavily through the many ailments

with which he was punished (*Metzudas David*).

Nathan's prophecy of doom was uttered, and immediately took effect. *Your hand came down upon me,* and *HASHEM struck the child that Uriah's wife bore to David* [*II Samuel* 12:15] (*Sforno*).

4. אֵין מְתֹם בִּבְשָׂרִי — *There is no perfection in my flesh.*

Radak explains that מְתֹם is derived from the root תָּמַם, *complete, perfect;* thus the מ at the beginning of this word is a prefix rather than a root letter. The Psalmist laments, 'There is no perfection in my body for every organ is afflicted.'

However, *Radak* quotes his father, *Rav Yosef Kimchi,* who maintains that מְתֹם is related to מתה (and the opening מ is indeed part of the root which means *people, persons* as in מְתֵי מִסְפָּר, *few in* [numbers of] *people* (105:12). [See also 17:14, 26:4]. Thus David means to say that his flesh has been so mutilated by sickness that it has lost its human form and he no longer resembles other people.[1]

מִפְּנֵי זַעְמֶךָ — *Because of Your wrath.*

Because of Your righteous anger

---

1. Before Adam sinned, his flesh was the essence of perfection — a radiant garment of spiritual splendor described as כָּתְנוֹת אוֹר, *robes of light* (not עוֹר *skin*). But Adam's transgression aroused God's זַעַם, *wrath* which reduced his flesh to mere בָּשָׂר, *flesh*, which inherently lacks מְתֹם, *perfection.* The *Talmud (Sotah* 5a) states that the letters of בָּשָׂר form an acrostic which alludes to בּוּשָׁה, *shame,* שְׁרוּחָה, *decay,* רִמָּה, *wormy rot* (*Tehillos Hashem*). [*See also Overview* to *Bircas Hamazon,* ArtScroll Edition, p. 19.]

ה מִפְּנֵי חַטָּאתִי: כִּי עֲוֹנֹתַי עָבְרוּ רֹאשִׁי

ו כְּמַשָּׂא כָבֵד יִכְבְּדוּ מִמֶּנִּי: הִבְאִישׁוּ נָמַקּוּ

ז חַבּוּרֹתָי מִפְּנֵי אִוַּלְתִּי: נַעֲוֵיתִי שַׁחֹתִי עַד־

ח מְאֹד כָּל־הַיּוֹם קֹדֵר הִלָּכְתִּי: כִּי־כְסָלַי

ט מָלְאוּ נִקְלֶה וְאֵין מְתֹם בִּבְשָׂרִי: נְפוּגֹתִי

which was provoked by my sins
(Radak, Malbim).

אֵין שָׁלוֹם בַּעֲצָמַי מִפְּנֵי חַטָּאתִי — [There is]
no peace in my bones because of my sin.

[After David sinned, his realization
of the enormity of his error was more
than mere intellectual conception. He
was physically ill, particularly in the
limb which performed the sin. שָׁלוֹם also
means whole (שָׁלֵם). David bewailed the
fact that every transgression leaves an
indelible imprint on the perpetrator as is
taught in Maseches Kallah Rabbasi
Chapter 3: Every sin a person commits
is engraved and recorded on his bones.
David moans that his every bone has
been carved out with a chisel of guilt
and he remains eternally scarred. Similarly the prophet warns וַתְּהִי עֲוֹנֹתָם
עַל עַצְמוֹתָם, And their iniquities
remained on their bones (Ezekiel
32:27)].

5. כִּי עֲוֹנֹתַי עָבְרוּ רֹאשִׁי — For my
iniquities have inundated me [lit. gone
over my head].

David compares his sins to swirling
sea waters which rose above his head
and threatened to drown him (Radak).

[רֹאשִׁי, my head, symbolizes the intellectual capacity which provides the
ability to control passions. Unfortunately, my lustful flesh, overcame my
better judgment.]

כְּמַשָּׂא כָבֵד יִכְבְּדוּ מִמֶּנִּי — Like a
heavy load they are burdensome ...

I do not possess sufficient mitzvos
and merits with which to bolster my
soul which staggers under a massive
burden of guilt (Radak).

[I have lost all self-control, because
my innate tendency to sin far outweighs
my capacity for self-discipline].

The Sages say that King Menashe of
Judah sinned for many years, but finally repented. He was so ashamed of his
iniquitous past that he dared not raise
his face towards the sky. He wore a
heavy copper helmet which forced his
face to be turned earthward. Similarly
the Psalmist says that the burden of his
sin is so crushing that it forces him to
bow his head in shame (Tehillos Hashem).[1]

6. הִבְאִישׁוּ נָמַקּוּ חַבּוּרֹתָי — Putrid and
rotted are my sores.

חַבּוּרָה sometimes refers to a bruise
caused by the blood which collects under the skin. Here it means a pus-filled
blister. Eventually the blister will burst
and the pus will ooze out (Radak).

מִפְּנֵי אִוַּלְתִּי — Because of my folly.

My foolishness led me to the sins
which caused my affliction. As the
Talmud (Sotah 3a) says: A person does
not sin unless he is overwhelmed by a
spirit of foolishness (Migdal David).

1. Rabbi Yehudah the Prince expounded: Great is the power of repentance, for, should the
slightest thought of it flicker in a man's heart, immediately it rises before the heavenly throne.
This is true no matter how guilty the penitent. David said, 'For my iniquities have inundated
me'. Ezra also said, 'For our iniquities have multiplied far above our heads and our guilt has
increased greatly, up to the heavens' (Ezra 9:6). But the Holy One, Blessed be He, responded,
'Fear not! Even if your sins should reach until the very foot of my heavenly throne, I will
forgive you if you repent (Pesikta Rabbasi 45:9).

because of my sin.

⁵ For my iniquities have inundated me;
   like a heavy load, they are burdensome
      beyond me.
⁶ Putrid and rotted are my sores,
   because of my folly.
⁷ I am bent and bowed exceedingly,
   all day long in bleakness I go.
⁸ For my self awareness is full of futility,
   and there is no perfection in my flesh.
⁹ I am faint and crushed exceedingly.

---

7. נַעֲוֵיתִי — *I am bent.*

As in וְהִתְעַוְּתוּ אַנְשֵׁי הֶחָיִל, *And the powerful men will be bent* [*Ecclesiastes* 12:13] (*Metzudas Zion*).

שַׁחֹתִי — *And bowed* [*down*]. By the burden of my sickness (*Radak*).

כָּל הַיּוֹם קֹדֵר הִלָּכְתִּי — *All day long in bleakness* [lit. *in blackness*] *I go.*

My facial characteristics have drastically changed. My countenance is so dark that it seems as if I have been exposed to the blazing sun all day (*Ibn Ezra*).

[Black clouds of sorrow and anxiety darken my brow and sink me into melancholy.]

8. כְּסָלַי — *My self awareness* [lit. *my flanks*].

The Translation follows *Rashi* who interprets the word as a reference to inner thoughts because the כְּסָלִים, *flanks*, are near the כְּלָיוֹת, *kidneys*, which are often considered the center of counsel and reflection (*Ibn Yachya*).[See commentary to 7:10.]

Literally, however, כְּסָלִים refer to the lower spine near the kidneys as in *Leviticus* 3:4 (*Metzudas Zion*), a delicate area which is susceptible to illness (*Radak*).

Or, David refers to his mind as כֶּסֶל

because when he sinned he acted like a כְּסִיל, *fool,* [as mentioned in verse 6 David cites the reason for sin as commentary ibid.).]
Yeibi).

מָלְאוּ נִקְלֶה — *Is full of futility.*

I have no illusions of grandeur. I am fully aware that I am, קַל *insignificant, worthless* (*Rashi*).

[I sinned because my mind was קַל, *lighthearted, frivolous* and thus easily overcome by my passions which *are like a heavy load, beyond my strength* (see commmmentary ibid)].

Literally, נִקְלֶה, *inflamed* derives from קָלוּי, *roasted* (*Metzudos*). My kidneys are inflamed as a result of my sickness (*Targum, Rav Yosef Kimchi*).

וְאֵין מְתֹם בִּבְשָׂרִי — *And there is no perfection in my flesh.*

These words are a repetition of verse 4, for the distraught man weeps incessantly in his anguish and recounts his woes over and over again (*Radak*).

9. נְפוּגֹתִי — *I am faint.*

My internal organs have lost their strength (*Malbim*), as we read concerning Jacob:

וַיָּפָג לִבּוֹ, *And his heart became faint* (*Genesis.* 45:26) (*Rashi, Radak, Ibn Ezra, Metzudas Zion*).

וְנִדְכֵּיתִי עַד־מְאֹד שָׁאַגְתִּי מִנַּהֲמַת לִבִּי:
י אֲדֹנָי נֶגְדְּךָ כָל־תַּאֲוָתִי וְאַנְחָתִי מִמְּךָ לֹא־
יא נִסְתָּרָה: לִבִּי סְחַרְחַר עֲזָבַנִי כֹחִי וְאוֹר־
יב עֵינַי גַּם־הֵם אֵין אִתִּי: אֹהֲבַי | וְרֵעַי מִנֶּגֶד
נִגְעִי יַעֲמֹדוּ וּקְרוֹבַי מֵרָחֹק עָמָדוּ:

וְנִדְכֵּיתִי — *And [I am] crushed.*
All of my limbs are broken and splintered (Malbim).

שָׁאַגְתִּי מִנַּהֲמַת לִבִּי — *I roar because of the groaning of my heart.*
The feeble invalid, *faint and crushed,* feels his strength ebbing as he slips toward death. Then he marshals his last traces of vitality for a final effort, like the final flicker of a dying candle. Although his heart groans (נוֹהֵם) from infirmity, he still has strength for one last שְׁאָגָה, joyous, triumphant *roar,* a demonstration of his faith that although his body may perish his soul will live on (Malbim).

10. אֲדֹנָי נֶגְדְּךָ כָל־תַּאֲוָתִי — *My Lord, before You is all of my yearning.*
These are the words of the heart's final cry: 'My Lord, as I stand ready to return my soul to You, my bodily needs and desires fade into insignificance' (Malbim).
For now I have but one wish, and that is to stand נֶגְדְּךָ, *before You* (Meiri).
Some people are inspired to serve God only after they observe others who are diligent in the performance of commandments. David declares, however, that the attainments of others do not move him. He is motivated exclusively by a pure yearning for God (Rabbeinu Yonah, Avos 4:21).

וְאַנְחָתִי מִמְּךָ לֹא נִסְתָּרָה — *My sighing is not concealed from You.*
To You it makes no difference whether or not I openly express my innermost feelings, for all is revealed to You (Radak).

The only reason for me to sigh over leaving this material world is the fear that I have not adequately prepared my soul to stand before You in the Hereafter (Meiri).
I only hope and pray that לֹא מִמְּךָ נִסְתָּרָה, *It* [my soul] *should not be concealed from You* and Your presence in the Hereafter (Tehillos Yisroel).
Rabbeinu Yonah in *Shaarei Teshuva* (1:12-14) cites יָגוֹן, *sorrow,* as the third principle of repentance. The sinner must be saddened by the enormous evil of disobedience to his Creator. He must sigh in bitterness and despair as King David said: 'My Lord, before You is all of my yearning, my sighing is not concealed from You. You know that my sole desire is to serve You. I groan only because of my sins and inadequacies in Your service.'

11. לִבִּי סְחַרְחַר — *My heart is engulfed.*
Misery and woe encircle me from all sides (Rashi).
Or *my heart goes around in circles,* as we find the *Targum* of סָבִיב, *around,* to be סְחוֹר. The tranquil man can concentrate and think clearly. Not so the troubled man whose thoughts dart here and there in an endless, confusing circle (Radak).
My mind goes around in circles searching and probing for my sins (Alshich).

עֲזָבַנִי כֹחִי — *My strength has forsaken me.*
The Torah is the strength of Israel. Because I forsook the Torah, the Torah abandoned me and left me helpless

XXXVIII   *I roar because of the groaning of my heart.*

¹⁰ *My Lord, before You is all my yearning,*
    my sighing is not concealed from You.
¹¹ *My heart is engulfed,*
    my strength has forsaken me,
The light of my eyes —
    that, too, has left me.
¹² *My friends and companions stand aloof from*
    my affliction,
    and my close ones stand at a distance.

(*Maharam Markado*). [*See Targum to* 29:11 *where* עֹז, *strength, is translated* אוֹרַיְיתָא, *Torah.*]

וְאוֹר עֵינַי גַּם הֵם אֵין אִתִּי — *The light of my eyes — that, too, has left me'.*

It is no coincidence that my heart is in turmoil and that my eyes have failed me. The Torah warns וְלֹא תָתוּרוּ אַחֲרֵי לְבַבְכֶם וְאַחֲרֵי עֵינֵיכֶם, *And you shall not stray after your heart and after your eyes* (*Numbers* 15:39). The heart and the eye are two agents that seek out sin (*Rashi, ibid.*). The heart is mentioned first, for the eyes follow the desires of the heart [and preceive what the heart wants them to perceive] (*Sifri ibid.*). Now that sickness has removed lust and craving from my heart, my eyes no longer search out evil (*Tehillos Hashem*).

12. אֹהֲבַי וְרֵעַי מִנֶּגֶד נִגְעִי יַעֲמֹדוּ — *My friends and my companions stand aloof from my affliction.*

Those who pretend to be my friends when it is beneficial for them, desert me in my time of need. They stand at a distance refusing to step closer to offer assistance (*Rashi*).

Many sick unfortunates find themselves forsaken by their former friends. Sympathy and compassion, give way to estrangement as people tire of observing another's misery. As Solomon said: כָּל אֲחֵי רָשׁ שְׂנֵאֻהוּ אַף כִּי מְרֵעֵהוּ רָחֲקוּ מִמֶּנּוּ, *All the brethren of the poor despise him, how much more so his companions who go far away from him* (*Proverbs* 19:7). Nothing strengthens the soul of the ill as much as a visit by a friend, but my 'friends' refuse to come near (*Radak*).

Instead of encouraging me, they convey to me their own conviction that I will not survive. Even when they visit me, they slowly draw away from my bedside, not wishing to be near a doomed man (*Malbim*), and because they cannot bear the stench of my festering sores (*Ibn Ezra*).

וּקְרוֹבַי מֵרָחֹק עָמָדוּ — *And my close ones stand at a distance.*

The קָרוֹב, *close one,* may be a friend, neighbor, or a blood relative (*Radak*).

The *Vilna Gaon* offers a homiletical interpretation: After the sick man discovers that his family, friends, wealth, and influence are of no avail, he realizes that only one hope remains — the merit of his *mitzvos.* He had imagined such merits to be stored away for the Hereafter, and inaccessible in his time of need, but behold — they alone now stand by his bedside. Thus: My truly close ones whom I thought were far away — only they stood up for me (*Sheiris Yisroel*).

יג וַיְנַקְשׁוּ | מְבַקְשֵׁי נַפְשִׁי וְדֹרְשֵׁי רָעָתִי
יד דִּבְּרוּ הַוּוֹת וּמִרְמוֹת כָּל־הַיּוֹם יֶהְגּוּ: וַאֲנִי
כְחֵרֵשׁ לֹא אֶשְׁמָע וּכְאִלֵּם לֹא יִפְתַּח־פִּיו:
טו וָאֱהִי כְּאִישׁ אֲשֶׁר לֹא־שֹׁמֵעַ וְאֵין בְּפִיו
טז תּוֹכָחוֹת: כִּי־לְךָ יהוה הוֹחָלְתִּי אַתָּה
יז תַעֲנֶה אֲדֹנָי אֱלֹהָי: כִּי־אָמַרְתִּי פֶּן־

13. וַיְנַקְשׁוּ מְבַקְשֵׁי נַפְשִׁי — *They lay snares, the seekers of my life.*

While my former friends shun me, my enemies have not been idle. With their slanderous accusations they lay traps to destroy my soul (*Radak*).

Now that there is no one left at my bedside to protect me, my enemies draw near to assure my swift demise by poisoning or stabbing me (*Malbim*).

דִּבְּרוּ הַוּוֹת וּמִרְמוֹת...יֶהְגּוּ — *They speak treacheries ... and contemplate deceit.*

[See *commentary* to 5:10].

Sforno explains: They incessantly taunt me with their treacherous words of self-righteous deceit. *Midrash Shocher Tov (Psalm 3)* records the solemn moral dissertations which they delivered to David: 'He who stole the lamb [Bath Sheba], and killed the shepherd [Uriah], has no salvation in God'.

They spread lies about me in order to gain public support for their campaign against me (*Malbim*).

14. וַאֲנִי כְחֵרֵשׁ לֹא אֶשְׁמָע — *But I, like a deaf man, [I] do [lit. will] not hear.*

As they plot my death while standing at my bedside I pretend not to hear. (*Malbim*).

I make myself oblivious to the treacherous lies they spread regarding me (*Radak*).

[David was eager to pay attention to his critics when their charges contained some truth, as he said בַּקָּמִים עָלַי מְרֵעִים תִּשְׁמַעְנָה אָזְנָי, *When evil ones rise up against me my ears hear* (92:12). From such criticism, he could learn to repent. But to their slanders, he turned a deaf ear.]

Rashi interprets these words as referring to the nation of Israel as a whole which hears insults, yet remains silent.[1]

וּכְאִלֵּם לֹא יִפְתַּח פִּיו — *Like a mute who opens not his mouth.*

I do not respond to their false accusations in order to justify myself (*Radak*).

[From this verse the *Talmud (Chagi-*

---

1. *Pesikta Rabbasi* (41:6) quotes the following request which Abraham made of God after showing his willingness to successfully withstand his most difficult test and was prepared to sacrifice his beloved son Isaac to God. [See *Bereishis II*, Artscroll ed., Ch. 22 and *Overview*]:

'Sovereign of the Universe! It is clearly revealed before You that when You commanded me to sacrifice my son Isaac I had strong arguments to counter Your command; arguments which You would have had to accept. I could have asked: Yesterday, You promised me, — *"In Isaac shall your seed be called"* (Genesis 21:12), but today You tell me to slaughter that very same Isaac? But I held my tongue; *I was like a deaf man, I did not hear, like a speechless man who opens his mouth.* Therefore, in this merit I request that when the offspring of Isaac stand before You in judgment on this day (of *Rosh Hashana*) every year, even if many prosecuting angels accuse them, please do not hearken to their accusations but answer the prayers of my offspring!'

XXXVIII
13-17

13 *They lay snares,*
   the seekers of my life;
Those who seek my harm speak treacheries,
   all day long they contemplate deceit.
14 *But I, like a deaf man I do not hear,*
   like a mute who opens not his mouth.
15 *I became like a man who cannot understand*
   and in whose mouth there are no rebuttals.
16 *Because for You, HASHEM, I waited,*
   You will answer, my Lord, my God.
17 *For I thought, 'Perhaps they will be glad about me,*

gah 2b) derives a principle: Wherever Scripture mentions a חֵרֵשׁ it refers to someone who is deaf but can speak. An אִלֵּם is a mute who can hear. In Talmudic Hebrew, however, the word חֵרֵשׁ describes a deaf-mute]

15. וָאֱהִי כְּאִישׁ אֲשֶׁר לֹא שֹׁמֵעַ — *I became like a man who cannot understand.*

[At first, I only pretended not to hear their insults, but after a while I became so oblivious to their false accusations that I actually did not even hear their remarks.]

From this we can deduce the intensity of David's devotion to God. And the very essence of his humility is clearly reflected in those words. His sole concern is for the honor of his Creator, so he has no regard for his own dignity. Therefore, he is oblivious of insults hurled at him. David demonstrated this level of intense devotion when Shimi ben Gera cursed him maliciously and yet he (David) paid no attention (*Reishis Chochma, Shaar HaAhava, II*).

וְאֵין בְּפִיו תּוֹכָחוֹת — *And in whose mouth there are no rebuttals.*

[I was offended by their insults and I composed rebuttals in my mind, but I restrained myself. Eventually, however, I stopped thinking of rebuttals because I no longer heard their words].

16. כִּי לְךָ ה׳ הוֹחָלְתִּי — *Because for You, HASHEM, I waited.*

I pay no heed to their threats for I have complete confidence in Your ability to save me (*Rashi*).

אַתָּה תַעֲנֶה אֲדֹנָי אֱלֹהָי — *You will answer my Lord, my God.*

I do not respond to their insults because I wait for You to take up my cause and to answer them far more effectively than I can (*Radak*).

I await Your response, for You are ה׳, HASHEM, the Dispenser of Mercy. Yet I will regard it as a kindness even if *You will answer for me my Lord, my God* [i.e., as אֱלֹהִים, the Dispenser of Strict Justice] (*Eretz HaChaim*).

17. כִּי אָמַרְתִּי פֶּן יִשְׂמְחוּ לִי — *For I thought* [lit. *I said*] *'Perhaps they will be glad about me'.*

I fervently await Your aid lest I succumb to my illness, thus giving my enemies cause for rejoicing (*Radak*).

We, the people of Israel, never dared answer our tormentors audaciously. We feared that we were unworthy of Your aid and that our failure to prevail would cause our oppressors to rejoice even more (*Rashi*).

[This brief comment provides us with an insight into the so-called *golus-* [exile-] *mentality* of the Jew who has so

יח יִשְׂמְחוּ-לִי בְּמוֹט רַגְלִי עָלַי הִגְדִּילוּ: כִּי-

יט אֲנִי לְצֶלַע נָכוֹן וּמַכְאוֹבִי נֶגְדִּי תָמִיד: כִּי-

כ עֲוֹנִי אַגִּיד אֶדְאַג מֵחַטָּאתִי: וְאֹיְבַי חַיִּים

כא עָצֵמוּ וְרַבּוּ שֹׂנְאַי שָׁקֶר: וּמְשַׁלְּמֵי רָעָה

תַּחַת טוֹבָה יִשְׂטְנוּנִי תַּחַת °רדופי-טוֹב:

°רָדְפִי ק'

often been despised for his cowardly submission to his gentile masters. *Rashi* proclaims that the Jew never was *intimidated* by the gentile. His lack of response was not an admission that he was at a loss for a reply. The Jew was silent only because he feared that his spiritual shortcomings would cause God to punish him with continued subjugation. *Rashi's* commentary on the subsequent verses will serve to amplify and clarify this concept.]

בְּמוֹט רַגְלִי עָלַי הִגְדִּילוּ — *At the faltering of my foot they will gloat over me.*

Having already witnessed that they reacted with joy to my slightest faltering, I can imagine their haughty response should I collapse completely (*Radak*).

18. כִּי אֲנִי לְצֶלַע נָכוֹן — *For I am set always to limp.*

This translation follows *Radak* who renders צֶלַע as *limp*. Because I am always limping in pain I cannot stop thinking of my sickness and my imminent death.

According to *Rashi* it would be best to render צֶלַע as *collapse*. Israel again

explains why it is silent before diatribes. Although we always hope for the best, we are prepared for the worst; for *collapse* and devastation.

צֶלַע also means *rib* and has a special connotation in reference to the wife whom God has pre-ordained for each man. As we read: וַיִּבֶן ה' אֱלֹהִים אֶת הַצֵּלָע אֲשֶׁר לָקַח מִן הָאָדָם לְאִשָּׁה, *And HASHEM, God, fashioned the rib which He took from Adam into a woman* (Genesis 2:22).[1]

19. כִּי עֲוֹנִי אַגִּיד אֶדְאַג מֵחַטָּאתִי — *Because of my iniquity, I think* [lit. *tell*], *I fret about my sin.*

Therefore I fear the specter of death (*Radak*). All of Israel fears suffering and degradation at the hands of the enemies. (*Rashi*).

Rabbeinu Jonah in *Shaarei Teshuva* (1:16) sets down the fifth principle of repentance as דְּאָגָה, *Worry.* The third principle, יָגוֹן, *Sorrow,* pertains to the past [see *commentary v.* 10], whereas דְּאָגָה, *Worry,* applies to the future. The sinner should worry over the punishments which are in store for him. He should also worry lest he has not

1. According to the Talmud (*Sanhedrin* 107a) David here shares with us a fact which puts his entire relationship with Bath Sheba in a different perspective. It was pre-ordained during the Six Days of Creation that David the son of Jesse should wed Bath Sheba the daughter of Eliam. כִּי אֲנִי לְצֶלַע נָכוֹן, *For I am prepared* [i.e., predestined] *for this rib* [i.e., his wife]. However, he was too hasty in uniting with her. Therefore the road to wed Bath Sheba was strewn with misfortune and pain, וּמַכְאוֹבִי נֶגְדִּי תָמִיד, *and my pain is continually before me'.*

[This is a key verse in this psalm, which seeks to demonstrate how David never forgot his sins and sings here for the purpose of לְהַזְכִּיר, *For remembrance.* David keeps his sin in mind at all times, and his enemies do not let him forget it either. Even as he fled from Absalom, we read, וְשִׁמְעִי הֹלֵךְ בְּצֶלַע הָהַר ... וַיְקַלֵּל, *And Shimi went along the mountain-side* [lit. *the ribs of the mountain*] ... *and cursed* [David] (II Sam. 16:13). *Midrash Shocher Tov* comments: He came to taunt him and remind him of the incident of *the rib* (i.e., Bath Sheba.]

*at the faltering of my foot they will gloat
over me!'*

¹⁸ *For I am set always to limp,
and my pain is always before me.*
¹⁹ *Because of my iniquity, I think,
I fret about my sin.*
²⁰ *But my foes abound with life,
and great are those who hate me without cause.*
²¹ *Those who repay evil for good
harass me for my pursuit of good.*

repented completely, and has been deficient in his suffering, bitterness, fasting, and weeping, as David said, *'Because my heart tells me of my iniquity, I worry about my sin.'*

20. וְאֹיְבַי חַיִּים עָצֵמוּ — *But my foes abound with life.* I decline steadily yet they constantly thrive and flourish *(Radak, Rashi).*

Another reason why I dare not oppose my oppressors is because they now enjoy abundant success, and the *Talmud* cautions against quarreling with the wicked during a period of their good fortune [cf. *commentary* to 37:1] *(Maharam Markado).*

The words of the Psalmist describing the degradation of Israel in the face of the success of her enemies echoes the words of the prophet, הָיוּ צָרֶיהָ לְרֹאשׁ, *Her tormentors have become leaders (Lamentations* 1:5), which the *Midrash (ibid.)* explains, Whosoever comes to torment Israel [being utilized by God as His agent to punish] becomes a great [world] leader *(Shaarei Chaim).*

וְרַבּוּ שֹׂנְאַי שָׁקֶר — *And great are those who hate me without cause.*

They have waxed mighty and prosperous as a result of their שָׁקֶר, *lie (Rashi),* while I have sunk into poverty *(Radak).*

21. וּמְשַׁלְּמֵי רָעָה תַּחַת טוֹבָה — *Those who repay evil for good.*

These enemies should love me because of the many kindnesses I have shown them, but instead they repay my benevolence with evil *(Radak).*

יִשְׂטְנוּנִי — *They harass me.*

They bear a malicious grudge against me as we read וַיִּשְׂטֹם עֵשָׂו אֶת יַעֲקֹב, *And Esau carried malice against Jacob (Genesis* 27:41) *(Metzudas Zion).*

תַּחַת רָדְפִי טוֹב — *For of my pursuit of goodness.*

Their hatred is motivated by envy. They see that I am dedicated to the pursuit of perfection while they are involved only in their quest for yet more evil. The קְרִי, *reading,* of the word is רָדְפִי, *my pursuit,* whereas the כְּתִיב, *spelling,* is רְדוּפִי, *my exclusive pursuit (Radak).* [This is to emphasize that I am alone, in my single-minded quest for goodness, *it is pursued by me alone*].

These vicious people are masters of perversion. Just as they repay kindness with treachery, so do they misinterpret my good as being evil. My many good deeds performed should have changed their low opinion of me. Instead, they claim that my righteousness is a deceitful masquerade, an effort to conceal my crimes *(Alshich).*

כב אַל־תַּעַזְבֵנִי יהוה אֱלֹהַי אַל־תִּרְחַק
כג מִמֶּנִּי: חוּשָׁה לְעֶזְרָתִי אֲדֹנָי תְּשׁוּעָתִי:

Israel declares: Because we stubbornly cling to the Holy One, Blessed be He,
and His commandments the nations
eternally hate us! (Rashi).

22. אַל תַּעַזְבֵנִי ה׳ — Forsake me not,
HASHEM.

They hope that I am eternally forlorn
and abandoned. Do not let their wish
come true (Radak).

אֱלֹהַי אַל תִּרְחַק מִמֶּנִי — My God, be not
far from me. As I lay on my sickbed, my
close ones stand far away (v. 12) but

You will take their place and stand at
my side (Ibn Ezra).

23. חוּשָׁה לְעֶזְרָתִי — Hasten to my
assistance. These words are an appropriate ending for this psalm which is
dedicated to the lonely exile of Israel
which drags on interminably. In this exile we continue to suffer from constant
slander and insults hurled at us personally and at our religious convictions.
Moreover, we are constrained to witness
the tremendous success and prosperity
of our enemies who repay our kindness

XXXVIII
22-23

²² *Forsake me not, HASHEM,*
   my God, be not far from me.
²³ *Hasten to my assistance,*
   O my Lord, my Salvation.

with evil. How fitting then that the
Psalmist should conclude with an
anguished plea that God hasten our
redemption from this bitter exile *(Meiri)*.

And how can we cause the redemption to come about swiftly? The *Talmud
(Sanhedrin* 98a based on Isaiah 60:22)
says: זְכוּ אַחִישֶׁנָּה, *If they are worthy, I
shall hasten it.* Therefore the Psalmist
beseeches God to seek out our merits so
that we may witness our speedy salvation *(Chazah Zion).*

אֲדֹנָי תְּשׁוּעָתִי — *O my Lord, my Salvation.*

Tehillas Hashem differentiates
between עֵזֶר, *assistance,* which is temporary and תְּשׁוּעָה, *salvation,* which is a
permanent solution to an oppressing
problem. When God dispatches an
agent to alleviate distress, the assistance
is as short-lived as is the agent.
However, says the Psalmist, if אֲדֹנָי, *my
Lord,* Himself will intervene, then He
will bring about my permanent תְּשׁוּעָה,
salvation.

[483]   *Tehillim*

39 מזמור לט

This psalm, dedicated לידותון, to Yedusun, conveys the dismal mood of the crushed man (or nation) shrouded in the gloom of failure and defeat. Rashi cites the Midrash (Shir HaShirim Rabbah 4:3) which derives יְדוּתוּן from the word דָּת, decree. Every psalm introduced with the word יְדוּתוּן refers to דָּתוֹת וְדִינִים, the [evil] decrees and [oppressive] laws which the enemy imposes upon the individual or the community of Israel. The persecuted man who witnesses his life's work going up in smoke, embarks upon an agonizing expedition of self-examination, searching for meaning in a life which appears to have been robbed of all purpose.

לַמְנַצֵּחַ °לִידִיתוּן מִזְמוֹר לְדָוִד: אָמַרְתִּי
אֶשְׁמְרָה דְרָכַי מֵחֲטוֹא בִלְשׁוֹנִי אֶשְׁמְרָה־
לְפִי מַחְסוֹם בְּעֹד רָשָׁע לְנֶגְדִּי: נֶאֱלַמְתִּי

א-ב
א-ג °לִידוּתוּן ק׳
ג

1. לִידוּתוּן — *To Yedusun.*

[See Prefatory Remarks]. *Radak* explains that David composed this psalm and gave it to Yedusun, the Temple singer, to chant.

[David divided the Levite families into twenty-four watches to serve as singers in the Temple on a rotating weekly basis. Of these, six families were headed by the six sons of Yedusun, and they in turn, *were under the charge of their father, Yedusun, who prophesied with a Kinnor to give thanks and to praise HASHEM. (I Chronicles 25:3)].*

Rashi adds that there was also a musical instrument called a *Yedusun* which was used by the Levites in the Temple.

2. אָמַרְתִּי אֶשְׁמְרָה דְרָכַי מֵחֲטוֹא בִלְשׁוֹנִי — *I said: 'I will guard my ways from sinning with my tongue'* [cf. comm. 38:14.]

I made up my mind that no matter how intense my afflictions will be, I will take care not to impugn God's ways with skeptical thoughts or with irreverent words (*Rashi*).

Binah L'Ittim notes that this is the basis for the words of the *Chovos Halevovos* who stresses that if a person seeks self-discipline he should begin by controlling his tongue. This mastery should reach the point where the heaviest bodily organs can be more easily moved than the tongue. The tongue is the key to the treasury of self-control in all areas of life.

[Silence is the initial reaction of the good man persecuted by what he perceives as harsh, unjust רָתוֹת, *decrees.*

He struggles to accept his divinely ordained lot. This resembles Job's initial reaction to his afflictions: *Despite all this Job did not sin, and he uttered not a base word against God (Job 1:22)].*

Radak and *Sforno* are of the opinion that this psalm describes David's reaction to a severe illness, specifically a plague of leprosy. [Leprosy is the punishment for the person who has spoken slanderously.]

אֶשְׁמְרָה לְפִי מַחְסוֹם — *I will guard my mouth with a muzzle.*

I will take such diligent care not to make an improper utterance that my mouth will seem to have a מַחְסוֹם, *muzzle,* on it (*Metzudas David*).

People wracked with sickness and fever usually scream out deliriously, but I guard my tongue at all times (*Ibn Ezra*).

Malbim differentiates between לָשׁוֹן, *tongue,* and פֶּה, *mouth. Tongue,* the internal organ of speech, symbolizes the expression of deeply felt intellectual concepts. On the other hand *mouth,* the external aspect of vocalization (from the lips outward), symbolizes words spoken without prior thought. David stresses that not only will he refrain from questioning God's ways intellectually, (with his internal לָשׁוֹן), but he also will take care to make no utterance (with his external פֶּה) which might be interpreted as displaying dissatisfaction with God's actions.[1]

בְּעֹד רָשָׁע לְנֶגְדִּי — *Even while the wicked one stands before me.*

Even at the height of my distress,

1. *Midrash Shocher Tov* illustrates the importance of the tongue with a parable: Once the King of Persia was on the verge of death. His physicians told him that his only chance for a cure was to drink the milk of a lioness. One of his physicians volunteered to undertake the task of obtaining such milk. He took ten goats with him and entered the den of a nursing lioness. On the first day he stood far off and threw one goat to her. The next day he edged up

XXXIX 1-3

For the director, for Yedusun,
        a song unto David.
²I said: 'I will guard my ways
        from sinning with my tongue,
I will guard my mouth with a muzzle
        even while the wicked one stands before me.'
³I became mute with stillness,

---

while my oppressors still torment me, I remain silent *(Rashi)*. [In this interpretation the wicked one is the direct cause of the Psalmist's suffering.]

Other commentator's interpret that the wicked one is not the cause of the pain, but that he has come to visit an ailing righteous person. 'At *that* time,' the Psalmist says, 'I take special care not to let the slightest groan of agony escape my lips lest this cause the wicked to rejoice over the afflictions of the righteous' *(Radak, Metzudas David)*.

[According to these commentaries, בְּעֹד would be rendered *only while*, for the patient can allow himself to groan only when he is *not* in the presence of evildoers.]

Rav Yitzchak Chajes draws our attention to the incident of Shimi ben Gera who cursed David to his face. Nevertheless, the king refused to exercise his royal prerogative to have him killed. In his last will and testament, however, David *did* instruct Solomon to have Shimi punished. This teaches that one must especially muzzle his tongue while the wicked man stands before him, because then he is apt to speak from uncontrolled anger, thus harming himself and adding unnecessary fuel to the flames of dissension and dispute.

3. נֶאֱלַמְתִּי דוּמִיָּה — *I became mute with stillness.*

I kept silent for so long that I began

somewhat closer and threw her another goat. So he continued until he became familiar enough to play with her and she let him take her milk. On the way home to the palace, he fell asleep and dreamt that his organs were debating over which had played the most important role in the his success. The physician's legs insisted that without them the milk could not be transported. His hands argued that they had milked the lioness. His eyes said that they had shown the way. His heart declared that it thought of the idea. Suddenly, his tongue spoke up and said: 'If not for me, where would you be?'

All of the organs laughed. 'How dare you compare yourself to us, you lowly tongue, locked away in the darkness of the mouth and not even possessing a hard bone like the rest of us?' The tongue warned them, 'On this very day I shall prove that I am sovereign over you all!'

The physician awoke and *proceeded* to the palace. As he handed the milk to the grateful king, his tongue said, 'Here is the milk of a dog.' The king was furious and commanded that this physician be hung.

All of the physician's organs wept and wailed until the tongue addressed them: 'If I save you all, will you admit that I am king?'

They all agreed. The tongue began to scream, 'Take me back to the king!' In the presence of the king the tongue complained, 'Why do you give orders to have me killed, is this my reward for serving you! Why don't you at least try to drink the milk, maybe it will work. Not only that, don't you know that a לְבִיָא, lioness, is also called a כְּלָבִיָא, the same word used for a female dog?' They tested the milk and found it to be genuine and healing. Whereupon all the organs proclaimed the tongue as their sovereign.

Therefore David said, 'I will guard my ways from sinning with my tongue.'

ד דּוּמִיָּה הֶחֱשֵׁיתִי מִטּוֹב וּכְאֵבִי נֶעְכָּר: חַם־
לִבִּי | בְּקִרְבִּי בַּהֲגִיגִי תִבְעַר־אֵשׁ דִּבַּרְתִּי
ה בִלְשׁוֹנִי: הוֹדִיעֵנִי יהוה | קִצִּי וּמִדַּת יָמַי

to seem like an אָלֵם, *one who has lost his power of speech* (*Radak*).

הֶחֱשֵׁיתִי — *I kept still.*
Malbim makes this differentiation between דּוּמָה and הֶחֱשֵׁיתִי: דְּמָמָה describes the silence of one who has stopped speaking. חָשָׁה refers to the silence of the person who has never spoken.

מִטּוֹב — *From the good.*
I.e., the greatest good possible, which is Torah study. The pain which the wicked foes inflicted upon me were so fearful that they disturbed my concentration on Torah study and this made the situation unbearable (*Rashi*).
In a homiletical sense, the *Talmud* (*Berachos* 5a) derives from our verse that whoever has the opportunity to engage in Torah study but does not do so, will be afflicted with distressing maladies. Thus, הֶחֱשֵׁיתִי מִטּוֹב, *I was silenced* [i.e. prevented from studying] from the good [Torah]. Therefore, וּכְאֵבִי נֶעְכָּר, *my pain was intensified.*

וּכְאֵבִי נֶעְכָּר — *And my pain was intensified.*
According to *Rashi*, without the opportunity to concentrate on Torah, the pain becomes so unbearabe that David is compelled to break his silence.
Radak, however, holds that David is saying that despite all of his intolerable pains he still remained mute. He even refrained from saying something good about God [הֶחֱשֵׁיתִי מִטּוֹב] for fear lest he might attempt to qualify his praise with a critical comment.

4. חַם לִבִּי בְּקִרְבִּי — *My heart grew hot within me.*
[At this point a change occurs. As a result of terrible illness (*Radak*) and the

frustration of remaining mute (*Malbim*), the man who previously suffered in silence moves slowly toward speech. This resembles the example of Job, who accepted everything with heroic patience at first. Later, however, his calm vanished, although his outward silence endured. *Despite all this, Job did not sin with his lips* (Job 2:10), but he did sin with complaints against God in his heart (*Rashi*).]

בַּהֲגִיגִי — *In my contemplations.*
Malbim defines הֶגְיוֹן as the mid-point between thought and speech, i.e. an idea on the verge of expression.
Sforno also says that הֶגְיוֹן is more than mere thought, rather it refers to the words which a person articulates privately. [See *comm.* Psalms 1:2 and 37:30].

תִבְעַר אֵשׁ — *A fire blazed.*
This idea demands urgent expression, just as a blazing fire requires immediate attention (*Rashi*).
My illness gives rise to a burning temperature which resembles a roaring fire (*Radak*).

בִלְשׁוֹנִי — *Then I spoke out openly* [lit. *with my tongue*].
I gave in to my burning desire for self-expression and allowed myself to ask the following question (*Rashi*).
My very breath was fiery as I finally spoke out (*Radak*).

5. הוֹדִיעֵנִי ה' קִצִּי — *Let me know, HASHEM, my end.*
How long will I continue to be in distress? When will my suffering come to an end? (*Rashi*).
When Israel was suffering in exile, the people refused to be consoled, saying, 'If You HASHEM will inform us

I was silent from the good;
and my pain was intensified.
⁴ *My heart grew hot within me,*
in my contemplations a fire blazed,
then I spoke out openly.
⁵ *Let me know, O HASHEM, my end,*
and the measure of my days, what is it?

when the misery will come to an end we will be consoled.' This may be likened to the father who told his son, 'You will receive ten lashes'. Each lash included an element of relief to the son for he knew that each blow was bringing him closer to the conclusion of his punishment (*Midrash Shocher Tov*).

Similarly, Job asked, מַה כֹּחִי כִּי אֲיַחֵל וּמַה קִצִּי כִּי אַאֲרִיךְ נַפְשִׁי, *What is my strength that I should hope, and what is my end that I should prolong my soul's*

existence? (*Job* 6:11). Job said: 'If I can still expect to live a normal lifetime, then I can patiently endure my grave illness, reinforced by the hope of recovery and better times to come. But if my days are few and there is no hope of recovery, then I ask that my end come swiftly for I cannot bear the excruciating pain' (*Radak*).[1]

וּמִדַּת יָמַי מַה הִיא — *And the measure of my days, what is it?*

1. The *Talmud* (*Shabbos* 30a) relates: David requested of the Holy One, Blessed be He, '*Let me know* HASHEM, *my end*'. God replied, 'I have already established a rule that no creature of flesh and blood shall know his end.' But David persisted, asking '*the measure of my days, what is it?*' [i.e. in what season of the year — when the days are of short measure or long? (*Maharsha*)]. Again God replied, 'I have already established a rule that no man will be informed of the measure of his days.' Finally David pleaded, '*Let me know when I will be deficient* [i.e., *dead*]'. God answered, 'Your life will come to an end on the Sabbath day'. David asked, 'Let me die on the day after the Sabbath [so that there will be ample time to make funeral preparations and proper eulogies (*Rashi*)]. God denied this request saying, 'By then, the reign of your son Solomon will have commenced, and one kingdom may not encroach on another one by even as little as a hair's-breadth.' David then asked to die on the day before the Sabbath, and God refused this too, saying, '*One day in your courtyard is worth more than one thousand* (84:11). One day of Torah study is worth more than a thousand burnt-offerings which your son Solomon will offer up in the Temple courtyard'.

From then on, David dedicated every Sabbath exclusively to the study of Torah. When the Sabbath on which he was destined to die arrived, the Angel of Death could not take his soul for he was protected by virtue of his incessant Torah study. So the Angel of Death went down into the garden behind the royal palace and made a tremendous crashing noise among the trees. David went out to determine the cause of the commotion [and continued to study Torah orally even as he walked]. However, a step suddenly broke under his foot and, startled, he momentarily stopped learning. At that moment, the Angel of Death claimed his soul!'

[What motivated David to inquire after his final day? Every man has a unique mission to accomplish on this earth. God gives him the talent, resources and opportunity to fulfill a specific quota of good deeds in an allotted time. The expression קֵץ, *end*, refers to the conclusion of that period. Most people lose sight of theirmission and stray from the path leading to their pre-ordained goal. ('The day is short, the work is great, and the laborers are lazy' [*Avos* 2:15]). Therefore, David pleaded, 'Let me know the extent of my capabilities, and what is expected of me, and how much time I have to realize the quota. Thus, I will constantly be goaded onward.' Furthermore, the nature of man is that while he is alive he cannot envision himself as ever being dead. He considers death as reserved for others. Therefore, David sought to be made aware of the fact that his life is indeed limited by a קֵץ, *end*.]

ו מַה־הִיא אֶדְעָה מֶה־חָדֵל אָנִי: הִנֵּה
טְפָחוֹת | נָתַתָּה יָמַי וְחֶלְדִּי כְאַיִן נֶגְדֶּךָ
ז אַךְ־כָּל־הֶבֶל כָּל־אָדָם נִצָּב סֶלָה: אַךְ־
בְּצֶלֶם | יִתְהַלֶּךְ־אִישׁ אַךְ־הֶבֶל יֶהֱמָיוּן

[Note that David does not ask to know מִסְפַּר יָמַי, *the number of my days*, rather he seeks to be informed of *the measure of my days*, i.e. how is my accomplishment measured according to what is expected of me at my קֵץ, end?

Another point: Most people measure themselves by their years, for a year represents a sizeable amount of time worthy of reckoning, whereas a month or a week and certainly a day, is of small significance and of little consequence. Not so the righteous. They cherish each *day* as a short but precious opportunity which must be measured and appraised. David asked about his *days* similar to Abraham of whom Scripture says, *And Abraham was old, well on in days* (Genesis 24:1)].

אֶדְעָה מֶה חָדֵל אָנִי — *Then I will realize how deficient I am.*

[חָדֵל literally means *to cease, to be missing*. In the context of this verse it means that David wants to know how his accomplishment measures up to final expectations so that he will realize his deficiencies and how far he is from his ultimate goal].

Ibn Ezra, Metzudas Zion, and *Malbim* identify חָדֵל as synonymous with חֶלֶד, *a lifetime, (v.* 6) with the letters transposed. Thus, they render 'So that I may know how long I will remain in this life.'

6. טְפָחוֹת נָתַתָּה יָמַי — [Like] *handbreadths have You made my days.*

My days are so few that they can be measured with one of the smallest of measures: the טֶפַח, *handbreadth* (*Rashi*).

The righteous man is acutely aware of the fleeting nature of life which vanishes before his very eyes. He feels how every breath he breathes brings him closer and closer to his last one, and how every step he takes, every small טֶפַח, *handbreadth*, of space which he traverses brings him nearer to the grave (*Yaavetz Hadoresh*).

וְחֶלְדִּי — *My lifetime.*

The translation follows *Radak* and *Metzudos* who render this word as synonymous with חָדֵל (*v.* 5) which also refers to the termination of a lifetime.

However, according to *Rashi*, חֶלֶד is a metaphor for old age which is likened to חֲלוּדָה, *turning rusty* [cf. *comm.* to מֵחֶלֶד (17:14).]

[Life is futile because it is no more than a prolonged process of 'rusting out.' From the moment man is born, he is already deteriorating and headed toward the grave.]

כְאַיִן נֶגְדֶּךָ — *Is as naught before You.*

The fleeting moments of our lives cannot compare to Your eternal, infinite existence (*Radak*)[1]

אַךְ כָּל הֶבֶל — *All is total* [lit. *nothing but*] *futility.*

Human existence is the sum total of all futile, worthless pursuits, as Solo-

1. *Ohel Yaakov* explains this phrase with a parable. A rich man refused to make a loan to a beggar. Even though he was sure that the honest pauper would eventually pay him back, he was equally certain that the manner of repayment would be unsuitable. The rich man argued that the beggar would reimbuirse him one penny at a time at intervals, and so, by the time the second penny was paid, the first would surely be gone and thus the full sum would never be

XXXIX *Then I will realize*
6-7 *how deficient I am.*
⁶ *Like handbreadths have You made my days,*
and my lifetime is as naught before You.
All is total futility —
all human existence, Selah.
⁷ *In total darkness does man make his way,*

mon taught in his wisdom, הֶבֶל הֲבָלִים אָמַר קֹהֶלֶת הֲבֵל הֲבָלִים הַכֹּל הָבֶל *'Futility of futilities! — Said Koheles — Futility of futilities! All is futile!' (Koheles 1:2) (Radak).*

However, *Metzudos David* renders this particular usage of הֶבֶל as *pain, sorrow,* as we find כִּי בַהֶבֶל בָּא וּבַחֹשֶׁךְ יֵלֵךְ *For he [man] arrives [is born] in pain and departs [to the grave] in darkness (Koheles 6:4).*

כָּל אָדָם נִצָּב — *All human existence* [lit. *All men stand erect.*]

[Not only when man is merely עוֹמֵד, *standing* (casually), is his existence precarious, but even when he reinforces his position in life by being נִצָּב, *standing erect* and firm, all his efforts are still futile.]

[At this point the persecuted man is overwhelmed by his tragedy, and questions the value of life itself. Since all is futile it is indeed better not to have been born. Again, this resembles Job who was finally compelled by his sufferings to hurl blasphemous complains against the heavenly design of life. *And Job replied and said: 'If only the day of my birth had been lost, and also the night on which they announced, "A man has been conceived"' (Job 3:1-2).*]

7. אַךְ בְּצֶלֶם יִתְהַלֶּךְ אִישׁ — *In total darkness does man make his way.*

He lives out his life בְּצַלְמָוֶת, *under the shadow of death,* constantly fearing the sudden, unknown death which may be lurking just around the corner *(Dunash quoted by Rashi, Radak, Metzudos).*

[Job too, spurned human existence, considering it worthy only of dark misery. הַיוֹם הַהוּא יְהִי חֹשֶׁךְ, *Let that day* [of my birth] *always be dark* (ibid 3:3) יִגְאָלֻהוּ חֹשֶׁךְ וְצַלְמָוֶת, *Let it be made despicable with darkness and the shadow of death* (ibid 3:4).

Ibn Ezra renders צֶלֶם in its more common translation, 'image'. Man's image is his situation and fortune which is in constant flux (similar to the shape of a flowing body of water which never remains quite the same). This incessant change is reflected in the צֶלֶם, *image,* of the heavenly bodies; the stars and astrological formations which are divinely endowed with the power to affect the future [under God's supervision] and are in perpetual motion.

Thus, when God wishes to change man's fortune, He effects His wish by the agency of the heavenly bodies; in turn, man becomes their 'image'.

[This concept may be broadened, for as *Nefesh HaChaim* and others expound, God can be the צֶלֶם, *image,* or צֵל, *shadow,* of man, as it were. If a person molds himself into a model of kindness, God will follow suit and treat

amassed intact again! Similarly, man considers his life to be long and significant, thinking he possesses many years. But this is not so. For the past is gone, and the future may never come. All man really possesses is the one moment of the present in which he is living now, and even that fleeting second, *is as naught before You.*

ח יִצְבֹּר וְלֹא־יֵדַע מִי־אֹסְפָם: וְעַתָּה מַה־
ט קִוִּיתִי אֲדֹנָי תּוֹחַלְתִּי לְךָ הִיא: מִכָּל־
פְּשָׁעַי הַצִּילֵנִי חֶרְפַּת נָבָל אַל־תְּשִׂימֵנִי:
י נֶאֱלַמְתִּי לֹא אֶפְתַּח־פִּי כִּי אַתָּה עָשִׂיתָ:
יא הָסֵר מֵעָלַי נִגְעֶךָ מִתִּגְרַת יָדְךָ אֲנִי כָלִיתִי:

---

him kindly, in turn. Thus man can shape God's manifestation in creation.][1]

אַךְ הֶבֶל יֶהֱמָיוּן — *Total futility does he lustfully pursue.*

[Man, the crown of creation, endowed with the unlimited opportunity to control the shape of God's revelation on earth, squanders his assets in the pursuit of petty lusts. Not only is it highly doubtful that he will attain his desires, but even if he does eventually succeed in realizing some of his fond wishes, he will discover that they were empty and futile (הֶבֶל), completely unworthy of his great efforts.]

Rashi and *Radak* both derive the word יֶהֱמָיוּן from the verb הָמְיָה, *yearning, lusting.* However, *Ibn Ezra* and *Metzudos* relate it to the noun הָמוֹן, *mass.* The Psalmist laments, 'man amasses great fortunes which prove to be futile'.

יִצְבֹּר וְלֹא יֵדַע מִי אֹסְפָם — *He amasses* [lit. *makes heaps*] *riches, yet knows not who will harvest them.*

Throughout the harvest season the farmer toils to make countless צְבּוּרִים, *piles* of his crops, yet he has no assurance that he will live to gather this bounty into his house (*Rashi*).

Slowly but surely bit by bit, man painstakingly amasses his treasures, yet he has no idea where they will go after his death (*Radak*).

The *Talmud* (*Bava Basra* 11a) relates that it was for this reason that King Monabaz donated to charity all his own treasures accumulated by himself and his many ancestors. He explained, 'They gathered treasures which cannot be protected from the hands of plunderers, but I gather mitzvos (spiritual treasures) stored away in heaven, safe from any foreign hand!' (*Shaarei Chaim*).

8. [Having concluded his vivid portrayal of the worthlessness of material pursuits, the Psalmist commences to outline the true mission of life.]

וְעַתָּה — *And now.*

Only now, after my terrible illness which convinced me of the frailty of man (*Radak*), and after having thoroughly analyzed the futility of wealth (*Rashi*).

מַה קִוִּיתִי אֲדֹנָי — *For what do I hope, my Lord.*

To whom can I turn for salvation from my raging fever since all medical efforts have proven utterly futile? (*Radak*). [What can I wish for in this world that is of meaningful, enduring value?]

תּוֹחַלְתִּי לְךָ הִיא — *[What is] my expectation of you?*

The translation follows *Rashi* who interprets this phrase as the conclusion

---

1. When a Torah lesson is taught in the name of its deceased author, his lips move along, even in the grave. Furthermore, whoever transmits a Torah lesson in the name of its author should keep a mental image of the teacher before his eyes [thus the lesson will be taught with greater clarity and faithfulness to the source], as it says, *Only with the image* [of the teacher before him], *does man* [the disciple] *make his way* (*Yerushalmi, Shekalim* 2:5).

total futility does he lustfully pursue,
He amasses riches,
yet he knows not who will harvest them.
⁸ *And now, for what do I hope, my Lord?*
What is my expectation of You?
⁹ *From all my trangressions rescue me;*
a disgrace before the degenerate do not make me!
¹⁰ *I was mute, I opened not my mouth,*
because You did it.
¹¹ *Remove from me Your plague;*
by the hostility of Your hand am I devastated.

---

of the question begun earlier.

Radak, however, takes this as the answer to the question: My expectation is [only] to You!

[To know You and to imitate Your ways is the only opportunity in life really worth striving for. Only from this pursuit can I expect to derive genuine satisfaction, as it says, *HASHEM is good to those who hope for Him, to the soul which seeks Him out* (Lamentations 3:25).]

9. מִכָּל פְּשָׁעַי הַצִּילֵנִי — *From all my transgressions rescue me.*

[But before I can know You intimately, O God, I must first remove the barriers which separate me from You. I am a captive, chained to my old, sinful ways and far removed from Your presence. Please rescue me from that way of life. Furthermore, I now abandon the blasphemies of Job and I recognize that all of my persecutions were well deserved results of my sins].

חֶרְפַּת נָבָל אַל תְּשִׂימֵנִי — *A disgrace before the degenerate do not make me.*

[נָבָל literally means *worn out,* for the faith which the heretic once possessed has been worn away by the tribulations of life which have stripped him of his appreciation of God's justice (cf. *comm.* 14:1). When Job's wife severely criticized him for accepting God's wrath

with perfectly innocent faith, and encouraged him to curse God, Job reprimanded her harshly, saying: כְּדַבֵּר אַחַת הַנְּבָלוֹת תְּדַבְּרִי, *like the speech of one of the degenerates do you speak* (*Job* 2:10).]

The man of faith knows that all of his sufferings are justified. He does not ask to be released from his pain, for he recognizes their value. He requests only that the wicked ones be punished also, so that they should not disgrace the righteous by saying, 'We must be right, for God punishes only you'. Heathen nations suffer in this world as a result of God's response to this request (*Rashi*).

10. נֶאֱלַמְתִּי לֹא אֶפְתַּח פִּי — *I was mute, I opened not my mouth.*

There was no one at whom to scream or to blame for my suffering, for I recognized that all my afflictions came from You as a result of my sins (*Radak*).

11. הָסֵר מֵעָלַי נִגְעֶךָ — *Remove from me Your plague.*

This refers to the plague of leprosy which afflicted David (*Sforno*) [and to which he also referred in 38:12 (*Radak*)].

[Now that I recognize my sins, there is no reason to prolong my agony for I have learned my lesson.]

מִתִּגְרַת יָדְךָ אֲנִי כָלִיתִי — *By the hostility of Your hand am I devastated.*

יב בְּתוֹכָחוֹת עַל־עָוֹן | יִסַּרְתָּ אִישׁ וַתֶּמֶס
כָּעָשׁ חֲמוּדוֹ אַךְ הֶבֶל כָּל־אָדָם סֶלָה:
יג שִׁמְעָה תְפִלָּתִי | יהוה וְשַׁוְעָתִי | הַאֲזִינָה
אֶל־דִּמְעָתִי אַל־תֶּחֱרַשׁ כִּי גֵר אָנֹכִי עִמָּךְ
יד תּוֹשָׁב כְּכָל־אֲבוֹתָי: הָשַׁע מִמֶּנִּי וְאַבְלִיגָה
בְּטֶרֶם אֵלֵךְ וְאֵינֶנִּי:

This translation follows *Rashi,
Radak,* and *Metzudos* who relate תִּגְרַת
to תִּגֶּר, *hostility* or *war* as in וְאַל
תִּתְגָּר בָּם מִלְחָמָה *Do not arouse
hostilities of war against them*
(Deuteronomy 2:9).

Rashi also quotes *Menachem* who
renders תִּגְרַת as *fear,* as in וַיָּגָר מוֹאָב
And Moab was frightened (Numbers
22:3).

12. בְּתוֹכָחוֹת עַל עָוֹן יִסַּרְתָּ אִישׁ — *With
rebukes for iniquity have You
chastened man.*

You warned us not to sin and
threatened us with harsh rebukes. You
have lived up to Your words by
punishing us for iniquity (*Rashi*).

The plagues which You send upon us
are like 'translators' who interpret Your
displeasure into afflictions which convey to us the message that You are
angered by our deeds (*Radak*).

וַתֶּמֶס כָּעָשׁ — *You rot like a moth.*

The עָשׁ is the moth [or the worm]
which eats clothing and causes it to rot
(*Metzudas Zion*).

חֲמוּדוֹ — *His precious* [flesh].

A person's flesh is precious to him
(*Rashi*).

You wasted away the precious fat of
his flesh and the power of his torso, just

as the עָשׁ, *moth,* swiftly devours a garment (*Radak*).

אַךְ הֶבֶל כָּל אָדָם סֶלָה — *Total futility is all
mankind, Selah!*

If man holds his own flesh so
precious and dear although it decays
and putrifies so easily and swiftly, what
better proof could there be of human
futility and worthlessness (*Radak*).[1]

13. אֶל דִּמְעָתִי אַל תֶּחֱרַשׁ — *To my tears,
be not mute.*

I shed tears not because of my pain
but because of my inability to serve You
with Torah study and prayer (*Sforno*).

The combination of prayers and tears
is like a liquid medicine prescribed by
an expert physician (*Ibn Ezra*).

The *Talmud* (*Bava Metzia* 59a) says:
Since the day that the Temple was
destroyed all of the gates of prayer are
locked, however, the gates of tears are
not locked as it says, *To my tears, be not
mute.* [This proves that tears enter into
heaven under all circumstances, because
the only request which the Psalmist
made was that they be heard and acted
upon (*Rashi*).]

[*Hirsch* calls a tear 'the sweat of the
soul!' Indeed, a tear of repentance is an
overflow of feeling which demonstrates
that he who weeps has overcome his

1. Rav Aharon 'Artchik' Bakst zt''l, one of the great leaders of pre-World War II Lithuanian
Jewry, would bang his fist on the table in the course of a *Mussar Shmuess* (a discourse on
ethics) shouting, 'What is superior, a man or a table? Certainly a table! If you don't wash this
table for a month it won't start to smell foul, but don't wash a man for a month and he will be
infested with lice and stench'.

XXXIX ¹² *With rebukes for iniquity have You chastened man,*
12-14   *You rot like a moth his precious flesh,*
     Total futility is all mankind, Selah.
     ¹³ *Hear my prayer, HASHEM;*
          to my outcry, lend an ear;
          to my tears, be not mute;
     For an alien am I with You,
          a settler like all my forefathers.
     ¹⁴ *Release me that I may regain my strength,*
          before I depart and I am no more.

normal, calm nature and is exerting himself to be more receptive to change and renewal. If man opens the gates of his heart in order to welcome God, certainly God reciprocates by opening all the gates of heaven before his tears.

The question has been asked: If the gates of tears are never locked why did God have to make them in the first place? The *Gerrer Rebbe* said that although sincere tears always gain admission above, the gates are sealed shut in the face of false tears. We might also add that although these gates are not locked, nevertheless they are closed and can be opened only as far as the forceful flow of tears will push them!]

כִּי גֵר אָנֹכִי עִמָּךְ — *For an alien am I with You.*

Man wanders the earth like a stranger who strays about in a foreign land. He travels from place to place constantly, lacking permanence. The Psalmist adds the word עִמָּךְ, *with You,* to stress that only in the hands of God lies the decision whether an individual will remain settled peacefully in one place or if he will be exiled and disturbed. Similarly, David himself said, (I *Chronicles* 29:15) *For we are aliens before You and settlers like all of our forefathers* (I *Chronicles* 29:15) (*Radak*).

David is alluding to his ancestress,

Ruth the Moabitess, who was a גִּיוֹרֶת, convert (*Rabbi Menachem Azariah of Pano.*).

תּוֹשָׁב כְּכָל אֲבוֹתָי — *A settler like all my forefathers.*

Despite the temporary nature of his stay on earth, man deludes himself into thinking that he is a settler because he follows in the footsteps of his forefathers, but they, too, were only transitory migrants in comparison with God's eternal existence (*Metzudos*).

If a person considers himself to be an alien in עוֹלָם הַזֶּה, *This World,* then he will join his forefathers, the Patriarchs, Abraham, Isaac and Jacob, and be permanently settled in the bliss of עוֹלָם הַבָּא, *the World to Come* (*Toldos Aharon*).

14. הָשַׁע מִמֶּנִּי — *Release me.*

The translation follows *Rashi, Ibn Ezra,* and *Radak.* However, *Metzudos* and *Malbim* render 'turn away from me.'

וְאַבְלִיגָה — *So that I may regain my strength.*

And thus be able to serve You as an able-bodied servant who can fulfill Your will (*Radak*).

בְּטֶרֶם אֵלֵךְ — *Before I depart.*

To the grave (*Radak*).

וְאֵינֶנִּי — *And I am no more.*

When I leave This World for the World to Come I will no longer have the opportunity to serve You, for that is the place of reward, not of good deeds (*Radak*).[1]

---

1. As his holy life was ebbing away, the *Vilna Gaon* called his disciples to his bedside. He held up his *tzitzis* and said: 'Behold the tremendous opportunities of This World. For a scant few *kopecks* one can purchase *tzitzis* which will afford him with thousands upon thousands of *mitzvos* as he wears them constantly. But in the Hereafter, even if a person should desire to give away a fortune he no longer has the privilege to add the smallest *mitzvah* to his account!' Then the saintly *Gaon* burst into tears at the thought that he would soon have no more opportunities to serve God.

תהלים [496]

The preceding Psalms described David in the throes of his debilitating malady. This Psalm is the joyous Song he composed when he returned to full health (Radak; Sforno). It is not an ordinary composition; but rather a very special שִׁיר חָדָשׁ, a new song (v. 4), for it describes David's unflagging faith which he renewed and refreshed (v. 2).

The first twelve verses of this Psalm would indicate that David was at the height of bliss when he uttered these words. [The ecstasy and the eloquence justify the description 'a new song' used in v. 4.] But, if we read beyong v. 12, we see that the song was written when the Psalmist was beset by many dangers and sorely in need of deliverance. In the midst of these woes David finds strength and inspiration in the many previous occasions when God rescued him. Thereby HASHEM demonstrated to David that He is the real מְנַצֵּחַ, one who grants victory, by endowing man with spiritual fortitude with which to withstand all earthly tribulations. This illustrates the unique power of David to extract rapturous joy from the depths of adversity (Hirsch).

Rashi and the Midrash emphasize another important dimension of this psalm, which addresses itself to all of Israel. In the Egyptian bondage, the nation was crippled by harsh slavery. Only by virture of their intense, enduring faith were the Israelites liberated and given the opportunity to sing a new song at the sea.

In addition, this Psalm alludes to the future Messianic redemption which will be the result of Israel's extraordinary faith and which will stimulate unprecedented waves of fresh song and jubilation.

א-ב לַמְנַצֵּחַ לְדָוִד מִזְמוֹר: קַוֹּה קִוִּיתִי יהוה
ג וַיֵּט אֵלַי וַיִּשְׁמַע שַׁוְעָתִי: וַיַּעֲלֵנִי | מִבּוֹר
שָׁאוֹן מִטִּיט הַיָּוֵן וַיָּקֶם עַל־סֶלַע רַגְלַי
ד כּוֹנֵן אֲשֻׁרָי: וַיִּתֵּן בְּפִי | שִׁיר חָדָשׁ תְּהִלָּה

1. לַמְנַצֵּחַ לְדָוִד מִזְמוֹר — *For the Conductor, unto David, a song.*

The superscription לְדָוִד מִזְמוֹר, *a song unto David*, always implies that David utilized the medium of song as a means to elevate himself sufficiently to attain the rapture of God's presence. The heading לְדָוִד מִזְמוֹר, however, indicates that first he was inspired by God's spirit which came לְדָוִד, *to David*, whereupon he composed the מִזְמוֹר, *song* to express the soaring emotion engendered by that inspiration. (Cf. *commentary* to 3:1).

2. קַוֹּה קִוִּיתִי ה' — *I have hoped and hoped for HASHEM.*

Israel does not possess sufficient merit to warrant redemption. Only because of their exceptional faith in God's redemption are they deserving of God's help, as the Prophet declares וְאָמַר בַּיּוֹם הַהוּא הִנֵּה אֱלֹהֵינוּ זֶה קִוִּינוּ לוֹ וְיוֹשִׁיעֵנוּ זֶה ה' קִוִּינוּ לוֹ נָגִילָה וְנִשְׂמְחָה בִּישׁוּעָתוֹ, *And he shall say on that day, 'Behold this is our God, we hoped for Him and He saved us this is HASHEM, we hoped for Him, we shall rejoice and be glad in His salvation* (Isaiah 25:9).

Similarly, it says טוֹב ה' לְקֹוָו, *Hashem is good to those who hope for Him* [Lamentations 3:25] (*Midrash Shocher Tov*).

If your hopes have not been realized, hope and hope again! In Egypt, the Israelites in bondage cried out again and again, *and God heard their cries* [Exodus 2:24] (*Shemos Rabbah* 23:12).

More than the results of his faith in God, David sought the inspiration of the hope itself. The means meant more to him than the end. Thus he says, 'It is for their ability to *hope* [קַוֹּה] to

HASHEM that *I* (truly) *hope* [קִוִּיתִי] (*Tehillos Hashem*).

וַיֵּט אֵלַי וַיִּשְׁמַע שַׁוְעָתִי — *So He inclined to me and heard my cry.*

Sometimes God does not 'bend down to hear', meaning that He, in His infinite wisdom, chooses not to interfere with the normal course of events in order to effect salvation (*Malbim*).

3. מִבּוֹר שָׁאוֹן — *For the pit of turbulent waters.*

The translation of שָׁאוֹן as a reference to *turbulent waters* follows *Rashi*. However, *Metzudas Zion* renders מִבּוֹר שָׁאוֹן, *from a dark pit*.

David describes his illness as a watery grave which threatened to swallow him alive (*Radak*).

God rescued Israel from the בּוֹר, *pit*, of Egyptian bondage, and from the שָׁאוֹן, *turbulent waters*, of the Sea of Reeds (*Rashi*).

מִטִּיט הַיָּוֵן — *Out of the filthy mire.*

יָוֵן is synonymous with רֶפֶשׁ, *filth*. It refers to the mud of the seabed which Israel crossed at the Sea of Reeds [and which God miraculously hardened for them] (*Rashi*).

Shemos Rabbah (ibid.) explains that this describes the muck and clay which the Israelite slaves used in manufacturing their daily quota of bricks.

Radak interprets יָוֵן as a collection of many types of mud, both solid and watery [cf. *Mikvaos* 9:2]. Here the word is used as a metaphor for a variety of ailments which afflicted David.

Malbim maintains that טִיט הַיָּוֵן is *quicksand* from which there is no escape as it sucks the victim downward.

XL
1-4

For the Conductor, unto David, a song.
² I have hoped and hoped for HASHEM,
so He inclined to me, and heard my cry.
³ He raised me from the pit of turbulent waters.
out of the filthy mire;
He set my feet upon a rock,
He firmed my steps.
⁴ He put in my mouth a new song,

[This corresponds to the *Talmud* (*Eruvin* 19a) which notes that טִיט הַיָּוֵן is one of the seven Scriptural expressions used for describing Gehinnom (purgatory). Thus, the word *quicksand* is used to imply that there is no escape from the consequences of sin.]

וַיָּקֶם עַל סֶלַע רַגְלִי — *He set my feet upon a rock.*

This salvation refers to the threat of בּוֹר שָׁאוֹן, *the turbulent, watery pit.* The man drowning therein desperately clutches for something solid, i.e., a rock, to which he can cling. *(Be'er Avraham).*

Rashi explains: God endowed Israel with wealth: the booty taken in Egypt and the spoils taken at the Sea.

[וַיָּקֶם alludes to יְקוּם, *substance.* Elsewhere we read: וְאֵת כָּל הַיְקוּם אֲשֶׁר בְּרַגְלֵיהֶם, *And all the substance at their feet* (Deut. 11:6), which the *Talmud* (*Sanhedrin* 110a) explains as the wealth and substance which give someone the ability to stand on his own feet without relying on others for support].

God completely restored my health and my strong constitution *(Sforno).*

When Saul seemed to have me in his grasp, God miraculously saved me at the סֶלַע הַמַּחְלְקוֹת, *the Rock of Division* (cf. *commentary* to 18:3) *(Alshich).*

Just as all of the winds in the world cannot overturn a great rock, so is it impossible to overthrow the kingdom of David for all times, because God Himself promised David an eternal monarchy *(Nir L'David).*

[According to *Yalkut Shimoni* (*Tehillim* 736), סֶלַע refers to the Temple as we find in *Jeremiah* 33:16. David exults that he was uplifted by the opportunity to prepare for its construction. The Temple's central point was the Holy Ark situated in the Holy of Holies on top of a סֶלַע, *rock,* — the אֶבֶן שְׁתִיָּה, the rock from which the world was created (*Yoma* 53b)].

כּוֹנֵן אֲשֻׁרָי — *He firmed my steps.*

This corresponds to the victim who is completely immobilized in the טִיט הַיָּוֵן, *the filthy mud* (quicksand), and who lacks solid ground on which to steady himself *(Be'er Avraham).*

My ailment left no scars or infirmities upon my body. God healed me completely without leaving any trace of my illness *(Sforno).*

4. וַיִּתֵּן בְּפִי שִׁיר חָדָשׁ — *He put in my mouth a new song.*

Radak notes that David is not content to thank God merely for His salvation. He perceives that even the inspiration to sing was a divine gift [cf. *commentary* to v. 1]. Indeed, it is incumbent upon man to create an original hymn of praise to God in recognition of every new miracle from which he benefits.

Malbim adds that when God saves through natural means, it is sufficient to express gratitude by means of an existing song of praise. But when the Creator effects salvation through a

לֵאלֹהֵינוּ יִרְאוּ רַבִּים וְיִירָאוּ וְיִבְטְחוּ
ה בַּיהוָה: אַשְׁרֵי־הַגֶּבֶר אֲשֶׁר־שָׂם יהוה
מִבְטַחוֹ וְלֹא־פָנָה אֶל־רְהָבִים וְשָׂטֵי כָזָב:
ו רַבּוֹת עָשִׂיתָ | אַתָּה | יהוה אֱלֹהַי

miraculous phenomenon, a *new song* is called for.[1]

A *new song* is particularly appropriate here because David was on the threshold of death and God endowed him with new life (*Tehillas Hashem; Norah Tehillos*).

Rashi explains that שִׁיר חָדָשׁ also alludes to שִׁירַת הַיָּם, *the Song at the Sea*, composed by the newly redeemed nation of Israel.

תְּהִלָּה לֵאלֹהֵינוּ — *A hymn to our God.*

David refers to Him as *our God* because he is calling upon everyone, the entire congregation, to join him in this song of praise (Radak).

Let them not only praise HASHEM, i.e. His manifestation of Mercy, but even God, i.e., His manifestation of strict Justice (Pa'amonei Zahav).

יִרְאוּ רַבִּים וְיִירָאוּ — *Multitudes shall see and be awed.*

Because the verse speaks of Israel as *seeing* and *fearing*, the *Midrash* interprets it as an allusion to the rescue of Israel at the Sea from destruction at the hands of the Egyptians as we find in *Exodus 14:31, And Israel saw the great hand which HASHEM used against the Egyptians, and the nation feared HASHEM, and they believed in HASHEM and in Moses His servant* (*Midrash Shocher Tov*).

Only the revealed miracle brings men to fear God's might. When He merely

manipulates nature, however, in a concealed manner not really discernible to unthinking people, His greatness is not appreciated (*Malbim*).

David's life serves as a lesson even for non-believers. All will learn to fear sin when they witness His former afflictions and the extent to which God helped him (*Radak*).

Midrash Shocher Tov echoes this theme: 'Whoever wishes to repent should study David's life, as the Prophet says, *Behold, I have placed him [David] as a testimony for the nations (Jeremiah 55:4).*

[According to *Maharam Markado* David's *new song (v. 4)* begins with the words of this verse. However, *Ibn Ezra (v. 6)* maintains that this verse is an introduction to the song, which begins with the next verse.]

5. אַשְׁרֵי הַגֶּבֶר — *Praises to the man.*

[For the explanation of אַשְׁרֵי, see *commentary* to 1:1.]

[The גֶּבֶר is more than just an ordinary man. He is a גִבּוֹר, *a mighty warrior*, who is self-sufficient and does not need the assistance of others. If such a secure person denies his own powers and his faith rests solely on God, he is surely praiseworthy.]

אֲשֶׁר שָׂם ה' מִבְטַחוֹ — *Who made HASHEM his trust.*

Similarly we find בָּרוּךְ הַגֶּבֶר אֲשֶׁר יִבְטַח בַּה' וְהָיָה ה' מִבְטַחוֹ, *Blessed is the*

---

1. The *Midrash* teaches that all Scriptural songs are called שִׁירָה in the feminine gender, because each victory of Israel gives birth to fresh sorrows and persecutions. However, the song of victory in the future is שִׁיר, in the masculine gender, for then our salvation will be complete and there will be no further sorrows. Therefore, wherever Scriptures refer to the composition which is חָדָשׁ, *new* — i.e. an allusion to the song of the future — it is called שִׁיר (see 33:3, 96:1, 98:1, 149:1, *Isaiah 42:10*).

a hymn to our God,

Multitudes shall see and be awed,

and they shall trust in HASHEM.

⁵ Praises to the man

who made HASHEM his trust,

And turned not to the arrogant,

and to strayers after falsehood.

⁶ Much have You done — You HASHEM, my God,

man who trusts in HASHEM, and makes HASHEM his trust (Jeremiah 17:7).

Some people, while trusting that God is the ultimate source of success, nevertheless turn to other forces as the vehicles to achieve that success. They put their efforts into commerce or professions in order to gain the divinely ordained prosperity. Therefore, although they trust in HASHEM they do not make HASHEM their [lit. his] trust i.e. the sole medium through which their trust is manifested. But the true believer turns to no force but HASHEM Himself even in his efforts to attain material fortune. He is the person who does make HASHEM his trust (Malbim).

רְהָבִים — The arrogant.

The word רַהַב is related to רָחָב wide, extended, and to רַב, much, great. [The arrogant have an over-inflated ego] (Hirsch).

As in יִרְהֲבוּ הַנַּעַר בַּזָּקֵן 'The youth will act arrogantly against the elder' [Isaiah 3:5] (Rashi).

He who trusts in HASHEM asks for no assistance from mighty warriors who are excessively reliant on their own strength (Radak). Arrogant men make commitments which far surpass their ability to fulfill (Malbim).

וְשָׂטֵי כָזָב —And strayers after falsehood.

שָׂטֵי is derived from שׂוֹט, to turn away treacherously. It refers to deceptive sorcerers (Radak) and to pagan idolators (Rashi).

According to Hirsch, it describes the arrogant men of might. At first glance, they inspire trust. However, when their help is needed they are of no avail. They disappoint those who rely on them, as they turn away fickly.

Whereas the boastful man cannot live up to his promises, the man of כָזָב does indeed achieve results. However, he lacks the ability and the consistency to maintain these results permanently [cf. commentary to 4:3]. Consequently, he is מְכַזֵב, he disappoints, those who depend on him (Malbim).[1]

6. רַבּוֹת עָשִׂיתָ אַתָּה ה' אֱלֹהַי — Much have You done — You HASHEM, my God.

---

1. The Midrash (Bereishis Rabbah 89:8) seems to contradict itself. First it presents Joseph as the perfect example of the man of sincere faith: 'Praises to the man who made HASHEM his trust'; this describes Joseph! The Midrash continues: 'And turned not to the arrogant'; this refers to the sin of Joseph in turning to Pharoah's שַׂר הַמַּשְׁקִים, butler, for assistance in being released from prison. For this lack of trust in God, Joseph was punished with two additional years of imprisonment.

The Beis HaLevi (Parshas Mikeitz) reconciles these two statements. For the ordinary person it would not be a breach of faith to hope for the intervention of an influential officer, as this is the customary procedure. But when one attains Joseph's plateau of faith, he is expected to turn to none but God for all assistance. Therefore, precisely because Joseph was the paragon of faith, it was improper for him to depend on a human being for his rescue from prison.

נִפְלְאֹתֶיךָ וּמַחְשְׁבֹתֶיךָ אֵלֵינוּ אֵין | עֲרֹךְ
ז אֵלֶיךָ אַגִּידָה וַאֲדַבֵּרָה עָצְמוּ מִסַּפֵּר: זֶבַח
וּמִנְחָה | לֹא־חָפַצְתָּ אָזְנַיִם כָּרִיתָ לִּי עוֹלָה

You HASHEM, are not like human rulers and leaders whose performance varies with the size of their audience. Such leaders seek popularity and public good-will, and therefore will do much for the multitudes, but little for the few. You HASHEM are different. You have done many things for me alone, for You are truly my God; concerned with my welfare, though I am but an individual (*Alshich*).

נִפְלְאֹתֶיךָ וּמַחְשְׁבֹתֶיךָ אֵלֵינוּ — *Your wonders and Your thoughts are for* [lit. *to*] *us*.

The נִפְלָאוֹת are the actual wonders which God put into action and the מַחְשָׁבוֹת are the divine thoughts which precede the execution of these miracles. Of course, to describe God as thinking prior to action is an anthropomorphism, for He has no need to consider and plan as do humans. As is common, Scripture merely speaks of God in human terms (*Radak*).

Alshich delves more deeply into this thought: The Psalmist uses the word אֵלֵינוּ [lit. *to us*] in order to emphasize that the interval between God's thought and the implementation of His wish is only *to us* — i.e. as we, with our limited human intellect, perceive events to occur. Unable to grasp God's true nature, we imagine Him to be subject to the limitations of time and to other impediments preventing the execution of His decree. As for God Himself, however, thought and deed are simultaneous. Furthermore, to God, both natural events and miracles are the same. He controls both with equal authority and ease. Only אֵלֵינוּ, *to us*, do certain events appear to be 'natural' phenomena while others are supernatural miracles.

Rashi renders אֵלֵינוּ as *for us*, and

adds: For our sake You created this world and for our sake You split the Sea. Furthermore, Your thoughts were occupied with long term plans for our welfare. You saw that the inhabitants of Canaan had exercised a scorched-earth policy when they learned of Israel's imminent conquest. They felled their trees and devastated their land. Therefore You detained us in the desert for forty years, so that the Canaanites would have ample time to forget us and our threat and so be aroused to develop their land again. Thus we eventually conquered a productive country.

The *Midrash (Bereishis Rabba* 65:8) amplifies this theme and stresses that God's concern for the ultimate success of Israel is the guiding force behind all events in history, even those which originally seemed to be detrimental. For example, Isaac became blind only so that Jacob should later be able to take the blessings which Isaac had intended for Esau. [All dark spots in history are for the sake of future light.]

The *Talmud* (*Yevamos* 77a) relates how God planned David's birth many years before he was born. The Torah prohibits the Ammonite and the Moabite from entering the Congregation of God, but the restriction applies only to males, not to females. This is because God foresaw that David was destined to descend from Ruth the Moabite and that Rechavam, King of Judah, grandson of David and progenitor of the Davidean line, was to be born from Solomon's wife, Na'amah the Ammonite.

David sang *You released my bonds* (117:16). He said, 'Sovereign of the Universe, two prohibitions restricted me and You released them, i.e. the Moabite and Ammonite, Ruth and Na'amah.

Your wonders and Your thought are for us,
none can compare to You.
Can I relate or speak of them?
They are too mighty to recount.
⁷ Neither sacrifice nor offering did You desire,
but receptive ears You opened for me;

This is the meaning of the verse, *Many things You Yourself have done HASHEM, my God* (singular), *Your wondrous works and Your thoughts are for us* (plural).

David did not say *for me*, he said *for us*: Rechavam was sitting in David's lap and the grandfather told his young grandson 'These verses [permitting the females] were said for the benefit of us both.'

אֵין עֲרֹךְ אֵלֶיךָ — *None can compare with You.*

No king or savior can match Your deeds *(Rashi)*. Similarly we find: *There is none like You among the gods, my Lord, and there is nothing to match Your deeds* (86:8).

Or, עֲרֹךְ can mean *to account*. No one can adequately attribute אֵלֶיךָ, *to You* all of Your miracles because they are innumerable *(Radak)*.

Or, עֲרֹךְ can be rendered *value*: To the human who beholds Your wonders these are deeds of significance. But, *to You* they are of no special '*value*', for You control the natural and the supernatural with equal facility *(Malbim)*.

אַגִּידָה וַאֲדַבֵּרָה עָצְמוּ מִסַפֵּר — *Can I relate or speak of them? They are too mighty to recount.*

The *Talmud (Berachos* 33b) cautions us not to attempt to recite all of God's praises, for we are limited in what we can express, but the praises of God are infinite *(Alshich)*.

7. זֶבַח וּמִנְחָה לֹא חָפַצְתָּ — *Neither sacrifice nor offering did You desire.*

זֶבַח refers to the שְׁלָמִים i.e. the animal brought as a *peace-sacrifice*. מִנְחָה refers to the *meal-offering* of fine flour mixed with oil *(Radak)*.

Although Your benign attention is permanently riveted upon us, You have no desire for repayment of any sort, not even in the form of sacrifices, because Your sole concern is for our welfare. *(Ibn Ezra; Malbim)*.

HASHEM said: On the day when the Torah was given at Sinai I demonstrated no desire for offerings, as the Prophet says, *For I spoke not to Your fathers, nor commanded them on the day that I brought them out of the land of Egypt, concerning burnt-offerings or sacrifices. But this I commanded them, saying, 'Heed My voice and I will be Your God and You will be My people* (Jeremiah 7:22-23).

Furthermore, when I spoke of sacrifices in the Scriptures, I mentioned the subject only in voluntary terms: *When any man of you shall bring an offering unto HASHEM* [of his own free will] *(Leviticus 1:2)*, but I did not impose them upon you as an obligatory burden. Even the תָּמִיד, *daily* sacrifices and the מוּסָפִין, *additional* sacrifices of the Sabbath and festivals, although obligatory, are merely to cause satisfaction and pleasure to Me and they are a relatively insignificant obligation upon Israel. *(Rashi)*.[1]

אָזְנַיִם כָּרִיתָ לִי — *But receptive ears You opened* [lit. 'You dug'] *for me.*

Ears which were attuned to God were a major factor in the success of the

---

1. *Radak* provides an introduction to the institution of sacrifice:
   God's primary concern was that Israel should obey Him. In the Ten Commandments,

ח וַחֲטָאָה לֹא שָׁאָלְתָּ: אָז אָמַרְתִּי הִנֵּה־
ט בָאתִי בִּמְגִלַּת־סֵפֶר כָּתוּב עָלָי: לַעֲשׂוֹת־

House of David and the lack of such attentive ears brought about the downfall of David's predecessor, King Saul. Samuel the Prophet chastised Saul, the disobedient King who sought to appease God's wrath with sacrifices, הַחֵפֶץ לַה׳ בְּעֹלוֹת וּזְבָחִים כִּשְׁמֹעַ בְּקוֹל ה׳, הִנֵּה שְׁמֹעַ מִזֶּבַח טוֹב לְהַקְשִׁיב מֵחֵלֶב אֵילִים, *Does HASHEM desire offerings and sacrifices as much as He desires the hearkening to the voice of HASHEM? Behold, to heed is better than to sacrifice, to listen attentively surpasses* [offering of] *the fat of rams'* [I Samuel 15:22] *(Radak; Ibn Ezra; Alshich).*

This also alludes to the fact that David's ears were receptive to the rebuke and admonition of the prophet Nathan. God appreciated David's sincere repentance and confession far more than any sacrifice *(Sforno).*

The *Zohar* notes that David achieved the highest level of atonement when his ears heard the curses of Shimi ben Gera and he accepted his insulting words with the utmost humility and contrition. David could have easily silenced the vile Shimi by allowing his eager bodyguards to slay him as they considered themselves duty-bound to do. Yet he displayed enormous restraint and listened attentively. David attributes to his Maker this ability to listen humbly, for God created him with a nature so receptive to rebuke *(Chazah Zion).*

עֹלָה וַחֲטָאָה לֹא שָׁאָלְתָּ—*Burnt- and sin-offerings You did not request.*

The עֹלָה, *burnt offering,* atones for

הִרְהוּרֵי חֵטְא, *sinful thoughts,* and for neglecting the performance of מִצְוֹת עֲשֵׂה, *positive commandments.* The חַטָּאת, *sin-offering,* atones for the commission of unintentional sins provided the sins are so severe that the transgressor would be liable to the penalty of כָּרֵת, *extirpation,* had he committed them intentionally. God would prefer that we transgress no sins at all and hence render needless the entire institution of atonement sacrifices. *(Radak).*

But if one is not careful, he will first neglect a seemingly 'small' mitzvah or contemplate just one sinful thought, for which he should bring an עֹלָה. This negligence will eventually bring him to more serious infractions for which he must sacrifice a חַטָּאת hence the wording of the verse עֹלָה חֲטָאָה *(Chazah Zion).*

8. אָז אָמַרְתִּי הִנֵּה בָאתִי — *Then I said, 'Behold I have come.'*

David speaks on behalf of the collective Israel, saying: *Then,* at the time of מַתַּן תּוֹרָה, *the Giving of the Torah,* we came to You with the tradition of Your divine covenant, and declared, נַעֲשֶׂה וְנִשְׁמָע, *We shall do and we shall listen* [Exodus 24:7] (Rashi, Ibn Ezra). [We fully understood at the very outset of our relationship that Your only wish was that we should obey Your commandments faithfully.]

Then, when You healed my illness, I fully comprehended Your preference for obedience rather than sacrifices *(Radak).*

therefore, there is no mention of service through sacrifice. Only after Israel strayed did God enjoin animal sacrifices, in order to help them onto the road to repentance.

Then He required individual sinners to bring private sacrifices and He obligated the entire congregation to offer up two תָּמִיד, *continual,* sacrifices every day. The purpose of the communal sacrifices was because, after Israel sank to a lower moral level, it became inevitable that in the course of each day there would be many incidents of inadvertent sins. The communal sacrifices atone for all those unrecognized sins [and demonstrate that unless they elevate themselves, Israel will be inextricably mired in sin.]

Burnt-offerings and sin-offerings
You did not request.
⁸ Then I said, Behold I have come!'
In the Scroll of the Book is written of me.

בִּמְגִלַּת סֵפֶר כָּתוּב עָלָי — *In the scroll of the Book it is written about me.*

Our declaration of נַעֲשֶׂה וְנִשְׁמָע is recorded for all time in *the Book* — i.e. the Torah Scroll — as an eternal testimony to Israel's unwavering faith *(Rashi).*

Or: Now that I have completely recovered from my illness, I scrupulously observe every commandment of the Torah, recorded on *the scroll of the book.* This form of dedicated service surpasses all sacrifices *(Radak).*

Ibn Ezra suggests: When David was wracked with pain and sickness he vowed to compose a *new song* to God if he survived *(v. 4).* To make his vow more binding he had his solemn oath recorded on a scroll.

Now, as he sings his *new song* he is fulfilling that obligation which he inscribed in the scroll.

Malbim identifies *the scroll of the* book as the heart of the Jew [of which Scripture says: 'Write it upon the tablet of your heart' *(Proverbs* 3:3, 7:3, *Jeremiah* 17:1)] which has a natural inclination to perform in a moral and righteous manner. Even if God had never demanded of His people any display of appreciation or sacrifice *(v. 7),* the heart of the nation would nevertheless feel that it must do something to cause Him great satisfaction *(v. 9).*

Sforno observes that David is referring to the special Torah Scroll which the king must write for himself. The *Talmud (Sanhedrin* 21b) says that this Sefer Torah was fashioned like an amulet which could conveniently be hung upon the king's right hand so that it would accompany him wherever he went. Thus the king might continually study the word of HASHEM wherever he went and thereby come to fear Him.[1]

1. The commentaries *(Sanhedrin ibid.)* question how a complete Sefer Torah could be made small and light enough to dangle conveniently from the King's arm at all times. Another problem is that the dangling of a Sefer Torah is specifically forbidden by the *halachah* because it is disrespectful. For these reasons, *Rashash (ibid.)* ventures that the king carried a small scroll which contained only a brief synopsis of the 613 commandments. The *Arukh* quotes *Rav Nachshon Gaon* who is of the opinion that this scroll contained only the Ten Commandments which consist of 613 letters. These opinions lend themselves well to *Sforno* who renders our verse as referring to the King's special Sefer Torah described as *the scroll* (synopsis, abridgement, cf. *Gittin* 60a) *of a book* (of the entire Sefer Torah) *written* (especially) *for me* (cf. *Sanhedrin* 21b: *The king must write a Sefer Torah specifically for his own sake).*

Further support for the interpretation that our verse refers to the Sefer Torah may be derived from the fact that this psalm is dedicated to a *new song.* In *Deuteronomy* 31:19 the obligation to write a Sefer Torah is couched in similar terms *And now write for yourselves this 'song'* (cf. *Rambam Hilchos Sefer Torah* 7:1).

These words also allude to David personally. The *Talmud (Yevamos* 77a) mentions that when David was anointed he thought that he had only recently come to God's attention (cf. *footnote v. 6).* David descended from the elder daughter of Lot, the mother of Moab. The daughters of Lot were saved from the holocaust of Sodom only because God wished to assure that David would emanate from their line.

In describing these daughters the Torah uses an extra word *your two daughters* הַנִּמְצָאֹת

רְצוֹנְךָ אֱלֹהַי חָפָצְתִּי וְתוֹרָתְךָ בְּתוֹךְ מֵעָי:
בִּשַׂרְתִּי צֶדֶק | בְּקָהָל רָב הִנֵּה שְׂפָתַי לֹא

---

9. חָפָצְתִּי אֱלֹהַי רְצוֹנְךָ לַעֲשׂוֹת — *To fulfill Your will, my God, have I desired.*

My natural inclination, my genuine desire, is to serve You of my own volition and to bring You pleasure (Malbim).

[This concept that it is a Jew's ingrained desire to fulfill God's will is given halachic application by *Rambam (Hilchos Geirushin* 2:20): 'In a situation where it is incumbent upon a husband to give his wife a bill of divorce, the Jewish court may resort to the exercise of force in order to compel the husband to discharge his obligation. Although in all cases a bill of divorce must be given with the free will and consent of the husband, the coercive method does not detract from the husband's willingness. For, despite his apparent refusal to comply with the law, the husband truly wishes to live like an Israelite and desires to perform the mitzvos and refrain from transgressions. It is merely the perversity of his evil inclination which has overwhelmed the uncooperative husband at this time. The chastisement applied by the court will serve to weaken the grip of his evil in-

clination and when he cries out [while being coerced] 'I consent' then his true self has come to the fore and the Bill of Divorce is considered as one given willingly.]

וְתוֹרָתְךָ בְּתוֹךְ מֵעָי — *And Your Torah is in my innards.*

It is constantly on my mind and it never slips from my attention (Radak).

My will is so inextricably bound up with Yours that I need not search through a scroll of parchment and ink to discover Your wish. I need only scrutinize my own innermost parts, my heart and mind and conscience, and they will inform me of the the Torah's commands (Malbim).

Even that which enters into מֵעָי [lit. *my intestines*] is controlled by Torah legislation. I am careful not to eat forbidden foods or untithed produce (Rashi).

He who desires to gain Torah knowledge must make this his exclusive pursuit. To the extent that he yearns for other pleasures, his desire and capacity for Torah is diminished. In Rabbinic lore, the Torah scholar is described as

---

that are found, this extra word corresponds with the verse מְצָאתִי דָוִד עַבְדִּי בְּשֶׁמֶן קָדְשִׁי מְשַׁחְתִּיו, *I have found My servant David, with My holy oil I anointed him* (89:21).

When David realized this he exclaimed: *Then* [at first] *I said, 'Behold I have come!'* [only recently to God's attention. But I now realize that] *In the scroll of the book* [i.e., the Torah] *it is* [already] *written about me.*

Yalkut Shimoni (Bereishis 41) traces David's roots, to an even earlier book. It is written, *This is the Book of the generations of Adam (Genesis* 5:1). God showed Adam all future generations. He showed the soul of David to Adam, saying 'He is inscribed to live for only three hours.'

Said Adam, 'Sovereign of the Universe, how many years have been alloted to me?'

'One thousand', was the reply.

'Does the heavenly order allow a man to make a gift of his years?'

'Yes', answered God.

'If so, I give seventy of my years to this soul of David!' Adam then took a scroll of parchment and recorded his gift as a binding transaction. He signed his name to it with the signatures of God and the angel Mitatron as witnesses.

Therefore, David sang, 'Behold I have come! [To the world for seventy years, because] *In the scroll of the book* [of the generations of Adam] *it is written about me.'* [See Chapter I of *Overview* to Vol. 1.]

9 *To fulfill Your will, my God, have I desired*
and Your Torah is in my innards.
10 *I proclaimed Your righteousness*
in a vast assembly.
Behold my lips I do not restrain;

one who מִילָא כְּרֵיסוֹ, *has filled up his innards* [*with knowledge*]. The *Midrash*
(quoted in *Tosafos Kesubos* 104a s.v.
לֹא נֶחְנֵתִי) warns, Before you pray that
Torah should enter into your innards,
pray first that delicacies should not
enter into your innards [and distract
you]' (*Chomas Anoch*).

The Sages warn us: Do not say, 'I do
not relish eating pork.' Instead say, 'I
would enjoy eating pork, but what shall
I do, my Creator has prohibited it'
(*Rashi, Leviticus* 20:26). *Harav Gifter*
explains that every God-fearing Jew actually loathes swine meat and finds it
repulsive. Does this revulsion run
counter to the above dictate of the
Sages? No! What the Sages are saying is
this. Do not say that pork is abhorrent
to you for health reasons or because of
gastronomic preferences. Say rather
that if you were permitted to, you
would enjoy this delicacy. Why then do
you not eat pork? Only because you are
a subject of your Creator! However,
now that He has forbidden this food it is
indeed repulsive and loathsome, for its
consumption represents a rebellion
against the revered Master.

[Based on this we can explain this
verse: *To fulfill Your will, HASHEM, is*

my desire. Your will controls my tastes
and appetites, my likes and dislikes to
the point where *Your Torah is in my innards* and influences my gastronomic
preferences.]

10. בְּשַׂרְתִּי צֶדֶק בְּקָהָל רָב — *I proclaimed*
[lit. *heralded (Your) righteousness to a
vast assembly.*

Not only do I fulfill Your commands
which are recorded on *the scroll of the
book*, but I also feel obliged to publicly
announce the many acts of kindness
that You have performed for my benefit
so that the masses will be inspired to
trust You. I call myself a מְבַשֵׂר, *a herald
of news* because I always hasten to inform the public of every new kindness
which You bestow (*Radak*).[1]

Speaking for the entire nation, the
Psalmist says: We, the children of
Israel, announced Your kindness by
singing the Song of the Sea, the Song of
Miriam's Well and the Song of Deborah
(*Rashi*).

הִנֵּה שְׂפָתַי לֹא אֶכְלָא — *Behold, my lips I
do not restrain*

I take advantage of every opportunity
to glorify Your Name in order to attract
the masses towards Your service
(*Sforno*).

1. The *Talmud* (*Eruvin* 63a) relates that as long as David's teacher, Iyra Hayairi was alive,
David himself would not teach a Torah lesson nor issue a halachic decision for this would be
disrespectful to his master as David said, '*In my heart I hid Your sayings so that I should not
sin towards You*' (119:11). But after the passing of his teacher, David opened up the wellsprings of his wisdom as he said, '*I proclaimed righteousness* [I taught new lessons of Torah]
in the vast assembly' [before multitudes of students].

Similarly, *Yalkut Shimoni* 408 asks, 'What type of בְּשׂוֹרָה, *good news* did they need to hear
in the days of David? Were not the years of his reign a semblance of the future reign of the
Messiah when all will be blissful and tranquil? Rather the *news* which David announced was
Torah *news*, for he lectured and expounded before the people such original novellae as had
never before been heard.'

יא אֶכְלָא יהוה אַתָּה יָדָעְתָּ: צִדְקָתְךָ לֹא־
כִסִּיתִי בְּתוֹךְ לִבִּי אֱמוּנָתְךָ וּתְשׁוּעָתְךָ
אָמַרְתִּי לֹא־כִחַדְתִּי חַסְדְּךָ וַאֲמִתְּךָ לְקָהָל
יב רָב: אַתָּה יהוה לֹא־תִכְלָא רַחֲמֶיךָ מִמֶּנִּי
יג חַסְדְּךָ וַאֲמִתְּךָ תָּמִיד יִצְּרוּנִי: כִּי אָפְפוּ־
עָלַי | רָעוֹת עַד־אֵין מִסְפָּר הִשִּׂיגוּנִי
עֲוֹנֹתַי וְלֹא־יָכֹלְתִּי לִרְאוֹת עָצְמוּ
יד מִשַּׂעֲרוֹת רֹאשִׁי וְלִבִּי עֲזָבָנִי: רְצֵה יהוה

11. צִדְקָתְךָ לֹא כִסִּתִי בְּתוֹךְ לִבִּי — *Your righteousness I have not concealed within my heart.*

I do not allow myself to forget it for a moment and I always make it known to others *(Radak)*.

Your righteousness is so evident to all that no man can keep it a secret within his heart as we find, צִדְקָתְךָ כְּהַרְרֵי אֵל, *Your righteousness is like the mighty mountains* [Psalms 36:7] *(Chazah Zion)*.

אֱמוּנָתְךָ וּתְשׁוּעָתְךָ אָמַרְתִּי לֹא כִחַדְתִּי חַסְדְּךָ וַאֲמִתְּךָ לְקָהָל רָב — *Of Your faithfulness and salvation have I spoken; I have not withheld Your kindness and Your truth from* [lit. *to*] *vast assemblies.*

[This verse seems to be a repetition of v. 10, but David adds a new thought. He stresses that he seized every opportunity to expound on the essential topic of faith. Even when the assembly was convened to hear a lecture on a different subject, he would not refrain from directing discussion towards of faith. (See *Rambam, Berachos* 9:5.)

12. אַתָּה ה׳ — *You HASHEM.*

You, Yourself, not Your agent or messenger *(Tehillos Hashem)*.

לֹא תִכְלָא רַחֲמֶיךָ מִמֶּנִּי — *Withold not Your mercy from me.*

David reasoned that since *I do not hold back my lips* [from announcing Your righteousness] *(v. 10)*, therefore I

deserve that You, too, should not withhold Your compassion from me *(Norah Tehillos)*.

Furthermore, the *Talmud (Shabbos 151b)* states: Whoever has compassion for others will be treated with compassion by God. Therefore David asks to be inspired with a sense of compassion for his fellow man so that he will merit God's compassion *(Ohel Yaakov)*.

חַסְדְּךָ וַאֲמִתְּךָ תָּמִיד יִצְּרוּנִי — [May] *Your kindness and Your truth always protect me*

I am protected by the fact that *I have not refrained from telling of Your kindness and Your truth to vast assemblies* [v.11] *(Ibn Ezra)*.

13. אָפְפוּ — *Encircled.*
[See *commentary* to 18:5.]

רָעוֹת עַד אֵין מִסְפָּר — *Evils without number.*

The course of normal, everyday living is strewn with countless pitfalls and potential causes of injury. Yet, somehow man navigates each day unscathed. This is due to his merits which insulate him from lurking danger. But sin can remove the protective shield of merit. When that occurs the sinner will immediately be beset by the *evils without number* which had always encircled him, but had been hitherto held at bay *(Radak)*.

11-13   ¹¹ *Your righteousness I have not concealed*
                within my heart,
        Of Your faithfulness and Your salvation
                have I spoken;
        I have not withheld Your kindness and Your truth
                from the vast assembly.
        ¹² *You, HASHEM—withhold not Your mercy from me;*
                may Your kindness and Your truth
                always protect me.
        ¹³ *For evils without number encircled me,*
                my sins had overtaken me, and I could not see;
        They were more than the hairs on my head
                and my heart failed me.

הֵשִׂיגוּנִי עֲוֹנֹתַי — *My sins had overtaken
me.*

I am beset by innumerable evils
because my wicked past has finally
overtaken me *(Radak).*

Not only the sin is called עָוֹן, but its
punishment as well, as Cain said, גָּדוֹל
עֲוֹנִי מִנְּשֹׂא, *My punishment is greater
than I can bear* [Genesis 4:13] *(Ibn
Ezra).*

וְלֹא יָכֹלְתִּי לִרְאוֹת — *And I could not see.*

Midrash Shmuel explains that if a
person is beset with pain and affliction
he should take note of the specific organ
which is affected to determine whether
he has sinned with that particular limb.
Ordinarily such scrutiny will reveal the
source of the pain, because God punishes measure for measure. Here the
Psalmist bemoans the fact that he is
overwhelmed by such an onslaught of
pain in all of his limbs that he cannot
possibly scrutinize each one minutely to
discover each particular shortcoming
Dorash Moshe).

עָצְמוּ מִשַּׂעֲרוֹת רֹאשִׁי—*They were more
than the hairs of my head.*

The *Talmud (Succah* 51a) states that
the righteous refrain from sin because
they realize the gravity of transgression.
To them the evil inclination which attempts to persuade them to transgress
appears to be a great mountain, i.e., a
formidable force to be reckoned with.
The wicked, however, take sin lightly
and consider it to be a minor, trivial
matter. They visualize the evil inclination as a flimsy hair with which they
need not bother to contend.

Therefore, the Psalmist who laments
his many sins attributes them to his
failure to treat the specter of sin with
due seriousness. Now these individual
sins which he once considered to be
more worthy of note than *the hairs of
my head,* have become too numerous to
count *(Dorash Moshe).*

וְלִבִּי עֲזָבָנִי — *And my heart failed* [lit.
forsaken] me.

I have been deprived of my peace of
mind, hence I can no longer properly
concentrate on my Torah studies
(Sforno).

טו לְהַצִּילֵנִי יהוה לְעֶזְרָתִי חוּשָׁה: יֵבֹשׁוּ
וְיַחְפְּרוּ| יַחַד מְבַקְשֵׁי נַפְשִׁי לִסְפּוֹתָהּ
טז יִסֹּגוּ אָחוֹר וְיִכָּלְמוּ חֲפֵצֵי רָעָתִי: יָשֹׁמּוּ
עַל־עֵקֶב בָּשְׁתָּם הָאֹמְרִים לִי הֶאָח| הֶאָח:
יז יָשִׂישׂוּ וְיִשְׂמְחוּ| בְּךָ כָּל־מְבַקְשֶׁיךָ יֹאמְרוּ
יח תָמִיד יִגְדַּל יהוה אֹהֲבֵי תְּשׁוּעָתֶךָ: וַאֲנִי|
עָנִי וְאֶבְיוֹן אֲדֹנָי יַחֲשָׁב לִי עֶזְרָתִי
וּמְפַלְטִי אַתָּה אֱלֹהַי אַל־תְּאַחַר:

14. רְצֵה ה׳ לְהַצִּילֵנִי — *Will it, HASHEM, to rescue me.*

Spare me from illness and injury (*Radak*), from my enemies (*Alshich*), and from the evil inclination which blinds me (*Rav Yeibi*).

ה׳ לְעֶזְרָתִי חוּשָׁה — *HASHEM, to my assistance hasten.*

Help me to comprehend the words of Your Torah (*Sforno*).

15. מְבַקְשֵׁי נַפְשִׁי — *Those who seek my life* [lit. *soul*].

This refers to the evil inclination which wishes to destroy my holy spirit (*Alshich*).

Or: these are the shameless enemies who pursue me openly. Let them be put to shame openly (*Malbim*).

לִסְפּוֹתָהּ — *To put an end to it* [i.e., they seek to put an end to my life].

To make it cease to exist, as in עַד תֹּם כָּל הַדּוֹר, *until the entire generation ceases to be* (Deuteronomy 2:14) which Onkelos renders עַד דְּסָף כָּל דָּרָא (*Rashi*).

חֲפֵצֵי רָעָתִי — *Those who wish me evil.*

These are my hidden enemies who as yet have not dared to show their true wickedness. I pray that יִסֹּגוּ אָחוֹר, *let them fall* (be held) *back*, so that they should never be able to attack me (*Malbim*).

16. יָשֹׁמּוּ — *Let them be astounded.*

The translation follows *Rashi*. However, *Radak* and *Metzudas Zion* render *desolate*, from שִׁמָּמוֹן, *desolation.*

עַל עֵקֶב בָּשְׁתָּם — *By their deserved shame* [lit. *on the heel of their shame.*]

The shame which stuns and bewilders them should come as no surprise. It follows on the heels of their wicked ways, and they receive only what they justly deserve, measure for measure (*Rashi*).

Radak maintains that the word עֵקֶב itself may be translated as *reward*, as we read וְהָיָה עֵקֶב תִּשְׁמְעוּן, *And it shall come to pass as a reward if you listen* (Deut. 7:12).

הֶאָח הֶאָח — *Aha! Aha!*

These are the exclamations of my enemies who gloat with merriment over my misfortune (*Sforno*).

Similarly, we read, וַיַּרְחִיבוּ עָלַי פִּיהֶם אָמְרוּ הֶאָח הֶאָח רָאֲתָה עֵינֵנוּ, *They opened their mouths wide against me, they said, 'Aha! Aha! Our eyes have seen!'* [35:21] (*Malbim*).

17. יָשִׂישׂוּ וְיִשְׂמְחוּ בְּךָ כָּל מְבַקְשֶׁיךָ — *Let them rejoice and be glad in You, all who seek You.*

It was only to accomplish this that I took the pains to *proclaim Your righteousness in the vast assembly*[v. 10] (*Ibn Ezra*).

Those who seek worldly fortunes are

¹⁴ *Will it, HASHEM, to rescue me;*
HASHEM, to my assistance, hasten.
¹⁵ *Let them be put to shame and disgrace,*
those who seek my life, to put an end to it.
Let them fall back and be humiliated,
those who wish me evil.
¹⁶ *Let them be astounded by their deserved shame,*
those who say to me 'Aha! Aha!'
¹⁷ *Let them rejoice and be glad in You,*
all who seek You.
Let the always say, 'HASHEM be magnified!'
those who love Your salvation.
¹⁸ *As for me, I am poor and needy.*
My Lord think of me, You are my assistance
and He who causes my escape.
My God — do not delay.

worried until they actually find the object of their search. Not so the man who seeks God. His quest is not merely a means to an end, it is an end in itself, and so even while he still seeks he is glad (*Malbim*).

יֹאמְרוּ תָמִיד יִגְדַּל ה׳ אֹהֲבֵי תְּשׁוּעָתֶךָ — *Let them always say 'HASHEM be magnified!' — those who love your salvation.*

May ה׳, the *Attribute of Mercy*, be greater than the *Attribute of Strict Justice* (*Sforno*).

Those who truly love HASHEM do not mind the advent of misfortune, for it provides them with an opportunity to seek out God's mercy and to witness His salvation; an event which inevitably adds to God's prestige and magnifies His Name (*Malbim*).

Rabbeinu Bachya to Numbers 14:17 (see also 70:5 and 35:27) comments: The potency of God's benevolence in this world depends on Israel. If they are faithful in obeying His commands, they give Him the power, so to speak, to shower an abundance of good upon them. Conversely, when Israel sins, they weaken God's power to be magnanimous. After Israel flagrantly disobeyed God by ignoring His words and believing the spies who slandered Eretz Yisrael, God disassociated Himself from them. Therefore Moses exerted himself to induce God to increase His influence in this world saying, *And now, may the strength of my Lord be magnified.* This was also David's intention when he prayed, *May all those who desire Your salvation continually say, 'HASHEM be magnified'..*

18. וַאֲנִי עָנִי וְאֶבְיוֹן — *As for me, I am poor and needy.*

Throughout the Book of *Psalms,* the expression *poor and needy* refers to the nation of Israel (*Rashi*).

אֲדֹנָי יַחֲשָׁב לִי — *My Lord think of me.*

Let Him be cognizant of me, to be aware of my poverty (*Rashi*).

Also, יַחֲשָׁב can be translated *reckon,*

account i.e., 'May my Lord reckon my poverty as an atonement for my sins'. Or, יַחֲשָׁב may be related to חָשׁוּב, *worthy, important* i.e., 'May I be considered worthy in the eyes of my Lord' (*Radak*).

עֶזְרָתִי וּמְפַלְטִי אַתָּה אֱלֹהַי אַל תְּאַחַר — *You are my assistance and He who causes my escape. My God — do not delay.*

David said: 'Sovereign of the Universe! Pay attention to my poverty and need and hasten to my assistance, because You alone are my helper and rescuer. Eventually it is You who must redeem me; sooner or later, today or tomorrow! So why tarry? Do it now! (*Midrash Shocher Tov*).

With this chapter David closes the series of psalms in which he expresses gratitude to God for having healed him. He dedicates this work to the Lord 'Who cares wisely for the sick'.

A human physician confines his diagnosis to physical symptoms. God alone has the understanding to detect the deeper spiritual deficiency which saps the sinner's vitality. Sickness is inflicted upon a person to make him aware of God's displeasure with his moral shortcomings.

Rabbeinu Yonah (Shaarei Teshuvah 2:3, 4:1) sets forth this principle: 'Just as the body is susceptible to sickness, so is the soul. The illness afflicting the soul stems from its evil traits and its sins. God heals the soul through the ailments of the body as David said, HASHEM, show me favor, heal my soul for I have sinned against You (41:5).

David was particularly upset because his illness prevented him from realizing the great ambition of his life — the construction of the Temple (see comm. to v. 11).

God cured the ailing king, allowing him the privilege of preparing the plans and materials for Solomon's construction of the Temple. This was the pinnacle of David's career, therefore, this psalm comes as the climax and conclusion of the First Book of Psalms, his first compilation of God's praises.

[A close study of Psalm 30 is invaluable to the full appreciation of this psalm, since both works discuss David's return to health which allowed him to prepare for the construction of the Temple.]

אׁ-ב לַמְנַצֵּחַ מִזְמוֹר לְדָוִד: אַשְׁרֵי מַשְׂכִּיל אֶל-
ג דָּל בְּיוֹם רָעָה יְמַלְּטֵהוּ יְהוָה: יְהוָה |
°וְאַשֵּׁר ק' יִשְׁמְרֵהוּ וִיחַיֵּהוּ °יֻאַשַּׁר בָּאָרֶץ וְאַל-
ד תִּתְּנֵהוּ בְּנֶפֶשׁ אֹיְבָיו: יְהוָה יִסְעָדֶנּוּ עַל-

2. מַשְׂכִּיל אֶל דָּל — *He who cares wisely* [lit. *acts wisely*] *for the sick.*

The verse praises one who shows wise concern by visiting the sick. The word דָּל, to refer to a patient, is used similarly in the verse מַדּוּעַ אַתָּה כָּכָה דַּל בֶּן הַמֶּלֶךְ, *Why are you so sickly, O son of the king? (II Samuel 13:4).* דַּל literally means *lean.* It is used to describe the sick man who is usually thin and wasted away *(Rashi).*

[David, the bed-ridden patient who cannot stand, is called דַּל. Therefore in 30:2, when praising God for curing him, he used the words כִּי דִלִּיתָנִי, *for You have elevated me from the lowly status of the* דַּל (cf. comm. v. 1 ibid. and Ibn Ezra v. 2 ibid.).]

In the context of this verse, מַשְׂכִּיל refers to one who closely observes the condition of a sick man to have an understanding of his needs *(Radak; Ibn Ezra).*

[דַּל, also means *impoverished.* The theme of this verse is not limited to caring for the sick. It covers the broad spectrum of philanthropic activities for those in need.]

Rambam lists seven levels in the performance of charity, the very best way being to offer the poor man a loan so that he can help himself and save his dignity. The מַשְׂכִּיל, by planning his benevolence with intelligence and understanding, will see to it that his charity is provided in the fashion best suited to the circumstances *(Dorash Moshe).*

In this sense, מַשְׂכִּיל can also mean *to teach intelligence* i.e. to help the poor man understand the reason for his poverty or to comfort the sick man with an explanation of the causes of his ailment *(Ibn Ezra).*

The poor man can be made aware that his poverty is in punishment for a shortcoming such as treating food disrespectfully, or neglecting to wash his hands before meals *(Yoseif Tehillos).*

Furthermore, the considerate person will try to make the patient understand that the affliction of poverty is for his good because it serves to purge him of his sins and saves him from worse punishments *(Tehillos Hashem).*[1]

Malbim translates מַשְׂכִּיל אֶל דָּל, as 'he who learns from the poor (or sick)'. This means that the intelligent person will notice the miraculous care which God provides for the pauper who has no tangible means of support, yet survives through God's mercy and constant intervention.

בְּיוֹם רָעָה יְמַלְּטֵהוּ ה' — *On the day of disaster HASHEM will surely cause him to flee.*

1. Fortunate is the man who withstands his personal test, for there is no creature whom God does not test. God tests the rich man to see if his hands will open generously to the poor. He tests the poor man to see if he will bear his afflictions patiently without complaining against God's ways. If the rich man succeeds in his examination he will enjoy the fruits of wealth in This World and its principle will be conserved for his enjoyment in the Hereafter. Furthermore, he will be saved from the terrible fury of Gehinnom, as it says, *Praiseworthy is he who cares wisely for the poor, on the day of disaster HASHEM will surely cause him to flee.* But if the rich man fails his test, his wealth will vanish, while the possessions of the pauper who bears his poverty with patience, will double *(Midrash Shemos Rabbah 31:3).*

For the Conductor, a song unto David.
² Praiseworthy is he
who cares wisely for the sick,
On the day of disaster
HASHEM will surely cause him to flee.
³ HASHEM will preserve him
and keep him alive.
He will be made praiseworthy on earth,
and He will not present him to the will of his foes.
⁴ HASHEM will fortify him on his bed of misery;

This can be interpreted as a declarative statement in reference to the sick patient, emphasizing that when the illness reaches a crisis point, only God can provide a cure and all the ministrations of the physicians are futile (*Radak*). Or it can be understood as a prayer and a word of comfort which the visitor offers at the bedside of the invalid, fortifying the sick man's confidence with the assurance that God's aid is close at hand (*Radak* quoting his father).

Sforno interprets it as a promise of future reward to the person who attends to the sick and poor.

[Reb Shrage Feivel Mendelowitz ל"ז would encourage his students to make sacrifices for charity not only when they prospered, but even more so when foundering in dire financial straits. He based this on his unique interpretation of this verse, *Praiseworthy is he who cares wisely for the poor*, בְּיוֹם רָעָה, *on the day of his* [i.e., the philanthropist's] *personal financial disaster*. In reward, God will surely deliver the generous benefactor from evil.]

3. ה' יִשְׁמְרֵהוּ וִיחַיֵּהוּ — *HASHEM will preserve and keep him alive.*

According to *Rashi* and *Sforno*, this refers to the life of the benefactor who is promised life and security as his reward for nursing another.

Since a poor man is considered as if he were dead (*Nedarim* 65a), one who assists him back to financial health and 'life' is repaid (measure for measure) with life (*Yoseif Tehillos*).[1]

וְאֻשַּׁר בָּאָרֶץ — *He will be made praiseworthy on earth.*

God will provide the pauper with sustenance in his own locality and he will not be forced to wander to distant lands to earn his livelihood (*Malbim*). [See *comm.* to 37:3.]

He will have the good fortune to outlive his contemporaries and so his enemies will never have the pleasure of seeing him die (*Ibn Ezra*).

4. ה' יִסְעָדֶנּוּ — *HASHEM will fortify him.*

The *Talmud* (*Shabbos* 12b) derives from this verse that God supplies the invalid with strength and nutrition.

1. Not only will the philanthropist's life be preserved, it will also be prolonged. The *Talmud* (*Bava Basra* 11a) tells the story of Binyamin HaTzaddik who single-handedly supported a mother and her seven sons in the years of famine. Once, when he was sick and on the verge of death, the ministering angels came before God to plead his cause. 'Sovereign of the Universe, did You not say that whoever preserves even one Jewish life is as if he preserved the entire world? Shall this man who kept alive a mother and seven sons die so young?' Immediately his death sentence was torn to pieces and twenty-two years were added to his life.

ה עֶרֶשׂ דְּוָי כָּל־מִשְׁכָּבוֹ הָפַכְתָּ בְחָלְיוֹ: אֲנִי־
אָמַרְתִּי יהוה חָנֵּנִי רְפָאָה נַפְשִׁי כִּי־
ו חָטָאתִי לָךְ: אוֹיְבַי יֹאמְרוּ רַע לִי מָתַי
ז יָמוּת וְאָבַד שְׁמוֹ: וְאִם־בָּא לִרְאוֹת שָׁוְא
יְדַבֵּר לִבּוֹ יִקְבָּץ־אָוֶן לוֹ יֵצֵא לַחוּץ יְדַבֵּר:
ח יַחַד עָלַי יִתְלַחֲשׁוּ כָּל־שֹׂנְאָי עָלַי | יַחְשְׁבוּ

Consequently, we know that the שְׁכִינָה, Divine Presence, rests at the head of every sick man. Therefore, the visitor should not sit on the sick man's bed [for in doing so he would be acting irreverently towards the *Shechinah* which rests on the bed].

עַל עֶרֶשׂ דְּוָי — *On his bed of misery.*

This refers specifically to the seventh day of the illness when the patient is especially miserable (*Rashi* from *Midrash Shocher Tov*). According to *Tanchuma*, the crisis point is the fourth day.

כָּל מִשְׁכָּבוֹ הָפַכְתָּ בְחָלְיוֹ — *All his restfulness has been upset by his illness.*

This follows *Rashi* and *Radak* who interprets חָלְיוֹ as the severe stage of *his illness*, and מִשְׁכָּבוֹ as *his restfulness*.

Radak offers another interpretation: Despite the severity of the illness, You have given him the power to turn from side to side on his bed.

Malbim notes that the invalid usually soils his bedding and so it must frequently be changed and *turned over*. God sees to it that the patient is attended to and that this vital service is performed.

5. אֲנִי אָמַרְתִּי ה' חָנֵּנִי — *As for me, I said: 'O HASHEM show me favor.'*

Until now the well-meaning visitor has been speaking. Now begin the words of the sick man who seeks help only from God (*Radak*).

The forsaken patient laments: 'As for me personally, no one ever came to visit me with helpful intentions. All I can do is call to HASHEM for help' (*Rashi*).

רְפָאָה נַפְשִׁי כִּי חָטָאתִי לָךְ — *Heal my soul for I have sinned against You.*

He does not ask for his body to be healed, for he realizes that his ailment stems from his sins which are a malady of the soul. If his soul can be cured by receiving divine forgiveness, then the recovery of the body is inevitable (*Radak*).

The soul which has become desecrated by sin has lost its sensitivity to all things sacred and divine. The possessor of this soul loses his awareness of God's presence and is deadened to all experiences of the spirit (*Reishis Chochmah*).

6. אוֹיְבַי יֹאמְרוּ רַע לִי — *My foes, however, speak evil of me.*

The wise, caring person (*v.* 1) blessed me and cared for my needs, but my foes only await my doom (*Radak*).

Midrash Shocher Tov raises a basic question: Did David really have foes? Is it not written: וְכָל יִשְׂרָאֵל וִיהוּדָה אֹהֵב אֶת דָּוִד, *And all of Israel and Judah loved David* (I Samuel 18:16). Who then were his enemies? Only those who wished to cheat and rob, but were prevented from doing so by David — it was they who hated him!

Alshich observes that when God makes the righteous suffer as an atonement for the sins of their generation, their ordeal is not only a shield for their contemporaries whose sins were responsible for these afflictions. It is also a benefit to the righteous for they become instrumental in atoning for so many others. However, this is true only

all his restfulness has been upset by his illness.

⁵ *As for me, I said: 'O HASHEM, show me favor!*
    Heal my soul for I have sinned against You!'
⁶ *My foes speak evil of me:*
    'When will he die and his name perish?'
⁷ *And if one comes to see,*
    insincerely does he speak.
He desires to gather himself malicious information;
    upon going out he reveals it.
⁸ *United against me, all my enemies whisper,*

when the sinners admit their guilt and recognize the great kindness the *tzaddik* does by suffering for them. David laments that his personal suffering will not accomplish this because his wicked contemporaries attribute the evil to his sins, rather than to theirs. Therefore they do not appreciate his sacrifice on their behalf. Furthermore, they would prefer to see him dead.

מָתַי יָמוּת וְאָבַד שְׁמוֹ — *'When will he die and his name perish?'*

When my enemies hear me crying out,'*Show me favor'*, they rejoice over my agony and anxiously look forward to the day when I will perish (*Rashi*).

The Brisker Rav cites numerous verses from *Psalms* to prove that the establishment of the Temple in Jerusalem and the perpetuation of the Davidic dynasty are interdependent. David's enemies rejoice over his illness which prevents the construction of the Temple for they know that in the absence of the Temple, David's name and royal line will sink into oblivion. (See *Pref. Remarks* and *comm. v.* 11).

7. וְאִם בָּא לִרְאוֹת — *And if one comes to see.*

I.e., if one of my enemies comes to visit me in my illness (*Radak*).

He does not come to visit me or care for my needs, he comes merely to observe my misery and gloat over my agony (*Alshich*).

שָׁוְא יְדַבֵּר — *Insincerely does he speak* [lit. *He speaks in vain*].

With his lips he speaks of his concern for my well-being, but in his heart he seeks only my injury (*Radak*).

לִבּוֹ יִקְבָּץ אָוֶן לוֹ — *He* [lit. *his heart*] *desires to gather himself malicious [information]*.

While he speaks sympathetically to me in my sick room, his mind absorbs everything detrimental about me, which he will use against me later (*Rashi; Radak*).

יֵצֵא לַחוּץ יְדַבֵּר — *Upon going out, he reveals it* [lit. *he goes outside and speaks*].

He has filled himself with so many vicious thoughts that he can hardly wait to run outside and blurt out his venom to anyone who will listen (*Alshich*).

This enemy has come as an agent for all of my foes. His mission is to appraise my condition, whether I am about to die or not. Should I appear to be recovering, the spy will call together my enemies to plot my assassination (*Malbim*).

8. יַחַד עָלַי יִתְלַחֲשׁוּ כָּל שֹׂנְאָי — *United against me, all of my enemies whisper.*

This verse continues the thought of the previous one. After my malicious

ט רָעָה לִי: דְּבַר־בְּלִיַּעַל יָצוּק בּוֹ וַאֲשֶׁר
י שָׁכַב לֹא־יוֹסִיף לָקוּם: גַּם־אִישׁ שְׁלוֹמִי |
אֲשֶׁר־בָּטַחְתִּי בוֹ אוֹכֵל לַחְמִי הִגְדִּיל עָלַי
יא עָקֵב: וְאַתָּה יהוה חָנֵּנִי וַהֲקִימֵנִי

---

visitor leaves, he assembles my enemies to hear his evil report (Radak).

Alshich, however, comments that this verse begins a new thought. It discusses a group of vicious visitors who observe all the evil they can and then, while yet in the sickroom, eagerly whisper their evil impressions among themselves, speaking softly so that the patient should not hear.

9. דְּבַר בְּלִיַּעַל יָצוּק בּוֹ — *The result of his lawlessness is poured over him.*

This is what they think and say about me. They claim that my illness is a result of my crimes and sins (Rashi).

בְּלִיַּעַל is a contraction of בְּלִי עוֹל, *without a yoke* [of fear of heaven] (Metzudas Zion).

Yaavetz HaDoresh calls attention to the fact that David tried, sentenced, and executed the evil Naval who is described as בֶּן בְּלִיַּעַל, *a lawless person* (I Samuel 25:17). David's enemies now accuse him of murdering Naval unjustly. They interpret His illness as a sign from heaven, proving that he, David, is the true בְּלִיַּעַל, *lawless person*, and Naval was his innocent victim.

According to *Midrash Shocher Tov*, בְּלִיַּעַל may be understood as בְּלִי עַל, *with nothing upon him*. David's enemies claimed that he was not really ill. He feigned sickness in order to test the reactions of his visitors and discover who were his foes.

Finally, *Malbim* maintains that these words contain the secret of the assass-

ination plot. They plan to use דְּבַר בְּלִיַּעַל, *an evil thing* [poison] which they will יָצוּק בּוֹ, *pour into him.*

וַאֲשֶׁר שָׁכַב לֹא יוֹסִיף לָקוּם — *'And now that he lies ill may he rise no more.'*

May the poison serum accomplish its lethal work, without the interference of any antidote (Malbim).

May David not have the power to stand up to transmit the Temple scroll [see *comm.* to v. 11] (Brisker Rav).

10. גַּם אִישׁ שְׁלוֹמִי אֲשֶׁר בָּטַחְתִּי בוֹ — *Even my ally* [lit. *man of my peace*] *in whom I trusted.*

The invalid laments that in his hour of distress not only do his enemies attack him, but even his trusted friends betray him (Radak).

I cannot trust my most faithful servants to reveal to me the plot of my enemies, for all have abandoned my cause (Malbim).

אוֹכֵל לַחְמִי — *Who ate my bread.*

[Even more painful is the ingratitude of the person upon whom I have lavished so much kindness. Now he bites the hand which fed him].

My most trusted servant, the attendant who tastes my food before I eat it, even he cannot be trusted to warn me of the poison put into my meal (Malbim).[1]

הִגְדִּיל עָלַי עָקֵב — *Develops* [lit. *makes large*] *an ambush against me.*

This translation of עָקֵב follows

---

1. Rabbi Yochanan said: At first David referred to Achitophel as his master, for he had learned Torah from him. Later, after Achitophel began to sin and fall, David referred to him merely as his colleague. Finally, when Achitohel lost all of his status, David called him *my disciple*, as we learn from the verse *Even my ally, in whom I trusted* [Achitophel] *and who ate my bread*, [who partook of my Torah knowledge *(Rashi)*] *even* [this student] *develops an ambush against me (Sanhedrin* 106b).

against me they devise my harm.

⁹ *'The result of his lawlessness is poured over him —*
and now that he lies ill, may he rise no more!'

¹⁰ *Even my ally in whom I trusted, who ate my bread —*
develops an ambush against me.

¹¹ *But as for You, HASHEM, show me favor*
and raise me up —
then I shall repay them.

Rashi who bases his opinion on the verse in *Joshua* 8:13: וְאֶת עֲקֵבוֹ מִיָּם לָעִיר, *And his ambush was from the west of the city. Radak*, however, renders this phrase literally: *He raised his heel high above me* to trample me.

According to *Ibn Ezra* David bemoans the fact that his friends did not visit him at all in his sickness. Rather, they turned their heels away from his house and in their pride they held themselves aloof from him.

11. וְאַתָּה ה' חָנֵּנִי וַהֲקִימֵנִי — *But as for You HASHEM, show me favor and raise me up.*

They claim that I will not arise from my illness (v. 9), therefore I ask that You refute their claims by raising me up (*Radak*).

[With these words David expresses the true cause of his distress, God's unwillingness to permit him to construct the Temple. The following *Midrashim* elaborate on this theme.]

The Holy One, Blessed be He, transmitted to Moses the מְגִילַת בֵּית הַמִּקְדָּשׁ, *Scroll of the Beis Hamikdash*, [which described the Temple in detail and revealed its many secrets].

Moses received the scroll while standing. He stood up and gave it over to Joshua who was standing. [Because of the great holiness of the document, both parties engaged in its transmission were required to stand, as a sign of reverence and awe.] Joshua stood up and gave it to the elders as they stood.

The elders gave it to the prophets as they stood. The prophets [specifically Samuel] gave it to David as he stood. But when David fell sick he could not stand up to transmit it. He prayed, *But as for You, HASHEM, show me favor and raise me up* in order that I may transmit it to them in its entirety [וַאֲשַׁלְּמָה לָהֶם is derived from לְהַשְׁלִים, *to complete.*]

God heard his plea, *And King David stood up on his feet* (I Chronicles 28:2). At that time he transmitted the scroll to Solomon (*Midrash Samuel* Ch. 15; *Aggadas Bereishis* ch. 38; *Yalkut Shimoni, Chronicles*, 1081).

וַאֲשַׁלְּמָה לָהֶם — *Then I shall repay them.*

Radak observes that David threatened to repay their evil measure for measure. He awaits the moment of their sickness when he will hurt them by showing no concern for their misery.

Many commentators are troubled by this uncharacteristic and inappropriate vengefulness. However, *Sforno* explains, that as king, David was required to act in this unforgiving fashion. The *Talmud* (*Yoma* 22b) severely criticizes David's predecessor, King Saul, for being unconcerned over the preservation of his honor, as Scripture testifies, *And they degraded him and brought him no gifts, but he made himself mute* (I Samuel 10:27). [This was one of the reasons why Saul was eventually removed from the throne, for a king's dignity is not his personal concern, but

יב וָאֲשַׁלְּמָה לָהֶם: בְּזֹאת יָדַעְתִּי כִּי־חָפַצְתָּ

יג בִּי כִּי לֹא־יָרִיעַ אֹיְבִי עָלָי: וַאֲנִי בְּתֻמִּי

יד תָּמַכְתָּ בִּי וַתַּצִּיבֵנִי לְפָנֶיךָ לְעוֹלָם: בָּרוּךְ
יהוה | אֱלֹהֵי יִשְׂרָאֵל מֵהָעוֹלָם וְעַד־
הָעוֹלָם אָמֵן | וְאָמֵן:

a reflection of the national honor.]

Radak quotes *Rav Saadya Gaon* who interprets David's vow to repay his enemies in a merciful light. Indeed David vows to reciprocate their animosity — but not with vengeance. He pledges to pay them with kindness and charity [which will change their malicious attitude toward him]. This was typical of David's generous spirit.

This view is supported by *Midrash Shocher Tov*: God asked David, 'With what do you wish Me to repay them, with evil?' 'Heaven forbid' David replied. 'Is it not true that *when they* (my enemies) *were sick my clothing was sackcloth?* (35:13). Despite the fact that when I was sick they prayed that I perish, I fervently pleaded for their recovery. Furthermore, *I afflicted myself with fasting (ibid.)*. And lest someone suspect that I was insincere and really prayed for their injury, then *As for my prayer, upon my own bosom let it return (ibid.)*, and let that harm come upon me.' Therefore, David prayed here, HASHEM *show me favor and raise me up* [for if I fall they will interpret this as a sign that I did not pray on their behalf].

Finally, *Shaarei Chaim* suggests the following interpretation of David's request. As we have commented on the verse: *Many are the pains of the wicked* (32:10), the most intense and annoying pain is experienced by the wicked man who sees the success of *one who trusts in* HASHEM (ibid.).

Similarly, David asks here, HASHEM *show me favor and raise me up*, and this display of my good fortune will frustrate my enemy so greatly that in this fashion *I shall repay them*.

12. בְּזֹאת יָדַעְתִּי כִּי חָפַצְתָּ בִּי — *By this shall I know that You are pleased with me.*

When You will lift me from my sick-bed and will not allow my enemies to triumph over me (*Rashi*).

Midrash Shocher Tov continues (see v. 11): God said to David, 'Since you do not desire revenge against your enemies, your generosity of spirit is a sign *by which I know that you are pleased with Me* and that you truly desire to follow in My merciful ways.

כִּי לֹא יָרִיעַ אֹיְבִי עָלָי — *That You will not let my foe applaud* [lit. *shout triumphantly*] *over me.*

You will not allow him to rejoice while he casts derision against me with arrogant words of scorn (*Radak*).

Sforno explains: Although David did not win every battle in his long military career, he was never defeated so decisively that his enemies could blow their trumpets triumphantly to applaud his defeat.

13. וַאֲנִי בְּתֻמִּי תָּמַכְתָּ בִּי — *Because of my integrity You have supported me.*

After You found my integrity and faith to be flawless *You supported me* to help me rise from my sick-bed (*Radak*).

I fulfilled the dictates of the Torah which is perfect (19:8) and I asked יְהִי לִבִּי תָמִים בְּחֻקֶּיךָ, *Let my heart be perfect in fulfilling Your statutes* [119:80] (*Midrash Shocher Tov*).

[Similarly, David said וַאֲנִי בְּתֻמִּי אֵלֵךְ, *As for me, I go in my perfect*

XLI
12-14

¹² *By this shall I know that You are pleased with me;*
that You will not let my foe applaud over me.
¹³ *Because of my integrity You have supported me,*
and let me stand erect before You forever.
¹⁴ *Blessed be HASHEM, the God of Israel,*
from This World to the World to Come,
Amen and Amen!

---

innocence, redeem me and show me favor (26:11).]

The man who studies religion philosophically admits to faith only because it appeals to his personal logic and mentality. Therefore his 'faith' is a mere delusion, for essentially he worships only his own intellect! It stands to reason that since he believes only in himself, he must help himself. But the perfectly innnocent believer who trusts in God with simple, unquestioning faith, certainly deserves divine support, for God alone is the pillar of his existence *(Shaarei Chaim).*

וַתַּצִּיבֵנִי לְפָנֶיךָ לְעוֹלָם — *And let me stand erect before You forever.*

לְעוֹלָם, *forever,* refers to the full term of a normal human lifetime. The sick man asks to live out all of his days fortified with divine support *(Radak).*

You gave me the strength to stand erect while transmitting the scroll of the Beis HaMikdash *(Brisker Rav).*

[The word לְעוֹלָם alludes to the Temple. The *Noda B'Yehuda* (II *Orach Chaim* 87) cites many sources to prove that whenever Scripture uses the phrase חֻקַּת עוֹלָם it should not be translated as *An eternal statute* but rather as, *A*

statute for the Eternal House, meaning the Temple.]

14. בָּרוּךְ ה' אֱלֹהֵי יִשְׂרָאֵל — *Blessed be HASHEM, the God of Israel.*

The invalid vows to bless God in these terms when he arises from his sickbed *(Rashi).*

With this verse David concludes the first of the five Books of *Psalms.* Therefore he offers thanks to the Lord for providing him with the inspiration and strength to accomplish this great undertaking *(Metzudas David; Ibn Yachya, Yaavetz Hadoresh).*

Furthermore, David prays that all of the praises and blessings which he included in this Book should reverberate from the lips of all Israel from now until the Hereafter *(Malbim).*

מֵהָעוֹלָם וְעַד הָעוֹלָם — *From This World to the World to Come.*

From the beginning of time until the very end of time *(Radak).*

Hashem, who is only God of Israel in This World is destined to be acknowledged and blessed by all mankind in the World to Come *(Zera Yaakov).*[1]

אָמֵן וְאָמֵן — *Amen and Amen!*

[אָמֵן is derived from the word אֱמוּנָה,

---

1. *Rashi* (*Berachos* 63a, s.v. וְיְבָרְכוּ שֵׁם כְּבוֹדֶךָ) quotes the *Tosefta* which explains: This phrase is a proclamation that This World is merely a פְּרוֹזְדוֹר, *corridor,* leading to the טְרַקְלִין, *main chamber,* which is the World to Come. Therefore, practice and accustom yourself to recite God's praises in this temporary world so that you will be prepared to praise Him eternally in the permanent world which has no end! [The entirety of our brief earthly sojourn is no more than a preparation for the meaningful life of the Hereafter. The perfection of our existence there depends on the quality of our preparations here.]

Rabbi Chaim of Volozhin, in a gloss to *Nefesh haChaim* 1:6, explains that the Temple is the point where the two worlds meet. Since the Divine Presence dwells there, this world of matter

faith. By saying *Amen*, one declares, 'I firmly believe all of the aforementioned to be true.']

From the repetitive *Amen* of our verse, Rabbi Yehuda derives: Whoever answers *Amen* in This World will be privileged to answer *Amen* in the World to Come! *(Midrash Tanchuma).*

[Similarly, the *Talmud (Berachos* 4b) promises, Whoever recites תְּהִלָּה לְדָוִד, *the Hymn of David,* three times a day in This World will certainly merit a place in the World to Come. For the Hereafter is an endless hymn dedicated to our Maker, and the *Psalms of David* are the text of that eternal hymn.]

and the future world of the spirit blend there and become one. For that reason one of the benedictions recited during the service in the First Temple concluded with the words בָּרוּךְ ה׳ אֱלֹהֵי יִשְׂרָאֵל עַד הָעוֹלָם, *Blessed be HASHEM, the God of Israel until* [the End of] *the World* [singular]. This alluded to the above-mentioned fusion of both worlds in the Temple.

Second Book / ספר שני

מזמור מב 42

Ten men contributed songs to the Book of Psalms: Adam, Malchizedek, Abraham, Moses, Heiman, Yedusun, Assaf and the three sons of Korach (Rashi, Psalms 1:1). The entire First Book of Tehillim (Psalms 1-41) is attributed to David. The Second Book of Tehillim begins with a series of eight psalms (42:49) ascribed to the sons of Korach. In the Third Book of Tehillim, another four psalms (84, 885, 887, 88) appear in their name. The sons of Korach were Assir, Elkanah and Aviassaf (Exodus 6:24).

Rashi (v. 1) states that Korach's sons initially joined their father's infamous mutiny against Moses and Aaron. In the midst of the rebellion, however, they realized their folly and repented. When the earth opened its mouth to swallow the entire assembly of Korach and to transport them to Gehinnom, God miraculously provided a place of refuge for Korach's three sons. They landed on an elevated niche within the earth, high above the flames of purgatory. It was on that precarious ledge that they composed these psalms.

When they ascended to the earth's surface, a holy spirit descended upon them and they prophesied concerning the exiles of Israel, the destruction of the Temple, and the advent of the Davidic monarchy.

Centuries later the descendants of Korach's sons still retained the divine inspiration created by this miraculous deliverance. Korach's descendants staunchest advocates of that very work of Moses which Korach had planned to destroy by his mutiny. (Hirsch).

According to the Vilna Gaon, this psalm is the Song of the Day for the second day of the Sukkos festival (Maaseh Rav 234). [The שִׂמְחַת בֵּית הַשּׁוֹאֵבָה, The Festival of the Water Drawing, began on this day in the Temple. The eighth verse refers specifically to this celebration; many other references to water-springs and Temple celebrations are found throughout the psalm.]

לַמְנַצֵּחַ מַשְׂכִּיל לִבְנֵי־קֹרַח: כְּאַיָּל תַּעֲרֹג א־ב
עַל־אֲפִיקֵי־מָיִם כֵּן נַפְשִׁי תַעֲרֹג אֵלֶיךָ

1. לַמְנַצֵּחַ מַשְׂכִּיל — *For the conductor, a Maskil* [see *comm.* to 32:1].

This psalm is of such universal significance that it is dedicated as a מַשְׂכִּיל *instruction*, for all to hear (*Hirsch*).

לִבְנֵי קֹרַח — *By the sons of Korach* [See Prefatory Remarks].

The Prophet Samuel was a descendant of Korach. Samuel's grandson was Heiman ben Yoel (I *Chronicles* 6:18) and he had fourteen sons, who were the Levites chosen by David to be the nucleus of the Temple choir and orchestra (I *Chronicles* 25:4-6). *Ibn Ezra*, suggests that they are the *sons of Korach* mentioned throughout the Book of *Psalms*. [See 88:1: — *A song with music ... for the sons of Korach, A Maskil unto Heiman Haezrachi.*]

Radak cites *Ibn Ezra's* opinion and asks why these Levites should identify themselves with the evil Korach when they could trace their genealogy to their illustrious ancestor Samuel the prophet? *Meiri* explains that despite his tragic quarrel with Moses, Korach had been the most distinguished of all the Levites; therefore it was a great honor to be his descendant.

If we assume that these *sons of Korach* were indeed David's contemporaries, it is very possible that they were not the *composers* of these psalms, but merely the performers. Perhaps David himself wrote them and gave them to the *sons of Korach* for inclusion in the Temple service. Some say that David created these psalms while he was a forlorn fugitive in the land of the Philistines [see Prefatory Remarks to Psalm 34]. Others say that he foretold future exiles of the entire Jewish nation. (*Radak*).

In reference to the opinion that בְּנֵי קֹרַח are the actual *sons of Korach* who lived at the time of Moses, *Ibn Yachya*

explains that when David was composing the *Book of Tehillim* he found manuscripts from centuries earlier including the works of the *sons of Korach*. David chose the most appropriate psalms and rewrote them in his own universal style.

Radak raises a question concerning the joint authorship of these psalms: How is it possible that these three men were inspired to say the same words at the same time? *Ibn Yachya* explains that when David found old manuscripts, the individual authors of the respective psalms were not recorded, so David attributed the psalms to Korach's sons as a group. *Midrash Shocher Tov* reveals that when Korach's sons were snatched at the last moment from the flames of Gehinnom, they repented simultaneously with equal fervor and sincerity. Thus united, their hearts were inspired with identical prophecies and psalms.

2. כְּאַיָּל תַּעֲרֹג — *As the hart entreats.*

Rashi notes the grammatical inconsistency in these words: אַיָּל is the male *hart*, but the verb תַּעֲרֹג is feminine.

This intentional discrepancy alludes to the longing cries of both the אַיָּל (male) *hart* and the אַיָּלָה (female) *hind.*

The Rabbis said that the hart is the kindest and most devout of all animals. When the other beasts and animals are thirsty, they gather around the hart, prodding him to supplicate Heaven. The hart then digs a hole in the earth, inserts his horns, and screams in anguish. The Holy One, Blessed be He, takes pity on him and sends water from the תְּהוֹם *the watery deep* [see verse 8].

The hind possesses an anatomical peculiarity. Its womb and birth canal are too small to allow for the birth of its young. During labor the helpless hind cries out in agony. The Holy One, Blessed be He, has mercy on her; he dispatches a snake to bite her in the area of

F or the Conductor,
   a Maskil by the sons of Korach.
² As the hart entreats by the springs of water,
   so does my soul entreat You, O God.

her womb. This sudden stab of pain causes a muscle spasm which opens her womb so that the fawn can emerge safely.

Hirsch observes that the female gender is used to indicate that the hart's thirst has caused him to become extremely weak.

Rashi points out that the verb ערג refers specifically to the unique cry of the hart. The Hebrew language has specific words to describe the sounds peculiar to individual animals; examples include: נהֵם *roar* [lion], שׁוֹקֵק *growl* [bear], גָּעָה *low* [cattle], and צִפְצוּף *chirp* [bird].

Hirsch notes that ערג is used in reference to animals in general in the verse גַּם בַּהֲמוֹת שָׂדֶה תַּעֲרוֹג אֵלֶיךָ כִּי יָבְשׁוּ אֲפִיקֵי מָיִם, *Also, the animals of the field entreat You, for the springs of water have gone dry (Joel 1:20)*. Here too, ערג is the cry of the animal thirsting for water.

Tzofnas Pa'aneach explains that although all creatures long for water, the hart becomes more parched than the others because it dwells in the arid wilderness.

עַל אֲפִיקֵי מָיִם — *By* [lit. *on*] *the springs of water*.

This refers to the springs of water which the thirsty hart digs out with his horns *(Rashi)*.

The root of this word is פוק, *to emerge, to come forth*, which describes the water gushing forth from the ground *(Hirsch)*.

The hart often swallows snakes whose poison causes an intense heat within its stomach. Therefore, it seeks out a spring of water in a desperate attempt to cool off. Some say that the harts are relentlessly pursued by packs of dogs. The pitiful deer run until they find a deep stream of water. They cry out and plunge into the cool water, which refreshes them and provides concealment from the dogs *(Radak)*.

The poisonous snakes which the hart reputedly swallows symbolize the venomous hatred of the gentiles which Israel is forced to 'swallow' and endure in the exile *(Maharam Markado)*.

כֵּן נַפְשִׁי תַעֲרֹג אֵלֶיךָ אֱלֹהִים — *So does my soul entreat You, O God*.

[The sons of Korach were singularly qualified to express such feelings. When they descended toward Gehinnom, they were as alienated from God as man can possibly be. They were truly exiled to the most arid, barren wilderness.]

This psalm echoes the cries of Israel in exile and in captivity. Their yearning for freedom is not prompted by a desire to exercise political power or to take revenge on their enemies. Their sole desire is to refresh themselves in the pure waters of God's Torah *(Mahari Yaavetz Hadoresh)*.

At that same time the soul of Israel will be released from its shackles and will soar heavenward like a gushing geyser *(Hirsch)*.

Although the hart is very thirsty, it unselfishly seeks enough water to quench the thirst of the other animals, as well. Similarly, the exiles of Israel do not seek redemption solely for their own sake. They yearn to bring all of mankind close to God in order to satisfy the universal thirst for the divine *(Alshich)*.

ג אֱלֹהִים: צָמְאָה נַפְשִׁי ׀ לֵאלֹהִים לְאֵל חָי
ד מָתַי אָבוֹא וְאֵרָאֶה פְּנֵי אֱלֹהִים: הָיְתָה־לִּי
דִמְעָתִי לֶחֶם יוֹמָם וָלַיְלָה בֶּאֱמֹר אֵלַי
ה כָּל־הַיּוֹם אַיֵּה אֱלֹהֶיךָ: אֵלֶּה אֶזְכְּרָה ׀
וְאֶשְׁפְּכָה עָלַי ׀ נַפְשִׁי כִּי אֶעֱבֹר ׀ בַּסָּךְ

3. צָמְאָה נַפְשִׁי לֵאלֹהִים — *My soul thirsts for God.*

Israel's craving is described as *thirst* rather than as *hunger*, because water is more essential than food for the maintenance of life. A man can live without food for a few days, but he cannot survive without water. And the soul's thirst for God is even more intense than the body's craving for water (*Radak*).

The perception of God achieved through Torah study is likened to drinking water. As the prophet says: הוֹי כָּל צָמֵא לְכוּ לַמַּיִם, *Ho, every one who thirsts, go to water* (Isaiah 55:1).

The congregation of Israel called out these words during the Babylonian Exile (*Rashi*).

For what do I thirst? Not for food and not for drink — only to see Your face, O God! (*Midrash Shocher Tov*).

I yearn to return to the level of sanctity which I attained at Sinai, when God Himself testified that I [Israel] merited the title אֱלֹהִים: *I said you are* אֱלֹהִים, *angels* [lit. 'gods'] [82:6] (*Pesikta Rabbasi* 1:2).

I yearn to see You exercise Your Divine Attribute of Justice (symbolized by Your Name אֱלֹהִים) against the gentiles on the final day of reckoning (*Pesikta Rabbosi*).

לְאֵל חָי — *For the living God.*

Our soul craves contact with the *Living God* as opposed to the lifeless idols of the surrounding peoples (*Radak; Hirsch*).

Hashem Himself is the source of Israel's vitality, as Scripture testifies: וְאַתֶּם הַדְּבֵקִים בַּה׳ אֱלֹהֵיכֶם חַיִּים כֻּלְּכֶם הַיּוֹם,

But you who cleave unto Hashem your God, are alive all of your today (Deut. 4:4). The yearning for God is as strong as the lust for life itself (*Malbim*).

מָתַי אָבוֹא — *When shall I arrive?*

When shall I ascend to Jerusalem as a pilgrim celebrating the three annual festivals close to God? The Psalmist prophetically foretells the three nations destined to disrupt the Temple service: Babylon, Greece, and Rome. In all three instances, Israel will cry out for salvation and God will respond affirmatively (*Rashi*).

וְאֵרָאֶה פְּנֵי אֱלֹהִים — *And appear before God* [lit. *and be seen before the face of God*].

At the time of the festival, Israel comes to 'see' God's presence in the Beis Hamikdash and to 'be seen' by God. Hashem reciprocates the intensity of a person's desire to see God in the extent to which He grants that individual His הַשְׁגָּחָה, *Providence* (*Nora Tehillos*).

Maharam Almosnino translates thus: *and cause the face of God to be seen through me.* The יָשָׁר *upright man*, is a reflection of God's image. All who gaze at this man will glimpse the perfection of the Almighty.

Scripture attests to the fact that certain people are a reflection of God: רָאִיתִי פָנֶיךָ כִּרְאֹת פְּנֵי אֱלֹהִים, *I have seen your face as if it were the face of God* (Genesis 33:10).

4. הָיְתָה לִּי דִמְעָתִי לֶחֶם — *For me, my tears were sustenance* [lit. *My tear was bread for me*].

From here we learn that weeping satisfies a person's hunger so that he no

XLII   ³ *My soul thirsts for God, the living God.*
3-5   *When shall I come and appear before God?*
         ⁴ *For me my tears were sustenance*
                day and night,
         As they taunt me all day long,
             'Where is your God?'
         ⁵ *These do I recall and pour out my soul within me,*
              how I passed with the throng,

longer desires to eat. Similarly, when Chana cried bitterly because of her barreness, וַתִּבְכֶּה וְלֹא תֹאכַל, *She cried and did not eat* [*I Samuel* 1:7] (*Rashi*).

Israel's desire for God is so all-encompassing that we yearn for no other nourishment (*Hirsch*).

Two of Israel's most significant spiritual acts are likened to bread. The Temple sacrifices are termed קָרְבָּנִי לַחְמִי, *My sacrifice, My bread* (*Num.* 28:2) and Torah study is compared to the staff of life, לְכוּ לַחֲמוּ בְלַחְמִי,*Go forth and partake of my bread* (*Proverbs* 9:5). In exile Israel is deprived of three prime sources of spiritual nourishment. Then the desolate nation has nothing but bitter tears to satisfy its hunger for God (*Malbim*).

In 80:6 we read הֶאֱכַלְתָּם לֶחֶם דִּמְעָה וַתַּשְׁקֵמוֹ בִּדְמָעוֹת שָׁלִישׁ, *You fed them the bread of tears, You had them drink — the tears of a third*. Rashi quotes two interpretations. The first: this describes the seventy years of the Babylonian exile, which lasted only one-third of the duration of the Jews' 210 year bondage in Egypt. According to the second explanation (based on *Midrash Shocher Tov*), the verse refers to the exile imposed by the Romans, who were descendants of Esau. Three tears came to Esau's eyes (when he realized that Jacob had received Isaac's blessings). One teardrop fell from each eye, but the שָׁלִישׁ, *the third one*, remained unshed. The congregation of Israel exclaimed, 'Sovereign of the Universe, because

Esau cried but three tears Your pity was aroused and You gave him a pleasant existence and mastery over the entire world. When You recognize the humiliation of Your sons, who cry incessantly [as attested by this verse: *My tears are my sustenance by day and by night*], You will certainly be overwhelmed with pity for their terrible plight.

בֶּאֱמֹר אֵלַי כָּל הַיּוֹם — *As they taunt me all day long* [lit. *when it is said to me all the day*]

The foe taunts me incessantly throughout the long period of exile (*Radak*).

אַיֵּה אֱלֹהֶיךָ — *Where is your God?*

If He is truly the Almighty God and if you sincerely serve Him, then why does He allow you to languish in the misery of exile? (*Radak*).

5. אֵלֶּה אֶזְכְּרָה — *These do I recall.*

The Psalmist speaks for all the exiles, even though many of them were born on foreign soil and didn't personally witness the splendor of the main pilgrimage to the Holy Temple. This is because those exiles became the repository of their forefathers' experiences in the Land of Israel (*Radak*).

וְאֶשְׁפְּכָה עָלַי נַפְשִׁי — *And pour out my soul within me* [lit. *And I pour my soul over me*].

Anguish causes my heart, the sanctuary of my soul, to melt like soft wax (*S'forno*).

[527]   *Tehillim*

אֶדַּדֵּם עַד־בֵּית אֱלֹהִים בְּקוֹל־רִנָּה וְתוֹדָה
הָמוֹן חוֹגֵג: מַה־תִּשְׁתּוֹחֲחִי | נַפְשִׁי וַתֶּהֱמִי ו
עָלָי הוֹחִלִי לֵאלֹהִים כִּי־עוֹד אוֹדֶנּוּ

Israel laments, 'I am in exile because my body rebelled against God and refused to do His bidding. Therefore I now pour out my soul in order to permeate my body with a new spirit of sanctity and obedience to God.' (Tehillas Hashem).

כִּי אֶעֱבֹר בַּסָּךְ — How I passed with the throng.

The word סָךְ, has several meanings: It has been translated as a partition, referring to separate groups of pilgrims (see Hirsch below). סָךְ also means a sum, a total, again referring to vast numbers of people on their pilgrimage route. It is also related to סְבָךְ and סוּכָּה, a covering and refers to the covered wagons in which people traveled to Jerusalem (Rashi).

Hirsch elaborates on Rashi's first translation rendering the words כִּי אֶעֱבֹר בַּסָּךְ as How I passed over all partitions. Israel remembers the pinnacle of its ancient glory, when the whole nation assembled for its pilgrim festivals in God's Holy Sanctuary in Jerusalem. Unified by this mandatory pilgrimage, Jews from all walks of life paid homage to God and to His Torah. Their unity transcended all barriers of social status, wealth, ability, and occupation which usually divide citizens. Thus the festival pilgrimages created a cohesive Jewish community which literally passed over all partitions.

אֶדַּדֵּם — Walking gingerly with them.

A mother's efforts to help her baby take his halting first steps are described

as מְדַדֶּה. The same term is used to describe the assistance given a newborn calf or foal to attempt its first wobbly paces (Rashi).

Menachem contends that this is a cognate of יָדִיד, dear friend, and indicates the bonds of friendship which united the pilgrims.

Dunash relates אֶדַּדֵּם to דְּמָמָה, silence, as in דּוֹם לַה׳ be mute before HASHEM (37:7). The throngs kept silent until they neared the Temple Mount. Then, they suddenly burst into ecstatic song.

הָמוֹן חוֹגֵג — A celebrating multitude.

According to Sforno, this describes those who returned from the Babylonian exile to witness the newly-rebuilt Beis Hamikdash, which was vastly inferior to the grandeur of the First Temple. The הָמוֹן, the multitude, i.e. the younger people who were born in exile after the destruction of the First Beis Hamikdash, were unaware of the differences between the two Temples, so they were חוֹגֵג, celebrating joyously at the time of the Second Temple's inauguration. But the few elders who remembered the splendor of the original Temple wept (Ezra 3:13; see comm. to 30:1).

The pilgrims came to offer the קָרְבַּן חֲגִיגָה, the Sacrifice of Festival Celebration, in the Temple (Radak).

The word חוֹגֵג is related to מָחוֹג, a circle. It refers to dancing in circles and celebration, as in Eating and drinking and חוֹגְגִים, dancing [I Sam. 30:16] (Metzudas David, Malbim, Radak).

1. The congregation of Israel laments before the Holy One, Blessed be He:
In the past, I ascended to Jerusalem on well-paved roads, but now I travel on a neglected path of thorns, as the prophet says, Behold, I will hedge your way with thorns' (Hosea 2:8). In the past, great trees were סוֹכֵךְ, shading, the roads to the Holy City, but now the path is barren and open to the blazing sun. In the past, I went in the shadow of God's protection, but now I

Walking gingerly with them up to
the House of God
With joyous song and thanks
a celebrating multitude.
⁶ *Why are you downcast, my soul,*
and why do you yearn for me? Anticipate God!
For I shall yet thank Him

6. תִּשְׁתּוֹחֲחִי — *Downcast* [lit. *Bowed down, bent over*] (*Metzudas Zion*).

This is a cognate of שָׁחָה, as in כִּי שָׁחָה לֶעָפָר נַפְשֵׁנוּ, *For our souls are cast down to the dust* (44:26). Here it is in the passive form, as the Psalmist inquires of his soul, 'What is the outside force which has cast you into despair?' (*Rashi*).

When my soul was stricken with grief because of its estrangement from its homeland, I sought to console it, asking, 'Why are you so downcast? Wait for God's imminent salvation!' (*Radak*).

Rashi to v. 3 notes that in this psalm and the next, the query מַה תִּשְׁתּוֹחֲחִי appears three times (42:6, 42:12, and 43:5), corresponding to the three nations which were to subjugate Israel and make the Jews *downcast*. Babylon, Greece, and Rome would put a halt to the Temple service, but each time the Jewish people will cry out to God and be redeemed.

וַתֶּהֱמִי עָלָי — *And* [*why do*] *you yearn for me* [see *comm.* of *Rashi* and *Radak* to 39:7].

Some say that the Psalmist is chastising his own soul for its selfishness. You cry and yearn all day for your own welfare and salvation, but never consider the glory of God, which is sunk in disgrace because His nation suffers in exile! Stop thinking only about yourself! הוֹחִילִי לֵאלֹהִים, *wait for God* and be concerned about His redemption from ignominy (*Shevet M'Yisroel*).[1]

הוֹחִלִי לֵאלֹהִים — *Anticipate God!* Wait hopefully for God's ultimate redemption (*Rashi*).

Do not yearn only for 'ה *the Attribute of Mercy*, but wait also for אֱלֹהִים, *the Attribute of Strict Justice.* You will, *thank Him for the salvation which comes from His Presence* through the afflictions which He sends to cleanse you (*Tehillas Hashem*).

am at the mercy of the gentile government. *Alas! These things do I recall!*

'In the past, I arose early and ascended with a basket of בִּכּוּרִים, *first fruits*, on my head and with God's praise on my lips. But now these same roads are desolate and still. I ascend in dead silence and I descend in dead silence. *Alas! These things do I recall!*

'In the past, I went up with *loud rejoicing and thanksgiving*, but now I ascend and descend in tears. In the past, I traveled with throngs and multitudes of people. But now I walk alone. *Alas! These things do I recall!' (Midrash Eichah Rabbasi 1:52)*.

1. [In his rapturous Sabbath poem לְכָה דוֹדִי, *L'cha Dodi, Rabbi Shlomo HaLevi Alkavetz* paraphrases the words of this verse in the stanza:

לֹא תֵבוֹשִׁי וְלֹא תִכָּלְמִי מַה תִּשְׁתּוֹחֲחִי וּמַה תֶּהֱמִי בָּךְ יֶחֱסוּ עֲנִיֵּי עַמִּי וְנִבְנְתָה עִיר עַל תִּלָּהּ, *You shall not be put to shame, nor shall you be disgraced! Why are you downcast, and why do you moan in yearning? The poor of my people find protection with You, and the city shall be rebuilt upon its ruins!*]

מב
ז-ח

ז יְשׁוּעוֹת פָּנָיו: אֱלֹהַי עָלַי נַפְשִׁי תִשְׁתּוֹחָח
עַל־כֵּן אֶזְכָּרְךָ מֵאֶרֶץ יַרְדֵּן וְחֶרְמוֹנִים
ח מֵהַר מִצְעָר: תְּהוֹם־אֶל־תְּהוֹם קוֹרֵא
לְקוֹל צִנּוֹרֶיךָ כָּל־מִשְׁבָּרֶיךָ וְגַלֶּיךָ עָלַי

יְשׁוּעוֹת פָּנָיו — [For] salvations of His Presence [lit. countenance; face.]

At the end of this psalm, we find a variation of this phrase יְשׁוּעֹת פָּנַי, [literally the salvation (which comes from) 'my' countenance]. This implies that there are two possible causes of redemption. If Israel is worthy, then the salvation comes from my [Israel's] Presence. But if the Jewish Nation is not worthy, then it must rely on God in His mercy to send the salvations which come from His Presence (Otzar Nechmad).

7. אֱלֹהַי עָלַי נַפְשִׁי תִשְׁתּוֹחָח — O my God, within me my soul is downcast.

The congregation of Israel said, 'I am filled with envy when I see the gentile nations dwelling in tranquility although they anger You with their wicked deeds. They remain undisturbed while my soul is poured out in tragedy and misfortune' (Midrash Shocher Tov).

The Talmud (Kesubos 110b) states: Whoever lives outside of Eretz Yisrael is like a man who has no אֱלוֹהַ, God [i.e., in exile one does not enjoy God's direct supervision and interest.] Therefore I yearn to return to Eretz Yisrael so that I can again address You as אֱלֹהַי, my God! As long as I cannot do so, my soul is downcast (Chazah Zion).

עַל כֵּן אֶזְכָּרְךָ מֵאֶרֶץ יַרְדֵּן — Because I remember you — from the land of Jordan [i.e., I am downcast because I remember how kind You were to us when we came from across the Jordan].

[When I witness Your generosity towards the gentiles] I remember that we, the Children of Israel also angered

You with our misdeeds when we were on the eastern banks of the Jordan. Nevertheless, You mercifully overlooked these offenses and miraculously split the Jordan so that we could cross into the Land of Israel. [Why do You now treat us with such severity and unbending strictness?] (Rashi).

I remember how the pilgrims would gather from the distant communities located on the other side of the Jordan and on the peaks of Hermon to ascend to Jerusalem for the festival (Radak).

וְחֶרְמוֹנִים — And Hermon's peaks (Targum).

The people of Sidom called Hermon, Sirion, and the Amorites called it Senir (Deut. 3:9). [This is the snow-capped mountain range in northern Eretz Yisroel which is located on the present day border with Lebanon and Syria (see Song of Songs 4:8).]

מֵהַר מִצְעָר — From Mount Mitzor.

This describes Mount Sinai, which is low and young (צָעִיר) in comparison with other mountains (Targum; Rashi).

[The Talmud (Sotah 5a) elaborates: God prefers the lowly, for He passed over the high mountains and set His Holy Presence to rest only on Mount Sinai. Nevertheless, Mount Sinai did not become proud. (See also Bamidbar Rabbah 13:4). Furthermore, Sinai was responsible for making Israel young (צָעִיר) again, as the Midrash (Shir HaShirim Rabbah 8:1) says: Scriptures refer to Mount Sinai as בֵּית אִמִּי, My mother's house (Song of Songs 3:4) because it was there that Israel became purified like a new-born child.]

for salvations of His Presence.
⁷ O my God, within me my soul is downcast,
because I remember You —
From the land of Jordan and Hermon's peaks,
from Mount Mitzor.
⁸ Watery deep to watery deep
calls out to the roar of Your torrents,
All Your breakers and Your waves
have swept over me.

Although we angered You at Sinai with the construction of the Golden Calf, You forgave our sins and accompanied us. Why then do you forsake us now that we are in exile? *(Rashi).*

8. תְּהוֹם אֶל תְּהוֹם קוֹרֵא — *Watery deep to watery deep calls out.*

One deep misfortune calls out to the next [which follows in rapid succession] *(Rashi).*

Before I have a chance to extricate myself from one problem, another problem develops *(Metzudas David).*

The Psalmist often likens tragedies to streams of water, as we read: וְנַחֲלֵי בְלִיַּעַל יְבַעֲתוּנִי, *And torrents of Godless men frighten me (Psalms 18:5).* These are the anguished feelings of the Psalmist as he pours out his soul over the plight of Israel in exile *(Radak).*

The *Targum* renders:, 'The upper [celestial] waters call to the lower [terrestrial] waters.'

[This alludes to the water cycle which governs all of human existence. Precipitation gathers and falls to earth as rain, which is absorbed into the earth. Later this moisture evaporates and rises upward again. On the Festival of Sukkos a water libation (נִיסוּךְ הַמַּיִם) symbolizing the *upper celestial waters* is poured from a spout in the side of the Temple altar and descends to the depths of the Temple Mount, to mingle with the *lower terrestrial waters.* This demonstrates that these two water

sources are inextricably interwined. The *Talmud (Taanis 25b)* bases the ritual on our verse *(Maharsha, ibid.)*

לְקוֹל צִנּוֹרֶיךָ — *To the roar of Your torrents* [lit. *To the sound of Your water canals.*]

[A צִנּוֹר is a duct, pipe, or gutter which channels a flow of water in a certain direction. *Rashi* renders it in old French as 'canals.']

Punishments rain down on me as from a flowing pipeline *(Rashi).* This torrent of punishment resembles rainwater which descends with great force and with a loud noise from gutters on the roofs. Also, the rainclouds with precipitation gushing down from them resemble water channels. The abundance of my woes, too may be likened to the gushing rain descending from these clouds *(Radak).*

כָּל מִשְׁבָּרֶיךָ — *All Your breakers.*

These are the towering waves which at first rise high above the surface and then smash down into foam and spray *(Rashi).*

[This refers figuratively to the violent catastrophes which shatter Israel in its exile.]

וְגַלֶּיךָ — *Your waves.*

[These are the calm waves which roll in smoothly like a גַּלְגַּל, *wheel.* Their flow is not tempestuous, but constant. This refers to the incessant discrimination which hounds Israel.]

ט עָבְרוּ: יוֹמָם | יְצַוֶּה יהוה | חַסְדּוֹ וּבַלַּיְלָה
שִׁירֹה עִמִּי תְּפִלָּה לְאֵל חַיָּי: אוֹמְרָה לְאֵל
י סַלְעִי לָמָה שְׁכַחְתָּנִי לָמָה-קֹדֵר אֵלֵךְ
יא בְּלַחַץ אוֹיֵב: בְּרֶצַח | בְּעַצְמוֹתַי חֵרְפוּנִי

[The outpourings from the heart of King David struck responsive chords in every Jew in distress. The prophet Jonah, for example, drew on significant portions of the idioms and phrases from *Psalms* in his prayer to God from the belly of the fish. See specifically *Jonah* 2:5: *Your breakers and Your waves all swept over me.*

9. יוֹמָם יְצַוֶּה ה' חַסְדּוֹ — *Let dawn Arrive!* — *May HASHEM command His loving-kindness.*

Let the dawn of redemption shine forth and let God bestow His mercy upon us! (*Rashi*).

The Psalmist heartens the exiled and persecuted Nation of Israel by foretelling its bright future (*Radak*).

These words also refer to the pilgrims during the time of the Temple. As the masses marched all day towards Jerusalem, God provided for their needs. When they encamped at night, each one would sing of the Divine God's, חֶסֶד, *lovingkindness,* which he had experienced during the day.[1]

וּבַלַּיְלָה — *But by night.*

Although we pray for the *dawn* of redemption, we pray that even while we are still submerged in the *night* of exile, may God allow His Presence to rest upon us (*Rashi*).

שִׁירֹה עִמִּי — *May His resting place be with me.*

Rashi bases this translation upon the מְסוֹרֶת הַגְּדוֹלָה, *the Great Tradition,* which, among the lists of homonyms, cites the word שִׁירֹה, as in our verse, with the word שִׁירוֹ (I *Kings* 5:12 where it definitely means *his song*). Thus, it is clear that שִׁירֹה does not refer to song; another meaning must, therefore, be sought. We find that the *Targum* of וַיִּחַן שָׁם יִשְׂרָאֵל, *'And Israel camped there,'* (*Exodus* 19:2) is וּשְׁרָא יִשְׂרָאֵל. Therefore, in our verse, שִׁירֹה can be interpreted as a noun meaning *place of rest.*

Rashi also quotes the *Midrash* which renders שִׁירֹה as *song.* Israel says to the Holy One Blessed be He: 'We recall what You did for us in Egypt; You commanded us to fulfill just one *mitzvah* on the day before Passover, [*By day Hashem commands His loving-*

1. The *Talmud* (*Avodah Zarah* 3b) derives a number of lessons from this verse:

1) By day God Himself engages in acts of *lovingkindness,* i.e. He sustains the world and provides it with food, and teaches Torah to the young. By night He listens to the 'Songs' of the sacred heavenly angels. 2) The devoted scholar who studies Torah deep into the night and *Sings with Me,* i.e. with God, enveloped in an aura of *loving-kindness* throughout the day. 3) One who engages in Torah study in this world, which resembles night, will be enveloped in *loving-kindness* in the Hereafter, which resembles the light of day.

[The earlier two statements may be explained in light of the *Zohar* quoted here by the *Minchas Shai.* 'During the day, God created those angels appointed to perform acts of loving-kindness. At night, He created the angels appointed to sing songs. Men worthy of hearing this celestial song will be enlightened in Torah and will understand the secrets of the past and of the future.' Thus, he who learns Torah deep into the night and in the darkness of this world is blessed with special intellectual illuminations, granted by God's great loving-kindness.]

⁹ *Let dawn arrive!*

— May HASHEM command His lovingkindness,
But by night, may His resting place be with me;
a prayer to the God of my life!
¹⁰ *I will say to God:*
'My Rock — Why have You forgotten me?
Why must I walk in gloom
because of the foe's oppression?'
¹¹ *Like a sword in my bones*
are the taunts of my tormentors

---

kindness]. We fulfilled the mitzvah [of the sacrifice of the lamb], and You redeemed us that very night. Therefore we sang Hallel. Now [during our exile] we fulfill not one, but many commandments — yet You do not redeem us!''

Radak, however, renders שִׁירֹה as *His song.* Thus the Psalmist proclaims that even in the dark night of exile, we sing to God concerning the many acts of loving-kindness which He performed for our forefathers and which He continues to perform for us in exile [although He has not yet redeemed us].

תְּפִלָּה לְאֵל חַיָּי — *A prayer to the God of my life!*

We pray to the God Who has guarded our lives *(Targum)* to keep us alive until the advent of the Redeemer, so that we may witness His salvation *(Radak).*

10. אֹומְרָה לְאֵל — *I will say unto God.*

When I address *A prayer to the God of my life* (v. 9) this is what I will say to Him *(Metzudas David).*

סַלְעִי — *My Rock.*

You were my Rock and my tower of might in the past; why do You now abandon me? *(Radak, Sforno).*

לָמָה שְׁכַחְתָּנִי — *Why have You forgotten me?*

Why is this exile so very long? It must be that You have forgotten me! *(Ibn Ezra).*

לָמָה קֹדֵר אֵלֵךְ — *Why must I go about in gloom*

I am like a mourner who wears dark clothes [and a gloomy expression] *(Ibn Ezra).*

11. בְּרֶצַח בְּעַצְמֹותַי חֵרְפוּנִי צֹרְרָי — *Like a sword* [lit. *as a murder weapon*] *in my bones are the taunts* [lit. *they have taunted or insulted me*] *of my tormentors.*

The taunts they hurl at me fall like a knife jabbed into my body *(Rashi).*

When they blaspheme You, O God, and mockingly ask 'Where are You?' I myself am wounded to the core. The עֲצָמֹות *'bones, skeletons'* are the body's foundation and epitomize man's essence. רֶצַח is a noun denoting a murder weapon *(Radak).*

Ibn Yachya interprets the opening words of this verse as a reference to the annihilation of the Torah leaders of Israel who are its עֶצֶם, *skeleton and support.* In the preceding verse, the Psalmist declares, *I will say unto God 'My rock! Why have You forgotten me?'* That question will be posed when the gentiles murder Israel's Torah leaders.

צוֹרְרָי בְּאָמְרָם אֵלַי כָּל־הַיּוֹם אַיֵּה
אֱלֹהֶיךָ: מַה־תִּשְׁתּוֹחֲחִי | נַפְשִׁי וּמַה־
תֶּהֱמִי עָלָי הוֹחִילִי לֵאלֹהִים כִּי־עוֹד
אוֹדֶנּוּ יְשׁוּעֹת פָּנַי וֵאלֹהָי:

בְּאָמְרָם אֵלַי כָּל הַיּוֹם אַיֵּה אֱלֹהֶיךָ — *When
they revile me* [lit. *say to me*] *all day
long: 'Where is your God?'*

[The second part of this verse corresponds to the latter half of the previous
verse. After the slaughter of the Torah
leaders who guide Israel towards God,
the gentiles will cruelly taunt us with
the challenge, *'Where is your God?'* It is
that vicious taunt which stirs my soul to
ask God, *'Why must I go about in
blackness because of the oppression of
the foe?'* (v. 10).]

12. מַה תִּשְׁתּוֹחֲחִי נַפְשִׁי — *Why are you
downcast, my soul?*

[Again the Psalmist comforts his soul,
which is the collective soul of all Israel,
with promises of future good fortune.]

יְשׁוּעֹת — *My salvation* [lit. *'the salvations'*].

פָּנַי — *'My countenance'.*

Since God's Presence still illuminates
my countenance, whom should I fear
and what should I mourn?

The salvation will take place when I
turn *my countenance* towards God, i.e.,

and return to Him with sincere repentance (*S'forno*).

Radak notes that פָּנַי may be
translated *in my lifetime*, as in the verse
עַל פְּנֵי תֶּרַח אָבִיו, *In the lifetime of
Terach his father* (*Gen*. 11:28). I still
wait for God to demonstrate this
ultimate salvation in my own lifetime.'

In verse 6 the Psalmist uses the word
פָּנָיו, *His countenance*, whereas here he
uses פָּנַי, *my countenance*. This alludes
to the two tragedies of the long exile.
The first and foremost tragedy is
spiritual: the concealment of פָּנָיו *His*
(God's) *countenance*. Thus, the main
salvation will be the restoration of
God's Presence to the world. Therefore,
in verse 6 יְשׁוּעֹת, *salvations*, is spelled
out in full, to emphasize the primary
significance of the return of God's
Presence. The second tragedy of the exile is the physical catastrophe which
befell Israel. Although Jewish suffering
is a terrible misfortune, the man of faith
realizes that this tragedy is dwarfed by
Israel's even greater spiritual devastation. Therefore, Israel's physical salvation, פָּנַי, *my countenance*, is written
חָסֵר, *incomplete* (יְשׁוּעֹת) to allude to its

When they revile me all day long:
    'Where is your God?'
¹² *Why are you downcast, my soul,*
    and why do you yearn for me?
Anticipate God!
    For I shall yet thank Him — my salvation
    the light of my countenance and my God.

secondary importance *Kehilas Ephraim).*

Hirsch explains the variant readings with profound insight. Often man deludes himself into thinking that God's imperatives are in contradiction to his personal aspirations for a successful life. Man views פָּנָיו, i.e., God's purpose for creation, as incompatible with פָּנַי, i.e., his own personal goals, although man may subordinate his own desires to Hashem's Will with painful resignation. Israel will ultimately realize that there has never been any conflict between man's own genuine goals and the goals established by God. When Israel fully understands that Hashem is אֱלֹהָי, *My God,* Whose sole interest is Israel's welfare, then they will see clearly that the direction of *His face* and *my face* are one.

וֵאלֹהָי — *And my God.*

The agony of the exile was greatest when the gentiles taunted us, *'Where is your God?'* (v. 11). The climax of redemption will arrive when Hashem reveals Himself as our God and the nations see it *(Radak; Ibn Ezra).*[1]

This moment will occur when He will accept my repentance and my prayer *(Sforno).*

1. On the twentieth of Tammuz, 1941, the Nazis ordered the Jewish inhabitants of Telshe, Lithuania, to dig their own graves. As they stood in the open pits, the Rav and Rosh Yeshiva of Telshe, HaGaon Rav Avrohom Yitzchak Bloch ל״צז, led the martyrs of his community in their final declaration of eternal faith, the Shema. *'Hear O Israel, Hashem is our God, Hashem is One!'*
The nazi beasts gleefully taunted the Rav, *'Where is your God now?'*
The Rav replied courageously *'Not only is He my God, He is also your God, and the day will come when you too will realize it!'*

*T*his *psalm is a direct continuation of the preceding one* (Radak v. *5). Once again the Psalmist expresses his deep yearning for redemption from the agony of exile.*

The devout Jew who mourns the destruction of the Temple and the long exile of our people arises at midnight to recite Tikkun Chatzos, *a collection of psalms and prayers which reflect the intensity of our grief.*

Tikkun Chatzos *is divided into two sections. The first half,* Tikkun Rachel, *is a dirge of sorrow and despair, echoing the bitter tears of Mother Rachel who weeps for her exiled sons [See Pref. Remarks to Psalms 79 and 137.]*

The second section, Tikkun Yaakov *and* Leah, *reveals a ray of hope for Israel's future* (Siddur Otzar HaTefillos). *The Patriarch Yaakov was never separated from his first wife, Leah; even in death the couple did not part, for their remains were interred, side by side, in the Cave of Machpelah.*

This symbolizes the inseparable ties which link Israel to God. Even the apparent death of the nation, its exile from its homeland, has not severed the bond of love which unites Israel with the Almighty.

Therefore, Tikkun Yaakov *and* Leah *begins with Psalms 42 and 43 which tell of Israel's thirst for God, a thirst which goes undiminished and unquenched throughout the endless years of exile. Israel awaits with hope the day when it will publicly be wed to its Eternal Partner in the Holy Temple.*

א שָׁפְטֵנִי אֱלֹהִים | וְרִיבָה רִיבִי מִגּוֹי לֹא־
ב חָסִיד מֵאִישׁ־מִרְמָה וְעַוְלָה תְפַלְּטֵנִי: כִּי־
אַתָּה | אֱלֹהֵי מָעוּזִּי לָמָה זְנַחְתָּנִי לָמָּה־
ג קֹדֵר אֶתְהַלֵּךְ בְּלַחַץ אוֹיֵב: שְׁלַח־אוֹרְךָ
וַאֲמִתְּךָ הֵמָּה יַנְחוּנִי יְבִיאוּנִי אֶל־הַר־

---

1. שָׁפְטֵנִי — *Avenge me* [lit. *'judge me'*].

Judge me rigorously [without mercy] (*Targum*); [then you will become convinced that I am superior to my oppressors] and you will avenge the terrible injustices I have suffered at the hands of my enemies (*Rashi; Radak*).

וְרִיבָה רִיבִי — *And champion my cause* [lit. *'and fight my fight'*].

I ask this of You because I lack the strength to defend myself (*Radak*).

מִגּוֹי לֹא חָסִיד — *Against a people without kindness.*

The Psalmist alludes to people like Ishmael who grew up among Abraham and Isaac, but did not learn from them (*Rashi*). [See *Ramban* to *Genesis* 16:6 for an explanation of why the sons of Ishmael (the Arab nations) treat the descendants of Abraham with extraordinary cruelty.] .

The Psalmist does not describe these men merely as 'wicked', because they are worse than wicked. They are, in fact, deceitful hypocrites who try to appear kind, although they are actually cruel (*Sforno*).

The hypocrites are the most dangerous villains. On his deathbed, King Yannai warned his wife, 'Beware of the צְבוּעִים, *'the camouflaged ones'* whose inner motives are as heinous as those of Zimri [who was so brazen that he committed adultery in front of Moses and the elders], but who hypocritically behave as though they merit the reward due to the righteous Pinchas [who courageously slew Zimri and his companion, thereby stopping the Heavenly

plague that had taken the lives of twenty-four thousand Jews (*Numbers* 25:1-15)] (*Tehillos Hashem*).

We find such hypocrisy in Nebuchadnezzar, who destroyed the First Temple. Daily, a heavenly voice would exhort the Babylonian king to destroy the Temple of the Jews, for they had angered God. God even called Nebuchadnezzar עַבְדִּי, *my servant*, because he fulfilled God's mission. But, in truth, Nebuchadnezzar was not at all concerned with doing God's will. His actual motive was a secret hatred for Israel (*Alshich*).

The Romans, who destroyed the Second Temple, were also masters of deception, which was part of their spiritual legacy from their ancestor, Esau. Esau deceived his father, Isaac, by asking him questions about minute points of Jewish law, in order to create the false impression that he was scrupulously observant and extremely pious, when he was, in fact, a depraved evildoer. The *Talmud* (*Avoda Zara* 3a) relates that in the future, the Romans will also try to fool God by claiming that every material advantage which they introduced to the world was done only for the benefit of Israel (*Eretz HaChaim*).

Hirsch explains that although the nations pay lip service to the concept of humane ethics [and although they do practice a measure of charity among themselves], they do not consider the *'alien'* Jewish people worthy of common decency. When the nations recognize an opportunity to take advantage of Israel's powerlessness, their underlying

XLIII
1-3

Avenge me, O God, and champion my cause
against a people without kindness,
Help me to escape
from a man of deceit and iniquity.
² For You are the God of my might,
why have You abandoned me?
Why must I walk in gloom
because of the foe's oppression?
³ Dispatch Your light and Your truth —
they will guide me,

---

tendencies toward violence and depravity are exposed, and they treat us with the utmost inhumanity.

מֵאִישׁ מִרְמָה וְעַוְלָה — *From a man of deceit and iniquity.*

Although the Psalmist is speaking of a multitude of fraudulent gentiles, he refers to them in the singular i.e., מֵאִישׁ, because they are all alike. Another explanation is that he is alluding to the one man who rules over all gentiles; the king (*Ibn Ezra*).

2. אֱלֹהֵי מָעוּזִּי — *The God of my might.*

In the past, when I was at the height of my glory, You defended me with your *might.* Why do You abandon me now, when I am in exile? (*Radak; Sforno*).

My forefathers called you their *might* only after You redeemed them; after the miracle at the Sea of Reeds, they sang יָהּ עָזִּי וְזִמְרָת, *my might and my song is HASHEM* (*Exod.* 15:2). But I call You *my might* even though You have not yet redeemed me! (*Midrash Shocher Tov*).

The Jews who left Egypt were fully cognizant of God's power even before the Splitting of the Sea; they knew of it by tradition and had seen it during the Ten Plagues. However, when their redemption was completed following the crossing of the sea, they recognized God as their own Savior and, for the

first time, called Him *my might.* The Psalmist, however, uses that description even while he is in exile. This is not to imply that he is superior to his illustrious ancestors. Rather it is because our forefathers imbued their progeny with a legacy of faith in God's salvation that later generations can call Him *my might* even though they had never witnessed His acts of salvation (*Tehillas Hashem*).

לָמָה קֹדֵר אֶתְהַלֵּךְ בְּלַחַץ אוֹיֵב — *Why must I walk in gloom because of the foe's oppression?*

You were not oblivious to the misery of our forefathers in Egypt, for Scripture states, וְגַם רָאִיתִי אֶת הַלַּחַץ, *and also I have seen the oppression (Exodus* 3:9). Why then do you allow me to sink into oppression at the hands of my present foe? (*Midrash Shocher Tov*).

3. אוֹרְךָ — *Your light.*

Send the King Messiah, who is likened to light, as we read in (132:17), עָרַכְתִּי נֵר לִמְשִׁיחִי, *I prepared a candle for my Messiah (Rashi; Sforno).*

Restore the light of prophecy to Israel, as we pray daily: אוֹר חָדָשׁ עַל צִיּוֹן תָּאִיר וְנִזְכֶּה כֻלָּנוּ מְהֵרָה לְאוֹרוֹ, *shine a new light upon Zion and may we all speedily merit to see its light* (*Rashbam*).

The plea for light refers to the

ד קָדְשְׁךָ וְאֶל־מִשְׁכְּנוֹתֶיךָ: וְאָבוֹאָה | אֶל־
מִזְבַּח אֱלֹהִים אֶל־אֵל שִׂמְחַת גִּילִי וְאוֹדְךָ
ה בְכִנּוֹר אֱלֹהִים אֱלֹהָי: מַה־תִּשְׁתּוֹחֲחִי |
נַפְשִׁי וּמַה־תֶּהֱמִי עָלָי הוֹחִילִי לֵאלֹהִים
כִּי־עוֹד אוֹדֶנּוּ יְשׁוּעֹת פָּנַי וֵאלֹהָי:

previous lament, 'Why must I go about in gloom?' (v. 2) (Ibn Ezra; Radak).

וַאֲמִתְּךָ — And Your truth.

Send Elijah the Prophet [to herald the advent of Messiah], for he is a trustworthy messenger (Rashi).[1]

Because I am in the clutches of the man of deceit and iniquity, I ask you to rescue me with your truth (Ibn Ezra).

Rabbi Yonasan Eyebeschuvetz, in a final note to his work Kreisi U'pleisi on Yoreh Deah, notes that according to tradition, if the Messiah is to come at the pre-ordained time, Elijah will precede his arrival by three days in order to announce him. If Israel is especially virtuous, however, they will merit that the Messiah and Elijah will both arrive simultaneously, without any prior announcement. The Psalmist prays for this swift redemption: 'Send forth your light (Messiah) and your truth (Elijah), send them together without delay!' (Tosafos Yom Tov).

הַר קָדְשְׁךָ — The mount of Your Sanctuary.

This is Mount Moriah, upon which the Temple was built (Ibn Ezra).

This alludes to the actual Sanctuary constructed on earth (Nir L'David).

1. [Compare I Kings 17:24. After Elijah resuscitated the dead son of the widow of Tzorfas, she exclaimed, עַתָּה זֶה יָדַעְתִּי כִּי אִישׁ אֱלֹהִים אָתָּה וּדְבַר ה' בְּפִיךָ אֱמֶת, Now I know that you are a man of God and that the word of God in Your mouth is true. The Zohar (Shemos 197a) says that the revived boy was the prophet יוֹנָה בֶן אֲמִתַּי, Jonah the son of Amittai. Furthermore, says the Zohar, Amittai was the prophet Elijah, who was Jonah's 'second' father and who attained a new title of honor as a man of אֱמֶת, truth, for accomplishing the wonder of bringing Jonah back to life.]

Elijah is a symbol of truth because he will be the final arbiter of an halachic questions (Sforno). [In describing unresolved questions, the Talmud frequently uses the contraction תיקו, an acrostic for תִּשְׁבִּי יְתָרֵץ קוּשְׁיוֹת וְאִיבַּעְיוֹת, The Tishbite (Elijah) will solve all questions and dilemmas.]

They will bring me to the mount of Your Sanctuary
and to Your dwellings.
⁴ That I may come to the altar of God,
to God the gladness of my joy,
And praise You on the Kinor,
O God, My God.
⁵ Why are you downcast, my soul,
and why do you yearn for me?
Anticipate God! for I shall yet thank Him,
my salvation, the light of my countenance
and my God.

מִשְׁכְּנוֹתֶיךָ — *Your dwellings.*

These are the courtyards which are destined to be built in the Third Temple *(Ibn Ezra).*

This refers to the spiritual Temple, which must be restored in heaven before its corresponding earthly edifice can be rebuilt *(Nir L'David).*

4. וְאָבוֹאָה אֶל מִזְבַּח אֱלֹהִים — *That I may come to the altar of God.*

At that time I will have the opportunity to offer sacrifices to God as in days of yore *(Radak).*

The previous altar was constructed by men, but the future altar will descend miraculously from heaven. [See *Sukkah* 41a, *Rashi* and *Tosafos ibid.* s.v. אִי נָמֵי]. Thus the *altar* will truly be of God *(Alshich).*

שִׂמְחַת גִּילִי — *The gladness of my joy* *(Radak; Hirsch).*

Although the future redemption will be filled with signs of rejoicing, I will remember that God is the sole true source of my joy *(Hirsch).*

אֱלֹהִים אֱלֹהָי — *O God, my God.*

Although You are אֱלֹהִים, *God,* Whose majesty and power extend over the entire universe, nevertheless, to me You have a special role as אֱלֹהָי, *my* [personal] *God (Be'er Avraham).*

In the future *the people who are not kind* (v. 1) will come to recognize my special relationship with God *(Ibn Ezra).*

5. מַה תִּשְׁתּוֹחֲחִי נַפְשִׁי — *Why are You downcast, my soul?*

The Psalmist now repeats a refrain from the preceding psalm (vs. 6,12), because the two psalms have the same theme. [See *commentary ibid.*] *(Radak).*

T his psalm, the third composition of the sons of Korach, is a
memoir dedicated to their beloved country, Eretz Yisrael. They
describe vividly the Divine assistance which allowed Israel to conquer
the land, and they lament the Divine displeasure which caused Israel
to lose it.

Arvei Nachal (Parshas Shelach) outlines the strategy for a permanent conquest of the Holy Land. God fashioned the earth in general
and Eretz Yisrael in particular in accordance with His universal
blueprint, the Torah. The spiritual essence of every square inch of
soil is related to Torah laws. Through Torah study and the performance of its laws, Israel seizes the spiritual cone of each 'objective,'
and thereby the conquest of the external physical terrain as a matter
of course.

The sons of Korach depict the early triumphs of our people as they
entered the Promised Land — invincible, and armed with Torah Laws.
They mourn the bitter defeat which our people suffered when they
abandoned these divine weapons. Nevertheless, these inspired singers
are filled with hope, for even in the exile, the Jewish people have displayed undaunted loyalty to Torah by sacrificing their lives for the
sanctification of God's Name. Surely this merit will unlock the gates
of redemption.

לַמְנַצֵּחַ לִבְנֵי־קֹרַח מַשְׂכִּיל: אֱלֹהִים | א־ב
בְּאָזְנֵינוּ שָׁמַעְנוּ אֲבוֹתֵינוּ סִפְּרוּ־לָנוּ
פֹּעַל־פָּעַלְתָּ בִימֵיהֶם בִּימֵי קֶדֶם: אַתָּה ג
יָדְךָ גּוֹיִם הוֹרַשְׁתָּ וַתִּטָּעֵם תָּרַע לְאֻמִּים

2. בְּאָזְנֵינוּ שָׁמַעְנוּ — *With our ears we have heard.*

Korach's sons had no need to hear about these miracles with their ears for they had been present when the wonders occurred. They witnessed the Splitting of the Sea and of the Jordan River, they were sustained by God for forty years in the Wilderness, and they participated in Joshua's miraculous conquest of Canaan. Therefore, the sons of Korach must be speaking for later generations of Jews who did not experience these miracles, but learned about them from their fathers (*Rashi*).

אֲבוֹתֵינוּ סִפְּרוּ לָנוּ — *Our fathers have recounted to us.*

[Although the Jews who witnessed the miracles could not personally recount them to their descendants born centuries later, the Psalmist implies that the transmission of this tradition remained broken.]

This tradition was transmitted from father to son through the generations, until it reached the generation which went into exile (*Radak*).

Because our forefathers were righteous, their testimony is reliable. Furthermore, since a father loves his child, he teaches him nothing but the truth (*Ibn Ezra*).

When the Jews were redeemed from Egypt Moses said to them: 'You are not being saved because of your personal merit; rather, God is granting you this salvation in order that you recount these wonders to your children.' In this way, God would be glorified, for Israel would recount His praises among the nations.

The sons of Korach retorted, 'Of what benefit is the account of ancient wonders to those who are now exiled among the nations? The exiles will benefit only when You actually perform similar miracles for them!' (*Midrash Shocher Tov*).

בִימֵיהֶם בִּימֵי קֶדֶם — *In their days, in days of old.*

This seems to be redundant, for events which occurred *in their days* obviously took place *in days of old*. By this apparent repetition, the Psalmist alludes to a major principle in the interpretation of Jewish history: Events which occurred early in the life of the nation have lasting significance. The events of Israel's formative years foreshadow the nation's future. The beginning of Jewish history is seen as the spiritual seed from which future generations germinated [cf. *Ramban, Genesis* 2:3]. Therefore, the Psalmist emphasizes that those were not ordinary times; they were יְמֵי קֶדֶם, *days of old* [קֶדֶם also means *prior*, i.e., those days were the prelude to the future].

We can expect the miraculous events of that period to be repeated later in our history. The double expression, פֹּעַל פָּעַלְתָּ, *the deeds which You performed* [lit. *the performance which You performed*], suggests, therefore, that God's performance [of miracles such as those about to be recounted] will be repeated. (*Ohel Yaakov*).[1]

3. אַתָּה יָדְךָ — *With Your own hand* [lit. *You Your hand ...*].

The word יָדְךָ should be interpreted as if it included the prefix ב: בְּיָדְךָ, *with Your hand (Ibn Ezra, Radak).*

Israel's military might is not credited with driving the Canaanites from the

XLIV
1-3

For the Conductor, by the sons of Korach
a Maskil.
² God, with our ears we have heard,
     our fathers have recounted to us,
The deeds which You performed in their days,
     in days of old.
³ You, with Your own hand, drove out peoples,
     and emplanted them.

Land. The *hand* of God alone was responsible for this feat (*Radak*).

גּוֹיִם הוֹרַשְׁתָּ — *You drove out peoples.*

This translation follows the *Targum, Radak,* and *Metzudos* who relate הוֹרַשְׁתָּ to גֵּרַשְׁתָּ, *You chased out.* However *Rashbam* contends that גּוֹיִם refers to the Twelve Tribes, of Jacob, whom God promised: גּוֹי וּקְהַל גּוֹיִם יִהְיֶה מִמֶּךָ, *A people, and a congregation of peoples shall come forth from you* (Genesis 35:11). Thus, הוֹרַשְׁתָּ is cognate with יְרוּשָׁה, *inheritance, estate,* meaning: *You bequeathed this land as an estate for the Tribes.*

וַתִּטָּעֵם — *And You emplanted them.*

Them refers to our fathers; as *Targum* renders this verse: *You drove out the peoples of Canaan and es-*

tablished the House of Israel in their stead.

The establishment of the Children of Israel in the Holy Land is compared to planting, to indicate that God has granted the Jews perpetual possession of the Land. Just as the tree is permanently rooted in its soil, the Jews are eternally bound to the Promised Land. Other verses which refer to the 'planting' of the Jews in *Eretz Yisrael* include תְּבִאֵמוֹ וְתִטָּעֵמוֹ בְּהַר נַחֲלָתְךָ, *You shall bring them and You shall plant them in the mountain which is Your estate* (Exodus 15:17), and וּנְטַעְתִּים עַל אַדְמָתָם וְלֹא יִנָּתְשׁוּ עוֹד מֵעַל אַדְמָתָם, *I will plant them on their land, and never again will they be uprooted from their land* (Amos 9:15).

This metaphor further alludes to the

---

1. *Alshich* notes that these few words contain the key which will unlock Israel's chains of exile. Before Israel can return to its land it must defend itself against the nations which challenge its claim to *Eretz Yisrael.* These nations cry לְסְטִים אַתֶּם, *You are bandits.* [They accuse Israel of having illegally driven out the Land's rightful owners.] *Rashi* begins his commentary to *Genesis* (1:1) by quoting Rav Yitzchak, who explains that the Torah — which is essentially a book of laws, not of history — begins with the narrative of Creation in order to provide Israel with a reply to the charge of banditry.

'The entire universe belongs to God, He created it and He granted it to whomever was fit in His eyes. It was His desire to give it to them and it was His desire to take it back from them, ceding it to us!'

The Sages teach us that the universe was created through עֲשָׂרָה מַאֲמָרוֹת, *Ten Utterances.* In *Avos 5,* the Mishnah lists many other series of ten. *Maharal* and others find a relationship between them. The ten plagues, which God brought upon Egypt, correspond to these 'Ten Utterances.' Since the plagues totally defied the laws of nature, they proved dramatically that the forces of nature are subject solely to the will of God, Who created them. By demonstrating God's total mastery of even the minutest detail of nature, the plagues renewed the lesson of the Ten Utterances: that God is the Creator and Master of the universe. Thus, Israel's claim to *Eretz Yisrael* was reinforced, for if God the Creator did not give up his mastery of the world, then He could determine to whom its territories should be assigned.

ד וַתְּשַׁלְּחֵם: כִּי לֹא בְחַרְבָּם יָרְשׁוּ אָרֶץ
וּזְרוֹעָם לֹא־הוֹשִׁיעָה לָּמוֹ כִּי־יְמִינְךָ
ה וּזְרוֹעֲךָ וְאוֹר פָּנֶיךָ כִּי רְצִיתָם: אַתָּה־הוּא
ו מַלְכִּי אֱלֹהִים צַוֵּה יְשׁוּעוֹת יַעֲקֹב: בְּךָ

higher degree of holiness present in the Land. When a Jew returns to *Eretz Yisrael*, his soul draws renewed strength as if it had experienced a new birth. In this sense, it resembles a tree that was transplanted to more fertile soil *(Dorash Moshe).*

תָּרַע לְאֻמִּים — *You afflicted* [lit. *did bad to*] *the nations.*

This translation follows *Rashi* and *Metzudas David,* who relate תָּרַע to רַע, *evil. Targum* and *Rashbam* render תָּרַע, *to break,* [as in תְּרֹעֵם בְּשֵׁבֶט בַּרְזֶל, *smash them with a rod of iron (2:9)].*

Malbim notes that this verse records two forms of Divine action against the gentile inhabitants of *Eretz Israel,* for the nations which were to be displayed by Israel fell into two distinct categories.

The גּוֹיִם are the native *people,* unified by purely physical factors, such as geographic proximity and ethnic similarity. A גּוֹי is a physical and territorial rather than an ideological entity. The גּוֹיִם must be displaced from *Eretz Yisrael* because God has reserved that territory for the Jewish people. Therefore, *You drove out the people and planted Israel in their place.*

The second group of gentiles are the לְאֻמִּים, *nations,* united by an ideological and spiritual bond. They actively deny God's sovereignty and scoff at Him.

Such people must be removed from *Eretz Yisrael* not only to clear the territory for Jewish habitation but also to eliminate the spiritual threat which the scoffers pose to the sacred chosen people. Because the לְאֻמִּים are willfully רַע, *evil,* You brought misfortune (תָּרַע) upon the nations and banished them — to demonstrate clearly the futility of their beliefs [cf. comm. of *Malbim,* to 2:1].

וּזְרוֹעָם לֹא הוֹשִׁיעָה לָּמוֹ — *Nor did their own arm help them.*

Malbim here develops a major principle of Torah *Hashkafa.* The זְרוֹעַ refers to the upper arm, which moves the forearm and hand. The upper arm is the source of the hand's strength.

Scripture refers to this relationship between the upper arm and the hand to symbolize God's actions on behalf of Israel. When the children of Israel are righteous enough to merit Divine intervention they are described as the זְרוֹעַ, *(upper arm)* and God's actions are described as יַד ה', the hand of HASHEM, which derives its strength from Israel's worthiness.

When the children of Israel fail to merit Divine intervention, God's deeds are described as זְרוֹעַ ה', *the upper arm*

---

1. The Rabbis said: Sichon, King of the Emorites, was as indestructable as a fortified town. When Sichon sat on a high wall, his feet would reach the ground! How did the Holy One, Blessed be He, vanquish him? He took Sichon's guardian angel, bound him, and gave him to Moses. Why? God foresaw that none of Sichon's descendants, would be God-fearing; therefore, He completely eradicated Sichon and his posterity.

How did the Emorites die? Rabbi Levi said: God sent two poisonous flying insects to assault each Emorite. The insects attacked the Emorites in the eye, and they died. If not for this Divine assistance, Israel could never have overcome them. Even Moses was so awed by their might that Hashem reassured him *'Do not fear them'* (Deuteronomy 7:18). King David referred to this when he said, *'For not by their sword did they possess the land.'* (Tanchuma, D'varim 8).

XLIV
4-5

You afflicted nations and banished them.
⁴ *For not by their sword did they possess the land,*
   nor did their own arm help them,
But by Your right hand, Your arm, and the light
   of Your countenance —
   for You favored them.
⁵ *Only You are my King, O God —*
   command the salvation of Jacob!

of HASHEM, which derives its strength not from Israel's worthiness but from God's own mercy.

The Psalmist states that when the Jews entered the Holy Land their victories were not a result of their own virtues, but of Divine kindness. Scripture attests לֹא בְצִדְקָתְךָ וּבְיֹשֶׁר לְבָבְךָ אַתָּה בָא לָרֶשֶׁת אֶת אַרְצָם, *Not because of your righteousness or because of the uprightness of your heart are you coming to possess their land* (Deuteronomy 9:5).

The Psalmist echoes this theme: *Their own upper arm did not bring them salvation,* i.e. they did not fully deserve God's help. *Rather it was ... Your upper arm,* i.e God's mercy was the sole source of their salvation.

יְמִינְךָ — *[But by] Your right hand.*

You battled against the pagans of the land and annihilated them (S'forno).

[We find battle ascribed to the right hand in the verse, יְמִינְךָ ה׳ נֶאְדָּרִי בַּכֹּחַ יְמִינְךָ ה׳ תִּרְעַץ אוֹיֵב, *Your right hand HASHEM is mighty in strength, Your right hand, HASHEM, shatters the foes* (Exodus 15:6)].

וּזְרוֹעֲךָ — *[And] Your arm.*

You destroyed them with Your right hand. Moreover, the mere threat of Your might terrified them, as we read: תִּפֹּל עֲלֵיהֶם אֵימָתָה וָפַחַד בִּגְדֹל זְרוֹעֲךָ יִדְּמוּ כָּאָבֶן, *Fear and dread will fall upon them, the greatness of Your arm will make them as still as stone* (Exodus 15:16) (Sforno).

וְאוֹר פָּנֶיךָ — *And the light of Your countenance.*

This refers to God's *Attribute of Mercy* (Sforno).

The miracles which You enacted for them were not נִסִּים נִסְתָּרִים (hidden miracles), cloaked by the laws of nature. Rather, they were openly revealed wonders which publicly demonstrated Your presence in Israel (Malbim).

Thus God fulfilled the promise He had made to Moses and to all of Israel, וַיֹּאמַר פָּנַי יֵלֵכוּ וַהֲנִחֹתִי לָךְ, *And He said, My presence will go before you and I will lead you* (Exodus 33:14) (Alshich).

כִּי רְצִיתָם — *For You favored them.*

As long as they engaged in Torah study, they found favor in Your eyes (Targum).

[Israel's conquest of Canaan was not merely a military campaign. It was a spiritual crusade to cleanse the land of pagan influence and to replace paganism with a spirit of Godliness. Therefore, when Israel abandoned the diligent pursuit of Torah study, God immediately turned His sword against them and their leader, Joshua (cf. Joshua 5:13; Megillah 3a).]

5. אַתָּה הוּא מַלְכִּי אֱלֹהִים — *Only You are my King, O God.*

You, Who performed wonders for my ancestors, have remained my sovereign and God to this very day (S'forno). Therefore, please repeat the miracles which You performed in the past (Radak).

ז צָרֵינוּ נְנַגֵּחַ בְּשִׁמְךָ נָבוּס קָמֵינוּ: כִּי לֹא
ח בְקַשְׁתִּי אֶבְטָח וְחַרְבִּי לֹא תוֹשִׁיעֵנִי: כִּי
הוֹשַׁעְתָּנוּ מִצָּרֵינוּ וּמְשַׂנְאֵינוּ הֱבִישׁוֹתָ:
ט בֵּאלֹהִים הִלַּלְנוּ כָל־הַיּוֹם וְשִׁמְךָ | לְעוֹלָם

Dorash Moshe adds: When You exhibited Your wonders in Egypt, You were not yet Israel's King, for Israel did not fully submit to Your sovereignty until they accepted the commands of Your Torah at Sinai. If my ancestors were worthy of Your kindness even before You became their King, how much more do I deserve Your kindness today, for I am totally subjugated to Your rule and You alone are *My King, O God.*

צַוֵּה יְשׁוּעוֹת יַעֲקֹב — *Command the salvations of Jacob*

The name of Jacob is associated with salvation because he blessed his descendants and prayed for their redemptions, saying: הַמַּלְאָךְ הַגֹּאֵל אֹתִי מִכָּל רָע יְבָרֵךְ אֶת הַנְּעָרִים, *The angel who redeemed me from all evil should bless the young men* (Genesis 48:16) *(Ibn Ezra).*

6. בְּךָ צָרֵינוּ נְנַגֵּחַ — *Through You we shall gore our foes.*

This translation follows *Ibn Ezra* and *Radak.* The Targum renders בְּךָ as *by Your word.* בְּךָ is composed of the letters ב and כ, which have the combined numerical value of twenty-two. This sum alludes to the twenty-two letters of the Torah, which is the *word* of God *(Zerah Yaakov).* [צָר is usually translated as *tormentor,* but in the context of this Psalm, it means *foe.*]

Radak notes that Israel's triumph over the enemy is described as *goring* in the verse, בָּהֶם עַמִּים יְנַגַּח, *With them He gores nations* (Deuteronomy 33:17).

We have begged for a supernatural Divine intervention by *Your right hand* (v. 4) so that we would not be required to wage war. But, if we are not worthy

of miracles and if we must engage in battle, then please be with us and help us to gore our adversaries *(Malbim).*

בְּשִׁמְךָ — *By Your Name.*

This refers to the power of the Torah, which is composed of many different combinations of the letters of God's real name *(Yosef Tehillos).* [See *Ramban,* Introduction to *Commentary on Torah*].

Even if we do not merit Your direct intervention in our battles, then at least aid us by sending an angel who can wage war בְּשִׁמְךָ, *in Your Name (Malbim).*

נָבוּס קָמֵינוּ — *Shall we trample our opponents.*

The word נָבוּס means *to wallow, to trample,* as in the phrase מִתְבּוֹסֶסֶת בְּדָמָיִךְ, *Wallowing in your blood* (Ezekiel 16:6) *(Rashi).*

[The Psalmist requests divine assistance even after the battle is won and the enemy subdued, for the threat of insurrection always looms over the occupying army which must crush all pockets of enemy resistance.]

7. כִּי לֹא בְקַשְׁתִּי אֶבְטָח — *For I do not trust in my bow.*

[The commentaries cite the sudden transition from plural to singular in this verse.]

Radak explains that the Psalmist now prefers to speak of the entire nation as one person. According to *Ibn Ezra,* these are the words spoken by each archer and swordsman in the Israelites' army. Each individual soldier declares, 'I do not expect to be saved by my own power, but by Hashem's might' *(Radak).*

⁶ *Through You shall we gore our foes;*
by Your Name trample our opponents.
⁷ *For I do not trust in my bow,*
nor does my sword save me.
⁸ *For You saved us from our foes,*
and our haters You shamed.
⁹ *In God we glory all the day,*
and Your Name forever thank, Selah!

וְחַרְבִּי לֹא תוֹשִׁיעֵנִי — *Nor does my sword save me.*

What then does save me? My prayers! The Psalmist speaks here of *the salvation of Jacob (v. 5).* Jacob said that he conquered his enemies בְּחַרְבִּי וּבְקַשְׁתִּי, *With my sword and with my bow' (Genesis 48:22),* which the *Targum (ibid.)* renders *With my prayers and with my supplication.* Jacob's weapon could not have been an actual sword, for that implement had been taken away from him and given exclusively to the bloody hands of Esau, as it says, עַל חַרְבְּךָ תִחְיֶה, *And you [Esau] shall live by your sword (Genesis 27:40).* [See *Alshich* and *Malbim.*]

8. כִּי הוֹשַׁעְתָּנוּ מִצָּרֵינוּ — *For You saved us from our foes.*

We know that we need not rely on our own weapons for salvation (v. 8) not only because *we have heard with our ears* — i.e. from our forefathers — that You alone wage our wars (v. 2), but also because we personally witnessed Your intervention when You saved us from our tormentors *(Ibn Ezra, Radak).*

וּמְשַׂנְאֵינוּ הֱבִישׁוֹתָ — *And our haters, You shamed.*

You literally saved us *from our tormentors,* for You forced them to help us against their own will. Since Hashem forced *our haters* to foil their own plans, they were terribly humiliated *(Tehillos Hashem).*

9. בֵּאלֹהִים הִלַּלְנוּ — *In God we glory.*

We compose hymns of praise to You, and our souls glory in the fact that You are our King *(Ibn Ezra).*

We praise ourselves in the presence of our enemies by declaring that we place our full confidence in our God, who will save us from their hands *(Radak).*

We tell the gentiles that for our sake God will relate to them as אֱלֹהִים, *the Dispenser of Strict Justice* and will punish them according to the letter of the law *(Chazah Zion).*

כָּל הַיּוֹם — *All the day.*

This really means *all of the days,* as in 25:5, אוֹתְךָ קִוִּיתִי כָּל הַיּוֹם, *I have hoped for You all the days (Radak).*

וְשִׁמְךָ לְעוֹלָם נוֹדֶה — *And Your name forever thank.*

Although the exile seems to drag on endlessly, this has not discouraged us nor caused us to forget Your name *(Radak).*

You punish our enemies with the name אֱלֹהִים, *Elohim*__ (Which denotes the attribute of Divine judgment), but You relate to us with שִׁמְךָ, *Your (true) Name,* 'ה, *HASHEM,* which denotes the attribute of Divine mercy *(Chazah Zion).*

10. [Having concluded his review of Israel's glorious past, the Psalmist laments the bitter exile which the nation now endures.]

Hebrew text with verse numbers on right:

מד
י-יד

י נוֹדֶה סֶּלָה: אַף־זָנַחְתָּ וַתַּכְלִימֵנוּ וְלֹא־
יא תֵצֵא בְּצִבְאוֹתֵינוּ: תְּשִׁיבֵנוּ אָחוֹר מִנִּי־צָר
יב וּמְשַׂנְאֵינוּ שָׁסוּ לָמוֹ: תִּתְּנֵנוּ כְּצֹאן מַאֲכָל
יג וּבַגּוֹיִם זֵרִיתָנוּ: תִּמְכֹּר־עַמְּךָ בְלֹא־הוֹן
יד וְלֹא־רִבִּיתָ בִּמְחִירֵיהֶם: תְּשִׂימֵנוּ חֶרְפָּה

אַף זָנַחְתָּ וַתַּכְלִימֵנוּ — *Though You abandon and disgrace us.*

Nevertheless, we will always continue to give thanks to Your name forever (v. 9) (Radak).

[The Psalmist introduces his description of the exile by reaffirming the staunch faith which has sustained Israel even in its darkest hours.]

Other commentators translate אַף זָנַחְתָּ וַתַּכְלִימֵנוּ in the past tense, to signify, "You have not redeemed us as You have our forefathers; on the contrary, You have abandoned and disgraced us. In the past You saved us i.e., our forefathers] *from our tormentors;* (v. 8) therefore, *In God we gloried all of the days* (v. 9). Now our enemies taunt us, '*Where is the God in whom you gloried? He has abandoned you!'* In the past, *You shamed our enemies* (v. 8), but now *You disgrace us* when the enemies see that we are cast away (Ibn Ezra; Radak).

וְלֹא תֵצֵא בְּצִבְאוֹתֵינוּ — *And go not forth with our armies.*

Your Holy Spirit does not rest upon our troops (Targum).

[See 60:12 and comm. (ibid.) הֲלֹא אַתָּה אֱלֹהִים זְנַחְתָּנוּ וְלֹא תֵצֵא אֱלֹהִים בְּצִבְאוֹתֵנוּ.]

11. תְּשִׁיבֵנוּ אָחוֹר — *Caused us to retreat* [lit. *to turn back*].

You made us turn the back of our necks to them [when we fled] (Targum).

Not only did You fail to redeem us, but also You caused terror to melt our

hearts and our resolve. Therefore we lacked the courage to make a stand against the foe (Ibn Ezra).

12. תִּתְּנֵנוּ כְּצֹאן מַאֲכָל — *You delivered us like sheep for devouring.*

In exile, the murder of a Jew by a gentile was considered no more of a crime than killing a sheep (Hirsch).

Alshich points to the irony of our downfall: when we are in God's favor the prophet declares, וְאַתֵּן צֹאנִי צֹאן מַרְעִיתִי אָדָם אַתֶּם אֲנִי אֱלֹהֵיכֶם נְאֻם אֲדֹנָי ה', *And you my sheep, the sheep of my pasture, you are men, and I am your God says the Lord, HASHEM/Elohim* (Ezekiel 34:31).

In our relationship with God we are described as His tender *sheep*, but in comparison to all other nations, only the people of Israel are worthy of being called *men.* The barbaric atrocities of the gentiles cause them to be considered wild beasts, whereas Israel represents the epitome of civilization.

When Israel is in exile, however, the gentiles consider themselves the flower of mankind and view the Jews as outcasts of society. Moreover, we are deemed even more lowly than the animals, for *they delivered the corpse of Your servant to be consumed by the birds of the sky* (79:2), i.e. they treat us like foul, putrid carrion.

וּבַגּוֹיִם זֵרִיתָנוּ — *And among the nations scattered us.*

Those of us who were not slaughtered and devoured by the enemy were dispersed among the nations (Ibn Ezra).

*¹⁰ Though You abandon and disgrace us,
     and go not forth with our armies.
¹¹ You caused us to retreat from the foe,
     and our haters to plunder for themselves.
¹² You delivered us like sheep for devouring,
     and among the nations scattered us.
¹³ You sold Your nation for no fortune,
     and did not increase their price.
¹⁴ You made us a disgrace to our neighbors,*

In particular, we were scattered throughout the one hundred and twenty-seven provinces of the empire of Persia/Media (Alshich).

Because gentile law regarded us as no better than animals (sheep), we were constantly forced to search for new shelter, causing us to become increasingly dispersed. Our population in each country dwindled, and we became a weak, barely visible minority (Hirsch).

13. תִּמְכֹּר עַמְּךָ בְלֹא הוֹן — *You sold Your nation for no fortune.*

As the Prophet said, חִנָּם נִמְכַּרְתֶּם, *You were sold for nothing* (Isaiah 52:3). The men who sells his possessions usually does not expect to recover them. Similarly, You sold us into such a lengthy exile that it seems as if You will never take us back (Radak).

This sale was a great disgrace for us, for if an owner values his goods, he places a high price on them. Conversely, if he gives them away, he proves that he deems them worthless (Nora Tehillos).

When a master purchases a slave for a considerable sum, he treats the slave well in order to protect his investment. Since our captors acquired us at no cost, however, they have no concern for our welfare, and treat us with wanton cruelty (Malbim).

Even when our enemies are in a position to sell us, they regard us as so utterly devoid of value that they charge

nothing for our people. When Haman wanted to compensate Ahaseuros by paying 10,000 talents of silver for permission to annihilate the Jewish nation, Ahaseuros refused payment for he was content to get rid of the Jews at no royal expense. He said to Haman, 'The silver is given to you and the nation too, to do with it as you see fit' (Esther 3:11) (Alshich).

וְלֹא רִבִּיתָ בִּמְחִירֵיהֶם *And did not increase [through] their price.*

I.e., You, Hashem, made no profit from the sale of Israel to the nations. It is not unusual for a person to give a present without taking anything in return. But in such cases it is customary for the donor to praise his gift so that the beneficiary will appreciate it. But You, Hashem, remained silent concerning Israel's true worth; You did not inform the gentiles that their conquest of our nation greatly increased their own assets. (Baalei Bris Avrohom).

14. תְּשִׂימֵנוּ חֶרְפָּה לִשְׁכֵנֵינוּ — *You made us a disgrace to our neighbors.*

[Cf. 79:4, הָיִינוּ חֶרְפָּה לִשְׁכֵנֵינוּ לַעַג וָקֶלֶס לִסְבִיבוֹתֵינוּ.]

Malbim comments that these tragic verses describe the progressive deterioration of our status in society. At the beginning of our exile, we had slave-masters who were eager to keep us, although they treated us harshly. In time, our dishonor was such that no

טו לִשְׁכֵנֵינוּ לַעַג וָקֶלֶס לִסְבִיבוֹתֵינוּ: תְּשִׂימֵנוּ

טז מָשָׁל בַּגּוֹיִם מְנוֹד־רֹאשׁ בַּלְאֻמִּים: כָּל־

הַיּוֹם כְּלִמָּתִי נֶגְדִּי וּבֹשֶׁת פָּנַי כִּסָּתְנִי:

יז מִקּוֹל מְחָרֵף וּמְגַדֵּף מִפְּנֵי אוֹיֵב וּמִתְנַקֵּם:

יח כָּל־זֹאת בָּאַתְנוּ וְלֹא שְׁכַחֲנוּךָ וְלֹא־

יט שִׁקַּרְנוּ בִּבְרִיתֶךָ: לֹא־נָסוֹג אָחוֹר לִבֵּנוּ

כ וַתֵּט אֲשֻׁרֵינוּ מִנִּי אָרְחֶךָ: כִּי דִכִּיתָנוּ

one would come near us, as it says: וְהִתְמַכַּרְתֶּם שָׁם לְאֹיְבֶיךָ לַעֲבָדִים וְלִשְׁפָחוֹת וְאֵין קֹנֶה, *And you will attempt to sell yourselves to your foes for slaves and maidservants, and no one will buy you* (Deuteronomy 28:68).

[Since no one wanted to live in our proximity, isolated ghettos were established.]

לַעַג וָקֶלֶס לִסְבִיבוֹתֵינוּ — *The mockery and scorn of those around us.*

Malbim adds: As the duration of the exile lengthens, the circle of anti-semitism continues to expand. At first, only our immediate neighbors despised us and confined us to ghettos. Eventually this senseless hatred spread until all of our gentile compatriots found it repulsive to breathe the same air and to tread the same soil as the Jews. We were unanimously scorned and forcibly expelled from the entire land.

15. תְּשִׂימֵנוּ מָשָׁל בַּגּוֹיִם — *You made us a byword among the peoples.*

Among the gentiles, the word 'Jew' became a byword used to describe anything base and despicable (*Hirsch*).

After having expelled us so cruelly, the gentile nations could have purged all hatred of Israel from their memories, but this did not occur. Although our bodies were cast out, our name remained a permanent part of the gentiles' everyday vocabulary (*Malbim*).

מְנוֹד רֹאשׁ בַּלְאֻמִּים — *A cause for the nations to shake their heads.*

They shake their heads at us in derision, as we read: כָּל רֹאַי יַלְעִגוּ לִי יַפְטִירוּ בְשָׂפָה יָנִיעוּ רֹאשׁ, *All those who see me deride me, they open their mouths, they wag their heads* [22:8] (*Radak*).

When the nations discuss the welfare of their citizens, they reject the idea that the Jew deserves kindness or consideration. Throughout their deliberations, they *shake their heads* in negation and opposition, denying the Jew favor or advantage (*Hirsch*).

16. כְּלִמָּתִי נֶגְדִּי — *My humiliation is before me.*

Malbim explains that when a person is humiliated by others this is known as כְּלִימָה. The next verse ascribes this humiliation to קוֹל מְחָרֵף *the voice of the reviler* (of Israel) and the *blasphemer* (of God)

וּבֹשֶׁת פָּנַי כִּסָּתְנִי —*My shamefacedness covers me.*

Malbim continues: בֹּשֶׁת is the feeling of shame which arises from within man when he recognizes how disgracefully he has conducted himself.

[When the exiled Jews suffer כְּלִימָה, humiliation at the hands of others, they begin to feel *ashamed* for they recognize that their own sins and misconduct caused the exile.]

17. מִקּוֹל מְחָרֵף וּמְגַדֵּף — *At the voice of blasphemer and reviler.*

the mockery and scorn of those around us.
¹⁵ *You made us a byword among the peoples,*
     a cause for the nations to shake their heads.
¹⁶ *All day long my humiliation*
     is before me
And my shamefacedness covers me
     ¹⁷ *at the voice of reviler and blasphemer,*
     before enemy and avenger.
¹⁸ *All this came upon us*
     yet we did not forget You;
nor have we falsified Your covenant.
¹⁹ *Our heart has not drawn back,*
     nor our footsteps strayed from Your path.

They degrade us intentionally, viciously and publicly, with loud, audible voices *(Ibn Ezra).*

וּמִתְנַקֵּם — *And avenger.*
They seek to take revenge, as if we had actually harmed them first *(Radak).*

18. [We now enter the third portion of this Psalm. After completing his description of Israel's suffering and humiliation in the exile, the Psalmist declares that Israel remained undaunted. Their undying faith in their eventual redemption and restoration invested them with the courage to withstand the calamities of the exile.]

כָּל זֹאת בָּאַתְנוּ וְלֹא שְׁכַחֲנוּךָ — *All this came upon us yet we did not forget You.*
Despite our suffering we never forgot that we must praise and thank You for everything *(Metzudas David).*

וְלֹא שִׁקַּרְנוּ בִּבְרִיתֶךָ — *Nor have we falsified Your covenant.*
Even when under duress, we did not desert our faith and convert *(S'forno).*
Although we were persecuted and threatened, we never neglected to perform the Bris Milah, nor did we cease to

observe the covenant of the Sabbath *(Malbim).*

Alshich interprets: *Nor have we falsified Your covenant* by claiming that, in exile, the Torah is no longer valid or binding. God had promised וְאַף, *And yet despite all this, when they are in the land of their foes, I will not despise them nor will I reject them, to destroy them, nullify My covenant with them.* (Leviticus 26:44). When Israel suffers tremendously in exile and God's presence is nowhere to be seen, it would be natural for Israel to question the truth of the assurances contained in the Divine Covenant — yet we have never done so.

19. לֹא נָסוֹג אָחוֹר לִבֵּנוּ — *Our heart has not drawn* [lit. stepped] *back .*
Our hearts have not retreated from a position of firm faith *(Radak).*

20. כִּי דִכִּיתָנוּ — *Even when You crushed us.*
Rashi translates כִּי as בַּאֲשֶׁר, *when.*

בִּמְקוֹם תַּנִּים — *In the place of Tanim.*
[The word *Tanim* refers to a wild creature which lives in a place unfit for human habitation, but the exact identity

מד בְּמָקוֹם תַּנִּים וַתְּכַס עָלֵינוּ בְצַלְמָוֶת: אִם־

כא שָׁכַחְנוּ שֵׁם אֱלֹהֵינוּ וַנִּפְרֹשׂ כַּפֵּינוּ לְאֵל

כב זָר: הֲלֹא אֱלֹהִים יַחֲקָר־זֹאת כִּי־הוּא יֹדֵעַ

כג תַּעֲלֻמוֹת לֵב: כִּי־עָלֶיךָ הֹרַגְנוּ כָל־הַיּוֹם

of this creature is unknown. The word usually means reptile or fish, and in modern Hebrew, תַּן means *jackal*. Since we lack the specific guidance of Talmudic sources, the word has been left untranslated. (See comm. to *Eichah* 4:3 Artscroll edition).]

Ibn Ezra interprets the word as if the מ at the end of תַּנִּים was substituted with a נ, to create תַּנִּין, *sea giant*. This implies, we have been thrust down to the very depths of the sea, where the dangerous sea giants roam; and this dark, murky place surely resembles צַלְמָוֶת *the shadow of death*.

Ibn Ezra and *Radak* also offer an alternate interpretation for the original spelling of תַּנִּים, explaining that this is a vicious beast of the wilderness. This is an allusion to the Babylonians, who tormented their Jewish captives mercilessly.

וַתְּכַס עָלֵינוּ בְצַלְמָוֶת — *And shrouded us with the shadow of death*.

The gentiles sought to wrest us from our faith by their death threats (*Malbim*).

21. אִם שָׁכַחְנוּ שֵׁם אֱלֹהֵינוּ — *Have we have forgotten the Name of our God*.

... Then God Himself would investigate and discover it (*Rashi*). Ac-

tually, any such inquiry would reveal that the thought of betraying God never even entered our minds (*Radak, Sforno*), as it says *All this came upon us, yet we did not forget You* (v. 18) (*Ibn Ezra*).

The four commentators cited above construe this verse as a denial of any wrongdoing. However, *Alshich* interprets the verse as both a confession of betrayal and an apology. The Psalmist explains that the only cause of betrayal was torture worse than death, as we read, *Because You crushed us in the place of the [cruel] Tanim* (v. 20).

The *Midrash* echoes this concept: Rabbi Chanina bar Abba said, 'If someone would tell me to give up my life for the sanctification of God's name, I would do it, provided that he kill me instantly. But I could not endure the דּוֹר שֶׁל שְׁמַד, *the generation of persecution*. Then, the enemies took iron balls and heated them until they became white-hot. They placed these balls under the armpits of their pitiable victims and squeezed the life out of them. They took sharp splinters of reed and stuck them under their victims' fingernails, until they squeezed the life out of them.[1]

וַנִּפְ רֹשׂ כַּפֵּינוּ לְאֵל זָר — *And extended our hands [lit. palm] to a strange God?*

1. We find a similar idea in the *Talmud* (*Kesubos* 33b): The self-sacrifice of Chananya, Mishael and Azariyah is regarded as a classic example of martyrdom. They refused to bow down to the statue of Nebuchadnezzar, even though this refusal condemned them to be thrown into a raging inferno. The Talmud states, however, if the Babylonians had that beaten and tortured them incessantly, they would have yielded and bowed down to the statue.'

Rabbeinu Tam (ibid. *Tosafos s.v.* אלמלא) maintains that they would have bowed down rather than submit to torture only because Nebuchadnezzar's statue was not a true idol, but a glorification of the king.

[See conclusion of footnote on *v.* 23].

20 *Even when You crushed us in the place of* Tanim
and shrouded us in the shadow of death.
21 *Have we forgotten the Name of our God
and extended our hands to a strange god?*
22 *Would God not have discovered this?
for He knows the secrets of the heart.*
23 *Because for Your sake we are killed all day long*

Even when they forced us to worship their idols under pain of death, we did not succumb, and we gave up our lives as it says, *For Your sake we are slain all the time* (v. 23) *(Radak).*

22. הֲלֹא אֱלֹהִים יַחֲקָר זֹאת — *Would not God have discovered this?* [lit. *searched this out*].

[This is a continuation of the rhetorical question posed in the previous verse.] If we had forsaken God, if even the vaguest thought of apostasy had momentarily entered our minds, then, *Would God not have discovered this?*

Furthermore, the most compelling proof of our unquestioning faith is that we never *extended our hands to strange gods* and that we gladly died for God's sake. Only the man whose faith is firm can surrender his life without reservation or regret *(Radak).*

כִּי הוּא יֹדֵעַ תַּעֲלֻמוֹת לֵב — *For He knows the secrets of the heart.*

[*Tosafos (Shabbos* 12b s.v. שאין השרת מלאכי) holds that the ministering angels are aware of the thoughts of man's heart. *Maharitz Chayos (ibid.)* however, cites a number of Scriptural passages which indicate that only God is capable of this all-pervasive knowledge, as in 7:10, *O searcher of hearts and minds, O righteous God.* (Cf. citations in *Gilyon Rabbi Akiva Eiger* and *S'fas Emes, ibid.*)

The solution may be that angels know man's conscious thoughts but only God understands *the secrets of the*

heart, i.e. the sub-conscious complexities of the human mind.

23. כִּי עָלֶיךָ הֹרַגְנוּ כָל הַיּוֹם — *Because for Your sake we are slain all day long.*

[In every generation, the Jew has proudly surrendered his life to sanctify God's name. *Meshech Chochmah (Parshas Vayeira* 22:14) explains that martydom became ingrained in the Jewish character when the Patriarch Isaac readily encouraged his father, Abraham, to sacrifice him in accordance with God's command. (See *Overview* to *Breishis* II Artscroll ed.)

Therefore, in the preceding verse, the Psalmist calls upon God to acknowledge Israel's undying loyalty to Him, *for He knows the secrets of the heart.*]

Rashba asks how it is possible to be *slain all the time,* since a person can only die once. He comments that this verse actually refers to the Mitzvah of reciting the Shema every day. When the Jew declares, וְאָהַבְתָּ אֵת ה׳ אֱלֹהֶיךָ בְּכָל לְבָבְךָ וּבְכָל נַפְשֶׁךָ, *And you shall love HASHEM your God with all your heart and all your soul (Deuteronomy* 6:5), he should firmly resolve that he is prepared to give up his life if necessary, for the love of God's name. This sincere commitment is considered equivalent to actual martyrdom, and Jews who maintain this determination are credited with being *slain all the time* for God's sake.

Divrei Shlomo adds: The conclusion of this verse confirms *Rashba's* interpretation, for it says נֶחְשַׁבְנוּ [lit. *We are thought to be*] כְּצֹאן טִבְחָה *as sheep prepared for slaughter,* i.e., with our

כד נֶחְשַׁבְנוּ כְּצֹאן טִבְחָה: עוּרָה | לָמָּה תִישַׁן |
כה אֲדֹנָי הָקִיצָה אַל־תִּזְנַח לָנֶצַח: לָמָּה־פָנֶיךָ
כו תַסְתִּיר תִּשְׁכַּח עָנְיֵנוּ וְלַחֲצֵנוּ: כִּי שָׁחָה
כז לֶעָפָר נַפְשֵׁנוּ דָּבְקָה לָאָרֶץ בִּטְנֵנוּ: קוּמָה
עֶזְרָתָה לָּנוּ וּפְדֵנוּ לְמַעַן חַסְדֶּךָ:

thoughts alone we are considered
sacrifices for God's glory.[1]

נֶחְשַׁבְנוּ כְּצֹאן טִבְחָה — *We are considered
as sheep [prepared] for slaughter*
(*Targum*).

As animals prepared for slaughter,
the righteous submit to their executioners (*Midrash Koheles* 3:18).

Although we are superior to our executioners in every way, we act like
helpless animals and deliver ourselves
for slaughter, to sanctify Your Name
(*Ibn Ezra*).

[The Jew surrenders not because he is
cowardly or weak, but because he is
convinced that his death is the will of
God. With true heroism, he submits to
the Divine decree.]

Sacrificing one's life is not the only
form of martyrdom. The *Talmud* (*Gittin* 57b) cites numerous ways in which
Jews give of themselves כָּל הַיּוֹם, *all day*

long. For example, 1) Jews willingly cir-
cumcize their sons, despite the danger
involved. 2) The Sages speak in praise
of Torah scholars who endure such
hardship in the pursuit of their studies
that they may say figuratively of
themselves that they commit suicide for
the sake of Torah knowledge.

Sefer Chassidim adds: If a Jew is embarrassed by those who ridicule him
when he fulfills God's mitzvos, it is
considered a sacrifice of his blood for
God's name, because the blood rushes
to his face when he blushes in shame
and disappears as he pales.

24. עוּרָה — *Awaken!*

עוּרָה should not be understood
literally, as *Awaken!*, for the *Talmud*
(*Sotah* 48a) emphasizes that God never
sleeps. As stated in 121:4: *Behold the
Guardian of Israel does not sleep, nor
does He slumber.*

1. *Dorash Moshe* elaborates on this theme by citing the Talmud's description (*Berachos* 61b)
of the heroic death of Rabbi Akiva. As the Romans tore at his flesh with iron combs, Rabbi
Akiva calmly recited the Shema. His disciples were amazed by his fortitude, but Rabbi Akiva
attempted to minimize his heroic accomplishment. He explained, 'All of the days of my life I
recited the credo *And you shall love* HASHEM *your God with all your heart and all your soul*,
but I was grieved that I was never given the opportunity to fulfill this commitment. Now that
the opportunity has finally arrived should I not fulfill it (joyously)'?

The *Shaloh Hakodosh* reveals the profundity of Rabbi Akiva's statement. When reciting
the words, *With all your soul*, one should imagine the excruciating pain experienced when dying and try to feel the torment of an agonizing execution. If one conditions himself in such a
manner all the days of his life, then when he is actually confronted with the need to submit to
a violent death for God's sake, he will be so accustomed to the pain that it will hardly affect
him.

Therefore, Rabbi Akiva said, 'Since I was מִצְטַעֵר, *pained*, all my days over this verse, the
actual torture does not disturb my joy now.'

The *Maharam* of *Rottenburg* (*Responsa* 517) emphasizes this idea and promises that once a
person unconditionally resolves to surrender his life to sanctify God's name, he will feel no
pain despite any torture the enemy may inflict on him.

[Consequently, Jewish law does not differentiate between brief and prolonged torture, in
regard to the obligation to sanctify God's name. See conclusion of footnote to *v.* 21.]

XLIV   *we are considered as sheep for slaughter.*
24-27   ²⁴ *Awaken, why do You seem to sleep, O my Lord?*
       Arouse Yourself, forsake not forever!
   ²⁵ *Why do You conceal Your face*
       ignore our affliction and oppression?
   ²⁶ *For prostrated to the dust is our soul,*
       clinging to the earth is our belly.
   ²⁷ *Arise — assist us!*
       And redeem us by virtue of Your kindness!

Certainly, God's supervision of the world never ceases; however when He shows no reaction to the cruel persecution of the Jews, *it appears to mankind as if God 'slumbers.'*

The *Talmud (ibid.)* relates that in the Second Beis Hamikdash, there was a group of Levite singers known as the מְעוֹרְרִין *the Awakers.* They would stand on the courtyard stage and chant the verse *Awaken! Why do You [seem to] sleep my Lord?'* Yochanon, the High Priest, abolished this practice [because by interpreting the verse literally, the singers were blasphemously reproaching Hashem].

Maharsha (ibid.) stresses that even the figurative meaning of this verse applies only to the time when the Temple is destroyed and Israel is dispersed, but not to Yochanan's time, when the Temple still stood.

לָמָה תִישַׁן אֲדֹנָי — *Why do You seem to sleep, my Lord?*

We have no doubt that God is fully awake and that He is aware of all events. However, our gentile enemies taunt, 'Downtrodden Jew, where is your Saviour? Is He asleep?' *(Ibn Ezra).*

Minchas Shai notes that this verse is punctuated by a פְּסִיק, *line of interruption,* which separates לָמָה תִישַׁן *Why do You sleep from* אֲדֹנָי, *my Lord.*

This division indicates that God, being incorporeal, is not subject to physical needs, even though the Torah describes Him anthropomorphically.

הָקִיצָה — *Arouse Yourself!*

This form of awakening is more vigorous than that implied by the word עוּרָה *(Malbim).*

25. לָמָה פָנֶיךָ תַסְתִּיר — *Why do You conceal Your face?*

Vilna Gaon explains that הֶסְתֵּר פָּנִים *concealment of the Divine Presence,* constitutes a double punishment. We are imperiled physically because God no longer protects us; even worse, we are endangered spiritually, because God tests us by camouflaging his Providence so that preordained events appear to be mere accidents. This can mislead men to believing that God has abandoned the world to natural forces and that He no longer reigns as Master of the Universe *(Zera Yaakov).* [See *Overview* to *Megillas Esther,* ArtScroll ed.]

תִּשְׁכַּח עָנְיֵנוּ וְלַחֲצֵנוּ — *[And] ignore* [lit. *forget*] *our afflicion and oppression.*

[The Psalmist declares that if God had not cared for us in the past, then His present indifference would be less painful. But we are well-aware that God once bestowed His full affection on us and that our shameful conduct has made Him want to forget His special relationship with us.]

26. כִּי שָׁחָה לֶעָפָר נַפְשֵׁנוּ — *For prostrated to the dust is our soul.*

The long saga of Israel's woes nears its end. Like a dying man gasping for

his last breath, Israel groans, 'I stand at the brink of death; I am about to return to the dust from whence I came!' (*Radak*).

Alshich observes that these words allude to the cause of Israel's severe degradation. Man is composed of lowly matter and a lofty spirit; life's mission is to harness this matter and discipline it to serve the purposes of the spirit. Thus the *dust* can rise to the level of the *soul*. But the children of Israel failed to subordinate the material to the spiritual; instead they used their intellect and *soul* to satisfy the mundane desires of their *dust*. God is not to blame for Israel's decline; the nation buried itself.

דָּבְקָה לָאָרֶץ בִּטְנֵנוּ — *Our belly is pressed to the earth.*

This description also underscores Israel's acute degradation. When a person trips, he usually tries to break his fall, so that he hits the ground supported by his hands and feet. In this position he looks no worse than an animal, which goes about on all fours. But when the children of Israel stumble, the land on their faces with nothing to shield them from the impact of the

fall. They 'bite the dust' and lie flat on their bellies, in a position even lower than an animal's. They appear to have no 'hands', i.e., no means of self-support (*Midrash Shmuel*).

27. קוּמָה עֶזְרָתָה לָּנוּ — *Arise! Come to our assistance!*

Once Israel has descended to the lowest point, the nation immediately begins to ascend. As the Psalmist said, '*our soul is bowed down to the dust ... Arise!*' (*Shemos Rabbah* 1:9).

Alshich adds that it is not uncommon for a fallen man to rise, for, once he has reached the bottom, his situation can only approve. However, under normal circumstances his ascent is gradual. Therefore the Psalmist pleads on behalf of Israel, 'Arise swiftly, O God, and grant Israel a meteoric rise'.

וּפְדֵנוּ לְמַעַן חַסְדֶּךָ — *And redeem us by virtue of Your kindness.*

When Israel is restored to its former glory with supernatural swiftness, the world will recognize that you no longer conceal Your presence from the Jewish people. This will demonstrate that Israel is Your chosen nation, the beneficiary of '*Your kindness*' (*Alshich*).

This is a song of praise for the Sages of the Sanhedrin of Moses, composed prophetically by the sons of Korach (Targum).

Korach, supported by two hundred fifty leaders of the Congregation of Israel, challenged the Divine authority of Moses and slandered him with vicious accusations of selfishness and falsehood (Numbers 16:2). The sons of Korach repented and sought to undo their father's treachery by portraying Moses and all authentic Torah scholars in the light of truth, emphasizing their boundless generosity and scrupulous honesty.

Indeed, the salvation of Korach's sons, who originally collaborated with their rebellious father, was a direct result of their respect for Moses. While they were sitting with their father, Moses passed by. Korach's sons were in a quandary. They pondered: If we stand to honor Moses, we will disgrace our father; but if we sit, we will breach the Torah's command to rise in the presence of a Sage. Finally they decided that it was preferable to honor the scholar, Moses, despite the affront to their father. At that moment, the spark of sincere repentance began to flicker in their hearts (Yalkut Shimoni 752).

The Torah scholar resembles the שׁוֹשַׁנָּה, rose, a delicate flower surrounded by thorns, which seem ready to pierce the rose's fragile petals. Actually, these brambles protect the rose by discouraging the hands which try to pluck it. Similarly, those who originally oppose the Sages (who represent God) will ultimately recognize the Sages' truly splendid virtues and become their guardians and supporters.

The Midrash and commentaries relate this psalm to several individuals described in Scripture. At first Abraham was universally ostracized for his teachings, but he was later acclaimed as the leading citizen of the world. At first David was vilified and pursued, but he was finally accepted as ruler and king. At first Messiah will be challenged, but he will ultimately become the universal sovereign. Alshich and Malbim interpret this psalm as a description of the coarse body, which at first hinders the development of the soul, but is eventually trained to assist it.

Alshich and Hirsch also explain this psalm as a wedding song celebrating the marriage of a bride and groom, who begin marriage with two very different and sometimes conflicting personalities, but who ultimately blend together in perfect sublime harmony. In light of these interpretations, the Psalm's title, שִׁיר יְדִידֹת, A song of endearment, is highly appropriate.

אַ לַמְנַצֵּחַ עַל־שֹׁשַׁנִּים לִבְנֵי־קֹרַח מַשְׂכִּיל
בַּ שִׁיר יְדִידֹת: רָחַשׁ לִבִּי | דָּבָר טוֹב אֹמֵר

---

1. עַל שֹׁשַׁנִּים — *Upon Shoshanim* [lit. *the roses.*]

[See Artscroll *Songs* 2:1 for a complete discussion of why שֹׁשַׁנָּה is translated *rose*, rather than *lily.*]

Radak and *Malbim* identify the *Shoshanim* as the musical instrument which accompanied this psalm. Its name is derived from its rose-like shape *(Metzudas Zion)*.

According to *Rashi*, this psalm was composed in honor of the Torah scholars who are tender as the rose, beautiful as the rose and saturated with good deeds as the fresh, moist rose. Just as the rose contains many exquisite petals, so is the Torah sage composed of a variety of a scholarly attainments *(Ohel Yaakov)*.

[שֹׁשַׁנִּים may also be read שֶׁשָׁנִים, *who study and review*, alluding to the scholars who are constantly immersed in their lessons in order to fulfill the commandment וְשִׁנַּנְתָּם, *And you shall teach them diligently (Deuteronomy* 6:7). See *comm. v.6* חִצֶּיךָ שְׁנוּנִים.]

[*Targum* renders שֹׁשַׁנִּים as *Sanhedrin* as he does in 69:1 and 80:1, the only other instances where this title is used. However, *Rashi (Psalms* 60:1) identifies this name with Israel, which resembles a rose surrounded by menacing thorns and which needs a prayer for protection.]

Radak and *Ibn Ezra (v.* 2) maintain that this song was dedicated to Messiah. *Ibn Ezra* adds that it may refer to David himself; for the names of Messiah and David are one, as seen in the verse, *And David, My Servant, will be a* [Messianic] *prince for them forever (Ezekiel* 37:25).

Nora Tehillos notes that this psalm was placed after the previous one, which vividly describes the agony of Israel in exile, to foretell Israel's glorious redemption at the time of the Messiah.

לִבְנֵי קֹרַח — *For the sons of Korach.*

Just as the rose is encircled by thorns, so were the sons of Korach surrounded by their father and his followers. Just as the custom is to burn and destroy the thorns, so were Korach and his company obliterated, but his sons, who were like roses, were plucked out of the inferno and saved *(Midrash; Alshich)*.

The sons of Korach were actually swallowed by the earth together with their father and his cohorts. They said of themselves, *Our soul is bowed to the dust, our belly is pressed to the earth (44:26). But at the last moment they cried out, 'Arise! Come to our assistance! (44:27)*.

The Holy One, Blessed be He, responded, 'It all depends on you! Just as the rose which wishes to flourish turns itself towards the sky, so must you train your hearts towards heaven in sincere repentance. When Israel repents I will redeem them, as the prophet declares, *I will be as the dew for Israel, if they flourish like the rose,* [which lifts its head heavenward]' *(Hoshea* 14:6). Therefore this Psalm of Korach's son's is entitled, *Upon the roses. (Midrash Shocher Tov)*.

מַשְׂכִּיל — *Maskil* [lit. *for enlightenment* see *comm.* 32:1.]

The sons of Korach were *enlightened* in that they recognized that Moses was in the rights, therefore, they repented and sang *(Tehillos Hashem)*.

שִׁיר יְדִידֹת — *A song of endearment* [lit. *friendships.*]

[The term here is not the singular יְדִידוּת, *friendship* but the plural יְדִידוֹת, which alludes to a number of friends

For the Conductor, upon Shoshanim,
    for the sons of Korach, a Maskil,
    a song of endearment.
² My heart is astir with a good theme;

(feminine) or *endearments*. The commentaries suggest that this *endearment* takes several forms.]

This is a song of love [for the Torah scholars], a song of praise for them, a song intended to endear the scholars to all men and to make their Torah appreciated by all (*Rashi*).

The song arouses Israel's love for their Father in heaven, and His love for them (*Sforno*).

The song describes God's love for His ordained Messiah (*Radak*).

The psalm is prefaced with three special [musical] terms לַמְנַצֵּחַ, מַשְׂכִּיל, שִׁיר corresponding to the three sons of Korach. All were יְדִידֹת, *friends*, of God. Furthermore, Moses, Aaron and all of the great scholars who were *friends* of God came to hear the songs which the sons of Korach composed (*Midrash Shocher Tov*).

2. רָחַשׁ לִבִּי דָּבָר טוֹב — *My heart is astir with a good theme.*

This is the preface to the song of endearment. The Psalmist declares that his heart was stirred to create a fine composition in praise of the Torah scholar (*Rashi*). [Torah is described as טוֹב, as in *Psalms* 119:72, *Proverbs* 3:14, 4:2, and *Avos* 6:3].

רָחַשׁ — *Astir* [lit. stirred, moved.]

Hirsch notes that this is the only place in Scriptures where רחש is employed as a verb rather than as a noun meaning a creeping reptile.

Meiri defines this as a slight quivering motion which is almost imperceptible. The creeping reptile is called רחַשׁ because of its peculiar motion [cf. *Leviticus* 11:20-21 and 22:5, where the *Targum* of שֶׁרֶץ is רָחַשׁ]. In the language of the Talmud, we find that the faint murmuring of the lips is termed רְחוּשׁי מְרַחְשָׁן שִׂפְוָותֵיה (*Sanhedrin* 90b). Here it means, *My heart was stirred to compose this song by a spirit of prophecy.*

Sforno renders רחש as *proliferate*, thus: My heart gives birth to many good thoughts.

Midrash Shocher Tov observes that when the sons of Korach were swallowed in the earth, they were dumb — struck by the awesome sight of the fires of Gehinnom leaping from below. Although their tongues were mute, their hearts were *stirred* to repentance and God graciously accepted this minimal silent confession of guilt, and saved them. Furthermore, the Psalmist uses the singular form לִבִּי, *my heart*, to emphasize that the three sons were simultaneoulsy aroused and developed identical thoughts at the same time and their hearts were as one.

Hirsch notes the contrast between the ordinary poet and the inspired Psalmist. Authors typically seek out pretty words and polished phrases, assuming that once they discover the proper words, the right thoughts will follow automatically. Not so the Psalmist, whose hymns well up from the depths of his heart. His main concern is the sincerity and truth of his inner thought. The words needed for outward expression are but secondary vehicles of communication. Therefore, the first thing that happens is: *My heart is astir.* Afterwards: *my tongue is the pen.*

אָנִי מַעֲשַׂי לְמֶלֶךְ לְשׁוֹנִי עֵט | סוֹפֵר
ג מָהִיר: יָפְיָפִיתָ מִבְּנֵי אָדָם הוּצַק חֵן
בְּשִׂפְתוֹתֶיךָ עַל־כֵּן בֵּרַכְךָ אֱלֹהִים
ד לְעוֹלָם: חֲגוֹר־חַרְבְּךָ עַל־יָרֵךְ גִּבּוֹר הוֹדְךָ

אֹמֵר אָנִי מַעֲשַׂי לְמֶלֶךְ — I say: 'My
works befit a king.'

I declare that the song which I composed is fit for a king i.e., for a Torah
scholar — who is called a king,
(Proverbs 8:15) (Rashi). [See Gittin 62a:
Who are the true kings? The Rabbis!]

This song befits the King Messiah
(Radak).

לְשׁוֹנִי עֵט סוֹפֵר מָהִיר — My tongue is the
pen of a skillful scribe.

Rashi quotes Rabbi Moshe Ha-
Darshan who translates מָהִיר as בָּקִי,
well-versed, adept. This concurs with
the Targum.

Radak relates מָהִיר to מַהֵר, swift,
nimble, suggesting that this scribe
writes without delay or hesitation. He
takes pains to insure brevity and con-
ciseness (Sforno).

The Psalmist conveys his message in
the most succinct form to fulfill the dictum (Pesachim 3b): One should always
teach his students in the shortest way
possible (Imrei Shefer).

According to an ancient adage, the
tongue is the pen of the heart (Ahavas
Olam). [Only when the heart is free of
ambivalence and indecision can the
tongue articulate its sentiments without
hesitation.]

A person should remember that
whatever his tongue utters here [in this
world] is immediately inscribed in the

record book in heaven. Thus the tongue
truly functions simultaneously as a
'pen' (Alshich).

3. יָפְיָפִיתָ מִבְּנֵי אָדָם — You are beautiful
beyond other men.

You [the Torah scholar] are fairer
than the ordinary men who are immersed in temporal, material pursuits
(Rashi).[1]

Your extraordinary beauty is two-
fold (hence the compounded form of
(יָפְיָפִיתָ — יָפֶה): Both your outer appearance and the words which flow
from within you are attractive (Radak).

This refers to the all-inclusive excellence of Messiah, of whom the prophet
says: (Isaiah 52:13) Behold My servant
shall be enlightened, he shall be exalted
and lifted up and he shall be very high
(Ibn Yachya).

Kedushas Levi renders these words
literally, 'You have become beautiful
from the sons of man,' intimating that
the king should always bear in mind
that his majesty is derived from his subjects, for if they had not accepted his
rule, he would have nothing. [Therefore
the king should be humble. The Torah
scholar also derives the most beautiful
and significant part of his learning from
his students, as the Talmud (Taanis 7a)
notes, 'From my students I learned most
of all!']

1. [However, once the scholar begins to seek material benefits, he no longer appears attractive. The Talmud (Sanhedrin 52B) states: 'How does a Talmid Chacham (Torah Scholar) appear in the eyes of the Am Haaretz (unlearned man)? At first, he resembles a precious, golden
vase. Once he starts to talk freely to the Am Haaretz, the Sage seems like a mere silver vase.
And when the Talmid Chacham derives some benefit from the Am Haaretz, the ignorant man
loses respect for the Sage and regards him as a cheap earthenware jug, which breaks easily and
cannot be repaired.' (This refers to the scholars and leaders who joined Korach's revolt. They
were scholars, at first, but once they accepted favors and gifts from the wealthy Korach, he
lost all respect for them. Finally, he pressured them to join his evil conspiracy — Rashi,ibid.).]

I say: 'My works befit a king,
my tongue is the pen of a skillful scribe.'
³ *You are beautiful beyond other men,*
charm is poured upon your lips,
Accordingly God has blessed you
for eternity.
⁴ *Gird your sword upon your thigh,*

הוצק חֵן בְּשְׂפְתוֹתֶיךָ — *Charm is poured
upon your lips.*

The spirit of prophecy is placed upon
your lips *(Targum).*

The Torah scholar is the most attractive of all men because God has endowed him with the ability to issue
truthful and authoritative halachic decisions *(Rashi).*

[The Torah scholar is exhorted to
share his knowledge orally. The *Talmud*
(Eruvin 54a) advises, Scholar, open
your mouth and recite! Open your
mouth and study, that your knowledge
will be retained and your life will be
lengthened, as it says, *Torah is life for
those who spread it by their mouths*
(Proverbs 4:22).]

עַל כֵּן בֵּרַכְךָ אֱלֹהִים לְעוֹלָם — *Accordingly
God has blessed you for eternity.*

The Kingdom of Messiah shall endure forever *(Meiri).* He shall be eternally endowed with the greatest of
blessings: he will find favor in the eyes
of all men *(Radak).*

4. חֲגוֹר חַרְבְּךָ עַל יָרֵךְ גִּבּוֹר — *Gird your
sword upon your thigh, O mighty one.*

Radak notes that sometimes the
sword is girded on the מָתְנַיִם, *loins*
[above the thigh; see *Exodus* 28:42] as
in *II Samuel:* 20:8 [see *Rashi, ibid.*], and
sometimes, as in this verse, it is fastened
on the יָרֵךְ, *thigh.*

Rashi explains this phrase as an allegory describing מִלְחַמְתָּה שֶׁל תּוֹרָה, *the
battle of Torah study.*[1]

1. [In many instances we find that intensive Torah study is compared to deft swordsman-
ship.]
See *Song of Songs* 3:8 Artscroll edition כֻּלָּם אֲחֻזֵי חֶרֶב מְלֻמְּדֵי מִלְחָמָה, *All of them gripping
the sword of tradition, skilled in the battle (of Torah).* Compare this with *Chagigah* 14a:
Mighty Man refers to a master of tradition; *Man of War* refers to one who can dispute in the
intellectual 'warfare' of Torah (i.e., he is a mentally agile debater who knows how to deal with
the argumentation essential to the study of Torah).
Specifically, the girding of the mental sword denotes preparation to render a judgment or
halachic decision. The *Talmud,* *(Sanhedrin* 36a) notes the words David used in bidding the
members of the Sanhedrin to ready themselves for Judgment: *And David said to his men: Let
every one of you men gird his sword. And every man girded his sword, and David also girded
his sword* (I Samuel 25:13).
The *Talmud* *(Sanhedrin* 7a) emphasizes the extreme caution which the magistrate must exercise when approaching a ruling: The judge should always imagine a sword poised on his
thigh [or, at his throat, *(Rambam, Sanhedrin* 23:8)] and the fires of Gehinnom roaring
beneath him.
Rav Yosef Yitzchak interprets the girding of the sword on the loins as a simile describing
self-control and restraint. The Psalmist teaches that the greatest victory is not won by the man
who conquers others with his unsheathed sword, but by the man who refrains from drawing
his sword. This form of self-mastery is a real triumph; it truly bespeaks *a majesty and a splendor.*

ה וַהֲדָרְךָ: וַהֲדָרְךָ | צְלַח רְכַב עַל־דְּבַר־
אֱמֶת וְעַנְוָה־צֶּדֶק וְתוֹרְךָ נוֹרָאוֹת יְמִינֶךָ:

הוֹדְךָ וַהֲדָרֶךָ — *Your majesty and your splendor.*

Your Torah knowledge is your praise (*Rashi*); Specifically, the knowledge which you amassed for yourself is *your majesty* and that which you teach to others is *your splendor* (*Sforno*). [The above explanation complements the commentary of *Malbim* on *Psalms* 104:1 which defines הוֹד as private and personal *majesty*, and הָדָר as external *splendor* displayed to the public eye.]

[On the Sabbath a person may not carry objects in the public domain, but he is permitted to wear garments and adornments. The *Talmud (Shabbos* 63a) debates whether or not the girded sword is classified as an adornment (which would permit one to wear it on the Sabbath). One opinion maintains that a sword can be considered an adornment on the basis of this verse, which describes the sword as a *majesty and splendor.* An opposing view refutes this by citing the verse in *Isaiah* (2:4), *And they shall beat their swords into plowshares and their spears into pruning hooks.* If, the argument goes, the sword is an adornment, then why should it be destroyed in the future? The *sword* in our verse is a metaphor to denote Torah knowledge.]

In consonance with his opinion that this psalm describes Messiah, *Radak* understands the *sword* as a real weapon. Although the prophets always portray the Messianic era as a time of universal peace, this tranquility will be achieved only after the terrible war of Gog and Magog [see *Prefatory Remarks, Psalms* 2]. During this cataclysmic confrontation, the Messiah's martial skills will be his *splendor.*

[See *Psalms* 21:6 הוֹד וְהָדָר תְּשַׁוֶּה עָלָיו, *majesty and splendor You conferred*

upon him which *Midrash Shocher Tov* interprets as a reference to Messiah who is endowed with *two* forms of excellence: beauty and strength. Also, see above v.3, describing Messiah as possessing a two-fold excellence: יָפְיָפִיתָ.

5. וַהֲדָרְךָ — *And [this is] your splendor.*

Your most prominent attribute is not the military prowess depicted in the previous verse but the intellectual achievements described here (*Malbim*).

Radak understands *verses* 4 and 5 to mean: After You (Messiah) achieve Your splendid triumph over the enemies, as described in the preceding verse, do not subjugate them (*ride over them*) with pride and haughtiness. Rather be guided always by truth and sincere humility.

צְלַח — *Gain success.*

Radak renders this as *go over, trample,* referring to the conquest of the enemy. [See *Radak* on *II Samuel* 19:18:וְצָלְחוּ הַיַּרְדֵּן לִפְנֵי הַמֶּלֶךְ, *And they passed over the Jordan before the king.*]

[Concerning Solomon, the son of David, it is written וַיִּצְלַח, *And he succeeded* (I Chronicles 29:23). According to the *Talmud (Sanhedrin* 93b) David, too is described as מַצְלִיחַ, *successful* (see gloss ibid.]

רְכַב עַל דְּבַר אֱמֶת — *And ride [high] on truthfulness.*

Rashi explains that the Torah scholar will issue true and honest decisions, unaffected by external factors. This is also a distinctive feature of the Messiah, as Scripture says: *And the spirit of Hashem will rest upon him, the spirit of wisdom and understanding, the spirit of counsel and might, the spirit of knowledge.... and he shall not judge after the sight of his eyes nor decide*

XLV
6-8

O mighty one — your majesty and your splendor.
⁵ And this is your splendor: gain success,
ride high on truthfulness and righteous humility.
May it guide you to awesome deeds
with your right hand.

after the hearing of his ears (Isaiah 11:2,3)

True faith and sincere belief in Hashem are hallmarks of the Messiah as Isaiah (11:5) says: *And righteousness shall be the girdle of his loins and faith the girdle of his body* (Ibn Yachya; Norah Tehillos).

Targum interprets: [Messiah] will ride on a unique royal steed.

וְעַנְוָה צֶדֶק — *And right and humility.*
This alludes to the excellent characteristics of the Messiah (*Isaiah 11:4*): *And with righteousness he will judge the poor, and decide with equity for the humble of the earth* (Ibn Yachya).

[*Rambam, Hilchos Melachim* 2:6 describes humility as the hallmark of the Jewish King: Although the Torah accorded the King great honor, nevertheless he must feel himself small and insignificant...He must deal compassionately with both the lowly and the great ... concern himself with the dignity of all ... speak softly to the people ... and act with extreme humility ... and untiring patience ... as a shepherd who tends to his flock.]

[In reference to the scholar, the Sages say: עֲנָוָה סְיָג לְחָכְמָה, *Humility is the safeguard of knowledge* (Kallah Rabbassi 3). Also, we find that the dimensions of the golden Ark of the Sanc-

tuary, the repository of the Torah were given in fractions, whereas the dimensions of the other sacred vessels were given in whole numbers. *Baal Haturim* (*Exodus 25:10*) emphasizes that this teaches the Torah scholar humility: 'Never consider yourself whole and complete but rather a mere fraction of what you should be!']

וְתוֹרְךָ נוֹרָאוֹת יְמִינֶךָ — *May it guide you to awesome deeds with your right hand.*
Addressing the scholar, the Psalmist continues to speak of Torah study in militaristic terms: 'Your dedication to Torah and to truth will guide you to such an amazing strategy that your right hand will succeed in performing awesome deeds' [i.e., you will be endowed with an unerring perception of the true and fitting halachic decision.] Continuing his symbolism of war, the Psalmist refers to the scholars accomplishments as if he were a mighty warrior holding a weapon in his right hand (*Rashi*).

Norah Tehillos comments that Messiah will be endowed with an unerring genius for 'sniffing out' the truth, as it says: *And he shall smell with the fear of HASHEM* (Isaiah 11:3). According to *Rashi* (ibid.), the Messiah will be able to detect a person's innocence or guilt merely by observing his face.[1]

---

1. The Talmud (*Sanhedrin 93b*) relates: Bar Kuziva reigned two-and-one-half years. He declared to the Sages, 'I am the Messiah!' They said to him 'It is written of the Messiah that he has the ability to smell the truth and render judgment accordingly. Let us see whether you possess this power!' When the Sages proved that Bar Kuziva lacked this ability and that he was a false messiah, they executed him. [See *Ravad's* gloss on *Rambam, Hilchos Melachim* 11:3]

[565]   *Tehillim*

ו חִצֶּיךָ שְׁנוּנִים עַמִּים תַּחְתֶּיךָ יִפְּלוּ בְּלֵב

ז אוֹיְבֵי הַמֶּלֶךְ: כִּסְאֲךָ אֱלֹהִים עוֹלָם וָעֶד

ח שֵׁבֶט מִישֹׁר שֵׁבֶט מַלְכוּתֶךָ: אָהַבְתָּ צֶּדֶק

וַתִּשְׂנָא רֶשַׁע עַל־כֵּן | מְשָׁחֲךָ אֱלֹהִים

ט אֱלֹהֶיךָ שֶׁמֶן שָׂשׂוֹן מֵחֲבֵרֶךָ: מֹר־וַאֲהָלוֹת

6. חִצֶּיךָ שְׁנוּנִים ... בְּלֵב — *Your arrows ... sharpened ... in the heart.*

First, the metaphor of the *sword* is employed (*v. 4*); now the Psalmist uses the metaphor of *arrows* (*Ibn Ezra*).

Our translation follows *Rashi* who instructs us to read the first and last phrases of this verse as one continuous statement viewing the middle phrase עַמִּים תַּחְתֶּיךָ יִפְּלוּ as a parenthetical interruption (מִקְרָא מְסוֹרָס). Thus *Your arrows are sharpened i the heart of the foes of the king; nations fall beneath you. Ibn Ezra* maintains that יִפְּלוּ, *they fall*, refers to the *arrows*. Thus *Your arrows are sharpened...they fall into the heart of the foes of the king.*

Rashi continues to explain that the Psalmist elsewhere likens *arrows* to students, as we read, כְּחִצִּים בְּיַד גִּבּוֹר כֵּן בְּנֵי הַנְּעוּרִים, *As arrows in the hand of the warrior, so are the children of one's youth* (127:4). Furthermore, the Torah scholars who are engaged in heated discussion and dispute are considered temporary *foes* as the Psalmist (*Psalms* 127:5) concludes: לֹא יֵבֹשׁוּ כִּי יְדַבְּרוּ אֶת אוֹיְבִים בַּשָּׁעַר *They shall not be put to shame rather they shall speak with their enemies in the gate.* [See *Talmud, Kiddushin* 30a) for elaboration on this theme. There the Sages exhort the scholars, וְשִׁנַּנְתָּם 'Let the words of Torah be sharp and clear in your mouth! If someone asks you a question, do not hesitate or stammer; rather, respond immediately with clarity!']

עַמִּים תַּחְתֶּיךָ יִפְּלוּ — *Nations fall beneath you.*

In the merit of Torah study, the gen-

tile nations are vanquished by Israel (*Rashi*).

As the *Talmud* (*Gittin* 57b) says: when the voice of Jacob is raised [in Torah study], the hands of Esau are subdued (*Tehillos Hashem*).

The clarity and sharpness of Israel's Torah teachings will overwhelm the erring gentile nations to the point that they will feel compelled to admit that the truth is with the Jews (*Sforno*).

Abarbanel writes that Jerusalem is now in the hands of the Ishmaelites (Arabs), but that Edom is destined to capture the city. The Ishmaelites will not tolerate this and will gather to battle the Edomites. The redemption of Israel [and the downfall of all our enemies who slay each other] will result from this war (*Rav Vidal HaTzorfati*).

בְּלֵב אוֹיְבֵי הַמֶּלֶךְ — *In the heart of the foes of the king.*

[The initial downfall of Israel's foes does not take place on the field of battle. Our enemies defeat themselves by surrendering to the destructive passions of their hearts.]

7. כִּסְאֲךָ אֱלֹהִים — *Your throne, O judge.*

According to *Rashi*, אֱלֹהִים refers to the scholar in his role as judge. Even a mortal man of flesh and blood can merit this divine title if he sincerely seeks to administer God's justice on earth, as we read concerning Moses רְאֵה נְתַתִּיךָ אֱלֹהִים לְפַרְעֹה, *Behold I have placed you as judge* [lit. *master*] *over Pharoah* (*Exodus* 7:1). [See also *ibid.* 21:6; 22:7.]

Ibn Ezra [cited in *Radak*] is of the opinion that אֱלֹהִים refers to God. He

XLV
6-8

⁶ *Your arrows are sharpened,*
nations fall beneath you,
in the heart of the foes of the king.
⁷ *Your throne, O judge,*
is forever and ever,
The scepter of equity
is the scepter of your kingdom.
⁸ *You love righteousness*
and hate wickedness,
Accordingly has God, your God, anointed you
with oil of joy above your peers.

renders: *Your throne [O King] is the throne of* אֱלֹהִים, *God,* as it is written וַיֵּשֶׁב שְׁלֹמֹה עַל כִּסֵּא ה׳, *And Solomon sat on the throne of HASHEM (I Chronicles 29:23).*

Rav Saadia Gaon (quoted by *Ibn Ezra* and *Radak*) translates: *Your throne [O King] is prepared and established by God.*

שֵׁבֶט מִישֹׁר שֵׁבֶט מַלְכוּתֶךָ — *The scepter of equity is the scepter of your kingdom.*

...Therefore your throne is *forever and ever (Rashi),* because things Divine do not deteriorate with the passage of time [and truth and Divinity are synonymous] *(Malbim).*

8. אָהַבְתָּ צֶּדֶק וַתִּשְׂנָא רֶשַׁע עַל כֵּן מְשָׁחֲךָ — *You love righteousness and hate wickedness accordingly has ... God anointed you.*

[Other monarchs gain their thrones as a result of savage power struggles in which all law, order, and decency are callously discarded. The unpopular king who rules only by brute force oppresses and tyrannizes his subjects,

plunging them into misery. Not so the king of David's line. His throne is divinely established by virtue of the king's equity and righteousness. Therefore his enthusiastic subjects welcome his anointment as a cause for national gladness.]

אֱלֹהִים אֱלֹהֶיךָ — *God, your God.*

Although אֱלֹהִים, *God,* is Master of the entire universe, He watches over you [His Chosen King] with special providential care, which makes Him אֱלֹהֶיךָ, *your* [personal] *God (Meiri).*

שֶׁמֶן שָׂשׂוֹן — *Oil of joy.*

Most subjects despise those who have the authority to rule over them, but your anointment was greeted with joy *(Otzar Nechmad).* [1]

Ahavas Olam raises a halachic question: If we interpret this Psalm as referring to Messiah, then this verse teaches us that the future Messiah will actually be anointed with sacred oil. This seems to run counter to the Talmudic dictum, 'A King who is the son of a King is not anointed ... because the monarchy is his

1. *Yalkut Shimoni (Samuel 124)* relates that the oil itself rejoiced when anointing David. When Samuel attempted to pour the oil on the heads of each of David's seven brothers, instead of flowing downward, the oil recoiled back up to the horn. But before Samuel even had a chance to pour the oil on David, the oil spurted forth from the horn on its own and anointed David. It turned into pearls and precious gems on his head, for God had observed David's righteousness and deemed him eminently worthy of monarchy.

by inheritance ... unless his rule is disputed' *(Horios 11b: Rambam, Hilchos Melachim 1:12)*. Since Messiah is a direct scion of the House of David and inherits the throne as his rightful estate, why will he be anointed?

The answer is that God wishes to demonstrate to the entire world that Messiah reigns on his own merit and that even if he were *not* heir to the throne, he would be fit to rule. This is the message of our verse: *You, Messiah, personally love righteousness and hate wickedness: therefore God has personally anointed you with a special anointment.*

[*Minchas Chinuch* (107) explains that when the ten tribes rebelled against Rechavam, the son of Solomon, he lost sovereignty over them. In order for Solomon or his heirs to regain royal status over the ten tribes, a new anointment is needed. Therefore, Messiah will require a new anointment if he wishes to reign over all of Israel, including the ten tribes.]

מֵחֲבֵרֶךָ — *Above your peers.*

Ibn Ezra comments that if this psalm is dedicated to David himself, then חֲבֵרֶךָ would refer only to Saul. [*Samuel* warned Saul that his monarchy would be taken away by God saying: *And He will give it to your friend who is worthier than you (I Samuel 15:28).*] If, however, the psalm refers to Messiah, then חֲבֵרֶךָ would refer to Messiah's peers, the other devout sages of his generation.

Radak maintains that חֲבֵרֶךָ is plural, despite the fact that the customary י before the ךָ (the required spelling in the plural) is deleted.

9. מֹר — *Myrrh.*

Rav Hai Gaon identifies this as the fragrant sap of a tree, called *luvni* in Arabic *(Radak)*. [See *Ramban* on *Exodus 30:23*.]

[This also alludes to the Torah scholar, as we read *(Song of Songs 5:13)* שִׂפְתוֹתָיו שׁוֹשַׁנִּים נֹטְפוֹת מוֹר עֹבֵר, *His* [the Torah scholar's *(Targum)*] *lips are roses, they drip flowing myrrh.*

The *Talmud (Shabbos 88b)* comments: 'With every word which the Holy One, Blessed be He, spoke, the whole world became filled with the fragrance of spice.' For God's words spiritually purify and refresh the soul, just as fragrant spices revive the body *(Alshich)*.]

וַאֲהָלוֹת — *Aloes.*

Aloes are plants of the lily family. Rav Adda explained in the name of Rav Yehuda that it is called *ahalos* because it comes to us by way of אֹהָלִים [ohalim], *tents* [i.e., it is imported by Bedouin tent-dwellers *(Matanos Kehunah)*]. However, the Rabbis say that it was called *ahalos* because it spreads in the tent [i.e., when used as incense in the Holy Service, its smoke spread in the אֹהֶל מוֹעֵד, *Tent of Meeting' (Radak)*]. It was with this fragrance that the Jews perfumed themselves during their forty years in the desert. [See *Midrash* and ArtScroll *commentary* to *Song of Songs 4:14*.]

קְצִיעוֹת — *[And] cassia.*

This is an exceptionally fragrant spice whose odor pervades the air. We find that one of Job's unusually beautiful daughters was called קְצִיעָה *(Job 42:14)* because her fragrance spread out like that of the cassia [*Bava Basra 16b*] *(Alshich).*

Rashi, Radak, and *Alshich* identify קְצִיעוֹת as the name of one of the spices, but *Ibn Ezra* disagrees. He argues that the absence of a ו, *vov* before this word indicates that it is not preceded by the article *and;* he takes this as evidence that the word is not connected with the two previous words (מֹר וַאֲהָלוֹת). *Ibn Ezra* interprets that the word is an adjec-

XLV   ⁹ *Myrrh, aloes, and cassia*
9   *are all your garments —*
          Finer than ivory palaces
            will be Mine that will gladden you.

tive (related to קָצַע *cut*) which modifies כָּל בִּגְדֹתֶיךָ. His translation is: *well cut and tailored are all your garments.*

כָּל בִּגְדֹתֶיךָ — *Are all your garments.*

All your garments are permeated with a pleasant fragrance (Rashi).

It is imperative that the Torah scholar wear only fresh, clean clothing (*Ibn Yachya*). [The Talmud (*Shabbos* 114a) says that a Torah sage who wears stained garments deserves to die. *Rav Yaakov Emden* comments that if the scholar ignores visible stains on his garments, he cannot be concerned about an unseen character flaw on his soul!]

Radak and *Meiri* interpret the *garments* as a metaphor for a person's character traits. This usage is seen throughout Scripture, as in *Ecclesiastes* 9:8, *At all times let your garments be white*. Refined character and good deeds weave an intangible 'garment' which surrounds the soul with glory (*Alshich*). [The poetic figure of fragrances and spices is used because the sense of smell is considered the most spiritual of the senses (see *Berachos* 43b).]

Rashi concludes his commentary with the observation that allegorically, this word may be read בְּגִידֹתֶיךָ, *your treacheries*, suggesting that even your sins and transgressions, which betray God and emit a foul stench, are atoned

for [through repentance], permitting your former fragrance to return.

מִן הֵיכְלֵי שֵׁן — *Finer than* [lit. *from*] *ivory palaces*.

The palaces which are prepared to gladden you in the Garden of Eden surpass the finest ivory palaces on earth (*Rashi*).

According to *Otzar Nechmad*, מִן is rendered literally as *from* and the *ivory palaces* refer to the paradise of Eden itself. The Psalmist informs us that the fragrances mentioned above come *from* Eden, as *Baal HaMaor* testifies: *Myrrh* and *aloes* are native only to Eden. The wind tears leaves and branches from these trees and casts them into the River Pishon which flows out of Eden. Arabs later gather these leaves from the river and enjoy their heavenly fragrance.[1]

Meiri identifies the *ivory palaces* as the upper heavens. From there God sends man the inspiration to cloak his soul in good deeds and splendid character traits.

מִנִּי שִׂמְּחוּךָ — *Will be Mine that will gladden you.*

Rashi renders מִנִּי as an abbreviated form of מִמֶּנִּי, *from Me.* The figurative palaces with which I [God] will reward you in the World to Come, will be far superior to even the most lavish ivory trappings of this world.

1. The *Talmud* (*Bava Metza* 114b) tells of the Sage, Rabbah bar Avuha whose dire economic straits hampered his advancement in Torah study. In order to alleviate his poverty, Elijah once took Rabbah to the Garden of Eden where he told Rabbah to remove his mantle and fill it with the wonderfully fragrant leaves of the Garden. As Rabbah was leaving Eden with his precious load, a heavenly voice proclaimed, 'Woe! Who had devoured and squandered his eternal reward as wantonly as Rabbah bar Avuha' [i.e., these leaves were reserved for the righteous in the Hereafter.] Upon hearing this, Rabbah promptly threw the leaves back into the Garden. Nevertheless, his cloak had absorbed such an extraordinary fragrance from the leaves that he sold it for 12,000 dinars and divided the profits among his sons-in-law.

י שִׂמְחוֹךְ: בְּנוֹת מְלָכִים בְּיִקְּרוֹתֶיךָ נִצְּבָה
יא שֵׁגַל לִימִינְךָ בְּכֶתֶם אוֹפִיר: שִׁמְעִי־בַת
וּרְאִי וְהַטִּי אָזְנֵךְ וְשִׁכְחִי עַמֵּךְ וּבֵית
יב אָבִיךְ: וְיִתְאָו הַמֶּלֶךְ יָפְיֵךְ כִּי־הוּא אֲדֹנַיִךְ

However, *Radak* and *Meiri* translate מְנִי as an emphatic form of the word מִן, *from* (see *Judges* 5:14, מְנִי אֶפְרַיִם...מְנִי מָכִיר): *The fragrance of your garments comes from the ivory palaces, from the very same palaces which gladden you.*

10. בְּנוֹת מְלָכִים בְּיִקְּרוֹתֶיךָ — *Daughters of kings visit you.*

This translation follows *Rashi*, who derives this word, from בִּקּוּר, *visit*. Princesses from all over the world come to attend to you and, to join your royal retinue.

The *Midrash* (*Bereishis Rabbah* 45:1) relates that both Pharoah [the father of Hagar] and Avimelech gave their daughters to the Patriarch Abraham, saying, 'Far better that they should be servants in the house of Abraham than noble princesses elsewhere.'

However, *Ibn Ezra, Radak,* and *Menachem* (quoted in *Rashi*) relate בְּיִקְּרוֹתֶיךָ to יָקָר, *precious, dear.* Thus: *Among your dearly beloved wives are the daughters of kings,* who are deeply honored to present their daughters to you.

Targum seems to incorporate both translations, rendering: They come to *visit* [בִּיקּוּר] you and to give you *honor* [יְקָר].

נִצְּבָה — *Erect stands.* [See *commentary* to 2:2, s.v. יִתְיַצְּבוּ.]

שֵׁגַל לִימִינְךָ — *The queen at your right.*

The *daughters of kings* are the foreign princesses who only enter the king's presence when they receive a special summons [i.e., although they have converted according to the prescribed halachic ritual, they are nevertheless mere concubines]. However, the שֵׁגַל is the Jewish queen, the king's con-

stant consort. Only she is bedecked in the most splendid crown jewels from Ophir (*Radak*).

Targum renders this allegorically: *the scroll of the Torah is in your right hand* [referring to the halachah that the king must carry a Sefer Torah with him at all times (*Deuteronomy* 17:19), attached to his right arm like a jeweled ornament (*Sanhedrin* 21b; see *footnote* to 16:8).]

בְּכֶתֶם אוֹפִיר — *In the golden jewelry of Ophir* (*Rashi*).

[The land of Ophir is reknowned for the quality and abundance of its gold, as seen in *I Kings* 9:28; 22:49 and in *I Chronicles* 29:4.]

11. שִׁמְעִי בַת — *Hear, O maiden* [lit. *daughter.*]

Radak says that *daughter* refers to the *daughters of kings* in the previous verse. *Listen to my words of discipline.*

Ibn Ezra suggests that if this psalm is for David, then *daughter* means his שֵׁגַל, *queen*; If this psalm is for Messiah, then the *daughter* is the entire congregation of Israel described elsewhere (*Lamentations* 2:6) as בַת יְהוּדָה, *the daughter of Judah* (see *Targum* and *Rashi*).

וּרְאִי — *See.*

'Understand my words once you have heard them.' Intellectual perception is often referred to as רְאִיָה *vision* (*Radak*).

From these words we arrive at an essential credo of Torah faith: man's idea of what is right does not necessarily concur with God's. *Every way of man is straight in his own eyes* (*Proverbs* 21:2). *There is a way which appears straight before a man yet its end is the ways of death* (*Proverbs* 14:12).

Since man's eyes are easily misled

10 *Daughters of kings visit you,*
erect stands the queen at your right
in the golden jewelry of Ophir.
11 *Hear, O maiden, see and incline your ear,*
forget your people and your father's house—
12 *Then the King will desire your beauty,*
for He is your Master — submit to Him.

[see *Overview, Tehillim I*], the Jew must first listen to the Oral Tradition handed down from Sinai, which will provide him with the basis of truth, i.e., *Hear, O daughter!* Only then will he be able to use his eyes properly to interpret visual data — וּרְאִי, *And see!* (*Ohel Yaakov; Beis HaLevi, Parshas Ki Sisa*)

וְהַטִּי אָזְנֵךְ — *And incline your ear.*

Beis HaLevi (Parshas Ki Sisa) continues that the Jew should first blindly accept the tradition which he receives (*hears*) from his parents and teachers. *Hear* refers to the development of this unquestioning faith in the complete truth of God's word. After his faith is firmly established, a Jew may apply his individual intelligence to Torah study and try to comprehend the logic and wisdom of each commandment; this process is suggested by the word וּרְאִי, *see.* Nevertheless, the scholar should never delude himself into thinking that his limited mind can totally grasp (*see*) the complete meaning of every *mitzvah.* Even after he studies Torah independently, he should still base his faith on what he hears and receives — וְהַטִּי אָזְנֵךְ, *And* [continue to] *incline your ear.*

וְשִׁכְחִי עַמֵּךְ — *Forget your people.*

This refers to the Samaritans, who dwell in your midst (because they ostensibly converted to Judaism and joined the Chosen People) and among whom you grew up (*Rashi*). [The Samaritans, who are known as כּוּתִים, *Kuthim*, rejected the Oral Tradition of Torah Law, תּוֹרָה שֶׁבְּעַל פֶּה and accepted only the

written tradition of תּוֹרָה שֶׁבִּכְתָב. Thus they failed to follow the prescribed path of placing שְׁמְעִי, *hear*, before רְאִי, *see.* Their detrimental influence must be shunned.]

Metzudas David interprets this entire verse in reference to the Messiah. The Psalmist exhorts all of the nations (*the daughters*) to listen to the commands of Messiah and to *forget* the wicked conspiracy of *the nations* of Gog and Magog, who plan to battle God's chosen king.

וּבֵית אָבִיךְ — *And your father's house.*

Forsake the idols worshiped by your forefathers. [Specifically, this indicates Terach, father of Abraham, who followed the pagan gods of Chaldea.]

Similarly we find that the pious Levites who refused to join the rest of Israel in the idolatrous service of the Golden Calf are praised: *Who said of his father and of his mother: 'I have not seen him', neither did he acknowledge his brethren, nor knew his own children* (*Deuteronomy* 33:9). Their loyalty and devotion to God transcends all personal considerations and relationships (*Olelos Ephraim*).

12. וְיִתְאָו הַמֶּלֶךְ יָפְיֵךְ — *Then the King will desire your beauty.*

If you follow the instructions set down in the previous verse, then the King [God] will yearn for the perfection of your deeds (*Rashi*).

כִּי הוּא אֲדֹנַיִךְ וְהִשְׁתַּחֲוִי לוֹ — *For He is your Master — submit to Him* [lit. *and you should prostrate yourself.*]

יג וְהִשְׁתַּחֲוִי־לֽוֹ: וּבַת־צֹר | בְּמִנְחָה פָּנַיִךְ
יד יְחַלּוּ עֲשִׁירֵי עָם: כָּל־כְּבוּדָּה בַת־מֶלֶךְ
טו פְּנִימָה מִמִּשְׁבְּצוֹת זָהָב לְבוּשָׁהּ: לִרְקָמוֹת
תּוּבַל לַמֶּלֶךְ בְּתוּלוֹת אַחֲרֶיהָ רֵעוֹתֶיהָ

Metzudas Zion, explaining these words in reference to Messiah, renders: If you, (the nations) follow his commands, then Messiah will reciprocate by acting as your guardian and dedicated protector. Then you may submit yourselves [*prostrate yourself*] to him without any fear or reservations, for he will take you under his wings.

13. וּבַת צֹר — *As for the daughter of Tyre.*

Tyre is the [prosperous] city which is very close to the Land of Israel. Its inhabitants always bring presents to each of the wives of the King [of Israel] (*Radak*).

[Indeed, Tyre symbolizes Israel's arch-enemy, Edom. The Sages teach that Israel and Edom will never share equal stature, for the balance of power will shift in favor of only one nation at a time. 'If one is filled with abundance, the other must be desolate' (*Pesachim* 42b; *Rashi* on *Megillah* 6a). In the Messianic era, Israel will gain eternal superiority and Tyre will humbly come to Jerusalem to pay tribute.]

בְּמִנְחָה פָּנַיִךְ יְחַלּוּ — *With homage will they seek Your presence.*

Our translation follows *Rashi*. The scholar need not seek the financial aid of the wealthy, [symbolized by Tyre] because [if he is truly worthy] the rich will [deem it a privilege to] support him, and they will seek him out in order to offer him their gifts (*Sforno*).

Radak punctuates the verse differently: וּבַת צֹר בְּמִנְחָה, *And the daughter of Tyre — with homage* / פָּנַיִךְ יְחַלּוּ עֲשִׁירֵי עָם, *The rich of the nation seek your presence*, i.e., Not only the people of Tyre, but also the wealthy men of every

nation will bring gifts to the daughters of the kings (who are married to the Jewish Monarch).

14. כָּל כְּבוּדָּה בַת מֶלֶךְ פְּנִימָה — *The complete glory of the princess is within.*

Those courtiers who are part of the royal retinue are the epitome of dignity, nobility and glory. They shun ostentation and seek privacy (*Rashi*).

[Throughout Rabbinic literature, the Sages cite this verse as a description of the chastity and modesty of the Jewish woman, who is no less a princess than the king's daughter. The glory of the Jewish wife and mother is to hold court in the inner chambers of her own home, which is her palace and royal domain.

Rambam (*Hilchos Ishus* 13:11) writes: Every woman should go out to visit her parents or to console the mourners or to rejoice at weddings or to perform acts of kindness for her friends, for a wife is not to be imprisoned in her home, as if it were a dungeon ... But it is a disgrace for a woman always to go into public places and main streets and a husband should restrain his wife from acting thus ... For the essence of a wife's beauty is to be enthroned in the corner of her home, as it says, *The complete glory of the princess is within.*]

מִמִּשְׁבְּצוֹת זָהָב לְבוּשָׁהּ — *Surpassing golden settings is her raiment.*

מִשְׁבְּצוֹת are the settings for precious gem (*Metzudas Zion*). [In particular, they were used in the garments of the High Priest, as in *Exodus* 28:11,13 et al. *Rashi* (ibid. 28:20) explains that the מִשְׁבֶּצֶת, *setting*, is expertly designed to perfectly cover the gem — neither too little nor too much. Similarly the rami-

13 *As for the daughter of Tyre,*
with homage will they seek your presence,
those richest of the nation.
14 *The complete glory of the princess is within;*
surpassing golden settings is her raiment.
15 *In embroidered apparel*
she is brought to the king,
The virgins in her train are her companions,

ment of the modest Jewish woman, who resembles a precious jewel, is carefully tailored and measured to cover her properly.][1]

Because the courtiers acted with privacy and modesty, they merit garments which are even more exquisite than those of the High Priest, which are adorned with golden settings *(Rashi)*.

15. לְרִקְמוֹת תּוּבַל לַמֶּלֶךְ — *In* [lit. *to*] *embroidered apparel she is brought to the king.*

While wearing beautifully stitched garments they will bring gifts to the Master of the Earth, as the prophet *(Isaiah 66:20)* says: *And they shall bring all of your brothers out of all the nations — an offering to HASHEM (Rashi).* [Perhaps the usage of the relatively uncommon verb תּוּבַל in our verse alludes to the fact that one of the distant nations which will come to God at that time is תּוּבַל, as mentioned in the previous verse in *Isaiah (66:19)*].

According to *Targum*, this refers to the priests who bring offerings to God in the Temple while wearing embroidered clothes [מַעֲשֵׂה רֹקֵם, see *Exodus 28:39*].

Radak, Ibn Ezra, and *Malbim* render תּוּבַל literally as *she is brought* i.e., the *daughter of the king* [referred to in the previous verse] is taken into the presence of the king. *Malbim* also translates לְרִקְמוֹת literally as *to embroider,* i.e. she is brought to an embroidered (wedding) canopy.

בְּתֻלוֹת אַחֲרֶיהָ רֵעוֹתֶיהָ — *The virgins in her train* [lit. *behind her*] *are her companions.*

According to *Rashi*, the *maidens* are the *companions* of the daughter of the king. This alludes to the future, when the gentiles will follow in the train of Israel [they will suddenly relinquish their age-old animosity and become our bosom companions], as the prophet *(Zechariah 8:23)* foretells: *In those days it shall come to pass that ten men out of all the languages of the nations shall take hold and shall seize the skirt of he who is a Jew, saying, 'We will go with you for we have heard that God is with you.'* [Perhaps because the gentiles will undergo a complete change of attitude towards Israel and renew their friendship, they are described as pure, untouched *maidens.*]

1. There was a pious woman named Kimchis who had seven sons, each of whom served in the office of High Priest. The Sages asked her, 'By virtue of which good deeds did you merit such honor?'

She replied, 'Not even the walls of my home ever saw a hair of my head uncovered. Neither did they ever see as much as the hem of my undergarments!'

In reference to Kimchis, the Sages recited this verse; *The complete glory of the princess is within* [because she acts with extraordinary modesty, she merits sons who are High Priests] *whose raiment is set with gold (Yerushalmi, Yoma 1:4).*

טז מוּבָאוֹת לָךְ: תּוּבַלְנָה בִּשְׂמָחֹת וָגִיל
יז תְּבֹאֶינָה בְּהֵיכַל מֶלֶךְ: תַּחַת אֲבֹתֶיךָ יִהְיוּ
בָנֶיךָ תְּשִׁיתֵמוֹ לְשָׂרִים בְּכָל־הָאָרֶץ:
יח אַזְכִּירָה שִׁמְךָ בְּכָל־דֹּר וָדֹר עַל־כֵּן עַמִּים
יְהוֹדֻךָ לְעֹלָם וָעֶד:

Radak (v.16) explains the metaphor of the בְּתוּלוֹת: just as maidens have no intimate knowledge of men before they marry, so do the nations remain completely ignorant of God and Torah until they heed the commands of Messiah and accept the dictates of the Torah, either by converting to the religion of Israel or by fulfilling the seven Noachide laws.

Metzudas David, differentiates between the maidens who are maidservants, who walk behind the princess, and the companions, who walk at her side.

מוּבָאוֹת לָךְ — Are led [lit. brought] to You.

The entire retinue is brought before the presence of God (Rashi) or before the Messiah (Metzudas David).

16. תּוּבַלְנָה בִּשְׂמָחֹת וָגִיל — They are brought with gladness and joy.

They all come voluntarily, without coercion (Ibn Ezra).

The nations gather eagerly around the Messiah to follow his orders and teachings (Radak).

תְּבֹאֶינָה בְּהֵיכַל מֶלֶךְ — They enter the palace of the King.

[They will be welcomed into the inner chambers.]

17. תַּחַת אֲבֹתֶיךָ יִהְיוּ בָנֶיךָ — Succeeding your fathers will be your sons.

According to Rashi, this statement [which appears to be a blessing] was addressed to all of Israel.

[An unbroken tradition of Torah study transmitted from father to son is a special blessing in regard to Torah scholarship. The Talmud (Bava Metzia 85a) teaches, 'Whoever is himself a scholar, has a son who is a scholar, and a grandson who is a scholar is guaranteed by God Himself that Torah will never depart from his descendants, … for the Torah always returns to its established dwelling place.']

Radak, however, interprets it as a declaration concerning Messiah, who inherits his throne from his forebears, who possessed it for generation after generation. Similarly, Messiah will transmit the monarchy to his progeny, who will continue to rule for uninterrupted generations. Thus, of each reigning member of this royal family we can say, Succeeding your fathers will be your sons.

The Midrash (Shir Hashirim Rabbah 1:6) observes that this blessing was especially apparent in Solomon, who took the place of his father in every way: A king, son of a king. A scholar, son of a scholar. A righteous man, son of a righteous man. David reigned forty years, and Solomon reigned forty years. David laid the Temple foundations; Solomon built the Temple above them. David authored books; so did Solomon. David composed songs; so did Solomon. David built an altar; so did Solomon. David brought up the Ark; so did Solomon.

are led to you.

¹⁶ *They are brought with gladness and joy,*
they enter the palace of the King.
¹⁷ *Succeeding your fathers*
will be your sons.
You will appoint them
as leaders throughout the land.
¹⁸ *I will commemorate Your Name*
through all generations,
Therefore the nations will acknowledge You
forever and ever.

תְּשִׁיתֵמוֹ לְשָׂרִים בְּכָל הָאָרֶץ — *You will ap-point them as leaders throughout the land.*

This statement is addressed to God: You will place the scions of Messiah in positions of authority everywhere *(Me-tzudas David).*

This is a blessing: May your sons develop the competence which will enable them to assist you in ruling the land for the benefit of your subjects *(Hirsch).*

18. אַזְכִּירָה שִׁמְךָ בְּכָל דֹּר וָדֹר — *I will commemorate Your Name through all generations.*

Rashi maintains that the Psalmist is referring to God. *Radak* is of the opin-ion that the verse is speaking of Mes-siah. In every generation we make con-stant mention of his name and await his arrival with longing.

Chazah Zion notes the use of the poetic feminine form אַזְכִּירָה rather than the proper masculine אַזְכִּיר. He explains that the extra letter ה alludes to the Four-Letter Name which represents God's Attribute of Mercy. Thus: In all generations, at all times, both good and

bad, I will make the name of Hashem memorable, reminding myself and others that even when God punishes harshly, He has my best interests in mind and is motivated solely by His *At-tribute of Mercy.*

Yaavetz HaDoresh observes that these words allude to the Sages' view that God exiled Israel and scattered them among the nations so that the Jews should promulgate His name in the farthest reaches of the globe and produce sincere converts *(Pesachim 87b).*

עַל כֵּן עַמִּים יְהוֹדֻךָ לְעוֹלָם וָעֶד — *Therefore the nations will acknowledge You forever and ever.*

Because I praise Your name inces-santly even in this generation, all na-tions will be prepared to acknowledge You when Your full glory is ultimately revealed *(Sforno).*

Radak concludes that since Israel yearned for Messiah in every genera-tion, therefore all nations will eventual-ly acknowledge his [universal, absolute] sovereignty, which will be un-precedented in the annals of history.

T his psalm was composed by the sons of Korach who became inspired by a spirit of prophecy when their father disappeared before their eyes (עֲלָמוֹת=נֶעְלָם, hidden). Korach's sons were saved; therefore, they recited this song' (Targum).

Hashem delivered Korach's sons from the earth which opened and threatened to swallow them with their father. This event taught Korach's sons that Divine salvation is never distant from those who deserve it, no matter how hopeless their plight may appear.

During their moment of inspiration, Korach's sons foresaw occasions in which Israel was destined to be endangered by armies and cataclysms which would threaten to tear the earth asunder. One such occasion occurred when the mighty Sennacherib and his hordes convulsed the entire globe and uprooted all of the nations (Rashbam). Another will occur during the War of Gog and Magog, when the peoples of the earth will gather to devastate Jerusalem (Yaavetz HaDoresh). In each case, God will foil the enemy's plots and miraculously rescue His Chosen People from danger.

This song is titled עֲלָמוֹת (which alludes to עוֹלָמוֹת many worlds), to indicate that God's salvation is expressed constantly, throughout the world (Dorash Moshe). Furthermore, we are obliged to trust God's guidance, which controls every aspect of life, although His deeds are נֶעְלָמוֹת, hidden and concealed (Divrei Shlomo).

א לַמְנַצֵּחַ לִבְנֵי־קֹרַח עַל־עֲלָמוֹת שִׁיר:
ב אֱלֹהִים לָנוּ מַחֲסֶה וָעֹז עֶזְרָה בְצָרוֹת
ג נִמְצָא מְאֹד: עַל־כֵּן לֹא־נִירָא בְּהָמִיר
ד אָרֶץ וּבְמוֹט הָרִים בְּלֵב יַמִּים: יֶהֱמוּ
יֶחְמְרוּ מֵימָיו יִרְעֲשׁוּ־הָרִים בְּגַאֲוָתוֹ

---

1. עֲלָמוֹת — *Alammos*

This is a musical instrument used in the Temple, as we read in *I Chronicles* 15:20 (*Rashi, Radak*).

Alshich explains that this is a song which expresses Israel's powerful love for God. Israel is referred to as עֲלָמוֹת, as we read עַל כֵּן עֲלָמוֹת אֲהֵבוּךָ, *Therefore do young maidens love You* (*Song of Songs* 1:3). [The *Midrash* (ibid.) comments: *The maidens* (i.e., Israel) *love You with youthful energy* (עֲלָמוֹת) *and vigor. ...*]

Meiri [in keeping with his theory that the names of instruments reflect their special musical characteristics (see *commentary* to 5:1 and 22:1)] explains that this instrument had the unique ability to arouse an extraordinary joy, found only in עֲלָמוֹת, *young men* or *maidens*.

[We may also interpret עֲלָמוֹת as עַל מָוֶת, *even unto death*, which alludes to Israel's irrepressible love for God, which remains steadfast even in the face of persecution and martyrdom. (See *commentary* to 9:1 and 48:15).]

2. אֱלֹהִים לָנוּ מַחֲסֶה וָעֹז — *God is for us refuge and strength*

Hashem not only defends us but also strengthens us during battle. He is our *refuge* when He protects us from the enemy's onslaught. Then He is our *strength* when we counter-attack and destroy the foe.

עֶזְרָה — *Help*

The Psalmist here refers to God as *refuge, strength,* and *help*. These three designations allude to the three sons of Korach who received Divine assistance (*Chazah Zion*).

בְצָרוֹת — *In distress* [lit. *distresses*]

This refers to the distress of חֶבְלֵי מָשִׁיחַ, *the travails of the* [*advent of*] *Messiah* (*Radak*).

The plural form of this word affords us a glimpse of God's *help*, for even if He must punish someone He does not bring distress upon him all at once. Instead He makes the punishment bearable by dividing it into a number of smaller, less overwhelming צָרוֹת, *distresses* (*Tehillas Hashem*).

נִמְצָא מְאֹד — *Very accessible* [lit. 'much to be found']

Our translation follows *Radak* who interprets מְאֹד, *much*, as the description of the עֶזְרָה, *help*, which God gives. Since He saves tiny, weak Israel from the threat posed by many mighty nations, God's help is indeed great (*much*).

According to *Metzudas Zion*, these words describe God Himself who is always available and present to lend assistance in difficult times.

Sforno maintains that נִמְצָא מְאֹד [*much to be found*] describes our צָרוֹת, which are extremely frequent because we so often incur God's wrath by choosing to do evil.

3. עַל כֵּן לֹא נִירָא — *So we shall not be afraid*

Since we have witnessed God's merciful salvation in the past, we do not fear the future, no matter how menacing it seems (*Sforno*).

בְּהָמִיר אָרֶץ — *At earth's transformation.*

The prophet (*Isaiah* 51:6 warns of that cataclysmic day [and simultaneously offers hope to those whom God

XLVI
1-4

For the Conducter, for the sons of Korach,
on the Alammos, a song.
² God is for us refuge and strength,
a very accessible help in distress,
³ So we shall not be afraid at earth's transformation,
and at mountains' collapse in the heart of the sea.
⁴ Its waters will rage and be muddied,
mountains will roar in His glory, Selah.

favors]: *For the heavens shall vanish like smoke and the earth shall wear out like a garment and they that dwell therein shall die in like manner; but my salvation shall be forever [for the righteous] and My righteousness shall not be withdrawn.*

The sons of Korach witnessed a terrible transformation of the earth; they were swallowed in the ground, yet were saved from doom by being suspended in the air. Therefore, they could assure Israel that similar miracles would occur in the future (*Rashi*).

According to *Ibn Ezra*, the Psalmist assures us that God Himself promised that no threatening global transformation will occur, because He has permanently established the boundaries of the earth and has decreed that the seas will never again cover the land mass. Thus *we have no fear that the earth will be transformed.*[1]

Indeed, *Radak* renders בְּהָמִיר אָרֶץ not as an upheaval of natural forces but political and military turmoil which will turn the entire globe into a battlefield, as the prophet warns: *Many tumultuous disorders come upon the inhabitants of the earth. They are shattered — nation*

against nation, city against city for God confused them with all manners of distress (*II Chronicles* 15:6).

וּבְמוֹט הָרִים בְּלֵב יַמִּים — *And at mountains' collapse in the heart of the sea*
This is metaphorical; *mountains* refers to the well-established kings who will be swept into the maelstrom [i.e., *the heart of the sea*] of the global war of Gog and Magog (*Sforno*).

Chazah Zion interprets the verse as a figurative description of the re-establishment of Jewish sovereignty. According to this view, we have no fear because there *will* indeed be a transformation, for the land will change from Arab rule to Jewish rule. The land will become transformed from desolate desert to fertile reconstructed territory. Then the *mountains*, i.e., the distinguished, righteous men, will uproot themselves from the exile and travel over *the heart of the sea* to make their way to the Holy Land.

4. יֶחְמְרוּ מֵימָיו — *Its waters...muddied.*
This refers to the waters' turbulence, which stirs up mud and slime from the sea floor [as in *Isaiah* 57:20] (*Rashi*).

1. *Ibn Ezra* makes use of this verse to negate a theory that was popular among the scientists of his day. Astronomers claimed that the orbit of the sun fluctuates a number of degrees in the sky. Therefore, they predicted, the sun would assume a new position which would have a disastrous effect on the earth's climate. Seas would evaporate into dry land and deserts would be flooded!

Nevertheless, *Ibn Ezra* points to our verse which assures mankind that it need have no fear, for God has promised to interfere with this cataclysmic course of nature, preventing a global catastrophe.

ה סֶלָה: נָהָר פְּלָגָיו יְשַׂמְּחוּ עִיר־אֱלֹהִים
ו קְדֹשׁ מִשְׁכְּנֵי עֶלְיוֹן: אֱלֹהִים בְּקִרְבָּהּ בַּל־
ז תִּמּוֹט יַעְזְרֶהָ אֱלֹהִים לִפְנוֹת בֹּקֶר: הָמוּ
גוֹיִם מָטוּ מַמְלָכוֹת נָתַן בְּקוֹלוֹ תָּמוּג

Thus יַחְמְרוּ is derived from חֵמָר, *slime*, [see *Genesis* 14:10] (*Radak*).

Radak also suggests that חָמָר can mean *heaps, piles*, as in חֳמָרִם חֳמָרִם, *piles upon piles* (*Exodus* 8:10). Here the raging sea waters are seen as piling up in towering waves.

Metaphorically, the armies of Gog and Magog will surge forward like a raging sea, only to be defeated and covered with slime and rubble (*Sforno*).

יִרְעֲשׁוּ הָרִים — *Mountains will roar.*

The mighty nations who joined Gog and Magog now roar in the anguish of defeat (*Sforno*).

בְּגַאֲוָתוֹ — *In His glory* [lit. *pride*].

This defeat of the wicked will come about when God will display His glorious might, as described in verse 2 (*Rashi*).

5. נָהָר — *The river.*

Rashi comments that this river flows from the Garden of Eden. *Ibn Ezra* identifies it as *Gichon*, which is the river of Jerusalem.

[*Rashi* notes in *Berachos* 10b that, although the Sages refer to the waters of Jerusalem (*II Chronicles* 32:4) as *Gichon*, that stream is not the same as the large river flowing out of Eden (*Genesis* 2:13). The river mentioned in *Genesis* does not lie in *Eretz Yisrael*. The *Gichon* of *Chronicles* is the שִׁילוֹחַ, the *Siloam Pool*, near Jerusalem, which is also called *Gichon* in *I Kings* 1:33 (see *Targum, ibid.*).]

פְּלָגָיו יְשַׂמְּחוּ עִיר אֱלֹהִים — *Its streams will gladden the City of God.*

As opposed to all the *waters* which *rage and grow murky*, one *river* will continue to flow tranquilly out of Jerusalem, the *City of God*. [This city will be unaffected by the surrounding turmoil.] The prophet [*Zechariah* 14:8] foretells, *And it shall come to pass on that day that living waters shall go out of Jerusalem half of them toward the eastern sea and half of them toward the western sea.* [That is, the Divine influence emanating from Jerusalem shall bring peace to both halves of the turbulent world, east and west] (*Radak*).

The main current of Torah knowledge flows into the world from the *Beis HaMikdash*, the Divine fountainhead. From there the *river* branches out into streams of intellectual enlightenment which flows into every *Beis HaMidrash* [House of Study] throughout the entire world. As the prophet proclaims [*Isaiah* 2:3], כִּי מִצִּיּוֹן תֵּצֵא תוֹרָה, *For out of Zion, Torah comes forth* (*Sforno*).

The prophet exhorts us to utilize these *waters*, saying [*Isaiah* 12:3], וּשְׁאַבְתֶּם מַיִם בְּשָׂשׂוֹן מִמַּעַיְנֵי הַיְשׁוּעָה, *And you shall draw up water with rejoicing from the wellsprings of Salvation* (*Radak*).[1]

קְדֹשׁ מִשְׁכְּנֵי עֶלְיוֹן — *Sanctified dwelling place of the Most High.*

Although the *entire* land of Israel is God's dwelling place, the holiest place of all [where His spirit rests with the

---

1. *Targum* renders the verse in *Isaiah*, וּתְקַבְּלוּן אוּלְפַן חֲדַת בְּחֶדְוָה מִבְּחִירֵי צַדִּיקַיָּא, *And you shall receive a new lesson, joyously, from select righteous men.* Rambam (*Guide* 1:30) explains that the *Targum* translates in this fashion because water is a metaphor for wisdom, which will then flow abundantly from the Sages, who are *the eyes of the congregation*. The word מִמַּעַיְנֵי, *from the wellsprings*, shuld be read מֵעֵינֵי, *from the eyes*. This will bring the true יְשׁוּעָה, *salvation*.

⁵ *The river — its streams will gladden*
the City of God,
sanctified dwelling place of the Most High.
⁶ *God is within it, it shall not falter,*
God will help it at the break of dawn.
⁷ *Nations roar, kingdoms totter,*
He raised His voice and the earth will dissolve.

greatest intensity] is Jerusalem (*Radak*); and the Holy Temple (*Sforno*).

6. אֱלֹהִים בְּקִרְבָּהּ בַּל תִּמּוֹט — *God is within it, it shall not falter.*

Although other mountains collapse and fall (v. 3), Mount Zion in Jerusalem will remain standing (*Ibn Ezra*).

This alludes to a statement in *Avos d'Rabbi Nassan*: Ten wondrous things occurred to our forefathers in Jerusalem ... Never did a building collapse [as a result of an earthquake] (*HaChaim Yoducha*).

יַעְזְרֶהָ אֱלֹהִים לִפְנוֹת בֹּקֶר — *God will help it at the break of* [lit. *facing*] *dawn.*

Targum renders: God will assist us in the merit of Abraham, who prayed for [assistance] at the break of dawn [see Genesis 19:27].

Radak notes the special symbolism of the word *dawn*. He explains that a battle will rage around Jerusalem, *I will gather all of the nations against Jerusalem to do battle, and the city shall be taken and the houses plundered* (Zechariah 14:2). That period [of defeat] will be known as עֶרֶב, *night*.

However, the ensuing era of victory will be called אוֹר, *light*, as the prophet (ibid. v. 7) foretells, וְהָיָה לְעֵת עֶרֶב יִהְיֶה אוֹר, *And it shall come to pass that at the time of night there will come a light.*

Tehillos Hashem interprets these words as a reference to the miraculous destruction of the host of Sennacherib, King of Assyria [see prefatory remarks]: *And it came to pass that night that the angel of Hashem went out and smote in the Assyrian camp one hundred and eighty-five thousand, and when they arose early in the dawn, behold, they were all dead corpses* (II Kings 19:35).

7. הָמוּ גוֹיִם מָטוּ מַמְלָכוֹת — *Nations roar, kingdoms totter.*

The nations which gather around Jerusalem begin roaring and boasting of their might, but eventually they will totter in defeat (*Sforno*).

נָתַן בְּקוֹלוֹ — *He raised His voice* [lit. *He gave with His voice*].

This refers to the great shofar which will be sounded at the time of the future redemption (*Chazah Zion*).

According to *Targum*, this alludes to the voice of God which thundered at Sinai, causing all of the nations to tremble and to roar in fear. [See *Zevachim* 116a. See also *commentary* to 29.11.] *Alshich* notes that his tremendous voice was heard לִפְנוֹת בֹּקֶר, *at the break of dawn* (v.6).[See Exodus 19:16.]

תָּמוּג אָרֶץ — *The earth will dissolve* [or: *melt.*]

This translation follows *Menachem*,

As *Shem Tov Falaquera* explains, true salvation is the liberation of the mind from the shackles of falseness and fantasy, which imagine that lust and gratification are meaningful and valuable. At the present time, a student can experience the bliss of having a personal *Messiah* if he allows his teacher (*Rebbe*) to teach him how to release his mind from its prison of personal desires. We still await the advent of the universal Messiah, who will grant this intellectual redemption to all men.

ח אָרֶץ: יהוה צְבָאוֹת עִמָּנוּ מִשְׂגָּב לָנוּ
ט אֱלֹהֵי יַעֲקֹב סֶלָה: לְכוּ־חֲזוּ מִפְעֲלוֹת
י יהוה אֲשֶׁר־שָׂם שַׁמּוֹת בָּאָרֶץ: מַשְׁבִּית

who relates this to נָמֹגוּ כֹּל יֹשְׁבֵי כְנָעַן, *All the inhabitants of Canaan melted* (*Exodus* 15:15). *Dunash*, however, defines תָּמוֹג as a term for *motion*, as in הֶהָמוֹן נָמוֹג, *The multitude moves* [*I Samuel* 14:16]; he translates this verse as *the earth moves* (*Rashi*).

Sforno draws our attention to the words of the prophet (*Zechariah* 14:12) which foretell disaster of consumption and *melting: And this will be the plague with which Hashem will smite all the peoples that have gathered against Jerusalem; their flesh shall melt while they stand upon their feet, and their eyes shall melt away in their sockets and their tongues shall melt away in their mouth.*

8. ה׳ צְבָאוֹת עִמָּנוּ — *HASHEM of Legions is with us.*

When the nations totter and melt, and Israel stands firm, everyone will recognize that *HASHEM of Legions is with us,* — but not with them (*Ibn Ezra*).

It will then be evident that God relates to us with His name HASHEM, i.e., *the Divine Attribute of Mercy* (*Alshich*).

Shaarei Hayashar observes that the gentile nations are supervised and controlled by a host of angels in heaven; only Israel is supervised directly by God. Thus, Hashem, who is master of legions of angels [which control the gentiles], is personally involved only *with us.*

מִשְׂגָּב לָנוּ — *A stronghold for us.*

The numerical value of לָנוּ equals eighty-six, which is the value of אֱלֹהִים. Thus, the verse esoterically signifies that HASHEM, *the Divine Attribute of Mercy*, is a stronghold to subdue His

Aspect of אֱלֹהִים, *the Dispenser of Strict Justice* (*Yoseif Tehillos*).

אֱלֹהֵי יַעֲקֹב — *The God of Jacob.*

More than any other patriarch, Jacob suffered a life filled with trials and afflictions; he survived only because God acted as his stronghold. Therefore it is most appropriate that when God is termed מִשְׂגָּב, *stronghold*, His name is associated with our father Jacob (*Norah Tehillos*). [Similarly we read (20:2) יְשַׂגֶּבְךָ שֵׁם אֱלֹהֵי יַעֲקֹב, *May the name of Jacob's God make you impregnable (see commentary there).*

[Simple mercy is extended only to men of meager faith. One who truly trusts in God realizes that strict judgment is the truest form of mercy, for it cleanses man of his shortcomings and propels him to higher levels of faith.]

Jacob was a man of complete faith who aspired to the level of וְהָיָה ה׳ לִי לֵאלֹהִים, *And HASHEM will be to me as God,* (*Genesis* 28:21); i.e., he asked that ה׳, *the Divine Attribute of Mercy,* should become for him אֱלֹהִים, *the Dispenser of Divine Justice* (*Sforno*). To Jacob, the names ה׳ and אֱלֹהִים were as one, for he understood that God's justice *is* mercy. Therefore, whenever Jacob's name is mentioned, both names of *God* are used together, as we read above (20:2) שֵׁם אֱלֹהֵי יַעֲקֹב...וְיַעַנְךָ ה׳ and here again ה׳ צְבָאוֹת עִמָּנוּ ... אֱלֹהֵי יַעֲקֹב.]

סֶלָה — *Selah!*

Many translate סֶלָה as *forever* [see commentary to 3:3]. The verse ends with יַעֲקֹב סֶלָה *Yaakov — forever*, because Jacob has indeed been immortalized. His face is etched into the throne of God Himself and will remain engraved there forever (*Ibn Yachya*).

XLVI
8-9

⁸ HASHEM of Legions is with us,
    a stronghold for us is the God of Jacob, Selah.
⁹ Go and see the works of HASHEM,
    Who has wrought devastation in the land.

9. לְכוּ חֲזוּ — *Go [and] see*

Sforno says that the Psalmist addresses his exhortation to the people of Jerusalem who will survive after the War of Gog and Magog. [Since Jerusalem will be left unscathed, they must *go* (לְכוּ) into the land of Israel which surrounds the city to witness the devastation.]

Hirsch defines חֲזוּ as the vision of the mind and soul, which perceive the full spiritual import of God's deeds and do not remain content with a superficial glance. [Thus the usage of לְכוּ *go* is justified because it suggests that in order to truly perceive the inner truth of God's works, one must make the effort to *go* and delve into the depths of events.

In 66:5 we read לְכוּ וּרְאוּ מִפְעֲלוֹת אֱלֹהִים, *Go and see the accomplishments of God*. It is relatively easy to perceive God in the role of אֱלֹהִים, *the Dispenser of Divine Justice*, for we often see men suffering for their sins. In that verse, therefore, the Psalmist uses the word רְאוּ, *see*. But here he encourages us to recognize the Creator as ה' *The Dispenser of Mercy*, even while He is inflicting punishment on the land. To perceive that such harsh punishments are truly motivated by Hashem's merciful concern for His erring creations is most difficult and requires the concentrated internal perception of חֲזוּ, *Behold'.*]

מִפְעֲלוֹת ה' — *The works of HASHEM.*[1]

Whatever wonders you may witness, be assured that they were wrought by none other than Hashem (*Radak*).

It may be difficult to attribute the awesome devastation to God, since He is the Creator Who desires the perpetuation of His creatures rather than their destruction. Although He is a God of peace who generally shuns violence, these devastating accomplishments are His, for He alone knows what is best for His world (*Kiflayim L'Sushiya*).

אֲשֶׁר שָׂם שַׁמּוֹת בָּאָרֶץ — *Who has wrought* [lit. *placed*] *devastation in the land.*

Many mighty armies will crowd around beseiged Jerusalem, yet the handful of Jewish inhabitants will utterly destroy them. Let it be known that this is the act of God, as it says, *The remainder of the people shall not be cut off from the city. Then shall Hashem go forth and fight against those nations, as*

---

1. *Minchas Shai* confides that he finds this phrase one of the most difficult challenges in all of his studies of Scripture. The problem is whether God's name here should read ה' or אֱלֹהִים.
In 66:5 we find a very similar passage לְכוּ וּרְאוּ מִפְעֲלוֹת אֱלֹהִים. There is no question that אֱלֹהִים is the proper version there. Here however, the traditional manuscripts read ה', and thus is the name rendered in *Targum* and in many *Midrashim*. However, there is overwhelming evidence from other old manuscripts, *Midrashim*, *Zohar*, grammatical works, lexicons, and Masoretic texts that the proper version here should be אֱלֹהִים.
In conclusion, *Minchas Shai* leaves it to the great scholars to render a final, authoritative decision, based upon the sources.

מִלְחָמוֹת עַד־קְצֵה הָאָרֶץ קֶשֶׁת יְשַׁבֵּר
וְקִצֵּץ חֲנִית עֲגָלוֹת יִשְׂרֹף בָּאֵשׁ: הַרְפּוּ
וּדְעוּ כִּי־אָנֹכִי אֱלֹהִים אָרוּם בַּגּוֹיִם אָרוּם
בָּאָרֶץ: יהוה צְבָאוֹת עִמָּנוּ מִשְׂגָּב לָנוּ
אֱלֹהֵי יַעֲקֹב סֶלָה:

יא

יב

when He fights on the day of battle [Zechariah 14:2-3] (Radak).[1]

10. מַשְׁבִּית מִלְחָמוֹת עַד קְצֵה הָאָרֶץ — *He makes cessation of wars to the end of the earth.*

The conclusion of the wars of Gog and Magog will mark the end of warfare for all time. When the nations finally come to realize that everything is in the hands of Hashem, they will subjugate themselves to His service [and refrain from all hostilities which are in defiance of His will]. Thus will the words of the prophet be fulfilled: *And HASHEM will be king over all of the earth, on that day HASHEM will be one and His Name one* [Zechariah 14:9] (Radak).

קֶשֶׁת יְשַׁבֵּר וְקִצֵּץ חֲנִית — *The bow will He break, [and] sever the spear.*

As the prophet forewarned Gog [Ezekiel 39:3]: *I will strike the bow out of your left hand and cause the arrows to fall out of your right hand* (Radak).

[When all nations realize that their arms are useless against God — as will be demonstrated by the annihilation of the all-powerful Gog and Magog — they will destroy their own weapons, as the Prophet envisions: *And they shall beat* their swords into plowshares and their spears into pruning-hooks (Isaiah 2:4)].

עֲגָלוֹת יִשְׂרֹף בָּאֵשׁ — *And wagons consume in [the] fire.*

Scripture states: *I will rain down upon him (Gog) fire and brimstone, and upon his bands and upon the many nations who are with him* [Ezekiel 38:22] (Radak).

[Similarly the prophet predicts (*ibid.* 39:9-10): *And they that dwell in the cities of Israel shall go forth and set fire to the weapons* [of Gog] *and burn them, both shield and armor, bow and arrows, and the clubs and the javelins and they shall make fires with them for seven years. They will take no wood out of the field nor cut down any out of the forests, for they shall make fire with the weapons.*

11. הַרְפּוּ — *Desist!*

Desist from your assault on Jerusalem (Rashi).

These are the final words of warning which God addresses to the nations before *breaking their bow and spear* (Ibn Ezra).

Sforno notes that God always attempts to warn the wicked to change

1. The *Talmud* (*Berachos* 7a) interprets this verse homiletically (rendering שַׁמּוֹת as שֵׁמוֹת, names) and teaches that the name by which a person is called is not arbitrary, but a result of Divine inspiration. A name describes a person's true nature and affords us a glimpse into his future accomplishments. This we learn from a homiletical reading of our verse. Instead of שַׁמּוֹת, *devastation*, read שֵׁמוֹת, *names.* Thus, *Go out and behold the accomplishments of HASHEM, for He has placed names* (שֵׁמוֹת) *in the land.*

For example, the name רוּת, *Ruth* foretells that she would merit to have as her descendant David [her great-grandson], who would sate [רְוָהוּ=רוּת=sate] his Creator with songs and praises.

*10 He makes cessation of wars
to the end of the earth,
The bow will He break, sever the spear,
and wagons consume in fire.
11 Desist! Know that I am God,
I shall be exalted among the nations,
exalted upon the earth.
12 HASHEM of Legions is with us,
a stronghold for us is the God of Jacob, Selah.*

their evil ways, יַעֲזֹב רָשָׁע דַּרְכּוֹ וְאִישׁ אָוֶן מַחְשְׁבֹתָיו, *Let the wicked forsake his way, and the man of iniquity, his plans* (Isaiah 55:7).

Shir HaShirim Rabbah (5:3) interprets הַרְפּוּ homiletically, relating it to הֶרֶף עַיִן, *the batting of an eyelash.* This implies: Desist from evil immediately and repent instantly, within the brief moment required for the batting of an eyelash.

וּדְעוּ כִּי אָנֹכִי אֱלֹהִים — [And] *know that I am God.*

Know that all efforts against My will are futile, for only *I* possess the power to elevate men and to crush them (*Radak*).

אָרוּם בַּגּוֹיִם אָרוּם בָּאָרֶץ — *I shall be exalted among the nations, exalted upon the earth.*

The Prophet (*Isaiah 26:5*) describes the decline of God's estate, Judea and Jerusalem, in double terms, יַשְׁפִּילֶנָּה יַשְׁפִּילָהּ עַד אֶרֶץ יַגִּיעֶנָּה עַד עָפָר, *He lays it low, laying it low even to the ground, bringing it even to the dust.* Corresponding to this, the future elevation of God's kingdom is depicted in double terms. First God will utterly destroy the sovereignty of the nations: *I shall be ex-*

alted among the nations. Then, He will assume total mastery over the world: [*And HASHEM will be King over all of the earth* [*Zechariah 14:19*]; *I shall be exalted among the nations, exalted upon the earth.*] (*Chazah Zion*).

12. ה' צְבָאוֹת עִמָּנוּ — *HASHEM of Legions is with us.*

This verse repeats verse 8 to emphasize that when the eagerly awaited salvation finally arrives we will never desist from extolling God, as the Psalmist exclaims (41:14), *Blessed is HASHEM, God of Israel, from this world to the next — Amen and Amen'* (*Maharam Markado*).

מִשְׂגָּב לָנוּ אֱלֹהֵי יַעֲקֹב סֶלָה — *A stronghold for us is the God of Jacob, Selah.*

All nations are destined to recognize God's sovereignty, but their comprehension will be weak and unclear. Israel, however, will enjoy a vivid perception of incomparable clarity. This is because the Gentiles never sought out God previously, whereas the twelve tribes of Israel received a tradition from Jacob to search incessantly for the divine. Their quest endures סֶלָה, *forever* (*Ibn Yachya*).

T *his Psalm is a sequel to the preceding one which describes the defeat of all the nations who unite against God and His Chosen People (Radak). After the earth returns to order and tranquility, the nations will recognize God's universal mastery and will seek His presence in Jerusalem (Malbim).*

Another theme is woven into the fabric of the text: the ability of the shofar blast to inspire mankind and to arouse God's mercy. The shofar blast described here refers to the horn of redemption which the Messiah is destined to blow. However, the Rabbis teach us that it also alludes to the shofar blown every Rosh Hashanah, which symbolizes the individual soul's redemption from its sins. Rav Saadiah Gaon enumerates ten reasons for the sounding of the shofar on Rosh Hashanah. (Most of these reasons are included in the Commentary to this Psalm). On Rosh Hashanah, this Psalm is recited seven times prior to the sounding of the shofar. The Name אֱלֹהִים, which refers to God's manifestation as the Dispenser of Strict Justice appears here seven times. Thus the Name אֱלֹהִים is recited a total of forty-nine times.

The Sages teach that there are forty-nine levels of spiritual impurity before the lowest depth from which no redemption is possible. Correspondingly, there are forty-nine ascending levels of sanctity which man can attain. The forty-nine times which the Name is recited allude to the power of these verses to transform the forty-nine possible levels of spiritual uncleanliness into forty-nine corresponding levels of sanctity and purity. When Israel is inspired to purify and perfect itself with such intensity, surely God's strict justice will be changed to His Attribute of Mercy (Matteh Ephraim, Elef HaMagen 585:5).

לַמְנַצֵּחַ לִבְנֵי־קֹרַח מִזְמוֹר: כָּל־הָעַמִּים א־ב
תִּקְעוּ־כָף הָרִיעוּ לֵאלֹהִים בְּקוֹל רִנָּה:
כִּי־יהוה עֶלְיוֹן נוֹרָא מֶלֶךְ גָּדוֹל עַל־כָּל־ ג

1. לַמְנַצֵּחַ — *For the Conductor.*

Most commentators agree that this psalm is dedicated to the era of the Messiah. However, *Ibn Ezra* quotes *Rabbi Moshe*, who ascribes this chapter to the exile of Babylon [reflecting Israel's yearning for redemption and return to Jerusalem]. *Ibn Ezra* cites another opinion which links this psalm to a great event in David's life, the carrying of the Ark of God up to Jerusalem.

מִזְמוֹר — *A song.*

[Although this was first composed by Korach's sons, David adopted the Psalm as his own and endowed it with universal dimensions. The *Yalkut* asserts that David's harp was related to the Messianic Shofar and the future redemption: Rabbi Chanina said, Every part of the ram which Abraham sacrificed instead of his son Isaac on Mount Moriah was used for a good purpose. Its sinews were fashioned into harpstrings for David. Its hide became the belt which girded Elijah's loins. Its left horn was sounded on Mount Sinai. Its right horn will be sounded by the Holy One, Blessed be He, at the time of the future redemption].

2. כָּל־הָעַמִּים — *All [you] nations.*

This is an exhortation. The Psalmist addresses the survivors of the war of Gog and Magog [which was described vividly in Psalm 46] (*Sforno*).

If the psalm is dedicated to David himself, then the nations are those which were conquered and ruled by this king of Israel (*Ibn Ezra*).

תִּקְעוּ כָף — *Join hands.*

This translation follows *Rashi*, who interprets this as a call to assimilate for the purpose of praising God [see *commentary. to v. 6*, בְּקוֹל שׁוֹפָר 'ה]. The ex-

pression תָּקַע כָּף is used in this sense in *Proverbs* (6:1, 17:18, 22:26). Thus, All you nations join hands in an alliance to collectively *call out to God!*

However, *Radak, Meiri,* and *Sforno* render תִּקְעוּ כָף as *clap your hands for joy,* as in יִמְחֲאוּ כָף, *they clap hands* (98:8).

Chazah Zion notes that the numerical value of כָּף is one hundred. On Rosh Hashanah, *all of the nations* pass before God in judgment (*Rosh Hashanah* 16a; see 33:15), and at that time we are commanded: תִּקְעוּ, *blow* (on the shofar) כָּף, one hundred blasts.

הָרִיעוּ לֵאלֹהִים — *Call out to God.*

[This may also be translated as *sound blasts of the horn,* i.e., sound a תְּרוּעָה, *broken note*].

Malbim observes that it is customary to sound the trumpets during a royal coronation ceremony. This is what the nations will do when they appoint God as their sovereign.

[Similarly, *Rav Saadiah Gaon* lists ten reasons for blowing the shofar on Rosh Hashanah. His first explantion is that since Rosh Hashanah corresponds to the first day of man's (Adam's) creation, humanity is obliged to coronate God as king with fanfare on this day, as David says, בַּחֲצֹצְרוֹת וְקוֹל שׁוֹפָר הָרִיעוּ לִפְנֵי הַמֶּלֶךְ ה', *With trumpets and the sound of the horn blast forth before the king, HASHEM* (98:6)].

Chazah Zion renders הָרִיעוּ as *break yourselves,* referring to the words of the prophet (*Isaiah* 24:19) who depicts the future downfall of the nations as רֹעָה הִתְרֹעֲעָה הָאָרֶץ, *Broken and shattered is the land.* With the sound of the broken *Teruah*-blast of Rosh Hashanah, the heart of the sinner is broken and so is God's wrath. [This corresponds to *Rav*

XLVII **F**or the Conductor,
1-3   by the sons of Korach, a song.
        ² All you nations, join hands!
          Call out to God with a cry of joy.
        ³ For HASHEM is Most High, awesome,
          a great king over all of the earth.

Saadiah Gaon's seventh reason for blowing the shofar].

בְּקוֹל רִנָּה — With a cry of joy.

[Why should the nations rejoice after their downfall?] Radak explains that the nations will rejoice in the realization that their downfall was instrumental in helping Creation attain its purpose. Once they realize that Hashem is the only God and Israel is His chosen nation, they will know that their defeat was necessary to bring about the revelation of these historic truths.

Tehillos Hashem emphasizes that the nations are commanded to rejoice even לֵאלֹהִים, to God in his Aspect as Strict Judge, i.e., they must rejoice even after He has harshly, but justly, punished them with defeat.[1]

3. כִּי ה׳ עֶלְיוֹן נוֹרָא — For HASHEM is Most High, awesome.

This is the cry of joy which the nations are urged to shout out (Ibn Ezra).

He is Most High because He controls everyone; He is awesome because He performs wonders that cause the nations to fear Him (Radak).

Malbim explains that these two descriptions refute the two main arguments of the heretics. Some heretics deny God's reality entirely and attribute

the entire Creation to the activities of celestial bodies and cosmic forces. In the future, everyone will realize that God is Most High, i.e., the prime Cause and first Source of Creation.

Other idolators admit God's role as Creator, but claim that God later abandoned this world to the influences of the blind forces of nature, no longer caring about the earth's lowly creatures [see Rambam, Hilchos Avodah Zarah 1:1]. They claim that God no longer cares enough to punish or reward; they contend, therefore, that there is no need to fear Him. This heresy will also be abandoned in the future, when everyone witnesses the awesome punishments which God inflicts upon those who defy Him. These public punishments will serve as a warning to all.

[Rav Saadiah Gaon's second reason for sounding the shofar is that before a king punishes his subjects for neglecting his decrees,he gives them a final warning. Rosh Hashanah initiates the Ten Days of Repentance, culminating in the final judgment of Yom Kippur. The shofar blast represents Hashem's last warning to His people].

מֶלֶךְ גָּדוֹל עַל כָּל הָאָרֶץ — A great king over all of the earth.

Shaarei Chaim's explanation seems to

1. Alshich introduces a deep concept:
   Man lives by the grace of heaven, which constantly sends energy and sustenance to earth. This sustenance may come from the hand of God, or it may come through His appointed celestial angels. Before the defeat of Gog and Magog, the nations were not subjugated, but were far removed from God, (who turned them over to the jurisdiction of the angels). After their defeat they will lose their physical freedom, but gain Godliness by becoming the vassals of Israel. For Israel's bountiful sustenance, provided by Hashem Himself, will overflow to encompass the nations as well. Thus, they will experience for the first time the ecstasy of being sustained by God, therefore, they rejoice!

ד הָאָרֶץ: יְדַבֵּר עַמִּים תַּחְתֵּינוּ וּלְאֻמִּים
ה תַּחַת רַגְלֵינוּ: יִבְחַר־לָנוּ אֶת־נַחֲלָתֵנוּ אֶת
ו גְּאוֹן יַעֲקֹב אֲשֶׁר־אָהֵב סֶלָה: עָלָה

lead directly from the *Malbim's* interpretation (cited above):

In 99:2 we read גָּדוֹל וְרָם בְּצִיּוֹן 'ה, הוּא עַל כָּל הָעַמִּים, *HASHEM is great in Zion, and He is high above all the nations.* Something גָּדוֹל, *great*, resembles a tower, which rises to the sky, but is based on earth. Thus does the Jewish people (*Zion*) view God: He is *great* and *lofty*, yet He is also involved with the world. The word רָם, *high above*, refers to an elevated object which is completely divorced from the earth, such as a soaring bird. Thus do the gentile nations conceive of God: He is deemed aloof and remote!

In then future, however, the nations will recognize that God is indeed involved in our earthly affairs. Therefore He is described as מֶלֶךְ גָּדוֹל עַל כָּל הָאָרֶץ, *A great king over all of the earth.*

4. יְדַבֵּר עַמִּים תַּחְתֵּינוּ — *He plagues the nations in our stead.*

This translation generally follows *Targum* and particularly *Rashi,* who relates יְדַבֵּר to דֶּבֶר, *pestilence, plague.* God vents His wrath on the nations; and thus His anger abates and Israel escapes unscathed. Similarly, God tells Israel נָתַתִּי כָפְרְךָ מִצְרַיִם, *I have made Egypt your ransom'* (Isaiah 43:3).

However, the other major commentators render יְדַבֵּר as יְנַהֵג, *He will lead,* indicating that God will lead the nations from the ends of the earth to Jerusalem, to bring them under Israel's rule.

Hirsch interprets יְדַבֵּר as *to gather together* [see I *Kings* 5:23].

וּלְאֻמִּים תַּחַת רַגְלֵינוּ — *And kingdoms beneath our feet.*

The translation of לְאֻמִּים as *Kingdoms* (see *Genesis* 25:23 וּלְאֹם מִלְאֹם יֶאֱמָץ) follows *Tehillos Hashem* who

emphasizes that the wicked nobles who control the hierachy of *kingdoms* will suffer much more than the simple peasants who are described above as עַמִּים, *nations,* meaning *followers.* Because the nobles conspired to tyrannize and oppress Israel, they are condemned to be crushed *beneath our feet.* The common folk who did not initiate any persecutions but merely followed their cruel leaders, will now be led (יְדַבֵּר) under the guidance and rule of Israel.

Sforno believes that this Jewish domination will be entirely beneficial to the nations. They will be *under* our intelligent guidance and will follow the path of *our feet,* as the prophet foretells: *You will be named the priests of HASHEM, men shall call you the ministers of our God* (Isaiah 61:6).

[In the Messianic era, even if the nations seek to repent and convert to Judaism, they will remain under the authority of Israel. For the *halacha* stipulates, converts are not accepted during the days of Messiah (*Yevamos* 24b), because they are assumed to be insincere and attracted only by Israel's rise to power. Converts can join our nation as equals only if they enter our ranks when we are downtrodden and despised. Those who are willing to take part in our misery can later share the fruits of our glory.]

5. יִבְחַר לָנוּ אֶת נַחֲלָתֵנוּ — *He will choose for us our heritage.*

In the days of Messiah, Hashem will return us to our estate, the Holy Land, and to the Temple, which is the pride of Jacob (*Radak*).

Sforno stresses that despite the Jew's complete domination of the nations, Israel will not harm them nor drive

XLVII
4-5

4 *He plagues the nations in our stead,*
and kingdoms beneath our feet.
5 *He will choose for us our heritage,*
the pride of Jacob which He loved, Selah.

them from their lands. Rather, Israel will choose to dwell only in its rightful ancestral estate, the Holy Land, which is hospitable only to Jewish inhabitants, as it says, *And your enemies who dwell therein shall be made desolate (Leviticus 26:32).*

Ibn Ezra (v.1) notes that there are those who maintain that this Psalm was an accompaniment for the Ark as it was carried to its permanent quarters. It is evident that the exact location of Mount Moriah, the site of the future Temple, was not yet known, for they said, *He will [yet] choose for us our estate.* [Thus, they walked blindly, waiting for God to guide their steps, just as Abraham had journeyed to sacrifice Isaac on Mount Moriah without advance knowledge of his destination.]

אֶת גְּאוֹן יַעֲקֹב — *The pride of Jacob.*

This is the Holy Temple, where God's spirit resides in splendor. The Jewish nation views the fact that God dwells in its midst with great גָּאוֹן, *pride,* and sees the Divine Presence as its most remarkable advantage over other nations (*Radak*).[1]

[See *Leviticus* 26:19 and *Rashi* ibid.; and *Ezekiel* 24:21 אֶת מִקְדָּשִׁי גְּאוֹן עֻזְּכֶם, *My Temple, your mighty pride*].

Why does the Psalmist here refer to all of Israel as *Jacob? Ibn Yachya* ex-

plains that the third Patriarch is singled out because only his face is 'etched into God's celestial Throne' as representative of Israel and mankind.

Rav Shlomo Atiya notes that Jacob demonstrated a very special reverence for the Temple. It was he who was completely overwhelmed by the magnificence of God's Presence on Mount Moriah, exclaiming *How very awesome is this place (Genesis 28:17).* He vowed to erect a monument on the site and to serve God there. The Almighty reciprocated and took special pride in Jacob from that time onward.

[We even find that God takes the name of Jacob as His own and calls Himself גְּאוֹן יַעֲקֹב (*Amos* 8:7, *Radak* ibid.)]

Alshich comments that the first two Temples, which were temporary, were identified with Abraham and Isaac respectively. However, the third and final Beis Hamikdash, which will endure eternally, is ascribed to the merit of Jacob, who also lives forever [Our forefather Jacob never (really) died. (*Taanis* 5b; see *Ramban Genesis* 49:33)]. The immortal *Jacob* is the one whom He [*God*] loved [סֶלָה] *forever* [see *commentary* to 3:3].

[*Rav Saadiah Gaon's* fifth reason for sounding the shofar is to remind us of the *Beis HaMikdash,* which lies in

1. After the destruction of the *Beis Hamikdash,* God transferred His abode from the Holy Temple to the study hall. The *Talmud (Berachos* 8a) states: Since the day of the destruction, God has no interest in This World other that the four cubits of *halachah.* The houses of study became the main גָּאוֹן, *pride,* of God and Israel. Perhaps this is why the title given the heads of the Torah academies in Babylon was גָּאוֹן, *Gaon* [lit. *pride*].

Meiri (introduction to *Avos*) suggests a different reason. The heads of these *yeshivos* had to be completely fluent in all sixty trctates of the Talmud — by heart! The numerical value of גָּאוֹן is sixty, an allusion to this prodigious accomplishment. [There are various traditions regarding the number of tractates in the Talmud. See *Z'man Nakat* by *Rabbi David Cohen* (chapter 2), for a complete discussion.

ז אֱלֹהִים בִּתְרוּעָה יהוה בְּקוֹל שׁוֹפָר:
ח זַמְּרוּ אֱלֹהִים זַמֵּרוּ זַמְּרוּ לְמַלְכֵּנוּ זַמֵּרוּ:

ruins. The gentile marauders blew their horns and trumpets in battle as they vanquished Israel and destroyed the Temple. The sound of the shofar should arouse us to beseech God to rebuild the *Beis HaMikdash*, which is our pride.]

אֲשֶׁר אָהֵב — *Which He loved.*

Jerusalem is the city which God chose for His abode (see *I Kings* 11:13) and Zion is His desire, as it says (87:2) *God loves the gates of Zion* (*Radak*).

6. עָלָה אֱלֹהִים בִּתְרוּעָה — *God ascended with the blast.*

Sforno paraphrases: When אֱלֹהִים, the Dispenser of Strict Justice, rises up and executes His judgement against Gog and Magog, the horn of victory will sound a triumphant blast.

Radak continues: That victory will fulfill the prophecy *I shall be exalted amongst the nations* (46:1) and then God will be recognized as *Most High and awesome.*

According to *Pirkei d'Rabbi Eliezer* (Chapter 46), these words allude to the transmission of the Second Tablets at Sinai. The original Tablets were destroyed because of the Golden Calf, which was made as a result of confusion concerning the precise time of Moses' ascent and descent from the mount. When Moses went up the second time, the days were clearly marked off and recorded by the daily blast of the shofar. At that time, the faith of the people rose high above the threat of idolatry; therefore, *God ascended with the blast.* For this reason, the custom is to sound the shofar publicly from the first of Elul, the day of Moses' third ascent (*Tur Orach Chaim* 581).

[*Rav Saadiah Gaon's* third reason for sounding the shofar on Rosh Hashanah is to recall the blasts sounded at Sinai].

Ibn Ezra and *Radak* interpret this

with reference to the Holy Ark, which was concealed in the depths of Mount Moriah as the era of the First Temple drew to a close. In the future, when the great horn of redemption is blown, this Ark will *ascend* from its concealment. The Ark is called אֱלֹהִים because God's spirit rests upon it between the cherubs. Similarly, we read (*Numbers* 10:35) *And when the Ark began to journey forth Moses said, 'Arise HASHEM'* Then, too, the Ark arose to the sound of trumpets (*Yaavetz haDoresh*).

Many *Midrashim* suggest that the Psalmist is alluding to the blast of the shofar on Rosh Hashanah. Specifically the תְּרוּעָה, *teruah,* is the broken blast which symbolizes the harsh, shattering punishments of אֱלֹהִים, *the Dispenser of strict Justice.* When the Jew hears the sound of the *teruah,* he realizes that he deserves shattering punishment for his sins and is inspired to repent. Having felt remorse for his sins, he is forgiven and the verdict of אֱלֹהִים is nullified. Thus, *God* (אֱלֹהִים) *ascends and departs because of the Teruah blast.*

Also, it is taught that the sound of *tekiah* corresponds to Abraham; *shevarim,* to Isaac; and *teruah,* to Jacob and David, because the lives of both were marked by shattering tragedies, which they overcame with their complete faith (*Elef HaMagen* 585:4)].

The *Midrash* says: *Praiseworthy is the nation which knows the Teruah blast* (89:16). This is the nation of Israel which knows how to appease its Maker with the *teruah* blast, whereupon He arises from His Throne of Strict Judgement and sits down on His Throne of Mercy where He converts harsh justice to compassion (*Vayikra Rabba* 29).

ה׳ בְּקוֹל שׁוֹפָר — *HASHEM, with the sound of the shofar*

Sforno observes that this is the long

XLVII
6-7

⁶ *God ascended with the blast,*
HASHEM, with the sound of the shofar.
⁷ *Make music for God, make music,*
make music for our King, make music.

awaited blast signalling the ingathering of exiles, *'And it shall come to pass on that day that a great horn shall be blown; and they shall come — those who were lost in the land of Assyria, and those who were dispersed in the land of Egypt — and they shall prostrate themselves before HASHEM in the holy mountain, Jerusalem. (Isaiah 27:13).*

[The eighth reason for the sounding of the shofar offered by *Rav Saadiah Gaon* reflects this verse. He stresses that when one hears the shofar on Rosh Hashanah, he should pray for the day of the קִבּוּץ גָלוּיוֹת, *the Ingathering of the Exiles.*]

Alshich, pursuing the theme of Rosh Hashanah, explains that after the broken *teruah* blast, אֱלֹהִים, God's strict justice is tempered with the Name 'ה, *HASHEM.*

Hirsch identifies the *sound of the shofar* as the unbroken sound of the *tekiah* blast. This symbolizes God's unwavering, unending love for Israel. In his commentary to *Leviticus* 23:24, *Hirsch* explains that תָּקַע means *to bring something forcefully into something else, to ram, to thrust into.* The term is also used for the handshake, which symbolically binds the parties to a transaction, as one party thrust his hand into the hand of the second party. With reference to a wind instrument, the *tekiah* is a sustained unbroken note which attracts and keeps one's attention.

Ramban relates the word, שׁוֹפָר to שֶׁפֶּר, *beauty.* The blast of the shofar arouses Israel to repent and beautify its ways so that it may serve as an example of rectitude for all nations.

7. זַמְּרוּ אֱלֹהִים זַמֵּרוּ — *Make music for God, make music.*

Radak (v. 8) explains that this is not an exhortation to play music, but a command to compose new, fresh melodies.

[Throughout the *Book of Psalms* מִזְמוֹר is translated as *song.* However, as explained in the *commentary* to 30:1, the root word זמר, is more accurately translated as *the instrumental accompaniment* to lyrics, which are called שִׁירָה. Since the previous verse speaks of a musical instrument, the shofar, the word זַמֵּרוּ is best rendered *make music.*]

This opinion is supported by *Alkabetz (Divrei Shlomo)* and by *Hirsch* who refers us to his *commentary* to *Genesis* 43:11 [German and Hebrew editions, deleted in English], where he explains that זמר is not the chanted word, but the melody, the tune arising from the soul.

Hirsch notes that זֶמֶר is related to זְמוֹרָה, *vine, branch.* Inside the branch, the sap gathers long before the fruit emerges. When a sufficient amount of this nutritious liquid accumulates, the tree is ready to burst forth with fruit.

So, too, with song. All feelings and emotions are gathered into the strains of the wordless melody. When these feelings reach a crescendo, they overflow into original words of praise. The well-chosen, inspired word of שִׁירָה is thus the fruit of the זִמְרָה.

Chazah Zion perceives זִמְרָה as a cognate of זְמֹרָה, *pruning.*

Through ecstatic song, a person can remove or *prune* God's strict judgment [see *Overview*, Vol. I.]

זַמְּרוּ לְמַלְכֵּנוּ זַמֵּרוּ — *Make music for our King, make music!*

This repetition indicates that one melody inspires the next (*Divrei Shlomo*).

Yaavetz Hadoresh notes that the

כִּי מֶלֶךְ כָּל־הָאָרֶץ אֱלֹהִים זַמְּרוּ מַשְׂכִּיל: מָלַךְ אֱלֹהִים עַל־גּוֹיִם אֱלֹהִים יָשַׁב | עַל־ ט כִּסֵּא קָדְשׁוֹ: נְדִיבֵי עַמִּים | נֶאֶסְפוּ עַם י

word זַמְּרוּ is repeated five times in these two verses, alluding to the Five Books of Moses. The Torah was enshrined in the Ark which David was escorting to Jerusalem.

[This procession was accompanied by an unprecedented outburst of music and song. *And David and all of the House of Israel played before HASHEM with all manner of instruments made of cypress wood and with harps and flutes and with timbels and with rattles, and with cymbals ... So David and all of the House of Israel brought up the Ark of HASHEM* [בִּתְרוּעָה וּבְקוֹל שׁוֹפָר] *with shouting and with the sound of the shofar (II Samuel 6:5,15).*]

8. כִּי מֶלֶךְ כָּל־הָאָרֶץ אֱלֹהִים — *For God is King of all the earth.*

Although God is Master of the entire universe, and has at His disposal the legions of heavenly minstrels, in His humility He desires to hear the music of man (*Otzar Nechmad*).

HASHEM will be acknowledged as king over the entire earth (Zechariah 14:9). At that time the shofar blast will herald universal peace. But today the shofar is used as an instrument of war. Then Joshua said to the people, *'Blow (the shofar) for HASHEM has given you the city.'*

[The *Talmud* (*Berachos* 56b) states that the same dream may be interpreted as a good or as a bad omen. The prophecy of the dream is determined by the interpreter. Thus if one sees a shofar in his dream he may interpret it as a call to battle or as a herald of peace.]

זַמְּרוּ מַשְׂכִּיל — *Make music, O enlightened one.*

Even the ordinary people are exhorted to *clap hands* and *shout out to God a cry of joy* (v. 2), for these simple forms of merriment are within their ability. However, the composition of music is a complex art reserved for the מַשְׂכִּיל, *enlightened man* of superior intelligence (*Radak*).

Otzar Nechmad draws our attention to a grammatical inconsistency. The singular form מַשְׂכִּיל, *enlightened one*, follows the plural verb זַמְּרוּ. This implies that although many intelligent men are urged to compose, each should purse the task individually, for each man's comprehension of God's glory is unique.

Rav Yeibi notes that the appelation *enlightened one* reflects our Sages' statement (*Sanhedrin* 91b): Whoever recites songs (to God) in this world will be given the privilege of reciting songs in the World to Come. That is, only the מַשְׂכִּיל, who is discerning enough in this world to praise God, will be able to make music in the future.

According to *Rav Yoseif Kimchi* (quoted by his son, *Radak*) and *Meiri*, מַשְׂכִּיל is not a description of the composer but of the composition [rendering: *make enlightened music.*] This is not a mere folk tune, but a work of the highest excellence which wins the listener's attention and stimulates him to use his mental facilities to recognize the dominion of God.

9. מָלַךְ אֱלֹהִים עַל גּוֹיִם — *God reigns over the peoples.*

Until now, God ruled only over Israel; henceforth, He shall reign over

XLVII
8-10

8 *For God is King of all the earth,*
     make music, O enlightened one!
9 *God reigns over the peoples,*
     God sits upon His holy throne.
10 *The nobles of the nations gathered,*

all peoples [see Zechariah 14:9]
(Radak).

אֱלֹהִים יָשַׁב עַל כִּסֵּא קָדְשׁוֹ — *God sits upon
His holy throne* [lit. *throne of His
holiness.*]

Hostility to God will no longer exist.
He will be welcomed everywhere in the
world, for *He reigns over all peoples.*
Nevertheless, He will choose to rest His
Holy Presence only in the sacred Tem-
ple of Israel *(Sforno).* [כִּי בָחַר ה' בְּצִיּוֹן
אִוָּהּ לְמוֹשָׁב לוֹ, *for God has chosen Zion,
desired it as His dwelling place*
(132:13).]

Eretz HaChaim comments that God's
name and His throne will be incomplete,
until the Messianic era, when God's
enemies (particularly Amalek) will be
vanquished. [See *Exodus* 17:16, *Rashi
ibid.*] Only then will *God sit upon His
holy throne.*

Shevet MiYisroel views this as an allusion to the *Midrash (Bereishis Rabbah*
82:9), which states: When God judges
Israel He does it hastily, while standing
[as it were], so that their examination
will be brief and superficial and their
verdict lenient. When judging the nations, however, He sits, in order to conduct a lengthy and exacting investigation of their deeds. Then He adopts the
role of a prosecutor and accuses them.

Thus, the Psalmist foretells that when
אֱלֹהִים rules the gentiles *He will sit down*
[for lengthy review] *upon His holy
throne* [of judgment].

[Rav Saadiah Gaon's eighth reason
for the sounding of the Shofar is to
bring to mind the awesomeness of the
Final Judgment, as the prophet says, *For
the great day of HASHEM is near, it is
near and swiftly draws close ...* יוֹם שׁוֹפָר
וּתְרוּעָה, *A day of the shofar (sound) and
the shout (Zepheniah* 1:14,16).].

10. נְדִיבֵי עַמִּים — *The nobles of the
nations.*

Radak and *Ibn Ezra* identify these as
the great nobles of the gentile nations.
Sforno describes them as the outstanding philanthropists. According to
Rashi, the נְדִיבִים are the non-Jews who
nobly submitted to slaughter and martyrdom in order to sanctify God's
Name.

[Abraham is considered the paragon
of נְדִיבוּת, martyrdom, nobility, self-
sacrifice. Israel, more than any other nation, is called בַּת נָדִיב, *daughter of
nobility (Songs* 7:2). This designation
applies especially when Israel is
prepared to sacrifice the comforts of
home in order to make the arduous
festival pilgrimage to Jerusalem *(Chagigah* 3a). At these times the Jews
resemble Abraham, who gave up
everything in order to follow God to the
land of Canaan. The noble gentiles who
gather in Israel are following in the
footsteps of Abraham and deserve to be
called נְדִיבִים.[1]

Rav Saadiah Gaon's sixth reason for

---

1. The *Midrash (Devarim Rabbah* 2:24) relates that when the Sages, Rabbi Eliezer, Rabbi
Yehoshua, and Rabban Gamliel were in Rome, the Senate decreed, 'Thirty days hence no Jew
may exist anywhere in the entire world '.

There was one God-fearing senator, the councillor of the Emperor, who revealed this plot to

אֱלֹהֵי אַבְרָהָם כִּי לֵאלֹהִים מָגִנֵּי־אֶרֶץ
מְאֹד נַעֲלָה:

the sounding of the shofar is to remind us of *Akeidas Yitzchak*, when Abraham's son Isaac was prepared to give up his life for God. So should every Jew be ready to sacrifice himself for God.]

Rabbeinu Yonah (Sha'arei Teshuvah III: 168) identifies the נְדִיבֵי עַמִּים as the tribal heads of Israel, for the twelve tribes of Israel are called עַמִּים, *nations* (see *Deuteronomy* 33:19). When the entire congregation gathers to serve God, they are deemed stalwart followers of Abraham, who sanctified God. Anyone who deserts the congregation desecrates the Divine Service which it represents; therefore he is classed among those who despise God's Name.

נֶאֱסָפוּ — *Gathered.*

They congregate in the Holy Land *(Sforno)* in order to accept the complete sovereignty of God *(Otzar Nechmad).*

עַם אֱלֹהֵי אַבְרָהָם — *The nations of the God of Abraham.*

These martyrs are identified as the nation of *Abraham's* God because Abraham was the first man to sacrifice his entire being for the sake of God, by becoming the first convert [for Abraham incurred the wrath of Nimrod, who threw him into a blazing furnace] *(Rashi).*

[These martyrs are presumably converts to Judaism, and Abraham was the first to proselytize. Scripture considers these proselytes creations of Abraham, referring to them as *the souls he made in Haran (Genesis* 12:5).The very name Abraham is a contraction of אַב הֲמוֹן גּוֹיִים, *Father of a multitide of nations* [*Gen.* 17:4]. For this reason, the *halachah* stipulates that the proselyte may refer to the patriarchs as *his* forefathers and that he is considered the

the Rabbis. They were terribly distraught, but the senator encouraged them, saying confidently, 'Fear not! The God of the Jews will save them within these thirty days!'

After twenty-five days elapsed, the senator told his wife of the planned genocide. She exclaimed,'Woe, there are only five days left to nullify this decree!' This righteous woman conviced her husband to commit suicide, so that the Senate would adjourn for thirty days of mourning; thus the evil decree would expire unfulfilled.

When the Sages consoled the senator's widow, they were very upset that he had martyred himself without having had the spiritual benefits of circumcision and conversion. The widow

the nation of the God of Abraham,
For God's are the shields of the earth —
He is exceedingly exalted.

descendant of our father Abraham (*Rambam, Hilchos Biccurim* 4:3).]

כִּי לַאלֹהִים מָגִנֵּי אֶרֶץ — *For God's are the shields of the earth.*

[After the world witnesses God's might in protecting Israel from Gog and Magog], everyone will realize that He truly possesses the power to shield those who trust in Him (*Rashi*). [Thus they will no longer deny God's omnipotence by asking, 'If God is truly All-Powerful, how could He permit heathens to kill the martyrs?' They will realize that although God could have shielded the martyrs, He wished to grant them the incomparable privilege of sanctifying His holy name.]

Ibn Ezra and *Radak* render מָגִנֵּי as *nobles, kings* [who provide their subjects with physical protection] as in *Psalm* 89:19 and *Hosea* 4:18. This description

corresponds with נְדִיבֵי, *nobles.*

Sforno also connects both titles, explaining that these men are philanthropists who provide shelter for their neighbors and shield the souls of their people by teaching them the proper way to serve God. [Thus they emulate Abraham.] These men, chosen by God to fill this role in society, now gather around Him.

מְאֹד נַעֲלָה — *He is exceedingly exalted.*

According to *Rashi, Radak,* and *Ibn Ezra,* this describes God, who is no longer degraded as impotent but recognized as the Omnipotent Protector of His faithful.

Sforno interprets this as praise for Abraham, who fathered a nation which faithfully adheres to his actions and beliefs. This feat has never been duplicated by any other man.

---

comforted them by offering proof that the Senator had, in fact, undergone a secret circumcision and conversion.

The Rabbis then applied our verse to him, explaining, *the nobles of the nations gathered, the nation of the God of Abraham* (the converts), *for God's are the shields of the earth;* your husband deserves many shields from God, because Abraham put his life in danger only after God promised *I am your shield* (*Genesis* 15:1), but this noble martyr sacrificed his life without any divine assurance. *He is greatly exalted* — even more exalted than Abraham!

T he previous psalm describes the defeat of all the nations hostile to
  God, which will take place in Messianic times. It concludes with a call
to all who were faithful to God to gather together in the Holy Land and
in the chosen city of Jerusalem.

Here the Psalmist describes the future glory of this city which now
lays in ruins. Its reconstruction will be no mere architectural feat of mortar and stone. Rather, the restoration of the sacred city will signal an era
of national renewal. We will be like children returning to their father's
home, and God, our father, will invest us with new energy and vitality to
lift our souls to immortality (v. 15).

This psalm is the שִׁיר שֶׁל יוֹם, Song of the Day, during the Temple service of the second day of the week, for on the second day of Creation,
God separated between the heavenly and earthly components of the universe and ruled over both (Rosh Hashanah 31a).

Furthermore, the Midrash explains that on the second day, division
[מַחֲלוֹקֶת, schism; strife] was created, when the upper and lower waters
were separated against their will, so to speak.

Rabbeinu Bachya explains that this schism was the root of all subsequent strife and defiance in the world. The Talmud (Shabbos 156a)
states: 'One who is born on the second day will be bad-tempered,
because on that day the waters were divided.' Rashi comments that as a
result of his bad temper, he will become 'divided' — i.e., estranged —
from other people.

Resisei Layla explains that this division between heaven and earth ini-
-tiated the eternal strife between the physical and the spiritual.
Therefore, it was fitting that the psalm for the second day was composed
by the sons of Korach, for he was the instigator of strife against Moses
in the Wilderness. (See ArtScroll Genesis 1:7, commentary and footnote).

According to the Zohar, Korach's sons composed the psalm while tottering on the brink of Gehinnom where, had they not repented, they
would have descended with their father. [The Talmud (Pesachim 54a)
states that the Torah omits the words כִּי טוֹב, that it was good, from the
narrative of the second day of Creation because on that day the fire of
Gehinnom was created.] Therefore, concludes the Zohar, this psalm is
the appropriate daily song for the second day of the week.

א-ב שִׁיר מִזְמוֹר לִבְנֵי־קֹרַח: גָּדוֹל יהוה
וּמְהֻלָּל מְאֹד בְּעִיר אֱלֹהֵינוּ הַר־קָדְשׁוֹ:
ג יְפֵה נוֹף מְשׂוֹשׂ כָּל־הָאָרֶץ הַר־צִיּוֹן

1. שִׁיר מִזְמוֹר — *A song with musical accompaniment.*

[*Ibn Ezra* states that the titles שִׁיר מִזְמוֹר and מִזְמוֹר שִׁיר share the same meaning; therefore, our translation here follows that used for מִזְמוֹר שִׁיר in 30:1. See *commentary* there for futher explanation.]

The *Zohar (Acharei Mos)* explains that this apparent redundancy emphasizes the great significance of this psalm. Similarly, *Psalm 92* begins with the repetition מִזְמוֹר שִׁיר לְיוֹם הַשַּׁבָּת and the word שִׁיר, *song*, is repeated in the title of שִׁיר הַשִּׁירִים, *the Song of Songs*, in both cases to indicate their importance.

2. גָּדוֹל ה' וּמְהֻלָּל מְאֹד — *Great is HASHEM and much praised.*

Indeed, HASHEM's greatness is universal and unchanging. During the exile, however, this greatness is not readily apparent; therefore, the very name יהו"ה has been reduced to י"ה [*Eruvin* 18b] (*Eretz HaChaim*).

In the future, however, God's Name will be restored to its former size and greatness, and He will be *much praised* (*Sforno*).

This is especially so in the city of Jerusalem and particulary on the Temple Mount, which is the only place where God's complete name is pronounced properly in its entirety (*Zerah Yaakov*).

Shevet MiYisrael explains that not only will God's name be magnified in this city, but also the city will be enlarged to demonstrate the greatness of the God who dwells there. The *Midrash* says: In the future, the Temple will expand to cover the entire area of Jerusalem and Jerusalem will expand over all of Eretz Yisrael (see *Maharsha*, *Bava Basra* 75b s.v. ירושלים).

בְּעִיר אֱלֹהֵינוּ הַר קָדְשׁוֹ — *In the city of our God, Mount of His Holiness.*

When *the city of our God* is inhabited and built up, God is recognized as גָּדוֹל, *great*. But when it is destroyed and the Temple lays in ruins, and all that remains is the bare *Mount of His Holiness*, then God is *much praised*, i.e.,He is praised even more than previously, because the sanctity the Temple Mount which still remains even while the Temple itself is in ruins, demonstrates the intensity of God's holy spirit, which can never be blotted out or chased away (*Alshich*) [see *Rambam, Beis HaBechirah* 6:16.]

Malbim observes that, generally speaking, awe is best cultivated and maintained at a distance. As one grows closer and more intimate with the object of wonder, the awe steadily diminishes for 'familiarity breeds contempt.' With HASHEM it is not so. The closer we draw to Him — living together in *His city* and constantly visiting *His mount of Holiness*, the more convinced we become that *Great is HASHEM and much praised.*

3. יְפֵה נוֹף — *Fairest of sites.*

This translation of נוֹף follows *Menachem* (in *Rashi*), *Ibn Ezra*, and *Radak* who render נוֹף as *section, area*, as in שְׁלֹשֶׁת הַנָּפֶת, *three districts* (*Joshua* 17:11).

Rav Yoseif Kimchi (quoted by his son, *Radak*) draws our attention to the fact that the globe is divided into seven distinctly different climate zones. Ordinarily, a change of climate has an adverse affect on one's health. However, those who move to Israel suffer no harmful effects. Moreover, if they move into the holy atmosphere of Jerusalem, they feel not the slightest

XLVIII A song with musical accompaniment
1-3 by the sons of Korach.
² Great is HASHEM and much praised,
in the city of our God,
Mount of His Holiness.
³ Fairest of sites, joy of all the earth, Mount Zion

trace of discomfort, for the air of this city is the world's finest.

Similarly, the Sages (*Bava Basra* 158b) said in praise of the atmosphere of the Holy Land, 'The very air of the land of Israel makes one wise' (*Sforno*).

Dunash (quoted in *Rashi*) renders נוֹף as a *branch* of a tree, referring to the prominent mountain of the holy city, Mount Olives [which symbolizes the fertility and abundant wealth of Jerusalem.]

Indeed, the נוֹף is not a thin twig, but a very large branch or tree trunk which supports and nourishes many smaller twigs to sprout. So is Jerusalem the fountainhead of the blessings which God showers on the earth. Every tree needs roots, and the roots of Jerusalem emanate from יְרוּשָׁלַיִם שֶׁל מַעֲלָה *the celestial Jerusalem*, which is the ultimate source of the blessings of this world (*Yaavetz haDoresh*).

Similarly, *Ramban* in the introduction to his commentary on the Torah cites the Rabbinic tradition that King Solomon successfully cultivated every type of fruit, vegetable and plant in Jerusalem; even exotic and rare spices thrived in his gardens. This accomplishment defies all established rules of agriculture, for different plants normally require extremely diverse climate and soil conditions in order to grow.

Ramban explains that at Creation, God first created the substance of Jerusalem. He then expanded that substance and enlarged it to the dimensions of the world. Thus, all nutrients and forces invested in the earth emanate

from Zion. That the soil of one area is suited to a particular fruit, is an indication that a rich vein of nutrients is branching off from the main trunk in Jerusalem in the direction of that specific country. Solomon knew which location in Jerusalem was the source of each individual vein of fertility; thus he successfully planted all growing organisms on that site [see *Tosafos Rabbeinu Peretz, Pesachim* 8b.]

A number of additional interpretations of נוֹף are offered:

— This is derived from the Greek word *nymph*, meaning *bride*, hence, יָפֶה נוֹף, *a beautiful bride* (*Rashi*).

— This alludes to the הֲנָפָה, *raising up*, of the Omer barley offering on the second day of Passover [to symbolize that the Temple is the source of fertility.] Also, the nations of the world are destined to be *raised up*, (i.e., spiritually elevated) in Jerusalem in the future (*Tanchuma, Pikudei* 8).

— Jerusalem is as sweet and desirable as נוֹפֶת *honey* [see 19:11] of the highest grade, made of the tastiest nectar (*Zohar Chadash*).

— Egypt is the most fertile of all lands and *Nof*, נֹף (= מֹף, *Memphis*) is the richest of Egypt's cities [see *Jeremiah* 46:19, *Isaiah* 19:13], for it is embellished with 395 Divine adornments. Nevertheless, the beauty of Jerusalem surpasses it, for the Holy City is יְפֵה נוֹף, *fairer than Nof* (*Midrash Ha Ne'elam*).

— All of this is true because the יְפֵה נוֹף of Jerusalem is an all-encompassing *fairness*. Jerusalem is כְּלִילַת יֹפִי *perfect in beauty* (*Lamentations* 2:15), and all

ד יַרְכְּתֵי צָפוֹן קִרְיַת מֶלֶךְ רָב: אֱלֹהִים

ה בְּאַרְמְנוֹתֶיהָ נוֹדַע לְמִשְׂגָּב: כִּי־הִנֵּה

ו הַמְּלָכִים נוֹעֲדוּ עָבְרוּ יַחְדָּו: הֵמָּה רָאוּ כֵּן

ז תָּמָהוּ נִבְהֲלוּ נֶחְפָּזוּ: רְעָדָה אֲחָזָתַם שָׁם

of the nations recognize this (*Shemos Rabbah* 36:1). [1]

מְשׂוֹשׂ כָּל הָאָרֶץ — [*The*] *joy of all the earth.*

[Cf. *Lamentations* 2:15: מָשׂוֹשׂ לְכָל הָאָרֶץ, *a cause for joy for the whole earth.*]

What manner of joy did Jerusalem offer? A man arrived in the city downcast and deeply troubled by the burden of sin which he carried. In the Temple he sacrificed a sin-offering or a guilt-offering; this atonement absolved him of his sins. Thus he left cleansed and brimming with joy. Futhermore, the [communal] sacrifices of the Temple were a source of blessing for [Israel and] the entire world (*Rashi*).

The sacred atmosphere of Jerusalem is conducive to producing scholars of the highest caliber, who then go forth to guide the entire world towards truth, which is the epitome of joy (*Sforno*).

[When the Sages first established a system of public Torah education for youngsters, they wanted the central school to be in Jerusalem, for they knew that if the children witnessed the Priests totally immersed in the divine service and sensed the sanctity which envelopes the city, they would advance tremendously in their studies, thus fulfilling the verse [*Isaiah* 2:3]: *from Zion, Torah*

goes forth (*Bava Basra* 21a; *Tosafos* s.v. כִּי מִצִּיּוֹן).]

[No melancholy or depressed spirits were tolerated in this city of joy.] The *Midrash* (*Shemos Rabbah* 52:5) relates: Outside of Jerusalem there was a large rock, כִּיפָּה שֶׁל חֶשְׁבּוֹנוֹת *The Rock of Calculations*. Whenever a person needed to analyze his financial affairs he would leave the city to make is computations at this rock [lest his account prove unfavorable, thus causing him anguish (*Zerah Ephraim*) which cannot be tolerated in Jerusalem, intended as it is to be '*the joy of all the earth*.']

הַר צִיּוֹן— *Mount Zion.*

A צִיּוֹן is a *marker* or *monument* used as a memorial for the dead (*II Kings* 23:17). Spelled צִיּוֹן, it refers to the site of God's Sanctuary, a timeless memorial for the preservation of truth for the benefit of mankind. Even after the Temple was destroyed the mountain and its symbolism remain to remind mankind of the presence of the true God (*Hirsch*).

יַרְכְּתֵי צָפוֹן — *By the northern sides* [lit. *The sides of the north.*]

Sforno explains that the Land of Israel and Jerusalem are strategically located in the center of the middle east, between the two great northern land masses of Europe, on one side, and Asia,

1. Ten measures of beauty were allotted to the world. Jerusalem took nine and one measure remains for the remainder of the world (*Kiddushin* 49b).

The Sages took great pains to preserve this beauty and place many restrictions on the city to protect its environment (*Bava Kamma* 82b). For example, no garbage dumps were allowed within the city; no large ovens or kilns were permitted, because they produce smoke which blackens the white walls of the city; while the rose gardens which were planted in the days of the early prophets were allowed, other gardens and orchards were prohibited, lest people throw weeds and undesirable plants in the streets and lest the air be polluted by the stench of the manure used as fertilizer.

by the northern sides, city of the great king.
God, in her palaces is known
as the stronghold.
⁵ For behold the kings assembled,
they came together.
⁶ They saw and were forthwith astounded,
they were terrified and fled in haste.

on the other (hence the description *the sides of the north*). These two continents, the cradles of civilization, derived their cultural and intellectual treasures from the spiritual riches flowing from Jerusalem.

Rashi stresses that the prime gladness emanating from Jerusalem is the joy of atonement obtained through sacrifice, The sin-offerings and the guilt offerings were slaughtered on *the northern side* of the altar.

קִרְיַת מֶלֶךְ רָב — *The city of the great king.*

This refers to the city of David, as in קִרְיַת חָנָה דָוִד, *the city of David's encampment* [Isaiah 29:1], and the city of the Messiah *(Radak)*.

4. אֱלֹהִים בְּאַרְמְנוֹתֶיהָ נוֹדַע לְמִשְׂגָּב — *God, in her palaces, is known as the stronghold.*

This fact will only be fully appreciated in the future, when God's presence will be very close to the inhabitants of the city *(Rashi)*.

Ordinarily the prowess of a warrior is not known until he leaves the security of his fortress, for only then can he display his courage and strength. With God it is not so. Even when He dwells within the safe haven of the palace, He is still famous as a *stronghold* of might *(Yaavetz haDoresh)*.

Others say that אַרְמְנוֹתֶיהָ *her palaces* refers to Jerusalem's two bastions of Jewish faith, i.e., the First and Second Temples *(Dorash Moshe; Chazah Zion)*.[The Temple was the *stronghold*

of Jewish might, as we read, *May He dispatch your help from the Sanctuary and support you from Zion* (20:3).]

5. כִּי הִנֵּה הַמְּלָכִים נוֹעֲדוּ — *For behold, the kings assembled.*

The armies of Gog and Magog assemble to attack Jerusalem *(Rashi)*.

At that time, they will recognize that God is the *stronghold* (v. 4) of this city [for their mighty assault will be to no avail] *(Radak)*.

עָבְרוּ יַחְדָּו — *They came* [lit. *passed over*] *together.*

The *Midrash* (Bereishis Rabbah 93:2) renders עָבְרוּ as *they were angered* [from עֶבְרָה *wrath*] יַחְדָּו *at each other*, referring to the terrible feud between Judah and the ten tribes of Israel, which brought their kings *together* to clash in battle.

6. הֵמָה רָאוּ כֵּן תָּמָהוּ — *They saw and were forthwith astounded.*

When the kings who attacked Jerusalem witnessed the wondrous feats which God performed in His battle against their armies, they were astounded and terrified *(Radak)*.

According to *Midrash Shocher Tov*, this refers to the many potentates who came to *pass over* (v. 5) and tour the ruins of Jerusalem after her destruction. They were amazed and shocked by the utter desolation.

Sforno says that this describes the monarchs who came to visit the holy city in its glory. They were astonished by the wealth of scholarship and

ח חִיל כַּיּוֹלֵדָה: בְּרוּחַ קָדִים תְּשַׁבֵּר אֳנִיּוֹת
ט תַּרְשִׁישׁ: כַּאֲשֶׁר שָׁמַעְנוּ | כֵּן רָאִינוּ בְּעִיר־
יהוה צְבָאוֹת בְּעִיר אֱלֹהֵינוּ אֱלֹהִים
י יְכוֹנְנֶהָ עַד־עוֹלָם סֶלָה: דִּמִּינוּ אֱלֹהִים

wisdom which they discovered. They began to fear that the brilliant inihabitants of Jerusalem would decide to conquer the world (which they could have done with ease); therefore, *they were terrified and trembling*.

רְעָדָה אֲחָזָתַם שָׁם — *Trembling gripped them there.*

I.e., in the very place where the enemy sought to slaughter multitudes of Jews and to plunder vast treasures, *there* they were gripped with terror before the awesome might of God (*Radak*).

8. בְּרוּחַ קָדִים — *With an east wind.*

This is th wind which is reserved for God's punishments, as seen during the destruction of the Egyptians at the Sea: *And God swept the sea with a strong eastern wind* (Exodus 14:21) and during the downfall of Tyre: *The eastern wind smashed you in the midst of the seas* (Ezekiel 27:26) (*Rashi*).

Ibn Ezra comments that this refers to the mighty storm wind which will stir up turbulence in the sea, causing *convulsions like a woman in birth travail* (v. 7).

תְּשַׁבֵּר אֳנִיּוֹת תַּרְשִׁישׁ — *You smashed the ships of Tarshish.*

[Tarshish is mentioned frequently in Scripture as a flourishing distant seaport from which many valuable and exotic goods were imported to Israel.] As for its exact location, *Rashi* here offers these enigmatic directions: 'They are neighbors of Tyre which is in Africa [and was founded by] a descendant of Edom.'

Some identify it with Tartessus in ancient Spain, beyond the Rock of Gibraltar. *Kesses HaSofer* claims that this identification is without basis because the description of Tarshish in *Ezekiel* 27:12 places it amid countries of Asia Minor. Perhaps it refers to Tarzia in the Balkans. [See comm. to ArtScroll *Gen*. 10:4, and *Jonah* 1:3.]

Radak observes that throughout Scriptures we find Tarshish described as a major seaport which sent out great fleets of ships [throughout the Mediterrannean Sea] as in *Jonah* 1:3 and *Ezekiel* 27:25.

[The prophet (*Ezekiel* 27:25-26) echoes the Psalmist in predicting that the naval might of Tarshish is doomed. *The ships of Tarshish were your caravans for your wares; you were replenished and heavily laden in the heart of the seas. Your rowers brought you into great waters; the east wind has broken you in the heart of the Seas.*]

Hirsch explains that since תַּרְשִׁישׁ was west of *Eretz Yisrael*, her ships could reach the Holy Land only if they were propelled eastward by a strong wind from the west. Therefore, the Almighty sends an eastern wind against this fleet, driving it westward, away from its destination.

9. [On that day, when Israel will witness the downfall of the enemy as described in *vs.* 5-8, they will pay homage to Hashem:]

כַּאֲשֶׁר שָׁמַעְנוּ — *As we heard.*

We heard from our forefathers the wonders which You performed for them (*Rav Shlomo Atiyah*), and we listened to the prophets who foretold

XLVIII   7 *Trembling gripped them there,*

7-10   *convulsions like a woman in birth travail.*

     8 *With an east wind*
        You smashed the ships of Tarshish.

     9 *As we heard, so we saw —*
        in the city of HASHEM of Legions,
in the city of our God —
        may God establish it to eternity, Selah!
    10 *We hoped, O God, for Your kindness*

the doom of Gog and Magog (*Radak*), and we were well aware of the passage in the Torah [*Deuteronomy* 28:1] which promises: *and God will place you as most high above all the peoples of the earth* (*Sforno*).

כֵּן רָאִינוּ — *So we saw.*
All the prophecies of consolation which the prophets envisioned came true (*Rashi*).[1]

בְּעִיר ה' צְבָאוֹת — *In the city of HASHEM of legions.*
The Almighty is master of the celestial Legions above and the earthly legions below. It is He Who allows the legions of Gog and Magog to assemble against Jerusalem and it is He Who causes their defeat (*Radak*).

בְּעִיר אֱלֹהֵינוּ — *In the city of our God.*
In this war God acts as אֱלֹהִים שֶׁלָּנוּ *our Judge,* to render a verdict in our

favor against our enemies and to destroy them (*Radak*).

10. דִּמִּינוּ אֱלֹהִים חַסְדֶּךָ — *We hoped, O God, for Your kindness.*
This translation follows *Rashi* and *Metzudos,* who relate דִּמִּינוּ to דּוֹם, as in דּוֹם לַה', *hope for HASHEM* (*Psalms* 37:7). As *Rashi* explains, the Psalmist now launches into a fervent prayer to God, (yearning to see the fulfillment of the victories described in the preceding verses). He says, 'We have always placed our hopes in Your kindness, awaiting Your salvation which will appear in the midst of Your Sanctuary.'
Others derive this word from דמה *to think, imagine, conceive* (*Menachem; Ibn Ezra; Radak; Sforno*) [for Israel will say in the future: 'the wondrous events which we just witnessed live up to the conception of triumph which we imagined long ago.']

1. The *Vilna Gaon* detects here an allusion to the verse in the portion of תּוֹכָחָה *Admonition* in *Deuternomy* 28:63: *And it shall come to pass, just as* (כַּאֲשֶׁר) *God rejoiced over you to do you good and to increase you, so* (כֵּן) *will He rejoice over you to doom you and to destroy you.*
Here tha Psalmist states: The first part of the aforementioned prophecy which tells of the good reward reserved for the Jews is introduced with the word כַּאֲשֶׁר. Our downtrodden people has not been fortunate enought to *see this,* i.e., the blessing of כַּאֲשֶׁר has remained in the realm of שָׁמַעְנוּ, *we heard,* for we have *heard* of ancient blessings, but not *seen* them in our time.
However, the second half of the prophecy contains a threat of severe punishment. This harsh warning begins with the work כֵּן. Unfortunately, these tragic sufferings are not mere hearsay; רָאִינוּ, *we have seen* them with our own eyes.

יא חַסְדְּךָ בְּקֶרֶב הֵיכָלֶךָ: כְּשִׁמְךָ | אֱלֹהִים כֵּן
תְּהִלָּתְךָ עַל־קַצְוֵי־אֶרֶץ צֶדֶק מָלְאָה
יב יְמִינֶךָ: יִשְׂמַח | הַר־צִיּוֹן תָּגֵלְנָה בְּנוֹת
יג יְהוּדָה לְמַעַן מִשְׁפָּטֶיךָ: סֹבּוּ צִיּוֹן
יד וְהַקִּיפוּהָ סִפְרוּ מִגְדָּלֶיהָ: שִׁיתוּ לִבְּכֶם |

בְּקֶרֶב הֵיכָלֶךָ — *In the midst of Your Sanctuary.*

Originally דִּמִּינוּ *we imagined* that Your kindness and benevolence would be confined to the limited area of *Your Sanctuary.* But now we see that Your spirit overflows to the extent that *Your praise is to the end of the land* (v. 11) [i.e., the land of Israel.] Therefore *Mount Zion will rejoice over the good fortune of the Temple area and the daughters of Judea will be glad* (v. 12), i.e., the other cities of Israel [which are considered Jerusalem's children.] will also have cause for joy (*Abarbanel*).

Others punctuate the verse differently, to read דִּמִּינוּ אֱלֹהִים — *We imagined* (when we witnessed the past destruction of Israel) that You were acting as אֱלֹהִים, *the Dispenser of Strict Justice.*

But now, when we see the final outcome of history, we are convinced that in *Your Sanctuary* above, i.e., in Your heavenly abode, which is the source of all Your thoughts and decisions, You were motivated by pure חֶסֶד, *kindness*, i.e., Your afflictions were truly for our good (*Otzar Yesharim*).

Thus we also appreciate the destruction which You brought into *the midst of Your Sanctuary* below, i.e., into the Temple. This too was kindness, for You partially vented Your rage on the wood and the stones, rather than unleashing Your full fury on the Children of Israel (*Zerah Yaakov*).

11. כְּשִׁמְךָ אֱלֹהִים כֵּן תְּהִלָּתְךָ — *Like Your Name, O God, so is Your praise.*

The prophets described Your might to Israel and gave You exalted names

and titles. We can now testify that Your praiseworthy deeds do indeed match those names and live up to Your reputation. Therefore, even those who were so far removed from belief in You, O God, that they were seen as having gone *to the ends of the earth*, can now proclaim that *righteousness fills Your right hand* (*Radak*).

A king of flesh and blood may be landed as a mighty warrior when he is actually weak. He may be praised as beautiful, when he is ugly. He may be hailed as merciful, when he is actually quite cruel. But the Holy One, Blessed be He, truly surpasses any possible praise, as it says (*Nechemiah 9:5*) *You are exalted above all blessing and praise* (*Tanchyuma Shemos* 2).

12. יִשְׂמַח הַר צִיּוֹן — *May Mount Zion be glad.*

[On the day of victory, when the inhabitants of Zion will rejoice.]

תָּגֵלְנָה בְּנוֹת יְהוּדָה — *May the daughters of Judea rejoice.*

Jerusalem is the 'mother' city, and the cities around her, are like her 'daughters' [who rejoice at their mother's success (*Ibn Ezra*).

לְמַעַן מִשְׁפָּטֶיךָ — *Because of Your judgments.*

This refers to the harsh punishments You meted out to the nations which assaulted Jerusalem (*Ibn Ezra*).

Some say that the *judgments* refer to the destruction of the Temple. This, too, is a cause for rejoicing, inasmuch as God vented His fury primarily on wood and stones, but spared the nation (*Shaarei Chaim*).

in the midst of Your Sanctuary.

¹¹ Like Your Name, O God, so is Your praise —
    to the ends of the earth.
Righteousness fills Your right hand.
¹² May Mount Zion be glad,
    may the daughters of Judah rejoice,
    because of Your judgments.
¹³ Walk about Zion and encircle her,
    count her towers.
¹⁴ Mark well her ramparts, raise up her palaces,

The Talmud (*Makkos* 23a) relates that when Rabbi Akiva saw foxes roaming amid the Temple ruins, he laughed for joy. He explained that there were prophecies of both destruction and renewal. When we see that the first promise, of devastation, was completely fulfilled, we can be confident that the second promise, of renewal, will be similarly fulfilled. Thus, Zion may joyfully anticipate reconstruction *because of Your judgments*, since the conclusion of the judgments heralds the dawn of the redemption (*Dorash Moshe*).

13. סבּוּ צִיּוֹן וְהַקִּיפוּהָ — *Walk about Zion and encircle her.*

Walk about the inside of the city; *encircle her* from without (*Chazah Zion*).

Rashi maintains that this verse is addressed to those who will be engaged in the reconstruction of Jerusalem. They are bidden to calculate exactly how many soaring towers are necessary for a city of such stature.

Ibn Ezra and *Radak* interpret this as a call to all *of the nations* to gather around Jerusalem [rebuilt] to marvel over her vastness, strength, and beauty.

Zera Yaakov calls our attention to the *Midrash Shocher Tov*, which says that the area of Jerusalem is destined to expand tremendously in the future (see *comm. v.* 2) and that thousand of structures will be added to the city. The Psalmist bids the people to encircle and measure the present small area of Jerusalem and to count its few houses and towers, so that we will properly appreciate its future expansion.

סִפְרוּ מִגְדָּלֶהָ — *Count her towers.*

Hirsch suggest that counting the towers is part of routine care and maintenance of the fortress. He notes that in *Isaiah* 33:18, the סֹפֵר אֶת הַמִּגְדָּלִים is listed among the officals who administer the operation of the city. [*Rashi'* there refers to our verse.][1]

14. שִׁיתוּ לִבְּכֶם — *Mark well* [lit. *put your hearts.*]

The *Midrash* (*Bereishis Rabbah* 48:11) teaches that the human heart should ordinarily be spelled with a double 'ב' as לְבָבְכֶם, because it is composed of two parts: — the good and the evil inclinations. However, the hearts of angels are called לִבְּכֶם (*Genesis* 18:5)

---

1. It was said of the renowned *tzaddik* Rabbi Yosef Zundel of Salant that he sought to fulfill this verse whenever he traveled about Jerusalem, by counting the number of houses in the holy city including those of the gentiles. It was also a time-honored custom of the pious to walk all around the outer wall of Jerusalem every Erev Rosh Chodesh (*Tenuas HaMussar* Vol. I, p. 108).

לְחֵילָה פַּסְּגוּ אַרְמְנוֹתֶיהָ לְמַעַן תְּסַפְּרוּ
לְדוֹר אַחֲרוֹן: כִּי זֶה אֱלֹהִים אֱלֹהֵינוּ
עוֹלָם וָעֶד הוּא יְנַהֲגֵנוּ עַל־מוּת:

with a single 'ב', because they possess only the good inclination. The Psalmist here addresses the people of the Messianic era; he uses לִבְּכֶם to teach us that at that time the evil inclination will no longer control the hearts of men. [Thus, men will resemble angels.]

לְחֵילָה — [To] her ramparts.]

In Lamentations 2:8, we read of the חֵל וְחוֹמָה, the rampart and wall, of the city. The Talmud (Pesachim 86a) describes חֵל as a low wall within a חוֹמָה, principle wall which is higher (Rashi, Pesachim 86a).

The verse in Lamentations suggest that originally HASHEM had resolved to destroy [only] the outer wall of Zion. Once the destruction was underway, however, He destroyed the low rampart as well (Lechem Dim'ah).

[Here the Psalmist stresses that Jerusalem will be reconstructed completely, down to the minutest, most insignificant detail, including the low rampart which is not an essential part of the fortifications.]

Targum renders חֵילָה as אוֹכְלוּסָהָא her vast populace: Take note of the teeming masses which inhabit this city and undoubtedly exceed the city's normal absorption capacity.

The fact that there is room for everyone in this metropolis defies rational explanation and can only be ascribed to a Divine miracle. The Mishnah (Avos 5:7) relates that one of the ten miracles which transpired in the Temple and Jerusalem was that no man ever said, 'It is too cramped for me to spend the night in Jerusalem' (Alshich).

Others render חֵילָה as her strength, to indicate, 'Take note of the unique strength of Jerusalem which is from God alone' (Tefillah L'Moshe).

פַּסְּגוּ אַרְמְנוֹתֶיהָ — Raise up her palaces.

פִּסְגָה, as in Deuternomy 3:27, is a height. Therefore פַּסֵּג means to raise aloft, i.e., to make eminent (Hirsch).

Since the city of Jerusalem would seem to be terribly cramped for space, it is enigmatic how so many massive palaces fit into the city. It therefore appears as if these palaces are raised up, i.e., 'floating on thin air' (Alshich).

לְמַעַן תְּסַפְּרוּ לְדוֹר אַחֲרוֹן — That you may recount it to succeeding generations [lit. the last generation.]

The translation follows Rashi who interprets the verse as an exhortation to each generation to tell its successors of Jerusalem's glory.

The previous exhortation to scrutinize the wonders of Jerusalem refers mainly to the city of the future. Nevertheless, this obligation is also in force regarding Jerusalem in its original state. The Talmud states (Succah 52b), 'Whoever never beheld Jerusalem in her glory, never saw a truly desirable city.' Therefore, recount to your descen-

that you may recount it
to succeeding generations,
¹⁵ *that this is God, our God,*
forever and ever,
He will guide us like children.

dants the beauty which you beheld in Jerusalem of old but which they were not privileged to see, so that they may anticipate the even greater splendor of the rebuilt Jerusalem. For the prophet (*Isaiah* 54:11-12) foretells, *Behold I will cover your stones with fair colors, and lay your foundations with sapphires. And I will make your windows of rubies and your gates of beryl and all your borders of the choicest stones (Radak).*

15. כִּי זֶה אֱלֹהִים אֱלֹהֵינוּ עוֹלָם וָעֶד — *That this is God, our God, forever and ever.*

What will be related to your descendants down to the last generation? *That this is God,* the Lord Who was with us in the past, in the former Jerusalem. He will never change and will continue to be *our God forever and ever* in the Jerusalem of the future (*Sforno*).

הוּא יְנַהֲגֵנוּ עַל־מוּת — *He will guide us like children.*

This translation follows *Targum* and *Rashi,* who render this as one word עַלְמוּת *youth* or *childhood,* meaning He will guide us with extreme caution and care, as a father who leads his young child.

Or: He will preserve our youthful energy and vitality so that even in old age we will be as vigorous as young children (*Meiri*).

Menachem exegetically reads the word as עוֹלָמִית, *forever,* i.e., in both עוֹלָמוֹת, *worlds:* This World and the World to Come.'

Ibn Ezra mentions the opinion that the word is related to הֶעְלֵם, *the unseen,* alluding to the fact that God's administration of the world's affairs is hidden from the eye and above human comprehension.

However, according to the correct *Masores* tradition, these are two separate words (*Ibn Ezra*) which mean עַד מָוֶת *until death (Radak).*

The *Midrash* interprets these words literally, to mean *above death,* i.e., He *leads us to immortatilty.* This will occur in the future, for when Israel beholds God's presence *eye to eye,* they will live forever (*Tanchuma, Bamidbar* 17). [This may also allude to the authors of this psalm, the sons of Korach, who, through penitence, transcended above a fiery death in Gehinnom.]

In the future, שִׁיתוּ לִבְּכֶם לְחֵילָה (*v.* 14) Rivet your attention upon God, Who will be in the center of the חוֹלָה *circle* surrounded on all sides by the righteous who dance around Him with עֲלָמוֹת *youthful energy* and sing: '*This is God our God forever and ever: He will lead us into* עוֹלָמוֹת — *this world and the next!'* (*Yerushalmi Megillah* 2:4).

Solomon, son of David, once said, 'There is a sickening evil which I have seen under the sun, riches hoarded by their owner to his misfortune' (Koheles 5:12). *This refers to the wealth of Korach, which led to his unrealistic ambitions and his eventual downfall* (Rashi, ibid. and Pesachim 119a).

The sons of Korach, who recognized monetary greed as the root of their father's evil, concluded their series of instructive psalms with a final hymn concerning the relationship between man's material goods and his spiritual and moral mission (Alshich).

They taught that man must utilize all of his material and physical resources to enhance his spiritual existence, so that his soul will survive its brief sojourn on earth and ascend to immortality upon the death of its body.

If, however, man mistakenly regards the acquisition of riches as an absolute good and as the primary aim of life, he then forfeits his aspirations for eternity in both worlds and his existence does not continue beyond the grave (Hirsch).

Therefore, it is customary to recite this psalm after the prayers in the house of mourning (during the seven days of the Shivah *period) to emphasize the true meaning of life — and death, for the benefit of those who have just suffered the loss of a relative.*

It is thus quite evident why this psalm is placed after the preceding one, which concludes הוּא יְנַהֲגֵנוּ עַל מוּת, He will lead us beyond death — to immortality.

לַמְנַצֵּחַ לִבְנֵי־קֹרַח מִזְמוֹר: שִׁמְעוּ־זֹאת א-ב
כָל־הָעַמִּים הַאֲזִינוּ כָּל־יֹשְׁבֵי חָלֶד: גַּם־ ג
בְּנֵי אָדָם גַּם־בְּנֵי־אִישׁ יַחַד עָשִׁיר וְאֶבְיוֹן:

1. מִזְמוֹר לִבְנֵי קֹרַח — *By the sons of Korach, a song.*

In the preceding psalms, the sons of Korach addressed themselves to the chosen people of Israel *(Hirsch)* and spoke of the Jews' exile and redemption. Now they offer a song of universal significance, a lesson to all people who are overwhelmed by the desire to amass riches *(Yaavetz HaDoresh).*

Meiri notes that this psalm is also addressed to Israel in exile. For the exiled Jews who behold the wealth of their oppressors and contrast it with their own wretched penury may grow envious. Therefore, the Psalmist depicts the dismal end of those who exist for the purpose of accumulating riches.

Ibn Yachya adds that this lesson will be of particular significance in the trying period of חֶבְלֵי מָשִׁיחַ, *the travails of Messiah,* when the poverty and oppression of Israel will be particularly desperate and discouraging.

2. שִׁמְעוּ זֹאת כָּל הָעַמִּים — *Hear this all you nations.*

People of all nations err by relying on their money; therefore, all must be admonished *(Rashi).*

Alshich differentiates between two ways of utilizing the ears. שְׁמִיעָה, *hearing,* is to hear a voice from afar. הַאֲזָנָה *giving ear,* is to hear a voice at very close range; by drawing quite close to the speaker in order to catch his low, intimate whisper [see *Deuteronomy* 32:1; *Daas Zekeinim, ibid.*]

Those who have not yet been overcome by the lust for wealth, the ordinary people represented by כָּל הָעַמִּים, require only a warning from afar (שִׁמְעוּ) concerning this evil. However, those who have already become infected with the passion for wealth, the יֹשְׁבֵי חָלֶד, the

permanent *inhabitants of the decaying earth, require more vigorous advice and admonishment. Therefore, they are encouraged to give ear* הַאֲזִינוּ, i.e., to pay close attention.

הַאֲזִינוּ — *Give ear.*

This reflects the words of the *Midrash:* When a man falls from a high ladder and suffers multiple injuries, the physician must bind each wound individually. However, when a man's sins cause him to plummet from his lofty spiritual peak and to 'bruise' all the 'organs' of his soul, God, the Great Healer of the human spirit does *not* need to treat each wound individually. He tells the sinner 'All I ask of you is one organ: your ear. Let your ear hearken to My advice and be cured, and the rest of the soul will swiftly regain its health' *(Yalkut Eliezer).*

חָלֶד — *Decaying earth.*

[See *Commentary* to 17:14 and 39:6.] *Rashi* relates חָלֶד to חֲלוּדָה, *rust.* It describes our transitory world which can readily *decay* and *rust* away.

[The prophet *Isaiah* (38:11) refers to יוֹשְׁבֵי חָדֶל, *the inhabitants of the world which ceases to exist.* The commentators *(Ibn Ezra; Metzudos; Radak;* and *Kara)* all identify that word as synonymous with חָלֶד, since we often find words in which the letters interchange.]

Why are the *inhabitants of decaying earth* likened to the 'weasel' [i.e., the word חָלֶד is related to חוּלְדָה, *weasel*]? This rodent incessantly snatches food and drags it away to hoard in hiding places, without ever wondering, 'For whom am I collecting all of these stores? Who will benefit from this surplus?'

In similar fashion, many men spend their lives busily earning and saving,

For the Conductor, by the sons of Korach,
a song.
² Hear this all you nations,
give ear all you dwellers of decaying earth.
³ Even sons of Adam, even sons of man;
together — rich man, poor man.

---

toiling and hoarding, without ever asking, 'For whom and for what do I slave?' Concerning such people, the Psalmist lamented (39:7), *In darkness only man makes his way, his lustful pursuits are completely futile, he heaps up riches yet he knows not who will gather them in* (*Yerushalmi, Shabbos* 14:1).

3. בְּנֵי אָדָם — [*Even*] *sons of Adam* (*Targum*).

Amudei Sheish observes that the Psalmist begins his condemnation of material lust by addressing Cain and Abel, the *sons of Adam*, who were the first ones to quarrel over worldly possessions. [See *Genesis 4:8* and *Tanchuma, ibid.*] Cain said to Abel: 'Let us divide the world. I am the oldest, so I get a double share.' Strife ensued, and Cain killed Abel.

The *Midrash* adds that when the two brothers divided the world, one took the immovable land and the other took the movable objects. The former said, 'You are standing on my land', while the latter said 'What you are wearing is mine!' One said, 'Disrobe!', while the other retorted, 'Fly! (off my land)'...]

According to *Rashi*, בְּנֵי אָדָם refers to the nations descended from Ishmael and the sons of Keturah. They are called sons of *Adam* [i.e. a great man] because their father, Abraham, was described as הָאָדָם הַגָּדוֹל בָּעֲנָקִים, *the man who was great among the giants* (*Joshua* 14:15).

בְּנֵי אִישׁ — [*Even*] *sons of man.*
Targum identifies these as the sons of Jacob [for Jacob's face is etched upon God's celestial throne, as representative

of all humanity. Jacob was called אִישׁ תָּם, *a perfect man* (*Genesis* 25:27).]

Rashi says that this refers to the sons of Noah who was titled אִישׁ צַדִּיק *a righteous man* (*Genesis* 6:9). *Amudei Sheish* explains this as a reference to Ham, the son of Noah, who castrated his father to prevent him from fathering any more children who would share in Noah's wealth and estate (*Genesis* 9:22; *Sanhedrin* 70a)

Hirsch explains that the *sons of man* are people who derive social and financial advantage through the fact that they can trace their ancestry back to men of distinction. *Sons of Adam* includes the vast majority of humans who know only that Adam was their forbear and who lack any other pedigree. The message of this psalm is of equal importance to both categories of men: Power and wealth are overrated and worshiped not only by those who possess and were born into them, but to the same extent — if not even more so — by those who lack them, and were born without them.

יַחַד עָשִׁיר וְאֶבְיוֹן — *Together — rich man, poor man.*
Both rich and poor alike are infatuated by money. Concerning the rich, Solomon said, '*A lover of money will never be satisfied with money* (*Koheles* 5:9). The impoverished אֶבְיוֹן is similarly תָּאֵב לַכֹּל, *desirous of everything* (*Ohr Olam*).

The *Targum* renders כַּחֲדָא זַכָּאָה וְחַיָּבָא, *Together as one — both those (rich) with merits and those (impoverished) with guilt.* This alludes to

ד פִּי יְדַבֵּר חָכְמוֹת וְהָגוּת לִבִּי תְבוּנוֹת:
ה אַטֶּה לְמָשָׁל אָזְנִי אֶפְתַּח בְּכִנּוֹר חִידָתִי:
ו לָמָּה אִירָא בִּימֵי רָע עֲוֹן עֲקֵבַי יְסוּבֵּנִי:

the words of *Midrash Shocher Tov*
which warn that it is possible that one
who is rich in Torah knowledge and one
who [in his extreme ignorance] is 'poor'
in Torah, may both descend to Gehinnom.

[Doeg and Achitophel were both *rich*
in Torah, were heads of Sanhedrin, yet
they did not put their knowledge into
practice; therefore they were doomed.
Others have the talent and oportunity
to study Torah but neglect it, remaining
poor and ignorant. All these men are
culpable and they will burn *together*.]

[Realizing the tremendous importance of Torah study, the sons of
Korach emphasized its predominance in
the verse immmediately following: *My
mouth shall speak wisdom* (i.e., Torah).]

4. פִּי יְדַבֵּר חָכְמוֹת —*My mouth shall
speak wisdom* [lit. *wise sayings, max-
ims*].

Wisdom refers to the *understanding*
which results from *the meditation of my
heart* (Radak).

Contemplation of things Divine
causes the Divine Spirit to descend
upon the prophet. Then his mouth
becomes a sacred instrument of God, as
David said of himself (*II Samuel* 23:2):
'*The spirit of Hashem spoke through
me and His word was on my lips*'
(Alshich).

וְהָגוּת לִבִּי תְבוּנוֹת — *And the meditations
of my heart are insightful.*

[Insight is a Divine reward
which the scholar merits when he exerts
himself to share his wisdom with others.
Thus, if his *mouth shall speak wisdom*
while transmitting his knowledge to
others, God will fill his heart with fresh
insights and abundant understanding

ensuring him an inexhaustible supply
of wisdom to share with his students.]

Tehillos Hashem draws our attention
to Rabbi Meir's formula for presenting
a popular Torah lecture: The speaker
should divide his discourse into three
parts: One part אַגָּדָה, *homiletics and
moral sayings*, referred to here as: *my
mouth shall speak wisdom*; one part
הֲלָכָה, *deep legal discussions*, namely:
*the meditations of my heart which are
insightful*; and one part מְשָׁלִים, *parables
and wise sayings*, as in the next verse: *I
will incline my ear to the parable*. [See
Sanhedrin 38b.]

5. אַטֶּה לְמָשָׁל אָזְנִי — *I will incline my
ear to the parable.*

Indeed, the parable par excellence is
nothing less than the Torah itself,
which David calls (*I Samuel* 24:13)
מְשַׁל הַקַּדְמֹנִי, *the parable of the Ancient
One* [i.e., God] (Rashi).

HaRav Gifter explains that a parable
is a story designed to help the listener
comprehend a deeper truth which
would be almost impossible to grasp if it
were communicated directly. God's being and His will are totally incomprehensible to the limited, mortal
mind of man. The Torah couches these
eternal, ineffable truths in human
terms, and, as such, the Torah resembles a parable.

[In this composition the Psalmist
searches for the meaning of life and of
man's mission on earth. Therefore, he
turns to God's blueprint for the world,
the Holy Torah, for guidance and direction.]

אֶפְתַּח בְּכִנּוֹר חִידָתִי — *I will solve* [lit.
open] *my riddle with the harp.*

[The ways of God and the complexities of life are often an unfathomable

⁴ *My mouth shall speak wisdom,*
and the meditations of my heart are insightful.
⁵ *I will incline my ear to the parable,*
I will solve my riddle with the harp.
⁶ *Why should I fear in days of evil? —*
The sin I trod upon surrounds me!

mystery. Only he who is blessed with Divine inspiration and enlightenment can solve these riddles. Sacred music is conducive to lifting the soul to the level of transcendental ecstasy which precedes such Divine revelation (*Shabbos* 30b).]

According to *Ya'aros Devash*, these words capture the essence of David's personality. To discover the secret of David's soul, study the workings of the harp: The more vigorously its strings are plucked, the louder its sound and the more resonant its tone. The more God 'plucked' David's heartstrings with pain and affliction, the louder and more beautiful his songs became. עוּרָה כְבוֹדִי עוּרָה הַנֵּבֶל וְכִנּוֹר, *Awake, my soul, awake O lyre and harp!* (57:9). The soul is aroused and stimulated in the very same way as the lyre and harp. (See *Overview* part III).

6. לָמָה אִירָא בִּימֵי רָע — *Why should I fear in days of evil?*

[This verse reveals the *riddle* which deeply troubled the Psalmist and succinctly records the answer which he discovered through the inspiration induced by his harp.

Man is beset with anxiety and self-doubt. He is perplexed and alarmed by an unknown danger which seems to dog his steps. Man, therefore, cries out in anguish, 'What is this dread which robs my soul of its natural serenity and destroys my peace of mind? Every small threat of evil suddenly seems to be magnified a thousand-fold, and I am terrified by my own shadow!']

In particular, man dreads the insecurity of old age, which *Koheles* (12:1) describes as יְמֵי הָרָעָה, *evil days* (*Ibn Ezra*). Old age is frightening because of its attendant infirmity and frail health (*Rashi, Koheles* ad loc.), and because it heralds the approach of death, which is followed by Divine punishment for one's sins (*Taalumos Chochmah, Koheles* ad loc.).

Radak observes that man's entire existence in this temporary world may be described as *days of evil*, for one who immerses himself in the pursuit of worldly goods brings misfortune and evil upon himself. According to *Radak*, the riddle continues: If the honest, thinking man realizes the futility of evil greed, why does he still brood over the acquisition of wealth and persist in hoarding his possessions, which he regards as a symbol of his success and status?

Even more bewildering, adds *Amudei Sheish*, is that when man actually reaches *the evil days* of old age, when all other lusts and cravings have ceased to affect the worn, brittle body, the passion for wealth remains relentless.

עֲוֹן עֲקֵבַי יְסַבֵּנִי — *The sin I trod upon* [lit. *my heels*] *surrounds me.*

The cause of dread are the sins which a person considers inconsequential. There are sins which some people consider so minor that they commit them with impunity, as if grinding them underfoot. Therefore they are called עֲבֵרוֹת שֶׁאָדָם דָשׁ בַּעֲקֵבָיו, *the sins which a person treads upon with his heels.* It is because of such sins that a person will

ז הַבֹּטְחִים עַל־חֵילָם וּבְרֹב עָשְׁרָם
ח יִתְהַלָּלוּ: אָח לֹא־פָדֹה יִפְדֶּה אִישׁ לֹא־

feel dread when his time of judgment
arrives (Rashi).

[In a single pithy statement, the
Psalmist now offers a solution to the
puzzle of human anxiety and insecurity.

This statement is not addressed to an
inveterate, deliberate evildoer, for the
cáuse of *his* troubled soul is easy to
diagnose. Rather, these words are
dedicated to the purportedly religious
individual who seems to be following
God's *parable*, i.e., the Divine blueprint
for life set down in the Torah. He does
not sin intentionally, yet his life contains countless, unintentional transgressions, which he ignores.

Thus, he is surrounded (יְסוּבֵּנִי) and
imprisoned by the unintentional sins to
which he attached no importance. In
this sense, his offenses, caused by
negligence, were 'crushed underfoot
with his heels' (i.e., עֲוֹן עֲקֵבַי), for the
heel is the most insensitive part of the
foot (Midrash; see *footnotes* and commentary 19:12, בְּשָׁמְרָם עֵקֶב רָב).]

Despite his external facade of righteousness, this man who treads casually
on 'minor' sins misunderstands the
basic concept of the Jew's responsibility
to his Maker and Master. Our
obedience to the command of God must
be based solely on the fact that each
commandment represents His will. We
have no right to weigh the comparative
value of each command to decide which
one deserves greater adherence and
which deserves less. All must be fulfilled equally, because all represent
God's will.

It is upon the men who serve their
own will and values that God brings the
sadness and anxiety of *evil days*, in
order to awaken them to earnest reflection concerning their careless lapses and
to teach them to be more mindful of
their true duty in life *(Hirsch)*.

7. הַבֹּטְחִים עַל חֵילָם — *Those who trust
in their riches* [lit. *strength*].

[Most men do not react properly to
the benign warnings of the *days of evil*.
They pay no heed to the call of God
which is contained in their afflictions, in
their anxiety, and in the stirrings of
their uneasy conscience. God cries out,
'You yearn for security and tranquility;
discover security by surrendering
yourself to the protective shield of My
will!'

[But man remains as insensitive as the
tough, thick skin of the עֵקֶב, *heel*. He
strives to still his pangs of insecurity by
building a financial fortress for himself.
His real Temple of worship is the bank,
not the House of Prayer.]

To people such as these, *Targum*
cries out: 'Woe unto those who put
their faith in their possessions!' Of
what avail is your wealth in the face of
death, the Angel of Death who relentlessly makes his rounds and does not
discriminate between the rich and the
poor? *(Meiri)*.

[Korach is a perfect example of a man
who trusted in his wealth and grew
over confident and over ambitious.
Korach was the treasurer of Pharoah's
palace and held the keys to all of the
king's vaults. But God warned him,
'Korach, what benefit will you derive
from this wealth? The money is
destined for the use of all Israel; you
shall not enjoy it' *(Bamidbar Rabbah
18:15)*.

Korach found the treasure troves full
of gold and silver which had been hidden away by Joseph, who had amassed
all the world's wealth during the years
of the famine. Korach sought to use
these riches to wipe Moses and Aaron
from the face of the earth *(Targum
Yonasan, Numbers 16:19; see also
Sanhedrin 110a and Pesachim 119a)*.

⁷ *Those who trust in their riches,*
and of their great wealth they boast —
⁸ *But a brother he cannot redeem,*
nor redeem himself;
nor give to God his ransom.

Finally, the *Midrash (Bamidbar Rab-bah 22:6)* states: Three wonderful gifts were created in this world, he who merits even one of them is blessed with the greatest fortune of life. Wealth is one of these divine gifts. But when is it a blessing? When this gift comes from heaven by virtue of one's Torah scholarship. However, the wealth and power which creatures of flesh and blood seize for themselves are worthless and will not endure—as happened with Korach!

Thus, Korach exemplifies those who trust in חֵילָם, *the strength of their riches.*]

וּבְרֹב עָשְׁרָם יִתְהַלָּלוּ — *And of their great wealth they boast.*

These men slowly sank from bad to worse. At first, they believed in God and His assistance and only placed a portion of *trust in their riches.* But, as their wealth increased, their faith in God diminished, until eventually the mention of the Name vanished from their lips. Then they denied God's assistance and glorified only themselves for their shrewd dealings and sharp business acumen. This is nothing less than total כְּפִירָה, *heresy (Maharam Almosnino).*

Jeremiah warned Israel not to get ensnared in this terrible heresy, crying out *(Jeremiah 9:22,23): Let not the rich man boast in his riches. But let he who boasts, boast in this, that he understands and knows Me (Radak).*

There is another disastrous tendency found in men of wealth. They will sin repeatedly without fear or misgiving, because, *they trust in their riches* and

plan to redeem their corrupted souls by 'bribing' God with *charity which saves from death (Proverbs 10:2,11:4).*

But here their greed backfires, ensnaring them in a trap of their own making.

First they promise enormous sums to charities, and publicly *boast of their great wealth.* But when the time comes to redeem their pledges, their greed is so overpowering that they simply cannot part with their precious wealth. Thus, *(v. 9) [Too] precious is the redemption of their soul, and unattainable forever (Dorash Moshe).*

8. אָח לֹא פָדֹה יִפְדֶּה אִישׁ — *[But] a brother he cannot redeem, nor redeem himself* [lit. *a man*].

This translation follows *Ibn Ezra* who identifies אִישׁ, *man,* as the subject and אָח, *brother,* as the object. The adverb לֹא, *cannot;* modifies both פָדֹה and יִפְדֶּה. Thus, 'The riches of the affluent man [אִישׁ] are useless for they cannot redeem [פָדֹה] a brother (i.e., his family and loved ones), and neither can the man save himself [וְיִפְדֶּה אִישׁ] with his wealth.'

This greedy, perverted man is classed with those *whose money is dearer to them than their own lives (Pesachim 25a).* Since the miser would rather die than spend his money to save his own life, he will certainly not give money to redeem a brother *(Kli Chemdah).*

לֹא יִתֵּן לֵאלֹהִים כָּפְרוֹ — *Nor give to God his ransom.*

Even if he would wish to ransom his soul from God, in whose hands rests the power of life and death — he could not,

ט יִתֵּן לֵאלֹהִים כָּפְרוֹ: וְיֵקַר פִּדְיוֹן נַפְשָׁם
י וְחָדַל לְעוֹלָם: וִיחִי־עוֹד לָנֶצַח לֹא יִרְאֶה
יא הַשָּׁחַת: כִּי יִרְאֶה | חֲכָמִים יָמוּתוּ יַחַד
כְּסִיל וָבַעַר יֹאבֵדוּ וְעָזְבוּ לַאֲחֵרִים חֵילָם:

for God does not accept bribes (Radak).

[Charity brings atonement only when it accompanies genuine repentance and reflects sincere concern for one's fellow man. It is worthless if given mechanically, as a 'pay-off,' by a remorseless sinner.]

Sifri (Haazinu 32) comments that the merits of righteous fathers will not save their wicked sons. Abraham cannot save Ishmael, nor can Isaac save Esau. Furthermore, since *a brother he cannot redeem,* Isaac cannot save Ishmael, nor can Jacob save Esau — even if they offered all the money in the world.

9. וְיֵקַר פִּדְיוֹן נַפְשָׁם — *For precious is the redemption of their soul.*

God very much desires that they liberate their souls from the shackles of lust, for the pure soul is *precious* to Him (*Sforno*). Yet since the soul is so priceless and *precious,* if man should damage it through sin, no amount of money can compensate for the damage (*Sifri*).

וְחָדַל לְעוֹלָם — *And unattainable* [lit. *ceased, halted*] *forever.*

Not only is *redemption* by means of mere money יֵקַר, *precious,* i.e., difficult to attain, it is truly impossible (*Metzudas David*).

In the event of sincere repentance, however, such *redemption* is not only possible, but it is also יֵקַר, *precious,* to God. This occurs when the penitent experiences such acute remorse over his sins that it becomes חָדַל, *impossible,* for him to return to his former erring ways (*Sforno*). [See *Rambam, Hilchos Teshuvah* 2:2.]

Targum echoes these sentiments: 'If

he will pay the precious ransom [of true penitence], then his disgrace and punishment will be חָדַל, *halted* forever.'

10. וִיחִי־עוֹד לָנֶצַח — *Shall he, then,* [lit. *and he will*] *live for eternity?*

It is *forever* unattainable (v. 9) that the sinner *should live on for eternity* (*Radak*), unless he repents; then his soul can and will *live on for eternity* (*Sforno*).

This opportunity to gain immortality is itself the greatest incentive spurring man to repentance, for if he renounces the petty pleasures of sin, *he will live on for eternity* (*Tehillos HaShem*).

לֹא יִרְאֶה הַשָּׁחַת — *And never see the pit?*

[Had Korach repented, he could have lived out his life in dignity and could have gained immortality in God's service. But he was remorseless, and his rebelliousness led to actual heresy: 'There is no Torah from heaven, Moses is no Prophet, Aaron is no High Priest! (*Yerushalmi Sanhedrin* 10:1).

Korach even denied that God was the Creator the world (*Zohar*).

God therefore invented a unique creation especially designed to deal with Korach. The pit inflicted extra punishment on Korach, as the *Midrash* (*Bamidbar Rabbah* 18:19) explains: Korach suffered devastation more than all the other sinners. While all were watching, the fire sprang at him and set him ablaze. The flames enveloped him, wrapping him in a fiery ball; he rolled around helplessly, until he sank into the pit with all his cohorts.]

11. כִּי יִרְאֶה חֲכָמִים יָמוּתוּ — *For he sees that wise men die.*

⁹ *For precious is the redemption of their soul,*
and unattainable forever.
¹⁰ *Shall he, then, live for eternity*
and never see the pit?
¹¹ *For he sees that wise men die;*
Together the foolish and the senseless perish,
and leave their wealth for others.

According to *Rashi* and *Radak*, it is this phenomenon which discourages the wealthy sinner, for when he observes the struggle on the battlefield of life, he notes that death always emerges as the victor. No one escapes death's grasp, not even the righteous and wise. Disheartened, the sinner makes no effort to redeem his own soul from sin or to redeem the body of his brother from mortal danger.

On the other hand, *Hirsch* suggests that the inescapable specter of the grave should be sufficient to shake the sinner from his stupor and arouse him to self-examination. For if even the meritorious [*the wise men*] eventually die, then certainly the sinners will share this fate. Therefore, it is only logical for a person to prepare his soul for death and for Divine judgment.

יַחַד כְּסִיל וָבַעַר יֹאבֵדוּ — *Together the foolish and the senseless perish.*

Wise men merely *die,* i.e., only their bodies fade away. Their souls live on and can expect a glorious future. Not so *the foolish* sinners who *perish* completely, leaving no trace of body or soul (*Radak, Rashi*).

Furthermore, only foolish people *leave their wealth to others,* for their only resources are material ones, which cannot accompany them to the grave. Not so the wise, however, who enrich their souls and intellect; therefore, they 'profit' from their 'earnings' forever, for their spiritual treasure accompanies them in the World to Come (*Yad Yosef*).

כְּסִיל וָבַעַר — *The foolish and the senseless.*

There is a marked difference between these two. The כְּסִיל is not unintelligent; in fact, he may very well have a brilliant mind, full of wisdom. Yet his intelligence is surpassed by his insatiable lusts and desires. The unbridled pursuit of gratification is so detrimental that the כְּסִיל eventually comes to despise moral and ethical wisdom, for he fears it will deprive him of his pleasures. As Solomon said, וּכְסִילִים יִשְׂנְאוּ דָעַת *And fools despise wisdom (Proverbs* 1:22; *Malbim, ibid.)*

Hirsch (to *Genesis* 45:17) explains that the כְּסִיל is one who tenaciously adheres to an unjustified point of view. He foolishly insists on his own opinion, regardless of contrary teachings or arguments. The בַעַר, however, lacks intelligence and resembles the בְּעִיר, animals, as we read, *I am senseless* (בַעַר) *and know nothing, I am like an animal with You* (73:22).

Hirsch also notes that the true root of this word is בער, *burning,* which describes the life of an animal who is 'ablaze' with Divinely implanted impulses and instinctive desires which cannot be bridled. Similarly, the men described as בַעַר heed only the sensual 'fires' of their flesh, totally disregarding their minds, which become blank and devoid of sensibility.

וְעָזְבוּ לַאֲחֵרִים חֵילָם — *And [they] leave their wealth* [lit. *strength*] *for others.*

[This is the most forceful argument against the rich who are intent on

יב קִרְבָּם בָּתֵּימוֹ | לְעוֹלָם מִשְׁכְּנֹתָם לְדֹר

יג וָדֹר קָרְאוּ בִשְׁמוֹתָם עֲלֵי אֲדָמוֹת: וְאָדָם

יד בִּיקָר בַּל־יָלִין נִמְשַׁל כַּבְּהֵמוֹת נִדְמוּ: זֶה

hoarding vast fortunes which they cannot possibly spend. What purpose is there in amassing wealth which will not serve its owner?] [1]

12. קִרְבָּם — [Yet] *they imagine* [lit. *their inner thoughts*].

This translation follows *Rashi, Ibn Ezra,* and *Radak.* The verse refers to the men who waste their intellectual endowments devising 'secure', 'indestructible' construction projects which are doomed to eventual decay and obsolescence. Nevertheless, they delude themselves into thinking that *their houses are forever.*

Other commentators transpose the letters so that this word reads קִבְרָם, *their grave,* (*Moed Katan* 9b). Because the wicked have no merits, they will not arise at the time of resurrection; therefore 'their grave' will remain בָּתֵּימוֹ לְעוֹלָם, *their houses forever* (*Ibn Ezra*).

מִשְׁכְּנֹתָם לְדֹר וָדֹר — *Their dwellings for generation after generation.*

Their main aspiration was that their

massive construction [for the public] should survive as a *house forever.* Failing this, they wished that at least their private מִשְׁכָּן, *dwelling,* would stay in their own family to perpetuate their illustrious name *from generation to generation* of their descendants and heirs (*Divrei Shlomo*).

[מִשְׁכָּן may also be translated as *Tabernacle. Harav Gifter* notes that when Korach challenged Moses, he did not stop at mere threats. He actually built his own tabernacle to vie with the one built by Moses and Aaron. Therefore, we find constant reference to מִשְׁכָּן קֹרַח, *the Tabernacle of Korach,* throughout the episode. (*see Numbers* 16:24,27 and *Pirkei Torah,* ibid).

Korach imagined that his מִשְׁכָּן would endure for generations, but it did not.]

קָרְאוּ בִשְׁמוֹתָם עֲלֵי אֲדָמוֹת — *They have proclaimed their names* [lit. *with their names*] *throughout* [lit. *upon*] *the lands.*

[Every man instinctively yearns for immortality. Those who deny the soul's immortality in the World to Come seek

1. The *Talmud (Eruvin* 54a) relates: Shmuel said, 'Snatch and eat, snatch and drink, for this temporary world from which we are destined to depart is like a wedding feast.' *Rashi* explains, that a wedding, although a great event, lasts for a short time. Therefore, do not waste this brief opportunity. If you possess money which you can use for your benefit and pleasure, don't save it for tomorrow, lest tomorrow find you in the grave, and your money unspent, fulfilling no purpose. For if God gave this money to you, He wanted you to spend it wisely, to purchase the necessities and amenities which would assist you in His service.

The *Talmud* continues: Rav said to Rav Hamnuna, 'My son, if you have money, enjoy it! For there are no pleasures in the grave and death is all but imminent; it does not delay! Perhaps you are concerned about leaving an estate for your children? Who can assure you that they will keep their portion after your death? [If it is God's will that they be poor, your bequests will be of no avail. If God has determined that they be rich, your efforts are not necessary.] People are like blades of grass. Some wither and die; others sprout to take their place. As the grass grows taller and its nutritional needs become larger, its source of sustenance increases proportionately. Similarly, as children grow and develop, their income grows proportionately. Since God provides, fathers need not leave their children with anything (*Rashi*).

Finally, the *Talmud (Gittin* 47a) relates that when Resh Lakish died, he left only one bushel of spices for his heirs; yet he mourned that he had wasted precious time to acquire a commodity which he would never use. Sadly, he described his wasted efforts with this verse, *And they leave their wealth for others.*

XLIX
12-13

¹² *Yet they imagine that their houses are forever,*
  their dwellings for generation after generation;
They have proclaimed their names
   throughout the lands.
¹³ *But as for man, in glory he shall not repose,*
   he is likened to the silenced animals.

ways to eternalize their names only in This World.]

The wicked build great metropolises in their own honor. Tiberius, the Roman Emperor built טְבֶרְיָא, Tiberias; Alexander the Great built Alexandria; Antiochus the Greek built Antioch (*Bereshis Rabbah* 23:1).

Alshich points out that Scripture recounts still another attempt at self-immortalization: *Absalom in his lifetime had taken and erected for himself the pillar which is in the King's Valley, for he said, 'I have no son to keep my name in remembrance,' and he called the pillar after his own name and it is called Absalom's Monument unto this day (II Samuel 18:18).*

[The *Talmud (Sotah* 11a) states that Absalom did indeed have children, three sons and a daughter *(II Samuel 14:27)*. But, because of his violent nature, they lacked the benefit of sound paternal guidance; therefore, they amounted to nothing. Having failed to erect a human monument of heart and spirit, Absalom constructed a lifeless shrine of stone *to proclaim his name throughout the lands.*]

13. וְאָדָם בִּיקָר בַּל יָלִין — *But as for man — in glory he shall not repose.*

[The preceding verse emphasized man's futile struggle to immortalize himself, *his memory* on earth. Now the Psalmist demonstrates clearly just how precarious a foothold man really has in this world.]

Man refers to the guilty man who is condemned *(Targum)*; he is immediately removed from his *glory.* On the sixth

day of creation, Adam was created. In the fifth hour of the day he stood on his feet. In the tenth hour he committed a sin. In the eleventh hour, he was judged. In the twelfth (and last) hour of that day he was driven out of Eden and never spent a single night of 'repose' in יְקָר, *the glory,* originally prepared for him in Eden *(Sanhedrin* 38a).

Ibn Ezra maintains that יקר also refers to money, which man imagines to be his *glory.* When a man is laid to rest in the grave, his money will *not repose* with him there.

In addition, suggests *Radak,* יקר describes the soul which is identified elsewhere as כָּבוֹד, *glory; honor* [see 16:9, 30:13 and *commentary ibid.*].

נִמְשַׁל כַּבְּהֵמוֹת נִדְמוּ — *He is likened to the silenced animals.*

Most commentaries derive the word נִמְשַׁל in our verse from מָשָׁל, *parable, comparison,* and note that the fate of the wicked is comparable to that of the animal after its death.

The man who squanders his life in pursuit of the useless vanities of This World will find, to his dismay, that when he slips into the *repose* of death, he will be stripped of the soul which he corrupted. His soul will have become so overwhelmed by his body that it will decay along with his moldering flesh. Thus this man will *not repose* with his *honor* i.e., his soul, because he spent his life *likened to the animals* who are *silenced* forever at death, since they leave no soul.

The introduction to *Sefer Mitzvos Hagadol* explains that man is composed

דַרְכָּם כֵּסֶל לָמוֹ וְאַחֲרֵיהֶם | בְּפִיהֶם יִרְצוּ
סֶלָה: טו כַּצֹּאן | לִשְׁאוֹל שַׁתּוּ מָוֶת יִרְעֵם

---

of two parts: angel and animal. The challenge of life is to determine which part will vanquish the other. After death, the struggle ends and the two contestants disengage. The animal descends to the grave, the angel ascends heavenward. Therefore, the כְּתִיב, *traditional spelling*, is נִדְמָה in the singular, for during life the two opponents are joined as one. But the קְרִי, *traditional pronunciation*, is נִדְמוּ in the plural which alludes to the separation of man's two aspects after death. [See *Minchas Shai* for a lengthy discussion of the קרי and כתיב of this word.]

The *Talmud (Sanhedrin* 38b) homiletically translates נִמְשַׁל as *ruled over, conquered* (from מוֹשֵׁל), and נִדְמוּ is rendered as *they appear*. Ordinarily, animals fear humans and accept man's mastery with docility, because man was created in God's image, the image of sovereignty. If however, animals attack men and *rule over* them, this signifies that the men have sinned and thereby distorted their Divine features to the extent that now *they appear* to be *animals* themselves.

נִדְמוּ — *Silenced.*

This translation follows *Rashi*: the soul of the sinner is *silenced* after death; thus he resembles the dead animal, which has no afterlife.

Radak comments that נִדְמוּ may be rendered *cut off* as in נִדְמֹה נִדְמָה מֶלֶךְ יִשְׂרָאֵל, *The king of Israel is completely cut off (Hoshea* 10:15).

Or נִדְמוּ may be related to דוֹמֶה,

similar in appearance, in which case this word is a repetition of נִמְשַׁל and means *he is comparable (to the animals).*

Maharam Almosnino suggests that נִדְמוּ describes the animals as creatures of דִּמְיוֹן, *confused, distorted imagination*, unlike man, who was meant to be a creature of שֵׂכֶל, *clear, rational logic*. If man would analyze life with his clear, objective mind, he would embrace faith and reject sin.

[This echoes the words of *Sotah* 5a: No man sins unless he is possessed by a spirit of foolishness.

Sforno (Genesis 3:6) explains that the evil inclination is powerless without the aid of the imagination, which distorts reality and magnifies the temptation of sin.] [1]

14. זֶה דַרְכָּם — *This is their way.*

[The wicked do not sin by chance or whim; rather they are convinced that *their way* is the right way. They are so confident of this that they even recommend their way to their descendants who follow them].

כֵּסֶל לָמוֹ — *Folly is theirs.*

They simply cannot travel the proper path of life because their כְּסִילוּת, *foolishness*, accompanies them wherever they go (*Radak*).

Rashi cites the *Talmud (Shabbos* 31b) which relates כֵּסֶל to חֵלֶב הַכְּסָלִים, *the fat on the flanks (Leviticus* 3:4) over the kidneys. The kidneys are the seat of understanding and sound advice [see *Berachos* 61a, and *Psalms* 7:10, 16:7].

---

1. [Korach too was a victim of his own imagination, which conjured illusions of grandeur and tempted him to stray. The *Midrash (Bamidbar Rabbah* 18:8, quoted by *Rashi)* observes that Korach was truly perceptive; if so, what prompted him to embark upon this madness? His eyes deceived him, for he saw in a vision the long line of his illustrious descendants. Therefore, he exclaimed, 'If such prestigious progeny will be descended from me, is it possible that I should sit by quietly?' However, he didn't see clearly; for these illustrious descendants were the offspring of his sons, who repented. Moses, however, knew the truth with prophetic clarity.]

14 *This is their way — folly is theirs,*
yet of their destiny their mouths speak soothingly,
Selah!
15 *Like sheep,*
for the Lower World are they destined.
Death shall consume them

Why then do the kidneys of the wicked fail to guide them? The wicked are fully aware that the folly of their ways will ultimately bring them down. But they allow their *fat* [i.e., their lust] to blind their common sense to cover the kidneys, as it were. Therefore, they plunge into sin (*Shabbos* 31b).

וְאַחֲרֵיהֶם בְּפִיהֶם יִרְצוּ סֶלָה — *Yet of their destiny, their mouths speak soothingly, Selah!*

The Talmud (*Shabbos* 31b) continues: Is it possible, perhaps, to attempt to minimize some of their evil by attributing it to the blindness resulting from the כֶּסֶל, fat which numbs their understanding? No! This is impossible, for they themselves constantly *speak of their afterlife* (אַחֲרֵיהֶם) and insist that it is reserved only for those who follow their wicked ways. This proves that their offenses are intentional and deliberate (*Rashi*).

Radak renders: וְאַחֲרֵיהֶם, *and their descendants* [lit., those who follow them], בְּפִיהֶם יִרְצוּ, *give approval* [to their parents] *with their mouths.*

The wicked foster a tradition of evil which they transmit to their children in such glowing terms that the children regard their parents with deep admiration and praise their parents' corrupt craving for wealth.

Meiri offers another interpretation: וְאַחֲרֵיהֶם, *their end,* implies the end of their days, when they see the shadow of death fast approaching. At that time בְּפִיהֶם, *with their mouths,* i.e., with insincere lip service, יִרְצוּ, *they will express a desire* for סֶלָה, *eternity* [see 3:3].

Their wish will be rejected, however, because they have no sincere interest in repentance. The proof is that even if you challenge them on their deathbeds to return their stolen riches to those whom they cheated and robbed, they will refuse, for wealth remains dearer to them than their own souls.[1]

15. כַּצֹּאן לִשְׁאוֹל שַׁתּוּ — *Like sheep, for the Lower World are they destined* [lit. placed, appointed].

The wicked are like senseless animals who give no thought to their fate, like unsuspecting sheep, huddled in the slaughter pen (*Rashi*).

Only at the last minute, when death looms before them, do they become alarmed; but then it is too late (*Rabbeinu Yonah, Shaarei Teshuvah* 2:17).

Hirsch, based on *Isaiah* 22:7, defines שַׁתּוּ as a turning of one's steps toward a certain path, which, in this verse, was

1. *Midrash Halsamari* perceives in this phrase an allusion to Rabba bar bar Chana's statement (*Sanhedrin* 110a): A Bedouin once offered to show me where Korach was swallowed up in the wilderness. He led me to two gaping craters belching forth smoke. When I bent my ear to the ground, I heard Korach's band screaming, 'Moses is true and his Torah is true, and we are liars.' The Bedouin testified [from his personal investigation and observation (*Rashi*)] that these sinners are perpetually roasted over the fires of Gehinnom, but that once every thirty days, they return to where they were swallowed, in order to make their proclamation.

In the light of this, the sons of Korach said: וְאַחֲרֵיהֶם, when in the end they come to their final punishment, בְּפִיהֶם יִרְצוּ, they try to make amends by confessing their guilt with their mouths. They follow this routine סֶלָה, *forever,* but to no avail, for their confession is too late!

וְצוּרָם קְרי וַיִּרְדּוּ בָם יְשָׁרִים | לַבֹּקֶר °וְצִירָם לְבַלּוֹת
טז שְׁאוֹל מִזְּבֻל לוֹ: אַךְ־אֱלֹהִים יִפְדֶּה נַפְשִׁי

not the path originally intended; i.e., the Lower World was certainly not intended to be man's final destination. However, the wicked have rerouted their lives away from heaven and towards Gehinnom.

מָוֶת יִרְעֵם — *Death shall consume them.*
This translation follows *Rashi* and *Rabbeinu Yonah* (*Shaarei Teshuvah* 2:17), who explain that the death of the wicked is not like that of the beasts. Beasts die once, but the wicked are consumed by death every day. The soul of the wicked is constantly prey to destruction and deterioration, until it decays, disintegrates, and disappears.

In addition, *Rashi* translates יִרְעֵם as 'He shatters them' [see 2:9].

Others suggest that this word is related to רֹעֶה, *shepherd.* The shepherd allows his flock to graze in lush meadows to fatten them for the kill, although the sheep fail to realize that with every tempting bite they are moving a bit closer to the butcher's knife.

So too, the wicked wallow in wealth and satiate themselves with luxuries, unaware that none other than the Angel of Death is stuffing them in This World so as to bring them closer to their doom in the next (*Maharam Almosnino*).

So said the prophet (*Hoshea* 4:16) Hashem shall pasture (the wicked) like sheep in a broad meadow. Elsewhere the Psalmist (37:20) reiterates his prophecy of their destruction: *The wicked shall perish, and the foes of HASHEM are like the fattened sheep, they vanish, like smoke they vanish* (*Vidal HaTzorfati*).

וַיִּרְדּוּ בָם יְשָׁרִים לַבֹּקֶר — *And the upright shall dominate them* [lit. *subdue them*] *at daybreak.*
Nowadays [in the dark night of the lonely exile] the wicked are brazen-faced and audacious, their confidence reinforced by their wealth and might.

Now they dare to dominate and oppress the upright. But when the Day of Final Judgment arrives, the righteous will overcome them, as the prophet Malachi (3:21) promises: *And you shall tread upon the wicked, for they shall be ashes under the soles of your feet, on the day when I shall act, so says HASHEM of Legions* (*Radak*).

Rabbeinu Yonah notes that the *Talmud* (*Rosh Hashanah* 17a), derives from the above verse that the wicked descend to Gehinnom for twelve months. After twelve months their bodies are destroyed, and their souls are burned, and they become ashes under the feet of the upright!

לַבֹּקֶר — *At daybreak.*
Rabbeinu Yonah explains that the time of the revival of the dead is compared to morning, when a man wakes from his sleep, as it is written, *And many of them that sleep in the dust of the earth shall awaken* (*Daniel* 12:2).

That day will shine for the righteous like a radiant dawn, as the prophet Malachi (3:20) said, *But unto you who fear My name shall the sun of righteousness arise with healing in its wings.* That very same sun shall set the wicked ablaze like a roaring furnce (*Rashi; Radak*).

[The prophetic statement *And the upright shall dominate them at daybreak* alludes to the episode of Korach. Immediately following Korach's initial assault on Moses, Moses was Divinely inspired and replied בֹּקֶר וְיֹדַע ה' אֶת אֲשֶׁר לוֹ, *At daybreak then HASHEM will make known the man who is His own* (*Numbers* 16:5)].

וְצוּרָם לְבַלּוֹת שְׁאוֹל — *And their form shall erode* [lit. *wear away*] *the Lower World.*
Rashi and *Rabbeinu Yonah* render

and the upright shall dominate them at daybreak,
And their form shall erode the Lower World
from being a shelter for them.
¹⁶ *But God will redeem my soul from the grip of*
the Lower World,

צוּרָם as צוּרָתָם, *their form, essence,* a
simile for soul. [*Rabbeinu Yonah* cites
Hoshea 13:2 as an example of a similar
linguistic peculiarity.]

This alludes to the statement of the
Talmud (*Rosh HaShanah* 17a) that
there is a class of the most vicious sinners for whom a twelve month sojourn
in Gehinnom does not suffice. This
group includes the heretics, apostates,
and those who deny the Torah and have
no faith in the resurrection of the dead.
Their punishment is everlasting. Even
after Gehinnom 'wears away' and its
fires are extinguished, they will continue to suffer (*Rashi*).

[Gehinnom is designated as a place of
re-formation. Those who warped
themselves with sin in this world resemble broken metal vessels which
are returned to the fiery kiln to be
melted down and reshaped. Our verse,
however, speaks of sinners who are so
hopelessly misshapen that nothing can
change them; even after ages in Gehinnom, they still retain צוּרָם, *their* (grotesque) *form.*

Korach is an example of a man condemned to burn forever, as is stated in
Sanhedrin 110a (see *commentary* to v.
15).]

Hirsch comments on the relationship
between the כְּתִיב, *traditional spelling,*
צִירָם, and the קְרִי, *traditional pronunci-*
ation, צוּרָם [lit. *their rock*].

This describes the soul of man, for a
rock is a symbol of that which is solid
and unchangeable. However, the צוּר,
soul, of man earns eternity only if it
regards itself as a צִיר, *messenger,* of
Hashem, an instrument dedicated to
Divine service.

It makes no difference to the faithful
messenger what powers or possessions
the Divine Dispatcher has provided him
for the fullfillment of his earthly mission. His only concern is to remain loyal
in fulfilling his Divinely assigned task.

מִזְּבֻל לוֹ — *From being a shelter* [lit.
habitation] *for them* [lit. *him*].

This alludes to Gehinnom, which will
wear away, leaving the guilty soul lost,
with no place to go (*Rashi*).

According to *Rabbeinu Yonah,* this
means that the wicked man has
deprived his soul of dwelling in the
celestial regions where it originated.
This heavenly abode is called זְבֻל קָדְשֶׁךָ,
Your holy habitation (Isaiah 63:15).

Rabbeinu Yonah continues: Through
his sins, the evildoer causes his
precious, exalted soul to forsake its sublime habitation and to decay in the
depths of the lower world. How hard
death is for the sinner who did not, during his lifetime, divorce the lusts of the
world from his soul. The Sages said
(*Derech Eretz*), 'Is it your desire not to
die? Die, so that you do not die'. That is,
one who wishes his day of death to lead
to eternal life will resolve within himself
that since in the end, he is destined to
leave the earth and his bodily desires,
and in fact to despise them, he will
abandon them in his lifetime and make
use of the earth only in the service of
the exalted God. Then, his day of death
will truly lead to eternal life.

16. אַךְ אֱלֹהִים יִפְדֶּה נַפְשִׁי מִיַּד שְׁאוֹל —
But God will redeem my soul from the
grip of the Lower World.

The Psalmist has concluded his
observations concerning the wicked and

יז מִיַּד שְׁאוֹל כִּי יִקָּחֵנִי סֶלָה: אַל־תִּירָא כִּי־

יח יַעֲשִׁר אִישׁ כִּי־יִרְבֶּה כְּבוֹד בֵּיתוֹ: כִּי לֹא

בְמוֹתוֹ יִקַּח הַכֹּל לֹא־יֵרֵד אַחֲרָיו כְּבוֹדוֹ:

יט כִּי־נַפְשׁוֹ בְּחַיָּיו יְבָרֵךְ וְיוֹדֻךָ כִּי־תֵיטִיב

---

the doomed. He now refers to his own soul with words of encouragement and confidence.

He declares, 'I have not allowed myself to be lulled into lethargy by the comforts and enticements of this world. I have been alert to *incline my ear to the instructive parable*; therefore, I *have solved the riddle (v. 5).* Thus I am certain that God will bring me close to Him, far from *the grip of the Lower World'* (Rashi).

כִּי יִקָּחֵנִי סֶלָה — *For He will take me, Selah.*

When my love for God is so all-consuming that the very letters of His name become indelibly etched in my heart (Ibn Ezra), and when I think of Him incessantly and my yearning soul cleaves to Him, then it is impossible that my spirit should not merge with the Divine Spirit (Rashbam).

Thus I shall never die; rather, my soul will be drawn upwards, until it disappears into the heavenly abode, as we read of the ancient *tzaddik (Genesis 5:24): And Chanoch walked with God, then he was no more, for God had taken him (Ibn Ezra).*

17. אַל־תִּירָא כִּי יַעֲשִׁר אִישׁ — *Fear not when a man grows rich.*

Now the Psalmist turns to the people who are sensible enough to listen to his sage advice. He admonishes them for being dejected and discouraged by the success of the wicked.

He argues, 'Will his riches assure the wicked man a longer, better life? Despite your poverty, you may very well outlive the prosperous! And if you fear that his riches will be an asset in the World to Come, rest assured that he will take nothing with him' (Radak).

According to *Targum,* this verse is addressed specifically to Moses, encouraging him not to be afraid of the wealth and might of Korach.

כִּי יִרְבֶּה כְּבוֹד בֵּיתוֹ — *When he increases the splendor* [lit. *honor*] *of his house.*

According to *Divrei Shlomo,* כִּי may be translated as *because,* i.e., you needn't fear the prosperity of the wicked 'because' he only increases the splendor of his earthly house and pays no attention to erecting a 'house' in heaven by means of charitable deeds. When he dies he will thus be left a pauper, and you will be the rich owner of a celestial palace.[1]

18. כִּי לֹא בְמוֹתוֹ יִקַּח הַכֹּל — *For upon his death he will not take anything.*

הַכֹּל is usually translated *all, every-*

---

1. *Yad Yoseif* pursues this thought further, explaining that even if the wicked *do* give charity, death will nonetheless strip them of their possessions. This idea is poignantly illustrated by the Talmudic tale (*Kesubos* 66b-67a) of the daughter of Nakdimon ben Gurion, a man of immense wealth. The Sages once found her scrounging in the dung of the animals belonging to the Arabs, searching for kernels of barley. So tattered were her garments that she had to wrap herself in her long, wild tresses of hair in order to stand in the presence of the Sages. The Sages remembered that her wedding dowry had been one million golden zuzim, and they were astonished at her tragic descent into abject poverty.

She herself explained the cause of the terrible reverse in her family's fortunes: 'The people of Jerusalem have a saying for it, מֶלַח מָמוֹן חָסֵר, *the salt* (preservative) *of money is depletion* (expenditure for charity).' [She thereby implied that her family had not given enough charity.

XLIX
17-19

for He will take me, Selah!
¹⁷ *Fear not when a man grows rich,*
  when he increases the splendor of his house.
¹⁸ *For upon his death he will not take anything,*
  his splendor will not descend after him;
¹⁹ *Because himself does he bless in his lifetime;*

thing; however, here it means *any-thing*, i.e., when he dies he shall not take *anything* (*Radak; Ibn Ezra*). [Combined with the negative לא, *not*, *everything*, becomes *nothing*.]

Rabbeinu Bachya (*Exodus* 25:23) records the custom of the devout Jews of medieval France who built their own coffins, using the wood from their dining table. In this way, they signify that, at death, man takes nothing with him; the charity which he gave and the kindness which he displayed to the poor guests at his table are the only remnants of his earthly toil which remain.

לֹא יֵרֵד אַחֲרָיו כְּבוֹדוֹ — *His splendor will not descend after him.*

[The demise of Korach would seem to refute the opening statement of this verse, for when he descended into the bowels of the earth, he and his followers *did* take *everything* with them: *their houses ... all of their possessions* (*Numbers* 16:32). Even their clothes which were in the hands of the launderers were ripped away, and rolled into the pit (*Bamidbar Rabbah* 18:13). Even their names which were inscribed in documents, even their needles which had been loaned to others, were swallowed

by the earth (*Yerushalmi, Sanhedrin* 10:1).

The answer, of course, is that since Korach could not use these possessions in the grave, they were, in effect, lost to him. Moreover, God decreed that these things be swallowed in order to erase Korach's name and honor, not to enhance it. Of Korach we can surely say, *His splendor shall not descend after him.*]

19. כִּי נַפְשׁוֹ בְּחַיָּיו יְבָרֵךְ — *Because himself does he bless in his lifetime.*

Rashi explains that the wicked brim with self-confidence until they are confronted with the harsh realities of the grave. Before that grim moment of truth, they lack even the most remote fear of retribution and declare, 'My soul will be at peace.'

There is, however, one peculiarity in the hymn of self-praise which the wicked man sings to himself: it is a solo. Only *he himself blesses his soul;* no one else joins in his hymn, for all others regard him with contempt and derision.

Radak interprets these words as a lament over the golden opportunity of life, which was wasted by the wicked: In his lifetime, man is given the chance

By not 'depleting' its resources for good causes, it doomed itself to lose its fortune.]

The *Talmud* questions the accuracy of this explanation, for Nakdimon ben Gurion was famed for his generosity: 'When he used to step out of his home to go to the House of Study, silk cloth was rolled out before him. After he passed, the poor were free to take the expensive cloth for themselves.'

The *Talmud* concluded with the insight: 'All the charity which he performed was solely for enhancing his own honor! (See *Maharasha*).

This is the lesson the Psalmist teaches here. There is no need to fear that the rich man will take his money with him, for even his charity is worthless because he gave it only to increase the honor of his own house.

כ לָךְ: תָּבוֹא עַד־דּוֹר אֲבוֹתָיו עַד־נֵצַח לֹא
כא יִרְאוּ־אוֹר: אָדָם בִּיקָר וְלֹא יָבִין נִמְשַׁל
כַּבְּהֵמוֹת נִדְמוּ:

to shower abundant blessings upon his soul, something which only *he himself* can accomplish. This can be achieved by concentrating on the enrichment of his spirit with Torah and *mitzvos* and by neglecting the petty desires of the body.

According to *Targum*, this verse describes a man who did take full advantage of the opportunities offered by life: The soul of Moses did bless You during his lifetime, and similarly וְיוֹדֶךָ, *all the righteous praise You,* תֵּיטִיב, *for You do good for those who serve (*לָךְ, *) You.*

וְיוֹדֶךָ כִּי תֵיטִיב לָךְ — *Others will praise you if you improve yourself.*

The Psalmist now addresses himself to the over-confident sinner and offers a suggestion which will help him to achieve universal acclaim: 'Straighten your crooked path, improve your deeds, and then others will also eagerly recite your praises' (*Rashi*).

20. תָּבֹא עַד דּוֹר אֲבוֹתָיו — *You shall come to the generation of his fathers.*

The Psalmist continues to encourage the wicked man to mend his ways, explaining that he will fully appreciate the

benefits of his repentance after his death. Then he will behold the generations of the wicked who are incarcerated in Gehinnom from long ago (i.e., the ancestors, the fathers of the wicked men of today) and who are doomed to darkness for all eternity (*Rashi*).

According to *Targum*, these words are a promise to the righteous: 'The good reputation of the upright shall ascend to the level of their righteous fathers'.

עַד נֵצַח לֹא יִרְאוּ אוֹר — *To eternity they shall see no light.*

Rabbeinu Yonah (Shaarei Teshuvah 2:18) describes the condemnation of the wicked most vividly: The soul which lusted only for the desires of the body will be severed from its roots, and descend at death to the earth, the place of its lust. But first it *does* ascend to the heights for Justice and Judgment, to witness how it bartered the heavens for the lower world. It resembles a stone flung from a sling, for after rising on high, it falls (in accordance with nature) to the earth.

Both the souls of the righteous and the wicked arise heavenward for Judgment. The souls of the righteous are

Others will praise you if you improve yourself.
²⁰ *You shall come to the generation of his fathers —*
to eternity they shall see no light.
²¹ *Man is in glory but understands not,*
he is likened to the silenced animals.

found to be worthy and are seated beneath the throne of God. The souls of the wicked are driven back to earth. There is no hope for them ever to emerge from the darkness, for, as the Psalmist said, *To eternity they shall see no light.*

21. אָדָם בִּיקָר וְלֹא יָבִין — *Man is in glory but understands not.*

The tragedy of the sinner can be perceived with dreadful clarity. For man, created in the image of God, possesses glorious potential *(Sforno)*. His soul which is made of the glorious substance of the heavens, is a splendor *(Radak)*. The world in which the soul is placed presents glorious opportunities for spiritual advancement and self-improvement *(Bris Avraham)*.

But alas, man, in his obsession with wealth, is oblivious to the glory and *understands it not (Rashi)*.

נִמְשַׁל כַּבְּהֵמוֹת נִדְמוּ — *He is likened to the silenced animals.*

The man who neglects his mission can only be likened to the dead animal, the silenced one. For the live animal is above this lowly perversion of humanity. As the prophet said *(Isaiah*

1:3), *The ox knows his owner and the ass, his master's feeding bag; but Israel does not know, My nation does not consider (Bris Avraham).*

According to *Midrash Shocher Tov*, this verse depicts Korach, who basked in glory as head of the Levites. He was a profound scholar and merited the unsurpassed privilege of carrying the אָרוֹן, *Ark of the Covenant (Bamidbar Rabbah* 8:3).

When Moses inaugurated the Levites for the Temple service, he shaved their heads. In the heavens, God and His ministering angels admired this symbol of purity and cleanliness, regarding it as a semblance of the Divine. Thus was Korach's name derived, for קְרַח literally means *bald.*

But Korach failed to appreciate this symbolic act and was deeply humiliated by his baldness. Therefore, he rebelled.

God announced: 'I sought to endow him with the glory of the heavenly heights, but now he shall sink to the lowest depths! *(Zohar).*

Truly, Korach *was in glory but understood it not.* Therefore he sank into oblivion and *is likened to the silenced animals.*

This psalm describes the intense desire of the Creator to reveal Himself to his beloved Israel. This powerful desire is truly the yearning of a father who wants to envelop his son in his protective embrace. Yet, God cannot indicate His Presence to His children until they, too, demonstrate a sincere desire to draw near to Him (v. 1-7).

For those who have strayed, one means of return is the sacrifice. The word קָרְבָּן derives from קרוב, close. By no means is God's favor won by the physical act of placing the parts of the offering upon the fire of the altar. It is the new awakening of the heart and soul accompanying the sacrifice which clothes the penitent with humility and makes him worthy of God's Presence (v. 8-15).

The Psalmist tells us that the most effective means of drawing close to God is by immersing the mind in His Torah. Rabbi Chaim of Volozhin would say: He who merely observes the commandments establishes a 'servant-master' relationship with God. But he who studies Torah makes himself worthy of being God's son. As we recite in the daily Amidah prayer, הֲשִׁיבֵנוּ אָבִינוּ לְתוֹרָתֶיךָ, Return us, our Father, to Your Torah.

Here, too, the student must be sincere and his motives pure. If his inner soul is decayed, his lips polluted with slander, and his eyes made venal with evil, of what value is his Torah?

Finally the Psalmist outlines the reward for each man in accordance with his efforts. Eventually, the gentiles and even the corrupt men of Israel, will perish (v. 16-22). But those who sincerely yearned for God, those who acknowledged and paid tribute to Him, will behold His Presence. He who offers acknowledgement honors Me, preparing the way and I will show him the salvation of God (v. 23).

א מִזְמוֹר לְאָסָף אֵל | אֱלֹהִים יְהוה דִּבֶּר
וַיִּקְרָא־אָרֶץ מִמִּזְרַח־שֶׁמֶשׁ עַד־מְבֹאוֹ:
ב־ג מִצִּיּוֹן מִכְלַל־יֹפִי אֱלֹהִים הוֹפִיעַ: יָבֹא

1. מִזְמוֹר לְאָסָף — *A song of Assaf.*

[This psalm introduces us to Assaf, one of the ten composers who contributed to the Book of *Tehillim (Bava Basra* 14b). In addition to this work, Assaf wrote eleven more psalms *(73-83)* making him the most prolific psalmist after David himself.

Assaf was the leading Levite musician of his times [*I Chronicles* 16:5,7; 25:1,2,6] and his name is often equated with that of David, [*Nehemiah* 12:46]. Assaf was more than a composer, he was also endowed with the spirit of prophecy [*I Chronicles* 25:2]. Many centuries later we find that when King Chizkiyahu rededicated the Temple he commanded the Levites to praise Hashem *With the words of David and Assaf the Seer* [*II Chronicles* 29:30, see *Tanna d'Bei Eliyahu Chap.* 30].

The Sages differ as to the precise identity of Assaf. Rabbi Yochanan says that Assaf is one of the three sons of Korach who jointly composed many of the psalms. However, since he was a devoted Torah scholar, he merited the privilege of composing songs himself as well as in collaboration with his brothers. Based on a series of verses (*I Chronicles* 6:22-28 citing the lineages of of Assaf and Aviassaf) Rav maintains that Assaf could *not* have been one of Korach's sons (*Shir HaShirim Rabbah* 4:4).

אֵל — *Almighty.*

This translation follows *Targum* which renders this title as תַּקִיפָא *powerful.*

[This translation is in consonance with *Sefer Hameonos* who explains that the Name אֵל alludes to God's mercy — not the relatively, mild mercy implied by the Name HASHEM — but rather an intense and powerful compassion which is reserved for the most righteous men who are lost in distress [see *footnote* to 22:2; and *Rashi* to *Exodus* 34:6].

The translation of אֵל as *Almighty* differs from our usual translation. Elsewhere in *Psalms* we render it as *God*, following *Targum* (ad loc.) who translates אֱלָהָא; see also 10:11 and 18:31.

Perhaps the deviation in this verse is because here the Psalmist enumerates three distinctly different names of God. For the sake of complete accuracy *Targum* here emphasizes the unique aspect of the Name אֵל which is best described as תַּקִיפָא, *powerful* of compassion. See also *Ibn Ezra* and *Rashbam.*]

אֱלֹהִים — *God.*

This psalm describes God as He will appear in His role of Supreme Judge in Messianic times, as the Prophet foretells: *When I shall return the captives of Judah and Jerusalem, I will gather all of the nations ... and I will enter into judgment with them (Joel* 4:1,2). The juxtaposition of אֵל to אֱלֹהִים serves to clarify the description of God as 'Judge of all judges, Mightiest of the mighty' *(Radak).*

ה' — *HASHEM.*

This describes the divine מִדַּת הָרַחֲמִים, *Attribute of Mercy* and completes the list of God's three primary forms of revelations to mankind: אֵל is the intense and powerful מִדַּת הַחֶסֶד, *Attribute of Almighty Mercy*, reserved for the completely righteous; אֱלֹהִים is the strong מִדַּת הַדִּין, *Attribute of Strict Justice*, which is administered to the wicked; ה', *HASHEM*, is reserved for the person who constantly vacillates

L
1-2

A song of Assaf,
Almighty, God, HASHEM spoke summoning the earth
from the rising of the sun to its setting.
² Out of Zion, consummation of beauty,
God appeared.

between good and bad. He is judged with the gentle מִדַּת הָרַחֲמִים *Attribute of Mercy*, but HASHEM does not overwhelm him with intense *Almighty Kindness (Eretz HaChaim)*.

Alshich delves yet deeper into the meaning of these three divine titles. In creating the world, אֵל, *the Almighty*, was inspired by a profound desire to do חֶסֶד, *kindness*, with all souls. Rather than allowing the souls to bask in un-earned celestial bliss, God sought to provide them with an opportunity to be challenged and tested so that they could earn their reward by adhering to rigid standards of conduct despite earthly temptation and distraction of sin. At first the implementation of this plan required that God be exacting in His evaluation of each soul's performance, applying His Name of אֱלֹהִים, indicating *the Attribute of Strict Justice*. But God realized that the בֵּינוֹנִי *the average man* — fallible and temptation-prone — could not survive such demands and so He tempered Strict Justice with Mercy. Thus the *Kindness* of אֵל together with the *Justice of* אֱלֹהִים fostered the concept of 'ה, HASHEM — *Mercy*.

דִּבֶּר וַיִּקְרָא אָרֶץ — *Spoke, summoning the earth.*

God issued a call to all mankind to enlist in His service. He did this at a time when the entire human race consisted only of individuals as when He issued commands to Adam and Eve and later to Noah and his sons, instructing them in the seven Noahide laws (*Sforno*).

And in the future He will once again

call out to mankind. But then He will judge them for having neglected His commands. He will summon them from all the corners of the earth, *from the rising of the sun to its setting*, arousing in them militant spirits to gather and make war upon Jerusalem (together with Gog and Magog) so that He may destroy them (*Radak*).

[At that epic moment in history, the Almighty will exercise great חֶסֶד, *kindness*, with the righteous nation of Israel, and דִין, *Strict Justice*, with the wicked nations of the world. Thus, he will appear as אֵל and אֱלֹהִים at one and the same time.]

מִמִּזְרַח שֶׁמֶשׁ עַד מְבֹאוֹ — *From the rising of the sun to its setting.*

All of creation cries out to the wicked who are spread over the face of the earth: 'Since you sinned you must be judged with severity, but let it be known that this was not God's intention! עוֹלָם חֶסֶד יִבָּנֶה, *the world is built for kindness'* (89:3).

Even the daily orbit of the sun attests to this truth, for morning is the time of special kindness as the Psalmist says לְהַגִּיד בַּבֹּקֶר חַסְדֶּךָ, *To tell in the morning of Your kindness* (92:3). Whereas the dark night is reserved for harsh justice (*Chazah Zion; Eretz Hachaim*).

2. מִצִּיּוֹן מִכְלַל יֹפִי אֱלֹהִים הוֹפִיעַ — *Out of Zion, consummation of beauty, God appeared.*

Because the nations of the earth did not hearken to God's call, He abandoned them and chose the one beautiful nation who paid heed, Israel (*Sforno*).

אֱלֹהֵינוּ וְאַל־יֶחֱרַשׁ אֵשׁ־לְפָנָיו תֹּאכֵל

ד וּסְבִיבָיו נִשְׂעֲרָה מְאֹד: יִקְרָא אֶל־

הַשָּׁמַיִם מֵעָל וְאֶל־הָאָרֶץ לָדִין עַמּוֹ:

[God bestowed *mitzvos* upon men to enlighten their souls that they may reflect the splendor of the divine. All the nations rejected this opportunity, but the obedient people of Zion polished their souls to be the *consummation of beauty;* in them the reflection of *God appeared.*][1]

Rabbeinu Bachya interprets this psalm as a prophecy of the future תְּחִיַת הַמֵּתִים, *Resuscitation of the Dead.* God originally created the world from Zion, the rock upon which the Holy Ark was later emplaced, and He continued to pour His blessings of life and sustenance down through the channel of Zion. Therefore, it is from this place that all of life is destined to be resurrected. [See 48:3 for complete discussion of Zion as the source of the earth's abundance based on this verse.]

3. יָבֹא אֱלֹהֵינוּ וְאַל יֶחֱרַשׁ — *May our God come and not be silent.*

God has chosen to conceal Himself in This World. He neither appears to administer well-deserved punishment to the wicked, nor bestow rewards upon the deserving righteous ones. He even seems to remain silent in the face of atrocities — such as the wanton murder of His faithful followers (*Rashi*).

But we hope with faith and pray with confidence that this silence will be broken in the future (*Sforno*).

אֵשׁ לְפָנָיו תֹּאכֵל — *A fire consuming* [lit. *will consume*] *before Him.*

In the future a fiery wrath will emanate from Him and consume the wicked who hitherto went unscathed (*Radak*).

וּסְבִיבָיו נִשְׂעֲרָה מְאֹד — *And His surroundings exceedingly turbulent.*

The question arises — Why indeed does God wait for the future to punish the nations while He allows them to tyrannize Israel in her times of exile? Why does He seem to be oblivious to their heinous crimes while at the same time being fearfully accurate and demanding in enforcing the most minute subtleties of the law with regard to Israel?

The answer is that one always pays much closer attention to that which is right before his eyes. God's gaze is fixed on Israel, His beloved people, so even their slightest flaws are readily discernible. Thus *His surroundings* [i.e., Israel which is near Him] *is exceedingly turbulent* [because He exacts judgment upon His near ones]. (*Yaavetz HaDoresh*).

So said the Sages (*Yerushalmi, Shekalim* 5:1): To those who stand close, סְבִיבָיו, *surrounding Him,* God is נִשְׂעֲרָה i.e., He disciplines them scrupulously even for a deviation as minute as a שַׂעֲרָה, *a hair's-breadth.* The Psalmist repeats this principle elsewhere too, saying, וְנוֹרָא עַל כָּל סְבִיבָיו, *He is awesome over all those surrounding Him* (89:8).

The *Yerushalmi* continues: Do not think that God is lax or forgiving towards the enemy nations. Whosoever dares to insinuate that God's justice is lax — let that man's innards be severed and loosened! With the nation God bides His time, waiting for the opportunity to administer final devastating retribution.

The *Mechilta* (*Beshalach* 15:11)

---

1. History will bear testimony to four divine appearances: God appeared in Egypt to perform miracles for Israel, and at Sinai to transmit the Torah. He is destined to reveal Himself a third time in the War of Gog and Magog and finally in the Epoch of Messiah, as it says, *Out of Zion the consummation of beauty, God appeared* (*Sifri, Parshas Brocho,* 33:2).

L
3-4

³ *May our God come and not be silent.*
A fire consuming before Him,
and His surroundings exceedingly turbulent.
⁴ *He will summon the heavens above and the earth,*
that He may avenge His people.

derives from these words how different the ways of God are from those of man. A king, in order to be held in awe by the masses, must keep his distance from them. Those close to him soon learn that he is a mere mortal — no better nor worse than they. Not so with the Almighty God. The more one knows Him and aspires to be close to Him — the greater the awe, to the point where the most intimate tremble, for *His surroundings are exceedingly turbulent.*

4. יִקְרָא אֶל הַשָּׁמַיִם מֵעָל — *He will summon the heavens above.*

[Every nation on earth is represented above in the heavenly *family* by a spiritual force which is known as its מַלְאָךְ, *angel*, or שַׂר, *prince*. All relations which God has with the nation on earth begin with the שַׂר above, and so the *Talmud* teaches that when Hashem seeks to punish a nation He begins by afflicting their *angel*, as it says: (*Isaiah 24:21*) *On that day HASHEM will punish the legions of the high ones on high* [and afterwards] *the kings of the earth upon the earth*].

In the time to come, God will initiate His retribution against the nations by summoning their *angels* in heaven (*Rashi; Ibn Ezra*). [See Targum here and in verse 6 who renders שָׁמַיִם as אַנְגְלֵי, *angels*].

Radak notes that in the past God has also called upon an *angel* to smite a nation as we read: *And the angel of HASHEM went out and smote in the camp of Assyria, one hundred and eighty five thousand* (*II Kings 19:35*).

Others suggest that we may interpret these words literally, i.e. that God will

actually call upon the heavens to testify on behalf of Israel, as the Torah says: (*Deuteronomy 31:28*) *And I will call upon heaven and the earth to bear witness on them* [cf. *Avoda Zara* 3a] (*Yaavetz HaDoresh*). Both heaven and earth will declare that even when Israel was swept into the depths of exile they continued to fulfill the Torah and its *mitzvos* (*Sforno*).

וְאֶל הָאָרֶץ לָדִין עַמּוֹ — *And* [to] *the earth that He may avenge* [lit. *to judge*] *His people.*

The punishment visited upon the heavenly *angels* will descend to the earth where the kings and nations will be afflicted as well. This will fulfill the prophecy (*Deuteronomy 32:36,43*) כִּי יָדִין ה' עַמּוֹ .... כִּי דַם עֲבָדָיו יִקּוֹם, *For HASHEM will judge* [for the sake of] *His nation ... for He will avenge the blood of His servants* (*Rashi*).

Radak observes: The peoples of the earth will actually participate in bringing their own punishment upon themselves. God will sweep all of them into a storm of chaos and confusion which will bring men to slaughter their own brothers as is predicted by the prophets [*Ezekiel 38:21; Zechariah 14:13*].

Radak also cites the opinion of the *Talmud* (*Sanhedrin* 91b) that *the heavens* refers to the soul and *the earth* refers to the body. Both will be called to account on the day of reckoning.

In this vein the *Rokeach* (*Hilchos Rosh Hashana* 201) notes that הַשָּׁמַיִם, *the heavens* is the numerical equivalent of נְשָׁמָה, *soul* = 395; and לָדִין, *to avenge*, [which follows the word הָאָרֶץ

ה אִסְפוּ־לִי חֲסִידָי כֹּרְתֵי בְרִיתִי עֲלֵי־זָבַח:
ו וַיַּגִּידוּ שָׁמַיִם צִדְקוֹ כִּי־אֱלֹהִים | שֹׁפֵט
ז הוּא סֶלָה: שִׁמְעָה עַמִּי | וַאֲדַבֵּרָה יִשְׂרָאֵל

the earth], is the equivalent of הַגּוּף *the body* = 94.[1]

5. אספו לי חֲסִידָי — *Gather Me My devout.*

God will call upon the natural forces of heaven and earth (*Rashi*) and He will demand of the gentile nations as well (*Radak*), that they all assist in gathering the scattered exiles of Israel into Jerusalem. Only the children of Israel can be considered God's *devout ones* for they alone struck an eternal pact of allegiance to the Almighty.

כֹּרְתֵי בְרִיתִי עֲלֵי זָבַח — *Sealers of My covenant through sacrifice.*

At Sinai, Israel entered into an eternal covenant with God and commemorated this solemn pact with the offering of שְׁלָמִים, *peace-offerings* (*Exodus* 24:5). Moses sprinkled half of the sacrificial blood on the altar and half on the people (*Rashi, Radak*). [This ritual was the official ceremony of conversion which accorded the Israelites the status of complete Jews (*Krissus* 9b). The sprinkling of the blood symbolized Israel's willingness to uphold the divine covenant even to the point of sacrificing its own life-blood to do so!]

It must be remembered that when they left the bondage of Egypt, the devout men of Israel endangered themselves by swiftly performing the hazardous covenant of circumcision in

order to partake of the Passover lamb. Circumcision is the basis of Israel's special covenant with God (*Radak; Shemos Rabbah* 19:5. See ArtScroll *Bereishis* 17:1-14).

At that time the Children of Israel were truly taking their lives into their hands, for the lamb was the deity of Egypt and to slaughter it was an act of total defiance which was sure to infuriate the Egyptians and provoke bloody vengeance. Moreover, at that very crucial moment when the Jewish people required all the strength they could muster in their own self-defense, they incapacitated themselves instead by performing an operation that would exhaust them — the *Bris Milah!*

Thus, they submitted themselves completely to the protection of God and sealed their Divine Covenant with total surrender and sacrifice (*Alshich*).

Eretz HaChaim observes that the covenant of *Milah*, even today, is still sealed *through sacrifice*, i.e., with a costly feast, which demonstrates how joyous and precious the *Bris Milah* is to Jews [*Shabbos* 130a].

The *Talmud* (*Sanhedrin* 108a) identifies those in history who epitomize the ideals set forth in this verse: *sealers of My covenant* — this refers to Chananya, Mishael, and Azarya who refused to betray their covenant with God by bowing to Nebuchadnezzar's idol and were

1. The Roman Emperor Antoninus mentioned to Rabbi Judah the Prince that both the body and the soul can present an argument which will exempt them from future judgment. The body can claim, 'All my sins must be due to the soul for since the soul has departed from me [at death] I repose in the grave like a silent, lifeless rock [which proves that I am completely incapable of any sin when left to myself].' The soul retorts, 'From the moment I left the body I wander aimlessly and helplessly like a bird [and I have done no evil].'

Rabbi Judah replied that the solution to this dilemma may be illustrated with a parable. A king cultivated a splendid orchard and entrusted its safekeeping in the hands of two watchmen — one was crippled and the other was blind. Once, the cripple said to the blind

⁵ *Gather Me My devout ones,*
sealers of My covenant through sacrifice.
⁶ *And the heavens will proclaim His righteousness,*
for God is the Judge, Selah!
⁷ *Pay heed, My people, and I shall speak;*

therefore thrown into the blazing furnace.

עָלֵי זָבַח — *Through sacrifice.*

This refers to Rabbi Akiva who joyfully sacrificed his life for the sanctification of God's Name.

Targum emphasizes that in everyday life the Jew has the opportunity to renew this covenant daily with sincere prayer which is likened to sacrifice.

וַיַּגִּידוּ שָׁמַיִם צִדְקוֹ — *The heavens will proclaim* [lit. *will relate*] *His righteousness.*

No transient creature whose sojourn in the world is brief can bear true witness to the righteousness of God. For history is in a constant state of flux, and no situation is static or enduring.

Therefore, only the heavens and the celestial legions which exist forever can attest to the past, present, and future, and confirm that God never betrayed His covenant with Israel. These permanent observers of world events are the only ones who can testify that God never failed ultimately to take revenge upon those who oppressed Israel (*Radak*).

כִּי אֱלֹהִים שֹׁפֵט הוּא סֶלָה — *For God is the Judge, Selah.*

The heavens will also testify that even when God smote us harshly in His role of אֱלֹהִים, *the Dispenser of Strict Justice,* He acted with righteousness, and only for our ultimate benefit *(Tehillos Hashem).*

7. שִׁמְעָה עַמִּי וַאֲדַבֵּרָה — *Pay heed, My people and I shall speak.*

Radak explains: After God will condemn the wicked nations and seal their doom, He will turn His attention to Israel and He will not spare them from the rebuke which they deserve for their sinful deeds. God will remove the wicked men of the nation and obliterate them leaving only the righteous, whom He will admonish.

Many prophets foretold these events, Zephaniah (3:11,12) said: *For then I shall remove from your midst your proudly exulting ones. ... And I will leave in your midst an afflicted and poor people.*

Zechariah (13:8,9) predicted: *And it shall come to pass that of all the land, says HASHEM of legions, two parts within it shall be excised and die, and only the third part will be left within it. And I will bring the third part through the fire and will refine them as silver is refined.*

man, 'I see luscious first fruits in the orchard! Come, place me on your shoulders and I will pluck them'. The blind man consented, and the fruits were plucked and eaten by both men.

Soon the royal owner of the orchard arrived and demanded to know what had happened to his fruits. The blind man defended himself, 'Do I have eyes to see them?' And the cripple argued, 'Do I have feet to go get them?' What did the clever king do? He placed the cripple on the shoulders of the blind man and judged them both together as one!

Rabbi Judah concluded: Similarly, in the future, God will thrust the soul back into the lifeless body and judge them together, as it says: *He will summon the heavens above* (the soul) *and the earth* (the body), *that He may judge His people (Sanhedrin 91b).*

ח וְאָעִידָה בָּךְ אֱלֹהִים אֱלֹהֶיךָ אָנֹכִי: לֹא
עַל־זְבָחֶיךָ אוֹכִיחֶךָ וְעוֹלֹתֶיךָ לְנֶגְדִּי
ט תָמִיד: לֹא־אֶקַּח מִבֵּיתְךָ פָר מִמִּכְלְאֹתֶיךָ
י עַתּוּדִים: כִּי־לִי כָל־חַיְתוֹ־יָעַר בְּהֵמוֹת

יִשְׂרָאֵל וְאָעִידָה בָּךְ — **O Israel, and I shall bear witness against you.**

My people [עַמִּי] refers to the ordinary people of simple faith and devotion to whom God speaks simply [וַאֲדַבְּרָה]. *Israel* refers to the elite, the scholars and the very pious who bear greater responsibility for the faults of the people; thus they are treated with greater severity. God Himself bears witness against them and their shortcomings [וְאָעִידָה] (Alshich).

But, as *Radak* points out, all who survive God's initial purge of the truly wicked, will be men of basically fine character who deserve to be admonished only for relatively minor offenses as Isaiah (4:3) said: *And it shall come to pass that he who is left in Zion, and he who remains in Jerusalem, shall be called 'holy'.*

אֱלֹהִים אֱלֹהֶיךָ אָנֹכִי — **God, your God, am I.**

God declares to Israel: You have just seen me appear as אֱלֹהִים, *the Judge*, of the world, meting out strict, harsh justice to the nations. Fear not for yourselves! A special judgment is reserved for you, because you have remained faithful and have not abandoned My ways. I am אֱלֹהֶיךָ, your [personal] Judge who will find ways to remedy your sins without punishment for the past, but rather by instruction and warning for the future (Sforno).

8. לֹא עַל זְבָחֶיךָ אוֹכִיחֶךָ — **I shall not rebuke you for your sacrifices.**

Says God: I am not dismayed if you neglect to offer up to me זְבָחִים, *sacrifices* (Rashi), such as the חַטָּאת *sin-offering* or the אָשָׁם *guilt-offering* (Ibn Ezra). My only concern is for the sins

which you commit [which necessitate such acts of atonement and appeasement] (Radak).

Rabbi Moshe Isserlis points out that the קָרְבָּן, *sacrifice*, is merely a *means* towards an end. The root of the word is קָרַב, *close*, for the sacrifice is a means for the alienated to draw close to God once again. How? By entering into קְרָב, *battle* [lit. 'close combat'], with the forces of evil which the sinner himself created.

וְעוֹלֹתֶיךָ לְנֶגְדִּי תָמִיד — **[Nor] are your burnt-offerings My constant concern [lit. *before Me always*].**

Our translation follows *Rashi* and *Radak* who interpret the first word of the verse — לֹא, *not* — as referring to both parts of the verse.

Targum however, renders the verse differently: 'I shall not rebuke you for the many sacrifices which you failed to bring throughout your period of exile, *because* the burnt-offerings which your fathers offered up to Me in the past constantly occupy My attention [and appease Me].

9. לֹא אֶקַּח מִבֵּיתְךָ פָר — **I take not from your household any bull.**

Although the bull is in *your* possession, it is not truly yours. You must understand that whatever God claims from you is His, just as all the world is His (Rashi).

The Psalmist singles out the bull for it is the largest of the animals brought as a sacrifice (Ibn Ezra; Radak).

He refers to it in the singular because a person usually offers up no more than one at a time of these large and expensive animals (Chazah Zion).

Israel, and I shall bear witness against you.
God, your God, Am I.

⁸ I shall not rebuke you for your sacrifices,
nor are your burnt offerings
my constant concern.

⁹ I take not from your household any bull,
nor from your pens any goats.

¹⁰ For Mine is every beast of the forest
the Behemoth of a thousand mountains.

מִמִּכְלְאֹתֶיךָ — [Nor] from your pens.

The מִכְלָה is a כֶּלֶא, prison, lock-up for the sheep and goats [cf. Habakuk 3:17] (Ibn Ezra; Metzudas Zion).

עַתּוּדִים — Goats.

The עַתּוּדִים specified here are representatives of the entire goat family because they are its largest members (Radak).

Nevertheless, in comparison to the bullock the goat is small, so people customarily offer up a few at a time, hence the plural usage, goats (Chazah Zion).

10. כִּי לִי כָל חַיְתוֹ יָעַר — For Mine is every beast of the forest.

Not only the animals which 'seem' to belong to you really belong to Me, but even the animals which belong to no one, the wild beasts of the forest which appear to be totally independent — they, too, are Mine (Radak).

Before the giving of the Torah, when offerings were made voluntarily, all clean animals were fit for Divine sacrifice, as is evidenced by Noah who sacrificed from all the clean species. However, at Sinai when God commanded that sacrifices be offered to Him, He did not demand that Israel offer every beast of the forest — which is Mine. Rather He narrowed the obligation to very few species — the cow family, the sheep family, and the dove family

— which shows that the purpose of all sacrifices is for the betterment and atonement of Israel not for the benefit of God (Sforno).

Midrash Tanchuma (Pinchas 12) amplifies this theme: God says: Not to satisfy my appetite did I command you to offer sacrifices, for all that you bring is already Mine ... Ten species of clean animals exist, three are domesticated, seven are not. Did I then, for My sake, burden you to exert yourself to comb the hills and mountains for the seven inaccessible species? No! I asked you only to offer the three animal species which are readily available — oxen, sheep, and goats.

בְּהֵמוֹת בְּהַרְרֵי אָלֶף — The Behemoth of [lit. in] a thousand mountains.

Targum and Rashi identify בְּהֵמוֹת as the ox that is designated for the feast of the righteous which is destined to take place in the Garden of Eden. From Rashi [based on Tanchuma, Pinchas 12] it seems that although the plural form is used, i.e. בְּהֵמוֹת, in truth, this is really only one very huge animal called Behemoth. It grazes upon a thousand lush mountains, every day and strips them bare. Nevertheless, a miracle occurs and immediately, upon every mountain, there sprouts forth a new growth of fresh green grass. [See Akdamus Millin, Artscroll ed. v. 75 for a discussion of Behomoth.]

יא בְּהַרְרֵי־אָלֶף: יָדַעְתִּי כָּל־עוֹף הָרִים וְזִיז
יב שָׂדַי עִמָּדִי: אִם־אֶרְעַב לֹא־אֹמַר לָךְ כִּי־
יג לִי תֵבֵל וּמְלֹאָהּ: הַאוֹכַל בְּשַׂר אַבִּירִים
יד וְדַם עַתּוּדִים אֶשְׁתֶּה: זְבַח לֵאלֹהִים
טו תּוֹדָה וְשַׁלֵּם לְעֶלְיוֹן נְדָרֶיךָ: וּקְרָאֵנִי בְּיוֹם

Rashi also suggests that אָלֶף, a thousand, may refer to the number of animals, not mountains, or it may describe the height of one mountain — a formidable one thousand *parsas*.

11. יָדַעְתִּי כָּל עוֹף הָרִים — *I know every bird of the mountains.*

God continues: There are so many different species of birds which fly the skies that it is impossible for man to know them all (*Ibn Ezra*). Also, many are completely inaccessible to man for they live on remote mountains (*Radak*), and yet all of these myriad species are well-known to Me (*Targum*).

וְזִיז שָׂדַי עִמָּדִי — *And what creeps upon fields is with Me.*

I know clearly every reptile, every creeping thing which זָז, *moves*, from place to place. They are עִמָּדִי, *with me* i.e. within the range of my knowledge (*Rashi*).

According to *Vayikra Rabbah* 22:10, the זִיז is a huge bird with a wingspan so enormous that it blots out the light of the sun. It feeds on the grasses of many fields which taste differently, therefore its flesh contains many flavors. *Targum*, based on *Bava Basra* 73b, also identifies זִיז as a giant bird whose feet are planted on earth [i.e. *my fields*] and whose head pierces the heavens where it sings before God, i.e. עִמָּדִי *with Me.*

Meiri however, in an entirely different interpretation translates זִיז as *the choicest grain* of שָׂדַי, *my fields*. This alludes to the מְנָחוֹת, *meal offerings*, which are brought before God in the Temple.

12. אִם אֶרְעַב לֹא אֹמַר לָךְ — *Were I hungry I would not tell you.*

God says: Even if I possessed the properties of a frail man who becomes hungry, I would never ask to be fed with sacrifices. I lack nothing since the entire world is Mine (*Ibn Ezra; Radak*).

Moses, whose mission it was to live on Mount Sinai for forty days and forty nights in order to receive the Torah, had no need for food and drink throughout that time. If he who was merely God's agent did without food, then surely God himself, whom Moses served, never experiences thirst or hunger (*Tanchuma Pinchas* 12).

כִּי לִי תֵבֵל וּמְלֹאָהּ — *For Mine is the world and its fullness.*

Although God is Master of the world, nevertheless, He desires the sacrifices of Israel and He describes them as רֵיחַ נִיחוֹחִי, *My pleasant savor* (Numbers 28:2).

Why did God desire that Israel sacrifice two communal lambs every day, one in the morning and one in the afternoon? So that their remembrance and the remembrance of their forefathers should rise up before Him!

So said the Holy One, Blessed be He, to Israel: 'My sons, My beloved ones, am I lacking anything that I need to make demands of you? All that I ask is that you should love each other, honor each other, and respect each other ... (*Tanna d'Bei Eliyahu Rabbah*, 28).

13. הַאוֹכַל בְּשַׂר אַבִּירִים — *Need I eat the flesh of bulls?*

This refers back to the פָּרִים, *bullocks,*

11 *I know every bird of the mountains,*

   and what creeps upon My fields is with Me.

12 *Were I hungry I would not tell you,*

   for Mine is the world and its fullness.

13 *Need I eat the flesh of bulls?*

   Or the blood of goats need I drink?

14 *Offer God confession —*

   then redeem to the Most High your vows.

---

and עַתּוּדִים, *goats,* of verse 9. Once again God emphasizes that He does not demand these offerings in order to satisfy His hunger (*Ibn Ezra*).

Although the halachah requires a person to bring sacrifices in specific instances, it is not the flesh which I desire. Rather, My pleasure derives from the fact that you heed My words and fulfill My wish (*Rashi*).

וְדַם עַתּוּדִים אֶשְׁתֶּה — *Or the blood of goats need I drink?*

Targum perceives this phrase as a euphemism for the זְרִיקַת הַדָם *the sprinkling of the blood* of the sacrifice on the walls the altar.

14. זְבַח לֵאלֹהִים תּוֹדָה — *Offer God confession* [lit. *thanks*].

The translation follows *Rashi* who renders תּוֹדָה as *confession* [of sin] rather than in its more common translation of *thanksgiving offering.* Thus: acknowledge your errors and sincerely repent — this is the sacrifice which I truly desire. After you have discharged this primary obligation you can proceed to *redeem to the Most High your vows,* i.e. to offer the animal sacrifices which you pledged. Only then will those sacrifices find favor before Me (*Rashi*).

Offer sacrifice by placing your Evil Inclination before God and this will be reckoned as if you had brought an actual קָרְבַּן תּוֹדָה, *thanksgiving offering* (*Targum*).

Alshich comments: Not only must you thank the Holy One, Blessed be He when He appears as ה', with His *Attribute of Mercy,* but even when He is revealed as אֱלֹהִים in His *Attribute of Strict Justice,* you must acknowledge His kindness. To recognize God's goodness even in the harshest of situations requires a great humbleness of the spirit as it says זִבְחֵי אֱלֹהִים רוּחַ נִשְׁבָּרָה, *The sacrifices of God are the broken spirit* (51:19).

Ibn Yachya concludes that since the קָרְבַּן תּוֹדָה reflects the achievement of deep perception and appreciation of the ways of God and indicates a true humility of the spirit, this sacrifice is preferable to all the other offerings which are presented to God. Small wonder, then, that the Sages tell us that even though all sacrifices will be discontinued in the post-Messianic era, the *thanksgiving offering* will still be brought, and prayers of thanksgiving and acknowledgement of God's mercy will still be recited (*Tanchuma Emor 14*).

וְשַׁלֵּם לְעֶלְיוֹן נְדָרֶיךָ — *And redeem to the Most High your vows.*

Tehillos Hashem explains that this alludes to the vow which every infant makes at the behest of the angel before he is allowed to leave his mother's womb (*Niddah* 30b): Swear that you will be righteous and not wicked!

טז צָרָה אֲחַלֶּצְךָ וּתְכַבְּדֵנִי: וְלָרָשָׁע | אָמַר
אֱלֹהִים מַה־לְּךָ לְסַפֵּר חֻקָּי וַתִּשָּׂא בְרִיתִי

15. וּקְרָאֵנִי בְּיוֹם צָרָה — *Beseech Me* [lit. *call upon me*] *in day of distress.*

If you have protected and sanctified your speech by fulfilling your vows (v. 14) then God will pay your words close attention and surely listen to your call in the day of distress (*Ibn Ezra*).

It will not be necessary for you to engage in prolonged prayer. The moment you merely *call out* to God, He will respond (*Alshich*).

אֲחַלֶּצְךָ וּתְכַבְּדֵנִי — *I will release you and you will honor Me.*

God says: 'Since you are trustworthy and sincere I am proud to associate with you. I will not give to an angel the privilege of redeeming you on the day of your distress. Instead, I will be honored to do this Myself (*Alshich*).

You honored Me in the past by scrupulously observing My commandments. In response I will honor you now (*Radak*).

After I release you, you will continue to *honor Me* by fulfilling the vows you made (v. 14) in your distress (*Ibn Ezra*), and by offering me praise and acknowledgement (v. 14; *Sforno*).

But, if you present sacrifices that are not accompanied by sincere repentance, they will be not an honor but a true disgrace to Me [God] for then it will that seem you imagine that you can deceive Me and conceal from My vision the secret evil which lies in your heart (*Radak*).

16. וְלָרָשָׁע אָמַר אֱלֹהִים — *But to the wicked, God said.*

In introduction to this verse, *Radak* defines the *wicked* one as a scholar whose outward piety is a mask for a failure to practice what he learns. This form of hypocrisy is dangerous both to the sinner and to those around him.

[There is hope for the man whose evil is unconcealed; his concerned neighbors and friends have the opportunity to admonish him for his sinful ways. But one who sins in secrecy in order to avoid the criticism of his peers, denies the omnipresence of God who sees everything. He fears only the probing eyes of man. Outwardly he displays devoutness, therefore no one can admonish him (see *Bava Kama* 79b).

Moreover, this pseudo-sage cannot deceive all men indefinitely. Eventually, people will recognize his immorality and will react in one of two ways. Some ignorant people will be influenced to emulate his sins, arguing that if a scholar performs such deeds, they cannot be evil in the eyes of God. Others will be outraged by his conduct and blame his hypocrisy and insincerity on the Torah he has studied.]

God tells these unscrupulous masters of deception to desist from their Torah studies which, in their results, are detrimental!

The Sages (*Sanhedrin* 106b) cite Doeg the Edomite, David's archenemy, as a classic example of the great Torah scholar whose teachings were riddled with hypocrisy. It was he who mercilessly slandered David to Saul and incited the melancholy king to massacre the entire priestly city of Nob. The Holy One, Blessed be He, asked of Doeg: 'When you arrive at the Torah portion of לָשׁוֹן הָרָע, *slanderous talk*, and the portion of רְצִיחָה, *murder*, what lesson can you expound?'

[Another tragic example is Elisha ben Avuya who was reknowned as a brilliant Torah master. Yet, while he seemed to studying diligently he was secretly studying heretical books which he hid in his bosom (*Chagigah* 15b). Finally he shed his masquerade and openly defied the Torah earning the title

L
15-16

¹⁵ Beseech Me in day of distress,
I will release you and you will honor Me.
¹⁶ But to the wicked, God said,
'To what purpose do you recount My decrees
while bearing My covenant upon your lips?'

אַחֵר, the Other One i.e. the man who changed from his former self.]

מַה לְּךָ לְסַפֵּר חֻקָּי — To what purpose do you recount My statutes.

This scholar is well-versed in the vastness and complexity of the Torah. He speaks glibly of the many duties incumbent upon the loyal Jew and prates of his staunch faith. Yet, all of this display of knowledge is nothing but a סִפּוּר, the recounting of a tale which he takes lightly. It has no personal effect on him. To this corrupt man, Torah study is merely a pleasant intellectual exercise for the mind (Hirsch).

The חֹק is a decree which has no apparent rational reason, such as the law of the Red Heifer or shatnez. These unfathomable statutes are designed to provide man with an opportunity to sacrifice his logic and intellect before the will of God and to display his total submission to the will of his Maker. The arrogant, wicked sage does not pay homage to a superior being. He worships only his own intellect. Therefore, the חֹק decree is the special target of his scorn, and he never misses an opportunity to recount and mock the decrees (Ibn Yachya; Shevet Mussar).

Kesef Mezukak suggests that this verse continues the earlier discussion of sacrifices. Even when guilt stirs the conscience of the wicked man and prods him to offer a sacrifice, he performs this ritual with improper intentions.

The sacrifices are really not חוקים, decrees; their purpose can be understood. Instead, of allowing his human

intelligence to guide his actions, the sinner acted like a mindless, lustful animal, thus forfeiting his privilege of continuing in life. But, the merciful Creator presented man with a means of atonement. He said, 'Slaughter an animal in your place and recognize that such a fate should have been yours, for you have acted like the dumb beast.' It is easy to understand how the renewed awareness brought about by the sacrifice is a forceful means of repentance and ultimate atonement.

But the wicked go through the motions of the sacrificial ritual and remain indifferent and unaffected. They claim that this ancient ceremony is a meaningless decree to be performed without any reason or feelings of contrition. Therefore, God angrily challenges them here, demanding, To what purpose do you recount My ritual of sacrifice if you regard it as no more than an empty decree?'

וַתִּשָּׂא בְרִיתִי עֲלֵי פִיךָ — While bearing [lit. you bore] My covenant upon your lips.

The teachings of the Torah do not affect the inner feelings of the wicked scholar. His heart is not in his studies, He bears the covenant of God only upon his lips, but his soul is oblivious of it (Hirsch).

In Sanhedrin 106b, the Sages declare that Doeg's knowledge was merely 'from the lips outward'. But God rejects, this for He desires only the sincerity of the heart (רחמנא ליבא בעי). [See 5:6-11 and Psalm 52 for a lengthy discussion of Doeg's shallow, perverted scholarship].

יז עֲלֵי־פִיךָ: וְאַתָּה שָׂנֵאתָ מוּסָר וַתַּשְׁלֵךְ

יח דְּבָרַי אַחֲרֶיךָ: אִם־רָאִיתָ גַנָּב וַתִּרֶץ עִמּוֹ

יט וְעִם מְנָאֲפִים חֶלְקֶךָ: פִּיךָ שָׁלַחְתָּ בְרָעָה

כ וּלְשׁוֹנְךָ תַּצְמִיד מִרְמָה: תֵּשֵׁב בְּאָחִיךָ

17. וְאַתָּה שָׂנֵאתָ מוּסָר — *For you hate discipline.*

This refers to the study of proper conduct between man and his fellow man (*Radak*).

The covenant of God (*v.* 16) places limitations upon man's actions and speech, but you despise this מוּסָר [lit. *chain, restraint*] because it inhibits your pursuit of gratification (*Hirsch*).

[This alludes to Doeg, for the *Talmud* (*Sanhedrin* 106b) says, 'Doeg did not die until he forgot his Torah learning as it says, הוּא יָמוּת בְּאֵין מוּסָר, *He will die without discipline* (*Proverbs* 5:23). Although he was a brilliant student of the wisdom of the Torah, Doeg despised the Divine discipline imposed by it, so ultimately he abandoned his Torah studies].

וַתַּשְׁלֵךְ דְּבָרַי אַחֲרֶיךָ — *And you threw My words behind you.*

This refers to all other commands of the Torah [specifically those controlling the relationship between man and God] (*Radak*).

The rebellion of the wicked who totally reject God did not erupt overnight. Their heresy is the result of a drawn out process of alienation which began even while they were still observing God's commandments. Their very first step towards heresy was taken when they made God's service secondary in their lives and ceased to give God their attention. Once they tossed God's words behind them and treated them as insignificant, they eventually sunk to the point where they *hate discipline* (*Tehillos Hashem*).

18. אִם רָאִיתָ גַנָּב וַתִּרֶץ עִמּוֹ — *If you saw a thief you sanctioned him.*

The word וַתִּרֶץ derives from רָצוֹן, *approval, sanction*. You agree to join the criminal in his lawless acts (*Rashi; Radak*).

Even though you are not a thief or an adulterer, nevertheless you approve of these crimes in principle. You rejoice when you see that the Torah's statutes do not subdue the passions of men and you sanction the wanton and licentious conduct of others for it excuses your own lack of discipline (*Hirsch*).

Targum relates וַתִּרֶץ to רָץ, *running* i.e. you run to join the thief in his crime. *Tehillos Hashem* adds that the man described here, originally set out to make a rendezvous with others for an immoral purpose i.e. *and with adulterers is your lot.* However, on the way he saw an opportunity to profit by joining in a theft. He *runs* to complete the robbery so that he will not miss his rendezvous for adultery.

וְעִם מְנָאֲפִים חֶלְקֶךָ — *And with adulterers is your lot.*

At first the hypocrite sought to justify himself by claiming that he rejected merely decrees that make no sense to him (*v.* 16). But eventually the true extent of his heresy is revealed when he transgresses even the universally understood prohibitions against theft and adultery. This proves that he is concerned only with satisfying his selfish desires and whims and has no interest in submitting to Divine authority (*Ohel Yaakov*).

The path of crime begins when a sinner participates in one theft which in itself is a relatively minor wrongdoing. He deludes himself that his career of lawlessness will stop there. He is mistaken, for once a man has forfeited his

¹⁷ *For you hate discipline*
    and you threw My words behind you.
¹⁸ *If you saw a thief you sanctioned him*
    and with adulterers was your lot.
¹⁹ *You dispatched your mouth for evil,*
    and your tongue adheres to deceit.
²⁰ *As you sit — against your brother you speak;*

self-control and submitted to his passions he is no longer his own master. Ultimately, he will surrender even to the lust for adultery, and be doomed. Therefore, we find that in the Ten Commandments the prohibitions against theft and adultery are written together, side by side (*Exodus* 20:13) to emphasize that a minor infraction leads to a major offense (*Alshich*).

19. פִּיךָ שָׁלַחְתָּ בְרָעָה — *You sent forth your mouth for evil.*

You accustomed your mouth to spread slanderous tales about others (*Radak*) and to teach false ideas and beliefs (*Sforno*).

Slander is described as dispatching the words of evil, for the disastrous effects of tale-bearing soar beyond all geographic boundaries and limitations. A man can sit in Jerusalem and spread slander about his enemy in Rome (*Kesef Mezukak*)!

וּלְשׁוֹנְךָ תַּצְמִיד מִרְמָה — *And your tongue adheres to deceit.*

Slander eventually leads to deceit, for when the slanderer is confronted by the man whose reputation he has tainted, he seeks to cover up his actions with lies (*Tehillos Hashem*).

Be'er Avraham explains that the verb roots דבק and חבר describe the joining of two objects which maintain their separate identities even after they are brought together. But צמד refers to a complete merging of two units into one

indivisible whole as in צָמִיד פָּתִיל עָלָיו, *the covering bound tightly upon it* (*Numbers* 19:15). [The slanderer's tale is repeated so often that to utter falsehood becomes the ingrained, habitual behavior of his tongue. This conduct becomes an irrevocable part of his personality].

Since he seeks to corrupt the masses by disseminating evil ideas, this man fears that the intelligent leaders will detect his sinister plot. Therefore, he resorts to treachery and deceit in order to conceal his true intentions (*Sforno*).

Furthermore, he becomes a master at composing and *joining together* false tales (*Rashi*) and he usually *joins together* with other liars and slanderers to share their company (*Radak*).

20. תֵּשֵׁב — [*As*] *you sit* [lit. *you will sit*].

The company of slanderers and scoffers is referred to as a session of people who *sit*, as in מוֹשַׁב לֵצִים, *the session of scorners* (1:1). In such company, you dispatch your words of ridicule and slander (*Ibn Ezra*).

בְּאָחִיךָ תְדַבֶּר — *Against your brother you speak.*

Radak explains that this is a paternal brother. This implies that your motive in disparaging your *father's son* is because you share the same inheritance; thus there is a rivalry between you (*Radak*).

כא תְּדַבֵּר בְּבֶן־אִמְּךָ תִּתֶּן־דֹּפִי: אֵלֶּה עָשִׂיתָ|
וְהֶחֱרַשְׁתִּי דִּמִּיתָ הֱיוֹת־אֶהְיֶה כָמוֹךָ
כב אוֹכִיחֲךָ וְאֶעֶרְכָה לְעֵינֶיךָ: בִּינוּ־נָא זֹאת
כג שֹׁכְחֵי אֱלוֹהַּ פֶּן־אֶטְרֹף וְאֵין מַצִּיל: זֹבֵחַ
תּוֹדָה יְכַבְּדָנְנִי וְשָׂם דֶּרֶךְ אַרְאֶנּוּ בְּיֵשַׁע
אֱלֹהִים:

בְּבֶן אִמֶּךָ — *Against your mother's son.*
If you permit your tongue to grow accustomed to slander for profit as in your dispute with your paternal brother who is a fellow heir, you will come to slander even those with whom you have no reason to quarrel such as your maternal brother with whom you share no estate (*Rashi; Radak*).

The Sages stress that there is no innocent slander; any form of gossip corrupts the character and leads to more serious offenses: 'If you have allowed your tongue to grow accustomed to slandering your colleague who is not of your people you will ultimately degrade your fellow Jew' (*Devarim Rabbah* 6:9).

'If you speak against Esau who is the son of your brother you will eventually sink to the point where you will speak against a son of your own nation who is as distinguished as Moses, the Master of all Prophets' (*Tanchuma Pikudei* 7).

תִּתֶּן דֹּפִי — *You spread* [lit. *you will give*] *contempt.*
Rashi relates דֹּפִי to לַהֲדֹף, *to reject.* The slanderer causes his victim to become a social outcast, a pariah, by heaping disgrace upon him and ruining his reputation.

21. אֵלֶּה עָשִׂיתָ וְהֶחֱרַשְׁתִּי — *These have you done and I kept silent.*
You were guilty of all these crimes, yet I patiently kept silent and ignored your sins (*Ibn Ezra; Radak*) so as to give you an opportunity to repent of your own accord (*Targum*).

You perverted your role and mission as a Torah scholar. Instead of guiding

the people toward goodness and truth, you set an example of evil — and yet I was merciful and held back punishment (*Sforno*).

דִּמִּיתָ הֱיוֹת אֶהְיֶה כָמוֹךָ — *You thought I would be like you.*
[The repetition of הֱיוֹת אֶהְיֶה lit. 'it would be, I would be' denotes a complete state of being i.e. 'I would be altogether'].

You misinterpreted my patient silence and deluded yourselves with the false assumption that My silence was proof of My unawareness of your concealed crimes. You compared Me to yourselves and imagined that just as mortals are ignorant of conspiracies, so, too, is God (*Ibn Ezra; Sforno*).

Radak adds in the name of 'an old scholar': I kept silent despite all the things you have done to anger Me, but for this sin I can no longer keep still. If you imagine that I am a corporeal body like yourself, finite and fallible — this gross misconception is intolerable, and must be refuted!

Targum renders: דִּמִּיתָ, *you harbored illusions of immortality* and imagined that הֱיוֹת, *you would exist* peacefully forever. אֶהְיֶה כָמוֹךָ, you said in your heart, *I will be mighty like You, O God!*

Imrei Yehuda notes that the numerical value of כָמוֹךָ is 86 which is equal to the numerical value of אֱלֹהִים.

אוֹכִיחֲךָ וְאֶעֶרְכָה לְעֵינֶיךָ — *I will rebuke you and indict you* [lit. *prepare it*] *before your eyes.*
God warns: my patience will come to an end and I will rebuke you and set

against your mother's son you spread contempt.
²¹ *These have you done and I kept silent;*
 You thought I would be like you —
I will rebuke you
 and reveal it before your eyes!
²² *Understand this please,*
 you who have forgotten God,
Lest I tear you asunder and
 there be none to set you free.

²³ *He who offers confession, honors Me,*
 then preparing the way,
I will show him the salvation of God.

---

forth the case against you. I will then enumerate every one of your concealed sins, clearly demonstrating that I always knew your secrets. Malachi (3:18) foretold the day when hypocrites will be unmasked and their evil revealed, *Then you shall come back and differentiate between the righteous and the wicked, between him that serves HASHEM and him who serves Him not* (Radak).

22. בִּינוּ נָא זֹאת שֹׁכְחֵי אֱלוֹהַ — *Understand this now, you who are oblivious to God.*

You robbers, adulterers, and slanderers who have erased God from your consciousness, understand the clear rebuke which is addressed to you and return to a new awareness of God (Ibn Ezra; Radak).

This teaches that the person who engages in לְשׁוֹן הָרָע, *slander*, will eventually become so corrupted that he will come to deny the existence of God Himself, for the Psalmist addresses the slanderers as *you who are oblivious to God* (Yerushalmi, Peah 1:1).

פֶּן אֶטְרֹף וְאֵין מַצִּיל — *Lest I tear asunder there is no rescuer.*

In this world I can wait patiently for

you to return (*v.* 21) but when the day of final judgment arrives, there will be no way to avoid the wrath of My strict justice. If you have not prepared yourself with a *rescuer* i.e., repentance and good deeds, then you are doomed to be *torn asunder* by My righteous fury (Radak; Alshich).

The word טֹרֵף, *tear asunder,* is often used to describe an attack by a lion from which there is no rescue. However, when the flock is attacked by a wolf and a bear, the shepherd can still save his sheep (Ibn Ezra). [See 7:3 *Lest he tear my soul asunder like a lion, dismembering without rescuer.*]

23. זֹבֵחַ תּוֹדָה יְכַבְּדָנְנִי — *He who offers confession, honors Me.*

The choicest sacrifice is brought by him who repents and acknowledges his errors. This sincere penitent truly honor me (Rashi).

So said Solomon in his wisdom (Proverbs 21:3), *To do righteousness and justice is more acceptable to HASHEM than sacrifice* (Rav Shlomo Alkabetz).

The word תּוֹדָה can also be taken in its literal sense of a *thanksgiving*

sacrifice. If so, the Psalmist declares that God prefers such an expression of sincere appreciation of His goodness far more than all other offerings which come to atone for sin. *Midrash Tanchuma*, *(Tsav 7)* notes that David alludes to this in the peculiar spelling of יְכַבְּדָנְנִי in which the suffixial נ, *nun*, is repeated although grammatically there should be but a single *nun* — יְכַבְּדֵנִי. This implies that in God's eyes, a תּוֹדָה, *thanksgiving sacrifice*, honors Him doubly.

וְשָׂם דֶּרֶךְ — *Then, preparing the way* [lit. *and set the way*.]

All I ask of the sinner is that he should make the first move towards repentance by acknowledging his shortcomings, then I will immediately respond and prepare the way for him to return to Me completely. [In this interpretation, וְשָׂם דֶּרֶךְ, *preparing the way*, refers to God Who eases the path of the penitent] *(Rashi)*.

According to *Sforno* the one who prepares the way is not God, but the penitent who struggles to find the path of righteousness which leads to the World to Come.

The Sages say that the title דֶּרֶךְ שָׂם, i.e., one who engages in *preparing the way*, befits anyone who exerts himself to make the path of Torah observance easier and smoother for all people *(Vayikra Rabbah 9:2)*.

— This is the teacher who faithfully guides his young pupils on the path of Torah.

— This is the merchant who deals honestly and separates the tithes properly from his produce so as to provide his customers with permissible food.

— This is the man who removes the rocks, thorns, and obstacles from the public highway.[1]

אַרְאֶנּוּ בְּיֵשַׁע אֱלֹהִים — *I will show him the salvation of God.*

God declares: On the future day of judgment and reward, I will reveal the good fortune which was always reserved for the righteous, but which had remained concealed until then. At that time I will display the glory of the truly deservant ones who will be granted the eternal bliss of divine illumination *(Radak)*.

---

1. The *Midrash* cites as an example of the public benefactor, *who prepares the way* a person who kindles lights to illuminate the streets for passersby. Reish Lakish said: Saul was granted the royal throne only in the merit of his pious grandfather who lit lamps on the dark streets leading to the House of Study. Because of this he was called (*I Chronicles* 8:33) נֵר, *lamp*, and saw the *salvation of God* through his grandson, Saul *(Radal)*.

Moed Katan (5a) homiletically reads וְשָׂם (with a שׁ, *shin*), *he who appraises*, i.e., the person who acts intelligently in all situations and can evaluate the benefits or drawbacks of a given action. The *Talmud* cites as an example, a disciple of Rav Yannai who always posed difficult questions during his master's lectures. However, he would raise his challenging queries only during private lectures attended by the close disciples who fully appreciated Rav Yannai's greatness. During public lectures for the unlearned masses, the student would sit in silence lest his question be one which Rav Yannai could not answer. Were that to happen, Rav Yannai's stature would be diminished in the eyes of the unsophisticated audience.

51 מזמור נא

In his monumental work, Shaarei Teshuvah, Rabbeinu Yonah devotes the entire first section to a comprehensive discussion of the twenty principles of repentance. He quotes frequently from this psalm, which he calls פֶּרֶק הַתְּשׁוּבָה, the Chapter of Repentance, because it is יְסוֹד מוּסָד לְעִקְרֵי הַתְּשׁוּבָה, 'the basic foundation of all the principles of repentance' (Shaarei Teshuvah 1:23).

Indeed, every fiber of David's being was immersed in the spirit of repentance. Our Rabbis teach, 'Whoever wishes to repent should scrutinize the deeds of David' (Midrash Shocher Tov 4:4).

David is described as 'the man who made the yoke of repentance sublime' (Moed Katan 16b).

By virtue of David's devotion to constant self-improvement, his efforts merited special Divine assistance. God sent the prophet Nathan to inform him of his sin and to guide him on the path of return. [See Overview, chapters 4-5 for a deeper understanding of David's sin and repentance.] David composed this psalm at that time.

Since the theme of this chapter is penitence and purity, it is customary to recite it on the Sabbath when פָּרָשַׁת פָּרָה, the Portion of the Red Heifer is read, in order to remind the congregation to purify itself in anticipation of the Passover festival.

לַמְנַצֵּחַ מִזְמוֹר לְדָוִד: בְּבוֹא־אֵלָיו נָתָן א־ב
הַנָּבִיא כַּאֲשֶׁר־בָּא אֶל בַּת־שָׁבַע: חָנֵּנִי ג
אֱלֹהִים כְּחַסְדֶּךָ כְּרֹב רַחֲמֶיךָ מְחֵה

1. לַמְנַצֵּחַ מִזְמוֹר לְדָוִד — *For the Conductor, a song of David.*

Indeed, when Nathan came to David a dirge and a lament would have been more suitable (*Alshich*) [for the prophet rebuked David severely and warned him of the harsh punishment he could expect. Nevertheless, even in that moment of wrath, God treated David kindly; therefore, he sang].

Midrash Shocher Tov comments that this psalm illustrates the verse, *Death and life are in the power of the tongue* (*Proverbs* 18:1), for David merited life in the World to Come because of his tongue, which said to Nathan, *I have sinned against HASHEM* (II *Samuel* 12:13). As soon as Nathan said to David, *HASHEM also has forgiven your sin, you shall not die* (II *Samuel* ibid), David composed this psalm.

Zera Yaakov points out that after the incident with Bath Sheba, רוּחַ הַקּוֹדֶשׁ, *the holy spirit*, departed from David. The penitent king composed a מִזְמוֹר, *song*, in order to reach a state of ecstasy, so that the holy spirit could again descend לְדָוִד *unto David* [see comm. to 3:1].

Finally, *Shaarei Chaim* explains that repentance which is spurred by אַהֲבָה, *love* is far superior to that which is motivated by יִרְאָה, *fear* of punishment. David composed this psalm to uplift his spirit to that level of love which is a prerequisite for the *teshuvah* of אַהֲבָה.

2. בְּבוֹא אֵלָיו נָתָן הַנָּבִיא — *When Nathan the prophet came to him.*

[In this phrase, we detect three elements of Divine kindness.]

First, the prophet came *to him* i.e., Nathan came to David privately, when he was alone, and thereby saved him great embarassment (*Alshich; Toras Chesed*).

Second, God's agent was the distinguished Nathan, rather than an ordinary man. In the Talmud (*Berachos* 10a) we find that when God wanted Isaiah to chastise King Chizkiyahu, the question arose whether the king should go to the prophet (and thus honor him) or whether the prophet should go to the king (and thus honor *him*). Despite David's sin, God still honored him by sending His prophet to the king (*Tehillos Hashem*).

Third, David's sin concerning Bath Sheba is one of the most misunderstood incidents in all of Scripture. Within this puzzling episode lies the mystery of David's נְשָׁמָה, soul . [It is essential to emphasize that David sinned solely for the sake of God (see *v.* 6).] David rejoiced that God had sent a man of penetrating prophetic vision to rebuke him, for an ordinary man would be ignorant of the true nature of the king's sin (*Tehillos Hashem*).

[Indeed, David praised God as מֵרִים רֹאשִׁי, *He who raises up my pride* (3:5), — alluding to the fact that God saved his reputation through the words of the prophet Nathan (*Midrash Shocher Tov, ibid.*).]

כַּאֲשֶׁר בָּא אֶל בַּת שָׁבַע — *When he came to Bath Sheba.*

Dorash Moshe emphasizes that, in fact, Nathan did not go to David until after Bath Sheba bore David her first son (II *Samuel* 11:27, 12:2), almost a year after David's sin. Until then, David did *not* repent, because he excused his conduct with a number of 'righteous' rationalizations. However, when Nathan voiced God's displeasure, the king was immediately filled with deep remorse [see *Shaarei Teshuvah* 1:3]. Therefore it is considered as if David repented immediately after his sin,

LI
1-3

For the Conductor,
a song of David.
² When Nathan the prophet came to him,
when he came to Bath Sheba.
³ Show me favor, according to Your kindness,
according to Your vast compassion
erase my transgressions.

although it occurred a year earlier.

In his commentary to *II Samuel* 12:2, *Alshich* explains that since God loved David and had mercy on him, he did not send Nathan to rebuke him until long after the sin. If David had been accused immediately, his life would have been forfeited, because it was ordained in heaven that only death could atone for David's offense. After his son was born, only to become ill and die soon after, the infant's life took the place of his father's.[1]

חָנֵּנִי אֱלֹהִים כְּחַסְדֶּךָ — *Show me favor, according to Your kindness.*

This request appears to be self-contradictory. First David implies that his merits are totally inadequate, for he appeals for God's *favor* and *kindness.* Yet he calls upon אֱלֹהִים *Elokim,* the Divine name which characterizes God as the Enforcer of Strict Justice, rather than upon ה' *HASHEM,* the Divine name which characterizes God as the Dispenser of Mercy. The fact that David chose to use the former Divine Name would seem to imply that he is righteous enough to withstand the

strictest Divine judgment *(Shevet Mussar, Tehillos Hashem).*

[We can reconcile this apparent contradiction with the explanation that David considers himself only *partially* deservant; therefore, he asks for Divine *kindness* in addition to his own righteous merits. This idea is illustrated by *Midrash Shocher Tov:* David's situation is comparable to that of a wounded man who sought treatment from a physician. The doctor told him, 'I cannot treat your wound, for it is large, and the amount of money in your hand is small.' The wounded man pleaded, 'Take all the money I possess as your payment, and concerning the balance of my bill, show me kindness!']

כְּרֹב רַחֲמֶיךָ מְחֵה פְשָׁעָי — *According to Your vast compassion erase my transgressions.*

Radak notes that the plural form *transgressions* implies that two offenses were involved; the taking of Bath Sheba and the death of Uriah.

Beis Elokim explains the use of the word מְחֵה, *erase.* An intentional transgression adheres to the soul like a

---

1. The *Midrash* relates that at the time David slew Goliath, Uriah the Hittite had not yet converted to Judaism. David was unsuccessful in his attempt to strip the chain-mail armor from the dead giant so that he could decapitate him, because David couldn't find the knotted end of the metal thread which' linked all the chain-mail hooks together. Then Uriah approached David and asked, 'If I show you the knot, will you give me an Israelite woman for a wife?' When David consented, Uriah showed him the knot, which had been tied on Goliath's sole.

God was angry with David for promising a daughter of Israel to a gentile. He decreed that Bath Sheba, the woman who had been preordained to be David's wife, should be Uriah's wife first. [The Sages say *(Sanhedrin* 107a), 'Bath Sheba was designated as David's mate from the six days of Creation, but David took her before the proper time (see *Maharal* and *Toras Chaim, Sanhedrin ibid).]*

פְּשָׁעָי: °הרבה כַּבְּסֵנִי מֵעֲוֹנִי וּמֵחַטָּאתִי
טַהֲרֵנִי: כִּי־פְשָׁעַי אֲנִי אֵדָע וְחַטָּאתִי נֶגְדִּי
תָמִיד: לְךָ לְבַדְּךָ חָטָאתִי וְהָרַע בְּעֵינֶיךָ

clinging substance. It resembles dirt adhering to surface of a fabric which must be thoroughly scraped and *erased* if the soul is to regain its cleanliness.

4. הֶרֶב כַּבְּסֵנִי מֵעֲוֹנִי — *Abundantly cleanse me from my iniquity.*

Sforno explains that David's iniquity was that he did not confess and repent [for almost a year], until Nathan the prophet came to rebuke him. For a man of David's spiritual stature, such a delay was a serious offense.

Radak notes that the word is written (כְּתִיב) הַרְבֵּה, *many*, but is pronounced הֶרֶב *thoroughly; much.* David said 'You have performed *many* kindnesses for me in the past; therefore I ask You to continue Your mercy now by *thoroughly* washing off my iniquity.'

Beis Elokim states that the spiritually defiling 'residue' created by *iniquity* penetrates deeper than that which is created by *transgression. Transgression* is a clear-cut offense which is readily identified. *Iniquity* is more subtle and covert. Therefore it is comparable to dirt so deeply absorbed into a fabric that it can be removed only by repeated, 'thorough' laundering.

וּמֵחַטָּאתִי טַהֲרֵנִי — *And from my sin purify me.*

David accepted responsibility for the deaths of all the other soldiers who died in the battle in which Uriah was killed. Although he had never sought their deaths, David blamed himself for the casualties, considering each death to be his own [unintentional] *sin (Sforno).*

Beis Elokim observes that the unintentional *sin* is comparable to dust which clings lightly to the surface of a garment. Brushing or shaking the garment will suffice to *purify* the fabric; no

vigorous scraping or laundering is necessary.

Malbim draws the following distinction between the two forms of transgression: עָוֹן *iniquity* describes an עוות *distortion* of the intellect which causes a person to err and neglect a Torah command. The חֵטְא, *sin* is an (unintentional) offense, a superficial deed which is comparable to contracting טומאה, impurity through contact with an unclean object. Purity is easily regained by immersion in a ritual bath (mikvah).

Atonement for חֵטְא is relatively easy to obtain; all David asks is: *From my sin purify me.* But even after the sin is gone, the spiritual damage remains. The blemish on the soul, the intellectual distortion(עוות), these are deeply ingrained.For this David vigorously pleads, *Abundantly cleanse me of my iniquity.*

5. כִּי פְשָׁעַי אֲנִי אֵדָע — *For my transgressions I recognize.*

I readily acknowledge my wrongdoing and make no attempt to deny or hide it. I am not like Cain, who feigned ignorance ofhis brother's murder, saying (*Genesis* 3:9) לֹא יָדַעְתִּי, *I do not know* (*Radak*).

This admission of guilt is in itself a virtue which makes me worthy of forgiveness (*Sforno*).

Alshich notes that David does not use the past or present tense, but the future tense אֲנִי אֵדָע, *I will know.* He suggests: As long as I live this knowledge will be with me and I shall never forget it!

וְחַטָּאתִי נֶגְדִּי תָמִיד — *And my sin is before me always.*

Since my sin fills me with perpetual regret and constant anxiety, it looms

⁴ *Abundantly cleanse me from my iniquity,*
    and from my sin purify me.
⁵ *For my transgressions I recognize,*
    and my sin is before me always.
⁶ *Against You alone did I sin,*
    And evil in Your eyes did I do,

before me incessantly *(Rashi)*. Thus, I am constantly reminded never to repeat such an error again, even unintentionally *(Sforno)*.

In the *Talmud (Yoma* 86b) we find a difference of opinion. The Rabbis maintain that when a person confesses to a sin, repents on Yom Kippur, and does not repeat his offense, it is despicable for him to confess and repent the same sin the following Yom Kippur. To do so is like 'a dog who returns to its vomit.'

Rabbi Eliezer ben Yaakov, however, claims that repeated confession and repentance are highly desirable, for David said, *And my sin is before me always,* i.e., 'I never feel that it is washed away and forgotten; it looms before my eyes constantly' *(Rashi)* [*Rambam (Hilchos Teshuvah* 2:8) decides in favor of Rabbi Eliezer.][1]

Alshich comments: every sin creates an evil spiritual force in heaven which acts as a קָטֵיגוֹר, an *'accusing angel'* which spreads a negative and detrimental influence against the sinner. David mourns: חַטָּאתִי, 'the harmful force of my own creation' נֶגְדִּי 'works against me', תָמִיד 'always interfering with my spiritual growth and enrichment'.

6. לְךָ לְבַדְּךָ חָטָאתִי — *Against You alone did I sin.*

[As David said to Nathan, חָטָאתִי לַה',

I have sinned to HASHEM (II *Samuel* 12:13), for I violated the spirit of the law, thereby creating a climate of disregard for God's mitzvos (see II *Samuel* 12:4 and *Rashi*). In other respects, I did not actually transgress, for Bath Sheba was legally divorced and Uriah was condemned to die because of insubordination against me, the king (see *Overview* Part IV).]

Radak provides additional insight into David's apology: David admitted, 'Since I realized that my actions might be misinterpreted, I took pains to exercise discretion. My servants, unaware of my intentions, brought Bath Sheba to me in secrecy. I sent Joab a secret message, urging him to make Uriah's death seem to be a chance casualty of war. I sinned only in the privacy of my heart, for my intentions were tainted with lust.'[See *Rashi* and *Maharsha* on *Shabbos* 56 a]. 'Although I harmed no innocent man, I realize that, to You, my thoughts were offensive; for this, I readily admit my guilt.'

Therefore, my forgiveness is exclusively in Your hands *(Rashi)*. Even if I wished to ask forgiveness of Uriah and the other soldiers killed with him, I could not, for they are all dead *(Sforno)*.

וְהָרַע בְּעֵינֶיךָ עָשִׂיתִי — *And evil in Your eyes did I do.*

1. The Torah *(Leviticus* 9:7) relates that when the Tabernacle was dedicated, Moses had to coax Aaron to enter it to perform the service. *Ramban (ad loc.)* explains that Aaron, God's consecrated servant, had never committted a sin other than that of participating in the Golden Calf. The specter of that sin was deeply etched into his consciousness and he constantly saw the image of the calf before his eyes, preventing him from feeling worthy, just as David said *And my sin is before me always.* Therefore, Moses had to allay Aaron's fears to persuade him that he was indeed worthy of the priesthood.

עָשִׂיתִי לְמַעַן תִּצְדַּק בְּדָבְרֶךָ תִּזְכֶּה
בְשָׁפְטֶךָ: הֵן־בְּעָווֹן חוֹלָלְתִּי וּבְחֵטְא יֶחֱמַתְנִי אִמִּי: הֵן־אֱמֶת חָפַצְתָּ בַטֻּחוֹת וּבְסָתֻם חָכְמָה תוֹדִיעֵנִי: תְּחַטְּאֵנִי בְאֵזוֹב

ז

ח

ט

[As Nathan thundered against me, 'Why have you despised the word of HASHEM to do that which is evil in His eyes' (II Samuel 12:9).]

Beis Aharon explains that עֵינֶיךָ, your eyes, in our verse does not refer to the eyes of God, but to David's eyes, i.e., David confesses that he has misused Your eyes — the ones which God provided him along with all the parts of his body.

[See Overview, Part II, where it is explained that God endowed David with a unique attribute: יְפֵה עֵינַיִם beautiful eyes (I Samuel 16:12), which represented a clarity of vision focused exclusively on God's will and completely unaffected by lust and temptation. David failed his trial with Bath Sheba because desire for her blurred his clear vision.]

לְמַעַן תִּצְדַּק בְּדָבְרֶךָ — So that You would be justified when You speak.

Rashi (based on Sanhedrin 107b) explains that David had asked God to test his ability to withstand temptation. God told him that he was as yet unprepared for such a trial and would surely fail. After the sin, David addressed God, saying, 'It is clearly revealed and known to You that if I had tried to subdue my lust I could have done so, but I gave in to temptation purposely so that You would be justified, lest people say that the servant has bested his Master. For had I passed the test, Your divine prediction would have been proven in-

accurate.' [The commentaries emphasize that, in reality, David did fail to conquer his passions; the excuse he offered was a rationalization. See Publisher's Preface to Levush Mordecai on Bava Kama and Ha'amek Davar, Numbers 22:33.]

Radak and Sforno interpret these words as David's argument as to why God should accept his repentance: 'You spoke of repentance to Cain and promised, surely if you improve yourself you will be forgiven (Genesis 4:7). To Moses You revealed Yourself as, forgiving iniquity and transgression and sin (Exodus 34:7). Now I beg You to justify those words by forgiving me!'

תִּזְכֶּה בְשָׁפְטֶךָ — And be in the right when You judge.

'Forgive me, so that when You judge, condemn, and punish the wicked who refused to repent their evil ways, they won't be able to protest, "What good would our repentance have done, for You would not have forgiven us anyway?" ' (Rashi; Radak; Sforno).

7. הֵן בְּעָווֹן חוֹלָלְתִּי — Behold, in iniquity was I fashioned.

Rashi explains: 'I was formed by a male and a female, both creatures of flesh and blood who were full of sin.' [Even the most devout have some contact with sin (Vayikra Rabbah 14:5). עָווֹן iniquity is written מָלֵא 'full' (with two 'vavs' וֹ), in order to emphasize man's great tendency towards sin.][1]

1. [Although the Talmud (Bava Basra 17a) counts Jesse, the father of David, as one of the rare individuals who were completely innocent of any act of personal sin, nevertheless as a descendant of Adam and Eve, he too had the instinctive human tendency towards passion and error which resulted from their sin in the Garden of Eden (see Overview, I). David laments that this basic human weakness was passed on to him at conception although he imputes no sinful deed to Jesse.]

So that You would be justified when You speak,
and be in the right when You judge.
7 Behold, in iniquity was I fashioned,
and in sin did my mother conceive me.
8 Behold, You desire truth
in the concealments,
And in my innermost heart
You revealed to me wisdom.

Beis Elokim explicates, 'From the moment of my birth, I was affected by the Evil Inclination, or it attached itself to me at the moment I left my mother's womb, as Scripture says, לַפֶּתַח חַטָּאת רֹבֵץ, *Sin rests at the door* (*Genesis* 4:7).

[At the time of birth, the Evil Inclination displaces the Good Inclination, which does not return until the child reaches maturity (*Piskei Tosafos, Nedarim* 62).]

Maharal emphasizes that David never used these arguments as an excuse to allow himself to sin. Rather after he *did* stumble into sin, he pleaded with God to take into consideration the natural human tendency towards iniquity, and to judge him with understanding and compassion [see *Sforno*].

וּבְחֵטְא יֶחֱמַתְנִי אִמִּי — *And in sin did my mother conceive me.*

Rashi observes יֶחֱמַתְנִי is derived from חוֹם, *warmth*, referring to a woman's heat at the time of procreation and conception (see *Genesis* 30:38).

Maharam Arama adds, that by the process of elimination, David attributes *sin* to his mother, because his father, Jesse, was one of the four men in all history who died without any trace of personal sin (*Shabbos* 55b; *Targum Ruth* 4:22; see *footnote*).

Ibn Ezra comments this alludes to the fact that Eve, the mother of all mankind, did not bear children until after she sinned. [This would appear to be the case according to the order of events set forth in the third and fourth chapters of *Genesis*. However, according to the *Talmud* (*Sanhedrin* 38a), Eve bore children before the sin.]

8. הֵן אֱמֶת חָפַצְתָּ בַּטֻּחוֹת — *Behold You desire truth in the concealments.*

The commentaries identify the טֻחוֹת as the kidneys, which are טָחוֹת, *concealed* [see *Leviticus* 14:43] with protective fat (*Metzudas David*; *Rashi*). [The kidneys are considered to be the seat of human intellect, as in *Job 38:36* and *Psalms 7:10, 16:7.*] David said, 'Although I have sinned, O God, nevertheless my true faith in You is still intact deep within the *concealments* of my being. This strong conviction and *truth* is what *You desire*. Therefore, please forgive my sin, which was spurred only by momentary, external temptation and was not an integral part of my inner being.

The most convincing argument which I can offer to prove that I never meant to rebel against You or deny Your sovereignty is that I now regret my sin so bitterly and beseech You to guide me towards the path of truth (*Ibn Ezra; Radak*).

וּבְסָתֻם חָכְמָה תוֹדִיעֵנִי — *And in my innermost heart You revealed to me wisdom.*

Inside the concealed chambers of my heart You have taught me how to [recognize and] confess my sins; such awareness requires great wisdom (*Rashi*).

[As explained previously (*v.* 6) David's transgressions were violations

וְאֶטְהָר תְּכַבְּסֵנִי וּמִשֶּׁלֶג אַלְבִּין:
תַּשְׁמִיעֵנִי שָׂשׂוֹן וְשִׂמְחָה תָּגֵלְנָה עֲצָמוֹת ‹ י
דִּכִּיתָ: הַסְתֵּר פָּנֶיךָ מֵחֲטָאָי וְכָל־עֲוֹנֹתַי יא

of the spirit, not the letter, of the law. On the surface, his actions could be justified; the crime lay concealed in the impure intentions of his innermost heart, deep in his unconscious mind. David himself was hardly aware of these concealed motivations.]

I ask that in the future You grant me the wisdom to recognize the true nature of סָתֻם the *innermost*, so that I will not misinterpret them again. [I.e., until Nathan rebuked me, I had felt that my motives for taking Bath Sheba were completely noble and pure] (*Radak*).

9. תְּחַטְּאֵנִי בְאֵזוֹב וְאֶטְהָר — *Purge me with hyssop and I shall be pure.*

David compared the taint which sin placed on his soul to a leprous spot afflicting the body (*Ibn Ezra*). Indeed, the *Talmud* (*Sanhedrin* 107b) says that for six months, David was actually plagued with leprosy because of his transgressions [cf. *Yoma* 22b; *Tosafos*; *Rabbeinu Chananel*; and *Tosafos Yeshanim* 22b].

The hyssop [together with the cedar wood] is used to sprinkle the pure waters on the leper during his final process of purification [see *Leviticus 14:6*] (*Rashi; Radak*).

Leprosy is a punishment for arrogance; therefore, the man who proudly lifts himself above others like the towering cedar tree is afflicted. But when he modestly lowers himself to the height of the humble *hyssop*, he is cured (*Bamidbar Rabbah 19:3*).

David displayed excessive pride and extreme over-confidence when he demanded that God test him (*Harav Melamed*). Moreover, he acted in a high-handed manner when he exercised his royal perogative to seize Bath Sheba at will to dispose of Uriah. The punishment for this arrogance was leprosy (*Tefillah L'Moshe*).

תְּכַבְּסֵנִי וּמִשֶּׁלֶג אַלְבִּין — *Cleanse me and I shall be whiter than snow.*

[As the prophet *Isaiah* (1:18) says concerning the penitent, *Though your sins be as scarlet, they shall be as white as snow.*]

Malbim explains that the most prominent form of leprosy is the בַּהֶרֶת, which is as white as snow (*Negaim 1:1*). When such a spot erupts on the surface of the skin, it indicates a black, evil character trait which must be cleansed by repentance and 'whitened' like snow. מְצוֹרָע is a contraction of מוֹצִיא רַע, *to remove the evil*]. The halacha is that if the leprosy spreads until it covers the entire body, then the leper is considered as clean, because this shows that this man has mobilized his entire body to sincerely regret his ways. Thus, David declares: מִשֶּׁלֶג, *from the snow* [— colored] growth which covers all of my skin on the outside, אַלְבִּין I shall be whitened — on the inside as well.'

10. תַּשְׁמִיעֵנִי שָׂשׂוֹן וְשִׂמְחָה — *Make me hear joy and gladness.*

Please inform me that I am forgiven (*Rashi*).

At first, David's soul was shrouded in a dark spirit of mourning because of his sins *It begs for release from this gloom* (*Ibn Ezra; Radak*).

Malbim adds that the leper is plunged into intensive mourning. He must isolate himself from society and rend his garments. He is obliged to publicly bemoan his uncleanliness and sorrow. Thus, David yearned to return to the normal joys of healthy life.

[The day preceding Yom Kippur is designated as a day of joyous feasting (*Rosh Hashonah 9a*). *Rabbeinu Yonah* (*Shaarei Teshuvah 4:8*) explains that this rejoicing displays genuine gladness at the arrival of this opportunity for

⁹ *Purge me with hyssop and I shall be pure,*
    cleanse me and I shall be whiter than snow.
¹⁰ *Make me hear joy and gladness,*
    may the bones which You crushed, exult.
¹¹ *Hide Your face from my sins,*
    and all my iniquities erase.

atonement, and bears testimony to sincere worry over our guilt and our deep sorrow over our transgressions. Similarly, David seeks this joy of Divine forgiveness.[1]

תָּגֵלְנָה עֲצָמוֹת דִּכִּיתָ — *May the bones which You crushed, exult.*

Solomon taught: *Good tidings make the bones fat (Proverbs 16:30),* but mourning crushes them *(Tefillah L'Moshe)*. Moreover, the imprint of each wrongdoing is stamped [i.e., *crushed*] indelibly on the organ which committed the sin, until the sinner is forgiven *(Eretz HaChaim)*.

Radak explains that upon hearing Nathan's accusations, David immediately confessed his sin. Nathan said: *God also has forgiven Your sin; you shall not die (II Samuel 12:13)*. However, the prophet told David that his life would be plagued by many miseries and sufferings *(II Samuel 12:10-14)*. David never asked to be exempted from these afflictions, for he realized that he deserved them and that they were essential for his repentance. Here he longs for the day when his ultimate atonement will bring him joy and when 'the crushing of his bones' will no longer be necessary.

11. הַסְתֵּר פָּנֶיךָ מֵחֲטָאָי — *Hide Your face from my sins.*

Ibn Ezra maintains that David is speaking euphemistically, as if to say 'Shield *my* face from *Your* wrath, which was aroused by *my* sins'; allow my repentance to erase their unpleasant memory from Your presence *(Radak)*.

Alshich (based on his commentary to *v.4*) interprets: Please disregard the 'accusing angel' which I created, with *my sin*.

וְכָל עֲוֹנֹתַי מְחֵה — *And all my iniquities erase.*

Alshich explains that in the fourth verse, David spoke in the singular; *my iniquity, my sin* because he was referring to the one great sin of his lifetime, the incident with Bath Sheba. Here, however, he speaks in the plural asking forgiveness for all other *sins* and *iniquities* which he committed. Therefore, David makes no mention here of פֶּשַׁע, *transgression*, for he never committed another intentional offense. [See commentary on *v.3*, concerning the plural, פְּשָׁעַי, *my transgressions*. This form was used because David was guilty of *two* counts of intentional wrongdoing during this *one* episode: taking Bath Sheba and killing Uriah.]

---

1. *The Vilna Gaon* says that שִׂמְחָה describes the *gladness* experienced at the beginning of an undertaking, and that שָׂשׂוֹן denotes the *joy* of completion, as we sing in the Sabbath אֵל אָדוֹן hymn — שְׂמֵחִים בְּצֵאתָם וְשָׂשִׂים בְּבוֹאָם 'Glad as they set out and joyous when they return'.
    Similarly, we sing, שָׂשׂוּ וְשִׂמְחוּ בְּשִׂמְחַת תּוֹרָה 'Rejoice and be glad on Simchas Torah'. On that day, שָׂשׂוֹן precedes שִׂמְחָה because we experience first the joy of ending the Torah reading and then the gladness of beginning the reading anew.
    In view of this, we may interpret David's words as '*Make me hear joy,* i.e., the joy of knowing that my atonement is complete, *and gladness,* i.e., allow me to make a fresh, pure beginning in Your service.

יב מְחֵה: לֵב טָהוֹר בְּרָא־לִי אֱלֹהִים וְרוּחַ

יג נָכוֹן חַדֵּשׁ בְּקִרְבִּי: אַל־תַּשְׁלִיכֵנִי מִלְּפָנֶיךָ

יד וְרוּחַ קָדְשְׁךָ אַל־תִּקַּח מִמֶּנִּי: הָשִׁיבָה לִּי

שְׂשׂוֹן יִשְׁעֶךָ וְרוּחַ נְדִיבָה תִסְמְכֵנִי:

טו אֲלַמְּדָה פֹשְׁעִים דְּרָכֶיךָ וְחַטָּאִים אֵלֶיךָ

---

12. לֵב טָהוֹר בְּרָא לִי אֱלֹהִים — *A pure heart create for me, O God.*

Until now, David was struggling to purify his heart of past sins. Now he calls for Divine assistance to protect his future integrity (*Rashi; Ibn Ezra*). He deserves this aid for 'He who strives to purify himself merits God's assistance' (*Yoma 38a*). Thus fortified against future sins, his heart would resemble a new creation (*Radak*). If the heart is pure, then the entire body (which depends on the heart) will be pure (*Reishis Chochmah*).

[*Rambam (Hilchos Teshuvah 2:4)* emphasizes that a fundamental of total repentance is to consider oneself as a newborn creature, totally divorced from the errors of the past: Among the techniques of *teshuvah* are to ... change one's name, as if to say, I am someone else, I am not the man who committed those offences! and he reforms his actions and goes out into exile ... '

We can also understand David's concern for preserving the purity of his heart in light of the *Rambam's* teaching (*Hilchos Melachim 3:6*) that the Torah was especially concerned lest the king's heart be distracted [by women],...for the heart of the king is the collective heart of the entire congregation of Israel (see *Overview* Part IV).]

וְרוּחַ נָכוֹן חַדֵּשׁ בְּקִרְבִּי — *And a steadfast spirit renew within me.*

This refers to an upright spirit (*Metzudas David*) [which does not bend or succumb to temptation].

S'forno renders נָכוֹן as synonymous with מוּכָן, *prepared*, i.e., Grant me an intellect (soul) capable of understanding God's ways and equipped to communicate these truths to others.

13. אַל תַּשְׁלִיכֵנִי מִלְּפָנֶיךָ — *Cast me not away from Your Presence.*

The servant who betrays his master may be forgiven, but never again will he enjoy the confidence of his master or be included in his counsel. David says, Although I have sinned, do not end our intimate relationship, for I am like a creature reborn, endowed with a pure, new heart; I am no longer the same person who offended You! (*Yaavetz HaDoresh*).

וְרוּחַ קָדְשְׁךָ אַל תִּקַּח מִמֶּנִּי — *And Your holy spirit take not from me.*

Ibn Ezra notes that David was endowed with God's holy spirit, as he himself said, רוּחַ ה' דִּבֶּר בִּי וּמִלָּתוֹ עַל לְשׁוֹנִי, *The spirit of HASHEM spoke through me and His word was on my lips* (II Samuel 23:2).

Radak adds that it was under the inspiration of this sacred ecstacy that David composed his songs and psalms. When he sinned, this spirit abandoned him. Now he pleads that it should return and never leave him again.

14. הָשִׁיבָה לִּי שְׂשׂוֹן יִשְׁעֶךָ — *Restore to me the joy of Your salvation.*

The Talmud (*Sanhedrin 107b*) infers from this that during the six month period of David's leprosy, the holy spirit abandoned him [as did all the members of the Great Sanhedrin]. He now pleads that the holy spirit be restored (*Rashi*).

Ibn Ezra says that before this incident, David was always happy because

12 A pure heart create for me, O God,
and a steadfast spirit renew within me.
13 Cast me not away from Your Presence,
And Your Holy Spirit take not from me.
14 Restore to me the joy of Your salvation.
and with a generous spirit sustain me.
15 Then I will teach transgressors Your ways,
and sinners shall repent to You.

at no other time had he sinned [intentionally] (see *Alshich, v. 10*).

Alshich translates יִשְׁעֶךָ as 'Your victory' explaining that although *II Samuel*, Chapter 2 is devoted to the episode of David and Bath Sheba, the opening verse of the chapter describes David's victory over Ammon [which, it would seem, should have been included in the preceding chapter]. This juxtaposition serves to teach that David's pride concerning his military triumph encouraged his Evil Inclination to sin.

Nevertheless, David now asks God to help him in his future battles and to *restore the joy of 'Your victory'*.

He argues that his only motivation for waging war was to alleviate the misery of his harassed and impoverished subjects [see *Berachos 3b*]. David's warfare was inspired by a רוּחַ נְדִיבָה *a spirit of charity* rather than by a desire for personal glory.

וְרוּחַ נְדִיבָה תִסְמְכֵנִי — *And with a generous spirit sustain me.*

This refers to the holy spirit, which generously suffuses the heart with songs of praise for God (*Radak*).

Rashbam translates רוּחַ נְדִיבָה as 'a ruling spirit' (as in נְדִיבֵי עַמִּים *the rulers of nations,* 47:10); i.e., 'Uphold my resolve to repent by strengthening my intellect so that it may rule over and subdue my passions.'

'Furthermore, let no obstacle arise which would interfere with my repentance' (*Rambam, Hilchos Teshuvah 6:4*).

15. אֲלַמְּדָה פֹשְׁעִים דְּרָכֶיךָ — *[Then] I will teach transgressors Your ways.*

When You will forgive me I will be able to serve as an example for others, who will recognize the efficacy of repentance. Then, they too will be encouraged to mend their ways (*Radak*).

Indeed this is why I requested *a pure heart created for me* (*v. 12*), because the admonition of a teacher can affect the hearts of his students only if his words come from a pure heart (*Alshich*). [Compare *Berachos 6b*, 'Whoever has a fear of heaven merits that his words be heeded'.]

Rabbeinu Yonah (*Shaarei Teshuvah 1:50*) lists this as the twentieth and final principle of repentance: 'Turn back as many people as possible from transgression, as Scripture says, *Return and turn back others from all your transgressions* (Ezekiel 18:30). Furthermore, if one does not rebuke others, he himself is punished for their sins. David said in the Psalm of Repentance, *I will teach transgressors Your ways.*

וְחַטָּאִים אֵלֶיךָ יָשׁוּבוּ — *And sinners shall repent to You.*

[The *Talmud* (*Avodah Zarah 4b*) states that, considering David's lofty level of personal piety, it is inconceivable that he should have sinned as he did, except for the fact that God decreed that his sin should come to pass (see *Rashi*).]

Maharsha (ad. loc.) and *Alshich* (*Ps. 131*) explain that God never forces any man to sin; the Sages mean to say

טז יָשׁוּבוּ: הַצִּילֵנִי מִדָּמִים | אֱלֹהִים אֱלֹהֵי
יז תְּשׁוּעָתִי תְּרַנֵּן לְשׁוֹנִי צִדְקָתֶךָ: אֲדֹנָי
יח שְׂפָתַי תִּפְתָּח וּפִי יַגִּיד תְּהִלָּתֶךָ: כִּי | לֹא־
תַחְפֹּץ זֶבַח וְאֶתֵּנָה עוֹלָה לֹא תִרְצֶה:
יט זִבְחֵי אֱלֹהִים רוּחַ נִשְׁבָּרָה לֵב־נִשְׁבָּר

that God usually protects the devout
and helps them to subdue their lusts and
passions. Here, this customary סַיְיעְתָּא
דִשְׁמַיָּא, *Divine assistance* was not
granted to David.]

This happened in order that an individual who commits an offense and
despairs of repentance can be told, 'Go
learn from King David, who repented
and was completely forgiven'.]

16. הַצִּילֵנִי מִדָּמִים אֱלֹהִים — *Rescue me
from blood-guilt — O God.*

'Let me not die violently by the
sword, as a punishment for having
caused the death of Uriah' (*Rashi*).

'I call upon You as אֱלֹהִים, the
*Supreme Judge Who has the final
authority to decide whether to condemn
or whether to exonerate me*' (*Radak*).

תְּרַנֵּן לְשׁוֹנִי צִדְקָתֶךָ — *Let my tongue sing
joyously of Your righteousness.*

Spare me the task of eliminating my
enemies through violence so that no
blood-guilt will taint my hands. In
return *my tongue will sing joyously of
Your righteousness* and kindness
(*Chazah Zion*).

Fill my mouth with the sweet words
of Torah and my tongue *will sing
joyously of Your righteousness. Thus,
my tongue, so well occupied, will have
no opportunity for spreading words of
slander and I will be rescued from
blood-guilt* (*Na'avah Tehillah*).

17. אֲדֹנָי שְׂפָתַי תִּפְתָּח — *My Lord, open
my lips.*

*Open my lips so that I may speak
words of Torah* (*Targum*). Forgive me
now and provide me with cause to
recite Your praises (*Rashi*). Cleanse me

of sin so that I will be worthy of
teaching others Your ways (*Sforno*).

Return to me Your holy spirit, which,
before my sin, stirred my lips to compose Divinely inspired melodies,
(*Radak*).

Ramban (Emunah U'Bitachon,
Chapter 5) maintains that שְׂפָתַי is
related to שְׂפַת הַנָּהָר the river bank, i.e.,
the barriers which confine the river in
its narrow channel. *Harav Gifter* explains that man is self-centered and
limited. His soul is restricted and stifled
within the narrow confines of his finite
body. But when man stands before the
infinity of his Maker, his eternal soul
surges until it 'overflows' the 'banks' of
his body. For this reason, the Sages
(*Berachos* 4b) decreed that this verse
should be recited before a person stands
in God's presence to pray.

וּפִי יַגִּיד תְּהִלָּתֶךָ — *That my mouth may
declare Your praise.*

[When man, so frail and insignificant, stands before his Maker and contemplates His praises, he should be
struck silent with awe. Therefore he
must pray for Divine assistance to open
his mouth and grant it the ability to
declare God's praises.]

18. כִּי לֹא תַחְפֹּץ זֶבַח וְאֶתֵּנָה — *For You
desire no offering, else I would give it.*

According to the letter of the law,
David did not sin at all (*Shabbos* 56a),
but David, in his piety, considered
himself a sinner (*Arvei Nachal*).
Therefore he says, 'If I had committed
this crime unintentionally, I could atone
for it with a חַטָּאת, *sin offering, but my
sin was a* מֵזִיד, *an intentional transgression* (*Rashi; Ibn Ezra*). Therefore, all I

¹⁶ *Rescue me from blood-guilt — O God,*
God of my salvation.
Let my tongue sing joyously of Your righteousness.
¹⁷ *My Lord, open my lips,*
that my mouth may declare Your praise.
¹⁸ *For You desire no offering, else I would give it,*
A burnt-offering You do not favor.
¹⁹ *The offerings of God*
are a broken spirit,
A heart broken and crushed

can offer is a broken heart, subdued in sincere repentance *(Radak).*

עוֹלָה לֹא תִרְצֶה — *A burnt-offering You do not favor.*

Rather You hope that the burning of the sacrificial flesh will inspire the sinner to 'burn out' the animal lusts which corrupt his heart *(Radak).*

19. זִבְחֵי אֱלֹהִים רוּחַ נִשְׁבָּרָה — *The offerings of God are a broken spirit.*

The name אֱלֹהִים appears six times in this psalm, but the name ה', HASHEM appears not once *(Chazah Zion).* Animal sacrifices are offered to ה', the Divine Name indicating God's attribute of Mercy, in order to obtain forgiveness for unintentional errors. But intentional transgressions require that one offer extreme remorse and complete repentance in order to appease אֱלֹהִים, the Divine Name indicating God's Attribute of Strict Justice *(Tanya).*[1]

לֵב נִשְׁבָּר וְנִדְכֶּה — *A heart broken and crushed.*

[See *Commentary* to 34:19: HASHEM is close to those who are broken at heart, and those who are crushed in spirit He saves.]

Rabbeinu Yonah (Shaarei Teshuvah 1:33) explains that *a broken heart* connotes a modest and humble spirit; *A crushed heart* connotes the breaking of physical lust, for the heart is the repository of desire. If one breaks his physical urges, he accrues a great advantage for when he is tempted to transgress, he will reason, 'I did not even succumb to my desire for what is permitted, how then shall I stretch forth my hand for what is forbidden?' *(Shaarei Teshuvah 1:32).*

Furthermore, the Psalmist makes an analogy here to the breaking of impure vessels which by rendering them unfit for their precious service, purifies them,

1. The Talmud *(Sotah 5b)* states that Rabbi Joshua ben Levi said: 'How great are those who subdue their spirits, for when the Temple stood, if a person gave a burnt-offering, he gained the merit of only that single burnt-offering. If he donated a meal-offering, he was given credit only for that single meal-offering. But he who sacrifices his pride and subdues his spirit with genuine humility is considered as if he offered every form of sacrifice, for it says *the offerings* [the plural indicates many offerings'] *of God are a broken spirit* [the singular form of רוּחַ, *spirit* indicates that this single act of submission is as precious as many sacrifices]. In addition, this man's prayer is never rejected, as the verse continues, *a heart, broken and crushed, O God, You despise not.*

Maharal (Nesiv HaTeshuvah, Chapter 2) explains that קָרְבָּן literally means *a way of drawing near.* Passion and pride separate man from his Maker; when these are removed by means of sincere repentance and genuine submission, man draws as near to God as humanly possible.

כ וְנִדְכֶּה אֱלֹהִים לֹא תִבְזֶה: הֵיטִיבָה
בִרְצוֹנְךָ אֶת־צִיּוֹן תִּבְנֶה חוֹמוֹת יְרוּשָׁלָם:
כא אָז תַּחְפֹּץ זִבְחֵי־צֶדֶק עוֹלָה וְכָלִיל אָז
יַעֲלוּ עַל־מִזְבַּחֲךָ פָרִים:

as Scripture commands, *(Leviticus 11:35) Whether oven or stove, it shall be broken in pieces* (Shaarei Teshuvah 1:23).

אֱלֹהִים לֹא תִבְזֶה — *O God You will despise not.*

You despise the animal sacrifice when it is not accompanied by a broken heart, but You do not despise the broken heart even though it is not accompanied by an animal sacrifice (Radak).

Rambam (Hilchos Matnos Aniyim 10:5) rules that it is prohibited to display anger or shout at an impoverished beggar because his spirits have already been shattered, and Scripture teaches, *A heart broken and crushed, O God, You despise not* [i.e., God is concerned for the welfare of these unfortunate people, and will be angered if they are abused.]

20. הֵיטִיבָה בִרְצוֹנְךָ אֶת צִיּוֹן — *Benefit with Your grace unto Zion.*

Radak explains that David previously pleaded for the return of the holy spirit, which had left him when he sinned be returned to him, saying: *Restore unto me the joy of Your salvation, v. 14).* The two final verses of this Psalm are evidence that his request will ultimately be fulfilled; the verses foretell the destruction of the First and Second Temples. The multitude of sacrifices in them could not avert the destruction, for the people were debased with evil and sin.

However, in the Messianic era, God will delight in the sacrifices of Israel, for they will all unite to serve God devotedly as one. Concerning that utopian

epoch, the psalmist prays, *Benefit with Your grace unto Zion.*

Ibn Yachya perceives in the word הֵיטִיבָה a request for the return of God's Presence, which is called טוֹב, *good*, as Scripture states, אֲנִי אַעֲבִיר כָּל טוּבִי עַל פָּנֶיךָ, *I will make all My goodness pass before You (Exodus 33:19).*

תִּבְנֶה חוֹמוֹת יְרוּשָׁלַיִם — *Build the walls of Jerusalem.*

Ibn Yachya notes that David was concerned about the building of the First Temple. He prayed that God should grant him, or one of his sons, the privilege of building the Temple and the walls of the city, and should not deem him unworthy because of his sins.

The *Zohar (Parshas Mishpatim)* observes, How different are the ways of God from the ways of man. Men first construct the outer walls of the city for protection and then they build the houses inside. But God will first build the future Beis HaMikdash, called Zion, and only afterwards *build the walls of Jerusalem.*

21. אָז תַּחְפֹּץ זִבְחֵי צֶדֶק — *Then You will desire the sacrifices of righteousness.*

Then, in the days of the Messiah, when *the earth shall be full of the knowledge of Hashem, as the waters cover the sea (Isaiah 11:9),* no man will sin; therefore, no sin or guilt offerings will be sacrificed. Only שְׁלָמִים, *peace offerings* will be donated voluntarily by the righteous (Metzudas David).

These offerings will be accompanied by the most desirable of all sacrifices, *the heart broken and crushed (Sforno).*

O God, You will despise not.

²⁰ *Benefit with Your grace unto Zion,*
build the walls of Jerusalem.
²¹ *Then You will desire*
the sacrifices of righteousness,
burnt-offering and whole-offering.
Then they will offer bullocks
upon Your altar.

עוֹלָה — *Burnt-offering.*

This refers to the עוֹלַת תָּמִיד, *the daily burnt-offering,* which was offered in the morning and in the afternoon *(Ibn Ezra).*

The prophet Isaiah (56:7) envisions this future era. God promises, *I will bring them to My holy mountain and make them joyful in My House of Prayer; their burnt-offerings and sacrifices shall be favorably accepted upon My altar* (Abarbanel).

וְכָלִיל — *And whole-offering.*

According to *Ibn Ezra,* this refers to the meal-offering brought by the priest, which is burned whole. [It is called כָּלִיל in *Leviticus* 6:15-16].

Sforno identifies this as the incense offering, which is called כָּלִיל in *Deuteronomy* 33:10.

However, *Rashi* and *Ibn Ezra* (based on *Yoma* 26a) identify כָּלִיל as an עוֹלָה,

burnt-offering (see *Baal HaTurim Deuteronomy 3:10*). In *I Samuel 7:9* we find the term עוֹלָה כָּלִיל. Thus, in our verse, עוֹלָה and כָּלִיל may be considered synonymous.

אָז יַעֲלוּ עַל מִזְבַּחֲךָ פָרִים — *Then they will offer bullocks upon Your altar.*

According to *Rabbeinu Yonah* (*Shaarei Teshuvah* 1:4), bullocks symbolize deep repentance. The prophet *Hoshea* (14:3) said, *we shall render the words of our lips to be as bullocks,* i.e., 'accept our confessions of sin and let them be considered as sin-offerings.' Bullocks are mentioned specifically because the blood of a bullock *sin-offering* was sprinkled on the inner curtain and on the golden altar. [Therefore, the bullock symbolizes repentance which penetrates to the inner core of the man and uproots the very source of the sin].[1]

---

1. *Shaarei Chaim* renders the verse, 'Then the bullocks will [voluntarily] go up upon Your altars. He offers a explanation, based on *Yalkut Shimoni (Melachim 214)*, which relates the story of Elijah on Mount Carmel. The prophet selected two identical twin bullocks. The one chosen for Elijah's sacrifice eagerly ran after him to be slaughtered on the altar of this righteous person. The other twin, designated for the priests of the idol Baal, refused to budge; all nine hundred and fifty pagan priests could not move an inch.

In the first two Temples, the bullocks did not voluntarily run to the slaughter because the poeple of Israel were not worthy. But in the future, when all of Israel will be sanctified and purified by repentance, the entire world will be eager to serve them, including 'the bullocks, who will go up [וְיַעֲלוּ] by themselves upon your altar.'

Once again David addresses himself to the most critical moral problem of his generation: the jealous enmity between men which undermines their principles to the point that they are willing to spread slander and fabricate evil tales in order to destroy their rivals. David cites a painful incident from his personal life which illustrates this theme.

David is forced to flee like a beggar from the blind, jealous wrath of his father-in-law, Saul. Starving and unarmed, David comes to Nob, the city of Priests, in which the Tabernacle was situated, and asks Achimelech the priest to give him bread and a sword. Assuming that David is on a mission in the loyal service of King Saul, the unsuspecting Achimelech supplies the fugitive with his needs.

But, at that time, Doeg the Edomite, the head of Sanhedrin and Saul's closest adviser, was in spiritual retreat at the Tabernacle of God. He reported the transaction to Saul in such a manner as to implicate Achimelech as a conspirator against the insecure king. This treacherous slander incited the despairing King to condemn the entire city of Nob to death, as rebels against the monarchy, a horrible sentence which was eagerly carried out by Doeg himself (I Samuel, Chapters 21-22).

These tragic events moved David to compose this Maskil, (an instructive psalm), to inform the people of the treachery of Doeg and slanderers like him.

1. לַמְנַצֵּחַ — *For the Conductor*

Maharal (*Nesivos Olam, Nesiv Ha-lashon*, Chapter 4), comments that David sought to combat the moral degeneration of his time with the songs he composed for the Temple. This idea is based on *Midrash Shocher Tov* (12:7):

Even children living in the days of Saul, David, and Samuel knew those subtle distinctions of תּוֹרָה שֶׁבְּעַל פֶּה, *the Oral Law*, which elaborate forty-nine arguments by which a creature may be proven clean and forty-nine other arguments by which it may be proven unclean. Yet despite their intellectual achievments, David's scholarly subjects fell before their enemies in battle because they were corrupted by the vice of tale-bearing (*Yerushalmi, Peah* 1:1). [See Prefatory Remarks to Psalm 15].

The Evil Inclination tempts a man to sin in the very area in which he excels. Therefore, since David's contemporaries were distinguished in their speech, which were devoted to the study of the Oral Law, their Evil Inclination concentrated his advances on the sins of the mouth. The nation succumbed to the temptation and sinned with its tongue. David sought to atone for this transgression by composing *Tehillim*, songs of praise designed to purge and purify their twisted tongues.

מַשְׂכִּיל לְדָוִד — *A Maskil, by David.*

The *Maskil* is a psalm composed with special intellectual effort to teach an essential lesson. Since the sin of לָשׁוֹן הָרַע, *evil speech*, is so widespread and tempting and the laws governing speech

are so complex, great שֵׂכֶל,*wisdom*, is needed to fulfill the teachings of the Torah in this area (*Eretz Hachaim*).

Chazah David notes the relationship between this psalm and the preceding one. Solomon said, *Death and life are in the power of the tongue* (*Proverbs* 18:21). In the previous psalm, David was condemned to die, until he confessed, חָטָאתִי, *I have sinned*. Immediately, he was forgiven and granted eternal life. This psalm depicts the opposite situation, for Doeg's wicked tongue brought him to eternal damnation.

Chazah David continues:

David was אַדְמוֹנִי, *ruddy*, i.e., passionate and sensual [see *Overview* I] and Doeg was אֲדֹמִי red. The numerical value of דָוִד is fourteen, as is that of the name דּוֹאֵג. These similarities show that essentially David and Doeg were once equals who could be differentiated only by their divergent modes of speech.[1]

Concerning Doeg and his kind, Solomon observed, *Permit not your mouth to bring your flesh into guilt* (*Koheles* 5:5).

2. דּוֹאֵג — *Doeg.*

[The name דּוֹאֵג literally means *the worrier*, revealing the defect in Doeg's character. Torah study should fill the scholar's heart with complete confidence and faith in God, whose Torah he studies. The scholar who devotes himself to the daily study of the Word of God should feel as serene as a child cradled in his father's arms. Doeg, however, studied Torah without feel-

---

1. Throughout *Chronicles*, David's name is spelled דָּוִיד which has the numerical value of twenty-four, alluding to David's great achievement of setting up twenty-four priestly watches in the Temple. *Chida* in *Rosh David* explains that this change of spelling was in response to David's request that even the numerical value of his name not be the same as Doeg's. Homiletically, this is the intent of David's prayer: עֲשֵׂה עִמִּי אוֹת לְטוֹבָה וְיִרְאוּ שֹׂנְאַי וְיֵבֹשׁוּ, *Make for me an [extra] אוֹת, letter [lit. sign] for the good, so that my enemies may see and be shamed* (86:17).

For the Conductor.
a Maskil, by David,
² Upon the arrival of Doeg the Edomite,
who informed Saul, saying to him,

ings of faith, as an empty cultural or academic pursuit. Selfishly, he used his knowledge as a tool, by which to elevate his own position. He found security in his status rather than in God. Jealous and fearful of rivals, he was tormented by anxiety and worry [see *Ben Yehoyada, Sanhedrin* 106b). How different was David, whose name is spelled דוד, *lover*, symbolizing his deep trust in, and love of, God.]

Midrash Shocher Tov explains that an entire psalm is dedicated to Doeg because God reveals the evil of the hypocrite in order to make the nature of his deeds understood. Otherwise, the punishment that befalls him would cause men to question God's justice. In this case, Doeg, who was well-known as the Head of Sanhedrin [אֲבִיר הָרֹעִים, *chief of the shepherds (I Samuel* 21:8)], possessed considerable knowledge of the Torah. Therefore, Scripture publicizes the fact that he was a slanderer.

הָאֲדֹמִי — *The Edomite*.

According to *Radak*, Doeg lived in the land of Edom.

Midrash Shocher Tov offers six explanations for this name:

First, Doeg was called *the Edomite* [derived from אָדֹם, *red*] because he was envious of David, who was called אַדְמוֹנִי, *ruddy (I Samuel* 16:12). Nor was Doeg alone in his envy of David: all the members of his clan, the Ziphites, Nabal the Carmelite, and the men of Keilah, were envious of him.

Second, he was called *the Edomite* [related to דָּם, *blood*] because he *perverted the truth in order to bring about the shedding of the blood of Nob, city of Priests, which he exterminated*

singlehandedly, as it says: Doeg the Edomite turned, and he fell upon the priests, and he slew that day eighty-five men (I Samuel 22:18).

Third, it was he who called for the shedding of the blood of David, saying to Saul, *'he deserves to die' (I Samuel* 20:31).

Fourth, Doeg the Edomite forbade Saul to shed the blood of Agag, King of Amalek. Because of Doeg's ruling, Saul was judged guilty of the heavenly death penalty for having spared the life of a guilty Amalekite.

Fifth, he was called *the Edomite* because his superior scholarship enabled him to מַאֲדִים, *redden with shame*, the faces of those who argued the law with him. During debates, Doeg would use his superior arguments to reduce his opponent to silence [דוֹמֵם, *silent*, is also related to אֲדֹמִי].

Sixth, in that he sullied the attainments of David, he was like Edom who disparages Israel. Just as Edom seeks vengeance, so did Doeg seek vengeance against David.

וַיַּגֵּד לְשָׁאוּל — *Who informed Saul*.

Midrash Shocher Tov relates וַיַּגֵּד to the root word אָגַד, *joined, bound*; i.e., when Doeg recounted the episode, he *added* his own opinions and ideas in such a way that Saul was aroused to burning fury.

He said, 'Achimelech has made David king even while you are still living. For, although inquiry may not be made of the Urim V'Tumim on behalf of any man except the king, members of the court, or one upon whom the needs of the public depend; nevertheless, inquiry was made on behalf of David!'

When Doeg said this, a spirit of

malicious envy entered Saul. Achimelech sought to defend himself, saying, *Who amongst all of your servants is so trusted as David, who is the king's son-in-law? Have I only today begun to inquire of God for him? (I Samuel 22:14-15).* 'This was not the first time, for it has long been my custom to inquire on behalf of David!'

[See *Parashas Derachim, Derech HaRabbim* 13 for a discussion of the halachic background of Doeg's argument and Achimelech's justification.]

This explanation infuriated the King even more, and he issued a death sentence against Achimelech (*I Samuel* 22:17). However, Saul's guards, Abner and Amasa, refused to harm the priests.

In desperation, Saul turned to Doeg, and said, 'Why do you stand still? You already smote the priests of Nob with your tongue; rise now and smite them with the sword!' Doeg then single-handedly slaughtered the entire city of Priests.

וַיֹּאמֶר לוֹ — *Saying to him.*

The phrases *'he informed Saul saying to him'* seem to be redundant. In order to understand the purpose of this double wording, *Shaarei Chaim* applies *Rashi's* comment (*Exodus* 19:3) that יַגֵּד means to speak words which arouse the listener, whereas אָמַר means to speak gently and soothingly.

The sly Doeg did not wish to appear as a vicious prosecutor of the priests. Therefore, once he incited Saul's wrath and was confident that his accusations had struck home (וַיַּגֵּד), he cunningly

changed his tone of voice in an insincere 'attempt' to assuage Saul's anger by seeking apologies in defense of the priests (וַיֹּאמֶר). By concluding his inflammatory denunciation with soothing words of conciliation, he hoped to shift the blame for the slaughter from himself to Saul.

Doeg was motivated by the desire to punish and injure everyone who associated with David. As the *Talmud* (*Shabbos* 149b) states, 'Whoever causes his fellow to be punished on his account is barred from entering the presence of God ... for he who is a cause of evil is himself considered evil.' Doeg was jealous primarily because David enjoyed God's intimate closeness (cf. *Sanhedrin* 93b, *Shabbos* 56a) [See *comm. v.* 9, which indicates that Doeg did partially succeed in his ambition to damage David.] [1]

בָּא דָוִד אֶל בֵּית אֲחִימֶלֶךְ — *David came to the house of Achimelech.*

Alshich explains that Doeg happened to be visiting the Tabernacle when David arrived. If David had merely spoken to Achimelech in the Tabernacle itself, in full view of Doeg, the king's trusted confidant, then there could be no suspicion of conspiracy. But Doeg emphasized that the two men had retired to the privacy of Achimelech's personal residence, charging that they spoke of treacherous plots which had to be concealed from Doeg, the supporter of King Saul.

It is hard to understand why Doeg went to such lengths to implicate

---

1. We can also understand Doeg's mad desire to destroy the priests by noting that the Tabernacle was at the root of Doeg's jealousy. The *Talmud* (*Zevachim* 54b) relates that on the night when David first fled from Saul, Samuel chose David as Saul's successor and gave him a scroll containing secret traditions concerning the construction of the Temple in place of the Tabernacle, 'It was this privilege which kindled Doeg's jealousy', the *Talmud* concludes.

Fittingly, the cause of Doeg's death also emanated from the Tabernacle. 'A fiery shaft sprang out of the Holy of Holies and burned all around him [Doeg]' (*Yerushalmi, Sanhedrin* 10:2).

'David came to the house of Achimelech.'
³ Why do you pride yourself with evil
O mighty warrior?
The kindness of God
is all day long.

Achimelech in this fabricated con-spiracy. *Parashas Derachim (Derech Hamelech* 11 and *Derech Harabbim* 13) explains that Doeg bore no particular grudge against Achimelech. Rather his intention was to use Achimelech as a pawn to bring punishment upon David, for if the priests were to suffer because of David's association with them, then he would be held liable by God for hav-ing been a cause of another's misfortune [see *comm.* to *v.* 10].

3. מַה תִּתְהַלֵּל בְּרָעָה הַגִּבּוֹר — *Why do you pride yourself with evil, O mighty warrior?*

David cries out to Doeg with the vocative form הַגִּבּוֹר, *O mighty warrior!* 'You are not an ordinary scholar, a mere גִּבּוֹר [i.e., warrior in the battlefield of learning]; you are, in fact, הַגִּבּוֹר *the greatest scholar' (Radak).*

Why then do you, a distinguished and universally acclaimed Torah sage, prefer to be honored for your evil deeds? *(Rashi). Strangely, you continue to boast of the feat of physical might which you performed when you single-handedly massacred the entire city of Nob (Midrash)* [see *comm.* 5:6.]

The Torah in which you excel is called תּוֹרַת חֶסֶד, *the law of kindness (Proverbs* 31:26). Why then do you boast of your cruelty?

David asked Doeg, 'Is a man truly mighty when he sees his fellow at the edge of a pit and pushes him in, when he sees his fellow on top of a roof and pushes him off? On the contrary, a man

deserves to be called *a mighty warrior* when his fellow is about to fall into a pit and he grasps his hand to prevent his fall or when he lifts the fallen man from the pit. But when you saw that Saul was angry at me, you persisted in vilifying me' *(Midrash Shocher Tov).*

Had you subdued your Evil Inclina-tion [רָעָה], and refrained from slander-ing me, then you would truly be con-sidered a mighty גִּבּוֹר, for the Sages said: *Who is mighty? He who conquers his Evil Inclination! (Avos* 4:1). But now that you have so disgracefully sur-rendered yourself to your own evil in-clination, how dare you pride youself as a גִּבּוֹר? *(Os HaBris).*

חֶסֶד אֵל כָּל הַיּוֹם — *The kindness of God is all the day long.*]

Your might and slander were powerless, because God's kindness enveloped me continually. His kindness saved me from Saul again and again and will continue to preserve me in the future *(Radak).*

Furthermore, why do you consider Achimelech's kindness the evidence of complicity? Do you really think that without his aid I would have died of starvation? Don't you realize that a Divine spirit of mercy hovers over Israel all day long, inspiring all Jews to perform acts of kindness? If Achimelech had not helped, many others would certainly have eagerly come to my rescue! *(Rashi).*[1]

[Since Doeg was selfish and cruel, he was truly amazed even by relatively

1. Ironically, the tragedy of Nob came about because David's dearest friend, Jonathan, inad-vertently neglected to do kindness with his comrade. The *Talmud (Sanhedrin* 104a) lauds one who provides food for his wayfarers and guests, and emphasizes the terrible harm which can result from missing an opportunity for kindness: If Jonathan had lent David only two loaves

ה   לְשׁוֹנֶךָ כְּתַעַר מְלֻטָּשׁ עֹשֵׂה רְמִיָּה: אָהַבְתָּ

ו   רָע מִטּוֹב שֶׁקֶר | מִדַּבֵּר צֶדֶק סֶלָה: אָהַבְתָּ

ז   כָל־דִּבְרֵי־בָלַע לְשׁוֹן מִרְמָה: גַּם־אֵל

יִתָּצְךָ לָנֶצַח יַחְתְּךָ וְיִסָּחֲךָ מֵאֹהֶל וְשֵׁרֶשְׁךָ

ח   מֵאֶרֶץ חַיִּים סֶלָה: וְיִרְאוּ צַדִּיקִים וְיִירָאוּ

---

minor acts of hospitality; thus, he considered Achimelech's actions to be extraordinary and hence, suspicious.]

Finally, ought a man who practices mercy towards God (so to speak) engage in cruelty? For he who occupies himself with Torah study is considered to be practicing mercy towards God! (*Midrash Shocher Tov*).

The man who recognizes God's mercy should permit his mouth to engage in nothing but the recounting of *the kindness of God all day long (Ibn Ezra).*

6. לְשׁוֹן מִרְמָה — *A tongue of deceit.*

Had Doeg had sincerely sought the welfare of Saul and Achimelech, he would have confronted Achimelech and warned him that if he assisted David he would arouse Saul's wrath. But Doeg preferred to be deceptive; therefore, he allowed Achimelech to help David so that he could later slander him *(Radak).*

Malbim explains that Doeg was ultimately destroyed by his own *deceitful tongue.*

In *II Samuel* (Chapter 1) we read that Saul's Amelekite attendant informed David of the king's death and claimed responsibility for it, expecting that this would earn him David's favor. The truth was that Saul had mortally wounded himself by falling on his own sword. Nevertheless, David slew the Amalekite because he claimed to have harmed the anointed king of God.

Rashi (II Samuel 1:2 and 1:9) quotes

the *Pesikta* which identifies this Amalekite as Doeg the Edomite! After David's attendant stabbed Doeg to death, David said (*II Samuel* 1:16): *The guilt of your blood is upon yourself alone, for your own mouth testified against you, saying, 'I have slain the anointed of HASHEM.'*

Malbim explains David's words thus; Even though your *deceitful tongue* is now lying in regard to the death of Saul (for you only sought to gain my favor by claiming to have avenged me upon my enemy), nevertheless, you shall die because of your earlier crime of slaughtering Achimelech the High Priest, *the anointed of HASHEM.*

7. גַּם אֵל יִתָּצְךָ לָנֶצַח — *Likewise, God will smash you for eternity.*

[Doeg, the war which you wage is not merely a campaign against David; rather you are challenging God Himself who has chosen David.] Furthermore, you dared to massacre God's chosen servants, the priests, in the very House of God *(Radak).*

'You teach a distorted version of God's own Torah in order to justify your wicked deeds. Therefore, *God Himself will smash you! (Sforno).*

[The *Mishnah (Sanhedrin* 11:1) lists Doeg among the individuals who forfeited their share in the World to Come.]

Midrash Shocher Tov observes that even in this world Doeg was afflicted with leprosy, which is the punishment

---

of bread [before David set out in flight from Saul] then David would have had no reason to ask Acimelech for food. Nob the city of priests would not have been destroyed, Doeg would not have been ruined, and Saul and his sons [including Jonathan] would not have been slain.

⁴ *Treachery does your tongue devise,*
　　like a sharpened razor working deceit.
⁵ *you love evil more than good,*
　　falsehood more than speaking righteousness,
　　Selah.
⁶ *You love all devouring words,*
　　a tongue of deceit.
⁷ *Likewise, God will smash you for eternity,*
　　He will shatter you and tear you from the tent,
　　and uproot you from the land of life, Selah.
⁸ *The righteous will see it and be frightened,*

---

reserved for slanderers. His leprosy is indicated by the fact that here it says *God will smash you,* just as it says of the leper's house, *He will smash the house* (Lev. 14:45).

יַחְתְּךָ — *He will shatter you.*

This translation follows *Rashi* and *Targum. Radak* renders *He will take you away,* for he maintains that the word is related to חוֹתֶה אֵשׁ, *raking away fiery coals.* His father *Rav Yosef Kimchi,* also derives יַחְתְּךָ from חוֹתֶה, but translates *He will burn you.*

וְיִסָּחֲךָ — *And He will tear you.*

Again the translation is according to *Rashi,* however *Radak* renders *He will destroy you.*

מֵאֹהֶל — *From the tent.*

God will not allow you to dwell in His tent, the Tabernacle *(Targum),* [for your visit to the Tabernacle resulted in the massacre of Nob.] Nor will you have the privilege of studying in the tent of Torah, the Beis Hamidrash *(Sforno).*

Furthermore, your teachings on the Torah will never be taught in the schools of Jewish learning *(Sanhedrin* 106b).

Yalkut Shimoni (I Samuel 131) describes Doeg's last moments: 'Doeg was teaching his students; as they absorbed what he said, he forgot his own wisdom, bit by bit. When his students finally

realized that he was falsifying and distorting the law, they tied ropes to his feet and dragged him away.' [Cf. *Pesikta's* version of Doeg's death cited in *v.* 6 above.]

According to the *Talmud,* three angels of destruction accosted Doeg: One caused him to forget his learning; one burned his soul; and one took his ashes and scattered them in every synagogue and house of study *(Sanhedrin* 106b) [see comm. to 5:11.]

וְשֵׁרֶשְׁךָ מֵאֶרֶץ חַיִּים סֶלָה — *And He will uproot you from the land of life, Selah.*

Even your roots will be ripped out of the earth so that no remembrance of you will remain. You will not leave any sons who are worthy Torah scholars *(Sanhedrin* 106b). This punishment is fitting because you uprooted the entire family of Achimelech, leaving no infant alive *(Ibn Ezra).*

8. וְיִרְאוּ צַדִּיקִים וְיִירָאוּ — *The righteous will see it and be frightened.*

When they witness the revenge which God will take on behalf of the slain priests, their fear of the Almighty will increase *(Radak),* [compare 40:4 רָאוּ רַבִּים וְיִירָאוּ.]

At first, the righteous men feared Doeg's slander, for his vicious barbs were aimed at all men of good will. After his downfall, however, righteous

ט וְעָלָיו יִשְׂחָקוּ: הִנֵּה הַגֶּבֶר לֹא יָשִׂים
אֱלֹהִים מָעוּזּוֹ וַיִּבְטַח בְּרֹב עָשְׁרוֹ יָעֹז
י בְּהַוָּתוֹ: וַאֲנִי | כְּזַיִת רַעֲנָן בְּבֵית אֱלֹהִים
יא בָּטַחְתִּי בְחֶסֶד־אֱלֹהִים עוֹלָם וָעֶד: אוֹדְךָ
לְעוֹלָם כִּי עָשִׂיתָ וַאֲקַוֶּה שִׁמְךָ כִי־טוֹב
נֶגֶד חֲסִידֶיךָ:

men laughed in relief (*Sanhedrin* 106a, *Maharsha, ibid.*).

[Throughout the generations *the righteous* Sages were *afraid* and anxious lest one of their students develop into a Doeg-like scholar. The *Talmud (Berachos* 17b) relates that when the Rabbis took leave of each other after the lesson they would pray: May our group not resemble Saul's group, from whose ranks there came forth Doeg the Edomite.]

וְעָלָיו יִשְׂחָקוּ — *But [lit. and] they will jeer at him.*

They will laugh when they detect the irony of Doeg's fate. His mouth, which caused the death of so many innocent men, finally confessed his own guilt and sealed his doom when he told David that he had killed Saul *(Malbim).*

9. הִנֵּה הַגֶּבֶר לֹא יָשִׂים אֱלֹהִים מָעוּזּוֹ — *Behold this is the man who did not make God his stronghold.*

This is the proclamation people will make when they see Doeg's ignominious end *(Radak).*

He will serve as an everlasting example of the futility of seeking success through evil *(Ibn Ezra).*

[The man who protects his personal interests by resorting to slander thereby denies that God is a *stronghold* with the ability to ensure the security of those who trust in Him.]

וַיִּבְטַח בְּרֹב עָשְׁרוֹ — *But trusted in his abundance of wealth.*

Doeg was confident that Saul would

reward him handsomely for the zealous loyalty he displayed in annihilating an entire city accused of treason *(Sforno).*

יָעֹז בְּהַוָּתוֹ — *And drew strength from his treachery.*

Doeg sought to strengthen his own postion by finding favor in Saul's eyes when he denounced the *treachery* of Nob *(Metzudas David).*

10. וַאֲנִי כְּזַיִת רַעֲנָן — *But I am like an evergreen olive.*

The leaf of the olive tree remains green and moist throughout the year; it never withers *(Radak).* [See 1:3 where the righteous man is described as one *whose leaf never withers.*]

David said, 'Although I now flee like a fugitive who appears to have no future, I am confident that I will become as productive as the olive tree and that I will sire children and grandchildren who will dwell in the House of God *(Rashi).*

Futhermore, I hope to be a source of enlightenment and illumination for my people, just as kindled olive oil lights up the darkness *(Sforno).* [See *Shemos Rabbah* 36:2].

Alshich notes that the olive, noted for its bitter taste, symbolizes the difficulties and afflictions of life [see *Eruvin* 18b.] The Rabbis [*Menachos* 53b] say, Just as the olive discharges the oil only after being crushed, the Jew extracts the full measure of piety from within himself only after experiencing suffering and affliction *(Shevet*

but they will jeer at him:
⁹ Behold this is the man
who did not make God his stronghold,
But trusted in his abundance of wealth,
drew strength from his treachery.'
¹⁰ But I am like an evergreen olive
in the House of God,
I trust in the kindness of God
forever and ever.
¹¹ I will thank You forever when You do it,
and put hope in Your name;
For You are good to Your devout ones.

M'Yisroel). Here David states that, because of the bitter suffering which he experienced [as a result of Doeg's slander and persecution], *I trust* [that these afflictions will enable me to merit] *the kindness of God forever and ever.*

בְּבֵית אֱלֹהִים — *In the House of God.*

Concerning Doeg, David said earlier (v. 7), *God ... will pluck you from the tent* [i.e., the Tabernacle] *and uproot you from the land of life.* In contrast, David hopes that by virtue of his own complete trust in God, he will deserve to be rooted in the House of God forever (Ibn Ezra; Radak).

Scripture describes the visit of Doeg to the Tabernacle, *And he was detained before HASHEM* (I Samuel 21:8), implying that the House of God was not his true home and source of existence, but that he was merely *detained* there momentarily. David, in contrast, sunk the roots of his being into the holy soil of God's Sanctuary (Malbim).

בָּטַחְתִּי בְחֶסֶד אֱלֹהִים עוֹלָם וָעֶד — *I trust in the kindness of God forever and ever.*

Alshich explains that the *kindness* of אֱלֹהִים, *the Arbiter of Strict Justice,* reforms the sinner and brings him to the World to Come.

Chomas Anoch interprets this verse

in light of the *Talmud (Sanhedrin 95a),* which reveals how much God demands of intimate devotees such as David. The Talmud notes that although David was the innocent victim of Doeg's vehemence and Saul's jealousy, David was responsible, in a sense, for having aroused the worst in these men. It was because of David that the city of Nob was massacred, that Saul and his sons were slain in battle, and that Doeg was killed. Any person who is the cause of so much bloodshed, albeit inadvertently, cannot be considered totally guiltless. [*Chamra V'Chaia (Sanhedrin 102b)* says that David should have generously and wholeheartedly forgiven his enemies and thereby spare them from punishment.]

The use of the name אֱלֹהִים, *Dispenser of Strict Justice,* in our verse, indicates that David was to be punished. Nevertheless, David trusted בְּחֶסֶד אֱלֹהִים, *in the 'kindness' of God,* with which His Judgment was tempered. God offered David a choice of punishments, and David finally accepted the punishment that his own descendants would be annihilated. [See *comm.* to 7:1.] This occurred when Ataliah slaughtered the entire royal family, with the exception of the infant

Yoash, who was hidden in the attic above the Holy of Holies in the Temple [see *II Kings* 11:1-2 and Prefatory Remarks, *Psalms* 12.]

In this psalm, David foretells the doom of Doeg and recognizes that ultimately his own descendants will be threatened as a result of this enmity. Therefore, David prays that his offspring will flourish *like an evergreen olive in the House of God*, i.e., in the attic of the Holy of Holies where the last remnant of his seed will be replanted. Also, says David, *I trust in the kindness of God forever and ever* that my progeny will never be completely destroyed.

11. אוֹדְךָ לְעוֹלָם כִּי עָשִׂיתָ—*I will thank You forever when You do it.*

I.e., when You take revenge against my enemies and defend my rights (*Targum; Radak*).

When You help me to become a flourishing olive, thriving in Your House (*Sforno*).

וַאֲקַוֶּה שִׁמְךָ כִי טוֹב נֶגֶד חֲסִידֶיךָ — *And [I will] put hope in Your Name; You are good to Your devout ones* (*Targum*).

Radak כִי טוֹב: *that You are good,* i.e., 'This is what I shall tell those who are devoted to You of Your kindness, and I will hope for the טוֹב, *goodness,* of the World to Come' (see *Sforno*).

53 מזמור נג

T his psalm is almost an exact replica of Psalm 14. Both
compositions speak of the exile and the future redemption.
However, as explained in the Prefatory Remarks to Psalm 14, the
earlier work focuses on the destruction of the First Temple at the
hands of Nebuchadnezzar, whereas this psalm describes the destruction of the Second Temple by Titus (Rashi).

Radak and Meiri explain that this position in the Book of Tehillim
was chosen with great care in order to emphasize its theme.

The founding of the royal house of David met with fierce opposition from those who denied David's right to rule. They resorted to the
most devious and treacherous means to prevent David's ascent to the
throne. In Psalm 52, we read of Doeg's evil machinations and slander.
In Psalm 54, we learn of the Ziphites who mercilessly betrayed David
to Saul. In both cases, God foiled the plots of those who attempted to
disrupt the establishment of David's reign.

Psalm 53 depicts the climax and the conclusion of the Davidean
line, which will occur with the advent of Messiah, who will end the
exile and clear the ruins of the Second Temple by dedicating the
Third. Like his ancestor David, Messiah will suffer persecution at
the hands of sceptics and scoffers, who will refuse to recognize his
sovereignty and will scheme to assassinate him to destroy his
monarchy. Furthermore, throughout Jewish history, we will be
threatened by wicked men, such as Titus, who will attempt to destroy
Israel, the nation of David. However, all of these villains will share
the fate of Doeg and the Ziphites: utter failure and terrible misfortune.

1. מָחֲלַת — *Machalas.*

Rashi identifies the *Machalas* as a special type of musical instrument. In addition, he relates this word to מַחֲלָה, *malady, affliction,* referring to the downtrodden state of Israel after the destruction of the Second Temple, when the Jews were plagued with countless tragedies.

Meiri, following his customary approach [see 5:1; 22:1], demonstrates how this unique musical accompaniment complements the special theme of this psalm: It is known to those who are well-versed in the science of musicology that certain strings and chords are tuned to give forth a depressing, mourning sound which evokes feelings of anxiety, sorrow and weeping. The *Machalas* instrument had the ability to draw forth such tragic emotions from the depths of the heart.

[This word does not appear in Psalm 14, suggesting that the *malady* and *afflictions* of the second destruction far surpassed those of the first. The First (Babylonian) exile lasted but seventy years, whereas the Second, (Roman) exile has continued for almost two thousand years (see *Yoma* 9b).]

Chazah Zion renders מָחֲלַת as מְחִילָה, *forgiveness,* [thus, this psalm would be related to Psalm 51, which speaks of repentance, atonement and reconciliation with God.] The *degraded man* who denies God's presence sees nothing wrong with sin; therefore, he never seeks *forgiveness.* But the מַשְׂכִּיל [lit. *wise man*] realizes that *from heaven God gazes down upon mankind (v. 3).*

God recounts man's sins and requires those who transgress to seek forgiveness.[1]

מַשְׂכִּיל — *A Maskil.*

[This word, too, is absent from Psalm 14. As explained in 32:11, the term *Maskil* denotes a psalm composed with special intellectual effort to serve as an instructive essay devoted to heightening Israel's comprehension of God's ways.

After the terrible events of the second destruction and the ensuing exile, Israel felt very alienated from God. It was extremely difficult for the Jews to appreciate the divine plan and purpose which guided their destinies as they wandered aimlessly from persecution to persecution. Groping blindly in the gloom of an apparently endless *galus,* Israel felt abandoned and forlorn. Therefore, this psalm of intensive instruction seeks to help Israel gain an understanding of God's ways in the Second Exile.]

According to *Sforno,* this psalm is a direct continuation of the previous one and represents a diagnosis of the מַחֲלַת מַשְׂכִּיל, [lit. *the malady of the intellectuals*]. This refers to the Torah scholars who have healthy minds but sick hearts; they must improve their character and conduct. Doeg and those who resemble him are prime examples of this *'malady'.*

[In truth, *Sforno's* interpretation of this psalm complements that of *Rashi.* The malady of the exile will reach its most agonizing proportions when the

1. In describing Israel's celebration around the Golden Calf, Scripture says, *And he* [Moses] *saw the calf and the mecholos (Exodus 32:19).*

Rabbeinu Bachya (ibid.) points out that nine different types of musical instruments are mentioned in Scripture. Undoubtedly, many instruments were used to encourage the pagan festivities around the calf, but the Divine Will ordained that Moses should notice only the *mecholos* instrument. This was meant to signify to him that despite the severity of the offense, the nation would merit *mechilah,* forgiveness.

LIII
1-2

For the Conductor upon the Machalas,
  a Maskil of David.
  ² *The degraded man says in his heart,*
    'There is no God!'
  They acted corruptly and despicably
    through iniquity;
  Not one does good.

nation of Israel falls under the leadership of irresponsible pseudo-scholars who suffer from a moral and spiritual *malady*.

The *Talmud (Sotah* 49b) states that this problem will plague Israel in the chaotic times preceding the advent of Messiah when there will be no rebuke or discipline, the wisdom of the Sages will fall into ruin, and truth will completely vanish.]

2. אָמַר נָבָל בְּלִבּוֹ — *The degraded man* [or: *'degenerate'*] *says in his heart.*

Rashi maintains that the *degraded man* described here is Titus. The *Talmud (Gittin* 56b) relates the story of the atrocities which this Roman general perpetrated: Titus hurled words of blasphemy and curses heavenward. He dragged a prostitute into the Holy of Holies where he performed a lewd act upon an open Torah Scroll. He then grasped his sword and slashed the *Paroches*, the curtain in front of the Holy of Holies. A miracle occurred and blood spurted from the gash. Titus imagined this to be a sign that he had killed God Himself (ח״ו)! [Actually, this blood showed that God's heart was 'bleeding', as it were, because of the destruction, *(Tosafos ibid)*.]. Gloating over his success, Titus then made the *Paroches* into a sack and stuffed it with the precious vessels of the Temple, which he loaded on a ship for display at the time of his triumphant entry into Rome.

According to *Midrash Shocher Tov*, נָבָל in this verse is not an adjective

meaning *degenerate*, but a proper noun referring to *Nabal the Carmelite* [*I Samuel* 25], *a wealthy man so selfish that he refused David's plea to provide food and drink for his hungry troops.*

Norah Tehillos explains that this psalm was purposely placed directly after *Psalm* 52 in order to emphasize the stark contrast between Achimelech (*Psalm* 52:2) and Nabal. Achimelech gladly sacrificed his life in order to extend hospitality to David. He generously supplied David with everything he desired. Nabal, however, not only vehemently denied David's request but also insulted him.

Sforno identifies the נָבָל as the insincere scholar whose external piety and wisdom cloak a heart which questions the very existence of God! As the *Talmud (Sanhedrin* 106b) says: 'All of Doeg's Torah knowledge was from the lips outward [i.e., insincere] ... but what God truly desires is the heart!'

אֵין אֱלֹהִים — *There is no God!*

When Titus slashed the *Poroches* and blood flowed, he exulted 'God is dead!' *(Rashi).*

[Nabal the Carmelite denied David's authority and his claim to the throne (see *I Sam.* 25:10). Thus he is considered to have denied the authority of God Himself! (*Midrash Shocher Tov;* see Article 12 of *Rambam's* 'Thirteen Principles of Faith' cited in *comm.* to 2:2).]

הִשְׁחִיתוּ — *They acted corruptly.*

[This term is used to describe lewd

ג עָוֶל אֵין עֹשֵׂה־טוֹב: אֱלֹהִים מִשָּׁמַיִם
הִשְׁקִיף עַל־בְּנֵי־אָדָם לִרְאוֹת הֲיֵשׁ
ד מַשְׂכִּיל דֹּרֵשׁ אֶת־אֱלֹהִים: כֻּלּוֹ סָג יַחְדָּו

acts of unchastity, as in *Genesis* 6:12. It alludes to the abominable behavior of Titus and his prostitute in the Holy of Holies. According to *Midrash Shocher Tov*, Nabal the Carmelite was also guilty of such corrupt wanton acts.]

וְהִתְעִיבוּ עָוֶל — *And despicably* [*through*] *iniquity.*

Their total corruption and depravity rendered them despicable in the eyes of others (*Radak*).

[We often find in Scriptures that *iniquity* is considered *despicable*, as in *Deuteronomy* 25:16 and *Proverbs* 29:27.]

Chazah Zion observes that עָוֶל refers specifically to dishonesty in monetary affairs (see *Lev.* 19:15, 35).

[In the very beginning of the era of the Second Temple, the children of Israel underwent a major transformation: no longer were they plagued by the desire to worship idols (*Yoma* 69b), but by the desire to amass wealth. It is well known that the Second Temple was destroyed as a result of שִׂנְאַת חִנָּם, *unwarranted hatred*. *Yerushalmi Yoma* (1:9) explains: 'Since they loved their money, they came to hate one another!' Thus it was a fitting punishment that the Second Temple was destroyed by Rome, an empire which was particularly notorious for avarice. The *Midrash* (*Shemos Rabbah* 35:5) relates that no wheel moved in Rome unless it was well oiled with money: מִתְרַפֵּס בְּרַצֵּי בָּסֶף, *submitting to pieces of silver* (68:31) This describes the government of Rome!]

3. אֱלֹהִים — *God.*

The essential difference between this psalm and *Psalm* 14 is the Name used to refer to God. In *Psalm* 14, the name *HASHEM* predominates, while in *Psalm*

53 the designation אֱלֹהִים, *God* occurs throughout (*Hirsch*).

[The moral decay and *malady* (מַחֲלָת) which afflicted the Jewish people during the Second Temple brought about a spiritual degeneration. Only the harsh remedies meted out by אֱלֹהִים, '*the Dispenser of Strict Justice*', could serve as an effective cure for this alarming spiritual disease. After the first destruction, however, the spiritual caliber of the people was such that they still deserved the manifestation of God's Mercy represented by the Name HASHEM.]

מִשָּׁמַיִם הִשְׁקִיף — *From heaven* [*God*] *gazed down.*

[In general, the term הִשְׁקִיף, *He gazed*, denotes a critical observation for the sake of meting out punishment. [See *Rashi Gen.* 18:16 and *Yerushalmi Maaser Sheni* 5:5. See *Torah Temimah* on *Deut.* 26:15, suggesting that this rule applies only to the Pentateuch and not to other Scriptures such as *Psalms*, as evidenced by *Psalms* 85:12, 102:20, and *Songs* 6:10.]

Dorash Moshe explains that רְאִיָה *looking*, means enlargement of the span of vision to encompass the broadest possible area, whereas הַשְׁקָפָה, *gazing*, means to reduce the focus of vision in order to scrutinize a single object. Naturally, if a person seeks to find fault with someone he must use הַשְׁקָפָה to study his subject closely.

לִרְאוֹת הֲיֵשׁ מַשְׂכִּיל — *To see if there be one who reflects.*

This refers to a person who ponders the words of the Torah, seeking guidance (*Targum*).

[David exemplified this quality, as it says, וַיְהִי דָוִד לְכָל דְּרָכָיו מַשְׂכִּיל, '*And David was intellgent in all of his ways*'

³ *From heaven God gazed down upon mankind*
   to see if there be one who reflects;
   one who seeks out God.
⁴ *They are all dross,*
   together become depraved;

(*I Samuel* 18:14). He succeeded in following the upright ways of God; therefore, וַה׳ עִמּוֹ, *and HASHEM was with him* (*ibid.*). It was David's genius for acting wisely which stirred Saul's jealousy, *And Saul saw that he was most intelligent and he stood in fear of him* (*ibid. v.* 15).

The conflict between these two men is a symbol of the larger conflict between Israel and the nations. Their hatred is aroused because they see that Israel has made the wise choice of following God, whereas they have failed to do so. (See *Prefatory Remarks, Psalm* 68.) The depraved culture of Rome demanded that the intellectual and spiritual heritage of Israel be eradicated, lest the arguments of the Torah uncover the inherent worthlessness of Roman thought.]

דֹּרֵשׁ אֶת אֱלֹהִים — *[One] who seeks out God.*

I.e., one who seeks out God by clinging to the Sages of His Torah, in order to learn from them the will of the Almighty. Prior to the destruction of the Temple, God sought such devoted disciples of the rabbis, but found none in whose merit the Temple could be spared. The *Talmud* (*Shabbos* 119b) says that Jerusalem was destroyed only because its inhabitants disgraced Torah Sages (*Yoseif Tehillos*).

4. כֻּלּוֹ סָג — *They are* [lit. *he is*] *all dross.*

This translation follows *Rashi* who sees סָג as cognate with סִיגִים, *impurities; dross.*

Ibn Yachya and *Metzudas David* define סָג as a verb related to נָסוֹג, *to turn back; retreat* [i.e., since the destruction, Israel has made no progress but has remained in a state of perpetual failure and decline.]

Targum renders: 'They all scatter' [i.e., the exile has dispersed Israel to every corner of the earth.]

In Psalm 14, we have a variant reading, הַכֹּל סָר, *they have all gone astray. Midrash Shocher Tov* comments: At first they merely *had all gone astray.* Thus, there was still hope, for the man who deviates from the path can be brought back in repentance. Now, however, everyone has become totally *filled with dross;* therefore, the situation is hopeless.

Hirsch explains that they degenerated to the point that any former spark of nobility and refinement disppeared. As a result, they seem to be beyond return, just as base dross can never be converted into refined metal.[1]

יַחְדָּו נֶאֱלָחוּ — *Together become depraved.*

They are rotten from without [in their affairs with other men] and from

1. *Yoseif Tehillos* observes that in the word סָג we can detect an allusion to the root of their spiritual malady, i.e., excessive pride which is known as רוּחַ גַּס, *haughtiness of spirit.* The *Talmud* (*Sotah* 5a) allows the Torah scholar to display a minute trace of pride (גֵּסוּת) in order to demonstrate his authority to his community. The *Talmud* prescribes that only 'one-eighth of an eighth', i.e., one-sixty-fourth of one's pride may be expressed. No more than this minute fraction of pride can be tolerated. The numerical value of גַּס or סָג equals sixty-three, corresponding to the sixty-three parts of pride which must be suppressed [even by one who is thoroughly familiar with ס״ג, the *sixty-three* volumes of the *Talmud.*].

ה נֶאֱלָחוּ אֵין עֹשֵׂה־טוֹב אֵין גַּם־אֶחָד: הֲלֹא
יָדְעוּ פֹּעֲלֵי אָוֶן אֹכְלֵי עַמִּי אָכְלוּ לֶחֶם
אֱלֹהִים לֹא קָרָאוּ | שָׁם פָּחֲדוּ־פַחַד לֹא־ ו
הָיָה פָחַד כִּי־אֱלֹהִים פִּזַּר עַצְמוֹת חֹנָךְ
הֲבִשֹׁתָה כִּי־אֱלֹהִים מְאָסָם: מִי יִתֵּן ז
מִצִּיּוֹן יְשֻׁעוֹת יִשְׂרָאֵל בְּשׁוּב אֱלֹהִים
שְׁבוּת עַמּוֹ יָגֵל יַעֲקֹב יִשְׂמַח יִשְׂרָאֵל:

within [in their inner feelings toward
God] (Midrash Shocher Tov).

אֵין עֹשֵׂה טוֹב אֵין גַּם אֶחָד — None does
good, not even one.

There is not a single man among the
legions of Titus who protests this
atrocity (Rashi).

[The historian Josephus makes an attempt to apologize for Titus, claiming
that he actually tried to stop his troops
from burning down the Beis Hamikdash
but could not hold back the wild hordes
who were bent on destruction.

Maharal in Be'er Hagolah (באר השׁשׁי
ד׳ה עוד אסף) stresses that, beyond any
doubt, the intentions of Titus were far
more savage and blasphemous than
those of Nebuchadnezzar. The
Babylonian king destroyed the Temple
only as a military action to suppress the
Jewish revolt which flared against him.
Titus, however, sought to vanquish
God Himself by destroying His holy
Sanctuary.

Maharal continues that even if we accept the testimony of Josephus, Titus
will not be vindicated. For the Sages, in
their holy vision, saw that Titus' true
motive for sparing the Temple was his
desire to desecrate it with his
abominable actions while it still stood in
all its glory and grandeur! (see Netzach
Yisroel, Chap. 5).]

5. הֲלֹא יָדְעוּ פֹּעֲלֵי אָוֶן — Do they not
realize [lit. know], those evildoers?

If they are not aware of the doom

which faces them for devouring my
people, then someone should forewarn
them of the impending disaster (Rashi).

According to Sforno, this incredulous
query is addressed to the corrupt
scholars and judges, who should realize
the impact of their depravity.

אֹכְלֵי עַמִּי אָכְלוּ לֶחֶם — They who devour
my people [as they would] devour
bread.

These corrupt sages and magistrates
put a price on their decisions and sold
their rulings in exchange for a bribe.
This is the prime source of their lavish
income. Thus, they unjustly devour the
innocent people so that they can earn
their sustenance and devour bread
(Sforno).

אֱלֹהִים לֹא קָרָאוּ — They who do not call
upon God.

[In Psalm 14, the name 'ה appears instead of אֱלֹהִים.]

The Sages should lead the people in
prayer, penitence, and Torah study,
calling upon God for salvation. Instead
they lead others into crime (Sforno).

Targum renders this entire verse, All
those men of deceit know full well that
it is I [God] Who supply their bread;
why then do they devour bread and
refuse to call upon My Name by
reciting a blessing?

6. שָׁם פָּחֲדוּ פַחַד לֹא הָיָה פָחַד — There
they will be stricken with terror, a terror
such as never was.

LIII   *None does good, not even one.*

5-7   *⁵ Do they not realize, those evil doers? —*
         They who devour my people
         as they would devour bread,
    They who do not call upon God.
       ⁶ They will be stricken with terror;
         a terror such as never was.
For God scatters the bones of those encamped
         against you.
      You shamed them for God has rejected them.
    ⁷ O, that out of Zion
         will come Israel's salvations!
When God returns the captivity of His nation,
         Jacob will exult,
         Israel will rejoice.

Even the sheer terror experienced by Belshazzar on the night of his downfall [see *Daniel* 5:1 and *comm. to* 14:5] cannot compare to the horror which awaits this enemy *(Rashi).*

At the 'End of Days', the armies which assemble with Gog and Magog will panic when they witness that the host of weapons arrayed against them includes pestilence and blood, torrential floods and devastating hailstones *(Meiri).*

Dorash Moshe interprets this homiletically: The wicked will be terrrified by the fires of Gehinnom in the future only because they never had any fear of God in the past.

כִּי אֱלֹהִים פָּזַּר עַצְמוֹת חֹנָךְ — *For God scat-*

ters the bones of those encamped against you.

This refers to the armies which will encamp around Jerusalem and beseige it *(Radak).*[1]

הֱבִישֹׁתָה כִּי אֱלֹהִים מְאָסָם — *You shamed them for God has rejected them.*

In Psalm 14, this verse is very brief and reads: *There they will be stricken with terror, for God is with the righteous generation. Rashi* (ibid.) explains that even during the exile, God's holy spirit never departed from the righteous men of Israel. This refers to Babylon, where God's presence accompanied King Yechanyah and his myriad Torah scholars. However, in the Second (Roman) Exile, this was not the case.

1. [We can also perceive here an allusion to the ignominious fate of Titus. The Talmud (*Gittin* 56b) relates that on his deathbed Titus gave the following instructions: 'After death, cremate my body and scatter the ashes over the seven seas, so the the God of the Jews will not be able to find me to bring me before His Tribunal of Justice.'

Titus did not succeed in his attempt to escape Divine retribution. Indeed, the very sentence which he passed upon himself is meticulously fulfilled. Every day his ashes are gathered and he is judged and condemned to another cremation, and once again his ashes are scattered over the seven seas (see *comm. to* 21:10).]

Therefore the Psalmist deletes that statement from this psalm and substitutes a description of the humiliation which eventually came upon our persecutors.[1]

7. יְשׁוּעַת יִשְׂרָאֵל — *Israel's salvations.*

In Psalm 14, we read יְשׁוּעַת יִשְׂרָאֵל, *Israel's salvation*, in the singular form because that psalm speaks of one event: the redemption from the First (Babylonian) Exile. However, that redemption was not really a total one, for many people remained in the diaspora and the Second (Roman) Exile was already in the making. The return to Israel at that time was not a final rest, but a mere interlude.

The final redemption of the future will be a complete one, marking the end of all exiles. This redemption will put an end to the countless exiles and expulsions which the Jews have endured throughout history; the culmination of an ever-repeating, vicious cycle. Therefore, it is most appropriately described as *the* (many) *salvations of Israel (Chazah Zion).*

Our nation can merit a swift and early redemption in either of two ways: by virtue of exceptionally meritorious conduct, or by virtue of excessive sufferings, for the intensity of our pain can compensate for the lack of the exile's completion. Thus the Psalmist wishes, '*O that out of Zion would come the salvations* which are not caused by extra suffering but rather may be attributed to the merits *of Israel' (Panim Yofos).*

בְּשׁוּב אֱלֹהִים — *When God returns.*

Here *Israel's salvations* [plural] are many and complete, because they come about at the hands of אֱלֹהִים, indicating God as the *Dispenser of Strict Justice.* If Israel merits salvation by its good deeds, then this salvation will endure forever. However, in Psalm 14 we read בְּשׁוּב ה', *When HASHEM returns*, indicating that *God as the Dispenser of Mercy* took pity on them and redeemed them, although they did not deserve it. Such a redemption is incomplete and short-lived, merely יְשׁוּעַת יִשְׂרָאֵל an isolated instance of a single salvation of Israel *(Midbar Kedemos; Mikdash Me'at).*

יָגֵל יַעֲקֹב יִשְׂמַח יִשְׂרָאֵל —*Jacob will exult, Israel will rejoice.*

The name *Jacob* always describes the Jewish masses, the common-folk. However, *Israel* denotes the elite, the scholars and saints who guide the masses [see *comm.* to 14:7.] All of them together will rejoice at the final redemption *(Malbim).*

---

1. Ultimately, God rejected the proud tyrant Titus and humiliated him. The Talmud (*Gittin* 56b) relates that a great storm threatened Titus' ship as he sped back to Rome from Jerusalem. He roared, 'The God of the Jews has power only over the seas! Let Him challenge me on dry land, where I will surely vanquish him!'

A heavenly voice went forth, 'You wicked villain, I placed a tiny, insignificant creature in this world, the gnat. I will dispatch this weak insect to do battle with you on dry land!'

A gnat flew by, entered Titus' nose, penetrated his skull and pecked at his brain for seven years. The relentless pain was maddening. Once Titus passed by a blacksmith and the sound of the hammer crashing down on the anvil silenced the gnat. Henceforth, Titus had a blacksmith bang before him every day. If the smith was a gentile, he was paid for his work. If the smith was a Jew, Titus would say, 'You deserve no pay! Let it suffice that you have the pleasure of witnessing the humiliation of your enemy.'

This remedy helped for but thirty days. When Titus finally died after seven years of agony, they opened his head, releasing a giant gnat the size of a bird, armed with a sharp beak of copper and nails of iron.

54 מזמור נד

I n Psalm 52 we read of Doeg, an individual, who became corrupted
because he engaged in slander; in Psalm 54 we learn of an entire
community which was ruined because it engaged in talebearing.
Psalm 53 was placed between these two compositions because it
related to them both. It describes the נָבָל, the degraded man; who
blasphemes, There is no God!' Despite his vehement protestations of
innocence, the slanderer described in this psalm, personified by the
men of Ziph, is no better than the heretical נָבָל, for the Sages said, 'He
who slanders is considered as if he denied the existence of God'
(Baalei Bris Avraham).

The treachery of the Ziphites surpassed that of Doeg, for the
Ziphites, who were of the tribe of Judah, were David's own relatives.
Even Saul was amazed that the Ziphites would betray their kinsman
to a king from the tribe of Benjamin. But these treacherous men willingly sacrificed their integrity in the hopes of satisfying their greed
and ambition by currying favor with King Saul.

David was so depressed by their abominable conduct that he
employed special נְגִינת, musical instruments, (verse 1) to accompany
this psalm, in order to lift his spirits to a level of prophetic ecstasy
(Alshich).

לַמְנַצֵּחַ בִּנְגִינֹת מַשְׂכִּיל לְדָוִד: בְּבוֹא
הַזִּיפִים וַיֹּאמְרוּ לְשָׁאוּל הֲלֹא דָוִד
ג מִסְתַּתֵּר עִמָּנוּ: אֱלֹהִים בְּשִׁמְךָ הוֹשִׁיעֵנִי
ד וּבִגְבוּרָתְךָ תְדִינֵנִי: אֱלֹהִים שְׁמַע תְּפִלָּתִי
ה הַאֲזִינָה לְאִמְרֵי־פִי: כִּי זָרִים | קָמוּ עָלַי
וְעָרִיצִים בִּקְשׁוּ נַפְשִׁי לֹא שָׂמוּ אֱלֹהִים

---

1. מַשְׂכִּיל — *A Maskil* [lit. *instruction*].

This psalm of *instruction* teaches a vital lesson. Although David was in mortal danger as a result of the treachery of the Ziphites, he did not despair but prayed for Hashem's mercy in this apparently hopeless situation. This illustrates David's credo (*Berachos* 10a), 'Even when a lethal sword is poised at a person's throat, he should not refrain from beseeching God's mercy' (*Nora Tehillos*).

[David and his men escaped from Saul into the wilderness of Ziph. When the Ziphites discovered David's hideaway, they promptly sped to Saul's headquarters in Givah to inform him of David's exact location. They boasted proudly, *'Therefore, O King, according to your heart's desire to descend* (i.e. attack) *— descend; and our responsibility shall be to deliver him (David) into the hands of the King' (v.20)*]

Rabbi Yochanan says: They were called זִיפִים, *Ziphites*, because they *falsified* (מְזַיֵּיף) their words (*Sotah* 48b).

Maharsha (ibid.) explains that they lied by claiming that they could easily deliver David into Saul's hands, despite the fact that David was actually far removed from their grasp.

וַיֹּאמְרוּ לְשָׁאוּל — *And* [they] *said to Saul*.

Solomon said, *'If a ruler pays heed to lies, all his servants will be wicked'* (Prov. 29:12). So it was in Israel. When the Ziphites noticed that Saul was influenced by the slander he heard about David, they also felt encouraged to

betray him. Saul was eager to hear evil reports from others; for example, *'Doeg the Edomite came and told Saul* [slanderous reports]' (52:2), and Nabal also mocked David [and supported Saul (53:2).]. Observing this, the Ziphites did not hesitate to slander David to Saul, (*Midrash Shocher Tov*).

הֲלֹא דָוִד מִסְתַּתֵּר עִמָּנוּ — *Is not David in hiding among* [lit. *with*] *us?*

Eretz Hachaim notes that it would seem that they should have said, מִסְתַּתֵּר אֶצְלֵינוּ, *He hides near us*, because עִמָּנוּ, *with us*, implies that David and the Ziphites were hiding together.

He explains that the Ziphites were in fact saying to Saul, 'We tricked David by pretending that we too are your enemies. We purported to hide from you, so that David would feel secure among us.'

3. אֱלֹהִים בְּשִׁמְךָ הוֹשִׁיעֵנִי — *O God, save me by Your Name*

David said to the Holy One, Blessed be He, 'Master of the Universe, when an officer persecutes a man, the man can complain to the prefect. If the prefect persecutes him, he can complain to the Emperor. But if the Emperor persecutes a man, to whom can he complain? Saul is king. To whom shall I complain about him? I can complain only to You!' (*Midrash Shocher Tov*).

וּבִגְבוּרָתְךָ תְדִינֵנִי — *And by Your might vindicate me*.

'Treat me according to the dictates of

For the Conductor; with instrumental music, a Maskil to David

2 When the Ziphites came and said to Saul
'Is not David in hiding among us?'
3 O God, by Your Name save me,
and by Your might vindicate me.
4 O God, hear my prayer
give ear to the utterances of my mouth.
5 For strangers have risen up against me
and powerful men sought my soul.
They have not set God before themselves, Selah.

Your might (the Torah), for You have written therein: *You shall not deliver to his master a slave who escaped his master and came to you* [for refuge] (*Deut.* 23:16). If You display such concern for the slave who only yesterday served idols, then certainly You will care for me and guard me from Saul. For I am a prince, the son of a prince from the royal family of Judah!' (*Midrash Shocher Tov*).

4. אֱלֹהִים שְׁמַע תְּפִלָּתִי — *O God, hear my prayer.*

Radak and *Ibn Ezra* explain that the 'prayer' mentioned here is the inner, unspoken request of the heart.

The *Zohar (Parshas Metzora)* teaches that God rejects the prayers of those who spread evil tales. Therefore David asks God to hear his prayers but not those of the Ziphites, who are tainted by slander (*Dorash Moshe*).

הַאֲזִינָה לְאִמְרֵי פִי — *Give ear to the utterances of my mouth.*

'Please pay close attention to my words so that You can respond to my entreaty even before I voice the entire supplication (*Alshich*).

Doeg and the Ziphites came to Saul and he gave ear to their slander. I shall not go to Saul, but to You. Hear me, give ear unto me (*Midrash Shocher Tov*).

5. כִּי זָרִים קָמוּ עָלַי — *For strangers have risen up against me.*

Ibn Ezra and *Radak* identify these as the alien gentiles; *Metzudas David* maintains that the verse refers to the Ziphites, who estranged themselves from their relative, David, by supporting Saul, who was a stranger to them.

וְעָרִיצִים בִּקְשׁוּ נַפְשִׁי — *And powerful men sought my soul.*

This refers to Doeg and Achitophel. Whereas the Ziphites threatened only my body, they assaulted my soul, as well. Not only did then challenge me with weapons, but they attacked me with arguments from the Torah, claiming that, as a result of my sins, my soul would never merit the World to Come (*Chazah Zion*).

לֹא שָׂמוּ אֱלֹהִים לְנֶגְדָּם — *They have not set God before themselves.*

Their deeds are not inspired by a desire to please God (*Sforno*).

ו לְנֶגְדָּם סֶלָה: הִנֵּה אֱלֹהִים עֹזֵר לִי אֲדֹנָי

בְּסֹמְכֵי נַפְשִׁי: °יָשׁוּב הָרַע לְשֹׁרְרָי

ח בַּאֲמִתְּךָ הַצְמִיתֵם: בִּנְדָבָה אֶזְבְּחָה־לָּךְ

ט אוֹדֶה שִּׁמְךָ יהוה כִּי־טוֹב: כִּי מִכָּל־צָרָה

הִצִּילָנִי וּבְאֹיְבַי רָאֲתָה עֵינִי:

ו־ט   ז יָשִׁיב קרי

They curry favor with Saul because he is the king, ignoring God's promise that Saul will be replaced by a worthier monarch (*Vidal HaTzorfati*).

They fail to consider the warning contained in the Torah (*Deut.* 27:24), *Cursed be he who smites his friend in secret* [through slander]. Instead they rely on Saul's blessing to them: בְּרוּכִים אַתֶּם לַה׳, *Blessed be you unto HASHEM* (I *Sam.* 23:21). Obviously, Saul's blessing is useless if they are accursed by God (*Midrash Shocher Tov*).

6. הִנֵּה אֱלֹהִים עֹזֵר לִי —*Behold! God is my helper.*

Therefore, slander cannot harm me (*Radak*).

What was the outcome of the Ziphite's treachery? Saul and his army surrounded David in a trap from which there seemed no possible escape. Suddenly, however, a messenger appeared, summoning Saul to depart immediately to protect the land from a surprise Philistine invasion (I *Sam.* 23:27-28; see footnote to 18:3).

David declares that he recognizes that it was God Himself who rescued him from this death-trap by sending an angel to serve as the messenger (*Maharam Markado*).

אֲדֹנָי בְּסֹמְכֵי נַפְשִׁי — *My Lord is with supporters of my soul.*

David prays for the welfare and success of those who do not slander but support him (*Ibn Ezra*).

[Furthermore, David recognizes that any help he receives from men is actually a manifestation of Hashem's favor.]

7. יָשִׁיב הָרַע לְשֹׁרְרָי — *May He repay the evil to those who watch for me.*

The word is written (כְּתִיב) יָשׁוּב, *It* [the evil] *will return*, but it is read (קְרִי) יָשִׁיב, *He* [God] *will repay*, [i.e., cause to be returned.] David prayed: 'May the evil which they planned recoil upon them (יָשׁוּב) but let their punishment come in such a way that it is clearly an

⁶ *Behold! God is my helper,*
   my Lord is with supporters of my soul.
⁷ *May He repay the evil to those*
   who watch for me.
Because of Your truths cut them down!
⁸ *With a free-will offering I will sacrifice to You,*
   I will thank Your Name, HASHEM, *for it is good.*
⁹ *For from every distress has He rescued me,*
   and upon my foes has my eye looked.

act of divine retribution, for God Himself *will return* (יָשִׁיב) their evil to them' (*Hirsch*).

בַּאֲמִתְּךָ הַצְמִיתֵם — *Because of Your truths cut them down.*

It is true that You decreed that I will survive to replace Saul as king. Therefore, those who wish to interfere with Your solemn decree must be cut down and removed (*Radak*).

8. בִּנְדָבָה אֶזְבְּחָה לָּךְ — *With a free-will offering I will sacrifice to You.*

I cannot bring a קָרְבָּן תּוֹדָה, *a thanksgiving offering*, because that is appropriate where a dangerous situation has been resolved to the satisfaction of all involved. In this case, however, God is saddened because He must destroy those of His creatures who threaten me. Therefore, I will merely sacrifice a *free-will offering* to demonstrate my appreciation for my personal salvation (*Sforno*).

9. כִּי מִכָּל צָרָה הִצִּילָנִי — *For from every distress has He rescued me.*

[God has mercifully saved me from myriad misfortunes of which I will always remain unaware. For this, too, I must render Him thanks.]

וּבְאֹיְבַי רָאֲתָה עֵינִי — *And upon my foes has my eye looked.*

The Sages teach that the person who deserves salvation is granted the privilege of witnessing the downfall of his enemies, as when Israel saw the destruction of Egypt at the Red Sea. But he who is saved by the merits of others does not deserve this privilege. Therefore, Lot, who was saved by virtue of Abraham's merit, was forbidden to look back upon the destruction of Sodom.

David exults that he is privileged to witness his enemies' defeat because this indicates his righteousness (*Nava Tehillah*).

In the preceding Psalms, David recounts his early suffering at the hands of Saul, Doeg, and the Ziphites, malicious adversaries who were bent on his destruction. Nevertheless, the grief they caused David cannnot compare to the suffering inflicted by Achitophel, an intimate friend who later became his archenemy.

As Alshich (v. 13) observes, the pinprick inflicted by a friend is far more painful than the sword wound dealt by an enemy.

Late in David's life he was betrayed by Achitophel, the wisest sage of the realm, the brilliant strategist, the unerring statesman, who had skillfully guided the fortunes of David's monarchy throughout the most crucial period of his reign.

Their strong bond of friendship had been forged not only by political considerations, but also by spiritual communion. For David and Achitophel studied the Word of God together, sharing the secrets of the holy Torah.

How utterly bereft David was when Achitophel abruptly ruined this remarkable relationship by inciting David's son Absalom to launch an assassination plot against his father! Bitterly, David surveys the past and realizes too late, that Achitophel's 'friendship' had never been inspired by love or admiration. A selfish opportunist, he was motivated solely by envy and by a passion to ascend to the throne. Actually, Achitophel planned to depose Absalom in order to seize the crown for himself. [See Prefatory Remarks, Psalms 4 and 5].

Distraught and disillusioned, David flees Jerusalem before his foes. As he sinks into despair, he yearns to abandon the society of all men, for, whom can he now trust? If someone would but give me wings like the dove! I would fly off and find rest! (v. 7). Ultimately, however, David realizes his responsibility to remain at the head of his people, despite his personal anguish. He asks only for peace and for the eradication of chief enemy, Achitophel, who treacherously robbed him of life's most precious treasure: faithful friendship.

לַמְנַצֵּחַ בִּנְגִינֹת מַשְׂכִּיל לְדָוִד: הַאֲזִינָה
אֱלֹהִים תְּפִלָּתִי וְאַל־תִּתְעַלַּם מִתְּחִנָּתִי:
הַקְשִׁיבָה לִּי וַעֲנֵנִי אָרִיד בְּשִׂיחִי
וְאָהִימָה: מִקּוֹל אוֹיֵב מִפְּנֵי עָקַת רָשָׁע
כִּי־יָמִיטוּ עָלַי אָוֶן וּבְאַף יִשְׂטְמוּנִי: לִבִּי
יָחִיל בְּקִרְבִּי וְאֵימוֹת מָוֶת נָפְלוּ עָלָי:
יִרְאָה וָרַעַד יָבֹא בִי וַתְּכַסֵּנִי פַּלָּצוּת:

1. לַמְנַצֵּחַ בִּנְגִינֹת — *For the Conductor, with musical instruments.*

David composed this Psalm as he fled from Absalom his son [see 3:1] (*Maharam Markado*). As agony and despair threatened to envelop him, he employed cheerful *musical instruments* to dispel the gloom and to lift himself to the ecstatic level of Divine inspiration (*Alshich*).

2. הַאֲזִינָה אֱלֹהִים תְּפִלָּתִי — *Give ear, O God, to my prayer.*

Rav Yehuda bar Yitzchak taught that David had no greater friend than Achitophel who was the king's counselor (I Chronicles 27:33).

Rav Nachman taught that David was not afraid of any man except Achitophel. Hence David beseeched, *Give ear, O God, to my prayer.* The Holy One, Blessed be He, asked David: 'Haven't you said, "Though an army would besiege me, my heart would not fear"?' (27:3)?

David replied, 'Master of the Universe, give me such enemies of whom I can say, "I pursued my foes and overtook them and returned not until I had annihilated them" (18:38). This Achitophel is not such an enemy, for he is greater than I am!' (*Midrash Shocher Tov*).

וְאַל תִּתְעַלַּם מִתְּחִנָּתִי — *Do not disregard my pleas.*

When David heard that Achitophel was with Absalom and his conspirators, he pleaded (*II Samuel 15:31*), *Please HASHEM, turn the counsel of Achitophel into foolishness* (*Midrash Shocher Tov*).

3. אָרִיד בְּשִׂיחִי — *I lament as I speak.*

This translation, based on *Genesis 27:40*, follows *Rashi*, *Ibn Ezra*, and *Radak*. *Menachem*, however, relates אָרִיד to רָדָה *rule, dominate* as in *Genesis 1:28* and renders this phrase, *I control (my fate) with my words* (of prayer).

וְאָהִימָה — *And I moan.*

This alludes to the description of David's flight (*II Samuel 14:30*): *And David went up by the ascent of the Mount of Olives and wept as he went up, and he had his head covered and went barefoot, and all the people who were with him covered their heads [in mourning], and they ascended, weeping as they went up* (*Maharam Markado*).

4. מִקּוֹל אוֹיֵב — *At the shout* [lit. *voice*] *of the foe.*

Alshich explains that this alludes to the loud curses and threats which Shimi ben Gera hurled at David as the king fled before Absalom (*II Samuel 16:5-13*).

מִפְּנֵי עָקַת רָשָׁע — *On account of the oppression of the wicked.*

They not only curse me, but also they

LV

1-6

For the Conductor,
   with musical instruments, a Maskil by David.
² Give ear, O God, to my prayer,
   do not disregard my pleas.
³ Pay me heed and answer me.
   I lament as I speak, and I moan.
⁴ At the shout of the foe,
   on account of the oppression of the wicked,
for they accuse me of evil and passionately hate me.
⁵ My heart shudders within me,
   and the terrors of death have befallen me.
⁶ Fear and trembling penetrate me,
   and I am overcome with horror.

oppress me physically by pursuing me
(Kiflayim L'Tushiya).

כִּי יָמִיטוּ עָלַי אָוֶן — For they accuse me
[lit. they drop on me] of evil.

They claim that I desecrated the holy
Name of God by my sins and that the
scales of justice are tipped against me.
Accordingly, they dropped the balance
of the scales against me and declared me
completely guilty (Eretz Hachaim).

וּבְאַף יִשְׂטְמוּנִי — And passionately hate
me.

The people of Israel once wholeheartedly pledged their allegiance to me
and gladly accepted me as their king,
but today their love has changed to passionate hatred, and they have crowned
my son in my place (Radak).

According to Hirsch, יִשְׂטוֹם is related
to סָתוּם, locked up, and refers to hatred
previously concealed in the heart, but
now unleashed in its full fury.

5. לִבִּי יָחִיל בְּקִרְבִּי — My heart shudders
within me.

Even when no immediate danger
looms before my eyes, I am still uneasy.
Anxiety and fear of the unknown

agitate my spirit and give me no rest.
This is a signal of impending doom, as
the Talmud (Megillah 3a) says: Even
though his eyes do not see, his soul
senses calamity (Shaarei Chaim).

וְאֵימוֹת מָוֶת נָפְלוּ עָלָי — And the terrors of
death have befallen me.

Radak observes that the specter of
death loomed over David in particular
when Achitophel advised Absalom: 'Let
me now choose out twelve thousand
men and I will arise and pursue David
this night. And I will come upon him
while he is weary and weak-handed,
and I will make him afraid, and all the
people who are with him shall flee, and I
will smite only the king. I will bring
back all of the people to you and when
all have returned except the one man
whom you seek then all the people will
be in peace.' And this saying pleased
Absalom well and all the elders of Israel
(II Samuel 17:1-4).

6. יִרְאָה וָרַעַד יָבֹא בִי — Fear and
trembling penetrate me.

The vague anxiety of my heart (v. 5)
grows and increases (Shaarei Chaim),
until [mental] fear and [physical] trem-

ז וָאֹמַר מִי־יִתֶּן־לִי אֵבֶר כַּיּוֹנָה אָעוּפָה
ח וְאֶשְׁכֹּנָה: הִנֵּה אַרְחִיק נְדֹד אָלִין בַּמִּדְבָּר
ט סֶלָה: אָחִישָׁה מִפְלָט לִי מֵרוּחַ סֹעָה
י מִסָּעַר: בַּלַּע אֲדֹנָי פַּלַּג לְשׁוֹנָם כִּי־רָאִיתִי
יא חָמָס וְרִיב בָּעִיר: יוֹמָם וָלַיְלָה יְסוֹבְבֻהָ

---

bling become part of my very being (*Ibn Ezra*).

7. וָאֹמַר — *Then I said.*

[The terrible anguish within David's heart surges outward, until the bitterness bursts forth from his lips in this powerful plea.]

מִי יִתֵּן לִי אֵבֶר כַּיּוֹנָה — *If someone would but give me wings like the dove!*

Ibn Ezra suggests that David is familiar with *the dove* because it is synonymous with the carrier pigeon, which kings were accustomed to use for sending messages.

The *Midrash*, (*Bereishis Rabbah* 39:8) offers the explanation that all other birds, when they are exhausted, stop to rest on a boulder or a tree, but when the dove grows weary, it merely folds one wing to give it rest and continues to fly with the other wing.

'With wings like the dove', says David, 'I would flee from my pursuers and be assured of a successful escape' (*Sforno*).

אָעוּפָה וְאֶשְׁכֹּנָה — *[Then] I would fly off and find rest.*

I would fly until I found a secure haven, where I could finally rest from the fear and trembling which overcame me (*Radak*).

Norah Tehillos notes that David's words seem to be self-contradictory. If he *flew*, then he would not be at *rest*; and if he seeks *rest*, why does he ask to *fly*? Actually, this statement alludes to the *Midrash* cited above, which explains that even while the dove *flies* with one wing, it is at *rest* with the other.

8. הִנֵּה אַרְחִיק נְדֹד — *Behold, I would wander afar.*

I would make my way to some distant wilderness where there would be no possibility for my enemies to send spies to discover my whereabouts (*Sforno*).

אָלִין בַּמִּדְבָּר — *And [I would] dwell in the wilderness.*

[*Rambam* (*Hilchos Deos* 6:1) recommends this as the proper course of action for anyone who feels that civilization is a threat to both his body and his soul: Man's nature is that he is influenced by his environment and the society of people ... Therefore, if a man finds himself in a country whose inhabitants are evil, he must remove himself to a different land where righteous men dwell. If all countries are corrupt, as is the case in our times, then he should live all alone. If he is not allowed to live in isolation, then he must flee to the caves, the badlands, and the wilderness to escape the detrimental influence of the sinners.']

9. אָחִישָׁה מִפְלָט לִי — *I would speed myself to shelter.*

This alludes to the time when David was trapped by Saul in the wilderness of Maon. Scripture states (*I Samuel* 23:26), *And David made great haste to escape for fear of Saul, for Saul and his men encircled David and his men round about to seize them* (*Sforno*).

מֵרוּחַ סֹעָה — *From violent wind.*

The word סֹעָה is related to נֹסַע, *to journey*, suggesting that this wind travels great distances (*Menachem*).

The violent wind uproots mighty

⁷ *Then I said, 'If someone would but give me wings*
like the dove! I would fly off and find rest!
⁸ *Behold! I would wander afar,*
and dwell in the wilderness, Selah.
⁹ *'I would speed myself to shelter*
from violent wind, from tempest.'
¹⁰ *Consume, my Lord, and confuse their tongue,*
for I saw violence and strife in the city.
¹¹ *Day and night they encircle it upon its walls,*

trees and makes them 'travel' to a new position (*Rashi*).

This describes David's enemies, whose passionate hate resembles a violent storm [for they threaten to uproot him from his throne] (*Radak*).

10. בַּלַּע אֲדֹנָי — *Consume* [lit. *swallow up*], *my Lord.*

['May Achitophel and his henchmen who spout words of evil treachery against me be forced to *swallow up* their own words!']

פַּלַּג לְשׁוֹנָם — *And confuse* [lit. *divide*] *their tongue.*

Cast a spirit of dissension and discord among them, so that they will be split into many conflicting factions. Let them be paralyzed by dispute (*Radak; Sforno*).

[Indeed, David's wish was immediately fulfilled, for Chushai the Arkite (who secretly supported David) offered advice to Absalom which contradicted that of Achitophel. He claimed that it would be preferable to wait until a tremendous force of soldiers could be gathered, so that Absalom's massive army could overwhelm David's tiny force. *And Absalom and all the men of Israel said, 'The counsel of Chushai the Arkite is better than the counsel of Achitophel'; for HASHEM had ordained to defeat the good counsel of Achitophel so that HASHEM might bring evil upon Absalom (II Samuel 17:14).*

Furthermore, the counsel of Achitophel was literally *swallowed up* when he strangled himself and died in utter disgrace.]

כִּי רָאִיתִי חָמָס וְרִיב בָּעִיר — *For I saw violence and strife in the city.*

'Already I see that they are quarreling among themselves in *the city* of Jerusalem (*Radak*) concerning how they should share the spoils' (*Sforno*).

[The Psalmist stresses that the *strife* occurred in *the city* of Jerusalem, for such dissension is a radical departure from the placid nature of this center of שָׁלֵם (שָׁלוֹם) *Peace.* Elsewhere, David himself described Jerusalem as *The city where all of Israel become good friends* (122:3; *Yerushalmi, Chagiga* 3:6).]

This internal discord assures their ultimate downfall, for the Sages say (*Bamidbar Rabbah* 11:7): Even when men worship idols, if they act with peace and brotherhood, they will be spared the harsh sentence of strict justice. But if men are embroiled in feuds, then, even if they are righteous, they are doomed (*Tehillos Hashem*).

11. יְסוֹבְבֻהָ עַל חוֹמֹתֶיהָ — *Encircle it upon its walls.*

The Psalmist likens *the city* to a large circle. *Violence* and *strife* are on the circumference. Thereby, the wicked protect the inner core of *iniquity* and *mischief* which is at the heart of the city (*Ibn Ezra*).

יב עַל־חוֹמֹתֶיהָ וְאָוֶן וְעָמָל בְּקִרְבָּהּ: הַוּוֹת
בְּקִרְבָּהּ וְלֹא־יָמִישׁ מֵרְחֹבָהּ תֹּךְ וּמִרְמָה:
יג כִּי לֹא־אוֹיֵב יְחָרְפֵנִי וְאֶשָּׂא לֹא־מְשַׂנְאִי
יד עָלַי הִגְדִּיל וְאֶסָּתֵר מִמֶּנּוּ: וְאַתָּה אֱנוֹשׁ
טו כְּעֶרְכִּי אַלּוּפִי וּמְיֻדָּעִי: אֲשֶׁר יַחְדָּו נַמְתִּיק

12. הַוּוֹת בְּקִרְבָּהּ — *Treachery is within it.*

[The very essence of the city has become treachery. The lives of her citizens are dedicated to crime and guile.]

וְלֹא־יָמִישׁ מֵרְחֹבָהּ — *Never leaving its square.*

It is in the broad, main street of the city that all of Absalom's supporters gather to hatch their plots of *fraud and deception (Radak).*

[They openly engage in malicious conspiracy and make no attempt to conceal their shameful treachery. Similarly, a prophet of another era describes the decline of Jerusalem and laments (*Isaiah* 59:14), *Justice is turned away and righteousness stands far off, for truth has stumbled in her broad avenue and uprightness cannot enter.*]

תֹּךְ — *Fraud.*

This word is synonymous with מִרְמָה *deception;* they are also used together in 10:7. Literally, תֹּךְ (תּוֹךְ) means *inside,* and suggests that the deceitful man uses friendly words to camouflage the malice concealed inside his heart. This describes Absalom and his supporters, who originally disguised themeselves as admirers of David, in order to catch him unawares *(Radak).*

We also find this word used in connection with חָמָס, *violence* (see 72:14), for the ultimate purpose of this masquerade was to facilitate brutal plundering and looting *(Rashbam).*

13. כִּי לֹא אוֹיֵב יְחָרְפֵנִי וְאֶשָּׂא — *For no foe can revile me that I can endure.*

This translation follows *Rashi* David states that if any other than Achitophel had cursed and betrayed him, he would not have *endured* (i.e., overlooked) such calumny. However, at first David felt compelled to show Achitophel special consideration, despite his rages, for, David venerated him as an extraordinary scholar and teacher (*v.* 14).

Radak offers a totally different interpretation: David says, 'If any other foe had cursed me, I *would* have gallantly accepted his insults and ignored their vicious intent. But you, Achitophel, were לֹא אוֹיֵב, 'not a foe', but a trusted intimate. Now that you suddenly *revile me,* I am so utterly shocked by your betrayal that I cannot *endure it.'*

לֹא מְשַׂנְאִי עָלַי הִגְדִּיל וְאֶסָּתֵר מִמֶּנּוּ — *No enemy can grow so great against me that I be put in hiding from him.*

The translation follows *Rashi.* 'I would not cower or hide from any enemy, rather I would stand up and fight. Only you, Achitophel, did I avoid out of respect for your Torah scholarship.'

Radak offers a different interpretation: 'With a different enemy, who made his malice known, I would have protected myself or gone into hiding. But you, Achitophel, caught me completely by surprise!'

Alshich paraphrases, 'I could silently bear the curses of Shimi ben Gera, and I could calmly accept the threats of King Saul, who *made himself great against me.* Only your treachery, Achitophel, is too much for me to bear, — for the pin-

iniquity and mischief are within it.

¹² *Treachery is within it,*
    never leaving its square are fraud and deception.
¹³ *For no foe can revile me that I can endure,*
    no enemy can grow so great against me
  that I be put in hiding from him.
¹⁴ *But you are a man, of my measure,*
    my guide, and my intimate friend,
¹⁵ *With whom together we would share*
    sweet counsel,

---

prick inflicted by a friend is far more painful than the sword wound dealt by an enemy!'

14. וְאַתָּה אֱנוֹשׁ כְּעֶרְכִּי — *But you are a man of my measure.*

[David now explains why Achitophel differs from all other adversaries.] 'You are a great man whose stature is equal to my own. I always treated you as an equal, despite the fact that I am a king and you are a commoner' (Radak).

[*Midrash Shocher Tov* relates עֶרְכִּי to עוֹרֵךְ, *to place in order,* suggesting that Achitophel's academic role was to arrange Torah laws in proper order so as to facilitate David's program of studies.]

Alshich emphasizes that despite Achitophel's academic brilliance, he did not surpass David's scholastic achievements, for David was the greatest sage of his time and and an essential link in the chain of מְסוֹרָה, *Tradition,* which was transmitted from generation to generation. [See Introduction of *Rambam* to *Yad Hachazakah.*]

אַלּוּפִי — *My guide* [lit. *leader*].

'Although you, Achitophel, were only my equal and peer, I treated you as my superior, and as one who had authority over me' (Radak).

According to *Targum* and *Midrash Shocher Tov,* this is related to אלף, *to*

teach, implying, 'You were my mentor and guide in Torah studies.'

וּמְיֻדָּעִי — *And my intimate friend.*

'You were my closest confidante, the one with whom I shared my most intimate secrets' (Radak).

15. אֲשֶׁר יַחְדָּו נַמְתִּיק סוֹד — *With whom together we would share sweet counsel* [lit. *secret*].

Together we would delve into the intricacies of the Torah (Rashi).

Our relationship was idyllic, a model of sweet comradery and perfect trust (Sforno).

Moreover, no plan or counsel seemed *sweet* and acceptable to me until I consulted Achitophel and received his approval (Radak).

According to the Rabbis, David was particularly indebted to Achitophel for having instructed him on two occasions. Once, when Achitophel found David alone, engaged in Torah study, He asked, 'David why do you delve into Torah alone? Its wisdom will be revealed to you and endure only if you study, together with friends! Let us therefore take *sweet counsel* together and engage in Torah learning' (*Avos* 6:3; *Rashi* and *Mechzor Vitry,* ibid.; and *Kallah Rabbosi*). [The second instance in which Achitophel offered im-

סוֹד בְּבֵית אֱלֹהִים נְהַלֵּךְ בְּרָגֶשׁ:
טז ‏יְשִׁימוֹת | עָלֵימוֹ יַרְדּוּ שְׁאוֹל חַיִּים כִּי־
יַשִּׁיא מָוֶת קרי
יז רָעוֹת בִּמְגוּרָם בְּקִרְבָּם אֲנִי אֶל־אֱלֹהִים
יח אֶקְרָא וַיהוה יוֹשִׁיעֵנִי: עֶרֶב וָבֹקֶר

portant guidance to David is described below.]

בְּבֵית אֱלֹהִים נְהַלֵּךְ בְּרָגֶשׁ — *In the House of God we would walk with multitudes.*

The word רָגֶשׁ means *a great assemblage,* as in לָמָּה רָגְשׁוּ גוֹיִם, *Why do the nations gather?* (2:1). We would walk together to the House of God to study or pray (*Rashi; Radak*).

When a king goes out, he usually walks alone at the head of the royal procession, with his retinue following behind. However, David accorded Achitophel an unprecedented honor by allowing him to walk beside the king, as his equal. Achitophel 'repaid' this generosity by betraying David (*Alshich*).

The second significant recommendation which Achitophel made to David occurred when Achitophel found David going to the House of Prayer alone. He asked, 'Don't you realize that *amid a great company of people is the* [divine] *king's glory* (Proverbs 24:28)?' [God's honor is enhanced when a multitude of people pray in unison.]

Others translate רָגֶשׁ as *speed;* accordingly Achitophel said, 'When you go

to pray, go swiftly, like a man hastening after his sovereign.'

According to the variant version propounded by *Rashi* (Avos 6:3), once Achitophel found David entering the House of Study with an erect, military bearing [suggesting a trace of pride]. He admonished him, 'A person should enter the House of God with רָגֶשׁ *feelings of awe,* so that the fear of heaven might rest upon him when he studies.'[1]

16. יַשִּׁיא מָוֶת עָלֵימוֹ — *May He incite death against them.*

The translation follows *Rashi,* who relates it to הַנָּחָשׁ הִשִּׁיאַנִי, *the serpent incited me* (Genesis 3:13). [Although this phrase is written (כְּתִיב) as one word (ישימות), it is read (קְרִי) as two words (יַשִּׁיא מָוֶת).]

Ibn Ezra and *Radak* render יַשִּׁיא as command (see 89:23), which is also related to נָשָׁה, *to demand payment of a debt* (see *Exodus* 22:24), indicating: 'May God command the Angel of Death to demand that this villain pay his debt with his life.

An alternative interpretation in *Ibn Ezra* defines יַשִּׁיא as 'make them forget' (see *Genesis* 42:51; *Deuterony* 32:18),

1. If one learns one chapter, one halacha, one verse, one expression, or even one letter from his fellowman, he should treat him with esteem. This can be derived from the conduct of David, king of Israel, for he learned from Achitophel only two things, yet he called him his *master,* his *guide* and his *intimate friend.* A logical inference (*kal Va-chomer*) can be drawn: If David, king of Israel, (who learned only two things from Achitophel) called him *master, guide,* and *intimate friend,* then when someone learns from his fellow man one chapter, one halacha, one verse, one expression or even one letter, he has an even greater obligation to treat the teacher with respect (*Avos 6:3*).

Many commentaries puzzle over the 'logic' of this deduction. From David's example we know only that one should honor his teacher after learning *two things* from him. It has not yet been proven that one should accord his teacher respect after learning as little as *one letter* from him.

in the House of God we would walk
with multitudes.

¹⁶ May He incite death against them,
let them descend to the Lower World, alive,
for evil is in their dwelling and within them.
¹⁷ As for me, upon God shall I call,
and HASHEM will save me.

suggesting that the best deterrent against sin is constant fear of the day of death [see *Berachos* 5a.] Thus: Make these men oblivious to the specter of death, so that it should pounce on them suddenly and take them by surprise!

Malbim notes that this wish was soon fulfilled when Achitophel, (whose counsel had never before been rejected), suddenly found his advice ignored; he committed suicide rather than live on in shame.

יֵרְדוּ שְׁאוֹל חַיִּים — *Let them descend to the Lower World, alive.*

Let them die suddenly, without any previous warning. Let them not be sick before they depart; rather allow them to be robust and *alive* when they are abruptly swallowed up *(Radak).*

[This punishment fit Achitophel's crime perfectly, for the most painful aspect of his treachery was not the actual rebellion but the traumatic shock which David suffered at this sudden betrayal by his trusted companion.]

כִּי רָעוֹת בִּמְגוּרָם בְּקִרְבָּם — *For evil is in their dwelling and within them.*

This translation follows *Rashi* and *Targum.* However, *Radak* and *Ibn Ezra* render מְגוּרָם as *their place of assembly,* to signify: The evil plots which are within them (against David) are revealed when they all gather in their place of assembly in Jerusalem.

17. אֲנִי אֶל אֱלֹהִים אֶקְרָא — *As for me, upon God shall I call.*

When danger and suffering threaten me, I am prepared to accept the affliction graciously as just punishment for my sins. I call upon אֱלֹהִים, *the Divine Attribute of Strict Justice,* declaring that I recognize the equity of His verdict against me *(Tehillos Hashem).*

וַה׳ יוֹשִׁיעֵנִי — *And HASHEM will save me.*

This recognition of God's perfect justice is in itself a great merit, by virtue of which God softens the harsh sentence against me and treats me with

Meiri and Rabbi Chaim of Volozhin in *Ruach Chaim* resolve this problem with the perception that 'one letter' is no trifle, for every letter contains the entirety of the Torah, as each part of God's wisdom is a reflection of and a link to the whole body of sacred knowledge. However, 'one letter' has significance only if it is learned from a truly God-fearing man whose teachings are infused with the spirit of the entire Torah.

Achitophel had no fear of God. His lessons, despite their logic and intellectual appeal, were truly hollow, profane, and secular. The *Tanna* chooses his words with utmost care. From Achitophel, David learned שְׁנֵי דְבָרִים *two ideas,* rather than genuine Torah teachings; the word בִּלְבָד, *only,* implies that these teachings stood alone, totally divorced from the entire body of Torah wisdom. Nevertheless, David showed tremendous gratitude even for Achitophel's limited 'secular' advice. Thus a student should certainly venerate the person who links him to the entire Torah, albeit through the vehicle of a single letter!

וְצָהֳרַיִם אָשִׂיחָה וְאֶהֱמֶה וַיִּשְׁמַע קוֹלִי:
יט פָּדָה בְשָׁלוֹם נַפְשִׁי מִקְּרָב־לִי כִּי־בְרַבִּים

the compassionate name 'ה, *the Divine Attribute of Mercy (Tehillos Hashem)*.

18. עֶרֶב וָבֹקֶר וְצָהֳרַיִם אָשִׂיחָה וְאֶהֱמֶה — *Evening, morning, and noon [I] supplicate and I moan.*

These three periods of prayer correspond to the three times of day when the position of the sun changes most noticeably: in the evening the sun vanishes, at dawn it appears, at noon it reaches its zenith *(Radak)*.

[This serves as an inspiration. First, the sight of the ever-changing sun should teach man not to remain static and stagnant but to strive for self-improvement and self-transformation. Second, the inexorable passage of time and the change of seasons should heighten man's awareness and appreciation of his Creator, who is the Prime Force behind this constant movement, although He Himself never changes.][1]

The *Kuzari* (3:5) describes the significance of the prescribed times of prayer: The three times of daily prayer are the real produce of the day and night; they are the spiritual center of a man's time, while the other hours serve merely as the path which leads to this center. Man eagerly anticipates the approach of this time, for during prayer he resembles the spiritual, celestial beings and removes himself from mere animal existence.

Prayer sustains the soul, just as food nourishes the body. The blessed influence of one prayer endures until the time of the next, just as the strength derived from the morning meal lasts until dinner. The further the soul is removed from the time of prayer, the more it is darkened by coming into contact with the mundane world.

The great Kabbalist, *Rabbi Menachem Azarya of Pano* makes a calculation that relates David's own prayers to his role as the spiritual heir of Adam [see *Overview*]: *Adam lived to be 930 years of age (Genesis 5:5).* After his sin, he dedicated his life to repentance, engaging in prayer at the three designated times, עֶרֶב וָבֹקֶר וְצָהֳרַיִם, *evening, morning, and noon.* These three words have the numerical value of 930. He also engaged in *fasting,* תַּעֲנִית which also has the numerical value of 930.

19. פָּדָה בְשָׁלוֹם נַפְשִׁי — *He redeemed my soul in* [lit. *with*] *peace.*

In the merit of my incessant daily prayer (v. 18), HASHEM redeemed me from Absalom long before the decisive encounter on the battlefield. While peace still reigned, before the hostilities

---

1. From this verse, the Rabbis learn that a person should not pray more than three times a day. The Emperor Antoninus once asked Rabbi Judah the Prince, 'May one pray continually?'

'No', the Rabbi replied, 'for one who acts in this manner will come to treat God's presence with levity.' The Emperor refused to accept this answer [convinced that more frequent prayer was preferable].

The next day, the holy Rabbi arose early and stood before the monarch shouting, 'Hail Caesar!' After a brief interval he approached again, proclaiming, 'A salute to the Emperor!' Next he declared, 'Peace to you, O king!'

The Emperor was very annoyed because these constant salutations seemed ludicrous. He said, 'Rabbi, you are disgracing the royal name!'

Rabbi Judah replied, 'Listen to your own words! You are merely a mortal king of flesh and blood and yet you feel that constant praise to your name is a mockery, rather than an honor. To an even greater extent would constant prayer be a ridiculous show before the Master of the Universe!' *(Tanchuma, Mikeitz 9)*

¹⁸ *Evening, morning, and noon I supplicate*
and moan — and He hears my voice.
¹⁹ *He redeemed my soul in peace from battles*
drawing near me,
for the sake of masses who were with me.

actually began, God had already prepared my victory and salvation (*Alshich*).

Tehillos Hashem suggests that the Psalmist is referring to David's last blessing to Absalom, which proved to be a fatal curse. The *Talmud (Berachos 64a)* states: He who takes leave of his friend should wish him לֵךְ לְשָׁלוֹם, *Go on to peace'* [which implies that he has a long life of accomplishment still ahead of him] and not לֵךְ בְּשָׁלוֹם, *Go with peace'* [which implies that he has already acquired peace and fulfillment and therefore no longer needs to continue his life]. This lesson may be learned from David who said to Absalom, לֵךְ בְּשָׁלוֹם, *go with peace'* (II *Samuel* 15:9), and Absalom was killed.'

When David bid Absalom farewell, he had no idea of his son's plotplot. David innocently believed that Absalom's purpose in going to Hebron was to offer his annual Nazirite sacrifice to God (II *Samuel* 15:7-8). In truth, Absalom went to Hebron in order to rally his conspirators and begin his revolt against his father. Although David was caught unprepared, God was not! God put into David's mouth the fatal words לֵךְ בְּשָׁלוֹם *Go with peace*, which sealed Absalom's doom. Therefore, David gives thanks here, *He redeemed my soul* [by causing me to say, 'Go בְּשָׁלוֹם] *with peace.'*

מִקְּרָב לִי — *From battles drawing near me.*

The word קְרָב means *battle (Radak).* [It also means *close, near,* implying fighting at close range in hand-to-hand combat.] God prevented such a fierce

battle from *drawing near* to harm me, *(Ibn Ezra)* and redeemed me even before the battle began *(Alshich).*

כִּי בְרַבִּים הָיוּ עִמָּדִי — *For the sake of masses who were with me.*

This translation follows *Rashi,* who explains that David attributes his ultimate victory to the prayers of the masses who petitioned God on his behalf.

[In truth, the *masses* of Israel and their leaders seemed to support Absalom. Nevertheless, the Rabbis note (*Yerushalmi, Sotah* 1:8), that the followers of Absalom grew disillusioned with their leader's arrogance and lack of sympathy. They secretly began to sympathize with David, praying, 'May we fall into the hands of David and not he into ours, because if we fall into David's, he will surely have mercy on us, but if he falls into our hands, we will not (be allowed to) show him any mercy!

Perhaps this explains the usage of the word בְרַבִּים (literally, *within the masses*), rather than simply רַבִּים, *the masses,* because ostensibly the masses were *not* with David. However, 'within them', i.e., deep in their hearts, they prayed secretly for David.]

Our translation, which follows *Rashi,* is supported by *Berachos* 8a, which derives from here that the prayers of the masses are never rejected by God.

Radak, however, was troubled by the fact that the masses were overtly hostile to David, differs with *Rashi* and translates, *from the masses who were against me.*

Midrash Shocher Tov, following the

כ הָיוּ עִמָּדִי: יִשְׁמַע | אֵל | וְיַעֲנֵם וְיֹשֵׁב קֶדֶם
סֶלָה אֲשֶׁר אֵין חֲלִיפוֹת לָמוֹ וְלֹא יָרְאוּ
כא אֱלֹהִים: שָׁלַח יָדָיו בִּשְׁלֹמָיו חִלֵּל בְּרִיתוֹ:
כב חָלְקוּ | מַחֲמָאֹת פִּיו וּקְרָב־לִבּוֹ רַכּוּ
כג דְבָרָיו מִשֶּׁמֶן וְהֵמָּה פְּתִחוֹת: הַשְׁלֵךְ עַל־

translation of *Rashi*, interprets this verse in a mystical vein, as an allusion to the never-ending battle of daily life. When a person sins, he creates evil forces which literally saturate the atmosphere around him. These detrimental forces seek to harm the sinner who created them, yet God, in His mercy, provides salvation. Every good deed which man performs brings even greater 'masses of angels', i.e., good influences and positive forces, into the world; they overwhelm the evil and *redeem the soul with peace.*

20. יִשְׁמַע אֵל וְיַעֲנֵם — *May God hear and answer them.*

[This plea is a direct continuation of the preceding verse.] According to *Rashi* this verse means: May God hear the prayers of the masses who sympathize with me and answer them. However, *Radak*, who understands the previous verse to mean that the masses were against David, relates יַעֲנֵם to עִנּוּי, *suffering*, rather than to עָנָה, *answering*, translating: *May God hear me and cause them* [the masses] *to suffer.*

וְיֹשֵׁב קֶדֶם סֶלָה — *He who is enthroned from days of old, Selah.*

Your existence, O God, preceded that of all Your creations, for You are enthroned from the dawn of the world. Since, Your strength undoubtedly surpasses that of any creature, You have the power to humble the wicked (*Radak*).

Targum translates *Selah* as *forever*; thus the word serves to emphasize God's eternal existence [see 3:3].

אֲשֶׁר אֵין חֲלִיפוֹת לָמוֹ — *Against those who ignore their own demise* [lit. *transfer.*]

These are the wicked, who deem themselves immortal and never consider the day of death, when they will be 'transferred' from the living to the dead (*Rashi*).

Neither do they fear that their good fortune may be 'transferred' to bad (*Ibn Ezra*).

Therefore, they stubbornly refuse to repent and 'transform' their ways (*Sforno*).

Radak, however, interprets these words as a continuation of the description of God, *Who is enthroned from days of old*. It is He Who *ignores* the specter of *demise* or *transformation*.

וְלֹא יָרְאוּ אֱלֹהִים — *And fear not God.*

Since good fortune persistently smiles upon these wicked men, they have no fear of אֱלֹהִים, *the Enforcer of Strict Justice.*

21. שָׁלַח יָדָיו בִּשְׁלֹמָיו — *He stretched out* [lit. *sent forth*] *his hands against his peaceful ones.*

This refers to Achitophel, for he attempted to harm David who trusted him implicitly and who desired to live in peace and harmony with him (*Rashi; Radak*).

[The term שְׁלֹמָיו fits David perfectly, because he was the quintessence of peace. The *Midrash* (*Bamidbar Rabbah* 11:7) states that the blessing, *And may He give you peace* (Numbers 6:26) refers to the kingship of the House of David, which is the epitome of peace.]

²⁰ *May God hear and answer them* —
  He Who is enthroned from days of old, Selah —
*against those who ignore their own demise
  and fear not God.*
²¹ *He stretched out his hands against His peaceful ones,
  he profaned his covenant.*
²² *Smoother than butter were the words of his mouth,
  but his heart was at war;*
*his words were softer than oil,
  yet they were curses.*
²³ *Cast upon HASHEM your burden*

חִלֵּל בְּרִיתוֹ — *He profaned his covenant.*
Achitophel contemptuously broke his pact of friendship with David (*Radak*).

22. חָלְקוּ מַחֲמָאֹת פִּיו — *Smoother than butter were the words of his mouth.*

David now contemplates the polished phrases of Achitophel and realizes, in retrospect, that the convincing words of this treacherous counselor were no more than deceitful 'smooth talk' designed to cause David to relax his guard (*Radak*).

וּקְרָב לִבּוֹ — *But his heart was at war* [lit. *battle*].

When Achitoplel finally revealed his battle-plan to pursue David immediately with 12,000 men and to capture the weak and exhausted king, his logical, convincing strategy seemed flawless, an operation as 'smooth as butter.' It was universally acclaimed: *And the plan found favor in the eyes of Absalom and in the eyes of all the Elders of Israel* (II Samuel 17:4).

When David saw that everyone was pleased with Achitophel's strategy, he was terrified. But the Holy One, Blessed be He, said to him, 'Fear not, for I am with you!' (*Midrash Shocher Tov*).

Words of peace flowed smoothly from his lips, but his heart planned a war (*Radak*).

רַכּוּ דְבָרָיו מִשֶּׁמֶן — *His words were softer than oil.*

[Butter generally smoothes over the outer surface, whereas oil is used to penetrate into the pores of the skin, to saturate and thoroughly soften it. Achitophel hoped that his reassuring words would be not only *smoother than butter*, but also *softer than oil*. Achitophel hoped to penetrate and to soften David's heart so that later he could stab it with a dagger.]

וְהֵמָּה פְתִחוֹת — *Yet they were curses.*

The translation follows *Rashi*. However, *Targum, Menachem,* and *Ibn Ezra* render this as *a sharpened, lethal dagger* called פְּתִיחוֹת [literally, *open ones*] because it is open, unsheathed, and prepared for the kill.

23. הַשְׁלֵךְ עַל ה' יְהָבְךָ — *Cast upon HASHEM your burden.*

Sforno and *Alshich* explain that whenever David began to suspect that a conspiracy was forming against him, Achitophel would attempt to drive away his misgivings with 'smooth words' of faith. 'Dismiss every fear from your mind;' he would say, '*cast your burden* of anxiety *upon HASHEM,* who will surely protect you.'

Although this credo is very true, Achitophel did not himself believe it; he

יְהוָה ׀ יְהָבְךָ וְהוּא יְכַלְכְּלֶךָ לֹא־יִתֵּן
כד לְעוֹלָם מוֹט לַצַּדִּיק: וְאַתָּה אֱלֹהִים ׀
תּוֹרִדֵם לִבְאֵר שַׁחַת אַנְשֵׁי דָמִים וּמִרְמָה
לֹא־יֶחֱצוּ יְמֵיהֶם וַאֲנִי אֶבְטַח־בָּךְ:

offered this advice only to deceive the king *(Norah Tehillos).*

According to *Rashi,* the Holy Spirit is speaking to David at the conclusion of this doleful and depressing Psalm, dedicated to David's disillusionment with man. The hopeful message is clear: 'Even if every man on earth betrays you, you can always place your trust in God!.'

Radak adds that David now transmits this encouraging message to all other pious men.

Midrash Shocher Tov observes: When a mortal who has a patron goes to him for the first time, the patron receives him; the second time, he also receives him; the third time, he does not welcome him personally; and the fourth time, he cannot spare a moment for him. Not so the Holy One, Blessed be He; every time you impose yourself upon Him, He receives you personally. Hence, *Cast upon* HASHEM *your burden and He will sustain you.*[1]

וְהוּא יְכַלְכְּלֶךָ — *And he will sustain you.*

[The word כַּלְכָּלָה is a repetitious form of כָּל, *everything.* It implies that not only will God supply פַּרְנָסָה, *livelihood,* i.e., the basic requirements of life, but He will also generously provide everything a person needs.]

לֹא יִתֵּן לְעוֹלָם מוֹט לַצַּדִּיק — *He will never allow faltering of the righteous.*

[Not only does God sustain the body, He also provides for the soul. Even when the righteous man is pursued and harassed, God instills within him the spiritual fortitude to overcome every obstacle and to retain his faith.

Thus, David consoles his wounded soul: 'Although I have been bitterly disappointed by men, I am confident that God will never disappoint me.']

24. וְאַתָּה אֱלֹהִים תּוֹרִדֵם לִבְאֵר שַׁחַת — *But You, O God, shall lower them into the well of destruction.*

[Whereas God invites the righteous to draw near to Him and to cast their burdens upon Him, he utterly despises the wicked and casts them away to the

1. The *Dubno Maggid* illustrates our verse with a parable: A weary tramp was walking on the road, carrying his heavy pack. A wagon driver passed by and offered him a lift, which was eagerly accepted. After traveling a while, the wagon driver noticed that his passenger still kept his heavy load on his shoulders, even though there was plenty of empty space in the wagon. Upon the driver's inquiry, the considerate tramp explained, 'I appreciate your kindness, but really it's enough that you are carrying me on your wagon; should I bother you to carry my load as well?'

'Fool', exclaimed the driver, 'don't you realize that if I am carrying you, I am also carrying your load?'

So, too, many people spend their entire lives bent under the tremendous burden of providing themselves with a livelihood. Of course, they believe in God, but they are satisfied with His generosity in providing life and health. How can they bother Him to sustain them financially as well?

They fail to realize that the Creator who maintains the life of His creatures also provides their livelihood. Man's sole responsibility is to remember that he himself does not 'make a living' he merely 'takes a living' from God. Therefore, *Cast upon* HASHEM *your burden and He will sustain you.*

and He will sustain you,
He will never allow
the faltering of the righteous.
24 But You, O God, shall lower them
into the well of destruction,
men of bloodshed and deceit shall not live out
half their days;
but as for me, I will trust in You.

place furthest removed from His Presence, the *well of destruction* i.e., Gehinnom.]

Hirsch notes that David does not call it בּוֹר שַׁחַת, *the pit of destruction*, but בְּאֵר שַׁחַת, *the well of destruction*. A pit is a receptacle which passively collects water from an outside source, it symbolizes the followers who only take orders. A well is a source from which waters spring, signifying the leader who initiates schemes and strategies. Achitophel and Doeg were leaders, initiators of evil, rather than mere imitators. Each one resembled a well, constantly spewing forth malice and hate! Eventually, they were both undone by their own devices of destruction.

אַנְשֵׁי דָמִים וּמִרְמָה — *Men of bloodshed and deceit.*

[These men were intent on shedding innocent blood and did not hesitate to use devious means to achieve their ends.]

לֹא יֶחֱצוּ יְמֵיהֶם — [They] *shall not live out half their days.*

Rabbi Yochanan said that Doeg and Achitophel never met each other, Doeg lived during the reign of Saul [when David was in his late twenties

(*Maharsha*)] and Achitophel lived during the reign of David.

[David lived to the age of seventy, and he reigned forty years. Absalom and Achitophel rebelled when David was sixty-five.]

These men did not live out even half of a lifetime [a normal lifespan is seventy years, see 90:10] Doeg lived to be no more than thirty-four years old, and Achitophel lived to be no more than thirty-three. [This demonstrates God's kindness to David, for had his adversaries been contemporaries, David could not have survived their combined onslaught (*Sanhedrin* 106b; *Maharsha*).]

וַאֲנִי אֶבְטַח בָּךְ — *But as for me, I will trust in You.*

I trust that You will save me from my enemies (*Sforno*).

Furthermore, I am confident that just as You destroyed the bodies of my enemies in this world, You will consume their souls in the lower world of Gehinnom, *the well of destruction* (*Radak*).

And, although each is doomed to live less than half of a lifetime, I am confident that You will fulfill the number of *my days*, (*Ibn Ezra*) [indeed, David lived a full seventy years] and establish my kingdom firmly for all time.

We first read of David's sojourn in the court of the Philistine king, Achish of Gath, in Psalm 34. There, speaking in retrospect, David exults over his miraculous escape from the Philistines. Here, however, his mood is somber as he records his initial shock and dismay upon realizing the terrible danger which faced him so unexpectedly in Achish's palace.

Hounded by Saul and his army, the fugitive could no longer evade his relentlessly determined pursuers. He was forced to flee to a hostile foreign kingdom in the hope that perhaps these gentiles would afford him the haven that was tragically unavailable to him in his own homeland.

How bitter was David's disappointment when he was recognized by the king's bodyguard, who was none other than the giant Yishbi, the brother of Goliath, David's most famous victim! David seemed to be on the very brink of death as Yishbi stormed before Achish and demanded the right to avenge the blood of his slain brother.

The holy spirit which enveloped David at that moment stirred him not only to bemoan his personal grief, but also to relate the woeful tale of his persecuted people, who were also fated to wander from land to land as hunted refugees. In this sense both the king and his people truly resembled יוֹנַת אֵלֶם רְחֹקִים, A silenced dove in wandering, whose salvation is far away (v.1).

א לַמְנַצֵּחַ ׀ עַל־יוֹנַת אֵלֶם רְחֹקִים לְדָוִד
ב מִכְתָּם בֶּאֱחֹז אֹתוֹ פְלִשְׁתִּים בְּגַת: חָנֵּנִי
אֱלֹהִים כִּי־שְׁאָפַנִי אֱנוֹשׁ כָּל־הַיּוֹם לֹחֵם
ג יִלְחָצֵנִי: שָׁאֲפוּ שׁוֹרְרַי כָּל־הַיּוֹם כִּי־רַבִּים

1. יוֹנַת אֵלֶם רְחֹקִים — *Upon* Yonas Eilem Rechokim.

Literally, this means *the silenced dove of those that are far away;* it refers to David, who was in the territory of the Philistines, outside of Israel, his native land. Threatened by Goliath's hostile brother Yishbi, David was helpless as a trapped dove, whose song is muted by fear (*Rashi*).

David saved himself by pretending to be a madman who could not possibly be the hero of Israel [See *comm.* to 34:1]. Thus, his characteristically intelligent speech became *silenced;* his hysterical raving resembled the cooing of the dove, which the prophet considers as a silly bird, as in the verse, כְּיוֹנָה פוֹתָה אֵין לֵב, *like a foolish dove without understanding* (Hosea 7:11) (*Radak*).

Meiri identifies the *Yonas Eilem Rechokim* as a musical instrument which reproduces the cooing of the dove. *Meiri* notes that the dove has two different calls. When this gentle bird is frightened, it repeats its moaning cry frantically, without respite. However, when at ease, the dove coos only at long intervals leaving a *silent* (אֵלֶם) pause between the cries which are *distant* (רְחֹקִים) from each other. [Thus, the musical accompaniment of this psalm underscores its theme, to suggest that David resembles a dove who is silenced for long intervals.]

The positioning of this psalm after the preceding one serves to emphsaize its theme. In the preceding psalm, David laments that the society in which he lives is corrupt and that no man can be trusted. Therefore, he yearns to abandon his land, saying *'O that I would have wings like the dove, then I would fly away and find a place of rest'* (55:7).

Now that sheer desperation has forced David to 'sprout' the wings of a *dove* and flee to Gath, he finds that there, too, he is betrayed and realizes that he resembles a helpless *silenced dove* (*Norah Tehillos; Tehillas Hashem*).

Even in the midst of this deep personal tragedy, David's thoughts transcended his individual situation to encompass the Jews who would be forced into exile throughout the centuries, for Israel resembles a flock of *doves* spread out רְחֹקִים, *far away* (*Tehillas Hashem*).

לְדָוִד מִכְתָּם — *By David, a* Michtam.

[See *comm.* to 16:1 for full discussion of the various definitions of *Michtam;* according to one opinion, it is a combination of two words, מָךְ and תָּם as follows:]

Midrash Shocher Tov comments that the threats of Goliath's brother rendered David אֵלֶם, *silent,* for he realized that he was helpless, since his own warriors were רְחֹקִים, *far away.* As a result of this sobering experience, David truly became מָךְ, *humble,* and תָּם, *perfect.*

בֶּאֱחֹז אֹתוֹ פְלִשְׁתִּים בְּגַת — *When Philistines seized him in Gath.*

As explained in the Prefatory Remarks, most commentaries attribute this psalm to David's first encounter with Achish in Gath (I *Samuel* 21:11-16). However, *Be'er Avraham* maintains that it refers to David's second encounter with Achish.

When Saul first began to persecute him, David fled to Achish for the first time all alone. Many months later, weary of running from Saul, David again attempted to escape from the jealous king. Accompanied by six hundred great warriors and their

56
1-3

F*or the Conductor,*
    upon Yonas Eilem Rechokim,
By David, a Michtam
    when Philistines seized him in Gath.
² *Favor me, O God,*
    for men yearn to swallow me,
Every day
    the warrior oppresses me.
³ *Every day my watchful foes*
    aspire to swallow me,

---

families, David pretended that he wished to enter into an alliance with Achish. This ruse enabled David to dwell safely in Philistia for more than four months (*I Samuel* 27).

Achish was firmly convinced that David despised his own people, Israel, and considered David to be a loyal vassal. David became filled with horror and dismay, however, when Achish appointed him to serve as his personal aide and bodyguard during a military campaign against Israel (*I Samuel* 28:1-2). David was trapped; he could never consent to wage war against his own people, but to refuse would mean certain death.

At that moment of crisis, God sent salvation: Achish's own generals refused to trust David, the Hebrew alien, to join them in their assaults against the Hebrew people (*I Samuel* 29:3-10). David now praises God for his miraculous escape.

2. חָנֵּנִי אֱלֹהִים — *Favor me, O God.*

Let Me find favor in Your eyes even though I have been forced to abandon Israel, Your favored country, and to flee to Philistia, a land which You despise (*Sforno*).

כִּי שְׁאָפַנִי אֱנוֹשׁ — *For men* [lit. *man*] *yearn to swallow me.*

I abandoned the Holy Land only under duress, when it became impossible for me to escape Saul's

relentless pursuit (*Sforno*). Even here in Philistia, Achish and his men are eager to destroy me (*Radak*).

כָּל הַיּוֹם לֹחֵם יִלְחָצֵנִי — *Every day the warrior oppresses me.*

Saul's determination and persistence were incredible for he did not interrupt his pursuit of David even for a moment (*Radak; Sforno*).

3. שָׁאֲפוּ שׁוֹרְרַי כָּל הַיּוֹם — *Every day my watchful foes aspire to swallow me.*

Wherever I turn, in Israel or in foreign lands, I am confronted by *watchful foes* who do not let me out of their sight (*Radak*).

Norah Tehillos and *Yaavetz Hadoresh* render שׁוֹרְרַי as *my singers.* David traces the source of his woes back to the people who sang his praises after his triumph over Goliath by saying, '*Saul has slain his thousands and David his ten thousands.*' [Immediately, *Saul was very angry and the saying sorely displeased him . . . and Saul viewed David with enmity from that day onwards* (*I Samuel* 18:7-9).

It was this very song which endangered him when he fled to Achish! *And the servants of Achish said to him, 'Is this not David the King of the land? Did they not sing of him to one another in dances, saying, "Saul has slain his thousands and David his ten thousands"?'* (*I Samuel* 21:12) Achish's generals repeated this (ibid. 29:5) when

ד לֹחֲמִים לִי מָרוֹם: יוֹם אִירָא אֲנִי אֵלֶיךָ

ה אֶבְטָח: בֵּאלֹהִים אֲהַלֵּל דְּבָרוֹ בֵּאלֹהִים

בָּטַחְתִּי לֹא אִירָא מַה־יַּעֲשֶׂה בָשָׂר לִי:

ו כָּל־הַיּוֹם דְּבָרַי יְעַצֵּבוּ עָלַי כָּל־מַחְשְׁבֹתָם

לָרָע ז °יָצֻפִּינוּ יָגוּרוּ | °יִצְפּוֹנוּ הֵמָּה עֲקֵבַי יִשְׁמֹרוּ

---

they expressed their suspicions about David's facade of apparent loyalty (Be'er Avraham).

כִּי רַבִּים לֹחֲמִים לִי מָרוֹם — *For many war with me, O Most High!*

Although many yearn to swallow me, their aspirations will never be fulfilled, for You, O Most High, do battle for me (Ibn Ezra).

The words לֹחֲמִים לִי may also be translated: *they fight for me, on my behalf*, referring to the celestial (מָרוֹם) angels whom God has commanded to protect David from his foes (Yaavetz HaDoresh).

4. יוֹם אִירָא אֲנִי אֵלֶיךָ — *The day when I fear - I will trust in You.*

Midrash Shocher Tov (Psalm 34) comments: The Philistines and Goliath's brother demanded of Achish, 'Let us kill this man who killed our brother!'

Achish replied, 'Didn't David kill your brother in a fair fight? Had your brother Goliath killed David, instead, wouldn't that also have been in a fair fight? Furthermore, Goliath stipulated "If he will be able to battle me, then we will all be your servants" '(I Samuel 17:9).

Upon hearing this, the Philistines said to Achish, 'If this is true, get up from your throne, for your kingship rightfully belongs to David! In fact, since David is a subject of Saul, aren't we actually all servants of Saul?' Thus, they confounded Achish.

At that instant, David became afraid; but nevertheless, he declared, 'On the day when I fear I will trust in You.' Then God saved him by giving him a touch of madness, which disguised his identity.

5. בֵּאלֹהִים אֲהַלֵּל דְּבָרוֹ — *In God['s strict justice]—I [still] praise His word.*

Even when He acts towards me as אֱלֹהִים, *the Dispenser of Strict Justice*, I appreciate His verdict and accept it gladly (Rashi) [see v. 11]. I rejoice in affliction, for thus do I repay the debt incurred through my sin (Mikdash Me'at).

Some interpret this as an oath: 'By God! I swear to praise Him under all circumstances' (Yaavetz HaDoresh; Ibn Yachya).

בֵּאלֹהִים בָּטַחְתִּי לֹא אִירָא — *In God['s strict justice] I have trusted.*

God promised me through the prophet Samuel that I would someday be king. Since that promise was made, I have suffered terribly, yet my faith in God's word remains unshaken, for I console myself, saying: 'Just as אֱלֹהִים strictly and persistently adheres to His rules of Justice, so will He be unyielding in fulfilling His promise to me' (Radak).

כָּל הַיּוֹם דְּבָרַי יְעַצֵּבוּ — *Every day they turn my words sorrowful.*

Their relentless pursuit has transformed my normal conversation into an endless stream of sorrowful pleas for salvation (Rashi).

According to *Ibn Ezra* and *Radak*, it is the words of David which bring sorrow to his foes. David says: 'Because דְּבָרַי, *my words*, never fail to reiterate my faith in דְּבָרוֹ, *His word* (v. 5) [i.e., His promise to make me king], my enemies are sad.'

Alshich perceives in this the true cause for David's grave concern when he raved madly before Achish. As a man of deep faith, David realized that so long as he trained his thoughts upon God and incessantly expressed His

For many war with me,
O Most High!
4 The day when I fear —
I will trust in You.
5 In God's strict justice —
I still praise His word,
In God's strict justice I have trusted,
I shall not fear, what can flesh do to me?
6 Every day they turn my words sorrowful,
about me all their thoughts are for evil.
7 They assemble,
they lie in ambush,
they watch my every tread

praises, no man could possibly harm him. As he declared in the previous verse: 'In God... I praise His word', therefore, 'In God, I trusted, I shall not fear'; for the man totally involved in praising God can boast, 'What can flesh do to me?'

Now David laments that the very vehicle of his escape could become his undoing. Since his mind and mouth were filled with thoughts and words of madness, he lost his greatest merit for salvation. Thus instead of joyous praise, they bring sorrow to my words, by forcing me to feign madness.

עָלַי כָּל מַחְשְׁבֹתָם לָרָע — About me all their thoughts are for evil.

In the opinion of Saul and his cohorts, all of my words and my aspirations to be king are motivated exclusively by evil intentions (Tehillas Hashem).

Alshich interprets these words as a reference to Achish's hostile bodyguard. When David feigned madness, the king was inclined to fall for the ruse, but these sceptical men remained unconvinced. They were determined to prove that David's sole intention was to perpetrate an evil fraud.

According to Be'er Avraham, this refers to the Philistine generals who suspected David of evil in his alliance with Achish.

7. יָגוּרוּ — They assemble.
[This refers to Saul's three thousand men who searched for David.]

In order to carry out their aggressive intentions against me, they gather together their sympathizers and bring them to places where I will be vulnerable to attack (Rashi; Radak; Metzudas David).

יִצְפֹּנוּ — They lie in ambush [lit. they wait].

This translation follows the קְרִי, pronunciation. However, the כְּתִיב, spelling, is יַצְפִּינוּ, they place in hiding, i.e., not only do they lie in ambush themselves, but also they take the trouble to place other men in concealed vantage points (Radak).

The Philistines who suspect that my madness is a ruse hide spies everywhere to scrutinize my words and actions. They hope that during this intensive surveillance they will catch me acting sane and sober (Alshich).

הֵמָּה עֲקֵבַי יִשְׁמֹרוּ — They watch my every tread [lit. my footsteps].

The Philistines claim that close scrutiny of my footsteps will expose my

ח כַּאֲשֶׁר קִוּוּ נַפְשִׁי: עַל־אָוֶן פַּלֶּט־לָמוֹ בְּאַף

ט עַמִּים | הוֹרֵד אֱלֹהִים: נֹדִי סָפַרְתָּה אָתָּה

שִׂימָה דִמְעָתִי בְנֹאדֶךָ הֲלֹא בְּסִפְרָתֶךָ:

י אָז | יָשׁוּבוּ אוֹיְבַי אָחוֹר בְּיוֹם אֶקְרָא זֶה־

יא יָדַעְתִּי כִּי־אֱלֹהִים לִי: בֵּאלֹהִים אֲהַלֵּל

יב דָּבָר בַּיהוה אֲהַלֵּל דָּבָר: בֵּאלֹהִים

---

true mental status. If, upon being released from the palace of Achish, I walk straight back to *Eretz Yisrael*, this will prove my sanity; but if I aimlessly stumble and wander to and fro, this will lend credence to my claim of mental instability (*Alshich*).

כַּאֲשֶׁר קִוּוּ נַפְשִׁי — *Whenever they anticipate* [lit. *hope*] *my soul.*

They lay in ambush whenever they anticipate an opportunity to capture me and thereby take my life (*Rashi; Radak*).

8. עַל אָוֶן פַּלֶּט לָמוֹ — *For inquity shall rescue be theirs?*

Radak interprets this as a question: Is it possible that they should ever be *rescued* [i.e., absolved] from the terrible iniquity which they perpetrate?

Rashi, however, renders this as an indignant statement describing the baseness of David's pursuers: The men who follow Saul to assist in my pursuit are selfish. They desire פַּלֵּט, *to snatch* [lit. *rescue*] a handsome reward for their participation in this *iniquity*.

בְּאַף עַמִּים הוֹרֵד אֱלֹהִים — *In anger cast down the nations, O God!*

This Philistine nation has built up a scheme to trap me. Please, O God, *cast down* that evil design and shatter it (*Rashi*).

נֹדִי סָפַרְתָּה אָתָּה — *My wanderings have You Yourself counted.*

You are well aware of all the places in which I have been forced to seek refuge (*Rashi*). Since גָּלוּת, *exile*, atones for a person's sins, please erase my guilt according to the measure of my

wanderings and suffering (*Chazah Zion*).

[Note the correspondence between verse 7 and verse 9. The Philistines *watch my every tread* for evil *as they anticipate for my soul* (v. 7). Therefore David now asks God to protect him by *counting* these very same steps of wandering in his merit.]

שִׂימָה דִמְעָתִי בְנֹאדֶךָ — *Place my tears in Your flask.*

When You assess my suffering, consider not only my wanderings, but also the many tears which I have shed. Surely You cannot neglect these, for the Sages say (*Bava Metzia* 59a): 'Even when all the gates of heaven are locked, the Gate of Tears is never shut' (*Sforno*).

[David was not moved to tears by his personal woes but by a larger, noble concern for *Eretz Yisrael*. As a devoted servant of God, David realized that he and God were inseparable. Thus, when David abandoned the land of Israel God 'accompanied' David and 'absented' Himself as well. David lamented this loss of sanctity in the Holy Land.]

From these words the *Talmud* (*Shabbos* 105a) derives that it is meritorious to shed tears over the loss of a worthy man. The tears shed for him are not forgotten. God counts them and safeguards them in His treasure room, as it says: *Place my tears into Your flask. Are they not in Your record?*

God preserves these holy tears because they will become the fresh dew which He will use to revive the dead at the time of תְּחִיַת הַמֵּתִים, *Resurrection* (*Mahari Pinto*).

whenever they anticipate my soul.
⁸ For iniquity shall rescue be theirs?
In anger cast down the nations, O God!
⁹ My wanderings have You Yourself counted;
place my tears in Your flask.
Are they not in Your record?
¹⁰ Then will my foes retreat on the day I cry out,
thereby will I know that God is with me.
¹¹ In God's strict justice — I praise His word.
In HASHEM's mercifulness — I praise His word.

הֲלֹא בְּסִפְרָתֶךְ — *Are they not in Your record?*

Radak explains that the word הֲלֹא is always used when there is a need for special emphasis [see v. 14].

According to *Rashi*, סִפְרָתֶךְ is derived from מִסְפָּר, *number, account;* but *Menachem* and *Radak* relate it to סֵפֶר, *book,* to imply, *Record all of my sufferings in Your ledger* so that they will never be forgotten.

10. אָז יָשׁוּבוּ אוֹיְבַי אָחוֹר בְּיוֹם אֶקְרָא — *Then will my foes retreat* [lit. *will return backward*] *on the day I cry out.*

[When You accept my prayers in the merit of my wandering and my tears (v. 9), then my foes will surely be routed.]

Furthermore, when I enter battle, I shall reinforce my merits *when I call out* (אֶקְרָא) the *Shema*. The *Talmud* (Sotah 42a) assures the armies of Israel: Even if you engage your enemies empty-handed, with nothing more than the merit of the *Shema* in your favor, you will overcome the foe! (*Sh'eiris Yaakov*).

זֶה יָדַעְתִּי כִּי אֱלֹהִים לִי — *Thereby will I know that God is with me.*

I.e., My victory will prove that God came to my aid (*Radak*).

Ibn Yachya prefers a different interpretation: זֶה יָדַעְתִּי, *This I know already,* i.e., that my triumph is assured, כִּי אֱלֹהִים לִי, *for I am for God,* i.e., my entire being is dedicated to His service,

therefore He Shall not forsake me!

11. בֵּאלֹהִים אֲהַלֵּל דָּבָר — *In God['s strict justice] — I praise His* [lit. *the*] *word.*

Even if God is strict and harsh with me, I joyously accept His decisions; and I will praise Him always (*Rashi; Midrash Shocher Tov*).

No matter what happens to me, I will remember the greatest kindness which You granted me: דָּבָר, *the word* i.e., the commitment You gave me when You promised to make me king (*Radak; Ibn Ezra;* see v. 5 דְּבָרוֹ).

בַּה' אֲהַלֵּל דָּבָר — *In HASHEM['s mercifulness] — I praise His* [lit. *the*]

The Sages of the *Mishnah* taught that a person is obligated to bless God in the time of misfortune just as he blesses God in the time of good fortune. According to Rav Shmuel bar Nachmani, this obligation is derived from the verse: *As HASHEM* (i.e., the Name signifying the Divine Attribute of Mercy) — *I praise His word, As ELOHIM* (i.e., the Name signifying the Divine Attribute of Strict Justice) — *I praise His word,* to indicate that man's praise for God should remain unchanging and uninterrupted (*Berachos* 60a).

[In quoting this verse, the Sages reversed its actual order to emphasize that God's mercy is foremost and to teach that even when He is strict, His prime motivation is mercy and concern for His creations].

בָּטַחְתִּי לֹא אִירָא מַה־יַּעֲשֶׂה אָדָם לִי:
עָלַי אֱלֹהִים נְדָרֶיךָ אֲשַׁלֵּם תּוֹדֹת לָךְ: כִּי
הִצַּלְתָּ נַפְשִׁי מִמָּוֶת הֲלֹא רַגְלַי מִדֶּחִי
לְהִתְהַלֵּךְ לִפְנֵי אֱלֹהִים בְּאוֹר הַחַיִּים:

יג-יד

12. בֵּאלֹהִים בָּטַחְתִּי לֹא אִירָא — *In God I trust, I fear not.*

When *God* afflicts a person with *Strict Justice* it is possible that he will not be able to endure the pain and suffering. David therefore proclaims that he is completely confident that God Himself will reinforce his strength; thus he has no fear that he will collapse beneath the burden of his punishment (*Tehillas Hashem*).

מַה יַּעֲשֶׂה אָדָם לִי — *What can man do to me?*

This question is asked in verse 5 with one variation: there the word בָּשָׂר, *flesh,* is substituted for אָדָם, *man.* *Radak* defines these words as synonyms, but according to *Alshich,* אָדָם is a title of honor reserved for Jews [*Yevamos* 61a] and refers to David's Israelite enemies, whereas בָּשָׂר, *flesh,* is a derogatory reference to David's heathen enemies in general, and to Achish in particular.

13. עָלַי אֱלֹהִים נְדָרֶיךָ — *Uon me, O God, are Your vows.*

According to many commentaries

(*Radak; Ibn Ezra; Sforno*) נְדָרֶיךָ, *Your vows,* refers to the vows which David made to God while he was in exile.

Alshich, however, maintains that *Your vows* refers to the vows which God made to the royal tribe of Judah, promising that the family of David would emanate from Judah and that its sovereignty would be unsurpassed. These Divine vows were expressed in the Patriarch Jacob's final blessing to his sons.

David declares that these *vows* buoyed his spirits even in the gloom of exile, for he realizes that 'Everything promised to the tribe of Judah really devolves עָלַי, *upon me,* and represents a special commitment to give me the throne.'

אֲשַׁלֵּם תּוֹדֹת לָךְ — *I shall render* [lit. repay] *thanksgiving offerings to You.*

When I was in danger, I promised that once rescued, I would sacrifice offerings of thanksgiving to God (*Radak*). [1]

14. כִּי הִצַּלְתָּ נַפְשִׁי מִמָּוֶת — *For You rescued my soul from death.*

1. *Midrash Shocher Tov* comments that this verse also alludes to Messianic times, because in the future, all forms of sacrifice are destined to become obsolete [since men will be righteous, no sacrifices will be required to atone for their sins (*Radak*)], with the exception of the thanksgiving offerings. [This will be retained so that men may show their appreciation to God for providing a utopian world (*Radak*).] Similarly, prayers of petition will be discontinued, (since God will provide men with all their requirements, they will no longer plead for their needs), but prayers of praise and thanks will still be recited (in recognition of God's kindness).

¹² *In God's strict justice have I trusted,*
      I shall not fear.
    What can man do to me?
¹³ *Upon me, O God, are Your vows,*
      I shall render thanksgiving offerings to You.
¹⁴ *For You rescued my soul from death —*
      even my feet from stumbling —
    To walk before God
      in the light of life.

This refers to death at the hands of Saul (*Yalkut Shimoni*) and to the death reserved for sinners who forfeit their claim to life (*Targum*).

Yaavetz HaDoresh comments: Although the Torah usually discourages men from making vows (*Ecclesiastes* 5:4), the *Midrash* (*Bereishis Rabbah* 70:1) learns from the example of the Patriarch Jacob (*Genesis* 28:20) that it is advisable to make a vow to God in a time of mortal danger. [See *Tosafos Chullin* 2b s.v. אבל and *Ritva* and *Rashba* to *Nedarim* 9a.]

David now explains that he too has obligated himself to God with vows (*v.* 13), because God delivered him from death.

הֲלֹא רַגְלַי מִדֶּחִי — *Even my feet from stumbling.*

I.e., Not only did You save me from death, but You even prevented my feet from stumbling into the snares set by the wily Achitophel (*Yalkut Shimoni*); and from being enmeshed in sin by the Evil Inclination (*Targum*).

Thus I am assured that I will not stumble into the fires of *Gehinnom* (*Alshich*).

Yaavetz HaDoresh continues: In addition to his human enemies, David was threatened by the terrible menace of a hostile environment. Often he was forced to take refuge in the inhospitable

desert or in the forbidding wilderness. The *Talmud* (*Berachos* 54b) rules that surviving a trip across the uninhabited desert (or surviving any of three other dangerous situations) obligates a person to bring a קָרְבָּן תּוֹדָה, *a thanksgiving offering.*

Therefore David says: *I shall render thanksgiving offerings to You* (*v.* 13) because *You rescued ... my feet from stumbling* into the deadly pitfalls of the desert.

לְהִתְהַלֵּךְ לִפְנֵי אֱלֹהִים — *To walk before God.*

Before God means in the Land of Israel (*Midrash; Radak*) and in the *Beis Hamikdash* (*Metzudas David*).

There I will have the opportunity to study God's Torah in peace of mind, without harrassment by my enemies (*Sforno*).

בְּאוֹר הַחַיִּים — *In the light of life.*

This refers to the Garden of Eden (*Midrash; Radak*). *Sforno* identifies it as the World to Come.

This is congruent with the *Talmud's* statement (*Sanhedrin* 102a) that God said, 'Come, let us stroll together with [David] the son of Jesse in the Garden of Eden' (*Alshich*).

[This is the most sublime reward to which a man can aspire and it represents the goal of David's entire career.]

T*he narrative of I Samuel, chapter 24, serves as the background for this psalm. Saul and three thousand men search for David in the rocky caves of the wilderness of En-Gedi. All alone, Saul inadvertently entered the cave in which David and his men were hiding. Instead of yielding to his men's demands that he kill Saul, David contented himself with cutting off a corner from a garment, which Saul had momentarily removed. In this manner, David sought to impress upon Saul that he was not his enemy and that Saul was unjustified in hating and pursuing him.*

This highly dramatic moment, fraught with danger for both Saul and David, prompted David to compose this psalm.

This is the first of three psalms (57-59) which refer to Saul's pursuit of David; all begin with the plea Al Tashcheis — Do not destroy!

א לַמְנַצֵּחַ אַל־תַּשְׁחֵת לְדָוִד מִכְתָּם בְּבָרְחוֹ
ב מִפְּנֵי־שָׁאוּל בַּמְּעָרָה: חָנֵּנִי אֱלֹהִים | חָנֵּנִי
כִּי בְךָ חָסָיָה נַפְשִׁי וּבְצֵל־כְּנָפֶיךָ אֶחְסֶה
ג עַד יַעֲבֹר הַוּוֹת: אֶקְרָא לֵאלֹהִים עֶלְיוֹן
ד לָאֵל גֹּמֵר עָלָי: יִשְׁלַח מִשָּׁמַיִם | וְיוֹשִׁיעֵנִי
חֵרֵף שֹׁאֲפִי סֶלָה יִשְׁלַח אֱלֹהִים חַסְדּוֹ

1. לַמְנַצֵּחַ אַל תַּשְׁחֵת — *For the Conductor,* Al Tashcheis [lit. *do not destroy*].

This psalm is entitled *Al Tashcheis* because David composed it when he was on the brink of destruction and death; thus, he was pleading to God for salvation *(Rashi)*.

David's righteousness and humility were truly astounding. Despite Saul's threat and his implacable hatred, David persisted in accepting him as his king and refused to injure his sovereign in any way. David's primary concern was not for his own life, but for Saul's. David's men forcefully insisted that it would be suicidal not to exploit this God-given opportunity to slay their pursuer, Saul; but David held them back, shouting, *Al Tashcheis* — *do not destroy!'* (*Alshich*).

[In a deeper sense, David implored his followers not to fall into the state of moral decay which had already corrupted a major portion of the nation under Saul's influence. David pleaded: 'Saul seeks to accomplish his desires through hatred, violence, and murder. Let us not allow ourselves to fall into this destructive syndrome. Rather, let us seize this opportunity to demonstrate to the nation that unity must be achieved through clemency, mercy, and pardon. Therefore, I beg you, *Do not destroy!'*]

בְּבָרְחוֹ מִפְּנֵי שָׁאוּל בַּמְּעָרָה — *When he fled from Saul, in the cave.*

Inside the cave it was Saul who was in danger, not David. Nevertheless, David is described as *fleeing* even while

he was safe, because he *fled* from the temptation to kill his trapped, helpless enemy *(Alshich)*.

The *Midrash* (*Bereishis Rabbah* 51:7) notes that centuries earlier, David's ancestor, Lot, was saved from the destruction of Sodom by hiding in a cave. Thus David prayed, 'Master of the Universe! Even before I entered this cave, You showed kindness to others for my sake and saved them in a cave! Therefore, now that I myself am in a cave, I beg of You, be kind and *do not destroy!'*

2. חָנֵּנִי אֱלֹהִים חָנֵּנִי — *Favor me, O God, favor me.*

A double request: 'Favor me by strengthening me not to kill others and by not allowing others to kill me!' *(Rashi)*.

[Saul posed a double threat. Thus: 'Save me from both physical destruction and moral corruption.']

כִּי בְךָ חָסָיָה נַפְשִׁי — *For in You my soul took refuge.*

[In the past I have always sought to protect myself through You and not by means of violence and destruction.]

וּבְצֵל כְּנָפֶיךָ אֶחְסֶה — *And in the shadow of Your wings I shall take refuge.*

[Even now, as I am concealed in the shadowy depths of the dark cave, I realize that Your presence is my only true protection. By refusing to exploit this opportunity to slay Saul I will demonstrate that I reject the security of human might.]

עַד יַעֲבֹר הַוּוֹת — *Until treachery passes by.*

For the Conductor, Al Tashcheis,
    by David, a Michtam,
When he fled from Saul, in the cave.
² Favor me, O God, favor me,
    for in You my soul took refuge,
And in the shadow of Your wings I shall take refuge
    until treachery passes by.
³ I will call upon God, Most High,
    to the God Who fulfills for me.
⁴ He will dispatch from heaven
    and save me;
From the disgrace of those
    who desire to swallow me, Selah,
God will dispatch His mercy
    and His truth.

I will continue to act in such a conciliatory fashion until I succeed in erasing the feelings of treachery and animosity which poison Saul's heart (Meiri).

3. אֶקְרָא לֵאלֹהִים עֶלְיוֹן — *I will call upon God, Most High.*

My situation seems hopeless. To whom can I appeal for justice if I am pursued by the king himself, since he is the supreme authority in the land? Nevertheless, I am not afraid; for I call upon God whose, authority is even higher! (Radak).

לָאֵל גֹּמֵר עָלָי — *To the God who fulfills for me.*

[The desperate man who feels compelled to resort to violence in order to achieve his goals is misled by a false conception. He is convinced that man is responsible for assuring his own success and that he must take matters into this own hands if he wishes to bring his schemes to completion.

David declares: 'I know differently! It is incumbent upon man to have the courage to take the first step to reach his goal, no matter how difficult that step may be. I firmly believe that a man need do no more, once he has taken this initiative. Upon recognizing a man's good intentions, God assumes responsibility for bringing his noble ideas to fruition.

'I call upon God to effect my salvation as He sees fit; I shall not end Saul's threat to me with an act of physical violence.']

4. יִשְׁלַח מִשָּׁמַיִם וְיוֹשִׁיעֵנִי — *He will dispatch from heaven and save me.*

The numerical superiority of the enemy forces does not intimidate me, for God will send down His ministering angels to rescue me (Radak; Targum).

חֵרֵף שֹׁאֲפִי — [*From*] *the disgrace of those who desire to swallow me.*

This punishment is appropriate because if Saul would respect the word of God, as transmitted through the prophet Samuel, he would recognize my Divinely ordained claim to the throne. By ignoring the word of God, he disgraces it; therefore, he himself deserves to be disgraced (Radak).

יִשְׁלַח אֱלֹהִים חַסְדּוֹ וַאֲמִתּוֹ — *God will dispatch His mercy and His truth.*

May He act with *mercy* towards me and with strict *truth* and justice towards my enemies (Sforno).

ה וַאֲמִתּוֹ: נַפְשִׁי | בְּתוֹךְ לְבָאִם אֶשְׁכְּבָה
לֹהֲטִים בְּנֵי־אָדָם שִׁנֵּיהֶם חֲנִית וְחִצִּים
ו וּלְשׁוֹנָם חֶרֶב חַדָּה: רוּמָה עַל־הַשָּׁמַיִם
ז אֱלֹהִים עַל כָּל־הָאָרֶץ כְּבוֹדֶךָ: רֶשֶׁת |
הֵכִינוּ לִפְעָמַי כָּפַף נַפְשִׁי כָּרוּ לְפָנַי שִׁיחָה
ח נָפְלוּ בְתוֹכָהּ סֶלָה: נָכוֹן לִבִּי אֱלֹהִים נָכוֹן

---

5. נַפְשִׁי בְּתוֹךְ לְבָאִם — *My soul is among lions.*

My soul is threatened by such heroic *lions* of Torah scholarship as Saul's generals Abner and Amassa, who make no protest against Saul's violent pursuit of an innocent man such as myself (*Rashi; Yerushalmi, Peah 1:1*).

Radak explains that although David was running away from these men he describes himself as בְּתוֹךְ, *among* them, because he never succeeded in eluding them; they were always following close behind him.

Alshich however, identifies these *lions* as David's own followers who were with him in the cave, for they resembled hungry, ferocious lions, roaring to tear Saul apart. David barely succeeded in restraining them.

אֶשְׁכְּבָה לֹהֲטִים — *I lie with fiery men.*

Once I sought refuge in the vicinity of the Ziphites, who proved to be vicious men, aflame with the desire to slander me to Saul (*Rashi*).

They sought to burn me alive with the fiery breath of their wicked mouths (*Radak*).

The malicious slanderer is far more dangerous than the hungriest lion (*Sforno*).

בְּנֵי אָדָם שִׁנֵּיהֶם חֲנִית וְחִצִּים — *People whose teeth are spears and arrows.*

These are the people of Keilah, who betrayed David to Saul (*Yerushalmi, Peah 1:1*).

Their scathing tales and evil reports were like *spears and arrows*, which kill even from a distance. Similarly, slander

spoken in one place can injure someone far away (*Tanchuma Metzora 2*).

וּלְשׁוֹנָם חֶרֶב חַדָּה — *And whose tongue is a sharp sword.*

According to *Yerushalmi (Peah 1:1)*, it is this description which refers to the Ziphites; the description *fiery men* (inflamed with a passion for slander) refers to Doeg and Achitophel. *Yerushalmi* concludes that because there were so many slanderers in the time of David, his armies would suffer many losses in battle.

6. רוּמָה עַל הַשָּׁמַיִם אֱלֹהִים — *Be exalted above the heavens, O God.*

Depart, O God, from this lowly world of men consumed by base passions and a lust for cheap slander. They do not deserve to have Your exalted, holy presence in their midst. Preserve Your glory in the heavens above where it belongs (*Rashi*).

עַל כָּל הָאָרֶץ כְּבוֹדֶךָ — *Above all the earth be Your glory.*

In heaven, where You rule over the many forces and angels (*Targum*) which control this world, please manipulate the universal order in such a way as to foil my enemies and to render me victorious so that *Your glory will be above all the earth* (*Radak; Sforno*).

7. רֶשֶׁת הֵכִינוּ לִפְעָמַי — *A snare they prepared for my footsteps.*

Saul said to the treacherous Ziphites (*I Samuel 23:22*), 'Go, I pray you; make yet even more sure, and know and observe the place where his foot treads and who has seen him there, for I am

5 *My soul is among lions,*
   I lie with fiery men,
People whose teeth are spears and arrows,
   and whose tongue is a sharp sword.
6 *Be exalted above the heavens, O God,*
   above all the earth be Your glory.
7 *A snare they prepared for my footsteps,*
   they bent down my soul,
They dug a pit before me —
   they fell into it, Selah.
8 *My heart is steadfast, O God, my heart is steadfast,*

---

told that he [David] deals very subtly' (Radak).

כָּפַף נַפְשִׁי — *They bent down my soul.*
[Saul sent messengers to all of the cities of Israel in his search for me. I was deeply depressed by the fact that so many of my countrymen responded readily to Saul's call and my soul was bent in shame.]

כָּרוּ לְפָנַי שִׁיחָה נָפְלוּ בְתוֹכָהּ — *They dug a pit before me, they [themselves] fell into it.*
[See 7:16, *He digs a pit, digs it deep, only to fall into his own trap.*]
Saul imagined that he had finally dug my grave when he surrounded me at the rock of division (I *Samuel* 23:28). In truth, he brought about his own downfall, because in order to stop Saul from pursuing me, God sent a murderous Philistine attack against him which diverted his attention and forced him to abandon me *(Sforno).*
Earlier, Saul had tried to bring about David's death by sending him on an impossibly hazardous mission: he ordered David to bring him the foreskins of no

less than one hundred Philistines (I *Samuel* 18:25). With God's help, David succeeded and did not fall into Saul's pit. However, Saul eventually met his own final defeat at the hands of that same Philistine nation *(Rashbam).*

8. [The first seven verses of this psalm reflect David's anxiety and fear. However, once he has recounted the downfall of his enemies in the very trap which they had set for him (*v.* 7), he is imbued with a new spirit of confidence and ecstasy, which inspires the following rapturous verses of praise for God.]

נָכוֹן לִבִּי אֱלֹהִים נָכוֹן לִבִּי — *My heart is steadfast, O God, my heart is steadfast.*
[The final verses of this psalm are almost an exact replica of the opening verses of Psalm 108. Compare this verse with 108:2.]
My heart and faith are steadfast at all times *(Ibn Ezra)*, both when You treat me with kind mercy and when You treat me with strict justice *(Rashi).*
I am confident of my ultimate success in this world and in the World to Come *(Ibn Yachya).*[1]

---

1. *Midrash Shocher Tov* observes that the episode in the cave convinced even Saul of the legitimacy of David's claim to the throne. According to one view cited by *Rashi* to I *Samuel* 15-27, after Samuel rebuked Saul for his sins, the prophet grasped Saul's cloak and tore it. Samuel told him, *'This symbolizes that God has torn the monarchy away from you'* (ibid. 15:28).
Saul asked, 'And who is my successor?'
Samuel replied, 'The man who will rip away the corner of your cloak (as I did) is the one

ט לִבִּי אָשִׁירָה וַאֲזַמֵּרָה: עוּרָה כְבוֹדִי עוּרָה

י הַנֵּבֶל וְכִנּוֹר אָעִירָה שָּׁחַר: אוֹדְךָ בָעַמִּים |

יא אֲדֹנָי אֲזַמֶּרְךָ בַּלְאֻמִּים: כִּי־גָדֹל עַד־

יב שָׁמַיִם חַסְדֶּךָ וְעַד־שְׁחָקִים אֲמִתֶּךָ: רוּמָה

עַל־שָׁמַיִם אֱלֹהִים עַל כָּל־הָאָרֶץ כְּבוֹדֶךָ:

אָשִׁירָה — *I will sing.*

[I will sing because I was delivered from the physical harm which Saul had intended to inflict on me.]

וַאֲזַמֵּרָה — *And I will make music.*

[See *comm.* to 30:1 מִזְמוֹר שִׁיר].

Not only was my body saved, but also my soul was rescued from ruination. I thank God for helping to restrain me from shedding Saul's blood. For this additional kindness I will add special musical accompaniment to my songs (*Malbim*).

9. עוּרָה כְבוֹדִי — *Awake, O my soul* [lit. *my honor*].

[The soul is the כָּבוֹד, *glory*, of man, as is explained in 8:6 and 30:13.]

Malbim explains that this verse vividly depicts the metamorphosis which took place within David's soul.

Saul's malicious jealousy and relentless pursuit had left a deep, dark blot on David's soul. As an innocent man condemned and vilified, as a helpless fugitive hunted and threatened, David suffered greatly and became withdrawn. The full radiance of David's brilliant personality went into eclipse. His senses and emotions were deadened by disgrace and pain; his lively talents became faded and dull.

David's primary fear had been that he might sink into a bitter melancholy similar to Saul's and that he might become a man obsessed with violence and revenge. This unexpected encounter with Saul instantly dissolved

his fears. First, by refraining from harming Saul, David proved to himself that he had successfully preserved his own integrity, despite Saul's moral collapse. Second, Saul himself now publicly admitted his own folly and David's righteousness, thus restoring David's reputation.

David's soul now surged with renewed strength: *Awake, O my soul!* Once again David felt himself to be an instrument of God, dedicated to singing His praises *Awake, O Neivel and Kinnor!* He now anticipated a personal renaissance; his sun was rising, heralding a fresh morning of growth and success: *I shall awaken the dawn!*

עוּרָה הַנֵּבֶל וְכִנּוֹר — *Awake, O* Neivel *and* Kinnor.

[See *footnote* to 33:2 for a complete discussion of the precise nature and identity of these musical instruments, which were used more than any others to accompany David's psalms. Compare this verse with 108:3.]

Radak explains that David, speaking figuratively, calls upon these instruments to play by themselves, joining him in his moment of ecstatic release from sorrow.

[See *commentary* to 49:5 אֶפְתַּח בְּכִנּוֹר חִידָתִי.]

אָעִירָה שָּׁחַר — *I shall awaken the dawn.*[1]

10. אוֹדְךָ בָעַמִּים אֲדֹנָי — *I will thank You among the peoples, my Lord.*

I.e., among the tribes of Israel, who

destined to take away your kingdom.'

When David cut the corner of Saul's cloak in the cave, Saul immediately remembered Samuel's fateful prophecy and declared, 'וְעַתָּה הִנֵּה יָדַעְתִּי כִּי מָלֹךְ תִּמְלוֹךְ, *Behold now I know that you will indeed be king* [I Samuel 24:20]. You will be the monarch in This World and in the World to Come.'

57 I will sing and I will make music.

9-12 ⁹ Awake, O my soul, awake, O Neivel and Kinnor;
I shall awaken the dawn.
¹⁰ I will thank You among the peoples, my Lord.
I will sing to You among the nations.
¹¹ For great until the very heavens is Your kindness,
and until the upper heights is Your truth.
¹² Be exalted above heaven, O God,
above all the earth be Your glory.

---

are called עַמִּים, *peoples*, (see *Deuteronomy* 33:19; *Ibn Ezra*; *Radak*). [Cf. 108:4.]

אֲזַמֶּרְךָ בַּלְאֻמִּים — *I will sing to You among the nations.*

I.e., the gentile nations of the world (*Ibn Ezra*).

[May the praises of God which spring forth from Israel overflow onto the lips of all the nations, who will learn from Israel's example.]

11. כִּי גָדֹל עַד שָׁמַיִם חַסְדֶּךָ — *For great until the very heavens is Your kindness.*

Malbim refers us to his comment on 36:6, where he explains in detail the two categories of heavenly order: חֶסֶד, *kindness,* and אֱמֶת, *truth.*

The *Talmud* (*Pesachim* 50b) notes an apparent contradiction between these words and those in 108:5, where it is written: כִּי גָדֹל מֵעַל שָׁמַיִם חַסְדֶּךָ, *for Your kindness is great even above the heavens.* The *Talmud* explains that for people who perform the *mitzvos* לִשְׁמָה, *for the sake of God,* God's kindness extends מֵעַל, even *beyond* the heavens. But for those who act שֶׁלֹּא לִשְׁמָה, *not* [completely] *for the sake of God,* God's kindness extends only עַד, *until* the heavens.[2]

וְעַד שְׁחָקִים אֲמִתֶּךָ — *And until the upper heights is Your truth.*

[שְׁחָקִים is the name of one of the seven heavenly spheres. See *Chagigah* 13a.]

12. רוּמָה עַל שָׁמַיִם אֱלֹהִים — *Be exalted above heaven, O God.*

This verse is practically a duplicate of

---

1. Based on this verse, the *Talmud* (*Berachos* 3b-4a) relates that David took only a short nap every night. Precisely at midnight the north wind would blow through the *Kinnor* (harp) over his bed, rousing him so that he could study Torah until the dawn.

Midrash (*Eichah Rabbasi* 2:27) adds: When the people of Israel heard their monarch studying Torah in the middle of the night, they said, 'If David, the [busy] king of Israel, is studying Torah, certainly we, too, must do so.' Immediately they engaged in Torah study [cf. *Overview* part IV].

Some commentaries interpret this story homiletically. Often the terrible tragedies of David's life would deaden his spirit to the extent that his faculties became dormant. Yet within the depths of his being, there remained a רוּחַ צְפוּנִית, *a hidden* (צָפוּן) *spirit* (רוּחַ), which never died. It was the spirit which awakened his soul to greet the dawn of spiritual renewal (*Yetev Lev*).

2. The *Chofetz Chaim* illustrates this Talmudic passage in *Ma'amar Toras Habayis*, ch. 8:

The performance of each and every *mitzvah* creates good angels and sacred forces which accompany a man to heaven when his soul departs from this earth. How fortunate the soul will feel when it sees itself surrounded by tens of thousands of angels of its own creation! However, to its utter dismay, as the soul enters the heavenly gates, it sees that the angels are left

v. 6 and 108:6. However, in *v. 6* we read עַל הַשָּׁמַיִם, *above* **the** *heavens.*

Hirsch explains that the definite article ה, *the*, is added there *(v. 6)* to indicate *the heavens*, par excellence. A devout servant of God merits special considerations in the workings of Divine Providence. Therefore, David first asked that God should arise and exalt Himself to act with the unique Divine Providence and control reserved for the chosen servants of God. This special celestial involvement is called הַשָּׁמַיִם, *the heavens.*

Now David concludes the psalm with a plea for the sake of all men — *Arise, O God,* and control this world from שָׁמַיִם, *heaven* above, and implement justice and order for the sake of all of humanity.

עַל כָּל הָאָרֶץ כְּבוֹדֶךָ — *Above all the earth be Your glory.*

May it become apparent when You overthrow all the monarchs of the earth that You are the Supreme Ruler above *(Sforno).*

[This is a most appropriate conclusion for this psalm dedicated to David's relationship with King Saul. David prays: At times it appears as if You are far removed from human affairs and events. But when You manipulated affairs so wondrously that Saul put himself into my hands in the cave, then Your special concern for me in *the heavens (v. 6)* became gloriously apparent on earth. Now I ask that even Your general supervision in *heaven (v. 12)* become a clear manifestation of Your presence over all the earth.]

behind, unable to enter the celestial paradise, for the myriads of *mitzvos* which created those angels were not done purely for the sake of God, but were motivated in part by mundane personal considerations. Therefore, these *mitzvos* must remain within the earthly sphere; they can rise no higher. Only those *mitzvos* performed purely 'for the sake of heaven,' soar above the heavens and accompany the soul for eternity.

This psalm is the second in the Al Tashcheis trilogy. It describes the abrupt end of Saul's short-lived benignity toward David.

Psalm 57 (based on the narrative of I Sam. 24) told how David restrained his men from killing Saul. Instead, David cut off a corner of Saul's robe which he later showed the king as proof of his loyalty. Saul was convinced that he had misjudged David and his warm feelings of old returned.

But Saul's underlings conspired to destroy this good will. They came to Saul and argued: 'Is David to be esteemed as a righteous man simply because he did not slay you in the cave? He knew that if he dared harm you, we would have torn him limb from limb. He was afraid to do you harm!' (Midrash Shocher Tov).

Abner, Saul's leading general, scorned David's claim, saying that Saul's garment had been torn by a thorn and that David found the severed piece of cloth and fabricated the claim that he had had Saul at his mercy (Yerushalmi Sotah 1:8).

Abner's charge rekindled Saul's fury against David. The king resolved to hunt down his younger rival: And he [Saul] arose and went down to the Wilderness of Ziph with three thousand chosen men of Israel to seek David in the Wilderness of Ziph (I Sam. 26:3). This psalm is based on the events of that pursuit.

נח א-ב לַמְנַצֵּחַ אַל־תַּשְׁחֵת לְדָוִד מִכְתָּם: הַאֻמְנָם אֵלֶם צֶדֶק תְּדַבֵּרוּן מֵישָׁרִים תִּשְׁפְּטוּ בְּנֵי

1. אַל תַּשְׁחֵת — *Al Tashcheis* [lit. *do not destroy*].

While pursuing David, Saul and his men made camp in the desert. God cast a deep slumber on the company which enabled David and Avishai ben Zeruyah to enter the camp safely.

Saul lay sleeping with his spear thrust into the ground near his head. Avishai pleaded with David for permission to kill Saul with his own spear, but David restrained him, saying, 'אַל תַּשְׁחִיתֵהוּ, *do not destroy him — who can extend his hand against HASHEM's anointed and be pardoned?' (I Sam. 26:9).*

As he had done earlier when he cut off the corner of Saul's robe, David sought proof by which he could later show that he had not harmed the king even when he had the opportunity to do so.

He took the spear and the jug of water which were near Saul's head, and departed.[1]

מִכְתָּם — *A Michtam.*
Rashi (16:1) translates this as *a crown.* *Alshich* comments that this title is well deserved because David's noble conduct in all his dealings with Saul, especially in the incident of the spear and the jug, proved beyond any doubt that he was worthy of the royal *crown.*

[The incident of the spear and jug provided an unsurpassed glimpse into

David's greatness of character, for after he cut Saul's robe, the king solemnly swore to cease his pursuit of David, but he went back on his word. Nevertheless, David did not lose faith in God's anointed, and he released Saul once again. This represents the *crown* of David's tolerance and magnanimity.]

2. הַאֻמְנָם — *Is it true?*
This word is derived from אָמֵן, *true,* and אֱמוּנָה, *belief.* With the addition of the suffix, ם, *mem,* it means *in truth.* (Similarly, the word חֵן, *grace, favor,* becomes *free of charge* when it is given the suffix, *mem*). When the interrogative prefix ה, *he,* is added, we have the question הַאֻמְנָם, *Is it true?* (Hirsch).

Rashi perceives this as the opening of a rhetorical question: David turns to his pursuers and asks incredulously, 'Can it be true that you are silent?'

The Sages, interpreting this verse homiletically, relate אֻמְנָם to אוּמָן, *craftsman:* 'Which craft should man pursue in this world? He should strive to emulate an אִלֵּם, *a mute* (in order to avoid evil talk). Should one refrain from speaking even words of Torah? Certainly not! For the verse continues: צֶדֶק תְּדַבֵּרוּן, *justice should you speak* [i.e., of Torah, which is the ultimate justice] (*Chullin* 89a).

אֵלֶם — [*That you are*] *silent?*
This translation follows *Rashi.* David

---

1. Psalms 56, 57, and 58 describe three incidents when David was saved from mortal danger. *Chazah David* relates the proximity of the three narratives to an incident cited in the *Midrash* (*Otzar Midrashim* I p. 47).

David sat in his garden and watched a flea attacking a spider. A madman came and chased both insects away with a stick. David asked of God, 'Master of the Universe, of what value are these three creatures? The flea only bites, but contributes nothing. The spider weaves and weaves all year, yet no one can wear its web. The madman causes damage to others, and he has no concept of Your greatness?

God replied, 'David! The time will come when you will need all three and then you will realize their purpose!'

Psalms 56-58 demonstrate how David came to understand God's reply. Psalm 56 tells how David saved himself from Achish by feigning madness. Psalm 57 refers to David's attempt to elude Saul's pursuit by hiding in a cave. God sent a spider to spin a web across the cave's

For the Conductor, Al Tashcheis, by David, a Michtam.

² Is it true that you are silent?
Justice should you speak!
With fairness should you judge people!

demands of his antagonists: 'When you sought to convince Saul of my guilt, you spoke loudly and lengthily. Why have you suddenly fallen silent now that you can establish my innocence?'

However, *Ibn Ezra, Radak,* and *Meiri* relate אֵלֶם to אֲלֻמִּים, *sheaves, bundles.* In the context of this verse it means *an assembly* of the magistrates of the land. David calls upon them to live up to their responsibilities: 'Why do you allow innocent men like me to be unjustly persecuted? *Assemble* your courts. Evaluate my recent compassion towards Saul and declare me innocent of treachery.'

Meiri adds that אֵלֶם alludes to the אוּלָם, *chamber,* in which the court convenes.

צֶדֶק תְּדַבֵּרוּן — *Justice should you speak!* *Midrash Shocher Tov* comments: After David took Saul's spear and jug, *he stood upon a distant mountain... and called...,* הֲלוֹא תַעֲנֶה אַבְנֵר, *will you not answer, Abner?... You are a man of valor* [charged with protecting the king, but now you deserve to die for] *you did not watch over God's anointed... Where are the king's spear and his jug?'* [ibid. v. 13-16].

But Abner could not answer. He was

like a man struck dumb, and he refused to concede David's righteousness.

David asked further: 'Have you pursued me with צֶדֶק, *justice,* as the Torah says, צֶדֶק צֶדֶק תִּרְדֹּף, *Justice, justice shall you pursue (Deut. 16:20)?* [In that verse which is addressed to the courts, צֶדֶק has the connotation of justice. The verse to be cited next is addressed to the individual. There, the word צֶדֶק has the connotation of righteousness and fairness.] Have you judged me with righteousness, as the Torah says, בְּצֶדֶק תִּשְׁפֹּט עֲמִיתֶךָ, *In righteousness shall you judge your neighbor (Lev. 19:15)?'*

מֵישָׁרִים תִּשְׁפְּטוּ בְּנֵי אָדָם — *With fairness should you judge people* [lit. *the sons of man*]!

Abner was indeed unfair in his assessment of David's actions. When David offered the spear and jug as proof that Saul had been in his grasp, Abner refuted him by arguing that one of Saul's own men might have stolen the articles and delivered them to David; or Saul's armor bearer might have taken the spear and the jug down to a well to fetch water and forgotten them where David later found them.

When David heard these far-fetched arguments he challenged Abner, 'How

entrance. Seeing the unbroken web, Saul was convinced that no one could have entered. He went in to rest, giving David the opportunity to cut off a piece of the royal robe and flee undetected. Later David found the spider and kissed it, exclaiming, 'Blessed is your Creator Who fashioned such wondrous creatures for this world!'

Our psalm tells how David was saved thanks to a flea. When He and Avishai secretly entered Saul's camp, they saw the mighty Abner sleeping next to Saul's head. His legs surrounded the king protectively, but his knees were bent and elevated. David slipped beneath them and took Saul's spear and jug. Suddenly, the sleeping Abner stretched out his legs flat on the ground, trapping David beneath them. Had David attempted to move, he would have aroused Abner. David silently cried to God for mercy. God sent a flea which bit Abner's leg causing him to draw them up once again, allowing David to escape.

Thus, David's life was saved by the very creatures and conditions he had maligned. As a result, he perceived as never before the greatness of God's creation.

ג אָדָם: אַף־בְּלֵב עוֹלֹת תִּפְעָלוּן בָּאָרֶץ

ד חֲמַס יְדֵיכֶם תְּפַלֵּסוּן: זֹרוּ רְשָׁעִים מֵרָחֶם

ה תָּעוּ מִבֶּטֶן דֹּבְרֵי כָזָב: חֲמַת־לָמוֹ כִּדְמוּת

חֲמַת־נָחָשׁ כְּמוֹ־פֶתֶן חֵרֵשׁ יַאְטֵם אָזְנוֹ:

ו אֲשֶׁר לֹא־יִשְׁמַע לְקוֹל מְלַחֲשִׁים חוֹבֵר

do you explain the edge which I cut from the king's garment?'

Abner replied, 'The edge was ripped off by a thorn!'

Because Abner resorted to such tortured rationalizations rather than admit David's innocence and seek to heal the breach between David and Saul, he was condemned (by Heaven) to die. This incident is the source of the *Talmudic* saying: Abner died because of the well and the thorn (*Sanhedrin 49a, Rashi* and *Rabbeinu Chananel* ibid.).

3. אַף בְּלֵב עוֹלֹת תִּפְעָלוּן — *Even in your heart you do wrongs.*

Rashi and *Radak* explain that עוֹלֹת is the plural of עַוְלָה, *offense, wrong.* The corrupt judges of Saul's kingdom never cease to think of new ways to commit *wrongs.* So intense was their concentration on these misdeeds that their thoughts had the force of deeds that were actually committed.

Chomas Anoch suggests that עוֹלֹת may be interpreted in its literal sense as the plural of עוֹלָה, *a burnt sacrifice.* The Sages say that a person should bring such an offering to atone for הִרְהוּרֵי עֲבֵירָה, *sinful thoughts.* Therefore, the psalmist urges the corrupt foe not to minimize the power of an evil thought, for an obligation to atone with a burnt offering can be incurred *even in the heart.*

בָּאָרֶץ חֲמַס יְדֵיכֶם תְּפַלֵּסוּן — *In the land you weigh out the violence of your hands.*

According to *Rashi,* תְּפַלֵּסוּן bears the connotation of precise weighing and measuring. Saul's cunning magistrates cloak their crime in a robe of justice, claiming that their every verdict is based on the exact, precise weighing of the letter of the law.

[David's argument is that Abner and the rest of Saul's officers, judges, and advisors have perverted their minds to the point where they cannot differentiate between good and evil. Therefore it is no wonder that they distort David's clear-cut evidence of his peaceful intentions.]

4. זֹרוּ רְשָׁעִים מֵרָחֶם — *Estranged are the wicked from the womb.*

Even while still in their mother's womb, the evil are estranged from God. As our Sages tell us, while he was still an unborn fetus, Esau strained towards pagan temples (*Rashi*).

The opposite is true of the righteous. In the earliest stages of their development they are already inclined towards sanctity. Thus we find that when Rebeccah passed by the house of study, Jacob struggled to leave her womb. Of the righteous, the prophet says (*Jeremiah 1:5*), *Before I formed you in the belly I knew you, and before you came out of the womb I sanctified you* (*Midrash Shocher Tov*).

Alshich paraphrases David's argument: The difference between a robe ripped unevenly by a thorn and one cut clearly by a knife is readily apparent. How can anyone confuse a well planned act executed with smooth precision, with an accident? Such a distortion is the fruit of a mind *estranged* from truth and logic from the very moment of its conception.

תָּעוּ מִבֶּטֶן דֹּבְרֵי כָזָב — *Astray from birth* [lit. *from the belly*] *go the speakers of falsehood.*

The translation follows *Metzudas*

³ *Even in your heart*
you do wrongs,
In the land you weigh out
the violence of your hands.
⁴ *Estranged are the wicked from the womb,*
astray from birth go the speakers of falsehood.
⁵ *They have venom like the venom of a snake,*
like a deaf viper that closes its ear.
⁶ *So as not to hearken to the voice of charmers,*
of the most cunning spellbinder.

David, who perceives *from the belly* as a metaphor for the time of birth and onwards. *Malbim*, however, interprets מִבֶּטֶן literally, and stresses that these wicked people were perverted even before birth, while they were still embryos. Therefore they are permanently alienated from righteousness and integrity.

[This verse does not indicate a belief in a preordained fate which is beyond man's control. Although everyone is endowed with free will to choose between good and evil, he is also born with certain handicaps which hinder his ability to choose good. The challenge of life is to overcome these obstacles. Some have physical handicaps, others have social or economic ones. The people described here had mental and emotional tendencies toward evil which made it difficult for them to think objectively. Nevertheless, by applying themselves to the task of channeling their evil tendencies towards good, they could have achieved righteousness.]

5. חֲמַת לָמוֹ כִּדְמוּת חֲמַת נָחָשׁ - *They have venom like the* [lit. *image of*] *venom of a snake.*

When these evil men are incited to rage, their דְמוּת, *image* [i.e., their facial features], is contorted with hate and their mouth seems to spit out poisonous venom (*Radak*).

When the serpent caused Eve to sin he injected into her and her seed a

וְזֻהֲמָה, *defilement*, which pollutes mankind to this very day (*Shabbos* 146a). The righteous man neutralizes the negative effects of this *defilement*, but the wicked one allows this vile poison to numb his intellect so that the lessons of Torah and ethics leave no impression on him (*Sforno; Alshich*).

כְּמוֹ פֶתֶן חֵרֵשׁ יַאְטֵם אָזְנוֹ — *Like a deaf viper that closes its ear.*

As a serpent ages, it becomes deaf in one ear. Then it stuffs its other ear with dirt in order not to hear the incantations of the snake charmer who wishes to render it harmless (*Rashi*).

The passion for evil burns strongly within this man, compelling him to act criminally, even as the serpent is driven to bite because of its instinctive urge to do harm. Therefore this man deliberately deafens himself to reproach in order to foil any attempt to influence him to mend his ways (*Hirsch*).

אֲשֶׁר לֹא יִשְׁמַע לְקוֹל מְלַחֲשִׁים - *So as not to hearken* [lit. *hear*] *to the voice of charmers* [lit. *whisperers*].

David complains that no matter how convincing his arguments were, Abner adamantly refused to be swayed or *charmed* by them (*Alshich*).

חוֹבֵר חֲבָרִים מְחֻכָּם — *Of the most cunning spellbinder.*

This man refuses to listen to reason. He closes his ears so that logical arguments will not penetrate his mind, fear-

ז חֲבָרִים מְחֻכָּם: אֱלֹהִים הֲרָס־שִׁנֵּימוֹ
בְּפִימוֹ מַלְתְּעוֹת כְּפִירִים נְתֹץ | יהוה:
ח יִמָּאֲסוּ כְמוֹ־מַיִם יִתְהַלְּכוּ־לָמוֹ יִדְרֹךְ חִצּוֹ
ט כְּמוֹ יִתְמֹלָלוּ: כְּמוֹ שַׁבְּלוּל תֶּמֶס יַהֲלֹךְ
י נֵפֶל אֵשֶׁת בַּל־חָזוּ שָׁמֶשׁ: בְּטֶרֶם יָבִינוּ

ful lest he fall under the *spell* of truth and be stayed from the perpetration of evil. Just as the embryo is *estranged* from the outside world while *in the womb (v.4)*, so does the wicked man seek to insulate himself from any benign outside influences (*Migdal David*).

7. אֱלֹהִים הֲרָס שִׁנֵּימוֹ בְּפִימוֹ — *O God, smash their teeth in their mouth.*

This verse continues to use the allegory of the snake charmers. After their spell has rendered the serpent temporarily harmless, they swiftly extract the snake's poisonous fangs (*Alshich*).

In the preceding psalm (57:6), David said of the wicked, *their teeth are spears and arrows,* i.e., their slanderous barbs are sharp and piercing. Now he calls to render them harmless by breaking the power of their slanderous bite (*Radak*).

[God hearkened to David's plea and Abner did become a victim of his own crime, as the Sages say (*Yerushalmi Peah* 1:1): In Saul's time four men died as a result of slander — Doeg, Saul, Achimelech, and Abner.]

מַלְתְּעוֹת כְּפִירִים — *The molars of the young lions.*

These are the large molars with which lions grind their food (*Rashi*).

The slanderer resembles the ferocious young lion which vigorously rips its prey apart and chews it to pieces (*Radak*).

Indeed, Abner with his legendary strength, resembled a mighty lion. The Sages teach that it was easier to move a massive wall six cubits wide than to move one of Abner's feet (*Koheles Rabbah* 9:11).

Yalkut Shimoni (Jeremiah 285) adds that Abner was the tallest man in the Israelite army. So confident was he of his strength, that he declared, 'If only the globe had a handle — I would grab the earth and shake it!'

8. יִמָּאֲסוּ — *Let them be despicable.*

Let them be so overcome by failure that anxiety and worry may plague their hearts and their lives become מָאוּס, *despicable* (*Rashi*).

However, *Radak* and *Ibn Ezra* render יִמָּאֲסוּ as a form of יִמַּסּוּ, *let them melt;* the א, *aleph,* is added for extra emphasis, taking the place of the doubled consonant, the extra ס (יְמָסְסוּ).

כְמוֹ מַיִם יִתְהַלְּכוּ לָמוֹ — *As if in water, let them wade.*

Let them be inundated by a flood of sorrow and tears (*Rashi*)

Radak and *Ibn Ezra* render: [Let them melt] *and be as running water.*

יִדְרֹךְ חִצּוֹ — *Let Him [i.e., HASHEM] aim* [lit. *tread on*] *His arrows.*

Rashi comments that this plea is addressed directly to God, asking Him to attack the enemy and to *cut him down.*

According to *Radak,* this verse is a continuation of David's prayer for the failure of his foes: When any of them *treads on* his bow to prepare it for stringing and shooting, may the *arrows* crumble and fall apart as if *cut to pieces.*

9. כְּמוֹ שַׁבְּלוּל — *Like the snail.*

The meaning of שַׁבְּלוּל is uncertain. *Rashi* first suggests that it is a *snail. Hirsch* explains that as the snail moves, it leaves behind it a trail of mucous matter. Thus the name שַׁבְּלוּל may derive

⁷ O God, smash their teeth
    in their mouth;
The molars of the young lions —
    shatter, HASHEM.
⁸ Let them be despicable,
    as if in water, let them wade,
Let Him aim His arrows
    to cut him down.
⁹ Like the snail that melts and slithers away,
    the stillbirth of a mole that never saw the sun.

from שְׁבִיל, path. (Rashi here renders שַׁבְלוּל in Old French as a limtza. In Leviticus 11:30, Rashi applies the same term to the חֹמֶט, another creeping reptile.)

Alternatively Rashi explains שַׁבְלוּל as שִׁבֹּלֶת מַיִם, a great wave of water (see 69:16), which washes away (melts) the foe.

תֶּמֶס יַהֲלֹךְ — That melts and slithers [lit. goes] away.

Because a slimy trail of mucous oozes from the snail, it appears to be melting away. David says, 'It is my prayer that my foes should continually melt away and disappear in similar fashion' (Sforno).

Midrash Shocher Tov observes that just as the snail disappears, yet leaves behind a visible trail, so too with evil slander; long after the actual sound of the words vanish, the damage which they caused still remains!

נֵפֶל אֵשֶׁת — The stillbirth of a mole.

The Talmud (Moed Kattan 6b) describes the אֵשֶׁת as a field pest which, together with mice and other rodents, damages crops. The most prominent feature of the אֵשֶׁת is that it cannot see. [Most translations identify אֵשֶׁת as the mole which lives mainly in the undergound darkness and has poor eyesight.]

Rashi here identifies the אֵשֶׁת as the תִּנְשֶׁמֶת which is listed among the unclean creeping animals (Leviticus 11:30) and which Targum (ibid.) renders as אַשׁוּתָא.

Among the unclean birds, we also find the תִּנְשֶׁמֶת (ibid. 11:18) which Rashi identifies as the bat which flies blindly in the night and closely resembles the creeping rodent תִּנְשֶׁמֶת which has no eyes.

Hirsch comments: The stillborn animal never sees the light of the sun, nor does a mole, although born alive, ever behold the light because its habitat is underground. Similarly these evil men stray in darkness, for their minds were never illuminated by the brilliant light of Torah knowledge (Sforno).

Rashi also suggests that נֵפֶל אֵשֶׁת may be translated as the stillborn child of an אִשָׁה, woman.

Radak observes that both the stillborn child in the mother's womb and the snail ensconced within its shell have never seen the sun.

בַּל חָזוּ שָׁמֶשׁ — That never saw the sun.

Midrash Shocher Tov interprets this homiletically with reference to the slanderers. They are destined to fall (נֵפֶל) into the fires (אֵשֶׁת) of Gehinnom, from which they shall never emerge to see the sun of the World to Come.

סִירֹתֵיכֶם אָטָד כְּמוֹ־חַי כְּמוֹ־חָרוֹן
יא יִשְׂעָרֶנּוּ: יִשְׂמַח צַדִּיק כִּי־חָזָה נָקָם
יב פְּעָמָיו יִרְחַץ בְּדַם הָרָשָׁע: וְיֹאמַר אָדָם
אַךְ־פְּרִי לַצַּדִּיק אַךְ יֵשׁ־אֱלֹהִים שֹׁפְטִים
בָּאָרֶץ:

10. בְּטֶרֶם יָבִינוּ סִירֹתֵיכֶם אָטָד — *Before your tender briars develop into* [lit. *understand*] *hardened thorns.*

Rashi explains this as a simile: סִירָה is a young briar shoot which is still relatively soft; it symbolizes the young offspring of the wicked who still lack the בִּינָה, *understanding*, to be mature, hardened criminals who are symbolized by אָטָד, *hardened thorns.*

However, *Radak, Sforno,* and *Malbim* render סִירֹתֵיכֶם as *your cooking pots,* which are heated by a fire made of אָטָד, *dry thorns.* [Similarly we find כְּקוֹל הַסִּירִים תַּחַת הַסִּיר, *Like the sound of crackling thorns under the pot* (*Koheles* 7:6).] By the use of the example of a pot, the psalmist alludes to the *swiftness* with which the wicked will be destroyed. Ordinarily, the fire burning beneath a pot heats the metal quickly; but the destruction of the wicked will occur with extraordinary dispatch, even before the pot *understands,* i.e., feels, the effect of the flames.

Sforno interprets this allegorically: God will not delay the punishment of the wicked until after they die and the flames of *Gehinnom* are felt by them. The punishment of the wicked will come much sooner — כְּמוֹ חַי, *even while they live,* כְּמוֹ חָרוֹן, *with unbridled wrath,* God will sweep them away.

Returning to *Rashi's* original translation of סִירֹתֵיכֶם as *tender briars,* *Alshich* detects a special allusion to Abner's folly. David asks, 'בְּטֶרֶם יָבִינוּ, *Do you still fail to understand?* The *tender briar* which you claim ripped Saul's robe surely could not cut better than אָטָד, *a hardened thorn.* Thus, how do you explain the fact that the cut was straight, and neat כְּמוֹ חַי, *as if done*

by a live person? If, indeed, a thorn tore the robe, then the rip should have been jagged, כְּמוֹ חָרוֹן, *resembling* [a cloth torn in] *anger!'*

כְּמוֹ חַי — *As if with might.*

חַי, *life,* is another term for גְּבוּרָה, *might* (*Rashi*).

Malbim observes that the prophets often compare the punishment of the wicked to cooking them in a pot, as in *Ezekiel* 24:3, שְׁפֹת הַסִּיר שְׁפֹת, *Set down the pot, set it down.* If God brings their suffering upon them only after patiently allowing them time to fill the measure of their evil, they are compared to well cooked flesh, but if their evil is so great that God is compelled to punish them sooner than anticipated, they are likened to בָּשָׂר חַי, *raw meat,* which has not had time to cook.

כְּמוֹ חָרוֹן יִשְׂעָרֶנּוּ — *As if with wrath He will storm at them* [i.e., He will sweep them away like a whirlwind].

God will not wait for these men to grow old and weak. Rather, while they are still חַי, *lively, robust,* and *mighty,* He will swoop down upon them in a turbulent burst of *wrath* (*Radak*).

11. יִשְׂמַח צַדִּיק כִּי חָזָה נָקָם — *The righteous one shall rejoice when he sees vengeance.*

I.e., when he witnesses God's wrath as He *sweeps them* [the wicked] *away in a storm* (*Radak*).

The Sages teach that often a person is saved from danger thanks to the merit of others who are more righteous than he. Such a person does not deserve to see the destruction of his enemies and God will prevent him from doing so. If someone is allowed to watch the down-

¹⁰ *Before your tender briars develop*
        into hardened thorns,
As if with might, as if with wrath
        He will storm at them.
¹¹ *The righteous one shall rejoice*
        when he sees vengeance,
His feet shall he bathe
        in the blood of the wicked.
¹² *And mankind shall say,*
        'There is, indeed, a reward for the righteous;
        there is, indeed, a God judging the land.'

fall of his adversaries, it proves that he is a truly righteous man. Therefore *The* [genuinely] *righteous one shall rejoice when he sees vengeance*, not because he gloats over the suffering of his enemy, but as a sign from God that he has been saved by virtue of his own merit (*Panim Yafos*).

פְּעָמָיו יִרְחַץ בְּדַם הָרָשָׁע — *His feet* [lit. *footsteps*] *shall he bathe in the blood of the wicked.*

Hirsch emphasizes that this phrase should not be understood literally, as a gruesome orgy of revenge. Rather the verse allegorically expresses the concept that righteous people should draw a lesson from the punishment of the wicked. When the wicked drown violently in their own blood, the righteous are inspired to avoid evil even more meticulously than before. Thus they *wash their own footsteps* because of the lesson they derive from *the blood of the wicked*.

[These words, which seem to make light of the blood of the wicked, allude to Abner. *Yerushalmi Peah* 1:1 lists the factors which sealed Abner's doom. Paramount was the accusation, 'He made the bloodshed of the youths into a game, therefore he forfeited his own blood.' This refers to the time when Abner met his rival general, Joab, who commanded David's army. Abner sug-

gested, '*Let the young soldiers arise and play* (i.e., engage in swordplay) *before us'* (II Samuel 2:14). The duel resulted in fatalities, yet Abner considered it a sport. Because he was unconcerned with bloodshed, his own blood was spilled].

12. וַיֹּאמַר אָדָם אַךְ פְּרִי לַצַּדִּיק — *And mankind shall say, 'There is, indeed, a reward* [lit. *fruit*] *for the righteous.'*

When the world will see that God avenges the righteous, all will admit that the good deeds of the devout do not go unrewarded (*Rashi*).

Sforno adds: They will see the truth of the *Mishnah (Peah* 1:1) which teaches that although the primary reward for good deeds is reserved for the World to Come, God benefits the righteous with פֵּירוֹת, *fruits*, of their labor in this world.

אַךְ יֵשׁ אֱלֹהִים שֹׁפְטִים בָּאָרֶץ — *'There is, indeed, a God judging the land.'*

The translation of אֱלֹהִים as God (in His role of Judge), follows *Targum* and *Radak*. *Radak* and *Ibn Ezra* also suggest that אֱלֹהִים are the *ministering angels* [see also *comm*. 27:6] whom God has appointed as His agents to supervise the world and administer justice to mankind. [Saul and his judges failed to do justice to David, but David informs them that they have no monopoly on

justice. If human judges fail to discharge their duties, then the Supreme Judge has many agents through whom justice will be rendered ultimately.]

The Sages comment (*Avos d'Rabbi Nathan*, 29): He who diligently pursues his Torah studies is supplied with heavenly assistance in the form of angels who aid his diligence (by removing obstacles and difficulties from his path); but he who wastes his opportunity to study Torah is afflicted with many heaven-sent agents who interfere with his studies. Lions, wolves, leopards, tigers, snakes, soldiers, and bandits — all of these surround this man and punish him. As the verse states,

'Indeed there are ministering angels in the land.'

[This is David's final message to Abner and the others who hunt him. They refused to acknowledge David's involvement in the cutting of the robe and the removal of the spear and jug. They attribute everything to chance. Probing deeper into their hearts, David reveals that they attribute all events to chance, and not to Divine intervention. Therefore their final punishment will come about in such a way as to demonstrate clearly that *there is a God who judges the land* and that nothing is left to chance.][1]

1. [Abner died a violent death and the events which led to it indicate that he was punished measure for measure.

Assael ben Zeruyah pursued Abner. Defending himself, Abner hurled his spear at Assael, striking him a mortal blow near the fifth rib where the bladder and the liver meet. Joab, Assael's brother, accused Abner of murder, arguing that Abner could have defended himself by wounding Assael. Abner protested his innocence, pleading that he killed Assael accidentally, that the spear struck the victim by chance.

Joab refuted this claim, saying, 'Only a skilled marksman who aims with unerring accuracy can hit this small, vulnerable spot. This did not happen by chance! Abner, you are a murderer!' The Sanhedrin condemned Abner, and Joab slew him.

As Abner lay dying, he conquered his own desire for revenge, in an act of strength that surpassed all his conquests on the battlefield. *Yalkut Shimoni, Jeremiah* 285, relates:

When Joab stabbed him, Abner grasped Joab and twisted his body around into a complete circle. Immediately, all the men of Israel pleaded with Abner, 'Sire, if you kill Joab, then we will be like orphans without a father to protect them, for the Philistines will surely attack and defeat us.'

Abner asked, 'But what shall I do! This man extinguished the bright candle of my life.'

The people replied, 'Bring your case before the דַּיָּין הָאֱמֶת, *The Judge of Truth,*and let Him decide.'

Abner released Joab from his death grip and fell. One man lived and the other went to his death.

Behold, Abner had finally learned that *Indeed there is a God who judges the land.*]

This psalm is the third and last composition in the Al Tashcheis series. It is based on the very first incident in which Saul pursued David (recorded in I Samuel 19).

As David's star gained ascendancy, Saul's dark and troubled spirit sank to the lowest depths. Once, when David played music before the king in an attempt to soothe his anguish, a spirit of evil descended on Saul. He flung his deadly spear at David's head, barely missing his mark. David fled from the palace.

Saul sent soldiers to David's home to watch him that night and to slay him in the morning. David was Saul's son-in-law, for his wife was Saul's daughter Michal. She loved her noble husband more than she did her bitter father, so she helped David to escape through a side window.

Michal then placed a lifelike mannequin (teraphim) in David's bed as a ruse. At first she was able to restrain Saul's men by claiming David was sick, but then Saul dispatched his messengers again, saying: 'Bring him back to me in his bed so that I myself can slay him.' By the time Saul's soldiers discovered the deception, David had disappeared, leaving only the mannequin in his place.

David composed this psalm of entreaty and thanksgiving upon his narrow escape from Saul.

א לַמְנַצֵּחַ אַל־תַּשְׁחֵת לְדָוִד מִכְתָּם בִּשְׁלֹחַ
שָׁאוּל וַיִּשְׁמְרוּ אֶת־הַבַּיִת לַהֲמִיתוֹ:
ב הַצִּילֵנִי מֵאֹיְבַי | אֱלֹהָי מִמִּתְקוֹמְמַי
ג תְּשַׂגְּבֵנִי: הַצִּילֵנִי מִפֹּעֲלֵי אָוֶן וּמֵאַנְשֵׁי
ד דָמִים הוֹשִׁיעֵנִי: כִּי הִנֵּה אָרְבוּ לְנַפְשִׁי
יָגוּרוּ עָלַי עַזִּים לֹא־פִשְׁעִי וְלֹא־חַטָּאתִי
ה יהוה: בְּלִי־עָוֹן יְרֻצוּן וְיִכּוֹנָנוּ עוּרָה

1. לַמְנַצֵּחַ — *For the Conductor.*

[We cannot fail to be amazed at David's awesome capacity to create music and song even in times of severe adversity. The *Talmud (Sotah* 48a) states that when the Sanhedrin, the High Court, was dissolved, song and music vanished from people's lips, as Scripture says (*Lamentations* 5:14) *The elders have gone from the gate* (where the court convened), *the young men* (have desisted) *from their music.*

The helpless victim of injustice is usually preoccupied with his own misery; he is oblivious to the joy which also exists in the world. Although David realized that there was not one honest magistrate to whom he could appeal and from whom he could demand justice, he would not allow the melody which always welled up in his heart to be stilled.

David appealed to the Supreme God of Justice, and sang of His fair verdict, which he awaited with perfect faith.]

אַל תַּשְׁחֵת — Al Tashcheis [lit. *Do not destroy*].

David composed this psalm while on the verge of death; therefore he pleaded with God, '*Do not destroy me*' (Rashi).

בִּשְׁלֹחַ שָׁאוּל וַיִּשְׁמְרוּ אֶת הַבַּיִת לַהֲמִיתוֹ — *When Saul dispatched, and they guarded the house to kill him.*

[I.e., when Saul dispatched troops to guard David's house to prevent his escape so that Saul could later have him killed (see *prefatory remarks*).]

Alshich observes that God inspired Saul to handle this affair in a most inefficient manner, thus affording David an opportunity to escape. Saul should have given immediate orders for his men to break into David's home and slay him. By waiting outside all night, Saul's men not only allowed David to escape but also enabled him to gain a substantial head start in his flight.

2. הַצִּילֵנִי מֵאֹיְבַי ... מִמִּתְקוֹמְמַי — *Rescue me from my foes... those who rise against me.*

Norah Tehillos observes that David was already plagued by his old *foes,* the marauding gentiles and Philistines who attacked Israel. He bemoans the fact that he must fight on two fronts — against the gentiles and against his own countrymen, former friends, who now *rise up against me.*

Hirsch attaches special significance to this description of David's enemies: David was completely innocent, for he had done absolutely nothing to offend Saul's supporters. His only 'crime' was that God was with him and had caused him to *rise* to spectacular success. Because David's star was rising, his jealous rivals sought *to rise up* themselves in order to engineer David's downfall.

3. הַצִּילֵנִי מִפֹּעֲלֵי אָוֶן — *Rescue me from evildoers.*

These are the men who lay in ambush outside the gates of David's home (*Radak*).

59
1-5

For the Conductor, Al Tashcheis,
    by David, a Michtam
When Saul dispatched,
    and they guarded the house to kill him.
² Rescue me from my foes, O my God;
    over those who rise against me, strengthen me.
³ Rescue me from evildoers;
    and from bloody people, save me.
⁴ For, behold! they lie in ambush for my soul,
    around me gather impudent ones —
Not for my transgression
    and not for my sin, O HASHEM!
⁵ Without iniquity they run and prepare —

וּמֵאַנְשֵׁי דָמִים הוֹשִׁיעֵנִי — *And from bloody people, save me.*

The *evildoers* were appointed to capture David, whereas the *bloody people* were those who were assigned to kill him (*Radak*).

4. יָגוּרוּ עָלַי — *Around me* [lit. *upon me*] *gather.*

This translation follows *Rashi* and *Radak* [see 56:7]. *Ibn Ezra* suggests that it may be rendered *they settle around me* to suggest they establish a permanent guard post outside my house to ensure uninterrupted surveillance.

עַזִּים — *Impudent ones.*

Sforno identifies these impudent enemies of David as seven members of Saul's family who were later hung in order to appease the Gibeonites (II Samuel Chapter 21). [The reason that they were singled out for death is explained in *Yevamos* 79a.]

לֹא פִשְׁעִי וְלֹא חַטָּאתִי — *Not for my transgression and not for my sin.*

These killers do not stalk me because of any crime which I have committed (*Radak*). [They are spurred only by jealousy.]

ה' — *HASHEM!*

This is an exclamation. David cries out: 'HASHEM, save me — You know the truth!' (*Radak*).

5. בְּלִי עָוֹן — *Without iniquity.*

Not only am I innocent of any sin towards God (v. 4), but I am also guiltless of committing any iniquity against these foes which could justify the hatred they feel for me (*Radak*).

And yet they attack me without the slightest compunction. Even as they wrong me, they persistently declare בְּלִי עָוֹן, *'We are without iniquity'* (*Malbim*).

יְרוּצוּן וְיִכּוֹנָנוּ — *They run and prepare.*

Their audacity has no limits! Even if they commit their crimes with cold-blooded indifference, one might expect them to be ashamed to perpetrate them publicly. Yet, they bustle about and make a tremendous public commotion while they prepare for the kill (*Norah Tehillos*).

Furthermore, as they spy on me, they hurry to run back to Saul with slanderous reports about my behavior (*Maharam Markado*).

וֹ לִקְרָאתִי וּרְאֵה: וְאַתָּה יהוה־אֱלֹהִים |
צְבָאוֹת אֱלֹהֵי יִשְׂרָאֵל הָקִיצָה לִפְקֹד כָּל־
הַגּוֹיִם אַל־תָּחֹן כָּל־בֹּגְדֵי אָוֶן סֶלָה:
ז יָשׁוּבוּ לָעֶרֶב יֶהֱמוּ כַכָּלֶב וִיסוֹבְבוּ עִיר:
ח הִנֵּה | יַבִּיעוּן בְּפִיהֶם חֲרָבוֹת

עוּרָה לִקְרָאתִי וּרְאֵה — *Awaken towards me and see.*

[See 44:24 where we find that עוּרָה implies: Show that You are awake. Certainly, God's personal supervision over the righteous never ceases; however, when He does not react to the persecution which they suffer at the hands of their pursuers, it appears as if He slumbers and must be awakened.]

6. [In this verse, David abruptly shifts his attention from Saul to the gentiles, whom he now asks God to destroy. The commentaries attempt to explain this sudden change of theme.]

וְאַתָּה ה' אֱלֹהִים צְבָאוֹת אֱלֹהֵי יִשְׂרָאֵל — *And You, HASHEM, God of Legions, God of Israel.*

David seeks to arouse God in all of His vast glory; in all of His attributes which include kindness and justice; and in all of His power, which rules both the celestial forces above and the nation of Israel below *(Ibn Ezra).*

According to *Radak*, David abandoned hope of receiving justice in his own time. He surveyed the society around him and saw only corruption and dishonesty. The land of Israel did not lack judges and sheriffs, yet none of them protested Saul's outrageous conduct. In despair, David trains his hopes on the future, when God will appear as the all-powerful אֱלֹהִים, *Judge,* of the entire world. Then God will mete out true justice to all men, including Saul and his bloodthirsty cohorts.

Malbim, however, views David's plea as a request for the present. David was the mighty champion of Israel, the foremost defender against the Philistine

host. Here David displays a great sense of responsibility towards his people, for now that he must go into hiding, he can no longer publicly lead their defense against the foe. Therefore, he turns over his command to another General, *the God of Legions, the God of Israel,* and begs Him to continue the fight.

הָקִיצָה לִפְקֹד כָּל הַגּוֹיִם — *Arouse Yourself to remember all the nations.*

According to *Rashi, the nations* actually refers to Saul and his minions. *Yaavetz Hadoresh* explains that they resemble the gentiles, for just as *the nations* hate Israel, without any real reason, so do Saul and his men hate David without cause. Therefore, the verdict issued against them should resemble that of the gentile nations.

[The comparison of Saul and his supporters to *the nations* alludes to the basic defect which undermined the foundation of Saul's monarchy. When Israel first demanded that Samuel appoint a king for them, they were motivated by a sense of inferiority and by a desire to imitate the gentiles. They cried, *'Appoint for us a king who will rule us like all the nations'* (I Samuel 8:5). Saul's ill-conceived reign was doomed from its very inception (see *comm.* to 4:9). Consequently, this monarchy was plagued by the kinds of machinations, intrigues, and jealousies with which the royal palaces of the gentiles are rife. This jealousy was the source of David's woes and Saul's ultimate destruction.]

Malbim, following his previous comment, interprets: 'Now that I [David] must relinquish my command of Israel, please, God, take charge *and remember*

awaken towards me and see.
⁶ *And You, HASHEM, God of Legions,*
God of Israel,
Arouse Yourself to remember all the nations,
favor not any evil traitors, Selah.
⁷ *They return toward evening,*
they howl like the dog and go round about
the city.
⁸ *Behold! they spew with their mouths,*

---

to wage war against *the nations* who threaten Israel.'

אַל תָּחֹן כָּל בֹּגְדֵי אָוֶן — *Favor not any evil traitors.*

David concludes his request: 'Although I ask You to combat the gentiles, I also ask You to remember that the *evil traitors* of Israel must also be punished without undeserved mercy' (*Malbim*).

7. יָשׁוּבוּ לָעֶרֶב — *They return toward evening.*

This alludes to the soldiers who stood guard around David's house from evening until the following morning (*Radak*).

יֶהֱמוּ כַכָּלֶב — *They howl like the dog.*

[Although there were many soldiers, David refers to them in the singular, as כֶּלֶב, one dog, for they all repeated the same slanderous tales in Saul's ears, so their voices were as one.]

Just as the dog tends to howl in the darkness of night, the cowardly talebearer slanders his foes in dark secrecy rather than denouncing them publicly (*Rashbam*).

[Moreover, the *Talmud* (*Bava Kama* 60b) states that when the Angel of

Death comes to a city to claim someone's soul, the dogs sense his presence and howl. Saul's men played a dual role; they lurked in the night as agents of death, and they howled like dogs.]

[See *Chafetz Chaim, Shmiras HaLashon*, 1:4-9, for a detailed comparison of the talebearer and the dog.

וִיסוֹבְבוּ עִיר — *And go round about the city.*

The guards resembled a pack of hungry dogs, surrounding its prey.

In addition to the armed guards stationed outside David's house, Saul dispatched search parties to go around and comb the city in the event that David managed to slip through the cordon around his home (*Radak*).[1]

8. הִנֵּה יַבִּיעוּן בְּפִיהֶם — *Behold! they spew with their mouths.*

Rashi explains that this is a direct continuation of the preceding verse. Towards evening my foes assembled to besiege my home, but in truth, their wickedness had already begun by day, when they *spewed forth* evil tales about me in the ears of Saul and incited his wrath.

[Although common sense dictates

---

1. [This alludes to the *Talmud* (*Eruvin* 61a) which says that a killer is dangerous only in his own city, where his confidence is bolstered by the familiar environment. Put him in a strange city and he will feel too insecure and frightened to do much harm. As the folk saying goes: 'Take a dog away from his hometown and he won't bark even once in seven years!'

Therefore, David says, 'Because these killers roam around the city, their hometown, at will, they feel a sense of mastery, and howl menacingly like dogs!']

ט בְּשִׂפְתוֹתֵיהֶם כִּי־מִי שֹׁמֵעַ: וְאַתָּה יהוה
י תִּשְׂחַק־לָמוֹ תִּלְעַג לְכָל־גּוֹיִם: עֻזּוֹ אֵלֶיךָ
יא אֶשְׁמֹרָה כִּי־אֱלֹהִים מִשְׂגַּבִּי: אֱלֹהֵי
°חסדי חַסְדּוֹ יְקַדְּמֵנִי אֱלֹהִים יַרְאֵנִי בְשֹׁרְרָי:
יב אַל־תַּהַרְגֵם | פֶּן־יִשְׁכְּחוּ עַמִּי הֲנִיעֵמוֹ

that men who are laying a trap should exercise the utmost caution and secrecy in order to catch their prey by surprise, Saul's men carelessly publicized their plot to every passer-by. They were so thrilled by the thought of David's impending doom that they could not contain their excitement, but spewed forth the details of their strategy.

In addition, they were proud that the king himself had appointed them to execute this mission. While they gloried in their great prestige, they failed to consider the enormity of their intended crime (see Sforno).]

חַרְבוֹת בְּשִׂפְתוֹתֵיהֶם — Swords are on their lips.

Their razor-sharp words of slander are as murderous as the blade of a sword (Targum).

כִּי מִי שֹׁמֵעַ — For 'Who listens?'

They proudly boast of their 'courageous' campaign against David, but, in truth, they are cowards. They dare to speak so boldly only because they think that David does not hear. If they realized that he could overhear them, they would immediately fall silent, for fear that David might someday ascend to the throne and punish them (Radak).

9. וְאַתָּה ה' תִּשְׂחַק לָמוֹ — But as for You, HASHEM — You laugh at them.

David said: 'These men imagine that since I do not hear of their plots, I am defenseless and at their mercy. O God, foil their schemes and show them how greatly they err! For You, my Protector, hear every word they utter. You can ridicule them as no one else can, for You realize the emptiness of their threats' (Radak).

They strut about and boast that they have the entire city under the tightest security. You laugh at this presumption (Sforno).

תִּלְעַג לְכָל גּוֹיִם — You mock all nations.

Just as You mock all nations which threaten to harm Israel [see 2:4], so will You ridicule these enemies of mine [and undo their schemes] (Rashi).

10. עֻזּוֹ — Power is his [lit. his power].

The translation follows Rashi, who refers this to the enemy, who has the upper hand in this conflict with David; and Radak who applies this to Saul.

Hirsch perceives in these words the rule which influenced all of David's actions towards Saul: 'As long as all the royal might and power remain in the hands of Saul, I [David] shall refrain from any belligerent action against him. Patiently and faithfully I wait for You, O God, to take the initiative. It was You who invested Saul with his royal powers, and You alone will decide when to divest him of them.'

Ibn Ezra interprets עֻזּוֹ as a reference to God Himself, of whom we can say Power is His alone. Therefore, says David, 'For You [alone] do I wait.'

אֵלֶיךָ אֶשְׁמֹרָה — For You do I wait.

I.e., to deliver me from the threat of my foes.

Patiently, I await the end of the time which You have destined for the duration of Saul's reign (Hirsch).

Until that time, not only will I not attack Saul but also אֶשְׁמֹרָה, I shall guard, him even from my own men who wish to slay him (Sforno). [See I Samuel, chapters 24 and 26.]

swords are on their lips — for 'Who listens?'

⁹ But as for You, HASHEM — You laugh at them,
You mock all nations.
¹⁰ Power is his —
for You do I wait, for God is my stronghold.
¹¹ The God of my kindness — He will anticipate me,
God will show me my watchful foes.
¹² Slay them not,
lest my nation forget.

כִּי אֱלֹהִים מִשְׂגַּבִּי — *For God is my stronghold.*

[David says: 'I am determined to defend myself from Saul only passively, despite the tremendous risk involved in such a dangerous course of action. I do not consider this to be suicidal because I firmly believe that I am well protected, *for God is my stronghold.*']

11. אֱלֹהֵי חַסְדִּי יְקַדְּמֵנִי — *The God of my kindness — He will anticipate me.*

God will *anticipate* my need and extend His help before my enemies can vanquish me *(Rashi).*

Sforno comments that God promised the kings of Israel special kindness in their struggles and wars. David says: 'Although I am not yet the king, I hope that God will *anticipate* my ascension to the throne by kindly granting me special power to emerge triumphant from conflicts, even before my coronation.'

[The word is spelled חַסְדּוֹ (כְּתִיב), *His kindness,* but is pronounced חַסְדִּי (קְרִי), *my kindness.* This duality suggests, 'Because I am assured of His [God's] protective kindness towards me, I can be kindly towards Saul.'

David's use of the Name אֱלֹהִים, denoting God as Dispenser of Justice indicates his confidence that if his pursuer deserves punishment, then יְקַדְּמֵנִי, *God will anticipate me,* by meting out justice so that I need not take action (see *Radak; Rashi; Ibn Ezra).*]

As *Hirsch* explains, the discrepancy between the spelling and pronunciation serves to emphasize that the actions of God and man are intertwined. The psalmist declares: God's actions towards me are a reflection of my own deeds. To the degree that I practice lovingkindness (חַסְדִּי) towards others, God will act kindly towards me (חַסְדּוֹ).

Olelos Yehudah points out that these words, *The God of my kindness — He will anticipate me,* teach a general rule of God's conduct with man: First, He displays kindness and showers a person with the means to perform the commandments. Only then, does God obligate man to respond. As the *Midrash* says, 'Did I [God] ever ask anyone to put up a *mezuzah* before giving him a house? Did I ever require a circumcision before blessing a person with a son? Did I ever demand tithes before supplying a man with fruits?'

אֱלֹהִים יַרְאֵנִי בְשֹׁרְרָי — *God will show me my watchful foes.*

Radak explains: God will show me the downfall of those who dog my steps and watch me with hatred, as Scripture says, *And Saul watched David with an evil eye (I Samuel 18:9).*

12. אַל תַּהַרְגֵם פֶּן יִשְׁכְּחוּ עַמִּי — *Slay them not, lest my nation forget.*

[David's prime concern was neither his own safety nor revenge; rather, he sought to counter the bad influence

יג בְּחֵילְךָ וְהוֹרִידֵמוֹ מָגִנֵּנוּ אֲדֹנָי: חַטַּאת־
פִּימוֹ דְּבַר־שְׂפָתֵימוֹ וְיִלָּכְדוּ בִגְאוֹנָם
יד וּמֵאָלָה וּמִכַּחַשׁ יְסַפֵּרוּ: כַּלֵּה בְחֵמָה כַּלֵּה
וְאֵינֵמוֹ וְיֵדְעוּ כִּי־אֱלֹהִים מֹשֵׁל בְּיַעֲקֹב
טו לְאַפְסֵי הָאָרֶץ סֶלָה: וְיָשֻׁבוּ לָעֶרֶב יֶהֱמוּ

which his foes exercised over the people of Israel. He desired that God publicize the downfall of the wicked as an object lesson for the benefit of those who harbored any wish to follow in their ways.]

David asked: 'Do not destroy them with one quick blow, which is hardly noticed and swiftly forgotten' (Rashi, Radak). [Instead, reduce their power gradually, so that people will marvel at their protracted and irreversible decline and will witness the utter helplessness of these once powerful men.]

הֲנִיעֵמוֹ בְחֵילְךָ — *Deprive them of Your wealth* [lit. *Impoverish them with Your might*].

This translation follows *Rashi*, who renders הֲנִיעֵמוֹ as *remove them* from their property, for it is truly *Your wealth* which You had graciously bestowed upon them. [Man's 'ownership' of goods is an illusion, for God actually owns everything. One's material goods should be viewed as a Divine trust which is to be properly disbursed.]

Radak, however, interprets הֲנִיעֵמוֹ as *make them wander about* (from נָעוּ) to search for their daily bread. *Ibn Ezra* adds that in this manner they will resemble the dog which strays around the city and sniffs for scraps of food. This punishment is particularly fitting, for *they howl like the dog and go round about the city* (v. 7).

[The dog is a symbol of extreme poverty, as the *Talmud* (*Shabbos* 155b) says: There is no creature as poor as the dog for his food supply is very scarce.]

The *Chafetz Chaim* in *Shmiras Halashon* 1:6 explains that arrogance is the root of the desire to slander and degrade one's fellow man. Therefore, poverty is its most appropriate punishment, for it serves to humble the proud. Even today, although the punishment of צָרַעַת, *leprous spots*, no longer strikes the arrogant slanderer, poverty still does!

Rashbam perceives yet another moral lesson here: The slanderer drifts around peddling his gossip (הוֹלֵךְ רָכִיל), and therefore, he is ultimately condemned to wander about in search of a livelihood.

וְהוֹרִידֵמוֹ — *And cast them down.*

[Let them descend not only from their financial position but also from their high level of social prestige.]

13. חַטַּאת פִּימוֹ דְּבַר שְׂפָתֵימוֹ — *The sin of their mouth is the word of their lips.*

Let their punishment be so clear that not only will others learn from it, but also they themselves will recognize the evil of their slanderous words (*Radak*).

Let them admit *with the words of their own lips* to the *sin of their mouth* (*Alshich*).

וְיִלָּכְדוּ בִגְאוֹנָם — *And they shall be ensnared by their pride.*

In their arrogance, they declared, *'Who listens?' (v. 8)* and disregarded the threat of Divine retribution. They will be trapped in this very arrogance, [for You, O God, *listen* closely to every proud word they utter] (*Ibn Ezra*).

וּמֵאָלָה וּמִכַּחַשׁ יְסַפֵּרוּ — *Because of curses and falsehoods which they recount.*

[The word כַּחַשׁ literally means *denial*. The slanderer is eventually rebuked by his victim for his vicious tales. If the slanderer fears the victim, he will feel

*Deprive them of Your wealth, and cast them down,
O our Shield, my Master.*

¹³ *The sin of their mouth is the word of their lips,
and they shall be ensnared by their pride,
Because of curses and falsehoods
which they recount.*
¹⁴ *Destroy them in wrath,
destroy them until they are no more!
And then shall they know that God rules Jacob,
to the ends of the earth, Selah.*
¹⁵ *And they return toward evening,
they howl like the dog*

compelled to resort to *falsehood* to deny that he had ever slandered him. If the slanderer has no fear of the man whom he wronged, he will contemptuously *curse* him in response to his accusation.]

14. בַּלֵּה בְחֵמָה בַלֵּה — *Destroy them in wrath, destroy them.*

Eradicate them by degrees *(Radak).* The repeated use of the word בַּלֵּה implies the gradual process of their downfall *(Hirsch).*

Norah Tehillos perceives here an allusion to the suffering of Gehinnom, which is not limited to one isolated punishment. After the wicked are consumed by the flames, they are repeatedly re-created so that they can be returned to the fire again and again. [See *commentary* to 6:11 and 21:18.]

וְאֵינֵמוֹ — *Until they are no more.*

[Although it is desirable that their terrible fate should long be remembered, they themselves must be completely destroyed and obliterated.]

וְיֵדְעוּ כִּי אֱלֹהִים מֹשֵׁל בְּיַעֲקֹב לְאַפְסֵי הָאָרֶץ — *And then shall they know that God rules Jacob, to the ends of the earth.*

God pays more attention to His Chosen People, Israel, than He does to the other nations. Nevertheless, when the world sees the intensity of His ex-

acting supervision over Jacob, they will recognize His ability to control mankind in general, even *to the ends of the earth (Radak).*

['Israel' is the title applied to our people when they are meritorious; the designation 'Jacob' is employed when the Jews are less deserving of Divine favor.

God is called מוֹשֵׁל, *ruler,* when He must force His sovereignty on His subjects against their will. He is referred to as מֶלֶךְ, *king,* when the people readily accept His dominion.

David addresses himself to the wicked Jews who pursue him; he refers to them as *Jacob* because of their evil ways. God will force His will upon them as their מוֹשֵׁל, *ruler,* which will be a lesson to all of the far-flung nations who are also estranged from God and refuse to recognize His authority.]

15. וְיָשֻׁבוּ לָעֶרֶב יֶהֱמוּ כַכָּלֶב — *And they return towards evening, they howl like the dog.*

This is a repetition of *v. 7.* There, however, David spoke only to his Jewish enemies, who were of his generation, whereas here he addresses himself to all the nations who will gather with Gog and Magog at the end of days, as the sun of history sets before the Mes-

כַּכֶּ֑לֶב וִיס֥וֹבְבוּ עִֽיר׃ הֵ֤מָּה °יְנוּע֣וּן לֶֽאֱכֹ֑ל ׳יְנִיע֣וּן טז

אִם־לֹ֥א יִ֝שְׂבְּע֗וּ וַיָּלִֽינוּ׃ וַאֲנִ֤י | אָשִׁ֬יר עֻזֶּ֗ךָ יז

וַאֲרַנֵּ֣ן לַבֹּקֶר֮ חַ֫סְדֶּ֥ךָ כִּֽי־הָיִ֣יתָ מִשְׂגָּ֣ב לִ֑י

וּ֝מָנ֗וֹס בְּי֣וֹם צַר־לִֽי׃ עֻ֭זִּי אֵלֶ֣יךָ אֲזַמֵּ֑רָה כִּֽי־ יח

אֱלֹהִ֥ים מִ֝שְׂגַּבִּ֗י אֱלֹהֵ֥י חַסְדִּֽי׃

---

sianic era. They will howl at Israel like
mad dogs *(Sforno)*.

[This alludes to the *Talmudic* statement *(Sotah* 49b) that in the era
preceding the advent of Messiah 'the
face of the generation will resemble the
face of a dog.' Their deeds will resemble
the treachery of Saul's cohorts, as will
their ultimate punishment.]

וִיסֹ֥בְבוּ עִֽיר — *And go round about the
city.*

The armies of Gog and Magog will
encircle Jerusalem and besiege the Holy
City *(Sforno)*.

According to *Meiri*, both verses
refer to Saul's men. However, verse 7
tells of their wicked deeds, while this
verse describes their punishment,
measure for measure. Since they roamed

the city to find David, they are doomed
to wander about the city forever as beggars and scavengers.

16. הֵ֤מָּה יְנוּע֣וּן לֶֽאֱכֹ֑ל — *They wander
about to eat.*

They resemble the starving dog,
whose hunger does not let him sleep.
Until he is sated, he wanders about in
search of food *(Rashi)*.

[Saul's men sought to satisfy their
lust for power and revenge by 'feasting'
on David's corpse, therefore they are
doomed to eternal poverty and starvation.]

17. וַאֲנִ֤י אָשִׁ֬יר עֻזֶּ֗ךָ — *But as for me, I
shall sing of Your might.*

This is a repetition of David's
previous declaration, *Power is His (v.*

59

16-18   *and go round about the city.*

¹⁶ *They wander about to eat,*
if they are not sated that they may sleep.
¹⁷ *But as for me, I shall sing of Your might,*
and rejoice before dawn in Your kindness,
For You have been my stronghold
and a refuge in the day of my distress.
¹⁸ *My Power — to You shall I sing,*
for God is my stronghold, God of my kindness.

10); i.e., *Power* belongs to God alone, and He alone may be praised for it *(Ibn Ezra)*.

Joy will return when God displays His *might* against the foe *(Radak)* and when He finally bestows His *might* upon David, by publicly crowning him king *(Sforno)*.

וַאֲרַנֵּן לַבֹּקֶר חַסְדֶּךָ — *And rejoice before dawn in Your kindness.*

When dawn will begin to break and I see that my escape from Saul's men (last night) was successful, then I shall rejoice *(Rashi)*.

18. עֻזִּי אֵלֶיךָ אֲזַמֵּרָה — *My Power — to You shall I sing.*

This concluding verse contrasts with *v.* 10, עֻזּוֹ אֵלֶיךָ אֶשְׁמֹרָה, *Power is his —*

for You do I wait. Rashi to verse 10 translates עֻזּוֹ, *power is his*, and applies it to David's enemies. However, *Rashi* refers עֻזִּי, *my Power*, in this verse to God who is the source of my strength.

Radak, who refers עֻזּוֹ, *Power is his*, to Saul, here translates עֻזִּי as *power is mine*. As long as the royal power was in the hands of Saul, I could only wait in silence. However, now that עֻזִּי, *power is mine*, I can sing joyously.

כִּי אֱלֹהִים מִשְׂגַּבִּי אֱלֹהֵי חַסְדִּי — *For God is my stronghold, God of my kindness.*

[No matter how powerful I become, I shall never abuse my power and privileges as Saul did. I will never forget that I owe all that I am to Your *kindness*, for You alone are *my stronghold* and my strength.]

[743]   *Tehillim*

60

This psalm presents David's inspired vision of a universal order of nations united in complete harmony. This was his dream. True, Scripture describes David as a mighty warrior endowed with extraordinary martial skills; nevertheless, he was not a belligerent man of war, but an ambassador of peace.

The concept of universal peace is a manifestation of monotheism, the belief in one Almighty God. Pagan mythology depicts a chaotic heaven torn asunder by jealous, warring 'gods' who are no more than an exaggerated reflection of their human creators. Struggle, conflict, and polarization are basic elements of the idolator's weltanschauung.

The Jew, who believes in one Creator, believes that all of the diverse elements of this universe are basically united to serve the purposes of the one God, Who gives order to the world. Israel is at the center of this world order, and the supreme tribunal of this nation, the Great Sanhedrin, convenes in the Temple, which is the spiritual center of the earth. Each of the seventy members of this august body is symbolic of one of the world's seventy nations and the seventy-first member, the chief justice, represents Israel, the nation which controls the order of all other peoples (Ramban, Numbers 11:16).

David dedicated this psalm of war to Sanhedrin, because he fought only upon the advice and consent of this high court. He waged war only to establish Israel's mastery over the seventy nations and to establish a harmonious world order of nations dedicated to divine peace.

א לַמְנַצֵּחַ עַל־שׁוּשַׁן עֵדוּת מִכְתָּם לְדָוִד
ב לְלַמֵּד: בְּהַצּוֹתוֹ | אֶת אֲרַם נַהֲרַיִם וְאֶת־

1. לַמְנַצֵּחַ — *For the Conductor.*

[It is essential to be aware of the background and the setting of this composition. In *II Samuel*, Chapter 7 and again in *I Chronicles*, Chapter 17, Nathan, the prophet, informs David that his life's dream will indeed be realized, and that a Temple will be built to serve as the focal point of God's Holy Presence in the world. The actual construction of this edifice would be executed by David's son; nevertheless, David was charged with making all preparations necessary for this universal center of sanctity.

[In *II Samuel*, Chapter 8 and *I Chronicles*, Chapter 18, we read of David's preparations (see *Rashi, I Chronicles* 8:1). Until now, David's wars were purely defensive campaigns to counter foreign assaults. Henceforth David takes the offensive (*Malbim, I Samuel* 8:11), for now he must subjugate the nations in order to prepare for universal peace.

[First David smote the Philistines; then he subjugated Moab. Finally he was victorious over Hadadezer, the king of Aram Tzovah.]

עַל שׁוּשַׁן עֵדוּת — *Upon* Shushan Eidus [lit. *the rose of the testimony*.]

Many commentaries suggest that this is a special type of musical instrument shaped like a rose (*Metzudas Zion*). It produced exquisite music, and thus resembled the rose, which is the most lovely of flowers (*Meiri*). עֵדוּת, *Eidus*, is related to the word עֲדִי, *jewel, adornment* [see Ezekiel 16:7], and describes the beauty of this instrument (*Ibn Ezra; Meiri*).

Rashi, following *Midrash Shocher Tov*, renders עֵדוּת as *testimony*, an allusion to the Great Sanhedrin, which accepts testimony and has final jurisdiction over legal affairs.

Sanhedrin is also called שׁוּשַׁן as in בִּטְנֵךְ עֲרֵמַת חִטִּים סוּגָה בַּשּׁוֹשַׁנִּים, *Your belly is like a heap of wheat hedged about with roses (Songs* 7:3). [As the *Talmud (Sanhedrin* 37a) comments, 'Just as all men benefit from a heap of nutritious wheat, so do all benefit from the decisions of Sanhedrin. The Sanhedrin also protects Israel from sin, by erecting legal barriers and moral deterrents which safeguard Israel just as a thorny hedge protects the roses.][1]

מִכְתָּם — *A* Michtam.

Targum renders this as פֵּרְשָׁגֵן, *an explanation;* i.e., Sanhedrin examined the terms of the covenant with Aram and explained that since Aram had initiated hostilities twice, the pact was void (*Targuma d'HaTargum*).

According to the *Midrash (Bereishis*

1. The *Midrash* relates that when Joab, David's general, went to wage war on Aram, the Arameans confronted him and asked, 'Are you not the descendant of Jacob, and therefore does not a covenant exist between us?' For Laban, our forebear, said, *"Now come let us make a covenant, you* [Jacob] *and I"*... *And Jacob took a stone and set it up for a monument*... *and Laban said, "This stone is a testimony* (עֵד) *between me and you this day"* ' (*Genesis* 31:44, 45, 48).

[This incident is the basis for the *Targum* on our verse, which translates שׁוּשַׁן as יָשָׁן, *the ancient*, עֵדוּת, *monument of testimony*, which was rerected by Jacob and Laban.]

Joab had no answer for this claim and so he returned to consult with David, who assembled the Sanhedrin. It ruled that Joab should reply: 'The Arameans themselves nullified this covenant of peace! Indeed, Bilaam [on his way to curse Israel] admitted, *"Balak, the King of Moab, brings me from Aram"* (*Numbers* 23:7). This was not the only time the Arameans betrayed their pact with the intent of harming Israel, for Scripture testifies, *The children of Israel served Cushan-Rishasaim the King of Aram-Naharaim* (*Judges* 3:8). Aram is guilty on two counts!'

F or the Conductor, upon Shushan Eidus,
    a Michtam *by David, to instruct.*
² *When he made war against*
    Aram Naharaim and Aram Tzovah,

Rabbah 74:15), מִכְתָּם is a contraction of two words: מַכּוֹת תַּמּוֹת, *total beatings,* referring to the license Sanhedrin gave David to wage a total war against Aram.

The *Midrash* also relates that when Joab informed David of the problem with Aram, David was determined to resolve this question immediately. He forsook the customary pomp and protocol befitting a king, removing the imperial robes from his shoulders and the royal crown from his head. He wrapped himself in a simple *talis* and came humbly before Sanhedrin with his halachic question concerning the interpretation of the covenant.

[This alludes to two other translations of מִכְתָּם discussed in the commentary to 16:1. First, the *Talmud (Sotah* 10b) says that even at the height of his imperial splendor, David remained מִכְתָּם, i.e., מָךְ, *humble,* and תָּם, *innocent,* to all. Second, although David removed his מִכְתָּם, *crown,* as a sign of submission to the court's ruling, nevertheless, his sterling character invested him with an aura of majesty which far surpassed that provided by his royal crown.]

לְלַמֵּד — *To instruct.*
Sanhedrin taught David that he was justified in fighting Aram, and David composed this work to make known this fact (see *Radak*).

In addition, David taught this composition to the Temple singers and instructed them to publicize it, for it speaks of God's mercy in aiding David's army to vanquish Aram despite Israel's relative weakness and military inferiority *(Ibn Ezra).*

Meiri concludes that this psalm has the power to instruct mankind and instill in them the faith and recognition that all human affairs and events are directed by a Divine order and with a purpose.

2. בְּהַצּוֹתוֹ — *When he made war.*
This translation follows *Rashi, Radak* and *Metzudos,* based on *Numbers* 26:9.

Ibn Ezra suggests that it means *when he destroyed.*

Midrash Shocher Tov here offers additional interpretations of בְּהַצּוֹתוֹ.

— It means that Joab set Aram on fire (לְהַצִּית אֶת הָאוֹר).

— When the ה is midrashically interchanged with a ח, the word reads בְּחַצּוֹתוֹ, *when he split in two,* meaning that David divided and mixed up the nations, for he took the people of Aram-Naharaim and settled them in Aram-Tzovah, and placed the people of Aram-Tzovah in Aram-Naharaim [cf. *Radak*]. בְּחַצּוֹתוֹ also means that David riddled Aram with חִצִּים, *arrows.*

אֲרַם נַהֲרַיִם — *Aram Naharaim* [lit. *Aram of the pair of rivers.*]

[*Rashi (Genesis* 24:10) says that this city is situated on *two rivers,* one of which is פְּרָת, *the Euphrates* (cf. *Targum* here and in *Genesis* 24:10). This river is called *the great river (Genesis* 5:18) because it is the eastern border of *Eretz Yisrael,* the greatest of all lands (*Shavuos* 47b; *Rashi, Genesis* 2:14). Possibly the name נַהֲרַיִם (lit. *pair of rivers)* is an honorific title for the Euphrates River itself, indicating its distinguished status.]

Midrash Shocher Tov (on Psalm 1) relates this name to the preceding word [בְּהַצּוֹתוֹ =] בְּחַצּוֹתוֹ, *when he split in two,* stating, 'We find that whatever Moses did, David did as well... Moses split the sea and David split the river, as it says, *when he split Aram of the two*

אֲרַם צוֹבָה וַיָּשָׁב יוֹאָב וַיַּךְ אֶת־אֱדוֹם
ג בְּגֵיא־מֶלַח שְׁנֵים עָשָׂר אָלֶף: אֱלֹהִים
זְנַחְתָּנוּ פְרַצְתָּנוּ אָנַפְתָּ תְּשׁוֹבֵב לָנוּ:
ד הִרְעַשְׁתָּה אֶרֶץ פְּצַמְתָּהּ רְפָה שְׁבָרֶיהָ

rivers [i.e., he miraculously caused the Euphrates River to split into two so that it would not block his army when he went out to attack Aram.]

אֲרַם צוֹבָה — *Aram Tzovah.*

[There were two separate kingdoms of Aram, located in present-day Syria (see ArtScroll *Bereishis I* p. 328 for a description of the geographical locations referred to in our verse). First David smote Hadadezer, the king of Aram Tzovah (Aleppo), who was attempting to expand the boundaries of his own country by conquering and annexing land on the other side of the Euphrates River (*Rashi, I Chronicles* 18:3). The king of Aram-Damascus then came to aid Hadadezer; both met with disastrous defeat.]

וַיָּשָׁב יוֹאָב וַיַּךְ אֶת אֱדוֹם ... שְׁנֵים עָשָׂר אָלֶף — *And Joab returned and smote Edom ... twelve thousand* [*men.*]

Scripture records this event in three different places; the commentaries point out discrepancies among the three accounts in regard to (1) the victorious general, (2) the vanquished nation, and (3) the extent of the enemy's loss.

Here the victorious general is Joab ben Zeruyah; in *II Samuel* 8:13, it is David; in *I Chronicles* 18:12, it is Joab's brother, Avishai.

Both here and in *Chronicles* the defeated nation is described as Edom, but in *II Samuel* it is identified as Aram.

Here, the enemy loss is put at twelve thousand, but the other two sources recorded it as eighteen thousand.

From the commentaries of *Rashi* and *Radak*, we can develop the following reconciliation of the various sources:

Edom and Aram joined their armies in order to defend themselves against David; therefore their force is

sometimes called Aram and sometimes Edom. First Avishai battled them and killed only six thousand men. Then his brother Joab *returned* (וַיָּשָׁב) and fought them again, killing an additional twelve thousand as recorded here. In *Chronicles*, Scripture credits Avishai with all eighteen thousand casualties; because he had the merit of beginning the campaign, the entire amount is attributed to him. In *II Samuel*, the victory is ascribed to David because, as king, he was commander-in-chief of *both* armies.

However, according to the *Midrash* (*Bereishis Rabbah* 74:15) Israel smote twelve thousand of Edom and set up a military government to rule the occupied land. Edom then rebelled against Israel and this uprising was put down at the cost of an additional eighteen thousand Edomite casualties [see *Alshich* and *Sforno* here and *Malbim* (*II Samuel* 18:13), based on *Midrash Tanchuma*.]

שְׁנֵים עָשָׂר אָלֶף — *Twelve thousand* [*men*].

[These words appear after the אתנחתא *separation* note, and thus appear not to refer back to the Edomite army, i.e., it is not a total of enemy losses. This justifies the opinion of the *Targum* that the reference is to the number of Jews who fell during the campaign against Edom and Aram. However, *Targuma d'HaTargum* says that our printed version of the *Targum* is erroneous and that it should read that David and Joab smote twelve thousand of the Edomites.]

3. אֱלֹהִים זְנַחְתָּנוּ פְרַצְתָּנוּ — *O God, You forsook us, You breached us.*

David said this at the very outset of the hostilities, when Hadadezer crossed the Euphrates and brazenly attempted

and Joab returned and smote Edom
     in the Valley of Salt,
          twelve thousand men.
³ *O God, You forsook us, You breached us,*
     You were angry with us, O restore us!
⁴ *You made the land quake, You broke it;*

to annex part of the land of Israel. Initially Hadadezer's penetration was successful and he broke through Israel's defenses; thus, with God's help, Hadadezer had *breached our defenses* and it seemed as if he might conquer the entire land, showing that *You forsook us (Radak).* [1]

[According to our version of *Targum* (but see comment above), David's lament may refer to the twelve thousand lives his army had to pay for its triumph (see the *Targum* on the preceding verse).]

Rashi maintains that at his moment of victory over Edom, David was deeply troubled by his prophetic vision of the future. He foresaw that Edom would strike back and dominate Israel with tyranny and harsh oppression. Now David turned to God and asked for Divine mercy during the future Edomite-Roman persecution.

אָנַפְתָּ תְּשׁוֹבֵב לָנוּ — *You were angry [with us], O restore us!*

Do not forsake us forever. Once You have vented Your anger on us [as punishment for our sins], restore us to our former glory *(Rashi).*

◄§The *commentary* to the coming verses will follow two separate lines of thought: *Radak* traces David's feelings concerning the present campaign against Aram-Edom, whereas *Rashi* relates David's statements to the Roman conquest of the future.

4. הִרְעַשְׁתָּה אֶרֶץ — *You made the land quake.*

Midrash Tanchuma (Vayeitzei 3) contends that this refers to the miraculous assistance which God gave to Joab and Avishai in their campaign against Aram. He caused an earthquake (רַעַשׁ) to shatter (פְּצַמְתָּהּ) the earth into pieces; these pieces (שְׁבָרֶיהָ) were brought close to each other, thus shortening the road to Aram considerably. This is called קְפִיצַת הָאָרֶץ, *a leaping of the earth.* This miracle was

1. Many nations attacked Israel previously but their intentions had only been to plunder, tax, or enslave the Jews; therefore, in retaliation, David merely subjugated and taxed these nations. But David's treatment of Aram was unique, for only this country was annexed to the Land of Israel; it was known as *Surya.* David attempted to invest this territory with the halachic status of the Holy Land proper. He did this as a punishment *measure for measure,* since Aram had sought to lay claim to and annex Jewish land (see *Sotah* 44b, *Rashi* s.v. ומלחמת בית דוד and *Gittin* 8a *Rashi* s.v. סוריא).

However, the halachah does not officially recognize the annexation of Aram, because it was not done with the sanction and authority of the Great Sanhedrin. They argued with David, saying 'Near your own palace there are still large tracts of land which have not yet been conquered from the Canaanites; why do you go out to conquer foreign lands?' (See the *Ran's* commentary on *Avodah Zarah* 21a).

Previously in this Psalm we saw that David's campaign against Aram was indeed officially sanctioned by Sanhedrin, who ruled that the ancient covenant with Laban was nullified. However, Sanhedrin had only authorized David to wage war against Aram, but not to conquer and annex it. David felt that the annexation was an integral part of the battle, for he wanted to punish them measure for measure for having dared to annex part of *Eretz Yisrael.* (עיין ויואל משה: מאמר ישוב א״י סימן י״ג ובמור וקציעה או״ח סימן ש״ו).

ה כִּי־מָטָה: הִרְאִיתָ עַמְּךָ קָשָׁה הִשְׁקִיתָנוּ
ו יַיִן תַּרְעֵלָה: נָתַתָּה לִירֵאֶיךָ נֵּס לְהִתְנוֹסֵס
ז מִפְּנֵי קֹשֶׁט סֶלָה: לְמַעַן יֵחָלְצוּן יְדִידֶיךָ

granted to only three other individuals: Abraham, Eliezer, and Jacob.

According to *Rashi*, David foresaw the droves of Roman legions who were destined to march through the land, causing it to tremble beneath their feet.

פְּצַמְתָּה — *You broke it.*

The translation follows *Rashi*, who also offers as an alternative the rendering of *Rabbi Moshe HaDarshon: You tore it open* (see *Meiri*).

According to *Radak*, this alludes to the breaches which Hadadezer made in Israel's borders. Following *Rashi's* interpretation, this foretells the time when Rome would establish colonies at strategic points throughout Israel in an effort to divide the Jewish populace, as the *Talmud* (*Megillah* 6a) states: The Roman city of Caesarea situated between the shores was like a sharp peg thrust into the midst of Israel [to fragment it] (*Rashi*). [1]

רְפָה שְׁבָרֶיהָ — *Heal its fragments.*

Although the word derives from רָפָא, *heal*, and should therefore be spelled with an א, *aleph*, we often find a ה, *he*, substituted for an א, *aleph* (*Rashi; Radak; Ibn Ezra*).

[The word רָפָה literally means *soft, weak*. This alludes to the request that the remedy for Israel's wounds be gentle rather than harsh.]

כִּי מָטָה — *For it totters.*

This alludes to the many *Talmudic*

statements (*Sanhedrin* 97a) testifying that the Messianic redemption from the Roman exile will not come until Israel totters and falls to the lowest possible level of degradation. At that point, the Jewish nation will rise again (*Zera Yaakov*).

5. הִרְאִיתָ עַמְּךָ קָשָׁה — *You showed Your nation harshness.*

This occurred in the war with Edom, when so many men of Israel were killed (*Sforno*).

הִשְׁקִיתָנוּ יַיִן תַּרְעֵלָה — *You made us drink benumbing wine.*

Rashi explains that רַעַל literally means *an envelopment, an enclosure*. Wine deadens the sensitivity and emotion of the heart and seals it off from external stimuli. [Thus, 'the shocking tragedy of our nation has paralyzed us with fear and killed all the feelings of our heart.' The *Talmud* (*Shabbos* 13b) says that since Israel is constantly plagued with the cruel persecutions of the Romans, the Jews have become completely numb and insensitive to the pain, just as a dead man's flesh cannot feel the sharp point of the dagger.]

Midrash Shocher Tov interprets תַּרְעֵלָה as a contraction of two sets of two words, thus finding a double meaning to the word: This wine מְתַעֵר, *arouses*, the עוֹלָם, *world*, to מַתִּיר, *undo*, עוֹלָה, *the burden*, of Torah. This intimates that the yoke of Torah has been

---

1. This concept of the earth being *broken* alludes to the idea that the world is only considered to be united when Israel is recognized by all nations as the center of world affairs for it says: יַעֲקֹב חֶבֶל נַחֲלָתוֹ , *Jacob is the bond* (which keeps together all the nations) *of His estate* (*Deuteronomy* 32:9).

The *Zohar* (*Parshas Balak*) says that of all the gentile nations, Moab, in particular, denied this principle of a Divine universal order. Therefore David punished them (measure for measure) and *measured them according to the* חֶבֶל, *bond* [line] (*II Samuel* 8:2).

Two-thirds of the nation were found to have denied this 'bond' and were put to death. The remaining third were spared. (See *comm. v.* 10 מוֹאָב סִיר רַחְצִי.)

heal its fragments for it totters.
⁵ You showed Your nation harshness,
You made us drink benumbing wine.
⁶ You gave those who fear You
a banner to raise themselves,
for truth's sake, Selah!
⁷ So that Your beloved ones may be released —

---

torn away from Israel through the sin of drunkenness.

6. נָתַתָּה לִּירֵאֶיךָ נֵּס לְהִתְנוֹסֵס — *You gave those who fear You a banner to raise themselves.*

You have given us the power to vanquish our enemies [Aram and Edom] and to wave our battle standards over them in triumph (*Radak; Meiri*).

Rashi (based on *Bereishis Rabbah* 55:1) renders נֵס homiletically as נִסָּיוֹן, *trial,* to suggest, 'You have tested us in many trying and oppressive situations [such as the tyrannical persecution of Edom-Rome] in order to provide us with the opportunity לְהִתְנוֹסֵס, *to be proven,* faithful under all circumstances. Each time we successfully pass such a test we rise higher and higher, like the נֵס, *banner,* which is unfurled on the highest mast of the ship.[1]

מִפְּנֵי קֹשֶׁט — *For truth's sake.*

You granted us victory against the invaders in order to be *true* to Your promise to let us live peacefully in our land *(Radak).*

Furthermore, our victories were granted by virtue of the fact that we studied the *truth* of Your Torah. As the *Talmud (Sanhedrin* 49a) says: If not for the merit of David, who stayed behind the battle lines to study Torah, his general, Joab, would not have emerged triumphant from his wars *(Sforno).*

According to *Rashi,* these words explain that God constantly puts Israel through difficult trials in anticipation of His final judgment, in which they will be generously rewarded. God wants the gentiles to admit wholeheartedly the *truth* and equity of His verdict and to say, 'It is only fair that Israel should be rewarded, for they withstood so many difficult trials.'

Hirsch explains that קֹשֶׁט in Chaldean is synonymous with אֱמֶת, *truth,* in Hebrew (cf. *Proverbs* 22:21 לְהוֹדִיעֲךָ קֹשְׁטְ אִמְרֵי אֱמֶת, *To inform you of the truth of true words*). Also, in Aramaic the word קשט means *to adorn* (see *Bava Basra* 60b); it is obviously related to תַּכְשִׁיט, *jewel, adornment.* [The נִסָּיוֹן uncovers a person's *true* inner qualities and displays them to the world as the most glorious of *adornments,* for no quality is more precious than truth.]

Finally *Targum* observes that the psalmist is requesting Divine assistance in the merit of the Patriarchs [each of whom endured difficult *trials* and was found to be *true*]. *Targuma d'HaTragum* notes that this verse recalls the merit of Abraham's קֹשֶׁט, *truth,* for Scripture says, *You found his heart true to You* (Nechemiah 9:8).

7. לְמַעַן יֵחָלְצוּן יְדִידֶיךָ — *So that Your beloved ones may be released.*

Meiri comments that this is a form of blessed tranquility, a release from ten-

---

1. The comparison of a נִסָּיוֹן, *trial,* to an unfurled *banner* is most appropriate. *Ramban* (*Bereishis* 22:1) explains that God Himself harbors no doubt as to the successful outcome of every trial, because God only 'tests' righteous people who will survive the challenge. Why, then, does He bother to 'test' them at all, if the results are assured? The answer is that God

ס
ח

ח הוֹשִׁיעָה יְמִינְךָ °וַעֲנֵנוּ: אֱלֹהִים | דִּבֶּר
בְּקָדְשׁוֹ אֶעְלֹזָה אֲחַלְּקָה שְׁכֶם וְעֵמֶק

°וַעֲנֵנִי

sion and care. [The *Talmud* (*Yevamos* 102b) comments on וְעַצְמֹתֶיךָ יַחֲלִיץ, *He shall release your bones* (*Isaiah* 58:11), that this is the most sublime blessing]. On the Sabbath we pray רְצֵה וְהַחֲלִיצֵנוּ, *Favor us and release us* (*Bircas Hamazon*) from our weekday worries.]

Malbim notes that חָלוּץ also has a military connotation: *to be armed* [see *Rashi* on *Numbers* 31:3], i.e., 'fortify Your beloved nation of Israel to go forth well armed and prepared for battle.'

יְדִידֶיךָ — *Your beloved ones.*

Most commentators (*Radak*, *Metzudas David*) render this as a reference to righteous people in general, for whose success the psalmist prays.

Targum, however, renders it as a specific reference to Isaac. Thus, the psalmist prays that Israel be saved in the merit of Isaac.

[In the special benediction offered at the circumcision ceremony, Isaac is called יָדִיד, *beloved*, because he was the cherished son of Abraham. See *Rashi* on *Shabbos* 137b, *Targuma d'HaTargum*.]

According to *Midrash Shocher Tov* (*Psalm* 84), this refers to the Temple of which it says, מַה יְּדִידוֹת מִשְׁכְּנוֹתֶיךָ, *how beloved are Your Tabernacles* (84:2). The Temple was built by Solomon, who was called יְדִידְיָה, *beloved of HASHEM.* (II *Samuel* 12:25). He built it in the territory of Benjamin, whom Moses called יְדִיד ה', *Beloved of HASHEM* (*Deuteronomy* 33:12). Therefore, for the sake of the Temple, David prayed *that Your beloved ones may be released.*

[According to *Radak's* interpretation, this alludes to the fact that David waged

these wars as a preparation for Solomon's construction of the Temple (as explained in *comm.* to *v.* 1). According to *Rashi*, this alludes to the destruction of the beloved Temple at the hands of Edom-Rome.]

הוֹשִׁיעָה יְמִינְךָ — *Save [with] Your right hand.*

Ibn Ezra and *Ibn Yachya* observe that this should be interpreted as בִּימִינְךָ, including the prepositional prefix ב, *with:* i.e., save with Your right hand.

Radak explains the literal reading of *save Your right hand:* When God ignores the atrocities perpetrated against Israel and refrains from protecting His nation, it appears as if He lacks the ability to react and as if His hands are 'tied'. The psalmist calls upon God to *release* His might against the foe in order to *save* His 'reputation.'

Norah Tehillos and *Malbim* note that David specifically asks for Divine action with the *right hand*, symbolizing God's attribute of Mercy, which performs miracles for those deserving of His grace.

The *Targum* adds, 'Save us by virtue of the חֲסִידוּת, *devotion*, of our Patriarch Jacob.'

Hirsch explains the request *save Your right hand* according to the verse עִמּוֹ אָנֹכִי בְצָרָה אֲחַלְּצֵהוּ, *I [God] am with him [Israel] in distress; I shall release him* (91:15). The Sages say that when Israel wanders in exile, God, is also considered to be in exile. God's true glory manifests itself in the world only when Israel dwells securely in its sovereign state, its homeland. Therefore, the psalmist

wishes to do a kindness to the righteous, extracting their hidden potential powers of faith and bringing them to fruition. The righteous will be fortified when the power of their faith is activated, and their example will serve as an inspiration for others [see *Ramban, Shaar HaGemul* and *comm.* to 12:5]. Thus, the נִסָּיוֹן truly resembles a banner which is unfurled on high in order to display the identity of its bearers. [See Overview to *Lech Lecha*, ArtScroll Bereishis, vol. II.]

save with your right hand and respond to me.
⁸ *God said in His sanctity*
that I would exult, divide portions;
and the Valley of Succos
would I measure out.

urges God to release His beloved nation so that His own splendor can be *released* and revealed to all.

וַעֲנֵנִי — *And respond to me.*

[The כְּתִיב, *spelling,* is וַעֲנֵנוּ, *respond to us,* but the קְרִי, *pronunciation,* is וַעֲנֵנִי, *respond to me.* This teaches us that as King of Israel, David transcended his individual personality and dedicated himself completely to the commonwealth. The requests which he made of God did not concern personal problems, but matters of general welfare. God's fulfillment of his wishes was not merely an *answer* to David, but an *answer* to all of Israel.

[108:7-14 is a repetition of this verse and of those immediately following. There, too, we have this discrepancy between the pronunciation and the spelling (see *Minchas Shai* (108:7-14) and *Hirsch.*]

8. אֱלֹהִים דִּבֶּר בְּקָדְשׁוֹ — *God said in His sanctity.*

Through His Holy Inspiration, God communicated to me that I would [now] rule over His nation, Israel (*Radak*) and that [in the future] all of the scattered exiles would be ingathered and placed once again under the rule of the House of David (*Rashi*). Scripture states, *For HASHEM has spoken of David saying, 'By the hand of My servant David I will save My people Israel from the hands of the Philistines and from the hands of all their enemies'* (II Samuel 3:18).

Targum renders בְּקָדְשׁוֹ, *from the holy Temple,* because God spoke to David there [concerning its construction and its future survival].

אֶעְלֹזָה — *[That] I would exult.*

This would occur when He fulfilled His promises by giving monarchy and victory to David (*Radak; Rashi; Metzudas David*).

אֲחַלְּקָה שְׁכֶם — *(I would) divide portions.*

Portions refers to enemy property which would be apportioned to the Jewish exiles returning from the Diaspora (*Rashi*). [See *Targum* and *Ibn Ezra* on *Genesis* 48:22 שְׁכֶם אַחַד, *one portion.*]

Rashi also suggests that שְׁכֶם may refer to the city of *Shechem,* which symbolizes Jacob's territorial claim over the Holy Land. [The city's significance is derived from the fact that Shechem was the first place where Jacob camped when he returned to Israel from Aram, and it was there that he made his first purchase of land from the Canaanite inhabitants (*Ibn Yachya*)] Thus, the psalmist prophesies that all Jacob's territorial possessions are destined to be returned to the Jewish nation.

Radak and *Meiri* interpret these words as a reference to David's personal experiences. After Saul's death, his son Ish-Boshes, supported by the mighty Abner, set up a kingdom in the province of Ephraim. All the places mentioned in this and the following verses were part of that domain. David now declares that God was true to His promise to grant David complete sovereignty over *all* of Israel, including the rival province of Ephraim and its cities (including Shechem). [This encourages David to place his full trust in God during the present campaign against Aram.]

וְעֵמֶק סֻכּוֹת אֲמַדֵּד — *And the Valley of Succos would I measure out.*

Rashi and *Ibn Yachya* observe that

ט סֻכּוֹת אֲמַדֵּד: לִי גִלְעָד | וְלִי מְנַשֶּׁה
וְאֶפְרַיִם מָעוֹז רֹאשִׁי יְהוּדָה מְחֹקְקִי:
י מוֹאָב | סִיר רַחְצִי עַל־אֱדוֹם אַשְׁלִיךְ נַעֲלִי
יא עָלַי פְּלֶשֶׁת הִתְרוֹעָעִי: מִי יֹבִלֵנִי עִיר

this also alludes to Jacob's initial claim to the Holy Land, because even before he came to Shechem he spent eighteen months at *Succos* (see *Rashi* on Genesis 33:17). When this territory is divided among the returning Jewish exiles, it will first be *measured out*.

According to *Radak* and *Meiri, Succos* was part of the territory of Ish-Boshes, who first challenged David's ascension to the throne, but later submitted to his reign.

לִי גִלְעָד וְלִי מְנַשֶּׁה וְאֶפְרַיִם מָעוֹז רֹאשִׁי **9.** — *Mine is Gilead, and mine is Menasheh, Ephraim is the stronghold of my head.*

David mentions Gilead and Ephraim, which both belonged to Ish-Boshes, and includes Menashe too, thus incorporating both sons of Joseph. This alludes to all of the tribes of Israel—with the exception of Judah (David's own tribe) — which were initially hostile. All of these eventually submitted to David's rule *(Meiri; Radak).*

יְהוּדָה מְחֹקְקִי — *Judah is my lawgiver.*

My officers, who are my main support and who enforce my authority, come from Judah *(Rashi).*

מְחֹקֵק literally means *lawgiver* who decides legislation and inscribes the rulings in the nation's law books [חֲקִיקָה means *to engrave or inscribe*]. This is the special privilege of the royal tribe of Judah, as we read, לֹא יָסוּר שֵׁבֶט

מִיהוּדָה וּמְחֹקֵק מִבֵּין רַגְלָיו, *The scepter shall not depart from Judah nor the lawgiver's staff from between his feet* (Genesis 49:10).

10. מוֹאָב סִיר רַחְצִי — *Moab is my washbasin.*

I will treat Moab with contempt, like the putrid water of the chamber pot which is cast away in disgust *(Radak).*

[סִיר may also be translated as *cooking pot*]. God said, 'For Moab, I set down on the stove a pot full of punishments!' *(Devarim Rabbah* 3:2) or 'I will clean their land thoroughly as one who scours a *cooking pot' (Ibn Ezra).*

David had good cause to despise Moab, as the *Midrash (Bamidbar Rabbah* 14:1) explains: When Saul's pursuit forced David to flee from the land of Israel, he placed his father and mother under the protection of the king of Moab [*I Samuel* 22:3-4]. David had more confidence in the Moabites than he had in Saul, because his grandmother was Ruth the Moabite; but the king of Moab killed the entire family.[1]

Therefore, Moab is likened to a *cooking pot,* for just as a pot dissolves meat, so was the flesh of David's family devoured in Moab. Only one of David's brothers escaped to Nachash, king of Ammon, who refused to heed the king of Moab's demands that the refugee be returned.

1. *Alshich* perceives in the phrase *Moab is my washbasin* an allusion to the taint of Moabite ancestry on David's lineage. David spent his life *washing* his soul and cleansing it from any trace of gentile association.

[The *Talmud (Yoma* 22b) states that no leader should be appointed to a position of authority over the community unless he has a basketful of 'creeping reptiles' tied to his back, meaning that his family tree should have some lowly ancestry. Then, if he grows excessively proud, people can taunt him, 'Turn around and see from whence you came.' The proof of this is that since Saul's pedigree was perfect, he disregarded admonition and fell; but David's Moabite ancestry always haunted him and caused him to be more humble and cautious in his affairs (see *Rashi, Yoma* 22b).]

⁹ *Mine is Gilead,*

and mine is Menasheh,

Ephraim is the stronghold of my head,

Judah is my lawgiver.

¹⁰ *Moab is my washbasin,*

upon Edom will I cast my lock,

Philistia, join together with me.

¹¹ *Who will bring me*

Later David punished Moab for their treachery, as we read (II *Samuel* 8:2), *And he smote Moab, and measured them with the line, making them lie down on the ground, and he measured out two lines* [two-thirds of the populace] *to be put to death and one full line* [one-third] *to keep alive.* [See footnote v.4 פִּצְמָתָה].

עַל אֱדוֹם אַשְׁלִיךְ נַעֲלִי — *Upon Edom will I cast my lock.*

The translation of נַעֲלִי follows *Rashi,* implying, 'I will *lock* Edom into my tight grip.' *Metzudas David* renders, 'I will cast iron chains on their feet in order to fetter them.'

Sforno adds that Moab was near *Eretz Yisrael.* Because it was under David's constant surveillance, he could humiliate Moab without fearing a revolt. Since Edom was further away, the threat of an uprising was greater in that country. Therefore, David *cast his lock* on all of Edom's fortifications and strongholds, in anticipation of armed resistance.

Radak, however, translates נַעֲלִי as *my shoe,* to indicate that David's armies trampled and subjugated the forces of Aram and Edom.

The *Midrash* (*Shemos Rabbah* 15:16) adds that in the future God will also grind Edom underfoot, as the prophet (*Isaiah* 63:3) foretells: *I* [God] *trod the winepress alone . . . I trod them* [Edom] *in my anger, and trampled them in my fury.* God will stamp on the rulers of Edom with special fury, as the psalmist

says, *Upon Edom I cast* נַעֲלִי, *my shoe.*

[It should be emphasized that the psalmist speaks of these enemies with contempt only because they are considered adversaries of God. As a matter of fact, from this very campaign against Edom we learn that the Jewish army accorded its foes great respect as human beings. Scripture states *And David made himself a great reputation when he returned from smiting Aram, in the Valley of Salt* (II *Samuel* 8:13). This refers to the fact that David buried all of the Edomite dead, which enhanced Israel's reputation. The Jews will also bury their fallen enemies in the future war of Gog and Magog (*Rashi; Radak; Kara;* II *Samuel* 8:13)]

עָלַי פְּלֶשֶׁת הִתְרוֹעָעִי — *Philistia, join together with me.*

This translation follows *Rashi,* who derives הִתְרוֹעָעִי from רֵעַ, *friend, companion.* [David calls upon Philistia to submit to his dominion voluntarily since it is destined to fall before David's conquering army anyway.]

Metzudas David interprets הִתְרוֹעָעִי to mean *blow the horn blast* (from תְּרוּעָה), i.e., 'Let Philisita recognize my sovereignty and blow a ceremonial blast on the trumpet to announce my coronation.'

Sforno however relates this word to תרע, *to smash* [see 2:9 תְּרֹעֵם], meaning, 'Philistia, be shattered and disintegrate before me!'

Hirsch translates this entire phrase as a taunt to this enemy of Israel *after its*

ספ
יב-יד

מָצוֹר מִי נָחַנִי עַד־אֱדוֹם: הֲלֹא־אַתָּה יב
אֱלֹהִים זְנַחְתָּנוּ וְלֹא־תֵצֵא אֱלֹהִים
בְּצִבְאוֹתֵינוּ: הָבָה־לָּנוּ עֶזְרָת מִצָּר וְשָׁוְא יג
תְּשׁוּעַת אָדָם: בֵּאלֹהִים נַעֲשֶׂה־חָיִל וְהוּא יד
יָבוּס צָרֵינוּ:

defeat: 'Now let Philistia dare to claim triumph over me' [see *Ibn Ezra* and *Radak*].

11. מִי יֹבִלֵנִי עִיר מָצוֹר — *Who will bring me to the fortified* [lit. *besieged*] *city.*

Rashi views this rhetorical question as a plea for future victories: 'Who will help me to conquer the mighty metropolis of Rome if not You?'

According to *Radak*, however, this is a rhetorical question concerning David's past victories (even though it is worded in future tense): 'Who brought me to victory over the fortified cities of Philistia, Moab, and Aram, if not You, O God?'

Targum identifies מָצוֹר as the city צוֹר, which is synonymous with Rome (see *Rashi, Genesis* 25:23, *Targuma d'HaTargum*).

12. הֲלֹא אַתָּה אֱלֹהִים זְנַחְתָּנוּ — *Did not You, O God, forsake us?*

According to *Radak*, this is the psalmist's reply to the question posed in the preceding verse: 'Who brought us victory over the fortified city? It was none other than You, O God! It was also You who had forsaken us and who

refused to go out with our legions; but when You decided to favor us, You granted us amazing success over enemy forces which vastly surpassed our small army both in numbers and in might.[1]

Sforno observes that David bemoans the great losses he suffered in his campaign against Edom [twelve thousand men (see *v.* 2,3)] and sees this as a sign of Divine displeasure and indifference.

וְלֹא תֵצֵא אֱלֹהִים בְּצִבְאוֹתֵינוּ — *And not go forth, O God, with our legions?*

[Under normal conditions, God *does* accompany our legions: *For HASHEM, Your God, walks in the midst of Your camp to deliver you and to give up your enemies before you; therefore your camp shall be holy* (Deuteronomy 23:15). *Ramban* equates the sanctity of the Jewish army camp to the holiness of the *Beis HaMikdash*, where God's *Shechinah* dwells.

[The Sages tell us (*Kiddushin* 70b) that God's holy spirit dwells only among the families of Israel who strive to preserve their pure lineage. *Sforno* (*Deuteronomy* 23:15) explains that since David wished to arouse God's presence in his camp, he demanded that any soldier who wished to join his army

1. The *Talmud* (*Gittin* 57a) describes Bar Deroma, a Jewish warrior whose great strength robbed the Romans of the courage to fight. Unfortunately, Bar Deroma's arrogance caused his own downfall, for he said to God: *'You, O God, have forsaken us; go forth no longer with our legions,'* as if to say that he could be victorious without God's help. God complied by abandoning Bar Deroma to the forces of nature. Soon afterwards, he was killed by a snake.

The *Talmud* explains that David was neither punished nor criticized when he uttered this very same verse, because his intention was different, for his question and answer were rhetorical as explained above in the commentary (see *Maharsha, Gittin* 57a).

Yerushalmi (*Taanis* 4:5) says that Bar Kochba was guilty of the same arrogance as Bar Deroma, for he proclaimed, 'O God, do not help us and do not hinder us!' i.e., Remove Yourself from this conflict, because we can fend for ourselves. In fact, Bar Kochba quoted our verse (60:12) in his request for Divine nonintervention.

to the fortified city,
who will lead me
unto Edom?
¹² Did not You, O God,
forsake us,
And not go forth,
O God, with our legions?
¹³ Grant us help against the oppressor;
futile is the aid of man.
¹⁴ Through God we shall form an army
and He will trample our oppressors.

provide evidence of his untarnished ancestry (See *Kiddushin* 76b).

In addition, only the most devout men of faith were allowed to remain in the ranks, while sinners were dismissed. Thus these pure souls clung to the pure spirit of God, Whose presence permeated the camp with holiness (*Chinuch* 566).

13. הָבָה לָנוּ עֶזְרָת מִצָּר — *Grant us help against* [lit. *from*] *the oppressor.*

Grant us a victory directly from Your hands, rather than through a human intermediary. Let this redemption resemble our liberation from Egypt, which You engineered without employing an angel or a celestial being (*Tehillos Hashem*).

וְשָׁוְא תְּשׁוּעַת אָדָם — *Futile is the aid* [lit. *salvation*] *of man.*

[David and his generals waged war guided by this principle. Joab arrayed his army against Aram, and Avishai pitted his forces against Ammon. Joab said: *If the Arameans be too strong for me, then you shall save me; but if the children of Ammon be too strong for you, then I will come and save you* (II Samuel 10:11). Joab realized, however, that, in the final analysis, one cannot rely on mere military strategies. Therefore, he continued (II Samuel

10:11): *Be of good courage and let us prove strong for our people . . . and HASHEM will do that which seems proper to Him,* i.e., although we will fight with all our might, we know that salvation is exclusively in God's hands (*Radak,* II *Samuel* 10:11).]

14. בֵּאלֹהִים נַעֲשֶׂה חָיִל — *Through God shall we form an army.*

This translation follows *Radak,* who explains that even if our numbers are few and our enemies are many, we will make God our army and He will defend us.

Rambam (*Hilchos Melochim* 7:15) offers the following words of encouragement to the Jewish soldier on the eve of battle: When the soldier is locked in combat, he should depend on none other than God, the Hope and Savior of Israel in times of distress. Let him recognize that he is fighting for the preservation of God's Name. Therefore, he must throw himself into mortal danger without fear or panic. Let him forget his wife and family and train his thoughts only on the battle.

The man who battles with all his heart without fear, solely for the sanctification of God's Name, is assured that he will not suffer any wound or harm. Furthermore, this man will establish a fine home in Israel. His merits will

protect his descendants forever, and he is assured of a portion in the World to Come.

The *Midrash (Eichah Rabbosi* 1:33) renders בֵּאלֹהִים נַעֲשֶׂה חָיִל, *In God we shall produce strength*, to teach that when Israel complies with God's will, the Chosen People 'strengthens' the Almighty, but when Israel abandons God's will, the Jewish people 'weakens' God.

וְהוּא יָבוּס צָרֵינוּ — *And He will trample our oppressors*. [See 44:6.]

Be'er Moshe (II Samuel 8) explains that David sought to subdue his adver-saries in order to prepare for the Messianic era of order and harmony. *Yerushalmi (Kiddushin* 1:8) explains that in its initial conquest of the Land, Israel inherited the territory of only the seven Canaanite nations, but that in the future, they will expand their posses-sions to the land of the three nations of Edom, Moab, and Ammon (see *Bereishis Rabbah* 44).

[David triumphed over these three peoples (*II Samuel* 8:2; 12:29), and now he prayed for their complete defeat in Messianic times, when the universal peace and order for which David yearned all his life will be realized.]

This psalm demonstrates that no distance or danger could diminish David's fervent love for God. Even when Saul pursued him to the furthest reaches of the realm, David's heart remained rooted in the spiritual center of the land — the House of God — and he yearned for the opportunity to serve God in the holy precincts (Malbim).

Sforno and Metzudos David maintain that this psalm was composed when David traveled to repel Aram, the nation which threatened to overrun and to annex the remote eastern boundaries of the land of Israel, the end of the land (v. 3). [That threat is discussed in the preceding psalm, to which this chapter is a sequel.]

Radak, based on the Midrash, adds that David's cries echo the collective prayers of Israel in exile. From the dismal loneliness and isolation of the Diaspora, the Jews cry out to their Redeemer to restore them to their national home.

The psalm concludes with a request for the continuity of the Davidic line of kings. The kings of the House of David are the precursors of the Messiah, who will gather the scattered remnants of Israel into the land of their fathers.

א־ב לַמְנַצֵּחַ | עַל־נְגִינַת לְדָוִד: שִׁמְעָה אֱלֹהִים
ג רָנָּתִי הַקְשִׁיבָה תְפִלָּתִי: מִקְצֵה הָאָרֶץ |
אֵלֶיךָ אֶקְרָא בַּעֲטֹף לִבִּי בְּצוּר־יָרוּם מִמֶּנִּי
ד תַנְחֵנִי: כִּי־הָיִיתָ מַחְסֶה לִי מִגְדַּל־עֹז
ה מִפְּנֵי אוֹיֵב: אָגוּרָה בְאָהָלְךָ עוֹלָמִים
ו אֶחֱסֶה בְסֵתֶר כְּנָפֶיךָ סֶּלָה: כִּי־אַתָּה

1. לַמְנַצֵּחַ עַל נְגִינַת — *For the Conductor, on* Neginnas.

This title לַמְנַצֵּחַ בִּנְגִינוֹת appears frequently in psalms; however, this specific variation, עַל נְגִינַת, is unique. *Meiri* maintains that the two terms are synonymous and refer to musical instruments in the Levite orchestra [see *comm.* 4:1]. Thus עַל means *on*, i.e., this psalm was composed to be played on the *Neginnas* instrument.

However, *Pesikta Rabbosi* (9:2) renders עַל נְגִינַת: *because of songs*. David said: 'Because God has kindly granted me the privilege of praising Him with songs, I now dedicate a נֶצַח, *an eternal tune*, to His benevolence!' [David is particularly pleased that despite the fact that he is so far removed from the center of God's Presence, he is still granted the inspiration to compose psalms (see Pref.).]

2. שִׁמְעָה אֱלֹהִים רִנָּתִי — *Hear, O God, my cry.*

This refers to the audible call which escapes from the lips (*Ibn Ezra*).

Israel pleads: 'Please hear me even though I am in exile and distant from You' (*Dorash Moshe*).

הַקְשִׁיבָה תְּפִלָּתִי — *Listen to my prayer.*

This indicates the unspoken yearning of the heart (*Ibn Ezra*).

I praised You aloud for Your past kindness and You heard *my cry*. Therefore, continue to heed *my prayer* for Your future assistance (*Sforno*).

3. מִקְצֵה הָאָרֶץ אֵלֶיךָ אֶקְרָא — *From the end of the land unto You I call.*

According to *Rashi*, David sent his armies out on distant foreign campaigns [while his royal duties forced him to stay behind]. When he grew concerned for their safety at the *end of the land,* he implored God to assist them.

Radak identifies *the end of the land* as Philistia, where David himself sought refuge from Saul.

Midrash Shocher Tov interprets these words as a reference to Israel in exile: Wherever and whenever Israel cries out to the Holy One, Blessed be He, He responds, as it says, *I called on Your name, HASHEM, from the depths of the pit. You heard my voice* (Lamentations 3:55,56). God replies [with regret], 'Now you begin to call upon Me *from the end of the land*, but when you were still in your land you neglected to call Me!' [This implies, had the nation only cried out then, it certainly would have been spared the misery of exile.]

בַּעֲטֹף לִבִּי — *When my heart grows faint.*

This translation follows the Targum בְּאִשְׁתַּלְהָיוּת לִבִּי, *when my heart is drained and exhausted.*

Metzudos David however, relates the word to עֲטִיפָה, *to be enveloped,* i.e., when my heart is shrouded in misery and suffering.

Radak notes that incessant prayer at the time of a crisis is called עֲטִיפָה, as in תְּפִלָּה לְעָנִי כִי יַעֲטֹף, *a prayer of the afflicted when he is shrouded* (102:1).

בְּצוּר יָרוּם מִמֶּנִּי תַנְחֵנִי — *To a rock which is too high for me—lead me!*

Place me upon the rocky pinnacle which, because of its towering height, is inaccesible to me unaided (*Rashi*).

61
1-5

For the Conductor, on Neginnas,
by David.

² Hear, O God, my cry,
listen to my prayer.

³ From the end of the land unto You I call,
when my heart grows faint.
To a rock which is too high for me —
lead me!

⁴ For You have been a refuge for me,
a tower of strength in the enemy's face.

⁵ I shall dwell in Your tent forever,
take refuge in the shelter of Your wings, Selah.

The rock symbolizes the much desired land of Israel, which lay beyond the reach of the fugitive, David, and which is still inaccessible to the far-flung exiles of Israel (Radak).

Sforno suggests that David's heart grew faint when he contemplated his invincible enemies. Therefore, he calls for Divine assistance against the adversaries who tower over him.

4. כִּי הָיִיתָ מַחְסֶה לִי — For You have been a refuge for me.

In the past, You brought glory to Your name by providing me with miraculous protection. Therefore, I beseech You to continue Your shelter as a tower of strength in the face [i.e., in the presence] of the enemy; for if You abandon me now, O God, I fear that the enemy will attempt to strip You of Your glory, saying, 'God's strength has failed Him!' (Sforno).

5. אָגוּרָה בְאָהָלְךָ עוֹלָמִים — I shall dwell in Your tent forever.

[Until now the psalmist primarily lamented his dismal situation in exile. Now he expresses his innermost wishes concerning the redemption and the return to God's presence.]

Radak comments that in reference to David, אָהָלְךָ, Your tent, indicates the

מִשְׁכָּן, Tabernacle [which then represented the focal point of sanctity]. In reference to the exiles of Israel, Your tent means the Beis HaMikdash [which the exiled Jews yearn to see rebuilt].

עוֹלָמִים — Forever [lit. worlds].

Grant me the privilege [of dwelling in Your Presence] not only in This World but also in the World to Come (Rashi).

Tehillos Hashem points out that the World to Come is actually composed of many עוֹלָמִים, worlds, as the Mishnah teaches: The Holy One, Blessed be He, is destined to bequeath to each tzaddik three hundred and ten worlds (Uktzin 3:12). These worlds will exist forever.

The Sages ask, 'Is it possible for a man to live עוֹלָמִים, forever?' They explain that David actually requested of God that Torah lessons be taught in his name, even after his death. As Rabbi Yochanan said in the name of Rabbi Shimon bar Yochai: Whenever the words of a Torah scholar are repeated in this world, his lips move along in the grave! In this manner, David hoped to achieve immortality (Rashi; Yevamos 96b).

Pesikta Rabbosi (2:4) adds that the Holy One, Blessed be He, swore to David: Even after you pass on, your name will not depart from My House.

אֱלֹהִים שָׁמַעְתָּ לִנְדָרַי נָתַתָּ יְרֻשַּׁת יִרְאֵי
שְׁמֶךָ: ז יָמִים עַל־יְמֵי־מֶלֶךְ תּוֹסִיף שְׁנוֹתָיו
ח כְּמוֹ־דֹר וָדֹר: יֵשֵׁב עוֹלָם לִפְנֵי אֱלֹהִים
ט חֶסֶד וֶאֱמֶת מַן יִנְצְרֻהוּ: כֵּן אֲזַמְּרָה שִׁמְךָ
לָעַד לְשַׁלְּמִי נְדָרַי יוֹם | יוֹם:

At every Temple offering, your name will be mentioned and your psalms will be sung!

Indeed, to this very day we proclaim, (Rosh Hashanah 25a) דָּוִד מֶלֶךְ יִשְׂרָאֵל חַי וְקַיָּם, David, King of Israel, lives on and endures (Yalkut Eliezer).

6. כִּי אַתָּה אֱלֹהִים שָׁמַעְתָּ לִנְדָרַי — For You, O God, have heard my vows.

[During his lifetime, David made a number of vows.]

At the moment of my birth, the angel adjured me [as he does all infants], 'Be righteous, and do not be wicked' (Niddah 30a; Klei Chemdah).

While I was in exile, I vowed to do many things for the sake of God, if He would return me safely to the Holy Land.

Throughout the centuries of exile, Jews have made similar vows (Radak).

Furthermore, I vowed that I would not rest until I found the proper site for the Temple (see 132:2-5).

Since God sees that I have dedicated my life to the fulfillment of all these vows, He grants me Divine protection (Alshich).

נָתַתָּ יְרֻשַּׁת יִרְאֵי שְׁמֶךָ — You have granted the heritage of those who fear Your Name.

Radak notes that although David speaks in past tense saying, 'You ... have heard my vows,' actually, God has not yet responded. The psalmist speaks this way to demonstrate his firm faith that his requests will be fulfilled.

Rashi and Radak advance different versions of the prayer to which David alludes here.

Grant my return to Eretz Yisrael, the homeland of the nation which fears Your Name! (Rashi).

Bless me with the privilege of dwelling in Your estate — the holy Tabernacle [or the Beis HaMikdash, where all who enter are awed by Your Name] (Radak).

Malbim points out that when David made his vows to God, the Almighty reciprocated with the promise that if David's descendants would fear His Name, then the monarchy would remain as their heritage forever (see 132:11, 12).

7. יָמִים עַל יְמֵי מֶלֶךְ תּוֹסִיף — May You add days on to the days of the king.

Kings usually die young for they are at the center of all dissension (Sforno). The Sages teach (Pesachim 87b) that the throne 'buries' its royal occupants, for Scripture relates that every prophet in Israel outlived four kings (Otzar Nechmad).

David requested, 'If it has been ordained that I should die young, please add to the predestined number of my days so that they reach at least seventy years, which is the customary lifespan for generation after generation (Rashi).

[See 90:10: The days of our years are seventy years.]

Radak observes that a similar incident occured when fifteen years were added to the life of King Chizkiyahu, who was initially destined to die young (Isaiah 38:5).

As Radak explains, this psalm echoes the cries of Israel in exile: The nation pleads that its redeemer, the Messiah, be granted long life.

שְׁנוֹתָיו כְּמוֹ דֹר וָדֹר — May his years be like generation after generation.

Pirkei d'Rabbi Eliezer (19) explains this as an allusion to the first man, Adam HaRishon, who donated seventy years of his life to David so that he

6 For You, O God,

have heard my vows,

You have granted the heritage

of those who fear Your Name.

7 May You add days on to the days of the king,

may his years be like generation

after generation.

8 May he sit forever before God.

Appoint kindness and truth,

that they may preserve him.

9 Thus shall I praise Your Name forever,

to fulfill my vows day after day.

---

could enjoy a normal lifespan. [See Overview in Vol. I].[1]

8. יֵשֵׁב עוֹלָם לִפְנֵי אֱלֹהִים — *May he sit forever before God.*

This refers to the king [David or Messiah] (*Rashi*).

May he spend his days in permanent pursuit of total wisdom and fear of God (*Radak; Sforno*).

May he remain in Your presence, in the *Beis HaMikdash*, and not be forced to go to distant places to fight the enemy (*Metzudas David*).

חֶסֶד וֶאֱמֶת מַן יִנְצְרֻהוּ — *Appoint kindness and truth, that they may preserve him.*

This translation follows *Rashi,*

Radak, Sforno, and *Metzudos,* who relate מַן to זַמֵן *appoint, prepare* (see *Jonah* 4:6), i.e., may God's *kindness* and the *truth* of His vow to guard the king preserve him from his foes, so that wars will be unnecessary (*Metzudas David*).

The *Midrash* (*Shemos Rabbah* 31:5) however, renders מַן as מִי, the interrogative pronoun *who*. David said to the Holy One, Blessed be He, יֵשֵׁב עוֹלָמְךָ, *equalize men in Your world*. [יֵשֵׁב is thus interpreted as יְשַׁוּ, *equalize*, i.e., David wanted all people to be equally wealthy (*Yefeh Toar*).] 'Why should there be such disparity between rich and poor?' God replied: 'If I make all men equal (שָׁוֶה), then מַן, *who*, will preserve חֶסֶד

---

1. *Otzar Nechmad* and *Eretz HaChaim* note that the *Zohar* (*Vayishlach*) attributes David's lifespan to a different source: [Abraham was allotted one hundred-eighty years (as was his son Isaac; see *Rashi, Genesis* 25:30), but lived only one hundred seventy-five. If Jacob was unworthy of a full allotment of his father's years, he should have at least lived as long as his grandfather, but he lived twenty-eight years less (147 years). Joseph also would have been expected to equal his father in lifespan, but he fell short by thirty-seven years (110 years).] Abraham contributed five years of his life to David; Jacob contributed twenty-eight years; and Joseph contributed thirty-seven years, for a total of seventy years. Why didn't the seventy years donated by Adam suffice?

Chida (*Midbar Kedeimos* 4:6) resolves this problem by explaining that since David was unique, he required a double measure of life. The *Talmud* (*Shabbos* 89b) teaches that in the average lifespan of seventy years, fifty percent of the time is expended on sleep and mundane pursuits; but David did not have a normal sleep schedule; he needed only brief naps (*Sukkah* 26b). Since David's days were completely dedicated to *full* life, he required *two* gifts of seventy 'normal' years; in combination, these provided David with his *full* years.

[This explains the repetition in the phrase, *May his years be as generation after generation.* This alludes to the fact that David's years resulted from a double contribution of lifespans.]

וֶאֱמֶת, the mitzvah of kindness and true charity?' [See Kol Yaakov on Megillas Esther 3:11.]

[Rav Yerucham Levovitz explained: God did not create the precept of charity because He saw that there were poor people in the world. Rather, God created poor people in order that there would be an opportunity to fulfill the mitzvah of charity. A world devoid of opportunities to show kindness to others is inconceivable, for compassion is the very purpose of This World.][1]

9. כֵּן אֲזַמְּרָה שִׁמְךָ לָעַד — *Thus shall I praise Your Name forever.*

Literally, כֵּן means *so*. Just as I praise You when You accord me victory in the battlefield, *so shall I sing praise of Your Name forever* when I no longer need to go out to battle *(Metzudas David).*

Rashi inteprets: Just as You reveal Your kindness to me, *so* shall I reciprocate with appropriate hymns of appreciation to fulfill my vows to You. I shall record these praises as a memorial for all time *(Sforno).*

לְשַׁלְּמִי נְדָרַי יוֹם יוֹם — *To fulfill my vows day after day.*

With the dawn of each new day, I shall add fresh praises to Your Name *(Sforno).*

This refers specifically to the *day* of Israel's salvation and to the *day* when the Messiah will be invested with his monarchy *(Targum).*

Then, in complete peace and tranquility, I will truly be able to fulfill my vow *(v. 5)*: אָגוּרָה בְאָהָלְךָ עוֹלָמִים, *I shall dwell in Your tent forever (Sforno).*

---

1. The *Talmud (Eruvin 85b)* relates that R' Judah the Prince displayed great respect for the rich. R' Akiva also accorded the rich much honor, based on a homiletical interpretation of this verse, which is understood as a question followed by an answer. חֶסֶד וֶאֱמֶת מַן, *When is the world properly settled in the eyes of God?* יֵשֵׁב עוֹלָם לִפְנֵי אֱלֹהִים יִנְצְרֻהוּ, *when the rich are kind and prepare ample provisions for the poor, thus preserving the world. (Rashi* explains that מַן means *provisions* [as in מָן, *manna*]. God Himself has honored the wealthy by appointing them as His agents for the preservation of the world. Therefore, the rich deserve respect).

Although he is pursued by murderous enemies who are both powerful and rich, David's complete trust in God remains unshaken. Indeed, the persecution by his enemies elicits new foundations of faith from David's soul. He lashes out against the very forces which threaten him and reveals their הֶבֶל, worthlessness.

Obviously, a mortal's might and money can never prevail against the decrees of the Almighty Master of the universe. All God asks of man is that he await the ultimate Divine victory with faith and patience.

Rashi identifies this as the hymn of Israel in exile. It depicts the supreme test of the nation's endurance throughout a seemingly interminable Golus. This psalm is a source of strength and courage to the beleaguered nation, for it counsels, 'Wait patiently. If you will place your hopes in God and in God alone — if you will relinquish your infatuation with money and political influence — then your swift redemption is assured!'

א־ב לַמְנַצֵּחַ עַל־יְדוּתוּן מִזְמוֹר לְדָוִד: אַךְ אֶל־
ג אֱלֹהִים דּוּמִיָּה נַפְשִׁי מִמֶּנּוּ יְשׁוּעָתִי: אַךְ־
הוּא צוּרִי וִישׁוּעָתִי מִשְׂגַּבִּי לֹא־אֶמּוֹט
ד רַבָּה: עַד־אָנָה | תְּהוֹתְתוּ עַל־אִישׁ
תְּרָצְּחוּ כֻלְּכֶם כְּקִיר נָטוּי גָּדֵר הַדְּחוּיָה:

1. עַל יְדוּתוּן — *On* Yedusun (cf. *Minchas Shai*).

[See *Prefatory Remarks* and *comm.* to 39:1.]

Rashi describes the *Yedusun* as a unique instrument in the Temple orchestra. Homiletically, the word is related to דָּתוֹת, *evil decrees*, suggesting that this psalm is the chant of the victim of persecution and oppression.

According to *Radak*, *Yedusun* was a prominent Levite, a leader of the Temple singers.

2. אַךְ אֶל אֱלֹהִים דּוּמִיָּה נַפְשִׁי — *Only for God does my soul wait silently.*

This translation combines the opinions of a number of commentaries. *Targum*, *Radak* and *Meiri* render דּוּמִיָּה as *silence*. *Rashi* and *Metzudas David* translate it as *await* [see *comm.* to *Psalms* 37:7 נֶאֱלַמְתִּי and 39:3 דּוֹם לַה׳ [דּוּמִיָּה].

[In fact, these two interpretations are related, because the man who sincerely *awaits* the salvation of God makes no attempt to secure assistance from any other source. He is *silent* like a דּוֹמֵם, *inanimate object*.]

The word אַךְ, *alone, only,* serves to exclude all power except God's. It recurs throughout this psalm, for the composer extols that pure conviction and unadulterated faith which recognize none but the Almighty (*Yaavetz; Hirsch*).

Even when God appears as אֱלֹהִים, the Divine Name representing the Attribute of Strict Justice, the faith of the psalmist remains firm (*Divrei Sholom*).

3. אַךְ הוּא צוּרִי וִישׁוּעָתִי — *Only He is my Rock and my Salvation.*

[Cf. *v.* 7 and *comm.* ibid.]

God is my sole shield against any mishap; He is my protective *Rock;* and if [I deserve that] misfortune should befall me, God is also *my Salvation* from suffering (*Alshich*).

Lechem Shlomo observes that man is a synthesis of חוֹמֶר, *shapeless physical matter,* and צוּרָה, *intelligent form.* Man's spiritual ascent depends on the extent to which his heavenly צוּרָה dominates his mundane חוֹמֶר by placing a Divine imprint on every aspect of his being. God molds and sculpts the צוּרָה of man with צָרָה, *suffering,* which teaches man to spurn physical attractions for the sake of enhancing his Divine intellect. Therefore, David refers to God as צוּרִי, meaning *He Who fashions and molds my* צוּרָה.

מִשְׂגַּבִּי — *My Stronghold.*

God does not rescue me from suffering and then desert me. After assuring my salvation, He elevates me and strengthens me with success (*Alshich*).

לֹא אֶמּוֹט — *I shall not falter.*

Since God is *my Stronghold,* He certainly will prevent me from falling (*Ibn Ezra*).

רַבָּה — *Greatly.*

[This word does not appear in verse 7. Here the psalmist is not yet imbued with total confidence in God's complete salvation. Although he feels secure that no major catastrophe will destroy him, he does feel vulnerable to minor failures.]

Rashi, based on *Midrash Shocher Tov,* interprets רַבָּה homiletically as *Gehinnom,* the great, eternal punishment from which there is no escape. David is confident that with God's help

For the Conductor, on Yedusun
a song of David.

² Only for God does my soul wait silently,
from Him comes my salvation.

³ Only He is my Rock and my Salvation;
my Stronghold,
I shall not falter greatly.

⁴ How long will you plot treacherously
against man?
May You all be slain —
like a leaning wall; like a toppled fence.

---

he will not sin so *greatly* as to deserve such a severe punishment (*Alshich*).

According to *Sforno's* unique interpretation of this psalm, it was composed as a threat to the nation of Ammon, who dared to act treacherously towards David and Israel. David has no fear of their might and he is confident that he *will not falter* when he attacks רַבָּה, *Rabbah*, the capital of Ammon.

4. [The psalmist now addresses himself to his tormentors and admonishes them.]

עַד אָנָה תְּהוֹתְתוּ עַל אִישׁ — *How long* [lit. *until when*] *will you plot treacherously against man?*

The translation of תְּהוֹתְתוּ follows *Rashi, Ibn Ezra, Ibn Yachya,* and *Metzudas David,* who identify its root as הַוּוֹת, *treachery,* [see 5:10]. However, *Targum* and *Menachem* (quoted in *Rashi*) relate the word to וַיֵּתֶא, *gather,* suggesting, 'How long will you persist in assembling for the sake of perpetrating evil?'

Rashi also cites commentaries which render this, 'How long will you speak slanderously — at great length?'

Finally, *Hirsch* derives תְּהוֹתְתוּ from חִתַּת, *frighten,* translating, 'How long

will you strike terror into a man?'

תְּרָצְּחוּ כֻלְּכֶם — *May you all be slain.*

This statement may be understood as a curse which the psalmist hurls at his bloodthirsty adversaries (*Ibn Ezra; Radak; Metzudas David*) or as a revelation of the treacherous plots of the enemy; according to the latter, David is exclaiming, 'You all plan to murder me!' (*Rashbam; Ibn Yachya*).

בְּקִיר נָטוּי — *Like a leaning wall.*

According to *Ibn Ezra, Radak,* and *Metzudos David,* this is a continuation of the preceding curse. It means, 'You should be murdered, but not with a quick and easy death. Rather, you should live in perpetual terror, always tottering on the brink of destruction, as does a weak leaning wall.'

However, other commentaries understand this as a description of the enemy's treacherous plot: 'You are cold-blooded murderers who kill without any qualms. You kill nonchalantly and effortlessly, like a man who gives a slight push to a tottering wall in order to knock it over' (*Ibn Yachya*).

The very wall in whose shade I took refuge you desire to topple on me! (*Rashbam*).[1]

---

1. The *Talmud (Sanhedrin* 109a) identifies the people of Sodom as the personification of the evils enumerated in this verse. When a wealthy traveler visited their city, they would cast

ה אַךְ מִשְּׂאֵתוֹ | יָעֲצוּ לְהַדִּיחַ יִרְצוּ כָזָב בְּפִיו
ו יְבָרֵכוּ וּבְקִרְבָּם יְקַלְלוּ־סֶלָה: אַךְ
לֵאלֹהִים דּוֹמִי נַפְשִׁי כִּי־מִמֶּנּוּ תִּקְוָתִי:
ז אַךְ־הוּא צוּרִי וִישׁוּעָתִי מִשְׂגַּבִּי לֹא
ח אֶמּוֹט: עַל־אֱלֹהִים יִשְׁעִי וּכְבוֹדִי צוּר־עֻזִּי
ט מַחְסִי בֵּאלֹהִים: בִּטְחוּ בוֹ בְכָל־עֵת | עָם

גֶּדֶר הַדְּחוּיָה — [Like] a toppled fence.

The קִיר is the *wall* of the house, upon which the heavy קוֹרוֹת, *rafters*, rest. The גֶּדֶר is a flimsy *fence* around the outer property. Since the קִיר is sturdier than the גֶּדֶר, pressure that causes the *wall* to lean will knock the *fence* down (*Norah Tehillos*).

5. אַךְ מִשְּׂאֵתוֹ יָעֲצוּ לְהַדִּיחַ — *Only because of his loftiness have they plotted to topple him.*

These murderers are so extraordinarily vicious because they are terrified lest some man challenge them by rising to a position of authority which would enable him to administer the punishment they so justly deserve. Therefore, they devise rash acts of terror to destroy any potential opposition (*Rashi*).

Ohel Yaakov observes that as a person's station in life rises, he grows more and more vulnerable to the attacks of antagonists who seek out his most minute errors. Thus, the wily hypocrite first lavishes praise on his victim, to increase his prestige; when the hypocrite later slanders him, the victim's fall from glory is doubly disgraceful.

Radak interprets the entire verse as a reference to God; each of the wicked seeks לְהַדִּיחַ, *to lure away*, his associates from recognizing the towering Omnipotence of God. These evil men deny that God knows the inner thoughts of man; therefore, they seek to deceive

with expressions of blessing, while cursing Him in their hearts.

6. אַךְ לֵאלֹהִים דּוֹמִי נַפְשִׁי — *For God alone my soul waits silently.*

[Although David realizes that his enemies are scheming against him (v. 4-5), he remains completely unafraid, for he recognizes that there exists no power on earth except *God alone*. Therefore, David maintains a tranquil silence.]

כִּי־מִמֶּנּוּ תִּקְוָתִי — *Because from Him is my hope.*

This verse is almost the same as verse 2. *Chovos Halevovos* and *Hirsch* explain that the differences between the verses serve to characterize two men on different levels of faith.

The first man retains his own private aims and desires and trusts that God will help him to achieve his goals. The second man, however, is so devoted to his Maker that he abandons all personal ambitions and preferences, accepting whatever lot God decides to grant him.

The first man is described in v. 2 as waiting אֶל אֱלֹהִים, *to God*, implying that God is distant from him. He looks forward to a particular event which he personally considers יְשׁוּעָתִי, *my salvation*. Since this person's faith is relatively weak, he may falter; he is only assured that (v. 3) he *will not falter greatly*.

In this verse, however, the man is

covetous eyes on his riches. They sat him beneath *a leaning wall* and toppled it over on him, so that they could seize his money.

Maharsha (ibid.) explains that they staged the 'accident' in such a way that it appeared as if the victim was responsible for tipping over the wall. Since the traveler was liable for the 'damage' he had caused, the Sodomites confiscated the dead man's money as 'payment.'

⁵ Only because of his loftiness
        have they plotted to topple him
        delighting in deceit.
With their mouth they bless;
        inwardly they curse, Selah!
⁶ For God alone my soul waits silently —
        because from Him is my hope.
⁷ He alone is my Rock and Salvation;
        my Stronghold,
I shall not falter.
⁸ Upon God rests my salvation
        and my glory,
the Rock of my strength —
        my refuge is with God.
⁹ Trust in Him at every moment,
        O Nation!

---

completely committed לֵאלֹהִים, *for God.* Since God Himself is the man's sole desire and תִּקְוָה, *hope,* he will not falter at all (*v.*8).

7. אַךְ הוּא צוּרִי וִישׁוּעָתִי — *He alone is my Rock and Salvation.*

The psalmist repeats this credo [cf. *v.* 3] in order to constantly reinforce his unswerving faith (*Radak*).

לֹא אֶמּוֹט — *I shall not falter.*

This verse means, 'I shall not be swayed in the least,' whereas in *v.* 3, the psalmist implied that he might falter slightly.

According to *Radak,* this psalm echoes the words of the Jews in exile. He comments that before Israel was redeemed (see *v.* 3), the Jews were in danger of suffering a decline. Once they leave the *golus* behind (*v.* 7), however, they are completely safe from any fall.

8. עַל אֱלֹהִים יִשְׁעִי וּכְבוֹדִי — *Upon God rests my salvation and my glory.*

God is so intimately involved with my affairs that there is no reason for me to be concerned with my personal welfare. He will surely determine *my salvation* and He will preserve *my glory,* i.e., my reputation (*Ibn Ezra*).

In exile, the *glory* of Israel is tarnished by disgrace; but when God provides the *salvation* of total redemption, Israel's renewed prestige is assured (*Radak*).

צוּר עֻזִּי מַחְסִי בֵּאלֹהִים — *The Rock of my strength — my refuge is with God.*

God will grant me this complete protection and concern only if I depend upon Him without reservations and without placing my trust in any other force. I must consider Him alone as *the Rock of my strength.* I may seek *refuge* only *in God* (*Alshich*).

9. בִּטְחוּ בוֹ בְכָל עֵת — *Trust in Him at every moment.*

After completing his admonition [which began in *v.*4] to the treacherous foes, the psalmist now addresses the masses, to fortify their faith (*Ibn Ezra*).

Radak notes that these inspiring

שִׁפְכוּ־לְפָנָיו לְבַבְכֶם אֱלֹהִים מַחֲסֶה־לָנוּ
סֶלָה: אַךְ | הֶבֶל בְּנֵי אָדָם כָּזָב בְּנֵי אִישׁ
בְּמֹאזְנַיִם לַעֲלוֹת הֵמָּה מֵהֶבֶל יָחַד: אַל־
תִּבְטְחוּ בְעֹשֶׁק וּבְגָזֵל אַל־תֶּהְבָּלוּ חָיִל |
כִּי־יָנוּב אַל־תָּשִׁיתוּ לֵב: אַחַת | דִּבֶּר
אֱלֹהִים שְׁתַּיִם־זוּ שָׁמָעְתִּי כִּי עֹז

words are especially appropriate for the Jews in exile, implying, 'No matter how long the bitter exile endures, never give up hope, for the redemption can come suddenly, at any time.'

Even in the darkest hour, when there appears to be no glimmer of hope, never forget the credo of faith handed down by the royal family of David (*Berachos* 10a): Even when a sharpened blade is poised at a person's neck [to kill him], he should not give up hope of deliverance and for God's mercy [which appears at all times] (*Tehillos Hashem*).

The *Midrash* (*Aggados Bereishis*) stresses that David was particularly fortunate. Other men pray and receive no response; God ignores them purposely, because He wants them to continue praying. However, since David's life was one of constant prayer, he was assured that he would be answered instantly, *at every moment.*

שִׁפְכוּ לְפָנָיו לְבַבְכֶם — *Pour out your hearts before Him.*

Repent before God with total sincerity [hide nothing from Him]. Then your redemption will be assured (*Radak*).

10. אַךְ הֶבֶל בְּנֵי אָדָם — *Naught but vanity are common men!*

Place no faith in their assistance (*Ibn Ezra*) and do not fear their threat, for God [alone] is a refuge for us (*Rashi*).

כָּזָב בְּנֵי אִישׁ — *Deceit are distinguished people.*

[Cf. *comm.* to 49:3 גַּם בְּנֵי אָדָם גַּם בְּנֵי אִישׁ.]

The בְּנֵי אָדָם are simple people who lack distinguished ancestry. Understandably, others place little faith in their ability to help. The בְּנֵי אִישׁ, however, are those who possess wealth and influence inherited from their prestigious forebears. The psalmist warns that even these apparently powerful and capable men are not worthy of our confidence, for they are כָּזָב, deceitful and disappointing.]

בְּמֹאזְנַיִם לַעֲלוֹת הֵמָּה מֵהֶבֶל יָחַד — *If they be lifted on the scales, they and vanity would be equal.*

This translation follows *Rashi*. However, *Ibn Ezra* and *Radak* explain that if all men were weighed, they would be found to be even *less* than vanity [מֵהֶבֶל], rather than *equal* to it.

According to *Metzudas David*, the psalmist claims that if the בִּטָחוֹן, *divine faith*, professed by all mankind (*v.* 9) were weighed on a scale, it would amount to less than הֶבֶל, *nothing.*

The Rabbis (*Kallah Rabbosi* 8) emphasize that human calculations and appraisals are הֶבֶל, *worthless.* People presumptuously decide that a woman is suitable for a certain man, that riches befit a certain person, that a house is appropriate for a certain family, but God

1. *Midrash Shocher Tov* points out that man's very existence proves God's constant mercy. The soul of man is a celestial, spiritual force which spurns its union with the mundane body and struggles for release to escape heavenward. Only God's never-ending intervention *at all times* preserves this precarious union and keeps the breath of life interwoven with the coarse flesh.

Pour out your hearts before Him,
God is a refuge for us, Selah!
¹⁰ *Naught but vanity are common men!*
Deceit are distinguished people!
If they be lifted on the scales,
they and vanity would be equal.
¹¹ *Trust not in oppression,*
and in robbery place not vain hope;
Though wealth flourishes,
pay it no heed.
¹² *Once has God spoken;*
twice have I heard this

---

has already weighed these questions *and lifted them on a scale,* arriving at different conclusions and matching other people יַחַד, *together.*

11. אַל תִּבְטְחוּ בְעֹשֶׁק — *Trust not in oppression.*

Just as it is *vanity* to trust in man (v.10), it is foolish to rely on wealth *(Ibn Ezra),* particularly when it is ill-gotten gain *(Radak).*

To the extent that man finds security in his riches, he deprives himself of complete trust in God *(Alshich).*

עֹשֶׁק — *Oppression.*

This refers to property which a person unlawfully withholds from its true owner and to wages or debts which a man refuses to pay *(Radak).*

Ibn Ezra identifies עֹשֶׁק as the money gained through deception and fraud. This includes excessive markup.

גֵּזֶל — *Robbery.*

This refers to money openly taken by force *(Radak; Ibn Ezra)* [see *Bava Kama* 79b].

The psalmist here depicts the unlawful man's descent into crime: at first, he merely fails to pay what he owes to creditors and to employees; eventually, however, he engages in active, violent robbery *(Migdal David).*

אַל תֶּהְבָּלוּ — *Place not vain hope.*

Man himself is empty *vanity* (v. 10), but when he places his hopes in criminal gains then he is doubly *vain (Ibn Ezra).*

חַיִל כִּי יָנוּב — *Though wealth flourishes.*

When you notice evil men who enjoy financial success and whose wealth grows daily *(Rashi),* like a tree which produces abundant fruit with no effort on the part of its owner, *pay no heed (Radak).*

אַל תָּשִׁיתוּ לֵב — *Pay it no heed* [lit. *do not set your heart upon them.*]

Their wealth will not endure, and it will not protect them when tragedy strikes *(Radak).*

12. אַחַת דִּבֶּר אֱלֹהִים שְׁתַּיִם זוּ שָׁמָעְתִּי — *Once* [lit. *one thing*] *has God spoken, twice* [lit. *two things*] *have I heard this.*

God has taught the truths of the Torah not only once but many times, through the prophets who speak in His Name *(Radak).*

God proclaimed the laws of the one Torah, and Moses, the great teacher, repeated them twice *(Targum).* The first four books of the Pentateuch are the original lesson. The fifth book is known as מִשְׁנֵה תוֹרָה, *the repetition of the Torah (Targum D'Matargum).*

יג לֵאלֹהִֽים: וּלְךָֽ־אֲדֹנָי חָ֑סֶד כִּי־אַתָּה
תְשַׁלֵּ֖ם לְאִ֣ישׁ כְּֽמַעֲשֵֽׂהוּ:

Moreover, each statement in the Torah conveys more than one message for every word has a dual meaning, the נִגְלָה, *revealed truth*, and the נִסְתָּר, *concealed truth*. Thus God pronounced אַחַת, *one word*, from which we heard שְׁתַּיִם, *two things* (*Rabbeinu Bachya*, comm. to *Exodus* 13:1).

Thus God fashioned the לֻחֹת, *tablets*, so that the script could be seen from both sides of the stones, alluding to the double dimension of the Torah (*Rabbeinu Bachya*, ibid. 32:16).

This is what the prophet *Jeremiah* (23:29) meant when he said that the word of God is וּכְפַטִּישׁ יְפֹצֵץ סָלַע — *like an anvil smashing a rock*. Just as a rock can be shattered into many fragments, each verse can be broken down into many lessons and interpretations (*Sanhedrin* 34a).

כִּי עֹז לֵאלֹהִים — *That strength belongs to God*.

From *one* of the Ten Commandments we heard and understood *two* Divine attributes. In the second commandment, God declared that פֹּקֵד עֲוֹן אָבֹת עַל בָּנִים — *He visits the sins of the fathers upon the children* (*Exodus* 20:5). This demonstrates God's מְדַת הַדִּין, *the Divine Attribute of Strict Justice*, from which we realize *that strength belongs to God* (*Rashi*).

Radak stresses that once we realize that *strength belongs to God* alone, we must place faith in Him exclusively.

Man must abandon his reliance on human power and wealth.

13. וּלְךָ אֲדֹנָי חָסֶד — *And Yours, my Lord, is kindness*.

Rashi continues to point out that the second commandment reveals another aspect of the Divine: מְדַת הַחֶסֶד, the *Divine Attribute of Mercy*.

Scripture says וְעֹשֶׂה חֶסֶד לַאֲלָפִים — *And I act kindly unto the two thousandth generation of them that love me and keep my commandments* (*Exodus* 20:6).

Thus we heard of *two* Divine attributes from *one* commandment.

כִּי אַתָּה תְשַׁלֵּם לְאִישׁ כְּמַעֲשֵׂהוּ — *For You reward each man in accordance with his deeds*.

[This seems to contradict the preceding statement, for, if God repays in strict accordance with a person's deeds, where is His *kindness*?]

The Talmud (*Rosh Hashanah* 17a) explains that God first attempts to adhere to the letter of the law, but if He sees that man cannot withstand this, He exercises His חֶסֶד, *kindness* [see *Tosafos*, ibid. s.v. בִּתְחִלָּה].

Other commentators detect a glimmer of *kindness* even in the word כְּמַעֲשֵׂהוּ. *Rashi* translates this *similar to his deeds*, indicating that God mercifully minimizes and softens the punishment so that it is *not* in complete accordance with the sin. Nevertheless, the punishment does

that strength belongs to God.

¹³ *And Yours, my Lord,*
is kindness, for You reward
each man in accordance with his deeds.

bear a similarity to the sin, measure for measure.

Alshich and *Metzudas David* observe that this mode of punishment is really a great boon, for often a person is unaware of his error, but the punishment then spurs him to self-awareness, for it reflects the nature of the offense.

Alshich adds that we can detect compassion even in God's *reward in* (precise) *accordance with his deeds*, for God takes man to task only for the actual act of sin and not for the thought which accompanied it. [See *Kiddushin* 40a; see also *comm.* and footnote to 66:18.]

Also, although an apparently isolated transgression may indirectly cause much more evil, God does not punish the sinner for the inadvertent results of his sin.

Rashi notes, however, that when a person does a *mitzvah*, the opposite is true; then God does *reward each man in accordance with his deeds.*

[God's reward is complete; it extends even to the good thoughts which accompanied the good deed and to the indirect good which results from the *mitzvah*.][1]

Radak concludes that these final words echo the hymn of Israel in exile, proclaiming, 'Despite the seemingly endless duration of the bleak exile, we remain undaunted and completely confident in Your חֶסֶד, *kindness*. We recognize that our suffering is truly our salvation, for it clears our account in this world so that we can fully enjoy the bliss of future redemption and perfect reward for our *mitzvah* without disturbance.'

1. *Midrash Shocher Tov* teaches that a sinful action bears no fruit, in that the sinner is not taken to task for the indirect outgrowth of his deeds; but a *mitzvah* is fertile and prolific, for all good things which sprout from the original deed are generously rewarded.

Moreover, God is scrupulous in His system of accounting. If a man sins ten times and then performs ten *mitzvos*, God does not use up the merit of the *mitzvos* in an attempt to cancel out the damage of the sins. Rather, He administers the complete punishment due for the offenses and then bestows the proper reward.

Rambam (comm. to Mishnah, *Avos* 4:22) echoes this theme, noting that the dictum, 'God accepts no bribes' seems odd, for what possible interest could God have in any human gift? He explains that this means that God will not be swayed even by gifts of the spirit; i.e., if a man is condemned to suffer for his sin, every myriad *mitzvos* will not make God overlook the man's single transgression [cf. *Ramban, Deuteronomy 10:16*].

The only 'spiritual bribes' which can divert God's attention from sin are תְּשׁוּבָה תְּפִילָה וּצְדָקָה, *penitence, prayer, and charity (Midrash Shocher Tov* 17:2).

[See *Margolios Hayam* to *Sanhedrin* 102b for a lengthy discussion of this entire theme.]

D avid sought refuge from his pursuers, but he became stranded and trapped in the parched wasteland of the Judean desert.

Outside, Saul and his army surrounded him. From within, David was attacked by a terrible thirst which utterly drained his energy.

Oblivious to these dangers, David erected a massive fortress of faith which insulated him from the ravages of his hostile physical environment. His vast intellectual powers were completely preoccupied with the desire to draw even closer to God.

David's thirst in the wilderness was essentially spiritual. He longed to gaze upon God's splendor and he yearned to hear the teachings of Torah scholars, who reveal the ways of God.

Indeed, David's soul was ablaze with love for his Maker. This flaming thirst could be quenched only by closeness to Hashem, as David states: In the shadow of Your wings I shall joyously sing (v. 8).

Midrash Shocher Tov observes that this psalm foretells that the exiled children of Israel will cry out, 'Our souls are weary and parched; we yearn for the refreshing words of Torah, but the gentiles will not allow us this.' Thus will the words of the prophet (Amos 8:11) be fulfilled: Behold the days are coming, says my Lord HASHEM / ELOHIM, when I shall send a famine in the land, not a famine of bread, nor a thirst for water, but a thirst for hearing the words of HASHEM.

א מִזְמוֹר לְדָוִד בִּהְיוֹתוֹ בְּמִדְבַּר יְהוּדָה:
ב אֱלֹהִים | אֵלִי אַתָּה אֲשַׁחֲרֶךָּ צָמְאָה לְךָ |
נַפְשִׁי כָּמַהּ לְךָ בְשָׂרִי בְּאֶרֶץ־צִיָּה וְעָיֵף

1. מִזְמוֹר לְדָוִד — *A song of David.*

The *Zohar (Parshas Terumah)* cites David's intense spiritual ecstasy and his special genius for composing hymns of praise even in situations of extreme danger and adversity.

Alshich adds that although David found himself in one of the most barren and desolate spots in Israel, he still rejoiced, for at least he was in the Holy Land rather than on alien soil.

The *Midrash* states that it is better to be in the wastelands of Israel than in the palaces of any foreign land. According to the *Talmud (Kesubos* 110b), a person who lives outside of the land of Israel is like a man without a God.

Therefore, in the next verse, David sings, *O God, You are* [still] *my God!* (*Dorash Moshe*).

בִּהְיוֹתוֹ בְּמִדְבַּר יְהוּדָה — *When he was in the wilderness of Judah.*

Radak identifies this as the wilderness of Ziph, where David was hiding from Saul.

Norah Tehillos notes that the setting of this psalm is not identical to that of Psalm 54, for the people of Ziph threatened David twice. David's first encounter in Ziph, recorded in *I Samuel* 23:19-29, took place when the Ziphites informed Saul of David's hiding place; then David narrowly escaped at the סֶלַע הַמַּחְלֹקֶת, *Rock of Division* [see footnote, 18:3]. Psalm 54 is dedicated to that incident; therefore, it begins (v.2), *When the Ziphites came and said to Saul, 'Indeed, David is hiding in our midst.'*

The Ziphites betrayed David a second time, as described in *I Samuel* 26:2-3. At that time, however, David was not as concerned about the physical threat which they posed; rather, he mourned the suffering of his soul,

which was exiled in a spiritual wilderness, completely cut off from the spiritual centers of Israel.

Since our psalm is based on the latter incident, David here makes no direct mention of the Ziphites. Rather he expresses anguish over his isolated location, *the wilderness of Judah.*

2. אֱלֹהִים אֵלִי אַתָּה — *O God — You are my God.*

See footnote to 22:2; אֵל is defined as the name of God which gives strength and power in times of distress to those who are completely righteous. *Targum* here renders אֵלִי as תֻּקְפִּי, *my might.*

Radak explains that a fugitive is highly vulnerable; God is his sole support and protection.

Chozeh David observes that David was particularly disillusioned by the treachery of the Ziphites, for they were his close kinsmen of the royal tribe of Judah. Not only did they betray David, but their perfidy even took place in the tribal territory which they shared with David, *the wilderness of Judah.*

Now David realized more than ever before the futility of putting trust in any man, however close he may seem. He proclaimed that, henceforth, *O God — You* [alone] *are my God* [and savior].

אֲשַׁחֲרֶךָּ — *I seek You.*

This translation follows *Rashi* and *Metzudas David. Targum* and *Ibn Ezra* suggest that this word may be related to שַׁחַר, *dawn,* implying that David renewed his quest for God with every new dawn [see 27:4 וּלְבַקֵּר בְּהֵיכָלוֹ].

צָמְאָה לְךָ נַפְשִׁי — *My soul thirsts for You.*

The psalmist does not describe himself as רָעֵב, *starving,* because that word does not adequately indicate the intensity of his passionate yearning.

63
1-2

A song of David,
  when he was in the wilderness of Judah.
² O God — You are my God,
  I seek You.
My soul thirsts for You,
  my flesh longs for You;
In a land barren,
  and weary with no water.

The agony of acute thirst far surpasses the pangs of hunger, for the need for water is the most intense and urgent of human needs (*Radak*; *Yaavetz HaDoresh*).

[Although David literally lacked water in this parched and torturous wasteland, he makes no mention of it, for his soul was ablaze with an ecstatic yearning for God which rendered him oblivious to all other desires and physical needs.]

Where then was the fresh wellspring which would have provided David with spiritual refreshment? According to *Radak*, David desired to be either in Kiryat Yearim, where the Holy Ark was kept, or in Givon, where the Tabernacle stood. Men who sought the presence of God would gather in these two spiritual centers to hear the teachings of the great scholars of Israel. David sorely missed the company of Torah scholars, for the fighters who joined David's band were not of high intellectual caliber; rather, they were bitter and broken men who had fled from their troubles (*I Samuel* 22:2).

בָּמַהּ לְךָ בְשָׂרִי — *My flesh longs for You.*
Rabbi Asher of Stolin (based on the words of *Rashi* and *Ibn Ezra*) explained that in all of Scripture, no word expresses such intense desire as the word בָּמַהּ. It is a longing of unsurpassed intensity.

Malbim traces this word to בָּמֶה, *how much*, to suggest, 'O, how much does my flesh long for You!' The man overcome with such longing concentrates all

of his senses on this one wish and becomes oblivious to all else. In the desert, the typical person would be preoccupied with his need for water, but David thought only of God (*Rabbeinu Bachya*).

The *Midrash* (*Bereishis Rabbah* 69:1) relates בָּמַהּ to בְּמֵהִין, *mushrooms*, for these plants derive no nourishment from the soil and survive exclusively on the moisture they absorb from the atmosphere. [Similarly, David recognizes that his survival depends only on the inspiration which he draws from above, rather than any mundane, physical sustenance.]

Norah Tehillos points out that David's body and soul achieved total harmony. Just as David's 'soul thirsted' for God, so did his 'flesh long' for God; his entire being was suffused with sublime spirituality.

בְּאֶרֶץ צִיָּה — *In a land barren.*
[It should be noted that the wilderness of Judah is not only hot and dry, but also highly saline. To the east, it borders on the Dead Sea, whose high salt concentration renders the surrounding area especially arid and desolate. The air is saturated with salt, which increases thirst immensely.]

וְעָיֵף בְּלִי מָיִם — [*And*] *weary with no water.*
According to *Radak* and *Ibn Ezra*, this describes the utterly parched earth of this wilderness.

However, *Metzudas David* and

ג בְּלִי־מָיִם: כֵּן בַּקֹּדֶשׁ חֲזִיתִךָ לִרְאוֹת עֻזְּךָ

ד וּכְבוֹדֶךָ: כִּי־טוֹב חַסְדְּךָ מֵחַיִּים שְׂפָתַי

ה יְשַׁבְּחוּנְךָ: כֵּן אֲבָרֶכְךָ בְחַיָּי בְּשִׁמְךָ אֶשָּׂא

ו כַפָּי: כְּמוֹ חֵלֶב וָדֶשֶׁן תִּשְׂבַּע נַפְשִׁי

ז וְשִׂפְתֵי רְנָנוֹת יְהַלֶּל־פִּי: אִם־זְכַרְתִּיךָ

Hirsch maintain that this refers to the man traveling through *the barren land.* It is he who grows *weary with no water.*

3. כֵּן בַּקֹּדֶשׁ חֲזִיתִךָ — *Thus have I beheld You in the Sanctuary.*

Rashi translates כֵּן, *thus* or *just as,* implying, 'To the extent that I thirsted and longed to witness Your splendor *just as* I once beheld it in Your Sanctuary, I am ultimately destined to see *Your might and Your glory.*

Radak renders: *Just as* a man in the desert thirsts for water, כֵּן, *thus,* do I long to behold Your sacred Presence in the holy shrine.

חֲזִיתִךָ — *I beheld You.*

Malbim points out that the root חָזָה denotes the spiritual perception experienced by the prophets. Such insight is called חָזוֹן, *a prophetic vision.*

Hirsch adds that חָזָה is derived from חָזֶה, *the breast,* for it alludes to vision of the heart, rather than of the eyes. The word רָאָה, in contrast, refers to ordinary physical eyesight.

Thus, 'now, while I am isolated and geographically distant, my heart perceives Your Sanctuary, and I envision the day when I will be privileged *to see* (לִרְאוֹת) *Your glory* face to face.'

לִרְאוֹת עֻזְּךָ וּכְבוֹדֶךָ — *To see Your might and Your glory.*

God's *might,* עֹז, refers to the holy Torah, as in 29:11 (*Alshich*), and to the Ark of the Law, called (132:8) אֲרוֹן עֻזֶּךָ (*Hirsch*).

כָּבוֹד refers to the *glory* of God's Presence, which rests upon the Ark (*Metzudas David*).

4. כִּי טוֹב חַסְדְּךָ מֵחַיִּים — *For better is Your kindness than life.*

The *kindness* which You will bestow upon the righteous in the World to Come far surpasses the good *life* which You grant the wicked in This World (*Targum*).

Radak explains: You displayed Your kindness to mankind when You endowed humanity with intelligence, for this faculty elevates man's existence above the life devoid of higher intelligence experienced by animals and other living things.

Metzudas David adds: The entire purpose of my *life* is to utilize Your *kindness,* intelligent speech, so that *my lips shall praise You.* If I am deprived of this opportunity, my *life* is bereft of all purpose. Therefore, *my soul thirsts for You* and *my flesh longs for You,* for every intelligent person yearns to fulfill his mission in life.

Radak suggests another interpretation, in which חַיִּים refers to the rich and powerful men [who possess all of the benefits of *life.*] According to this view, David here declares, 'These men promise to do charity and favors, yet, O God, Your *kindness* outshines theirs. Saul showed me kindness by accepting me into his court and by making me his general; he gave me his daughter in marriage and was my benefactor in many ways. Yet after all this kindness, he now seeks to kill me. [To escape his pursuit, I am exiled to this barren wilderness.] Therefore, it is fitting that *my lips shall praise* only *Your kindness* and not that of any חַיִּים, *living,* mortal man.

שְׂפָתַי יְשַׁבְּחוּנְךָ — *My lips shall praise You.*

In this manner, I shall accomplish my purpose in life (*Metzudas David*).

³ Thus have I beheld You in the Sanctuary;
to see Your might and Your glory.
⁴ For better is Your kindness than life;
my lips shall praise You.
⁵ Then I shall bless You all my life;
in Your Name I shall lift my hands.
⁶ As with fat and abundance
will my soul be sated;
And with joyous language
will my mouth give praise.

---

5. כֵּן אֲבָרֶכְךָ בְחַיָּי — *Then I shall bless You all* [lit. *with*] *my life.*

When I come before You in Your Sanctuary, כֵּן, *then* I shall dedicate my entire life to blessing Your Name (*Rashi*).

Radak translates כֵּן as *so* or *similarly*, suggesting 'just as *my lips praised You* (v.4) until now, so shall I continue to bless You forever.'

The *Talmud* (*Berachos* 16a) explains the declaration *I shall bless You with my life* to mean: I shall recite the *Shema* before You.

[When he recites the *Shema*, the Jew accepts the command to love God בְּכָל נַפְשְׁךָ, *with all your soul* (*Deuteronomy* 6:5); i.e., he vows to sacrifice his life, if necessary, for the love of God.]

The three sections which make up the *Shema* contain a sum of 248 words, alluding to the 248 organs of the human body (which form the basis for life). All of these organs are to be dedicated to the service of God (*Eretz HaChaim*).

בְּשִׁמְךָ אֶשָּׂא כַפָּי — *In Your Name I shall lift my hands.*

After spending a lifetime blessing You in This World, I shall lift up my hands to Your name, in the World to Come (*Targum*).

The *Talmud* (*Berachos* 16a) interprets this to mean, 'I shall pray to You.'

Yalkut Eliezer explains that the true

purpose of prayer is to *lift*, i.e., to elevate and exalt God's Name. Although the bulk of the benedictions of *Shemoneh Esrei* are requests for the welfare of the supplicant, the supplicant's motive for seeking personal success should be to add glory to God's Name.

6. כְּמוֹ חֵלֶב וָדֶשֶׁן תִּשְׂבַּע נַפְשִׁי — *As with fat and abundance will my soul be sated.*

David said, 'If You will grant me the opportunity to bless You and to exalt Your Name (v.5), then my thirsty, parched soul will be totally *satisfied*, just as the body is content after a *fat and abundant* meal.'

The *Kuzari* notes that the soul is sustained by a regimen of prayer, just as the body is maintained by ample meals at regular intervals (*Malbim*; see *comm.* to *Psalms* 55:18).

וְשִׂפְתֵי רְנָנוֹת יְהַלֶּל פִּי — *And with joyous language* [lit., *lips*] *will my mouth give praise.*

Here the word שִׂפְתֵי [lit. *lips*] is rendered as *languages* [cf. *Genesis* 11:1] (*Rashi*; *Metzudas David*) to imply 'I will use any language I know to express Your praise' (*Ibn Ezra*).

The words will be as sweet and pleasant to my lips as fat and abundant delicacies (*Radak*).

This spiritual joy is illustrated in the

ח עַל־יְצוּעָי בְּאַשְׁמֻרוֹת אֶהְגֶּה־בָּךְ: כִּי־
הָיִיתָ עֶזְרָתָה לִּי וּבְצֵל כְּנָפֶיךָ אֲרַנֵּן:
ט דָּבְקָה נַפְשִׁי אַחֲרֶיךָ בִּי תָּמְכָה יְמִינֶךָ:
י וְהֵמָּה לְשׁוֹאָה יְבַקְשׁוּ נַפְשִׁי יָבֹאוּ
יא בְּתַחְתִּיּוֹת הָאָרֶץ: יַגִּירֻהוּ עַל־יְדֵי־חָרֶב

Talmud (Berachos 9b) by Rav Bruna, whose devotion during morning prayer filled him with such rapture that he was smiling in ecstacy the whole day (*Yaavetz HaDoresh*).

7. אִם זְכַרְתִּיךָ עַל יְצוּעָי — *When I remember You upon my couch* [lit. *couches*].

Radak proves from various sources that אִם may be translated as *when*. In this verse, it implies: At night, *when my mind is free of daily concerns and distractions, I can concentrate my thoughts on You. At that time, my soul becomes satisfied as with fat and abundance* (*Ibn Ezra*).

Formerly, I would remember You while reclining on my soft, luxurious royal couch; now, lying on the cold, hard rocks in the wilderness, my thoughts are concentrated on You. Whenever I think of You, You draw near and Your Presence provides me joy and comfort (*Hirsch*).

Radak notes that David uses the plural יְצוּעָי, *couches*, because while David was fleeing from Saul, he slept in a different place every night.

בְּאַשְׁמֻרוֹת אֶהְגֶּה־בָּךְ — *In night watches meditating upon You.*

Radak cites the *Talmudic* dictum (*Berachos* 3a) that the night is divided

into three equal watches. At the end of every watch, the Holy One, Blessed be He, mourns for His Temple, which lies in ruins, and for His sons, the children of Israel, who are dispersed in exile. The *Shulchan Aruch* (*Orach Chaim* 1:2-3) accepts the ruling of the *Rosh* (*Berachos* 3a) that all God-fearing men should arise at the end of each night watch to join God in His lamentation.

Even in David's times, before the destruction of the Temple and the exile of Israel, the king would lament the misfortunes and problems of his people at the night watches. With his prophetic vision, David foresaw the future suffering of his people. Although David was awake almost all night (*Berachos* 3b; *Succah* 26b), he prayed with special inspiration and fervor at the אַשְׁמֻרוֹת.[1]

8. כִּי הָיִיתָ עֶזְרָתָה לִּי — *For You were a help for me.*

It is fitting that I should think of You at all times (*v. 7*) because You help me constantly (*Radak*).

וּבְצֵל כְּנָפֶיךָ אֲרַנֵּן — *In the shadow of Your wings I shall joyously sing.*

I am especially grateful to God for providing me with a place of refuge in *Eretz Yisrael* rather than in a foreign land [see *comm. v. 1*]. I sing with extra

---

1. אַשְׁמֻרוֹת also refers to the crack of dawn, the אַשְׁמֹרֶת הַבֹּקֶר [see *Exodus* 14:24]. The very first *halachah* in the entire *Shulchan Aruch* (*Orach Chaim* 1:1) is: A person should arise just before dawn to commence his daily service of God. *Ramoh* (ibid.) maintains that the Jew's Divine service actually begins at night: At bedtime, a man should think of God, in Whose Presence he will sleep, and immediately upon awakening, he should arise from bed with vigor and alacrity.

This teaches that a person's conduct upon retiring at night determines how and when he will arise. This is the message of this verse: '*If I remember You* [when I lay down to sleep] *on my couch*, [then] *I shall think of You* [and arise quickly] *at the* אַשְׁמֻרוֹת *of dawn.*'

7 *When I remember You upon my couch;*
in night watches meditating upon You.
8 *For You were a help for me;*
in the shadow of Your wings
I shall joyously sing.
9 *My soul cleaves after You;*
to me, Your right arm lent support.
10 *But as for them,*
they seek desolation for my soul;
They shall enter
the lowest depths of the earth.
11 *He shall drag him by the sword;*

---

joy, because I am still *in the shadow of Your wings* (Alshich).

9. דָּבְקָה נַפְשִׁי אַחֲרֶיךָ — *My soul cleaves after You.*

My spirit knows no desire other than the yearning for You *(Radak).*

[Although man cannot physically cleave to God, he can attain closeness to Him with his intellect and soul, by studying God's ways. The *Targum* here paraphrases: 'My soul is drawn after the pursuit of Your Torah.']

When Moses begged to understand God, He responded: *You cannot see My face, for no man can see Me and live ... You shall see,* אֲחֹרָי, *My back, but My face will not be seen (Exodus 33:20, 23).*

Here David says, 'I cannot see Your face directly; like Moses, I must approach You *from behind,* by cleaving *after You.* Moreover, You respond with kindness and *support me with Your right hand,* as if I were face to face with You *(Divrei Shlomo).*

בִּי תָּמְכָה יְמִינֶךָ — *To me, Your right arm lent support.*

I cleave to You tenaciously, just as the flame clings to the candlewick; my hold is strengthened by the Torah which You presented with Your right hand, as Scripture says *(Deuteronomy*

33:2): *From His right hand a fiery law was given to them (Zerah Yaakov).*

10. וְהֵמָּה לְשׁוֹאָה יְבַקְשׁוּ נַפְשִׁי — *But as for them, they seek desolation for my soul.*

[Cf. translation of שׁוֹאָה in *comm.* to 35:8, 17.]

According to *Radak,* this refers to the pursuers [Saul and his men] who seek to destroy David. They lie in ambush on a foggy day [when visibility is poor] in order to take David by surprise *(Rashi).*

Ibn Ezra, however, identifies these men as the informers [of Ziph] who revealed David's secret hideaway to Saul.

יָבֹאוּ בְּתַחְתִּיּוֹת הָאָרֶץ — *They shall enter the lowest depths of the earth.*

David prays: 'These lowly men attempted to condemn me and to drag me to *Gehinnom.* Let them sink to the lowest depths instead' *(Radak).*

11. יַגִּירֻהוּ עַל יְדֵי חָרֶב — *He shall drag him by the sword.*

Radak explains that the root הַגָּרָה, *to flow,* refers primarily to liquids [see *Lamentations* 3:49]. In this verse it means *the sword will cause* blood *to flow.* Since the word denotes the movement of objects from place to place, it

יב מְנָת שֻׁעָלִים יִהְיוּ: וְהַמֶּלֶךְ יִשְׂמַח
בֵּאלֹהִים יִתְהַלֵּל כָּל־הַנִּשְׁבָּע בּוֹ כִּי יִסָּכֵר
פִּי דוֹבְרֵי־שָׁקֶר:

also indicates that the corpse of the enemy will be dragged about ignominiously. The singular form is utilized because David is addressing his foremost enemy, Saul. [Saul, in fact, was finally killed by the sword and his corpse was disgraced.]

מְנָת שֻׁעָלִים יִהְיוּ — *A portion of foxes shall they be.*

Radak explains that David reverts to the plural יִהְיוּ, *they shall be*, because he is now addressing Saul's many followers. He asks that their corpses be abandoned to the wild beasts of prey.

According to *Rashi*, 'Let their homes and settlements become desolate, inhabited only by wild foxes.'

12. וְהַמֶּלֶךְ יִשְׂמַח בֵּאלֹהִים — *But the king shall be glad with God.*

Rashi contends that David here refers to himself as king, for although Saul still reigned, Samuel had already anointed David as his immediate successor.

My adversaries taunt me, predicting that I shall never ascend to the throne. Destroy them, I pray, and invest me with monarchy so that I may rejoice in God's choice *(Radak)*.

Sforno maintains that David is praying on King Saul's behalf. 'Although he pursues me relentlessly, I refuse to curse him [for he is still the anointed of God]. Rather I pray that his troubled, melancholy spirit should find joy in fulfilling God's command to vanquish our gentile foes, so that he will no longer have to seek joy in pursuing me.' [According to *Sforno*, the curse of the

a portion of foxes shall they be.

¹² *But the king shall be glad with God,*
glorified will be everyone who swears by Him;
For the mouth of falsifiers
will be stopped.

preceding verse was not directed at Saul, as *Radak* explains.]

יִתְהַלֵּל כָּל הַנִּשְׁבָּע בּוֹ — *Glorified will be everyone who swears by Him.*

When the world sees that You have saved me, all righteous men who cleave to You will be recognized as praiseworthy *(Rashi).*

These God-fearing men are those totally honest people who have the exclusive right to swear by Your Name *(Radak).*

As the prophet *(Jeremiah 9:22-23)* says, אַל יִתְהַלֵּל חָכָם בְּחָכְמָתוֹ, *Let not the wise man glory in his wisdom, neither let the mighty man glory in his might; let not the rich man glory in his riches;*

but let he who glories glory only in this: that he understands and knows Me *(Rashbam).*

כִּי יִסָּכֵר פִּי דוֹבְרֵי שָׁקֶר — *For the mouth of falsifiers will be stopped.*

This refers to those who swear falsely in the Name of God *(Radak).*

David said, 'I do not suffer most from Saul himself, but from liars who slander me to him and invite his wrath with false tales about me. When these villains are silenced, my men and I will rejoice' *(Metzudas David).*

[Then we will no longer be trapped in the wilderness of Judah; we will be able to *behold You in the Sanctuary, to see Your might and Your glory (v.3).*]

The preceding Psalm described David in exile. Although physically isolated from God, spiritually David remained completely absorbed in the service of the Almighty. This total concentration rendered David oblivious to all sinister threats.

Centuries later, in the exile of Babylon, Daniel, a descendant of the royal line of David, duplicated the selfless dedication of his illustrious ancestor. Midrash Shocher Tov and Rashi explain that this psalm is based on the events narrated in the sixth chapter of the Book of Daniel.

Immediately upon his ascension to the Babylonian throne, Darius the Mede appointed 120 satraps to govern the vast empire. The satraps were responsible to three ministers, of whom Daniel was the most capable and distinguished. Jealous of Daniel's prominence, the satraps and viziers plotted his downfall.

They convinced Darius to issue a decree prohibiting his subjects from addressing petitions to God or man for the first thirty days of the new king's reign. All requests would be addressed exclusively to Darius during this period, in order to enhance his authority and prestige at the very outset of his rule. The satraps decreed that anyone disobeying their edict would be cast into the lion's pit.

All obeyed the decree save Daniel, who continued to pray to God three times daily. No threat, not even the spector of the lion's pit, could divert Daniel from the service of God. Like David, Daniel thirsted only for God. Daniel's well deserved reward and his miraculous salvation will be described in the commentary to this psalm.

א-ב לַמְנַצֵּחַ מִזְמוֹר לְדָוִד: שְׁמַע־אֱלֹהִים קוֹלִי
ג בְשִׂיחִי מִפַּחַד אוֹיֵב תִּצֹּר חַיָּי: תַּסְתִּירֵנִי
ד מִסּוֹד מְרֵעִים מֵרִגְשַׁת פֹּעֲלֵי אָוֶן: אֲשֶׁר
שָׁנְנוּ כַחֶרֶב לְשׁוֹנָם דָּרְכוּ חִצָּם דָּבָר מָר:
ה לִירוֹת בַּמִּסְתָּרִים תָּם פִּתְאֹם יֹרֻהוּ וְלֹא

2. שְׁמַע אֱלֹהִים קוֹלִי — *Hear, O God, my voice expressing my woes.*

Radak and *Metzudas David* render שִׂיחִי as *my tale of woes* [cf. *Psalms* 55:3].

However, שִׂיחַ is often interpreted as a reference to fervent prayer [cf. *Berachos* 26b]. *Midrash Shocher Tov* explains that this alludes to Daniel, who ignored the decree of Darius by maintaining his regime of prayer. Daniel would pray daily in his upper chamber, open the windows facing Jerusalem, and kneel in supplication to God (*Daniel* 6:11).[1]

Many commentaries wonder why Daniel endangered his life in order to pray. This was not a case where יֵהָרֵג וְאַל יַעֲבֹר, *one must let oneself be killed rather than transgress.* This rule applies at all times only to three cardinal sins: idolatry, immorality, and murder. However, where coercion is aimed at conversion one must sacrifice his life for קִדּוּשׁ הַשֵּׁם, *Sanctification of God's Name,* even for a Jewish custom. Since the king's intent here was for his own glory, without intent to convert Jews, Daniel was not obligated or even permitted to jeopardize his life.

Alshich (comm. to *Daniel*) explains that for this reason Daniel prayed in the secrecy of his upper chamber and not in the synagogue where he had no doubt prayed previously. In order not to anger the king and endanger his own life, he chose to ostensibly abide by the king's decree, while furtively upholding his obligation to God.

Malbim (comm. to *Daniel*) interprets Daniel's defiance of the king's decree not as a conscious act of martyrdom, but as a miscalculation as to the danger of his actions. The king's decree prohibited *whoever shall make a request* (*Daniel* 6:8) to address himself to anyone but Darius. Daniel made no petition or request; he merely offered praise, blessing, and thanksgiving to God as was his daily custom.

However, because the satraps were determined to find Daniel guilty of transgressing the king's decree, they interpreted his prayer as a specific petition. [See *comm. Daniel* 6:11, ArtScroll ed. for lengthy discussion of Daniel's martyrdom.]

מִפַּחַד אוֹיֵב תִּצֹּר חַיָּי — *From dread of the foe preserve my life.*

According to *Midrash Shocher Tov,* this refers to the verse: *These men [his enemies] assembled and found Daniel praying and supplicating before his God* (*Daniel* 6:12).

R' Saadiah Gaon (*Daniel* 6:12) comments that they stealthily surrounded Daniel's home and asked Daniel's maidservant what he was doing. When she answered, 'He is kneeling and praying to his God,' they immediately entered and personally witnessed this 'crime,' which they swiftly reported to the king.

3. תַּסְתִּירֵנִי מִסּוֹד מְרֵעִים — *Hide me from the counsel* [lit. *the secret*] *of the wicked.*

[On the outside the satraps and

1. It is interesting to note that the house where Daniel prayed became a landmark and a holy site in Babylon. Many centuries after Daniel's death, the Sages of the *Talmud* would travel to pray at Daniel's home (see *Eruvin* 21a and *Rashi, ibid*).

F or the Conductor,
a song of David.

² *Hear, O God, my voice expressing my woes;*
from dread of the foe preserve my life.

³ *Hide me from the counsel of the wicked,*
from the assembly of evildoers,

⁴ *Who have sharpened their tongue*
like the sword,

And aimed their arrow —

a bitter word —

⁵ *To shoot in secrecy at the innocent;*
suddenly they shot, and they are unafraid.

---

viziers claimed to be deeply concerned with consolidating the power and prestige of the king; secretly, however, their sole desire was to destroy Daniel.]

מֵרִגְשַׁת פֹּעֲלֵי אָוֶן — *From the assembly of evildoers.* [Cf. 2:1 לָמָה רָגְשׁוּ גוֹיִם.]

Even after receiving the accusation against Daniel, King Darius wanted to forgive his beloved and highly respected prime minister; but all of the satraps הַרְגִּשׁוּ עַל מַלְכָּא, *assembled around the king (Daniel 6:16),* insisting that the law of the land must be strictly enforced and that Daniel must be punished (*Rashi*).

4. אֲשֶׁר שָׁנְנוּ כַחֶרֶב לְשׁוֹנָם — *Who have sharpened their tongue like the sword.*

The satraps spread לָשׁוֹן הָרָע, *slanderous tales,* about Daniel to deprive him of the king's favor (*Rashi*).

דָּרְכוּ חִצָּם דָּבָר מָר — *And aimed their arrow — a bitter word.*

Literally, דָּרְכוּ means to *step on* the bow in order to string it and prepare it for shooting (*Ibn Ezra*).

The arrows were smeared with poison to make them doubly lethal (*Targum*).

When the wicked slander their vic-tims at close range, the impact of the slander resembles the thrust of the sword. When they slander from a dis-tance their barbed words resemble poisoned arrows shot from a bow (*Norah Tehillos*).

5. לִירוֹת בַּמִּסְתָּרִים תָּם — *To shoot in secrecy at the innocent.*

The wicked slander their victims sur-reptitiously, in order to deprive them of an opportunity for self-defense (*Ra-dak*).

[Much to his dismay, King Darius was finally forced to accede to the de-mands of the satraps and ministers: Daniel was thrown into the lion's den. In *Daniel* 6:18 we read: *And a stone was brought and was placed over the opening of the pit, and the king sealed it with his signet ring and with the signet rings of his nobles, so that his will regarding Daniel not be changed.* The commentators explain that the king placed a stone barrier at the entrance of the den to circumvent the cunning of his nobles, for he feared that they would secretly throw stones or shoot arrows at Daniel and later falsely attribute his death to the lions (*R' Saadiah Gaon*).][1]

---

1. *Rashi* (*Daniel* 6:18) explains that in all of Babylon there are no stones; fences and buildings were made of clay bricks produced from mud (see *Genesis* 11:3). However, God summoned

ו יִירָאוּ: יְחַזְּקוּ־לָמוֹ | דָּבָר רָע יְסַפְּרוּ
לִטְמוֹן מוֹקְשִׁים אָמְרוּ מִי יִרְאֶה־לָּמוֹ:
ז יַחְפְּשׂוּ־עוֹלֹת תַּמְנוּ חֵפֶשׂ מְחֻפָּשׂ וְקֶרֶב
ח אִישׁ וְלֵב עָמֹק: וַיֹּרֵם אֱלֹהִים חֵץ פִּתְאוֹם
ט הָיוּ מַכּוֹתָם: וַיַּכְשִׁילֻהוּ עָלֵימוֹ לְשׁוֹנָם

6. יְחַזְּקוּ לָמוֹ דָּבָר רָע — *They urge an evil matter upon him.*

Feigning concern for the king's authority, the satraps deviously encouraged Darius to issue an evil decree (*Rashi*).

Otzar Nechmad renders יְחַזְּקוּ, *they intensify,* to suggest that whenever the wicked notice the slightest flaw in the behavior of the righteous, they purposely exaggerate its significance, to make it appear a very *evil matter.* [Thus, when the satraps sought to find fault with Daniel (*Daniel* 6:5-6), they could accuse him only of praying to God, for his general behavior was beyond reproach.]

יְסַפְּרוּ לִטְמוֹן מוֹקְשִׁים — *They speak of concealing snares.*

Ostensibly, the satraps were motivated purely by loyalty to the king; actually their sole intention was to set a trap for Daniel (*Rashi*).

אָמְרוּ מִי יִרְאֶה לָּמוֹ — *They say, 'Who will see them?'*

Foolishly, they ask, 'Who shall see us?', forgetting that God knows every thought and sees every deed (*Radak*).

7. יַחְפְּשׂוּ עוֹלֹת — *They search out pretexts.*

They seek libelous accusations to use against Daniel, as Scripture says (*Daniel* 6:5): *Then the viziers and the satraps tried to find a libel against*

Daniel with regard to the kingdom; but they could find neither fault nor corruption because he was faithful; and there was found neither error nor corruption in him (*Rashi*).

תַּמְנוּ חֵפֶשׂ מְחֻפָּשׂ — *They complete a diligent search.*

[The crafty nobles were undaunted by their inability to uncover a misdeed with which to accuse Daniel.] They strained their ingenuity to fabricate a complaint against their hated enemy, and finally *they accomplished* [i.e., *completed*] their goal (*Radak; Metzudas David*).

Our text reads תַּמְנוּ, *they complete,* but *Rashi's* version has טָמְנוּ, *they conceal.* This suggests that when the satraps finally devised their wily plot against Daniel, *they concealed* their true intentions deep within their hearts, to avoid arousing the king's suspicion (see *Minchas Shai*).

וְקֶרֶב אִישׁ וְלֵב עָמֹק — *Within man and deep in heart.*

[Although the nobles delved into the depths of their hearts to find fault with Daniel, their effort was futile, for Daniel had also searched the inner recesses of his soul as he prayed to God. The merit derived from this sincere self-scrutiny protected Daniel from the satraps' plot.

[*Midrash Shocher Tov* teaches that when Darius came to inquire about

angels to bring a huge stone from the Land of Israel to cover the mouth of the lion's den. According to some commentators, an angel in the form of a lion sat at the edge of the pit to frighten away intruders (*Midrash Shocher Tov*).

R' Saadiah Gaon (*Daniel* 6:23) adds that the prophet Habakuk and his Judean field workers miraculously appeared in the pit. They prepared a lavish banquet for Daniel, and together they sang songs praising God's wondrous mercy.

⁶ *They urge an evil matter upon him,*
they speak of concealing snares;
they say, 'Who will see them?'
⁷ *They search out pretexts,*
they complete a diligent search;
within man and deep in heart.
⁸ *Then God shot an arrow at them suddenly;*
suddenly their wounds appeared.
⁹ *They were caused to stumble*
by their very own tongue;

Daniel's welfare the next morning, Daniel did not respond immediately to the king's questions because he was in the midst of reciting the *Shema*. Daniel's devotion to God was so complete that no one, not even the king himself, could distract the prophet during his prayers (even though *halachah* permits one to interrupt *Shema* to greet one who might otherwise kill him. See *Berachos* 13a).]

8. וַיֹּרֵם אֱלֹהִים חֵץ פִּתְאוֹם — *Then God shot an arrow at them suddenly.*

This form of punishment was especially appropriate, for Daniel's wicked enemies had shot at him without warning (v. 5) *(Ibn Ezra).*

Daniel remained in the lion's den overnight; in the morning, he emerged unscathed. His enemies sought to deny the miraculous nature of his salvation by claiming that the lions did not molest Daniel because their appetites had been satiated by a previous meal.

The king, outraged by this allegation, announced that Daniel's enemies must spend the night in the lions' den in order to test the validity of their defamatory claim.

Darius took the nobles (120 satraps and 2 viziers), their wives (122 women),

and one child of each (122 children; a total of 366 people) and swiftly shot them like arrows into the den. The ferocious, hungry lions, who outnumbered the people four to one, devoured them instantly. The lions shattered their bones before they even touched the floor of the lion's den *(Rashi; Midrash Shocher Tov).*

הָיוּ מַכֹּתָם — *[Suddenly] their wounds appeared* [lit. *came to be*].

Radak explains that the word פִּתְאוֹם, *suddenly,* modifies both the clause which precedes it and the clause which follows it.

9. וַיַּכְשִׁילֻהוּ עָלֵימוֹ לְשׁוֹנָם — *They were caused to stumble by their very own tongue.*

The tongues which they had used to condemn Daniel ultimately turned against them *(Rashi).*

[Darius cast them into the lion's den only to test their own claim that the lions' appetites had already been satisfied. Had the satraps remained silent, Darius would not have subjected them to this trial.]

The punishment, too, was tailored to the satraps' plots against Daniel (v. 4), for they had *sharpened their tongue like the sword (Ibn Ezra).*

י יִתְנוֹדְדוּ כָּל־רֹאֵה בָם: וַיִּירְאוּ כָּל־אָדָם
וַיַּגִּידוּ פֹּעַל אֱלֹהִים וּמַעֲשֵׂהוּ הִשְׂכִּילוּ:
יא יִשְׂמַח צַדִּיק בַּיהוה וְחָסָה בוֹ וְיִתְהַלְלוּ
כָּל־יִשְׁרֵי־לֵב:

יִתְנוֹדְדוּ כָּל רֹאֵה בָם — *All who see them
shake their head.*

Observers shake their heads in scorn
and derision (*Rashi*).

10. וַיִּירְאוּ כָּל אָדָם וַיַּגִּידוּ פֹּעַל אֱלֹהִים —
*Then all men came to fear, and declared
the work of God.*

[Upon witnessing the miraculous
rescue of Daniel and the terrible revenge
visited upon his foes, King Darius
wrote: *To all the peoples, nations, and
languages that live in all the earth, your
peace should multiply! I hereby issue a
decree that: throughout the extent of
my kingdom let them tremble before,
and fear, the God of Daniel — Who is
the living God and everlasting; His
kingdom is that which will not be
destroyed, and His rule is till eternity.
He saves and rescues, and performs
signs and wonders in heaven and on
earth — Who has saved Daniel from
lions* (Daniel 6:26-28).

וּמַעֲשֵׂהוּ הִשְׂכִּילוּ — *And His deed they
comprehended.*

They realized that all of God's
punishments requite a person for his actions 'measure for measure', i.e., Divine

punishment always 'fits the crime'
(*Chozeh David*).

[God is Master of the universe in
general and Sovereign of the animal
kingdom in particular. Animals instinctively obey their master. Therefore,
when man successfully preserves the
Divine image in which he was created,
then he too commands the obedience of
the animals (see 49:13).

[The *Zohar* emphasizes that the lions
were totally subdued in the presence of
Daniel because the prophet embodied
the image of their Divine Master.

[Everyone who observed Daniel
glimpsed in him a reflection of God
Himself; in this way, they indirectly
gained an improved understanding of
God's deeds.]

11. יִשְׂמַח צַדִּיק בַּה' — *Let the righteous
one be glad in HASHEM.*

[Even after Daniel's miraculous
salvation, God continued to give Daniel
additional reasons for rejoicing, as
Scripture attests (*Daniel 6:29*): *And this
Daniel was successful throughout the
reign of Darius and in the* [subsequent]
reign of Cyrus the Persian.]

10-11   ¹⁰ *Then all men came to fear,*
             and declared the work of God;
             and His deed they comprehended.
         ¹¹ *Let the righteous one be glad in HASHEM,*
             and take refuge in Him;
         And let all the upright in heart find glory.

Migdal David notes that the final verse of this psalm resembles the last verse of Psalm 32: שִׂמְחוּ בַה׳ וְגִילוּ צַדִּיקִים וְהַרְנִינוּ כָּל יִשְׁרֵי לֵב, *Be glad in HASHEM and rejoice, O righteous. Cry out in joy, all upright of heart.*

The difference between the two verses is that the former is a command which exhorts the righteous to find joy in their faith, whereas the latter is a Divine promise that God will help those who seek this joy to find it.

וְחָסָה בּוֹ — *And take refuge in Him.*

When the righteous witness that the faith they placed in God was justified, they resolve to trust in God with even greater devotion in the future *(Radak).*

וְיִתְהַלְלוּ כָּל יִשְׁרֵי לֵב — *And let all the upright in heart find glory.*

They may glory in the fact that because of their integrity, they have merited Divine salvation *(Rashi).*

[The *Talmud (Sanhedrin* 93b) observes that Daniel was glorified in an extraordinary manner: an entire book of Scripture received his name. This fulfilled the prophecy of *Isaiah* (56:5): שֵׁם עוֹלָם אֶתֶּן לוֹ, *I will grant him an everlasting name,* for *Chida* notes that the numerical value of the word שֵׁם, *name* — 340 — is equal to that of סֵפֶר, *book.*]

Finally, *Bris Avraham* notes the difference between the צַדִּיק and the יָשָׁר (cf. comm. of *Malbim* to *Psalms* 33:1). The *righteous* (צַדִּיק) adheres to the commands of God in all of his actions, but in his mind he is still troubled by questions and doubts. Because of his intellectual uncertainty, he needs Divine aid to overcome the temptations posed by the Evil Inclination. Thus, *the righteous are glad in HASHEM,* i.e., in His assistance.

In contrast, the *upright* (יָשָׁר) recognizes God's truth so clearly that he needs no Divine assistance to overcome temptation. Since the upright themselves deserve credit for their accomplishments, *they find glory* 'independently,' without reference to God.

מִזְמוֹר סה 65

T his psalm is a prayer which David composed at a time of terrible
national disaster. In II Samuel 21, we read: And there was a
famine in the days of David for three years, year after year, and
David sought out the presence of Hashem. In this psalm, David
entreats God to send abundant rains and rich harvests (Malbim;
Norah Tehillos).

Ibn Ezra (v. 10) adds that at the moment the drought struck, the
nation was also invaded by a foreign army. Since this psalm was composed at a time when the nation was threatened both from within and
from without, the psalmist voices his longing for the advent of the
Messiah. Although the Messiah's arrival is eagerly awaited at all
times, anticipation of his coming is heightened at times of national
emergency, for the Messiah will solve all of Israel's problems, both
internal and external, economic and political (Yaavetz HaDoresh).

In conclusion, the psalmist expresses his wish for an agricultural
renaissance in which the Holy Land would flourish once more, free-
ing the children of Israel to concentrate on their true mission, the service of God.

א־ב לַמְנַצֵּחַ מִזְמוֹר לְדָוִד שִׁיר: לְךָ דֻמִיָּה
תְהִלָּה אֱלֹהִים בְּצִיּוֹן וּלְךָ יְשֻׁלַּם־נֶדֶר:
ג־ד שֹׁמֵעַ תְּפִלָּה עָדֶיךָ כָּל־בָּשָׂר יָבֹאוּ: דִּבְרֵי

1. מִזְמוֹר לְדָוִד שִׁיר — *With musical accompaniment, by David, a song.*

[See comm. to Psalms 30:1, where מִזְמוֹר is identified as the accompaniment of כְּלֵי זֶמֶר, *musical instruments*, and שִׁיר is described as the lyrics of the song.

Although plagued by starvation, David never ceased to praise God, anticipating his future salvation.

Hirsch notes that שִׁיר, the masculine form, refers to the final redemption of the future, while שִׁירָה, the feminine form, alludes to those acts by which the Almighty lays the groundwork for the ultimate salvation. [Cf. comm. to *Psalms* 33:3. Thus this psalm, which refers to the famine of David's times, also contains a deeper theme: the ultimate Messianic redemption.]

2. לְךָ דֻמִיָּה תְהִלָּה — *Silence is Your praise.*

This translation follows *Rashi*, who explains that any effort to recount all of God's virtues is utterly futile, since His wondrous attributes are infinite. Indeed, every attempt to completely enumerate His praises only detracts from His glory, for it implies that His praises are finite and within human understanding.

[Conversely, when man stands before his Creator in silent recognition of his own inadequacy, this constitutes the most eloquent testimony to God's magnificence, which defies human comprehension.]

The Sages of the *Talmud (Megillah 18a)* expressed this idea in the adage, מִלָּה בְּסֶלַע מַשְׁתּוּקָא בִּתְרֵין, *If a word is worth a silver coin, then silence is surely worth two,* and סַמָּא דְכוּלָּה מַשְׁתּוּקָא, *silence is the most potent of all formulas.*

Lachmei Todah renders לְךָ דֻמִיָּה תְהִלָּה: *Your silence is Your praise,*

alluding to God's patience, which restrains Him from punishing sinners immediately after they commit an offense.

Ibn Ezra, Radak, and *Sforno* render דֻמִיָּה as *waiting, hoping,* for the Holy Ark which was in Zion. The masses assembled there to pay homage. The words of praise which they prepared *waited* on their lips, hoping for an opportunity to be uttered in Your presence. Ever since the destruction of the Temple, the children of Israel have eagerly awaited the moment when they will be redeemed from exile to worship in Zion.

Indeed, this wholehearted yearning for God constitutes an unparalleled tribute to the Almighty, as the psalmist pledges (71:14), *And I shall await* [You] *continually and* [thus] *add to all of Your praises (Sefer Halkkarim).*

אֱלֹהִים בְּצִיּוֹן — *O God in Zion.*

This phrase refers to *God who dwells in Zion,* because it was there that the gentiles devastated the sacred Temple. Although this atrocity deserves to be avenged with unbridled Divine might and fury, God restrains Himself with amazing patience. This *silence is God's praise (Rashi;* see *Lachmei Todeh,* above).

Only in Zion is God's omnipotence revealed, as the psalmist declares (99:2), *HASHEM is great in Zion and He is exalted above all the nations.* It is in Zion, therefore, that Israel is awed into silence, recognizing that any attempt to enumerate God's praises is futile (*Beer Avraham*).

Even in Zion, where legions of Levites were available to chant hymns of praise, דֻמִיָּה, *silence,* surpassed all words (*Meir Tehillos*).

Yaavetz HaDoresh suggests that when drought and famine struck the

65
1-3

For the Conductor, with musical accompaniment, by David, a song.

² Silence is Your praise, O God in Zion,
    and for Your sake the vow is fulfilled.
³ O heeder of prayer,
    unto You does all flesh come.

land of Israel, the entire nation assembled in Zion to fast and pray for salvation.

וּלְךָ יְשֻׁלַּם נֶדֶר — And for Your sake the vow is fulfilled.

For centuries, the Jewish nation awaited the opportunity to serve You selflessly in the Temple, in order to fulfill the oath which they had taken at Sinai (Exodus 24:7): נַעֲשֶׂה וְנִשְׁמָע, We shall do [this refers to the performance of the Torah's precepts] and we shall listen [this refers to the understanding of the commandments] (Sforno).

Even when they are dispersed into exile, they vow to serve You once again in Zion (Radak).

[When the starving nation of Israel gathered to pray for rain and bountiful harvests, they made many solemn vows to God, which they hoped to fulfill shortly.]

3. שֹׁמֵעַ תְּפִלָּה — O Heeder of prayer.

God hears the prayers of all mankind in the Holy Temple, which is situated in Zion; the prophet (Isaiah 56:7) described the Beis HaMikdash as a בֵּית תְּפִלָּה, House of Prayer (Ibn Ezra).

No mortal can hear prayers as God does. A human king cannot even hear the words of two men who speak at the same time; certainly he cannot understand the pleas of the multitudes who cry out simultaneously. However, the Holy One, Blessed be He, hears the individual prayers of all mankind, even though they are uttered coinstantaneously (Midrash Shocher Tov).

This defies the normal laws of nature, for ordinarily the sound of a single voice can be understood by ten ears, but

the sound of ten voices cannot be understood by only one ear (Pesikta Rabbasi 21:6).

The Midrash (Shemos Rabbah 21:4) notes that the vast variety of prayers are described here in the singular form, as תְּפִלָה, because a special angel gathers the prayers offered in all of the synagogues and fashions them into one perfect entreaty, which crowns God like an עֲדִי, jeweled tiara. [According to Yefeh Toar, this word is related to עָדֶיךָ.]

עָדֶיךָ כָּל בָּשָׂר יָבֹאוּ — Unto You does all flesh come.

The Beis HaMikdash is a universal House of Prayer, dedicated לְכָל הָעַמִּים, to all the nations (Isaiah 56:7; Ibn Ezra).

In this sacred shrine, יָבוֹא כָל בָּשָׂר לְהִשְׁתַּחֲוֹת לְפָנַי אָמַר ה', 'All flesh shall come to bow before me, 'says HASHEM (Isaiah 66:23; Radak).

God is not like a human king, who discriminates between rich and poor, powerful and weak. The Holy One, Blessed be He, treats all flesh as equals. He listens attentively to the prayers of every individual (Shemos Rabbah 21:4).

Shevet M'Yisrael observes that the reference to בָּשָׂר, flesh, alludes to the Talmudic dictum (Sotah 5a): A man's plea is not heard unless he humbles himself by making his heart become soft flesh [rather than tough, insensitive muscle].

Furthermore, there are heretics who perpetuate the false claim that God hears only the prayers which request perfection of the soul and spirit, but not those which concern the body. The psalmist refutes this notion, declaring that our Father in heaven eagerly awaits every prayer, even those dedicated to

עֲוֹנֹת גָּבְרוּ מֶנִּי פְּשָׁעֵינוּ אַתָּה תְכַפְּרֵם:
ה אַשְׁרֵי | תִּבְחַר וּתְקָרֵב יִשְׁכֹּן חֲצֵרֶיךָ
נִשְׂבְּעָה בְּטוּב בֵּיתֶךָ קְדֹשׁ הֵיכָלֶךָ:
ו נוֹרָאוֹת | בְּצֶדֶק תַּעֲנֵנוּ אֱלֹהֵי יִשְׁעֵנוּ

mundane, material concerns of the *flesh* (*Mabit*).

[Therefore, the children of Israel can expect God to listen to their prayers in time of famine even though these petitions relate to the sustenance of the *flesh*.]

4. דִּבְרֵי עֲוֹנֹת גָּבְרוּ מֶנִּי — *Talk of sins overwhelms me.*

We fully recognize that this famine is not a chance happening, but a Divinely ordained punishment for our many iniquities (*Ibn Ezra*).

It is futile to attempt to catalog our countless errors and flaws. Therefore, we do not itemize our failings, but simply pray that You will pardon all of our transgressions (*Rashi*).

Alshich observes that David personally accepts the blame for this calamity, since he is the nation's leader. Because David occupies such a prominent position, even his minute flaws are noticed by the masses and thereby cause desecration of God's Name. David laments, *Even minor iniquities* (דִּבְרֵי עֲוֹנֹת) are magnified and *become overwhelming* (גָּבְרוּ מֶנִּי) *because they were performed by me* and thus assume grave importance.

פְּשָׁעֵינוּ אַתָּה תְכַפְּרֵם — *Our transgressions — You will pardon them.*

[The commentaries note that the verse begins in the singular, but ends in the plural.]

Radak explains that this inconsistency was intended to emphasize that the psalm speaks for the multitudes of Jews who have languished in exile throughout the generations.

Sforno perceives this as David's confession: 'Since I realize that my own ini-

quities are overwhelming, my merits are not sufficient to overcome them and bring forgiveness on behalf of the entire congregation. Therefore, I must beseech You, O God, to mercifully pardon our transgressions.'

In conclusion, *Sfas Emes* comments that the righteous leader is the heart of the nation. His private sin causes the public to transgress, for his offense triggers a decline in the spiritual level of the entire people [see *Overview, Tehillim* Vol. I, Section IV]. David pleads, 'Since my personal iniquities overwhelmed me, I caused our national transgressions. Since I am responsible, I beg You to *pardon them.*'

5. אַשְׁרֵי תִּבְחַר וּתְקָרֵב — *Praises to the one You choose and draw near.*

According to *Radak*, this alludes to the generation of exiles which God will *choose* for redemption. He will *draw* them *near* by causing their return to *Eretz Yisrael* and Jerusalem.

Bamidbar Rabbah (83:2) interprets this as a reference to God's devoted followers, the great men of Jewish history. Some were merely chosen, i.e., singled out for distinguished service, but some were also drawn near, thus being shown special Divine favor.

David was chosen as Scripture says (78:70), *He chose David His servant.* After David sinned, he was rejected; Absalom forced David to leave Jerusalem, God's city. However, under the influence and guidance of his revered teacher, Eira HaYari [who taught him to repent], David was drawn near once again.

יִשְׁכֹּן חֲצֵרֶיךָ — *To dwell in Your courts.*

⁴ *Talk of sins overwhelms me,*
*   our transgressions — You will pardon them.*
⁵ *Praises to the one You choose and draw near*
*   to dwell in Your courts,*
To be sated with the goodness of Your house,
*   the holiness of Your Sanctuary.*
⁶ *With awesome works of righteousness*
*   You answer us,*
O God of our salvation,

This alludes to the prohibition which forbids all men (except for David and his descendants) to sit and dwell in the Temple courtyard (*Sotah* 40b). This distinction indicates David's special favor in the eyes of God (*Alshich*).

נִשְׂבְּעָה בְּטוּב בֵּיתֶךָ — *To be sated with the goodness of Your house.*

Sforno interprets this as a prayer: O Lord, grant us an abundant flow of the sanctity which streams from Your Temple. Please overlook the fact that we are unworthy of such generosity.

Alshich adds that the Temple was the source of all spiritual satisfaction. The *Midrash* calls the *Beis HaMikdash* בֵּית הַשׁוֹאֵבָה, *the house of elevation,* because it was from this consecrated spot that Israel became spiritually elevated by the Holy Spirit [cf. *Succah* 50b and *Tosafos, s.v.* חד תני ibid.].

According to *Vidal HaTzorfati* and *Shaloh HaKodosh*, the psalmist here offers advice to the devoted man who seeks to *draw near* to God. David advises that this closeness can only be accomplished by spurning all material pleasures and by finding satisfaction solely in the *goodness* of God.

קְדֹשׁ הֵיכָלֶךָ — *The holiness of Your Sanctuary.*

It is customary to recite this verse during the circumcision (*Bris Milah*) ceremony. The *Zohar* (*Lech Lecha*) states that the ten words in this verse correspond to the ten Divine canopies which are granted to those who fulfill the *mitzvah* of circumcision.

Through the covenant of circumcision, the people of Israel were *chosen* and *drawn near* to God (*Iyun Tefillah*). The children of Israel ascend higher and higher, until they reach the *holiness* of the celestial *sanctuary*, where their souls cleave to God (*Sharbit HaZohar, Siddur Otzar Tefillos*).

6. נוֹרָאוֹת בְּצֶדֶק תַּעֲנֵנוּ — *With awesome works of righteousness You answer us.*

Your *righteousness* is evident because You defend us from the hostile pagans and drive them off with *awesome* blows (*Rashi*).

From this we learn that we need not fear, so long as we remain worthy of God's mercy. Just as You stave off the external threat of the enemy, You will protect us from the internal danger of famine and drought (*Ibn Ezra*).[1]

---

1. The *Talmud* (*Yoma* 69b) says that when the pagan hordes openly desecrated the sacred Temple, it seemed as if God were no longer נוֹרָא, *awesome.* Afterwards, however, when Israel managed to survive being scattered in exile among multitudes of murderous enemies, people wondered, 'How can one helpless sheep endure, surrounded by seventy hungry wolves?' This proves that the nations realize that we have remained the chosen people of God, despite our suffering. They don't destroy us, for they fear God's נוֹרָאוֹת, *awesome works.*

זְ מִבְטָח כָּל־קַצְוֵי־אֶרֶץ וְיָם רְחֹקִים: מֵכִין

חְ הָרִים בְּכֹחוֹ נֶאְזָר בִּגְבוּרָה: מַשְׁבִּיחַ |

שְׁאוֹן יַמִּים שְׁאוֹן גַּלֵּיהֶם וַהֲמוֹן לְאֻמִּים:

טְ וַיִּירְאוּ יֹשְׁבֵי קְצָוֹת מֵאוֹתֹתֶיךָ מוֹצָאֵי־

יְ בֹקֶר וָעֶרֶב תַּרְנִין: פָּקַדְתָּ הָאָרֶץ |

מִבְטָח כָּל קַצְוֵי אֶרֶץ וְיָם רְחֹקִים — *O Trust of earth's far ends and distant seas.*

All men, even those who inhabit the most remote locations, turn to You when in need, for Your kingdom stretches to the very ends of the earth (*Rashi*).

The exiles of Israel are scattered not only to קַצְוֵי אֶרֶץ, *the earth's far ends*, but also to קַצְוֵי יָם, *the distant seas*. This refers to the far-flung, isolated islands. They yearn to be gathered once again into the center of the world, Jerusalem (*Radak; Sforno*).

Midrash Shocher Tov interprets this homiletically: The celestial Gates of Prayer are not always open, but the Gates of Repentance are open forever.

Just as the sea is always accessible to everyone who wants to bathe there, we *trust* that the 'sea' of repentance is constantly open to the person who seeks to immerse himself in it.

Radak explains that a lesson may be derived from this natural phenomenon.

Our exiled nation may appear to be moribund or lifeless; the gentiles taunt us mercilessly, saying that the Jewish people will never experience a national renaissance. Nevertheless, the exile is actually a long, lonely incubation period, during which time God prepares the proper conditions for our future rebirth, which will inaugurate an era of unparalleled national growth and success.

7. מֵכִין הָרִים בְּכֹחוֹ — *Who readies mountains with His strength.*

Rashi observes that although the rocky surface of the mountainside does not appear to be arable, God prepares the ground with special weather conditions and rains; as a result even this

poor soil produces vegetation. (According to *Targum*, these plants sustain the mountain goats.) Elsewhere, the psalmist refers to God as the One *Who prepares rain for the earth, Who makes the mountains grow grass* (147:8).

נֶאְזָר בִּגְבוּרָה — *Who is girded with might.*

God can display His *might* whenever it becomes necessary, for the Almighty is constantly prepared and *girded* with His own unfailing strength (*Radak*).

Rashi explains that the psalmist refers here to God's גְבוּרָה, *might,* because he is marveling at the rainfall [which cures drought and famine and brings abundant crops]. The *Talmud* (*Taanis* 2a) describes the Divine system of watering the earth as גְבוּרוֹת גְּשָׁמִים, *the powers of the rain.*

8. מַשְׁבִּיחַ שְׁאוֹן יַמִּים — *Who calms the roar of the seas.*

All of the commentaries are in agreement as to this translation of מַשְׁבִּיחַ, *calms.* Similarly, we read (89:10) אַתָּה מוֹשֵׁל בְּגֵאוּת הַיָּם בְּשׂוֹא גַלָּיו אַתָּה תְשַׁבְּחֵם, *You rule the proud swelling of the sea; when its waves arise, You calm them* (*Rashi; Ibn Ezra*).

[Ordinarily, מַשְׁבִּיחַ is translated *improves.* It is possible to find a relationship between that rendition and the translation here, for whoever aspires to better himself feels unfulfilled and unsettled. Once he achieves the desired improvement, his uneasiness is stilled.]

שְׁאוֹן גַּלֵּיהֶם — *The roar of their waves.*

Just as You control the mighty forces of the sea, so do You control the mighty nations. The nations roar and threaten Israel, yet You restrain them and redeem Israel from their midst (*Radak*).

O Trust of earth's far ends and distant seas,
⁷ *Who readies mountains with His strength,*
   Who is girded with might,
⁸ *Who calms the roar of the seas,*
   the roar of their waves
   and the multitude of nations.
⁹ *Inhabitants of the furthest ends*
   are frightened by Your signs,
with the appearance of morning and evening
   You cause joy.
¹⁰ *You paid heed to the earth*

The roar of the seas refers to the gentile masses; *the roar of the waves* refers to their haughty rulers, who arrogantly place themselves above the common people (*Sforno*).

וַהֲמוֹן לְאֻמִּים — *And the multitude of nations.*

The translation follows *Targum* and *Ibn Ezra*.

However, *Metzudas David* and *Hirsch* render הֲמוֹן as *tumult, roar,* derived from הָמָה.

This denotes the loud sound of agitated motion created by a noisy multitude. *Ibn Ezra* observes that God is Master over both the forces of nature and the forces of mankind. Therefore, He will save Israel from famine and from foes.

Radak (v. 9) perceives this as an allusion to the exodus from Egypt: He who stilled *the roar of the seas* when He split the waters before the Children of Israel is destined to still the multitude of nations and rescue Israel from their midst.

9. וַיִּירְאוּ יֹשְׁבֵי קְצָוֹת מֵאוֹתֹתֶיךָ — *Inhabitants of the furthest ends are frightened by Your signs.*

Every day, God impresses His sovereignty upon all of mankind by displaying celestial signs which demonstrate His awesome mastery over the forces of nature. At times God

employs the supernatural in order to draw man's attention to His mighty rule. After He split the sea, God caused all of mankind to recognize the miracle, as Scripture says (*Exodus 15:14*). *The nations heard and were afraid; trembling took hold of the inhabitants of Philistia.* Similarly, all men shall fear Him in the future, when He gathers in the exiles of Israel (*Radak*).

According to *Metzudas David*, אוֹתֹתֶיךָ refers to the *signs* of rumbling thunder and flashing lightning, which strike fear in all hearts [cf. *Berachos* 59a].

מוֹצָאֵי בֹקֶר וָעֶרֶב תַּרְנִין — *With the appearance of morning and evening You cause joy.*

Mankind is awed by the precise routine of the celestial luminaries: the sun rises punctually every morning (*Radak*). The undeviating schedule of daily appearances fosters a sense of security in man (*Metzudas David*). Even the luminaries themselves seem to rejoice in their routine, as Scripture says (*Job* 38:7): בְּרָן יַחַד כּוֹכְבֵי בֹקֶר, *When the morning stars together sing for joy* (*Radak*).

Mankind pays homage to God for creating this flawless solar system. In their morning prayer, Jews recite the benediction בָּרוּךְ ... יוֹצֵר הַמְּאוֹרוֹת, *Blessed are You... Who fashions the*

וַתְּשֹׁקְקֶהָ רַבַּת תַּעְשְׁרֶנָּה פֶּלֶג אֱלֹהִים
מָלֵא מָיִם תָּכִין דְּגָנָם כִּי־כֵן תְּכִינֶהָ:
יא תְּלָמֶיהָ רַוֵּה נַחֵת גְּדוּדֶהָ בִּרְבִיבִים
יב תְּמֹגְגֶנָּה צִמְחָהּ תְּבָרֵךְ: עִטַּרְתָּ שְׁנַת

luminaries. At night, Jews say, בָּרוּךְ..., הַמַּעֲרִיב עֲרָבִים, *Blessed are You... Who causes nightfall to descend* (*Rashi*).

Sforno perceives in this verse a prayer for restoration of the earth's antediluvian perfection: May it be Your will that the sun return to its original axis (which was perfectly aligned with the rotation of our planet), so that the earth will again enjoy perpetual spring.

10. פָּקַדְתָּ הָאָרֶץ וַתְּשֹׁקְקֶהָ — *You paid heed to the earth and watered her.*

Some commentaries relate וַתְּשֹׁקְקֶהָ to תַּשְׁקֶה, *You water*, explaining: Whenever You desire to benefit mankind, You water the earth with extra rains (*Rashi*).

Indeed, immediately prior to the formation of Adam (and before he sinned), You improved the soil for his sake, as Scripture states (*Genesis* 2:6), *A mist ascended from the earth and watered the whole surface of the soil* (*Sforno*).

Ibn Ezra explains that during David's lifetime, Israel was simultaneously endangered by two threats: The foe laid siege to their land, but God *remembered the land* and rescued the people, drought and famine plagued Israel, but God *watered her* with rain.

Others relate תְּשֹׁקְקֶהָ to תְּשׁוּקָה, *craving* (*Ibn Ezra*). The *Midrash* (*Shir HaShirim Rabbah* 7:11) comments that a woman craves only her husband, Israel craves only its Father in Heaven, and rain desires only to descend to earth.

Radak renders וַתְּשֹׁקְקֶהָ, *You cause* [the earth] *to crave*, suggesting: When You punish the nations which defy You, You hold back the rains until the parched earth craves moisture. Only then do You mercifully water the land.

Similarly, Israel languishes in exile and longs to be revived by the fresh dew of redemption.

רַבַּת תַּעְשְׁרֶנָּה — *You enriched her abundantly.*

The root of this word is עָשִׁיר, *rich*, which suggests that God sends abundant rain so that the world will prosper (*Radak*); at the dawn of Creation, God cultivated the earth without any help from man, as Scripture (*Genesis* 2:9), *And HASHEM, God, caused to grow from the ground every tree that was pleasing to the sight and good for food* (*Sforno*).

In explicating the significance of the word עָשִׁיר, *Shir HaShirim Rabbah* (7:11) teaches that if man is worthy, the Creator will make the land עָשִׁיר, *rich*, but if he is unworthy, the earth will produce only עֲשִׂירִי, *one tenth*, of its capacity.

פֶּלֶג אֱלֹהִים מָלֵא מָיִם — *[From] the tent of God filled with water.*

The *Talmud* (*Taanis* 8b) describes פֶּלֶג as a קוּבָּה, *tent*, or *compartment*, in the heavens, where אֱלֹהִים, *God*, stores the rain which eventually descends to the earth [see *Targum*].

Radak, however, identifies פֶּלֶג as the *large pool of water* formed after it rains. The word אֱלֹהִים is utilized to emphasize the extraordinary size of this body of water, which was created in such a brief time. These pools provide water for man and beast and also moisten the dry soil.

תָּכִין דְּגָנָם — *You prepare their grain.*

Even after You water the earth, You continue to assure the success of the crop by channeling favorable winds to the fields and by protecting the tender

65

11-21

> *and watered her,*
> *You enriched her abundantly,*
> * from the tent of God filled with water.*
> *You prepare their grain,*
> * for thus do You prepare it.*
> ¹¹ *Her ridges You water generously,*
> * settling in her furrows.*
> *With showers You soften her,*
> * her growth You bless.*
> ¹² *You crown the year of Your goodness*

shoots from pestilence and blight (*Radak*).

כִּי בֵן תְּכִינֶהָ — *For thus do You prepare it.*

According to *Radak*, this refers to the protection of the grain, as described above. Obviously, generous rains are of no value if the crop is later devastated by blight or by storms.

Sforno maintains that this statement delineates God's original master plan for mankind: You fashioned the world in a way that would release man from all mundane pursuits, because the earth was intended to produce the staples of life (grains and fruits) without the need for human exertion. This utopian existence would *prepare* mankind to concentrate exclusively on the service of God.

[Here lies the solution to the threat of famine, for when climatic and agricultural conditions prove unfavorable to human survival, this indicates that mankind had forsaken its mission (i.e., Divine service). At these times, God ceases to *prepare* the earth for humanity. When men return to the pursuit of their ordained purpose and destiny, the earth will return to its normal pattern of productivity.]

11. תְּלָמֶיהָ רַוֵּה — *Her ridges You water generously.*

The psalmist continues to recount the blessings of the water cycle.

The תְּלָמִים, *ridges*, are the mounds of dirt which are formed by plowing. God causes these rows to be watered generously by the rains (*Radak*).

נַחֵת גְּדוּדֶהָ — *Settling in her furrows.*

Radak defines גְּדוּדִים, lit. *scratches*, as the deep furrows between the *ridges* created by plowing. [The rainwater *settles* in the *furrows* and nourishes the seeds planted there.]

Metzudas David translates גְּדוּדֶהָ as *her bands of men*, referring to the hungry people who wander around the earth in search of food. They derive נַחַת, *satisfaction*, from the rains, which banish drought and famine from the land.

בִּרְבִיבִים תְּמֹגְגֶנָּה — *With showers You soften her.*

The heavy rains come and soften the soil, which was formerly hard and untillable (*Radak*).

צִמְחָה תְּבָרֵךְ — *Her growth You bless.*

After the rains of Heavenly blessing, the crops flourish, growing to heights far surpassing those that would ordinarily be expected (*Sforno*).

12. עִטַּרְתָּ שְׁנַת טוֹבָתֶךְ — *You crown the year of Your goodness.*

When You decide to prosper a year,

יג טוֹבָתֶךָ וּמַעְגָּלֶיךָ יִרְעֲפוּן דָּשֶׁן: יִרְעֲפוּ
יד נְאוֹת מִדְבָּר וְגִיל גְּבָעוֹת תַּחְגֹּרְנָה: לָבְשׁוּ
כָרִים | הַצֹּאן וַעֲמָקִים יַעַטְפוּ־בָר
יִתְרוֹעֲעוּ אַף־יָשִׁירוּ:

You send the rains, which crown it with goodness *(Rashi)*.

This decision takes place on the first day of the year, *Rosh HaShanah*, when Israel crowns God as their sovereign *(Panim Yafos)*.

Meiri suggests that the wealth and prosperity described in these verses is no more than an allegory, alluding to genuine success, i.e., spiritual and intellectual development. Just as the finest earth lies fallow and dormant if not blessed with Heavenly rain, the powers of the mind and soul are locked up until Divine inspiration stimulates and releases them.

וּמַעְגָּלֶיךָ יִרְעֲפוּן דָּשֶׁן — *And Your paths drip with abundance.*

When You open the channels of rain, You graciously release all of the sources of Heavenly abundance, and they flow down the *path* to earth *(Alshich)*.

Radak identifies God's מַעְגָּל, *path*, as the clouds which *drip* down the rain which creates abundance on earth.

Ibn Ezra, however, maintains that מַעְגָּל refers to the countless new rivulets formed after heavy rainfall, for they testify to abundance.

It is significant, notes the *Panim Yafos*, that the letters of דָּשֶׁן are numerically equivalent to 354. The lunar year, on which the Jewish calendar is based, is composed of 355 days. On the first day *Rosh HaShanah*, God decides the degree to which He will bless the other 354 days with דָּשֶׁן, *abundance*.

13. יִרְעֲפוּ נְאוֹת מִדְבָּר — *They drip onto pastures of wilderness.*

Just as *Your paths drip abundance* onto inhabited areas for the sake of mankind, so do *they drip onto the wilderness*, to benefit the wild animals which pasture there *(Radak)*.

וְגִיל גְּבָעוֹת תַּחְגֹּרְנָה — *And the hills gird themselves.*

This is symbolic: when the rains cease and drought strikes the countryside, the scorched hills seem to be shrouded in sackcloth and mourning; but when the rains revive the soil and cover it with rich produce, the hills appear to be girded with happiness *(Radak)*.

14. לָבְשׁוּ כָרִים הַצֹּאן — *The meadows don sheep.*

and Your paths drip with abundance.
     ¹³ *They drip onto pastures of wilderness*
          and the hills gird themselves with joy.
     ¹⁴ *The meadows don sheep*
          and the valleys cloak themselves with fodder.
They shout for joy,
          they even sing!

The translation of בָּרִים, *meadows,* follows *Rashi, Radak,* and *Ibn Ezra.* [Only in one other place in Scriptures is כַּר rendered thus; in *Isaiah 30:23,* we read יִרְעֶה מִקְנֶיךָ ... כַּר נִרְחָב, *He will graze Your cattle ... in the broad meadow.*]

The lush vegetation which grows as a result of the rains attracts countless sheep to the meadows. They graze together so densely that they cover the earth like a swathe of thick cloth.

[Throughout Scripture, בָּרִים usually means *sheep.* See 37:20, *Deuteronomy* 32:14.]

Targum [based on *Rosh HaShanah* 8a] renders: The בָּרִים, *rams,* clothe [a euphemism for impregnate] the צֹאן, *ewes.* The mating season takes place sometime in early spring, when the *valleys cloak themselves with fodder.*

וַעֲמָקִים יַעַטְפוּ בָר — *And the valleys cloak themselves with fodder.*

Every inch of the surface will be productive, without any empty, fallow space *(Metzudas David).*

It seems superfluous to say that the valleys will be well watered, for we have already learned that even the high hills and mountains will receive adequate rainfall. With this apparently unnecessary clause, the psalmist indicates that the valleys will not be flooded by an overabundance of rain *(Radak).*

יִתְרוֹעֲעוּ אַף יָשִׁירוּ — *They shout for joy, they even sing.*

When a dry spell snaps, famine ends and prosperity returns. Therefore, men shout and sing for joy *(Rashi; Metzudas David).*

Ibn Ezra interprets this as a continuation of the preceding symbolism: When the hillsides burst forth with vigorous new growth, they seem to *shout for joy.*

According to *Radak,* this describes the fresh winds which blow gently through the full-grown stalks of grain, producing a soft, pleasant hum which sounds like a hymn of joy.

[Similarly, when Israel returns from exile they will be rejuvenated and invigorated to sing out of sheer ecstasy.]

מזמור סו 66

David composed this psalm in the twilight of his career, when God released him from the threat of the many hostile nations which surrounded him. Relieved of his concerns about the present, David was free to dream of the Messianic future (Ibn Yachya).

The psalmist first turns to Israel's glorious past, replete with wonders and miracles. The salvation of days gone by inspires the faith that such events are destined to be repeated on an even grander scale in the future, when God grants Israel its ultimate redemption (Meiri).

Meiri also suggests that the original version of this psalm was composed at the time of the exodus from Egypt. It foretells the splendor of the Temple, which was destined to be built by Solomon. Later, David adapted this work to the circumstances of his and future generations.

Indeed, Sforno observes that this psalm provides an eternal lesson in the art of supplication. David teaches the exiles to exert themselves in prayer to God and to emulate the example of their forefathers, who were granted redemption because of their unparalleled devotion in prayer.

In light of this, we can understand why the Vilna Gaon (Maaseh Rav 194) designates this as the 'Song of the day' for the sixth day of Passover: these verses serve as a most appropriate introduction to the climactic redemption at the sea, which occurred on the seventh of Passover.

א לַמְנַצֵּחַ שִׁיר מִזְמוֹר הָרִיעוּ לֵאלֹהִים כָּל־
ב הָאָרֶץ: זַמְּרוּ כְבוֹד־שְׁמוֹ שִׂימוּ כָבוֹד
ג תְּהִלָּתוֹ: אִמְרוּ לֵאלֹהִים מַה־נּוֹרָא
ד מַעֲשֶׂיךָ בְּרֹב עֻזְּךָ יְכַחֲשׁוּ־לְךָ אֹיְבֶיךָ: כָּל־
הָאָרֶץ | יִשְׁתַּחֲווּ לְךָ וִיזַמְּרוּ־לָךְ יְזַמְּרוּ

1. לַמְנַצֵּחַ שִׁיר מִזְמוֹר — *For the Conductor, a song with musical accompaniment.*

The psalmist begins with three musical instructions, thereby alluding to Israel's redemption from three countries: Babylon, Media, and Greece. Each of these joyous events merits its own musical composition (*Alshich*).

In addition, these three terms refer to the three Temples [where songs of praise were offered and will again be offered to God] (*Eretz HaChaim*).

הָרִיעוּ לֵאלֹהִים כָּל הָאָרֶץ — *Exult to God all the earth.*

The psalmist addresses himself to Israel: 'Conduct yourselves in a manner which will inspire love and respect in the eyes of the world. Then the nations will admire you and will shout for joy when God redeems you' (*Sforno*).

2. זַמְּרוּ כְבוֹד שְׁמוֹ — *Sing to the glory of His Name.*

When Israel is in exile, God's Name is disgraced and derided by the nations; they taunt us, 'Where is your God? Why does He not come to your aid?' Therefore, when you are redeemed make sure to proclaim God's true glory to the world! (*Radak*).

Earn the respect of the nations, for this will lead mankind to praise God for having chosen so glorious a nation as Israel (*Sforno*).

Tehillos Hashem notes that זַמְּרוּ is

related to זְמוֹרָה, *branch.* It signifies, 'disperse and disseminate God's glory,' just as a tree's branches spread out far from its trunk.

שִׂימוּ כָבוֹד תְּהִלָּתוֹ — *Make that glory His fitting praise.*

Sefer HaIkkarim observes that a human king depends upon the honor and acclaim of his subjects. If he were to reject it, the mortal king would be stripped of his power and majesty.

Only the Divine King of kings embodies true glory, which is eternal and does not depend on human bondage. Therefore, שִׂימוּ, *make* God's exclusive possession of genuine כָבוֹד, *glory,* תְּהִלָּתוֹ, *His praise* (*Shevet M'Yisrael*).

3. אִמְרוּ לֵאלֹהִים מַה נּוֹרָא מַעֲשֶׂיךָ — *Say unto God, 'How awesome are Your works!'*

Rashi explains that since מַעֲשֶׂיךָ, *Your works,* is plural, the plural adjective נוֹרָאוֹת would normally have been employed.

The use of the singular form נוֹרָא suggests the following interpretation: The vast number of *Your works* does not detract from the significance of each individual deed, for every act You perform is נוֹרָא, *awesome,* in its own right.

According to a different interpretation, the verse can be rendered: No mortal can perceive Your Divine essence directly. Only by studying *Your works* can man hope to gain insight into Your being, which is נוֹרָא, *awesome.*[1]

---

1. By limiting God's praise through the diminutive singular form נוֹרָא, the psalmist teaches us a significant lesson: only part of a person's praiseworthy attributes and accomplishments should be mentioned in his presence. Here God is addressed directly (*Say unto God*); thus, אוֹמְרִים מִקְצָת שְׁבָחוֹ בְּפָנָיו, *We recite only part of His praise in His Presence.* When He is not addressed directly, this restriction does not apply, as we see in 136:1; there God is not spoken to

66
1-4

For the Conductor,
    a song with musical accompaniment:
Exult to God all the earth!
² *Sing to the glory of His Name,*
    make that glory His fitting praise.
³ *Say unto God,*
    'How awesome are Your works!'
Because of Your abundant power,
    Your enemies acknowledge their lies to You.
⁴ *All the earth will bow to You*
    and they will sing to You,
    they will sing to Your Name, Selah.

בְּרֹב עֻזְּךָ יְכַחֲשׁוּ לְךָ אֹיְבֶיךָ — *Because of Your abundant power, Your enemies acknowledge their lies to You.*

When You demonstrate Your powerful control over the events of this world by causing cataclysms such as plagues of pestilence, famine, thunderstorms, and war, the wicked cringe with fear and confess the כַּחַשׁ, *lies*, and sins of which they are guilty' (*Radak*).

However, even this confession is an insincere כַּחַשׁ, *deception*, a homage motivated solely by fear. In their hearts, the wicked remain unfaithful to the Almighty (*Sforno; Rashbam*).

Their insincerity and opportunism were possible only because their humble confessions were not accompanied by the intellectual recognition of God and His sovereignty. Rather, יְכַחֲשׁוּ, the wicked became gaunt and emaciated by starvation and suffering, which compelled their feigned 'confessions' (*Rashbam; Tanchuma*).

Radak renders יְכַחֲשׁוּ literally as *they deny*, to indicate that when they ultimately realize Your ability to destroy them, the nations will *deny* that they ever persecuted Israel.

According to *Shemos Rabbah* (20:10), the gentile monarchs who originally denied Hashem's sovereignty were forced to retract and *deny* their blasphemy. Pharaoh, Nebuchadnezzar, and Sennacherib mocked God before they eventually admitted to His majesty and might.

4. כָּל הָאָרֶץ יִשְׁתַּחֲווּ לְךָ וִיזַמְּרוּ לָךְ — *All the earth will bow to You and they will sing to You.*

As the prophet *Zephaniah* (3:9) foretells, *Then I will transform the nations to a pure language, that they may all call upon the Name of HASHEM to serve Him with one consent* (*Radak*).

This transformation will take place in two stages. First, the nations will be totally crushed by their new-found awareness of their instrinsic degradation (יִשְׁתַּחֲווּ לָךְ). Later, their bowed spirits will be lifted in song (וִיזַמְּרוּ לָךְ) when they recognize God's exalted majesty (*Norah Tehillos*).

directly and He is praised more: הוֹדוּ לַה׳ כִּי טוֹב כִּי לְעוֹלָם חַסְדּוֹ, *O give thanks to HASHEM, for He is [completely] good, for His loving-kindness endures forever* (*Bereishis Rabbah* 32:3).

[This is one of the common cases in Scripture where God is used as an example to teach rules of propriety that apply not to Him, but to human beings. In our case, there is no essential difference between speaking *to* God or *of* Him, since He is Omnipresent.]

ה שִׁמְךָ סֶּלָה: לְכוּ וּרְאוּ מִפְעֲלוֹת אֱלֹהִים
ו נוֹרָא עֲלִילָה עַל־בְּנֵי אָדָם: הָפַךְ יָם |
לְיַבָּשָׁה בַּנָּהָר יַעַבְרוּ בְרָגֶל שָׁם נִשְׂמְחָה־
ז בּוֹ: מֹשֵׁל בִּגְבוּרָתוֹ | עוֹלָם עֵינָיו בַּגּוֹיִם
°יָרוּמוּ תִּצְפֶּינָה הַסּוֹרְרִים | אַל °יָרִימוּ לָמוֹ

יְזַמְּרוּ שִׁמְךָ סֶּלָה — *They will sing to Your Name, Selah.*

The songs which previous redemptions inspired were short-lived, interrupted by destruction and exile; but the tunes composed in honor of the ultimate redemption will continue סֶלָה, *forever* [see comm. 3:3] (*Tehillos Hashem*).

5. לְכוּ וּרְאוּ מִפְעֲלוֹת אֱלֹהִים — *Go and see the works of God.*

[Cf. *comm.* to 46:9 לְכוּ חֲזוּ מִפְעֲלוֹת ה׳.]

These words are what all men on earth are destined to say to one another (*Radak*).

Ibn Ezra renders לְכוּ as *come to me*, as in *Isaiah* 1:18, to indicate that every man will invite his neighbor to join in the discovery of God's ways.

נוֹרָא עֲלִילָה עַל בְּנֵי אָדָם — *Awesome in deed toward mankind.*

God may do as He pleases with mankind, for His actions have no external constraints. Therefore, all men stand in awe before Him (*Radak*).

Men are also terrified by God's omniscience. Since their every action is known to Him, they tremble lest He find fault with them (*Rashi*).

Rabbeinu Bachaya relates עֲלִילָה to עָלָה, *cause* for God Himself is the Prime Cause of all events.

Hirsch elaborates that even before the dawn of Creation, the Sovereign of the universe envisaged an ultimate goal for all worldly affairs. To realize this goal, God set into motion an awesomely complex series of interwoven causes and effects.

Throughout history, the Almighty guided and manipulated the development of events in order to reach the goals which He had originally set.

Midrash Tanchuma (Vayeshev 4) notes that the chronicle of Joseph's elevation to royal power has become a classical illustration of Divine orchestration of human affairs.

Countless, apparently unrelated incidents meshed in order to draw the entire House of Israel to Egypt, for God's original plan had ordained that the foundation of Jewish history would be set there, in the form of a cruel bondage and a miraculous redemption. Once the Divine wheels of history are set in motion, no earthly power can stand in their path.

6. הָפַךְ יָם לְיַבָּשָׁה — *He changed the sea into dry land.*

The psalmist now enumerates some of God's awesome accomplishments (*Radak*). [The splitting of the Sea of Reeds was an extraordinary miracle because it totally transformed nature.]

In addition, the entire makeup of the Egyptian nation was drastically changed at that time. Not only did the Egyptians perish on earth, but even their שַׂר לְמַעְלָה, *sovereign angel in heaven*, was slain [i.e, the nation was stripped of its spiritual essence and its unique role in the Divine scheme of universal history was altered] (*Alshich*).

בַּנָּהָר יַעַבְרוּ בְרָגֶל — *Through the river they passed on foot.*

This refers to Israel's miraculous crossing of the Jordan River (*Joshua* Chapter 3) as the Jews entered the Land of Canaan (*Targum; Radak*).

[Unlike the Sea of Reeds, the Jordan did not split open. Rather, as its waters

⁵ *Go and see the works of God,*
  awesome in deed toward mankind.
⁶ *He changed the sea into dry land,*
  through the river they passed on foot;
  there we rejoiced in Him.
⁷ *He rules the world with His might,*
  His eyes oversee the nations.
Let not the rebellious exalt themselves, Selah.

raced downstream they halted abruptly, their course dammed by a huge, invisible barrier, which caused the waters to pile up in a towering wall (*Joshua* 3:16) that reached a height of many miles (*Sotah* 34a). Further downstream, beneath the pillar, Israel crossed the completely dry river bed on foot.]

[Also בְּרָגֶל, lit. *by foot*, alludes to the fact that the waters of the Jordan only halted after the priests, who were carrying the Ark, dipped their feet into the edge of the river (*Joshua* 3:15).]

שָׁם נִשְׂמְחָה בּוֹ — *There we rejoiced* [lit. *we will rejoice*] *in Him.*

We rejoiced when we crossed over the Jordan (*Ibn Ezra*).

Rashi, however, interprets this as a reference to the Sea of Reeds, which rejoiced at the opportunity to fulfill God's wishes by splitting.

The Children of Israel were also gladdened at the sea, for God's Name was sanctified throughout the entire world in a manner which was unmatched by the damming of the Jordan River. At the sea, Israel expressed their joy with Song (*Exodus* 15:1), whereas at the Jordan they remained silent (*Chozah David*).

Radak renders נִשְׂמְחָה literally as *we will rejoice*, to indicate that our rejoicing will occur in Messianic times, when God *with His scorching wind will shake His hand over the river and will smite it into seven streams and cause men to cross over dry-shod. And there shall be a highway for the remnant of His people that shall remain from Assyria, just as there was for Israel in the day that they came up out of the land of Egypt* (*Isaiah* 11:15-16).

7. מֹשֵׁל בִּגְבוּרָתוֹ עוֹלָם — *He rules the world with His might.*

The translation of עוֹלָם as *world* follows *Targum* and *Metzudas David*. *Sforno* adds that God alone rules the world, not the ministering angels.

However, *Ibn Ezra* and *Radak* render עוֹלָם: *forever*, to indicate that after the final redemption of Israel, God's undisputed sovereignty over the world will endure *forever*.

Tehillas Hashem interprets גְּבוּרָתוֹ as a reference to God's *mighty* anger, which is aroused by Israel's transgressions: *He rules over* (or *controls*) *His anger forever.*

עֵינָיו בַּגּוֹיִם תִּצְפֶּינָה — *His eyes oversee the nations.*

God has always been lenient with the nations and overlooked their offenses. In the future, however, He will watch them closely and punish them strictly, in accordance with the letter of the law (*Radak; Sforno*).

When God is angered by the shortcomings of Israel, He need only turn His watchful gaze towards the gentiles. When compared with their depravity, Israel's offenses become insignificant, providing God ample justification to control His mighty anger (*Noam Megodim*).

הַסּוֹרְרִים אַל יָרוּמוּ לָמוֹ סֶלָה — *Let not the rebellious exalt themselves, Selah.*

Since God originally treated the wicked leniently, they misinterpreted

ח סֶלָה: בָּרְכוּ עַמִּים | אֱלֹהֵינוּ וְהַשְׁמִיעוּ
ט קוֹל תְּהִלָּתוֹ: הַשָּׂם נַפְשֵׁנוּ בַּחַיִּים וְלֹא־
י נָתַן לַמּוֹט רַגְלֵנוּ: כִּי־בְחַנְתָּנוּ אֱלֹהִים
יא צְרַפְתָּנוּ כִּצְרָף־כָּסֶף: הֲבֵאתָנוּ בַמְּצוּדָה
יב שַׂמְתָּ מוּעָקָה בְמָתְנֵינוּ: הִרְכַּבְתָּ אֱנוֹשׁ
לְרֹאשֵׁנוּ בָּאנוּ־בָאֵשׁ וּבַמַּיִם וַתּוֹצִיאֵנוּ

---

this as a sign of Divine weakness. They took advantage of His mercy and flouted the law with impunity. These rebels are destined to be vanquished (*Radak; Sforno*).

8. בָּרְכוּ עַמִּים אֱלֹהֵינוּ — *Bless our God, O Nations.*

Ibn Ezra suggests that *Nations* may refer to the Jebusites, who were under Israelite dominion and were thus obligated to obey such an exhortation, or it may refer to Israel itself [the chosen of all peoples].

Rashi and *Radak* explain this as an address to all non-Jews. When mankind realizes that the incessant persecution of the exile has failed to annihilate our nation, they should bless God for the miracles He wrought to assure our survival [i.e., they should thank God for aborting their schemes to exterminate His chosen people, for such a heinous crime would have aroused His unbridled wrath (cf. *comm.* to 117:1).]

Dorash Moshe interprets this exhortation in light of the Talmudic dictum that no proselytes will be accepted in Messianic times, for fear that the convert's professed love for God and Torah is insincere and that his true motive is the wish to share in Israel's glory (*Yevamos* 24b). According to this view, the psalmist teaches that if the nations wish to *bless our God* by joining His rank, they must do so now, while He is still אֱלֹהֵינוּ, *the Dispenser of Strict Justice,* who shows no special favor to Israel. Once He redeems Israel, conversion will no longer be possible.

9. הַשָּׂם נַפְשֵׁנוּ בַּחַיִּים — *He who set our soul in life.*

God preserved us throughout the travails of exile (*Radak*) in a manner which defies the laws of nature and of history (*Sforno*).

He *set our soul* on the righteous path which leads to eternal *life* in the hereafter (*Targum; Ibn Yachya*).

וְלֹא נָתַן לַמּוֹט רַגְלֵנוּ — *And did not allow our foot to falter.*

He reinforced our steadfast resolve to recognize no deity other than Him. He did not let us fall prey to the lure of strange gods and alien religions (*Sforno*).

10. כִּי בְחַנְתָּנוּ אֱלֹהִים — *For You examined us, O God.*

[Exile is the ultimate test of our loyalty to God. The pressure of this precarious, abnormal existence on alien, hostile soil has tested every fiber of our faith.]

We have passed this Divine examination, and our loyalty is clearly above reproach (*Sforno*).

צְרַפְתָּנוּ כִּצְרָף־כָּסֶף — *You refined us as if refining silver.*

Our exile has functioned as a crucible, enabling You to eliminate the undesirable dross from our midst. Many heretic, apostate, and defiant sinners have perished and disappeared from our ranks (*Sforno*).

Those who remain have been refined by the process of repentance [which was spurred by the dangers of the exile] (*Rashi*).

8 *Bless our God, O Nations,*
let the sound of His praise be heard.
9 *He who set our soul in life*
and did not allow our foot to falter.
10 *For You examined us, O God,*
You refined us as if refining silver.
11 *You installed us in the cage,*
You placed constraint upon our loins,
12 *You mounted a mortal over our heads;*
we entered fire and water

---

11. הֲבֵאתָנוּ בַמְּצוּדָה — *You installed us in the cage.*

You trapped us in a cramped prison (*Rashi*) so well fortified that only a miracle could permit us to escape from its confines (*Radak; Ibn Yachya*).

[The impregnable nature of this prison explains why the term מְצוּדָה, which really means *fortress* (see 18:3), is used to describe it.]

Hirsch observes that the existence which the exiled Jew has endured in his ghetto resembles that of a man enclosed in a cage in two respects:

First, the Jew has been barred from normal contact and relations with the outside world; second, the Jew has been a defenseless target, vulnerable to attacks from all sides. This unique test has revealed Israel's inherent moral nobility, from which there have been remarkably few defections throughout the millenia of our persecution. The salient fact of Israel's history is not the number of its defectors, but the inspiring steadfastness with which it has remained loyal to its mission.

שַׂמְתָּ מוּעָקָה בְמָתְנֵינוּ — *You placed constraint upon our loins.*

The root עָקָ means *painful oppression* (see 55:4) which restrains free movement (*Rashi; Ibn Ezra*).

The gentiles arbitrarily exercise their unlimited authority to restrict our privileges. We are constrained from actions which are permitted to all other citizens (*Hirsch*).

12. הִרְכַּבְתָּ אֱנוֹשׁ לְרֹאשֵׁנוּ — *You mounted a mortal over our heads.*

Prior to our exile, no frail mortal ruled us and we looked to You alone as our Sovereign (*Radak*); but in exile we are subject to the whim of the lowest of men, the scum of the earth (*Sforno*). Thus the prophet *Isaiah* (26:13) laments, *Other lords besides You have sovereignty over us.*

בָּאנוּ בָאֵשׁ וּבַמַּיִם — *We entered fire and water.*

Our suffering may be compared to fire, which consumes an object, and water, which drowns it. The tragedies of the exile should have overwhelmed us and obliterated our name; yet, with Your aid, we have survived (*Radak*).

R' Avraham Azulai notes that the psalmist likens adversity to fire and water, which are both vehicles of ritual purification [see *Numbers* 31:23], for *golus* has had the same cleansing effect on the spirit of the Jewish people.

The *Talmud* (*Megillah* 11a) teaches that the Babylonian Exile under the dominion of Nebuchadnezzar is signified by *fire* [because this tyrant intimidated Israel with the threat of death in a furnace]. The Egyptian exile under

יג לָרְוָיָה: אָבוֹא בֵיתְךָ בְעוֹלוֹת אֲשַׁלֵּם לְךָ

יד נְדָרָי: אֲשֶׁר־פָּצוּ שְׂפָתָי וְדִבֶּר־פִי בַּצַּר־

טו לִי: עֹלוֹת מֵחִים אַעֲלֶה־לָּךְ עִם־קְטֹרֶת

אֵילִים אֶעֱשֶׂה בָקָר עִם־עַתּוּדִים סֶלָה:

טז לְכוּ־שִׁמְעוּ וַאֲסַפְּרָה כָּל־יִרְאֵי אֱלֹהִים

---

the rule of Pharoah is connoted by *water* [since Pharoah attempted to drown all male infants in the Nile].[1]

וַתּוֹצִיאֵנוּ לָרְוָיָה — *And You withdrew us to abundance.*

[See *comm.* to 23:5, כּוֹסִי רְוָיָה, *my cup overflows.*] When God provides salvation, He does not merely bestow a meager measure of sustenance upon His beneficiaries. Rather, He generously provides them with more than they need or deserve.

13. אָבוֹא בֵיתְךָ בְעוֹלוֹת — *I shall enter Your house with burnt offerings.*

The psalmist now speaks in the singular, as the collective voice of the exiles who pledge to fulfill the vows they took in *golus*. This will be accomplished when God rebuilds His house, the Temple (*Radak*).

These future sacrifices will represent thanksgiving. Rather than complain about our exile, we will express our appreciation for the purifying effect which *golus* has had on our souls (*Norah Tehillos*).

אֲשַׁלֵּם לְךָ נְדָרָי — *I shall pay You my vows.*

The *Talmud* (*Chagigah* 7a) observes that in *Proverbs* (25:17), King Solomon discourages frequent visits to the *Beis HaMikdash*, saying, *Let your foot be*

seldom in your neighbor's house, lest he be sated with you and hate you, whereas here David seems eager to bring offerings constantly.

The *Talmud* explains that Solomon was referring to sin and guilt offerings. It is certainly preferable that no offenses be committed, making such sacrifices rare. However, David was eager to dedicate voluntary burnt offerings and peace offerings, which are a desirable display of intense love for God.

14. אֲשֶׁר פָּצוּ שְׂפָתָי — *Which my lips uttered* [lit. *opened* (*Targum*)].

This refers to extraordinary pledges prompted by situations of great distress, as exemplified by Yiftach, who said (*Judges* 11:35) of the vow he took when entering battle, וְאָנֹכִי פָּצִיתִי פִי, *for I have opened my mouth* (*Ibn Ezra; Hirsch*).

The duress of exile prompts Israel to utter vows of equal gravity [for *golus*, too, is a continuous battle] (*Radak*).

15. עֹלוֹת מֵחִים אַעֲלֶה לָּךְ — *Burnt offerings of fat animals I shall offer up to You.*

Rashi and Radak indentify מֵחִים as a cognate of מוֹחַ, *bone marrow*, the vital substance which symbolizes robust health and corpulence.

Vayikra Rabbah relates מֵחִים to מָחָה, *wipe out*, teaching that this verse may

---

1. The *Talmud* teaches that if misfortune drives a desperate man to lower himself before another person when requesting charity, this humiliation is considered as painful as death by *fire and water* together (*Berachos* 6b).

Furthermore, the Sages (*Bava Metziah* 75a) perceived that even the man who is forced to swallow his pride by soliciting a loan is extremely sensitive because of the damage done to his self-respect. Therefore, if the creditor knows that the debtor does not yet possess the means to repay the loan, he may not even pass in front of him, lest the debtor interpret this as a hint that payment of the debt is due, for this will cause the debtor anguish which equals the suffering inflicted by *fire and water*.

and You withdrew us to abundance.
¹³ I shall enter Your house with burnt offerings,
   I shall pay You my vows,
¹⁴ Which my lips uttered,
   and my mouth spoke in my distress.
¹⁵ Burnt offerings of fat animals
   I shall offer up to You,
With the burning of rams,
   I will prepare bulls with goats, Selah.
¹⁶ Go and hearken, all you who fear God,
   and I will relate what He did for my soul.

be illustrated by the example of the king who was served a sumptuous repast. The monarch was so delighted by the very first course that he 'wiped his plate clean.' [Similarly, the supplicant prays that the intense devotion which accompanies his עוֹלָה should render it exceedingly desirable to God. If the holy fires of the altar quickly consume every fragment of the animal's flesh, this will indicate Divine pleasure and acceptance of the supplicant's offering.]

עִם קְטֹרֶת אֵילִים — With the burning of rams.

The translation follows Radak and Metzudas David, who interpret this as a reference to the הַקְטָרַת הַחֲלָבִים, the burning of the fat, of the ram offering.

However, Targum understands these words to denote two separate offerings: קְטֹרֶת, burnt incense, and אֵלִים, rams.

Tanchuma (Tetzavah 15) states that David yearned to emulate the deeds of the נְשִׂיאִים, princes, of the twelve tribes, who offered incense as the first part of their special sacrifice at the dedication of the Tabernacle (Numbers Chap. 7).

אֶעֱשֶׂה בָקָר עִם עַתּוּדִים סֶלָה — I will prepare [lit. make] bulls with goats, Selah.

This phrase supports the opinion (see Tanchuma above) that David was patterning his offering after the offering of

the נְשִׂיאִים, princes, of the twelve tribes; for these were the only individuals who brought such a vast variety of offerings, including bullocks, goats, rams [and incense] (Vayikra Rabbah 88:3).

16. לְכוּ שִׁמְעוּ ... כָּל יִרְאֵי אֱלֹהִים — Go and hearken, all you who fear God.

Each and every God-fearing man will exhort his comrade with this advice (Radak).

Rashi identifies the יִרְאֵי אֱלֹהִים as the sincere proselytes who converted to the Jewish faith. [See Rashi to 115:13.]

[In verse 5, the psalmist declared לְכוּ וּרְאוּ מִפְעֲלוֹת אֱלֹהִים, Go and see the works of God. That declaration served as an introduction for an overview of Jewish history (vs. 6-12) as it is visible to the mortal eye of בְּנֵי אָדָם, the sons of man.

Now, however, the psalmist delves even deeper and calls upon the truly God-fearing to hearken, i.e., to understand (Sforno) what effect the Almighty's guidance of history has had on the development of the Jewish soul (לְנַפְשִׁי).]

וַאֲסַפְּרָה ... אֲשֶׁר עָשָׂה לְנַפְשִׁי — And I will relate what He did for my soul.

The order of this verse is interrupted. According to Sforno, this interruption indicates that this deeply significant

יז אֲשֶׁר עָשָׂה לְנַפְשִׁי: אֵלָיו פִּי־קָרָאתִי
יח וְרוֹמַם תַּחַת לְשׁוֹנִי: אָוֶן אִם־רָאִיתִי
יט בְלִבִּי לֹא יִשְׁמַע│אֲדֹנָי: אָכֵן שָׁמַע אֱלֹהִים
כ הִקְשִׁיב בְּקוֹל תְּפִלָּתִי: בָּרוּךְ אֱלֹהִים
אֲשֶׁר לֹא־הֵסִיר תְּפִלָּתִי וְחַסְדּוֹ מֵאִתִּי:

message must be repeated: First *I will relate* to all of Israel and then *I will emphasize* to *all who fear God* exactly *what He has done* to develop the boundless spiritual resources of *my soul.*

17. אֵלָיו פִּי קָרָאתִי — *Unto Him (with) my mouth I called.*

Ibn Ezra notes that the grammatically proper reading would have been בְּפִי, *with my mouth.*

Binah L'ittim explains that David loved God with such intensity and selfless devotion that he feared lest he use his most precious organ, his mouth, improperly. Therefore, he dedicated his entire power of speech to the Almighty and begged Him to choose the proper words of prayer and praise. Thus, this clause should be understood as follows: אֵלָיו פִּי, *Unto Him* [is consecrated] *my mouth,* [therefore, the prayers which God composed] קָרָאתִי, *I called out.*

וְרוֹמַם תַּחַת לְשׁוֹנִי — *And He was extolled by* [lit. *beneath*] *my tongue.*

Throughout the duration of the exile, we never ceased to call out to God in supplication, and we extolled His majesty [without pause] (*Rashi*).

Our translation renders רוֹמַם as a verb: *I extolled Him,* thus He was extolled, מְרוֹמָם, *extolled,* תַּחַת לְשׁוֹנִי, *by my tongue* (*Rashi; Radak*).

Literally, תַּחַת לְשׁוֹנִי means *beneath my tongue,* alluding to the heart, which fashions words and provides the intellectual support *beneath* verbal statements (*Radak*). In addition, hidden deep *beneath my heart* are splendid ideas for extolling God, but these sublime insights cannot be articulated (*Ibn Ezra*).

Noam Elimelech stresses David's selflessness. Even when *unto Him I called,* requesting my personal needs, the underlying motive *beneath my tongue* was to have the opportunity וְרוֹמָם, *to extol* God for my success. No matter how desperate my situation, I always addressed God in a low, calm voice, whispering and suppressing the words *beneath my tongue,* for I firmly believe that God is Omnipresent and draws near to the prayers of every supplicant. The Sages (*Berachos* 24b) said that someone who raises his voice in prayer resembles the false prophets [who screamed and ranted to their deaf idols] (*Beis Elokim*).

18. אָוֶן אִם רָאִיתִי בְלִבִּי — *If I perceived iniquity in my heart.*

[I know that it is impossible for thoughts of iniquity to be harbored in my heart, for it is filled only with love for the Almighty; its bursts with extolment which defies expression (v. 17).]

לֹא יִשְׁמַע אֲדֹנָי — *My Lord would not have listened.*

Even if a sinful thought stole into my heart, God graciously overlooked it and ignored it (*Rashi; Radak*).

From this the Sages of the *Talmud* (*Kiddushin* 40a) derived the important principle that מַחֲשָׁבָה רָעָה אֵין הקב״ה מְצָרְפָהּ לְמַעֲשֶׂה, *The Holy One, Blessed be He, does not consider an evil thought to be an evil deed.* He pardons the iniquitous thought as long as it does not result in an evil deed. However, when it does lead to sin, then the offender is punished for both his forbidden action and his sinful thought.

The *Shaloh Hakodosh* maintains that

¹⁷ *Unto Him with my mouth I called*
and He was extolled by my tongue.
¹⁸ *If I perceived iniquity in my heart,*
my Lord would not have listened.
¹⁹ *In truth, God has heard,*
He has hearkened to the sound of my prayer.
²⁰ *Blessed be God, Who has not withdrawn*
my prayer or His loving-kindness from me.

this amnesty applies only to adventitious thoughts of sin; but if a person deliberately concentrates his mental capabilites upon iniquitous machinations, then his sinful scheming cannot be condoned by God. The Rabbis (*Yoma* 29a) condemned this serious offense in the dictum: הִרְהוּרֵי עֲבֵירָה קָשִׁים מֵעֲבֵירָה, *The thought of sin is more pernicious than sin itself.*

[This is because thought affects the intellect, which is the enduring essence of man, whereas a physical deed may affect only the body, which is merely man's temporary shell. When sin is etched into the mind, eternal damage may result.][1]

19. אָכֵן שָׁמַע אֱלֹהִים — *In truth [Targum* בְּקוּשְׁטָא; *see Exodus* 2:14] *God has heard.*

His favorable response to my petition attests to the *truth* and sincerity of my plea. For, although God would pardon *the iniquity in my heart* (v. 18), such improper thoughts would taint the purity of my supplication and render it unacceptable (*Ibn Ezra*).

As the psalmist declares (145:18), קָרוֹב ה׳ לְכָל קֹרְאָיו לְכֹל אֲשֶׁר יִקְרָאֻהוּ בֶאֱמֶת, *HASHEM is close to all who call upon Him, to all who call upon Him sincerely (Rashbam).*

הִקְשִׁיב בְּקוֹל תְּפִלָּתִי — *He has hearkened to the sound of my prayer.*

My anguish and the desperation of my plight were not sufficient cause to enlist the aid of God. What aroused Him was the ring of truth — the sincere קוֹל, *sound,* of my prayers. Thus, even judging me strictly in His role as אֱלֹהִים, *the Dispenser of Strict Justice,* He deemed me truly worthy of His salvation (*Norah Tehillos*).

20. בָּרוּךְ אֱלֹהִים — *Blessed be God.*

[He is blessed not only when merciful, but even when He acts as אֱלֹהִים, *the Dispenser of Strict Justice.*]

אֲשֶׁר לֹא הֵסִיר תְּפִלָּתִי וְחַסְדּוֹ מֵאִתִּי — *Who has not withdrawn my prayer or His kindness from me.*

Even while אֱלֹהִים afflicted me and my heart grew faint from agony, He continued to lift my spirits and inspired *my prayer* (*Kli Chemdah*).

This inspiration was the unique *loving-kindness* which God displayed to me (*Ibn Ezra*).

The *Talmud* (*Berachos* 5a) teaches that sometimes God ordains that pious men of extraordinary devotion undergo suffering and tribulations known as יִסּוּרִים שֶׁל אַהֲבָה, *afflictions of* [Divine] *love.* This suffering is not sent as a

1. The *Talmud* qualifies this rule, which grants pardon for casual thoughts of iniquity:
(1) It only applies to a God-fearing Jew whose soul is basically good. Thus, if he even considers doing a *mitzvah*, he is rewarded as if he actually accomplished that good deed. Evil, however, is completely alien to the Jewish soul; therefore, adventitious sinful thoughts can be disregarded.

On the other hand, the evil thoughts of an idolater, whose soul is corrupted, *are punished;*

punishment or as atonement for past sins (for its recipients are righteous men), but as an opportunity to increase future reward. When the devout accept their afflictions with joy and praise of the Divine Will which ordained them, their merits increase in direct proportion to the severity with which their faith in God has been tested.

These *afflictions of* [Divine] *love* can be distinguished from the afflictions of Divine punishment in that the former do not interfere with the afflicted man's pursuit of Torah study or with his prayer, for this verse says, *Blessed be ELOHIM* [for His strict judgment] *Who has not allowed my prayer* [which tells of] *His loving-kindness to depart from me.*

The psalmist concludes on a hopeful note: When all of Israel witnesses the many acts of kindness which God performed for me, they will gain confidence in God's determination to redeem them from the long exile *(Metzudas David).*

since these evil thoughts reflect the idolater's true nature, they cannot be overlooked by God. However, the idolater's occasional noble impulses and good intentions are not rewarded until they result in meritorious conduct, and the thought is authenticated by concrete action.

(2) If a Jew becomes so perverted that he starts to think of serving idols, then these thoughts cannot be dismissed casually and are accorded the status of an actual deed.

(3) If a Jew sins once and then repeats the sin once again, הוּתְּרָה לוֹ, it becomes permissible to him, in the sense that his conscience no longer recoils from this offense, but begins to tolerate it. Lacking restraint, even a casual impulse to sin will lead to actual transgression; therefore, the thought itself is deemed a sin.

Panim Yafos observes that the psalmist alludes to this by adopting the singular form, אָוֶן, *iniquity,* saying, *Had I perceived iniquity in my heart,* for if a person sins only once, then iniquity is not detected in his heart, but after the sin is repeated, iniquity does become apparent.

The Holy One, Blessed be He, revealed this extraordinary psalm to Moses and later to David. Both men were granted a holy vision, in which this psalm was engraved on a sheet of the purest gold, which was fashioned in the shape of a seven-branched candelabrum (menorah).

David duplicated this psalm in its menorah design and etched it onto his shield, so that he could study its teachings before entering into battle; this meritorious conduct assured David's victory (Chida, Midbar Kedeimos מערכת ד׳ אות כ״א. Chida notes that he copied this statement from the original manuscript of Rabbi Shlomo Luria, the Maharshal). A diagram of the psalm in its traditional menorah form appears in an appendix at the end of this volume.

Avodas HaKodesh says that whoever concentrates daily on this menorah and its message is considered as if he actually kindled the menorah in the Beis HaMikdash; such a person is surely destined to inherit the World to Come. Whoever recites it while concentrating on its menorah design will surely be safeguarded from all evil and enjoy great success.

It is customary to recite this psalm before Sefiras HaOmer on the forty-nine days between Passover and Shavuos (Alshich; Akeidas Yitzchak; Kesef Mezukak).

In addition, many congregations chant this psalm with a special tune immediately preceding the evening prayer at the conclusion of the Sabbath.

א־ב לַמְנַצֵּחַ בִּנְגִינֹת מִזְמוֹר שִׁיר: אֱלֹהִים
יְחָנֵּנוּ וִיבָרְכֵנוּ יָאֵר פָּנָיו אִתָּנוּ סֶלָה:
ג לָדַעַת בָּאָרֶץ דַּרְכֶּךָ בְּכָל־גּוֹיִם יְשׁוּעָתֶךָ:
ד יוֹדוּךָ עַמִּים | אֱלֹהִים יוֹדוּךָ עַמִּים כֻּלָּם:

1. לַמְנַצֵּחַ בִּנְגִינֹת מִזְמוֹר שִׁיר — *For the Conductor, upon* Neginos, *a song with musical accompaniment.*

Alshich emphasizes that this psalm has a universal message. The four musical instructions of this introductory verse correspond to the four realms (mineral, vegetable, animal and human) which make up the world; all four kingdoms were in a state of imperfection until the Torah was given at Sinai.

The following seven verses, which make up the body of this psalm, contain forty-nine words, corresponding to the seven weeks (49 days) which precede the giving of the Torah on Shavuos. On each of these days, Israel entered another one of 'the forty-nine gates of wisdom' (*Yosef Tehillos*).

The seven verses also allude to the seven branches of the menorah, which are the source of intellectual illumination for Israel.

This psalm describes the bounteous blessings and the redemption which await the children of Israel if they dedicate themselves to cultivating the rich spiritual and intellectual heritage contained in the Torah.

2. אֱלֹהִים יְחָנֵּנוּ וִיבָרְכֵנוּ — *May God favor us and bless us.*

Radak interprets this as a special request made by the Jews in exile: [Since our fortunes steadily decline] may God increase His blessings for us every day!

Sforno adds: *Favor us* although we are undeserving; bless us with fertility, for the terrible persecutions of *galus* have decimated our ranks.

Hirsch explains that חָנַן refers to the granting of intellectual abilities, as in the first request in the daily silent prayer, the *Shemoneh Esrei*, which begins אַתָּה חוֹנֵן לְאָדָם דַּעַת, *It is You*

Who favor man with wisdom. [Even during the harsh exile, when so many basic needs are unmet, intellectual advancement always remains the prime concern of the Jewish people.]

Rashbam observes that this request reflects the style of the priestly blessing: יְבָרֶכְךָ ה', *May HASHEM bless you*; וִיחֻנֶּךָּ, *And show you favor (Numbers 6:24, 25).*

יָאֵר פָּנָיו אִתָּנוּ סֶלָה — *May He display His luminous countenance with us, Selah.*

May He grant us success in all of our endeavors (*Radak*).

May He illuminate our minds so that we may perceive the wondrous lessons of the Torah (*Sforno*).

May we forever be a reflection of the Divine intellect, and thus display the צֶלֶם אֱלֹהִים, *the image of God*, which makes man capable of knowing God's will and endowing his physical existence with Divine holiness (*Tehillos Hashem*).

Rashbam observes that this wish alludes to the priestly benediction (Numbers 6:25) יָאֵר ה' פָּנָיו אֵלֶיךָ, *May HASHEM shine His face towards you.*

3. לָדַעַת בָּאָרֶץ דַּרְכֶּךָ — *To make known Your way on earth.*

We ask for intellectual enlightenment so that we may be equipped to spread Your teachings throughout the world. We yearn to guide mankind toward an appreciation of *Your way*, which refers to Your beneficence (*Rashi; Sforno*).

Mankind is baffled by the seemingly chaotic development of human affairs. If You will shine Your countenance upon Israel, this will demonstrate to all men that You do in fact guide world events upon a well defined path towards a clear-cut goal. Then mankind

67
1-4

For the Conductor, upon Neginos
a song with musical accompaniment.
² *May God favor us*
and bless us,
May He display His luminous countenance
with us, Selah.
³ *To make known Your way on earth,*
among all the peoples Your salvation.
⁴ *Then nations will acknowledge You,*
O God,
The nations will acknowledge You —
all of them.

will come to recognize דַּרְכֶּךָ, *Your way,*
in all affairs בָּאָרֶץ, *on earth (Hirsch).*

Hirsch notes that God's *way* is a dual concept, for it includes both the manner in which God guides world events and the pattern of conduct which God has directed man to follow. By shining His countenance upon the Jewish nation, God will make known both facets of His *way:* Mankind will recognize that human history is guided along Divinely designed paths towards the fulfillment of Divinely ordained goals; the blessings with which God favors the Jewish people will also lead mankind to adhere to the pattern of human conduct prescribed by God's Law and exemplified by the Jews.

This will fulfill the prophecy (*Isaiah* 11:9): *The earth shall be full of the knowledge of HASHEM, as the waters cover the sea (Radak).*

בְּכָל גּוֹיִם יְשׁוּעָתֶךָ — *Among all the peoples Your salvation.*

God's interest is not confined to Israel; He is also concerned with the welfare and salvation of the other peoples. One purpose of Israel's exile and dispersion was to expose all of the nations to the Torah's teachings, so that they might have an opportunity to accept the truth and be saved. The Sages (*Pesachim* 87b) taught that the Holy One, Blessed be He, exiled Israel among the nations in order to add proselytes to the Jewish people (*Shaarei Chaim*).

4. יוֹדוּךָ עַמִּים אֱלֹהִים — *[Then] nations will acknowledge You, O God.*

Gradually, Israel's benign influence will spread the Divine teachings amongst the nations, until every nation will acknowledge God and pay Him homage (*Hirsch*).[1]

1. *Rav Yosef Engel* (*Droshos Otzros Yosef* 8) demonstrates that the purpose of the *mitzvah* of סְפִירַת הָעוֹמֶר, *counting the Omer,* is to foster a heightened appreciation of God and of one's fellow man. The climax of this awareness is on the thirty-third day, *Lag B'Omer.*

The *Omer* period is designated as a time of mourning for the twenty-four thousand disciples of R' Akiva who died at this time; they suffered this punishment because they neither respected nor appreciated each other properly (*Yevamoos* 62b).

The plague which struck them ceased on the thirty-third day because it was then that they finally absorbed the lesson of the *Omer* and increased their appreciation for God and man.

The psalmist alludes to this here, because אֱלֹהִים is the thirty-third word in this composition of forty-nine words. It marks the climax: יוֹדוּךָ עַמִּים אֱלֹהִים, *The nations will acknowledge You, O God.*

ה יִשְׂמְחוּ וִירַנְּנוּ לְאֻמִּים כִּי־תִשְׁפֹּט עַמִּים
מִישֹׁר וּלְאֻמִּים | בָּאָרֶץ תַּנְחֵם סֶלָה:
ו יוֹדוּךָ עַמִּים | אֱלֹהִים יוֹדוּךָ עַמִּים כֻּלָּם:
ז אֶרֶץ נָתְנָה יְבוּלָהּ יְבָרְכֵנוּ אֱלֹהִים
ח אֱלֹהֵינוּ: יְבָרְכֵנוּ אֱלֹהִים וְיִירְאוּ אוֹתוֹ
כָּל־אַפְסֵי־אָרֶץ:

יוֹדוּךָ עַמִּים כֻּלָּם — *The nations
acknowledge You—all of them.*

Ultimately, the message of God will
penetrate every corner of the land and
all nations will worship Him (Hirsch).

5. יִשְׂמְחוּ וִירַנְּנוּ לְאֻמִּים — *Nations will be
glad and sing for joy.*

עַם and לְאֹם both mean *nation.* לְאֹם
refers to the *state* which governs a people and represents to the outside world
the particular striving of that people. So
long as nations are selfish and ac-
quisitive, their outside stance, their
nationalistic posture, will reflect
selfishness; but ultimately, all national
governments will discard their present
policy of selfish isolation and recognize
that the welfare of all men depends on
the establishment of a harmonious community of nonaggressive nations
joyously united in the worship of God.

עַם is *a unified national community,*
separate from all other nations. International dissension and animosity are
inevitable, so long as each nation seeks
only its own welfare (Hirsch).

Kli Chemdah comments that the
tolerant לְאֻמִּים, *states,* respected the exiles of Israel as their equals; they
regarded them as representatives of a
worthy fellow nation, rather than as
despised foreigners. Since these states
with their enlightened goals of world
unity and mutual respect are compatible
with Israel's Messianic aspirations, they
will rejoice upon the advent of the
Redeemer.

כִּי תִשְׁפֹּט עַמִּים מִישֹׁר — *Because You will
judge the nations with fairness.*

[Each individual עַם, *national com-*

munity, considers itself superior and
refuses to treat Israel as its equal. They
are destined to undergo Divine judgment for their failure to ensure מִישֹׁר,
fairness, equity.]

וּלְאֻמִּים בָּאָרֶץ תַּנְחֵם סֶלָה — *And the nations on earth You will guide, Selah.*

[In this world, the לְאֻמִּים, *states,*
strive to achieve מִישֹׁר, *equity* and
fairness, as a means toward the creation
of a stable world balance of power.
They seek to create an international
order whose benefits would exceed the
advantages experienced by the self-
seeking, uncooperative עַמִּים, *national
communities.* Although their motives are
to further their own ends rather than to
serve God, they nevertheless move in
the direction of establishing a moral,
ethical order; for that they deserve to be
rewarded. The *states* will receive their
reward when God openly guides human
affairs to the establishment of an eternal
human brotherhood which recognizes
no borders or nationalities.]

6. יוֹדוּךָ עַמִּים אֱלֹהִים — *[Then] nations
will acknowledge You, O God.*

This is a repetition of verse 4. According to *Sforno* and *Rashbam,* verse 4
introduces verse 5, signifying that the
nations will given thanks when You
judge them with fairness [and restore
the harmony of the social order]. Verse
6 introduces verse 7, indicating *the nations will acknowledge* [i.e., give
thanks] — when *the earth has yielded its
produce* [and the earth's original agricultural abundance is restored].

According to *Hirsch,* the use of the
word *Selah* to conclude verses 2, 5, and

⁵ Nations will be glad
   and sing for joy
Because You will judge the nations
   with fairness,
And the nations on earth
   You will guide, Selah.
⁶ Then nations will acknowledge You,
   O God,
The nations will acknowledge You —
   all of them.
⁷ The earth has yielded its produce,
   may God, our own God, bless us.
⁸ May God bless us
   and may all the ends of the earth fear Him.

8 indicates that the psalm is divided into three parts. They correspond to the three distinct phases in which mankind will fulfill its ultimate Divinely ordained mission. First (vs. 1-2), only the Jewish people will come to recognize and to obey God's will. Second (vs. 3-5), the leaders of all the nations will submit to God's authority and worship Him. Third and finally (verses 6-8), all people will learn to worship God directly; at this point, their national leaders will become superfluous and give up their positions of privilege and power.

As Hirsch explains the repetition of this verse, the general populace will be initially incapable of recognizing God's majesty and His Law on their own. Only under the guidance and influence of their intelligent leaders will they develop sufficient insight to offer thanks to God and to serve Him.

Later, when the recognition of God's sovereignty spreads worldwide, all men will submit to God and render homage to Him without any intermediary. Then the newly enlightened nations (i.e., the general populace) will acknowledge God of their own accord, without re-quiring their leaders' example and instructions.

7. אֶרֶץ נָתְנָה יְבוּלָהּ — The earth has yielded its produce.

[The political renaissance of the future will be accompanied by an agricultural rebirth, for the world's spiritual development will pervade the earth and affect the soil. The Talmud (Sanhedrin 98a) notes that the advent of Redemption will be heralded by agricultural changes: You mountains of Israel shall sprout forth your branches and yield your fruit to my people Israel, for they are at hand to arrive (Ezekiel 36:8).]

Radak explains that prior to the Redemption, sin will pollute the atmosphere and disturb the balance of the water cycle. God warned Israel not to stray after false gods, for the result would be וְעָצַר אֶת הַשָּׁמַיִם וְלֹא יִהְיֶה מָטָר וְהָאֲדָמָה לֹא תִתֵּן אֶת יְבוּלָהּ, He will hold back the heavens and there will be no rain, and the earth will not give forth its produce (Deuteronomy 11:17).

In the future, however, the earth will yield its bounty effortlessly without any human cultivation or labor. Moreover,

it will produce a finished product, not merely the raw, unprocessed crop. The Sages say (*Kesubos* 111b) that the trees are destined to grow baked loaves of the finest flour *(Tehillos Hashem)*.

יְבָרְכֵנוּ אֱלֹהִים אֱלֹהֵינוּ — *May God, our own God, bless us.*

It is in the power of Israel to transform אֱלֹהִים, the Divine Name which denotes God's sovereignty over all the nations, into their personal deity, אֱלֹהֵינוּ, *our God*, who attends to their needs with special concern. Israel turns to God with unreserved devotion. He reciprocates by vouchsafing His uniquely paternal Providence to the Jewish people *(Kedushas Levi)*.

8. יְבָרְכֵנוּ אֱלֹהִים — *May God bless us.*

After the Redemption, the nation of Israel will spread throughout the earth, as God had promised the Patriarch Jacob (*Genesis* 28:14): וְהָיָה זַרְעֲךָ כַּעֲפַר הָאָרֶץ וּפָרַצְתָּ יָמָּה וָקֵדְמָה וְצָפֹנָה וָנֶגְבָּה, *And your seed shall be like the dust of the earth and shall spread abroad to the west and to the east and to the north and to the south* (Sforno).

וְיִירְאוּ אוֹתוֹ כָּל אַפְסֵי אָרֶץ — *And may all the ends of the earth fear Him.*

Even the most remote civilizations, isolated at the ends of the earth, are destined to recognize God's glory *(Ibn Ezra)*.

When the nations witness the splendid fortunes of Israel after the Redemption, they will be imbued with awe before the Almighty for they will reason that God favored the Jewish people only because of their God-fearing behavior. The nations will conclude that they should follow Israel's example; thus, they will join Israel in rendering homage to God *(Rashi)*.

מזמור סח 68

The theme of this composition is the Revelation at Sinai, which the psalmist describes with unsurpassed eloquence and ecstasy. This Revelation at Sinai affected the whole world; it was a cataclysmic event, an upheaval second only to the Creation in its colossal proportions.

From this traumatic transformation, Israel emerged as the Chosen People, a nation rising heavenward in obedience to the Divine summons; and as this one nation ascended, the seventy alien societies fell, eternally estranged, for they had rejected God's invitation to join His ranks.

As God drew closer to Israel, the nations recoiled further from the Jewish people; each fresh outpouring of Divine love for the sacred nation was met with a new wave of bitter hatred from the gentiles. The Talmud explains (Shabbos 89b) that Mount Sinai (סִינַי) received this name because it is the source of the nations' hatred (שִׂנְאָה) for the Jews. It also was called Chorev (חוֹרֵב), the Talmud continues, because from this mountain, devastation (חוּרְבָּן), descended upon the nations. Therefore, the opening verses of this psalm describe the gentiles' many attempts to surround and destroy Israel.

The Gaon of Vilna (Maaseh Rav 196) designates this as the Song of the Day for the second day of Shavuos, which is the festival commemorating the Sinaitic Revelation.

א־ב לַמְנַצֵּחַ לְדָוִד מִזְמוֹר שִׁיר: יָקוּם אֱלֹהִים
יָפוּצוּ אוֹיְבָיו וְיָנוּסוּ מְשַׂנְאָיו מִפָּנָיו:
ג כְּהִנְדֹּף עָשָׁן תִּנְדֹּף כְּהִמֵּס דּוֹנַג מִפְּנֵי־אֵשׁ

1. לַמְנַצֵּחַ — For the Conductor.

Literally, this word may also be rendered: *To Him who causes victory* [see comm. 4:1]. The opening verses of this psalm are a plea for victory over the nations who assault and threaten Israel [see *Prefatory Remarks*].

Dorash Moshe points out that the first two letters of this word, ל, *lamed* and מ, *mem*, together have a numerical value of 70, indicating that the psalmist prays to be נָצָה, *victorious* over the seventy gentile nations of the world.

Rashi identifies Amalek as the specific foe here. [Amalek, a vicious, godless enemy, was the first nation to attack Israel as the Jews were journeying towards Sinai to accept the Torah.]

Ibn Yachya and *Malbim* contend that these introductory verses refer instead to Ammon, Moab, Edom, and Aram, which beleaguered Israel in the reign of David [see II *Samuel*, Chapter 8; see also *Ibn Ezra, Psalms* 68:1].

Radak maintains that this prayer alludes to Sennacherib of Assyria, who laid siege to Jerusalem, the citadel of King Chizkiyahu.

Meiri suggests that the psalmist here foretells the encircling of the Holy City which will occur during the Messianic battle of Gog and Magog.

2. יָקוּם אֱלֹהִים — Let God arise.

[This verse is based on *Numbers* 10:35, וַיְהִי בִּנְסֹעַ הָאָרֹן וַיֹּאמֶר מֹשֶׁה קוּמָה ה' וְיָפֻצוּ אֹיְבֶיךָ וְיָנֻסוּ מְשַׂנְאֶיךָ מִפָּנֶיךָ, *And it came to pass when the Ark journeyed forward that Moses said: 'Arise, HASHEM, and let Your foes be scattered and let those who hate You flee before You.'*

Since the Torah given at Sinai was the source of the gentiles' undying hatred of Israel (see *Prefatory Remarks*), it is fitting that the very same Torah, deposited in the Holy Ark,

should lead Israel into battle against its adversaries.]

Whereas Moses addressed God directly, in the second person, and described Him as the *Dispenser of Mercy*: קוּמָה ה', *Arise HASHEM*, David speaks indirectly, in the third person, and pleads with the *Dispenser of Strict Justice*: יָקוּם אֱלֹהִים, *Let God arise* (*Chazah Zion; Toras Chesed*).

Eretz HaChaim explains that Moses was primarily concerned with the merciful salvation of Israel and was content to have the militant gentile nations scattered. David, however, perceived that the nations of every generation posed a mortal danger to Israel, a threat which demanded a severe, final response. Therefore, he invoked God's strict justice to utterly destroy the enemies, saying (v. 3), *'Let the wicked perish in the face of God.'*

יָפוּצוּ אוֹיְבָיו — Let His enemies be scattered.

Rashi (*Numbers* 10:35) describes these enemies as massed in tight assault formation. [Thus David prays, 'Let their strong ranks be broken and their staunch fighters dispersed.']

According to *Malbim*, the אוֹיֵב is far more dangerous than the שׂוֹנֵא. The former actually demonstrates his hatred with malicious actions, whereas the latter merely harbors animosity in his heart [see *comm.* of *Malbim* to 18:18].

Since the אוֹיֵב actually engages in battle, he will be beaten and *scattered*. The שׂוֹנֵא, however, stands back in the rear, concentrating on battle strategy. When Israel triumphs, he *flees*.

וְיָנוּסוּ מְשַׂנְאָיו מִפָּנָיו — And let His foes [lit., *those who hate Him*] *flee before Him.*

Rashi (*Numbers* 10:35) comments that these are the pursuers [who chase

For the Conductor, by David,
  a song with musical accompaniment.
² Let God arise,
 let His enemies be scattered;
And let His foes
 flee before Him.
³ As smoke is dispersed,
 so disperse them;
As wax melts before the fire,

---

after Israel. David prays, 'Let them now take to their heels and flee before the might of Israel.']

Rashi goes on to explain that מְשַׂנְאָיו, *those who hate Him* (i.e., God), refers to whoever despises and attacks Israel. Similarly, we read (83:3-4): וּמְשַׂנְאֶיךָ נָשְׂאוּ רֹאשׁ, *And those who hate You have lifted [their] head.* How is their hatred demonstrated? עַל עַמְּךָ יַעֲרִימוּ סוֹד, *They take deceptive counsel against Your nation.* [1]

3. כְּהִנְדֹּף עָשָׁן תִּנְדֹּף — *As smoke is dispersed, so disperse [them].*

The success of the wicked is an illusion resembling the thick smoke billowing through a chimney. This seemingly solid mass will soon dissipate into a wisp, as the wind drives the smoke away. This echoes the verse (37:20) וְאֹיְבֵי ה' ... כָּלוּ בֶעָשָׁן כָּלוּ, *The foes of HASHEM ... they vanish, in smoke they vanish (Midrash Shocher Tov).*

Smoke and vapor, which always rise, symbolize the haughty man whose pride stirs him with aspirations to climb even higher on the ladder of power and success *(Sforno).*

Like a dark and ominous column of smoke rising heavenward, the wicked momentarily seem to represent real danger. Yet smoke's nature dictates that it must gradually fade away, a process hastened by the wind. Similarly, evil cannot long endure; it will fade away of its own accord, and its disintegration will be accelerated by God's hidden guidance of the events of human history. All evildoers will perish, because the very nature of evil is ephemeral and lacks enduring reality *(Hirsch).*

כְּהִמֵּס דּוֹנַג מִפְּנֵי אֵשׁ — *As wax melts before the fire.*

The psalmist does not use the simile of wax completely consumed בָּאֵשׁ, *in the fire,* but speaks only of the wax melted מִפְּנֵי אֵשׁ, *before the fire (Tehillas Hashem).*

Shaarei Chaim explains that in the previous verse, two categories of adversaries were described. The אוֹיֵב, *foe,* poses an actual physical threat. He must be completely destroyed, like smoke, which vanishes in the wind.

However, the שׂוֹנֵא, *enemy,* merely contemplates evil in his heart. If he changes his attitude, he can be saved.

---

1. [The root of anti-Semitism is *not* the instinctive loathing and revulsion which people feel for an alien. Rather, this perverse enmity manifests a deep strait of bitter antagonism against all that is truly sacred and representative of God's universal dominion. The enemy of Israel despises the burdensome authority of God.

This truth is illustrated by Hitler, who explained that he was motivated to obliterate the Jewish people 'because they cursed civilization with a conscience.'

Although the anti-Semite may espouse other religions with fanatic zeal, this is merely *deceptive counsel* (83:4), i.e., an attempt to cunningly disguise his godlessness.]

ד יֹאבְדוּ רְשָׁעִים מִפְּנֵי אֱלֹהִים: וְצַדִּיקִים
יִשְׂמְחוּ יַעַלְצוּ לִפְנֵי אֱלֹהִים וְיָשִׂישׂוּ
ה בְשִׂמְחָה: שִׁירוּ | לֵאלֹהִים זַמְּרוּ שְׁמוֹ סֹלּוּ
לָרֹכֵב בָּעֲרָבוֹת בְּיָהּ שְׁמוֹ וְעִלְזוּ לְפָנָיו:

Thus, he resembles melted wax which retains its substance, although its outer shape is transformed.

Malbim observes that this verse parallels the preceding verse, which repeated Moses' proclamation as the camp of Israel journeyed in the wilderness. By day, the camp was led by the עַמּוּד עָנָן, *Pillar of Cloud*, which cleared a path before them. Now the psalmist requests a similar salvation: *Disperse all obstacles and enemies in their path as smoke is dispersed.*

By night, the עַמּוּד אֵשׁ, *Pillar of Fire* went before them. Therefore, the psalmist makes a parallel request, that the present enemy melt *before the fire.*

יֹאבְדוּ רְשָׁעִים מִפְּנֵי אֱלֹהִים — *So let the wicked perish in the face of God.*

Rashi observes that in the days of Moses, God's wrath was kindled against the opponents of Israel. Moses addressed the Holy Ark as it returned from battle, וּבְנֻחֹה יֹאמַר שׁוּבָה ה' רִבְבוֹת אַלְפֵי יִשְׂרָאֵל, *And when it came to rest, he said: 'Rest, HASHEM, upon the myriads and thousands of Israel'* (Numbers 10:36).

[This implies, 'Let the enemy armies perish but allow the armies of Israel to return home unscathed, with their full regiments of myriads and thousands' (*Daas Zekeinim*, Numbers 10:36).]

4. וְצַדִּיקִים יִשְׂמְחוּ יַעַלְצוּ לִפְנֵי אֱלֹהִים — *But as for the righteous — let them be glad, let them exult before God.*

Eretz HaChaim comments that the Holy Ark scattered the enemies of the Almighty, but the devout unite and rejoice in the Ark's presence, as Scripture states, *And David danced before [the Ark of] HASHEM with all his might* (II Samuel 6:14). In addition, the Ark was

a source of joy for all in its vicinity; when the Ark was housed in the home of Oved Edom of Gat for three months, his family was greatly blessed by its presence (II *Samuel* 6:11).

[In *comm.* to 9:3, it was explained that עָלַץ is related to חָלַץ, *to release from bonds*; it is an expression of joyous release from depression and confinement.

The wicked feel cramped and very uneasy in the presence of God. The sight of the Temple or the Holy Ark inhibits their instinctive pursuit of the profane and restricts their promiscuous abandon.

The righteous, however, are inspired by the holy precincts. All of their dormant talents and energies are suddenly released, as they strive to serve their Creator. This sudden self-realization gives rise to an indescribable sense of exultation.]

Alshich and *Sforno* perceive here a reference to that fire which simultaneously melts the wicked like wax (v. 3), and strengthens the righteous. The *Talmud* (*Nedarim* 8b) teaches that in the future, God will remove the blazing sun from its protective sheath. Then, its fierce heat will consume the wicked, while it heals the righteous.

וְיָשִׂישׂוּ בְשִׂמְחָה — *Let them rejoice with gladness.*

The short-lived *gladness* derived from material pleasures eventually leaves a vacuum in the heart, but the spiritual *gladness* derived from God's service causes the devout to *rejoice* perpetually (*Binah L'ittim*).

Radak maintains that this psalm refers to the downfall of Sennacherib [see v. 1], which took place on the first night of Passover. He explains that

so let the wicked perish in the face of God.

⁴ But as for the righteous —

let them be glad,

Let them exalt before God;

let them rejoice with gladness.

⁵ Sing to God,

make music for His Name,

Extol Him

Who rides in Aravos, With YAH His Name

and exult before Him.

when King Chizkiyahu and his nation were saved from the Assyrian host they *rejoiced* over the Jews' redemption from Egypt [which is commemorated by the Festival of Passover] *with* [additional] *gladness* because of their deliverance from Sennacherib.

5. שִׁירוּ לֵאלֹהִים זַמְּרוּ שְׁמוֹ — *Sing to God, make music [for] His Name.*

[See *comm.* to 30:1.]

When the children of Israel *rejoice with gladness (v. 4),* every celebrant will encourage his comrade to exult and sing hymns of praise *(Ibn Ezra).*

They will say זַמְּרוּ [cognate with זוֹמֵר, *to prune*] שְׁמוֹ, implying, 'If you remove the distractions which distort clear perception of His Name and deeds, then you will be inspired to sing' *(Chasam Sofer).*

סֹלּוּ — *Extol (Rashi; Radak; Ibn Ezra; Rashbam).*

[Cf. *Proverbs* 4:8, סַלְסְלֶהָ וּתְרוֹמְמֶךָּ, *Extol her and she will elevate you.*]

Rabbi Moshe (quoted in *Ibn Ezra*), *Radak,* and *Hirsch* relate סֹלּוּ to סָלַל, *to raise up,* from which are derived מְסִלָּה, *highway,* and סוּלָּם, *ladder.* [Cf. *Isaiah* 62:10, סֹלּוּ סֹלּוּ הַמְסִלָּה, *Build up, build up, the road. See comm.* to 3:3.]

Chasam Sofer paraphrases this exhortation: 'Construct a mental highway upon which your spirits can rise towards God!'

לָרֹכֵב — *(To) Him Who rides.*

רֹכֵב denotes the total mastery of the horseman over his steed. The metaphor is used to describe the firm guidance with which God directs the events of the world *(Radak; Hirsch).* We find similar references later in this psalm, where we read of רֶכֶב אֱלֹהִים, *the chariot of God* (v. 18), which appeared at Sinai, and רֹכֵב בִּשְׁמֵי שְׁמֵי קֶדֶם, *The Rider upon the loftiest of primeval heavens (v. 34) (Ibn Ezra).*

[God manifests His mastery only to the extent that people recognize it. As man's comprehension increases, God's guidance expands, as Scripture states, רֹכֵב שָׁמַיִם בְּעֶזְרֶךָ, *He rides the heavens with your* [Israel's] *help (Deuteronomy 33:26).*]

בָּעֲרָבוֹת — *In Aravos.*

This is the highest heaven, where God sits upon [i.e., rides] His great throne *(Targum).*

This heaven controls the motions and orbits of all the lower spheres *(Radak).*

The *Talmud (Chagiga* 12a) describes the loftiest of the seven celestial heavens as עֲרָבוֹת, *Aravos,* where 'God stores righteousness, justice, and charity.' There rest the treasuries of life, peace, and blessing. The highest of the heavenly spheres also holds the souls of the *tzaddikim,* the souls which have not yet come to life, and the dew by means of which God will resuscitate the dead.

ו אֲבִי יְתוֹמִים וְדַיַּן אַלְמָנוֹת אֱלֹהִים בִּמְעוֹן
ז קָדְשׁוֹ: אֱלֹהִים ׀ מוֹשִׁיב יְחִידִים ׀ בַּיְתָה

God called it עֲרָבוֹת because the righteous deeds of the *tzaddikim* were עֲרֵבִים, *sweet and desirable*, to Him. He planted their accomplishments in this heaven, where they bear the fruit of providing the universe with spiritual enrichment (*Midrash Shocher Tov*, 114).

[This means that by virtue of the deeds and understanding of the righteous, God attains a higher degree of spiritual mastery. It was His will that His Presence be obscure on earth, but that it become revealed as a result of the spiritual achievements of virtuous people.]

בְּיָהּ שְׁמוֹ — *With YAH His Name.*

This signifies, *extol Him* with this unique designation (*Radak*). This Divine Name denotes God's awesomeness, as the prophet (*Isaiah* 26:4) says, כִּי בְּיָהּ ה' צוּר עוֹלָמִים which *Targum* renders: *Through the awesome might of HASHEM you will find Salvation.* This is similar to a previous exhortation of the psalmist (2:11), *Serve HASHEM in awe and rejoice with trembling* (*Rashi*).

The *Talmud* (*Menachos* 29b) interprets *Isaiah* 26:4 thus: With the letters of יָהּ, YAH, HASHEM fashioned (צוּר) *the worlds*. First, He created the World to Come with the smallest letter, י, *yud*, because that world is reserved for the humble people who minimize their worth. Their number is very small.

Then He made This World with the letter ה, *he*, which is open on the bottom, to symbolize that life offers many temptations to succumb to sin, and thus to descend to damnation. The small opening at the top of the left leg of the ה implies that only a fraction of mankind

will rise to heaven (*Maseches Heicholos*, Chapter 7).

וְעָלְזוּ לְפָנָיו — *And exult before Him.*

The verse begins with the Name אֱלֹהִים, which denotes God as the *Dispenser of Strict Justice*, but concludes with a reference to יָהּ, which is only half of the Name יְהוּ"ה, which denotes God as the *Dispenser of Mercy*. *Sforno's* commentary implies that God does not exercise His full mercy as long as He must dispense severe but just punishments. Nevertheless, even when the Divine mercy must be tempered, *exult before Him*, for He utilizes all His attributes only to benefit man.

6. [In the preceding verse, the people were encouraged to compose a hymn to praise and extol God. They responded with the following composition, which continues until the end of this psalm (*Rashi*).]

אֲבִי יְתוֹמִים וְדַיַּן אַלְמָנוֹת — *Father of orphans and Judge of widows.*

Radak comments that although God soars in the loftiest heights of *Aravos*, He remains intimately involved in the affairs of the weakest and least prominent people. He is a father to the orphan, who desperately needs a parent.[1] Since she is often beleaguered by those who encroach upon her estate and possessions, the אַלְמָנָה, *widow*, resembles an אָלֵם, *mute*, unable to plead on her own behalf (*Hirsch*). Therefore God protects the widow by defending her before the court.

The *Talmud* (*Megillah* 31b) notes that this juxtaposition of verses 5 and 6 illustrates the rule: כָּל מָקוֹם שֶׁאַתָּה מוֹצֵא גְבוּרָתוֹ שֶׁל הַקְּבָּ"ה שָׁם אַתָּה מוֹצֵא

1. When *Rambam* (*Hilchos Nachalos* 11:12) codifies the laws governing the אַפּוֹטְרוֹפּוֹס, *trustee*, whom the court appoints as guardian over the estate of the orphans, he concludes, 'Although the trustee is not required to render an exact accounting of his transactions, he should personally keep a scrupulously precise account for himself, bearing in mind that the protector of the orphans is none other than God Himself, *Who rides in Aravos* and Who is *Father of orphans.*

⁶ *Father of orphans and Judge of widows*
is God in the habitation of His holiness.
⁷ *God gathers the lonely into a family,*

עֲנְוְתָנוּתוֹ, *whenever Scripture refers to God's might, it immediately mentions His humbleness.*

Rashi interprets this verse as a metaphorical reference to Israel, a people abandoned by the world like a homeless orphan. Only God is our Father. At the time of the destruction, the tragedy was compounded because יְתוֹמִים הָיִינוּ וְאֵין אָב, *we have become orphans and fatherless* (Lamentations 5:3), implying that even our Father in Heaven rejected us.

At that time, Jerusalem was desolate: הָיְתָה כְּאַלְמָנָה, *it became like a widow* (Lamentations 1:1). In that bitter moment, God became *Judge of widows* (i.e., of Jerusalem).

Even in exile, however, we are not completely lost; we are not like orphans or widows whose protection is dead. Rather, God is only temporarily estranged from His people. He resembles the father and husband who journeyed to a distant land but will eventually return (*Midrash Shocher Tov*, 2).

אֱלֹהִים בִּמְעוֹן קָדְשׁוֹ — *Is God in the habitation of His holiness.*

Although God's glory soars to the celestial heights, He still cares for the lowest creatures on earth and guides their ways (*Ibn Ezra*).

7. אֱלֹהִים מוֹשִׁיב יְחִידִים בַּיְתָה — *God gathers* [lit. *settles*] *the lonely into a family* [lit. *house*].

[The word בַּיְתָה, *house*, does not refer to an architectural structure but to the family as a social unit.] When the children of Israel were isolated and scat-

tered throughout the land of Egypt, God gathered them together to create a unified nation (*Rashi*).

Meiri adds that in contrast to the Egyptian masses, the Jews were not nameless serfs. Each one was a יָחִיד, *individual*, outstanding, distinguished, and of unique merit. When the sons of Jacob descended to Egypt, they were a small band of extraordinary individuals; the Jews maintained their personal identity until they later departed in multitudes as עַם סְגוּלָה, *a treasured nation*.

Similarly, at the time of the future Messianic redemption, the Jews will be isolated and dispersed to the very ends of the earth. Yet, God will gather them בַּיְתָה, *to their ancient homeland*, the Land of Israel.

The Rabbis (*Sotah* 2a) interpret this passage homiletically as a reference to the Divine art of matchmaking, for it is a superhuman task to take יְחִידִים, *lonely individuals*, who may be strangers and emotional opposites with conflicting personal priorities and preferences, and to fuse them into one unit. God alone can *gather* [*them*] *into a family*, because at the moment of conception, a בַּת קוֹל, *heavenly voice*, proclaims the Divine decree that the body and soul of the future mates should develop in such a manner that they later become a single harmonious whole. Because the partners were intended and fashioned for one another, the marriage ceremony which takes place later is tantamount to the reunion of two temporarily separated parts of an organism which are being returned to their original unity.[1]

1. A Roman noblewoman once asked Rabbi Yose ben Chalafta how long it took God to create the world. 'Six days,' he replied.
  'And what has He been doing since then?', she inquired.
  'He sits and makes matches,' said Rabbi Yose.
  'What!' cried the matron incredulously. 'This is the Divine craft? Why, even I can make

מוֹצִיא אֲסִירִים בַּכּוֹשָׁרוֹת אַךְ סוֹרְרִים
שָׁכְנוּ צְחִיחָה: אֱלֹהִים בְּצֵאתְךָ לִפְנֵי עַמֶּךָ ח
בְּצַעְדְּךָ בִישִׁימוֹן סֶלָה: אֶרֶץ רָעָשָׁה | אַף־ ט

מוֹצִיא אֲסִירִים בַּכּוֹשָׁרוֹת — *He releases the prisoners at suitable moments.*

God redeemed Israel from Egypt in the most *suitable* (כָּשֵׁר) season of the year — springtime — for then the weather is optimal for traveling on the road; it is neither too hot nor too cold (*Rashi*).

Ibn Ezra, Radak, and *Meiri* translate כּוֹשָׁרוֹת as *bonds* (cognate with קוֹשָׁרוֹת with the כ, *kaf*, in place of the ק, *kuf*): *God releases the prisoners from their bonds.*

However, *Hirsch* notes that בַּכּוֹשָׁרוֹת literally means *with their bonds.* [This teaches that even though the Jews had been physically liberated from Egypt, spiritually, they remained in bondage, for they were enslaved by ignorance, doubts, and their personal desires. The Children of Israel achieved spiritual independence only after God enlightened their minds by the revelation of the Torah at Sinai.]

The Sages render בַּכּוֹשָׁרוֹת as a contraction of the words בְּכִי, *weeping,* and שִׁירוֹת, *songs.* When Israel was released from bondage, it was a time of *weeping* for the Egyptians and of *song* for the Jews, who were redeemed in the merit of their worthy forefathers (*Tanchuma, Boh* 1).

According to the *Midrash,* this phrase also relates to the formation of the family unit (mentioned at the beginning of this verse). When God matches a couple, their union is undoubtedly suitable and has the potential for hap-

piness. Ultimately, however, only the efforts of husband and wife determine whether or not the match will succeed. If they appreciate the wisdom of God's choice, the resulting happiness will cause them to sing שִׁירוֹת, *songs,* of joy and gratitude; but if they refuse to accept their Divinely designated mates, they will be engulfed in unhappy בְּכִי, *weeping* (*Bereishis Rabbah* 68:4).

Furthermore, if the couple is God-fearing, they will מוֹצִיא אֲסִירִים בַּכּוֹשָׁרוֹת, *bring forth* scholarly sons who are able to decide what is halachically אָסוּר, *prohibited,* or כָּשֵׁר, *permitted;* but if the couple is not meritorious, their son will be an ignoramus whose parched mind is barren of Torah knowledge.

אַךְ סוֹרְרִים שָׁכְנוּ צְחִיחָה — *Only the rebellious dwell in the thirsty land.*

When the Jews were redeemed from Egypt, they left behind a parched and barren land which had been ravaged by plagues. The erstwhile Jewish אֲסִירִים, *prisoners,* had been redeemed בַּכּוֹשָׁרוֹת, *at the suitable moment* — springtime, the most pleasant season of the year (*Rashi*).

[The verse implies that the Egyptians deserved this punishment because they were סוֹרְרִים, *rebellious,* against God.]

According to *Radak,* this entire verse refers to the downfall of Sennacherib, who besieged Jerusalem with his hordes. The Jews, trapped in the city, were a handful of יְחִידִים, *lonely individuals,* but God *released these*

matches!' [*Radal* explains that she denied that Divine Providence was a factor in the successful matching of men and women.]

'Perhaps it is easy for you to accomplish this,' declared Rabbi Yose, 'but in God's eyes, making matches is as difficult as splitting the sea.'

The noblewoman took one thousand manservants and one thousand maidservants and lined them up in two rows facing one another. She walked between the rows and arbitrarily decided, 'This one will marry this one; this one will marry this one.' She then sent the new couples home for the night.

[In line with the above-noted comment of *Radal,* she arrogantly attempted to demonstrate

He releases the prisoners

at suitable moments,

Only the rebellious

dwell in the thirsty land.

⁸ O God when You went forth

before Your nation,

When You marched through the wilderness, Selah.

---

prisoners from their bonds, with all the captives who had been kept in the camp of the Assyrians. An angel smote the Assyrian soldiers, burning their souls but leaving their bodies intact. Since these *rebellious* upstarts who challenged the sovereignty of God died without any bodily wounds, it appeared as if they died of thirst *in the thirsty land.*

8. אֱלֹהִים בְּצֵאתְךָ לִפְנֵי עַמֶּךְ — *O God, when You went forth before Your nation.*

In the wilderness, God's Pillar of Cloud went before them by day and His Pillar of Fire, by night *(Targum; Sforno).*

God's Holy Ark went out to battle before them to assure their victory *(Radak).*

According to *Pirkei d'Rabbi Eliezer* (Chapter 41), this alludes to the Jews' deep sleep on the night prior to the receiving of the Torah at Sinai. The night was very short, and the people overslept until two hours after daybreak. *God went forth* from heaven and arrived at Sinai *before the nation.* Moses hastily went through the camp to arouse the people, saying, 'Arise, for the Groom has already arrived, and He is waiting to escort His bride to the wed-

ding canopy! God is waiting to enter into a Torah covenant with Israel.'

[Ever since, it has been customary for Jews to stay awake the entire night of Shavuos, in order to atone for that first Shavuos night, when they overslept *(Mogen Avrhohom; Orach Chaim* 494).]

בְּצַעְדְּךָ — *When You marched.*

Hirsch defines צַעַד as a *slow, measured stride.* God did not hurry through the wilderness; He caused Israel to journey slowly and deliberately, so that the Jews would sense God's nearness and His guidance with their every step.

בִּישִׁימוֹן — *Through* [lit. *in] the wilderness.*

God directed His gracious providence towards Israel throughout their forty-year sojourn in the שְׁמָמָה, *desolation (Targum);* this Divine providence was especially evident when the Jews arrived at Sinai, which is also known as חוֹרֵב, *desolation (Sforno).*

[God gave the Torah in an uninhabited wilderness in order to emphasize that the authority of the Torah is not limited to one specific society or civilization. Torah life can flourish even in a forsaken wasteland.]

---

that such human relationships were random and unregulatd by God's wisdom. This being the case, God withdrew the guidance He normally extends to people engaged in matchmaking.]

The following morning, all the servants converged upon her. One had a head wound, another had an injured eye, a third had a broken leg. Each shouted that he could not tolerate his new mate.

Thereupon, the noblewoman summoned Rabbi Yose and admitted, 'There is no god like your God, and no truth comparable to your Torah. Your statement [that God alone makes fitting matches] is proper and just' *(Bereishis Rabbah* 68:4).

שָׁמַיִם נָטְפוּ מִפְּנֵי אֱלֹהִים זֶה סִינַי מִפְּנֵי
אֱלֹהִים אֱלֹהֵי יִשְׂרָאֵל: גֶּשֶׁם נְדָבוֹת תָּנִיף
אֱלֹהִים נַחֲלָתְךָ וְנִלְאָה אַתָּה כוֹנַנְתָּהּ:
יא חַיָּתְךָ יָשְׁבוּ־בָהּ תָּכִין בְּטוֹבָתְךָ לֶעָנִי

סֶלָה — *Selah* [lit. *forever;* see *comm.* 3:3].

In the wilderness, God demonstrated that He provides a deliverance from distress *forever*, i.e., at all times (*Rashi*).

9. אֶרֶץ רָעָשָׁה — *The earth roared.*

When the Torah was given, Mount Sinai quaked in the presence of God, as Scripture states (*Exodus* 19:18), *And the entire mountain trembled greatly.* The mighty nations of the earth also shuddered in awe as God's might was revealed at Sinai (*Radak*).

אַף שָׁמַיִם נָטְפוּ — *Even the heavens dripped.*

The skies over Sinai became dark and forbidding, as if they were about to *drip* with rain. Similar language is used in 18:12: *He made darkness His concealment ... dark waters and thick clouds* (*Radak*).

מִפְּנֵי אֱלֹהִים — *Before the Presence of* [lit. *because of*] *God.*

The earth and the heavens quaked in fear because of אֱלֹהִים, *the Dispenser of Strict Justice,* for He created the world on the condition [*Avodah Zarah* 5a] that the universe will endure only if Israel accepts the Torah. If the Torah is rejected, then the world has no purpose, and the entire universe will return to nothingness (*Tehillos Hashem*).

זֶה סִינַי — *This is Sinai.*

Clouds of smoke billowed from Sinai as from a fiery oven (*Targum*). [This signified God's awesome presence.]

מִפְּנֵי אֱלֹהִים אֱלֹהֵי יִשְׂרָאֵל — *Before the Presence of God, the God of Israel.*

Dorash Moshe points out that the numerical value of סִינַי, *Sinai,* (130) is equal to that of סֻלָּם, *ladder,* because

Sinai is the *'ladder'* upon which the souls of Israel ascend in order to stand *before the Presence of God.*

10. גֶּשֶׁם נְדָבוֹת תָּנִיף אֱלֹהִים — *A generous rain did You lavish* [lit. *pour*], *O God.*

Even as *the heavens dripped* afflictions and suffering upon the gentiles who rejected the Torah (*v.* 9), the skies lavished bountiful, blessed rains upon the Jews, who accepted the Torah (*Radak*).

The Children of Israel were overawed when they heard the voice of the Almighty at Sinai. Their souls soared heavenward, leaving their bodies limp and lifeless. God then showered them with the same life-giving dew with which He will revive tne dead at תְּחִיַּת הַמֵּתִים, *the Resurrection of the Dead,* and they came back to life (*Targum; Shabbos* 88a).

[God caused the Children of Israel to undergo this experience so that He could imbue them with a firm belief in the Resurrection of the Dead, for this is a cardinal principle of Jewish faith. At the very moment when He gave the Children of Israel the Torah, God implanted within them the faith that they could judge and anticipate the greatest reward not in This World, but following the Resurrection.]

נַחֲלָתְךָ וְנִלְאָה — [*When*] *Your heritage was weary.*

When *Your heritage* (the Holy Land and the Chosen People) — *was weary for rain,* You lavished it [rain] generously (*Targum; Rashi*).

אַתָּה כוֹנַנְתָּהּ — *You established it firmly.*

After the juggernaut of the Assyrian army swept through Judea, the

⁹ *The earth roared — even the heavens dripped*
before the Presence of God.
This is Sinai — before the Presence of God,
the God of Israel.
¹⁰ *A generous rain did You lavish,*
O God,
When Your heritage was weary
You established it firmly.
¹¹ *Your flock settled there.*
You prepare for the poor
with Your goodness, O God.

defenders of Jerusalem were *weary*. Yet, as always, You miraculously protected *Your heritage* and *You established it firmly (Radak)*, as Scripture states (*Exodus* 15:17), מִקְדָּשׁ אֲדֹנָי כּוֹנֲנוּ יָדֶיךָ, *The Temple, my Lord, Your hands established (Sforno)*.

11. חַיָּתְךָ יָשְׁבוּ בָהּ — *Your flock* [lit. *living creature*] *settled there* [lit. *in it*].
The translation of חַיָּתְךָ follows *Rashi, Ibn Ezra,*, and *Radak*. It is based on *II Samuel* 23:11. The psalmist compares the faithful of Israel to sheep who flock to their master.
They all assemble בָהּ, *therein*, i.e, in the Land of Israel *(Ibn Ezra)* and in Jerusalem *(Radak)*.
Alshich observes that these words explain what the Jews gained when their souls soared from their bodies at Sinai. God invested their spirits with new חִיוּת, *vitality*, for their strength had been sapped by the Egyptian bondage. Afterwards, יָשְׁבוּ בָהּ, the reinvigorated souls *settled* back into their original bodies.
תָּכִין בְּטוֹבָתְךָ לֶעָנִי אֱלֹהִים — *You prepare for the poor with Your goodness, O God.*
God actually benefited the Jews by

requiring them to wander in the wilderness for forty years, for when the Canaanites first heard that Israel was coming to *Eretz Yisrael* [after the Revelation at Sinai], they devastated their land to render it worthless to the Jewish people. However, when the Jews failed to arrive as expected, the Canaanites engineered a complete reconstruction. In this manner, God *prepare[d]* [the land] *with goodness for the poor* and homeless Jewish people *(Rashi)*.
In later years, *You prepare[d]* a victory *for the poor* remnants of Judea, who were miraculously saved from Sennacherib's army *(Radak)*.
The *Talmud (Eruvin 54a)* interprets this verse as an allusion to the Torah scholar who renounces the pleasures of this world to concentrate on his holy studies. The devout, dedicated scholar treats himself like a חַיָּה, *an animal*, which is not concerned with the manner in which its food is prepared, but swiftly devours whatever it needs in order to survive. If he lives with such perfect sincerity, then God assures him not only of success in his studies, but also in his material needs. Of him it is said, *You prepare for the poor with Your goodness, O God.*

יב אֱלֹהִים: אֲדֹנָי יִתֶּן־אֹמֶר הַמְבַשְּׂרוֹת צָבָא
יג רָב: מַלְכֵי צְבָאוֹת יִדֹּדוּן יִדֹּדוּן וּנְוַת־בַּיִת
יד תְּחַלֵּק שָׁלָל: אִם־תִּשְׁכְּבוּן בֵּין שְׁפַתָּיִם
כַּנְפֵי יוֹנָה נֶחְפָּה בַכֶּסֶף וְאֶבְרוֹתֶיהָ

12. אֲדֹנָי יִתֶּן אֹמֶר — *My Lord gave His* [lit. *the*] *word.*

He revealed the words of Torah to His nation, Israel (*Targum*), and simultaneously He *gave* [them] *His word* [i.e., His promise], as recorded in verse 14 (*Rashi*). [See 12:7 אִמְרוֹת ה׳.] אִמְרוֹת טְהֹרוֹת.]

הַמְבַשְּׂרוֹת צָבָא רָב — *Announcing to the great legion.*

[The commentaries note the peculiarity of the word הַמְבַשְּׂרוֹת, which is plural and in the feminine gender.]

Here the psalmist alludes to an ancient practice whereby women would announce the latest local news in their songs; similarly, God announced His word to the great legions (*Ibn Ezra; Radak; Sforno*).

God appointed two great מְבַשְּׂרוֹת, *announcers,* Moses and Aaron, to teach Torah to the legions of Israel (*Targum*).

Each word which God uttered at Sinai split [מְשַׁבְּרוֹת] into seventy מְבַשְּׂרוֹת, *announcements,* i.e., seventy languages, so that the *great legions* of the gentile nations could hear the Divine teachings (*Shabbos* 88b).[1]

Similarly, it was *announced* that the *great legion* of the Assyrian army besieging Jerusalem would be destroyed at the word of God (*Radak*).

At the time of the future Messianic redemption, too, God's word will herald the defeat of all who oppose His design (*Meiri*).

13. מַלְכֵי צְבָאוֹת יִדֹּדוּן יִדֹּדוּן — *Kings of legions flee, they flee.*

[The root of יִדֹּדוּן is נָדַד, *to wander* or *to move.* The repitition of the word signifies that at Sinai there were two directions of movement.]

Each word which God uttered at Sinai was so awe-inspiring that it caused the legions of Israel to *flee* [i.e., retreat] twelve *mil* [about 6 miles] from the mountain. Later the ministering angels helped them to *flee* [i.e., return] to their original position at Sinai (*Shabbos* 88a).

When Israel conquered Canaan, the kings of the gentile legions were forced to flee repeatedly (*Radak*).

וּנְוַת בַּיִת תְּחַלֵּק שָׁלָל — *And the dweller within apportions booty.*

[נְוַת is derived from נָוֶה, *dwelling.* The feminine form alludes to the wife, who is the homemaker and *dwells* in the privacy of the house.]

Radak notes that women are singled out in appreciation for their unique contribution to the war effort. It is they who soothe the battle-weary warriors and comfort the wounded with tender words.

This also refers to the Torah scholar's wife who tends to the needs of the household while her husband engages

1. The root of all languages in the world is Hebrew, the Holy Tongue. Hebrew was spoken exclusively, until God confused the tongues of mankind at the Tower of Babel. He then distorted the Holy Tongue in seventy different ways, and seventy derivatives of Hebrew emerged. These languages were so corrupt that it was impossible to recognize their holy source (*Shaloh Hakodosh*).

At Sinai, God desired to draw the seventy nations back to His sanctity. He sought to demonstrate to them that the essence of their language is also holy. Therefore, He split every Hebrew word He uttered into seventy languages to display the spark of holiness which is at the core of every foreign tongue (*Sfas Emes*).

¹² *My Lord gave His word,*

announcing to the great legion.

¹³ *Kings of legions flee, they flee,*

and the dweller within apportions booty.

¹⁴ *Were You to nestle between boundaries —*

dove's feathers plated with silver,

in the intellectual "battles" of Torah study. She is destined to share equally in her spouse's spiritual rewards; as Rabbi Akiva said to his disciples concerning his devoted wife, Rachel, 'Mine and yours [all of our Torah studies] are hers' (*Kesubos* 63a; *Chomas Anoch*).

A similar system is practiced in every Jewish war: the spoils are apportioned equally between those who go out to battle and those who are assigned to stay behind to guard the homefront (see *Numbers* 31:27; *Ibn Ezra*).

The Israelite conquerors of Canaan *apportioned* the spoils of their victories in this manner (*Rashi*).

When Israel received the Torah, the nations envied and admired Israel's selfless dedication to God. They *apportioned* honor to the Torah, which is called (119:162) precious שָׁלָל, *booty* (*Mechilta Yisro* 20:9).

14. אִם תִּשְׁכְּבוּן בֵּין שְׁפַתָּיִם — *Were you to nestle* [lit. *lie down*] *between boundaries.*

This alludes to the Torah scholar who sacrifices all physical comforts in his whole-hearted dedication to his studies. Issachar excelled in this virtue; Jacob praised him, saying (*Genesis* 49:14): *He resembles the beast of burden* [traveling continuously, day and night, with no permanent place of rest]. *He lies down (only) between boundaries* [of the cities]. This suggests that Issachar limits his sleep to brief naps at irregular intervals. (The words מִשְׁפְּתָיִם and שְׁפַתָּיִם are derived from שָׂפָה, *lip* or *riverbank*, signifying a border or limitation.)

The Lord gave His word and pledged to *the legion*[s] of Israel (v. 12) that if

they would dedicate themselves to Torah with similar self-sacrifice, bountiful joy and success would be theirs. See *Rashi* and *Bereishis Rabbah* 99:10.

Radak defines שְׁפַתָּיִם as the sooty oven into which a cooking pot is lowered. According to his rendition, the verse teaches that if the Children of Israel humble themselves, shunning social status and lofty positions in favor of their Divine service, then despite the dirt and soot which may cover them in the course of their duties, they will surely emerge as clean and white as *a dove plated with* [spotless] *silver.*

Targum renders שְׁפַתָּיִם as קִלְקַלְתָּא *dung heap* [related to אַשְׁפָּה]; thus the verse would mean: *The wicked kings sink into filth because they defy God, while Israel soars to the heavens like a dove.*

בְּנַפֵּי יוֹנָה — *Dove's feathers.*

Rashi translates בְּנַפֵּי as *plumes,* i.e., the outer feathers, which are primarily for ornament.

The *Talmud* (*Shabbos* 49a) explains that Israel is likened to a *dove*; just as the feathers of the dove protect the bird, so do the *mitzvos* protect Israel from danger.

נֶחְפָּה בְכֶסֶף — *Plated with silver.*

Reading the word שְׁפַתָּיִם as the word שְׂפַת יָם, *seashore, Rashbam* and *Targum* refer this verse to the abundance of silver and gold, lost by the drowning Egyptians, with which Israel was covered, at the shore of the Sea of Red.

According to *Radak*, this refers to the silver and gold which Israel plundered from the abandoned Assyrian camp.

טו בִּירַקְרַק חָרוּץ: בְּפָרֵשׂ שַׁדַּי מְלָכִים בָּהּ
טז תַּשְׁלֵג בְּצַלְמוֹן: הַר־אֱלֹהִים הַר־בָּשָׁן הַר
יז גַּבְנֻנִּים הַר־בָּשָׁן: לָמָּה | תְּרַצְּדוּן הָרִים

וְאֶבְרוֹתֶיהָ — *And her pinions.*

This is the actual אֵבֶר, *limb*, of the wing, which keeps the dove airborne, not merely the ornamental feathers (*Rashi*).

בִּירַקְרַק — *With brilliant gold.*

Rashi explains that although יָרֹק means *green*, the doubling of the final two letters to form יְרַקְרַק indicates a lack of greenness. The pure gold which comes from the lands of *Chavilah* and *Kush* (*Genesis* 2:11,12) does *not* have a reddish or greenish tint, as is often found in gold of lesser purity. [*Tosafos, Sukkah* 31b *s.v.* יָרוֹק כְּכַרְתִּי, describes יָרֹק (especially as used in this verse) as *yellow.*]

חָרוּץ — *Brilliant* [cf. *Proverbs* 8:19].

This word literally means *sharp*. In connection with intellectual capacity, it denotes initiative or diligence. It is also used to describe the worth of precious metals (*Hirsch*).

15. בְּפָרֵשׂ שַׁדַּי מְלָכִים — *When Shaddai prostrates kings.*

Literally, פָּרֵשׂ means *to spread out.* God vanquishes the kings and spreads them out flat on the ground, in a pose of total submission. Specifically, Scripture recounts such an occurrence after God smote the Assyrian camp (*II Kings* 19:35): *Behold, they were all dead corpses* [spread out on the face of the earth] (*Radak*).

Rashi perceives this as an allusion to the Torah scholars [the true *kings* of the world; see *Proverbs* 8:15] who unravel the knottiest halachic problems and *spread them out* [i.e., resolve them] like a smoothly pressed garment (see *Deuteronomy* 22:17).

שַׁדַּי — *Shaddai.*

The psalmist uses this particular Divine name because it designates God as the Master who triumphs over all

adversaries (*Ibn Ezra*).

Since the king of Assyria spoke with brazen arrogance against Shaddai, he therefore deserved to be crushed with the full force connoted by this mighty name (*Radak*).

The root of the Name שַׁדַּי is דַּי, *enough, desist.* Therefore, its use in the verse suggests, 'May the Almighty, Who called a halt to the process of Creation by shouting, 'דַּי, *Enough!'* (*Chagigah* 12a). bring an end to our suffering at the hans of the gentile kings (*Zerah Yaakav*).

בָּהּ תַּשְׁלֵג בְּצַלְמוֹן — *Those in shadowy darkness shall be whitened.*

When God sends salvation, the Jewish people, who were shrouded in a צֵל, *dark shadow,* of gloom, will become illuminated with bright joy (*Radak*).

Ibn Ezra identifies צַלְמוֹן as a mountain whose peak is always capped with snow. It is located on the eastern bank of the Jordan River. [Possibly, since the snow never melts there it seems as if the mountain peak is perpetually under a cool צֵל, *shadow.*]

Targum renders צַלְמוֹן as צַלְמָוֶת, *the shadow of death,* i.e., *Gehinnom, Hell,* which is the destination of the wicked kings.

16. הַר־אֱלֹהִים הַר בָּשָׁן — *The mountain of God, the mountain of Bashan.*

[The psalmist now demonstrates the superiority of Mount Sinai over all other peaks and explains why Sinai was the most suitable location for the Revelation.]

The word *Bashan* is used to praise any desirable geographic location because there was a specific place in *Eretz Yisrael* called *Bashan,* where the pasture land was exceptionally lush and abundant. Animals who grazed there were noted for their size and strength. [See *comm.* to 22:13 אַבִּירֵי בָשָׁן].

68   *And her pinions with brilliant gold.*

15-17   ¹⁵ *When Shaddai prostrates kings,*

those in shadowy darkness shall be whitened.

¹⁶ *The mountain of God,*

the mountain of Bashan;

the mountain of Gavnunim,

the mountain of Bashan.

¹⁷ *Why do you prance,*

you mountains of Gavnunim,

Although Mount Sinai was in a barren, parched wilderness, it was considered a הַר בָּשָׁן, *an exceptional mountain*, because the Holy Spirit came to rest upon it and it was designated as הַר אֱלֹהִים, *the Mountain of God (Radak)*.

[God chose Sinai precisely because it was the lowest and most insignificant mountain, to teach that Torah knowledge can only be acquired by the humble scholar who seeks no recognition for his accomplishments.]

הַר גַּבְנֻנִים הַר בָּשָׁן — *The mountain of Gavnunim, the mountain of Bashan.*

[Unlike Sinai, which is *exceptional* because of its spiritual excellence, the other great mountains are called בָּשָׁן, *exceptional*, because of their unusual physical dimensions.]

The word גַּבְנֻנִים is derived from גָּבוֹהַ, *tall*. The plural usage indicates exceptional height. Furthermore, the highest peak of this lofty mountain is surrounded on all sides by many lesser ridges called גַּבְנֻנִים (*Radak; Meiri*).

[The word גַּב also means *back*, signifying that these lower ridges serve

as a 'backdrop' setting off the lofty pinnacle, whose height is even more evident when compared to the lower surrounding mountains.

Indeed, because of the tall mountain's height, it was unacceptable as the place for receiving the Torah; for height symbolizes arrogance, the repugnant character flaw which disqualifies the student from achieving Torah excellence.][1]

17. לָמָה תְּרַצְּדוּן הָרִים גַּבְנֻנִים — *Why do you prance, you mountains of Gavnunim.*

Radak and *Menachem* (cited by *Rashi*) translate תְּרַצְּדוּן as תְּרַקְּדוּן, *dance* or *cavort*. The tall mountains are like proud creatures who *prance* about to display their beauty and height. Their efforts, however, do not avail, for God already designated Sinai as His chosen mountain.

The *Talmud* (*Megillah* 29b) perceives תְּרַצְּדוּן as a contraction of תִּרְצוּ דִין, *you desire judgment*, for God judged between all of the mountains and Sinai to decide which was most suitable for the giving of the Torah. Mount Tabor

---

1. The *Talmud* (*Megillah* 29b) notes that גַּבְנֻנִים alludes to גִּבֵּן, *elongated eyebrows*, a blemish which disqualifies a priest from serving in the Temple (*Leviticus* 21:20). [These eyebrows are so long that they droop down and cover the eyes (*Rashi, Leviticus* 21:20). Just as exceptional length renders the eyebrows unfit for the priestly services, so does exceptional height render the mountains unfit for receiving the Torah.]

The *Talmud* (*Megillah* 29b) concludes that this teaches us that a man whose soul is blemished by arrogance is as much of a cripple as a man whose body is maimed with a physical wound.

גִּבְנֻנִּים הָהָר חָמַד אֱלֹהִים לְשִׁבְתּוֹ אַף־
יח יהוה יִשְׁכֹּן לָנֶצַח: רֶכֶב אֱלֹהִים רִבֹּתַיִם
יט אַלְפֵי שִׁנְאָן אֲדֹנָי בָם סִינַי בַּקֹּדֶשׁ: עָלִיתָ
לַמָּרוֹם | שָׁבִיתָ שֶּׁבִי לָקַחְתָּ מַתָּנוֹת בָּאָדָם

and Mount Carmel both came to demand judgment; but God dismissed their claims, saying, 'Your peaks are defiled by the idols erected there. Only Sinai has preserved its purity' (*Bereishis Rabbah* 99:1).

According to *Rashi, Radak* and *Sforno,* this verse does not refer to Mount Sinai but to Mount Moriah, the location of the Holy Temple. *Rashi* translates תְּרַצְּדוּן as *attack from ambush,* indicating that the other mountains [i.e., the mighty gentile nations] assault the Temple Mount and seek to destroy it.

הָהָר חָמַד אֱלֹהִים לְשִׁבְתּוֹ — *[Towards] the mountain which God has desired for His abode?*

God chose Mount Sinai because of its low elevation, which symbolizes the desirable trait of humility (*Targum*).

Ramban (Exodus 25:1) explains that the main purpose of the מִשְׁכָּן, *Tabernacle,* and מִקְדָּשׁ, *Temple,* was to provide a suitable repository for the Torah given at Sinai. The stone tablets which were given on that mountain were safeguarded in the Holy Ark, which was enshrined in the Holy of Holies. Therefore the extraordinary love which God had for Sinai was later transferred to the Mount Moriah, which became His permanent abode.

אַף ה' יִשְׁכֹּן לָנֶצַח — *Even HASHEM will dwell there forever.*

Once God's holy spirit settled on Mount Moriah, it never departed. See *Rambam, Hilchos Beis HaBechirah* 6:16.

[The psalmist no longer designates God as אֱלֹהִים, *the Dispenser of Strict Justice,* but as ה', *the Dispenser of Mercy,* thereby suggesting that although it was necessary for God to ex-

ercise His strict justice by destroying the Temple Mount, we look forward to the day when the Almighty *will dwell there* as HASHEM of Mercy *forever.*]

18. רֶכֶב אֱלֹהִים רִבֹּתַיִם — *The chariot of God is twice ten thousand.*

When God revealed Himself to Israel at Sinai, He was escorted by *twice ten thousand, thousands of Shin'an,* which are angels. His use of this elaborate retinue displayed His great affection for His chosen people (*Rashi*).

A mortal king goes out to war with a great army, but sends much smaller delegations on peace missions. In contrast, the Holy One, Blessed be He, goes out to war alone, as Scripture states, ה' אִישׁ מִלְחָמָה, HASHEM *is a Man* [all alone] *of war (Exodus* 15:3); however, when He went to give Israel the Torah [the source of all contentment and peace], He was accompanied by many myriads of angels (*Sifri, BeHaaloscha* 12:5).

אַלְפֵי שִׁנְאָן — *Thousands of Shin'an.*

Rashi views שִׁנְאָן as cognate with שְׁנוּנִים, *sharp, prompt,* signifying thousands of efficient angels who speedily discharge their Divine mission.

Ibn Ezra renders שִׁנְאָן as שְׁנַיִם. Thus אַלְפֵי שִׁנְאָן should be rendered *two thousand,* which in combination with the plural רִבֹּתַיִם, *myriads,* gives a total of 22,000. *Ibn Ezra* comments that this may allude to the number of Levites in the wilderness.

God foresaw that all the tribes, with the exception of Levi, would eventually forsake the Torah; therefore, it was only in Levi's merit that God descended upon Sinai (*Tanchuma, Tzav* 10).

According to *Targum,* this means two thousand angels who were instructed

68

18-19

Towards the mountain
which God has desired for His abode?
Even HASHEM will dwell there forever.
¹⁸ *The chariot of God is twice ten thousand,*
thousands of Shin'an
My Lord is among them,
at Sinai in holiness.
¹⁹ *You ascended on high,*
having taken captives.
You took gifts for man,

[שׁוּנָה] by God directly, and *twice ten thousand* aflame with a celestial fire.

The *Midrash* (*Shemos Rabbah* 29:2) defines שַׁנְאָן as שְׁנָאִים, *that are beautiful,* referring to the ministering angels.

Sforno explains that these are angels שְׁנָאִים, *which move and change,* because they take on different forms when engaged in different missions. Each time they come in a prophetic vision, they take on a new appearance.

אֲדֹנָי בָם סִינַי בַּקֹּדֶשׁ — *My Lord is among them, at Sinai in holiness.*

According to Rabbi Yochanan, God descended at Sinai with six hundred thousand ministering angels who placed crowns on the head of each man of Israel as a reward for the holy zeal with which the Israelites accepted the Torah (*Tanchuma, Tetzaveh* 11).

19. עָלִיתָ לַמָּרוֹם — *You ascended on high.*

Rashi and *Targum* (based on *Shabbos* 89a) maintain that this refers to Moses, whose ascent on Mount Sinai was considered as an entry into the heavens.

When the ministering angels complained to the Holy One, Blessed be He, that a mortal did not belong among them, God replied, 'He ascended to take the Torah.'

The angels argued, 'This precious treasure, which was hidden away for the equivalent of 974 generations before the world was created, should not be given to mortal man.'

God then summoned Moses to counter the arguments of the angels. Moses reasoned with them, 'Angels do not need the Torah. You have no parents to honor, no possibility of conforming to the requirements of *kashrus,* and no Egyptian bondage to remember.'

The holy angels admitted the truth of Moses' words and consented to allow the Torah out of the heavenly domain, since its precepts apply only to man and to his world.

According to *Radak, Meiri* and *Sforno,* this verse refers to the conquest of *Eretz Yisrael* by the gentile armies who sent the Jews into exile. At that time it appeared as if God had completely forsaken the earth to the wicked *and [had] ascended on high.*

שָׁבִיתָ שֶּׁבִי — *Having taken* [lit. *You captured*] *captives.*

The angels sought to keep the Torah 'captive' in the heavens, until Moses captured it for mankind by his convincing arguments.

The length of the לֻחֹת, *tablets,* was six handbreadths. During the original struggle, the top two handbreadths were in the hands of God, the bottom two were grasped by the hands of Moses and two unclaimed handbreadths remained in the middle (*Shemos Rabbah* 28:1; *Yerushalmi Taanis* 4:5).

‏כ וְאַף סוֹרְרִים לִשְׁכֹּן | יָה אֱלֹהִים: בָּרוּךְ
אֲדֹנָי יוֹם | יוֹם יַעֲמָס־לָנוּ הָאֵל יְשׁוּעָתֵנוּ
‏כא סֶלָה: הָאֵל | לָנוּ אֵל לְמוֹשָׁעוֹת וְלֵיהוִֹה
‏כב אֲדֹנָי לַמָּוֶת תּוֹצָאוֹת: אַךְ־אֱלֹהִים יִמְחַץ

[Finally Moses *captured* all of the Torah for Israel].

Following the interpretation of *Radak*, *Meiri*, and *Sforno*, this means that the marauding gentile army overran the Holy Land and *took many captives*.

‏לָקַחְתָּ מַתָּנוֹת בָּאָדָם — *You took gifts for man.*

Moses brought the Torah down from heaven as a gift for mankind (*Targum; Rashi*).

In addition, when the angels accepted the truth of Moses' arguments, they displayed their friendship by giving him spiritual gifts. Even the Angel of Death was generous to Moses and revealed to him the secret of stopping a plague by burning incense (*Shabbos* 89b).

[According to the preceding interpretation, the word לָאָדָם, *for man*, would have been more appropriate. Literally, בָּאָדָם means *in man*, indicating that the Torah was presented to humanity because its precepts find their fulfillment only *in man* rather than in angels (see *Tanchuma Ki Sisa* 17).]

The degenerate nations, whose barbarity resembles that of the beasts, did not deserve the Torah. Only the Jews, who are the epitome of morality and civilization, merited it; they alone are called אָדָם, *man*, par excellence (*Ezekiel* 34:31). Thus Moses *took the gifts* בָּאָדָם, *by virtue of man*, i.e., Israel (*Pesikta Rabbasi* 48:4).

Radak interprets these words: You took *away* from man (i.e., Israel) the presents which You once bestowed upon him. After man sinned, Your holy spirit departed from him and You no longer protected him.

‏וְאַף סוֹרְרִים לִשְׁכֹּן יָה אֱלֹהִים — *That even rebels may dwell with YAH God.*

Since the Torah was given, God's Holy Spirit clings to Israel under all circumstances, even when they rebel and anger Him (*Rashi*).

Radak renders: When You were angered by Israel, even the rebellious gentiles such as the brazen king of Assyria sought to conquer and dwell with YAH God in the holy city of Jerusalem.

20. בָּרוּךְ אֲדֹנָי — *Blessed be my Lord.*
Rashi explains that the following is the song mentioned above (*v.* 5), *Sing to God, make music for His Name.* [Sing to God because of the gift He gave us at Sinai.]

Sing to God because of the victory He gave Israel over the Assyrian host (*Radak*).

יוֹם יוֹם — *Day by day.*
Bless Him for His past kindness and anticipate His future kindness with additional blessings (*Malbim*).

‏יַעֲמָס לָנוּ — *He burdens us.*
In addition to the basic precepts which are incumbent upon the Children of Israel, God daily adds new commands, trials, and challenges, thus increasing our *burden* (*Targum*).

He does this in order to reward us with maximum goodness every day; He seeks to *burden* us with all the kindness we can possibly bear (*Rashi*).

God's ultimate goal is not to *burden* us; rather, He desires that we be a burden [i.e., dependent] on Him, as Scripture states, (*Isaiah* 46:3) בֵּית יִשְׂרָאֵל הָעֲמֻסִים מִנִּי בֶטֶן, *the House of Israel who are borne by me from birth* (*Shemos Rabbah* 25:9).

‏הָאֵל יְשׁוּעָתֵנוּ סֶלָה — *The God of our salvation, Selah.*
This is how God acts toward us *day*

68　　　　*that even rebels may dwell with YAH God.*

20-22　²⁰ *Blessed be my Lord,*

day by day

He burdens us,

the God of our salvation, Selah.

²¹ *The God is for us*

a God of salvations.

Though HASHEM/ELOHIM, my Lord,

has many avenues toward death—

²² *God will cleave only the head of His foes,*

---

by day: for every threat and *burden*, He provides us with a *salvation (Rashi).*

[God saved Israel from Sennacherib, King of Assyria, because the nation assumed the full *burden* of Torah study. The *Talmud (Sanhedrin* 94b) explains that in the merit of this intense עוֹל, *burden*, of Torah study, God protected His nation against the conquest attempted by Sennacherib.]

21. הָאֵל לָנוּ אֵל לְמוֹשָׁעוֹת — *[The] God is for us a God of salvations.*

Even when God acts strictly with us, it is for the purpose of saving us from an even harsher punishment. The man who suffers from poverty must realize that this is the Lord's way of providing him an *avenue* of escape from *death*. Since the pauper is considered a dead man *(Nedarim* 64b), this bitter punishment can take the place of real death and provide salvation from it *(Kiflayim L'tushiya).*

וְלֵיהֹוִה אֲדֹנָי — *Though HASHEM / ELOHIM, my Lord.*

Alshich points out that although the Divine Name used here is HASHEM, the vowel dots appended to it are those of אֱלֹהִים, *Elohim.*

[This teaches that it is in His role of HASHEM, *the Dispenser of Mercy*, that He tempers His love with the seemingly harsh lessons associated with the Name אֱלֹהִים, *Elohim, the Dispenser of Strict*

Justice. Minor afflictions are intended to save a man from major tragedies by facilitating his recognition that he has displeased His Creator and by spurring him to repentance before he commits even graver offenses against God.]

לְמָוֶת תּוֹצָאוֹת — *Has many avenues toward death.*

Rashi translates תּוֹצָאוֹת as *paths or exits* [leading from life] to death. God saves Israel, but He opens before their enemies many avenues of death.

God has a vast arsenal of lethal weapons at His disposal for annihilating our foes. He smote the Egyptians with ten different plagues and then drowned them in the sea. He hurled deadly hailstones upon the Canaanites *(Joshua* 10:11) and incited such bedlam amidst the Philistine ranks that the soldiers slew each other (I *Samuel* 14:20). This variety of deaths is endless *(Radak).*

The *Talmud (Berachos* 8a) teaches that God created 903 different forms of death, corresponding to the numerical value of תּוֹצָאוֹת.

22. אַךְ אֱלֹהִים יִמְחַץ רֹאשׁ אֹיְבָיו — *God will cleave only the head of his foes.*

God will slay them unaided and alone, without spear or sword, as He did when His angel slew one hundred and eighty thousand Assyrians in one instant *(Radak).*

כ֠ג רֹאשׁ אֹיְבָ֑יו קָדְקֹ֥ד שֵׂעָ֗ר מִתְהַלֵּ֥ךְ
בַּאֲשָׁמָֽיו: אָמַ֣ר אֲדֹנָ֣י מִבָּשָׁ֣ן אָשִׁ֑יב אָשִׁ֗יב
כד מִֽמְּצֻל֥וֹת יָֽם: לְמַ֤עַן | תִּֽמְחַ֬ץ רַגְלְךָ֗ בְּדָ֑ם
כה לְשׁ֥וֹן כְּלָבֶ֗יךָ מֵאֹיְבִ֥ים מִנֵּֽהוּ: רָא֣וּ
הֲלִיכוֹתֶ֣יךָ אֱלֹהִ֑ים הֲלִיכ֥וֹת אֵלִ֗י מַלְכִּ֥י

The destruction will be direct and complete; it will be aimed at *the head*, which is the most important part of the body (*Meiri*).

Yaavetz HaDoresh translates רֹאשׁ אֹיְבָיו as *the first of His foes*, i.e., Esau's grandson Amalek, the first enemy to attack the Jews as they left Egypt. Of Amalek, Scripture says, רֵאשִׁית גּוֹיִם עֲמָלֵק, *the first of nations is Amalek* (*Numbers* 24:20).

קָדְקֹד שֵׂעָר — *The hairy skull.*
This refers to the skull of Esau, who is described as אִישׁ שֵׂעָר, *a hairy man* (*Genesis* 27:11; *Rashi*).

Esau seeks to conceal his wickedness beneath a facade of false piety. He resembles the swine which tries to prove that it is Kosher by displaying its split hooves (*Sforno*). [Therefore, Esau's skull will be split measure for measure.]

Meiri explains that the קָדְקֹד is the very center of the skull, where the hairline usually parts the hair into two separate sections. [Hence, this word is composed of two equal parts, קד and קד.]

Since the קָדְקֹד is the topmost point of the head, whenever Heavenly decrees descend upon a person, they are

described as falling upon this spot [see 7:17 and *Deuteronomy* 33:16-17].

מִתְהַלֵּךְ בַּאֲשָׁמָיו — *Of him who saunters with his guilt.*
The wicked man calmly follows his daily routine and is untroubled by his burden of *guilt*; he refuses to repent (*Radak*).

He continues to follow his evil ways and adds new offenses to his record of guilt (*Sforno*).

23. אָמַר אֲדֹנָי מִבָּשָׁן אָשִׁיב — *My Lord promised, 'I will bring back from Bashan.'*
Rashi renders: I will rescue them from exile among *the mighty ones of Bashan* [cf. 22:13].

According to *Radak*, this is a Divine pledge to *turn back* or thwart the Assyrian invasion of Israel. Since the enemy first infiltrated Jewish territory on the eastern side of the Jordan River, in the land once known as *Bashan*, the entire campaign was named *Bashan*.

אָשִׁיב מִמְּצֻלוֹת יָם — *I will bring back from the depths of the sea.*
I shall gather in the exiles of Israel from all over the land and even from the islands of the sea (*Rashi; Sforno*).[1]

1. When the Second Temple was destroyed, four hundred Jewish boys and girls were seized and transported by ship to Rome for immoral purposes. When the youths realized the foul fate which awaited them, they asked the oldest and wisest of their group, 'If we drown ourselves in the sea, will we still merit a portion in the World to Come?'
The wise youth cited this verse, '*My Lord promised 'I will bring back from Bashan* [i.e., those threatened by בּוּשָׁה, *immoral disgrace*], *I will bring back from the depths of the sea'* [i.e., those who drown themselves to preserve their purity and to sanctify God's Name]. Upon hearing this, the maidens all leaped into the sea without hesitation. The youths immediately followed their example. Concerning these young martyrs, the psalmist laments, כִּי עָלֶיךָ הֹרַגְנוּ כָל הַיּוֹם, *For Your sake we are killed all the time* (44:23).

the hairy skull of him who saunters with his guilt.

²³ My Lord promised,

'I will bring back from Bashan,

I will bring back from the depths of the sea;

²⁴ That your foot may wade

through blood;

That the tongue of your dogs

may have its portion from the enemies.'

²⁵ They saw Your ways, O God,

the ways of my God, my King, in holiness.

24. לְמַעַן תִּמְחַץ רַגְלְךָ בְּדָם — *(So) that your foot may wade through blood.*

Literally, מָחַץ means *to split* [see *Judges* 5:26]. Here it describes the parting of a liquid by wading through it: 'When the heads of our bitter foes are split, we shall wade in their blood' *(Rashi; Hirsch).*

Radak understands תִּמְחַץ as *to redden* [see *Isaiah* 63:1] the feet with the enemies' blood and *to redden* the tongues of the dogs who lick the blood.

לְשׁוֹן כְּלָבֶיךָ מֵאוֹיְבִים מִנֵּהוּ — *[That] the tongue of your dogs [may have] its portion from the enemies.*

Rashi (based on *Daniel* 1:10) translates מִנֵּהוּ as *its portion* of daily sustenance (from מָנָה, *a portion).* The Israelites' dogs shall find themselves amply provided with meat, bones, and blood from the remains of the enemy.

Midrash Shocher Tov comments that this refers to the drowned bodies of the Egyptians which were washed up on the shore of the Sea of Reeds. The Jews' dogs devoured the hands and limbs of the slave drivers who tortured the Israelites in Egypt.

25. רָאוּ הֲלִיכוֹתֶיךָ אֱלֹהִים — *They saw Your ways, O God.*

[At the sea, Israel *saw* Your way of

dealing justly with mankind, according to their deserts. They witnessed their dogs devouring the cruel hands which once beat the Jews. When they noticed that some Egyptians drowned swiftly and painlessly while others suffered slow, excruciating deaths, they realized that each man was punished in accordance with the extent of his wickedness.]

God revealed His ways so clearly at the Sea, the *Mechilta (Parshas Beshalach)* says, that the humblest maidservant at the sea witnessed more than Ezekiel ben Buzi saw in all his prophecies *(Ibn Yachya).*

Furthermore, they saw Your concern for their welfare. When You split the sea, You fashioned not one, but twelve separate הֲלִיכוֹת, *ways,* a specially designed path for each tribe *(Alshich).*

Years later, when Israel witnessed the death of the Assyrian camp, they fully recognized *Your ways* in guiding the fate of mankind *(Radak).*

הֲלִיכוֹת אֵלִי מַלְכִּי בַקֹּדֶשׁ — *The ways of my God, my King, in holiness.*

[The eyes of Israel scrutinized the annals of history wisely. In every event they searched out the hand of God. The Divine Hand is evident to those who desire to discover His holiness in order to emulate God's sacred ways.]

כו בַּקֹּדֶשׁ: קִדְּמוּ שָׁרִים אַחַר נֹגְנִים בְּתוֹךְ
כז עֲלָמוֹת תּוֹפֵפוֹת: בְּמַקְהֵלוֹת בָּרְכוּ
כח אֱלֹהִים אֲדֹנָי מִמְּקוֹר יִשְׂרָאֵל: שָׁם בִּנְיָמִן |
צָעִיר רֹדֵם שָׂרֵי יְהוּדָה רִגְמָתָם שָׂרֵי
כט זְבֻלוּן שָׂרֵי נַפְתָּלִי: צִוָּה אֱלֹהֶיךָ עֻזֶּךָ עוּזָּה

26. קִדְּמוּ שָׁרִים אַחַר נֹגְנִים — *First went singers, then musicians.*

At the sea, they first sang words of praise; only later were they joined by instrumental accompaniment (*Rashi*).

This demonstrates the intensity of their joy. Ordinarily, the orchestra begins the music in order to enliven the singers, who then join in. At the sea, the miracles which Israel witnessed sent their spirits soaring. The Jews broke into song before the musicians even had a chance to begin playing (*Yaavetz HaDoresh*).

Rashi, drawing upon the *Midrash* (*Shemos Rabbah* 23:7), identifies the שָׁרִים as the Children of Israel, who were given precedence over the angels. Although the angels were most eager to chant hymns of praise to the Almighty, He forced them to wait, explaining, 'It is not that I wish to make you appear inferior; rather, I must let the mortals sing first, lest those among them who are destined to die very soon lose their unprecedented opportunity to sing to Me. Since you angels are eternal, you are not threatened by sudden death.'

בְּתוֹךְ עֲלָמוֹת תּוֹפֵפוֹת — *In the midst of timbrel-playing maidens.*

The male singers were in the midst [of the camp], surrounded by the women, led by Miriam [who sang outside] (*Rashi; Radak*).

[*Exodus* 15:20 states, *And Miriam the prophetess, the sister of Aaron, took the timbrel in her hand, and all the women went out after her with timbrels and dancing.* The women left the camp because it is immodest to dance in the presence of men and it is forbidden for men to hear them singing (*Berachos*

24a). As an additional precaution, they drowned out their voices in the din of the crashing timbrels.

The tempo of the timbrel has a singularly irresistible effect, particularly on women. The *Talmud* (*Moed Kattan* 9b) says, 'A lady of sixty is rejuvenated into a little girl of six when she hears the sound of the timbrel; she runs (to dance). Therefore, all the women of Israel (including Miriam, who was eighty-six years old) are described here as nimble and graceful עֲלָמוֹת, *maidens*. (See *Pardeis Yosef, Shemos* 15:20).]

27. בְּמַקְהֵלוֹת בָּרְכוּ אֱלֹהִים אֲדֹנָי — *In congregations bless God, my Lord.*

[Israel did not cross the sea as a single קָהָל, *congregation*, but as twelve separate tribes or מַקְהֵלוֹת, *congregations*. Nevertheless, when it came time to sing God's praises, they all joined together as one.]

אֲדֹנָי מִמְּקוֹר יִשְׂרָאֵל — *From the source of Israel.*

Even the toddler on his father's knee and the infant at his mother's breast witnessed the glory of God at the sea and burst forth in song. Even the fetus in his mother's womb sang a hymn of praise, as it says, *In congregations bless God, my Lord — from the* מְקוֹר, *womb* [i.e., the *source* of human life] *of Israel* (*Berachos* 50b; *Yerushalmi Sotah* 5:4).

This alludes to the virtuous Jewish wives who fiercely protected their chastity, despite the fact that the Jews were at the mercy of the lewd Egyptians for hundreds of years. They kept the pedigree of Israel as pure as a fresh fountain by guarding the *source*, i.e.,

²⁶ *First went singers, then musicians;*

In the midst of timbrel-playing maidens.

²⁷ *In congregations bless God,*

my Lord — from the source of Israel.

²⁸ *There Benjamin, the youngest, rules them,*

the princes of Judah stoned them,

the princes of Zebulun,

the princes of Naphtali.

²⁹ *Your God decreed your might,*

---

the womb, from defilement. Since God's assistance enabled them to retain their purity, it is the subject of this song of praise *(Alshich).*

28. שָׁם בִּנְיָמִן צָעִיר רֹדֵם — *There Benjamin, the youngest, rules them.*

When Israel stood poised at the edge of the sea before it split, the tribes began to quarrel. Each argued that it deserved to be the first to plunge into the water. [Actually, the shore of the sea was long enough for everyone to have jumped into the water together, but each tribe wanted the honor of carrying the coffin of Joseph, for Israel had been assured that the sea would part in Joseph's merit *(Mahari Pinto).*] Suddenly, the tribe of Benjamin leaped into the sea [without Joseph's coffin], as the verse states, *Benjamin* רֹדֵם, i.e., רַד יָם, *went down into the Sea! (Sotah* 36b).

Because the tribe of Benjamin courageously assumed the role of leadership at the Sea, one of its members, King Saul, later became the first Jewish monarch. This is also alluded to in the word רֹדֵם, which is cognate with רֹדֶה, *to rule (Targum; Rashi).*

שָׂרֵי יְהוּדָה רִגְמָתָם — *The princes of Judah stoned them.*

Since Judah was the tribe Divinely ordained for the monarchy, Judah reacted forcefully to Benjamin's apparent usurpation of its royal power.

Judah stoned Benjamin, forcing the tribe to return to shore. Then, led by their prince, Nachshon ben Aminodov, the true tribe of monarchy jumped into the sea *(Sotah* 36b; *Alshich).*

Although the monarchy was later transferred from the House of Saul the Benjaminite to the House of David the Judean, the Temple was constructed predominantly on the territory of Benjamin and only partially on the estate of Judah. Since Benjamin descended to the sea first, the Holy Spirit descended upon his territory first *(Mechilta Beshalach,* 14).

שָׂרֵי זְבֻלוּן שָׂרֵי נַפְתָּלִי — *The princes of Zebulun, the princes of Naphtali.*

[They assisted Judah in stoning Benjamin.]

According to *Radak,* the verse alludes to the Assyrian attack on the Jewish nation. The Ten Tribes of Israel were already in exile; all that remained were a few scattered individuals, primarily from the tribes of Zebulun and Naftali. The noble men of these remnants came to Jerusalem to assist the tribes of Judah and Benjamin רִגְמָתָם, *gathered,* there. At that time, Benjamin courageously רֹדֵם, *overwhelmed,* the enemy in battle. When victory was achieved, all the different tribes, i.e., מַקְהֵלוֹת, *congregations,* united to bless God.

29. צִוָּה אֱלֹהֶיךָ עֻזֶּךָ — *Your God decreed* [lit. *has commanded] Your might.*

[At the moment of Israel's miraculous

ל אֱלֹהִים זוּ פָּעַלְתָּ לָּנוּ: מֵהֵיכָלֶךָ עַל־
לא יְרוּשָׁלָםִ לְךָ יוֹבִילוּ מְלָכִים שָׁי: גְּעַר חַיַּת
קָנֶה עֲדַת אַבִּירִים | בְּעֶגְלֵי עַמִּים מִתְרַפֵּס
בְּרַצֵּי־כָסֶף בִּזַּר עַמִּים קְרָבוֹת יֶחְפָּצוּ:

triumph, all recognized that God had decreed that Israel be invincible.]

Some attribute these words to the tribe of Judah, who declared that its might and royal power were from God (Dorash Moshe).

According to other commentators, these are the words of King David (Ibn Ezra) or King Chizkiyahu (Radak).

עוּזָה אֱלֹהִים זוּ פָּעַלְתָּ לָּנוּ — *This might, O God, You have wrought for us.*

The translation follows Radak. Rashi, however, interprets this as Israel's grateful blessing to God: 'Be mighty, for You have wrought all this good for our sake!'

30. מֵהֵיכָלֶךָ עַל יְרוּשָׁלָםִ — *Out of Your Temple on to Jerusalem.*

Your majesty overflows out of Your Sanctuary in the *Beis HaMikdash* and spreads over the entire city of Jerusalem. This was particularly evident at the time of the downfall of Assyria, which had conquered the world. Only Jerusalem remained impregnable, for it was fortified by the sanctity emanating from the *Beis HaMikdash* (Radak).

לְךָ יוֹבִילוּ מְלָכִים שָׁי — *To You the kings shall deliver tribute.*

Hirsch points out that the word שָׁי is only found here, in 76:12, and in *Isaiah* 18:7. In each case, the word signifies a special gift which the nations will some-day offer as tribute to God.

Just as God's glory is spread over Jerusalem, it shall eventually cover the entire earth. Then all the nations will pay tribute to Him and to the Messiah (*Esther Rabbosi* 1:4).

31. גְּעַר — *Destroy.*

When followed by a noun prefixed

with a ב, *beis*, this verb means *to rebuke harshly* [see *Targum*]. Here, however, it is translated *destroy* (Radak and Ibn Ezra, Psalms 9:6).

חַיַּת קָנֶה — *The beast of reed[s].*

This describes the greedy and overbearing nation which tramples the peoples of the world just as a wild boar crashes through flimsy reeds. Many Talmudic and Midrashic sources iden-tify this conqueror as the Roman Em-pire [see 80:14]. However, *Rashi* main-tains that this verse refers to Ishmael, i.e., to the Arabs.

According to the *Zohar (Parshas Pinchos)*, this alludes to the humble origin of the mighty Roman Empire. When Solomon sinned with his wives, God began to transfer the sovereignty, of Israel to Rome. To symbolize this, the Almighty sent the angel Gabriel to thrust a lone קָנֶה, *reed* into the Mediter-ranean Sea; eventually, debris collected around this reed and formed the Italian Peninsula (*Shabbos* 56b). [This signifies that Rome was essentially weak; its strength lay in its diplomatic skill in fashioning powerful alliances. Basically these nations were like debris or waste which clings together and solidifies into a strong position.]

This enemy attacks with long spears resembling *reeds* (Radak; Meiri).

Everything which Rome does is recorded with the very same 'reed pen' (*Pesachim* 118a). [Rome laid claim to being the epitome of culture and civilization. However, her 'pen' created not only Western law, literature, and art, but also the most inhuman decrees of torture and death against Israel and other nations (*Midrash Shocher Tov, Psalm* 2). At the core, the Romans were

this might, O God, You have wrought for us.
30 *Out of Your Temple on to Jerusalem —*
to You the kings shall deliver tribute.
31 *Destroy the beast of reeds,*
the assembly of bulls
among the calves of nations,
who ingratiates himself for pieces of silver;
Who scatters nations and desires battles.

ruthless, militaristic barbarians, no better than the wild *beast of the reeds.*]

עֲדַת אַבִּירִים בְּעֶגְלֵי עַמִּים — *The assembly of bulls* [lit. *mighty ones*] *among the calves of nations.*

Meiri cites 22:13, where the mightiest of nations are compared to *bulls.* They intimidate the weaker nations, who resemble tender calves.

מִתְרַפֵּס — *Who ingratiates himself.*
This corrupt nation would stoop to the lowest depths and grovel for love of money (*Meiri; Radak; Rashi*).

Hirsch notes that the root of this word is רֶפֶשׁ or רֶפֶס, *mud, mire,* indicating that the sophistication and culture of Rome are a crude facade. They would sell their pride and wallow in filth and *mud* for the sake of money. *Midrash Shocher Tov* (Psalms 2) understands מִתְרַפֵּס as a contraction of מַתִּיר פַּס, *they open the palm* of their hand to accept bribes.

בְּרַצֵּי כָסֶף — *For pieces of silver* (*Radak*).
Hirsch comments that רַצֵּי is related to רָצַץ, *to break into pieces.* [Since this nation lacks the slightest trace of self-respect, they would sell their souls for a mere scrap of silver.]

Rashi translates רַצֵּי as רְצוּי, *appeasement,* i.e., they are pleased only by money.

בִּזַּר עַמִּים — *Who scatters nations.*
The ב should be read as a פ, changing the word to פִּזַּר, *scatters* (*Rashi; Radak*).

קְרָבוֹת יֶחְפָּצוּ — [*Who*] *desires battles.*
This militaristic nation lives by the sword and constantly seeks an excuse to enter into hostilities with other nations (*Rashi*). [1]

1. The word קְרָבוֹת may also be identified with קָרוֹב, *close relative.* Based on this verse the Sages of the *Talmud* (*Pesachim* 118b) discovered the formula for comprehending Israel's erratic fortunes in exile.
Israel will prosper in exile only as long as the Jews safeguard their unique identity as God's chosen nation, a people set apart. When Israel seeks to assimilate into its gentile environment, however, it is violently rejected by its host nation. Just as the human body cannot tolerate the intromission of foreign matter and rejects it violently, so does the body of nations forcibly expel Israel when the Jewish nation attempts to enter its midst.
Thus, בִּזַּר עַמִּים, God *scatters* Israel *among* the far-flung *nations.* He drives them out of the country where they have wrongly come to feel 'at home ' because their sense of equality has caused them to forget that they are alien. They are rejected because קְרָבוֹת יֶחְפָּצוּ, *they desire closeness* [from קָרוֹב, *relative*] with the gentiles.
This lesson was vividly illustrated by Israel's first exile in Egypt. As long as the Jews voluntarily segregated themselves from the Egyptians and cloistered themselves in Goshen, they were held in esteem; but once they spread throughout the land and attempted to assimilate into Egyptian society, they were oppressed and threatened with annihilation (*Beis HaLeivi, Parshas Shemos*).

לב יֶאֱתָיוּ חַשְׁמַנִּים מִנִּי מִצְרָיִם כּוּשׁ תָּרִיץ
לג יָדָיו לֵאלֹהִים: מַמְלְכוֹת הָאָרֶץ שִׁירוּ
לד לֵאלֹהִים זַמְּרוּ אֲדֹנָי סֶלָה: לָרֹכֵב בִּשְׁמֵי
לה שְׁמֵי־קֶדֶם הֵן יִתֵּן בְּקוֹלוֹ קוֹל עֹז: תְּנוּ עֹז
לֵאלֹהִים עַל־יִשְׂרָאֵל גַּאֲוָתוֹ וְעֻזּוֹ
לו בַּשְּׁחָקִים: נוֹרָא אֱלֹהִים | מִמִּקְדָּשֶׁיךָ אֵל
יִשְׂרָאֵל הוּא נֹתֵן | עֹז וְתַעֲצֻמוֹת לָעָם
בָּרוּךְ אֱלֹהִים:

32. יֶאֱתָיוּ חַשְׁמַנִּים מִנִּי מִצְרָיִם — *Nobles shall come from Egypt.*

Menachem explains that חַשְׁמַנִּים are the inhabitants of the land of חַשְׁמוֹנָה.

However, *Radak* and *Ibn Ezra* identify them as the *nobles* of all the nations. Similarly, we find that the aristocratic family of Matisyahu, the high priest, was called חַשְׁמוֹנָאִי.

The *Talmud* (*Pesachim* 118b) says that in the future, the degrading exile will end. Israel will no longer strive to come close to the nations [see footnote v. 31]; rather, the nations will attempt to ally themselves with Israel. Even our archenemy, Egypt, will offer tribute (see v. 30).

Although the Messiah's first reaction will be to reject the gifts proffered by the nation which once oppressed us so cruelly, God will insist that the tribute be accepted, since Egypt had provided the family of the Patriarch Jacob hospitality in time of famine.

According to *Midrash Shocher Tov*, the name חַשְׁמַנִּים is a contraction of חָשׁוּ, *they hastened*, to bring מָנִים, *costly gifts*. Also they are מְמוּנִים, *completely prepared* to join our nation as proselytes.

כּוּשׁ תָּרִיץ יָדָיו לֵאלֹהִים — *Kush shall hasten its hands to God.*

Kush [commonly identified with Ethiopia] will eagerly follow the example set by Egypt and immediately bring tribute to the Messiah (*Pesachim* 118b).

According to *Radak*, before Sennacherib besieged Jerusalem, he conquered the empires of Egypt and Kush; he then held their noblemen captive in his camp while he encircled the Holy City. When these princes witnessed the wondrous destruction of the Assyrian host, they recognized the greatness of our God. They survived the plague, threw themselves into the hands of God's chosen people, and converted to Judaism.

33. מַמְלְכוֹת הָאָרֶץ שִׁירוּ לֵאלֹהִים — O *Kingdoms of the earth, sing to God.*

In this world, the gentile kingdoms fail to appreciate the greatness of the Almighty, who allows His chosen people to suffer so much at their hands. In the future, however, the kingdoms will realize that God only afflicted the Jews in His role as אֱלֹהִים, *the Dispenser of Strict Justice*, i.e., for their own benefit. At that time, the gentiles will sing God's praises (*Alshich*).

34. לָרֹכֵב בִּשְׁמֵי שְׁמֵי קֶדֶם — *To the Rider upon the loftiest of primeval heavens* [lit. *the heavens of heavens of old*].

This refers to the highest of the seven heavens, *Aravos*, as mentioned earlier in v. 5, *Extol Him who rides in Aravos.* Unlike this temporary world and its mortal inhabitants, the highest heavens and the angels who dwell there have existed from antiquity and will continue to exist forever (*Radak*).

³² *Nobles shall come from Egypt*

Kush shall hasten its hands to God.

³³ *O Kingdoms of the earth,*

sing to God,

make music to my Lord, Selah!

³⁴ *To the Rider upon*

the loftiest of primeval heavens

Behold He bestows with His voice,

a mighty voice.

³⁵ *Attribute might to God,*

Whose majesty hovers over Israel

And Whose might is in the clouds.

³⁶ *You are awesome, O God,*

from Your sanctuaries, O God of Israel —

It is He Who grants might and power

to the nation, blessed be God.

Previously, the kingdoms of earth attributed their sovereignty and success to the celestial signs, the heavenly bodies which they thought controlled man's fate and fortune; but when Israel ascends above all of the nations, they will recognize that God alone rules the heavens, just as the rider determines the path of his horse (*Sforno*).

הֵן יִתֵּן בְּקוֹלוֹ קוֹל עֹז — *Behold He bestows with His voice, a mighty voice.*

In the future, God will proclaim His complete sovereignty over all the earth. He will sweep away the lesser celestial forces which had previously been His agents and His intermediaries (*Sforno*).

35. תְּנוּ עֹז לֵאלֹהִים — *Attribute might to God.*

The *mighty voice* which will go forth (v. 34) will proclaim (*Ibn Ezra*) that the power which the nations previously exercised over Israel was not their own but was a Divine endowment (*Alshich*). The

strength of the Messiah will also be ascribed to the Almighty (*Sforno*).

In a sense, the source of all God's might is Israel: When the children of Israel follow the wishes of the Omnipresent, they reinforce the strength of the One above (see *Mechilta Beshalach* 15:6). The Divine wisdom had ordained that God's actions be a reflection of Israel's deeds; the strength of Israel's commitment *give[s] might to God* (*Rashbam; Binah L'ittim*).

עַל יִשְׂרָאֵל גַּאֲוָתוֹ — *Whose majesty* [lit., *pride*] *hovers over Israel.*

God can only be proud, so to speak, when Israel is faithful and obedient to His word (*ARIzal*). Then, He displays the extent of His majesty and pride by acting generously to His precious people (*Ibn Ezra*), and by making them triumphant over their foes (*Rashbam*). Similarly, the prophet (*Isaiah 49:3*) spoke of *Israel, in whom I will be glorified* (*Sforno*).

וְעֻזּוֹ בַּשְּׁחָקִים — *And Whose might is in the clouds.*

[When God's sovereignty is recognized on earth, He is empowered, so to speak, to exercise His might over the celestial forces above.]

36. נוֹרָא אֱלֹהִים מִמִּקְדָּשֶׁיךָ — *You are awesome, O God, from Your sanctuaries.*

Radak and *Ibn Ezra* perceive the plural form *Your sanctuaries* as an allusion to the dual existence of the *Beis Hamikdosh:* there is a spiritual Temple in the heavens which corresponds to the Temple on earth [the one below cannot be destroyed until its heavenly counterpart is obliterated].

In addition, *Radak* suggests that the plural form alludes to the various sections and chambers of the *Beis Hamikdosh.* The *Sanctuary* was divided into different levels of holiness.

The entire world was awestruck when God destroyed His most sacred and cherished place. This impressed upon all men the exacting demands of God's strict justice.

The *Talmud (Zevachim* 115b) says that the word may also be read מִמְּקֻדָּשֶׁיךָ, *from Your holy people,* meaning that God is especially demanding of His most pious and devout nation. When they are punished for even the slightest deviation from scrupulous adherence to the law, the world is filled with fear and awe.

O — אֵל יִשְׂרָאֵל הוּא נֹתֵן עֹז וְתַעֲצֻמוֹת לָעָם *God of Israel — it is He Who grants might and power to the nation.*

God will grant royal *might* to the Messiah and extraordinary *power* to the entire nation, as the prophet (*Micah* 5:7) foretells: *And the remnant of Jacob shall be among the nations in the midst of many peoples like a young lion among the flocks of sheep (Sforno).*

בָּרוּךְ אֱלֹהִים — *Blessed be God.*

This psalm begins with the prayer (v. 2) יָקוּם אֱלֹהִים, *Let God arise,* and it concludes with a response to this impassioned plea. In the future, God will demonstrate that the Divine justice which He had dispensed with such apparent harshness was actually disguised beneficence.

At that time, the entire world will enthusiastically bless אֱלֹהִים, *God, Dispenser of Strict Justice,* for everything He has done (*Yaavetz HaDoresh*).

מזמור סט 69

The great irony of Jewish history is that our exiled nation has spent more time on foreign soil than in its own homeland. Uprooted violently from their natural setting, the Jewish people have wandered for almost twenty centuries. Our people have not merely survived without a country to call their own — they have even flourished during the exile.

The fact of Jewish survival grows even more amazing when one considers the hostile environments into which our people have been thrust. Israel resembles a delicate and vulnerable rose. Just as the rose is protected by its thorns, the Jewish people are protected by the Torah, which fortifies us so that we may endure the hardships and dangers of our exile (Hirsch). This concept of exile provides the theme of this psalm.

Hirsch observes that the psalmist, David, has a prophetic vision of generations of brave Jews surviving the dark centuries of exile, sustained by the thoughts contained in this psalm. First, the downtrodden outcasts recount the tragic tale of their wanderings and woes (v. 2-30). Finally however, they draw on the deep reserves of faith which permeate the Jewish heart, and they shout out a triumphant hymn of everlasting devotion to God (v. 31-37). Thus, from the crucible of suffering emerges a mold of ironclad faith which has withstood the tests of the ages.

Another major theme, David's ancestry, is discussed at length in Overview to Megillas Ruth, ArtScroll edition, and in The Book of Our Heritage (Vol. 3), 'Sivan,' by Eliyahu Kitov.

א-ב לַמְנַצֵּחַ עַל־שׁוֹשַׁנִּים לְדָוִד: הוֹשִׁיעֵנִי
ג אֱלֹהִים כִּי בָאוּ מַיִם עַד־נָפֶשׁ | טָבַעְתִּי
בִּיוֵן מְצוּלָה וְאֵין מָעֳמָד בָּאתִי בְמַעֲמַקֵּי־
ד מַיִם וְשִׁבֹּלֶת שְׁטָפָתְנִי: יָגַעְתִּי בְקָרְאִי
ה נִחַר גְּרוֹנִי כָּלוּ עֵינַי מְיַחֵל לֵאלֹהָי | רַבּוּ
מִשַּׂעֲרוֹת רֹאשִׁי שֹׂנְאַי חִנָּם עָצְמוּ

1. עַל שׁוֹשַׁנִּים — *Upon Shoshanim.*

[See 45:1; 60:1.]

Here David sings of the exile of Israel, which began with the exile of the members of Sanhedrin, who are likened to שׁוֹשַׁנִּים, *roses (Targum).*

In exile, the seventy nations attack Israel, just as the thorns which surround the *rose* prick its delicate petals (*Rashi*).

The chief characteristics of the *rose* are its bright red color and its remarkable fragrance. These symbolize the main features of exile: Israel's wanderings have been stained with the blood of martyrdom, but the soul of our people has become permeated with the sublime fragrance of purity (*Alshich*).

2. הוֹשִׁיעֵנִי אֱלֹהִים — *Save me, O God.*

[Although Israel is accustomed to harsh treatment in the exile (for God manifests Himself to His people as אֱלֹהִים, *Dispenser of Strict Justice*), nevertheless, Divine salvation is to be expected when the very existence of the Jewish nation is endangered by the enemy.]

כִּי בָאוּ מַיִם עַד־נָפֶשׁ — *For the waters have reached until the soul!*

The nations are likened to water, as the psalmist says (18:17), *He drew me out of deep waters* (*Ibn Ezra*). Israel, up to its neck in troubles, is on the verge of death (*Radak*).

[Israel can endure the physical suffering of exile; but the nation cannot tolerate the erosion of its unique spiritual values by the heresy and immorality which pervade the exile.]

3. טָבַעְתִּי בִּיוֵן מְצוּלָה — *I am sunk in deep mire* [lit. *quicksand of the shadowy deep; cf. Psalms 40:3* טִיט הַיָּוֵן].

Israel laments: The exiled nation has a double problem; not only is it drowning in the waters of the מְצוּלָה, [lit. *shadowy deep*], but also it cannot extricate itself, because it is mired in יָוֵן [lit. *quicksand*] (*Radak*).

Contact with the gentile world introduced me to enticing new lusts. I am drawn into their grip, like a man sucked into quicksand (*Migdal David*).

Sforno says that מְצוּלָה refers to the Babylonian exile. This land was so low and muddy that the prophet (*Isaiah 44:27*) calls it צוּלָה, *shadowy deep.*

[*Sforno* analyzes every word in this psalm, demonstrating how each phrase refers to a different incident in Israel's long exile. However, we have omitted most of his comments because they would require excessive explanation and background material.]

וְאֵין מָעֳמָד — *(And) there is no foothold.*

[Assimilation threatens from all sides. There appears to be no way to maintain a separate, independent identity on an equal footing with other nations. Israel seems to be doomed.]

בָּאתִי בְמַעֲמַקֵּי מַיִם — *I have entered deepest waters.*

[Another double threat is mentioned here: Not only is Israel drowning in *deep waters*, but also a *swift current* is sweeping the nation, preventing its escape.]

וְשִׁבֹּלֶת שְׁטָפָתְנִי — *(And) a rushing current sweeps me away.*

69
1-5

For the Conductor, upon Shoshanim,
by David.

² Save me, O God,
for the waters have reached until the soul!
³ I am sunk in deep mire,
there is no foothold.
I have entered deepest waters;
a rushing current sweeps me away.
⁴ I am wearied by my crying,
my throat is parched,
My eyes failed
as I waited for my God.
⁵ More abundant than the hairs of my head
are those who hate me groundlessly.
Mighty are those who would cut me off,

[שִׁבֹּלֶת is related to שְׁבִיל, path. The gentile lifestyle runs counter to the Jewish way of life. It makes a strong impression upon the Jew who is struggling to survive in a hostile environment, and it threatens to 'sweep him away' from his Jewish tradition.]

4. יָגַעְתִּי בְקָרְאִי — I am wearied by my crying [lit. calling].

Like a drowning man screaming desperately for help, I called out until my throat became dry [and my cries were of no avail] (Radak).

נִחַר גְּרוֹנִי — My throat is parched.

Esau's prowess lies in his sword, but the power of Jacob rests in his throat. When Jacob raises his voice in prayer, he usually is answered. Yet, in the gloom of exile, God did not respond to the Jews' supplications; therefore, their voices grew hoarse from incessant prayer (Chozeh David).

כָּלוּ עֵינַי מְיַחֵל לֵאלֹהָי — My eyes failed as I waited for my God.

[Although I waited continuously for the dawn of redemption, and strained

my eyes until they grew weak, God did not even show me a glimmer of hope or communicate the slightest response to my plea.]

5. רַבּוּ מִשַּׂעֲרוֹת רֹאשִׁי שֹׂנְאַי חִנָּם — More abundant than the hairs of my head are those who hate me groundlessly.

Countless enemies have eagerly searched for an opportunity to attack Israel without any provocation, because they see that history bears out the Talmudic prognosis (Gittin 56a): Whoever afflicts Israel attains a position of world leadership (Tehillos Hashem).

עָצְמוּ מַצְמִיתַי — Mighty are those who would cut me off.

If the enemies merely multiplied like hairs, then their threat would not be overwhelming, for each hair is but a flimsy wisp which is easily bent back. However, my peril is truly great, because the strength of each individual enemy has increased, so that each has become a mighty and formidable adversary which threatens to raze me (Beer Avraham).

מַצְמִיתַי אֹיְבַי שֶׁקֶר אֲשֶׁר לֹא־גָזַלְתִּי אָז

ו אָשִׁיב: אֱלֹהִים אַתָּה יָדַעְתָּ לְאִוַּלְתִּי

ז וְאַשְׁמוֹתַי מִמְּךָ לֹא־נִכְחָדוּ: אַל־יֵבֹשׁוּ בִי |

קֹוֶיךָ אֲדֹנָי יֱהֹוִה צְבָאוֹת אַל־יִכָּלְמוּ בִי

ח מְבַקְשֶׁיךָ אֱלֹהֵי יִשְׂרָאֵל: כִּי־עָלֶיךָ

ט נָשָׂאתִי חֶרְפָּה כִּסְּתָה כְלִמָּה פָנָי: מוּזָר

י הָיִיתִי לְאֶחָי וְנָכְרִי לִבְנֵי אִמִּי: כִּי־קִנְאַת

אֹיְבַי שֶׁקֶר — *My falsehood-seeking foes.*

I dedicate my life to truth and refuse to join my foes in their pursuit of lies and false ideals. For this they cannot forgive me (*Rashi*).

שׂנְאַי חִנָּם, *those who hate me groundlessly*, pose much less of a threat. Since their hatred is groundless, they fabricate no slanderous tales to besmirch my reputation; but אֹיְבַי שֶׁקֶר, *my falsehood-seeking foes*, justify their bitter enmity by spreading false, malicious accusations against me (*Beer Avraham; see Targum*).

אֲשֶׁר לֹא גָזַלְתִּי אָז אָשִׁיב — *What I never stole I will then return.*

When the gentile mobs gather to do me harm, I have no choice but to appease them with bribes. Thus, I am compelled to *return that which I never stole*, i.e., I give them money which I do not owe them (*Rashi*).

According to *Radak:* The gentiles accuse me of thefts which I never committed and force me to repay money which I never stole.

6. אֱלֹהִים אַתָּה יָדַעְתָּ לְאִוַּלְתִּי — *O God, You know my folly.*

In the previous verse, Israel vigorously denied the false charges hurled by the gentiles. Israel now hastens to admit that she has indeed been guilty of sins — but not of those invented by the malicious enemy. God alone is aware of the full extent of these wrongdoings, but He also knows that these sins were caused by ignorance and foolishness (*Hirsch*).

The אִוֶּלֶת is the sin committed for no reason. [The Sages teach: A man does not sin unless he is seized by a spirit of madness (*Sotah* 5a).] Therefore, a senseless offense is punished by the senseless attack of שׂנְאַי חִנָּם, *those who hate me without cause* (*Beer Avraham*).

וְאַשְׁמוֹתַי מִמְּךָ לֹא נִכְחָדוּ — *And my guilty acts from You are not hidden.*

God recognizes that the hidden root of my *acts of guilt* is the lust for pleasure and gratification; but now, I realize that I was enticed by false fantasies, for the pleasures I so eagerly anticipated were truly harmful and evil. Since I lied to myself, I was plagued by (v. 5) אֹיְבַי שֶׁקֶר, *my enemies who lie* (*Beer Avraham*).

7. אַל יֵבֹשׁוּ בִי קֹוֶיךָ — *Let them not be shamed through me, those who wait for You* [cf. 25:3].

Israel has long awaited Divine redemption; if their hopes are ultimately dashed, then all other men awaiting Divine salvation will also be disappointed (*Radak; Rashi*).

According to *Malbim*, בּוּשָׁה is the inner *shame* one feels for himself whereas כְּלִמָּה is public *disgrace* suffered at the hands of others [see *comm.* to 35:3]. When those who wait for God see that their hopes go unfulfilled, they are personally 'shamed' by the realization that they have been unworthy of Divine assistance.

אֲדֹנָי ה' צְבָאוֹת — *My Lord HASHEM/ELOHIM of Legions.*

69

6-9

> *my falsehood-seeking foes.*
> *What I never stole*
> *I will then return.*
> ⁶ *O God You know my folly,*
>   *and my guilty acts from You are not hidden.*
> ⁷ *Let them not be shamed through me,*
>   *those who wait for You;*
> *My Lord HASHEM/ELOHIM of Legions,*
>   *let them not be disgraced through me,*
> *those who seek You,*
>   *O God of Israel.*
> ⁸ *Because for Your sake humiliation*
>   *I have borne,*
> *Disgrace covered my face.*
> ⁹ *I became a stranger to my brothers,*
>   *and an alien to my mother's sons.*

[When the ineffable four-letter Name of God follows אֲדֹנָי, it is vowelized and read as אֱלֹהִים, *Elohim*.]

You are the Master of the celestial legions above, and Lord of the legions of Israel below. Since You can manipulate all creation at will, we beg You to redeem Israel *(Radak)*.

אַל יִכָּלְמוּ בִי מְבַקְשֶׁיךָ — *Let them not be disgraced through me, those who seek You.*

Malbim continues: If those who seek You publicly are not answered they will suffer public בְּלִמָה, *disgrace,* by being embarrassed before others.

אֱלֹהֵי יִשְׂרָאֵל — *O God of Israel.*

Israel beseeches God to remember His promise that he would accompany them into exile: *When they are in the land of their enemies I will not reject them, neither will I abhor them, to destroy them utterly and to break my covenant with them, for I am HASHEM their God* (Leviticus 26:44; Hirsch).

8. כִּי עָלֶיךָ נָשָׂאתִי חֶרְפָּה — *Because for Your sake humiliation I have borne.*

Humiliation is the most intense form of insult and degradation suffered at the hands of others [see *comm.* to *Psalms* 35:4].

This *humiliation* would have ended in a moment had I only accepted the religion of my tormentors; but *for Your sake* I have gladly borne the burden of the Jewish faith *(Radak)*.

כִּסְּתָה כְלִמָּה פָנָי — *Disgrace covered my face.*

All the nations know that if Israel were to repent her sins she would immediately be redeemed. The continuation of the exile is therefore a public *disgrace*, because it reveals Israel's stubborn refusal to mend her ways *(Beer Avraham)*.

9. מוּזָר הָיִיתִי לְאֶחָי — *I became a stranger to my brothers.*

Beer Avraham differentiates between the נָכְרִי, *alien,* and the זָר, *stranger;* the former is a citizen of a foreign nation. The latter is someone from one's own nation who had been close but has become estranged.

בֵּיתֶךָ אֲכָלָתְנִי וְחֶרְפּוֹת חוֹרְפֶיךָ נָפְלוּ
עָלָי: וָאֶבְכֶּה בַצּוֹם נַפְשִׁי וַתְּהִי לַחֲרָפוֹת
לִי: וָאֶתְּנָה לְבוּשִׁי שָׂק וָאֱהִי לָהֶם לְמָשָׁל:
יָשִׂיחוּ בִי יֹשְׁבֵי שָׁעַר וּנְגִינוֹת שׁוֹתֵי שֵׁכָר:

Rashi explains that Esau was a very close relative of Israel, a full brother sharing the same father and mother. In exile, Israel *became a stranger* to Esau, for he refused to recognize their family bond.

Radak, however, contends that *stranger* refers to Ishmael, who was only a half-brother to the Jews, through the Patriarch Abraham. [See *comm.* to verse 22 for a description of how the Ishmaelites betrayed the exiled Jews.]

וְנָכְרִי לִבְנֵי אִמִּי — *And an alien to my mother's sons.*

According to *Radak* this describes Esau, who, unlike Ishmael, is a full brother to Israel. [Despite their close blood relationship, Esau was completely alienated from his Jewish brethren. The *Talmud (Kiddushin* 18a) describes Esau as an apostate Jew.]

10. כִּי קִנְאַת בֵּיתְךָ אֲכָלָתְנִי — *Because envy of Your House devoured me.*

The gentiles saw the great love which You displayed for us while Your House, the *Beis HaMikdash* stood [see *Yoma* 54a]. It was this love that aroused their envy *(Rashi)*.

Olellos Ephraim perceives in these words an allusion to the moral decay which undermined the social and spiritual fabric of the Jewish nation and caused the Temple to be destroyed. *Envy* and senseless hatred caused the House of God to be *devoured* [*Yoma* 9b], and the Temple will only be rebuilt when mutual consideration and brotherly love prevail.

According to the *Talmud (Zevachim* 54b), this is a reference to David's personal life. On the night that David first fled from Saul, Samuel designated David as Saul's successor. The prophet then gave David a scroll containing secret instructions concerning the construction of the Temple. (At that time, the nation was still using the temporary, portable Tabernacle.) The privilege of receiving these secrets kindled the jealousy of David's archenemy, Doeg the Edomite, which is referred to here [see footnote to 52:2].

וְחֶרְפּוֹת חוֹרְפֶיךָ נָפְלוּ עָלָי — *And the humiliations of those who scorn You have befallen me.*

O God, You proclaimed that You will surely redeem Israel. The gentiles mock us, however, for we continue to writhe in their clutches, with no salvation in sight. They deny Your ability to redeem us. This insult to You is reflected in the humiliation they heap upon us. They also place their faith in false idols, which is another form of insult to You *(Radak)*.

11. וָאֶבְכֶּה בַצּוֹם נַפְשִׁי — *And I wept while my soul was fasting.*

My soul is constantly shrouded in gloom and mourning *(Radak)*. This is especially so on the fast days which commemorate our national tragedy *(Hirsch)*. Other conquered nations bemoan only their physical suffering, but Israel laments her spiritual losses *(Alshich)*.

וַתְּהִי לַחֲרָפוֹת לִי — *And it was humiliating* [lit. *humiliations*] *for me.*

I was embarassed by my weeping, for it produced no results. You ignored my tears and left me in exile *(Metzudas David)*.

You Yourself, O God, became a source of humiliation to me, when the gentiles reviled me in an attempt to shatter my faith in You and to draw me to their false beliefs *(Radak)*.

¹⁰ *Because envy of Your House devoured me,*
and the humiliations of those who
scorn You have befallen me
¹¹ *And I wept while my soul was fasting*
and it was humiliating for me.
¹² *I made sackcloth my garment,*
I became for them a byword.
¹³ *They gossip about me, those who sit*
by the gate;
The drinking songs of drunkards.

---

12. וָאֶתְּנָה לְבוּשִׁי שָׂק — *I made sackcloth*
my garment.

The donning of sackcloth made of
coarse animal hair is a sign of humiliation and repentance. The wearer symbolically chastises himself for having
behaved as an impulsive, uncontrolled
animal. In general, this display of contrition is too extreme for the common
man; it is practiced only by men of extraordinary piety. The *Midrash* teaches
that Jacob introduced the practice of
wearing sackcloth. This tradition has
been maintained by Jews throughout
the generations. Scripture (*I Chronicles*
21:16) indicates that this practice is
reserved only for great men: *And David*
and the Sages, all robed in sackcloth,
fell down on their faces (*Shnei Luchos*
HaBris, Maseches Rosh HaShanah, first
gloss).

וָאֱהִי לָהֶם לְמָשָׁל — *I became for them a*
byword.

[See 44:15: תְּשִׂימֵנוּ מָשָׁל בַּגּוֹיִם, *You*
made us a byword among the peoples.]

Among the gentiles, the word 'Jew'
became a byword used to describe
anything base and despicable (*Radak;*
Hirsch).

13. יָשִׂיחוּ בִּי יֹשְׁבֵי שָׁעַר — *They gossip*
about me, those who sit by the gate.

[Any mass gathering is termed
'sitting by the gate,' for the gate was the

public area of the city.] When the
heathens assemble in their theaters and
circuses, the Jews are the butt of their
vile jokes (*Pesicha, Eichah Rabbasi* 17).

[Furthermore, שַׁעַר also means *the*
price of commodities sold at *the gate* of
the marketplace. Anti-Semites attribute
inflation to the Jews, whom they
falaciously accuse of exploiting the
consumer and driving up the prices.
The Jew-haters spread absurd rumors to
support their libels.] They allege: 'The
Jews squander all their weekly earnings
on their Sabbath. They have no
firewood for cooking, so they smash
their beds and burn the boards. This
forces them to sleep on the floor. Since
the hard ground makes them ache they
massage their sores with large quantities
of oil, which is why oil has become so
expensive!' (*Eichah Rabbasi* 17 and
3:5).

וּנְגִינוֹת שׁוֹתֵי שֵׁכָר — *The drinking song of*
drunkards [lit. *And the songs of beer*
drinkers].

Not only do the dignitaries who sit
prominently *by the gate* of the city
ridicule the Jews, but even the lowest
drunkards dare to deride us (*Midrash*
Chachomim).

They celebrate their holidays by
emphasizing our sorrows. Gleefully
they sing, 'The Jews wait forever for
Messiah, but he never comes!' (*Maha-*
ram Markado).

יד וַאֲנִי תְפִלָּתִי־לְךָ | יהוה עֵת רָצוֹן אֱלֹהִים

טו בְּרָב־חַסְדֶּךָ עֲנֵנִי בֶּאֱמֶת יִשְׁעֶךָ: הַצִּילֵנִי

מִטִּיט וְאַל־אֶטְבָּעָה אִנָּצְלָה מִשֹּׂנְאַי

טז וּמִמַּעֲמַקֵּי־מָיִם: אַל־תִּשְׁטְפֵנִי | שִׁבֹּלֶת

מַיִם וְאַל־תִּבְלָעֵנִי מְצוּלָה וְאַל־תֶּאְטַר־

יז עָלַי בְּאֵר פִּיהָ: עֲנֵנִי יהוה כִּי־טוֹב חַסְדֶּךָ

14. וַאֲנִי תְפִלָּתִי לְךָ ה׳ — *But as for me, my prayer is to You, HASHEM.*

David declared to the Holy One, Blessed be He, 'Master of the Universe, when the gentiles celebrate their festivals they eat, drink, and sing at their feasts all day long, without once mentioning Your Name. We are different. On the Jewish Sabbath, we do not forget You. We interrupt our eating, drinking, and relaxation to gather in the sacred House of God for the Afternoon Prayer, in which we praise you for all that you have provided' *(Midrash).* [1]

Furthermore, whenever the gentiles ridicule and threaten me, my only defense against them is *my prayer unto You,* pleading for *kindness* and *salvation (Radak; Meiri).*

עֵת רָצוֹן — *At an opportune time* [lit. *a time of favor*].

Part of my prayer is the wish that the timing of such prayer be favorable to You *(Rashi; Yerushalmi, Makkos 2:6).*

If he engages in incessant prayer, the supplicant can be certain that he will eventually arrive at a propitious moment *(Radak).*

One should take care to pray with the congregation, for whenever they gather to pray is *a favorable time* before God *(Berachos 7b).*

Israel's most fervent prayer is that God hasten the advent of Messiah and bring about the redemption at the most *favorable time (Meiri).*

Siddur Otzar Hatefillos (Sabbath Afternoon) explains that the era of chaos preceding the final redemption will span nine months, similar to the duration of pregnancy and birth. The agony will come to its climax on the late afternoon of the last Sabbath. Then we will find favor in the eyes of God, and He will begin to turn our suffering into joy.

אֱלֹהִים בְּרָב חַסְדֶּךָ עֲנֵנִי בֶּאֱמֶת יִשְׁעֶךָ — *O God, in the abundance of Your kindness, answer me with the truth of Your salvation.*

The redemption and the reconstruction of the *Beis HaMikdash* are extraordinary gifts which cannot become a reality through ordinary Divine *kindness.* They require רָב חַסְדֶּךָ, *an abundance of Your kindness,* as in וַאֲנִי בְּרֹב חַסְדְּךָ אָבוֹא בֵיתֶךָ (5:8): *As for me, through Your abundant kindness, I will enter Your House (Tefilloh L'Moshe).*

15. The following verses comprise the text of David's prayer to HASHEM *at a favorable time (Radak).*

1. Because we interrupt our festivities with the Torah reading during the *Minchah* service of the Sabbath afternoon it is customary to recite this verse at that time *(Tur, Orach Chaim 292).* However, it is not recited on the afternoon of a יוֹם טוֹב, *festival,* because the Torah is not read then. This verse is reserved for an עֵת רָצוֹן, *a favorable time,* when Israel pleases God by reading His holy Scriptures *(Beis Yosef, Orach Chaim 292).*

Since the gentiles ridicule Jewish Sabbath observance, it is particularly appropriate that this verse is read on the Sabbath as a retort to them *(see Perisha, Orach Chaim 292).*

¹⁴ *But as for me, my prayer is to You, HASHEM,*
at an opportune time,
O God, in the abundance of Your kindness,
answer me with the truth of Your salvation.
¹⁵ *Rescue me from the mire*
so that I sink not;
let me be rescued from my enemies
and from the deep waters.
¹⁶ *Let no swift current sweep me away,*
nor let the shadowy depths swallow me,
and do not let the pit close its mouth over me.
¹⁷ *Answer me, HASHEM,*
for Your kindness is good;

הַצִּילֵנִי מִטִּיט וְאַל אֶטְבָּעָה — *Rescue me from the mire so that I sink not.*

Radak observes that this verse and the following one, which describe Israel as being on the brink of tragedy, seem to contradict verse 3, which pictures Israel as a doomed nation, already engulfed in woe: *I am sunk in deep mire ... I have entered deepest waters; a rushing current sweeps me away.* Radak explains that the earlier verse depicts the immediate emergency, in which Israel is indeed sunk in the mire of exile and inundated with countless miseries. This verse, however, represents Israel's concern for the future. Israel entreats that she not be damned to an eternal exile from which there is no escape.

16. אַל תִּשְׁטְפֵנִי שִׁבֹּלֶת מַיִם — *Let no swift current sweep me away.*

Let no mighty king drag me away into foreign exile (*Targum*).

וְאַל תִּבְלָעֵנִי מְצוּלָה — *Nor let the shadowy depths swallow me.*

[In verse 3, מְצוּלָה is merely translated as *deep,* but a more accurate rendition takes note of the word's relation to צֵל, *shadow.* At this depth, the sun's rays do not penetrate, and the area is shrouded in a dark shadow. This symbolizes a desperate situation of bleak exile, without even a ray of hope for redemption.]

וְאַל תֶּאְטַר עָלַי בְּאֵר פִּיהָ — *And do not let the pit close its mouth over me.*

תֶּאְטַר is related to אִטֵּר יַד, *the left-handed man,* who cannot use his right hand because it is אָטֵר, *closed off,* from normal functions (*Rashi; Radak; Ibn Ezra*).

[Similarly, the exile seals Israel off from normal existence; the nation resembles a prisoner incarcerated in a deep well.]

Targum identifies the בְּאֵר, *well,* as Gehinnom (Purgatory). [Cf. *Eruvin* 19a and *comm.* to 16:11.]

17. עֲנֵנִי ה' כִּי טוֹב חַסְדֶּךָ — *Answer me, HASHEM, for Your kindness is good.*

Divine kindness is not merely a temporary benefaction, but an eternal good which has no injurious aftermath. You kindly designated us as Your Chosen People, but if we will be doomed in exile forever, then Your original kindness was short-lived and not truly *good* (*Yaavetz HaDoresh*).

יח כְּרֹב רַחֲמֶיךָ פְּנֵה אֵלָי: וְאַל־תַּסְתֵּר פָּנֶיךָ
יט מֵעַבְדֶּךָ כִּי־צַר־לִי מַהֵר עֲנֵנִי: קָרְבָה אֶל־
כ נַפְשִׁי גְאָלָהּ לְמַעַן אֹיְבַי פְּדֵנִי: אַתָּה
יָדַעְתָּ חֶרְפָּתִי וּבָשְׁתִּי וּכְלִמָּתִי נֶגְדְּךָ כָּל־
כא צוֹרְרָי: חֶרְפָּה | שָׁבְרָה לִבִּי וָאָנוּשָׁה
וָאֲקַוֶּה לָנוּד וָאַיִן וְלַמְנַחֲמִים וְלֹא

כְּרֹב רַחֲמֶיךָ פְּנֵה אֵלָי — *According to the abundance of Your mercy turn towards me.*

Do not determine my fate on the basis of my merits, for they are lacking; rather relate to me with Your boundless mercy, which knows no limitations (*Radak*).

18. וְאַל תַּסְתֵּר פָּנֶיךָ מֵעַבְדֶּךָ — *(And) hide not Your face from Your servant.*

[Exile must be understood as a new condition of Israel's eternal mission, rather than purely as a punishment. When Israel is banished from its own land, it assumes the challenge of serving as an example to its neighbors of how to live in accordance with God's will despite adverse circumstances. When it does so, it reflects its role as a people fashioned in God's image.

Therefore, the banished people asks, 'O God, if You conceal Your countenance from Your servant, Israel — thus making it difficult for us to fathom Your will — how can we be a reflection of Your sacred image?']

כִּי צַר לִי מַהֵר עֲנֵנִי — *Because I am distressed — answer me quickly.*

Since my situation is desperate, Your immediate response is imperative if I am to survive (*Radak*).

19. קָרְבָה אֶל נַפְשִׁי גְאָלָהּ — *Draw near to my soul — redeem it.*

Israel declares, 'My body will remain imprisoned in foreign hands as long as My soul is captivated by the allure of alien ideologies. Therefore, I pray, *redeem* my soul, for only this spiritual

liberation will assure the פִּדְיוֹן, *ransom of my body'* (*Beis Elokim*).

The Torah states (*Leviticus 25:25*): *If your brother becomes poor and sells some of his estate then his near kinsman shall come to redeem it.* This teaches that the closer the relative, the greater his obligation to redeem his kin. No one is more closely related to the human soul than God, for the soul of man is חֵלֶק אֱלוֹהַּ מִמַּעַל, *part of the Divine Being.* Thus, God, so to speak, is obligated to redeem His 'close relative,' Israel (*Malbim*).

לְמַעַן אֹיְבַי פְּדֵנִי — *Because of my foes, ransom me.*

Radak paraphrases: Release me from exile, for if You fail to do so, my foes will deny Your omnipotence and question Your ability to direct the affairs of the world.

Malbim differentiates between *redemption* and *ransom* as follows: a person is *redeemed* by relatives because of his close ties with them; someone is *ransomed* because of his intrinsic worth.

Unlike the human soul, which is considered akin to God, the body is not a close 'relative' of the Divine Spirit. Nevertheless, the body does deserve to be 'ransomed' on its own merits, lest it be wantonly destroyed by the threatening foe.

20. אַתָּה יָדַעְתָּ חֶרְפָּתִי וּבָשְׁתִּי וּכְלִמָּתִי — *You know my humiliation, my shame, and my disgrace.*

You know that I have suffered every

according to the abundance of Your mercy
    turn towards me.
      ¹⁸ Hide not Your face from Your servant,
        because I am distressed —
        answer me quickly.
      ¹⁹ Draw near to my soul — redeem it;
        because of my foes, ransom me.
      ²⁰ You know of my humiliation,
        my shame, and my disgrace;
          before You are all my tormentors.
      ²¹ Humiliation has broken my heart
        and I am deathly sick.
      I longed for comfort,
        but there was none,
      and for consolers,
        but I found none.

---

type of degradation during my exile (Radak).

נֶגְדְּךָ כָּל צוֹרְרָי — *Before You are all my tormentors.*

Often my tormentors cunningly sought to conceal their plots, not realizing that everything is revealed נֶגְדְּךָ, *before You (Radak).*

נֶגְדְּךָ can also be translated *against You,* to suggest: You know that the disgrace and humiliation which I suffer is on Your account, because I am Your representative. *All of my tormentors are actually against You (Vidal HaTzorfati).*

21. חֶרְפָּה שָׁבְרָה לִבִּי וָאָנוּשָׁה — *Humiliation has broken my heart and I am deathly sick.*

אָנוּשָׁה has been translated as *I am deathly sick* (Rashi); *I am pained* (Radak), or *I have given up hope* [derived from יָאוֹשׁ, *despair*] (Rav Shlomo Atiah).

Beer Avraham explains that the degradation and abuse heaped upon Israel robbed the people of their basic sense of human dignity. Thus, אָנוּשָׁה means *I have sunk to the level of* אֱנוֹשׁ, *frail, flimsy mortal.*

וָאֲקַוֶּה לָנוּד וָאַיִן — *I longed for comfort, but there was none.*

Literally, לָנוּד means *to shake* [see Job 2:11], for the person who comes to offer consolation usually shakes his head as a sign of compassion for the mourner (*Metzudas David*). [Israel bitterly recollects that throughout the exile, no gentile nation ever felt sympathy for her sorrow.]

וְלַמְנַחֲמִים וְלֹא מָצָאתִי — *And for consolers, but I found none.*

[Even if no nation truly felt our pain, at least the gentiles could have offered words of sympathy and solace in order to lighten our misery. Yet even this minimal display of human kindness was not forthcoming from our callous neighbors.]

כב מָצָאתִי: וַיִּתְּנוּ בְּבָרוּתִי רֹאשׁ וְלִצְמָאִי
כג יַשְׁקוּנִי חֹמֶץ: יְהִי־שֻׁלְחָנָם לִפְנֵיהֶם לְפָח
כד וְלִשְׁלוֹמִים לְמוֹקֵשׁ: תֶּחְשַׁכְנָה עֵינֵיהֶם
כה מֵרְאוֹת וּמָתְנֵיהֶם תָּמִיד הַמְעַד: שְׁפָךְ־
כו עֲלֵיהֶם זַעְמֶךָ וַחֲרוֹן אַפְּךָ יַשִּׂיגֵם: תְּהִי־
טִירָתָם נְשַׁמָּה בְּאָהֳלֵיהֶם אַל־יְהִי יֹשֵׁב:
כז כִּי־אַתָּה אֲשֶׁר־הִכִּיתָ רָדָפוּ וְאֶל־מַכְאוֹב

22. וַיִּתְּנוּ בְּבָרוּתִי רֹאשׁ — *They put poison in my meal.*

[בָּרוּתִי, *my meal*, is cognate with בִּרְיָה, described in II *Samuel* 13:7 as the special meal prepared to nurse a sick person back to health (בְּרִיאוּת). It also is the first meal prepared for mourners returning from the burial of a relative (סְעוּדַת הַבְרָאָה).

Not only did the gentiles fail to console the Jews, but even when Israel sought to comfort herself by nursing her own wounds and soothing her own suffering, the gentiles disturbed the Jews and poisoned their spirits with fresh insults and attacks (see *Radak*).]

וְלִצְמָאִי יַשְׁקוּנִי חֹמֶץ — *And for my thirst they gave me vinegar.*

Instead of quenching my thirst, they sought to intensify my agony by making me even thirstier.

This alludes to an incident of treachery documented by the *Midrash (Eichah Rabbah 2:2):* When the Jewish captives were led through their land, the Ishmaelites greeted the Jews with apparent friendliness and sympathy. First, the Ishmaelites gave them well salted food. Then they handed them leather bags which seemed to be full of water, to slake their burning thirst. However, when the unsuspecting Jews raised the bags to their lips, nothing but hot, dry air entered their weakened bodies and they fell dead. [See footnote to *Eichah* 1:19, ArtScroll edition.]

23. יְהִי שֻׁלְחָנָם לִפְנֵיהֶם לְפָח — *Let their table become a snare before them.*

Let them fall victim to their own attempt on my life! They put poison into the meal set on my table, but let them be so involved in their wicked scheming that they mix up their own meal with mine and eat the poison they prepared for me *(Beer Avraham).*

וְלִשְׁלוֹמִים לְמוֹקֵשׁ — *Let their very peace become a trap.*

May the very conditions which they long for as their goal of selfish peace become the source of their misfortune *(Rashi; Radak).*

[They seek to deny me tranquility while retaining their own composure and serenity. Deny them their wish; instead, trouble them and trap them in a web of anxiety and frustration.]

24. תֶּחְשַׁכְנָה עֵינֵיהֶם מֵרְאוֹת — *Let their eyes be too darkened to see* [lit. *from seeing*].

The vision of the wicked is distorted and dim. It leads them to failure and ruination; but the vision of the righteous is straight and true, guiding them in their spiritual ascent *(Midrash Esther Rabbah 7:9).*

וּמָתְנֵיהֶם תָּמִיד הַמְעַד — *And as for their loins, let them falter continually.*

Since the wicked do not see properly, they will stumble and falter. They will lose their high positions of power and prestige. The psalmist refers to the loins, because they support the body's upright posture *(Radak).*

25. שְׁפָךְ עֲלֵיהֶם זַעְמֶךָ — *Pour Your wrath upon them.*

²² *They put poison in my meal,*
and for my thirst they gave me vinegar.
²³ *Let their table become a snare before them;*
let their very peace become a trap;
²⁴ *Let their eyes be too darkened to see;*
and as for their loins,
let them falter continually.
²⁵ *Pour Your wrath upon them,*
and let the fierceness of Your anger
overtake them.
²⁶ *Let their palace be desolate,*
in their tents let there be no dweller.
²⁷ *For the nation You smote,*
they pursued,

Even when God chastises the righteous, He does so with love and concern. He does not drown them in one huge wave of agony, but metes out their suffering in small doses [see footnote to 6:2]. However, since He seeks to obliterate the wicked, He pours out His wrath over them in a single overwhelming torrent (*Yaavetz HaDoresh*).

God mercifully diverted His anger from the Jews themselves. He poured out his wrath upon the sticks and stones of the Temple rather than upon the Jewish nation. [See ArtScroll *Eichah, comm.* to 2:5,6; and 4:11.] The cruel gentiles, though, do not deserve the Divine compassion. Therefore, unleash the full measure of Your fury upon them! (*Shaarei Chaim*).

וַחֲרוֹן אַפְּךָ יַשִּׂיגֵם — *And let the fierceness of Your anger overtake them.*

If they should attempt to flee before Your wrath, do not let them escape. *Overtake them* with Your anger (*Radak*).

26. תְּהִי טִירָתָם נְשַׁמָּה — *Let their palace be desolate.*

They laid waste to Your palace, the *Beis HaMikdash*; therefore, let their splendid castles be desolate (*Norah Tehillos*).

בָּאָהֳלֵיהֶם אַל יְהִי יֹשֵׁב — *In their tents let there be no dweller.*

Throughout the centuries of exile, the gentiles never let us dwell peacefully in our tents; therefore, let them also be driven from their homes (*Norah Tehillos*).

27. כִּי אַתָּה אֲשֶׁר הִכִּיתָ רָדָפוּ — *For [the nation] You smote they pursued.*

God wanted to discipline His errant children of Israel through the gentiles, but they overstepped their authority. The Divine plan permitted the gentiles to smite Israel with restraint, in order to prod the Jews to mend their ways; but the cruel nations were filled with malicious zeal for their mission. Their unbridled, vicious persecution of the Jews was totally unauthorized (*Rashi; Radak*).

Therefore, God's fury is now aroused against these gentiles, as the prophet (*Zechariah* 1:15) warns: *I am greatly enraged by the nations who are at ease, for I was but a little displeased* [with Israel] *but they* [the nations] *helped to increase the evil* (*Yaavetz HaDoresh*).

כח חֲלָלֶיךָ יְסַפֵּרוּ: תְּנָה־עָוֹן עַל־עֲוֹנָם וְאַל־
כט יָבֹאוּ בְּצִדְקָתֶךָ: יִמָּחוּ מִסֵּפֶר חַיִּים וְעִם
ל צַדִּיקִים אַל־יִכָּתֵבוּ: וַאֲנִי עָנִי וְכוֹאֵב
לא יְשׁוּעָתְךָ אֱלֹהִים תְּשַׂגְּבֵנִי: אֲהַלְלָה שֵׁם־
לב אֱלֹהִים בְּשִׁיר וַאֲגַדְּלֶנּוּ בְתוֹדָה: וְתִיטַב

It was for this reason that Pharaoh and his people were punished for oppressing the Jews in Egypt, for God had only permitted him to enslave the Jews, but not to torture and kill them (*Otzar Nechmad*).

וְאֶל מַכְאוֹב חֲלָלֶיךָ יְסַפֵּרוּ — *And they relate the pain of Your mortally wounded.*

[In their cruel glee, they proudly tell of the suffering they inflicted on those whom You have permitted them to punish.]

Radak explains that although חָלָל usually means a *corpse*, that cannot be the correct translation here, because dead men feel no pain [see *Shabbos* 13b]. Here חָלָל means *mortally wounded*, on the brink of death.

If not for the Divine decree, the gentiles could not harm Israel in the least. If they were to realize that they are no more than human agents fulfilling a Divine command, all would go well; but they deny the Divine source of their power and boast of *the pain* which they think they have inflicted on the Jews whom, in truth, You, O God, have wounded — not they (*Tehillos Hashem*).

28. תְּנָה עָוֹן עַל עֲוֹנָם — *Add iniquity to their iniquity.*

Radak understands the word עָוֹן as an alternate for עוֹנֶשׁ, *punishment.* Thus, cause them to suffer new punishment, in addition to that which they already deserve.

Not only should they be condemned for the iniquity of pursuing Israel (v. 27), but also they must be judged guilty for bragging about the pain they added to Israel's wounds (*Ibn Ezra*).

Since their boasting proves that everything they did to Israel was motivated exclusively by cruelty, rather than by disinterested obedience to the Divine command, even pain which they *were* authorized to inflict on us is considered an *iniquity* which is added to their major sin [persecuting Israel excessively] (*Ibn Yachya*).[1]

וְאַל יָבֹאוּ בְּצִדְקָתֶךָ — *And let them not be privy* [lit. enter] *to Your righteousness.*

'You are destined to deal righteously with Israel in the future, allotting them abundant good. Do not allow the undeserving gentiles to have access to that goodness, which should be reserved exclusively for the righteous (*Radak*).

29. יִמָּחוּ מִסֵּפֶר חַיִּים — *Let them be wiped away from the Book of Life.*

Rashbam illustrates this verse poetically: All of the earth is the Book of God and all its inhabitants are

---

1. The *Ramban* in *Genesis* 15:4 (cited in footnote to the ArtScroll edition of *Yonah* 1:14), discusses the philosophical implicaton of the murder of someone whose death had been predetermined on *Rosh HaShanah*. Because a murderer acted out of his own motives, unaware of the Divine decree, he cannot plead that he was carrying out God's will. Since he commits the crime out of personal vindictiveness or hopes of gain, he is guilty, despite the fact that he fulfills God's plan. Pharaoh deserved punishment because he enslaved the Jews solely out of personal vindictiveness. The same applies to Sennacherib (see *Isaiah* 10:5-6) and to Nebuchadnezzar (see *Isaiah* 14:23, 14 and 47:6, 8).

> *and they relate the pain*
>   *of Your mortally wounded.*
> ²⁸ *Add iniquity to their iniquity*
>   *and let them not be privy to Your righteousness.*
> ²⁹ *Let them be wiped away from the Book of Life,*
>   *and with the righteous let them not be inscribed.*
> ³⁰ *But I am afflicted and pain-racked,*
>   *Your salvation, O God, shall raise me high*
> ³¹ *I shall praise the Name of God with song,*
>   *and I shall magnify it with thanksgiving;*

inscriptions. At death, all are erased from the Divine rolls.

Radak maintains that the psalmist is referring to the 'Book of Eternal Life' in the World to Come. In that sacred volume, the wicked have no place.

וְעִם צַדִּיקִים אַל יִכָּתֵבוּ — *And with the righteous let them not be inscribed.*

The *Talmud (Rosh HaShanah* 16b) states that the fate of each person is recorded in one of three special books which are opened on Rosh HaShanah. The perfectly righteous men are immediately inscribed and sealed in the Book of Life. The completely wicked men are immediately inscribed and sealed is the Book of Death. The fate of the others hangs in the balance from Rosh HaShanah until Yom Kippur. If they prove to be worthy, they merit inscription in the Book of Life. If they prove to be unworthy, they are inscribed in the Book of Death.

30. וַאֲנִי עָנִי וְכוֹאֵב — *But I am afflicted and pain-racked.*

Take note of the intense pain caused by the suffering of the exile, and quickly send Your salvation *(Radak).*

Not only is he עָנִי, *afflicted,* by physical pain, he is also the victim of poverty. The chaotic times at the end of the centuries of exile will precipitate a world-wide economic crisis; therefore, the Sages *(Sanhedrin* 97a) say that the advent of Messiah will not come until the last penny vanishes from the purse *(Chazah Zion).*

יְשׁוּעָתְךָ אֱלֹהִים תְּשַׂגְּבֵנִי — *Your salvation, O God, shall raise me high.*

Only Your assistance can lift me from my dismal situation *(Radak).*

31. אֲהַלְלָה שֵׁם אֱלֹהִים בְּשִׁיר — *I shall praise the Name of God with song.*

[The psalmist now enters the final phase of his composition. After recounting the many pains visited upon Israel in exile by אֱלֹהִים, *God, the Dispenser of Strict Justice,* the nation comes to realize that these very blows reinforced the Jewish character and made it impregnable, protected against the incessant onslaughts of the hostile environment.

This God-given strength sends a wave of spiritual exaltation through the loyal and obedient nation of God and fills its soul with song.]

וַאֲגַדְּלֶנּוּ בְתוֹדָה — *And I shall magnify it with thanksgiving.*

When God delivers me from the exile [and returns me to the Holy Land], I shall dedicate a קָרְבָּן תוֹדָה, *thanksgiving offering,* in recognition of His kindness *(Radak).*

לג לַיהוה מָשׁוֹר פָּר מַקְרִן מַפְרִיס: רְאוּ
עֲנָוִים יִשְׂמָחוּ דֹּרְשֵׁי אֱלֹהִים וִיחִי
לד לְבַבְכֶם: כִּי־שֹׁמֵעַ אֶל־אֶבְיוֹנִים יהוה
לה וְאֶת־אֲסִירָיו לֹא בָזָה: יְהַלְלוּהוּ שָׁמַיִם

32. וְתִיטַב לַה' מִשּׁוֹר פָּר — *And it shall please HASHEM more than a full-grown bullock.*

The *Talmud* (*Chullin* 60a) states that during the creation of the world, all animals first appeared on earth at the peak of maturity. At that time, Adam sacrificed a newborn שׁוֹר, *bullock,* which was already as mature as a פָּר, *bull.* Our verse alludes to Adam's offering. The *Talmud* infers from *Leviticus* 22:27 that for the purpose of Temple offerings even on the day of birth, the newborn calf is called a שׁוֹר, *bullock,* but it is not called a פָּר, *bull,* until it is three years old (*Rashi*).

The songs of praise and thanksgiving which Israel will sing to God upon its redemption will surpass the exquisite offering which Adam dedicated to HASHEM (*Radak*).

מַקְרִן מַפְרִיס — *Possessed of horns and hoofs.*

The *Talmud* (*Avodah Zarah* 8a) relates that Adam sinned on the very day on which he had been created. When the sun began to sink beneath the horizon, Adam lamented, 'Woe unto me! Because of my sin, the world is doomed to drown in darkness and to return to chaos. This must be the death penalty which Heaven has ordained for me!'

Adam and Eve both wept bitterly throughout the night.

When the first rays of daylight appeared, Adam realized that the darkness of night was not a punishment but part of the earth's daily cycle. In relief and gratitude, Adam sacrificed a full-grown ox. The ox had been created fully grown on the sixth day of Creation. Like all animals, it emerged from the earth. Our phrase, *horns and hoofs,* indicates that the ox came into being in that order: first the horns emerged, followed by the rest of its body, ending with the hoofs (*Rashi*).

R' Yehuda said in the name of Shmuel: 'The ox which Adam sacrificed possessed but one horn growing out of the center of its forehead.' Adam sinned because his lower animal nature overcame his Divinely granted intellect and spirit. Thus, he distorted his priorities by giving precedence to the flesh before the soul. This was a revolt against the spiritual mastery of God, the Oneness of His Name.

The ox which Adam later sacrificed in repentance symbolized that he had put his values and priorities back into order.

The word קֶרֶן, *horn,* also means *principal,* denoting 'the main thing.' The one horn sprouting from the center of the ox's head signified that henceforth uppermmost in Adam's mind, at the center of his thoughts, Adam had but one concern — to recognize that God is the one and only authority. Only His will should be obeyed. Secondary are the physical needs of man, symbolized by the *hoofs,* which support the animal's entire body. The *hoofs* are פָּרוּס, *split,* a sign that the desires of the flesh are many and diverse (*Maharsha; Avodah Zarah* 5a, *Nefesh HaChaim* 1:20).

Alshich interprets the symbolism of the *ox* differently. Throughout Rabbinical literature, the קֶרֶן, *horn,* is always associated with goring and damage. In the case of Adam, the *horn,* i.e., the damage caused by the sin, came

³² *And it shall please HASHEM more than*
a full-grown bullock
possessed of horns and hoofs.
³³ *The humble shall see it*
— they shall be glad,
you who seek God,
let your hearts revive.
³⁴ *For HASHEM hearkens to the destitute,*
and His prisoners He does not despise.
³⁵ *Heaven and earth shall praise Him;*

first. Only afterwards did Adam offer the kosher animal (identified by its split *hoofs)* to appease God. The offering of Messianic times will surpass this. At that time, Israel will offer a sacrifice of thanksgiving only for the sake of expressing its love for God, without needing atonement for any prior sin.

33. רָאוּ עֲנָוִים יִשְׂמָחוּ — *The humble shall see it — they shall be glad.*

Only the humble will be gladdened by the future salvation, for they alone will witness it. The arrogant will be destroyed *(Radak).*

דֹּרְשֵׁי אֱלֹהִים וִיחִי לְבַבְכֶם — *You who seek God let your hearts revive.*

The heart enveloped in gloom is considered dead, whereas the joyous heart abounds with energy and life. Redemption will lift the faithful ones of Israel from the shrouds of misery and will revive their hearts with gladness *(Radak).*

[For centuries, God's presence was hidden in the shadows; His influence over human affairs remained unseen. Only the devout who searched for Him caught a glimpse of His veiled hand in the events of history. However, when human history draws to an end, God will reveal His ways for all to see. Those who persistently sought to discover God will truly rejoice, for their dream of comprehending His ways will be realized. See *Hirsch.*]

34. כִּי שֹׁמֵעַ אֶל אֶבְיוֹנִים ה' — *For HASHEM hearkens to the destitute.*

Although the poor man is helpless or fettered by pain, this does not mean that God has forsaken him. On the contrary, his very affliction attests to God's respect for him. The Almighty desires to hear his fervent prayers for salvation and to purify his spirit by means of his afflictions *(Hirsch).*

וְאֶת אֲסִירָיו לֹא בָזָה — *And His prisoners He does not despise.*

The nations hold Israel in utter contempt because they arrogantly regard the Jews as their prisoners. In truth, the Jews are only the prisoners of God, the proof being that the Almighty can release them at any moment He desires. Unlike the haughty gentiles, God *does not despise His prisoners.* He will graciously hearken to their plea for redemption *(Radak).*

35. יְהַלְלוּהוּ שָׁמַיִם וָאָרֶץ — *Heaven and earth shall praise Him.*

[In the darkness of exile, God's praises were hidden, but when Israel is redeemed, the world will recognize His greatness. Israel will faithfully publicize His goodness until it is known throughout the earth and is even echoed by the heavens.]

Elsewhere, David offers a similar paean to God (I *Chronicles* 16:31) יִשְׂמְחוּ הַשָּׁמַיִם וְתָגֵל הָאָרֶץ וְיֹאמְרוּ בַגּוֹיִם ה' מָלָךְ, *The heavens shall be glad, and the*

לו וָאָרֶץ יַמִּים וְכָל־רֹמֵשׂ בָּם: כִּי אֱלֹהִים |
יוֹשִׁיעַ צִיּוֹן וְיִבְנֶה עָרֵי יְהוּדָה וְיָשְׁבוּ שָׁם
לז וִירֵשׁוּהָ: וְזֶרַע עֲבָדָיו יִנְחָלוּהָ וְאֹהֲבֵי
שְׁמוֹ יִשְׁכְּנוּ־בָהּ:

---

earth shall rejoice and they shall
proclaim to the peoples, 'HASHEM
reigns!' (Radak).

יַמִּים וְכָל רֹמֵשׂ בָּם — The seas and all that
moves therein.

This too echoes the prophecy of the
psalmist concerning the day when all of
the univese shall acclaim God (96:11):
יִרְעַם הַיָּם וּמְלֹאוֹ, The sea and its fullness
shall shout for joy (Radak).

36. כִּי אֱלֹהִים יוֹשִׁיעַ צִיּוֹן וְיִבְנֶה עָרֵי יְהוּדָה
— For God shall save Zion and build the
cities of Judah.

The psalmist mentions Zion and
Judah because they are the most
prominent locations in the Holy Land.
Also, Judea is the territory of the royal
tribe. While these Holy places were
under gentile rule, they were themselves
considered exiles (Radak).

וְיָשְׁבוּ שָׁם וִירֵשׁוּהָ — And they shall settle
there and possess it.

When Israel first conquered the land,
it was only granted to the Jews
temporarily, as evidenced by their later
exile. In the future, however, Eretz
Yisrael will become their eternal
possession and estate (Zerah Yaakov).

the seas and all that moves therein;
³⁶ For God shall save Zion
and build the cities of Judah.
And they shall settle there
and possess it.
³⁷ The offspring of His servants shall inherit it,
and lovers of His Name shall dwell there.

37. וְזֶרַע עֲבָדָיו יִנְחָלוּהָ — *The offspring of His servants shall inherit it.*

This refers to the descendants of the Patriarchs Abraham, Isaac, and Jacob (*Metzudas David*).

This promise will be fulfilled in the days of Messiah (*Ibn Ezra*).

וְאֹהֲבֵי שְׁמוֹ יִשְׁכְּנוּ בָהּ — *And lovers of His Name shall dwell there.*

This alludes to the Talmudic dictum that no proselytes will be accepted into Judaism in Messianic times (*Yevamos* 24b). Only those who join Israel in the misery of exile are considered sincere converts, stirred by a genuine love for God and His word. Those who request conversion in Messianic times are suspected of ulterior motives, such as the desire to share in the glory and reward of Israel.

Therefore, the psalmist concludes, in the future era of triumph and redemption only the veterans of the tortuous exile will dwell in the Holy Land, for only they have proven that they are *those who love His Name* (*Yaavetz HaDoresh*).

In the preceding psalm, David begged God to redeem the entire Jewish nation from exile. Here he makes a personal plea for his own return. Midrash Shocher Tov illustrates David's wish with a parable:

David may be likened to the shepherd who grazed the flocks of the king. The king became vexed by the shepherd and so he chased away the flock, tore down the animal shed, and dismissed the shepherd. After a time, the king gathered in the sheep and rebuilt the shed, but he did not restore the shepherd to his position. The shepherd lamented, 'Behold the sheep are gathered in, the shed is rebuilt, but I am not remembered!'

In the preceding psalm, (v. 36) David said, God shall save Zion and build the cities of Judah, as if to say, 'Behold the shed is rebuilt'; and they shall settle there and take possession of it, as if to say, 'Behold the sheep are gathered in.' In this psalm, David, the shepherd, asks, 'Shall I not be remembered?' Therefore this composition is dedicated לְדָוִד לְהַזְכִּיר, unto David, For Remembrance.

David gazed prophetically into the future and rejoiced over the rebirth of the nation. However, he feared that God would hold the leaders solely responsible for the sins of the people. Thus, as king and founder of the royal line, he and his descendants would be eternally doomed to exile and oblivion. Fully acknowledging his responsibility for the errors of his subjects, David nevertheless asks God to remember to credit him also for the merits of the people, by virtue of which they are redeemed. If the sheep are worthy to return home, this certainly reflects credit on the faithful shepherd who guided the flock.

א-ב לַמְנַצֵּחַ לְדָוִד לְהַזְכִּיר: אֱלֹהִים לְהַצִּילֵנִי
ג יהוה לְעֶזְרָתִי חוּשָׁה: יֵבֹשׁוּ וְיַחְפְּרוּ
מְבַקְשֵׁי נַפְשִׁי יִסֹּגוּ אָחוֹר וְיִכָּלְמוּ חֲפֵצֵי

1. לַמְנַצֵּחַ לְדָוִד לְהַזְכִּיר — *For the Conductor, unto David, For Remembrance.*

[This superscription appears only at the beginning of one other composition, psalm 38:1, which commences מִזְמוֹר לְדָוִד לְהַזְכִּיר. See *comm.* there.]

Radak and *Meiri* comment that David may have composed this work when he fled from Saul or when he escaped from Absalom. A desperate fugitive, David felt forsaken by God. Therefore he pleaded *for Remembrance.*

[At that time, David foresaw that the entire nation of Israel was destined to experience a sense of abandonment in exile. Therefore, he also bore their future problems in mind when he composed this work. Specifically, David addressed the anguish of the Jewish leaders (see *Prefatory Remarks*).]

Midrash Shocher Tov records God's promise: 'If Israel remembers Me, I shall remember them, as the prophet says, *Ephraim is a darling son to Me, indeed a child of delight, for as often as I speak of him, I do remember him even more; therefore, My heart yearns for him, I will surely have mercy on him, says HASHEM (Jeremiah 31:19).'*

2. אֱלֹהִים לְהַצִּילֵנִי — *O God — to rescue me.*

Verses 2-6 of this psalm are almost identical to verses 14-18 of psalm 40.

Malbim determines that David composed psalm 40 while he was escaping from Saul. He composed psalm 70 at the age of sixty-five, when he was fleeing from Absalom [see *II Samuel* 15:7; *Radak; Mahari Kara*].

This chronology is supported by the fact that psalm 71, which is a continuation of this psalm, refers to David's old age in verses 9 and 19 [see *Radak* to 71:1].

According to *Malbim*, this background explains the superscription לְהַזְכִּיר, *for Remembrance:* David pleads with the Almighty, 'Remember the miraculous rescue from Saul which You provided when I was young and repeat it now, in my old age, as I flee from Absalom!'

[The differences between psalm 40 and psalm 70 can also be understood in the light of this chronology. In 40:14, David invoked the Divine Attribute of Mercy, crying out, רְצֵה ה' לְהַצִּילֵנִי, *Will it, HASHEM, rescue me!* Since David knew that he was innocent in all his dealings with Saul, he felt entitled to HASHEM's mercy. However, when David fled from the army of Absalom, he realized that he was being justly punished for his sin concerning Bath Sheba, for the Prophet Nathan had forewarned him: *I will raise up evil against you from out of your own house (II Samuel* 12:11).

Therefore, David used the Divine Name אֱלֹהִים, which refers to God as *the Dispenser of Divine Justice,* pleading 'Despite my sins, take note of my sincere penitence and contrition. Please hasten לְהַצִּילֵנִי, *to my rescue!'*

ה' לְעֶזְרָתִי חוּשָׁה — *O HASHEM, to my assistance, hasten!*

After You, אֱלֹהִים, *the Dispenser of Divine Justice,* have consented to rescue me, do not delay the day of my salvation. Arouse the Name of HASHEM the Dispenser of Divine Mercy to have compassion and to hasten to my assistance *(Otzar Nechmad).*

3. יֵבֹשׁוּ וְיַחְפְּרוּ מְבַקְשֵׁי נַפְשִׁי — *Shamed and disgraced be those who seek my life.*

[In 40:15, the words יֵבֹשׁוּ וְיַחְפְּרוּ are followed by the word יַחַד, *together,*

For the Conductor, unto David, For Remembrance.
² O God — to rescue me,
O HASHEM, to my assistance, hasten!
³ Shamed and disgraced
be those who seek my life,
repulsed and humiliated
be those who wish me evil.

implying that all the men who joined in Saul's pursuit of David were united (*together*) by one intention: *to seek my* (David's) *life* in order to protect Saul's kingdom. In our psalm, however, the word יַחַד, *together*, is omitted, because no such unity existed in the camp of Absalom. His followers were enmeshed in conflicting conspiracies which splintered them into several groups. David refers to this internal strife in 55:16: *I saw violence and strife in the city* of Jerusalem, Absalom's headquarters.

Absalom tried to fool the people and the Sanhedrin (see 35:11,12, *comm.* and footnote). However, Achitophel, Absalom's most intimate counselor, secretly plotted to overthrow the young prince and to seize the throne (see *Prefatory Remarks*, Psalm 3). Another advisor, Chushai HaArki, was an undercover agent representing David's interests; therefore he purposely misled Absalom. The masses became disillusioned with Absalom and secretly prayed for his downfall (*Yerushalmi Sotah* 1:8; see *comm.* to 55:19).

Also, in 40:15, מְבַקְשֵׁי נַפְשִׁי, *those who seek my life*, is followed by the word לִסְפּוֹתָהּ, *to put an end to*, which is excluded here. Again the reason is that *all* of Saul's men sought *to put an end to*

David's life, out of loyalty to Saul. However, the motives of Absalom's followers were varied].

יָסֹגוּ אָחוֹר וְיִכָּלְמוּ חֲפֵצֵי רָעָתִי — *Repulsed* [lit. *retreat*] *and humiliated be those who wish me evil.*

Shevet M'Yisrael explains that this is a reference to Shimi ben Gera, who cursed David as he fled from Absalom, saying: 'Hashem has given the monarchy to Absalom your son, וְהִנְּךָ בְּרָעָתֶךָ, *and behold you are caught in your own evil*' (II Samuel 16:8).[1]

David's request, *let them be repulsed*, was ultimately fulfilled, for after Absalom was slain, Shimi was repulsed and forced to retract his previous hostility to David. Scripture recounts: *And Shimi ben Gera hurried... and came down with the men of Judah to meet King David... And Shimi ben Gera fell down before the king... And he said to the king, 'Let my lord neither reckon my iniquity against me, nor remember that which your servant did perversely on the day that my lord king went out of Jerusalem... For your servant knows that I have sinned. Therefore, behold I am the first one of all the House of Joseph to come down today to greet my lord, the king'* (II Samuel 19:17-21).

1. The curse hurled by Shimi ben Gera provides us with an essential key to understanding much of David's suffering at the hands of his foes.

Yalkut Shimoni (II Samuel 151) says that Shimi was referring to the carriage of Bath Sheba, which enjoyed a prominent position in the royal entourage. Shimi viewed this as the height of audacity, since he considered Bath Sheba the root of all David's difficulties. How dare David

ד רָעָתִי: יָשׁוּבוּ עַל־עֵקֶב בָּשְׁתָּם הָאֹמְרִים
ה הֶאָח | הֶאָח: יָשִׂישׂוּ וְיִשְׂמְחוּ | בְּךָ כָּל־
מְבַקְשֶׁיךָ וְיֹאמְרוּ תָמִיד יִגְדַּל אֱלֹהִים
ו אֹהֲבֵי יְשׁוּעָתֶךָ: וַאֲנִי | עָנִי וְאֶבְיוֹן אֱלֹהִים
חוּשָׁה לִּי עֶזְרִי וּמְפַלְטִי אַתָּה יהוה אַל־
תְּאַחַר:

4. יָשׁוּבוּ עַל עֵקֶב בָּשְׁתָּם — *Let them be turned back by their deserved shame.*

The word עֵקֶב refers to deserved recompense, whether it is reward for good or punishment for evil. Thus, may their punishment fit their crime. Since these enemies intended to put me to shame, let them come to shame, (*Radak*).

[In 40:16, the verse reads יָשֹׁמּוּ, *Let them be astounded* (Rashi) by their *deserved shame.* Because David recognized Saul as God's anointed king, he had no desire to ascend to the throne during Saul's lifetime. David did seek to foil Saul's vigorous attempts to kill him; he wanted to *astound* Saul, demonstrating that he was invulnerable to the king's attempts on his life.

Absalom, on the other hand, had treacherously usurped David's throne. Therefore, David requested that Absalom be *turned back* (יָשׁוּבוּ), i.e., deposed from the throne which he had unlawfully assumed.]

עַל־עֵקֶב בָּשְׁתָּם — *By their deserved shame.*

[See commentary to 40:16 for discussion of עֵקֶב. *Targum* here renders

because they lay in ambush for me. The עֵקֶב, *heel,* is the lowest part of the body, hidden from view; thus, it is synonymous with an ambuscade (see *Joshua* 8:13). This alludes to the treachery of Absalom and his party. They feigned loyalty to David while secretly plotting against the aging king.]

הָאֹמְרִים הֶאָח הֶאָח — *Those who say, 'Aha! Aha!'*

As I fled, they cheered with glee, 'Aha! Aha! Rejoice! Rejoice!' (*Radak*).

[Similarly, 35:21 states: *They broadly opened their mouths against me. They say, 'Aha! Aha! Our own eyes have seen!'*]

Likewise, the nations of the world rejoiced over the destruction of Jerusalem and the exile of the Jews, as Scripture (*Ezekiel* 26:2) says, *Tyre spoke of Jerusalem saying, 'Aha!'* (*S'forno*).

[In 40:16, we read הָאֹמְרִים לִי הֶאָח הֶאָח, *those who say to me, 'Aha! Aha!'*. As explained in detail in *comm.* to *v.* 3, all of Saul's men were united by one purpose only — the desire to capture David. Therefore, their taunts were directed only לִי, *to me,* i.e., to David.

persist in keeping this very woman as his esteemed queen? 'Since you do not chase her out,' Shimi argued, '*Behold you are caught in your own evil!*'

Meshech Chochma (Parshas Nitzovim) explains the *Talmud's (Yoma 86b)* teaching that complete repentance for a particular sin requires that a person overcome temptation the next time he has a similar opportunity to commit the same sin. The greater the similarity of circumstances in the two instances of temptation, the greater the evidence that the sinner has repented when he avoids repeating his sin. David had 'sinned' with Bath Sheba when she was Uriah's wife, according to this prescription for repentance, David would have had to divorce Bath Sheba and have her remarry, in order to prove that he had conquered his passion for her. Since her remarriage would duplicate her original status as another man's wife, David's temptation would be similar to his original test.

However, the *Talmud (Sanhedrin 18a)* forbids a queen to remarry after her relationship with

⁴ *Let them be turned back by their deserved shame*
those who say 'Aha! Aha!'
⁵ *Let them rejoice and be glad in You,*
all who seek You,
And let them always say, 'God
be magnified' — the lovers of Your salvation.
⁶ *As for me, I am poor and destitute.*
O God, hasten to me!
You are my assistance and He Who causes my escape,
HASHEM, do not delay!

Absalom's camp, however, was splintered into a number of factions which did not share common goals. They rejoiced and they gloated over the prospects of victory, but not all of them directed their taunts toward David.]

5. יָשִׂישׂוּ וְיִשְׂמְחוּ בְּךָ כָּל מְבַקְשֶׁיךָ — *Let them rejoice and be glad in You, all who seek You.*

[Despite their protestations of righteousness, Absalom and his clique were selfish men who sought fortune and power. David's followers, in contrast, were motivated neither by personal ambition nor by hatred for Absalom. They were devout men dedicated to the sanctification of God's Name. They realized that by supporting the monarch, whose mission is to symbolize God's authority and majesty, they glorify God.

However, Absalom's group rejoiced only at David's downfall, as the psalmist laments, *But when I limped they rejoiced and gathered* (35:15).]

וְיֹאמְרוּ תָמִיד יִגְדַּל אֱלֹהִים — *And let them always say, 'God be magnified.'*

[The reading in 40:17 is יֹאמְרוּ תָמִיד. The ו, *vav*, is added here to denote additional praises which will be inspired by the victory over Absalom.

In 40:17, the exclamation is יִגְדַּל ה', *HASHEM be magnified!* (see *comm.*). As explained in *comm.* to v. 2 (אֱלֹהִים לְהַצִּילֵנִי), David here uses the Name אֱלֹהִים, *the Dispenser of Strict Justice*, because the rebellion of Absalom was a Divine punishment for David's sin.]

With time, one's love for a finite object will wane and disappear. Love for the eternal God, whose majesty is infinite, however, will steadily increase. Those who seek Him discover new attributes תָמִיד, *always*. As their awareness of God's glory increases, so does their love for Him, and they exclaim, *'God be magnified!'* This implies the request that their awareness of His splendor grow ever greater (*Sefer Halkkarim*).

the king is terminated. Thus, Bath Sheba's divorce would accomplish nothing; she would merely become a forsaken woman, prohibited to all other men, while David would be permitted to remarry her.

The tragedy of David's life, therefore, was beyond repair. Although he dedicated himself to repentance, he could never fully eradicate his sin. Consequently a trace of sin always remained, providing his enemies with ammunition to use in their attacks on him.

Actually, all those who hated David, hated God; they despised David because he represented God. By sinning, however, David provided these foes with an excuse to blaspheme God, who had chosen David as His anointed. Therefore, when the prophet chastised David, he stressed (II *Samuel* 12:14): אֶפֶס כִּי נִאֵץ נִאַצְתָּ אֶת אֹיְבֵי ה' בַּדָּבָר הַזֶּה, *behold, by this deed you have provided the foes of Hashem with an excuse to blaspheme Him.* It is this taint which can never be completely erased.

אֹהֲבֵי יְשׁוּעָתֶךְ — *The lovers of Your salvation.*

[In 40:11 we read אֹהֲבֵי תְּשׁוּעָתֶךְ. See *comm.* to 71:15 for an explanation of the difference according to *Hirsch*.]

6. וַאֲנִי עָנִי וְאֶבְיוֹן — *As for me, I am poor and destitute.*

Chased from his palace, toppled from his throne, despised by his own son, David was indeed as wretched and as impoverished as a desperate pauper (*Radak*).

[With these words, David reminds God of one of his greatest merits: his arduous preparations for the construction of the Holy Temple. David, the successful ruler of a prosperous people, the conqueror of rich nations, became *poor and destitute* because he dedicated his enormous treasures to the purchase of materials for the *Beis HaMikdash*.

David pleads that God reward his devotion by speedily returning him to his throne, so that he might continue his efforts for the glorfication of God's name.][1]

Chazah Zion says that these words allude to the future suffering of Israel. After the destruction of the First Temple, the Jews were like an עָנִי, *poor man*, who is only nominally impoverished; but after the devastation of the Second Temple, Israel was stripped of every asset. Then the nation resembled the אֶבְיוֹן who is תָּאֵב לְכָל, *in need of everything*, possessing not even the basic necessities for survival.

אֱלֹהִים חוּשָׁה לִי — *O God hasten to me!*

[In 40:18 we read אֲדֹנָי יַחֲשָׁב לִי, *My Lord, think of me*.

Radak (ibid.) identifies יַחֲשָׁב with

חָשׁוּב, *worthy, important*, i.e., 'May I be considered worthy in the eyes of my Lord.' That request could only be made when David fled from Saul because David knew that he was completely innocent in all his dealings with his tormentor. However, when Absalom pursued David, David knew that he was being justly punished for his sins and so he could not ask God to consider him חָשׁוּב, *worthy*, of assistance on his own merit.]

עֶזְרִי וּמְפַלְּטִי אַתָּה — *You are my assistance and He Who causes my escape.*

Our verse refers to God's assistance in the masculine form: עֶזְרִי. This is in contrast to 40:18 where we read עֶזְרָתִי, in the feminine form. *Minchas Shai* cites the *Midrash* (*Kohelles Rabbah* 7:27) which proves from this that the Holy Spirit which envelops the prophets form sometimes speaks in the masculine form and sometimes in the feminine form.

ה' אַל תְּאַחַר — *HASHEM, do not delay!*

[In Psalm 40, David addresses himself to the Dispenser of Strict Justice and says אֱלֹהַי אַל תְּאַחַר, *My God, do not delay!* Throughout *this* composition David recognized his guilt and therefore referred to God as the strict and just אֱלֹהִים. However, in conclusion he now pleads for the mercy of ה', *the Dispenser of Kindness*.

In *Psalm* 40 David considered himself innocent of Saul's terrible accusations and thought himself worthy of HASHEM's kindness; but he concludes with a plea that even if he is guilty and fit to be punished by אֱלֹהִים, God, nevertheless God should not delay His salvation.]

---

1. *Chida* in *Devash L'pi* (מַעֲרֶכֶת טו) explains that Adam was responsible for introducing poverty into the world; as a result of his sin, all men were cursed with the responsibility to support themselves, as Scripture states, *'By the sweat of your brow shall you get bread to eat'* (Genesis 3:19).

David's seventy years of life, a gift from Adam, were dedicated to rectifying Adam's sin [see *Overview Tehillim*, Vol. I, part I]. David could have been the world's most affluent man, but he gladly impoverished himself for the benefit of the rest of mankind suffering from Adam's curse. Since the greatest blessing which he could bestow on mankind was the construction of the Temple, David gave all his money for that cause.

מזמור עא 71

This composition is a continuation of the previous psalm; therefore, it does not require a superscription. These verses provide further insight into David's agitated feelings as he fled from his son, Absalom.

When he had fled from Saul as a youth, David had been sustained by the hope that a long life still lay before him, during which time he would ascend to the throne. Now, in his old age, as the specter of death loomed before him, David truly feared that he might not live to regain his royal crown. David therefore pleaded with God to rejuvenate him, to draw even closer to him, and to endow his final years with unprecedented splendor.

David's passionate words express the feelings of all those who have reached advanced age. This psalm is their special prayer — a fervent request that their venerable years be blessed with dignity and grace, a prayer that meaningful accomplishments will crown a lifetime of achievement. It is a plea that God banish the emptiness and boredom which atrophy the body and frustrate the soul.

In addition, says Meiri, David identified the afflictions of his own old age with the anguish of the entire Jewish nation, which was destined to grow worn and weary during the protracted exile. Here David prays not only for his own rejuvenation, but also for the spiritual revival of the entire Jewish people.

א בְּךָ־יהוה חָסִיתִי אַל־אֵבוֹשָׁה לְעוֹלָם:
ב בְּצִדְקָתְךָ תַּצִּילֵנִי וּתְפַלְּטֵנִי הַטֵּה־אֵלַי
ג אָזְנְךָ וְהוֹשִׁיעֵנִי: הֱיֵה לִי | לְצוּר מָעוֹן
לָבוֹא תָּמִיד צִוִּיתָ לְהוֹשִׁיעֵנִי כִּי־סַלְעִי
ד וּמְצוּדָתִי אָתָּה: אֱלֹהַי פַּלְּטֵנִי מִיַּד רָשָׁע
ה מִכַּף מְעַוֵּל וְחוֹמֵץ: כִּי־אַתָּה תִקְוָתִי אֲדֹנָי

---

1. בְּךָ ה' חָסִיתִי — *In You, HASHEM, I took refuge.*

[The first three verses of this psalm are very similar to 31:2-4, which refers to David's flight from Saul (see *comm.* there). These lines were composed thirty-five years later, as David fled from Absalom.

At that time, the vast majority of the people and most of the Sanhedrin abandoned David. Therefore, the forsaken king could turn to God alone for refuge. Similarly, Israel in exile has no one to turn to but God.]

אַל אֵבוֹשָׁה לְעוֹלָם — *Let me not be shamed, ever.*

Midrash Shocher Tov observes that even though the gentiles disgrace the exiled Jews in this world, the Jews are assured that they will not be shamed in the World to Come, as the prophet says, *Israel is saved by HASHEM, a salvation for all times; they will not be shamed or disgraced forever and ever* (Isaiah 45:17).

[David accepted humiliation at the hands of Absalom, for he viewed it as a Divine punishment for his sin. He was prepared to endure his exile until he repented sufficiently to find favor in God's eyes. He pleads only that his rejection not be לְעוֹלָם, *forever.*]

2. בְּצִדְקָתְךָ תַּצִּילֵנִי וּתְפַלְּטֵנִי — *In Your righteousness rescue me and give me escape.*

David does not claim to deserve Divine salvation from Absalom because of his own *righteousness;* rather, he invokes God's righteousness. David recognizes that this tragic episode represents Divine retribution for his sin with Bath Sheba, for the prophet Nathan had warned him (II *Samuel* 12:11), '*Behold, I will raise up evil against you from out of your own house'* (Radak).

הַטֵּה אֵלַי אָזְנְךָ וְהוֹשִׁיעֵנִי — *Incline Your ear to me and save me.*

David realizes that his sins have formed a barrier which prevents his prayers from ascending heavenward to God. Therefore, David begs God to show him special favor by 'bending His ear' to David's mouth, so that his prayers can reach God directly, without any obstacle (Yaavetz HaDoresh).

3. הֱיֵה לִי לְצוּר מָעוֹן — *Be for me a sheltering rock* [lit. *a rock of a palace*].

[In 31:3, we read הֱיֵה לִי לְצוּר מָעוֹז, *become for me a mighty rock,* because when David fled from Saul, he wanted only a *mighty rock* for protection. Here, though, David's gravest concern was not for his personal safety, but for the preservation of his kingship and of his unique role as God's anointed leader of Israel. He requests that his מָעוֹן, *palace,* in Jerusalem, which symbolizes his monarchy, be returned to him (Radak).]

לָבוֹא תָּמִיד — *To enter for all times.*

[Weary from a lifetime of incessant challenges and flight, David now seeks peace and security for all times.]

צִוִּיתָ לְהוֹשִׁיעֵנִי — *You ordered my salvation.*

Continue to protect me as in the past, by sending Your guardian angels to escort me, as Scripture says (91:11),

In You HASHEM I took refuge,
let me not be shamed, ever.
² In Your righteousness rescue me
and give me escape,
Incline Your ear to me
and save me.
³ Be for me a sheltering rock
to enter for all times —
You ordered my salvation,
for my Rock and my Fortress are You.
⁴ My God! Give me escape
from the wicked one's dominion,
From the hand of the scheming
and the violent.
⁵ For You are my hope,
My Lord HASHEM/ELOHIM —

כִּי מַלְאָכָיו יְצַוֶּה לָּךְ לִשְׁמָרְךָ בְּכָל דְּרָכֶיךָ, *He commands His angels for you, to guard you on all your ways* (Radak).

This may also refer to the Divine command which prohibits the males of Moab from entering the congregation of Israel, but permits the females to enter (see *Deuteronomy* 23:4). Because of this law, David's great-grandmother, Ruth the Moabite, was allowed to marry Boaz. Here David offers thanksgiving for that Divine command which enabled him לָבוֹא תָמִיד, *to enter* [the Jewish nation] *for all times* (*Yaavetz HaDoresh*). [See also Overview V to Ruth, ArtScroll ed.]

כִּי סַלְעִי וּמְצוּדָתִי אָתָּה — *For my Rock and my Fortress are You.*

[In 18:3, David uses the same words to thank God for delivering him from Saul.]

4. אֱלֹהַי פַּלְּטֵנִי מִיַּד רָשָׁע — *My God, give me escape from the wicked one's dominion* [lit. *hand*].

The wicked one refers to Absalom (*Radak*). [It was Absalom who

threatened his father's life and publicly violated David's ten concubines. (See *II Samuel* 16:20-17:2.)]

מִכַּף מְעַוֵּל וְחוֹמֵץ — *From the hand* [lit. *palm*] *of the scheming and the violent.*

The *Targum* renders מְעַוֵּל as מָרֵי עֵילָא, *the master of schemes*, a title which perfectly fits Achitophel, Absalom's treacherous advisor (see *Radak*). [It was he who incited Absalom to acts of חָמָס, *violence*.]

חוֹמֵץ is cognate with חוֹמֵס, *the violent robber*, because the letters צ and ס are often interchanged in Hebrew usage (*Rashi; Radak*).

[The word כַּף, *palm*, denotes a stronger grip than יָד, *hand* (see *comm.* to 18:1). Since Achitophel posed a greater threat to David than did Absalom, David asks to be freed from his clutches.]

5. כִּי אַתָּה תִקְוָתִי — *For You are my hope.*

I fully recognize Your omnipotence; therefore, I place my trust and hope in no power other than You (*Radak*).

ו יֱהוֹה מִבְטַחִי מִנְּעוּרָי: עָלֶיךָ | נִסְמַכְתִּי
מִבֶּטֶן מִמְּעֵי אִמִּי אַתָּה גוֹזִי בְּךָ תְהִלָּתִי
ז תָמִיד: כְּמוֹפֵת הָיִיתִי לְרַבִּים וְאַתָּה
ח מַחֲסִי־עֹז: יִמָּלֵא פִי תְּהִלָּתֶךָ כָּל־הַיּוֹם
ט תִּפְאַרְתֶּךָ: אַל־תַּשְׁלִיכֵנִי לְעֵת זִקְנָה

מִבְטַחִי מִנְּעוּרָי — *My security since my youth.*

Yaavetz Hadoresh explains that in order to appreciate the significance of these words, we must understand the tragic circumstances of David's youth. [See *The Book of Our Heritage, Vol. 3,* 'Sivan,' by Eliyahu Kitov for a full discussion of this topic.] David was misunderstood and despised even by his own father and brothers. This was all part of the Divine design by which David learned to find his security exclusively in God, rather than in men.

6. עָלֶיךָ נִסְמַכְתִּי מִבֶּטֶן — *On You have I relied from birth* [lit., *the belly*].

From the moment of birth, You watched over me and provided me with ample sustenance. Even before I emerged from the בֶּטֶן, *belly*, You prepared food for me מִמְּעֵי אִמִּי, *from the innards of my mother* [this refers to the milk produced within her breasts] (*Radak*).

מִמְּעֵי אִמִּי אַתָּה גוֹזִי — *From the innards of my mother You drew me.*

The translation of גוֹזִי follows *Rashi, Radak,* and *Metzudas David.*

Malbim however, relates גוֹזִי to גוֹזֵז, *shear or cut,* because one of the miracles of procreation is God's ability to fashion one body within another, while sustaining both as separate entities. As the embryo takes shape in the mother's womb, it is separated so that it can develop independently within the placenta. Thus, *from the innards of my mother you cut me off.*

According to the *Talmud (Niddah* 30b-31a), גוֹזִי is a term for taking an oath; while the child is still within the

mother's womb, the angels make him swear to lead a righteous life [see footnote to 24:4].

[This demonstrates that the enormity of God's compassion and concern extends to the very roots of human existence. The Divine spark is implanted even in the fetus, for as *Maharshah (Niddah* 30b-31a) points out, גוֹזִי, *my oath,* has the numerical value of 26, which is equal to the numerical value of HASHEM's name.]

בְּךָ תְהִלָּתִי תָמִיד — *Of You is my praise always.*

I feel myself to be blessed and praiseworthy at all times because of the goodness You bestow upon me (*Radak*).

7. כְּמוֹפֵת הָיִיתִי לְרַבִּים — *I became an example for the multitude.*

Many witnessed my tragic downfall and were chastened by my example. They began to mend their ways lest they too be condemned to share the ignominious fate which was my punishment for my sins (*Rashi; Radak*).

David's entire existence was meant to set the standard of piety and devotion for his people. Even his shortcomings were part of a Divine design to enlighten all of Israel, as the *Talmud (Avodah Zarah* 4b) says: David did not truly deserve to commit his sin concerning Bath Sheba, but God caused the sin so that David should set an example of penitence for the masses. If any man becomes discouraged and doubts his ability to atone for his sins, we reassure him, saying, 'Learn a lesson from David, who erred and spent the rest of his life in intensive, sincere repentance!' (*Tehillos Hashem*).[1]

71
6-9

My security since my youth.

⁶ *On You have I relied from birth;*
    from the innards of my mother You drew me,
Of You is my praise always.
⁷ *I became an example for the multitude,*
    for You were my mighty refuge.
⁸ *Let my mouth be filled with Your praise,*
    all day long with Your glory,
⁹ *Do not cast me off in time of old age,*

וְאַתָּה מַחֲסִי עֹז — *For You [were] my mighty refuge.*

I set a positive example for the people as I fled from Absalom because they saw that I counted on You alone and that You responded by giving me full support (*Ibn Ezra*).

Despite my sins, [You accepted my repentance and] You returned me to my throne (*Radak*).

8. יְמָלֵא פִי תְהִלָּתֶךָ — *Let my mouth be filled with Your praise.*

[No man can fill his mouth with joyous praise when he is overwhelmed with the anguish of exile. Such *praise* can only be uttered upon experiencing the triumph of final salvation. As the *Talmud* (*Berachos* 31a) says: One cannot fill his mouth with mirth in this world, for Scripture states, אָז יִמָּלֵא שְׂחוֹק פִּינוּ, (Only) *then* (at the final redemption), *shall laughter fill our mouths* (126:2).]

From the words of this verse, the *Talmud* (*Berachos* 50b) derives the law that blessings should not be recited while a person has food in his mouth. Rather, his *mouth* should literally *be filled with Your praise.*

כָּל הַיּוֹם תִּפְאַרְתֶּךָ — *All day long with Your glory.*

I find glory in naught but the fact that You deemed me worthy of Your salvation (*Radak*).

9. אַל תַּשְׁלִיכֵנִי לְעֵת זִקְנָה — *Do not cast me off in time of old age.*

[*Avos* 5:21 teaches that זִקְנָה, *old age*, begins at sixty. David was sixty-five when Absalom rebelled.]

Just as You were with me in my youth, please accompany me now, in my old age (*Ibn Ezra*).

Even if I have grown old, i.e., accustomed to my sinful ways, please do not reject me (*Rashi*).

David said to the Holy One, Blessed be He, 'When I was young and strong, I put my life in danger to lead Your sons, the children of Israel, into battle. But now that I have grown old, [they no longer appreciate me and] they say "when will [the old man] die and his name perish?" ' (41:6).

The Holy One, Blessed be He, responded in the words of the prophet (*Isaiah* 46:4), 'Even to old age I am the same, and even to white hairs I shall carry you, I have made and I shall carry

---

1. Indeed, when David fled from Absalom his main concern was that he might set a bad example for the people. The *Talmud* (*Sanhedrin* 107a) teaches that David was so distraught that he even decided to make it appear as if he were worshiping idols.

When David's wise counselor and confidant, Chushai HaArki, observed this, he asked in amazement, 'Shall it then be said that a devout king like you worshiped idols?'

David replied, 'It would be even worse for people to say, "A pious king like David was killed by his own sons" ' [for if such a calamity befalls a righteous king, people will question the value of righteous living. This doubt will greatly undermine the faith of the masses

י כִּכְלוֹת כֹּחִי אַל־תַּעַזְבֵנִי: כִּי־אָמְרוּ אוֹיְבַי

יא לִי וְשֹׁמְרֵי נַפְשִׁי נוֹעֲצוּ יַחְדָּו: לֵאמֹר

אֱלֹהִים עֲזָבוֹ רִדְפוּ וְתִפְשׂוּהוּ כִּי־אֵין

יב מַצִּיל: אֱלֹהִים אַל־תִּרְחַק מִמֶּנִּי אֱלֹהַי

יג לְעֶזְרָתִי °חִישָׁה: יֵבֹשׁוּ יִכְלוּ שֹׂטְנֵי נַפְשִׁי

°חוּשָׁה יג

the burden, indeed I shall bear and rescue (Aggadas Bereishis 35).

כִּכְלוֹת כֹּחִי אַל תַּעַזְבֵנִי — **When my strength fails forsake me not.**

The *Baal Shem Tov* would say that even a young man can find himself 'cast into old age' for if he loses his enthusiasm for life, and slows down in his energetic pursuit of God's service, then he is virtually an old man. Therefore, even the youth should pray that his strength not fail him, so that God's vibrant spirit will not forsake him, leaving him feeble and decrepit.

Shaar bas Rabbim explains these words in light of the *Talmudic* dictum (*Avodah Zarah* 19a): Praiseworthy is the man who repents when he is still in the prime of manhood. If the sinner conquers his turbulent passions during his youth, this is a sign of true contrition; but if the sinner delays repentance until he has become frail and impotent, devoid of temptation, what does his repentance prove?

The tragedy which David experienced with Absalom in his old age caused him to repent the sins of his earlier years; but he feared that his sincere remorse might be deemed insignificant, since he was already elderly and feeble. Therefore he prays, '*Do not cast away my repentance in the time of*

old age; when my strength gives out, do not forsake me.'

10. כִּי אָמְרוּ אוֹיְבַי לִי — **For my foes say of me.**

My foes take counsel together and say of me, 'God has forsaken him' (v. 11). 'We can deal with David as we please, for God has abandoned him as a result of his sins' (*Rashi*).

וְשֹׁמְרֵי נַפְשִׁי נוֹעֲצוּ יַחְדָּו — **And those who watch for my life** [lit. *soul*] **consult together.**

This refers to the stalwart nobles who were once David's comrades, and vigilantly guarded his welfare. Now they have turned against him, and plot his doom (*Rashi; Radak*).

In an alternative interpretation, *Radak* suggests that the description *those who watch out for my soul* fits David's veteran enemies, who spied on him, alert for the most opportune moment to attack the helpless fugitive.

11. לֵאמֹר אֱלֹהִים עֲזָבוֹ — **Saying, 'God has forsaken him.'**

David laments: My enemies celebrate because my own flesh and blood has challenged my rule. They claim that this proves that I have been utterly abandoned by both God and man (*Radak*).

The *Talmud* (*Sotah* 21a) notes that

(*Rashi*).] David said, 'It is preferable that I worship idols [and be disgraced personally] than that the name of God be publicly desecrated. [David reasoned, 'If my son kills me after my feigned idolatry, God's name will be sanctified, because people will say that I was justly punished, for my idol worship.']

Chushai assured David that this drastic step was unnecessary. He explained that it was well known to the people that David was condemned to suffer at the hands of his upstart son because he sinned.

Chushai explained that the Holy Torah purposely juxtaposes the portion dealing with the בֵּן סוֹרֵר וּמוֹרֶה, *the rebellious, insolent son*, and the portion discussing the יְפַת תּוֹאַר, *the woman*

תהלים [882]

when my strength fails — forsake me not.
¹⁰ *For my foes say of me, and those who watch*
for my life consult together,
¹¹ *Saying: 'God has forsaken him,*
pursue and catch him,
For there is no rescuer.'
¹² *O God, be not far from me,*
O My God, hasten to my assistance.
¹³ *Let them be shamed and consumed —*
the adversaries of my soul.

David's enemies lost sight of David's stature as a Torah giant. They forgot that although sin can counterbalance the merit gained by performing a precept, it cannot cancel out the merit acquired by engaging in Torah study. The *Talmud* concludes that had David's foes only realized the tremendous protection which David enjoyed by virtue of his Torah study, they would not have dared to antagonize him. God never forsakes the dedicated Torah student, for the student refuses to abandon his quest for God's teachings.

רְדְפוּ וְתִפְשׂוּהוּ כִּי אֵין מַצִּיל — *Pursue and catch him for there is no rescuer.*

With these words, each of David's adversaries and pursuers encouraged his comrades to intensify their efforts to kill the king. They declared, 'David's legendary military prowess is a thing of the past. God has spurned him; his might has vanished' *(Radak).*

12. אֱלֹהִים אַל תִּרְחַק מִמֶּנִּי — *O God, be not far from me.*

[Remember that despite my sins, I still represent You in the world. If I am defeated, Your Name will be besmirched together with mine.]

Hirsch paraphrases: Prove to my enemies that You are never far from those who diligently study the Torah. Even if Torah scholars sin, their study enables them to repent, as the Sages comment: 'If only they had continued studying My Torah when they abandoned Me!' for immersion in this holy pursuit would eventually have brought the sinners back to God *(Yalkut Shimoni to Jeremiah 16:11).*

אֱלֹהַי לְעֶזְרָתִי חוּשָׁה — *O my God, hasten to my assistance.*

[See *comm.* to 22:20.]

13. יֵבֹשׁוּ יִכְלוּ שֹׂטְנֵי נַפְשִׁי — *Let them be shamed and consumed — the adversaries of my soul.*

At first, defeat will merely shame them, but as they experience repeated disaster, they will ultimately be devastated and consumed *(Alshich).*

of beautiful appearance, the attractive gentile girl captured in battle and taken in marriage by the Jewish soldier. The Torah teaches that the man who follows his lusts and takes such a wife is doomed to reap bitter fruits from the union. He will sire a barbarian who seethes with unbridled passions and revolts against all authority.

David had taken the captured Princess Ma'achah, the daughter of Talmai, King of Geshur, as a war bride. Thus, it was clear to all that a seditious son such as Absalom was destined to bedevil David some day. Indeed, David was inadvertently setting a מוֹפֵת, *example,* which benefited the people, for they now witnessed the full extent of God's justice, which punishes even a person as righteous as David, if he fails to heed the Torah's warnings.

יד יַעֲטוּ חֶרְפָּה וּכְלִמָּה מְבַקְשֵׁי רָעָתִי וַאֲנִי
תָּמִיד אֲיַחֵל וְהוֹסַפְתִּי עַל־כָּל־תְּהִלָּתֶךָ:
טו פִּי | יְסַפֵּר צִדְקָתֶךָ כָּל־הַיּוֹם תְּשׁוּעָתֶךָ כִּי
טז לֹא יָדַעְתִּי סְפֹרוֹת: אָבוֹא בִּגְבֻרוֹת אֲדֹנָי
יז יֱהֹוִה אַזְכִּיר צִדְקָתְךָ לְבַדֶּךָ: אֱלֹהִים

יַעֲטוּ חֶרְפָּה וּכְלִמָּה מְבַקְשֵׁי רָעָתִי — *Let them be enwrapped in humiliation and disgrace — those who seek my harm.*

[My enemies sought to undermine the authority of the Torah and underestimated its efficacy in restoring the sinner to God. As a result, they considered my spiritual *hurt* incurable. Disgrace them by proving their analysis to be completely wrong.]

14. וַאֲנִי תָּמִיד אֲיַחֵל — *As for me, I shall always hope.*

Even when tragedy and despair threaten to engulf me, my confidence in You will not be shaken. I eagerly await an opportunity *to add to all of Your praises (Rashi; Radak).*

According to *Kli Yakar*, these words reflect Israel's incessant yearning for redemption. אֲיַחֵל is an acrostic of the twelfth of *Maimonides'* Thirteen Principles of Faith (Principle 12): אִם יִתְמַהְמֵהַּ חַכֵּה לוֹ, [Even though] he [Messiah] *may tarry, wait for him.*

וְהוֹסַפְתִּי עַל כָּל תְּהִלָּתֶךָ — *That I will add to all Your praises.*

I await Your salvation because it will provide me with the opportunity to add to Your many praises (*Radak*).

Sefer HaIkkarim comments that the most eloquent praise which man can offer to God is to *continually hope* with silent, uncomplaining faith for His salvation.]

Tehillah L'David notes that although David composed or edited one hundred and fifty תְּהִילוֹת for the *Book of Psalms*, He yearned to compose still more praises; however, his lifelong suffering and persecution prevented the realization of this dream. Therefore David and

all of Israel *continually* hope for the Messianic era, in which countless new psalms will be composed. The numerical value of עַל כָּל, lit. *beyond all*, is 150, suggesting that in the future, the number of psalms will be far *beyond all* of the original 150.

15. פִּי יְסַפֵּר צִדְקָתֶךָ — *My mouth shall tell of Your righteousness.*

My entire being is suffused with feelings of love and gratitude to You, to the extent that praises flow effortlessly from my mouth (*Alshich*).

David now begins a paean of praise in gratitude for the clemency which God granted him. In truth, he deserved to die following his sin with Bath Sheba. However, when David acknowledged his transgression, and confessed חָטָאתִי, *I have sinned* [II Samuel 12:13], his sentence was commuted to יִסּוּרִים, *suffering*, which purified his soul and atoned for his misdeed [see *Psalms* 51].

David describes this Divine mercy as צְדָקָה, *righteousness*, and views the pain inflicted upon him by Absalom as part of the compassionate Divine plan which leads transgressors back to God (*Hirsch*).

כָּל הַיּוֹם תְּשׁוּעָתֶךָ — *All day long of Your salvation.*

Hirsch points out the subtle difference between תְּשׁוּעָה and יְשׁוּעָה: the word יְשׁוּעָה, related to the word יֵשׁ, denotes a triumph over dangers which imperil one's very יֵשׁ, *being*. The word תְּשׁוּעָה, however (derived from שׁוֹעַ, *wealthy*, as in *Isaiah* 32:5), indicates deliverance from threats to one's property, influence, or power.

[Although Absalom did not destroy

*Let them be enwrapped in humiliation
and disgrace—those who seek my harm.*
*¹⁴ As for me, I shall always hope
that I will add to all Your praises.*
*¹⁵ My mouth shall tell of Your righteousness,
all day long of Your salvation
for I do not know their numbers.*
*¹⁶ I shall come with the mighty deeds
of my Lord, HASHEM/ELOHIM,
I will mention Your righteousness,
Yours alone.*

David's life, i.e., his יֵשׁ, *being*, he did temporarily succeed in usurping David's royal power and influence. Hence, David's final victory from Absalom is appropriately termed a תְּשׁוּעָה.]

כִּי לֹא יָדַעְתִּי סְפֹרוֹת — *For I do not know their numbers.*

I am forced to sing Your praises incessantly, and to *relate Your righteousness all day long,* because Your wonders are infinite and, therefore, impossible to count *(Radak).*

16. אָבוֹא בִּגְבֻרוֹת... — *I shall come with the mighty deeds of my Lord, HASHEM/ELOHIM.*

I *shall come* to offer hymns of praise inspired by HASHEM's mighty acts *(Rashi).*

When I go out to battle my enemies, I place my faith in God's *might,* rather than in human power *(Radak).*

Thus, when I emerge victoriously, I claim no glory for myself, but only *make mention of Your righteousness, Yours alone (Meiri).*

[David composed this psalm at the age of sixty-five (see *Prefatory Remarks* and *comm.* to *v.* 9). He looked forward to old age, as he says in 90:10, יְמֵי שְׁנוֹתֵינוּ בָהֶם שִׁבְעִים שָׁנָה וְאִם בִּגְבוּרֹת שְׁמוֹנִים שָׁנָה, *The days of our years are seventy, or if with might, eighty years* (see *Avos* 5:24).]

[Repentance endowed the aged David with tremendous new reservoirs of moral vigor, to which he never had access in his youth. Consequently, he sought renewed physical vigor so that he might reach previously unattainable heights in the service of God.]

אַזְכִּיר צִדְקָתְךָ לְבַדֶּךָ — *I will mention Your righteousness, Yours alone.*

Since Adam had presented seventy years of his life to David as a gift [see *Overview, Tehillim* vol. I, part I], David expressed appreciation to Adam. 'However,' reasoned David, 'If God will let me live until I reach גְּבֻרוֹת, *might,* i.e., eighty years, then for those ten additional years I am indebted to God *alone,* and I will make mention of His righteousness exclusively' *(Chazah Zion).* [1]

1. [In 39:5 we read David's plea, *Let me know, O HASHEM, my end and the measure of my days, what is it?* In the *footnote* to that verse, we learn that God refused to tell David when he would die.

My son, Eliyahu Meir, יי״נ, observes that since David knew that he had received exactly seventy years of life as a gift from Adam, (as explained in the *Overview* to *Tehillim* vol. 1, part I), he should have known precisely when his death would occur.

This verse, however, teaches that David *did* harbor hopes of living longer than seventy

יח אֱלֹהִים אַל־תַּעַזְבֵנִי עַד־אַגִּיד זְרוֹעֲךָ

לְמִדַּתַנִי מִנְּעוּרָי וְעַד־הֵנָּה אַגִּיד
נִפְלְאוֹתֶיךָ: וְגַם עַד־זִקְנָה | וְשֵׂיבָה

17. אֱלֹהִים לִמַּדְתַּנִי מִנְּעוּרָי — *O God, You have taught me from my youth.*

From my earliest youth, You taught me to accept You as אֱלֹהִים, *the Strict Dispenser of Divine Justice.* It was You Who raised me as a lonely shepherd in a harsh and hostile environment, for no tender parents ever sheltered me. As the Patriarch Jacob described the rugged lot of the shepherd, *'By day drought consumed me, and the frost by night, and my sleep departed from my eyes'* (Genesis 31:40).

Ferocious combat was my youthful pastime, rather than innocent child's play: *Your servant slew both the lion and the bear (I Samuel 17:36).* This conditioned me to fear no mortal danger. Scripture records that David said, 'HASHEM, *Who delivered me from the paw of the lion and the paw of the bear, He will deliver me from the hand of the Philistine (I Samuel 17:37).*

My tender mind was molded with trust in God; as I grew older this youthful faith became even firmer, imbuing me with unshakeable confidence to face the vicissitudes of life *(Chazah Zion).*

In addition, O God, You have endowed me from youth with the ability to discern Your generosity and Providence in all phases of life *(Radak).*

וְעַד־הֵנָּה אַגִּיד נִפְלְאוֹתֶיךָ — *And until this moment I declare Your wonders.*

[The Sage Elisha ben Avuyah taught that lessons mastered in childhood can be compared to ink written on fresh paper *(Avos 4:25).*

The vivid lessons of David's youth left an indelible imprint on his soul. His early psalms were like unfinished

symphonies; throughout David's life, he added new verses in praise of God.

Although the aged David's bones grew brittle and his skin turned dry, his spirit remained youthful and undaunted. He continued to extol each new Divine revelation with his original youthful sense of awe (see *Radak; Alshich*).]

18. וְגַם עַד זִקְנָה וְשֵׂיבָה אֱלֹהִים אַל תַּעַזְבֵנִי — *And even until old age and hoariness, O God, forsake me not.*

[*Avos* 5:24 states: The man of sixty has attained זִקְנָה, *old age.* Rashi comments that at sixty, a man's hair begins to turn white. *Meiri* notes that when one reaches this age, he tends to lose his interest in worldly matters. This being so, the *Mishnah* advises him to take advantage of this natural phenomenon and concentrate his remaining years on the worship of the Holy One, taking heed of his approaching death.

Sixty is the age of complete mental maturity, for the Sages (*Kiddushin* 32b) teach that the word זָקֵן (*zaken*), *old,* is a loose abbreviation of the words *zehkanah-chochma,* one who has acquired wisdom.

David hoped that God would remain near him in his old age and grant him that wisdom which is attainable only at the peak of maturity.]

עַד...שֵׂיבָה — *Until... hoariness.*

[The *Mishnah* in *Avos* 5:24 continues: The man of seventy has attained שֵׂיבָה, *hoary old age.* The Torah commands, *You shall stand up before the man of* שֵׂיבָה *(Leviticus 19:32).* Since Heaven has seen fit to grant him advanced age, he deserves honor *(Magen Avos).*

years, on his *own* merit. It is also possible that he feared that his life might be shortened to less than seventy years, because of his sins. For these reasons he sought to know the exact *measure of his days.*]

¹⁷ *O God, You have taught me from my youth,*
and until this moment
I declare Your wonders.
¹⁸ *And even until old age and hoariness*
O God, forsake me not
Until I proclaim
Your strength to the generation,

Seventy is considered the natural end to a full life (see 90:10), and David himself died at seventy, as Scripture states, וַיָּמָת בְּשֵׂיבָה טוֹבָה שְׂבַע יָמִים, *and he died in full, hoary old age, full of days (I Chronicles 29:28).*

Meiri (Avos 5:24) comments: The old man of seventy is no longer capable of any worldly pursuits. Therefore, he should dedicate his time and energy for God's sake.

Magen Avos quotes *Rabbeinu Yonah:* As a man approaches his end, let him stir himself to repentance, in the realization that his life will not continue indefinitely.

When a wise philosopher first noticed the white strands in his hair, he remarked, 'These are the messengers of death.' If a person ignores this opportunity for repentance, the prophet criticizes him: *Hoariness has cast* [its mark on him], *and he knows it not (Hosea 7:9).* David asks that God be with him in this critical period of his life, as he approaches his final destiny.]

According to *Yalkut Shimoni 804,*

the word שֵׂיבָה is cognate with יְשִׁיבָה, *sitting.* This would suggest: when I was young and powerful, I could stand on my own two feet — yet You came to my assistance and performed wonders to save me. Now that I am feeble and compelled to sit, please do not forsake me.[1]

עַד אַגִּיד זְרוֹעֶךָ — *Until I proclaim Your strength.*

When I was young, it was possible for people to be misled by my physical strength and to attribute my amazing victories to my personal prowess. Now, although I am old and weak, I still continue to be triumphant. This proves that it is *Your strength* alone which supports me *(Radak; Malbim).*

Malbim adds that זְרוֹעַ literally means *the upper arm,* which is the source of the lower hand's strength (see *comm.* to 44:4). God is the זְרוֹעַ, i.e., the ultimate source of all human strength manifested in the lower world.

לְדוֹר — *To the generation.*

Radak identifies this as the present generation, i.e., David's contemporar-

---

1. The *Midrash (Bereishis Rabbah 59:3)* quotes Abraham, who asked, 'Dear God, now that You have granted me זִקְנָה, *old age,* please also grant me שֵׂיבָה, *hoariness.'* Abraham's request can be explained by drawing upon the introduction of *R' Shimon Shkop* to *Shaarei Yosher:*

The *Talmud (Bava Metziah 87a)* states that until Abraham, no man showed the signs of old age. Fathers and sons looked exactly alike; thus, when someone wanted to speak to Abraham, he sometimes mistakenly spoke to Isaac, and vice versa. Therefore, Abraham requested that he be given the appearance of old age, as Scripture states *(Genesis 24:1),* וְאַבְרָהָם זָקֵן בָּא בַּיָּמִים, *And Abraham was old, advanced in age.*

Abraham wanted to look his age in order to arouse his student's respect for his teachings concerning the one true God. He was a זָקֵן, *elder scholar,* and he began the Torah tradition among the Jewish people by establishing and heading a Yeshiva *(Yoma 28b).* Abraham deemed it essential that he be endowed with the glorious dignity of old age in order to arouse his students' respect and thereby facilitate their acceptance of the revolutionary belief in one God, which he sought to instill in their hearts.

יט לְדוֹר לְכָל־יָבוֹא גְּבוּרָתֶךָ וְצִדְקָתְךָ
אֱלֹהִים עַד־מָרוֹם אֲשֶׁר־עָשִׂיתָ גְדֹלוֹת
אֱלֹהִים מִי כָמוֹךָ: אֲשֶׁר °הִרְאִיתָנוּ |
צָרוֹת רַבּוֹת וְרָעוֹת תָּשׁוּב °תְּחַיֵּינוּ
וּמִתְּהֹמוֹת הָאָרֶץ תָּשׁוּב °תַעֲלֵנוּ: תֶּרֶב |

°הִרְאִיתַנִי כ
°תְּחַיֵּנִי
°תַּעֲלֵנִי כא

---

ies. *Targum* renders this as לְדָר דָרֵי, *for generation after generation.* [David hopes that these lessons taught to his generation will be so powerful that they will leave an impression for generations to come.]

לְכָל יָבוֹא גְּבוּרָתֶךָ — *To all who will yet come — Your might.*

May the venerable remnants of the present generation recount Your greatness to the next generation. I shall perpetuate Your Name by recording *Your might* in the Book of *Psalms* for future generations to read (*Radak*).

[Inspired by these tales of *Your might*, future generations will have the fortitude to endure their exile.]

19. וְצִדְקָתְךָ אֱלֹהִים עַד מָרוֹם — *And Your righteousness, O God, is unto the high heavens.*

Here David continues to reveal the details of the promise he began in the preceding verse: *I will proclaim ... Your righteousness* which is *unto the high heavens* (*Rashi*). Your righteousness surpasses that of any human *tzaddik*. It defies description because it is far beyond human comprehension (*Ibn Ezra*).

According to *Pesikta Rabbosi (47:1)*, God's compassion and concern extend not only to the lowly denizens of this earth but also to the lofty heavenly bodies. Since the moon had no light of its own, it appeared to be doomed to shrouded oblivion. God mercifully positioned it in the heavens in such a way that it would reflect the sun's brilliance and thus assume a position of prominence in the skies.

Hirsch reminds us that David (who is

here fleeing from Absalom) speaks as a penitent lauding God for the extraordinary charity and righteousness which He demonstrates to the remorseful sinner.

Indeed, repentance rises to the high heavens, as the Sages note (*Yoma* 86b), *Teshuvah* (repentance) is of unsurpassed greatness for its effects rise to God's heavenly throne. God has provided the sincere penitent with the opportunity to eradicate the very roots of his transgression and to make a fresh start.

אֲשֶׁר עָשִׂיתָ גְדֹלוֹת — *You, [Who] have done great things.*

Your accomplishments are so great that they defy description (*Alshich*).

אֱלֹהִים מִי כָמוֹךָ — *O God, who is like You?*

Your greatness inspires all who witness it to extol Your virtues, as did Moses and all of Israel when they joyously proclaimed (*Exodus* 15:11), מִי כָמֹכָה בָּאֵלִם ה', *Who is like You among the mighty HASHEM?'* (*Radak*).

20. אֲשֶׁר הִרְאִיתַנִי צָרוֹת רַבּוֹת וְרָעוֹת — *You [Who] have shown me many and grievous troubles.*

Although the word is written הִרְאִיתָנוּ with a ו, *vav* (denoting the plural form), it is pronounced with a י, *yud,* (which) indicates the singular form. This discrepancy implies that David has applied his personal experience to the history of the entire nation. David traces his own transition from hunted fugitive to honored monarch and prophesies that the Jewish people will undergo a similar metamorphosis from exile to redemption. David foresees that just as he was

To all who will yet come —
Your might.
¹⁹ And Your righteousness,
O God, is unto the high heavens,
You, Who have done great things,
O God, Who is like You?
²⁰ You, Who have shown me
many and grievous troubles, revive me again.
And from the depths of the earth
raise me again.

chased from Jerusalem by his son before returning in triumph to the Holy City, so will Israel eventually return from the Diaspora to their cherished homeland (*Radak; Hirsch;* see *Pesikta Rabbosi* 34:6).

[Ironically, the Jews were exiled from Jerusalem because of the treachery of the 'sons' of Israel, who betrayed their fatherland and brought destruction upon their own people; similarly, David was chased from Jerusalem by the treachery of his son Absalom.]

תְּשׁוּב תְּחַיֵּינִי — *Revive me again.*

[The exile of a nation normally signifies its demise as a unified entity. Thus the redemption of an exiled people is comparable to the resurrection of the dead.

Death also haunted David's family. The infant born from his initial union with Bath Sheba died soon after birth. David's son Amnon was treacherously murdered by Absalom, and Absalom himself was eventually slain.]

וּמִתְּהֹמוֹת הָאָרֶץ תָּשׁוּב תַּעֲלֵנוּ — *And from the depths of the earth raise me again.*

David compares his woes to a deep abyss *(Ibn Ezra).* The word תַּעֲלֵנוּ, *bring us up* (referring to the entire nation) is written in the plural but the pronunciation is in the singular, תַּעֲלֵנִי, *bring me up* (referring to David himself) *(Radak).*

[This alludes to the fact that after death, Absalom sank to the lowest

depths of hell. When David learned of his son's demise, *the king was sorely distressed and went up to the chamber over the gate and wept, and as he went, he said: 'My son Absalom, my son, my son Absalom! I would have died for you, O Absalom, my son, my son!'* (II Samuel 19:1).

The *Talmud* (*Sotah* 10b) asks why it was necessary for David to cry out eight times on behalf of his deceased son, referring to him both as *Absalom* and *my son.* The *Talmud* explains that David's first seven cries raised Absalom from the seven levels of *Gehinnom.* With David's eighth cry, some Sages maintain, Absalom's severed head was rejoined to his body. Others say that this final prayer elevated Absalom's soul so that it became worthy to enter the World to Come.

Maharsha (*Sotah* 10b) explains that ordinarily, even a father's great merits cannot save his sinful child from punishment (see *Tosafos, Sotah* 10b). In this case, however, Absalom was suffering in part for the sins of David. The prophet had warned David that his sin concerning Bath Sheba would have bad influence on his family: *'I will raise up evil against you from out of your own house'* (II Samuel 12:11).

Therefore, Absalom was in *Gehinnom* partly because of his father. David recognized this when he screamed, *'I would have died for you, O Absalom,*

כב גְּדַלְתִּי וְתִסֹּב תְּנַחֲמֵנִי: גַּם־אֲנִי | אוֹדְךָ
בִכְלִי־נֶבֶל אֲמִתְּךָ אֱלֹהָי אֲזַמְּרָה לְךָ
כג בְכִנּוֹר קְדוֹשׁ יִשְׂרָאֵל: תְּרַנֵּנָּה שְׂפָתַי כִּי
כד אֲזַמְּרָה־לָּךְ וְנַפְשִׁי אֲשֶׁר פָּדִיתָ: גַּם־
לְשׁוֹנִי כָּל־הַיּוֹם תֶּהְגֶּה צִדְקָתֶךָ כִּי־בֹשׁוּ
כִי־חָפְרוּ מְבַקְשֵׁי רָעָתִי:

my son, my son!' Therefore, David's prayers succeeded, because by praying for Absalom he was, in reality, praying for himself.

This perhaps is the meaning of the double usage: From the depths of the earth תַּעֲלֵנִי bring me (David) up, and thereby תַּעֲלֵנוּ bring us, i.e., both David and Absalom, up].

21. גִּדַּלְתִּי — תֶּרֶב — Increase my greatness.

Increase my greatness to a level which even surpasses the glory I enjoyed before my decline. In reference to the Jewish nation, this means that when the Messiah redeems Israel, the Jews will enjoy tremendous prestige which will exceed any temporary preeminence which they had ever enjoyed in former times (Radak).

[After David recovered his throne from Absalom, he enjoyed greater power and recognition than ever before.]

וְתִסֹּב תְּנַחֲמֵנִי — And turn to comfort me.

[David asks that he be granted consolation for the death of his son and that Israel be comforted for the suffering it endures in exile.]

22. גַּם אֲנִי אוֹדְךָ בִכְלִי נֶבֶל ... אֲזַמְּרָה לְךָ בְכִנּוֹר — I too shall thank You on the Neivel instrument ... I shall sing to You on the Kinor.

[See comm. to 33:22 for a complete description of these musical instruments.]

Exile stifles all sounds of music and joy, but when You increase my greatness at the time of the Messianic redemption, I will respond by increasing my songs of thanks to you (Radak).

אֲמִתְּךָ אֱלֹהָי — For Your faithfulness, my God.

You promised to return us from exile, and we shall rejoice when You faithfully fulfill Your word (Radak).

קְדוֹשׁ יִשְׂרָאֵל — O Holy One of Israel.

[When the individual or the nation of Israel as a whole becomes defiled by sin, it is You Who inspires them to return to the heights of holiness, so that they become worthy of redemption.]

23. תְּרַנֵּנָּה שְׂפָתַי כִּי אֲזַמְּרָה לָּךְ — My lips shall rejoice when I sing to You.

When my lips sing to the accompaniment of the Neivel and Kinor (Rashi), the ecstatic phrases of song will echo the joy bursting from my heart, and every utterance will be completely sincere.

Similarly the psalmist declared (84:3), לִבִּי וּבְשָׂרִי יְרַנְּנוּ אֶל אֵל חָי, Both my heart and my flesh will rejoice towards the living God (Radak).

David implies, 'The fact that I enjoy the privilege of singing to You is ample cause to rejoice. Indeed, song is the very

²¹ *Increase my greatness,*
   and turn to comfort me.
²² *I, too, shall thank You, on the* Neivel *instrument,*
   for Your faithfulness, my God,
I shall sing to You on the Kinor,
   O Holy One of Israel.
²³ *My lips shall rejoice when I sing to You,*
   and my soul which You have redeemed.
²⁴ *My tongue, too, all day long*
   shall utter Your righteousness.
For they are shamed,
   for they are humiliated —
   those who seek my harm.

purpose of my entire existence, for Adam endowed me with seventy years of his life only so that my songs should rectify the damage inflicted by his sins' (Alshich).

וְנַפְשִׁי אֲשֶׁר פָּדִיתָ — *And my soul which You have redeemed.*

David continues, 'My soul, which is a fragment of the soul of Adam, finds serenity and redemption from sin only through inspired song' (Alshich).

[Furthermore, I was redeemed from the threat of Absalom only by virtue of my sacred compositions praising God.]

24. גַּם לְשׁוֹנִי כָּל הַיּוֹם תֶּהְגֶּה צִדְקָתֶךְ — *My tongue, too, all day long shall utter Your righteousness.*

Today I sing to the accompaniment of musical instruments, but even when such instruments are absent, my tongue

will continue to sing of Your righteousness (Ibn Ezra).

[In his commentary to 12:4, Malbim states that שְׂפָתַיִם, lips, always denote external communication, the spoken work which relates the desires of the flesh; but לָשׁוֹן, tongue, refers to internal speech, the intimate thoughts of man's heart which are expressed only to his Creator. David says, 'My (external) lips shall rejoice (v. 23) and my (internal, spiritual) tongue too shall speak of Your righteousness.']

כִּי בֹשׁוּ כִי חָפְרוּ מְבַקְשֵׁי רָעָתִי — *For they are shamed, for they are humiliated — those who seek my harm.*

My spirit soars as I sing, while they are covered with disgrace (Radak).

Absalom and his followers suffered every type of ignominy and disgrace; they met with total defeat and their revolt was crushed (Alshich).

72 מזמור עב

T his psalm concludes the second Book of Tehillim. It is also the
   final psalm dedicated to specific events in David's lifetime (see
comm. to v. 20).

Radak states that David was near death when he composed this
hymn. It was the most triumphant day of his career — the day on
which he crowned his beloved son, Solomon, as his successor to the
royal throne. This magnificent event represented the realization of
David's primary goal, the culmination of all his prayers.

That glorious day brought unprecedented celebration. David's
loyal followers blessed him, 'As HASHEM has been with my master,
the king, so shall He be with Solomon, and may He make his throne
even greater than the throne of my master the king, David' ... And
they blew the shofar, and all the people said, 'Long live King
Solomon!' ... And the people played the flutes and rejoiced with great
joy, so that the very earth was shattered by their voices ... And also,
thus said the king, 'Blessed be HASHEM, the God of Israel, Who has
today provided a successor to sit on my throne, and my own eyes see
it' I Kings 1:37, 39-40, 48).

David entertained great hopes for his son. As his death
approached, David reviewed the events of his life and realized that
many of his cherished plans for creating a perfect society based on the
laws of the Torah remained unfulfilled. With his last breath, David
charged his temporal and spiritual heir, Solomon, with the task of
creating a utopian world order predicated on Divine righteousness
and justice.

Solomon came very close to realizing his father's great ambition,
and to the extent to which he succeeded, his rule resembled the future
reign of Messiah. Thus, Sforno and Radak note, the verses of this
psalm apply both to Solomon and to his descendant, the long-awaited
Messiah.

א לִשְׁלֹמֹה ׀ אֱלֹהִים מִשְׁפָּטֶיךָ לְמֶלֶךְ תֵּן
ב וְצִדְקָתְךָ לְבֶן־מֶלֶךְ: יָדִין עַמְּךָ בְצֶדֶק
ג וַעֲנִיֶּיךָ בְמִשְׁפָּט: יִשְׂאוּ הָרִים שָׁלוֹם לָעָם

1. לִשְׁלֹמֹה — *For Solomon.*

Why was the great gift of wisdom and justice granted to Solomon? Scripture relates (I *Kings* 3:5-12): *In Givon HASHEM appeared to Solomon in a dream of the night, and God said, 'Ask of me what I shall give you.'*

And Solomon said, ' You have done great kindness to my father, David, because he walked before You with truth and righteousness and with uprightness of heart, and You kept for him this great kindness and gave him a son to sit on his throne, as it is this day. And now, HASHEM, my God, You have made Your servant king in the place of David, my father, and I am but a little child; I know not how to go out or come in. [Solomon was only twelve years old when he became king. (*Seder Olam Rabbah* 14).] *Give therefore to Your servant an understanding heart to judge Your nation, that he may discern between good and evil, for who is able to judge this, Your very numerous nation?'*

And it pleased HASHEM that Solomon had asked this thing. And God said to him, 'Since you have requested this and you have not requested for yourself long life and you did not request for yourself riches and you did not ask for the life of your enemies, but You did request for yourself discernment, to understand judgment, behold, I have acted in accordance with your words, and I have given you a wise and understanding heart, so that there has been none who compares to you before you, and after you none shall arise like you'.

Rashi explains that David composed this psalm when he foresaw that such extraordinary wisdom would be granted to his son.

Targum renders לִשְׁלֹמֹה, *by Solomon,* maintaining that this psalm is a prophetic hymn composed by Solomon, dedicated to the future Messiah.

Radak notes that the Messiah is referred to as שְׁלֹמֹה, which is a contraction of שֶׁהַשָּׁלוֹם שֶׁלוֹ, *peace is his,* as in (*Songs* 8:12) הָאֶלֶף לְךָ שְׁלֹמֹה, *the thousand is for you, Solomon.*

אֱלֹהִים מִשְׁפָּטֶיךָ לְמֶלֶךְ תֵּן — *O God, Your judgments to the king—do give.*

David prays, 'O God, please endow my son (and the future Messiah) with the wisdom to follow the laws of the Torah without error and to render equitable decisions, based exclusively on Torah dictates' (*Rashi; Radak*).

Perfect, total justice cannot be performed by a finite, mortal judge, unless he is guided by the wisdom of God, Who is the sole source of universal justice (*Malbim*).

According to *Midrash Shocher Tov,* David refers here to a specific request: 'O God, You can distinguish between innocence and guilt without the aid of witnesses or warnings; please grant Solomon this ability.'

David's request was fulfilled when two women came before Solomon, each claiming to be the mother of a certain infant. Solomon brilliantly proved the identity of the real mother, without the aid of witnesses (I *Kings* 3:16-28).

At that moment, a Divine proclamation corroborated Solomon's judgment. Thus all of Israel knew with certainty that God had granted wise judgment to this king (see *Maccos* 23b).

וְצִדְקָתְךָ לְבֶן מֶלֶךְ — *And Your righteousness to the prince!* [lit. *son of the king*].

This also refers to Solomon (*Rashi*) and to the Messiah (*Radak*).

It is insufficient for a king to base his ruling solely on a rigid code of law. The responsible magistrate should temper justice with mercy and should help the

72
1-3

For Solomon. O God,
Your judgments to the king — do give,
and Your righteousness to the prince!
² May he judge Your nation with righteousness,
and Your poor with justice.
³ May the mountains bring the nation peace,

litigants to fulfill the requirements of the law (Rashi; Zerah Yaakov).

[When a new king is establishing his rule and building his dynasty, he often cannot afford to be lenient, lest he undermine his royal authority. Thus, God, Your (authority for strict) judgment to the (first) king — do give; but that king's son, who has inherited a stable, secure throne, can often afford to show clemency and compassion. Thus, grant Your righteousness (and a spirit of mercy) to the son of the king.]

According to Rashi, David asks that any harsh Divine judgment to be meted out to his family be inflicted directly upon him, the king. Thus David's son Solomon, the son of the king, would enjoy righteousness and serene peace and would not be condemned to suffer for his father's sins.

2. יָדִין עַמְּךָ בְצֶדֶק — May he judge Your nation with righteousness.

Mishnas Rabbi Eliezer 4 says that Solomon's uncanny judgment frightened everyone, including hardened criminals, into acting with righteousness. When the people heard of the famous case of the two mothers (in which Solomon saw the truth unaided by any tangible evidence or witnesses), they said, 'We had better not steal or break the law, lest Solomon discover our crimes.'

The Zohar (II 78a) says that since the Holy Spirit rested upon Solomon's wondrous throne, all who approached it were frightened and awed. A threatening figure perched on the throne would shake violently when anyone lied. Thus Solomon could detect a deceiver without the aid of witnesses.

[See Targum Sheni to Megillas Esther Chapter 1.]

וַעֲנִיֶּיךָ בְמִשְׁפָּט — And Your poor with justice.

May Solomon treat the downtrodden and the poor in accordance with the law and show no favoritism to the powerful and the rich (Radak).

Hirsch explains that the paupers are called Your poor because God Himself has decreed that they be impoverished. The Divine order of the world, Hirsch notes, is predicated on the unequal distribution of wealth [see commentary and footnote to 61:8]. If all men were economically equal and self-sufficient, then there would be no opportunity for צֶדֶק, righteousness, and charity in this world.

3. יִשְׂאוּ הָרִים שָׁלוֹם לָעָם — May the mountains bring the nation peace.

Rashi interprets this literally: When the mountains are filled with abundant grain and crops, the people are satisfied. Prosperity creates contentment, which fosters feelings of friendship and brotherhood. Thus, peace will flourish in the land.

Radak understands this allegorically: The mountains refers to the mighty monarchs of the gentile nations. Awed by Solomon's wisdom and might, they will seek to make peace with him throughout his reign. This also will occur in the Messianic era, which will be devoid of hostility.

According to Sforno, the mountains alludes to the high government officials appointed by the king. These smug bureaucrats tend to become petty tyrants who exploit the people under

ד וּגְבָעוֹת בִּצְדָקָה: יִשְׁפֹּט | עֲנִיֵּי־עָם יוֹשִׁיעַ

ה לִבְנֵי אֶבְיוֹן וִידַכֵּא עוֹשֵׁק: יִירָאוּךָ עִם־

ו שֶׁמֶשׁ וְלִפְנֵי יָרֵחַ דּוֹר דּוֹרִים: יֵרֵד כְּמָטָר

ז עַל־גֵּז כִּרְבִיבִים זַרְזִיף אָרֶץ: יִפְרַח־בְּיָמָיו

---

their rule. Solomon, however, will choose his ministers and officials wisely; therefore, they will *bring peace* and good will to the populace, rather than dissension and animosity.

וּגְבָעוֹת — *And the hills.*

The low hills also *bring peace to the nation* by charitably providing their rich fruits and produce (*Rashi*).

According to *Sforno, the hills* refers to the lower echelons of governmental authority, including petty officials and the wives of the ministers. They too will be compassionate and charitable.

4. יִשְׁפֹּט עֲנִיֵּי עָם — *May He judge the nation's poor.*

In *v.* 2, the psalmist speaks of עֲנִיֶּיךָ, *Your* [i.e., God's] *poor,* whose lot was determined by the Divine design which ordained unequal distribution of wealth to provide an opportunity for kindness and charity.

However, *the nation's poor* mentioned in this verse refers to those whose poverty can be traced to unjust social conditions caused by national disregard for human rights and for man's responsibility to his fellow man. These underprivileged citizens are the victims of a national indifference to kindness and charity (*Hirsch*).

יוֹשִׁיעַ לִבְנֵי אֶבְיוֹן — *And save the children of the destitute.*

Sforno explains that this refers to the children of rich parents who have suddenly lost their wealth. Since the plight of such youngsters who had been accustomed to affluence and ease is particularly distressing, the king will provide them with a generous allowance.

וִידַכֵּא עוֹשֵׁק — *And crush the oppressor.*

This refers to a cowardly charlatan

who secretly deceives his victims and thus exploits them. These despicable men will cower before Solomon's extraordinary ability to unearth hidden lies (*Ibn Ezra*).

5. יִירָאוּךָ עִם שֶׁמֶשׁ — *So that they will fear You at sunrise* [lit. *with the sun*].

This translation follows *Targum* and *Metzudas David.*

The *Talmud* (*Berachos* 9b) teaches that the devout men called *Vasikin,* who sought to fulfill the Torah's precepts perfectly, would recite the *Shema* immediately before sunrise and recite the *Shemoneh Esrei* service as the sun came over the horizon, in order to fulfill this verse.

Midrash HaNeelam explains that God created the brilliant sun so that man could view the awesome wonders of creation and come to fear God, the Creator.

However, *Rashi, Radak,* and *Ibn Ezra* render: Let them learn from Solomon to fear You and let this fear endure forever, i.e., as long as the sun and the moon continue to shine.

Malbim adds: May their fear of God be consistent — just as the sun and moon remain stable in their orbits.

[David's greatest wish was to restore mankind to the utopian status it enjoyed before Adam sinned. *Ramban* (*Genesis* 2:9) teaches that Adam originally resembled the heavenly host, which the *Talmud* (*Sanhedrin* 42a) describes as creatures of truth, whose achievement is truth, and who do not deviate from their appointed mission. (See *Overview, Tehillim* Vol. I part 1).]

וְלִפְנֵי יָרֵחַ — *And before the moon's appearance.*

Again the translation follows *Targum* and *Metzudas David.* The *Talmud*

and the hills — through charity.

⁴ *May he judge the nation's poor,*
and save the children of the destitute;
and crush the oppressor.
⁵ *So that they will fear You at sunrise*
and before the moon's appearance,
generation after generation.
⁶ *May he descend like rain upon mown grass,*
like showers watering the earth.

(*Berachos* 29b) cites the view that it is commendable to recite the afternoon prayers (the *Minchah* service) immediately prior to sunset, just as the moon begins to appear. However, this practice is not generally followed, for fear that the proper moment may be missed. (The afternoon prayers should be completed before sunset.)

דּוֹר דּוֹרִים — *Generation after generation.*

Solomon's lesson will be transmitted from father to son; thus the tradition will continue unbroken (*Metzudas David*).

The teachings of Messiah will endure to an even greater degree. When he teaches the nation to fear God, the people's faith will never lapse (*Radak*).

6. יֵרֵד כְּמָטָר עַל גֵּז — *May he descend like rain upon mown grass.*

This verse teaches that the ideal king should *descend* to the level of the common people and concern himself with their lives. As a result, his words will penetrate deep into their hearts, like the rain which saturates the earth; but if the king serves only the elite members of society, then his influence on the nation as a whole will be minimal (*Rashi; Hirsch*).

The rain which falls after the grass is mown is especially beneficial (see *Amos* 7:1), for then the moisture can irrigate not only the roots, but also the fresh tips of the grass.

In an allegorical sense, the cut grass connotes people who have been admonished for their shortcomings. Since people are normally averse to receiving chastisement and rebuke, reproof must be given in a roundabout, tactful way; but if the king displays genuine concern for his subjects, then they will accept even blunt criticism from him, realizing that his remarks are motivated by his sincere concern for their welfare (*Malbim*).

[Even if the monarch's criticism is sharp and cutting, the people will drink up his words thirstily, like freshly mown grass which soaks up water.]

כִּרְבִיבִים זַרְזִיף אָרֶץ — *Like showers watering the earth.*

[רְבִיבִים, derived from רַב, *great*, and רְבָבָה, *a myriad*, denotes a great downpour of rain.]

Rashi states that זַרְזִיף means *raindrops* (see *Yoma* 87a). The words of the benevolent king will quench the spiritual thirst of the nation, just as a shower of raindrops provides lifegiving moisture for the parched earth and inspires tremendous joy (*Radak; Sforno*).

Radak says that Solomon's reign fulfilled David's great expectations of utopian bliss: *And Judah and Israel dwelt securely, each man under his vine and under his fig tree, from Dan to Beer Sheva, all the days of Solomon* (I *Kings* 5:5).

The Messiah's reign will not only be a paradise of material wealth, but also one

ח צַדִּיק וְרֹב שָׁלוֹם עַד־בְּלִי יָרֵחַ: וְיֵרְדְּ מִיָּם
ט עַד־יָם וּמִנָּהָר עַד־אַפְסֵי־אָרֶץ: לְפָנָיו
י יִכְרְעוּ צִיִּים וְאֹיְבָיו עָפָר יְלַחֵכוּ: מַלְכֵי

of spiritual truth. The term זַרְזִיף is a contraction of two words which describe the Messiah's times: זִיף (זִיּוּף) falsehood; deceit, will become זָר, alien; unknown, because Messiah will banish deception from the world (Sforno).

7. יִפְרַח בְּיָמָיו צַדִּיק — *In his days may the righteous man flourish.*

The righteous man refers to the entire nation of Israel. In Solomon's days, as long as the Jews remained righteous, they flourished, as Scripture states, (I Kings 4:20) *Judah and Israel are many, like the sand on the sea — a multitude, they eat and drink and are happy* (Rashi).

At that time the nation developed spiritually, blossoming both in brilliant Torah study and scrupulous *mitzvah* observance. This can only occur when the Jews are settled securely in their own land (Sforno). [Similar spiritual growth will take place in the time of the Messiah.]

וְרֹב שָׁלוֹם — *With abundant peace.*

And he had peace on all sides round about him. And Judah and Israel dwelt in safety ... [and Solomon said] 'Now HASHEM, my God, has granted me rest on every side, there is neither adversary nor evil attack' (I Kings 5:4-5, 18).

All of David's prayers on Solomon's behalf were completely fulfilled, except for this. David requested eternal peace, but God ordained that the reign of the House of David would endure only as long as David's descendants remained faithful to His word. When they betrayed God, he withdrew His protection from them (Rashi).

עַד־בְּלִי יָרֵחַ — *Till there is no moon.*

[These words describe the ultimate degree of serenity, stability, and success. The commentaries offer numerous interpretations for this enigmatic description.]

Peace will last until the end of time, until even the moon (an indicator of time) is no more (Rashi; Radak).

The prophet *Isaiah* (60:19,20) describes the Messianic redemption thus: *The sun will no longer serve you with light by day, and for brightness, the moon will no longer give you light; HASHEM will be your eternal light, and your God will be your splendor. Your sun will not set again, nor will your moon be gathered in, for HASHEM will be an everlasting light for you and your days of mourning will be completed.*

At that time, God's glory will outshine the sun and the moon; therefore, they will no longer be needed (Hirsch).

Even the idolaters, the worshipers of the moon, will be no more (Targum).

People will feel so secure that even if the moon does not shine and the night is pitch black, they will walk the streets without any fear (Vidal HaTzorfati).

In exile, the gentiles shine (with success) like the sun, while Israel resembles the moon, which has no light of its own. Peace and autonomy will bring the 'waning moon' status of Israel to an end (Eretz Hachaim).[1]

8. וְיֵרְדְּ מִיָּם עַד יָם — *May he dominate from sea to sea.*

Solomon (and Messiah) will have sovereignty over all of the territory of

1. The Midrash (Shemos Rabbah 15:26) derives from the verse הַחֹדֶשׁ הַזֶּה לָכֶם, *This month* [lit. *this new moon*] *shall be for you* (Exodus 12:2) that the royal dynasty of Israel will resemble the cycle of the moon: It will endure for thirty generations, just as the month lasts thirty days. The light of Jewish sovereignty began to rise in the time of the Patriarch Abraham, who was universally recognized as *the prince of God* (Genesis 23:6) followed by

⁷ *In his days may the righteous man flourish*
with abundant peace till there is no moon.
⁸ *May he dominate from sea to sea,*
and from river to the ends of the earth.
⁹ *May nobles kneel before him,*
and may his foes lick the dust.

Eretz Yisrael, from יַם סוּף, *Sea of Reeds* (in the south), to the יַם פְּלִשְׁתִּים *Sea of Philistines* (the Mediterranean, in the north and west. See *Exodus* 23:31) (Rashi; Radak).

Sforno explains that the dominion implied by the word וְיֵרְדְּ is not an impersonal government by proxy; rather it means that the king personally leads the people. [The word is related to רֵד, *go down,* meaning that the monarch descends to the level of the people and is intimately involved in their affairs.]

וּמִנָּהָר עַד אַפְסֵי אָרֶץ — *And from river to the ends of the earth.*

The boundaries of *Eretz Yisrael* also extend from נְהַר פְּרָת, *the Euphrates River,* on the northeast and the נְהַר מִצְרַיִם, *the River of Egypt,* in the southwest (see *Genesis* 15:18). This encompasses all of the territory which was promised to the Patriarchs (Alshich).

Solomon ruled over all this land, and beyond, as Scripture attests, (I Kings 5:4) He [Solomon] *had dominion over all the land beyond the river, from Tifsach to Azah, and over all the kings*

who were beyond the river (Rashi; Radak).

9. לְפָנָיו יִכְרְעוּ צִיִּים — *May nobles kneel before him.*

This translation of צִיִּים follows *Rashi,* who bases his view on the *Targum* to *Numbers* 24:24 [Similarly, *Targum* on this verse renders צִיִּים as אִיפַּרְכַיָא, *governors.*]

Others say that צִיִּים are the inhabitants of אֶרֶץ צִיָּה, *the parched desert,* suggesting: Even these isolated tribes will hear of Solomon's majesty and come to pay homage to him (Radak).

Ibn Ezra, however, relates צִיִּים to צִי, *the navy* (see *Isaiah* 33:21). Thus, ships from far and near will sail to Israel to serve Solomon.

וְאֹיְבָיו עָפָר יְלַחֵכוּ — *And may his foes lick the dust.*

Any attempt to challenge Solomon's authority will meet with failure and frustration. *His foes* will be forced to *lick the dust* in his presence, in fear of his power (Radak).

Isaac, Jacob, Judah, Peretz, Chetzron, Rom, Aminodov, Nachshon, Salmon, Boaz, Oved, and Jesse. Then came David (whose name, דָּוִד, has the numerical value of 14). He lived in the fourteenth generation (counting from Abraham) and resembled the moon, which is almost full on the fourteenth day of the month. Solomon was the fifteenth generation; in his days, the glory of David's line reached full perfection, comparable to that of the full moon on the fifteenth day of the month.

Then the decline began: The situation deteriorated from generation to generation. [See *Yechezkel,* ArtScroll ed. Appendix II.] The waning light of the Davidic line disappeared entirely in the thirtieth generation, with King Tzidkiyahu. Nebuchadnezzar blinded King Tzidkiyahu and sent him into exile, symbolizing the total eclipse of the monarchy. This is the meaning of this verse: [Because of Jewish sovereignty] *there will be an abundance of peace, until* [the thirtieth generation, when] *the moon is no more.* (see *Overview Tehillim* Vol. I, Part VIII).

תַּרְשִׁישׁ וְאִיִּים מִנְחָה יָשִׁיבוּ מַלְכֵי שְׁבָא

יא וּסְבָא אֶשְׁכָּר יַקְרִיבוּ: וְיִשְׁתַּחֲווּ־לוֹ כָל־

יב מְלָכִים כָּל־גּוֹיִם יַעַבְדוּהוּ: כִּי־יַצִּיל אֶבְיוֹן

יג מְשַׁוֵּעַ וְעָנִי וְאֵין־עֹזֵר לוֹ: יָחֹס עַל־דַּל

יד וְאֶבְיוֹן וְנַפְשׁוֹת אֶבְיוֹנִים יוֹשִׁיעַ: מִתּוֹךְ

10. מַלְכֵי תַרְשִׁישׁ וְאִיִּים מִנְחָה יָשִׁיבוּ — *The kings of Tarshish and the isles shall return with tribute.*

In I *Kings* 10:21-23 we read the fulfillment of David's prayer: *And all King Solomon's drinking vessels were of gold, and all the vessels of the house of the forest of Lebanon were of pure gold, none were of silver, because it was not considered of any worth in the days of Solomon. For the king had at sea the navy of Tarshish with the navy of Hiram; once every three years the navy of Tarshish arrived bringing gold and silver, ivory and apes and peacocks. So King Solomon surpassed all the kings of the earth in riches and in wisdom.*

[Throughout Scriptures, *Tarshish* is described as a major seaport which dispatched great merchant fleets to the ends of the earth. See *comm.* to 48:8, *Genesis* 10:4, and *Jonah* 1:3.]

יָשִׁיבוּ — [*They*] *shall return.*

This usage is unexpected; *they shall bring* would seem to be more appropriate here. *Radak* and *Ibn Ezra* explain that this verse means that the nations will return to offer tribute to Solomon every year.

According to the *Midrash* (*Bereishis Rabbah* 78:12), this refers to the Messiah. All the gifts which Jacob gave to Esau, all the bribes which Jews have used to still the animosity of their oppressors through the ages, [and all the property which the gentiles have forcibly plundered from us] will be

returned to the Messiah when the nations subject themselves to his sovereignty (*Tehillos Hashem*).

מַלְכֵי שְׁבָא וּסְבָא אֶשְׁכָּר יַקְרִיבוּ — *The kings of Sheba and Seba shall offer gifts.*

The fulfillment of this verse is described in I *Kings* (10:1, 2, 10): *And when the Queen of Sheba heard of the fame of Solomon, for the sake of HASHEM, she came to test him with riddles. And she came to Jerusalem with a great retinue, with camels that bore spices and very much gold and precious stones … And she gave the king one hundred and twenty talents of gold, and very many spices and precious stones; never again did such an abundance of spices arrive to compare with that which the Queen of Sheba gave to Solomon.*

[Perhaps אֶשְׁכָּר, translated by *Targum* as *gifts,* is related to שָׂכָר, *reward,* which would imply that the Queen of Sheba bestowed her *gifts* on Solomon as a reward for the knowledge he had shared with her so generously: *And King Solomon gave to the Queen of Sheba all her desire, whatever she asked,* (I *Kings* 10:13).][1]

11. וְיִשְׁתַּחֲווּ לוֹ כָל מְלָכִים — *All the kings shall prostrate themselves before him.*

David's prayer for his son was answered when *all the earth sought the presence of Solomon, to hear his wisdom which God had put in his heart. And every man brought his tribute, ves-*

1. The *Talmud* (*Bava Basra* 15b) maintains that מַלְכַּת שְׁבָא does not mean *the Queen of Sheba,* rather it means מַלְכוּת שְׁבָא, *the royalty of Sheba.* *Maharsha* (*ibid.*) explains that the Queen of Sheba was not merely the wife of the king, rather she herself was the ruling monarch and this was a rare phenomenon in history.

10 *The kings of Tarshish and the isles*
shall return with tribute,
The kings of Sheba and Seba
shall offer gifts.
11 *All the kings*
shall prostrate themselves before him,
All the peoples
shall serve him.
12 *For he will deliver the crying destitute one*
and the poor one with none to help him.
13 *He will pity the impoverished and destitute;*
the souls of destitute ones he will save.

sels *of silver and vessels of gold, and raiment and armor, and spices, horses and mules, each year according to its due (I Kings 10:24-35).*

כָּל גוֹיִם יַעַבְדוּהוּ — *All the peoples shall serve him.*

They will not serve him out of fear, but out of love and admiration (*Sforno*).[1]

All the homage and adulation paid to Solomon will be paid to the Messiah as well (*Radak*).

12. כִּי יַצִּיל אֶבְיוֹן מְשַׁוֵּעַ — *For he will deliver the crying destitute one.*

Solomon was to earn the love and admiration of the entire world because of his towering moral stature. His court was universally recognized as the international tribunal of justice; the needy regarded him as their defender; he was the friend of the weak and persecuted.

Princes turned to him to arbitrate national disputes; weak nations called upon him for salvation from their powerful neighbors. Even paupers, feeble and powerless individuals, felt

that Solomon cared for their personal problems; they too appeared before him (*Radak; Ibn Ezra; Hirsch*).

וְעָנִי וְאֵין עֹזֵר לוֹ — *And the poor one with none to help him* [lit. *without a helper for him*].

[Although others spurn the cries of the ragged paupers who seek justice against tyranny, Solomon courageously championed their unpopular, but just cause.]

13. יָחֹס עַל דַּל וְאֶבְיוֹן — *He will pity the impoverished and destitute.*

Solomon did not use the huge amount of tribute brought to him by all the nations for his own pleasure. He distributed all excess wealth to alleviate the plight of the deprived (*Alshich*).

[The Torah prohibits the king from amassing a fortune of silver and gold in excess of his annual expenses for supporting his army and retinue (*Deuteronomy 17:17*), lest too much wealth fill his heart with pride. Similarly he is constrained from having too many horses or too many wives (*Deuteronomy 17:16,17*).

1. The universal homage paid to Solomon was not restricted to human beings. *Targum Sheini* (1:1) to *Megillas Esther* states that the fish of the sea and the birds of the sky, domestic animals and wild beasts came to Solomon's palace and presented themselves for slaughter, so that they might merit to be part of Solomon's meal.

וּמֵחָמָס יִגְאַל נַפְשָׁם וְיֵיקַר דָּמָם בְּעֵינָיו:
טו וִיחִי וְיִתֶּן־לוֹ מִזְּהַב שְׁבָא וְיִתְפַּלֵּל בַּעֲדוֹ
טז תָמִיד כָּל־הַיּוֹם יְבָרֲכֶנְהוּ: יְהִי פִסַּת־בַּר |
בָּאָרֶץ בְּרֹאשׁ הָרִים יִרְעַשׁ כַּלְּבָנוֹן פִּרְיוֹ

The *Talmud (Sanhedrin 21b)* states that Solomon transgressed both the prohibition against too many wives and the law of limiting the size of the royal stables; but despite Scriptural reports of Solomon's enormous wealth, the *Talmud* does *not* accuse him of possessing an overabundance of riches. The reason, as *Alshich* explains, is that Solomon used all his extra funds either for the Temple or to benefit the underprivileged.]

Sforno comments that Solomon was particularly sensitive to the plight of those who became impoverished because of inflation. When the rich plundered the poor by inflating the prices of such staples as grain, Solomon combatted this practice.

וְנַפְשׁוֹת אֶבְיוֹנִים יוֹשִׁיעַ — *The souls of destitute ones He will save.*

The rich employer exploits his poor laborer and works him to death. Solomon saved these wretched slaves from their desperate plight (*Sforno*).

14. מִתּוֹךְ וּמֵחָמָס יִגְאַל נַפְשָׁם — *From fraud and from violence he will redeem their soul.*

Literally תּוֹךְ means *inside*, suggesting that the deceitful man tries to conceal the injury and damage which he inflicts on his victim. In contrast, חָמָס describes acts of open *violence* (*Rashi; Ibn Ezra; Radak;* see comm. to Psalms 55:12).

Specifically, says *Sforno*, Solomon used his might and prestige to prevent kings from tyrannizing their helpless subjects.

וְיֵיקַר דָּמָם בְּעֵינָיו — *And their blood will be precious in his eyes.*

[Solomon's acute sense of justice was stirred by his great esteem for human

life and by his sensitivity to human suffering. It was anathema for him to advance the cause of his monarchy at the expense of human misery.]

15. וִיחִי וְיִתֶּן לוֹ מִזְּהַב שְׁבָא — *So he will live! And He will grant him of the gold of Sheba.*

This translation follows *Rashi:* Solomon will live on, and God will provide him with the wealth he needs to pursue his universal philanthropy.

According to *Ibn Ezra, Radak,* and *Metzudas David,* the verse signifies that Solomon's charity will infuse the poor with new life. Not only will the poor live, they will be prosperous, for Solomon will generously bestow upon them the tribute of gold he received from Sheba.

וְיִתְפַּלֵּל בַּעֲדוֹ תָמִיד — *And He will pray for him continually.*

God's blessings will pour down upon Solomon incessantly (*Rashi*).

The poor, the beneficiaries of Solomon's magnanimity, will shower an endless flow of prayers and blessings upon him (*Radak; Ibn Ezra; Metzudas David*).

16. יְהִי פִסַּת בַּר בָּאָרֶץ — *May an abundance of grain* [lit. *a loaf of bread*] *be in the land.*

Rashi determines that פִסַּת is cognate with פִּסְיוֹן, *enlargement; increase* [see *Leviticus* 13:7]. This *abundance* will create unprecedented contentment, which, in turn, will foster the פִּיוּס, *reconciliation*, of those who became estranged from God.

Radak adds that, at that time, when a man plants a mere פַּס, *fistful*, of seeds, a

14 *From fraud and from violence*
       he will redeem their soul,
And their blood will be precious
       in his eyes.
15 *So he will live!*
       And He will grant him of the gold of Sheba,
And He will pray for him continually
       and bless him every day.
16 *May an abundance of grain be*
       in the land on the mountain tops,
May its fruit rustle
       like the Lebanon;

vast field of grain will sprout from it.[1]

Sforno interprets this as an allegory: the wise and just king will concentrate his full pedagogic skills on a פַּס, *handful* of devoted disciples, who will then disseminate his universal message of equity and decency.

בְּרֹאשׁ הָרִים — *On the mountain tops.*

[Not only will the rich soil bear fruit, even the barren and inaccessible mountain tops will become verdant and amazingly productive.]

The *Talmud (Kesubos* 111b) foretells that in the future, a stalk of wheat [planted in the valley *(Maharshah)*] will grow to incredible heights, until it towers above the mountaintops.

יִרְעַשׁ כַּלְּבָנוֹן פִּרְיוֹ — *May its fruit rustle like the Lebanon.*

Each kernel of wheat will be as large as the huge fruits growing in the lush forest of Lebanon. They will equal the size of the large kidneys of a cow *(Rashi).*

In order to harvest these giant kernels from the tremendously high stalks, HASHEM will send a wind to shake the finest flour from the kernels. When this floats gently to earth, people will gather fistfuls, which will sustain them generously *(Kesubos* 111b).

The *Talmud (Yoma* 39b) also relates that when Solomon built the Holy Temple, he planted a variety of golden fruit trees which miraculously produced golden fruits. The wind would rustle through the trees and shake the precious fruit making it fall to the earth, providing a generous income for the priests who worked in the Temple.

When the gentiles entered the Temple courtyard to destroy it, these wondrous trees shriveled and died. In the future, however, they will be restored to their former splendor.

1. The *Talmud (Shabbos* 30b) records Rabban Gamliel's teaching that in the days of the Messiah, the land of Israel will produce loaves of baked bread [every day], in fulfillment of this verse.

One incredulous student mocked this statement, retorting, 'Does Scripture not teach, *there is nothing new under the sun?'* (Koheles 1:9).

Rabban Gamliel replied, 'I will show you something very similar which is already in existence.' He showed the student mushrooms, which sprout to full maturity overnight.

[Actually the sceptic's question was unfounded, because before Adam's sin, the earth did produce perfect, finished loaves of bread, which stopped coming after the sin.]

יז וְיָצִיצוּ מֵעִיר כְּעֵשֶׂב הָאָרֶץ: יְהִי שְׁמוֹ |
°יִנּוֹן לְעוֹלָם לִפְנֵי־שֶׁמֶשׁ °ינין שְׁמוֹ וְיִתְבָּרְכוּ
יח בוֹ כָּל־גּוֹיִם יְאַשְּׁרֻהוּ: בָּרוּךְ | יהוה
אֱלֹהִים אֱלֹהֵי יִשְׂרָאֵל עֹשֵׂה נִפְלָאוֹת

וְיָצִיצוּ מֵעִיר כְּעֵשֶׂב הָאָרֶץ — *May they blossom forth from the city like the grass of the earth.*

In the same way that agricultural marvels will bloom in the fields, demographic miracles will abound in the cities: an unprecedented population explosion will fill the urban areas with teeming masses *(Radak).*

Jerusalem, in particular, will witness spectacular growth of her Jewish population *(Rashi,* based on *Kesubos* 111b).

Hirsch observes that David envisioned his son's rule as providing the guidance needed for the city to function properly as the basis of society, and he wished to see his people thrive in the city, just as grass blooms in the fields. In our culture, the harmony and beauty of creation are more apparent in unpopulated areas than they are in cities. However, when our national life is conducted with integrity and purity, and based on the service of God, then the city will radiate more breathtaking beauty and spiritual splendor than any 'natural wonder' of the physical world. The masses who are dedicated to the fulfillment of the Divine mission are truly God's greatest wonder.

17. יְהִי שְׁמוֹ לְעוֹלָם — *May his name survive forever.*

May Solomon be recognized forever as a paragon of wisdom and wealth

(Rashi). May his name be equaled only by the great name of the Messiah *(Ibn Ezra).*

With the mere mention of the Messiah's name, the resultant yearning for his appearance hastens his arrival *(Beis Elokim).*

לִפְנֵי שֶׁמֶשׁ יִנּוֹן שְׁמוֹ — *May his dynasty endure as long as the sun.*

Radak explains that יִנּוֹן is cognate with נִין, *descendant,* to indicate that just as descendants perpetuate the memory of their ancestors, so should the fame of the king endure for as long as the sun shines, until the end of time. *Rashi* adds that this term for descendants is usually reserved for the heirs of the royal line.

According to *Pirkei D'Rabbi Eliezer* (ch. 32), יִנּוֹן alludes to *youth,* intimating that the Messiah is destined to bring about the resurrection of the dead.[1]

The *Talmud (Sanhedrin* 98b) marshals a number of opinions concerning the name of the Messiah. Some interpret these words literally, maintaining that יִנּוֹן שְׁמוֹ, *Yenon will be his* [actual] *name.* Other suggested names are מְנַחֵם, *Menachem,* שִׁילֹה, *Shiloh,* and חֲנִינָה, *Chaninah.* [Some commentaries have observed that the initial letters of all four suggested names spell מָשִׁיחַ, *Messiah!*]

וְיִתְבָּרְכוּ בוֹ — *And may men bless themselves by him.*

A father will bless his son, 'May you

1. *Kovetz Shiurim* Vol. II:29 quotes the responsa of *Radvaz* (II: 644), who explains there will be *two* resurrections. The general resurrection for all men will take place after the Messianic era. However, at the advent of the Messianic era a limited revival of the dead will occur, bringing back to life the outstanding individuals, the great scholars and men of piety, of each generation. This is also the opinion of the *Ritva,* who explains that it is only right that these dedicated persons should enjoy the bliss and rewards of the Messianic times. [See *Ikrei Hadat, Yoreh Deah Hilchos Aveilus* appendix 66.]

The *Talmud (Yoma* 5b) indicates that in the Messianic era Moses and Aaron will be alive once again and they will be available to make halachic decisions. [See *Pesachim* 114b, *Tosafos*

May they blossom forth from the city
like the grass of the earth.
¹⁷ *May his name survive forever,*
may his dynasty endure as long as the sun,
And may men bless themselves by him;
may all peoples praise him.
¹⁸ *Blessed be HASHEM, God, the God of Israel,*
Who alone does wondrous things.

be as wise and wealthy as Solomon'
(*Rashi*).

כָּל גּוֹיִם יְאַשְּׁרְהוּ — *May all peoples praise*
him.

[The sterling qualities of Solomon
and the Messiah will be universally
admired.]

18. בָּרוּךְ ה' אֱלֹהִים אֱלֹהֵי יִשְׂרָאֵל —
Blessed be HASHEM, God, the God of
Israel.

In the final three verses of this
composition, the author offers praise
and thanks to God, not only for the
inspiration to complete this psalm, but
also for the privilege of completing the
second Book of *Tehillim* (*Radak*).

Blessed be 'ה, *the Dispenser of*
Kindness and blessed be אֱלֹהִים, *the*
Dispenser of Strict Justice (*Sforno*).

Blessed be the Almighty, Who,
despite His exalted position as *HASHEM*
and God of the entire universe, still
supervises us personally as *the God of*
Israel (*Ibn Yachya*).

עֹשֵׂה נִפְלָאוֹת לְבַדּוֹ — *Who alone does*
wondrous things.

God intervenes personally, rather
than through an intermediary

(*Malbim*). He performs miracles for
Israel exclusively (i.e., *alone*), thus
demonstrating that He alone, *the God of*
Israel, is the true Lord. All pagan deities
are false (*Radak*).

Radak contends that David here
refers to a specific miracle: He asks that
God send a heavenly flame to burn on
the altar of Solomon's Temple, in order
to demonstrate to the world that
Solomon was worthy of *wondrous*
things alone, i.e., in his own merit.

The *Talmud* (*Niddah* 31a) illustrates
these words with a parable: As two
merchants were about to board a ship, a
sharp thorn pierced one man's foot,
forcing him to miss the ship.
Disappointed, the merchant cursed his
luck. Soon however, word arrived that
the ship had sunk. All aboard were lost.
Now the wounded merchant burst forth
in song, thanking God for his good
fortune.

This is the meaning of the verse, *He*
does wondrous things alone: often God
acts *alone* in such hidden ways that
even the beneficiary of His miracles
doesn't immediately recognize his own
good fortune!

s.v. אֶחָד זֵכֶר לְפֶסַח and *Sanhedrin* 51b, *Rashi s.v.* הַלְכָה לָמָה לִי.] *Rav Saadiah Gaon* states that
Moses will be revived together with all other prophets of Jewish history, who will assist him.

The *Yalkut Shimoni* to Job, Chapter 38, 924 tells us of Rav Yoshiya's final wish: 'Dress me
in white shrouds. Put shoes on my feet and a staff in my hand and put me on my side [in the
grave] so I will be ready when Messiah comes and calls me to life.'

The *Talmud* (*Sanhedrin* 92a) says that the righteous ones who will be resurrected [in the
Messianic era, *Rashi*] will never be returned to their graves.

Finally the Sages (*Sotah* 48b) speak of the future and place the revival of the dead *before* the
advent of Messiah, the scion of David. In light of the above sources, this must refer to the
outstanding leaders, not to the masses.

יט לְבַדּוֹ: וּבָרוּךְ | שֵׁם כְּבוֹדוֹ לְעוֹלָם וְיִמָּלֵא
כ כְבוֹדוֹ אֶת־כָּל־הָאָרֶץ אָמֵן | וְאָמֵן: כָּלּוּ
תְפִלּוֹת דָּוִד בֶּן־יִשָׁי:

---

19. וּבָרוּךְ שֵׁם כְּבוֹדוֹ לְעוֹלָם — *Blessed be His glorious Name forever.*

God has but one real name, which is ה', *HASHEM.* All other references to Him are merely descriptions of his countless powers and abilities (*Ibn Ezra*).

[When men are only aware of God's actions, they may err and attribute these deeds to false deities.] The climax of the Messianic mission is to bring mankind to an awareness of God's true identity as the one and only Divine power. The prophet (*Zechariah* 14:9) foretells: *On that day HASHEM will be One and His Name will be One* (*Radak*).

וְיִמָּלֵא כְבוֹדוֹ אֶת כָּל הָאָרֶץ — *And may all the earth be filled with His glory.*

This verse will be fulfilled only when men are imbued with a keen awareness of God's majesty, as the prophet (*Isaiah* 11:9) foretells, *for the earth shall be filled with the knowledge of HASHEM,* as the waters cover the sea (*Radak*).

אָמֵן וְאָמֵן — *Amen and Amen.*

The word בָּרוּךְ, *blessed be,* is found in the previous verse and repeated here. Since God is blessed twice, a double *Amen* is needed to verify both benedictions (*Midrash Chachomim*).

The repetition of *Amen* expresses the hope that God be glorified both in This World and in the World to Come (*Zera Yaakov*).

20. כָּלּוּ תְפִלּוֹת דָּוִד בֶּן יִשָׁי — *The prayers of David, the son of Jesse, are ended.*

As was explained in the *Prefatory Remarks,* this psalm was composed by David on his deathbed. It commemorates the last significant act of David's lifetime, the coronation of Solomon.

The Book of *Tehillim* ends with this psalm only in the sense that it is the last of the psalms that were inspired by specific events in David's lifetime. The

¹⁹ Blessed be His glorious Name forever

And may all the earth be filled with His glory.

Amen and Amen

²⁰ The prayers of David,
the son of Jesse, are ended.

following three books are predominantly songs of general praise for God.

The psalmist purposely laid out his book in this fashion, so that this inspired work would end with a tremendous outpouring of Divine praise (*Radak, Psalms* 72:1).

Rabbi Meir, quoted in the *Talmud* (*Pesachim* 117b), explains that the entire Book of *Tehillim* was composed by David. He teaches that כָּלוּ should not be read *are ended*, but should be interpreted as a contraction of the two words כָּל אֵלוּ, *all of these*, are the prayers of David.

[Although a number of psalms are ascribed to ten other righteous men (see *Rashi*, to 1:1), in truth they composed their songs merely as a personal recollection. It was David who rewrote all of the psalms so that they would relate to the souls of all men at all times.

See *Overview Tehillim*, Vol. I, part IV, 'The sweet singer of Israel'.]

R' Yosef Kimchi, quoted by his son, *Radak*, points out that it does not say that David's זְמִירוֹת, *psalms*, or הוֹדָאוֹת, *songs of thanksgiving*, are ended; rather the verse mentions David's תְּפִלוֹת, *prayers*.

David's praises of God will never end, but his *prayers* were inspired by his sins, his failures and his tragedies. In his *prayers*, David begs for atonement for himself and for his entire people.

With the advent of the perfect king, the Messiah, Israel will finally rid itself of all folly and failure. A nation redeemed and restored to grandeur, Israel will then live in a utopia, with no need for anguished pleas. Therefore, although תְּפִלוֹת, *prayers*, will come to an end, songs of praise and thanksgiving will resound joyously forever.

APPENDIX:
The Menorah

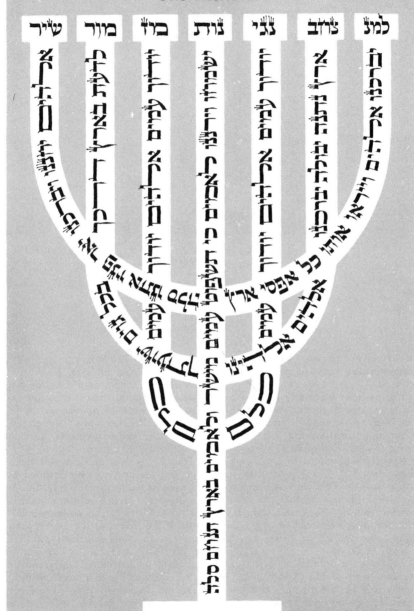